ELEVENTH EDITION

FINANCIAL INSTITUTIONS, MARKETS, AND MONEY

David S. Kidwell
University of Minnesota

David W. Blackwell
Texas A&M University

David A. Whidbee
Washington State University

Richard W. Sias
University of Arizona

WILEY

John Wiley & Sons, Inc.

VICE PRESIDENT AND EXECUTIVE PUBLISHER   George Hoffman

PROJECT EDITOR   Jennifer Manias

ASSISTANT EDITOR   Emily McGee

EDITORIAL ASSISTANT   Erica Horowitz

MEDIA EDITOR   Greg Chaput

CREATIVE DIRECTOR   Harold Nolan

SENIOR DESIGNER   Maureen Eide

SENIOR PHOTO EDITOR   Lisa Gee

PRODUCTION MANAGER   Dorothy Sinclair

SENIOR PRODUCTION EDITOR   Trish McFadden

PRODUCTION MANAGEMENT SERVICES   Aptara

COVER DESIGN   Wendy Lai

COVER PHOTO   Amy Uratsu/Photodisc/Getty Images

This book was set in 10.5/12 Janson Text by Aptara, Inc. and printed and bound by RRD/JC.
The cover was printed by RRD/JC.

This book is printed on acid free paper. ∞

Evaluation copies are provided to qualified academics and professionals for review purposes only,
for use in their courses during the next academic year. These copies are licensed and may not be sold
or transferred to a third party. Upon completion of the review period, please return the evaluation
copy to Wiley. Return instructions and a free of charge return shipping label are available at HYPERLINK
"http://www.wiley.com/go/return" www.wiley.com/go/returnlabel. Outside of the United States, please
contact your local representative.

ISBN 13: 978-047-056108-9
ISBN 10: 047-056108-4

Printed in the United States of America

10 9 8 7 6 5 4 3 2 1

PREFACE

TO THE STUDENT

We hope you are as excited about taking a course on financial institutions and markets as we were about writing the book. The core topics covered in the book are at the heart of what happens every day in the financial sector of the economy. When you have finished the course, reading the *Wall Street Journal*, the *Financial Times*, or the business section of the *New York Times* will be a piece of cake. Your friends, family, and fellow students will marvel at your insights into the financial system.

In the book, we stress fundamental concepts with an emphasis on understanding how things work in the real world. We hope that we have captured the vibrancy and excitement created by the dramatic changes taking place in the U.S. financial system. You are taking the course at a unique time in economic history, following the global financial crisis of 2007–2009 and the longest and most severe recession since the Great Depression of the 1930s. These events are radically reshaping the financial system.

Our goal is to provide a book that can guide you to a confident mastery and understanding of the U.S. financial system in an interesting and, hopefully, entertaining manner. The book is your passport to linking your classroom experience to what is happening in the economy and financial markets. What you learn will be applicable to your business career or in managing your personal financial affairs.

TO THE FACULTY

The focus of the eleventh edition of *Financial Institutions, Markets, and Money* is the same as that of the previous editions: to provide a balanced introduction to the operation, mechanics, and structure of the U.S. financial system. On the other hand, the book is remarkably different in that the global financial crisis of 2007–2009 resulted in major changes to the structure of the financial system, in regulation, and in how central banks operate. These changes have required major rewrites of nearly every chapter in the book. We hasten to add that changes in the financial system are still under way as we write this preface in July 2011. Economists and government officials are still sifting through the economic rubble from the financial crisis and the subsequent severe recession.

Though changes abound, the core coverage in the book still emphasizes financial institutions, markets, and instruments. Special attention is given to the Federal Reserve System and the impact of monetary policy on interest rates. We discuss how financial institutions manage risk caused by interest rate and economic changes.

Finally, the book is written with a strong historical perspective. Throughout the book we give attention to the historical development of financial institutions and markets and discuss important historical events. We believe that relating historical events to the book's fundamental concepts gives students a richer understanding of the material and a better perspective from which to evaluate current developments.

Teacher Friendly. In revising the book, we are mindful of the demands on faculty who are asked to do more with less. We want to help make your course on financial institutions and markets as successful as possible. To that end, we worked hard to write in a clear and understandable manner. Also, we put much effort into updating and improving the chapter learning features, several of which are new to the eleventh edition, such as Learning by Doing applications, the end-of-chapter Summary of Learning Objectives, and enhanced quantitative content. Finally, we provide first-rate teaching and learning aids such as the instructor's manual, test bank, study guide, and PowerPoint presentations that accompany each chapter.

The Book's Evolution. Our book, like the financial system, has had to adapt to the rapidly changing economic environment. When we published our first edition, the existing textbooks were primarily descriptive, merely describing the activities of financial institutions, or they were de facto money and banking texts, primarily focused on the banking system and monetary policy. In our first edition, we broke new ground by emphasizing both financial institutions and markets, and how monetary policy affected financial institutions. At that time, our "free-market" approach to regulation, which emphasized market-oriented rather than government-imposed solutions to problems, was not mainstream and, to some, was considered controversial.

As technology, regulation, and financial innovation changed the financial landscape, our book has had to evolve. In subsequent editions, we increased our emphasis on how interest rates are determined and on the structure of interest rates. We also increased our emphasis on the risks faced by financial institutions and on how institutions manage these risks using financial markets. Over the years, we expanded our coverage of financial markets, and now, for example, the book has separate chapters on equity markets, mortgage markets, derivatives markets, and international markets.

The Competitive Edge. Our approach to the topic made our book very successful in the early editions, and it continues to be successful today. Imitation is the sincerest form of flattery, and we have seen a number of imitators of our approach, which, apart from the wide use of this book, is the best evidence of its appeal to both students and faculty.

Our *competitive edge*, however, comes from our adherence to the approach for the book that was set in the first edition. First, we stress the mastery of fundamental material, placing an emphasis on how things really work in a market context. Second, we have a balanced coverage of the U.S. financial system, with strong emphasis on both institutions *and* markets. Third, we continually update the book to reflect major new developments in the financial system or to highlight changing trends. Finally, we focus on writing a book *for the students*, our most important audience, which facilitates learning and makes the study of financial institutions and markets an enjoyable experience.

Let Us Hear from You. We thank the faculty who adopted our book and the students who purchased our book. As you go through your course, we hope that we live up to our promise of providing a clear, concise, well-written, and academically sound text on the U.S. financial system. If you find a mistake or have concerns about a particular section, we would like to hear from you. Contact us via our e-mail addresses, which are listed at the end of the preface.

We believe this edition of the book is better than the tenth edition for a number of reasons. Apart from the customary detailed updating of facts and exhibits throughout the book, we worked painstakingly to improve the readability and the chapter features in this edition to better facilitate student learning. In this edition, especially in the chapters on financial markets, we continue our emphasis on how to read and interpret actual financial data, such as that reported in the *Wall Street Journal* or the *Financial Times*. We also continue to refine the chapter pedagogical features. We have also substantially revised the chapter contents to reflect the impact of the global financial crisis of 2007–2009.

WHY THIS EDITION IS BETTER THAN PREVIOUS ONES

PEDAGOGICAL FEATURES

This section summarizes the pedagogical features and highlights additions or improvements in the eleventh edition. The features that are new or have been substantially revised are indicated with an asterisk (*).

Chapter Opening Vignette. Each chapter begins with an opening vignette that describes a real company or business situation. The vignettes illustrate concepts that will be presented in the chapter and are also meant to heighten student interest and demonstrate the real-life relevance of the chapter material.

Learning Objectives. The opening vignette is accompanied by a set of learning objectives that identify the most important material for students to understand while reading the chapter. At the end of the chapter appears a feature, "Summary of Learning Objectives," highlighting the relevant chapter content.

Learning by Doing.* Chapters with quantitative content now have more in-text examples. These chapters now include a new feature: Learning by Doing. These applications contain quantitative problems with step-by-step solutions that provide guidance on how to approach similar problems. By including several exercises in each chapter where applicable we provide students with additional practice to hone their problem-solving skills.

Do You Understand? Each chapter includes several sets of Do You Understand? questions that usually appear at the end of a major section. These questions check student understanding of critical concepts in the material just covered, or ask students to apply what they have just read to real-world situations. To give students feedback on the Do You Understand? questions, we include the answers on the book's website (discussed later) and in the Instructor's Manual.

People & Events.* Each chapter includes at least one People & Events box. The People & Events boxes describe current or historical real-world situations to emphasize the applicability of one or more key concepts developed in the chapter. Over half of the People & Events boxes have been replaced and many others have been substantially revised. In the eleventh edition the People & Events boxes are particularly focused on the anatomy of the financial crisis of

2007–2009, the impact of the crisis on financial institutions and markets, and the emerging recovery from the crisis.

Exhibit Captions.   Where appropriate we provide captions for the exhibits to inform students of the exhibits' main points.

Summary of Learning Objectives.*   At the end of each chapter, you will find summaries of the key chapter content relevant to each of the Learning Objectives.

Key Terms.   We include a list of key terms at the end of each chapter. The terms appearing in the list are printed in boldface in the chapter. The definitions of all key terms appear in the glossary at the end of the book.

Questions and Problems.*   Each chapter ends with a set of questions and problems. Because students rely heavily on example questions and problems with solutions as a learning device, we have increased the number of end-of-chapter questions and problems. We have placed particular emphasis on increasing the number of quantitative problems or questions to correspond with the enhanced quantitative content as appropriate to the chapter. The answers to questions and problems are in the Instructor's Manual.

Internet Exercises.   We provide an Internet Exercise at the end of each chapter. These exercises direct students to websites from which they can obtain additional information about the chapter's topic or analyze data that illustrate key points from the chapter.

Glossary.*   The book contains an easy-to-use glossary defining the Key Terms listed at the end of each chapter.

SUMMARY OF CONTENTS AND MAJOR CHANGES

All chapters in the book have been updated to reflect recent events. A major change in the book is an increase in the quantitative content. We have noted that employers are increasingly expecting students to be well versed in problem-solving skills. As a result, we have increased the computational skill level, while maintaining our historic strength of being a conceptually focused book. Our goal is to provide students and instructors with a book that strikes a balance between helping students understand key financial and economic concepts and providing them with the necessary problem-solving skills. Below we summarize the contents and major changes to the eleventh edition.

Part 1: The Financial System.   **Chapter 1,** providing an overview of the U.S. financial system, has gone through a major *contextual update* reflecting changes in the financial system resulting from the 2007–2009 global financial crisis. The section on investment banking was expanded and now includes a new section on risk. A new section was added on the regulation of the financial system, which includes an analysis of the Financial Regulatory Reform Act of 2010. The section on the economics of financial intermediation was expanded and now includes a thorough discussion of transaction costs and the cost of asymmetric information in loan contracts and other financial contracts. We have significantly revised **Chapter 2,** which is about the Federal Reserve System and its impact on interest rates. We examine the Fed's new power to pay interest on reserves held at the Fed and its effect on monetary policy. We also discuss the impact of the financial system bailout on the Fed's balance sheet and the Fed's increase in regulatory power from the 2010 Regulatory Reform Act, including its power to manage systemic risk in the financial system. **Chapter 3** focuses on how the Fed conducts monetary policy. New to the chapter is a discussion of the Treasury Department's role in financing the expenditures made by the federal government, how the Treasury Department conducts fiscal policy, and the Treasury's role in stabilizing the economy. Until recently, monetary policy alone was employed to stabilize the economy.

Part 2: How Interest Rates Are Determined.   **Chapter 4** discusses the role of interest rates in the economy and how interest rates are determined. The discussion of the real rate of interest has been substantially expanded as has our discussion of the impact of inflationary expectations on the level of interest rates. We added sections on the realized real rate of return and on the purported phenomenon of so-called negative interest rates. **Chapter 5** focuses on the determinants of bond prices and interest rate risk. New to the chapter is material discussing the hazards and consequences of not properly managing interest rate risk. **Chapter 6** explores the reasons that interest rates vary among financial products on any given day and over the business cycle. We expanded our discussion of inverted yield curves and predicting recessions. We substantially expanded our discussion of how interest rates vary over the business cycle and analyzed a period during the 2007–2010 recession when expected inflation was zero, thus "exposing" the real rate of interest (it was 2.52 percent).

Part 3: Financial Markets.   The chapters in this part have been revised to reflect the new financial environment following the global financial crisis of 2007–2009, while maintaining their focus on the fundamental roles and functioning of the various markets. **Chapter 7** focuses on the economic role of money markets in the economy and the characteristics of money market instruments. Added to the chapter was a discussion of the impact of the financial meltdown on the money markets and the actions that the Fed took to stabilize the markets. The section on Treasury bills has been rewritten to reflect new Treasury auction procedures; the concept of a haircut was introduced in the section on repurchase agreements; and the concept of asset-backed commercial paper was introduced. **Chapter 8** analyzes the debt securities sold in the capital markets. The section on Treasury securities now explains how coupon rates are determined; the section on *financial guarantees* now includes a discussion of the role of insurance companies; and the section on international bond markets has been expanded. **Chapter 9** explains how the mortgage markets work and describes the major mortgage market instruments. New to the chapter is a thorough discussion of the government's takeover of the mortgage market that occurred in the aftermath of the subprime mortgage crisis and the failures of Fannie Mae and Freddie Mac. The chapter also includes a discussion of what the markets may look like moving forward. **Chapter 10** examines the market for equity securities. The chapter now includes a discussion of the changing structure and global consolidation of secondary markets, including NYSE's hybrid system and the increased competition between Nasdaq and the NYSE. Also new is an expanded discussion of valuation formulas, a section on short selling, and material on the government's renewed interest in insider trading by hedge funds. **Chapter 11** describes the most important markets for financial derivatives. New to the chapter is a revised and expanded discussion of swaps and the role of credit default swaps in the 2007–2009 financial crisis. The chapter also discusses the impact of the Dodd-Frank Wall Street Reform and Consumer Protection Act on swap trading. Also new to the chapter is an expanded discussion of option valuation. **Chapter 12** examines international financial markets, including foreign exchange markets and international money and capital markets. The chapter includes new discussion of the functions of foreign exchange markets and the determination of exchange rates. Also new to the chapter is a detailed example of how purchasing power parity affects exchange rate expectations.

Part 4: Commercial Banking.   Although the basic functions of commercial banks have not changed, the environment has been dramatically altered. **Chapter 13** has been completely updated and revised to reflect recent changes in the banking industry resulting from the financial crisis of 2007–2009. The chapter also incorporates coverage of bank earnings and performance previously included in the old Chapter 14 (tenth edition), "Bank Management and Profitability." Chapter 13 now provides comprehensive coverage of commercial bank operations and how those functions are reflected in a bank's financial statements in a single chapter. Remaining material on interest rate risk from the old Chapter 14 (tenth edition) is now part of a new chapter on risk management (Chapter 20 in the eleventh edition). **Chapter 14 (eleventh edition)** covers the role that banks play in the international financial system. The chapter updates the overseas operations of U.S. banks, foreign banking activities in the U.S., international banking trends, and U.S. international banking regulations. We also discuss cross-border bank mergers in the European Union countries and their impact on international banking markets. **Chapter 15** focuses on the regulation of financial institutions and has been revised significantly to reflect the aftermath of the financial crisis of 2007–2009. New to the chapter are discussions of the events leading up to the financial crisis and the establishment of the Troubled Asset Relief Program (TARP). Chapter 15 also discusses the *too-big-to-fail* issue, safety and soundness regulation, and the intent behind the Dodd-Frank Wall Street Reform and Consumer Protection Act of 2010. It also includes thorough discussions of recent bank failures, bailouts, moral hazard, and deposit insurance reform.

Part 5: Financial Institutions.   In addition to contextual updates, the chapters in Part 5 discuss the headline-grabbing events associated with the financial meltdown, including the Madoff scandal and the failures of Lehman Brothers, Bear Stearns, AIG, and Merrill Lynch. It also explains policy makers' decisions to save some institutions, while letting others fail. **Chapter 16** discusses thrift institutions and finance companies. The chapter was updated and revised to reflect recent changes in those industries. Where appropriate, the chapter has been shortened and streamlined for readability. **Chapter 17** on insurance companies and pension funds has been revised to reflect the role of the insurance industry in the financial crisis. In particular, the near-bankruptcy and subsequent bailout of American International Group (AIG), one of the largest insurers in the world, is thoroughly discussed. AIG's huge exposure to credit default swaps was potentially pivotal to the survival of the entire financial system. Also discussed are the major changes in the health insurance industry resulting from the 2010 Patient Protection and Affordable Care Act (so-called Obamacare). Quantitative examples addressing insurance company capital and profitability were added to the chapter. **Chapter 18** is about investment banks. During the financial crisis of 2007–2009 investment banks were "forced" (or "pressured") to adopt commercial bank charters and come under the regulation of the Federal Reserve System. The chapter chronicles these events. The chapter offers a new section on private equity firms and an expanded discussion of investment banks' proprietary trading and asset management operations, broker-dealer functions, and prime brokerage functions. **Chapter 19** on investment companies had a major reorganization with greater focus on the most important investment companies—open-end mutual funds and exchange-traded funds. We also incorporated into the discussions Morningstar Equity Style and Debt Style boxes. The chapter also expands treatment of hedge funds. **Chapter 20** "Risk Management in Financial Institutions" is a new chapter that incorporates some elements from the old Chapter 14 (tenth edition), "Bank Management and Profitability," with material on liquidity, credit, and interest rate risks. Chapter 20 also discusses the tradeoff between profits and risk faced by financial institutions. The chapter also includes an in-depth discussion of managing credit risk at the individual loan level and the loan portfolio level. It explains credit derivatives and how they are used.

KEEPING THE ATTIC CLEAN

Like an old house, a book entering its eleventh edition accumulates clutter. In the eleventh edition, we continue the process of thoughtfully "cleaning out the attic." With help from many of you, we continue to review all materials and retain only what we believe essential for students. We appreciate your comments and suggestions.

We organized this book to reflect a balanced approach to both financial markets and institutions, which reflects a typical course outline. However, depending on individual preference and course emphasis, there are alternative ways to organize the course, and our book is written to allow for a reorganization of the chapters for professors who wish to give primary focus to either institutions or markets. The only suggested constraint in our flexible design is that Parts 1 and 2 should be assigned first, because they provide the conceptual foundation and vocabulary for the financial system regardless of subsequent topic emphasis. The following

ORGANIZATION OF THE BOOK

diagram shows the balanced approach and an alternative sequence that emphasizes financial institutions:

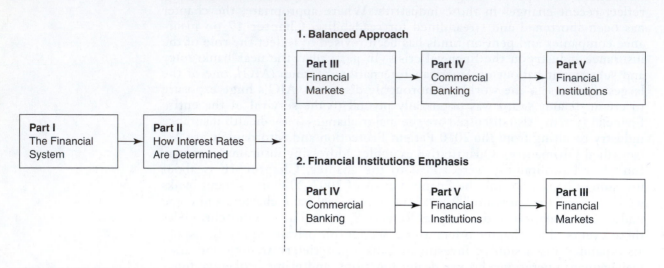

ANCILLARY PACKAGE

In the eleventh edition, we offer updated ancillary materials that will help both the students and the instructors optimize learning and teaching.

INSTRUCTOR'S MANUAL

Prepared by Vladimir Kotomin of Illinois State University, the Instructor's Manual contains a wealth of useful teaching aids, including chapter-by-chapter learning objectives, key points and concepts, answers to end-of-chapter questions and problems, and an outline of changes from the previous edition.

TEST BANK

Prepared by Wan-Jiun P. Chiou of Shippensburg University of Pennsylvania, the Test Bank, which includes at least 75 examination questions per chapter and has been updated to reflect the textbook's greater emphasis on numeric problems. It consists of true/false, multiple choice, and essay-type questions. A *Computerized Test Bank* is also available which consists of content from the Test Bank provided within a test-generating program that allows instructors to customize their exams.

POWERPOINT PRESENTATIONS

The PowerPoint presentations have been updated by Deniz K. Tudor of San Francisco State University so they reflect the updates within this revision. These chapter presentations are available on the companion website. The presentation for each chapter provides bulleted lecture notes and figures, tables, and graphs selected from the text, ready for classroom presentation. Instructors with the full version of PowerPoint have the ability to customize the lectures to reflect their personal course notes.

STUDY GUIDE

Lanny R. Martindale of Texas A&M University has revised the Study Guide to reflect the revisions made to the eleventh edition. Students will find this tool to be a valuable part of the learning package as they learn using this text. Each chapter provides a detailed chapter overview and list of learning objectives; topic outline; key terms review; completion, true/false, and multiple-choice questions; problems; and annotated solutions. Each chapter also includes a short Career Planning section designed to encourage students to begin thinking about their careers. There is a special Supplementary Material section that expands and applies each chapter's concepts to the real world by providing library references and assignments and flow-of-funds data analysis assignments. In addition, each of the early chapters features a How to Use the *Wall Street Journal* section intended to acquaint students with the organization of the *WSJ*. In later chapters, specific sections, data tables, and other features that pertain to specific chapters, such as futures and options, are discussed in the appropriate chapters.

STUDENT PRACTICE QUIZZES

Brand new Student Practice Quizzes have been prepared by Lanny R. Martindale of Texas A&M University to help students evaluate their individual progress throughout the chapter. Each quiz contains 15 multiple choice questions of varying difficulty so students can review key concepts and build test taking confidence chapter by chapter.

WEBSITE MATERIALS

A companion website for this text is located at www.wiley.com/college/kidwell. Here you can find the resources listed above as well as answers to the Do You Understand? questions found in each of the chapters of the text. There are additional supplemental materials available on the companion website as well. First is a chapter titled "History of the Financial System," which long-time users of the book will recall from previous editions. Second, the website contains technical notes on the deposit expansion process for instructors who wish to go into more detail about how to measure changes in the money supply resulting from Fed policy actions.

ACKNOWLEDGMENTS

As with any textbook, the authors, owe an enormous debt of gratitude to many people. First, we thank the reviewers who have contributed valuable suggestions for this eleventh edition:

Deanne Butchey, Florida International University
Wan-Jiun P. Chiou, Shippensburg University
Kenneth Daniels, Virginia Commonwealth University
Susan Flaherty, Towson University
Deniz K. Tudor, San Francisco State University
John Stansfield, University of Missouri
Ralph E. Steuer, University of Georgia

We also appreciate the many thoughtful comments we have received from reviewers over the previous ten editions. Although their names are too numerous to list here, we are nonetheless grateful for their efforts and credit them with helping the book to remain a success.

At John Wiley & Sons, we are grateful to Jennifer Manias, Senior Content Editor, who provided many helpful suggestions and much support, guidance, and motivation. We also applaud the efforts of Erica Horowitz, Editorial Assistant, for her diligence in guiding the manuscript through the production process. In addition, we appreciate the efforts of the other members of the Wiley team: Maureen Eide, who coordinated the design and layout of the book; and Valerie Vargas and Trish McFadden who performed superbly as senior production editors. We especially appreciate the strong contributions of our copy editor, Marianne L'Abbate of Double Daggers Editing Services, and the project manager, Jackie Henry of Aptara, who guided us through the final stages of production.

We gratefully acknowledge those who assisted us in revising and updating several of the book's key chapters. Each of these colleagues from the finance profession provided us with specialized expertise in their areas of teaching and research that keeps the book on the cutting edge: Vladimir Kotomin, Illinois State University (Chapters 7 and 8); Wei (Wendy) Liu, Texas A&M University (Chapters 12 and 14); and Mike McNamara, Washington State University (Chapter 17). Wendy Liu also substantially revised and improved the end of chapter key terms and the glossary. We also appreciate the efforts of those who assisted us with research and manuscript preparation: Babu Baradwaj, Chen Chen, Petra Kubalova, and Wenling Lu.

Finally, and most importantly, we thank our families and loved ones for their encouragement and for tolerating our many hours at the writing table. To all, thank you for your support and help.

David S. Kidwell
Minneapolis, Minnesota
david@dskidwell.com

David W. Blackwell
College Station, Texas
dblackwell@mays.tamu.edu

David A. Whidbee
Pullman, Washington
whidbee@wsu.edu

Richard W. Sias
Tucson, Arizona
sias@eller.arizona.edu

ABOUT THE AUTHORS

DAVID S. KIDWELL

Dr. David S. Kidwell is Professor of Finance and Dean Emeritus at the Curtis L. Carlson School of Management at the University of Minnesota. He holds an undergraduate degree in mechanical engineering from California State University at San Diego, an MBA from California State University at San Francisco, and a PhD in finance from the University of Oregon.

Before joining the University of Minnesota, Dr. Kidwell was Dean of the School of Business Administration at the University of Connecticut. Prior to joining the University of Connecticut, he held endowed chairs in banking and finance at Tulane University, the University of Tennessee, and Texas Tech University. He was also on the faculty at the Krannert Graduate School of Management, Purdue University, where he was twice voted the outstanding undergraduate teacher of the year. Dr. Kidwell has published research in the leading journals, including *Journal of Finance, Journal of Financial Economics, Journal of Financial and Quantitative Analysis, Financial Management,* and *Journal of Money, Credit, and Banking.*

Dr. Kidwell has been a management consultant for Coopers & Lybrand and a sales engineer for Bethlehem Steel Corporation. He is an expert on the U.S. financial system and is the author of more than 80 articles dealing with the U.S. financial system and capital markets. Dr. Kidwell has participated in a number of research grants funded by the National Science Foundation to study the efficiency of U.S. capital markets, and to study the impact of government regulations upon the delivery of consumer financial services.

Dr. Kidwell served on the board of the Schwan Food Company. He is the past secretary-treasurer of the board of directors of AACSB, the International Association for Management Education. He is a past member of the boards of the Minnesota Council for Quality, the Stonier Graduate School of Banking, and the Minnesota Center for Corporate Responsibility. He has also served as an examiner for the 1995 Malcolm Baldrige National Quality Award, on the board of directors of the Juran Center for Leadership in Quality, and on the board of the Minnesota Life Insurance Company.

DAVID W. BLACKWELL

Dr. David W. Blackwell is the James W. Aston/RepublicBank Professor of Finance and Associate Dean for Graduate Programs at Texas A&M University's Mays Business School. Prior to joining Texas A&M, Dr. Blackwell worked several years as a consultant with PricewaterhouseCoopers LLP and KPMG LLP. Before his stint in the Big 4, Dr. Blackwell served on the faculties of the University of Georgia, the University of Houston, and Emory University. He was also a visiting professor at the University of Rochester.

Dr. Blackwell's areas of expertise include corporate finance, commercial bank management, and executive compensation. His publications have appeared in the leading scholarly journals of finance and accounting such as *Journal of Finance*, *Journal of Financial Economics*, *Journal of Financial and Quantitative Analysis*, *Financial Management*, *Journal of Financial Research*, *Journal of Accounting Research*, and *Journal of Accounting and Economics*.

While in the Big 4, Dr. Blackwell consulted on a broad range of litigation matters including securities, breach of contract, and intellectual property infringement cases. He also consulted on matters involving securities and business valuation, corporate governance, and executive compensation. In addition, Dr. Blackwell has delivered executive education seminars in corporate finance and management of financial institutions for Halliburton, IBM, Kaiser Permanente, Chemical Bank, Southwire Company, Georgia Bankers Association, Warsaw Institute of Banking, Bratislava Institute of Banking, and the People's Construction Bank of China (PRC).

Dr. Blackwell earned his PhD in finance in 1986 and his BS in economics in 1981, both from the University of Tennessee, Knoxville. He is a past president of the Southern Finance Association, and a former associate editor of the *Journal of Financial Research*.

DAVID A. WHIDBEE

Dr. David A. Whidbee is an associate professor of finance and the Associate Dean for Faculty Affairs and Research in the College of Business at Washington State University. He received his PhD in Finance from the University of Georgia and his MBA and BS in finance from Auburn University. Dr. Whidbee has worked as a financial analyst in the Chief Economist's Office at the Federal Home Loan Bank Board and, subsequently, the Office of Thrift Supervision (OTS). While on the staff at these regulatory agencies, he performed research and analysis on the thrift industry and prepared congressional testimony concerning the problems the industry faced in the late 1980s.

In 1994, he joined the faculty at California State University, Sacramento, where he taught commercial banking and financial markets and institutions. In 1997, he left Cal State Sacramento to join the faculty at Washington State University, where he continues to teach commercial banking and financial markets and institutions. Dr. Whidbee's primary research interests are in the areas of financial institutions and corporate governance. His work has been published in several outlets, including the *Review of Financial Studies*, *Journal of Business*, *Journal of Accounting and Economics*, *Journal of Banking and Finance*, *Journal of Corporate Finance*, *Financial Management*, the *Financial Analysts Journal*, and the *Journal of Financial Services Research*. In addition, he has presented his research at numerous academic and regulatory conferences.

RICHARD W. SIAS

Dr. Richard W. Sias is the Tyler Family Chair in Finance and head of the Department of Finance at the Eller College of Management at the University of Arizona. He holds an undergraduate degree in finance, insurance and real estate from California State University, Sacramento, and a PhD in finance from the University of Texas. Prior to joining the Eller College, Dr. Sias served as the Gary P. Brinson Chair of Investment Management at Washington State University. He has also taught courses at Bond University in Australia and Cesar Ritz College in Switzerland.

Dr. Sias's research interests primarily focus on investments. He currently serves on the Editorial Board of the Financial Analysts Journal and has published numerous articles in the leading finance journals, including the *Journal of Financial Economics, Journal of Finance, Review of Financial Studies, Journal of Business, Financial Analysts Journal, Journal of Banking and Finance, Journal of Investment Management, Financial Review, Journal of Financial Research, Journal of Business Research, Review of Quantitative Finance and Accounting, Journal of Investing, and Advances in Futures and Options Research.*

Dr. Sias has also garnered a number of teaching and research awards and is member of the CFA Institute's Approved Speakers List, which provides him an opportunity to link his academic work with portfolio management in practice. In addition, Dr. Sias's work has been the focus of a number of popular press outlets, including articles in *Forbes, U.S. News and World Report,* and the *New York Times.*

CONTENTS

COMMERCIAL BANKING   403

PART IV

P A R T   I

THE FINANCIAL SYSTEM

CHAPTER ONE

An Overview of Financial Markets and Institutions

THIS BOOK IS ABOUT THE financial system, which consists of financial markets and institutions. The basic role of the financial system is to gather money from individuals and businesses that have more money than they need and route these funds to those who need money now. Businesses need money to invest in productive assets to expand their business, and consumers have a myriad of items they buy on credit, such as automobiles, personal computers, and iPhones. Money is the lubricant that makes an industrial economy run smoothly. Without money, the numerous financial transactions that businesses and consumers take for granted would grind to a halt.

Banks are a critical player in the financial system. Banks provide a place where individuals and businesses can invest their money to earn interest at low risk. Banks take these funds and redeploy them by making loans to individuals and businesses. Banks are singled out for special treatment by regulators and economists because most of what we call money in the economy is represented by deposits and checking accounts issued by banks. Thus, banks are the principal caretaker of the payment system because most purchases are paid by writing a check or making an online payment against a bank account.

The financial system is like a huge money maze—funds flow to borrowers from lenders through many different routes at warp speed. The larger and more efficient the flow, the greater the economic output and welfare of the economy.

The most powerful institutional player in the financial system is the Federal Reserve System (called the Fed). Its powers come from the Fed's role as the country's central bank—the institution that controls the nation's money supply. The Fed's primary responsibility is to stabilize the economy by conducting monetary policy by managing the money supply and interest rates.

Finally, the financial system is of great interest to politicians and government officials. Its health has a major impact on our economic well-being. The collapse of the financial system can be the harbinger of a recession or worse. A case in point is the 2008 financial crisis and near collapse of the global financial system that resulted in the most severe economic recession since the Great Depression of the 1930s. This book is your road map to understanding the financial system and the many financial issues that will affect your personal and professional life. ∎

Chapter 1 presents an overview of the financial system and how it facilitates the allocation of money throughout the economy. The chapter begins by describing the role of the financial system, defining surplus and deficit spending units, and describing characteristics of financial claims. It then explains how surplus and deficit spending units are brought together directly in financial markets or indirectly with the help of financial intermediaries. The chapter then identifies the types of financial institutions and markets that exist in the United States and the benefits they provide to the economy. We then discuss the five key risks faced by financial institutions: credit risk, interest rate risk, liquidity risk, foreign exchange risk, and political risk. The chapter closes with a high-level discussion of the regulation of the financial system.

LEARNING OBJECTIVES

1 Explain the role of the financial system and why it is important to individuals and to the economy as a whole.

2 Explain the ways that funds are transferred between surplus spending units (SSUs) and deficit spending units (DSUs).

3 Discuss the major differences between money and capital markets.

4 Explain the concept of informational asymmetry and the problem it presents to lenders.

5 Identify the major risks that financial institutions must manage.

6 Discuss the two main reasons that the financial sector is so highly regulated.

1.1 THE FINANCIAL SYSTEM

The financial system consists of *financial markets* and *financial institutions*. **Financial markets** are just like any market you have seen before, where people buy and sell different types of goods and haggle over prices. Financial markets can be informal, such as a flea market in your community, or highly organized, such as the gold markets in London or Zurich. The only difference is that, in financial markets, people buy and sell financial instruments such as stocks, bonds, and futures contracts rather than pots and pans. Financial market transactions can involve huge dollar amounts and can be incredibly risky. The dramatic changes in fortunes that occur from time to time because of large price swings make financial markets newsworthy.

Financial institutions are firms such as commercial banks, credit unions, insurance companies, pension funds, mutual funds, and finance companies that provide financial services to consumers, businesses, and government units. The distinguishing feature of these firms is that they invest their funds in financial assets, such as business loans, stocks, or bonds, rather than in real assets, such as manufacturing facilities and equipment. Financial institutions dominate the financial system worldwide, providing an array of financial services to large multinational firms and most of the financial services used by consumers and small businesses. Overall, financial institutions are far more important sources of financing than securities markets.

A PREVIEW OF THE FINANCIAL SYSTEM

Let's look at an example of how the financial system gathers money and channels it to those who need money. Suppose that Bob, who is a business major, receives an $8,000 scholarship loan for college at the beginning of the school year, but he needs only $3,000 of it right away. After checking out deals at different banks, Bob decides to deposit the $8,000 in the bank near campus: $3,000 in a checking account and $5,000 in a certificate of deposit (CD) that pays 5 percent interest and matures just as the spring semester begins. (CDs are debt instruments issued by banks that pay interest and are insured by the federal government.) Bob buys the CD because the interest rate is competitive, and the maturity date matches the time when Bob has to buy books and pay his tuition.

At the same time that Bob bought his CD, the bank received a loan request from Tony, who owns a local pizza shop near campus. Tony wants to borrow $25,000 to expand his home delivery service. The interest rate on the loan is 9 percent, which is a competitive rate and payable in 5 years. The money for Tony's loan comes from Bob and other persons who recently bought CDs from the bank. After careful evaluation, the bank decides to make the loan to Tony because of his good credit rating and because it expects the pizza parlor to generate enough cash flows to repay the loan. Tony wants the loan because the additional cash flows (profits) will increase the value of his pizza parlor. During the same week, the bank made loans to other businesses whose qualifications were similar to Tony's and rejected a number of loan requests because the applicants had low credit scores or the proposed projects had low rates of return.

From this example, we can draw some important inferences about the financial system:

- If the financial system is *competitive*, the interest rate the bank pays on CDs will be at or near the highest rate that you can earn on CDs of similar maturity and risk. At the same time, the pizza parlor and other businesses will have borrowed at or near the lowest possible interest cost, given their risk class. Competition among banks for deposits will drive CD rates up and loan rates down.

- Banks and other depository institutions, such as insurance companies, gather money from consumers in small dollar amounts, aggregate it, and then make loans in much larger dollar amounts, like the loan to Tony. Savings by consumers in small dollar amounts are the origin of much of the money that funds large business loans.

- An important function of the financial system is to allocate money to the most productive investment projects in the economy. If the financial system is working properly, only projects with high-risk adjusted rates of return are funded, and those with low rates are rejected.

- Finally, banks are profit-making organizations, and the bank in our example has earned a tidy profit from the deal. The bank borrowed money at 5 percent by selling CDs and lends money to the pizza parlor and other businesses at 9 percent. Banks and other lenders earn much of their profits from the spread between lending and borrowing rates.

BUDGET POSITION

Let's look in more detail at how money is channeled from lenders to borrowers. We begin with some basic facts.

In any economy, all economic units can be classified into one of four groups: (1) households, (2) business firms, (3) governments (local, state, and federal), and (4) foreign investors (nondomestic households, businesses, and government units). Each type of unit has different income sources and spending patterns. And just like you, every economic unit must operate within a budget constraint imposed by the unit's total income for the period. For a budget period such as a year, an economic unit can have one of three budget positions:

1. A *balanced budget*: Income and expenditures are equal.
2. A *surplus budget*: Income for the period exceeds expenses; these economic units have money to lend and are called **surplus spending units (SSUs)**.
3. A *deficit budget*: Expenditures for the period exceed revenues; these economic units need to borrow money and are called **deficit spending units (DSUs)**.

Households are the principal SSUs in the economy, but some businesses, state and local governments, and foreign investors and their governments periodically run surplus budgets. Taken as a group, businesses are the principal DSUs in the economy, followed by the federal government, but households, state and local governments, and foreigners at times borrow money to finance their purchases of homes, automobiles, and high-definition television sets.

FINANCIAL CLAIMS

One problem facing the financial system is the mechanism to transfer funds from SSUs to DSUs. Fortunately, the solution is simple. The transfer can be accomplished by the DSU writing out an IOU that the SSU is willing to accept. An IOU is a written promise to pay a specific sum of money (called the principal) plus a fee for the use of the money (called interest) and to have the use of the money over a period of time (called the maturity of the loan).

Promises to pay are called IOUs only in Western cowboy movies. In the real world, IOUs are called **financial claims**. They are claims against someone else's money at a future date. Financial claims also go by different names, such as *securities* or *financial instruments*; the names are interchangeable. Finally, note that financial claims (IOUs) are liabilities for borrowers (DSUs) and are simultaneously assets for lenders (SSUs), which illustrates the two faces of debt. That is, total financial liabilities outstanding in the economy must equal total financial assets.

HOW FUNDS FLOW THROUGH THE FINANCIAL SYSTEM

In the financial system, how does money move from SSUs (whose income exceeds their spending) to DSUs (whose spending exceeds their income)? The arrows in Exhibit 1.1 show schematically that there are two basic mechanisms by which

EXHIBIT 1.1
Transfer of Funds from Surplus to Deficit Spending Units

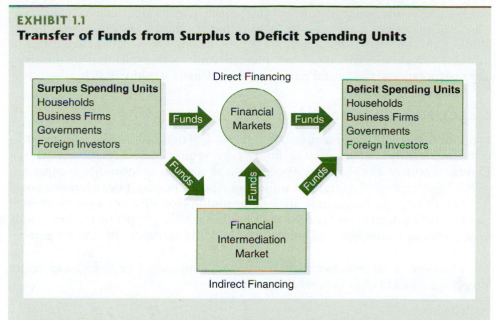

The role of the financial system—financial institutions and markets—is to facilitate the flow and efficient allocation of funds throughout the economy. The greater the flow of funds, the greater the accommodation of individuals' preferences for spending and saving. An efficient and sound financial system is a necessary condition to having a highly advanced economy like the one in the United States.

funds flow through the financial system: (1) **direct financing**, where funds flow directly through *financial markets* (the route at the top of the diagram), and (2) **indirect financing** (financial intermediation), where funds flow indirectly through *financial institutions* in the financial intermediation market (the route at the bottom of the diagram). The reason that financial institutions are often called **financial intermediaries** is because they are middlemen, facilitating transactions between SSUs and DSUs.

Regardless of the financing method, the goal is to bring the parties together at the least possible cost and with the least inconvenience. An *efficient financial system* is important because it ensures adequate capital formation for economic growth. Thus, if the financial system works properly, firms with the most promising investment opportunities receive funds, and those with inferior opportunities receive no funding. In a similar manner, consumers who can pay the current market rate of interest can purchase cars, boats, vacations, and homes on credit—and thus have them now rather than waiting until they have the money.

1.2 FINANCIAL MARKETS AND DIRECT FINANCING

Financial markets perform the important function of channeling funds from people who have surplus funds (SSUs) to businesses (DSUs) that need money. The top route in Exhibit 1.1 shows the flow of funds for direct financing. In direct financing, DSUs borrow money *directly* from SSUs in financial markets by selling them securities in exchange for money. Typical financial instruments bought and sold in the direct financial markets are stocks and bonds.

For most large business firms, direct financial markets are wholesale markets in which the minimum transaction size is $1 million or more. These markets provide funds at the lowest possible cost. The major buyers and sellers of securities in the direct financial markets are commercial banks, other financial institutions, large corporations, the federal government, and some wealthy individuals.

DIRECT FINANCING EXAMPLE

Suppose that Apple Computer (a DSU) needs $20 million to build a new manufacturing facility and decides to fund it by selling long-term bonds with a 15-year maturity. Let's say that Apple contacts a group of insurance companies, which have expressed an interest in buying Apple's bonds. The insurance companies will buy the bonds only after determining that they are a sound investment and are priced fairly for their credit risk. Likewise, Apple will sell its bonds to the insurance companies only after shopping the market to be sure it's getting a fair deal.

The flow of funds between the insurance companies (the SSUs) and Apple Computer (the DSU) is shown below:

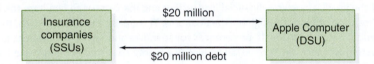

As you can see, Apple sells its bonds to the insurance group for $20 million and then gets to use the money for 15 years. For the use of the money, Apple pays the bondholders interest because the bonds are a liability. For the insurance companies, the bonds are an asset that pays interest to them.

OVERVIEW OF INVESTMENT BANKING

Two important players that deliver critical services in the direct credit markets are investment banking firms and large money center banks. **Investment banks** are firms that specialize in helping businesses sell *new* debt or equity in the financial markets. In addition, once the securities are sold, they provide a variety of broker-dealer services (buying and selling securities) for securities that have already been issued. Historically, the largest and most powerful investment banks were located in the Wall Street area of Manhattan in New York City. They are known for their willingness to take risk, creating new financial products through innovation, and their high executive salaries.

Money center banks are large commercial banks usually located in major financial centers who are major participants in the money markets. Some examples are Citicorp, Bank of America, and Wells Fargo Bank. These powerful firms are the flagship banks for the U.S. economy and provide funds and business loans to large multinational corporations. Money center banks are highly regulated by the Federal Reserve Bank to ensure that they take prudent risks with both their investment and loan portfolios. Money center banks may also have a large retail banking presence, providing consumers with personal and mortgage loans, checking and savings accounts, and credit cards.

HISTORICAL PERSPECTIVE

Banks have always desired to provide investment banking services to their customers and regulators, and many economists have expressed their doubts about whether banks should engage in such a risky activity. Historically, banks provided a safe haven for savings and transaction balances and they deployed these funds into business and consumer loans, taking prudent risks. Following the Great Depression, commercial banks were barred from engaging in investment banking activities. Without going into detail, the 1929 stock market crash was followed by widespread bank failures and a devastating depression. At the time, it was believed that excessive risk taking by commercial banks resulted in the large number of bank failures. Economists and politicians concluded that it was too risky for commercial banks to engage in investment banking and that the Great Depression was caused by the misbehavior of Wall Street and commercial banks. As a result, Congress passed the Glass-Steagall Act of 1933, which separated commercial banking from investment banking.

Beginning in 1999, bank regulators gradually allowed money center banks to engage in investment banking activities. There were two reasons for this change: (1) the 1990s were a period of time marked by a significant amount of deregulation in the economy and (2) recent research exonerated the banking system from being the primary culprit causing the Great Depression. By 2007, money center banks were well-established players in the investment banking markets.

INVESTMENT BANKING TODAY

In 2008, the financial system suffered a significant meltdown, which resulted in the worst financial crisis since the 1930s. The trigger point came in 2007, when banks and other mortgage lenders experienced a large number of defaults in the subprime mortgage market, which was a market for high-risk mortgage loans. These defaults caused numerous failures among banks, thrifts, and investment banks that held large portfolios of mortgage loans. The financial storm became more ominous with the failure of Bear Sterns and Lehman Brothers during 2008. Shortly thereafter, the remaining Wall Street investment banks were forced by regulators to merge with large money center banks, such as Merrill Lynch's merger with Bank of America. Goldman Sachs was forced to become a bank regulated by the Fed. The thrust of this regulatory action was to rein in excess risk taking by Wall Street investment banks and money center banks and thus stabilize them financially and reduce the risk of failures that could potentially destabilize the nation's economy.

Today, investment banking and its risk taking reside inside the banking system and are subject to strict oversight by the Federal Reserve Bank. We suspect that, sometime in the future, investment banks will reemerge as nonbank financial firms free of some of the strict banking regulations of the Fed. Because of investment banks' complicity in the 2008 market collapse, however, they will be subject to much more oversight and regulation than in the past, and their regulator will probably be the Fed. Now let's look at the types of services that investment banks provide to consumer and business firms.

INVESTMENT BANKING SERVICES

Bring New Securities to Market.   When management decides to expand a firm, they usually have a specific capital project in mind, such as building a new manufacturing facility. One important service that investment banks offer is to help firms bring their new debt or equity securities to market. There are three distinct tasks involved. First is *origination*, which is all the work necessary to prepare a security issue for sale. During the origination, the investment banker may also help the client determine the feasibility of a capital project and the amount of money that must be raised. Second is *underwriting*, which is the process whereby an investment banker helps a firm sell its new security issue in the direct financial markets. The most common type of underwriting arrangement is called a *firm commitment*. In a firm commitment deal, the investment banker assumes the risk of buying a new issue of securities from the issuing corporation at a guaranteed price. The guaranteed price is important to the issuer because the corporation needs a certain amount of money to pay for the investment project, and anything less than this amount is a serious problem. Finally, *distribution* occurs immediately after the securities are bought from the issuer and is the marketing and sales of securities to institutional and individual investors.

Trading and Brokerage Services.   Once financial claims have been issued, they may be resold to other investors in an aftermarket or a *secondary market*. There are two types of market participants that facilitate these transactions. **Brokers** help bring buyers and sellers together, acting as "matchmakers" and, if a sale takes place, they receive a commission for their services. Also note that brokers never own the securities they trade (buy or sell).

In contrast, **dealers** "make markets" for securities by carrying an inventory of securities from which they stand ready to either buy or sell at quoted prices. Dealers make profits by trading from their inventory *and* as a matchmaker. Most large investment banks have a significant portion of their overall business devoted to "brokerage" activities, with some part focused on wholesale sales to large institutional investors and another part devoted to retail sales devoted to consumers and small businesses.

HOW CONSUMERS ACCESS FINANCIAL MARKETS

Except for the wealthy, individuals do not participate in the direct financial markets because of their wholesale nature. That is, the transaction amounts are simply too large ($1 million or more) for most people to handle. Direct market participants are seasoned professionals who make their living trading in these markets, and most of us would be no match for them in making a deal. Individuals gain access to the financial markets indirectly by transacting with financial intermediaries, such as commercial banks or mutual funds, or through retail channels with investment banking firms.

DO YOU UNDERSTAND?

1. What is the role of the financial system?
2. What are financial claims?
3. Explain what is meant by the term *direct financing*.
4. What are investment banks, and what services do they provide?

Wall Street Faces Global Competition

Wall Street is the fabled financial district in New York City that is headquarters to some of the world's most powerful financial institutions, including Citigroup, JPMorgan Chase, Morgan Stanley, Merrill Lynch, and Goldman Sachs.[1] These firms, along with the financial markets centered in Manhattan—such as the New York Stock Exchange—do billions of dollars worth of business daily, making New York City the most important financial center in the world.

Recently, however, there has been some concern among U.S. politicians and business executives that Wall Street may be losing its grip on the world's financial markets. The first major shock was in 2005, when the European corporate debt market surpassed the U.S. debt market. The following year, the European market for initial public offerings surpassed the U.S. market. Then in 2008, the subprime market for mortgages collapsed, triggering a chain of events that resulted in a meltdown of global credit markets and a deep recession, the severity of which hadn't been seen since the 1930s. Much of the blame—fair or unfair—for the financial debacle fell on these Wall Street financial giants. Many felt that excessive risk taking and poor judgment led to the collapse of the financial system. Their industry leadership was in question.

Although most agree that Wall Street's preeminence is slipping, there are sharply different views regarding the causes and what, if anything, can be done to correct the problem. Some argue that government regulations have put Wall Street at a competitive disadvantage compared to European investment banks. Recently, for example, the high cost of compliance with the Sarbanes–Oxley legislation and with the Securities and Exchange Commission's (SEC's) mandated disclosure requirement are driving firms out of the U.S. capital markets. These and the passage of the Regulatory Reform Act of 2010 are driving the cost of doing business on Wall Street to intolerable levels, costing the typical firm millions of dollars per year. Many medium and small firms have abandoned the U.S. capital markets. This line of reasoning suggests that the solution to the problem is for Washington to lighten the regulatory and legal cost burdens so the playing field is level between U.S. and European investment banks. This argument is not compelling. Though regulatory cost arguments may be true in the short run, we find it highly unlikely that over the long term Washington will allow a major industry to wither away because of a negative regulatory differential.

We believe that there are more fundamental economic forces at work that may be difficult to alter in the short run. We believe that Wall Street's decline is part of a long-term trend of globalization and integration of the world's economies. Technological innovation has made information and capital more mobile and, as a result, investors are less concerned about where their trades and deals are done, as long as the price is right and the execution meets expectations. In addition, developing countries are industrializing rapidly and becoming wealthier; rather than transacting deals in the United States, they conduct them in emerging financial centers at home or in financial centers closer to home. For example, many Russian deals now happen in London, and Chinese deals are happening in Hong Kong. To overcome the slide, Wall Street must meet the competition with new and innovative financial products and become a thought leader in the applications of finance and technology. The federal government's role is to create a safe and sound financial system that is transparent and treats participants—buyers or sellers—fairly.

---

[1]As a result of the September 11, 2001, attack, most firms, for safety, redundancy, and reduction of risk from terrorism, no longer are headquartered in a single location. Most have executive and financial sales offices dispersed in the Wall Street and midtown areas of Manhattan. There is a trend to move information technology facilities out of Manhattan to several and diverse locations, such as New Jersey, Pennsylvania, and Connecticut.

1.3 TYPES OF FINANCIAL MARKETS

As one would expect, many different types of financial claims are issued in the primary markets by financial intermediaries and other economic units such as the federal government and large corporations. And it is no surprise that these claims are bought and sold in a large number of markets. In this and the following sections, we shall briefly describe the different types of financial markets and the more important financial instruments.

PRIMARY AND SECONDARY MARKETS

Financial claims are initially sold by DSUs in **primary markets**. All financial claims have primary markets. An example of a primary market transaction is IBM Corporation raising external funds through the sale of new stock or bonds.

People are more likely to purchase a primary financial claim if they believe they will not have to hold it forever (in the case of most common stock) or until its maturity date (in the case of bonds). **Secondary markets** are like used-car markets; they let people exchange "used" or previously issued financial claims for cash at will. Secondary markets provide liquidity for investors who own primary claims. Securities can be sold only once in a primary market; all subsequent transactions take place in secondary markets. The New York Stock Exchange (NYSE) is an example of a well-known secondary market.

Marketability.   An important characteristic of a security to investors is its marketability. **Marketability** is the ease with which a security can be sold and converted into cash. A security's marketability depends in part on the cost of trading and the search for information. The lower these costs, the greater a security's marketability. Because secondary markets make it easier to sell securities, their presence increases a security's marketability.

Liquidity.   A term closely related to marketability is **liquidity**. Liquidity is the ability to convert an asset into cash quickly without loss of value. In common usage, the two terms are often used interchangeably, but they are different. Liquidity implies that when a security is sold, its value will be preserved. Marketability does not carry this implication.

EXCHANGE AND OVER-THE-COUNTER MARKETS

Once issued, a financial claim (security) can be traded in the secondary market on an organized security exchange, such as the NYSE. Trades made through an exchange are usually made on the floor of the exchange or through its computer system. Organized security exchanges provide a physical meeting place and communication facilities for members to conduct their transactions under a specific set of rules and regulations. Only members of the exchange may use the facilities, and only securities listed on the exchange may be traded. The NYSE is the largest securities exchange for stocks. The Chicago Board of Trade (CBOT) and the Chicago Mercantile Exchange (CME) are the largest futures exchanges.

Securities not listed on an exchange are bought and sold in the **over-the-counter (OTC) market**. The OTC market differs from organized exchanges because the market has no central trading place. Instead, investors can execute OTC transactions by visiting or telephoning an OTC dealer or by using a computer-based electronic trading system linked to the OTC dealer. Traditional stocks traded over the counter have been those of small and relatively unknown firms, most of which would not qualify to be listed on a major exchange. However, electronic trading has become much more important in recent years, and many OTC stocks are issued by high-profile firms, especially technology firms.

PUBLIC AND PRIVATE MARKETS

Public markets are organized financial markets where securities registered with the Securities and Exchange Commission (SEC) are bought and sold. Public markets are highly regulated by the SEC to ensure that investors are treated fairly and that issuers fully disclose an investment's risk. Public markets are also wholesale markets where the transaction sizes are $1 million or more. Individual investors gain access to public markets through the retail division of commercial and investment banks. An example of a public market transaction is buying or selling of stock through your broker on the New York Stock Exchange.

The SEC has broad responsibility for overseeing the securities industry and it regulates all primary and secondary markets where securities are traded. Its primary regulatory responsibility is to protect investors of modest means from unscrupulous investment practices. Thus, the SEC focuses on ensuring that investors receive timely and accurate information and that the investment's risk is fully disclosed. The SEC offers no protection from investing in a bad deal or poor investment judgment as long as the investment's risk has been accurately disclosed. Most corporations want access to the public markets because they are wholesale markets where issuers can sell their securities at wholesale pricing, resulting in the lowest possible funding cost. The downside for corporations selling in the public markets is the high cost of complying with SEC regulations and the public information hassle that goes with it.

In contrast to public markets, a private market involves direct transactions between two parties. There is very little regulation in the private markets compared to public market transactions. Transactions in private markets are called **private placements**. Investors in the private markets are considered sophisticated investors and require little protection or have the means to hire adequate investment counsel. In private markets, a company contacts investors directly and negotiates a deal to sell them the entire security issue. Larger firms may be equipped to handle these transactions themselves. Smaller firms are more likely to use the services of an investment bank, which helps to locate investors, negotiate the deal, and handle the legal aspects of the transaction. Major advantages of a private placement are the speed at which funds can be raised and the low transaction costs. The disadvantage is that privately placed securities cannot legally be sold in the public markets because they lack SEC registration. As a result, private placement securities are less marketable than a comparable registered security.

FUTURES AND OPTIONS MARKETS

Markets also exist for trading in futures and options. Perhaps the best known futures markets are the New York Board of Trade and the Chicago Board of Trade. The Chicago Board Options Exchange is a major options market. Futures and options are often called *derivative securities* because they derive their value from some underlying asset. Futures contracts are contracts for the future delivery of assets such as securities, foreign currencies, interest rates, and commodities. Corporations use these contracts to reduce (hedge) risk exposure caused by fluctuation in interest rates, foreign exchange rates, or commodity prices. Options contracts call for one party (the option writer) to perform a specific act if called on to do so by the option buyer or owner. Options contracts, like futures contracts, can be used to hedge risk. Futures and options contracts are discussed in more detail in Chapter 11.

FOREIGN EXCHANGE MARKETS

The foreign exchange market is the market in which foreign currencies are bought and sold. Foreign currencies such as the British pound, the Japanese yen, the euro, and the Swiss franc are traded against the U.S. dollar or are traded against other foreign currencies. Foreign currencies are traded either for spot or forward delivery over the counter at large commercial banks or investment banking firms. Futures contracts for foreign currencies are traded on organized exchanges such as the Chicago Mercantile Exchange. The spot market is where currency, commodities, or financial instruments are sold for cash and delivered immediately. In contrast, forward markets are where dealers agree to deliver these financial claims at a fixed price at a future date.

INTERNATIONAL AND DOMESTIC MARKETS

Financial markets can be classified as either domestic or international markets depending on where they are located. Important international financial markets for U.S. firms are the short-term Eurodollar market and the long-term Eurobond market. In these markets, domestic or overseas firms can borrow or lend large amounts of U.S. dollars that have been deposited in overseas banks. These markets are closely linked to the U.S. money and capital markets.

1.4 THE MONEY MARKETS

Money markets are markets in which commercial banks and other businesses adjust their liquidity position by borrowing, lending, or investing for short periods of time. The Federal Reserve System conducts monetary policy in the money markets, and the U.S. Treasury uses them to finance its day-to-day operations. Also, in the money markets, businesses, governments, and sometimes individuals borrow or lend funds for short periods of time—from 1 to 120 days. Exhibit 1.2 shows the amount of various money market securities outstanding.

EXHIBIT 1.2
Major Money Market Instruments Outstanding (December 2010)

Instrument	$ billions
U.S. Treasury bills	1,772.5
Short-term municipal securities	129.3
Large, negotiable CDs	1,656.3
Commercial paper	1,050.5
Federal funds and security repurchase agreements	1,313.4

Money market instruments have maturities of less than 1 year, active secondary markets, and low default risk. Business firms and wealthy individuals use money market instruments to adjust their liquidity positions.

Source: Board of Governors, Federal Reserve System, Flow of Funds Accounts; Monthly Statement of the Public Debt of the United States.

The money market consists of a collection of markets, each trading a distinctly different financial instrument. In the simplest terms, the money markets are a wholesale market ($1 million) for financial claims that have characteristics very similar to money. Money market instruments typically have short maturities (usually 90 days or less), are highly liquid (active secondary markets), and have low risk of default. There is no formal organized exchange, such as the New York Stock Exchange, for the money markets. Central to the activity of the money markets are the dealers and brokers who specialize in one or more money market instruments. The major money market instruments are discussed below.

TREASURY BILLS

Treasury bills are direct obligations of the U.S. government and thus are considered to have no default risk. They are sold weekly and have maturities that range from 3 months to 1 year. Financial institutions, corporations, and individuals buy these securities for their liquidity and safety of principal.

NEGOTIABLE CERTIFICATES OF DEPOSIT

Negotiable certificates of deposit (NCDs) are large-denomination time deposits of the nation's largest commercial banks. Unlike other time deposits of most commercial banks, NCDs may be sold in the secondary market before their maturity. Only a handful of banks sell NCDs.

COMMERCIAL PAPER

Commercial paper is the unsecured promissory note (IOU) of a large business. Commercial paper typically has maturities ranging from a few days to 120 days and does not have an active secondary market. Corporations and finance companies are the major issuers of commercial paper.

FEDERAL FUNDS

Technically, **federal funds** are bank deposits held with the Federal Reserve bank. Banks with deposits in excess of required reserves may lend those excess reserves—called *fed funds*—to other banks. The bank that acquires the fed funds may use them to cover a deficit reserve position or can use the funds to make consumer or business loans. Fed funds loans are typically for 1 day or for over a weekend. At a more practical level, you may think of the fed funds market as the market in which banks make short-term unsecured loans to one another, and the fed funds interest rate is the interbank lending rate.

1.5 THE CAPITAL MARKETS

Individuals own real assets to produce income and wealth. Thus the owner of a machine shop hopes to profit from the sale of products from the shop, and the owner of a factory hopes to earn a return from the goods produced there. Similarly, owners of apartments, office buildings, warehouses, and other tangible assets hope to earn a stream of future income by using their resources to provide services directly to consumers or to other businesses. These assets are called *capital goods*; they are the stock of assets used in production. **Capital markets** are where capital goods are financed with stock or long-term debt instruments. Compared to money market instruments, capital market instruments are less marketable; default risk levels vary widely between issuers and have maturities ranging from 5 to 30 years.

Financial institutions are the connecting link between the short-term money markets and the longer-term capital markets. These institutions, especially those that accept deposits, typically borrow short term and then invest in longer-term capital projects either indirectly through business loans or directly into capital market instruments. We will now briefly describe the major capital instruments. Exhibit 1.3 shows the amounts outstanding for selected capital market instruments.

COMMON STOCK

Common stock represents an ownership claim on a firm's assets. Also referred to as *equity securities*, stock differs from debt obligations in that equity holders have the right to share in the firm's profits. The higher the firm's net income, the higher the return to stockholders. On the other hand, stockholders must share in any of the losses that the company may incur. And in the event of bankruptcy, creditors and debt holders have first claim on the firm's assets. Most stock market transactions take place in the secondary markets.

CORPORATE BONDS

When large corporations need money for capital expenditures, they may issue bonds. **Corporate bonds** are thus long-term IOUs that represent a claim against the firm's assets. Unlike equityholders' returns, bondholders' returns are fixed;

EXHIBIT 1.3
Selected Capital Market Instruments Outstanding (December 2010)

Instrument	$ billions
U.S. government securities	
Treasury notes	5,571.7
Treasury bonds	892.6
Inflation-indexed notes and bonds	616.1
State and local government bonds	2,259.1
Corporate bonds	11,427.8
Corporate stock (at market value)	20,986.5
Mortgages	13,947.3

Capital market instruments are used to finance real assets that produce income and wealth. They are bought and sold in the direct credit markets and typically have maturities greater than 1 year. Financial institutions are the connecting link between the money and capital markets.

Source: Board of Governors, Federal Reserve System, Flow of Funds Accounts; Monthly Statement of the Public Debt of the United States.

they receive only the amount of interest that is promised plus the repayment of the principal at the end of the loan contract. Even if the corporation turns in an unexpectedly phenomenal performance, the bondholders receive only the fixed amount of interest agreed to at the bonds' issue. Corporate bonds typically have maturities from 5 to 30 years, and their secondary market is not as active as for equity securities.

MUNICIPAL BONDS

Municipal bonds are the long-term debt obligations of state and local governments. They are used to finance capital expenditures for things such as schools, highways, and airports. The most distinguishing feature of municipal bonds is that their coupon income is exempt from federal income taxes. As a result, individuals or companies that are in the highest income tax brackets purchase municipal bonds. Although the bonds of large municipalities have secondary markets, most municipal bonds have limited secondary markets and thus are not considered liquid investments.

MORTGAGES

Mortgages are long-term loans secured by real estate. They are the largest segment in the capital markets in terms of the amount outstanding. More than half of the mortgage funds go into financing family homes, with the remainder financing business property, apartments, buildings, and farm construction. Mortgages by themselves do not have good secondary markets. However, a large number of mortgages can be pooled together to form new securities called *mortgage-backed securities*, which have an active secondary market.

DO YOU UNDERSTAND?

1. What are primary and secondary markets?
2. What are private placements?
3. How do money and capital markets differ?
4. What is the over-the-counter market and how does it differ from an exchange?

1.6 FINANCIAL INTERMEDIARIES AND INDIRECT FINANCING

As we mentioned earlier, many business firms are too small to sell their debt or equity directly to investors. They have neither the expert knowledge nor the money it takes ($1 million or more) to transact in wholesale markets. When these companies need funds for capital investments or for liquidity adjustments, their only choice may be to borrow in the *indirect* market from a financial institution. These financial institutions act as intermediaries, converting financial securities with one set of characteristics into securities with another set of characteristics. The bank's conversion of Bob's CD into a loan for Tony's pizza is an example of this conversion process. This process is called financial intermediation.

In indirect financing, a financial institution—an intermediary—stands between the SSU and the DSU. This route is shown at the bottom of Exhibit 1.1. The hallmark of indirect financing is that the financial intermediary transforms financial claims in a way that makes them attractive to both the SSUs and the DSUs. For indirect financing to take place, the DSU must be willing to issue a security with a denomination, maturity, and other security characteristics that match exactly the desires of the SSU. Unless both the SSU and the DSU are satisfied simultaneously, the transfer of money will not take place.

INDIRECT FINANCING EXAMPLES

At the beginning of the chapter, we worked through an example of indirect financing. In that situation, Bob, a college student, had $5,000 to invest for 3 months. A bank sold Bob a 3-month consumer CD for $5,000, pooled this $5,000 with the proceeds from other CDs, and used the money to make small-business loans, one of which was a $25,000 loan to the pizza parlor owner. Following is a schematic diagram of that transaction:

The bank raises money by selling services such as checking accounts, savings accounts, and consumer CDs, and then uses the money to make loans to businesses or consumers.

On a larger scale, insurance companies provide much of the long-term financing in the economy through the indirect credit market. Insurance companies invest heavily in corporate bonds and equity securities using funds they receive when they sell insurance policies to individuals and businesses. Here is the schematic diagram for intermediation by an insurance company:

Notice an important difference between the indirect and direct financial markets. In the direct market, as securities flow between SSUs and DSUs, the form of the securities remains unchanged. In the indirect market, however, as securities flow between SSUs and DSUs, they are repackaged and thus their form is changed. In the example above, money from the sale of insurance policies becomes investments in corporate debt or equity. By repackaging securities, financial intermediaries tailor a wide range of financial products and services to meet the needs of consumers, small businesses, and large corporations. Their products and services are particularly important for smaller businesses that do not have access to direct financial markets.

THE ECONOMICS OF FINANCIAL INTERMEDIATION

Financial intermediaries are firms that operate to make a profit. They buy financial claims (held as assets), such as business loans, consumer installment loans, and corporate bonds from DSUs. These claims have characteristics designed to meet the needs of the DSUs that buy them. Financial intermediaries finance the purchase of these financial claims by selling financial claims (IOUs) on themselves that are held as assets by others, assets such as checking and saving accounts, life insurance policies, and mutual fund shares to SSUs. These financial claims have characteristics that are attractive to SSUs.

To earn profits, financial intermediaries buy financial claims from DSUs whenever the income generated by the financial claims covers all of their borrowing and production costs. In the example about Bob presented earlier, the local bank charged the pizza shop owner 9 percent for the business loan, and the bank's cost of money for the CDs averages 5 percent. Thus, the bank's gross interest rate margin is 4 percent (9 − 5) from which the bank has to cover the cost of manufacturing the loan, its overhead expenses, and the risk of not being paid back (default risk).

One question we might ask is, Why don't consumers or businesses "manufacture" their own banking services and pocket the profits? Banks and other financial intermediaries are middlemen, and who needs a middleman? To understand why financial intermediaries exist, we need to understand the role of two important *market imperfections*—transaction costs and information costs. Let's turn to a discussion of transaction costs.

TRANSACTION COSTS

By **transaction costs** we mean all fees and commissions paid when buying or selling securities, such as search costs, cost of distributing securities to investors, cost of SEC registration, and the time and hassle of the financial transaction. In general, the greater the transaction cost, the more likely it is that a financial intermediary will provide the financial service. Banks and other financial intermediaries are experts in reducing transaction costs. Much of the cost savings come from economies of scale and from the use of sophisticated digital technology.

Transaction costs are particularly high when dealing with consumers and small businesses because the dollar amount of the transactions is small. Thus, the transaction costs of selling securities in small dollar amounts are often prohibitively expensive. As a result, financial intermediaries are almost always able to produce financial services at a lower cost than can individuals or small businesses. This is not always true for larger firms that have sufficient size to capture economies of scale and access to sophisticated technology. These large firms transact primarily in the direct credit markets for most of their financial service needs. Regardless of their size, however, almost every firm maintains some banking relationship, at a minimum, a transaction account to have access to the national payment system.

Let's look at an example to illustrate why financial intermediaries enjoy a comparative cost advantage over individuals and small businesses when producing financial services. Let's say that Tony, the pizzeria owner, learns that the bank is willing to loan him the $25,000; however, he thinks that the 9 percent loan rate is too high. Thus, Tony seeks an individual investor who might offer a lower loan rate.

Suppose that you have money to invest and are looking for some investment opportunities. You do not know Tony personally, but you have frequented the pizza shop when you were in college. You are currently a business consultant but not a financial expert. To keep the example simple, we assume the loan is for 1 year and your profits are earned from the gross interest rate spread, which is $1,000 ($25,000 × 0.04).

Let's look at the basic transactions needed to make the loan, and the bank's costs and your costs:

- **Loan contract.** You hire a lawyer to draw up a loan agreement: cost $600. The bank hires a topflight lawyer who draws up an airtight contract that is used at all the bank's branches: cost $3.00 per contract.
- **Credit reports.** You purchase an "economy" credit report to help you evaluate the firm's creditworthiness: cost $550. To ensure that your analysis is correct, you hire a neighbor who is the credit manager of a small manufacturing firm for $200: cost $750 ($500 + $250). The bank uses an expensive and sophisticated credit scoring model that generates a credit report and a recommended decision: cost $10 per credit report.
- **Monitoring the loan.** You gather the data and your neighbor reviews the quarterly financials for $200. The bank has a computer automated system for monitoring monthly loan payments and quarterly financials: the bank's cost for the year $25.

The total cost for the loan transaction score card looks like this:

Transaction Task	Bank Cost ($)	Your Cost ($)
• Loan contract	$3.00	$600.00
• Credit report	10.00	750.00
• Monitoring loan	25.00	200.00
Total cost	$38.00	$1,550.00

If you took the deal, you would lose $550 (i.e., $1,000 − $1,550). Though the bank's automated systems were expensive, the bank can spread the cost over a large number of loans. Thus, the bank's transaction costs, through a combination of scale economies, technology, and expertise, are much lower than you can generate as an individual. The bank's profit is $1,512 (i.e., $1,550 − $38). We conclude, therefore, that because financial intermediaries can reduce transaction costs substantially, they can provide loans and other financial services for people like Tony and Bob at favorable prices.

ASYMMETRIC INFORMATION

The presence of transaction costs explains some of the reasons why financial intermediaries play such an important role in financial markets. Financial intermediaries are major contributors to *information production*. They are especially good at selling information about a borrower's credit standing. The need for information about financial transactions occurs because of asymmetric information. **Asymmetric information** occurs when buyers and sellers do not have access to the same information; sellers usually have more information than buyers. This is especially true when the seller owns or has produced the asset to be sold to the buyer.

The classic asymmetric information situation is when you buy a used car from an individual. Clearly, the seller (the car's current owner) knows a lot more about the car's condition and problems than you do. Sellers typically are also reluctant to divulge a list of problems to potential buyers. The typical seller's response when asked about the car's quality is to claim, "She is a beauty." The key to reducing or solving the problem of asymmetric information is to gather more information. In the case of a used car, you can ask to test-drive the car or, better yet, you can hire a skilled mechanic to examine the car.

For financial transactions, *asymmetric information* refers to the fact that issuers of securities (the borrowers) know more than investors (the lenders) about the credit quality of the securities being issued. As you might expect, informational asymmetry is larger for loans to consumers and small businesses because little information is publicly available. Informational asymmetry is much less of a problem for large public corporations because so much information is readily available.

Adverse Selection.   Asymmetric information problems occur in two forms: adverse selection and moral hazard. **Adverse selection** problems occur *before* a financial transaction takes place. For example, say that the owner of a woodworking shop goes to a local bank for a business loan. The company is in financial trouble and may fold unless the owner is able to secure a loan for working capital. What is the owner to say when asked if he can repay the loan? He needs the money, and divulging the truth may jeopardize his chances to get the loan.

The adverse selection problems are more severe for small business and consumers because of the lack of publicly available information. Small businesses or consumers who need to borrow money will paint a positive picture about their financial situation. It's human nature. Ironically, firms or consumers with the most severe financial problems also have the greatest incentive to lie and "cook the books" to get a loan. The key to the deadlock is to gather more information about a business's or individual's credit situation. However, gathering additional information is not free. The bank must decide if the cost of gathering additional information is warranted. Loan pricing is particularly difficult when you don't know who is a good or bad credit risk. Let's assume for a moment that a bank lacks reliable information. If the bank sets the loan rate too high, the good credit risks will look elsewhere, leaving only bad borrowers. If the loan rate is too low, the bank will be inundated with borrowers of low credit standing, and the bank stands a good chance of losing more money on the bad credit risks than it will earn on its good borrowers. As a result, if reliable information is not available at a reasonable cost, the banker may decide not to make any loans to businesses or consumers in a particular market. This condition is known as **market failure**.

Moral Hazard.   **Moral hazard** problems occur *after* the transaction (loan) takes place. They occur if borrowers engage in activities that increase the probability that the borrower will default. In other words, the loan's default risk is much higher than the lender was led to believe at the time the loan was made. Let's return to our example of the woodworking shop owner who requested a loan for additional working capital. Let's say that the bank made the loan. Rather than using the money for working capital, however, the owner takes half the money and puts 10 percent down to buy a new high-tech machine that will increase his shop's operating efficiency, design capability, and (he hopes) sales. But it's a lot of money for one machine, and the monthly payments are large given current sales.

Clearly, the large monthly payment, which is a fixed cost, increases the loan's default risk above the original deal.

Why would a business owner take on additional risk that would increase the firm's probability of default? The reason is that owners (borrowers) share disproportionately in the upside gains while the lenders share disproportionately in the downside losses. To see this, note that a lender (the bank) is no better off whether the firm makes a small profit or a huge profit. In either situation, the payment to the bank is the same—limited to interest plus the repayment of principal. The owners are much better off if the firm is a huge success rather than a modest success because the owners keep the additional profits. Also, if the loan contract is for limited liability, the maximum loss the owner can incur is the dollar amount of equity invested in the firm. The decision whether to take on additional investment is a risk-return trade-off and depends ultimately on the owner's appetite for risk.

PROTECTION AGAINST MARKET FAILURES

If good solutions are not available for adverse selection and moral hazard problems, lenders will decrease the number of loans they make in a particular market. In the extreme case, the market will fail. To protect themselves against market failures, financial institutions become specialists in the production of additional information. With respect to adverse selection, banks are specialists in the origination of loans and determining a borrower's creditworthiness. For example, for consumer credit and small-business loans, banks have developed sophisticated credit-scoring models to determine prospective borrowers' creditworthiness. The customer fills out the credit application; the information is then scanned into a data bank, and in a matter of seconds the credit risk profile is displayed along with a credit recommendation. If the recommendation is to grant credit, the bank then verifies critical data; most of the verification can be automated by computer search. Thus, through the use of technology, banks have dramatically reduced adverse selection costs and have achieved significant economies of scale.

Moral hazard problems occur after the money is lent. Business loan contracts are detailed documents designed to provide incentives for borrowers to behave in a manner consistent with the intent of the loan contract. For example, the contract may spell out a series of performance measures with rewards and/or penalties, depending on the firm's performance over time. The performance measures are typically financial ratios. For example, if the firm's current ratio declines below 1.5, the loan rate increases 0.5 percent. Loan contracts can also be very restrictive: They can prohibit certain asset purchases or require that expenses be reduced by a certain percentage by some date. Banks have developed expertise in monitoring loan contracts and reducing costs through technology, thus achieving significant economies of scale.

CONCLUSIONS

Banks and other financial institutions have become experts in reducing transaction and information costs. Examples include originating new security issues, evaluating credit risk, writing restrictive loan contracts, and monitoring bond and loan contracts. If financial institutions are unable to find satisfactory solutions to transaction and information cost problems, lenders will make fewer loans to individuals and small businesses. Transaction and information costs are usually largest for individuals and small businesses and, as a result, they typically find it more economical to access the credit markets using the services of a financial intermediary. For large businesses, transaction and information costs tend to be much lower, and these firms do most of their financial transactions in the direct credit markets. Finally, as you read through the book, we will point out common adverse selection and moral hazard problems and how financial intermediaries try to mitigate their effects.

TYPES OF INTERMEDIATION SERVICES

In "transforming" direct financial claims into indirect ones, financial intermediaries perform five basic intermediation services.

Denomination Divisibility. Financial intermediaries are able to produce a wide range of denominations—from $1 to many millions. They can do this by pooling the funds of many individuals and investing them in direct securities of varying sizes. Of particular importance is their acceptance of deposits from individuals who typically do not have money balances large enough to engage in the wholesale transactions ($1 million or more) found in direct financial markets.

Currency Transformation. Many U.S. companies export goods and services to other countries, but few individuals living in the United States are willing to finance the overseas activities of these companies by buying direct financial claims denominated in a foreign currency. Financial intermediaries help to finance the global expansion of U.S. companies by buying financial claims denominated in one currency and selling financial claims denominated in other currencies.

Maturity Flexibility. Financial intermediaries are able to create securities with a wide range of maturities—from 1 day to more than 30 years. Thus, they are able to buy direct claims issued by DSUs and issue indirect securities with precisely the maturities (usually shorter) desired by SSUs. For example, savings and loan associations obtain funds by issuing passbook accounts and savings certificates and investing the funds in long-term consumer mortgages.

Credit Risk Diversification. By purchasing a wide variety of securities, financial intermediaries are able to spread risk. If the securities purchased are less than perfectly correlated with each other, the intermediary is able to reduce the fluctuation in the principal value of the portfolio.

Liquidity. For most consumers, the timing of revenues and expenses rarely coincides. Because of this, most economic units prefer to hold some assets that have low transaction costs associated with converting them into money. Many of the financial commodities produced by intermediaries are highly liquid. For example, a checking account permits consumers to purchase an asset or repay a debt with minimal transaction cost.

Financial intermediaries, therefore, tailor the characteristics of the indirect securities they issue to the desires of SSUs. They engage in one or more distinct types of intermediation: (1) denomination intermediation, (2) currency intermediation, (3) risk intermediation, (4) maturity intermediation, and (5) liquidity intermediation. They provide these and other services to earn a profit. SSUs and DSUs use these services as long as the cost of doing so is less than providing the services for themselves through the direct credit markets.

SSUs' or DSUs' choice between the direct credit market and the intermediation market depends on which market best meets their needs. Typically, consumers whose transactions are small in dollar amount (retail transactions) find that the intermediation market is most cost-effective. In contrast, economic units that deal in large dollar amounts (wholesale transactions) can switch back and forth between the two markets, selecting the market that offers the most favorable interest rate. For example, many large businesses take out loans from commercial banks, an intermediation transaction, and also raise money by selling commercial paper in the direct credit market.

DO YOU UNDERSTAND?

1. Explain what is meant by the term *indirect financing* and how it is related to *financial intermediation*.
2. Explain the concept of asymmetric information and illustrate it through a discussion of a business loan to a small company.
3. What is moral hazard and how does it apply to a corporate bond issue sale?
4. Thrift institutions specialize in what type of intermediation service?

1.7 TYPES OF FINANCIAL INTERMEDIARIES

Many types of financial intermediaries coexist in our economy. Although different, financial intermediaries all have one function in common: they purchase financial claims with one set of characteristics from DSUs and sell financial claims with different characteristics to SSUs.

Exhibit 1.4 shows the major financial intermediaries in our economy and their long-term growth rates between 1980 and 2009. During this period, the assets of all financial intermediaries totaled $45.5 trillion, and their assets grew at a compound annual rate of 8.5 percent. This rate of growth was faster than the economy as a whole, which grew at 5.8 percent. The largest financial intermediaries in the U.S. economy are commercial banks, but the fastest growing intermediaries are private pension funds (16.7 percent annual growth rate) and state and local government pension funds (13.1 percent annual growth rate). The rapid growth of financial intermediaries reflects the growth in indirect securities issued and the increase in the proportion of funds being channeled through the intermediation market.

Financial intermediaries are classified as (1) deposit-type institutions, (2) contractual savings institutions, (3) investment funds, or (4) other types of intermediaries. Exhibit 1.5 lists the major types of financial institutions and their balance sheet accounts. Notice that both their assets and liabilities are financial claims. A nonfinancial firm like Ford Motor Company also holds financial liabilities (e.g., long-term debt), but the primary assets held are real assets like the plant and equipment. As you read through this section, you should carefully follow along and note the asset and liability holdings of each institution as shown in Exhibit 1.5.

EXHIBIT 1.4
Size and Growth of Major Financial Intermediaries

Intermediary	Rank	2009 Total Assets ($ billions)	% of Total	1980 Total Assets ($ billions)	% of Total	Annual Growth Rate (%)
Commercial banks	1	14,133.0	31.0	1,482.0	35.1	8.1
Mutual funds	2	6,961.6	15.3	513.0	12.1	9.4
Private pension funds	3	5,471.0	12.0	62.0	1.5	16.7
Life insurance companies	4	4,825.5	10.6	464.2	11.0	8.4
Money market funds	5	3,258.6	7.2	196.8	4.7	10.2
Government-sponsored enterprises	6	3,013.8	6.6	195.1	4.6	9.9
Government pension funds	7	2,685.8	5.9	76.3	1.8	13.1
Finance companies	8	1,662.5	3.7	196.7	4.7	7.6
Casualty insurance companies	9	1,369.3	3.0	182.0	4.3	7.2
Savings institutions	10	1,253.7	2.8	791.6	18.7	1.6
Credit unions	11	882.7	1.9	68.4	1.6	9.2
Total		45,517.5	100.0	4,228.1	100.1	8.5
GDP		14,256.3		2,788		5.8

Commercial banks are the largest and most important financial intermediaries in the U.S. economy. Since 1980, private pension funds and government pension funds have been the fastest growing. The rapid growth of financial intermediaries, especially those involved in investment, reflects the tremendous wealth generated by the U.S. economy and the growing proportion of funds being channeled into the intermediation market.

Source: Board of Governors, Federal Reserve System, Flow of Funds Accounts (http://www.federalreserve.gov/releases/). Debt of the United States.

DEPOSIT-TYPE INSTITUTIONS

Deposit-type financial institutions are the most commonly recognized intermediaries because most people use their services on a daily basis. Typically, deposit institutions issue a variety of checking or savings accounts and time deposits, and they use the funds to make consumer, business, and real estate loans. The interest paid on deposit accounts is usually insured by one of several federally sponsored insurance agencies. Thus, for practical purposes, the deposits are devoid of any risk of loss of principal. Also, these deposits are highly liquid because they can be withdrawn on very short notice, usually on demand.

As the 2008 financial crisis worsened, Congress raised the federal deposit insurance limits at depository institutions from $100,000 to $250,000. The increase was designed to bolster ebbing public confidence in the banking system. The action to reinforce money market funds was precipitated when a multibillion-dollar fund closed and liquidated its assets. The insurance limit was last increased in 1980. The proportion of insured deposits in the banking system had fallen from an 82 percent peak in 1991 to 62 percent at the end of 2007.

EXHIBIT 1.5
Primary Assets and Liabilities of Financial Intermediaries

Type of Intermediary	Assets (Direct Securities Purchased)	Liabilities (Indirect Securities Sold)
Deposit-type institutions		
Commercial banks	Business loans Consumer loans Mortgages	Checkable deposits Time and savings deposits Borrowed funds
Thrift institutions	Mortgages	NOW accounts and savings deposits
Credit unions	Consumer loans	Share accounts Time and savings deposits
Contractual savings institutions		
Life insurance companies	Corporate bonds Corporate stock	Life insurance policies
Casualty insurance companies	Municipal bonds Corporate bonds Corporate stock	Casualty insurance policies
Private pension funds	Corporate stock Government securities Corporate bonds	Pension fund reserves
State and local government pension funds	Corporate stock Government securities Corporate bonds	Pension fund reserves
Investment funds		
Mutual funds	Corporate stock Government securities Corporate bonds	Shares in fund
Money market funds	Money market securities	Shares in fund
Other financial institutions		
Finance companies	Consumer loans Business loans	Commercial paper Bonds
Federal agencies	Government loans	Agency securities

This exhibit presents a summary of the most important assets and liabilities issued by the financial institutions discussed in this book. Notice that deposit-type institutions hold liability accounts that are payable upon demand. This makes liquidity management a high priority for these firms.

Source: Board of Governors, The Federal Reserve System, Flow of Funds Accounts.

Commercial Banks.   Commercial banks are the largest and most diversified intermediaries on the basis of range of assets held and liabilities issued. At the end of 2003, commercial banks held almost $7.8 trillion in financial assets. Their liabilities are in the form of checking accounts, savings accounts, and various time deposits. The Federal Deposit Insurance Corporation (FDIC) insures bank deposits up to a maximum of $250,000. On the asset side, commercial banks make a wide variety of loans in all denominations to consumers, businesses, and state and local governments. In addition, many commercial banks have trust departments and leasing operations. Because of their vital role in the nation's monetary system and the effect they have on the economic well-being of the communities in which they are located, commercial banks are among the most highly regulated of all financial institutions.

Thrift Institutions. Savings and loan associations and mutual savings banks are commonly called *thrift institutions*. They obtain most of their funds by issuing checking accounts (NOW accounts), savings accounts, and a variety of consumer time deposits. They use these funds to purchase real estate loans consisting primarily of long-term mortgages. They are the largest providers of residential mortgage loans to consumers. In effect, thrifts specialize in maturity and denomination intermediation because they borrow small amounts of money short term with checking and savings accounts and lend long term on real estate collateral. The FDIC insures deposits in thrifts in amounts up to $250,000.

Credit Unions. Credit unions are small, nonprofit, cooperative, consumer-organized institutions owned entirely by their member-customers. The primary liabilities of credit unions are checking accounts (called *share drafts*) and savings accounts (called *share accounts*); their investments are primarily devoted to short-term installment consumer loans. Credit union share accounts are federally insured to a maximum of $250,000. Credit unions are organized by consumers having a common bond, such as employees of a given firm or union. To use any service of a credit union, an individual must be a member. The major regulatory differences between credit unions and other depository institutions are the common bond requirement, the restriction that most loans are to consumers, and their exemption from federal income tax because of their cooperative nature.

CONTRACTUAL SAVINGS INSTITUTIONS

Contractual savings institutions obtain funds under long-term contractual arrangements and invest the funds in the capital markets. Firms in this category are insurance companies and pension funds. These institutions are characterized by a relatively steady inflow of funds from contractual commitments with their insurance policyholders and pension fund participants. Thus, liquidity is usually not a problem in the management of these institutions. They are able to invest in long-term securities, such as bonds, and in some cases in common stock.

Life Insurance Companies. Life insurance companies obtain funds by selling insurance policies that protect against loss of income from premature death or retirement. In the event of death, the policyholder's beneficiaries receive the insurance benefits, and with retirement the policyholder receives the benefits. In addition to risk protection, many life insurance policies provide some savings. Because life insurance companies have a predictable inflow of funds and their outflows are actuarially predictable, they are able to invest primarily in higher-yielding, long-term assets, such as corporate bonds and stocks. Life insurance companies are regulated by the states in which they operate and, compared to deposit-type institutions, their regulation is less strict.

Casualty Insurance Companies.   Casualty insurance companies sell protection against loss of property from fire, theft, accident, negligence, and other causes that can be actuarially predicted. Their major source of funds is premiums charged on insurance policies. Casualty insurance policies are pure risk-protection policies; as a result, they have no cash surrender value and thus provide no liquidity to the policyholders. As might be expected, the cash outflows from claims on policies are not as predictable as those of life insurance companies. Consequently, a greater proportion of these companies' assets are in short-term, highly marketable securities. To offset the lower return typically generated by these investments, casualty companies have substantial holdings of equity securities. Casualty insurance companies also hold municipal bonds to reduce their taxes.

Pension Funds.   Pension funds obtain their funds from employer and employee contributions during the employees' working years and provide monthly payments upon retirement. Pension funds invest these monies in corporate bonds and equity obligations. The purpose of pension funds is to help workers plan for their retirement years in an orderly and systematic manner. The need for retirement income, combined with the success of organized labor in negotiating for increased pension benefits, has led to a remarkable growth of both private pensions and state and local government pension funds since World War II. Because the inflow into pension funds is long term, and the outflow is highly predictable, pension funds are able to invest in higher-yielding, long-term securities.

INVESTMENT FUNDS

Investment funds sell shares to investors and use these funds to purchase direct financial claims. They offer investors the benefit of both denomination flexibility and default-risk intermediation. The uses of funds attracted by investment funds are shown in Exhibit 1.5.

Mutual Funds.   Mutual funds sell equity shares to investors and use these funds to purchase stocks or bonds. The advantage of a mutual fund over direct investment is that it provides small investors access to reduced investment risk that results from diversification, economies of scale in transaction costs, and professional financial managers. The value of a share of a mutual fund is not fixed; it fluctuates as the prices of the stocks in its investment portfolio change. Most mutual funds specialize within particular sectors of the market. For example, some invest only in equities or debt, others in a particular industry (such as energy or electronics), others in growth or income stocks, and still others in foreign investments.

Money Market Mutual Funds.   A money market mutual fund (MMMF) is simply a mutual fund that invests in money market securities, which are short-term securities with low default risk. These securities sell in denominations of $1 million or more, so most investors are unable to purchase them. Thus, MMMFs provide investors with small money balances the opportunity to earn the market rate of interest without incurring a great deal of financial risk. Most MMMFs offer check-writing privileges, which make them close substitutes for the interest-bearing checking accounts and savings accounts offered at most depository institutions. This advantage is limited, however, in that most MMMFs restrict the amount or frequency of withdrawals, and the federal government does not insure the funds.

During the 2008 financial crisis, the federal government took steps to restore confidence in the financial integrity of money market mutual funds and their ability to absorb losses. Many consumers have long considered the funds to be the near equivalent of a bank savings account. However, the recent financial crisis has put money market funds under increasing financial stress, which could lead to the failure and bankruptcy of some funds. As a result, the Treasury Department announced that, as of September 18, 2009, it would temporarily guarantee losses up to $50 billion. The federal guarantee was removed a year later.

Money market funds invest in short-term securities, such as Treasury and agency securities, bank certificates of deposit (CDs), asset-backed commercial paper, and other highly liquid securities with low default risk. Money market mutual funds differ from money market deposit accounts, which are offered by banks, thrifts, and credit unions. These are interest-bearing "bank accounts" insured up to $250,000 by the federal government and, as a practical matter, are free of risk. Money market fund shares carry the default risk of the individual securities that comprise the fund portfolio or trading loss the fund may incur.

OTHER TYPES OF FINANCIAL INTERMEDIARIES

Several other types of financial intermediaries purchase direct securities from DSUs and sell indirect claims to SSUs.

Finance Companies.　Finance companies make loans to consumers and small businesses. Unlike commercial banks, they do not accept savings deposits from consumers. They obtain the majority of their funds by selling short-term IOUs, called **commercial paper**, to investors. The balance of their funds comes from the sale of equity capital and long-term debt obligations. There are three basic types of finance companies: (1) consumer finance companies specializing in installment loans to households, (2) business finance companies focused on loans and leases to businesses, and (3) sales finance companies that finance the products sold by retail dealers. Finance companies are regulated by the states in which they operate and are also subject to many federal regulations. These regulations focus primarily on consumer transactions and deal with loan terms, conditions, rates charged, and collection practices.

Federal Agencies.　The U.S. government acts as a major financial intermediary through the borrowing and lending activities of its agencies. Since the 1960s, federal agencies have been among the most rapidly growing of all financial institutions. The primary purposes of federal agencies are to reduce the cost of funds and increase the availability of funds to targeted sectors of the economy. The agencies do this by selling debt instruments (called *agency securities*) in the direct credit markets at or near the government borrowing rate, then lending those funds to economic participants in the sectors they serve. Most of the funds provided by the federal agencies support agriculture and housing because of the importance of these sectors to the nation's well-being. It is argued that these and other target sectors in the economy would not receive adequate credit at reasonable cost without direct intervention by the federal government.

DO YOU UNDERSTAND?

1. Why do casualty insurance companies devote a greater percentage of their investments to liquid U.S. government securities than do life insurance companies?
2. What are credit unions and how do they differ from a commercial bank?
3. Why have mutual funds grown so fast compared to commercial banks?
4. For a consumer, what is the difference between holding a checking account at a commercial bank and holding a money market mutual fund?

1.8 THE RISKS FINANCIAL INSTITUTIONS MANAGE

Now let's turn our attention back to financial institutions, which, in providing financial intermediation services to consumers and businesses, must transact in the financial markets. Financial institutions intermediate between SSUs and DSUs in the hope of earning a profit by acquiring funds at interest rates that are lower than they charge when they sell their financial products. But there is no free lunch here. The differences in the characteristics of the financial claims financial institutions buy and sell expose them to a variety of risks in the financial markets.

As moot testimony to the importance of successfully managing these risks, the decade of the 1980s was a battleground now littered with the corpses of financial institutions that failed to adequately manage these risks. Managing these risks does not mean eliminating them—there is a trade-off between risk and higher profits. Managers who take too few risks sleep well at night but eat poorly—their slumber reaps a reward of declining earnings and stock prices that their shareholders will not tolerate for long. On the other hand, excess risk taking—betting the bank and losing—is also bad news. It will place you in the ranks of the unemployed with an armada of expensive Wall Street lawyers defending you.

In their search for higher long-term earnings and stock values, financial institutions must manage and balance five basic risks: credit risk, interest rate risk, liquidity risk, foreign exchange risk, and political risk. Each of these risks is related to the characteristics of the financial claim (e.g., term to maturity) or to the issuer (e.g., default risk). Each must be managed carefully to balance the trade-off between future profitability and potential failure. For now, we summarize the five risks and briefly discuss how they affect the management of financial institutions to provide a frame of reference for other topics in the book.

CREDIT RISK

When a financial institution makes a loan or invests in a bond or other debt security, the institution bears **credit risk** (or default risk) because it is accepting the possibility that the borrower will fail to make either interest or principal payments in the amount and at the time promised. To manage the credit risk of loans or investments in debt securities, financial institutions should (1) diversify their portfolios, (2) conduct a careful credit analysis of the borrower to measure default risk exposure, and (3) monitor the borrower over the life of the loan or investment to detect any critical changes in financial health, which is just another way of expressing the borrower's ability to repay the loan.

INTEREST RATE RISK

Interest rate risk is the risk of fluctuations in a security's price or reinvestment income caused by changes in market interest rates. The concept of interest rate risk is applicable not only to bonds but also to a financial institution's balance sheet. The savings and loan association industry is the prime example of how interest rate risk adversely affects a financial institution's earnings. In the volatile interest rate environment of the late 1970s and early 1980s, many savings and loan associations (S&Ls) failed because the interest rates they paid on deposits (liabilities) increased faster than the yields they earned on their mortgage loans (assets), causing earnings to decline.

LIQUIDITY RISK

Liquidity risk is the risk that a financial institution will be unable to generate sufficient cash inflow to meet required cash outflows. Liquidity is critical to financial institutions: Banks and thrifts need liquidity to meet deposit withdrawals and pay off other liabilities as they come due, pension funds need liquidity to meet contractual pension payments, and life insurance companies need liquidity to pay death benefits. Liquidity also means that an institution need not pass up a profitable loan or investment opportunity because of a lack of cash. If a financial institution is unable to meet its short-term obligations because of inadequate liquidity, the firm will fail even though the firm may be profitable over the long run.

FOREIGN EXCHANGE RISK

Foreign exchange risk is the fluctuation in the earnings or value of a financial institution that arises from fluctuations in exchange rates. Many financial institutions deal in foreign currencies for their own account, or they buy or sell currencies for their customers. Also, financial institutions invest in the direct credit markets of other countries, or they may sell indirect financial claims overseas. Because of changing international economic conditions and the relative supply and demand of U.S. and foreign currencies, the rate at which foreign currencies can be converted into U.S. dollars fluctuates. These fluctuations can cause gains or losses in the currency positions of financial institutions, and they cause the U.S. dollar values of non-U.S. financial investments to change.

POLITICAL RISK

Political risk is the fluctuation in value of a financial institution resulting from the actions of the U.S. or foreign governments. Domestically, if the government changes the regulations faced by financial institutions, their earnings or values are affected. For example, if the FDIC, which insures deposits at banks and thrift institutions, decided to increase the premium charged for deposit insurance, earnings at the affected institutions would likely decline. It is important for managers of financial institutions to monitor and predict as best as possible changes in the regulatory environment. Managers must be prepared to react quickly when regulatory changes occur.

Internationally, the concerns are much more dramatic, especially when institutions consider lending in developing countries without stable governments or well-developed legal systems. Governments can repudiate (i.e., cancel) foreign debt obligations. Repudiations are rare, but less rare are debt reschedulings in which foreign governments declare a moratorium on debt payments and then attempt to renegotiate more favorable terms with the foreign lenders. In either case, the lending institution is left "holding the bag." To grow and be successful in the international arena, managers of financial institutions must understand how to measure and manage these risks.

1.9 REGULATION OF THE FINANCIAL SYSTEM

The financial system is one of the most highly regulated sectors in the U.S. economy. There are two fundamental reasons for the high degree of regulation: (1) to protect consumers against industry abuses and (2) to stabilize the financial system. This section discusses both of these reasons and presents a high-level view of the regulatory environment that has prevailed since the 1930s.

CONSUMER PROTECTION REGULATION

There are a number of reasons for the pervasiveness of consumer protection regulations. Many of these regulations center on fair and equal access to credit markets. Federal regulations such as the Home Mortgage Disclosure Act of 1975 or the Community Reinvestment Act of 1977 are designed to prevent discrimination based on age, race, sex, and income.

Historically, the government has felt the need to protect consumers and small-business owners from the complexities of finance and its arcane decision-making rules. The concern is that finance professionals, with their superior knowledge of finance and market conditions, could exploit persons with little or no training in finance. Let's face it: Finance is a difficult subject to master.

Most of the consumer protection regulations focus on loan transactions, such as securing auto or home mortgage loans, or consumer deposit accounts, such as opening a savings account at a thrift institution or buying a certificate of deposit from a bank. For example, over the years the auto industry has developed a number of different ways to calculate the cost of financing a car. These techniques can give conflicting results when comparing alternative financing sources and may not correctly identify the lowest economic interest rate. The Truth-in-Lending Act of 1968 requires that lenders provide borrowers with the annual percentage rate (APR) when they apply for a loan. When comparing financing alternatives, the loan with the lowest APR is always the one with the lowest economic interest rate.

In addition, various laws protect investors against abuses such as insider trading, lack of disclosure, outright malfeasance, and breach of fiduciary responsibility. In general, the government tries to ensure that investors receive timely and accurate information about investments and receive full disclosure of the investment's risks. However, the government does not offer or provide any advice on the efficacy or soundness of a particular investment. Individual investors must take responsibility for their investment decisions.

STABILIZING THE FINANCIAL SYSTEM

The near collapse of the financial system in the fall of 2008 and the global credit crisis and recession that followed gave rise to a widespread call to insulate the real economy from the effects of future banking crises. Why are bank failures considered extraordinary events by economists? Why not let banks or other financial institutions fail like any other unsuccessful business? Let's look at a simple example.

When the local flower shop fails, the owners lose their investment in the business and Mom may not get her flowers on Mother's Day. When a bank fails, a large number of people in the community lose some or all of their life savings and businesses suffer losses to their cash and investment accounts at the bank. At the same time, local business and consumers may find it difficult to get credit. The result, at least temporarily, is a slowdown in economic prosperity and financial activity in the community.

If a number of banks fail simultaneously, people may lose confidence in the banking system, and a bank panic may occur. In the past, bank panics often started with bank runs. A bank run occurs when a large number of depositors simultaneously want to convert their deposits into cash and many of the deposits, such as checking accounts, are payable on demand. Because banks hold only a small amount of vault cash, it is not possible to satisfy all requests immediately. Most of a bank's assets are held as loans, which are difficult to convert into cash. As withdrawals start to mount, a bank's management "squeezes the banking system" for cash to pay depositors who want cash now. To get more cash and to improve their liquidity, banks are less interested in renewing loans as they come due; instead, they pressure borrowers to pay off loans early, and they reduce or do not renew lines of credit. The lack of available credit causes businesses to begin to contract and weaker businesses to fail. But rumors may become rampant, whether true or malicious scandal, and once a run on a bank starts, it is hard to save the bank from failure. The establishment of federal deposit insurance and the Fed's role as lender of last resort have eliminated most bank runs, but when they occur, especially with large banks, they can pose a serious threat to the economy.

A **bank panic** is the simultaneous failure of many banks during a financial crisis. If the panic spreads to other financial institutions, the decline in economic activity may be worse. For example, if an insurance company fails, people may lose all or part of their retirement income, health care coverage, or life insurance benefits. Regardless of how the financial panic proceeds, the failure of banks and other financial institutions creates doubts in the minds of people regarding the safety and soundness of the financial system. If nothing is done to restore public confidence, a widespread bank panic can ensue.

Once the financial system begins to unravel, it is generally not possible to stop a financial panic. When the financial system collapses, large numbers of individuals and businesses suffer losses to their wealth and find it difficult or impossible to obtain loans. As consumer wealth declines, uncertainty in the economy increases and consumers decrease their spending, which reduces the demand for goods and services in the economy. Soon factories begin laying off workers, unemployment begins to rise, and domestic gross national product declines. The net result is that the real economy is thrust into a recession by the collapse of the financial system, which is devastating to the social and economic fabric of society. This is the scenario that led to the Great Depression in the 1930s and the deep recession that began in December 2007. Typically, significant recessions are preceded by a financial panic.

HISTORICAL VIEW OF BANK REGULATION

It should be clear that the primary reason banks and other financial firms are so highly regulated is to prevent contagious bank failures and other types of market failures that ultimately result in a recession. The financial regulatory structure that prevailed for the last 80 years was conceived during the Great Depression (1929–1933) and reflects the economic thinking, the political problems, and the state of technology of the times.

By the beginning of the new millennium, critics charged that bank regulations in the United States were out of date. The financial system had become highly fragmented compared to other major industrial countries, most of which have just one bank regulator. The United States has three or more potential regulators. At the same time, some economists believed that the so-called competition among regulators for financial institutions to regulate resulted in regulation at the lowest common denominator, thus weakening the regulatory system. Other critics of U.S. bank regulations contended that regulations did not focus enough on safety

EXHIBIT 1.6
Highlights of the Financial Regulatory Reform Act of 2010

Consumer Protection Agency: Creates a new independent watchdog with the authority to protect consumers from hidden fees, abusive terms, and deceptive practices when purchasing financial services such as credit cards and mortgages. The agency is housed at the Fed and its dedicated budget is paid by the Fed.

Too big to fail problem: Legislation is designed to end the possibility that tax payers will be asked to bail out large financial firms whose failure threatens the overall economy: the so-called too big to fail problem. The Fed gains power to impose stricter operating standards; regulate nonbank financial firms, if necessary; and break up large, complex firms if they pose a risk to the financial system.

Advanced risk warning system: Establishes the Financial Stability Oversight Council, which has the sole responsibility for identifying and responding to emerging systemic risks posed by large, complex financial firms. The council will make recommendations to the Fed on how to decrease the risk.

Tougher regulation for large banks: The Federal Reserve will now regulate all bank- and thrift-holding companies with assets over $50 million. Smaller financial institutions, with assets less than $50 million, will be supervised by other regulators. This move protects the interest of the nation's community banks, which serve consumers. For large banks, it means tougher standards.

Executive compensation: A firm's shareholders now have a say about executive pay, with the right to a nonbinding vote on executive compensation.

Better protection for investors: Legislation was spurred by the Madoff scandal, which revealed that the SEC failed to provide aggressive oversight of the investment industry. New legislation encourages whistleblowers; creates the Investment Advisory Committee, which advises the SEC on its regulatory practice; and establishes the Office of Investor Advocate within the SEC to identify areas where investors have significant problems dealing with the SEC.

Transparency and accountability financial products: Eliminates the loopholes that allow risky and abusive practices to continue to be unregulated. Areas that currently need to be monitored and regulated are over-the-counter derivatives, asset-backed securities, hedge funds, mortgage brokers, and payday lenders.

In the wake of a global financial crisis, economists have called for a complete overhaul of banking regulations to insulate the real economy from the effects of future banking crises. How effective the act will be is difficult to say. Senator Chris Dodd (D-Conn.), the bill's primary sponsor, sounded a cautionary note when he said, "We won't know for another decade how successful the bill will be." In a moment of candor, Dodd went on to say, "This legislation will not stop the next crisis from coming." Dodd's point is that regulatory reforms may protect us against today's problems, but they may not protect us against future unforeseen problems.

and soundness of the financial system but instead focused on privacy disclosure, fraud prevention, anti–money laundering, anti-terrorism, anti–usury lending, and lending to low-income segments of the economy. Finally, critics contended that the regulations failed to account fully for the impact of technology on innovation and development of new financial products, such as the derivative securities. The stage was ripe for change.

REGULATORY REFORM

Facing the most serious financial collapse since the 1930s, President Obama proposed sweeping changes to the nation's financial system in June 2009. After more than a year of political wrangling, Congress passed the Financial Reform Act of 2010. (The act's official name is Restoring American Financial Stability Act of 2010.) The act is the most extensive reworking of financial regulations since the 1930s. It represents significant political compromise, but nonetheless the main contours of the plan will dramatically revamp everything, from the operation of large, complex bank-holding companies to consumer protection. As a preview to your study of bank regulations in Chapter 15, Exhibit 1.6 lists the most important regulatory issues addressed by the act. It's no surprise that it focuses on the safety and soundness of the financial system and the protection of consumers when they transact with financial services firms.

DO YOU UNDERSTAND?

1. Explain the concept of default risk and how a bank manages it.
2. Why is liquidity risk such a problem for commercial banks?
3. Why are bank failures considered extraordinary compared to the failure of businesses in other sectors of the economy?
4. Explain why major bank panics often affect the real sector of the economy.

SUMMARY OF LEARNING OBJECTIVES

1 Explain the role of the financial system and why it is important to individuals and to the economy as a whole. The role of the financial system is to gather money from SSUs and transfer it to DSUs in the most efficient manner possible. The larger the flow and the more efficiently the funds are allocated, the greater the accommodation of individual preferences for current spending and savings and the more likely that businesses will allocate money to the most productive investment projects in the economy.

2 Explain the ways that funds are transferred between surplus spending units (SSUs) and deficit spending units (DSUs). There are two basic ways that the transfer of funds between SSUs and DSUs takes place in the economy: (1) *direct financing* (financial markets) and (2) *indirect financing* (intermediation market). The direct credit markets are wholesale markets for financial claims where DSUs and SSUs trade financial claims among themselves; brokers, dealers, and investment bankers facilitate these transactions.

In the indirect credit markets, financial institutions intermediate, or stand between, transactions between DSUs and SSUs. The hallmark of indirect financing is that the financial intermediary transforms financial claims so that they are attractive to both SSUs and DSUs. Financial intermediaries, such as commercial banks, life insurance companies, and pension funds, facilitate indirect financing.

3   **Discuss the major differences between money and capital markets.** The *money markets* are a collection of markets where commercial banks and businesses adjust their liquidity by borrowing or lending for short periods of time. The Federal Reserve System conducts monetary policy in the money markets, and the Treasury Department uses the money markets to finance the day-to-day operations of the federal government. The most important money market securities are Treasury bills, negotiable certificates of deposit, and commercial paper. The *capital markets* are where business firms obtain funds for long-term investment projects and where consumers finance the purchases of long-term assets, such as real estate. Capital market securities have a long term-to-maturity and typically involve more risk than money market securities. The most important capital market instruments are corporate stocks and bonds, Treasury bonds, and residential mortgages.

4   **Explain the concept of informational asymmetry and the problem it presents to lenders.** When entering into financial contracts, such as a bank loan, one important risk factor that can influence the types of contracts agreed upon is the information gap that exists between the buyer and seller—called asymmetric information. Informational asymmetry occurs because buyers and sellers are not equally informed about the true quality of the financial claim. Generally the seller (borrower) knows more about the product than the buyer (lender). There are two forms of asymmetric information: adverse selection and moral hazard.

Adverse selection occurs *before* the transaction is completed and the lender cannot tell the difference between high- and low-quality loans. Moral hazard problems occur *after* the loan is made. They occur because borrowers deploy funds into projects of higher risk than originally agreed upon. The easiest way to reduce adverse selection and moral hazard costs is to gather more information and monitor the loan.

5   **Identify the major risks that financial institutions must manage.** Financial institutions are profit-maximizing businesses that earn profits by acquiring funds at interest rates lower than the rates they earn on their assets. The nature and characteristics of the financial claims they hold expose them to a variety of risks. The major risks that financial institutions face are credit risk, interest rate risk, liquidity risk, foreign exchange risk, and political risk.

6   **Discuss the two main reasons that the financial sector is so highly regulated.** The financial system is the most highly regulated sector in the U.S. economy. There are two fundamental reasons for the regulation: (1) to protect consumers from abuses by the industry and (2) to stabilize the economy. Historically, government officials have taken a paternalistic view toward consumers, believing that they need protection from the financial services firms, who possess superior knowledge of finance and market conditions. Thus, government groups are concerned that the average consumer may be victimized by unscrupulous firms. The failures of banks and other financial firms are treated as extraordinary events because their failures can lead to an economic recession. If a number of banks fail simultaneously, people lose confidence in the banking system, and a bank panic can occur. If nothing is done to restore public confidence, the bank panic spreads and the financial system collapses. The result is that the real sector of the economy is thrust into a recession by the collapse of the financial sector.

KEY TERMS

Financial markets	Surplus spending unit (SSU)	Financial claim	Investment bank
Financial intermediary (or financial institution)	Deficit spending unit (DSU)	Direct financing	Money center bank
		Financial intermediation (or indirect financing)	Broker
			Dealer

Primary market	Treasury bills	Municipal bonds	Commercial paper
Secondary market	Negotiable certificates of	Mortgages	Credit risk
Marketability	deposit (NCDs)	Transaction costs	Interest rate risk
Liquidity	Federal funds	Asymmetric information	Liquidity risk
Over-the-counter market	Capital markets	Adverse selection	Foreign exchange risk
Public market	Common stock	Market failure	Political risk
Private placement	Corporate bonds	Moral hazard	Bank panic

QUESTIONS AND PROBLEMS

1. Does it make sense that the typical household is a surplus spending unit (SSU) while the typical business firm is a deficit spending unit (DSU)? Explain.

2. Explain the economic role of brokers, dealers, and investment bankers. How does each make a profit?

3. Why are direct financing transactions more costly or inconvenient than intermediated transactions?

4. Explain how you believe economic activity would be affected if we did not have financial markets and institutions.

5. Explain the concept of financial intermediation. How does the possibility of financial intermediation increase the efficiency of the financial system?

6. How do financial intermediaries generate profits?

7. Explain the differences between the money markets and the capital markets. Which market would General Motors use to finance a new vehicle assembly plant? Why?

8. What steps should bank management take to manage credit risk in the bank's loan portfolio?

9. Metropolitan Nashville and Davidson County issues $25 million of municipal revenue bonds to finance a new domed stadium for the Tennessee Titans football team. The bonds have a face value of $10,000 each, are somewhat risky, and have a maturity of 20 years. Enterprise Bank of Nashville purchases one of the bonds using the $5,000 received from Sarah Levien and Ted Hawkins, who each purchased a 6-month certificate of deposit from the bank. Explain the intermediation services provided by Enterprise Bank in this transaction. Illustrate with T-accounts.

10. Explain the statement, "A financial claim is someone's asset and someone else's liability."

11. Why are banks singled out for special attention in the financial system?

12. Explain why households are the principal SSU unit in the economy.

13. Explain why direct financial markets are wholesale markets. How do consumers gain access to these important markets?

14. What are money center banks and why were they not allowed to engage in investment banking activities following the Great Depression?

15. What is the difference between marketability and liquidity?

16. Municipal bonds are attractive to what type of investors?

17. Why do corporations issue commercial paper?

18. Explain what is meant by moral hazard. What problems does it present when a bank makes a loan?

19. Explain the adverse selection problem. How can lenders reduce its effect?

20. Why is the financial system so highly regulated?

INTERNET EXERCISE

The government agencies that regulate financial institutions provide an array of statistics on their Web sites. Much of the data is available as downloadable files, making it easy for students, analysts, and researchers to learn about financial intermediaries by examining current and historical data on the different types of intermediaries. For example, several of the exhibits in this chapter were derived from data available from the Board of Governors of the Federal Reserve System (http://www.federalreserve.gov/releases/). The Federal Reserve Board's Z.1 statistical release (*Flow of Funds Accounts of the United States*) contains current and historical flow-of-funds accounts data. Your task in this Internet Exercise is to find data on the level of financial assets held by commercial banks. You will be looking for current and historical data from Table L.109.

1. Once you have located the data, enter them into a spreadsheet. The Web site provides instructions for downloading the data into a spreadsheet file, such as an Excel file. Create a chart using the following categories of financial assets: government securities, municipal bonds, corporate and foreign bonds, consumer loans, business loans, real estate loans, and other assets. Consider making the chart a 100-percent stacked-area chart. On the chart, show the percentage of assets in each category for the previous 3 to 5 years. This will show you the percentage of commercial banks' portfolios devoted to the various types of financial assets. You will notice some short-term trends and some long-term trends.

2. Also make a standard stacked-area chart showing the dollar amounts. It will show the aggregate increase in banks' lending and investing activities.

3. Using the two charts, identify the short-term trends in banks' lending and investment activities. What are the long-term trends?

4. Can you relate any of the long-term trends in banks' lending and investing activities to any long-term economic or societal trends? Can you relate any of the short-term fluctuations in banks' lending and investing activities to fluctuations in economic activity? To answer these questions, you might need to get some economic data such as gross domestic product (GDP) from the Federal Reserve Bank of St. Louis's FRED database (http://www.stls.frb.org/fred/).

The Federal Reserve and Its Powers

CHAPTER 2 IS ABOUT THE FEDERAL Reserve System (the Fed) and its impact on interest rates and the economy. It is often said that the chair of the Federal Reserve Board is the second most powerful person in the United States. Only the president, who is commander in chief of our armed forces, is more powerful. Where does all this power come from? It comes from the Fed's role as the nation's central bank and its responsibilities and powers to conduct monetary policy. The Fed's monetary policy actions have a direct effect on the level of interest rates, the availability of credit, and the supply of money, all of which have a direct impact on financial markets and institutions and, more important, on the level of economic activity and the rate of inflation.

To make the story even more interesting, with all of this awesome power, the Fed is "privately" owned by the banks that are members of the Federal Reserve System. As a result, the Fed is not a government agency and is remarkably free from presidential and congressional pressure. As you can tell, we have a lot of important issues to work through and explain in this chapter, so let's get down to the Fed's business—the business of money. That's what the Fed is all about! ■

This is foreign gold being counted by *sitters* in the bottom-most vault (80 feet below the busy financial district) of the Federal Reserve Bank of New York. Each gold bar weighs between 27 and 28 pounds. When this photo was taken, gold traded for about $32 an ounce. As of July 2010, gold traded for about $1,200 per ounce, making each bar worth about $518,000. The gold is stored in 120 compartments held by more than 70 countries and watched constantly by sitters. Sales require frequent transfers, and gold is shifted bar by bar from one to another of the compartments.

The purpose of this chapter is to explain what the Federal Reserve (the *Fed*) is, what it does, and why it is so powerful. The Federal Reserve System is the most important financial institution in our country. As our nation's central bank, it regulates our major financial institutions and controls the nation's money supply. The Fed has three basic tools to conduct monetary policy, which are implemented by controlling key accounts on its balance sheet. In Chapter 3, we will examine in detail the Fed's ability to affect the level of interest rates and how monetary policy affects various sectors in the economy. ∎

LEARNING OBJECTIVES

1 Explain the problems leading to the establishment of the Federal Reserve bank in 1914.

2 Explain the Fed's primary responsibilities as a central bank.

3 Identify the most powerful policy group within the Fed and discuss its powers.

4 Explain how the Fed conducts monetary policy and the various policy tools at its disposal.

5 Explain why open-market operations is the Fed's primary tool to conduct monetary policy.

2.1 ORIGINS OF THE FEDERAL RESERVE SYSTEM

A central bank regulates a nation's money supply and financial institutions in an attempt to provide the nation with a stable economic environment and an effective payment system. Early in its history, the United States had two central banks that operated reasonably well by the standards of the day. However, American politics has always feared centralization of power and economic concentration, and central banks were a prominent symbol of these fears. Both of these early central banks engaged in some minor political peccadilloes and lost their charters. The First Bank of the United States was disbanded in 1811 and the Second Bank of the United States died a quiet death after its charter was renewed but vetoed by President Andrew Jackson in 1832. Jackson's veto rendered a consummate political message that denounced the bank as unconstitutional, detailed the dangers of concentrated economic power that the bank posed, and denounced the bank as a menace and threat to American democracy. Jackson's powerful veto message was widely circulated as it was the death knell for central banking in the United States for over 80 years.

Between 1832 and 1914, the United States operated without a central bank. During this time, individual banks issued banknotes that served as the nation's money supply. Banknotes were IOUs (liabilities) of individual banks that looked and functioned like our present-day currency.

The major difference between the two systems was that when a bank made additional loans, the bank simply issued or printed more of its banknotes to fund the loans, thus increasing the money supply. Conversely, if the bank decreased the amount of loans it had outstanding, it would retire outstanding banknotes, decreasing the money supply. The fact that the banknotes were liabilities of the issuing bank and not the federal government was the cause of many problems, as we shall see.

Exhibit 2.1 shows a banknote issued by Canal Bank in New Orleans. The banknotes served as money to people who borrowed from banks or deposited money with them. Because banknotes were IOUs of individual banks, they carried the default risk of the bank that issued them. If a bank was viewed as too risky, its banknotes were exchanged in the market at a discount to their face value—so people would have to offer more money if they wanted to buy goods with risky banknotes. For example, if you had a banknote from a sound and well-managed bank like Wells Fargo Bank, an item priced at a dollar cost a dollar. But if you tried to make a purchase with banknotes issued by a bank that dealt in risky real estate developments, it might take $1.25 worth of that bank's notes to make the same purchase. And if you presented banknotes from a bank that was rumored to be about to fail, no one would take that bank's notes for purchases, unless they did not know any better. No wonder people preferred hard currency—gold or silver coins—over paper money. At one time in the United States, there were more than

EXHIBIT 2.1
Banknote Issued by Canal Bank, New Orleans, Louisiana

Historically, individual bank liabilities (called *banknotes*) served as money. The fact that so many different monies existed made commerce difficult. A person never knew if the banknote was from a sound bank or from a failed or disreputable bank. It's no wonder that banknotes from lesser-known banks were heavily discounted.

15,000 different banks issuing their own banknotes. You can see the obstacles and inefficiencies this made for commerce because it was difficult to know the good players from the bad.

Furthermore, from 1836 until the mid-1860s, the quantity of money varied widely in the United States as banks made more loans and issued more money during economic booms and contracted their lending and the money supply during recessions. Also, private banks failed with some regularity during recessions, further contracting the money supply. Thus, the nation's money supply not only was of varying credit quality but also expanded and contracted during economic cycles, thereby exaggerating the cycles.

NATIONAL BANKING ACTS

In the mid-1860s, the United States passed a series of national banking acts that tried to improve the soundness of the nation's money supply and to help finance the Civil War by allowing the sale of U.S. government bonds. State-chartered banks that issued banknotes were assessed a 10 percent annual tax on them—thereby making them prohibitively expensive to issue. However, banks were allowed to obtain charters as national banks and issue banknotes provided that they met certain conditions and agreed to be regulated by the newly authorized Comptroller of the Currency. Among the conditions necessary for issuing banknotes were (1) the requirement that each bank have its banknotes printed by the U.S. Mint to cut the risk of counterfeiting and (2) the requirement that each bank back its banknotes with holdings of U.S. government bonds that slightly exceeded the value of each banknote issued. In that way, each banknote could always be redeemed at face value even if the bank failed.

State banks were allowed to continue to operate after the National Banking Acts were passed. Federal bank regulators had expected the numbers of state banks to dwindle because the 10 percent tax on their banknotes would make it difficult for them to compete against national banks. However, they could issue demand deposit liabilities (checking accounts) instead of banknotes. To the surprise of federal bank regulators, checking accounts quickly became popular with the public. National banks also could issue checking accounts. Because demand deposits weren't insured and banks had some risk of failure, demand deposit liabilities, like individual banknotes before them, were often discounted when they were used to finance transactions. Furthermore, banks were still subject to failure if they issued too many demand deposits relative to the amount of "reserves" in the form of cash or deposits they held at other banks that were available to meet deposit withdrawals.

This problem was aggravated by the fact that the National Banking Acts let some banks count deposits held at other banks as part of their reserves. This **pyramiding of reserves** meant that many banks could run short of reserves simultaneously. This happened because as a bank ran short of cash to meet withdrawals, the bank would draw down its deposits at other banks to get cash, thereby making the other bank run short of cash. Because the nation's banknote currency supply was limited by the amount of government bonds outstanding, when the public demanded more cash, the banking system often ran short of cash and the economy experienced problems—called *bank panics*.

The scenarios preceding financial panics were similar. First the economy would enter a period of rapid expansion, creating heavy demand for bank credit. Banks would then issue more and more banknotes to satisfy their loan demand; this would increase the money supply, further stimulate the economy, and lead to inflation and higher interest rates. At some point, some banks had overextended themselves by issuing too many banknotes relative to their reserve holdings. A slight downturn in economic activity would cause overextended banks to fail and then people would panic! Why? The public knew that banks had small amounts of reserves relative to the amount of banknotes outstanding. When large numbers of people simultaneously demanded the conversion of their paper money into hard currency, banks were forced to *call* in loans from their customers. At that time, most bank loans were **call loans**, which are loans that are due when the bank calls and asks for repayment. When business loans were called unexpectedly, many businesses failed because they had purchased with their loan money inventory and capital equipment that could not be converted quickly to cash to pay the bank. Bank panics would spread, leading to large numbers of bank failures, which precipitated a large number of business failures as banks called more and more loans. The result was that the country would descend into a recession. The public and politicians began to suspect that there was some relationship between bank failures and the onset of a recession.

From the mid-1860s until the early 1900s, the economy suffered a number of serious recessions and financial panics, culminating in the crash of 1907. The 1907 panic resulted in widespread bank failures, substantial losses to depositors, and a crippling economic recession. The public and politicians were now convinced that a central bank was needed to prevent widespread bank failures and the resulting recessions. However, creating a structure for the new central bank that would be politically acceptable to the public was a challenge. The western and agricultural states, in particular, feared that the eastern industrial complex would control the central bank. These states preferred an **easy money** policy, which meant it was easy for banks to issue banknotes when businesses wanted loans (easy credit) and low interest rates. The eastern states preferred a stronger central bank that had the power to rein in inflation and put an end to the financial panic that led to the economic recessions that periodically crippled the country. As you will see, establishing our third central bank was not an easy task.

THE FEDERAL RESERVE ACT OF 1913

The passage of the Federal Reserve Act in 1913 was meant to correct some of the shortcomings of the national banking system that became apparent during the severe financial crisis of 1907. The goals of the legislation were to establish (1) a monetary authority that would expand and contract the nation's money supply according to the needs of the economy, (2) a **lender of last resort** that could furnish additional funds to banks in times of financial crisis, (3) an efficient payment system for clearing and collecting checks at par (face value) throughout the country, and (4) a more vigorous bank supervision system to reduce the risk of bank failures.

The Federal Reserve System's ability to provide currency was established to eliminate the financial panics that had plagued the country when the public feared currency would not be available on demand. An **elastic money supply** was achieved by authorizing the Federal Reserve banks to issue a new type of banknote—the Federal Reserve note. Member banks of the Federal Reserve System could obtain Federal Reserve notes whenever they needed extra currency. Today, Federal Reserve notes are the principal form of currency in circulation.

Because people were wary of centralized power, the Federal Reserve Act provided for twelve largely autonomous regional Federal Reserve banks coordinated

Free Banking and Wildcat Banks

The 26-year period from 1837 to 1863 is known as the Free Banking era in U.S. history. Banks operated with fewer laws and regulations than in any other period, and anyone who could meet minimum requirements could open a bank. Allowing such freedoms did not work very well; many free banks failed and their banknotes became worthless.

One of the most disastrous experiences with free banking occurred in Michigan. Early in 1837, the state legislature passed the first free banking law to encourage banking and promote economic stability. Unfortunately, it did not. Because banks created money by issuing banknotes, some dishonest people found that banking was an excellent way to "raise" money by printing banknotes to finance speculative or dishonest business ventures. By the end of 1839, most free banks had failed and the public was left with worthless banknotes.

Many of the financial shenanigans pulled by banks in Michigan were carried out by **wildcat banks**. Wildcat banks were opened by dishonest

bankers who intended to defraud the public by issuing banknotes far in excess of their reserves (gold or silver). The scam could work as follows: To discourage the public from redeeming banknotes, bank offices were set up in remote places "where only wildcats would dare tread." The bank would put the bogus banknotes into circulation by investing in assets that could be sold easily for hard currency or for the banknotes of a sound bank. As soon as the bank had the notes in circulation, it would close. The bank officers would then hop the stagecoach with all the assets they could carry and ride off with a tidy profit. Bank creditors were left with an empty vault and worthless banknotes.

Because many people had at one time or another been taken with worthless banknotes, the American vernacular developed many colorful names for paper money. Today, with strict bank regulation and federal deposit insurance, people no longer refer to paper currency as *shinplaster*, *stump rails*, *red dogs*, or *cow chips*.

by a Board of Governors in Washington, D.C. As originally conceived, each regional bank was responsible for the economic needs of a particular geographic area of the country and was owned by member commercial banks in each district that bought stock in the local Federal Reserve bank.

Over the years, the goals and role of the Federal Reserve System have changed with the changing political and economic environment. Originally, the structure of the Federal Reserve System was designed to diffuse power along regional lines; between the private and government sectors; and among bankers, businesspeople, and the public at large. This structure can still be seen today in the geographic boundaries of the district banks shown in Exhibit 2.2. Today, most authority in the system resides with the Board of Governors in Washington, D.C., rather than with the regional Federal Reserve banks, and the primary function of the Federal Reserve is economic stabilization through the management of the nation's money supply.

2.2 THE CURRENT STRUCTURE OF THE FED

The modern-day Federal Reserve System consists of a seven-member Board of Governors, twelve regional Federal Reserve banks (and their branches) located throughout the country, member banks, and a series of advisory committees. The structure also includes the powerful Federal Open Market Committee (FOMC), which conducts the nation's monetary policy.

EXHIBIT 2.2
The Federal Reserve System

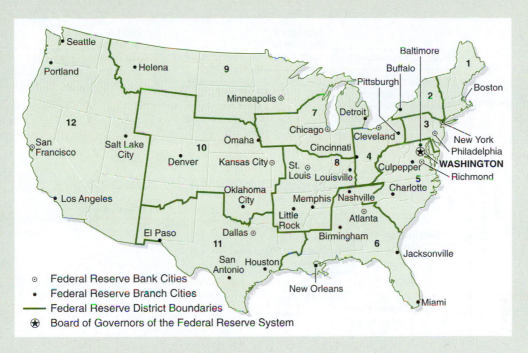

- ⊙ Federal Reserve Bank Cities
- • Federal Reserve Branch Cities
- — Federal Reserve District Boundaries
- ✪ Board of Governors of the Federal Reserve System

The Federal Reserve System consists of the Board of Governors and twelve Federal Reserve districts. Each district is served by a Federal Reserve bank that is named after its headquarters city. Historically, this unusual structure was necessary to calm the public's fear of concentration of political and economic power.

Note: Hawaii and Alaska are in the Twelfth Federal Reserve District.

Source: Federal Reserve Bulletin.

We will now discuss each of the major players in the Federal Reserve System and their responsibilities and powers. You might want to follow along with Exhibit 2.3, which shows the modern structure and policy organization of the Fed.

FEDERAL RESERVE DISTRICT BANKS

The twelve Federal Reserve banks in each region assist in clearing and processing checks and certain electronic funds payments in their respective areas of the country. They also issue Federal Reserve notes, act as a depository for banks in their respective districts, monitor local economic conditions, provide advice to the Federal Reserve Board, and participate in the making of monetary policy.

When first established, Federal Reserve district banks were intended to represent regional interests in Washington and to provide for the credit needs of their regions. Thus, they were given power to issue currency and establish discount rates applicable to all institutions in their regions that wished to borrow from them. Historically, discount rates have occasionally varied from one Federal Reserve bank to another. In recent years, however, the Federal Reserve Board used its power to review discount rates to enforce uniformity.

EXHIBIT 2.3

The Structure and Policy Organization of the FED

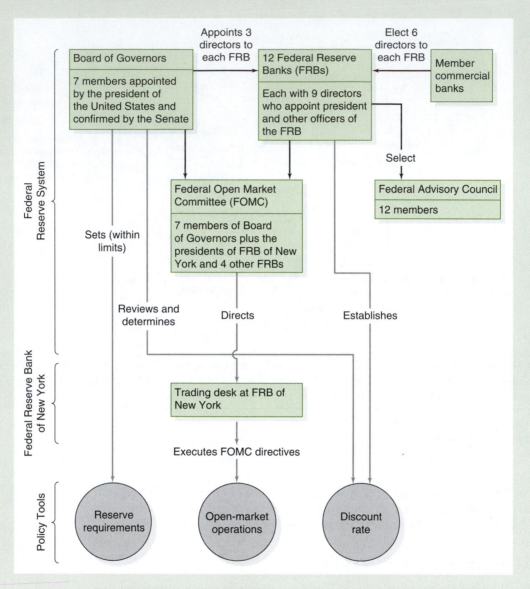

The Federal Reserve System has overlapping lines of authority. From this organizational chart, it is hard to tell who's in charge. Make no mistake about it, monetary policy is one of the big games in Washington, and the dominant person in forming the FOMC monetary policy directive is the chairman of the Board of Governors, currently Ben Bernanke. He chairs the Board of Governors and the FOMC meetings, sets the agenda for both meetings, and controls the flow of information.

Over time, the regional banks relinquished powers to the Board of Governors. Not only can the board review and disapprove the banks' discount rates, thereby causing the district banks to change their discount rates to satisfy the board, but the board also appoints the top officers of each district bank and determines their salaries. Nonetheless, through their periodic representation on the

Federal Open Market Committee (11 banks rotate 4 FOMC memberships, whereas the Federal Reserve Bank of New York has a permanent representative), Federal Reserve bank presidents help establish monetary policy.

MEMBER BANKS

Historically, all member banks were nationally chartered commercial banks, plus about 17 percent of state-chartered banks who chose to join the Federal Reserve System. The Financial Regulatory Reform Act of 2010, which we will discuss later in the chapter, eliminated the Fed's role in supervising small banks. Now the Fed regulates only large banks and bank holding companies with assets of more than $50 billion. Member banks buy stock in their regional Federal Reserve banks and help elect each regional bank's board of directors. The *stock* pays member banks a modest 6 percent dividend but does not carry the traditional powers of ownership, such as sharing in the profits and voting on important management decisions. Prior to 1980, only member banks had unrestricted access to the Federal Reserve's free check-clearing services. In 1980, Congress gave all depository institutions access to the check-clearing services, but it required that they pay service charges.

THE BOARD OF GOVERNORS

At the head of the Federal Reserve System is the seven-member Board of Governors headquartered in Washington, D.C. Because the Board of Governors sets the nation's monetary policy, the Board is among the most powerful of all governmental bodies. It is financially and administratively independent of both Congress and the president.

To promote the Fed's political independence, Congress established 14-year overlapping terms for Federal Reserve Board members, with one 14-year term expiring every 2 years. The governors, who are appointed by the president, are required to come from different Federal Reserve districts to prevent a concentration of power in one region of the country. The Senate confirms all presidential appointments. More recently, many governors chose not to serve the full 14 years, enabling some presidents to appoint a majority of the Board while in office. Whether this has reduced the Fed's independence has been a subject of occasional debate.

The chairman of the Board of Governors is chosen by the president from among the existing governors and serves a 4-year term. Also, it is expected that if a new chairman is chosen, the old chairman resigns from the board, regardless of the time remaining in the appointment.

THE FOMC

The **Federal Open Market Committee (FOMC)** consists of the seven members of the Board of Governors of the Federal Reserve System plus five presidents of Federal Reserve banks. The president of the Federal Reserve Bank of New York is a permanent member. This apparent inequity exists because the Federal Reserve Bank of New York implements monetary policy on a day-to-day basis. The FOMC is extremely important because this group of people actually determines monetary policy. The FOMC monetary actions directly affect the reserve balances of depository institutions and, ultimately, the country's level of economic activity.

THE FEDERAL RESERVE BANK OF NEW YORK

The Federal Reserve Bank of New York plays a special and important role in the Federal Reserve System. The bank is located in the heart of the fabled Wall Street financial district at 33 Liberty Street, a block away from Wall Street. The district is home to some of the largest commercial banks, investment banks, insurance companies, and financial markets in the world. The bank is known for its vast holdings of gold bullion and gold vault, which rest on Manhattan's bedrock 80 feet below street level. The vault contains 10 percent of the world's official gold reserves and holds 5,000 metric tons of gold bullion—$270 billion as of July 2010—more gold than Fort Knox. The gold is owned by many foreign nations, central banks, and international organizations.

The reason for the New York Fed's special status is its day-to-day responsibility of conducting monetary policy for the Federal Reserve System. This is done primarily through open-market operations—the buying and selling of U.S. Treasury securities. The trading desk is where the actual transactions take place, as spelled out in the FMOC's directive. The amount of securities bought or sold at the trading desk in any one day depends on current market conditions, the Fed's monetary policy objectives, technical market factors, and the price of securities across various maturities (the term structure). The Fed trades with a select list of firms from an approved list of government security dealers such as Citibank or Goldman Sachs. In addition, the New York Fed also houses the foreign exchange desk, which conducts foreign exchange interventions on behalf of the Fed and the Treasury Department.

Because of their proximity, Fed officials are in constant contact with key participants in the foreign exchange, bond, and equity markets. They are also in close contact with their counterparts at other central banks and key participants in international financial markets. Thus, New York Fed officials are an important source of intelligence and have significant input into important policy decisions at the Fed. Their intelligence-gathering skills are particularly important during times of financial crisis such as the recent collapse of the subprime mortgage market.

2.3 MONETARY POWERS OF THE BOARD OF GOVERNORS

The Board of Governors controls monetary policy because it controls the FOMC, which determines monetary policy. The reason is that there are only twelve voting members on the FOMC—seven governors and five district bank presidents—and, simply put, the board has the majority votes. The board also sets reserve requirements (within limits set by legislation) and effectively sets the discount rate. The board chair advises the president on economic policy; testifies on the state of the economy before Congress; and may, from time to time, represent the U.S. government in negotiations with foreign countries on economic matters. The board has a large staff of well-trained economists that advises it on economic policy matters and researches important economic questions. In recent years, many of the board members—and usually the chairman—have been trained economists.

REALITIES OF MONETARY POWER

The reality of power at the Fed is that the chairman of the Board of Governors is the dominant figure in the formulation and execution of monetary policy. Because of this power, the chair is often called the second-most-powerful person in the United States. The chairman controls the agenda and chairs the meetings of both the Board of Governors and the FOMC. The chair is the most prominent member of the board and is the official spokesperson for the board to Congress and the national press. Although not always the case in the past, today the chair is a trained economist with significant academic and/or practical experience on Wall Street or in the Federal Reserve System.

To lead the Fed, the chairman must have the leadership skills and intellectual credentials to gain the respect of his colleagues. If he does not, senior officials are less willing to defer to his judgment when the board or FOMC votes on important monetary or policy issues. These situations manifest themselves publicly when the board's votes are split rather than the normal consensus vote. However, there are times when board members or voting regional bank presidents have legitimate policy differences with the chairman and want to express those differences publicly and demonstrate their independence. However, if the truth be known, if you have a powerful chairman in the mold of Alan Greenspan or Paul Volcker, and you rack up too many votes contrary to those of the chairman, you quickly find yourself shut out of the corridors of power. Split votes also begin to occur near the time when the chairman is expected to step down and other board members begin to position themselves for the position of the chairman. As an example, at the September 24, 2003, board meeting, two board members openly broke with then-Chairman Greenspan's decision to hold monetary policy steady, the first time in 4 years there had been such dissent.

BOARD'S PROFESSIONAL STAFF

The board's professional staff of economic experts and advisers is a significant source of informal power within the Fed. Many of these staff have a long tenure in the Federal Reserve System, have in-depth knowledge of its operation and practices, and have a significant power base because of their expertise in some facet of monetary analysis. Furthermore, they interact daily with the Board of Governors, providing them with situational briefings, giving them access to and interpretation of research done at the Fed, and advising them on important decisions. Thus, the professional staff exerts an indefinable but significant influence on policy issues and in the decision-making process at the Fed.

Over the years, the Fed has been given a multitude of regulatory powers over commercial banks. Historically, many regulatory powers were granted following a major financial crisis, such as the Great Depression in 1929. More recently, the Fed has gained regulatory powers to protect consumers, to deal with discrimination in the marketplace, and to adjust to the changing structure of the financial system. To give you a feel for the scope of the Fed's regulatory powers, we discuss some of the more important regulations of the Fed. Exhibit 2.4, although admittedly dry, does a nice job of summarizing important regulatory powers of the Fed. The overall regulation of banks and other financial institutions is covered in detail in Chapter 15.

2.4 THE FED'S REGULATORY POWERS

EXHIBIT 2.4
Important Federal Reserve Regulatory Powers

Regulation	Topics of Regulations	Institutions Affected
A	Establishes Fed discount window policy	Borrowers from discount window
D	Establishes reserve requirements	All depository institutions
E	Regulates electronic funds transfer	All financial institutions
J	Regulates check collection and wire transfers of funds	All institutions using Fed facilities
K	Regulates international banking in United States and by U.S. banks abroad	Domestic and foreign banks
M	Regulates consumer leasing transactions	Institutions leasing consumer goods
G, U, T, X	Establishes securities margin requirements	Brokers, dealers, banks, and individuals
Y	Sets rules applicable to bank holding companies	Banks and their affiliates
Z, B, BB, C	Regulates consumer and mortgage credit transactions according to the following Acts: Z = Truth-in-Lending and Fair Credit Billing Acts B = Equal Credit Opportunity Act BB = Community Reinvestment Act C = Home Mortgage Disclosure Act	Institutions offering consumer and mortgage credit
P	Privacy of consumer financial information	All financial institutions
Q	Prohibits interest on demand deposits; formerly set interest rate ceilings on savings and time deposits	All commercial banks
DD	Regulates interest rate disclosures on deposits	All depository institutions offering interest-bearing deposits

REGULATORY POWERS

The Banking Act of 1933 (often called the *Glass–Steagall Act*) gave the Fed the power to regulate the maximum interest rate that banks could pay to depositors under **Regulation Q**. The Fed was given this power to prevent excessive and destructive competition among banks to attract funds from depositors. At the time, it was believed that excessive competition for deposits had contributed to bank failures and the Great Depression.

Over time, however, regulators discovered that Regulation Q periodically had adverse effects on banks and other depository institutions. The reason was that banks found it difficult to attract or retain deposits when the market rate of interest was higher than the maximum rate banks could pay for funds under Regulation Q. During these periods of time, banks would face disintermediation as depositors withdrew their funds from banks and reinvested their money in financial instruments that paid the market rate. In fact, money market mutual funds emerged in the early 1970s to provide an investment medium that paid the market rate of interest to consumers and investors with small dollar balances. Ultimately, Regulation Q was phased out by the Depository Institutions Deregulation and Monetary Control Act (DIDMCA) of 1980 and the Depository Institutions Act of 1982.

During the depression that followed the 1929 stock market crash, the Fed was given the power to regulate the purchase of stock on *margin*, which means using borrowed funds to purchase stock, which is then used as collateral for the loan. Under Regulations G, T, U, and X the Fed could regulate stock market margin credit requirements (or **margin requirements**), which determine the proportion of the stock's value that can be used as loan collateral. The Fed used these regulations to prevent what was then viewed as excessive speculation in the stock market. Prior to the crash, people could finance 90 percent or more of their stock purchases with the stock as collateral. Thus, if stock prices fell only by 10 percent, they might be unable to repay their debt. As a result, they had to sell quickly when stock prices started to fall, and their selling aggravated the stock price decline. By raising margin requirements, panic selling could be reduced or eliminated. At present, stock margin requirements are 50 percent.

Since the early 1940s, the Fed has been given expanded powers to protect consumers from the vagaries of the market. For example, during World War II and the Korean War, the Fed was given temporary powers to regulate down payment percentages and maximum payment terms on many types of consumer loans under Regulation W (currently lapsed). Further, with the passage of the Truth-in-Lending Act in 1968, the Fed acquired the power to mandate and regulate the disclosure of interest rates on consumer credit offered by banks, savings institutions, credit unions, retailers, finance companies, and other consumer lenders under Regulation Z. The Fed has also been given the power to write regulations mandating that financial institutions meet the requirements of the Equal Credit Opportunity Act (Regulation B), the Community Reinvestment Act (Regulation BB), the Fair Credit Billing Act (Regulation Z again), and many other consumer protection or *antidiscrimination* acts passed by Congress in the 1960s, 1970s, and 1980s.

In the DIDMCA of 1980, the Fed was given the power to assess reserve requirements on the transaction deposits of nonbank depository institutions (under Regulation D) and to allow all such institutions to borrow from its discount window (under Regulation A). Besides its domestic responsibilities, the Fed conducts U.S. interventions in foreign currency markets and is the primary regulator of foreign banks operating in the United States and U.S. banks operating overseas.

THE FINANCIAL CRISIS AND EXPANDED POWERS

To put the recent regulatory changes into perspective, it might be helpful to provide a brief overview of the economic conditions that prevailed during late 2000. As in the past, new regulations are often driven by a major financial crisis. The event was the 2007–2010 financial crisis, which sparked an 18-month recession that began December 2007 and officially ended June 2009. The recession was the longest and deepest downturn for the U.S. economy since the Great Depression (1929–1933). Indicators of a recession are visible declines in production, employment, and real income, and increases in defaults on loans by consumers and businesses.

The recession was global in scope and was spread around the industrial world by U.S. investment bankers marketing mortgage-backed securities. The financial crisis was linked to unintended consequences of changing lending practices by financial institutions. The federal government desired to increase homeownership and encouraged financial institutions to make high-risk mortgage loans to unqualified buyers. Another factor was the securitization of real estate mortgages in the United States that created highly marketable securities, but this securitization had underlying risks that were difficult to assess.

The collapse of the mortgage market began in the subprime lending market and quickly led to the collapse of the speculative bubble in the housing market.[1] Massive defaults on home mortgages, falling housing prices, and sharp and unexpected increases in commodity prices such as oil and food led to the failure and collapse of many of the United States' largest and most prestigious financial intuitions, such as Lehman Brothers, as well as a crisis in the automobile industry.

At the same time, millions of Americans lost their jobs, their savings were wiped out, and they saw few prospects for their future. The political consensus among the general public (voters) was that Wall Street and large businesses were out of control and needed to be reined in. Many economists felt that very large banks and nonbank business firms had the potential, if they failed, to threaten the stability of the overall economy.

The federal government responded with an unprecedented $700 billion bank bailout program to restore confidence in and stabilize the banking system, and a $787 billion fiscal stimulus bill that was designed to reduce unemployment and revitalize the U.S. automobile industry. Fiscal and monetary policies have somewhat stemmed the recession. As we approach the summer of 2011, however, unemployment remains at 9 percent and uncertainty remains about the future.

NEW REGULATORY POWERS

Because of regulatory failure, Congress passed a major overhaul of the regulatory structure for the U.S. financial system—the Financial Regulatory Reform Act of 2010 (the official name of the act is Restoring American Financial Stability). The biggest "winner" among the regulatory agencies with respect to power and influence was the Federal Reserve System. This result was not unexpected because the Fed is the only regulatory agency with the policy tools (monetary policy) at its disposal and the intellectual capital to manage the economy's systemic risk effectively. The overall thrust of the new regulations is to provide the Fed with the authority to monitor and, when necessary, intervene in the business affairs of large complex bank and nonbank holding companies that pose substantial risk to the national economy. Let's look at some of the Fed's gains from the 2010 Regulatory Reform Act.

Managing Systemic Risk.   The Fed's most important gain from the Regulatory Reform Act was to expand its ability to manage **systemic risk** in the economy (risk of the failure of the entire financial system resulting from the interdependencies among financial institutions). The act provides the Fed with unprecedented power to intervene in the business activities of large nonbank firms so it can better monitor and control systemic risk across the economy. This power is shared jointly with the Financial Stability Oversight Council (FSOC), which was created by Congress to identify and monitor systemic risk posed by large firms. The desired outcome from the legislation is for the Fed to take appropriate action before these large firms threaten the stability of the economy. In addition, if a large nonbank financial firm currently regulated by another entity, such as an insurance company, poses a threat to the national economy, the Fed has the power to take over the regulation

---

[1]Speculative bubbles are spikes in asset prices within a particular industry or commodity class, caused by exaggerated expectations of future price appreciation that cannot be supported by the asset's intrinsic value. Once investors realize the folly of their ways, prices fall back to a level supported by the asset's intrinsic value. The decline in prices usually involves a period of steep price declines (the bubble bursts) during which most investors panic and sell out of the assets.

of the firm. And in extraordinary circumstances, it has the power to break up firms or to require them to divest themselves of certain assets.

The Too Big to Fail Problem. The 2010 act contained legislation designed to reduce the possibility that tax payers will be placed in the position to bail out financial firms whose failure threatens the overall economy; the so-called **too big to fail** problem. The FSOC has the authority to make recommendations to the Fed to improve standards for capital, leverage, risk taking, and other performance measures. Thus, one of the legislation's goals is to strengthen large financial firms so they can better withstand financial stress and control their growth. The growth rate of a firm is important to monitor because economists believe that, as companies grow in size and complexity, their failure poses a greater risk to the financial system.

Why were these changes needed? Economists have long held the view that the federal government cannot allow giant financial firms to fail, especially large bank holding companies. To let them go bankrupt would cause irreparable damage to the economy, resulting in a banking panic, recession, or worse. As a result, the federal government steps in to bail out these firms if they get into serious financial trouble.

Of course, the theory of too big to fail is no longer idle speculation because that's what the $700 billion Emergency Economic Stabilization Act of 2008 was all about. The act, more commonly known as the *bailout of the U.S. financial system*, provided up to $700 billion for the U.S. Treasury to acquire distressed assets from banks, especially mortgage-backed securities, and to make capital injections into banks. The bailout of the financial system was the right course of action, but it has not proven to be a popular issue with the general public.

Tougher Regulations for Large Banks. The new bill also realigned regulatory reporting lines. Of interest, the 2010 bill strips the Fed of its oversight of more than 5,000 small bank holding companies and state-chartered banks with assets of less than $50 billion. Now, the Fed will regulate only large financial institutions, banks, and thrift holding companies with assets greater than $50 billion.

The reason for the realignment of regulators was to align small financial institutions with regulators who were more supportive of and sympathetic to their core mission of providing financial service to consumers. The Fed, on the other hand, with its extensive capital market experience, is better equipped to oversee the business activities of large, complex bank holding companies than other regulators. These oversight activities are also consistent with the Fed's responsibility to help identify and manage systemic risks in the economy.

2.5 INDEPENDENCE OF THE FED

One of the controversial aspects of the organization of the Federal Reserve System is the issue of its independence. Although the Fed is the key player in the management of the nation's economy through the conduct of monetary policy, it is not directly under the authority of Congress or the president. The Fed's independence is a result of the historical legacy of how it was founded and organized. The term *Fed independence* means that the Fed is free from political and bureaucratic pressures when it formulates and executes monetary policy.

In the short run, the Fed has a substantial degree of independence because it operates as a bank—in fact, a very profitable bank. Thus, unlike other government agencies, the Fed does not rely on Congress for funding. For example, in recent years the Fed's net earnings after expenses have been around $30 billion per year.

The Fed makes the lion's share of its earnings, about 85 percent, from its large portfolio of government securities. The balance of its earnings comes from loans to banks and nonbanks that borrow at the discount window and from miscellaneous fees it charges for services such as check clearing. Further promoting to Fed independence is the long 14-year terms of the governors, which insulates them from day-to-day political pressures. Assuming no resignations, incoming presidents can appoint only two governors in their first 4-year term and a majority of the board late in their second term.

Over the longer run, the Federal Reserve banks' independence is constrained. The Fed is well aware that it is our nation's third central bank. The two previous central banks lost their charters. The Fed is fully aware that Congress created the Federal Reserve System and that its charter can always be modified or terminated by Congress. Also, if the truth be known, it is unlikely that Congress would want the responsibility of setting monetary policy: Who would they have to blame when the economy performs poorly?

Finally, the Fed is subject to the laws of the United States, including the Employment Act of 1946 and the Full Employment and Balanced Growth Act of 1978, which come close to spelling out the economic responsibilities of the federal government. As a result, the Fed is keenly aware of political pressures and of secular changes in economic policy. A study of monetary policy after World War II indicates shifts in Fed economic policy whenever the presidency has changed hands. These shifts brought the Fed's policies more in line with the views of the new president, regardless of the personal views of the chairman or the president who originally appointed him.

In summary, overall the Fed has an extraordinary degree of independence for a government agency and is one of the most independent central banks in the world. And most interested parties agree that the Fed and, particularly, monetary policy should be insulated from short-run partisan politics. However, like the Supreme Court, the Fed recognizes the power of the political process and is not immune from the desires of the electorate. Thus, the Federal Reserve System is independent within, rather than independent of, the federal government.

IS INDEPENDENCE IMPORTANT?

Advocates of an *independent* central bank believe that independence from day-to-day political pressure allows the Fed to better manage their countries' national economies. By *better*, we mean that the central bank can take short-run policy actions that may be politically unpopular but in the longer run benefit the economy's overall macroeconomic performance. For example, this is often the case when inflationary pressures begin to build up in an economy during a period of rapid economic expansion. To dampen the inflation, a central bank raises interest rates to slow the rate of economic growth and, thus, dampen inflationary expectations. Needless to say, raising interest rates to slow down an economy rarely wins political applause.

Research supports the benefits of an independent central bank. When central banks for different countries are rank-ordered as to their degree of independence on a scale of 1 to 4 (1 being the least and 4 being the most independent), performance in controlling inflation is found to be best in countries with the most-independent central banks. As can be seen in Exhibit 2.5, the countries with the least-independent central banks, Spain and New Zealand, had average annual inflation rates for the study period of around 12 percent. In contrast, the two

EXHIBIT 2.5
Central Bank Independence and a Country's Rate of Inflation

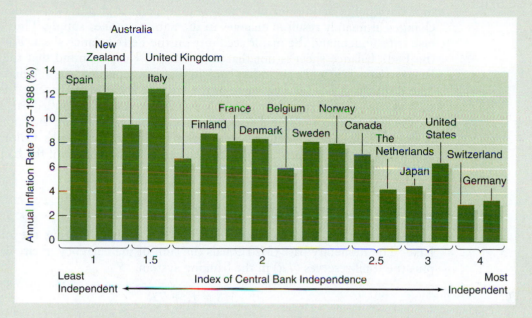

Countries with independent central banks have lower rates of inflation than countries with less independent central banks.

Source: Alberto Alesina and Lawrence Summers, "Central Bank Independence and Macroeconomic Performance, Some Comparative Evidence," *Journal of Money, Credit, and Banking* 25 (1993): 151–162.

countries with the most independent central banks, Switzerland and Germany, had average annual inflation rates around 3 percent. In the United States, whose central bank independence index was a 3, the average inflation rate was slightly more than 6 percent. Most economists agree that low rates of inflation are generally good for an economy. It is important to note that the study found that countries with independent central banks were no more likely to have high unemployment or greater fluctuation in national income than countries with less independent central banks.

DO YOU UNDERSTAND?

1. What were the problems posed by the National Banking Acts?
2. Why was the Fed initially established?
3. How did the Federal Reserve System try to solve problems from the National Banking Act period?
4. What is meant by "too big to fail"? What are the economic factors that drive this principle?

2.6 THE FED'S BALANCE SHEET

To gain an understanding of what the Fed does and how it implements monetary policy, it is useful to examine the Fed's balance sheet. As we see there, the Fed's monetary policy actions lead to changes in its balance sheet. These balance sheet changes ultimately result in changes to the nation's money supply. Thus, our first task is to understand the major accounts on the Fed's balance sheet. Fortunately, the Fed's balance sheet is not that complicated. Keep in mind that the Federal Reserve bank is just like any other bank in that it accepts deposits and makes loans. The difficulty arises because some of the balance sheet items have special names such as *reserves* or *discount borrowing*. Exhibit 2.6 presents a simplified balance sheet for the Fed. During our initial discussion, focus your attention on the January 2007 balance sheet, which occurred before the federal government's bailout of the financial system. The July 2010 balance sheet shows the effect of the bailout. We will discuss it at the end of the section.

LIABILITIES AND CAPITAL OF THE FED

Operationally, the Fed conducts monetary policy by changing the **monetary base**. The monetary base (MB) equals the sum of the currency in circulation (C) plus the total reserves (TR) in the banking system.

$$MB = C + TR \tag{2.1}$$

The Federal Reserve exercises control over the monetary base through the purchase or sale of government securities in the open market, called **open-market operations**. Holding everything constant, an increase in the monetary base leads to an increase in the money supply. As a practical matter, the Fed issues most of the currency in circulation, with the exception of a small percentage issued by the U.S. Treasury Department. However, we can ignore the monetary liabilities of the Treasury because the Treasury is not allowed to engage in monetary policy actions. Let's examine in more detail the most important monetary liabilities of the Fed.

Federal Reserve Notes.   As shown in Exhibit 2.6, by far the largest single liability of the Fed consists of Federal Reserve notes in circulation. Look at the bills (if any) in your pocket. You find that each has a seal of the Federal Reserve. You can take the bill to the Fed and ask for lawful money in exchange, but you get back only another Federal Reserve note. You do not get gold or any other precious metal. Federal Reserve notes are lawful money because they are "Legal tender for all debts, public and private." That means you can repay any debt in this country by offering the proper amount of Federal Reserve notes.

Depository Institution Reserves.   All banks and other depository institutions by law must hold deposits at the Federal Reserve banks, and these deposits are given the special name *reserves*. Reserves consist of all deposits held at the Fed and cash that is physically held in the bank's vault (called *vault cash*). These deposits are useful because they can be transferred from one institution to another when checks and wire transfers are *cleared* from one institution to another. Historically, the Fed has not paid interest on reserve accounts. It was granted the authority to pay interest on reserves because of technical problems it encountered implementing monetary policy during periods of extremely low interest rates. This issue will be discussed in greater detail later in the chapter.

EXHIBIT 2.6
Fed Balance Sheet

	January 2007 No Effect		July 2010 Bailout Effect	
	$Millions[a]	% of Total[a]	$Millions[a]	% of Total[a]
Assets				
Gold certificates	11,037	1.3%	11,037	0.5%
Special drawing rights certificates	2,200	0.3	5,200	0.2
Coin	797	0.1	1,958	0.1
U.S. government and agency securities	778,910	88.5	776,977	33.3
Federal agency debt securities	0	0.0	164,762	7.1
Mortgage backed securities	0	0.0	1,118,290	47.9
Loans	1,262	0.1	66,925	2.9
Net portfolio holdings through LLCs	0	0.0	93,235	4.0
Items in process of collection	6,773	0.8	763	0.0
Bank premises	1,945	0.2	2,230	0.1
Other assets	76,900	8.7	94,175	4.0
Total	$879,824	100.0%	$2,335,552	100.0%
Liabilities and capital				
Federal Reserve notes	781,347	88.8%	907,698	38.9%
Securities sold under agreements to repurchase	29,742	3.4	62,904	2.7
Deposits				
Depository institution reserves	20,044	2.3	1,061,239	45.4
U.S. Treasury	6,156	0.7	216,438	9.3
Foreign official	90	0.0	1,646	0.1
Other	239	0.0	10,593	0.5
Deferred availability cash items (DACI)	6,100	0.7	3,522	0.2
Other liabilities and accrued dividends	5,501	0.6	14,578	0.6
Capital	30,605	3.5	56,934	2.4
Total	$879,824	100.0%	$2,335,552	100.0%

Source: Board of Governors, Federal Reserve System, Federal Reserve Statistical Release, July 8, 2010. Available at http://www.federalreserve.gov/monetarypolicy/bst_fedsbalancesheet.htm

[a]Columns may not add up to totals because of rounding.

Reserves are also useful to the Fed for controlling the nation's money supply. Depository institutions are required to hold a certain amount of reserves at the Federal Reserve bank determined by the amount of transaction deposits their customers hold at their bank. Depository institutions can withdraw cash (Federal Reserve notes) from their reserve accounts at the Fed when they need it. As we explain later, any time there is an increase in reserves at the Fed, there is an increase in the money supply.

It is important to note that the **total reserves (TR)** held by a bank can be divided into two components: (1) reserves that the bank is required to hold by law, called **required reserves (RR)**, and (2) reserves in excess of those required, called **excess reserves (ER)**. Thus,

$$TR = RR + ER. \tag{2.2}$$

As mentioned previously, a bank must hold required reserves that are a specified percentage (fraction) of the total deposits at the bank. This fraction is called the *required reserve ratio* or *reserve requirement*, expressed as a percentage. For example, if the reserve requirement is 10 percent and the bank has \$10,000 in deposits, the bank's required reserves are \$1,000. Thus, the formula for required reserves is

$$RR = k \times DEP \text{ or } k = RR/DEP. \tag{2.3}$$

where k is the required reserve ratio and DEP is the total deposits held at the bank. Using Equation 2.2, if the bank has total reserves of \$1,500, the bank has excess reserves of \$500 (\$1,500 − \$1,000).

What does the bank do with the \$500 of excess reserves? Suppose the Fed does not pay interest on reserve accounts. The bank could leave the money at the Fed. However, there is an opportunity cost to holding non-interest-bearing assets. To put the money to work and earn some interest, the bank could lend the reserves to other banks in the Fed funds market or make business or consumer loans. The point here is that the bank has some options regarding what to do with its excess reserves. For most banks, the decision to hold excess reserves involves a risk-return trade-off; that is, the bank gives up some potential earnings for additional liquidity and bank safety.

When would a bank want to hold a substantial amount of excess reserves? Suppose that the nation is in a significant recession and credit markets are very unstable. With the risky environment, the bank will want to increase its liquidity (bank safety) and hold more excess reserves. All things being equal, the greater the uncertainty in the economy, the greater is management's desire to hold excess reserves. The decision by the Fed to pay interest on reserves will also affect the amount of excess reserves held by the bank. In general, all things being equal, the higher the interest rate the Fed pays on reserves, the more likely the bank is to increase its holding of excess reserves at the Fed.

Treasury Deposits.   Another important class of Federal Reserve deposits consists of U.S. Treasury deposits. The Federal Reserve acts as the *fiscal agent* for the U.S. Treasury Department, which simply means that the Fed acts as a bank for the Treasury, which can pay its bills by writing checks from its account at the Fed. If you ever get a check from the federal government, read the fine print and you find that the check was written on a deposit at a Federal Reserve bank. The Fed pays no interest on its checking accounts, and rarely provides free coffee and doughnuts for its depositors.

Deferred Availability Cash Items.   **Deferred availability cash items (DACI)** represent the value of checks deposited at the Fed by depository institutions that have not yet been credited to the institutions' accounts. For instance, if a bank in New York deposits a $200 check written on a bank in California, it gets a $200 deferred availability cash item for 2 days. At the end of that time, the New York bank's reserve deposit is increased by $200. The Fed does not give the New York bank instant credit because it takes time to ship the check to California and collect on it from the California bank. If all goes well, the Fed expects to collect the check in 2 days, and usually it is cheaper and more desirable to transfer the funds to the New York bank's account automatically than to wait for a message saying the check was finally collected from the California bank.

Capital.   Fed *capital* primarily represents money paid in by banks that are members of the Federal Reserve System (*member banks*) to purchase stock. The Fed pays a 6 percent dividend on that stock regardless of its earnings and returns the remainder (more than $25 billion a year) to the U.S. Treasury each year. As mentioned previously, stock in the Fed does not carry the typical rights of ownership as does stock in a corporation.

ASSETS OF THE FED

There are two important assets on the Fed balance sheet we must discuss. First, the Fed's loan accounts: changes in the loan accounts lead to changes in the reserve account and, hence, changes in the money supply. Second, the Fed's portfolio of government securities: the Fed earns billions of dollars every year on its large portfolio of government securities. Although most of these net profits are returned to the Treasury, they provide part of the foundation for the Fed's political independence from the president and Congress.

Loans.   Like any bank, the Fed can make loans, but it only makes loans to banks and other depository institutions. Loans from the Fed are for short periods of time, and the rate charged is referred to as the **discount rate**. When first established, the **discount window**, which is where banks borrow from the Fed, was designed to provide loans as a lender of last resort. Thus, when a bank was unable to attract the funds it needed in the market, it could borrow from the Fed. (In case you're wondering, there is no physical discount window; it's just an expression.) Historically, however, when banks wanted to borrow from the Fed, they had to provide bank loans as collateral for their borrowing. When the loans were brought to the "teller's" window at the Fed, the loans were collateralized at less than their face value, or discounted—hence, the term *discount window*.

Government Securities.   The Federal Reserve bank's largest asset category is its portfolio of U.S. Treasury and U.S. government agency securities. The Fed can buy and sell government securities in the market at will through its **open-market operations**. When the Fed buys government securities, it pays for them by providing the bank with additional reserves, thus immediately increasing the monetary base and ultimately increasing the money supply.

Cash Items in Process of Collection. **Cash items in process of collection (CIPC)** are items the Federal Reserve is clearing but for which it has not yet obtained funds. In our earlier example, the $200 check deposited by the New York bank is a CIPC item until it is actually subtracted from the account of the California bank on which it was written. Because the Fed clears many checks, the number of CIPC items is large.

Float. *Float* represents a net extension of credit from the Fed to depository institutions. It is the difference between CIPC and DACI. For instance, if it took the Fed 3 days to collect the check from the California bank instead of the 2 days assumed by the deferred availability credit schedule, the New York bank would receive a $200 deposit to its reserve account at the Fed the day before the money was withdrawn from the California bank's reserve account—so, DACI would fall but CIPC would not; as a result, float would rise by $200.

THE FINANCIAL SYSTEM BAILOUT

The Fed's balance sheet for July 2010 is distorted because it reflects aggressive monetary action—buying Treasury and other securities—by the Fed to stabilize the economy (see Exhibit 2.6). The financial crisis was the most severe since the 1930s. The balance sheet for January 2007 predates the financial crisis and thus is not affected. This section examines the effect of the Fed's monetary actions on key balance sheet accounts and some of the future consequences of the Fed's actions. To aid our discussion, the accounts we want to discuss are reproduced in the table below:

	Jan 2007	July 2010	Jan 2007	July 2010
Fed's Balance Sheet Items	**$Millions**	**$Millions**	**% of Total**	**% of Total**
U.S. government securities	778,910	941,759	88.5	40.4
Mortgage-backed securities	0	1,118,290	0.0	47.9
Loans	1,262	66,925	0.1	2.0
Depository institution reserves	20,044	1,061,239	2.3	45.4

The Emergency Economic Stabilization Act of 2008 was passed by Congress to respond to the collapse of the subprime mortgage market. The bill was motivated by a series of financial events precipitated by significant losses at large U.S. financial institutions during September 2008, including the federal government's takeover of Fannie Mae and Freddie Mac, the bankruptcy of Lehman Brothers, an emergency Federal Reserve loan to A.I.G. (American International Group), and the merger of Bank of America with the troubled investment firm Merrill Lynch.

The bailout plan authorized the secretary of the Treasury to spend up to $700 billion to purchase distressed and illiquid assets, especially mortgage-backed securities from impaired financial firms. Supporters of the plan argued that market intervention would reduce the uncertainty regarding these assets and prevent further erosion of confidence in the U.S. financial system. They also argued that a failure of Congress to act decisively could lead to a greater erosion of confidence in the financial system, resulting in a possible economic depression. On the other hand, opinion polls showed the American public had little tolerance for bailing out Wall Street investment firms. Some policymakers argued that $700 million was too much and some lower dollar amount would have sufficed.

The Fed's balance sheet exploded with mortgage-backed securities as the Fed went on a spending spree, purchasing distressed assets from financially impaired banks and other financial firms. Recall that in January 2007 there is no bailout effect, while July 2010 is a period affected by the bailout policy. From the table, you can see the following:

- The Fed's purchases of government securities increased $162.9 billion ($941.8 − $778.9) and mortgage-backed securities increased $1,118.3 billion ($1,118.3 − $0.0), for a total increase of $1,281.2 billion above a nonbailout year. Thus, the Fed was pumping massive amounts of liquidity—$1.28 trillion—into the financial system to stabilize it and gain public confidence.

- Using open-market operations, the Fed purchased Treasury and mortgage-backed securities from banks and credited their reserve account the amount of the transaction. Between the two balance sheet dates, the additional reserves held by banks increased by $1,041.2 billion ($1,061,239 − $20,044). As of July 2010, banks were holding much of their reserves and not lending them out to consumers or businesses. With the uncertainty in the economy, the Fed paying 0.25 percent on reserve balances, and the market Fed funds rate around 0.20 percent, most bankers felt it was in their best economic interest to "invest" in reserves at the Fed.

- The Fed's mortgage-backed securities portfolio carries substantial risk, and some of the assets may turn out to be worth much less than they are currently valued on the Fed's balance sheet. For example, the assets the Fed has taken from A.I.G. and Bear Stearns have resulted in some losses.

- So far the Fed continues to generate profits even with the losses to its mortgage-backed security portfolio. In 2009, the Fed earned a record profit of $45 billion, which was returned to the U.S. Treasury Department. This may not be the case in the future if large losses mount in the mortgage-backed security portfolio.

- Banks have substantially increased their borrowing at the discount window—by $65.7 billion ($66,925 − $1,262). These numbers are driven by smaller banks who are taking advantage of low-cost money from the Fed, a profit motive, and/or banks that have legitimate financial problems and cannot borrow in the open market. This is the Fed acting in its role of lender of last resort.

- Drawing down the Fed's balance sheet to levels before the crisis will require some agility and careful timing by the Fed. If the asset balances are drawn down too quickly, the Fed may drain critical liquidity out of the financial system and short-circuit the economic recovery. On the other hand, if the Fed waits too long to sell off the assets and the reserves spill over into the general economy, it will create a condition for massive monetary expansion, which could potentially lead to high levels of inflation.

LEARNING BY DOING 2.1
Computing a Bank's Excess Reserve Position

PROBLEM: A regional bank receives a new demand deposit (*DD*) of $5,000,000, in addition to existing demand deposits of $4,000,000. The current reserve requirement is 10 percent. The bank has $100,000 in vault cash and $350,000 in deposits at the Federal Reserve that are not yet invested. How much in excess reserves does the bank have available to make new loans?

APPROACH: This is an application of Equations 2.1 and 2.2. You first need to determine the amount of required reserves (*RR*) using the reserve requirement ratio (*k*) and the amount of deposits the bank has. Once *RR* is determined, you need to recognize that the bank has reserves already in the form of vault cash and deposits at the Fed. You can then use this information to compute the amount of excess reserves that the bank has available to loan out using Equation 2.1.

SOLUTION: Amount of required reserves (*RR*) needed by the bank:

$$RR = DD \times k = (\$5,000,000 + \$4,000,000) \times 0.10$$
$$= \$900,000$$

Total reserves (*TR*) at the bank in

$$TR = \text{cash} + \text{deposits at the Fed} + \text{new deposits}$$
$$= \$100,000 + \$350,000 + \$5,000,000$$
$$= \$5,450,000$$

Using Equation 2.1, the excess reserves (*ER*) available to the bank are:

$$ER = TR - RR$$
$$= \$5,450,000 - \$900,000$$
$$= \$4,550,000$$

The bank can use its excess reserves of $4.55 million to make new loans and/or invest in securities.

2.7 THE FED'S ROLE IN CHECK CLEARING

Many checks and electronic transfers are *cleared* by local banks exchanging them through local clearinghouse associations. Those clearinghouses net out the value of checks and transfers drawn on or received by each depository institution in the association and make only net payments of the net balances due among members in the association. This saves much time and expense because payments do not have to be made for each transaction individually.

The Fed also plays a major role in check clearing, particularly in clearing checks drawn on depository institutions located in other market areas or different parts of the country. The Fed clearing process is facilitated by the fact that most depository institutions either directly or indirectly hold reserve deposits or clearing deposit balances with the Fed. These deposits can then be transferred easily from one institution to another by making appropriate entries on the Fed's books.

It is important to remember that reserve balances are transferred from one bank to another when checks are cleared between them. They do not disappear from the banking system, only from the account of the bank on which the check was drawn. The total level of reserves at the Fed remains unchanged.

As noted earlier, the Federal Reserve is the most important financial institution in the economy because it controls the nation's money supply. The Fed has three major tools to either increase or decrease the money supply: (1) open-market operations, (2) changing the discount rate, and (3) changing the reserve requirement ratio.

2.8 FEDERAL RESERVE TOOLS OF MONETARY POLICY

OPEN-MARKET OPERATIONS

Open-market operations involve the buying and selling of government securities through the trading desk at the Federal Reserve Bank of New York. It is the most important policy tool the Fed has for controlling the money supply. The FOMC is the focal point for setting monetary policy at the Fed; it meets eight times per year in the main building of the Board of Governors in Washington, D.C. The purpose of the meeting is to set the target growth rate for the money supply, given past, current, and expected economic conditions.

The FOMC meeting starts at 9:00 A.M. sharp with the seven members of the Board of Governors and the twelve regional bank presidents, along with assorted senior staff members from the regional banks, the Board of Governors, and officers in direct charge of domestic and international securities operations. The board and the regional bank presidents (and a few key board staff members) sit around a large conference table. Other attendees are relegated to sitting around the sides of the room and, according to tradition, remain silent. Also, although only five of the regional bank presidents can vote, all are allowed to participate in the discussions.

The meetings have a predictable schedule. After housekeeping chores like approving the minutes of the last meeting, the first substantive report is a presentation on domestic open-market operations and foreign currency market operations since the FOMC's last meeting. Next is a briefing that is prepared by the board's economists on past and current economic conditions and then a 2-year national economic forecast. This report is often called the *green book forecast* because of the color of the folder it is bound in. Then regional bank presidents present their views of economic conditions in their districts. The information, contained in a report called the *beige book* (the cover color is beige), is derived from regional statistical data and extensive interviews with regional business and political leaders. The beige book is the only Fed briefing book distributed publicly and frequently receives considerable press coverage. The final formal presentation, contained in the *blue book*, is made by the board's director of monetary affairs. The presentation usually contains three alternative scenarios for monetary policy, given current and expected economic conditions.

After a discussion, the chairman of the Board of Governors presents his view on the state of the economy and what monetary policy actions are warranted. Then FOMC members and nonvoting regional bank presidents express their views on the appropriate monetary action. At some point, the chairman summarizes the

A Contrast in Style: Greenspan Versus Bernanke

Many consider the Federal Reserve chairman the second most powerful person in Washington behind the president. Every word the chairman utters, whether it be Ben Bernanke, the current chair, or Alan Greenspan, the past chair, is carefully gauged and calibrated for economic meaning. What is interesting about these two men are the differences in their career paths and the contrast in their management styles. They could not be more different.

Alan Greenspan set a record for longevity when he resigned as chairman of the Federal Reserve Board in January 2006, after 14 years in the position. Early in his career, he was an aspiring musician who attended the Juilliard School of Music and traveled with a swing band playing the clarinet. His passion for numbers and data served him well when he became a Wall Street veteran running his own economic consulting firm. He was also no stranger to the Washington power scene and was a seasoned player by the time he was appointed chairman of the Federal Reserve Board during June 1987. Greenspan's tenure spanned four presidents, a stock market crash, three foreign debt crises, and the onset of the War on Terror. Through it all, Greenspan won an iconic place in U.S. economic history for calming markets, controlling inflation, and invigorating the economy. Greenspan's only misstep in a long and illustrious career is that he may have kept interest rates too low, thus creating the asset bubble in real estate, which some experts believe led to the 2008 credit crisis.

Ben Bernanke succeeded Alan Greenspan as chairman when President Bush nominated him in October 2005. Bernanke holds a Ph.D. in economics from MIT and has a formidable reputation as a scholar. It's fair to say that Bernanke spent most of his career as a professor, first at Stanford University and then in the economics department at Princeton University, where he became the department chair. He was, however, no stranger to the highest levels of economic policymaking. Before becoming chairman of the Federal Reserve Board, he served

as a member of the Board of Governors (2002–2005) and as chairman of the President's Council of Economic Advisors (2006).

In contrasting the two individuals, Fed watchers consider Bernanke less ideological than former Ayn Rand disciple Greenspan, noting Greenspan's reluctance to weigh in on taxation and other public policy issues he considers to be outside the Fed's purview. Greenspan, never an economic theorist, believed in the power of the competitive market, favoring less regulatory intervention than Bernanke does. Greenspan's decisions were based on data analysis and intuitive instincts honed from years of experience on Wall Street.

In contrast, Bernanke relies on analytical academic models of markets and the economy to provide insight to policymaking decisions. Bernanke, always the professor, prefers open discussion of the issues with lots of give and take before making a decision, often stating his position last so as not to stifle discussion. Greenspan is more traditional and liked to control the discussion closely, often stating his views and position early in the discussion.

Finally, we should report that Bernanke has received much praise from fellow economists for handling the recession. On the firing line, his actions have been bold yet steady as the economy appears to be pulling out of its worst economic crisis since the 1930s. In many respects, he has tossed out the Fed's standard playbook and has orchestrated a number of innovative Wall Street financial rescues from shotgun weddings to emergency loan programs, and has provided the economy with vast amounts of new money. (In a shotgun wedding, The Fed "forces" some healthy Wall Street firms to acquire some failing firms via creation of financing deals or regulatory/political pressure.) Bernanke also knows that if the great recession turns into the Great Depression or if inflation runs rampant during the recovery, he will be blamed. On the other hand, if the economy recovers in a reasonable time, he's fast on his way to becoming a financial icon.

discussion and proposes a specific wording for the monetary policy directive that is given to the open-market desk to execute. The FOMC secretary then reads the proposed directive, and the twelve voting members vote. The policy directive is delivered to the manager of the Open-Market Account at the New York Fed, who uses it as a guideline to instruct traders at the open-market desk to buy or sell government securities. All of this is usually done by lunchtime.

In the afternoon of the same day, the Fed makes a public announcement of the outcome of the meeting: whether the Federal Reserve discount rate and target Fed funds rate is lowered, raised, or left unchanged. Historically, the Fed did not make public announcements after the meeting, and the markets had to guess what policy actions were taken. This led to intense speculation and, over time, a whole industry developed on Wall Street called *Fed watching*. The policy directives were published with a lag of 90 days. In 1994, however, the Fed decided to post meeting announcements to reduce the intense speculation and rumors that followed each meeting.

Changes to the Money Supply. The Fed changes the amount of reserves in the banking system on a day-to-day basis through the purchase or sale of government securities on the open market. The Fed is the only institution in the country that can expand or contract its liabilities at will. To expand them, it need only issue Federal Reserve notes or write a check on itself. The Fed can "print up" money whenever it needs it!

Let's do a simple example with T-accounts to see what happens when the Fed buys or sells government securities. Let's say the Fed decides to buy $1,000 in government bonds from Citibank in New York City. The T-accounts for Citibank and the Fed after the transaction are as follows (see upper portion of T-accounts):

Citibank		The Fed	
−$1,000 gov. bonds +$1,000 reserves at FRB		+$1,000 gov. bonds	+$1,000 Reserve deposit of Citibank
+$1,000 gov. bonds −$1,000 reserves at FRB		−$1,000 gov. bonds	−$1,000 reserves at Citibank

Notice that the Citibank balance sheet shows a reduction of $1,000 from its bond portfolio and an increase of $1,000 in its reserve deposit with the Federal Reserve bank (FRB). Essentially, the Fed has paid the bank $1,000 in reserves for the government bonds. As you can see in the upper portion of the T-accounts, the banking system as a whole now has an additional $1,000 in reserves because of the Fed's purchase of government bonds and the resulting expansion of the money supply.

Using similar reasoning, the sale of securities by the Fed leads to a contraction of the money supply. The lower portion of the T-accounts above illustrates what happens when desk traders at the Fed are instructed to sell government securities, with Citibank buying $1,000 of the bonds. Citibank pays for the bonds using its funds (reserves) at the Fed. As a result, the banking system has fewer reserves and, hence, the money supply has decreased.

DISCOUNT WINDOW BORROWING

The discount rate is the rate of interest that financial institutions must pay to borrow reserve deposits from the Fed. When the discount rate is low, financial institutions have an inexpensive source of funds for reserve requirement obligations, provided they don't mind the *discount window scrutiny*. That is, banks that frequently borrow from the discount window signal that they may have serious financial problems because they are not able to obtain funds in the market. Thus, when the discount rate is low, financial institutions prudently expand their assets and deposits more readily because it does not cost them as much to obtain the reserves required to back their new deposit or asset holdings. When the discount rate is high, the institutions are more reluctant to borrow reserves and are therefore more careful about expanding asset and deposit holdings if they must borrow from the Fed.

When banks borrow from the discount window, the funds they borrow are paid in reserves by the Fed. For example, suppose that Citibank borrows $1,000 at the discount window, resulting in the following T-account transaction:

Citibank		The Fed	
+$1,000 reserves at the FRB	+$1,000 discount loan	+$1,000 loan to Citibank	+$1,000 reserve deposits of Citicorp

Thus, when banks borrow at the discount window, there is an increase in reserves in the banking system and, hence, an increase in the money supply. The bank can hold the reserves if it is short of required reserves, it can make loans to businesses or consumers, or it can lend the reserves to other banks in the federal funds market. Similar reasoning suggests that when banks pay back loans at the discount window, the payment is made in reserves, thus decreasing the reserves in the banking system and resulting in a corresponding decline in the money supply.

The Fed can influence the extent of money supply expansion by changing the discount rate. All else being equal, if the Fed raises the discount rate, banks are inclined to borrow less at the discount window. Thus, banks make fewer loans or reduce their investments so they can repay their loans from the Fed, reducing the amount of reserves in the banking system and, hence, the money supply.

If the Fed cuts the discount rate, the opposite effect occurs. Banks that can do so will take advantage of the lower borrowing rate, especially banks with seasonal borrowing privileges at the Fed. The Fed's seasonal borrowing privilege plan allows smaller banks with large seasonal fluctuations in loan demand, such as banks in agricultural areas, to borrow at the Fed's discount window. By borrowing cheap funds at the discount window and lending them out at a higher rate, these banks can make more profits when the discount rate is low.

In the early days of the Fed, changing the discount rate was the primary way in which the Fed attempted to affect national monetary policy. Changing the rate affected a bank's willingness to borrow from the Fed, the total amount of Federal Reserve credit outstanding, and the nation's money supply. However, it is difficult to predict how much bank discount window borrowing increases or decreases when the discount rate is changed. Also, such changes may be misinterpreted by *Fed watchers*, who believe they foretell alterations in Fed policy. Thus, in recent years, the Federal Reserve has relied mainly on open-market operations to implement monetary policy. Today, changes in the discount rate are undertaken either in response to changes in other market interest rates or to send a message to the market of a change in Fed policy. If the Fed wants to have a psychological effect on the financial markets to show that it is serious about wanting to ease (or tighten) its policy, it often lowers (or raises) the discount rate to make sure its policy intent is not misunderstood.

RESERVE REQUIREMENTS

The Federal Reserve can establish reserve requirements within limits set by Congress. These requirements are important because they determine the amount of funds financial institutions must hold at the Fed in order to back their deposits. The Monetary Control Act of 1980 simplified the reserve process by bringing all depository institutions' reserve requirements under the control of the Fed, subject to the same reserve requirements. For instance, a depository institution that is subject to a reserve requirement of 10 percent on its transactions deposits must back every dollar of those deposits with 10 cents of reserve assets.

Exhibit 2.7 shows the reserve requirements for different types of deposit accounts. In addition to reserves on their transactions accounts, financial institutions may be required to hold small reserves, either in vault cash or in deposits at the Fed, against their holdings of short-maturity, nonpersonal time and savings deposits. Also, at the discretion of the Federal Reserve, banks may be required to hold reserves against certain other liabilities—such as Eurodollar borrowings from overseas branches or certain liabilities issued by bank holding companies.

The power to establish reserve requirements is one of the tools the Fed has to control the nation's money supply. Only the Fed can change reserve requirements for depository institutions. To show how changes in reserve requirements change the money supply, let's work through an example. Assume a bank has $5,000 in demand deposits (DD) and the reserve requirement for the bank is 20 percent ($k = 0.20$). Suppose the bank is fully *loaned up*, meaning it has no excess reserves ($ER = 0$). Also, for our example, DD is the money supply.

The top frame in Exhibit 2.8 (Initial Condition) shows the T-account for the bank's initial situation. Notice the bank's required reserves (RR) are $1,000 (0.20 × $5,000) and the bank has no excess reserves (ER); that is, $ER = TR - RR = $1,000 - $1,000 = 0. Also notice that $1,000 of reserves can support $5,000 in deposits and that the bank is fully loaned up with $4,000 in loans.

Now suppose that the Fed decides to reduce the reserve requirement on demand deposits from 20 percent to 10 percent. The mechanics of the process involves two steps. First, the reduction in the reserve requirement on the bank's existing deposits lowers the amount of required reserves to $500 and increases excess reserves by $500. That is, $RR = 0.10 × $5,000 = $500 and $ER = $1,000 - $500 = $500, as can be seen in the middle frame of Exhibit 2.8.

EXHIBIT 2.7
Reserve Requirements

Type of Liability	Requirement (percentage of liabilities)	Effective Date
Net transcation accounts		
$0–$10.7 million	0	December 31, 2009
More than $10.7 million to $55.2 million	3	December 31, 2009
More than $55.2 million	10	December 31, 2009
Nonpersonal time deposits	0	December 27, 2009
Eurocurrency liabilities	0	December 27, 2009

Source: Federal Reserve Board (http://www.federalreserve.gov/monetarypolicy/reservereq.htm).

EXHIBIT 2.8
How Changes in Reserve Requirements Change the Money Supply (Demand Deposits)

Initial Condition

Assets			Liabilities	
Reserves		$1,000	Demand Deposits	$5,000
	Required	1,000		
	Excess	0		
Loans		4,000		
	Total	$5,000	Total	$5,000

Reduction in Reserve Requirements

Assets			Liabilities	
Reserves		$1,000	Demand Deposits	$5,000
	Required	500		
	Excess	500		
Loans		4,000		
	Total	$5,000	Total	$5,000

New Equilibrium

Assets			Liabilities	
Reserves		$1,000	Demand Deposits	$10,000
	Required	1,000		
	Excess	0		
Loans		9,000		
	Total	$10,000	Total	$10,000

The second step is deciding what the bank should do with the $500 in excess reserves. It could just hold them at the Fed, but deposits at the Fed normally do not pay interest. More than likely, the bank makes loans and expands deposits to the point where all of the excess reserves are again absorbed as required reserves. At the reserve requirement level, $k = 10$ percent, the bank can support $10,000 of deposits ($DEP = RR/k = \$1,000/0.10 = \$10,000$). Thus, the Fed can expand the dollar amount of bank deposits by lowering reserve requirements on deposits, thereby increasing the money supply (see the lower frame of Exhibit 2.8). Similar reasoning indicates that when the Fed increases reserve requirements, the banking system contracts the amount of bank deposits and hence decreases the money supply.

LEARNING BY DOING 2.2

Calculating a Bank's Reserve Position

PROBLEM: A commercial bank has $1,000 in reserves, $9,000 in loans, and $10,000 of deposits. Answer the following questions: (a) If the reserve requirement is 10 percent, what is the bank's reserve position? (b) If the Fed raised the reserve requirement to 20 percent, how would this affect the bank's reserve position? (c) If the bank complies with the new reserve requirement (20 percent), what is the bank's new equilibrium reserve position?

APPROACH: This problem draws on your understanding of the application of Equations 2.2 and 2.3. The key to working this type of problem is to recognize that a bank's reserve level can only support a certain amount of deposits at a given reserve requirement, k.

SOLUTIONS: **(a)** The T-account below shows the bank balance sheet for the initial reserve position. The calculations to determine the bank's reserve position are straightforward. You are told that the bank's total reserves are $1,000 and deposits are $10,000. Applying Equation 2.3, the bank's required reserves (RR) are $1,000 ($0.10 \times \$10,000$) and, applying Equation 2.2, the bank's excess reserves are zero ($ER = TR - RR = \$1,000 - \$1,000 = 0$). Finally notice that a $1,000 reserve can support $10,000 in deposits and $9,000 in loans, given $k = 10$ percent. Thus, the bank is fully loaned up because excess reserves are zero.

(a) Initial Condition Balance Sheet, $k = 10$ percent

Assets		Liabilities	
Reserves	$1,000	Deposits	$10,000
Required	1,000		
Excess	0		
Loans	$9,000		
Total	$10,000	Total	$10,000

(b) The T-account below shows the bank balance sheet for the new reserve position when the reserve requirement (k) was increased to 20 percent from 10 percent. To generate the T-account, we assume that the Fed has just made the announcement and bank management has not reacted to the change. We are given all of the balance sheet numbers (e.g., total reserves, loans, and deposits) so we can compute the bank's reserve position. We use Equation 2.3 to calculate the bank's required reserves for the new environment: $RR = k \times \text{DEP} = 0.20 \times \$10,000 = \$2,000$. We are given the bank's total reserve and can compute excess reserves: $ER = TR - RR = \$1,000 - \$2,000 = -\$1,000$. As you can see, the bank is not in compliance and does not have enough reserves (negative reserve position). Bank management has two basic options: (1) Borrow reserves at the Fed's discount window or (2) let loans run off until the bank is in compliance; that is, do not renew loans as they mature.

(b) Balance Sheet New Reserve Requirement, $k = 20$ percent

Assets		Liabilities	
Reserves	$1,000	Deposits	$10,000
Required	2,000		
Excess	−1,000		
Loans	$9,000		
Total	$10,000	Total	$10,000

(c) The T-account below shows the bank balance sheet and reserves position after allowing loans to run off and using the proceeds from repaid loans to payoff depositors. The bank must comply with the new reserve requirement or suffer a reprimand from bank regulators. The bank has more deposits than the bank's reserves will support; thus, the bank will let loans run off until the bank is in compliance. At that time, excess reserves will be zero. Using Equation 2.3, we solve for the amount of deposits $1,000 of reserves will support. That is, bank deposits (DEP) = $RR/k = \$1,000/0.20 = \$5,000$. Because $TR = \$1,000$ and DEP $= \$5,000$, loans must equal $4,000. The bank's excess reserves are equal to zero because ER $= TR - RR = \$1,000 - \$1,000 = 0$, which means the bank is in compliance.

(c) Equilibrium Bank Reserve Position, $k = 20$ percent

Assets		Liabilities	
Reserves	$1,000	Deposits	$5,000
Required	1,000		
Excess	0		
Loans	$4,000		
Total	$5,000	Total	$5,000

PAYING INTEREST ON RESERVES

To better implement monetary policy, the Fed has wanted the authority to pay interest on reserves balances held at the Fed for a number of years. It received authorization from Congress during October 2008. Let's examine why the Fed desired this additional power.

As a practical matter, the Fed's primary tool for implementing monetary policy has been open-market operations, using the fed funds interest rate (the rate that banks charge each other for overnight loans) as the target rate. In practice, the FOMC prepares a policy directive that establishes the trading parameters and sets the fed funds target rates. The trading desk at the New York Fed implements the policy. The target rate is a short-term monetary objective that tells the Fed whether it is achieving the desired changes in the money supply. Of course, the Fed does not control the fed funds rate. The Fed *influences* the fed funds rate by affecting the supply and demand for reserves in the open market.

To see how monetary targets work, let's look at several examples. Suppose that the Fed wants to implement a higher interest rate. It would announce a new target rate, and the next day, the trading desk would reduce the supply of reserves—usually by open-market sales of securities from its security portfolio—which drains cash from the banking system. The fed funds rate usually responds to the announcement in anticipation of the actual sale of the securities. When the Fed wants a lower interest rate, it does the opposite—usually by purchasing securities—which injects cash into the banking system. Generally speaking, if the trading desk increases the target fed funds rate, the impact reverberates throughout the economy: The higher interest rates tend to discourage consumer and business borrowing, slowing down the rate of economic growth in the economy.

During August 2010, the fed funds target rate was near zero and the banking system was awash with reserves. Many of those reserves were not lent to other banks but were sitting as deposits at the Fed. If the Fed cannot pay interest on reserves, the concern is that, once the recession is over and the economy starts to grow, the Fed will try to raise interest rates to control the rate of economic growth and thus keep inflation in check. In fact, Fed officials have publicly announced their intentions to do this once economic growth is sustainable. The fear is that, with so many excess reserves in the banking system, the Fed will be unable to get the fed funds rate to rise by tightening the supply of money. This is no hypothetical problem. The Fed's trading desk has reported from time to time that it has been unable to prevent the fed funds rate from falling to very low levels. However, with the Fed's ability to pay interest on excess reserve, the interest payments provide an incentive to banks to put more reserves on deposit at the Fed and lend less of their reserves to other banks in the interbank market.

In summary, with the Fed's expanded power to pay interest on reserves, the trading desk now has two options when it wants to raise the fed funds rate: (1) It can *reduce the supply* of reserves by selling Treasury securities in the open market, or (2) it can influence the *demand* for reserves by raising the rate it pays on excess reserves, thus encouraging banks to put more reserves on deposit at the Fed and to lend less of their reserves to other banks.

COMPARING THE MONETARY TOOLS

Exhibit 2.9 summarizes how each of the three monetary policy tools—open-market operations, adjustments to the discount rate, and reserve requirement changes—affect the money supply. As you see, the Fed does not use all three tools to conduct monetary policy on a regular basis and, as a practical matter, each plays a different and important role in the Fed's monetary policy arsenal.

Open-market operations are the primary tool used by the Fed to conduct monetary policy on a day-to-day basis. The advantages are that open-market operations can be done easily, almost instantaneously, and with no announcement effect. In addition, any change to the money supply can also be easily reversed without an announcement effect. This is particularly important because one of the Fed's responsibilities is to ensure that the Treasury Department can sell and retire its debt in an orderly manner. This means that on a short-term basis, the

EXHIBIT 2.9
How Tools of Monetary Policy Affect the Money Supply

Monetary Policy Tool	Increase in Money Supply	Decrease in Money Supply
Open-market operations	FOMC directs the trading desk to purchase Treasury securities in the secondary market	FOMC directs the trading desk to sell Treasury securities in the secondary market
Adjust the discount rate	Board of Governors lowers the discount rate	Board of Governors raises the discount rate
Adjust bank reserve requirements	Board of Governors lowers the reserve ratio (within limits) to cause a higher money multiplier	Board of Governors raises the reserve ratio (within limits) to cause a lower money multiplier

Fed intervenes in the Treasury market to *smooth interest rates* (i.e., reduce interest rate volatility).

Adjustments to the discount rate have a number of shortcomings as a tool for monetary policy. First, changes to the discount rate affect the money supply only if banks are willing to respond. As mentioned previously, the Fed closely scrutinizes borrowing at the discount window; therefore, banks are reluctant to overuse this privilege. Furthermore, borrowing at the discount window is short term, and it is difficult to gauge the impact on the money supply for a given change in the discount rate. Thus, as a practical matter, changing the discount rate is not a viable tool for conducting monetary policy.

Finally, changes to reserve requirements are not used as a tool of monetary policy. The reason is that it is difficult to make a number of small adjustments to reserve requirements, as frequent changes are disruptive to the banking system. When the Fed does change reserve requirements, however, it is typically done to deal with a structural problem in the banking system.

SUMMARY OF LEARNING OBJECTIVES

1 **Explain the problems leading to the establishment of the Federal Reserve Bank in 1914.** Prior to the establishment of the Fed in 1914, pyramiding of reserves and lax state banking regulations allowed banks to issue too many banknotes (and other bank liabilities) relative to their reserve holdings. Then any downturn in the economy caused large numbers of depositors to simultaneously redeem their deposits or banknotes for hard currency, which was in short supply. The result was a large number of bank failures and business failures as banks called in business loans, which led to economic recession.

2 **Explain the Fed's primary responsibilities as a central bank.** The Federal Reserve System was established to provide an elastic money supply, be a lender of last resort, improve bank regulation, and improve the performance of the nation's payment system.

3 **Identify the most powerful policy group within the Fed and discuss its powers.** The most powerful policy group within the Fed is the Board of Governors. They set reserve requirements, set the discount rate, and control the FOMC because they have the majority of the votes.

4 **Explain how the Fed conducts monetary policy and the various policy tools at its disposal.** The Fed's most important duty is to establish the nation's monetary policy by changing reserve requirements, the discount rate, and its open-market operations that affect the amount of reserves in the banking system and, hence, the money supply.

5 **Explain why open-market operations is the Fed's primary tool to conduct monetary policy.** Over the years the Fed has come to rely more on open-market operations (directed by the FOMC) rather than the discount rate policy of individual district Federal Reserve banks when it wants to change monetary policy. Open-market operations can be implemented almost instantaneously with a great deal of precision, with no announcement effect, and can be easily reversed.

KEY TERMS

Pyramiding of reserves
Call loans
Easy money
Lender of last resort
Elastic money supply
Wildcat banks

Federal Open Market Committee (FOMC)
Regulation Q
Margin requirements
Systemic risk
Too big to fail
Monetary base

Open-market operations
Total reserves (*TR*)
Required reserves (*RR*)
Excess reserves (*ER*)
Deferred availability cash items (DACI)
Discount rate

Discount window
Open-market operations
Cash items in process of collection (CIPC)

QUESTIONS AND PROBLEMS

1. Explain why the banking system was so unstable prior to the establishment of the Federal Reserve System in 1914.

2. What is a call loan? How did call loans contribute to economic recessions?

3. What were the four goals of the legislation that established the Federal Reserve System? Have they been met today?

4. Explain why the Board of Governors of the Federal Reserve System is considered so powerful. What are its major powers and which is the most important?

5. Explain why the FOMC is the key policy group within the Fed.

6. Explain why Regulation Q caused difficulties for banks and other depository institutions, especially during periods of rising interest rates.

7. Explain the sense in which the Fed is independent of the federal government. How independent is the Fed in reality? What is your opinion about the importance of the Fed's independence for the U.S. economy?

8. A bank has $20,000 in reserves, $90,000 in bank loans, and $150,000 of deposits. If the reserve requirement is 10 percent, what is the bank's reserve position? What is the maximum dollar amount of loans the bank can make? What would happen to the nation's money supply if the Fed lowered the reserve requirement for banks to 6 percent? Demonstrate your results with a numerical example.

9. Why does the Fed not use the discount rate to conduct monetary policy? How does the Fed use the discount rate?

10. Explain how the Fed changes the money supply with an open-market purchase of Treasury securities.

11. Northwest National Bank received new demand deposits (*DD*) of $1,650,000. The current reserve requirement is 6 percent. The bank has $80,000 in vault cash and $110,000 in deposits at the Federal Reserve that are not yet invested. How much in excess reserves does the bank have available to make new loans?

12. Currently a community bank has $45,000 in reserves, demand deposits of $200,000, and loans of $145,000. It unexpectly receives an inflow of deposits of $50,000 into checking accounts and another $25,000 into time deposits. Current reserve requirements on demand deposits and time deposits are 10 percent and 3 percent, respectively. What is the bank's reserve position? What is the maximum dollar amount of loans that the bank could make?

13. Suppose the current reserve requirements set by the Federal Reserve are as follows:

Reserve Requirements

Type of Liability	Requirement (percentage of liabilities)
$0 to $10.7 million	0
More than $10.7 million to $55.2 million	3
More than $55.2 million	10
Nonpersonal time deposits	3
Eurocurrency liabilities	0

A bank has vault cash of $2 million, reserve deposits at the Federal Reserve of $25 million, transaction deposits of $275 million, and nonpersonal time deposits of $100 million. Calculate this bank's required reserves, excess reserves, and total reserves.

14. Refer to the table in Question 13. Now suppose the Federal Reserve raised the reserve requirements on deposits between $10.7 million and $55.2 million to 5 percent but eliminated the reserve requirement on nonpersonal time deposits. Calculate the bank's required reserves, excess reserves, and total reserves under these conditions.

15. The Fed decides to buy $10,000 of government bonds from Goldman Sachs. Using T-accounts, show the complete transaction. Did the money supply increase or decrease? Explain.

16. Why is the Federal Reserve Bank of New York granted special status? What is the special status?

17. What are three important regulatory powers that the Fed gained from the passage of the Financial Regulatory Reform Act of 2010? Explain each briefly.

18. With respect to the financial system, what is meant by "too big to fail"? Why is it an important issue?

19. What are the arguments that support having a strong and independent Federal Reserve Bank?

20. Why does the Fed want the ability to pay interest on reserve accounts?

21. If the country went into a recession, would you expect banks to increase or decrease their holding of excess reserves? Explain.

INTERNET EXERCISE

The Federal Reserve Board Web site contains valuable information and useful links to other Web sites. All the following questions can be answered by going to the Federal Reserve Board's Web site (http://www.federalreserve.gov) or to one of the sites linked to it.

1. First, go to the Federal Reserve Board's Web site, click on the monetary policy link and then the Federal Open Market Committee link. Identify when the most recent FOMC meeting occurred. Read the *Statement* issued after the meeting. What did the FOMC decide concerning the target fed funds rate? Briefly, what was the justification for that decision?

2. Next, while you are still on the monetary policy page, click on the beige book link. Then click on the *Report* link for the most recent FOMC meeting. Read the national summary page and the page for your Fed district. Discuss how the economy in your Fed district is performing. Is it faring better or worse than other districts? What sector of the economy in your district is driving your conclusions?

3. Finally, comment on whether you think the most recent FOMC decision benefits your Fed district more or less than other Fed districts.

The Fed and Interest Rates

FOLLOWING A FEDERAL OPEN MARKET Committee (FOMC) meeting, it is very common for newscasters to report something like, "The Federal Reserve lowered the fed funds interest rate today in an effort to stimulate the lagging economy." Although it's a great sound bite, in truth, there are a number of things wrong with this statement.

First, the Fed does not *set* the fed funds rate. The fed funds rate is a market-determined rate negotiated between borrowers and lenders in the fed funds market. The *fed funds rate* is the rate that banks charge to lend overnight funds to one another. The reason the newscaster may have made the statement is that the Fed, through open-market operations, is able to expand or contract the total reserves in the banking system, which in the short term, has an impact on the fed funds rate and other interest rates in the economy. However, on any given day there are many factors that affect interest rates. For the Fed to lower interest rates, it may have to persist in injecting additional reserves into the banking system.

Second, the only interest rate the Fed can set is the discount rate, which is the interest rate that the Fed charges banks that want to borrow from the Fed. The discount rate is often lowered (or raised)

In October 2005, Dr. Benjamin S. Bernanke succeeded the iconic Alan Greenspan as chairman of the Federal Reserve.

to signal the Fed's intent for monetary policy.

Finally, what the newscaster may have been reporting are comments contained in public releases by the Fed following an FOMC meeting. Given what the newscaster said, the statement may have contained language like, "The Federal Open Market Committee decided to lower its target for the fed funds rate." This means that the Fed will be increasing the amount of reserves in the banking system with the goal of increasing the money supply, which should put downward pressure on interest rates, ultimately stimulating business and consumer spending and increasing real gross domestic product (GDP). Overall, the newscaster's statement is incomplete and misleading. After you finish this chapter, you will be able to dissect the previous statement or similar statements with the precision of a financial surgeon. ■

In Chapter 2, we explained what the Federal Reserve is and how it controls the total reserves in the banking system by initiating changes to its balance sheet. The purpose of Chapter 3 is to explain how the Fed conducts monetary policy, which is the primary policy tool that the federal government uses to stabilize the economy over the business cycle. In the chapter, we discuss how the Fed adjusts the money supply, the role of the fed funds rate in the conduct of monetary policy, the goals for monetary policy, and how monetary policy is transmitted through the various sectors of the economy. We also discuss fiscal policy, how it's conducted, and its role in stabilizing the economy. Finally, to better understand the business cycle, we examine the 2008 financial crisis, the reasons it occurred, and the recession that followed. ∎

LEARNING OBJECTIVES

1 Explain how the Fed measures and manages the money supply.

2 Explain how the Fed influences the level of interest rates in the economy.

3 Describe the transmission process for monetary policy.

4 Discuss the goals of the Fed in conducting monetary policy.

5 Explain what fiscal policy is and how it works when there is a recession.

3.1 FEDERAL RESERVE CONTROL OF THE MONEY SUPPLY

As we discussed in Chapter 2, one of the most important powers of the Fed is its ability to control the monetary base. By controlling the monetary base, the Fed is able to control the money supply. The components of the monetary base—vault cash and reserve balances—are the only assets that financial institutions can use to satisfy reserve requirements. By controlling the monetary base, the Federal Reserve can control the total amount of assets that financial institutions can use to meet their reserve requirements. The Federal Reserve uses its power over these reserves to control the amount of money outstanding in the country.

MEASURES OF THE MONEY SUPPLY

Up to this point, we used the term *money supply* conceptually without providing a specific definition or measure. The reason for this is that there are many different definitions of money, and each measure has a role in monetary policy. Some of the definitions of money are based on theoretical arguments over

EXHIBIT 3.1 **Money Supply Measures**

M1	=	currency + checking deposits
M2	=	M1 + savings deposits, money market deposit accounts, overnight repurchase agreements, Eurodollars, noninstitutional money market mutual funds, and small time deposits

The M1 definition of money emphasizes money as a medium of exchange; M2 emphasizes money as a store of value. M1 and M2 are the most useful definitions of money when conducting monetary policy.

the definition of money—is money primarily transactional, or is money primarily a safe haven to store purchasing power? Putting theory aside, inside the Fed things are more practical; that is, what the Fed really wants to know is, when it increases or decreases the money supply, which definition of money has the greatest impact on interest rates, unemployment, and inflation.

The most widely used definitions of *money* are summarized in Exhibit 3.1. **M1** is the definition that focuses on money as a medium of exchange. M1 consists of financial assets that people hold to buy things with—transaction balances. Thus, the definition of M1 includes financial assets such as currency and checking accounts at depository institutions.

M2 is the definition of money that emphasizes the role money plays as a store of value. This means that if you hold these balances, your purchasing power will be protected to some extent if there is inflation. Recall that the value of money is its purchasing power—what you can buy with it. When there is inflation, you can buy less with a given amount of money; hence, there is a loss of purchasing power. Thus, M2 includes everything in M1 plus savings accounts, money market accounts, small time deposits, and some overnight money loans. Until recently, the Fed also tracked M3, an even more inclusive store of value monetary aggregate. However, in early 2006, the Board of Governors stopped publishing M3 after finding that it was not significantly more useful in monetary policy than M2.

MONETARY BASE AND MONEY SUPPLY CHANGES

When the Fed changes either the monetary base or reserve requirements, the money supply will usually change in a predictable manner. The reason is that banks are economically motivated to minimize their holdings of **excess reserves** because the Fed typically pays little or no interest on reserves. The Fed was authorized to pay interest on reserve accounts in October 2008. The reason it wanted this ability was to deal with a technical issue in the conduct of monetary policy during periods of very low interest rates, such as we experienced during the summer of 2008. Paying interest on reserve accounts is discussed in detail in Chapter 2. The Fed minimizes excess reserve holdings by making additional loans or buying investment securities. Let's first work through some examples to see how this mechanism works for the banking system as individual banks pursue their own economic self-interest. To keep our analysis straightforward, we initially assume that banks do not pay interest on reserves held at the Fed. Then we

EXHIBIT 3.2
Fed's Impact on the Money Supply with an Open-Market Purchase of Treasury Securities ($ billions)

Initial Condition

Assets		Liabilities	
Reserves	$60	Transaction Deposits	$600
Loans and Investments	540		
	$600		$600

Fed Injects $30 Billion of Reserves into Banking System

Assets		Liabilities	
Reserves	$90	Transaction Deposits	$600
Loans and Investments	510		
	$600		$600

Banking System Loaned/Invested Up

Assets		Liabilities	
Reserves	$90	Transaction Deposits	$900
Loans and Investments	810		
	$900		$900

relax this assumption to see the impact that paying interest on reserves has on the Fed's ability to control the money supply.

Our example begins in the top frame of Exhibit 3.2, which shows our initial condition for the banking system. Assume that the reserve requirement is 10 percent and that total reserves (**actual reserves**) in the banking system are $60 billion. Banks hold $540 billion in loans and investments, and demand deposits are $600 billion. Recalling our discussion in Chapter 2 (Equations 2.2 and 2.3), we see that the amount of **required reserves** is $60 billion ($RR = k \times DD = 0.10 \times$ $600 billion = $60 billion) and, hence, excess reserves equal zero ($ER = TR - RR$ = $60 billion − $60 billion = 0$). Thus, the banking system is fully "loaned" up— it cannot make any additional loans or investments because there are no excess reserves available. Banks are motivated to keep their excess reserves near zero because the Fed does not pay interest on reserves held at the Fed.

Now suppose the Fed buys $30 billion in government securities in an open-market transaction and pays for them by giving banks $30 billion more in reserve deposits at the Fed (see center frame of Exhibit 3.2). Thus, the total reserves held in the banking system increase from $60 billion to $90 billion, investments are reduced by $30 billion, and initially banks now hold $30 billion in excess reserves ($90 billion − $60 billion = $30 billion) because deposits are $600 billion. Being profit maximizers, banks try to spend any excess reserves they hold by making more loans and buying investments that pay an interest return. When a bank makes a loan, it gives a transaction deposit to the borrower or gives the borrower a check. When the check is cashed, either the borrower's transaction deposits increase or the transaction deposits of the person the borrower gave the check to increase. In all cases, total transaction deposits in the banking system increase when a bank uses some of its excess reserves to make a loan. Conversely, if a loan is repaid, the checking account of the person who repays the debt decreases when the bank cashes the check, and so do total transaction deposits unless the bank makes more loans.

When a bank uses excess reserves to expand investments, a similar process occurs. When a bank buys investments for its own account, it pays with a check or a wire transfer. When the check or wire transfer clears, the demand deposit of the person who sold the investment securities increases, and so do total deposits in the banking system. Conversely, when the bank sells some of its investment securities to the public in exchange for a check, and when the check clears, the public's transaction deposits decrease along with the bank's holdings of investment securities.

Therefore, banks expand their loans and investments so they can earn extra income. At the same time, by making more loans and by acquiring investments, they expand the public's holdings of transaction deposits. This process continues until they reach the state depicted in the lower panel of Exhibit 3.2. As shown, the banking system holds $900 billion in transaction deposits. Therefore, required reserves in the banking system are $90 billion, which equals total reserves and leaves no excess reserves with which to make additional loans or purchase additional investment securities. Thus, the deposit expansion stops at $900 billion. At that point, banks back their $900 billion in deposits with $90 billion in reserves and $810 billion in loans and investments.

What happens to our analysis if the Fed decides to pay interest on reserves? Fortunately, the logic and analysis are the same, except that for each of the three situations cited (see Exhibit 3.2), the banks will be motivated to hold excess reserves beyond what they would have otherwise held if the Fed paid no interest on reserves. All things being equal, the higher the interest rate paid on reserves the larger the bank's excess reserve holdings. Finally, note that the Fed's ability to control the money supply, as discussed here, depends on its ability to control the level of reserves and set reserve requirements. Paying interest on reserves provides the Fed with an additional tool to control the level of reserves.

The fed funds interest rate is one of the most closely watched interest rates in the economy. The market for fed funds consists of the borrowing and lending of overnight reserves among large banks and financial institutions on an unsecured basis. In simple terms, the **fed funds rate** is the *interbank lending rate* and represents the primary cost of short-term loanable funds. The rate on these overnight interbank loans is highly volatile: It is not unusual for the rate to fluctuate more than 25 basis points (0.25 percent) on either side of the average level in a day. The fed funds rate is of particular interest because (1) it measures the return on the most liquid of all financial assets (bank reserves); (2) it is closely related to monetary policy; and (3) it directly measures the available reserves in the banking system, which in turn influences commercial banks' decisions on making loans to consumers, businesses, or other borrowers.

3.2 THE FED'S INFLUENCE ON INTEREST RATES

MARKET EQUILIBRIUM INTEREST RATE

To give you an initial understanding of how the fed funds rate is determined, look at Frame A of Exhibit 3.3. The demand curve for reserves is primarily influenced

EXHIBIT 3.3
Impact of Monetary Policy on the Fed Funds Rate

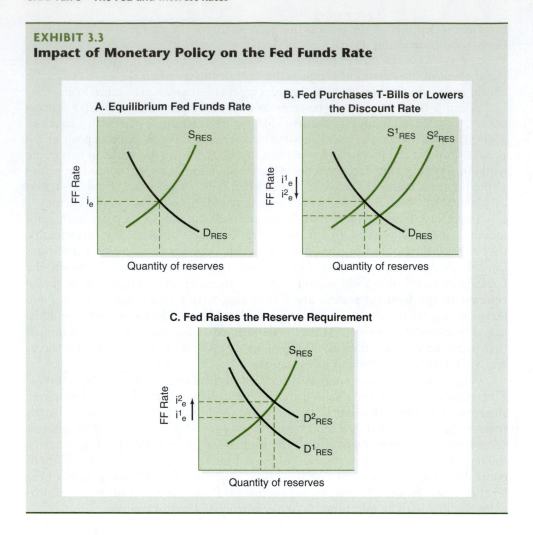

A. Equilibrium Fed Funds Rate

FF Rate

S_{RES}

i_e

D_{RES}

Quantity of reserves

B. Fed Purchases T-Bills or Lowers the Discount Rate

FF Rate

S^1_{RES} S^2_{RES}

i^1_e
i^2_e ↓

D_{RES}

Quantity of reserves

C. Fed Raises the Reserve Requirement

FF Rate

S_{RES}

i^2_e ↑
i^1_e ↑

D^2_{RES}

D^1_{RES}

Quantity of reserves

by the demand for excess reserves that are sensitive to interest rate changes. Thus, holding all other things constant, if the fed funds (FF) rate increases, the opportunity cost of holding excess reserves increases and the quantity of reserves demanded declines. As a result, the demand curve for bank reserves (D_{RES}) slopes downward.

The Federal Reserve bank controls the quantity of reserves in the banking system. However, as we discussed in Chapter 2, when the Fed lowers the discount rate, banks are more likely to borrow reserves from the discount window. The reason banks borrow these funds is to lend them out as commercial loans or, more likely, to lend to other banks in the fed funds market. Thus, holding all other things constant, if the fed funds rate increases, banks borrow more from the Fed, increasing the quantity of reserves in the banking system. Thus, the supply curve for reserves (S_{RES}) slopes upward, as shown in Exhibit 3.3, Frame A.

The market equilibrium rate of interest occurs when the quantity of reserves demanded by depository institutions is equal to the quantity supplied ($D_{RES} = S_{RES}$).

MONETARY POLICY AND THE FED FUNDS RATE

Now that we understand how the fed funds rate is determined, we want to see what impact the fed can have on the fed funds rate when it exercises the three tools of monetary policy: open-market operations, adjustments to the discount rate, and changes to the reserve requirement.

Open-Market Operations.   Given our previous discussions, the analysis is straightforward. Let's say the Fed plans to increase the amount of reserves in the banking system through open-market operations. To do this, the Fed instructs the trading desk at the Federal Reserve Bank of New York to purchase Treasury securities, thereby increasing the amount of reserves in the banking system. Thus, the open-market purchase shifts the supply curve to the right (S^1_{RES} to S^2_{RES}), as shown in Frame B of Exhibit 3.3, and, as a result, the market rate of interest declines from i^1_e to i^2_e. The same reasoning explains why interest rates rise when the Fed sells Treasury securities; a sale of Treasury securities shifts the supply curve to the left, causing the interest rate to rise. We conclude that an open-market purchase causes the fed funds rate to decline and an open-market sale causes the fed funds rate to increase. These changes can be seen in Frame B of Exhibit 3.3.

Adjusting the Discount Rate.   If the Fed decides to cut the discount rate, profit-maximizing banks may increase their borrowing from the Fed to make loans. Because banks borrow reserves when they borrow at the discount window, the supply curve for the quantity of reserves in the banking system shifts to the right (S^1_{RES} to S^2_{RES}), as seen in Frame B of Exhibit 3.3, and, as a result, the market rate of interest declines from i^1_e to i^2_e. We conclude that, all other factors held constant, when the Fed lowers the discount rate, the fed funds rate falls, and when the Fed raises the discount rate, the fed funds rate rises. The Fed's modern practice has been to move the fed funds target rate and the discount rate in tandem but to keep the discount rate higher. This encourages depository institutions to borrow existing reserves through the fed funds system (thus reallocating the existing monetary base), rather than borrow new reserves at the discount window (thus increasing the monetary base).

Adjusting the Reserve Requirement.   Let's say the Fed decides to increase the reserve requirement. When this occurs, required reserves held by banks increase and the quantity of reserves demanded therefore must increase at any given interest rate. Thus, the demand curve for reserves must shift to the right (D^1_{RES} to D^2_{RES}), as seen in Frame C of Exhibit 3.3, causing the fed funds rate to increase from i^1_e to i^2_e. Similarly, if the reserve requirement is decreased, the amount of excess reserves in the banking system is increased, causing the fed funds rate to decline. Thus, we conclude that when the Fed raises the reserve requirement, the fed funds rate increases and, similarly, when the Fed decreases the reserve requirement, the fed funds rate declines.

THE MARKET ENVIRONMENT

Many people believe that the Fed implements monetary policy by changing the fed funds rate. However, as we discussed, the fed funds rate is determined by negotiation between the private borrowers and lenders of reserves. In the fed funds market, banks and other institutions with immediately available excess reserves lend to other institutions that need reserve balances on an overnight basis only if the price—the fed funds rate—is agreeable to both the borrower and the lender of the funds.

The Fed can influence the fed funds rate only in the very short run by using its monetary policy to expand or contract the monetary base. For instance, if the Fed buys a large amount of government securities through its open-market operations, when it pays for them many banks find they have additional excess reserves. As they lend those reserves out to earn interest as quickly as possible, they may accept lower fed funds rates offered by borrowers, and the fed funds rate falls on an overnight basis. Conversely, if the Fed sells a large amount of government securities, when the buyers pay for those securities many banks and other depository institutions find that they have fewer reserves and excess reserves than they expected. To meet their reserve requirements, they may bid aggressively to borrow additional reserves in the fed funds market, and the fed funds rate rises.

LONG-TERM CONTROL OVER THE FED FUNDS RATE

Finally we should mention that most economists believe that the Fed cannot control the fed funds interest rate over the long term. Powerful macroeconomic forces will eventually overcome the Fed's monetary actions. For example, suppose that the Fed keeps the fed funds rate artificially high. If the rate is too high, few people will want to borrow, and so the fed funds rate will decline unless the Fed sells government securities to reduce the supply of bank reserves. As bank reserves decline, however, the monetary base and the money supply contract, and few people want to borrow in such a deflationary environment. If the Fed persists in keeping the fed funds rate too high, the process of contraction continues and financial panic ensues—as in the Great Depression of the 1930s.

Thus, it seems to be a reasonable conclusion that the Fed cannot control the fed funds rate in the long run. If it tries to do so, it may generate either excess inflation or a depression. The best the Fed can do in the long run is to try to run monetary policy so people expect very little change in price levels. Thus, interest rates will not fluctuate widely, reducing uncertainty in the economy, which should in turn stimulate economic growth.

THE IMPORTANCE OF THE FED FUNDS RATE

One may ask why the financial markets pay so much attention to changes in the fed funds rate if the Fed really can't control that rate in the long run. It is mainly because changes in the fed funds rate provide a clue to short-run changes in the Fed's monetary policy. On any given day, the Fed's actions can cause the fed funds rate to rise or fall. When the Fed is decreasing the growth rate of the monetary base and bank reserves, the fed funds rate tends to rise as more banks and other depository institutions find themselves short of reserves at the end of the day and rush to borrow their required reserves. Conversely, when the Fed is trying to encourage depository institutions to lend so the economy expands, it makes reserves readily available, so the fed funds rate tends to fall.

THE IMPORTANCE OF MONEY

The main reason the Fed changes the monetary base and, in the short run, interest rates, is to affect the level of output in the economy. *Monetarist economists*, led by the late American economist Milton Friedman, believe that a change in the money supply will alter aggregate spending and gross national product (GNP) by a predictable amount. The mechanism that drives this result is that, when people have more money to spend relative to their needs, they spend more freely and thus stimulate the economy directly. Conversely, if people have less money than they need given their income and expenditure levels, they spend less so they can accumulate more cash. Thus, for monetarists, the key variable that drives changes in the level of economic activity in the economy is the money supply as measured by the monetary base. The fed funds rate and other short-term interest rates serve primarily as a signal or guidepost as to how monetary policy is proceeding.

Keynesian economists, who follow macroeconomic theories developed by twentieth-century British economist John Maynard Keynes, tend to disregard the effects that changes in the money supply have on the purchases of goods and services. Instead, they focus on the impact that changes in the level of interest rates have on spending in the economy. They note that when people and banks have more money, they tend to buy more securities and make more loans, thereby driving down interest rates and increasing credit availability. Thus, in the Keynesian view, "expansive" monetary policy usually stimulates the economy by reducing interest rates and increasing the availability of credit so people and businesses can borrow more inexpensively and thus spend more freely. Conversely, Keynesian economists say that the reduction in bank reserves will cause banks to ration credit and increase interest rates; as a result, people will borrow less and therefore spend less. In sum, according to the monetarists, the key driver that changes economic output is *money*. According to the Keynesians, the key driver that changes economic output is interest rates or the availability of credit.

THE LIQUIDITY TRAP

In the Keynesian world, monetary policy always works unless the economy is in a **liquidity trap**, such as may have occurred during the Great Depression of the 1930s, when Keynes thought people already had so much money relative to their needs that any extra money would be hoarded and would no longer drive down interest rates. In its original conception, a liquidity trap results when the demand for money becomes infinitely elastic—the demand for money curve becomes horizontal—and further injection of money into the economy has no effect because interest can go no lower. Thus, if an economy enters a liquidity trap, further increases in the money supply cannot lower interest rates and stimulate economic output.

Though the concept had fallen out of favor with most economists, the concept became of interest in the 1990s when the Japanese economy fell into a decade of economic stagnation despite the presence of near zero interest rates. The new version of the liquidity trap does not require the existence of a horizontal demand for money curve. The new concept only requires the presence of a zero interest rate and the assertion that if interest rates are zero they can fall no further; thus, monetary policy would be impotent in those conditions. The liquidity trap concept is relevant today because U.S. and several European central banks have moved their target interest rate close to zero.

3.3 THE TREASURY DEPARTMENT AND FISCAL POLICY

Fiscal policy is the control over government spending and taxes by a central government to stabilize the economy's output over the business cycle. The two main tools of fiscal policy are government spending and taxation. In the United States, fiscal policy is undertaken at the federal level through acts of Congress and actions by the president. Fiscal policy is, for the most part, carried out by the Treasury Department.

DEPARTMENT OF THE TREASURY

The Treasury Department was established by an act of Congress in 1789 to manage the government's finances. The department is headed by the secretary of the Treasury, who is a member of the president's cabinet. The first secretary of the Treasury was Alexander Hamilton, who was asked to serve by President George Washington and was sworn into office in 1798. Hamilton is credited with almost single-handedly working out the nation's accounting and financial system.

Today, the Treasury Department's primary responsibility is to manage the federal government's finances once the president and Congress have agreed on what items will be included in the annual budget. The money for the budget comes from taxes collected by the Internal Revenue Service (IRS) and financing public debt through the sale of Treasury securities. The Treasury Department has responsibility for paying the bills of the federal government and for advising the president's office on financial, trade, tax, and fiscal policy matters.

The Treasury Department is also responsible for printing postage stamps, stamping coins, and printing paper money through the U.S. Mint. The department also enforces federal finance and tax laws and investigates and prosecutes tax evaders, counterfeiters, forgers, smugglers, and illicit spirits distillers.

FISCAL POLICY'S KEYNESIAN ORIGINS

Keynesian macroeconomic theory was developed by Keynes in the 1930s as a way for government policymakers to extract their country from the global depression of the 1930s. Keynes argued that some decisions made in the private sector led to undesirable economic outcomes. Thus, active responses by governments were required to stabilize output over the business cycle. Fiscal policy was Keynes's solution to the problem and, at the time, it was a radical departure from the prevailing economic thought. Fiscal policy focused on directing government spending into troubled areas of the economy or areas where there was a need for investment and development. President Roosevelt planned to pay for the investment in the U.S. economy by selling Treasury securities, which were liabilities of the federal government. Roosevelt broke rank from his economic advisers and took a chance to see if the new thinking would work. Fortunately for the country, it did work.

CHANGE OF FORTUNE

Fiscal and monetary policy advocates have both enjoyed periods of political favor when their doctrines had significant influence on policymakers. Both have also watched their doctrines fall out of favor. Fiscal policy took center stage during the Great Depression, which started with the stock market crash of 1929 and lingered for nearly a decade. Fiscal policy advocates were ebullient at its apparent success and saw it delivering full employment, economic growth, and stable prices. With government spending financed by issuing debt, Roosevelt built the basic infrastructure for American industrialization and beautification—the interstate highway and railway systems; bridges, such as the Golden Gate Bridge in San Francisco; hydroelectric dams and other energy projects, such as the Grande Cooley Dam; and national parks, such as Yellowstone National Park. During this time, monetary policy was relegated to the job of keeping bank reserves plentiful and interest rates low so the federal government could finance its deficit at the lowest possible cost.

Beginning in the 1950s, monetary policy made a dramatic resurgence. Milton Freidman, the late champion of the Chicago school of economic thought, presented impressive empirical evidence on the role of money and its impact on the economy. The empirical evidence suggested that money drove the economy and that sale of Treasury debt under fiscal policy was actually increasing the money supply. Thus, it was monetary policy that drove the recovery from the Great Depression and not government spending.

By the early 1970s, monetary and fiscal policies were on equal footing in the quest for a more stable business cycle. Fiscal policy lost some influence following its poor performance in dealing with stagflation (i.e., the combination of recession and inflation) of the 1970s. By the 1980s, fiscal policy had fallen out of favor. Monetary policy had become the stabilization policy of choice among government policymakers and influential academics. However, fiscal policy continued to play a role in the economy from time to time, notably in the 1980s Reagan tax cuts and the second Bush administration's 2000s tax cuts.

By the turn of the millennium, some economists were suggesting that monetary policy should be the primary instrument of economic stabilization and that fiscal policy was at best negligible. Some economists went as far as to declare that, with the policy tools available to central bankers, economists had the ability to stabilize the economy. The newspaper headlines read, *"the business cycle is dead."* Of course, those halcyon days are over. The global financial crisis of 2008 caused a resurgence of Keynesian thought as government leaders used Keynesian economics to justify government stimulus programs for their economies. We also learned that rumors about the "death" of the business cycles were premature.

THE GOVERNMENT EXPENDITURE MODEL

Unlike private expenditures, federal government expenditures are not usually related to economic determinants. Government expenditures are also not subject to the same budget constraints as other economic units because the federal government can print money. Governments make public expenditures over a wide range of goods and services: police and military protection, education, highways and bridges, healthcare, and the economic welfare of their citizens. Government officials are responsible for selecting the type and mix of expenditures, and these decisions are made in a political environment. Most government units face budget constraints and, if cutbacks are to be made, government officials must prioritize projects and the lowest-priority projects must be eliminated or reduced.

The government expenditure equation is straightforward. The amount of money government officials can spend is constrained by how much debt tax payers (voters) are willing to assume. Governments can finance their expenditures (G) with money raised either by taxation (T) or by incurring debt, usually through the sale of bonds (B).

$$G = T + \Delta B \tag{3.1}$$

Note in Equation 3.1 that the sale of new bonds in the primary market increases the outstanding stock of bonds, hence ΔB. Also note that only two of the variables in the equation are independent at any one time. The third variable is a residual. For example, if government officials set the level of expenditures (G) and set taxes (T) for a period, then $G - T$ is the amount of bonds the government must sell or retire.

Finally note that there are three possible budget positions:

1. If expenditures equal taxes, the government is in a balanced budget position and $G = T$.
2. If government expenditures exceed tax revenues, the government is in a deficit ($G > T$) position and bonds must be sold to balance the budget.
3. If government expenditures are less than tax revenues, the budget is in a surplus ($G < T$) position and bonds can be retired.

HOW FISCAL POLICY WORKS

To Keynesian economists, changes in government spending or taxation are the primary tools of fiscal policy. When the government spends money, it injects purchasing power into the economy; when the government collects taxes, it withdraws purchasing power from the economy. Keynesian economists further believe that both policy tools—government spending and taxation—have a direct and fairly predictable impact on gross national product (GNP). If there is an increase in government spending, GNP increases quickly and provides consumers with additional income. This induces additional income for consumers through a multiplier effect. The multiplier effect is caused by the initial rise in GNP, which provides consumers with additional income; they spend a fraction of this additional income, which causes GNP to go up even further. The process of receiving additional income and spending a fraction of the income will eventually stop as the successive increments in income and spending become smaller and smaller. The end result is that the increase in GNP will be some multiple of the original increase in government spending.

Changes in tax rates are seen to have similar multiple impacts on GNP. If tax rates are lowered, consumers are left with more disposable income. They spend a predictable fraction of this, causing a rise in GNP, which induces additional consumer spending.

FISCAL POLICY STANCES

Government officials use two basic stances for fiscal policy that affect the output of the economy. The simplest definitions of the two policy bromides are:

1. Expansionary fiscal policy is defined as an increase in government expenditures and/or a decrease in taxes that causes the government's budget deficit to increase or its budget surplus to decrease.
2. Contractionary fiscal policy is defined as a decrease in government expenditures and/or an increase in taxes that causes the government's budget deficit to decrease or its budget surplus to increase.

Combating a Recession. The Keynesian theories of economic output and employment were developed in the midst of the Great Depression of the 1930s. At that time, unemployment in the United States exceeded 25 percent, and the growth rate of real GNP declined steadily for most of the decade. The country was desperate for a solution to the economic malaise. Keynes believed that the way to combat the depression was not to wait for prices and wages to adjust but to engage in proactive expansionary fiscal policy. Keynesian economists also noted that wages were sticky downward and would not adjust quickly enough to deal with the reality of the high unemployment rate. As a result, the recessionary economy could persist for a long time.

A Budget Deficit. The solution to extracting the economy from the economic depression, according to the Keynesians, was to run a budget deficit by increasing government expenditures in excess of current tax receipts. The increase in government expenditures should cause an increase in aggregate demand in the economy to restore the economy to full employment equilibrium level. Because of the multiplier effect, the government needs to increase its expenditures by a small amount to achieve an equilibrium level of output. Thus, Keynesian fiscal policy offered a quick way out of a recession rather than waiting for wages and prices to clear. The primary aim of this policy action was to reduce unemployment.

DO YOU UNDERSTAND?

1. What is likely to happen to the monetary base if (a) the Treasury Department sends out Social Security checks payable from its account at the Fed, (b) the Fed buys more government securities, and (c) banks in general borrow less from the Fed's discount window and repay their past borrowings?

2. What is likely to happen to the fed funds rate if the Fed increases the reserve requirement? Explain.

3. Why do the financial markets pay so much attention to the fed funds rate given that the Fed doesn't really control that interest rate in the long run?

4. What is the basic difference between fiscal and monetary policy?

Over the last several decades, government policymakers have become increasingly aware of the social and economic cost of inflation, especially when inflation rates are high. High rates of inflation create uncertainty in the economy, making it difficult to plan or to make long-term investment decisions. The result is that the economy grows at a slower rate than it otherwise would. In the recent past, Argentina, Brazil, and Russia were examples of countries whose social and economic infrastructure was devastated by extremely high inflation rates (called hyperinflation, usually defined as an inflation rate exceeding 50 percent per month).

3.4 GOALS OF MONETARY POLICY

Because price stability is so critical to the overall workings of an economy, price stability is the primary goal of the Fed and most central banks throughout the world. There is some debate about how best to implement economic policies to achieve price stability. Over the last decade, one policy procedure that has received much attention for achieving price stability is *inflation targeting*.

INFLATION TARGETING

Inflation targeting is an economic policy where a central bank estimates and makes public a projected or target inflation rate, and then steers the actual rate of inflation in the economy toward the target rate through use of monetary policy tools. Once the target inflation rate is established, let's see how inflation targeting can be applied by the Fed. We'll look at two situations:

- **Inflation Rate Is Above the Target Rate:** The Fed is likely to raise interest rates by the open-market sale of Treasury securities (reduce the money supply). The higher interest rates reverberate through the economy and slow economic growth by choking off consumer and business spending, resulting in a lower inflation rate.
- **Inflation Rate Is Below the Target Rate:** The Fed is likely to lower interest rates by the open-market purchase of Treasury securities (increase the money supply). The lower interest rates reverberate through the economy and stimulate economic growth, resulting in a higher inflation rate.

Among the FOMC members, there is considerable disagreement about whether the Fed should adopt inflation targeting. Bernanke has written a number of academic articles favoring inflation targeting but has said that he will not consider adopting the policy unless a consensus supports the proposal. As a policy tool, inflation targeting has been successful in other countries because of its transparency, and it helps make inflation rates more predictable. Under an inflation targeting plan, investors know what the central bank considers the target inflation rate to be and can more easily factor it into their planning and investment decisions. It removes a great deal of uncertainty about the market inflation rate, which stimulates economic growth. Other economists counter that an inflation target policy would reduce the Fed's flexibility to stabilize economic growth or unemployment in the event of significant shock, such as the 2008 financial crisis. Currently, the FOMC makes public a statement of its desired range for inflation, usually around 1.5 to 2 percent. It does not have an explicit inflation target policy.

GOALS FOR MONETARY POLICY

In Western democracies, governments are charged with the responsibility to achieve certain social, political, and economic goals. Politically and socially, these goals center around preserving individual rights, freedom of choice, equality of opportunity, equitable distribution of wealth, individual health and welfare, and the safety of individuals and society as a whole. Economically, the goals typically center on obtaining the highest overall level of material wealth for society as a whole and for each of its members. For the U.S. government, the responsibility for achieving economic goals is spelled out in the Employment Act of 1946 and the Full Employment and Balanced Growth Act of 1978 (commonly called the

Humphrey–Hawkins Act). The centerpiece of these two bills commits the federal government to promoting high employment consistent with a stable price level. For the Fed, the two acts translate into six basic goals with two goals—high employment and stable prices—serving as primary goals.

The six goals for monetary policy are as follows:

1. Price stability
2. Full employment
3. Economic growth
4. Interest rate stability
5. Stability of the financial system
6. Stability of the foreign exchange markets

We now look briefly at the six goals and identify, where appropriate, some key measures.

PRICE STABILITY

In a **market economy** like that in the United States, consumers have a free choice to buy or not buy whatever goods or services they want. Price movements—up or down—signal to producers what consumers want by reflecting changes in demand. For example, if the price of a product rises, the product is more profitable, and producers increase production to gain the additional profits. **Price stability**, then, means that for some large market basket of goods, the average price change of all the products is near zero. Within the market basket, however, the prices of individual products can rise or fall, depending on supply and demand conditions.

The value of money is determined by the prices of a broad range of goods and services money buys in the economy. Simply put, the value of money is what you can buy with it. Changes in prices of goods and services that money can buy are measured by price indexes such as the Consumer Price Index (CPI), which are based on a market basket of goods or services purchased by consumers. There is an inverse relationship between price levels and the purchasing power of money. That is, if prices rise, fewer goods can be purchased with the same amount of money; thus, the purchasing power of money has declined. Conversely, if the prices of goods fall, one can buy more commodities with the same amount of money, so the purchasing power of money rises when prices fall.

Inflation is defined as a continuous rise in the average price level. Because the value of money is its purchasing power, inflation can affect a person's economic welfare. Thus, with inflation in an economy, over time, you have less and less purchasing power—your money buys less than it did before. The result is that you have suffered a loss in your economic wealth.

High rates of inflation present two problems in an economy. The first problem with inflation is that all economic units do not have the ability to adjust equally to price level changes. The result is that inflation causes unintended transfers of purchasing power between parties of financial contracts if the inflation is unanticipated or if the parties are unable to adjust to the anticipated inflation. For instance, people on fixed incomes may anticipate inflation but cannot alter their income stream if prices rise. Retired people on pensions are particularly likely to experience such difficulties. Of course, if inflation is anticipated correctly and the appropriate adjustments are made, no wealth transfer takes place. Unfortunately, in the real world, this is rarely the case.

The second problem caused by high rates of inflation is that they are a disruptive force in an economy. As was mentioned above, high inflation rates increase uncertainty, making it more difficult to plan for the future and make long-term investment decisions. There is evidence from academic studies that inflation leads to lower economic growth, especially in countries that have experienced a high rate of inflation, such as Argentina, Brazil, and Russia. The experience proved very damaging to the working of their economies and the social fabric of the countries.

What is the optimal inflation rate for an economy? There is no single optimal inflation rate because of cultural, political, economic, and life experience differences with inflation. For the U.S. economy, the Fed's current target rate for inflation is 2 percent annually.

FULL EMPLOYMENT

Full employment implies that every person of working age who wishes to work can find employment. Although most would agree that full employment is a desirable goal, in practice it is difficult to achieve. For example, a certain amount of unemployment in the economy is **frictional unemployment**, which means that a portion of those who are unemployed are in transition between jobs. Another reason for people not working is **structural unemployment**, meaning that there is a mismatch between a person's skill levels and available jobs or there are jobs in one region of the country but few in another region. Thus, a policy issue is whether workers should be required to move across the country for jobs or whether they should stay where their family and friends are located. As a result, government policymakers are willing to tolerate a certain level of unemployment—the **natural rate of unemployment**—a sort of "full employment unemployment rate." However, even this rate is subject to debate and change. For example, in the 1960s, full employment was considered to be 4 percent unemployment, but the comparable unemployment rate by 1980 was at least 5 percent.

Exhibit 3.4 illustrates the point that the acceptable rate of unemployment depends largely on the actual unemployment rate. The actual unemployment rate in the early 1980s was above 10 percent at times. Therefore, the politically acceptable rate of unemployment was also high. Today the acceptable rate of unemployment is around 5 percent, though unemployment did briefly dip below 4 percent in the late 1990s. During the recession that began in 2001, unemployment spiked upward to 6 percent; as the recovery picked up steam in 2004, unemployment declined. Currently, the politically acceptable unemployment rate is in the 5 to 6 percent range.

Exhibit 3.4 shows the unemployment rate from 1960 through 2010. Over the last half-century, unemployment typically spikes during a recession and then recovers rather quickly from the peak rate, once the economy has begun to recover. During the period shown in the exhibit, the average recession period was 9 months and the average period of expansion was nearly 5 years. The recent recession, which began in December 2007, lasted 18 months and ended in June 2009, has been troubling in that the unemployment rate shows no sign of abating from the 9 to 10 percent range. It comes as no surprise that the number one political issue is jobs, particularly in the manufacturing sector.

EXHIBIT 3.4
The U.S. Unemployment Rate (1960–2010)

Full employment doesn't mean zero unemployment. A certain amount of unemployment is acceptable because some people will be unemployed as they transition from one job to another and because others will not have the skills required for the available jobs. In addition, it is common for regional differences in the demand for labor to cause some unemployment. The acceptable rate of unemployment tends to fluctuate but is currently around 5 to 6 percent.

Source: U.S. Department of Labor, Bureau of Labor Statistics.
http://www.bls.gov/data/

ECONOMIC GROWTH

Economic growth is a fancy name that economists use for a rising standard of living, as measured by output per unit of input. Economic growth means you are living materially better today than in the past or better than your parents were, even though you are working the same hours per week they did. Economic growth is made possible through increased productivity of labor and capital. Typically, labor becomes more productive through education and training, and capital through the application of better technologies. Increases in economic growth may not always be desirable or benefit everyone. For example, it may not be desirable to have an increase in economic output if it results in significant degradation of the environment or our social infrastructure.

In recent years there has been some concern about the rate of economic growth in the United States. In the 1950s and 1960s the real gross domestic product grew at an annual rate in excess of 3½ percent. Since the early 1970s, **real GDP** has slowed down and has grown at only 2 to 2½ percent. This means the standard of living for American families was increasing at a slower rate of growth than in the past. What has puzzled economists during this dry spell is that there did not seem to be any payoff in increased productivity from the extensive investment that American businesses made in technology. In the late 1990s and very early 2000s, however, economic growth rebounded to the 3½ percent annual growth rate levels, and Alan Greenspan, then-chairman of the Federal Reserve Board, attributed the return to application of technology, especially computers and other digital technologies. From 2002 through 2005, real GDP grew by an average of about 3.2 percent per year, substantially confirming Greenspan's prediction in the near term. To check out recent GDP and productivity numbers at the Fed's Web site, go to the Internet Exercise at the end of the chapter.

INTEREST RATE STABILITY

Interest rate stability refers to the swings or volatility of interest rates over time. Large interest rate fluctuations introduce additional uncertainty into the economy and make it harder to plan for the future. Furthermore, periods of high interest rates inhibit consumer and business spending. In particular, purchases of big-ticket items that tend to drive and support economic expansions are highly sensitive to interest rates. For business, these are capital expenditures like plant and equipment purchases, and for consumers, the purchase of a home. Interest rate stability is also important for financial institutions that deal in long-term bond contracts, such as mortgages. An increase in interest rates produces a large loss on long-term bonds and mortgages. Exhibit 3.5 shows the level and volatility of interest rates since 1960. Fluctuation in interest rates during the 1980s and early 1990s resulted in serious financial losses at thrift institutions (savings and loan associations and mutual savings banks) and led to a collapse of the industry. Low interest rates over the last decade may have contributed to record housing sales and home renovation work. Many experts blame former Federal Reserve chairman Alan Greenspan for keeping interest rates too low, which created an asset bubble in real estate and precipitated the 2008 financial crisis and recession that followed.

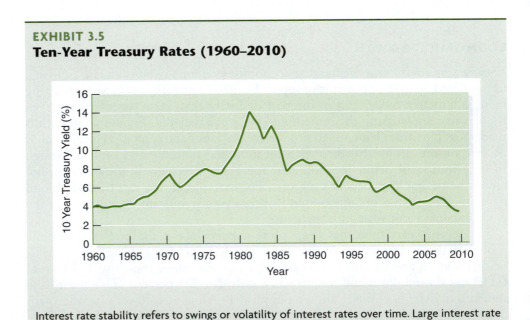

EXHIBIT 3.5
Ten-Year Treasury Rates (1960–2010)

Interest rate stability refers to swings or volatility of interest rates over time. Large interest rate fluctuations create additional uncertainty in the economy and make it hard to plan for the future. Periods of high interest rates retard consumer and business spending. Both factors slow down economic growth in an economy.

Source: Federal Reserve Board of Governors, H.15 Statistical Release.
http://www.federalreserve.gov/releases/H15/data.htm#fn13

STABILITY OF THE FINANCIAL SYSTEM

One of the major responsibilities of the Federal Reserve is to stabilize the financial system. Disruptions in the financial system can inhibit the ability of financial markets to channel funds efficiently between surplus spending units and deficit spending units. Any reduction in the flow of funds reduces consumer spending and business investment, which leads to slower economic growth. Also, individuals may find it more difficult or expensive to borrow and, thus, may have to postpone certain purchases such as buying a new car.

Another major responsibility of the Fed is the stabilization of the banking system—primarily depository institutions. Widespread failure of banks and other depository institutions can have a debilitating effect on the economy. Without going into detail, the 1929 stock market crash was followed by widespread bank failures and a devastating depression. Using the best analysis of the day, economists and politicians coalesced around the notion that somehow the Great Depression was caused by the misbehavior of Wall Street and the nation's banks. The Glass-Steagall Act of 1933 and other banking legislation of the period separated investment banking from commercial banking to remove various conflicts of interest, regulated margin requirements to reduce speculative investing, and introduced a number of anticompetitive measures in banking, such as Regulation Q, to reduce competition and, hence, bank failures. As one might expect, the number of bank failures dropped dramatically after this legislation, and the country has not had a depression since.

Today, the Fed tries to strike a balance between keeping the banking system competitive without risking widespread bank failures. One important way the Fed stabilizes the banking system is in its role as the "lender of last resort." The Fed accomplishes this by providing massive amounts of liquidity (bank reserves) to depository institutions when any economic or political issue threatens the integrity or safety of the banking system.

Two examples of the importance of the Fed's role as the lender of last resort are featured in the two People & Events features in this chapter. The first discusses the Fed's role in forestalling a financial panic in the days and weeks following the September 11, 2001, plane crashes into the World Trade Center and the Pentagon. The second deals with how the Fed stabilized the financial sector following Black Monday: the October 19, 1987, stock market crash, which was the largest one-day percentage decline in stock market prices in history. The two events were very different in their origin and destructive mechanism, but both had the potential to unravel the financial sector of the economy. Decisive actions by the Fed in both situations averted a financial panic.

STABILITY OF FOREIGN EXCHANGE MARKETS

Barring a major political setback, the globalization of business will continue well into the future. There are a number of forces that drive global economic integration. The most important of these are the emergence of global communications and other digital technologies, business firms' desire to become global suppliers, increasingly uniform business practices and standards, and the continued movement worldwide to free-market economies. As you would expect, international trade is an increasingly important sector of the U.S. economy and, as a result, stability of exchange rates is a major concern at the Fed.

PEOPLE & EVENTS

The Fed as Lender of Last Resort: Preventing a Financial Panic

In the days that followed September 11, 2001, the Federal Reserve played an important part in preventing a financial panic. The federal government essentially shut down after planes crashed into the World Trade Center and Pentagon, but the Federal Reserve System remained open. In fact, the Fed was very busy trying to forestall a financial meltdown.

The Fed has learned from previous crises that providing liquidity is the best way to calm financial markets and instill confidence in the banking system. By September 12, the Fed had added $38.25 billion to the banking system using repurchase agreements. The typical size of such operations is $2 billion to $6 billion. In addition, discount window borrowing far exceeded normal levels.

There are several reasons why banks demanded liquidity in the days after September 11. One reason is that many uncleared checks were stuck on grounded airplanes. Therefore, many banks borrowed at the discount window to finance the uncleared checks. A second reason is that the demand for cash by banks' customers surged. For example, the Chicago Fed reported that cash requirements were 10 to 15 percent above normal for banks in that district. Wells Fargo and other banks went so far as to impose limits on the size of cash withdrawals. Fortunately, the Fed's actions calmed fears of a panic and the financial system stabilized quickly.

Exchange rates determine the value of the dollar relative to foreign currencies. (Exchange rates are discussed in Chapter 12.) A rising value of the dollar means that U.S. dollars buy more foreign goods abroad but foreign currency buys fewer goods in the United States. The rising value of the dollar makes U.S. firms less competitive abroad and thus reduces exports. At the same time, the rising dollar stimulates imports because imports become less expensive. Clearly, widely fluctuating exchange rates introduce uncertainty into the economy and make it harder to plan and make international transactions in the future. Similarly, stabilizing exchange rates makes it easier for firms and individuals to purchase or sell goods abroad. Thus, stabilizing extreme fluctuations in the value of the dollar relative to other currencies is an important goal for the Fed.

POSSIBLE CONFLICTS AMONG GOALS

Fortunately, most of the goals of the Fed are relatively consistent with one another. The goals that have often been perceived as being in conflict are full employment and stable prices, at least in the short run. It is not the only conflict, but it is the one that has historically gained more attention from academic journals, policymakers, and the popular financial press.

The conflict revolves around the perception that, as unemployment decreases, inflation usually increases. The argument goes like this. At high levels of unemployment, there is substantial unused industrial capacity, and one would tend to believe that the most productive workers and most efficient manufacturing facilities are being utilized. As the economy begins to expand, unemployment starts to decline as workers are called back to work, and capacity utilization increases as more goods and services are produced. As the expansion continues, less efficient workers are called back to work, and wages begin to rise as labor becomes scarce;

EXHIBIT 3.6
Possible Trade-Off Between Unemployment and Inflation

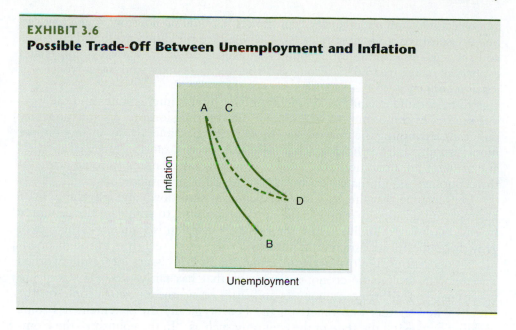

also, less efficient manufacturing facilities are brought on line, and raw materials supplies become scarce, leading to an increase in the rate of inflation that ultimately reaches the consumer.

Exhibit 3.6 shows a graph of this perceived trade-off between unemployment and inflation over time and how adjustments may take place. In the early to mid-1960s, the relationship between unemployment and inflation was fairly predictable and stable. However, in the 1970s, the economy experienced periods of both high inflation and high unemployment, and since then, the relationship between unemployment and inflation has not been stable or predictable. Thus, curves such as those shown in Exhibit 3.6 are currently not believed to be useful as policy tools. Nonetheless, some public policymakers and members of the press continue to be concerned about the so-called trade-off between inflation and unemployment. Through the 1990s and the 2000s, the U.S. economy experienced both moderate inflation and moderate unemployment, and no trade-off has been apparent.

Turning again to Exhibit 3.6, curve AB illustrates the possible trade-off between unemployment and inflation. Notice that as unemployment declines, the rate of inflation increases. Curve CD in the exhibit shows the trade-off curve that might exist if inflation is prolonged in the economy. In other words, after a prolonged period of inflation, inflation expectations become imbedded in the economy. Thus, as unemployment decreases, inflation only declines to point D, which then forms a new unemployment–inflation trade-off curve CD.

3.5 THE FED AND THE ECONOMY

Monetary policy is thought to affect the economy through three basic expenditure channels: (1) business investment, (2) consumer spending, and (3) net exports. Businesses spend for investment in plant, equipment, new buildings, and inventory accumulation. Consumer spending is typically divided into two categories: (1) consumer spending on durable goods such as automobiles, boats, appliances, and electronic equipment; and (2) consumer spending on housing, which tends to be very sensitive to interest rates. Net exports are the difference between goods and services imported into the country and those exported. Clearly, imports and exports are sensitive to the exchange rate between the dollar and the currencies of foreign countries.

To better understand how monetary policy affects interest rates and the various sectors of the economy, we examine the transmission process for monetary policy. By examining the transmission process, it is possible to trace changes in the money supply and see how the changes affect interest rates in financial markets and at financial institutions, the impact of money on spending in four sectors of the economy, and ultimately its impact on the GDP and inflation.

Let's assume that the economy has begun to slow down and that the FOMC has met and decided that now is the appropriate time to stimulate the economy by easing monetary policy. Thus, the FOMC's decision is to increase the rate of growth of the money supply by purchasing Treasury securities through open-market operations. Following the meeting, the FOMC issues a carefully worded statement in diplomatic economic language that has fairly precise meaning to experienced Wall Street economists and little or no meaning to people on the street or newscasters who report on the Fed. Typically the statement has some wording conveying the state of the economy such as, "In the context of the Committee's long-run objectives for price stability and sustainable economic growth, information that has become available since the last meeting suggests the economy is beginning to slow." The FOMC may also specify a lower target for the fed funds rate with a statement such as, "The FOMC decided to reduce the fed funds target rate to 6¼ percent from 6½ percent," and on occasion it may make a statement about the expected rate of growth of the money supply such as, "Contemplated reserve conditions are expected to be consistent with moderate to slightly faster growth in M2 over the coming months."

As shown in Exhibit 3.7, the process starts with the open-market purchase of Treasury securities at the trading desk at the New York Fed. The open-market purchase injects additional reserves in the banking system and, hence, leads to an increase in the money supply. As you recall, this happens because banks expand their deposits (money supply) until they have no excess reserves by making loans or purchasing securities.

An increase in the money supply also means an increase in the quantity of funds available to lend. All else staying the same, an increase in the supply of loanable funds causes a decline in interest rates in financial markets as well as a decline in lending rates at financial institutions. A decline in interest rates in financial markets increases the market value of fixed income securities like corporate bonds, mortgages, and mortgage-backed securities. This increase in the value of investment securities adds to the wealth of investors. At the same time, the reduced lending rate at financial institutions encourages borrowing by consumers. Consequently, consumer spending tends to increase in response to an increase in the money supply. There are several channels through which an increase in the money supply can cause an increase in consumption expenditures. First, greater (or lesser) holdings of money may cause the public to spend more (or less) freely. Second, when credit becomes more readily available and interest rates decline, consumers may borrow more readily to buy cars and other durable goods. Third, when consumers perceive that their current purchasing power has increased (or decreased) because of changes in their wealth holdings or in the

EXHIBIT 3.7
How Monetary Policy Affects Economic Variables

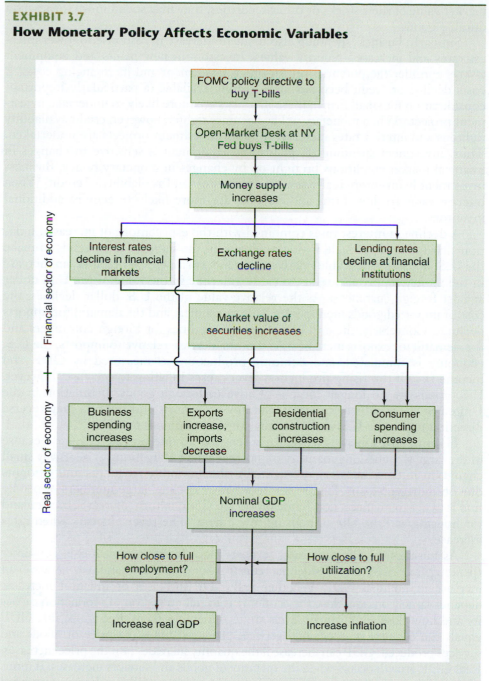

The real and financial sectors of the economy are closely related. The Fed attempts to manage the relation by controlling the monetary base and the money supply.

market value of their stocks or other securities, they may spend more (or less) on durable goods.

Similarly, business spending also tends to increase in response to lower interest rates and increased security values. Investors in new plants and equipment always consider the potential return on an investment and its financing costs. If costs decline or credit becomes more readily available (a particularly important consideration for small firms), these investors are more likely to undertake investment projects. When monetary policy becomes tighter, however, credit availability tightens and interest rates increase, so fewer investment projects are undertaken. Thus, investment spending on plants and equipment is sensitive to changes in financial market conditions brought on by changes in monetary policy. Business investment in inventory is also sensitive to the cost and availability of credit. When interest rates are low, firms and retailers are more likely to acquire additional inventory.

A decline in interest rates combined with the expectations of increased inflation that typically coincide with an increase in the money supply tends to make the U.S. dollar less desirable relative to foreign currencies. Therefore, an increase in the money supply also tends to cause a decline in the value of the U.S. dollar against foreign currencies. As the relative value of the U.S. dollar declines, the cost of imported goods increases for U.S. consumers and the demand for imports declines. Conversely, the cost of U.S. goods declines for foreign consumers and the demand for exports increases. As exports increase relative to imports, the U.S. economy is stimulated, and domestic production, as measured by GDP, and income rise. If the rising production level causes inflation to increase, however, U.S. goods are no longer cheaper relative to foreign goods. If inflation in the United States is sufficiently great, the flow of exports and imports may reverse direction unless the U.S. dollar's exchange rate continues to fall.

Housing investment is particularly sensitive to interest rate changes because of the large size and long maturity of mortgage debt obligations. A relatively small change in interest rates can substantially alter monthly payments and amounts due on mortgage loans. Hence, if interest rates decline, large numbers of people find it easier to finance a new home mortgage. This, in turn, increases the demand for housing and the rate of housing investment. The reverse occurs when rates increase.

As business spending increases, exports increase, imports decrease, consumer spending increases, and residential construction increases, and we observe an increase in nominal GDP. Whether real GDP increases or inflation increases depends largely on how close the economy is to full utilization of production capacity and how close employment levels are to full employment. Recognize that GDP equals the quantity of goods and services produced times the price of goods and services produced. GDP can increase if the quantity increases or if the price increases. Real GDP growth occurs when the quantity of goods and services increases. If monetary policy is overly expansive and the economy nears full employment and full utilization, inflation may increase to the point that it dominates the nominal increase in GDP. In other words, the price level has increased faster than the quantity of goods and services. An extreme example of this effect would be if the quantity of goods and services decreased while prices were increasing rapidly. It would then be possible to observe an increase in nominal GDP from the price level increase, even though the quantity of goods and services went down. An overly restrictive monetary policy, however, can limit both the real and the nominal GDP growth.

PEOPLE & EVENTS

Black Monday

In finance, Black Monday refers to Monday, October 19, 1987, a day that will go down in history as the largest one-day percentage decline in stock market history. The Dow Jones Industrial Index (DJIA) declined by more than 500 points, a decline of nearly 25 percent. The crash was global, starting in Hong Kong, spreading west through international time zones to Europe, and then hitting the United States. The stock market crash in Hong Kong declined 45 percent; Australia, 42 percent; Spain, 31 percent; and the United Kingdom, 26 percent.

There is no consensus on what caused the crash. The most popular reason places much of the blame on technology: program trading strategies that blindly sold stock as the market declined and computers that execute program trading commands in the blink of an eye. The fear was that the financial market meltdown had the potential of unraveling the financial sector of the economy and leading to a cataclysmic decline in economic activity—another 1929 Great Depression.

On the day following the crash, then-Fed-chairman Alan Greenspan and New York Federal Reserve bank president Gerald Corrigan expressed grave concerns about the viability of the banking system. The stress level and uncertainty facing market participants was staggering; a banking panic was possible. On October 20, the Fed announced it stood ready to provide massive amounts of liquidity to the financial system, both to banks and securities firms. Before the Fed's involvement, many brokerage houses and dealers were unable to find additional credit during the crisis. Without the additional funding, many firms and security dealers would have had to liquidate their positions at a loss. Fortunately, the Fed stepped in to provide discount loans to banks willing to lend to the security industry. Because of this decisive action, a real crisis was averted.

3.6 COMPLICATIONS OF MONETARY POLICY

The Fed's job of controlling the money supply is not easy. For one thing, there are a number of so-called **technical factors** that affect the monetary base. For example, although the Fed supplies the monetary base to the banking system, it cannot control cash drains. Cash drains cause a "leakage" between the change in the monetary base and the change in banks' holdings of actual reserves. In particular, cash holdings by the public use up the monetary base so it is not available to banks as actual reserves. Because cash drains from the banking system reduce actual reserves held by banks, the Fed must try to anticipate when people are likely to withdraw cash from banks. The Fed then tries to expand the monetary base to offset the cash drains so depository institutions' reserves do not fall and their loans, investments, and deposits do not contract as cash leaves the banking system. Conversely, the Fed must anticipate when people will put cash back in depository institutions and offset that addition to reserves, lest depository institutions expand their loans, investments, and deposits in an inflationary manner. Because seasonal fluctuations in cash flows are large, particularly around holidays, the Fed often must engage in open-market operations to offset these flows.

Similarly, the Fed must engage in open-market operations to offset the effects of float. Recall that float represents the difference between deferred availability cash items (DACI) and cash items in process of collection (CIPC). By its very nature, the level of float at the Fed changes on a daily basis.

A third technical factor is changes in Treasury deposits at the Fed. Large payments into or out of Treasury deposits at the Fed cause large shifts in depository institutions' reserves as the checks are deposited and collected. Thus, the Treasury tries to minimize fluctuations in its deposits at the Fed. It also tries to coordinate any large fluctuations in its deposits with the Fed so that depository institutions' reserve deposits do not fluctuate violently.

A final factor that, although not a technical factor, complicates the Fed's ability to influence the level of economic activity is the **velocity of money**, which is the relationship between the money supply and economic activity. Velocity (V) is computed as the ratio of national income (or GDP), Y, to the money supply, M:

$$M \times V = Y \quad \text{or} \quad V = Y/M \tag{3.2}$$

By knowing V, the Fed could predict by how much GDP would change for a given change in the money supply, M. Unfortunately for the Fed, the velocity of money changes over time and is difficult to predict. Therefore, even though the money supply and the level of economic activity tend to be correlated, the correlation may be sufficiently variable that it is difficult to use changes in the money supply to influence the economy in the short run. As shown in Exhibit 3.7, the transmission process of monetary policy is extremely complex; therefore, it is difficult to predict exactly what impact a given monetary policy will have on the economy by using a simple concept like velocity.

The trading desk at the New York Fed makes permanent adjustments to the monetary base by buying or selling Treasury securities. To offset the effects of technical factors, however, the trading desk uses repurchase agreements and reverse repurchase agreements. A *repurchase agreement* consists of the sale of a short-term security (collateral) with the condition that, after a period of time, the original seller will buy it back at a predetermined price. The collateral used most frequently is U.S. Treasury or agency securities. However, it is possible to use any of the better-known money market instruments. By using these agreements, the Fed can make very short-term, temporary adjustments to the monetary base. Chapter 7, which covers money market instruments in detail, discusses repurchase agreements as well.

3.7 ANATOMY OF A FINANCIAL CRISIS

In the previous sections, we discussed how monetary policy affects the output of the economy. Too much money in the economy leads to inflation and too little money leads to a recession. It all sounds so simple and predictable. Yet the 2008 fiscal crisis led to the most severe recession since the Great Depression. In testimony before Congress, former Fed chairman Alan Greenspan referred to the subprime financial crisis as a "once-in-a-century credit tsunami."

How did the 2008 financial crisis occur? What economic or psychological factors spun out of control to cause the collapse? In this section, we want to better understand why the 2008 financial crisis occurred, and why in most instances, a financial crisis leads to a recession. Before we start, we need to review the major events that comprise the financial crisis.

THE 2008 FINANCIAL CRISIS

The crisis had its roots in the real estate and the subprime lending markets. The year 2008 was tumultuous by any standard. An early signal that something was terribly wrong in the financial sector was the government-backed takeover of Bear Sterns by JPMorgan Chase during March 2008. Bear Sterns, the smallest of the Big 5 Wall Street investment banks, had invested heavily in below-prime-rate mortgage securities and had suffered substantial losses. (Investment banks, from largest to smallest, are Lehman Brothers, Merrill Lynch, Morgan Stanley, and Goldman Sachs.) JPMorgan agreed to take the deal *only* if the Fed would shield it from much of the risk of Bear's troubled assets. The administration hoped that this unusual step would restore confidence in the financial system and calm the market. Rather than having a calming effect, the banking system became increasingly wary and began tightening credit availability. During July, Fannie Mae and Freddie Mac, the nation's two mortgage giants, were hit hard by the escalating volume of mortgage foreclosures; by September 2008 both firms were taken over by the federal government. The bailout of Fannie and Freddie, which put taxpayers' money at risk, was not politically popular.

In a time span of about 45 days, the structure of the banking and investment banking industries was radically altered beyond most participants' wildest imagination. Beginning around September 2008, Bank of America agreed to purchase financially troubled Merrill Lynch, one of the world's leading investment banks, which had invested heavily in high-risk securities backed by subprime home mortgages. American International Group (AIG), one of the nation's largest insurance companies and heavily involved in the mortgage-based derivative markets, was saved from bankruptcy by an $85 billion capital injection by the federal government. Shortly thereafter, JPMorgan Chase agreed to purchase the assets of Washington Mutual in what was the largest bank failure in U.S. history. Also during September, Citigroup acquired Wachovia Bank. Goldman Sachs, who had arguably been the most successful Wall Street investment bank for decades, was humbled when it was forced to turn itself into a commercial bank to survive the 2008 meltdown and take on federal assistance. Though many of the failed financial firms were in different lines of business, the one characteristic they had in common is that they were all significant players in some part of the real estate markets.

A number of economists believe that the defining moment in the financial crisis may have occurred on September 15, when Lehman Brothers, the largest and much-storied Wall Street investment bank, declared bankruptcy after regulators were unable to find a suitable buyer for the firm. Lehman was the biggest bankruptcy in U.S. history. It was brought down by bad bets in the housing market made during the real estate boom. Like Bear Sterns, Lehman Brothers was a major participant in the subprime mortgage market. After the Lehman failure, the financial sector found itself in shambles, and a crisis of confidence made banks reluctant to loan money among themselves or, for that matter, to anyone else.

SUBPRIME LENDING MARKET

The subprime lending market was the epicenter of the 2008 financial crisis. Thus, it's necessary to understand how the market works. The term *subprime* refers to borrowers whose credit quality is less than stellar and who have a greater risk of default than prime borrowers. The size of the subprime mortgage market was huge. As of March 2007, it was estimated at $1.3 trillion. One reason for the market's growth was that, for nearly a decade, owners of commercial and residential properties saw their values increase uninterruptedly in a real estate boom. The housing boom coincided with a period of government deregulation.

To many consumers, buying a home was a "can't lose investment." The relaxation of credit standards, fueled in part by the government's core value that homeownership is desirable, made it possible for many more below-prime-rate borrowers to qualify for mortgage loans under one of the government-sponsored mortgage programs. In the past, these borrowers would not have qualified for a conventional mortgage loan.

Historically, after a mortgage was originated, the banks' and thrifts' only option was to hold the loan until maturity. There was no active secondary market for mortgage loans. One of the major innovations in finance was securitization, which is the process of distributing risk by aggregating individual mortgages into a pool, then issuing a new security backed by the pool. Investors are paid interest and principal from the mortgages in the pool. Because the securitized debt has a secondary market, it unlocks the value of illiquid assets, providing consumers with lower borrowing costs. Banks and thrifts who originated securitized mortgages no longer have to hold them to maturity. By selling the mortgages to investors, banks can replenish their funds, thus allowing them to issue more loans and generate additional transaction fees. Most securitized subprime mortgages are brought to market as mortgage-backed securities (MBSs), which are debt instruments backed by the mortgage pool.

Initially, the market for subprime mortgages worked well. Banks made lots of money. Consumers enjoyed cheap credit and lax credit terms. For example, in 2005 the median down payment for first-time home buyers was 2 percent, with 43 percent of those buyers making no down payment. Nearly 50 percent of first-time home buyers purchased variable rate mortgages, which carry substantial interest rate risk. Brushing aside the question of risk, politicians from both political parties fought for bragging rights: "Never have so many Americans owned their own home," they crowed.

Unfortunately, the subprime lending market is subject to the vagaries of the marketplace. The market worked well until home prices started to decline and interest rates began to rise in mid-2006. Depending on the borrower's circumstance and type of mortgage held, many homeowners were unable to keep up with their payments, defaulting on their mortgages. Financial institutions who owned these securities were forced to take huge write-downs and write-offs, and many were forced to raise more capital or go bankrupt. On Wall Street, subprime mortgages were called **toxic securities** because of their toxic effect on a firm's capital and ultimately its solvency.

FACTORS CAUSING A FINANCIAL CRISIS

We noted in Chapter 1 that a well-functioning financial system channels money to the best investment opportunities in the economy. When this occurs, the needs of consumers and businesses are met, and the output of the real economy is near its peak level. This happens when banks and other financial institutions have resolved asymmetric information problems—adverse selection and moral hazard. Many of these problems are solved by information that financial institutions produce.

A financial crisis occurs when there is a severe shock to the financial system that disrupts its ability to function normally. By "normal," we mean the ability to channel money to the most productive investment opportunity. The financial system ceases to function properly when adverse selection and moral hazard problems become significant. When this happens, commercial banks and other financial institutions make fewer loans and provide fewer financial services, consumer and business spending is reduced, cash flows become smaller, and the level of economic activity contracts.

We have identified five factors that may have caused or contributed to the 2008 financial crisis. These factors—(1) deterioration in financial institutions' balance sheets, (2) the bursting housing bubble, (3) abnormally low interest rates, (4) an increase in uncertainty in the economy, and (5) a banking crisis—will provide a starting point for our discussion.

DETERIORATION IN FINANCIAL INSTITUTIONS' BALANCE SHEETS

Earlier in the book, we mentioned that banks and other financial institutions play an important role in the financial system because they engage in information production activities that resolve information asymmetry problems. Some examples are credit reports, credit ratings, and systems that monitor a borrower's business activities and credit risk after a loan is made.

The financial health of financial firms also affects their ability to provide financial services to the economy. Suppose, for example, that banks suffer large loan losses in a particular type of loan. As these losses are written off against capital, banks have diminished resources and a restricted ability to make loans. There also may be pressures from bank regulators to tighten lending standards and perform more rigorous due diligence on loan applicants. These restrictions reduce consumer and business borrowing, which lead to a slowdown in economic activity.

Deregulation.   Increasing homeownership has been a political goal of several presidents, including Roosevelt, Reagan, Clinton, and G. W. Bush. Ironically, some economists believe that the cause of the 2008 financial crisis can be traced to 1992 deregulation legislation by the Bush administration. The legislation reduced some of the regulation over Fannie Mae and Freddie Mac, with the goal of making more money available for subprime borrowers. Similarly, in 1999, the Clinton administration pressured Fannie Mae to expand mortgage loans to low- and moderate-income households. The motivation behind both of these plans was to increase the number of subprime borrowers who could qualify for mortgage loans under government-sponsored programs. The resulting loans were high risk, and banks and others who had significant holdings of these loans through mortgage-backed securities incurred large losses.

Pricing Credit Risk.   The 2008 financial crisis exposed serious flaws in the credit rating process for mortgage securities. Most of the ratings are done by three rating agencies: Moody's, Standard & Poor's, and Fitch. When rating agencies assign a credit rating, they estimate the likelihood that the debt will be paid back—the security's risk of default. Once a security's credit risk is established, it is assigned a letter ranking on a scale of AAA, AA, A, BBB, BB, B, and so on. Any rating BBB and above is investment grade, and any ranking below BBB is considered speculative grade. AAA is the highest grade available. The division between investment and speculative grade is huge because banks and other financial institutions can purchase only investment grade securities.

Individual subprime mortgages are by definition speculative grade securities. However, when subprime mortgages were securitized and sold as MBSs, the securitized debt was rated AAA. The key question is, How did the securitization process take individual mortgages that are ranked subprime and transform them into MBSs rated AAA. There are two basic arguments provided by practitioners. First, the investment community believed that securitization provided lenders a more efficient way to manage credit risk. Second, the credit rating agencies believed that the AAA ratings were justified because of the credit risk reduction practices that were employed, such as purchasing credit risk insurance for the security issue.

However, as defaults on MBSs mounted above the rate expected for AAA debt, an interesting discovery was made. Because of complexities, the credit rating agencies had developed a mathematical model to rate securitized mortgage debt, which depended heavily on assumptions derived from limited historical data. The discovery was that the model underestimated the securities' actual default risk. The AAA credit rating was critical because it allowed MBSs to be sold to banks and other financial institutions in the United States and all over the world. Unfortunately, this serious error did not become apparent until many hundreds of billions of dollars of mortgage-backed securities had been sold—it was a problem of epic proportion. As of July 2008, credit rating agencies had to downgrade $1.9 trillion in mortgage-backed securities. Banks and other financial institutions that held sizable holdings of these securities suffered heavy losses. The heavy losses reduced their ability to make loans and deliver financial services, resulting in a decrease in the level of economic activity.

ASSET BUBBLE BURSTS

An asset bubble is formed when the price of assets is overinflated due to excess demand. It usually occurs when investors flock to a particular asset class, such as real estate or technology stocks, with the belief that they can earn higher than normal returns. Asset bubbles are often driven by low interest rates and a credit boom. When the bubble bursts, the price of assets declines over time to their true market value, and individuals and companies that own the asset suffer losses to their net worth. The loss of wealth means that these economic units will borrow and spend less, which will cause the economy to contract.

In the United States a number of asset bubbles began to appear: in real estate in mid-2006 and in oil and food prices in late 2007. Turning to the housing bubble, between 1997 and 2006 the price of a typical American home increased 124 percent. A contributing factor was the Fed's policy of maintaining lower interest rates. Low interest rates and rising housing prices resulted in a large number of homeowners refinancing their homes. Much of this money was used to finance consumer spending or to pay down existing debts.

By mid-2006, housing prices peaked; by September 2008, the price of the average U.S. house had declined by over 25 percent. As prices continued to decline, borrowers with adjustable rate mortgages could not refinance to avoid higher payments because interest rates were now beginning to rise. Of subprime borrowers, nearly 50 percent of the mortgages were variable rate. Beginning in 2007, lenders began to foreclose on nearly 1.3 million properties, and by 2008, the number was 2.3 million. By September 2009, nearly 15 percent of all mortgages were in default. Total losses were estimated in the trillions of dollars.

ABNORMALLY LOW INTEREST RATES

A number of economists have blamed former Federal Reserve chairman Alan Greenspan for keeping interest rates abnormally low, creating an asset bubble in housing that led to the financial crisis of 2008. The Fed pursued a low interest rate policy early in the decade. From 2000 to 2003, the Fed lowered the fed funds target interest rate from 6.5 percent to 1.0 percent. This was done to soften the effects of the dot-com bubble and the September 2001 terrorist attacks, and to combat the perceived risk of deflation. Lower interest rates encourage consumer and business borrowing. The Fed then raised the fed funds rate significantly between July 2004 and July 2006, which made homeownership much more expensive and put financial pressures on families who had variable rate mortgages.

INCREASE IN UNCERTAINTY

A dramatic increase in uncertainty in the financial sector or the economy can literally halt trading or lending activities. This happens when adverse selection and moral hazard problems are extreme. For example, if lenders cannot differentiate between good and bad credit, the market for loans fails. Some examples of major shocks are the failures of money center or Wall Street investment banks, a banking panic, and a sharp increase in commodity prices. We conclude that a significant increase in uncertainty leads to an increases in adverse selection and moral hazard problems. As these costs rise, the ability of the financial sector to make loans and deliver other financial services is diminished, which leads to reduced economic output.

BANKING CRISIS

If a bank suffers a significant loss in its loan or investment portfolio, the bank will fail. Depositors at other banks may worry about the safety of their deposits (in the absence of deposit insurance). If there is any concern, depositors will typically withdraw their funds as quickly as possible. If rumors, whether true or false, start about other banks, there will likely be a run on the banks. A bank run occurs because banks have a small amount of vault cash relative to their total deposit accounts, and many of these accounts are payable on demand. If the run is large enough, the bank can fail even though the bank's loan portfolio is sound. Because deposits can be withdrawn quickly, banks are prone to a contagion effect, which means rumors about bank financial soundness or potential insolvency spread from one bank to another and can cause widespread bank failures.

A bank panic is the simultaneous failure of many banks during a financial crisis. The source of the contagion is asymmetric information. Depositors do not know the quality of the bank's loan or investment portfolio (they lack reliable information) and, to be safe, they assume the worst. As bank failures become widespread, adverse selection and moral hazard problems become severe, and the banking system comes to a halt because everyone assumes the worst and lacks reliable information. A banking crisis can lead to a decline in the availability of credit in the economy, which results in a decline in business and consumer spending, and eventually a contraction in the economy.

Bank runs do occur still, and when the bank or financial institution is large, it is a serious economic event. Take, for example, the run on Wachovia Bank. The run started the morning of September 26, 2008. The North Carolina bank had been struggling on the edge of failure for several months under a mountain of bad debt, much of it mortgage related. The day before, the Federal Deposit Insurance Corporation (FDIC) had just seized the assets of Washington Mutual (WaMu). At WaMu, the run lasted 10 days and depositors had withdrawn $17 million before regulators closed the bank. At Wachovia, once the run was under way, regulators moved quickly to close the bank. Citigroup ultimately acquired it.

As you would expect, the 2008 financial crisis precipitated a number of bank failures: 25 banks failed in 2008 and 140 failed in 2009. In contrast, only 11 banks had failed in the 5 years preceding 2008. To help stabilize the financial system and reduce the likelihood of bank runs, the Emergency Economic Stabilization Act of 2008 authorized the FDIC to raise the deposit insurance limit to $250,000, per insured bank, from $100,000.

ANALYSIS OF THE 2008 FINANCIAL CRISIS

No two economists will agree on the precise factors that caused the 2008 financial crisis and subsequent recession. Here is our take on the causal factors. First, we do not see the financial crisis as a tsunami event, where a single factor is causal. We see the financial crisis as the perfect storm, where three or four large storms join together to form a category 5 hurricane. If any one of the factors had not been present, there still may have been a recession but one lesser in scope.

The Housing Bubble.   The most important factor in the 2008 financial crisis and the subsequent recession was the housing bubble, which peaked mid-2006. The size of the housing bubble was huge, and it was driven by a number of key factors that came together to form the perfect storm. First, a large number of below-prime borrowers were eager to get a mortgage through one of the government-sponsored mortgage loan programs. Their numbers were large because of the deregulation that made it easier to qualify for a government mortgage program. They also flocked to variable rate mortgages because of lower monthly payments; however, these loans were much more risky than conventional fixed rate mortgages. Second, easy money helped finance the housing construction boom. The artificially low interest rates also encouraged consumers to purchase homes and other debt-financed consumption, such as automobiles; boats; and large-screen, high-definition televisions. Finally, the securitized mortgage debt, with its AAA credit rating and secondary market, allowed it to be sold to financial institutions and investors in the United States and overseas.

Central Bank's Credit Policies.   As mentioned above, the low interest rate policy followed by Fed chairman Alan Greenspan contributed to the financial crisis. The Fed's easy money policy financed homeownership and the housing construction boom. It also encouraged consumers to run up record levels of consumer debt, which made them vulnerable to defaulting on their mortgage loans. Finally, the abundance of money in the market encouraged lax lending policy, such as no money down and sloppy due diligence work when validating loan applications.

Pricing Credit Risk Incorrectly.   MBSs were an ideal investment medium because they provided an active secondary market and carried a AAA credit rating, even though the underlying mortgages were subprime. Unfortunately, the credit rating model developed by the credit rating industry understated the actual credit risk for MBSs. This created an enormous problem because the MBSs were sold to investors as AAA rated debt, but their actual credit risk was something less than AAA. When the error was realized, the credit rating agencies were forced to downgrade nearly $2 trillion in mortgage-backed securities.

Lehman Brothers Bankruptcy.   The bankruptcy of Lehman Brothers on September 15, 2008, was a pivotal event that some economists believe increased uncertainty in the financial markets and changed the course of the recession. More specifically, it pushed the recession from a serious but manageable economic event to a major recession of a magnitude that had not been seen since the early 1930s. Once Lehman failed, the economy went into a frenzied free fall that brought the financial system to the brink of collapse.

The morning of the Lehman bankruptcy announcement, the fed funds rate jumped 6 percent, tripling the Fed's target rate of 2 percent. It was widely reported in the popular press that the market had frozen; that is, trading came to a near standstill. There were also unsubstantiated rumors that the crisis might precipitate runs on some large banks and/or additional failures were likely to occur. The fed funds market reaction was carefully watched because it's the market where large money center banks buy and sell reserves, the most liquid of all financial assets. Rumors about the banking system and the economy persisted even after the Federal Reserve Bank added $20 billion of temporary reserves to the banking system. What appeared to have actually occurred in the fed funds market was a significant decline in trading volume, and firms that did transact became very selective in choosing trading partners.

The Lehman failure was a public relations and operational disaster for the Bush administration. The signals from the market were very negative at best. It was no secret that Lehman had financial problems, but market participants were shocked that the government would allow it to fail, and no suitable buyer could be found. The signal was that losses in the subprime mortgage market were materially larger than people believed. Others believed that the serial failure of large banks and other financial institutions signaled that the government had lost control of the situation. An environment of uncertainty occurs when there is no objective information to resolve the adverse selection and moral hazard problems, rumors are rampant, and people assume the worst.

Preventing the Collapse.   President Bush's Treasury secretary was Henry Paulson, the former head of Goldman Sachs. He was one of Goldman's most accomplished global deal makers and negotiators. He was asked by the president to lead the administration's struggle to contain the credit crisis caused by the collapse of the housing market. Paulson was teamed with Fed chairman Ben Bernanke and New York Federal Reserve Bank president Timothy Geithner. Three days after the Lehman failure, in a dramatic meeting with key legislators, Paulson unveiled a proposal for a $700 billion program to purchase MBSs whose value had declined sharply or had become impossible to sell, the so-called toxic assets. The emergency legislation, called the Troubled Asset Relief Program (TARP), was viewed as a bank bailout program, and its reception was less than enthusiastic. After much venting and hostile questioning, Bernanke turned to stunned legislators and reportedly told them, "If we don't do this, we may not have an economy on Monday."

As expected, the proposed legislation attracted a political firestorm. There were concerns over the vast discretion the bill gave Treasury Secretary Paulson and the lack of controls over politically sensitive issues, such as executive compensation. After much public wrangling, name calling, and several failed votes, the legislation seemed doomed. Then, the jittery stock market took a deep plunge and key legislators realized the enormity of the risk. Both the Senate and the House quickly passed the legislation. The bill was signed by President Bush on October 3, 2008.

After leaving office on January 20, 2009, Paulson was criticized by Republicans and Democrats alike for moving too slowly in responding to the crisis. He worked closely with Bernanke and Geithner; the three of them as a team did more than a credible job of managing a complex problem in a highly charged political environment with huge financial risk for the country. The paradox of TARP was that rarely has a government program been so unpopular with the general public and reviled by so many lawmakers, even those who voted for it. Yet economists generally agree that the massive government bailout that began in 2008 averted a collapse of the financial system and saved the economy from coming to a grinding halt.

Postscript.   One always has to ask, What if the Lehman Brothers bankruptcy could have been avoided? Could the country have escaped some of the dire economic consequences it faced? Lehman's collapse came about because its customers and lenders feared they would not get paid the money owed to them. The only way to stave off the run on Lehman was for someone with deep pockets—the federal government—to stand behind Lehman's obligations. This guarantee would allow time for management to restructure the firm and to inject additional capital into the firm. Something like this was done for AIG or General Motors. Paulson, Bernanke, and Geithner (PBG) focused their efforts on a private solution in search of a buyer for Lehman. They nearly succeeded with the English bank Barclays, but at the last minute the deal was nixed by British bank regulators. The down side to the public solution is that financial markets and firms collapse quickly, so preexisting authority would have been required. Given the political environment, a bailout for Lehman would have been difficult.

THE 2007–2009 RECESSION

The 2007–2009 recession was global, sparked by the financial crisis of 2008. The recession was marked by a sharp drop in international trade, rising unemployment, and slumping commodity prices. The National Bureau of Economic Research (NBER)—the official arbiter of economic turning points—declared that the country entered into a recession during December 2007, and the recession was officially over in June 2009. The 19-month recession confirms what a number of economists have speculated; that the recession was the longest and also the deepest since the post–World War II period.

The declaration of recovery was heralded as good news, but many economists questioned its veracity. The country was mired with an unemployment rate of 9.6 percent that was expected to get worse before it got better. Some experts are predicting that the 9+ percent unemployment rate could extend through the next presidential election and that much of the unemployment problem is structural, meaning that job applicants do not have the right skills for the jobs that are available. A second factor that suggests a slow recovery from the recession is the market overhang from the housing bubble. Some economists believe that it will take several years, if not longer, for the excess supply of housing to clear the market.

DO YOU UNDERSTAND?

1. Describe the likely consequences for GDP growth when the FOMC directs the trading desk at the New York Fed to sell Treasury securities.

2. What defensive actions do you suppose the Fed takes during periods when cash holdings by the public increase? In other words, how does the Fed offset these cash drains?

3. As a college student who will soon enter the workforce, if you have not already, which of the objectives of monetary policy would you like the Fed to focus on in the coming years?

4. What causes an asset bubble? When a bubble bursts, what impact can it have on the economy?

SUMMARY OF LEARNING OBJECTIVES

1 Explain how the Fed measures and manages the money supply. The Fed has different measures of the monetary base (M1, M2), which reflect the continuum between a transactional view of the money supply and the view that money is primarily a store of value. The Fed attempts to manage the monetary supply primarily through open-market operations. When the Fed wants to increase the money supply, it purchases Treasury securities on the open market through the trading desk at the New York Fed. When it desires a decrease in the money supply, the Fed sells Treasury securities on the open market.

2 Explain how the Fed influences the level of interest rates in the economy. To influence monetary policy, the Fed targets changes to the fed funds rate, which is the interest rate on overnight loans of reserves among banks. Through its open-market operations, the Fed influences the amount of reserves in the banking system. When the Fed purchases Treasury securities on the open market, reserves tend to increase. A greater supply of reserves puts downward pressure on the fed funds rate. When the Fed sells Treasury securities, the opposite occurs.

3 Describe the transmission process for monetary policy. When the Fed increases the money supply by purchasing Treasury securities on the open market, there is downward pressure on interest rates. Lower interest rates make it more attractive for businesses to spend money on long-term investments and for consumers to spend on durable goods and housing. Increases in business and consumer spending lead to increases in GDP. How close the economy is to full capacity utilization and full employment determines whether a portion of the increase in nominal GDP is due to increases in the average price level (or inflation).

4 Discuss the goals of the Fed in conducting monetary policy. The six objectives of the Fed in conducting monetary policy are full employment, economic growth, stable prices, interest rate stability, stability of the financial system, and stability of foreign exchange markets.

5 Explain what fiscal policy is and how it works when there is a recession. The main instruments of fiscal policy are government expenditures and the government's power to tax. Fiscal policy is the use of government expenditures and revenue collections to affect economic output over the business cycle. During a recession, the government uses expansionary fiscal policy, which includes increasing government expenditures and/or decreasing tax collections. This fiscal policy alternative is intended to stimulate the economy by increasing aggregate expenditure and aggregate demand.

KEY TERMS

M1	Liquidity trap	Inflation	Natural rate of
M2	Inflation targeting	Full employment	unemployment
Excess reserves	Humphrey-Hawkins	Frictional	Real GDP
Actual reserves	Act	unemployment	Technical factors
Required reserves	Market economy	Structural	Velocity of money
Fed funds rate	Price stability	unemployment	Toxic securities

QUESTIONS AND PROBLEMS

1. What are the differences between M1 and M2? Why are there different measures of money?

2. What would happen to the monetary base if the U.S. Treasury collected $4 billion in taxes, which it deposited in its account at the Fed, and the Fed bought $2.5 billion in government securities? Do you now know why the Fed and Treasury try to coordinate their operations in order to have minimal effects on the financial markets?

3. If the Fed bought $3.5 billion in government securities and the public withdrew $2 billion from their transaction deposits in the form of cash, by how much would the monetary base change? By how much would financial institutions' reserves change? By how much would financial institutions' required reserves change if all proceeds from bond sales and all withdrawals from transaction accounts were deposited in or taken from accounts subject to a 10 percent reserve requirement? By how much would depository institutions' net excess reserves change?

4. If a country named Lower Slobovia decided to use U.S. dollars as a medium of exchange and therefore withdrew $10 billion in cash from its transaction deposits in the United States, what would happen to the U.S. monetary base? What would happen to depository institutions' actual reserve holdings? What would happen to U.S. financial institutions' net excess reserves if the Lower Slobovians withdrew their money from bank deposits subject to a 10 percent reserve requirement? What would probably happen to the U.S. money supply?

5. Assume a depository institution holds vault cash of $3 million and reserve deposits at the Fed of $25 million, and has borrowed $2 million from the Fed's discount window. If that institution holds $300 million in transactions deposits and is subject to a 3 percent reserve requirement on the first $50 million of those deposits and to a reserve requirement of 10 percent on all transactions deposits over $50 million, what are its required reserves? What are its excess reserves?

6. What is the essential difference between the Keynesian and the monetarist view of how money affects the economy?

7. What effects are decreases in reserve requirements likely to have on (a) bank reserves, (b) federal funds rates, (c) bank lending, (d) Treasury bill rates, and (e) the bank prime rate? Explain your answers.

8. Given your answers to Question 7, what, if anything, would you expect to happen to (a) housing investment, (b) plant and equipment investment, (c) intended inventory investment, (d) government expenditures, (e) consumption, (f) exports, and (g) imports? Why?

9. Explain the concepts of frictional unemployment, structural unemployment, and the natural rate of unemployment. How do these affect what is considered full employment?

10. What are some of the potential conflicts between the goals of monetary policy? Explain.

11. What are technical factors? How do they affect the implementation of monetary policy?

12. Why do security traders pay so much attention to the fed funds rate? Why is the fed funds rate so important?

13. Why is the concept of a liquid trap important to the conduct of monetary policy?

14. What is fiscal policy? How does fiscal policy compare to monetary policy?

15. Explain the fiscal policy stance that you would deploy if the economy were in a recession. How would you implement the policy?

16. What is the government expenditure equation? Explain the three budget positions.

17. What are the six goals the Fed is required by government legislation to achieve? Which two goals are the most important? Why?

18. Explain why stable prices are so important to an economy.

19. Assume the Fed undertakes open-market operations and buys Treasury securities. Explain what should happen to interest rates. What is the expected change in nominal GNP? How is nominal GNP then partitioned off between inflation and real GNP?

20. In your opinion, what were the three most important causes of the 2008 financial crisis?

INTERNET EXERCISE

The Federal Reserve Board Web site contains valuable information and useful links to other Web sites. All of the following questions can be answered by going to the Federal Reserve Board's Web site (http://www.federalreserve.gov) or to one of the sites linked to it. This is a long but interesting exercise. Get to work and you will learn a lot about the Fed!

1. As you know from this chapter, the Fed controls bank reserves, which are part of the monetary base. At the Federal Reserve Board Web site, go to its *Statistical Releases* and find release H.3. From that release, obtain the data needed to calculate the ratio of bank reserves to the monetary base for the most recent reporting period. Compute the ratio as a percentage and subtract it from 100 percent to find the portion of the monetary base that is held outside financial institutions. That is the end of your assignment, but here are some additional thought questions:

   (a) Can you see now why it is hard for the Fed to control the money supply precisely?

   (b) Where do you think the rest of the monetary base is, and under what conditions might it return to the banking system?

2. Find the most recent press release of the Federal Open Market Committee (FOMC) from the Web site (see the Internet Exercise in Chapter 2). What action did the FOMC take with respect to the target fed funds rate? What is the FOMC's current thinking about the state of the economy? Find an article from the *Wall Street Journal*, the *New York Times*, or your local newspaper that discusses the outcome of the recent FOMC meeting. How does the discussion in the article compare to the FOMC press release? Did the reporters get it right? Did the articles mention any impact of the announcement on the stock market or bond market? If so, what was the impact and how did the article explain it? Again, did the reporter get it right?

3. Find the Fed's Monetary Policy Report to Congress. Read Section 1, "Monetary Policy and the Economic Outlook." What was the Fed trying to do with monetary policy from 2009 to 2010? What was the economic basis for the Fed policy actions? What impact did the policy actions have on the fed funds rate, the 2-year Treasury rate, and the 10-year Treasury rate? Did the Fed change the discount rate during this period? What was the justification?

PART II

HOW INTEREST RATES ARE DETERMINED

The Level of Interest Rates

IF YOU READ THE *Wall Street Journal* or watch CNN on a regular basis, you know that interest rates are constantly in the news. During the 2007–2010 recession, there were fears that interest rates would become so low that the Fed's ability to stimulate the economy might be jeopardized. Journalists sounded the alarm over the perils of low interest rates as rates hovered near zero and consumers complained that they were earning almost no interest on their savings accounts. However, with the economy stalled at 9½ percent unemployment, the Fed continued to pump more money into the financial system in an effort to reinvigorate the stalled economy.

Even though we understand the factors that cause interest rates to change, only people who have a crystal ball can predict interest movements well enough to make consistent profits. The gutters of Wall Street are littered with failed interest rate prediction models.

The fundamental question addressed by this chapter is, Why are Interest rates considered such an important economic variable? They're important because they directly affect consumer and business spending. Interest rates are the cost of borrowing someone else's money to purchase goods and services, which must be paid back at a later date. The total cost of any credit purchase is the price of the product plus the interest payments. Thus, when interest rates are high, purchases become more expensive, business and consumer spending slows down, inflation is typically curbed, and economic expansion and job creation are choked off. In contrast, lower interest rates tend to encourage spending by consumers and businesses and to stimulate business expansion and job creation; however, under certain conditions, lower interest can overstimulate demand, which in turn can lead to inflation.

This chapter explains the role of interest rates in the economy and provides a basic explanation of the fundamental determinants of interest rates. The chapter serves as a foundation for Chapters 5 and 6, which also deal with interest rates. ◼

We begin this chapter by explaining the role of interest rates in the economy. Our discussion of interest rates begins with an examination of the determinants of the real rate of interest. The factors that determine the real interest rate are the underlying determinants of all interest rates in the economy. Next we focus on the loanable funds framework of interest rates, which is widely used by Wall Street economists because of its intuitive appeal and its ease of use in developing interest rate forecasting models. We then highlight the effect of inflation on the level of interest rates and discuss negative interest rates. Finally, we describe how investors and financial institutions forecast interest rate movements. ■

LEARNING OBJECTIVES

1 Define the concept of an interest rate and explain the role of interest rates in the economy.

2 Define the concept of the real interest rate and explain what causes the real interest rate to rise and fall.

3 Explain how inflation affects interest rates.

4 Calculate the realized real rate of return on an investment.

5 Explain how economists and financial decision makers forecast interest rates.

4.1 WHAT ARE INTEREST RATES?

For thousands of years, people have been lending goods to other people, and on occasion they have asked for some compensation for this service. This compensation is called *rent*—the price of borrowing another person's property. Similarly, money is often loaned, or rented, for its purchasing power. The rental price of money is called the **interest rate** and is usually expressed as an annual percentage of the nominal amount of money borrowed. Thus, an *interest rate* is the price of borrowing money for the use of its purchasing power.

To a person borrowing money, interest is the penalty paid for consuming income before it is earned. To a lender, interest is the reward for postponing current consumption until the maturity of the loan. During the life of a loan contract, borrowers typically make periodic interest payments to the lender. On maturity of the loan, the borrower repays the same amount of money borrowed (the principal) to the lender.

Like other prices, interest rates serve an **allocative function** in our economy. They allocate funds between surplus spending units (SSUs) and deficit spending units (DSUs) and among financial markets. For SSUs, the higher the rate of interest, the greater the reward for postponing current consumption and the greater the amount of saving in the economy. For DSUs, the higher the yield paid on a particular security, the greater the demand for that security by SSUs but the less willing they are to supply the security. Therefore, SSUs want to buy financial claims with the highest yield, whereas DSUs want to sell financial claims at the lowest possible interest rate.

4.2 THE REAL RATE OF INTEREST

The **real rate of interest** is one of the most important economic variables in the economy. It is the rate of interest determined by the returns earned on investments in productive assets (capital investment) in the economy and by individuals' time preference for consumption. The factors that determine the real rate of interest are the underlying determinants of all interest rates observed in the economy. For this reason, an understanding of the real rate of interest is important.

The real interest rate is determined in the absence of inflation and, as a result, it more accurately reflects the true cost of borrowing. The real rate of interest is rarely observable because most industrial economies operate with some degree of inflation, and periods of zero inflation are rare. The interest rate that we observe in the marketplace at any given time is called the **nominal rate of interest**. Its value reflects the factors that determine the real rate of interest plus the market's estimate of the degree of inflation in the economy. *Inflation* is the amount that aggregate price levels rise over time.

Let's now examine how the forces—the productivity of capital investments and individuals' time preference for consumption—interact to determine the real rate of interest.

RETURN ON INVESTMENT

Recall from your introductory finance course that businesses invest in capital projects that are expected to generate positive cash flows by producing additional real output. By more *real output*, we mean more automobiles, houses, high-definition TVs, and so on. The output generated by a capital project constitutes its **return on investment**, which is usually measured as a percentage. For example, if a firm has a capital project that costs $1,000 and it produces $200 in cash flows each year, the project's return on investment is 20 percent ($200/$1,000).

For a capital project to be approved by management, its return on investment must exceed the firm's cost of funds (debt and equity)—often called the cost of capital. Intuitively, this makes sense because if an investment earns a return greater than the firm's cost of funding, it should be profitable and thus increase the value of the firm. Continuing the example above, if the firm's cost of capital is 15 percent, the $1,000 capital project would be accepted by management because the project's return on investment exceeds the firm's cost of capital (20 percent > 15 percent). If the capital project earned only 12 percent, the project would be rejected because its rate of return is less than the firm's cost of capital (12 percent < 15 percent). Thus, a firm's cost of capital is the minimum acceptable rate of return on capital projects. Also notice that the level of interest rates affects the number of projects that can be funded in the economy. As interest rates increase, fewer capital projects are funded because fewer projects can earn an expected return that exceeds the firm's cost of capital.

TIME PREFERENCE FOR CONSUMPTION

People have different preferences for consumption over time. All things being equal, however, people prefer to consume goods today rather than tomorrow. This is called a **positive time preference** for consumption. For example, most people who want to buy a new car prefer to have it now rather than wait until they have earned enough cash to make the purchase. When people consume today, however, they realize that their future consumption may be less because they have forgone the opportunity to save and earn interest on their savings.

Given people's positive time preference for consumption the interest rate offered on financial instruments determines whether they will save or spend. At low interest rates, most people postpone very little consumption for the sake of saving—the reward for saving is low so they continue to buy TVs and video games. To coax people to postpone current spending, interest rates must be raised. At higher interest rates, people save more and spend less.

EQUILIBRIUM CONDITION

Exhibit 4.1 shows how the real rate of interest is determined in a supply and demand framework. Surplus spending units (SSUs) are willing to supply more funds to borrowers as interest rates go up because lending is more profitable. As interest rates go up, however, deficit spending units (DSUs) pull back on spending because it becomes too expensive to borrow.[1] Thus, when interest rates are higher, people spend less and save more, and business investment is choked off by the higher cost of funds.

The equilibrium rate of interest (r^*) is the point where the desired level of borrowing (B) by deficit spending units (DSUs) equals the desired level of lending (L) by surplus spending units (SSUs). At this point, funds are allocated in the economy in a manner that fits people's preference between current and future consumption, and all capital projects whose return on investment exceed the firm's cost of capital are funded.

The equilibrium rate of interest is called the real rate of interest. The real rate of interest is the fundamental long-run interest rate in the economy. The real rate is closely tied to the rate of return on capital investments and people's time preference for consumption. It is called the *real* rate of interest because it is determined by real output factors in the economy.

FLUCTUATION IN THE REAL RATE

Using the supply and demand framework in Exhibit 4.1, you can see how economic factors that cause a shift in the desired lending or desired borrowing curves will change the equilibrium rate of interest.

Demand Factors.   A major breakthrough in technology will shift the desired borrowing schedule to the right, thus increasing the real rate of interest. This makes

---

[1]The terms *surplus spending units (SSUs)* and *deficit spending units (DSUs)* are defined in Chapter 1.

EXHIBIT 4.1
Determinants of the Real Interest Rate

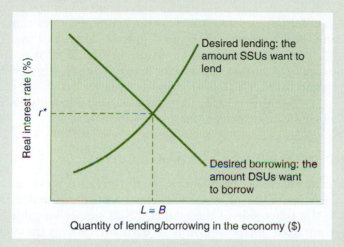

The real rate of interest is the base interest rate for the economy. It is closely tied to the productivity of capital investments in the economy and people's time preference for consumption. The equilibrium rate of interest is the point where the desired level of borrowing (*B*) equals the desired level of lending (*L*). The real rate of interest historically has been around 3 percent for the U.S. economy and has varied between 2 and 4 percent.

intuitive sense because the new technology spawns an increase in investment opportunities, increasing the desired level of borrowing. Similarly, a reduction in the corporate tax rate provides business firms with more money to spend on investments, which increases the desired borrowing schedule and causes the real rate of interest to increase. Other demand factors that could shift the desired borrowing schedule to the right and increase the real interest rates are an increase in the productivity of existing capital; an increase in expected business product demand, such as a big jump in the demand for efficient electric cars; or a demographic change such as a younger population, who tend to be heavy borrower-spenders (DSUs).

Supply Factors.   A supply factor that would shift the desired level of lending to the right, and hence lead to a decrease in the real rate of interest, would be a decrease in the tax rate for individuals. Lower individual tax rates would leave lender-savers with more money to lend and hence a lower real rate of interest. Another factor affecting the real rate of interest would be monetary policy actions by the Federal Reserve Bank. An increase in the money supply increases the funds available for lending, which should decrease the real interest rate. Another supply-side factor that could decrease the real rate of interest is a shift in consumer attitudes about saving, such as may have occurred following the 2007–2010 recession. The real rate of interest has historically been around 3 percent for the U.S. economy and has varied between 2 and 4 percent because of changes in economic conditions.

4.3 LOANABLE FUNDS THEORY OF INTEREST

Although the trade-off between productivity and thrift is the underlying force that determines interest rates, it is difficult to use this framework to explain short-run changes in the level of interest rates observed in a monetary economy (where money is the medium of exchange) such as ours. Interest rates can be viewed as being determined by the demand for and supply of direct and indirect financial claims during a particular time period. Thus, in the short run, interest rates depend on the supply of and the demand for loanable funds, which in turn depend on productivity and thrift. The loanable funds framework is widely used by financial analysts and economists because of its intuitive appeal and because it is easily employed as a basis for interest rate forecasting models.

SUPPLY AND DEMAND FOR LOANABLE FUNDS

DSUs issue financial claims to finance expenditures in excess of their current income. The need to sell these financial claims constitutes the demand for loanable funds. On the other side of the market, SSUs supply loanable funds to the market. SSUs purchase financial claims to earn interest on their excess funds. Exhibit 4.2 shows the major sources of the demand for and supply of loanable funds in the economy.

The scheme outlined in Exhibit 4.2 is, for the most part, disaggregated—it shows the sources of the gross supplies of and demands for loanable funds in the economy. Households, businesses, and governmental units operate on both sides of the market. For example, consumer personal savings are a major source of funds and, simultaneously, most households are demanders of funds as they engage in a wide variety of consumer credit purchases. Similarly, business firms supply loanable funds through depreciation and retained earnings, and they demand loanable funds to invest in plant, equipment, and inventories. State and local governments can run surplus budgets (tax revenues exceed expenditures)

EXHIBIT 4.2
Sources of Supply of and Demand for Loanable Funds

Supply of Loanable Funds (SSU)
Consumer savings
Business savings (depreciation and retained earnings)
State and local government budget surpluses
Federal government budget surplus (if any)
Federal Reserve increases in the money supply (ΔM)

Demand for Loanable Funds (DSU)
Consumer credit purchases
Business investment
Federal government budget deficits
State and local government budget deficits

Notice that households, businesses, and governmental units are both suppliers and demanders of loanable funds. During most periods, households are net suppliers of funds, whereas the business sector is almost always a net demander of funds.

that act as a supply of funds, whereas budget deficits (expenditures exceed tax revenues) create a demand for loanable funds as governmental units issue debt to cover the shortfall in revenues. The federal government historically has been a demander of loanable funds because it typically runs a deficit budget. The Federal Reserve is shown as a source of loanable funds. The supply of loanable funds is increased whenever the Federal Reserve increases the money supply (ΔM is positive) through an open-market purchase of Treasury securities. Likewise, an open-market sale of Treasury securities decreases the money supply (ΔM is negative).

The supply of loanable funds schedule is shown in Exhibit 4.3, Frame A. The aggregate schedule shown is a composite of all suppliers of loanable funds in the economy, and it is drawn sloping upward to the right. Hence, at higher interest

EXHIBIT 4.3
Interest Rate Determination in a Loanable Funds Framework

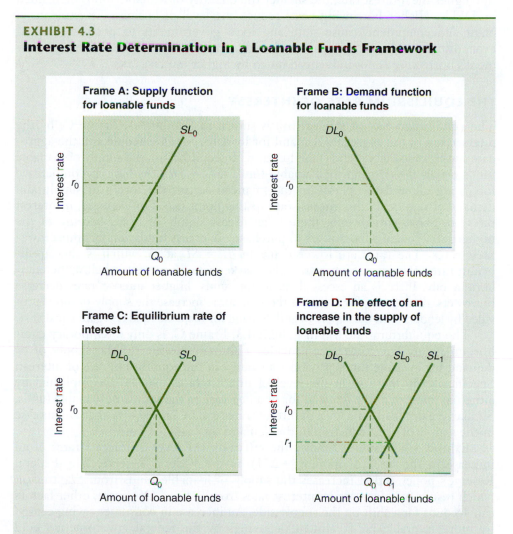

In the loanable funds framework, the equilibrium interest rate occurs at the intersection of the supply of loanable funds function and the demand for loanable funds function. At the intersection point, the supply equals the demand for loanable funds. All else equal, an increase in demand results in a higher interest rate. An increase in supply reduces the interest rate, as can be seen in Frame D.

rates, SSUs are willing to provide greater amounts of loanable funds. However, not all suppliers of loanable funds are equally sensitive to changes in interest rates.

In general, consumers save more as interest rates rise. Higher interest rates also stimulate business to finance investments out of internal sources (retained earnings and depreciation) rather than by issuing new debt or equity. This can be accomplished by reducing dividend payments to increase retained earnings or by switching to an accelerated depreciation method. Furthermore, at higher interest rates there is a decrease in the demand to hold money balances because of the greater opportunity cost of holding non-interest-bearing money. Thus, as interest rates rise, the quantity of loanable funds supplied to the market increases.

The aggregate demand schedule for loanable funds is shown in Exhibit 4.3, Frame B. It is drawn as a downward-sloping function of interest rates. In general, the higher the interest rate, the smaller the quantity of loanable funds demanded by DSUs. Higher borrowing costs reduce the level of business investments in plant and equipment, cause state and local governments to postpone capital expenditures, and reduce consumer installment purchases. The federal government's borrowing is not influenced much by higher interest rates.

THE EQUILIBRIUM RATE OF INTEREST

The equilibrium rate of interest (r_0) is shown in Exhibit 4.3, Frame C, by the intersection of the aggregate demand for loanable funds schedule and the aggregate supply of loanable funds schedule at r_0. In equilibrium, the supply of loanable funds equals the demand for loanable funds ($SL = DL$). As long as competitive forces are allowed to operate in the financial sector, the forces of supply and demand always bring the interest rate to this point (r_0). For example, if interest rates are above equilibrium, there is an excess supply of funds because of the higher rate. To entice borrowers to purchase the excess funds, lenders must lower their rates. The rates are lowered until $DL = SL$ at r_0, which is the equilibrium rate of interest. However, if the market rate of interest is below the equilibrium rate, there is an excess demand for funds. Higher interest rates decrease borrowers' demand for funds and at the same time increase the supply of funds provided by lenders until the supply of and demand for loanable funds is again equal at r_0.

The equilibrium rate (r_0) in Exhibit 4.3, Frame C, is only a temporary equilibrium point. Any force that provides a shift in position of the supply of or demand for loanable funds produces a change in the equilibrium rate of interest. Specifically, an increase in the level of interest rates may be accomplished by either an increase in the demand for or a decrease in the supply of loanable funds. Similarly, a decline in the level of interest rates can be caused by either an increase in the supply of or a reduction in the demand for loanable funds.

Exhibit 4.3, Frame D, shows the effect on the level of interest rates of an increase in the stock of money ($+\Delta M$) by the Federal Reserve. The Federal Reserve's policy action increases the supply of loanable funds from SL_0 to SL_1, which results in a decrease in interest rates from r_0 to r_1. Of course, other factors can account for a shift on the supply side. An increase in consumer saving caused by more favorable tax treatment of savings by the federal government would increase the supply of loanable funds and bring down interest rates. So would an increase in business saving as a result of high business profits. A change in state or federal government policy from a deficit budget to a surplus budget position because of reduced government expenditures also shifts the supply of loanable funds schedule to the right. On the demand side, downward pressure on interest rates results from a decline in expectations about future business activities. This results in a shift to the left in the demand schedule because of both reduced business investments and consumer credit purchases. Likewise, an increase in taxes reduces government deficits and the government's demand for loanable funds.

DO YOU UNDERSTAND?

1. Explain why the interest rate depends on the rate of return business firms expect to earn on real investment projects.

2. How does a consumer's time preference for consumption affect the level of savings and consumption? How does the interest rate affect the consumer's decision to spend or save?

3. How do you think an increase in personal tax rates would affect the supply of loanable funds, other things being equal? Why? How would the equilibrium interest rate be affected?

In our discussion so far, we have not mentioned the influence of price-level changes—inflation or deflation—on the level of interest rates. The real rate of interest is determined by real factors; thus, changes in price levels are not an issue. For other interest rates discussed, we assumed that price levels remained constant over the life of the loan contract. In the real world, however, price-level changes are common and they affect the value of loan contracts, for that matter, the value of any financial contract.

To account properly for price-level changes in a loan contract, there are two important relationships that we need to draw on from basic economics: (1) the *value of money*, which is its purchasing power—that is, what you can buy with it, and (2) the inverse relationship between changes in the price level and the value of money. We conclude that, as the price level increases (inflation), the value of money decreases. This makes sense because when we have rising prices (inflation), a dollar buys less. Likewise, if prices decrease (deflation), the value of money increases because a dollar buys more. Note that *deflation* is just the reverse of inflation; it should not be confused with *disinflation*, which is the slowing down in the rate of price increases (inflation).

4.4 PRICE EXPECTATIONS AND INTEREST RATES

LOAN CONTRACTS AND INFLATION

If borrowers and lenders do not adjust the loan contract to address the impact of expected price-level changes, there can be unexpected transfers of purchasing power between borrowers and lenders. For example, if prices rise during the life of a loan contract, the purchasing power of money decreases and the borrower repays the lender in inflated dollars—dollars with less purchasing power. Thus, borrowers receive a windfall gain at the expense of lenders. If prices decrease, the purchasing power of the money increases and lenders receive a windfall of more purchasing at the expense of borrowers.

CHAPTER 4 The Level of Interest Rates

124

Protection against changes in purchasing power can be incorporated into the interest rate on a loan contract. Suppose that you decided to loan a friend $1,000 for 1 year. After some discussion, you both agree that the fair rental price for loaning money is 5 percent and you both anticipate 7 percent inflation for the year. In the spirit of fair play, a contract fair to both you and the borrower would be as follows:

Items to Be Paid	Calculation	Amount
1. Principal		$1,000.00
2. Rent for 1 year on money loaned	$1,000 × 5%	50.00
3. Compensation for expected loss of purchasing power on the loan amount	$1,000 × 7%	70.00
Total Compensation to Lender		$1,120.00

For the use of $1,000 for 1 year, the loan contract calls for the payment of three items at maturity: (1) $1,000, which is the repayment of the amount borrowed; (2) $50, which is the interest, or rent, for the use of the money's purchasing power for 1 year; and (3) $70, which is the compensation to the lender for the loss of purchasing because of the 7 percent inflation expected during the 1-year period. It is clear from the example that the actual "interest" charged is *not* 7 percent, but 12 percent ($120): 5 percent ($50) compensation for forgoing current consumption and 7 percent ($70) for the anticipated loss of purchasing power due to inflation.

THE FISHER EQUATION

The preceding example suggests that protection against price-level changes is achieved when the nominal rate of interest is divided into two parts: (1) the real rate of interest, which is the rate of interest that exists in the absence of price-level changes; and (2) the anticipated percentage change in price levels over the life of the loan contract. This can be written as follows:

$$i = r + \Delta P_r \qquad (4.1)$$

where

i = the nominal rate of interest (the contract rate)
r = the real rate of interest
ΔP_e = expected annualized price level change
$= (P_{t+1} - P_t)/P_e$

For our fair contract example:

$i = 0.05 + 0.07 = 0.12 = 12.00\%$

Equation 4.1 is commonly referred to as the **Fisher equation**. It is named after economist Irving Fisher, who is credited with first developing the concept.

We should note a couple of important points about the Fisher equation. First, notice that the equation uses the *anticipated* (or *expected*) percentage price-level changes, not the observed or reported rate of inflation (or deflation). This way the lender is compensated for expected inflation (deflation) during the loan contract. Thus, to properly determine nominal interest rates, it is necessary to predict price-level changes over the life of the contract. Second, notice that ΔP_e is the *expected change* in *price levels*: price-level changes may be inflationary (rising prices) or they may be deflationary (declining prices). Most economies generally experience some rate of inflation most of the time. Deflation is not common; and when it does occur, it is usually during a deep or prolonged recession.

Third, notice that the nominal interest rate is defined as the rate of interest actually observed in financial markets—the market rate of interest. For real and nominal rates to be equal, the expected rate of price-level changes (inflation or deflation) must be zero ($\Delta P_e = 0$). Finally, as with all expectations or predictions, the actual rate of inflation, which can be determined only at the end of the loan contract, may be different from the expected rate of inflation, which is estimated by the market at the beginning of the loan contract.

A RESTATEMENT OF THE FISHER EQUATION

Our "derivation" of the Fisher equation above was an intuitive approach. Technically, if we want to adjust the real rate of interest (r) for changes in anticipated price levels (ΔP_e), we must multiply the real rate by ΔP_e. Thus, the proper mathematical expression for the Fisher equation is:

$$(1 + i) = (1 + r)(1 + \Delta P_e). \tag{4.2}$$

Solving the Fisher equation for i, we obtain the following equation:

$$i = r + \Delta P_e + (r \, \Delta P_e). \tag{4.3}$$

where $r \, \Delta P_e$ is the adjustment to the interest rate payment for loss of purchasing power due to inflation. If either r or ΔP_e is small, $r \, \Delta P_e$ is very small and is approximately equal to zero. Returning to the loan example, Equation 4.3 shows that the two parties should agree to the following contract rate:

$$i = 0.05 + 0.07 + (0.05 + 0.07) = 0.1235, \text{ or } 12.35\%.$$

Thus, for the 1-year loan for $1,000, the contract interest rate is 12.35 percent. The difference in the contract loan rate between the two variations of the Fisher equation (Equations 4.1 and 4.3) is 0.35 percent (12.35 − 12.00), less than a 3 percent error (0.35/12.35 = 2.83%). Thus, dropping $r \, \Delta P_e$ makes the insights from the Fisher equation easier to understand without creating a significant computational error.

PRICE-LEVEL CHANGES

Notice that ΔP_e is the percentage change in the price level and not the level of prices. Exhibit 4.4 illustrates this important statement. In our previous example, the real rate of interest was 5 percent and the rate of inflation increased from 0 to 7 percent. The nominal rate of interest thus went from 5 to 12 percent (see period 1 and 2). For the next time period, what happens to the nominal rate of interest if prices are expected to continue to rise at 7 percent annually? As Exhibit 4.4 shows, the nominal rate of interest stays at 12 percent (see period 3). This is

Irving Fisher (1867–1947): Economist

Irving Fisher was one of America's best-known economists. A man of exceptional talents and diverse interests, he was an economist, a statistician, a businessman, and a social reformer. The son of a Congregational minister, Fisher entered Yale University in 1884 and studied widely in the physical and social sciences throughout his academic career. His doctoral dissertation combined his love of mathematics and economics and is considered a classic today. On receiving his Ph.D., Fisher taught mathematics at Yale for 4 years and then switched to economics, the field in which he spent the rest of his academic career.

As an economist, Fisher is most acclaimed for his theory of the real rate of interest (presented in this chapter) and his analysis of the quantity theory of money. Regarding interest rates, Fisher articulated that two basic forces determine the real rate of interest in a market economy: (1) subjective forces reflecting the preference of individuals for present consumption over future consumption, and (2) objective forces depending on available investment opportunities and productivity of capital. Fisher also recognized the distinction between the nominal and the real rate of interest—the nominal rate of interest being composed of a real component and an inflation premium that compensates lenders for losses in purchasing power caused by inflation. Fisher's classic treatise on interest, *The Theory of Interest Rates*, was first published in the 1930s and is still reprinted today. Fisher's views on interest are the foundation for contemporary interest rate theory.

Outside the academic realm, Fisher had his share of wacky ideas, but he also met with some successes. One of his major achievements was a card index system he invented and sold; the company he formed merged in 1926 with other companies to form Remington Rand Corporation.

because, in each period, new loans are made with money already protected against past changes in purchasing power. However, if the expected annual inflation rate accelerates from 7 to 9 percent, the nominal interest rate will jump to 14 percent for all new loans (see period 4). Thus, the nominal interest rate will become larger only if the annual rate of inflation becomes larger.

EXHIBIT 4.4
Price Changes and Nominal Rates of Interest

Time Period	Real Rate	+	ΔP_e	=	Nominal Rate
1	5		0		5
2	5		7		12
3	5		7		12
4	5		9		14
5	5		−2		3
6	5		−5		0
7	5		−10		0

The nominal interest rate is affected by changes to the expected rate of inflation or rate of deflation. The higher the expected rate of inflation, the higher the nominal rate of interest. In the case of the expected rate of deflation, the higher the deflation rate, the lower the nominal rate of interest, but the nominal rate cannot decline below 0.

Finally, if prices begin to fall (deflation), the nominal rate will be below the real rate by the amount of the expected price rate decline. Thus, if prices are expected to decline 2 percent annually, the nominal rate in our example will be 3 percent (see period 5). Note if the annualized price decline equals the real rate of interest, the nominal interest rate will be zero (see period 6). If the expected rate of deflation is larger than the real rate, the nominal rate of interest will remain at zero (see period 7). The nominal rate of interest will never decline below zero—a negative interest rate—regardless of the rate at which the price declines. Negative interest rates say that the lenders pay the borrower to take their money and spend it however they wish and then return it free of charge. No economically rational person would enter into this type of agreement. Lenders would always prefer to retain their money and buy goods and service than pay someone else to do the same.

THE REALIZED REAL RATE OF RETURN

The Fisher equation (Equation 4.1) shows that the nominal interest rate is affected by inflationary expectations in the economy. As with all expectations, the actual rate of inflation over a loan contract will more than likely not equal the expected inflation rate that existed when the loan was originated. Hence, *the realized rate of return* on a loan may differ from the nominal rate that was agreed on at the time the loan was made. The **realized real rate of return** can be defined as the actual rate of return to the lender at the conclusion of the loan contract. Equation 4.1 can be modified so that the realized real rate of return can be formally expressed as follows:

$$r_r = i - \Delta P_a \qquad (4.4)$$

where

r_r = realized real rate of return on a loan contract
i = observed nominal rate of interest
ΔP_a = *actual rate of inflation* during the loan contract, where P are commodity prices
     = $(P_{t+1} - P_t)/P_t$

There are three possible outcomes for loan contracts and inflation. If the actual inflation rate at the end of the loan contract turns out to be higher than the expected inflation rate ($P_a > P_e$), the lender will earn a lower real rate of return because of an unintended transfer of purchasing power to the borrower from the lender. Conversely, if the actual inflation rate turns out to be less than the expected inflation rate ($P_a < P_e$), the lenders will earn a higher rate of return because of unintended transfer of purchasing power from the borrower to the lender. Finally, if the actual rate of inflation is equal to the expected inflation rate ($P_a = P_e$), expectations are realized and there is no transfer of purchasing power between the lender and borrower.

For example, the real rate of interest is 4 percent for a 1 year loan and the expected annual rate of inflation is 3 percent. Applying Equation 4.1, the nominal rate of interest on the loan is 7 percent (4 + 3). On this loan, the lender is expecting to earn 4 percent (7 − 3), after adjusting for inflation. However, if the actual inflation rate during the year is 5 percent, the realized real rate of return on the loan would be 2 percent (7 − 5) and not the 4 percent the lender had been expecting.

On the other hand, if the actual rate of inflation was 10 percent, the realized rate of return would be −3 percent (7 − 10); hence, a negative realized real rate. As can be seen from Equation 4.4, if actual inflation exceeds the nominal interest rate, i, the realized real rate of return will be negative, and there is wealth transfer (purchasing power) from the lender to the borrower. If the actual rate of inflation is 4 percent, there is no wealth transfer between the lender and the borrower because the initial inflation expectations were realized; that is, P_a equals P_e.

Finally, if there is deflation over the life of the loan contract, the realized return (r_r) is always a positive number and greater than the nominal interest rate (i), which is the expected return at the time the loan was originated. The reason is that if there is deflation, the borrower will be paying the loan back in dollars that are worth more because of deflation. Continuing the loan example above, suppose that over the loan contract period there was 10 percent deflation. The realized return: $r_r = i − P_a = 7 − (−10) = 7 + 10 = 17$ percent.

Exhibit 4.5 shows the nominal interest rate for 3-month Treasury bills plotted since 1970; also shown is the realized real rate of return on the 3-month bills for the same time period. As can be seen, the realized real rate was negative during most of the 1970s. Lenders underpredicted the rise in price levels and, in retrospect, charged too low a nominal rate of interest. Thus, unanticipated inflation caused unintended wealth transfers from lenders to borrowers. In the 1980s and 1990s the opposite was true. The realized real rate was high because actual inflation was lower than was anticipated. During the 2007–2010 recession, the realized rate of return was negative, with lenders underpredicting the rise in price levels. However, there is no evidence that as a group, borrowers or lenders are able to outpredict each other consistently.

EXHIBIT 4.5
Realized Rate of Return (1970–2010)

The realized rate of return can be positive or negative, depending on the extent to which the actual inflation rate exceeds the expected inflation rate. There is no evidence that lenders or borrowers are able to outpredict each other.

*The realized rate of return is the 3-month Treasury bill rate minus the actual percentage change in the Consumer Price Index (CPI) over the same year.

NEGATIVE INTEREST RATES

Can interest rates be negative? This is a difficult question to answer, especially with a simple yes or no. We observe negative interest rates from time to time, but as a practical matter, they are not common, usually occurring during times of severe economic stress. Until October 2010, the last time negative interest rates appeared in the United States was during the Great Depression.

A negative interest rate means that you pay someone to take your money! For example, if the prevailing interest rate was -2 percent and you decided to purchase a 1 year, $1,000 certificate of deposit (CD) from a bank, you would pay the bank $1,020 today and at the end of the year, the bank would pay you $1,000. You would have effectively paid your local bank $20 to keep your money.

Under what circumstance would such tomfoolery occur? The Fisher equation suggests that a negative nominal interest rate occurs when the expected rate of deflation (a negative term) exceeds the real rate of interest. The real rate of interest is always positive because we observe that human nature is such that nearly all market participants have a positive time preference for consumption. Then what causes negative interest rates to occur? They are typically caused by temporary imperfections in the marketplace. The negative interest rate is payment for something other than interest that the investor finds of value. Investors would not invest in negative interest rate securities unless they receive something of value— either money or a service. Let's look at two prominent negative interest rate situations to see if this is true.

Negative Interest Rates in Japan. A well-documented case of negative interest rates occurred in November 1998 in the Japanese Treasury bills market. At that time, the Japanese economy was in the depths of a 10-year recession, which ended in 2004. The Japanese Treasury rate became negative because investors with large cash balances did not want to buy bank liabilities due to their concerns over the stability of Japan's fragile banking system; there were persistent rumors that some large Japanese banks were about to fail, even though the government and bank regulators denied this. Investors were skeptical about the government's current economic recovery plans because a number of previous economic stimulus plans had failed. These investors had two viable investment options: (1) invest their money in Japanese bank liabilities, earning a modest interest return but incurring significant risk of default, and (2) invest in Japanese government treasury bills, incurring very little default risk but paying a negative interest rate to the Treasury. The negative interest rate was payment for storing money safely. At the November auction, the 6-month Treasury bills were priced to yield -0.004 percent. For $1 million in cash, the safe harbor storage cost is $200 $[1,000,000 \times (0.004/2)]$ for 6 months, which is a reasonable price to pay.

Negative Interest Rates on U.S. Treasury Securities. The negative yield on U.S. Treasury securities occurred during the last week of October 2010, attracting widespread newspaper coverage and headlines that read: "In Bond Frenzy, Investors Bet on Inflation." Many of the articles referred to the behavior by investors as "bizarre." However, the decision to purchase these Treasury bonds was a rational investment decision by investors who expected to earn a positive return on their investment. Let's see how they plan to do this.

The bonds in question were a special type of Treasury Security called (TIPS) Treasury Inflation-Protected Securities that provides investors with inflation protection. TIPS are Treasury securities issued at a fixed rate of interest, but with a principal adjusted every 6 months based on changes in the Consumer Price Index. At maturity, the bonds are redeemable at either their inflation-adjusted principal or their face value, whichever is greater. TIPS have lower yields than comparable traditional Treasury securities because of the inflation protection they provide.

The $10 billion of 5-year TIPS sold at auction highlights the difficult choice facing investors during the last week of October. Even though interest rates were at historic low rates, the Federal Reserve announced that it planned to purchase $600 billion in long-term bonds with the aim of stimulating the economy by lowering long-term interest rates and staving off deflation. At the Open Market Committee meeting a few days later, Chairman Bernanke justified the Fed's decision to stimulate the economy by noting that unemployment was high (9.7 percent) and inflation was low (less than 1 percent) and judged that the recovery "has been disappointingly slow." Thus, the possibility of a significant jump in inflation caused by aggressive monetary policy was deemed unlikely by the Fed. However, a number of economists and Wall Street investors felt that the Fed's bromide for the economy—flooding the economy with money—would cause inflation to soar.

The investors who purchased TIPS at a negative yield (−0.55 percent) were betting that inflation, currently running at 1 percent annually, would rise to a level that would more than compensate them for the premium paid for the bonds. So if inflation soared, as they expected, they would make a bundle. TIPS were a perfect vehicle to bet against the Fed's "no inflation promise."[2]

Conclusions.   Can interest rates be negative? In a classical economic system, interest rates are determined by the *return on real assets* and by society's positive time preference. Because the economic system is in real terms, the real rate of interest is always positive. In a monetary system where inflation/deflation can occur, the nominal interest rate can mathematically be negative when the deflation rate is larger than the real interest rate (see Exhibit 4.5). However, most economists would argue that the nominal interest rate can never be negative because investors are economically rational and would never pay someone to take their money.

Of course, we know that negative interest rates occasionally occur in financial markets. The negative "interest rate" payments are not interest payments in the classical definition. In fact, they are not really interest payments at all. They are cash payments made by investors for something of value they received. In the case of the Japanese Treasury bills, the negative interest rate was a de facto payment for the cost of safe harbor storage for cash. In the U.S. case, TIPS provided a convenient investment vehicle to bet against the Fed's no inflation promise.

INTEREST RATE MOVEMENTS AND INFLATION

The movements in short-term and long-term interest rates since 1970 are plotted in Exhibit 4.6. Plotted along with the interest rates is the rate of inflation

[2]The negative interest rate for TIPS in the primary market sales was no surprise because TIPS sold recently were already selling at negative yields in the secondary market as investors began hedging their portfolios against the risk of inflation.

EXHIBIT 4.6
Movements of Interest Rates and Inflation (1970–2010)

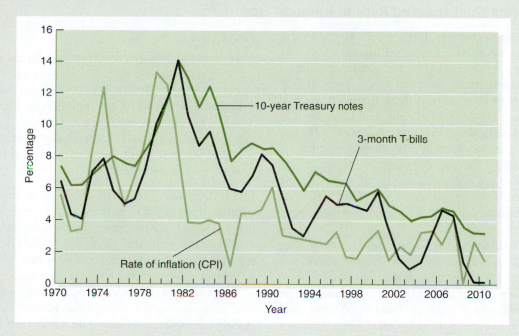

Interest rates change in response to inflation, as predicted by the Fisher equation. The rate of inflation is calculated based on the Consumer Price Index (CPI).

calculated from the Consumer Price Index (CPI). The exhibit shows that interest rates tend to change with changes in the rate of inflation, which is what we should expect, given the Fisher equation (Equation 4.1 or 4.3). Exhibit 4.6 also shows that short-term rates are more responsive to changes in inflation than long-term rates.

DO YOU UNDERSTAND?

1. If you believe that the real rate of interest is 4 percent and the expected inflation rate is 3 percent, what is the nominal interest rate?

2. If actual inflation turns out to be less than expected inflation, would you rather have been a borrower or a lender? Why?

3. During what period in the last 30 years were realized real rates of return negative? What causes negative realized real rates of return?

4. Explain why interest rates move with changes in inflation.

Estimating the Expected Rate of Inflation from TIPS

In 1977, the Treasury Department introduced a new security called, Treasury Inflation-Protected Securities (TIPS). TIPS are inflation-indexed bonds tied to the Consumer Price Index (CPI). Thus, investors who own these bonds earn a real return over the life of the bond. Unlike bonds that are fixed securities, the principal on a TIP can increase (or decrease) by the amount of inflation (or deflation) in the economy as measured by the CPI index every 6 months. At maturity, the bonds are redeemable at either their inflation-adjusted principal or their face value, whichever is greater.

The benefit of TIPS goes beyond protecting bondholders against inflation. It also provides a way to get market estimates of anticipated inflation and a measure of the real rate of interest. The model used by practitioners subtracts the real yield on TIPS from the nominal yield on a Treasury note of the same maturity, the yield difference provides a market-based measure of the expected inflation rate. In addition, several biases in the data require an adjustment, estimated to be about 50 basis points. Thus, the model is:

$$\Delta P_e = Y_{TB} - Y_{TIPS} + Adj$$

where

ΔP_e = annual expected percentage change in the price level
  = $(P_{t+1} - P_t)/P_t$
Y_{TB} = nominal yield on nonindexed Treasury bond, maturity n years
Y_{TIPS} = real yield on TIPS, maturity in years
Adj = 50-basis-point adjustment for inflation and liquidity risk

Using data from July 2010, the 10-year expected inflation rate is 1.935 percent (2.730 − 1.295 + 0.50), where 2.730 percent is the nominal yield and 1.295 percent is the real yield on a TIPS. The finding says that the public currently expects inflation to average 1.945 percent over the next decade.

Researchers at the Federal Reserve Bank of Cleveland have developed a more precise method for estimating the expected inflation rate. Of interest is that the findings from their model suggest that inflation will remain low, around 2 percent or less over the next decade, and is not expected to increase. If their model is correct, the Wall Street professionals who bet against Ben Bernanke's "no rise in inflation" promise are in trouble. You might want to follow up and see how investors in negative TIPS are doing.

4.5 FORECASTING INTEREST RATES

There has always been considerable interest in forecasting interest rate movements. The reason, of course, is that changes in the level of interest rates affect the present value of streams of future payments; that is, they affect the prices of financial assets—one's economic wealth! Beginning in the 1980s, interest rate movements became more volatile than in the past, and therefore firms and individual investors faced substantial exposure to interest rate risk. In general, economists use a variety of approaches to forecast interest rates. They range from naive forecasting models based on subjective adjustments to extremely complicated financial models of the economy. We will now examine two of the popular forecasting methods used by economists on Wall Street: statistical models of the economy and the flow-of-funds approach.

ECONOMIC MODELS

Economic models predict interest rates by estimating the statistical relationships between measures of the output of goods and services in the economy and the level of interest rates. The models range in complexity from single-equation models to those involving hundreds of simultaneous equations. The common element of all such models is that they produce interest rate forecasts assuming that the pattern of causality among economic variables is stable into the future.

Some of the larger economic models simultaneously forecast changes in spending on goods and services, wages and salaries, price levels, the balance of international trade, credit demand, supply of securities, capital goods, the money supply, the fiscal policy of the federal government, and interest rates. Once the relationships among these variables are modeled, expected *changes* in key economic variables are entered into the model; then changes in interest rates and output in various sectors of the economy are forecasted. For example, in the agricultural sector of the economy, changes in the prices of farm produce affect the balance of payments, farm machinery sales, the sales of capital goods used to produce farm machinery, personal income of farmers and other workers whose livelihood is tied to agriculture, and retail food prices. Increases in these factors ultimately lead to higher national income and rising price levels (inflation), which cause higher interest rates. Many of these models are difficult to use and employ hundreds of different financial and economic variables.

A more modest model is one developed by the Federal Reserve Bank of St. Louis. This model consists of only eight basic equations and generates quarterly forecasts for a number of key economic variables, such as the change in nominal and real GDP, the change in the price level (inflation), the unemployment rate, and the market rate of interest. The key input variables into the model are the change in the nation's money supply, the change in federal government expenditures, the potential full-employment output of goods and services in the economy, and past changes in price levels. At the very heart of the Federal Reserve Bank of St. Louis model is the effect of changes in the money supply on national income (or gross domestic product [GDP]), unemployment, and the rate of inflation. In case you have not guessed by now, the Fed of St. Louis model is a monetarist model of the economy. Exhibit 4.7 shows the linkage scheme for the model, with the key input variables shown on the left side of the exhibit.

FLOW-OF-FUNDS ACCOUNT FORECASTING

One of the most widely used interest rate forecasting techniques uses the flow-of-funds framework embedded within the loanable funds theory of interest rates. The flow-of-funds data show the movement of savings—the sources and uses of funds—through the economy in a structured and comprehensive manner. The flow-of-funds accounts are companion data to the national income accounts, which provide information about the flow of goods and services in the real economy. Since 1955 the Board of Governors of the Federal Reserve System has published quarterly and annual data on the flow-of-funds accounts.

In forecasting interest rates, analysts look for pressure points at which the demand for funds in a particular market exceeds the supply of funds, which should cause interest rates in that market to rise and ultimately spill over into other financial markets that are closely linked. Conversely, a low demand for funds relative to supply should drive interest rates down in a sector. The projections of changes in supply and demand factors are based in part on projections of changes in monetary policy, changes in fiscal policy, expected inflation, and other relevant economic variables. Clearly, a great deal of analysis, judgment, and luck are necessary for a good forecast. A number of studies over the years have assessed the accuracy of interest rate forecasts. Most of these studies conclude that interest rate forecasters perform poorly.

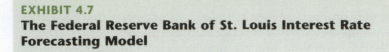

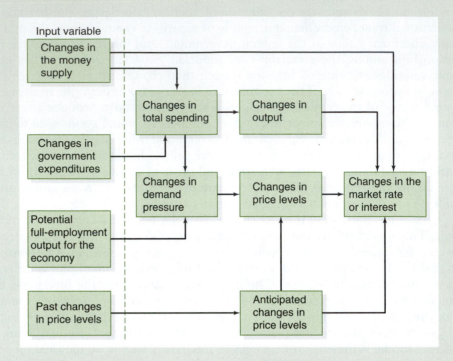

EXHIBIT 4.7

The Federal Reserve Bank of St. Louis Interest Rate Forecasting Model

In the St. Louis Fed model, as in most sophisticated interest rate forecasting models, changes in the money supply, government spending, economic activity, and inflation determine the interest rate.

SUMMARY OF LEARNING OBJECTIVES

1 **Define the concept of an interest rate and explain the role of Interest rates in the economy.** The interest rate is the price of "renting" an amount of money over a given period of time. Interest rates are similar to other prices in the economy in that they allocate funds between SSUs and DSUs.

2 **Define the concept of the real interest rate and explain what causes the real interest rate to rise and fall.** The real rate of interest is the fundamental long-run interest rate in the economy. It is the market equilibrium interest rate at which desired lending by savers equals desired borrowing by producers. It is the

rate of interest that prevails under the assumption that there is no inflation in the economy.

3 **Explain how inflation affects interest rates.** To protect borrowers and lenders from unwarranted transfers in purchasing power, the nominal (or stated) interest rate on a loan equals the real rate of interest plus compensation for changes in the purchasing power of money caused by price-level changes. This relationship is shown in the Fisher equation, which states that the nominal interest rate equals the real rate of interest plus the expected inflation rate.

4 Calculate the realized real rate of return on an investment. The return from a loan stated in terms of purchasing power of money is the realized real rate of return, which equals the nominal interest rate minus the actual rate of inflation. The realized real rate of return can be positive, zero, or negative, depending on how different actual inflation is from expected inflation.

5 Explain how economists and financial decision makers forecast interest rates. Investors and finan-cial institutions have a keen interest in forecasting the movements of interest rates because of the potential impact on their wealth. Interest rate forecasting models use expected economic activity and inflation expectations to predict interest rates. While models used to forecast interest rates are technically sophis-ticated and complex, the track record of forecasters in predicting the magnitude or direction of interest rate changes is weak.

KEY TERMS

Interest rate
Allocative function of
   interest rates

Real rate of interest
Nominal rate of interest
Return on investment

Positive time preference
Fisher equation

Realized real rate of
   return

QUESTIONS AND PROBLEMS

1. What factors determine the real rate of interest?

2. If the money supply is increased, what happens to the level of interest rates?

3. What is the Fisher effect? How does it affect the nominal rate of interest?

4. The 1-year real rate of interest is currently esti-mated to be 4 percent. The current annual rate of infla-tion is 6 percent, and market forecasts predict the annual rate of inflation to be 8 percent. What is the current 1-year nominal rate of interest?

5. The following annual inflation rates have been fore-cast for the next 5 years:

Year 1	3%
Year 2	4%
Year 3	5%
Year 4	5%
Year 5	4%

Use the average annual inflation rate and a 3 percent real rate to calculate the appropriate contract rate for a 1-year and a 5-year loan. How would your contract rates change if the year-1 inflation forecast increased to 5 percent? Discuss the difference in the impact on the contract rates from the change in inflation.

6. Under what conditions is the loss of purchasing power on interest in the Fisher effect an important consideration?

7. What is the track record of professional interest rate forecasters? What do you think explains their performance?

8. Explain how forecasters use the flow-of-funds approach to determine future interest rate movements.

9. An investor purchased a 1-year Treasury security with a promised yield of 10 percent. The investor expected the annual rate of inflation to be 6 percent; however, the actual rate turned out to be 10 percent. What were the expected and the realized real rates of return for the investor?

10. If the realized real rate of return turns out to be positive, would you rather have been a borrower or a lender? Explain in terms of the purchasing power of the money used to repay a loan.

11. Explain what the nominal rate of interest is and how it is related to the real rate of interest.

12. Explain what is meant by the term *positive time pref-erence for consumption*. How does it affect the rate of interest?

13. Explain how the equilibrium real rate of interest is determined.

14. Explain how the market rate of interest is deter-mined applying the loanable fund interest rate model.

15. What is the value of money? How does the value of money vary with aggregate price-level changes?

16. Explain why it's important to adjust financial contraction inflation. What is the relevant inflation factor?

17. Explain when the market rate of interest is equal to the real rate of interest.

18. Explain what is meant by the realized rate of return. How does it differ from the real rate of interest?

19. Explain what is meant by the term *negative interest rate*. Why can interest rate never be negative?

20. In financial markets, we occasionally observe negative interest rates. Reconcile the contradiction between the statement, "The nominal rate of interest will never decline below zero" and the negative interest that occurred in the Japanese Treasury bill market in November 1998.

INTERNET EXERCISE

The purpose of this exercise is to analyze the relationship between inflation and nominal interest rates. To complete this exercise, do the following steps:

1. Access the Web site of the Federal Reserve Bank of St. Louis at http://www.stls.frb.org/.

2. From the bottom of the home page, select FRED.

3. Then select Consumer Price Indexes.

4. Then select the nonseasonally adjusted Consumer Price Index (CPI) for All Urban Consumers and copy the most recent 3 years of data to a spreadsheet.

5. Calculate the monthly percentage change in the CPI.

6. Now, from FRED access Interest Rates.

7. Select 1-Year Treasury Constant Maturity Rate and copy the most recent 3 years of data to your spreadsheet.

8. Select 20-Year Treasury Constant Maturity Rate and copy the most recent 3 years of data to your spreadsheet.

9. Graph the Treasury rates and the monthly changes in CPI.

10. Use the graph to assess the impact of changes in inflation on short-term and long-term interest rates.

Bond Prices and Interest Rate Risk

BUSINESS EXECUTIVES ARE frequently asked to make decisions that require them to determine the value or price of cash flows over time. The value of the future cash flows depends not only on the size of the cash flow (the dollar amount), but also on when the dollars are received. It makes intuitive sense that a dollar received today is more valuable than a dollar received in the future. Dollars received today can be deposited in a bank and earn interest; future dollars cannot. Thus, the timing of when you receive money is important. Let's look at an example to illustrate the timing of money problem.

Suppose you won a $100 million jackpot. Does that mean your ticket is worth $100 million on the day you won the lottery? The answer is no! A Mega Millions jackpot winner is paid in one of two ways: (1) a series of 26 cash payments over 25 years, or (2) a lump sum cash payment. If you elect to take your winnings as annual cash payments over time, the

26 payments will total $100 million. On the other hand, if you elect the lump sum option, Mega Millions will pay you around $60 million (varies with market conditions), which is less than the stated value of $100 million.

Why is your ticket worth $60 million and not $100 million? The reason, of course, is the time value of money: a dollar in the future is worth less than a dollar today. To illustrate, if interest rates are at 5 percent, dollars paid to you that are 20 years into the future are worth only 37½ cents today and if they are 25 years into the future, they're worth only 29.5 cents today. Thus, because all of the

dollars, except the first payment, are dollars received in the future, the current value of the $100 million winning ticket is about $60 million.

This chapter and the next provide the knowledge and tools that you need to determine the value or price of financial assets and liabilities. We begin this chapter by explaining the concept of the time value of money, which is one of the most fundamental concepts in all of finance, and then we present a number of bond-pricing formulas that are mathematical applications of the time value of money. ■

The purpose of this chapter is to explain how interest rate movements affect the prices of assets and liabilities of investors and financial institutions. We focus on bonds because their behavior in the face of interest rate changes is similar to that of other financial instruments. Once you understand the mechanics of bond prices and how interest rates affect them, you can apply these concepts to understanding the critical management problems faced by individual investors and financial institutions.

We begin the chapter with a discussion of the time value of money, which provides the theoretical underpinning to the concepts of future value and present value. Next, we apply those concepts to develop a number formula for pricing bonds and explain how to calculate various bond yield measures. We then discuss the characteristics of a bond that influence its price volatility and develop the concept of interest rate risk. Finally, we discuss how financial institutions measure and manage interest rate risk and how the concept of duration is used to manage this risk. ■

LEARNING OBJECTIVES

1 Explain the time value of money and its application to the pricing of bonds.

2 Explain the different measures of yield that are important for analyzing a bond's performance:
   a. Yield-to-maturity
   b. Expected yield
   c. Realized yield
   d. Total return

3 Explain how changes in interest rates cause bond prices to change.

4 Describe interest rate risk and its two components: price risk and reinvestment risk.

5 Explain how interest rate risk can be measured.

6 Describe how investors and financial institutions manage interest rate risk.

5.1 THE TIME VALUE OF MONEY

Before we can understand how bonds are priced, we must review the concept of the time value of money. The **time value of money** is based on the belief that people have a positive time preference for consumption; that is, people prefer to consume goods today rather than consume similar goods in the future. Thus, the time value of money can be simply stated as *a dollar today is worth more than a dollar received at some future date*. This makes sense because if you had the dollar today, you could invest it and earn interest. In contrast, the further the dollar is in the future, the less it is worth because people prefer to consume today, all else being equal. Let's now examine how to place a value on both dollars today and dollars in the future.

FUTURE VALUE

Future value is the value of a given amount of money invested today (**present value**) at a given point in the future (**future value**) at a given rate of interest. The formula for calculating future value (**compounding**) is:

$$FV = PV(1 + i)^n \qquad (5.1)$$

where:

FV = future value of an investment n periods in the future
PV = present value of an amount of money (the value of money today)
i = interest rate
n = number of interest rate compounding periods

To illustrate, suppose you have $100 and put it in a savings account at a local bank, expecting to keep it there for 5 years. The bank pays 4 percent interest on savings accounts and compounds interest annually. Applying Equation 5.1, the future value is:

$$FV = \$100(1 + 0.04)^5$$
$$= \$100(1.2167)$$
$$= \$121.67$$

Thus, at the end of 5 years, the account has $121.67, which consists of the $100 original deposit plus $21.67 of interest.

If the bank decided to pay interest quarterly, the number of compounding periods increases to 20 periods (5 years × 4 quarters) and the annual interest rate converted to a quarterly interest rate is 1.00 percent (4 percent/4 quarters). Applying Equation 5.1 to the new situation, the future value is:

$$FV = \$100(1 + 0.01)^{20}$$
$$= \$100(1.2202)$$
$$= \$122.02$$

Notice that the dollar amount is slightly larger because we have increased the number of compounding periods and are now earning more interest on interest. For a given interest rate, the more frequent the compounding, the larger the future value. If you have a calculator available, it is easy to calculate the interest factor, $(1 + i)^n$, with just the touch of a few buttons and then multiplying the interest factor by the present value, PV, to determine the future value, FV. If you have a financial calculator, it is even easier.

PRESENT VALUE

Present value is the value today of a given sum of money to be received at a given point in the future. For example, suppose that you could buy a financial claim that would pay $121.67 in 5 years, and there is no doubt the amount will be paid (i.e., a risk-free cash flow). Furthermore, assume that your only other investment opportunity is to put your money in the bank at a risk-free interest rate of 4 percent. (Is this starting to sound familiar?) How much would you pay for this financial claim today? You know from the previous example that $100 deposited in the bank for 5 years at 4 percent will be worth $121.67—the same amount as the 5-year financial claim. Therefore, in a strictly financial sense, you would be indifferent to a choice between $100 today or $121.67 at the end of 5 years. In our example, the $100 amount is the *present value* (*PV*) of $121.67 to be received 5 years in the future.

Finding the present value of some future sum of money (called **discounting**) is simply the reverse of compounding. To illustrate this point, we use Equation 5.1:

$$FV = PV(1 + i)^n$$

The equation as it now stands allows us to solve for the future value (*FV*) of a given sum of money today (its present value). To solve for the present value (*PV*), we solve Equation 5.1 by dividing both sides of the equation by the interest factor, $(1 + i)^n$, which results in the following equation:

$$PV = FV\left[\frac{1}{(1 + i)^n}\right] \tag{5.2}$$

Going back to our original question, how much would we pay for $121.67 to be received 5 years in the future, if the interest rate on our next best alternative investment (i.e., your **opportunity cost**) were 4 percent? Using Equation 5.2, we compute the present value of $121.67 received in 5 years as:

$$PV = \$121.67\left[\frac{1}{(1 + 0.04)^5}\right]$$
$$= \$121.67(0.8219)$$
$$= \$100.00$$

The term in brackets in Equation 5.2 is called the *discount factor*, *DF*, and it is equal to the reciprocal of the interest factor (1/*IF*). Therefore, just as we were able to use a calculator to determine the future value if we were given the *PV*, *i*, and *n*, we can determine the present value if we are given the *FV*, *i*, and *n*.

DO YOU UNDERSTAND?

1. Why is a dollar today worth more to most people than a dollar received at a future date?
2. If you were to invest $100 in a savings account offering 6 percent interest compounded quarterly, how much money would be in the account after 3 years?
3. Your rich uncle promises to give you $10,000 when you graduate from college. What is the value of this gift if you plan to graduate in 5 years and interest rates are 10 percent?

This section focuses on how investors and financial institutions price bonds. The method employed involves the application of the present value formula. To find the present value, or *price*, of any financial instrument, we must first identify the timing and the magnitude of all cash flows we expect to receive from that instrument. These characteristics of the cash flows are determined by the terms of a bond contract, which we now define.

TERMS OF THE BOND CONTRACT

A **bond** is a contractual obligation of a borrower to make periodic cash payments to a lender over a given number of years. A bond constitutes debt, so there is a borrower and a lender. In the parlance of Wall Street, the borrower is referred to as the **bond issuer**. The lender is referred to as the investor, or the **bondholder**.

The bond consists of two types of contractual cash flows. First, on maturity, the lender is paid the original sum borrowed, which is called the **principal, face value**, or **par value**, of the bond. Note that these three terms are interchangeable. Second, the borrower or issuer must make periodic interest payments to the bondholders. These interest payments are called the **coupon payments** (C). The magnitude of the coupon payments is determined by the **coupon rate** (c), which is the amount of coupon payments received in a year stated as a percentage of the face value (F). For example, if a bond pays \$80 of coupon interest annually and the face value is \$1,000, the coupon rate is:

$$c = C/F$$
$$= \$80/\$1,000$$
$$= 8\%$$

To determine the timing of the cash flows we need to know the **term-to-maturity** (or maturity) of the bond, which is the number of years over which the bond contract extends. For example, a bond with 3 years to maturity and paying annual coupon payments has three coupon payments. The principal amount is repaid at maturity. Thus, a bond with a coupon rate of 8 percent and a face value of \$1,000 has \$80 coupon payments at the end of each of the 3 years and a principal payment of \$1,000 at maturity. Note that for most bonds it is assumed that the coupon and principal payments are received at the *end* of the year. In addition, many bonds pay coupon interest semiannually (or every 6 months) instead of once per year at the end of the year. We discuss how to deal with this type of bond a little later in the chapter.

It is important to keep in mind that for most bonds the coupon rate, the par value, and the term-to-maturity are fixed over the life of the bond contract. Most bonds are first issued in \$1,000 or \$5,000 denominations. Coupon rates are typically set at or near the market rate of interest or yield on similar bonds available in the market. A similar bond is one that is a close substitute, nearly identical in maturity and risk.

Also, note that the coupon rate and the market rate of interest may differ. The coupon rate is fixed throughout the life of a bond. The yield on a bond varies with changes in the supply and demand for credit or with changes in the issuer's risk. We discuss how to calculate a bond's yield later in this chapter. Because we now understand how the magnitude and timing of a bond's cash flows are determined, we can turn to a discussion of how to apply the present value formula to pricing bonds.

PEOPLE & EVENTS

Rogue Trader Incurs Huge Financial Losses for French Bank

In a country where market capitalism is often held in disdain, Société Générale was a Gallic success story—the Chateau Margaux of French banking. So it was a shock to their national pride when executives at Société Générale, one of Europe's largest banks, disclosed that Jerome Kerviel, a 31-year-old French trader at the bank, had incurred unauthorized trading losses valued at approximately $7.1 billion (€4.9 billion), the largest loss ever by a rogue trader.[1]

Like a number of other infamous rogue traders, Kerviel started with the bank in the back office of the trading division. There he learned how the bank's trading system and the complex internal control systems worked. After 5 years in the back office, in 2005, he was promoted to junior trader and, in late 2006, he began creating fictitious stock market trades. Citing Kerviel's extensive knowledge of the bank's operating and internal control systems, bank officials described how hundreds of thousands of trades were hidden behind offsetting, faked hedge trades. Kerviel knew that he had to close the trades in just 2 or 3 days so the bank's automated, timed controls would not trigger an "abnormality notice" from the internal control system. Kerviel would then shift those older trades to newly initiated trades.[2]

Unlike many rogue traders, Kerviel did not benefit personally from his illegal transactions and acted alone. He told officials his only motive was to be recognized as a star trader. But recent aca-demic research suggests the motivation may be more complex than that. Scientists are just starting to discover that some people's brains respond to high-risk situations, such as high-stakes trading, just as they do to the lure of sex. Brian Knutson, a professor of psychology and neuroscience at Stanford University, found when mapping the brain that some people get high on making lots of money. The larger the cash reward and the higher the risk, the more likely they were to take the risk.

Until recently, the propensity toward risky behavior was often unchecked by the possibilities of stiff penalties by the legal system. In the past, the business community and legal authorities would often dismiss corporate scandals as a few rotten apples in an otherwise sound barrel. Often there was no jail sentence for transgressions, just a monetary fine. This is no longer true today. Many believe the tipping point occurred in 2005, when Bernard Ebbers, the 63-year-old CEO of World Com, was sentenced to a harsh 25 years in prison; most courtroom observers had expected a light jail sentence, something less than 5 years. Students should be aware that penalties for fraud and unethical behavior are much harsher than they were in the past.

Jerome Kerviel, whose fraudulent trading nearly broke the bank, was sentenced on October 8, 2010, to 5 years in prison, with the sentence reduced to 3 years. He was also ordered to repay the bank for its losses, which, at his current salary, will take 16,000 years.

[1]A list of the five largest trading losses of all time: (1) Jerome Kerviel, loss $7.1 billion, Société Générale, 2008; (2) Brian Hunter, loss $6.5 billion, Amaranth Advisors, 2006; (3) John Meriwether, loss $4.6 billion, Long-Term Capital, 1998; (4) Yasuo Hamanaka, loss $2.6 billion, Sumitomo Corporation, 1996; and (5) Robert Citron, loss $1.7 billion, Orange County, 1994.

[2]In January 2008, when his fraud was revealed, bank officials divulged that at one point the dollar amount of unauthorized trades totaled as much as $70 billion—more than Société Générale's entire net worth.

THE BOND PRICE FORMULA

Because a bond is a borrower's contractual promise to make future cash payments, the pricing of a bond is an application of the present value formula. Thus, the price of a bond is the present value of the *future cash flows* (coupon payments and principal amount) discounted by the interest rate, which represents the time value of money. The formula for the present value, or *price*, of a fixed-coupon-rate bond with n periods to maturity is:

$$PB = \frac{C}{(1+i)^1} + \frac{C}{(1+i)^2} + \cdots + \frac{C+F}{(1+i)^n}, \tag{5.3}$$

where:

PB = the price of the bond or present value of the stream of cash payments
C = the periodic coupon payment
F = par value or face value (principal amount) to be paid at maturity
i = market interest rate (discount rate or market yield)
n = number of periods to maturity

In words, the formula says that the present value, or market price, of a bond is the sum of the discounted values of all future cash flows (coupon payments and principal). Don't be confused by the last term in the equation. Because the last coupon payment and the par or face value of the bond are both paid at maturity, the last term in Equation 5.3 includes both. Also, note that in applying the bond-pricing equation, there are five unknowns, and if we know any four of the variables, we can solve for the fifth. Fortunately, that task is made trivial if you have access to a financial calculator.

Consider a 3-year bond with a face value of $1,000 and a coupon rate of 8 percent. The coupon payments are $80 per year. If coupon payments are made annually and the current market rate of interest on similar bonds is 10 percent, the price of the bond, using Equation 5.3, is:

$$PB = \frac{\$80}{(1.10)^1} + \frac{\$80}{(1.10)^2} + \frac{\$1,080}{(1.10)^3}$$
$$= \$73.73 + \$66.12 + \$811.42$$
$$= \$950.27$$

Notice that to obtain the final cash payment, we have combined the final coupon payment ($80) and the face value of the bond ($1,000) to obtain $1,080. To determine the price of the bond, we can determine the present value of the individual cash flows and then sum them, or we can use a financial calculator.

Note that the price of this bond is *below* its face value. The bond is said to sell at a discount from face value and is known as a **discount bond**. In the next section, we discuss why bonds sell at prices other than their face values.

PAR, PREMIUM, AND DISCOUNT BONDS

One of the properties of the bond formula is that whenever a bond's coupon rate is equal to the market rate of interest on similar bonds (the bond's yield), the bond *always* sells at par. We call such bonds **par bonds** because they sell at par value. For example, consider a 3-year bond with a face value of $1,000 and an annual coupon rate of 5 percent when the yield or market rate of interest on similar bonds is 5 percent. The price of the bond, using Equation 5.3, is:

$$PB = \frac{\$50}{(1.05)^1} + \frac{\$50}{(1.05)^2} + \frac{\$1,050}{(1.05)^3}$$
$$= \$47.62 + \$45.35 + \$907.03$$
$$= \$1,000$$

As predicted, the bond's price equals its par value.

Now assume that the market rate of interest immediately rises to 8 percent. What is the price of the bond? Is it below, above, or at par? For i to equal 8 percent, the price of the bond declines to $922.69. The bond sells below par; such bonds are called *discount bonds*. Whenever the market rate of interest on similar bonds is above a bond's coupon rate, a bond sells at a discount. The reason is the fixed nature of a bond's coupon. If bonds with similar characteristics are yielding 8 percent and our bond is paying 5 percent (the coupon rate), no one will buy our bond at par because its yield is only 5 percent. To increase the bond's yield, the seller must reduce the price of the bond to $922.69. At this price, the bond's yield is precisely 8 percent, which is competitive with similar bonds. Through the price reduction of $77.31 ($1,000 − $922.69), the seller provides the new owner with additional return in the form of a capital gain.

If the interest rate on similar bonds were to fall to 2 percent, the price of our bond would rise to $1,086.52. The bond sells above par; such bonds are called **premium bonds**. Whenever the market rate of interest is below a bond's coupon rate, a bond sells at a premium. The premium price adjusts the bond's yield to 2 percent, which is the market yield that similar bonds are offering.

SEMIANNUAL COMPOUNDING

If coupon payments are made more than once a year, we modify Equation 5.3 as follows:

$$PB = \frac{C/m}{(1 + i/m)^1} + \frac{C/m}{(1 + i/m)^2} + \frac{C/m}{(1 + i/m)^3} + \cdots + \frac{(C/m) + F}{(1 + i/m)^{nm}}, \quad (5.4)$$

where m is the number of times coupon payments are made each year and the other terms are as previously defined. In the case of a bond with semiannual coupon payments (i.e., twice per year), $m = 2$. For example, if our 3-year, 5 percent coupon bond pays interest semiannually and the current market yield is 6 percent, the price of the bond would be:

$$PB = \frac{\$25}{(1.03)^1} + \frac{\$25}{(1.03)^2} + \cdots + \frac{\$1,025}{(1.03)^6}$$
$$= \$972.91$$

Note that the market yield is 3 percent semiannually (6 percent yearly), the coupon payment is $25 semiannually ($50 per year), and the total number of interest payments is 6 (two per year for 3 years). Quarterly and monthly compounding periods are computed in a similar manner.

ZERO COUPON BONDS

Zero coupon bonds have no coupon payment but promise a single payment at maturity. The interest paid to the holder is the difference between the price paid for the security and the amount received on maturity (or price received when sold). Common examples of zero coupon securities are U.S. Treasury bills and U.S. savings bonds. Generally, most money market instruments (securities with maturities of less than 1 year) are sold on a discount basis (issued at a price less than face value), meaning that the entire return on the security comes from the difference between the purchase price and the face value. In addition, some corporations have issued zero coupon bonds.

The price (or yield) of a zero coupon bond is simply a special case of Equation 5.4 in that all the coupon payments are set equal to zero. Hence the pricing equation is:

$$PB = \frac{F}{\left(1 + \dfrac{i}{m}\right)^{mn}} \tag{5.5}$$

where:

PB = the price of the bond
F = the amount of cash payments at maturity (face value)
i = the interest rate (yield) for n periods
n = number of years until the payment is due
m = number of times interest is compounded each year

For example, the price of a zero coupon bond with a $1,000 face value and 10-year maturity, and assuming semiannual compounding, when the market interest rate is 12 percent is calculated as follows:

$$PB = \frac{\$1,000}{(1.06)^{20}} = \$311.80$$

Notice that our calculation is based on semiannual compounding because most U.S. bonds pay coupon interest semiannually.

LEARNING BY DOING 5.1
Calculating the Price of a Bond Using a Financial Calculator

PROBLEM: Consider a 5-year bond with a face value of $1,000 and a coupon rate of 8 percent. If coupon payments are made semiannually, and the current market rate of interest on similar bonds is 10 percent, what is the price of the bond?

APPROACH: You can solve this problem using Equation 5.4, but that process can be tedious. Using a financial calculator simplifies the task. Prior to making the inputs into the financial calculator, recognize the following:

- While annual coupons will be $80, the semiannual coupons are worth $40.
- The number of periods is 10 (5 years × 2).
- The discount rate is half the current market rate on similar bonds, or 5 percent (10 percent × ½).

SOLUTION:

Semiannual coupon = C/2 = $40.00
Maturity of bond = n = 5 years = 10 semiannual periods
Number of compounding periods = m = 2
Number of coupon payments = $m \times n$ = 10
Current market rate = i = 10%

Enter	10	5%		$40	$1,000
	N	**i%**	**PV**	**PMT**	**FV**
Answer			**$922.78**		

The keys represent the following inputs:

N is the number of periods. The periods can be days, months, quarters, or years.
i is the interest rate per period, expressed as a percent.
PV is the present value, such as the price of a bond.
PMT is the amount of any recurring payment, such as a coupon payment.
FV is the future value, such as the par or face value of a bond received at maturity.

Given any four of these inputs, the financial calculator will solve for the fifth. Note that the interest rate key **i** differs with different calculator brands: Texas Instruments uses the **I/Y** key; Hewlett-Packard, an **i**, **%i**, or **I/Y**; and Sharp, **i**.

5.3 BOND YIELDS

The coupon rate on a bond reflects only the annual cash flow promised by the borrower to the lender. The actual rate of return the lender earns, however, depends on several key risks. First is the chance that the borrower fails to make coupon or principal payments in the amount or at the time promised. This is called **credit** or **default risk**. (We discuss the effect to default risk on bond returns thoroughly in Chapter 6. For the remainder of this chapter, we assume that borrowers make all cash flows as promised so that we can focus our attention on interest rate risk.) Second, market interest rates may change, causing the lender to have to reinvest coupon payments at interest rates different from the interest rate at the time the bond was purchased. This is called **reinvestment risk**. Finally, interest rate changes cause the market value of a bond to rise or fall, resulting in capital gains or losses to the investor.[1] This is called **price risk**.

   The purpose of this section is to explain various ways to measure bond returns or yields. In general, a yield on any investment, such as a bond, is the interest rate that equates the market price of an investment with the discounted sum of all cash flows from the investment. The ideal yield measure should capture all three potential sources of cash flow from a bond: (1) coupon payments, (2) interest income from reinvesting coupon payments, and (3) any capital gain or loss. We now discuss four yield measures: yield-to-maturity, expected yield, realized yield, and total return.

YIELD-TO-MATURITY

If a bond's purchase price is known, the bond-pricing formulas (Equations 5.3 and 5.4) can be used to find the yield of a bond. A yield calculated in this manner is called the **yield-to-maturity** or **promised yield**. It is the yield promised the

---

[1]More technically, a *capital gain* (or *loss*) is the difference between the purchase price and the principal if the bond is held to maturity or the difference between the purchase price and the sale price if the bond is sold prior to maturity.

bondholder on the assumption that the bond is held to maturity, all coupon and principal payments are made as promised, and the coupon payments are reinvested at the bond's promised yield for the remaining term-to-maturity. If the coupon payments are reinvested at a lower rate, the bondholder's actual yield is less than the promised yield (reinvestment risk).

An example of a yield-to-maturity calculation follows. If a person purchased a 3-year, 5 percent coupon (semiannual payments) bond for $951.90, the yield to maturity is found by solving the following equation for the interest rate (i):

$$\$951.90 = \frac{\$25}{(1 + i/2)^1} + \frac{\$25}{(1 + i/2)^2} + \cdots + \frac{\$1,025}{(1 + i/2)^6}$$

Unfortunately, the yield-to-maturity (i) cannot be determined algebraically but must be found by trial and error. That is, the calculation is done by selecting different values of i until the present value of the cash flows on the right side of the equation equals $951.90. Solving the preceding equation in this manner results in a yield of 3.407 percent semiannually, or 6.814 percent annually. The calculation of the final value of i (the yield) is cumbersome and difficult to make by hand because several iterations usually are required. Fortunately, most financial calculators (and spreadsheet programs) provide the answer at a touch of a button. We simply provide the current price, or present value; the number of periods over which the bond contract extends; the periodic coupon payments; and the par or face value to be received at maturity. Your financial calculator determines the periodic interest rate.[2]

LEARNING BY DOING 5.2

Calculating the Yield-to-Maturity on a Bond

PROBLEM: If a person purchased a 10-year, 5 percent coupon (semiannual payments) bond for $1,050.00, what is the yield-to-maturity?

APPROACH: You can solve this problem using Equation 5.4, but you would have to use trial and error. Using a financial calculator simplifies the task. Prior to making the inputs into the financial calculator, recognize the following:

- Annual coupons will be $50, but the semiannual coupons are worth $25.
- The number of periods is 20 (10 years × 2).
- The current price of the bond is $1,050.00.

SOLUTION:

Semiannual coupon = $C/2$ = $50/2 = $25
Maturity of bond = n = 10 years = 20 semiannual periods
Number of compounding periods = m = 2
Number of coupon payments = $m \times n$ = 10 × 2 = 20
Current market price = PB = $1,050.00

---

[2]Note that, for most financial calculators, you must enter the price, or present value, as a negative amount to reflect the fact that it is a cash outflow. The coupon payments and face value are cash inflows and are, therefore, entered as positive cash flows. In addition, if the bond pays semiannual coupon payments, you must convert the calculated semiannual interest rate to an annual yield-to-maturity by multiplying it by 2.

Enter	20		−$1,050.00	$25	$1,000
	N	**i%**	**PV**	**PMT**	**FV**
Answer		**2.189%**			

The semiannual yield is 2.189 percent, while the annual yield to maturity is 4.377 percent.

EXPECTED YIELD

The yield-to-maturity tells us what return we will earn on a bond if the borrower makes all cash payments as promised, if interest rates do not change over the bond's maturity, and if the investor holds the bond to maturity. Quite frequently, however, one or more of these events do not occur. For example, an investor may plan to sell a bond before maturity, the bond may be called prior to maturity, or the bond issuer may default. In any event, the return actually earned on a bond is likely different from the promised yield.

Investors and financial institutions that plan to sell their bonds before maturity would like to know the potential impact of interest rate changes on the returns of their bond investments ex ante (*before* the fact). They can use various forecasting techniques to estimate future interest rates based on information about the money supply, inflation rates, economic activity, and the past behavior of interest rates. Once armed with an interest rate forecast, an investor can predict the market price of a bond at the end of a relevant holding period. Given the prediction of the future price, the investor can calculate an **expected yield** that reflects the expected sale price.

Suppose you purchase a 10-year, 8 percent coupon (annual payments) bond at par and you plan to sell it at the end of 2 years at the prevailing market price. When you purchase the bond, your investment adviser predicts that similar bonds with 8 years to maturity will yield 6 percent at the end of 2 years. Your interest rate forecast implies that the bond's expected price is $1,124.20:

$$PB = \$1,124.20 = \frac{\$80}{(1.06)^1} + \frac{\$80}{(1.06)^2} + \cdots + \frac{\$1,080}{(10.6)^8}$$

Notice there are eight coupon payments and the principal payment remaining at the time of the planned sale. To calculate the expected yield over your 2-year holding period, you solve for the interest rate that equates the original purchase price (par, or $1,000, in this example) with the discounted sum of the cash flows you expect to receive (coupon payments and the *expected* sale price):

$$\$1,000 = \frac{\$80}{(1+i)^1} + \frac{\$80 + \$1,124.20}{(1+i)^2}$$

Solving the preceding equation, either by trial and error or with a financial calculator, results in an expected yield of 13.81 percent. In this case, the difference between the promised yield and the expected yield is accounted for by the expected capital gain of $124.20 received from selling the bond before maturity. Note that calculating the expected yield this way assumes we will be able to reinvest the coupon payments we receive at the expected yield of 13.81 percent. This may or may not be a reasonable assumption.

REALIZED YIELD

The **realized yield** is the return earned on a bond given the cash flows actually received by the investor and assuming that the coupon payments are reinvested at the realized yield. Suppose you purchased the bond in the previous example, a 10-year, 8 percent coupon (annual payments) bond at par. Rather than selling it in 2 years, however, you hold on to it for 3 years and sell it so that you can take a vacation to Cancún. At the time you sell the bond, 7-year bonds with similar characteristics (e.g., default risk) sell at yields of 10 percent.

In this case, the realized yield is different from the promised yield of 8 percent (or the expected yield of 13.81 percent calculated previously) because market yields on similar bonds increased to 10 percent. Similar to the calculation of expected yield, we calculate the yield actually earned on the investment by solving for the interest rate that equates the price you originally paid for the bond with the discounted sum of the cash flows you actually received.

The first step is to calculate the terminal price of the bond (i.e., the market price of the bond on the date you sell it). In the example, you paid $1,000 for the bond. You held the bond for 3 years and received three annual coupon payments of $80 each. The market price of the bond on the day you sell it is equal to the present value of the remaining seven coupon payments and final principal repayment:

$$PB = \$902.63 = \frac{\$80}{(1.10)^1} + \frac{\$80}{(1.10)^2} + \cdots + \frac{\$1,080}{(1.10)^7}$$

The next step is to set the original purchase price of $1,000 equal to the present value of the cash flows actually received (three coupon payments of $80 and the sale price of $902.63) and solve for the interest rate:

$$\$1,000 = \frac{\$80}{(1+i)^1} + \frac{\$80}{(1+i)^2} + \cdots + \frac{\$80 + \$902.63}{(1+i)^3}$$

Solving the preceding equation either by trial and error or with a financial calculator results in a realized yield of 4.91 percent annually. The difference between the realized yield and the promised yield in this case is accounted for by the capital loss of $97.37 ($1,000 − $902.63) suffered when the bond was sold before maturity. In sum, realized yield is useful because it allows an individual investor or financial institution to evaluate the return on a bond ex post (after the end of the holding period or investment horizon).

TOTAL RETURN

Unfortunately, both the expected yield and realized yield calculations assume that we will be able to reinvest the coupon payments at the calculated yield. It isn't easy to see this in the formulas shown here, but we'll prove it later. Fortunately, if we know (or if we are willing to make an explicit assumption about) the actual reinvestment rate, we can calculate something called the **total return** on a bond. It is the return we receive on a bond that considers capital gains or losses *and* changes in the reinvestment rate.

To calculate the total return for a bond, we must first determine two things: (1) the terminal value of the bond (the selling price if we sell the bond, the call price if the bond is called prior to maturity, or the par or face value of the bond if we hold it until maturity), and (2) the accumulated future value of all the coupon payments we received based on a known (or assumed) reinvestment rate. Once we know these two values, we determine the interest rate that equates our initial purchase price to the sum of these two values over the number of periods in our holding period.

Consider the previous example in which we purchased a 10-year, 8 percent coupon (annual payments) bond at par. We sold the bond after 3 years for $902.63 (see the previous calculations), so we know the bond's terminal value. To determine the accumulated future value of the coupon payments, we must find the reinvestment rate. If we are willing to assume that we reinvested the coupon payments at the initial promised yield of 8 percent, we would calculate the accumulated future value as follows:

$$FV_c = C\,[(1 + i)^n - 1]/i$$
$$= \$80\,[(1 + 0.08)^3 - 1]/0.08$$
$$= \$259.71$$

This is just an application of the future value of an annuity formula (as opposed to the future value of a lump sum calculation introduced earlier in the chapter). Notice that this is telling us that the accumulated future value of our coupon payments is equal to coupon payments, $240 (3 × $80), plus interest-on-interest, $19.71 ($259.71 − $240). Now, we just determine the interest rate that equates our initial purchase price, $1,000, to the sum of the $902.63 and $259.71:

$$\$1,000 = \frac{\$902.63 + \$259.71}{(1 + i)^3}$$

Solving for *i*, we learn that the total return for this investment is 5.14 percent. This is higher than the 4.91 percent we calculated earlier because our assumed reinvestment rate of 8 percent is higher than the implicitly assumed reinvestment rate of 4.91 percent in the realized yield calculation. This may not seem like a big difference to you, but in the professional bond investment world, it might be enough to determine whether you get an end-of-the-year bonus!

It is also worth mentioning that our assumed reinvestment rate of 8 percent, in this case, is probably more realistic than the implicitly assumed reinvestment rate of 4.91 percent in the realized yield calculation. Remember how we determined the terminal value (or selling price) of $902.63? It was based on an increase in the yield on the bond to 10 percent. If the yield on the bond increases to 10 percent, doesn't an 8 percent reinvestment rate seem more reasonable than a 4.91 percent reinvestment rate? The point is that, because of the way the expected yield and realized yield calculations handle the reinvestment rate, we might be better off using an explicitly assumed reinvestment rate (ex ante, or before the fact) or the known reinvestment rate (ex post, or after the fact).

DO YOU UNDERSTAND?

1. When a bond's coupon rate is less than the prevailing market rate of interest on similar bonds, will the bond sell at par, a discount, or a premium? Explain.

2. Under what conditions will the total return on a bond equal the promised yield?

3. Using the trial-and-error method, find the yield-to-maturity of a bond with 5 years to maturity, par value of $1,000, and a coupon rate of 8 percent (annual payments). The bond currently sells at 98.5 percent of par value.

4. An investor purchases a $1,000 par value bond with 15 years to maturity at $985. The bond pays $80 of coupon interest annually. The investor plans to hold the bond for 5 years and expects to sell it at the end of the holding period for 94 percent of its face value. What is her expected yield?

5.4 IMPORTANT BOND PRICING RELATIONSHIPS

There are three important relationships among bond prices and changes in the level of interest rates. These relationships are fundamental to understanding how to manage a bond portfolio. These relationships apply not only to bonds but also to all fixed-income securities. Recall that fixed-income securities are financial contracts whose interest or coupon payments are fixed for the life of the contracts. Typical fixed-rate contracts are most corporate, municipal, and Treasury bonds, as well as automobile loans and conventional home mortgage loans.

BOND PRICES AND YIELDS

Bond prices and yields vary inversely. Specifically, as the market rate of interest (or yield) rises, a bond's market price declines; or as the market rate of interest (or yield) declines, a bond's market price rises. This inverse relationship exists because the coupon rate or interest rate on a bond is fixed at the time the bond is issued. For example, when market interest rates rise, the only way to increase a bond's yield to be equal to the market rate of interest is to reduce the bond's price because the rate of interest the bond pays is fixed for the life of the bond contract. The investor in such a bond is "paid" the additional interest as a capital gain. Likewise, if market interest rates decline, the only way to reduce a bond's yield to the market rate is to increase the bond's price. For some numerical examples of the inverse relationship between bond price and yield, see the previous section of this chapter dealing with premium and discount bonds. The inverse relationship, one of the most important concepts discussed in this book, applies to bonds or any financial contract whose interest rate payments are fixed for the life of the contract.

BOND PRICE VOLATILITY AND MATURITY

The mathematics of the present value formula have some interesting implications for the relationship between bond price volatility and maturity. Specifically,

EXHIBIT 5.1

Relationship Among Price, Maturity, Market Yield, and Price Volatility for a $1,000, 5% Coupon Bond (Annual Payments)

(1) Maturity (years)	(2) Bond Price at 5% Yield ($)	Price Change if Yield Changes to 6%			Price Change if Yield Changes to 4%		
		(3) Bond Price ($)	(4) Loss from Increase in Yield ($)	(5) Price Volatility (%)	(6) Bond Price ($)	(7) Gain from Decrease in Yield ($)	(8) Price Volatility (%)
1	$1,000	$990.57	$9.43	−0.94	$1,009.62	$9.62	0.96%
5	1,000	957.88	42.12	−4.21	1,044.52	44.52	4.45
10	1,000	926.40	73.60	−7.36	1,081.11	81.11	8.11
20	1,000	885.30	114.70	−11.47	1,135.90	135.90	13.59
40	1,000	849.54	150.46	−15.05	1,197.93	197.93	19.79
100	1,000	833.82	166.18	−16.62	1,245.05	245.05	24.50

This exhibit shows that the longer the maturity of a bond, the greater the bond's price volatility. Thus, long-term bonds have greater interest rate risk than short-term bonds.

long-term bonds have greater price volatility than short-term bonds, holding other bond characteristics constant. **Bond price volatility** can be measured as the percent change in bond prices for a given change in interest rates.

Exhibit 5.1 demonstrates the relationship between bond price changes and maturity. The exhibit shows the price of a $1,000, 5 percent coupon bond when the market interest rate is 5 percent (column 2). The market rate of interest is then allowed to rise from 5 to 6 percent (column 3) and to fall from 5 to 4 percent (column 6). For both cases, the dollar price changes resulting from the given yield changes are recorded in columns 4 and 7. The percentage price changes (price volatilities) are recorded in columns 5 and 8.

As Exhibit 5.1 shows, when the market yield rises to 6 percent, a 1-year, 5 percent coupon bond falls to $990.57—a price decline of $9.43, or a price volatility of –0.94 percent. In contrast, the 20-year, 5 percent coupon bond sells at $885.30—a price decline of $114.70, or a price volatility of −11.47 percent. The 100-basis-point increase in interest rates causes a capital loss more than 12 times larger on the long-term bond than on the short-term bond.[3] Likewise, the price volatility of the long-term bond is 12 times greater than that of the short-term bond. Similar results are shown for an interest rate decrease in columns 7 and 8. In sum, the longer the term to maturity, the greater the price volatility; hence, long-term bonds have greater interest rate risk than similar short-term bonds.

[3]From now on, we will discuss changes in bond yields in terms of what investors and institutions on Wall Street call *basis points*. A basis point is 1/100 of 1 percent; that is, 100 basis points equal 1 percent. A change in yield of 25 basis points, for example, is equal to a change of 0.25 percent.

Calculating Bond Price Volatility.   As discussed above, a simple measure of bond price volatility is the percentage change in bond price for a given change in yield. More formally, the percentage change in a bond's price (price volatility) is calculated as:

$$\%\Delta PB = \frac{P_t - P_{t-1}}{P_{t-1}} \times 100 \qquad (5.6)$$

where:

$\%\Delta PB$ = the percentage change in price
P_t = the new price in period t
P_{t-1} = the bond's price one period earlier

For example, consider a bond selling at par with an 8 percent annual coupon. Suppose that yields on similar bonds increase by 25 basis points to 8.25 percent. In terms of dollars, the price of the bond falls from $1,000 to $983.41, a decline of $16.59. Applying Equation 5.6, the bond's price volatility is $\%\Delta PB$ = ($983.41 − $1,000)/$1,000 = $16.59/$1,000 = −16.6 percent. Thus, a bond's price volatility is a measure of how sensitive a bond's price is to changes in yields.

BOND PRICE VOLATILITY AND COUPON RATE

Another important factor that affects the price volatility of a bond is the bond's coupon rate. Specifically, the lower a bond's coupon rate, the greater the percentage price change (price volatility) for a given change in yield. This mathematical property of the bond-pricing formula is illustrated in Exhibit 5.2, which shows the prices of three 10-year bonds: a zero coupon bond, a 5 percent coupon bond, and a 10 percent coupon bond. Initially, the bonds are priced to yield 5 percent (see column 2). The bonds are then priced at yields of 6 and 4 percent (see columns 3 and 6). The dollar price changes for each bond given

EXHIBIT 5.2

Relationship Among Price, Coupon Rate, Market Yield, and Price Volatility for a $1,000, 10-Year Bond (Annual Payments)

		Price Change if Yield Changes to 6%			Price Change if Yield Changes to 4%		
(1) Coupon Rate %	(2) Bond Price at 5% Yield ($)	(3) Bond Price ($)	(4) Loss from Increase in Yield ($)	(5) Price Volatility (%)	(6) Bond Price ($)	(7) Gain from Decrease in Yield ($)	(8) Price Volatility (%)
0%	$613.91	$558.39	$55.52	−9.04%	$675.56	$61.65	10.04%
5	1,000.00	926.40	73.60	−7.36	1,081.11	81.11	8.11
10	1,386.09	1,294.40	91.69	−6.62	1,486.65	100.56	7.25

This exhibit shows that the lower the coupon rate of a bond, the greater the bond's price volatility. Thus, low-coupon bonds have greater interest rate risk than high-coupon bonds.

EXHIBIT 5.3
The Relationship Between Bond Price Volatility and the Coupon Rate

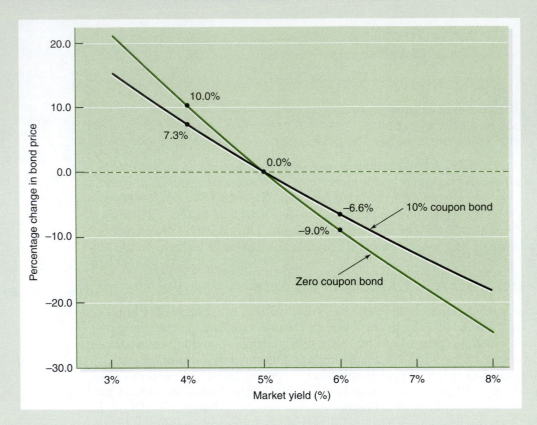

For two bonds with the same maturity, the bond with the lower coupon rate (0%) exhibits a larger percentage change in price for a given change in market yield and thus has more interest rate risk.

the appropriate interest rate changes are recorded in columns 4 and 7, and percentage price changes (price volatilities) are shown in columns 5 and 8. As column 5 shows, when interest rates increase from 5 to 6 percent, the zero coupon bond experiences the greatest percentage price decline, and the 10 percent bond experiences the smallest percentage price decline. Similar results are shown in column 8 for interest rate decreases. In sum, the lower a bond's coupon rate, the greater a bond's price volatility; hence, lower-coupon bonds have greater interest rate risk.

You can also see the effect of the coupon rate on bond price volatility using a price–yield profile. Exhibit 5.3 plots the percentage change in the bond's price (*y*-axis) versus the market yield (*x*-axis) for the zero and 10 percent coupon bonds in Exhibit 5.2. The exhibit shows that low-coupon bonds have a greater percentage change in price from par value than do high-coupon bonds when market interest rates change.

SUMMARY OF IMPORTANT BOND PRICING RELATIONSHIPS

You should remember three relationships between bond prices and yields:

1. Bond prices are inversely related to bond yields.
2. The price volatility of a long-term bond is greater than that of a short-term bond, holding the coupon rate constant.
3. The price volatility of a low-coupon bond is greater than that of a high-coupon bond, holding maturity constant.

We call on these relationships to help us explain interest rate risk in the next section, and later in the book they also help us explain how interest rate risk affects financial institutions.

5.5 INTEREST RATE RISK AND DURATION

By now, you should be catching on that investing in bonds can be risky. Market yields on bonds fluctuate on a daily basis, and these fluctuations cause bond prices to change through the mechanics of the bond-pricing formula (Equation 5.3). In this section, we formally present the concept of interest rate risk and show how investors and financial institutions attempt to manage it using a risk measure called duration.

INTEREST RATE RISK

Interest rate risk is the risk related to changes in interest rates that cause a bond's total return to differ from the promised yield or yield-to-maturity. Interest rate risk comprises two different but closely related risks: (1) price risk and (2) reinvestment risk. We now discuss these two risks.

Price Risk.   *Price risk* is defined by the first bond property described in the preceding section; namely, bond prices and bond yields are inversely related. Increases in interest rates lead to capital losses that cause total returns to decline. Conversely, decreases in interest rates lead to capital gains that cause total returns to rise. These fluctuations in total return caused by capital gains and losses constitute price risk.

Reinvestment Risk.   *Reinvestment risk* is a trickier concept. Remember, when we calculated yield-to-maturity, we noted that the bond pricing formula assumes that all coupon payments are reinvested at the bond's yield-to-maturity. Given that interest rates fluctuate, it is unlikely that an investor will reinvest all coupon payments at the promised yield. If, for example, interest rates increase over the life of a bond, coupons will be reinvested at higher yields, increasing reinvestment income.[4] The increase in reinvestment income increases the total return of the bond. If interest rates decline, the converse is true. The change in a bond's total return caused by changing coupon reinvestment rates is what constitutes reinvestment risk.

---

[4]We use future value mathematics to calculate reinvestment income, which is really just the interest-on-interest from a bond. Future values behave just the opposite of present values when interest rates change. When interest rates increase, future value increases. When they decrease, future value also decreases.

Price Risk Versus Reinvestment Risk.   It is very important to recognize that price risk and reinvestment risk partially offset one another. When interest rates decline, a bond's price increases, resulting in a capital gain (good news!), but the gain is partially offset by lower coupon reinvestment income (bad news!). However, when interest rates rise, the bond suffers a capital loss (bad news!), but the loss is partially offset by higher coupon reinvestment income (good news!).

DURATION AND BOND PROPERTIES

It is important for investors and financial institutions to be able to evaluate the effect of interest rate risk on their bond investments. How can we measure interest rate risk? The problem we have is that bond price volatility varies directly with maturity and inversely with coupon rate. A good measure of interest rate risk should account for both effects simultaneously. A measure of interest rate risk (or *bond price volatility*) that considers both coupon rate and maturity is **duration**. *Duration* is a weighted average of the number of years until each of the bond's cash flows is received. Using annual compounding, the formula for duration is:

$$D = \frac{\sum_{t=1}^{n} \frac{CF_t(t)}{(1+i)^t}}{\sum_{t=1}^{n} \frac{CF_t}{(1+i)^t}} = \frac{\sum_{t=1}^{n} \frac{CF_t(t)}{(1+i)^t}}{PB} \tag{5.7}$$

where:

   D = duration of the bond
   CF_t = interest or principal payment at time t
   t = time period in which principal or coupon interest is paid
   n = number of periods to maturity
   i = the yield to maturity (interest rate)

The denominator is the price of the bond (PB) and is just another form of the bond-pricing formula presented earlier (Equation 5.3). The numerator is the present value of all cash flows weighted according to the length of time to receipt. Admittedly, the formula for duration looks formidable. However, we will work through some examples and use them to illustrate the important properties of duration. We use the concept of duration throughout the book, so it is important that you grasp it now.

LEARNING BY DOING 5.3
Calculating the Duration of a Bond

PROBLEM: Let's illustrate the calculation of the duration of a bond. Say that you invested in a bond with a 3-year maturity, an 8 percent coupon rate paid annually, and a market yield of 10 percent. What is the bond's duration?

APPROACH: You can solve this problem using Equation 5.7. The bond has three coupon payments (CF) remaining and the face value of $1,000 due at the end of the third year (at maturity). With an 8 percent annual coupon, the first two cash flows are worth $80.00 and the final cash flow is worth $1,080.00 (the face value plus the final coupon payment). The discount rate is the market rate of 10 percent.

SOLUTION: While using the equation to solve for duration is viable for a small number of cash flows, longer periods can be more easily dealt with using Excel. Using Equation 5.7:

$$D = \frac{\dfrac{CF_1 \times 1}{(1+t)^1} + \dfrac{CF_2 \times 2}{(1+t)^2} + \dfrac{CF_3 \times 3}{(1+t)^3}}{\dfrac{CF_1}{(1+t)^1} + \dfrac{CF_2}{(1+t)^2} + \dfrac{CF_3}{(1+t)^3}}$$

$$D = \frac{\dfrac{\$80 \times 1}{(1.10)^1} + \dfrac{\$80 \times 2}{(1.10)^2} + \dfrac{\$1,080 \times 3}{(1.10)^3}}{\dfrac{\$80}{(1.10)^1} + \dfrac{\$80}{(1.10)^2} + \dfrac{\$1,080}{(1.10)^3}}$$

$$D = \frac{\$72.73 + \$132.23 + \$2,434.26}{\$72.73 + \$66.12 + \$811.42} = \frac{\$2,639.22}{\$950.27} = \mathbf{2.78 \ years}$$

We could also solve for duration using Excel. In fact, for longer-maturity securities, it would make the computation of duration easier.

To give you a chance to practice calculating duration, Exhibit 5.4 shows the duration for a group of bonds with different coupon rates (zero, 4 percent, and 8 percent) and different maturities (1 to 5 years); in all cases the bonds are priced to yield 10 percent, and coupon payments are paid annually. Now get your pad, pencil, and calculator and see if you can use the duration formula to obtain the durations in Exhibit 5.4. Alternatively, if you are good with the computer, it is relatively easy to set up the duration calculation in a spreadsheet.

Exhibit 5.4 and our previous examples illustrate some important properties of duration:

1. Bonds with higher coupon rates have shorter durations than bonds with smaller coupons of the same maturity. This is true because the higher coupon bonds receive more of the total cash flow earlier in the form of larger coupon payments. For example, for any given maturity, the 8 percent coupon bonds

EXHIBIT 5.4
Duration for Bonds Yielding 10% (Annual Compounding)

Duration in Years

Maturity (Years)	Zero Coupon	4% Coupon	8% Coupon
1	1.00	1.00	1.00
2	2.00	1.96	1.92
3	3.00	2.88	2.78
4	4.00	3.75	3.56
5	5.00	4.57	4.28

Duration is a measure of bond price volatility that considers both the coupon rate and term to maturity.

in Exhibit 5.4 always have a shorter duration than the 4 percent or zero coupon bonds.

2. There is generally a positive relationship between term-to-maturity and duration. The longer the maturity of a bond, the higher the bond's duration.[5] This is true because the bond's cash flow is received further out in time. Among the bonds in Exhibit 5.4 with the same coupon rate, you can see that those with longer maturities have longer durations.

3. For bonds with a single payment (principal with or without a coupon payment), duration is equal to term-to-maturity. Thus, for zero coupon bonds (the single payment is the principal), duration equals final maturity. Likewise, the 1-year bonds in Exhibit 5.4 have duration equal to 1 year because they pay coupon interest annually. Bonds with interim payments always have durations less than their final maturity.

4. All other factors held constant, the higher the market rate of interest, the shorter the duration of the bond. This stands to reason because the higher the market rate of interest, the faster coupon reinvestment income accumulates.

One property of duration that is particularly important to managers of financial institutions is the direct relationship between bond price volatility and duration. The greater a bond's duration, the greater the percentage change in a bond's price for a given change in interest rates. Thus, duration is a good measure of interest rate risk because, as noted previously, duration is positively related to maturity and inversely related to coupon rate.

USING DURATION TO CALCULATE BOND PRICE VOLATILITY

We have demonstrated that a direct relationship exists between bond price volatility and duration. In this section, we show how to use duration to estimate the percentage change in a bond's price resulting from a change in market interest rates using the following formula, which gives the relationship between bond price changes and duration:

$$\% \Delta PB \cong -D\left[\frac{\Delta_i}{(1 + i)}\right] \times 100 \tag{5.8}$$

Using the 3-year, 4 percent coupon bond in Exhibit 5.4, if the market interest rate increases 25 basis points from 10 percent to 10.25 percent, the percentage change in the value of the bond would be approximately:

$$\% \Delta PB \cong -2.88\left[\frac{0.0025}{1.10}\right] \times 100 = -0.65\%$$

For this bond, the actual price change is from \$850.79 to \$845.25, which results in a percentage change in price of −0.65 percent.[6] Therefore, we see that for this small change in the market rate, Equation 5.8 works well for estimating the

---

[5]For bonds selling at a discount (below par), duration increases at a decreasing rate up to a very long maturity, such as 50 years, and then declines. Because most bonds have maturities of 30 years or less, duration increases with maturity for most bonds we observe in the marketplace.

[6]To calculate \$850.79, use Equation 5.3 with an interest rate of 10 percent. Similarly, you can obtain \$845.25. To arrive at −0.65 percent, use Equation 5.6 with $P_t = \$845.25$ and $P_t - 1 = \$850.79$.

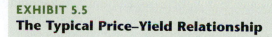

EXHIBIT 5.5
The Typical Price–Yield Relationship

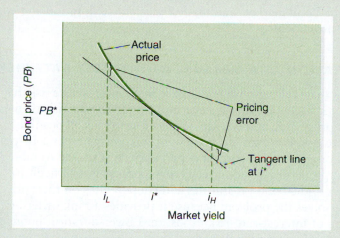

The tangent line to the price–yield profile can be used to estimate changes in bond prices due to changes in interest rates.

change in value of the bond. However, this equation may not work as well for large changes in interest rates. Using the same bond, let's see what happens if interest rates increase from 10 percent to 12 percent, an increase of 200 basis points. Equation 5.8 suggests the following change in value:

$$\% \Delta PB \cong -2.88 \left[\frac{0.02}{1.10} \right] \times 100 = -5.24\%$$

The *actual* price change is from \$850.79 to \$807.85, which is a 5.05 percent drop in the bond price.[7]

Our examples show that Equation 5.8 works well for small changes in interest rates but not for large changes. The shortcoming of Equation 5.8 is demonstrated in Exhibit 5.5. The curve, which is a representation of a price–yield profile, shows the relationship between a bond's price and the prevailing market yield (or market's required yield), and the straight line represents the price–yield relationship estimated by Equation 5.8. We see that for small changes in market yields around the tangent point, the straight line is a good estimate of changes along the price–yield profile. However, for large changes in market yields, the straight line is not a good estimate. Thus, Equation 5.8 requires a correction for the error in using the straight line to estimate the curve. Bond traders refer to the correction factor as **convexity** because the curve in Exhibit 5.5 is convex, which means that it curves away from the origin of the *x*–*y* axes. There is a complicated formula for convexity not presented here, but most bond traders have a good instinct for how bond prices will change given the maturity and the coupon rate of the bond.

---

[7]To calculate 5.05 percent, use Equation 5.3 to obtain the bond prices at 10 percent and 12 percent and then substitute the prices into Equation 5.6.

Although the formulas for duration and convexity are daunting, you should know that bond traders use these measures frequently to assess the interest rate risk of bonds and to estimate price changes. The computer screens that bond traders use to track the bond markets automatically calculate duration and convexity and feature them prominently.

USING DURATION AS A MEASURE OF INTEREST RATE RISK

We now know that (1) long-term bonds have more interest rate risk than short-term bonds and (2) low-coupon bonds have more interest rate risk than high-coupon bonds. These properties, however, do not allow us to rank all possible pairs of bonds on interest rate risk. For example, if we want to know whether a 10-year, 7 percent coupon bond or an 8-year, 5 percent coupon bond is exposed to more interest rate risk, the bond properties do not directly help because it is difficult to "eyeball" the relative impact of the bonds' maturities and coupon rates on their price volatilities.

Duration solves the problem because it provides a rank ordering of bonds on the dimension of interest-rate-risk exposure. Lower-duration bonds are exposed to less interest rate risk, and higher-duration bonds are exposed to more. Duration is related to the slope of the price–yield profile for a given bond. The steeper the price–yield profile, the greater the bond's duration and the greater the exposure to interest rate risk.

Given the two bonds described here, assume a current market yield of 5 percent. At the 5 percent yield, the duration of the 10-year, 7 percent bond is 7.71 years and the duration of the 8-year, 5 percent bond is 6.79 years. The 8-year, 5 percent bond has a shorter duration and thus is exposed to less interest rate risk. To test our conclusion, let's assume that the market yield increases from 5 percent to 5.5 percent, or an increase of 50 basis points. For this change in yield, the price of the 10-year, 7 percent bond falls 3.58 percent, whereas the price of the 8-year, 5 percent bond falls 3.17 percent. Thus, we see that duration properly ranked the bonds for their exposure to changes in interest rates.

DURATION OF BOND PORTFOLIOS

From our example, we see that duration ranks individual bonds based on their exposure to interest rate risk. We know, however, that investors seldom hold individual assets, and today investors often buy investment funds instead of individual securities. So can duration help with understanding the interest-rate-risk exposure of a bond portfolio or a bond mutual fund? The answer is yes. In fact, portfolio duration provides a rank ordering of portfolios by their exposure to changes in interest rates, just as it does for individual bonds.

To calculate duration of bond portfolios, we must recognize only that the duration of a bond portfolio is a weighted average of the individual bond durations. Each bond's duration is weighted according to the proportion of portfolio value accounted for by each bond. The formula for portfolio duration is

$$\text{Portfolio duration} = \sum_{i=1}^{n} w_i D_i \qquad (5.9)$$

where w_i is the proportion of the portfolio invested in bond i and D_i is the duration of bond i. In later chapters, we discuss how financial institutions use portfolio duration to manage their exposures to interest rate changes.

Let's work through a brief example to show how Equation 5.9 works. Suppose a bond portfolio contains four bonds, A, B, C, and D. Bond A has duration of 15.7 years and makes up 20 percent of the portfolio. Bond B has duration of 22.3 years and makes up 40 percent of the portfolio. Bond C has duration of 10.2 years and makes up 15 percent of the portfolio. Finally, Bond D has duration of 7.6 years and makes up 25 percent of the portfolio. You can calculate the duration of the bond portfolio with Equation 5.9:

$$
\begin{aligned}
D_{portfolio} &= D_A w_A + D_B w_B + D_C w_C + D_D w_D \\
&= 15.7(0.20) + 22.3(0.40) + 10.2(0.15) + 7.6(0.25) \\
&= 15.49 \text{ years}
\end{aligned}
$$

You can see from this example that financial institutions are able to change the durations of their bond portfolios by changing the proportions of bonds in the portfolios. For example, to make the duration of our example portfolio longer, a portfolio manager could decrease the proportion invested in Bond D and increase the proportion invested in Bond B.

USING DURATION TO MEASURE AND MANAGE INTEREST RATE RISK

Probably the most important use of duration is as a tool for reducing or eliminating interest rate risk over a given holding period. For example, suppose that you are in the beginning of your junior year in college and wish to plan for a well-deserved vacation 2 years from now. You have a 2-year investment horizon over which you must accumulate enough funds to take your vacation. You consider investing in bonds, but you are concerned about the potential impact of interest rate risk on the returns to your investment and, hence, your ability to afford the vacation. We now discuss the relative merits of three possible approaches to dealing with interest rate risk.

The Zero Coupon Approach.   The simplest way to avoid the interest rate risk in this situation is to invest in a zero coupon bond that matures in 2 years. This strategy eliminates price risk because the bond is held to maturity, and it eliminates reinvestment risk because there are no coupon payments to reinvest. The entire return from the zero coupon bond comes from the difference between the purchase price and the maturity value. Assuming default-free bonds, there is no risk in this strategy.

The Maturity-Matching Approach.   A more naive alternative is to invest in a coupon bond with a maturity equal to the 2-year holding period. With this strategy, you eliminate the price risk because you hold the bond to maturity, but there is still reinvestment risk because coupons are received. Consequently, interest rate changes could potentially wreak havoc with your vacation plans should interest rates decline dramatically over the 2 years.

The Duration-Matching Approach.   A surefire way of eliminating both price risk and reinvestment risk is to structure your bond investment such that the *duration* of the bond or a bond portfolio equals your holding period.[8] What happens with the duration-matching strategy that results in the elimination of both price and reinvestment risks? By matching duration with your holding period, you set up a situation in which capital gains or losses from interest rate changes are exactly offset by changes in reinvestment income. You are able to lock in on a given target return to your investment and thus ensure that you have enough money at the end of 2 years to take your vacation.

EXAMPLE OF THE DURATION-MATCHING STRATEGY AT WORK

Let's work through this example with some real numbers, so you can see exactly how duration can protect you from interest rate risk. Because you want to go on vacation to Cancún 2 years from now, your holding period or investment horizon (the period of time over which you invest) is 2 years. Assume that you expect the vacation to cost you approximately $1,210 2 years from now and the current market yield is 10 percent. If you purchase a zero coupon bond costing $1,000 with a maturity of 2 years and a maturity value of $1,210, you receive $1,210 2 years from now regardless of how interest rates move, assuming the issuer of the bond does not default.[9] For purposes of this example, we assume no risk of default. Now suppose that there are three possible interest rate scenarios: (1) the interest rate falls to 8 percent at the end of 1 year from now and remains at that level until the end of the second year, (2) the interest rate remains at 10 percent over the entire 2 years, or (3) the interest rate increases to 12 percent 1 year from now and remains there until the end of the second year. The maturity-matching strategy, which involves purchasing a 2-year bond with a 10 percent coupon rate, gives you the cash flows and the total returns shown next:

Cash Flows from the Maturity-Matching Strategy			
	Interest Rate Scenario		
Cash Flows 2 Years from Now	**8%**	**10%**	**12%**
(1) Principal	$1,000	$1,000	$1,000
(2) Proceeds from reinvesting the first coupon payment from the end of first year to the end of second year[1]	108	110	112
(3) Second coupon payment	100	100	100
Total cash flow	$1,208	$1,210	$1,212
Total return	9.9%	10.0%	10.1%

[1]The calculation is just a simple application of the future value formula. For example, assume you invest $100 for 1 year at 8 percent interest; you receive $100 × (1 + 0.08) = $108 at the end of the second year. The coupon reinvestment proceeds are calculated similarly for the other scenarios.

[8]Technically, this is true only when the term structure of interest rates is flat and moves in parallel shifts. Interest rates, unfortunately, do not usually behave this way in the real world. As a result, it is usually not possible to eliminate interest rate risk from a bond investment with this strategy, although many academic studies show that it is possible to obtain substantial *reduction* in interest rate risk. Furthermore, this strategy works only for one-time changes in interest rates. In practice, portfolio managers must adjust the duration of their bond portfolios (by buying and selling bonds of various durations) on an ongoing basis so that the duration of their portfolio constantly matches their investment horizon.

[9]The idea for this example and the numbers in it come from James C. Van Horne, *Financial Market Rates and Flows*, 6th ed., Upper Saddle River, NJ: Prentice Hall, 2001, pp. 109–110.

PEOPLE & EVENTS

Betting the Farm on Interest Rates and Losing

One lesson history has taught investors is that if an investment result is too good to be true, it's probably not. Just ask the citizens and investors in Orange County's investment fund. Orange County, once prime farmland, is a wealthy and conservative suburb south of Los Angeles. The county, which had an affluent tax base and high credit rating, filed for bankruptcy protection on December 6, 1994. It was the largest municipal bankruptcy in U.S. history.[1] How could this have happened?

During the 1970s and 1980s, the county's investment fund earned returns substantially above the average for similar funds. Orange County's treasurer, Robert Citron, developed a reputation as an aggressive and talented money manager. Because of his success, he became a star of municipal finance, touring the country, giving speeches on his esoteric investment strategies, and advocating that municipalities could pay some of their operating expenses from earnings on investments. Other municipalities were so impressed that they began investing in the county's investment fund. By 1994, the pool had grown rapidly, to about $8 billion in assets, and Citron was turning away some municipalities that wanted to invest.

The bond market was stunned when Orange County announced that its $8 billion investment fund faced losses of $1.6 billion, or 20 percent of the investment pool's value. What happened? In an effort to bolster the fund's sagging earnings, Citron borrowed an additional $14 billion from banks and other municipalities. He then invested the money in high-risk interest-sensitive investments, such as long-term bonds and derivative securities. He was "betting the farm" that interest rates would decline. If interest rates declined, bond prices would rise and the county's investment fund would earn a bundle of cash.

What Citron didn't know, however, was that the Fed had decided to restrict monetary growth and had initiated a series of interest rate hikes beginning in February 1994. As interest rates increased, Orange County's borrowing costs rose, and the fund was forced to pay out more interest than it earned on its investments. With mounting losses, creditors started asking for more collateral. At first, county officials tried to stonewall the market's requests for money and information as rumors of bankruptcy were rampant. The crisis played itself out quickly when the fund missed a $200 million payment on a $2.6 billion investment with First Boston Corporation. With no money to make payments, Orange County was forced to file for bankruptcy and, needless to say, Citron was fired as county treasurer. Meanwhile, county officials who had expected to earn $150 million in interest income to help finance part of the county's $3.7 billion annual budget now faced budget cuts and a reduction in government services.

The Orange County case illustrates three important facts about fixed income securities: (1) The price of fixed income securities decrease as the market rate of interest increases, (2) long-term debt has large price swings, and (3) the price swings inherent in long-term debt make it a high-risk investment. When interest rates go up, as they did in 1994, bond prices go down. This phenomenon gives rise to *price risk*. Unfortunately, the citizens of Orange County and investors learned about *price risk* as a result of Citron's unconscionable interest rate bets.

[1]For what it's worth, Robert Citron's loss of $1.7 billion in 1994 is ranked sixth in the list of biggest trading losses. Ranked first is Jerome Kerviel's trading loss of $7.1 billion in 2008 at Société Générale, France. Jerome Kerviel is featured in the other People & Events in this chapter.

The principal amount and the second coupon payment are fixed, regardless of which interest rate scenario occurs. What are affected by the interest rate change, however, are the proceeds from reinvesting the first coupon. When the level of interest rates remains the same at 10 percent, the total cash flow at the end of the second year is $1,210, exactly the amount you need to take your trip to Cancún. The bad news occurs when the interest rate falls to 8 percent. If that happens, the total cash flow falls short of what you need for your trip because you wouldn't be able to reinvest the intermediate coupon payment at the original yield-to-maturity of the bond, which is 10 percent. At a 12 percent market yield, you have enough for your trip and a little left over to buy a margarita on the airplane. You are exposed to interest rate risk because, over your investment horizon of 2 years, your total cash flow and your total return change as the market yield changes.

However, if you match the duration of your investment to the length of your holding period, you are protected from interest rate risk. Suppose you are able to find a bond that pays a 10 percent annual coupon payment and has 2.1 years to maturity. (There aren't too many 2.1-year bonds out there that pay one-tenth of a coupon payment at maturity. Recognize that this bond is hypothetical and contrived for purposes of the illustration.) Using the bond pricing formula, the value of this bond today would be

$$PB_{2.1} = \frac{\$100}{(1.10)} + \frac{\$100}{(1.10)^2} + \frac{\$1,010}{(1.10)^{2.1}} = \$1,000$$

Notice that the last coupon payment is only $10 because the bond is held only one-tenth of a year. Let's see what happens to your cash flows at the end of 2 years if you buy this bond. The cash flows are shown next:

Cash Flows from Buying the 2.1-Year Bond			
	Interest Rate Scenario		
Cash Flows 2 Years from Now	**8%**	**10%**	**12%**
(1) Proceeds from selling the 2.1-year bond after 2 Years	$1,002	$1,000	$998
(2) Proceeds from reinvesting the first coupon payment from the end of first year to the end of second year[1]	108	110	112
(3) Second coupon payment	100	100	100
Total cash flow	$1,210	$1,210	$1,210
Total return	10.0%	10.0%	10.0%

[1]The calculation is just a simple application of the future value formula. For example, assume you invest $100 for 1 year at 8 percent interest; you receive $100 × (1 + 0.08) = $108 at the end of the second year. The coupon reinvestment proceeds are calculated similarly for the other scenarios.

Notice that this strategy requires you to sell the 2.1-year bond 2 years from now, one-tenth of a year before it matures. At that point, the only cash flows remaining from the bond are one-tenth of a coupon payment and the principal repayment, both occurring in one-tenth of a year. Therefore, anyone purchasing the bond is willing to pay the present value of the remaining cash flows. For example, if rates fall to 8 percent, the bond is worth $1,002 at the end of 2 years, when the bond has one-tenth of a year remaining to maturity:

$$PB_{0.1} = \frac{\$1,010}{(1.08)^{0.1}} = \$1,002$$

You can do a similar calculation, which is just an application of the bond price formula, for the scenario in which rates increase to 12 percent.

There are several important observations in the preceding table. First, the cash flow at the end of 2 years is the same, regardless of which interest rate scenario occurs. This means that you have eliminated the interest rate risk from your position. Second, the total return is the same for each scenario, another indication that you have eliminated the interest rate risk. Finally, the strategy is structured such that the effects of price risk and reinvestment risk offset each other exactly. Notice that if interest rates rise to 12 percent, there is a price decrease of $2 on the bond (from $1,000 to $998) but an increase in reinvestment income of $2 (from $110 to $112). The bottom line is that you have enough money for your trip to Cancún, regardless of how interest rates change.

As it turns out, the *duration* of the 2.1-year bond is 2 years, so what you have really done is to match the duration of your bond investment with the length of your holding period or investment horizon. You can see the calculation of the bond's duration next:

$$D = \frac{\dfrac{\$100}{(1.10)} + \dfrac{\$100(2)}{(1.10)^2} + \dfrac{\$1,010(2.1)}{(1.10)^{2.1}}}{\dfrac{\$100}{(1.10)} + \dfrac{\$100}{(1.10)^2} + \dfrac{\$1,010}{(1.10)^{2.1}}} = 2.0$$

Thus, this example demonstrates that it is possible to eliminate interest rate risk by matching the duration of your investment with your holding period.

This example is admittedly somewhat contrived to make a teaching point, but the reality is that it is difficult to identify single bonds, such as the 2.1-year bond used here, whose durations equal a given holding period. What financial institutions do is form bond portfolios that have a given duration. They accomplish this by using Equation 5.9, the formula for portfolio duration, and varying the proportions (i.e., w_i) until they achieve the desired duration. This example works because we assumed that interest rates change at the end of the first year and then remain at that level until the bond is sold. After studying the duration formula, you should recognize that the duration of a bond also depends on the market yield. Every time the market yield changes, the duration changes. This means that real-world financial institutions must periodically adjust the duration of their bond investments to match the remaining holding period to keep the interest-rate-risk protection working.

HOW FINANCIAL INSTITUTIONS USE DURATION

The duration-matching strategy has many real-world applications. Managers of pension funds use the strategy to protect from interest rate risk the value of bond portfolios used to provide workers with retirement income in the distant future. By using duration combined with a strategy of "dedicating" a bond portfolio's assets to paying a particular stream of pension fund obligations, fund managers can ensure that they are able to pay retirees the contracted amount regardless of interest rate changes. In Chapter 20, we show how managers of commercial banks and thrift institutions can use duration to reduce fluctuations in net interest income (the difference between the average return of the assets minus the average cost of liabilities) resulting from interest rate changes. In addition, we show that banks can protect their net worth from interest rate risk by matching the average duration of the assets with the average duration of the liabilities.

DO YOU UNDERSTAND?

1. Consider a 4-year bond selling at par with a 7 percent annual coupon. Suppose that yields on similar bonds increase by 50 basis points. Use duration (Equation 5.8) to estimate the percentage change in the bond price. Check your answer by calculating the new bond price.

2. Define *price risk* and *reinvestment risk*. Explain how the two risks offset each other.

3. What is the duration of a bond portfolio made up of two bonds: 37 percent of a bond with duration of 7.7 years and 63 percent of a bond with duration of 16.4 years?

4. How can duration be used as a way to rank bonds on their interest rate risk?

5. To eliminate interest rate risk, should you match the maturity or the duration of your bond investment to your holding period? Explain.

SUMMARY OF LEARNING OBJECTIVES

1 **Explain the time value of money and its application to the pricing of bonds.** A given amount of money received today is worth more than the same amount of money received in the future in part because people prefer to consume goods today rather than consume similar goods in the future. Present value calculations determine how much a future cash flow is worth in today's dollars, given the rate of interest, which reflects the preference for current over future cash flow. Pricing a bond is a straightforward application of the present value formula. To price a bond, identify the timing and magnitude of its cash flows (principal and coupon payments) and use the market yield on similar bonds as the discount rate in the present value formula.

2 **Explain the different measures of yield that are important for analyzing a bond's performance:** (a) yield-to-maturity, (b) expected yield, (c) realized yield, (d) total return. Bond yield measures tell investors the rate of return on bonds under different assumptions. *Yield-to-maturity* is the rate of return assuming the bond is held to maturity and that all coupon payments are reinvested to earn the yield-to-maturity. Most investors want some idea of how a bond investment will perform in the future. The *expected yield* is the rate of return that reflects the anticipated

holding period and the anticipated coupon reinvestment income. The *realized yield* is the return earned on a bond given the cash flows actually received by the investor, assuming that the coupon payments are reinvested at the realized yield. Finally, many bonds are sold before maturity, and the reinvested coupon may not earn the yield-to-maturity due to interest rate changes. To determine the actual rate of return that was earned on a bond investment in the past, investors use *total return*, which accounts for the actual holding period and actual reinvestment income.

3 **Explain how changes in interest rates cause bond prices to change.** Bond prices and bond yields move inversely. When market yields increase, bond prices decrease, and vice versa. This effect is a mathematical property of the bond-pricing formula. The change in bond prices for a given change in market yield, also known as *bond price volatility*, is greater for bonds with longer maturities and lower-coupon rates, all other factors being equal.

4 **Describe interest rate risk and its two components: price risk and reinvestment risk.** *Interest rate risk* is the change in the value of a bond given a change in market yields. Changes in interest rates affect the price of the bond and the coupon reinvestment income.

Therefore, there are two types of interest rate risk: price risk and reinvestment risk. *Price risk* refers to changes in the market price resulting from changes in the market yield. *Reinvestment risk* is the variation in reinvestment income resulting from changes in the market yield. Price risk and reinvestment risk offset each other. When interest rates increase, bond prices fall, but coupon reinvestment income increases. The opposite occurs when market yields fall. Both types of risk can cause the total return to differ from the expected yield or the yield-to-maturity.

5 **Explain how interest rate risk can be measured.** Investors and financial institutions can measure interest rate risk using duration. Bonds with more interest rate risk have larger durations and those with less interest rate risk have smaller durations.

6 **Describe how investors and financial institutions manage interest rate risk.** Investors and financial institutions can manage interest rate risk using duration. By matching the duration of a bond investment with the length of the desired investment horizon or holding period, price risk and reinvestment risk offset each other. This strategy can eliminate the fluctuations in cash flow or total return over a given holding period.

KEY TERMS

Time value of money	Bondholder	Premium bond	Expected yield
Present value	Par value (principal, face value)	Zero coupon bond	Realized yield
Future value		Credit risk (default risk)	Total return
Compounding	Coupon payment		Bond price volatility
Discounting	Coupon rate	Reinvestment risk	Interest rate risk
Opportunity cost	Term-to-maturity	Price risk	Duration
Bond	Discount bond	Yield-to-maturity (promised yield)	Convexity
Bond issuer	Par bond		

QUESTIONS AND PROBLEMS

1. Julie Orzabal deposits $5,000 in a savings account offering 5.125 percent compounded daily. Assuming she makes no further deposits, what will be the balance in her account after 5 years?

2. Write the equation expressing the present value (or price) of a bond that has a 10 percent coupon (annual payments), a 5-year maturity, and a principal of $1,000 if yields on similar securities are 8 percent. Compute the price using a calculator.

3. Find the price of a corporate bond maturing in 5 years that has a 5 percent coupon (annual payments), a $1,000 face value, and an AA rating. A local newspaper's financial section reports that the yields on 5-year bonds are AAA, 6 percent; AA, 7 percent; and A, 8 percent.

4. What is the yield-to-maturity of a corporate bond with a 3-year maturity, 5 percent coupon (semiannual payments), and $1,000 face value if the bond sold for $978.30?

5. Explain why yields and prices of fixed-income securities are inversely related.

6. What is the relationship between bond price volatility and term-to-maturity? Between bond price volatility and the coupon rate?

7. Carol Chastain purchases a 1-year discount bond with a $1,000 face value for $862.07. What is the yield of the bond?

8. David Hoffman purchases a $1,000 20-year bond with an 8 percent coupon rate (annual payments). Yields on comparable bonds are 10 percent. David expects that, 2 years from now, yields on comparable bonds will have declined to 9 percent. Find his expected yield, assuming the bond is sold in 2 years.

9. Calculate the duration of a $1,000, 4-year bond with an 8 percent coupon rate (annual payments) that is currently selling at par.

10. Calculate the duration of a $1,000, 12-year zero coupon bond using annual compounding and a current market rate of 9 percent.

11. Define interest rate risk. Explain the two types of interest rate risk. How can an investor with a given holding period use duration to reduce interest rate risk?

12. Calculate the duration for a $1,000, 4-year bond with a 4.5 percent annual coupon, currently selling at par. Use the bond's duration to estimate the percentage change in the bond's price for a decrease in the market interest rate to 3.5 percent. How different is your answer from the actual price change calculated using Equation 5.6?

13. A bond with 3 years to maturity and a coupon of 6.25 percent is currently selling at $932.24. Assume annual coupon payments.

a. What is its yield to maturity?

b. Compute its duration using Equation 5.7 and the yield-to-maturity calculated above as the discount rate.

c. If interest rates are expected to decrease by 50 basis points, what is the expected dollar change in price? What is the expected percentage change in price?

14. Consider a bond that has a coupon of 8 percent paid semiannually and has a maturity of 5 years. The bond is currently selling for $1,047.25. Use Excel to do the following analysis.

a. What is its yield to maturity?

b. Compute its duration.

c. If interest rates are expected to increase by 75 basis points, what is the expected dollar change in price? What is the expected percentage change in price?

15. Identify the price of a Morgan Stanley bond from the *Wall Street Journal* section titled "Corporate Bonds"

or from Yahoo Finance. The bond should have a maturity of at least 4 years. Assume semiannual coupon payments. Using Excel, complete the following:

a. Compute its duration.

b. If interest rates are expected to increase by 45 basis points, what is the expected dollar change in price? What is the expected percentage change in price?

c. If interest rates are expected to decline by 35 basis points, what is the expected dollar change in price? What is the expected percentage change in price?

16. Explain the convexity of a bond. When pricing bonds, under what circumstances is convexity a problem?

17. When reducing interest rate risk, why is duration matching superior to maturity matching?

18. If two bonds are identical in all respects except that one bond compounds annually and the other semiannually, which bond has the higher price? Why?

19. If the coupon rate on a bond is equal to the market rate of interest on similar bonds, what is the price of the bond? What are these bonds commonly called?

20. Which of the following bonds has the largest price risk and why? Note that the bonds are identical in all respects except for the size of the coupon.

a. Zero coupon bonds

b. Par bonds

c. Discount

d. Premium

INTERNET EXERCISE

This exercise asks you to assess the volatility of interest rates in recent times by performing the following steps on the Internet:

1 Access the Web site of the Federal Reserve Bank of St. Louis at www.stls.frb.org.

2. Select FRED.

3. Select Interest Rates.

4. Select 1-year Treasury Constant Maturity Monthly Rates (GS1) and copy the data for the most recent 10 years to a spreadsheet.

5. Select 20-year Treasury Constant Maturity Monthly Rates (GS20) and copy the data for the same period as the 1-year rates.

6. Graph the data.

7. Calculate the mean and the standard deviation of the two data series.

Using the graphs and the calculations, assess the interest rate risk that bondholders of 1- and 20-year bonds were exposed to over the most recent 10-year period as compared to the previous 10-year period.

The Structure of Interest Rates

State and local governments issue tax-exempt municipal securities, often called "munis," to finance a multitude of capital projects. For example, munis finance athletic stadiums, bridges, college dormitories, parking facilities, and water and sewer treatment facilities.

ARMED WITH A BASIC understanding of the determinants of the general level of interest rates, we can now explore why interest rates vary among financial products and over the business cycle. To get an idea of how much interest rates differ across financial products, take a close look at the financial section of any major newspaper. On any given day, newspapers report yields on thousands of financial instruments, and almost every product has a different market rate of interest.

In the accompanying table, you see the diversity of interest rates that existed on February 3, 2011. For example, why do 3-month Treasury bills yield 0.14 percent and 10-year Treasury bonds yield 3.58 percent when both had the same issuer—the U.S. Treasury Department? Aren't Treasury securities the proxy for the risk-free rate? Why do Aaa rated municipal bonds yield 4.25 percent and Aaa corporate bonds yield 5.21 percent? Don't both securities have the same credit rating? Even more perplexing, why have interest rates declined so much in recent years? For example, in the last edition of the textbook, we reported that the 3-month Treasury bill yield was 4.98 percent (January 2007); in February 2011 it yielded 0.21 percent. What economic forces have driven short-term interest rates so low?

It all seems very confusing. If you read this chapter carefully, you will be able to explain how their characteristics, such as maturity, default risk, and tax treatment, cause the interest rates of securities to differ and how interest rates vary over the business cycle. ■

Selected Interest Rates, February 3, 2011	
Financial Instrument	**Interest Rate (%)**
3-month commercial paper	0.21
3-month certificate of deposit	0.28
U.S. government securities	
3-month Treasury bills	0.14
1-year Treasury bills	0.29
5-year Treasury notes	2.18
10-year Treasury bonds	3.58
Aaa municipal bonds	4.25
Aaa corporate bonds	5.21
Baa corporate bonds	6.19

Source: Federal Reserve Board of Governors, H.15 Statistical Release, and Bondsonline.com

Market analysts have identified five major characteristics that are responsible for most of the differences in interest rates among securities on any given day: (1) term-to-maturity, (2) default risk, (3) tax treatment, (4) marketability, and (5) special features such as call and put options. This chapter examines these factors separately and explains how each influences a security's yield. Finally, the chapter explains how interest rates behave over the business cycle. ■

LEARNING OBJECTIVES

1 Describe and explain the relationship between interest rates and the term-to-maturity of a financial instrument.

2 Explain the meaning and the measurement of default risk premiums.

3 Describe how tax treatment affects yield differences across different types of securities.

4 Explain the relationship between the marketability of a security and its yield.

5 Explain how special characteristics such as call provisions, put options, and conversion options affect a security's yield.

6 Explain how interest rates behave over the business cycle.

6.1 THE TERM STRUCTURE OF INTEREST RATES

The **term-to-maturity** of a loan is the length of time until the principal amount is payable. The relationship between a security's yield-to-maturity and term-to-maturity is known as the **term structure of interest rates**. We can view the term structure visually by graphically plotting yield-to-maturity and maturity for equivalent-grade securities at a point in time. The plots are then connected in a smooth line called the **yield curve**. It is important to note that, for yield curves to be meaningful, other factors that affect interest rates, such as default risk, tax treatment, and marketability, must be held constant.

Term structure relationships are best seen by examining yield-to-maturity relationships on U.S. Treasury securities. Exhibit 6.1 shows three yield curves for Treasury securities during the 2000s and the data to construct them. Treasury securities are ideal for constructing yield curves because, regardless of their maturity, the securities have similar tax treatment, default risk, and marketability. The yield curves were constructed by plotting term-to-maturity on the horizontal axis and the security's yield on the vertical axis. For example, when plotting the data for the January 2011 yield curve: 3-month securities yield 0.15 percent, 1-year securities yield 0.27 percent, 5-year securities yield 1.99 percent, and 10-year securities

EXHIBIT 6.1

Yield Curves on Treasury Securities in the 2000s

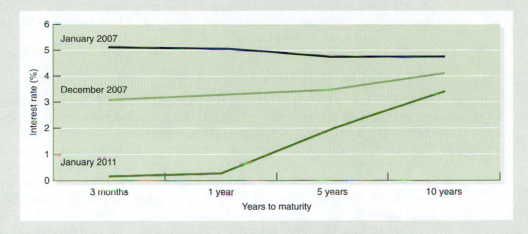

	Interest Rate (%)		
Terms to Maturity	**January 2011**	**December 2007**	**January 2007**
3 months (short-term)	0.15	3.07	5.11
1 year	0.27	3.26	5.06
5 years	1.99	3.49	4.75
10 years (long-term)	3.39	4.1	4.76

The shape of the yield curve varies over time. January 2007 is a downward-sloping yield curve. It is not frequently seen except prior to the start of a recession. December 2007 and January 2011 are both upward-sloping yield curves, which are the most commonly observed yield curves, usually seen during periods of economic expansion.

Source: Federal Reserve Board of Governors, H.15 Statistical Release.

yield 3.39 percent. The resulting yield curve shows that longer-term securities have higher yields than short-term securities.

As you can see in Exhibit 6.1, the shape and level of yield curves do not remain constant over time. As the general level of interest rates rises and falls, yield curves correspondingly shift up and down and have different slopes. We observe three basic shapes (slopes) of yield curves in the marketplace. First is the ascending or upward-sloping yield curve (January 2011 and December 2007), which is formed when interest rates are lowest on short-term securities, and it rises at a diminishing rate until the rates begin to level out on longer maturities. This is the yield curve most commonly observed. Flat yield curves (not shown in the exhibit) are not common but do occur from time to time. Descending or downward-sloping yield curves (January 2007) occur periodically and are marked by short-term rates (such as the 3-month Treasury bill rate) exceeding long-term rates (10- or 20-year Treasury bond yields). Downward-sloping yield curves usually occur at or near the beginning of an economic recession.

At this point you might be wondering what economic forces explain both the shape of the yield curve and its movement over time. You may also be asking yourself, Why is it important that I understand yield curves? We now discuss several theories that explain changes in the term structure. By studying these theories, you will come to a better understanding of how securities markets work and why prices and yields change.

THE EXPECTATION THEORY

The expectation theory holds that the shape of the yield curve is determined by the investors' expectations of future interest rate movements and that changes in these expectations change the shape of the yield curve.[1] The expectation theory is "idealized" because it assumes that investors are profit maximizers and that they have no preference between holding a long-term security and holding a series of short-term securities; that is, they are indifferent toward interest rate risk (or *risk neutral*). Nonetheless, economists believe the theory helps explain the shape of the yield curve.

To see how changing expectations of interest rate movements can alter the slope of the yield curve, let's look at an example. Suppose that an investor has a 2-year investment horizon and that only 1-year bonds and 2-year bonds are available for purchase. Because both types of securities currently yield 6 percent, the prevailing term structure is flat, as indicated by the yield curve shown below.

Now suppose that new economic information becomes available and investors *expect* interest rates on 1-year securities to rise to 12 percent within a year. This information, for example, might be an announcement by the Fed that it is targeting higher interest rates. Note that the 12 percent rate is a **forward rate** in that it is the interest rate that will exist 1 year in the future. Given this new information, what portfolio of bonds should profit-maximizing, risk-neutral investors hold?

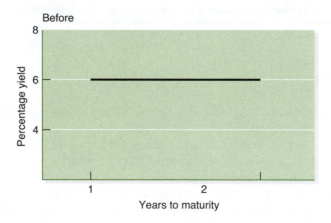

Under such circumstances, investors would want to buy 1-year bonds and sell any 2-year bonds they might own. Why? First, who would want to invest in long-term bonds and lock in the prevailing 6 percent yield when interest rates are

[1]The expectation theory was first stated by Irving Fisher (see Chapter 4, People & Events) and was further developed by the British Nobel laureate in economics, Sir John Hicks.

expected to rise to 12 percent in the future? Most investors would prefer to buy short-term securities, wait for interest rates to rise, and then buy long-term bonds and lock in the higher interest rate.

To invest over a 2-year investment horizon, a profit-maximizing investor in our example would examine the alternatives of (1) buying a 2-year bond or (2) buying two successive 1-year bonds. The investor would then select the alternative with the highest yield over the 2-year holding period. Specifically, if an investor buys a 1-year bond that currently yields 6 percent and at the end of the year buys another 1-year bond expected to yield 12 percent, the average expected holding-period yield for the 2-year period is 9 percent [$\frac{1}{2}$(6 + 12)]. (To keep things simple, we ignore interest-on-interest in the second year.) Alternatively, if the investor purchases a 2-year security, the 2-year holding-period yield is only 6 percent. Naturally, profit-maximizing investors begin to buy 1-year bonds, driving their price up and yield down. Simultaneously, investors sell 2-year bonds, driving their price down and yield up. The net effect of this portfolio adjustment is to shift the prevailing yield curve from flat to ascending, as shown in the following yield curve:

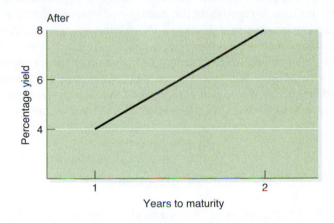

The process of buying 1-year bonds and selling 2-year bonds continues until any differential in expected returns over the 2-year investment period is eliminated. That condition *could* occur when the yields on 1-year securities equal 4 percent, the 2-year securities yield 8 percent, and the 1-year forward rate remains 12 percent. With this term structure, an investor who purchases a 2-year bond has a 2-year holding-period yield of 8 percent. This is identical to the investor who purchases a 4 percent 1-year security and then reinvests the proceeds at the end of the first year in the bonds expected to yield 12 percent. The expected yield for this strategy is 8 percent = [$\frac{1}{2}$(4 + 12)]. This is an equilibrium condition because under either alternative the investor's average holding-period return is the same. That is, investors are indifferent between the yield on a 2-year security and the average holding-period yield they can earn when investing in two successive 1-year securities.

THE TERM STRUCTURE FORMULA

Although simplified, the example in the preceding section illustrates that investors can trade among securities of different maturities and, if they are profit maximizers, obtain an equilibrium return across the entire spectrum of maturities. This implies a formal relationship between long- and short-term interest rates. Specifically, the long-term rate of interest is a geometric average of the current short-term interest rate and a series of expected short-term forward rates. More formally, the yield on a bond maturing n years from now is

$$(1 + {}_tR_n) = [(1 + {}_tR_1)(1 + {}_{t+1}f_1)(1 + {}_{t+2}f_1)\ldots(1 + {}_{t+n-1}f_1)]^{1/n} \quad (6.1)$$

where:

R = the observed (spot or actual) market interest rate
f = the forward, or future, interest rate
t = time period for which the rate is applicable
n = maturity of the bond

The postscript identifies the maturity (n) of the security, and the prescript represents the time period in which the security originates (t). Thus, ${}_tR_1$ is the actual market rate of interest on a 1-year security today (time t), also called the **spot rate**; similarly, ${}_tR_{10}$ is the current market rate of interest for a 10-year security. For the forward rates, the prescript still identifies the time period in which the security originates, but now it represents the number of years in the future; thus ${}_{t+1}f_1$ refers to the 1-year interest rate 1 year in the future; likewise, ${}_{t+2}f_1$ is the 1-year interest rate 2 years from now, and so on.

Do not panic—the geometric average is not as difficult to apply as it looks. Let's consider an example. Suppose the current 1-year rate is 6 percent. Furthermore, the market expects the 1-year rate a year from now to be 8 percent and the 1-year rate 2 years from now to be 10 percent. Using our notation,

$${}_tR_1 = 6 \text{ percent}$$
$${}_{t+1}f_1 = 8 \text{ percent}$$
$${}_{t+2}f_1 = 10 \text{ percent}$$

Given the market's expectation of future interest rates, we can calculate the current 3-year rate of interest by applying Equation 6.1:

$$(1 + {}_tR_3) = [(1.06)(1.08)(1.10)]^{1/3}$$
$${}_tR_3 = 1.0799$$
$${}_tR_3 = 0.0799, \text{ or } 7.99\%$$

Notice that an investor with a 3-year investment horizon will be indifferent about buying a 3-year security yielding 7.99 percent or three successive 1-year securities that also yield, on average, 7.99 percent.[2]

---

[2]For students who have difficulty understanding the behavioral implications of Equation 6.1, the geometric mean can be approximated with the following simpler arithmetic mean formula:

$${}_tR_n = \frac{1}{n}[{}_tR_1 + {}_{t+1}f_1 + {}_{t+2}f_1 \ldots {}_{t+n-1}f_1]$$

For our example,

$${}_tR_3 = \frac{1}{3}[6 + 8 + 10] = 8.0\%.$$

However, keep in mind that this approximation ignores the interest-on-interest.

The reason for developing Equation 6.1 was not to dazzle you with mathematical footwork but to show how investors' expectations of future interest rates determine the shape of the yield curve. For example, when short-term interest rates are expected to rise in the future (as in our previous example), the yield curve is upward sloping. This must be true because the long-term interest rate is an average of the current and the future expected short-term interest rates. Likewise, if the market expects future short-term interest rates to decrease, the yield curve is downward sloping. If no change is expected in future short-term rates, the yield curve is flat. The behavioral implications of the yield curve from the expectation theory are as follows:

Expected Interest Rate Movement	Observed Yield Curve
Market expects interest rates to increase	Upward sloping
Market expects interest rates to decline	Downward sloping
Market expects interest rates to stay the same	Flat

USING THE TERM STRUCTURE FORMULA TO CALCULATE IMPLIED FORWARD RATES

Under the expectations hypothesis, it is possible to calculate the forward interest rates implied by a set of spot interest rates. Suppose, for example, we know that the 1-year spot rate ($_tR_1$) is 6 percent, the 2-year spot rate ($_tR_2$) is 8 percent, and the 3-year spot rate ($_tR_3$) is 10 percent. Using this information, we can calculate the forward rates on a 1-year bond originating 1 year from now ($_{t+1}f_1$) and a 1-year bond originating 2 years from now ($_{t+2}f_1$). All we need to remember is that Equation 6.1 holds when the bond market is in equilibrium.

To find the **implied forward rate** on a 1-year bond originating 1 year in the future, set up Equation 6.1 as follows:

$$(1 + {_tR_2})^2 = (1 + {_tR_1})(1 + {_{t+1}f_1})$$

Substituting the known information, we obtain

$$(1.08)^2 = (1.06)(1 + {_{t+1}f_1})$$

Simplify and solve for $_{t+1}f_1$

$$_{t+1}f_1 = (1.1664/1.06) - 1 = 0.1004\,(10.04\%)$$

Thus, the set of spot rates implies that investors expect the 1-year interest rate 1 year from now to be 10.04 percent.

Similarly, we can solve for the implied forward rate on a 1-year bond originating 2 years from now using the information in the 2- and 3-year spot rates:

$$(1.10)^3 = (1.08)^2(1 + {_{t+1}f_1})$$

Solving for $_{t+2}f_1$, we obtain 14.11 percent. Thus, you can see the relationship between spot rates and forward rates.

In general, we can find the forward rate implied by two spot rates of adjacent maturities with the following formula, which is a straightforward simplification of Equation 6.1:

$$[(1 + {}_tR_n)^n/(1 + {}_tR_{n-1})^{n-1}] - 1 = {}_{t+n-1}f_1 \tag{6.2}$$

LEARNING BY DOING 6.1

Using the Term Structure Formula to Calculate Implied Forward Rates

PROBLEM: Suppose, for example, we know that the 1-year spot rate is 6 percent, the 2-year spot rate is 8 percent, and the 3-year spot rate is 10 percent. Calculate the forward rates on a 1-year bond originating 1 year from now and a 1-year bond originating 2 years from now.

APPROACH: You can solve this problem using Equation. 6.1 or Equation 6.2. Recognize that the 1-year spot rate can be designated as ${}_0R_1$, the 2-year spot rate as ${}_0R_2$, and the 3-year spot rate as ${}_0R_3$. You have been asked to compute the forward rates on a 1-year bond originating 1 year from now (${}_1f_1$) and a 1-year bond originating 2 years from now (${}_2f_1$).

SOLUTION: To find the implied forward rate on a 1-year bond originating 1 year in the future, set up Equation 6.1 as follows. Starting with the Equation 6.1, we have $n = 2$, and $t = 0$. Using our notation, the 2-year spot rate is ${}_0R_2 = 8$ percent and the 1-year spot rate is ${}_0R_1 = 6$ percent, and we solve for the implied 1-year forward rate ${}_1f_1$. We start by stating Equation 6.1 and modify for the equation as appropriate. Note the key to our solution is that we use two spot rates of adjacent maturity to solve for the forward rate.

$$(1 + {}_tR_n) = [(1 + {}_tR_1)(1 + {}_{t+1}f_1)(1 + {}_{t+2}f_1) \ldots (1 + {}_{t+n-1}f_1)]^{1/n}$$
$$(1 + {}_0R_2) = [(1 + {}_0R_1)(1 + {}_1f_1)]^{1/2}$$
$$(1.08) = [(1.06)(1 + {}_1f_1)]^{1/2}$$
$$(1 + {}_1f_1) = \frac{(1.08)^2}{(1.06)} = 1.10$$
$${}_1f_1 = 10\%$$

Thus, the set of spot rates implies that investors expect the 1-year interest rate 1 year from now to be 10 percent.

Similarly, we can solve for the implied forward rate on a 1-year bond originating 2 years from now using the information in the 2- and 3-year spot rates, ${}_0R_3 = 10$ percent and ${}_0R_2 = 8$ percent, and solving for the implied 1-year forward rate 2 years from now, ${}_2f_1$.

$$(1 + {}_0R_3) = [(1 + {}_0R_2)^2(1 + {}_2f_1)]^{1/3}$$
$$(1.10)^3 = [(1.08)^2(1 + {}_2f_1)]$$
$$(1 + {}_2f_1) = \frac{(1.10)^3}{(1.08)^2} = 1.14$$
$${}_2f_1 = 14\%$$

Solving for the 1-year forward rate 2 years from now, we obtain 14 percent. In the next section, we develop a general formula to compute the forward rate using a set of adjacent spot rates.

EXHIBIT 6.2
The Effect of Liquidity Premiums on the Yield Curve

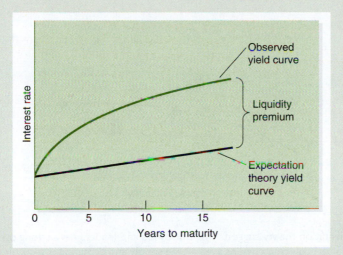

Liquidity premiums increase as maturity increases. Thus, liquidity premiums cause an upward slope in market yield curves.

TERM STRUCTURE AND LIQUIDITY PREMIUMS

We have seen that the expectation theory assumes that investors are indifferent about purchasing long-term or short-term securities. However, this usually is not true. Investors know from experience that short-term securities provide greater marketability (more active secondary markets) and have smaller price fluctuations (price risk) than do long-term securities. As a result, borrowers who seek long-term funds to finance capital projects must pay lenders a **liquidity premium** to purchase riskier long-term securities. Thus, the yield curve must have a liquidity premium added to it. The liquidity premium increases as maturity increases because the longer the maturity of a security, the greater its price risk and the less marketable the security. The liquidity premium therefore causes the observed yield curve to be more upward sloping than that predicted by the expectation theory. Exhibit 6.2 illustrates this effect.

THE MARKET-SEGMENTATION AND PREFERRED-HABITAT THEORIES

The **market-segmentation theory**, which differs sharply from the expectation approach, maintains that market participants have strong preferences for securities of a particular maturity, and that they buy and sell securities consistent with these maturity preferences. As a result, the yield curve is determined by the supply of and the demand for securities at or near a particular maturity. Investors who desire short-term securities such as commercial banks, determine the short-term yield curve; investors with preferences for intermediate maturities determine the intermediate-term yield curve; and investors who prefer long-term securities, such as pension funds and life insurance companies, determine the long-term

EXHIBIT 6.3
Market-Segmentation Yield Curve

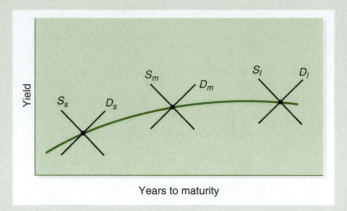

Market-segmentation theory suggests that borrowers and lenders have strong preferences for securities of a particular maturity. As a result, the supply and demand for securities at or near a particular maturity determine the yield for that maturity.

Note: Supply (*S*) and demand (*D*) for *s* = short-term maturities, *m* = intermediate-term maturities, and *l* = long-term maturities.

yield curve. On the supply side, security issuers tailor the maturities of their security offerings to the length of time they need the borrowed funds (see Exhibit 6.3). Thus, the market-segmentation theory assumes that both issuers and investors have a preference for securities with a narrow maturity range. Changes in interest rates in one segment of the yield curve, therefore, have little effect on interest rates in other maturities. Under the segmentation theory, discontinuities in the yield curve are possible. The segmentation theory is extreme because it assumes that certain investors are almost completely risk averse, which means that they do not shift the maturity of their holdings in exchange for higher yields.

The preferred-habitat theory extends the segmentation theory and explains why we do not observe discontinuities in the yield curve. The **preferred-habitat theory** asserts that investors will not hold debt securities outside their preferred habitat (maturity preference) without an additional reward in the form of a risk premium. Holding longer-term assets than desired exposes the investor to price risk, and holding shorter-term assets than desired exposes the investor to reinvestment risk; thus, leaving one's preferred habitat requires compensation for the additional risk. Unlike market-segmentation theory, the preferred-habitat theory does not assume that investors are completely risk averse; instead, it allows investors to reallocate their portfolios in response to expected yield premiums. The preferred-habitat theory can explain humps or twists in the yield curve but does not allow for discontinuities in the yield curve, as would be possible under the segmentation theory.

WHICH THEORY IS RIGHT?

Available evidence is not sufficiently persuasive to establish any one theory as being totally correct in explaining the term structure of interest rates. Market participants tend to favor the preferred-habitat theory, whereas economists tend to favor the expectation and liquidity premium approaches. Day-to-day changes in the term structure reveal patterns that are most consistent with the preferred-habitat theory. Changes in interest rates in one segment of the maturity spectrum appear not to be transmitted immediately to other segments. Furthermore, yield curves are not always smooth. For longer periods of time, such as month to month, interest rate changes in one maturity segment appear to be transmitted throughout the yield curve and yield curves appear relatively smooth. These observations are consistent with most published studies on the term structure that support the role of liquidity premiums and expectations of interest rates as important components of any interpretation of the term structure.

YIELD CURVES AND THE BUSINESS CYCLE

The *yield curve* is an analytical tool widely used by financial analysts and managers of financial institutions. As we previously discussed, the term structure of interest rates provides information about the market's expectations of future business activity. If the yield curve is upward sloping, it suggests that market participants believe that interest rates will increase in the future. Because interest rates and the business cycle are procyclical, increasing interest rates imply that market participants expect a period of economic expansion. The relationship between the yield curve and the business cycle is shown in Exhibit 6.4.

EXHIBIT 6.4
Interest Rate and Yield Curve Patterns over the Business Cycle

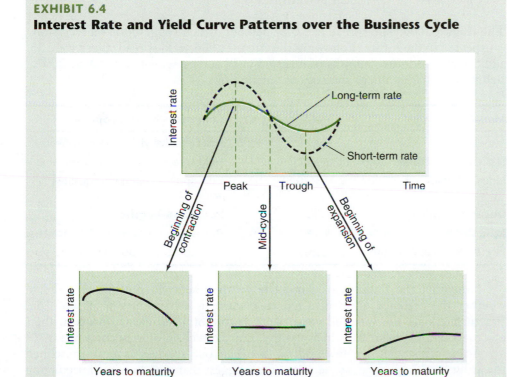

Yield curves are typically upward sloping during periods of economic expansion and turn downward when the economy begins to contract.

Similarly, if the yield curve is downward sloping, the market expects interest rates to decline in the future and therefore expects slower economic growth. In fact, descending yield curves are common near the final phase of a period of economic expansion. This fact has led many practitioners to believe that inverted yield curves can predict recessions. Although it is true that inverted yield curves have preceded many recessions during the postwar period, it can also be said that inverted yield curves have predicted more recessions than have actually occurred. In other words, this rule of thumb is not infallible.

Predicting Recessions.   The model used by practitioners to identify *inverted yield curves* computes the **yield spread (YS)** between the 10-year and 3-month Treasury securities or, alternatively, uses the fed funds rate as the short-term interest rate. To illustrate the process, we gathered the appropriate interest rate data for the 2007–2009 recession. The recession began during December 2007 and ended June 2009, lasting 18 months. It was the longest and most severe recession for the United States since the Great Depression.

We scanned the data to see if there were any inverted yield curves prior to December 2007. The first inverted yield curve appeared in August 2006. The yield spread calculation is shown below:

$$
\begin{aligned}
\text{Yield spread} &= \text{10-year Treasury yield} - \text{3-month Treasury yield} \\
&= 4.88 \text{ percent} - 5.09 \text{ percent} \\
&= -0.21 \text{ percent}^3
\end{aligned}
$$

The August 2006 yield spread is −0.21 percent, which suggests that a recession is expected in the future. Following the August 2006 yield spread, there were 15 additional consecutive months of inverted yield curves, which ended May 2007. Below are some summary statistics of our finding:

Month/Year	Yield Spread (%)	Comments on Yield Spreads
August 2006	−0.21	First negative yield spread appears.
September 2006/May 2007	−0.21/−0.12	Yield spreads have negative values.
June 2007/November 2007	0.36/0.80	Yield spread switches to positive values.
December 2007	**1.03**	**Recession begins.**
June 2009	**3.54**	**Recession ends after 18 months.**
July 2009/December 2009	2.35/2.39	Yield spreads all positive values.

Note that the findings of our ad hoc experiment do nothing to validate whether the presence of an inverted yield curve is a harbinger of a recession. Practitioners see the inverted yield curve as one of a number of tools in their macroeconomic toolkit to help assess the future direction of the economy.

Academic studies are few and far between but are less favorably inclined toward its use. In general, academic studies suggest that you do as well predicting

[3]The data come from the Federal Reserve Board of Governors: H.15 Statistical Release—Selected Interest Rates—various issues. The yield curves were constructed from monthly Treasury security yields figures generated by the Fed from daily yield values. The monthly yield data eliminate much of the random shock/white noise in the yield-spread computation.

recessions by chance (flipping a coin) as looking for inverted yield curves. One interesting finding is that inverted yield curves tend to overpick the number of recessions, but they rarely miss picking a recession.

Predicting Interest Rates. Everyone wants to predict the future. Some practitioners believe that the shape of the yield curve, which contains implicit consensus forecasts of future interest rates, can be used to predict the direction of interest rate movements and, hence, future economic activity. This subject is highly technical and controversial, with little agreement among practitioners.

To put the yield-curve prediction issue in perspective, yield curves do provide information about market expectations of future interest rate movements or business activity. As with any expectations, however, they may not be realized. The yield curve observed at any point in time represents the market's best interpretation of the economic data available. As new information becomes available, expectations are revised.

YIELD CURVES AND FINANCIAL INTERMEDIARIES

The slope of the yield curve is important in managing financial intermediaries such as commercial banks, credit unions, mutual savings banks, and finance companies. These and other intermediaries borrow funds in financial markets from surplus spending units and, after intermediation, lend the funds to businesses and consumers.

An upward-sloping yield curve is generally favorable for these institutions because they borrow most of their funds in the short term (transaction accounts and time deposits) and lend the funds at longer maturities, such as consumer loans, automobile loans, and home mortgages. For example, a bank borrows from consumers at 3 percent and makes 5-year automobile loans for 5 percent; the bank's gross profit margin is 2 percent (5 − 3). Clearly, the more steeply the yield curve slopes upward, the wider the *spread* between the borrowing and lending rates and the greater the profit for the financial intermediaries. At the beginning of a period of economic expansion, interest rates tend to be low and the yield curve is upward sloping.

When yield curves begin to flatten out or slope downward, different portfolio management strategies are called for. As the yield curve begins to flatten out, profits are squeezed, and management must institute a number of cost reduction measures to rein in costs to help restore profitability. Typical tactics are to reduce headcount, shorten banking hours, increase fee-based income, and eliminate the free coffee and doughnuts to customers in the lobby.

If the yield curve is near the top of the business cycle and is downward sloping, financial institutions typically try to shorten the maturity of their liabilities (sources of funds), thereby avoiding locking in relatively expensive sources of funds for a longer period of time; simultaneously, financial institutions try to lengthen the maturity of their loans. The key strategy here is to get borrowers to lock in relatively high borrowing rates for long periods of time in anticipation that interest rates will decline in the future.

Continuing our example, assume that we are now at the top of the business cycle: Interest rates are higher and the yield curve is inverted. Say that consumer deposit rates are now at $6\frac{1}{2}$ percent and 5-year auto loans are at 6 percent; the bank's gross margin is now a negative $\frac{1}{2}$ percent (6 − $6\frac{1}{2}$). This is bad news. However, if bank management believes that, in the short run, interest rates will return to their normal level (our original rate structure), they should continue to make auto loans at $6^1/_2$ percent. Then, when interest rates decline as expected, consumer funds will cost the bank 3 percent, and the bank's gross profit margin on its portfolio of auto loans will be close to 3 percent $(6 - 3)$. However, if interest rates do not decline, or worse, rise even higher, the bank could be in serious financial trouble. Our discussion of how the management of financial intermediaries reacts to changes in the yield curve over the business cycles is summarized next:

Business Cycle	Yield Curve Slope	Interest Rates	Strategy
Beginning of expansion	Upward	Low	Borrow short term. Lend long term.
Mid-cycle	Flat	High	Profits are squeezed. Implement cost reduction strategies.
Beginning of contraction	Downward	Higher	Shorten maturity of liabilities. Lengthen maturity of loans.

DO YOU UNDERSTAND?

1. If you know interest rates are going to rise in the future, would you rather own a long- or a short-term bond? Explain.

2. Suppose the spot rate on 4-year bonds is 11 percent and the spot rate on 5-year bonds is 12 percent. What forward rate is implied on a 1-year bond delivered 4 years from now?

3. What bond portfolio adjustments would investors make if interest rates are expected to decline in the future? How do these adjustments cause the yield curve to change?

4. How does the existence of a liquidity premium affect the shape of the yield curve?

5. Under the market-segmentation theory, why do investors not shift their holdings into the securities with the highest returns? Under the preferred-habitat theory, what is necessary for investors to shift their holdings away from their preferred maturities?

6.2 DEFAULT RISK

A debt security includes a formal promise by the borrower to pay the lender coupon payments and principal payments according to a predetermined schedule. Failure on the part of the borrower to meet any condition of the bond contract constitutes **default**. **Default risk** refers to the possibility of not collecting the promised amount of interest or principal at the agreed time.

It is believed that most investors are risk averse in that, if the expected returns from two investments are identical except for risk, investors prefer the security whose return is most certain. Therefore, to induce investors to purchase securities

EXHIBIT 6.5
Risk Premiums for Selected Corporate Bonds (2011)

Bond Ratings	Security Yield (%)	Equivalent Risk-Free Rate (%)*	Risk Premium (%)
Aaa	4.11	3.39	0.72
Aa	4.75	3.39	1.36
A	4.77	3.39	1.38
Baa	6.09	3.39	2.70

*10-year Treasury note yield.

Source: Federal Reserve Board of Governors, H.15 Statistical Release and Securities Industry and Fianancial Markets.

that possess default risk, borrowers must compensate lenders for the potential financial injury they may incur by purchasing risky securities. A security's default risk can be measured as the difference between the rate paid on a risky security and the rate paid on a default-free security, with all factors other than default risk being held constant.

The **default risk premium** may be expressed as

$$DRP = i - i_{rf} \qquad (6.3)$$

where DRP is the default risk premium, i is the promised yield to maturity on the security, and i_{rf} is the yield on a comparable default-free security. Yields on U.S. Treasury securities are the best estimates for the default-free rate. The larger the default risk premium, the higher the probability of default and the higher the security's market yield.

Market default risk premiums can be computed by comparing Treasury securities with risky securities of similar term to maturity and other issue characteristics. Exhibit 6.5 shows some typical risk premiums for corporate bonds of different credit quality. For example, the 72 basis-point default risk premium on Aaa-rated corporate bonds represents the market consensus of the amount of compensation that investors must be paid to induce them to buy risky bonds instead of default-free bonds (100 basis points = 1 percent). Also notice that as credit quality declines, the default risk premium increases.

Default risk premiums are not abstract notions, as can be attested by those who owned Penn Central debt securities when that company declared bankruptcy in June 1970. That bankruptcy was the largest corporate failure in American financial history at that time; it has since been eclipsed by many subsequent failures, including Enron ($63 billion in assets), Worldcom ($104 billion), and Conseco ($61 billion).

DEFAULT RISK AND THE BUSINESS CYCLE

Default risk premiums, as shown in Exhibit 6.6, vary systematically over the business cycle. They tend to widen during periods of economic decline and narrow during periods of economic expansion.

EXHIBIT 6.6
Default Risk Premiums (Yield Spreads Between Corporate and U.S. Treasury Notes)

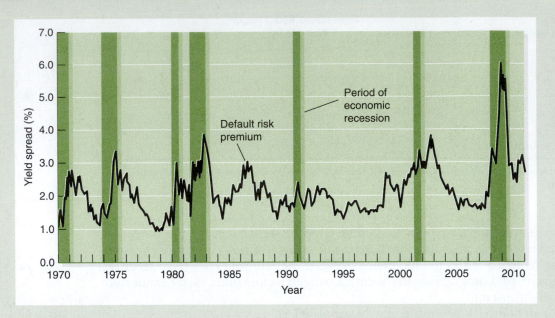

Notice that the default risk premium increases during periods of economic contraction and decreases during periods of economic expansion. Also notice that default risk premiums tend to peak near the end of a recession.

Note: Shaded ares indicate periods of economic recession. Corporate bonds are Baa rated. Treasury securities are 10-year notes.
Source: Federal Reserve Board of Governors, H.15 Statistical Release.

The pattern of behavior for default risk premiums is attributable to changes in investor willingness to own bonds of different credit ratings over the business cycle—the so-called **flight-to-quality** argument. Specifically, during periods of economic prosperity, investors are willing to hold bonds with low credit ratings in their portfolios because there is little chance of default, and these bonds normally have higher yields. During such times, investors tend to seek out the highest-yielding investments. However, during a recession, the prime concern of investors becomes safety. As a result, there is a flight to quality as investors adjust their portfolios—buying bonds with high credit ratings (low default risk) and selling from their portfolios bonds with low credit ratings. The increase in demand for high-grade bonds drives their price up and their yield down; correspondingly, a decrease in demand for bonds with low credit ratings drives their price down and their yield up. The result is the increase in default risk premiums during periods of economic recession.

BOND RATINGS

Bond ratings are published rankings of bonds based on relative default risk. Three major firms on Wall Street do bond ratings: Moody's Investors Service (Moody's), Standard & Poor's (S&P), and Fitch. All three agencies rank bonds in order of their perceived probability of default and publish the ratings as letter

EXHIBIT 6.7
Corporate Bond Rating Systems

Explanation	Moody's	Standard & Poor's/Fitch	Default Risk Premium
Best quality, smallest degree of risk	Aaa	AAA	Lowest
High quality, slightly more long-term risk than top rating	Aa	AA	—
Upper-medium grade, possible impairment in the future	A	A	—
Medium grade, lack outstanding investment characteristics	Baa	BBB	—
Speculative issues, protection may be very moderate	Ba	BB	—
Very speculative, may have small assurance of interest and principal payments	B	B	—
Issues in poor standing, may be in default	Caa	CCC	—
Speculative in a high degree, with marked shortcomings	Ca	CC	—
Lowest quality, poor prospects of attaining real investment standing	C	C	Highest

Investment-grade bonds are those rated Baa or above by Moody's (or BBB by Standard & Poor's and Fitch). Bonds below Baa are speculative grade. Financial institutions are typically allowed to purchase only investment grade.

Note: Moody's applies the modifiers 1, 2, and 3 to the ratings Aa to Caa, with a 1 indicating the issue is in the higher end of its rating, a 2 indicating it is in the mid-range, and a 3 indicating it is in the lower end. Similarly, Standard & Poor's and Fitch modify their ratings AA to CCC, with a + or − to indicate when an issue is in the higher or lower end of its rating category.

grades. The rating schemes they use are shown in Exhibit 6.7. The highest-grade bonds, those with the lowest default risk, are rated Aaa (AAA). As the default risk premium on the bonds increases, the bond rating becomes lower and lower. As shown in Exhibit 6.7, a bond rated Aa has a higher default risk premium than a bond rated Aaa, and a bond rated A has a higher default risk premium than a bond rated Aa, and so on. Individual investors and other retail customers of securities firms are the primary users of bond ratings. They do not have the skill to analyze a firm's credit standing and want credit information from an independent third party. Wholesale customers such as large corporations and the wealthy do their own credit analyses and therefore do not use the services of credit agencies.

Bonds rated in the top four rating categories—Aaa to Baa for Moody's and AAA to BBB for Standard & Poor's and Fitch—are called **investment-grade bonds.** Bonds rated below Baa (or BBB) are called **speculative-grade bonds** or **junk bonds.** The distinction between investment grade and speculative grade is huge because state and federal laws require commercial banks, insurance companies, pension funds, and other financial institutions to purchase only securities rated as investment grade.

Important questions to ask are how bond credit ratings do as a measure of default risk and whether investment-grade bonds have fewer defaults than bonds ranked below investment grade. Shown below is the percentage of bond issues that defaulted over the last 35 years.[4] The first column shows the bond rating at

---

[4]*Source:* U.S. Municipal Fairness Act, September 9, 2008.

the time the bond issue was sold. Notice that as bond credit quality decreases, the percentage of bonds defaulting increases monotonically. That is, 0.60 percent of the AAA-rated bonds defaulted over the 35-year period, 1.50 percent of the AA-rated bonds defaulted, 2.91 percent of the A-rated bonds defaulted, and so on. We conclude that bond credit ratings do a reasonable job of ranking bonds with respect to their underlying credit quality.

Rating at Time of Issue	Default Rate (%)
AAA	0.60
AA	1.50
A	2.91
BBB	10.29
BB	29.93
B	53.72
CCC	69.19

The default rates for investment-grade bonds—those ranked BBB or better—were significantly lower than any of the non-investment-grade categories. For example, the default rate on BBB-rated bonds, which is the lowest investment grade rank, was 10.29 percent, the default rate on BB-rated bonds—one ranking notch lower but speculative grade—was 29.93 percent, and the default rate for CCC-rated bonds was 69.19 percent. Overall, we conclude that bond ratings are a reasonable measure of default risk and that speculative-grade bonds have substantially more default risk than bonds rated investment grade.

HOW CREDIT RATINGS ARE DETERMINED

Moody's Investors Services (Moody's), Standard & Poor's (S&P), and Fitch Ratings (Fitch) are the main credit-rating agencies. Collectively, they provide almost all corporate and municipal debt credit ratings each year. The credit rating of a firm's debt is a measure of the firm's default risk in the opinion of the rating agency. In making this determination, bond-rating agencies consider a number of factors when assigning a bond rating. Among the most important are (1) the firm's expected cash flow; (2) the amount of the firm's fixed contractual cash payments, such as interest and principal payments or lease payments; (3) the length of time the firm has been profitable; and (4) the variability of the firm's earnings. Once a bond rating is assigned to a particular issue, the rating is periodically reviewed by the rating agency and is subject to change.

To give you an idea of how bond ratings work, we briefly describe the credit-rating process of Moody's. A first-time rating begins with a request from the debt issuer. The process starts with an introductory meeting in which Moody's discusses its procedures and the specific types of data most useful in understanding the credit quality of the issuer. Moody's does not do an exhaustive analysis of the issuer; instead, it focuses on elements relevant to the long-term and short-term credit risk of the issuer. An analytical meeting with the issuer's senior management follows the initial meeting.

The Credit-Rating Club

Following the Enron bankruptcy on December 2, 2001, credit-rating agencies found themselves under attack by investors and the target of congressional ire. What attracted all of the attention was the failure of the credit-rating agencies to recognize the extent of Enron's financial problems and the slow pace at which they downgraded the energy trader in its final months. Despite growing questions about its partnerships and other irregular deals, the rating agencies still had Enron at an investment-grade credit rating just 4 days before its final implosion!

As it turns out, only three credit-rating agencies are authorized by federal banking regulators and the Securities and Exchange Commission (SEC) to appraise the creditworthiness of corporate and government bond issues, creating a troika that wields enormous influence over the investment decisions of financial institutions and individual investors. How did this cozy arrangement come about, and what problems has it created?

The three credit-rating agencies—Moody's, Standard & Poor's, and Fitch—owe their elite status to two regulatory decrees. In 1936, the Comptroller of the Currency decreed that banks could hold only investment-grade securities, and the responsibility to assess default risk was delegated to credit-rating agencies. Other regulatory agencies followed suit, and soon insurance companies, mutual funds, and other financial institutions had to pay attention to bond ratings.

The result was that any company, municipality, or government unit that wanted access to the U.S. capital markets needed a credit rating, preferably an investment-grade rating, which is BBB or above. Further strengthening the position of the three rating agencies was a ruling in 1975 by the SEC that brokerage firms had to discount below-investment-grade bonds when calculating their assets, and that the bond rating had to come from an approved "nationally recognized statistical rating organization."

Criticism of the credit-rating agencies runs deep, and it is not new. Critics charge that the rating agencies are slow to downgrade a firm's credit standing and often fail to recognize firms that are in serious financial trouble before they default. Over the years, the demise of many large business firms has played out in a pattern of events similar to that of Enron, and some firms even retained their investment-grade status on the day they declared bankruptcy. Not helping matters politically have been the exceptionally high profits that the three franchise players have been able to extract from the market. Moody's recently released its earnings for the first time ever, and its 50 percent operating margin left little doubt why other firms would like to get into the rating business.

Critics argue that allowing additional credit-rating firms to expand the troika would increase competition, resulting in better, more accurate, and more timely credit ratings. The jolt of competition, they claim, would also stimulate more innovative solutions to problems. Other critics have suggested that the special status of rating agencies should be abolished altogether. They would put the responsibility of determining the creditworthiness of a bank's bond portfolio back on banks and bank regulators. Individual investors would then purchase bond credit ratings, if they desired, from any crediting agency they deemed to be reputable. Some suggest that ratings could be replaced by *credit spreads*—the difference between a yield on the security being evaluated and the yield on a risk-free security of similar maturity, such as a Treasury security.

Despite all the carping, it is probably unlikely that bank regulators or the SEC will dismantle the current regulatory structure and open up the gates to all comers. Regulators' biggest fear is that issuers would shop around for the highest credit rating. Furthermore, to gain the status and reputation to rate firms would require a substantial amount of capital and time. Small niche players would have little impact on the credit-rating market, and they are also vulnerable to market pressures. However, the threat of potential competition, bad publicity, and pressure from regulators has stimulated some changes by the major credit-rating agencies. More recently, they have been much more aggressive and quicker to downrate companies with deteriorating financial conditions. They also have begun using more sophisticated quantitative risk models that estimate the probability of default. These new models can be updated as new data become available.

The analytical meeting takes place at the issuer's headquarters and often takes as long as 2 days. Moody's focuses the meeting on five key subjects:

1. Background and history of the company
2. Corporate strategy and philosophy
3. Operating position—including competitive position, manufacturing capacity, distribution and supply networks, and marketing
4. Financial management and accounting policies
5. Other topics—derivatives usage, regulatory developments, investment opportunities, and major litigation

Through the discussion of these topics with senior management, Moody's develops an understanding of management's philosophy and plans for the future, which is considered a critical element of credit quality. The discussions also give senior management the chance to discuss the risks and opportunities of the firm that affect credit quality and outline their plans to address them.

The rating decision usually takes 4 to 6 weeks from the time of the analytical meeting, and the decision is made by a rating committee that analyzes all the information collected about the issuer. The committee generally has four or more members, including the lead industry analyst. When the committee makes its decision, it notifies the issuer of the rating and Moody's rationale for the rating. The rating is also distributed worldwide through the major financial media.

Obviously, the firm's default risk and thus its credit rating change over time. Because things change, Moody's continuously gathers information on all debt issuers that it has rated. When new information about an issuer suggests a possible change in default risk, Moody's forms a rating committee to review the issuer's credit rating. If the committee decides to change a credit rating, it notifies the issuer and the financial press.

From this process, it is obvious that there is not a right answer. Instead, credit rating requires expert analysts to reach an informed opinion about the default risk of the issuer. Also, for a rating to change, the new information about the issuer must be sufficient for the experts to change their opinion about the default risk of the issuer.

6.3 TAX TREATMENT

The interest rate most relevant to investors is the rate of return earned *after taxes*. Thus, the lower the taxes on the income from a security, the greater the demand for the security and the lower its before-tax yield. It is no surprise, therefore, that tax-exempt securities have lower market yields than similar taxable securities. Federal, state, and local governments impose a variety of taxes on income from securities, the most important of which is the federal income tax. Let us consider the effect that the tax structure has on the market yield of a security.

COUPON INCOME

All coupon income earned on state and local government debt is exempt from federal taxes. Thus, securities issued by state and local governments (called **municipal securities**) sell for lower market yields than comparable securities issued by the U.S. Treasury or private corporations. The exemption of coupon income from federal taxes stems from the separation of federal and state powers, and its primary purpose is to help state and local governments borrow at lower interest rates than would otherwise be possible.[5]

The decision by an investor to purchase either a taxable or a tax-exempt security depends on the relative yields between the two securities and the investor's marginal tax rate. To see how investors make this decision, consider the following example. Assume that the current yield-to-maturity on a taxable corporate bond is 10 percent, whereas the current tax-exempt yield on a municipal bond of comparable maturity and bond rating is 7 percent. The after-tax yield on the two securities can be compared using the following formula:

$$i_{at} = i_{bt}(1 - t) \tag{6.4}$$

where i_{at} is the after-tax yield on the security, i_{bt} is the before-tax yield, and t is the marginal tax rate of the investor. The equation assumes that the return on the securities is composed entirely of coupon income, with no capital gains. The after-tax yields on the two bonds are as follows for investors in a variety of different tax brackets:

Investors' Marginal Tax Rate (%)	Municipal Yield (%)	Corporate After-Tax Yield (%)
0	7	10 (1 − 0.00) = 10.0
10	7	10 (1 − 0.10) = 9.0
20	7	10 (1 − 0.20) = 8.0
30	7	10 (1 − 0.30) = 7.0
40	7	10 (1 − 0.40) = 6.0
50	7	10 (1 − 0.50) = 5.0

For example, an investor in the 20 percent tax bracket would buy a corporate security, because the after-tax return is 8 percent versus 7 percent for the municipal security. However, as the investor's marginal tax rate increases, the return on municipal securities becomes more favorable compared to the after-tax return on corporate bonds. An investor in the 40 percent tax bracket would prefer a tax-exempt security yielding 7 percent to the corporate security, for which the after-tax return is only 6 percent. The rule that emerges is that investors in high tax brackets, such as wealthy and fully taxed corporations (e.g., commercial banks), usually hold portfolios of municipal securities because of their higher after-tax yield compared to taxable securities of the same risk and maturity. In contrast, investors in lower tax brackets, such as persons with low incomes and tax-exempt institutions (e.g., pension funds), receive high after-tax yields from taxable securities because they pay fewer taxes. On a personal note, discussing your municipal

[5]During April 1988, the Supreme Court ruled that Congress is free to tax all coupon interest on state and local government bonds. Overturning a major 1895 precedent, the Court held that the Constitution does not protect state and local governments against federal taxation of interest received by a holder of municipal bonds. Currently, there is no movement in Congress to tax municipal bonds, but the potential to do so is now there. If the federal government were to tax municipal securities, it would most likely apply only to new bond issues and not to outstanding bonds.

EXHIBIT 6.8
Yields on Tax-Exempt and Taxable Securities

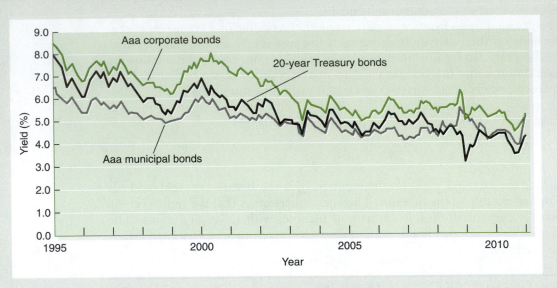

Because their coupon payments are tax exempt, the yields on municipal bonds are typically lower than the yields on similar taxable securities.

Source: Federal Reserve Board of Governors, H.15 Statistical Release.

bond portfolio at a cocktail party subtly identifies you as an upper-income person without your actually saying so.

Exhibit 6.8 illustrates how the differential tax treatment of long-term municipal bonds affects their yields relative to long-term corporate and Treasury bonds. As you can see from the exhibit, Aaa-rated municipal bonds have lower yields than either corporate bonds or Treasury bonds. It might seem odd that Aaa-rated municipal bonds have *lower* yields than those of Treasury bonds because municipal bonds have default risk and Treasury bonds do not. Don't forget, however, that the coupon income on Treasury bonds is subject to income tax, whereas municipal bonds are tax exempt. Apparently the tax benefit of owning the municipal bond offsets its increased default risk compared to the Treasury bond. Similarly, Aaa-rated municipal bonds have lower yields than Aaa corporate bonds because of the tax treatment of municipal bond income.

CAPITAL GAINS INCOME

From 1921 through 1986, long-term capital gains were taxed at substantially lower rates than ordinary income. For example, in 1986, long-term capital gains were taxed at 40 percent of the tax rate on ordinary income. During this period, taxable bonds trading at a discount from their par value had lower market yields than comparable bonds with coupon rates selling at or above par. The reason was that part of the income to the investor on the discounted bonds—the capital gain—was subject to the lower capital-gains tax rate. The tax law change that took effect in 1987 eliminated the tax differential, and thus capital-gains income was taxed as ordinary income. However, with the Taxpayer Relief Act of 1997 and the Reform Act of 1998, capital gains are once again taxed at a lower rate than ordinary income. Regardless of how the tax law treats capital gains relative to ordinary income, there is an advantage to capital gains in that the taxes are not paid until the gains are realized from the disposal of the security. Ordinary income such as coupon interest, however, is taxed on receipt. Because capital gains can be deferred, the present value of a capital-gains tax is less than an equivalent amount of ordinary income tax.

DO YOU UNDERSTAND?

1. Suppose the yield on a 30-year corporate bond rated Aaa is 8.86 percent and the yield on a 30-year Treasury bond is 8.27 percent. What is the default risk premium? Would you expect a higher or lower default risk premium on an A-rated bond?

2. How does the yield spread between Treasury bonds and risky corporate bonds vary over the business cycle? Can you provide a logical explanation for the cyclical behavior of the spread?

3. What factors do rating agencies consider when assigning bond ratings?

4. At what marginal tax rate would you be indifferent between an A-rated, 10-year corporate bond offering a yield of 10 percent and an A-rated, 10-year municipal bond offering a yield of 6 percent? Why does the municipal bond offer a lower rate if it has the same bond rating and maturity as the corporate bond?

6.4 MARKETABILITY

The interest rate on securities also varies with the degree of marketability. **Marketability** refers to the cost and quickness with which investors can resell a security. The greater the marketability of a security, the greater the demand for it and the lower its yield, all other characteristics, such as maturity, default risk, and tax treatment, held constant. Marketability depends on the costs of trade, physical transfer, search, and information. The lower these costs, the greater the security's marketability.

Marketability is often gauged by the volume of a security's secondary market. For example, short-term Treasury bills have the largest and most active secondary market and are considered to be the most marketable of all securities. Investors are able to sell virtually any dollar amount of Treasury securities quickly and without disrupting the market. Similarly, the securities of many other large, well-known issuers enjoy a high degree of marketability, especially those actively traded on the New York and American exchanges. For thousands of other securities not traded actively each day, however, marketability can pose a problem. The market for these may be confined to a region or a community. As a result, trading in them may occur infrequently, and it may be difficult to establish the securities' fair market price.

6.5 OPTIONS ON DEBT SECURITIES

Many bonds contain options that permit the borrower or lender to change the nature of the bond contract before maturity. More specifically, an *option* is a contract that gives the holder the right, but not the obligation, to buy or sell an asset at some specified price and date in the future. If the holder of the option has the right to buy the underlying security, the option is called a **call option** (**call provision**); if the holder has the right to sell the underlying security, the option is called a **put option**; and if the option holder has the right to convert the security into another type of security, the option is called a **conversion option**. Options that are traded separately from the underlying security are discussed in Chapter 11.

CALL OPTIONS

Most corporate and municipal bonds and some U.S. government bonds contain in their contracts a call option, or as it is often referred to, a *call provision*. A call option (or call provision) gives the bond issuer the option to buy back the bond at a specified price in advance of the maturity date. The price is known as the **call price**, and it is usually set at the bond's par value or slightly above par (usually 1 year's interest payment above par).

Bonds that contain a call option sell at a higher market yield than otherwise comparable noncallable bonds. The reason for the penalty yield on callable bonds is that the call option works to the benefit of the issuer (borrower) and to the detriment of investors. For example, if interest rates decline significantly below the coupon rate on a callable bond, the issuer can call (retire) the old bond issue and refinance it with a new one at a lower interest rate. The result of this action is that the issuer achieves an interest cost savings, but the investor is now forced to reinvest funds at the current lower market rate of interest, suffering a loss of interest income.

The difference in interest rates between callable and otherwise comparable noncallable bonds is known as the **call interest premium** and can be written as follows:

$$CIP = i_c - i_{nc} > 0 \tag{6.5}$$

where *CIP* is the call interest premium, i_c is the yield on a callable bond, and i_{nc} is the yield on a similar, noncallable bond. For proper comparison, the two bonds should be of similar default risk, term-to-maturity, tax treatment, and marketability. The *call interest premium*, therefore, is compensation paid to investors who own callable bonds for potential financial injury in the event their bonds are called. The greater the probability a particular bond will be called, the greater the call interest premium and the higher the bond's market yield. The call option is more likely to be exercised when interest rates are declining. Thus, the lower interest rates are expected to fall, the more valuable the option and, hence, the greater the *CIP*.

PUT OPTIONS

A *put option* allows an investor to sell a bond back (*put* the bond) to the issuer before maturity at a predetermined price. Investors typically exercise put options during periods when interest rates are rising and bond prices are declining. A put option sets a *floor*, or minimum price of a bond at the exercise price, which is generally at or below par value.

Because the put option is an advantage to investors, bonds that contain a put option sell at lower yields than comparable nonputable bonds. The reason for the lower yield is that investors can protect themselves against capital losses as a result of unexpected rises in interest rates. For example, if interest rates rise significantly above the coupon rate on a putable bond, the investor can sell (put) the bond back to the issuer at the exercise price (par or near par), then buy a new bond at the current market yield. The difference in yield between putable and similar nonputable bonds is called the **put interest discount** and can be expressed as follows:

$$PID = i_p - i_{np} < 0 \qquad (6.6)$$

where PID is the put interest discount, i_p is the yield on a putable bond, and i_{np} is the yield on a similar nonputable bond. The value of the put option depends on interest rate expectations; the higher interest rates are expected to rise, the more valuable the option and, hence, the greater the interest discount.

CONVERSION OPTION

Another factor that affects the yields on different securities is a conversion option. A *conversion option* allows the investor to convert a security into another type of security at a predetermined price. The most common type of conversion feature is the option to convert a bond into an issuer's stock; another popular option in volatile interest rate periods is the conversion of a variable-coupon bond into a fixed-coupon bond. The timing of the conversion is at the option of the investor. However, the terms under which the conversion may take place are agreed on when the security is purchased.

Because a conversion option is an advantage to investors, they pay higher prices (or require lower yields) for convertible securities. Thus, convertible bonds have lower yields than similar bonds without this option. This difference in yield is called the **conversion yield discount** and can be expressed as follows:

$$CYD = i_{con} - i_{ncon} < 0 \qquad (6.7)$$

where CYD is the conversion yield discount, i_{con} is the yield on a convertible bond, and i_{ncon} is the yield on a similar nonconvertible bond. The conversion yield discount is the price investors are willing to pay for the conversion option.

Convertible bonds have lower yields than similar nonconvertible bonds because the investor holding a convertible bond is granted a hedge against future risk. For example, if an investor owns a bond that is convertible into common stock and the stock price falls, the investor earns a fixed rate of return in the form of interest income from the bond. If the stock price rises sufficiently, the investor can exercise the option and earn a capital gain as the stock's current market price rises above the option's exercise price. Thus, the conversion option is most valuable during periods when stock market prices are rising and bond prices are declining.

For another example, suppose an investor owns a variable-coupon bond convertible into a fixed-coupon bond. If interest rates are rising, the investor would hold the variable-coupon bond and earn higher interest income as the coupon rates are adjusted upward in concert with the market rate of interest. Then, if the investor believes that interest rates are near their peak, the investor would exercise the option to convert into a fixed-coupon bond and thus lock in the higher rate of interest. The value of this conversion option depends on interest rate expectations; the higher interest rates are expected to rise, the more valuable the option and, hence, the greater the yield discount.

6.6 BEHAVIOR OF INTEREST RATES OVER THE BUSINESS CYCLE

In the final section on interest rates, we want to consolidate your knowledge of interest rates and examine some market data to explain how interest rates behave over the business cycle. Exhibit 6.9 plots the yield on the 10-year government bond since 1970 to represent nominal (or market) interest rate movements. In addition, we plotted the annual rate of inflation, represented by the annual percentage change in the Consumer Price Index (CPI). The CPI measures the goods and services that a typical family unit purchases during a year. Finally, the shaded areas on the chart identify time periods when the economy is in a recession. The shaded areas begin at the top of the business cycle and end at the bottom (or trough) of the recession.

EXHIBIT 6.9
Cyclical and Long-Term Trends in Interest Rates (1970–2011)

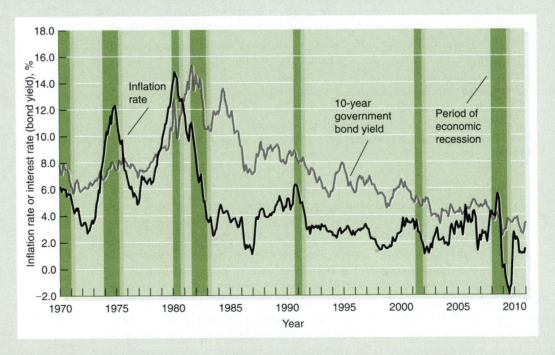

Three observations about interest rates can be drawn from the exhibit. First, the nominal (or market) rate of interest tends to rise and fall with the actual rate of inflation. This is consistent with the Fisher equation, suggesting that nominal interest rates rise and fall with the expected rate of inflation. Second, the nominal rate of interest tends to rise during periods of economic expansion and decline during economic contraction. Third, the real rate of interest is not directly observable unless prices are not expected to change; hence, price expectations are zero. During January 2009, inflation was zero and the 10-year Treasury rate was 2.52 percent. A value of 2.52 percent is a reasonable estimate for the real rate, given that the economy is in a recession and is consistent with the notion that the real rate varies with the business cycle.

Source: Federal Reserve Board of Governors, H.15 Statistical Release; www.inflationdata.com.

A recession is a business cycle contraction where macroeconomic indicators signal a slowdown in economic activity—gross domestic product (GPD), household incomes, business profits, consumer and business spending, and inflation all decline, while the unemployment rate and bankruptcies rise. Recessions typically occur when there is a precipitous decline in consumer and business spending, which is often followed by the bursting of an asset bubble, such as recently occurred in the real estate market, or an adverse supply shock, such as a spike in commodity or oil prices. In recent years, government remedies for recessions have primarily been monetary policy (increases in the money supply) and some mix of fiscal policy (increases in government spending and decreasing taxation).

Drawing on our discussion of the Federal Reserve System and of interest rates, we are able to reach some general conclusions:

- *The real rate of interest has historically averaged about 3 percent, rising during periods of business expansion and falling during periods of economic contraction (recession).* The real rate of interest is the fundamental long-term interest rate in the economy. The real rate focuses on investments in capital assets because they are the productive assets that create economic wealth in the economy. The underlying determinants of the real rate of interest are the return on capital projects and peoples' time preference for consumption. The real rate of interest measures the inflation-adjusted return earned by surplus spending units and represents the inflation-adjusted cost incurred by deficit spending units when they borrow to finance capital projects.

  The rate of interest observed in the marketplace is the nominal (or market) rate of interest. The real rate of interest is determined by the return on real assets; it is an interest rate determined in the absence of inflation. The real rate of interest is rarely the same as the nominal rate of interest, except at times when prices are not expected to change and thus price expectations are zero. The real rate usually cannot be observed directly.

  During the 2007–2009 recession, the economy briefly experienced a period of deflation, which is a decline in the prices of goods and services (see the 2007–2009 recession in Exhibit 6.9). Deflation should not be confused with disinflation, which is the slowing down in the rate of price increases. During January 2009, the rate of inflation was zero, thus the real and the nominal rate of interest were equal—the real rate of interest was 2.52 percent. Given that the country was in a recession, a real rate value of 2½ percent compared to an average value of 3 percent is a very plausible value. Given the economy was in a trough, the below 3 percent value is also consistent with the real rate varying cyclicly with the business cycle.

- *The nominal (or market) interest rates tend to rise and fall with changes in the actual rate of inflation.* The positive relationship between the rate of inflation and the level of interest rates is exactly what we would expect given the Fisher equation (Equation 4.1 in Chapter 4). Thus, we are comfortable with the conclusion that inflationary (price) expectations play an important role in determining the level of interest rates. The Fisher equation also highlights the fact that the nominal and real rate of interest are the same only when price expectations are zero. At times when price expectations are not zero, which is normally the case, the two rates are not equal, and any theory of market-determined interest rates, such as the loanable funds theory, must incorporate information on price expectations.

- *The nominal (or market) interest rates tend to rise during periods of economic expansion and decline during periods of economic contraction.* It makes sense that interest rates closely follow the business cycle. During periods of economic expansion, the Federal Reserve is likely to slow the growth rate of the money supply; the demand for funds increases as consumer and business spending increases because household incomes are higher and business profits are up; and, finally, price expectations are revised upward as the economy heats up and the demand for goods and services surges. All three forces act to exert upward pressure on interest rates. During periods of business contraction, the three forces operate in the opposite direction: Interest rates decline as the Fed stimulates the economy by increasing the money supply; credit demand decreases as business and household incomes decline; and prices are expected to increase at a slower rate, if at all.

The cyclical movements of interest rates are not as smooth as they appear in the chapter exhibits. A number of short-run forces, particularly seasonal forces, impinge on the cyclical forces and contribute to the irregular movement of interest rates. Nevertheless, over time, the cyclical forces dominate the temporary factors, and interest rates closely follow the business cycle.

Since the postwar period (1945–2011), there have been 11 business cycles with an average period of contraction (peak to trough) of 11 months and periods of expansion (trough to peak) of nearly 5 years. In general, periods of economic contraction tend to be short compared to periods of expansion, which tend to be longer. However, not every business cycle conforms to the average. To illustrate, the 1990–2000 period of economic expansion lasted 10 years (1990–2000), and the most recent recession lasted 18 months (2007–2009), which makes it the longest and deepest recession since the Great Depression (1929–1933).

DO YOU UNDERSTAND?

1. Which securities tend to have higher yields; those that are more marketable, or those that are less marketable? Why?

2. At what stage of the business cycle would you expect issuers to call in bonds? At what stage of the business cycle would you expect the call interest premium to be the highest? Explain.

3. Why do you think investors are willing to accept lower yields on putable bonds? Explain.

4. Holding the price of the firm's stock constant, would you be more likely to convert bonds into stock when interest rates are rising or falling? Explain.

SUMMARY OF LEARNING OBJECTIVES

1 **Describe and explain the relationship between interest rates and the term-to-maturity of a financial instrument.** Yield curves represent the relationship between yield and term-to-maturity of financial instruments. Yield curves may be upward sloping, downward sloping, flat, or humped. The shapes of the yield curve are explained by several theories:

a. The *expectations theory* suggests that if interest rates are expected to increase in the future, long-term rates will be higher than short-term rates, and the yield curve will slope upward. A downward-sloping curve occurs if market participants expect interest rates to decline.

b. *Liquidity premium theory* suggests that risk-averse investors require yield premiums to hold longer-term securities because of greater price or liquidity risk. These yield premiums cause an upward bias in the slope of the yield curve.

c. The *market segmentation theory* suggests that the shape of the yield curve is determined by the supply of and demand for securities within narrow maturity ranges.

d. The *preferred-habitat theory* suggests that investors will leave their preferred maturity range if they are adequately compensated for the additional risk.

2 **Explain the meaning and the measurement of default risk premiums.** The greater a security's default risk, the higher the interest rate that must be paid to investors as compensation for potential financial loss and risk bearing. Risk premiums can be measured as the difference between the yield on a risky security and that of a risk-free security with the same term-to-maturity. Yields on U.S. Treasury securities are the best proxies for risk-free interest rates.

3 **Describe how tax treatment affects yield differences across different types of securities.** Most investors are concerned with after-tax yields on securities. Thus, investors require higher before-tax yields on securities whose income is taxed at higher rates. We see lower before-tax yields on securities whose income is subject to lower tax rates.

4 **Explain the relationship between the marketability of a security and its yield.** *Marketability* is the ease and quickness with which investors can resell a security. The greater the marketability of a security, the lower its interest rate.

5 **Explain how special characteristics such as call provisions, put options, and conversion options affect a security's yield.** A number of special options, including call provisions, put options, and conversion features, cause yields to vary across otherwise similar securities:

a. A *call provision* allows an issuer to retire a security before its maturity date. Because the exercise of call options can injure investors, bonds with call options must offer higher interest rates than similar noncallable bonds.

b. A *put option* allows an investor to sell a bond back to the issuer before maturity at a predetermined price. Because put options protect investors against capital losses caused by rising interest rates, putable bonds offer lower yields than similar nonputable bonds.

c. A *conversion feature* allows the investor to convert a security into another type of security, allowing investors to hedge risk. Thus, convertible bonds offer lower yields than similar nonconvertible bonds.

6 **Explain how interest rates behave over the business cycle.** Interest rates tend to increase when the economy is growing (economic expansion) and to decrease when the economy is contracting (economic recession).

KEY TERMS

Term-to-maturity
Term structure of interest rates
Yield curve
Forward rate
Spot rate
Implied forward rate
Liquidity premium

Market-segmentation theory
Preferred-habitat theory
Yield spread (YS)
Default
Default risk
Default risk premium

Flight-to-quality
Bond ratings
Investment-grade bonds
Speculative-grade (junk) bonds
Municipal securities
Marketability

Call option (call provision)
Put option
Conversion option
Call price
Call interest premium
Put interest discount
Conversion yield discount

QUESTIONS AND PROBLEMS

1. Using the *Federal Reserve Bulletin*, the Federal Reserve Bank of St. Louis Web site (FRED), or the *Wall Street Journal*, plot the yield curve for U.S. Treasury securities on a quarterly basis for this year. Given your knowledge of the term structure of interest rates, what would be your economic forecast for next year?

2. Summarize the expectation theory and the preferred-habitat theory of the term structure of interest rates. Are these theories related, or are they alternative explanations of the term structure?

3. A commercial bank made a 5-year term loan at 13 percent. The bank's economics department forecasts that 1 and 3 years in the future the 2-year interest rate will be 12 percent and 14 percent, respectively. The current 1-year rate is 7 percent. Given that the bank's forecasts are reliable, has the bank set the 5-year rate correctly?

4. Define default risk. How does the default risk premium vary over the business cycle? Explain.

5. What do bond ratings measure? Explain some of the important factors in determining a security's bond rating.

6. Why do most commercial banks hold portfolios of municipal bonds and relatively few corporate bonds?

7. Explain the importance of a call provision to investors. Do callable bonds have higher or lower yields than similar noncallable bonds? Why?

8. Define marketability. Explain why the marketability of a security is important to both investor and issuer.

9. A new-issue municipal bond rated Aaa by Moody's Investors Service is priced to yield 8 percent. If you are in the 33 percent tax bracket, what yield would you need to earn on a taxable bond to be indifferent?

10. Historically, the yield curve typically has been upward sloping. Why would you expect this to be the case? (*Hint*: Historically, economic recessions typically last 9 to 12 months; expansions typically last nearly 5 years.)

11. Under which scenario, rising interest rates or falling interest rates, would a bond investor be most likely to exercise a put option on a bond? Explain.

12. Suppose the 7-year spot interest rate is 9 percent and the 2-year spot interest rate is 6 percent. The forecasted 3-year rate 2 years from now is 7.25 percent. What is the implied forward rate on a 2-year bond originating 5 years from now? (*Hint*: Under the expectations hypothesis, in equilibrium an investor with a 7-year holding period will be indifferent about investing

in a 7-year bond or a combination of securities over the same period.)

13. Suppose you hold a corporate bond that is convertible into the firm's stock. Stock prices are falling and interest rates are also falling. Would it be a good idea to exercise your conversion option under these conditions? Why?

14. Suppose you expect interest rates to increase in the future. You are not indifferent toward interest rate risk and the desire to maximize expected return. If you hold a portfolio consisting of 50 percent short-term bonds (<1 year to maturity) and 50 percent long-term bonds, how might you adjust your portfolio to maximize your profit? Explain carefully.

15. You are the holder of a variable-coupon bond that is convertible to a fixed-coupon bond. If you expect interest rates to rise, should you exercise your conversion option? Explain. What if you expect interest rates to fall?

16. Assume that the term structure of Treasury securities includes the following rates:

Security	Annual Yield (in %)
3-month bill	4.50
6-month bill	4.57
1-year note	4.52
2-year note	4.51
3-year note	4.48

Using this information calculate: (a) the 6-month annualized yield expected in the second half of the current year, and (b) the 1-year yield expected for year 3 [*Hint*: To answer (a) you will need to adjust the term-structure formula for semiannual compounding.]

17. The observed yields on a 1-year and 3-year security are 8 percent and 11 percent, respectively. What is the expected yield on a 2-year security 1 year from now?

18. An investor has an investment horizon of 4 years. The yield on a 2-year security today is 6 percent and the implied forward rate on a 2-year security 2 years from now is 6.75 percent. What should be the yield on a 4-year security today such that the investor is indifferent about investing in a 4-year security versus a combination of 2-year securities?

19. What is the preferred-habitat theory? Explain how it differs from the market-segmentation theory.

20. If interest rates are expected to *increase*, then identify what happens to the following factors using the expectations theory.

a. Demand for short-term securities by investors   **Increase / Decrease**

b. Supply of short-term securities by borrowers   **Increase / Decrease**

c. Price of short-term securities   **Increase / Decrease**

d. Yield of short-term securities   **Increase / Decrease**

e. Demand for long-term securities   **Increase / Decrease**

f. Supply of long-term securities   **Increase / Decrease**

g. Price of long-term securities   **Increase / Decrease**

h. Yield of long-term securities   **Increase / Decrease**

i. Shape of yield curve   **Normal / Inverted**

INTERNET EXERCISE

This exercise allows you to observe how the yield curve has changed over the past several years and to examine how changes in the yield curve are correlated with changes in the stock market.

1. Go to StockCharts.Com Dynamic Yield Curve at http://www.stockcharts.com/charts/YieldCurve.html.

2. By moving the red bar on the S&P chart or clicking the Animate button, you can see how the yield curve changed over time. At approximately what date does the yield curve first slope downward?

3. Do you see any relationship between when the stock market peaks and when the slope of the yield curve changes? Based on the discussion in this chapter, can you explain why the yield curve began to slope down?

4. What happened to the yield curve between December 2006 and December 2008?

PART III

FINANCIAL MARKETS

Money Markets

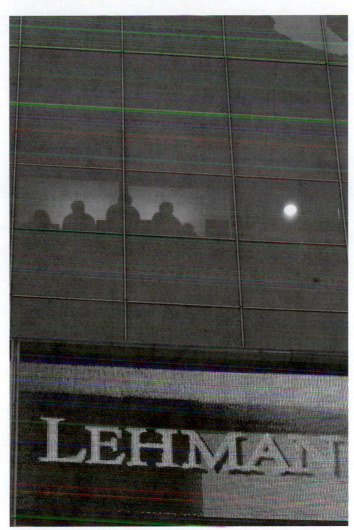

The Lehman bankruptcy put the financial markets on the brink of collapse.

ON SEPTEMBER 13, 2008, Henry Paulson, U.S. Secretary of the Treasury, and Timothy Geithner, president of the Federal Reserve Bank of New York, called a meeting on the future of Lehman Brothers, an embattled investment bank plagued by large losses and eroding confidence of counterparties who became unwilling to lend funds to Lehman even for the shortest periods of time. Two dozen of the world's most powerful bankers brought together by Geithner and Paulson failed to devise a rescue plan for Lehman. Two of the most interested potential acquirers, Bank of America and a U.K.-based Barclays PLC backed out as federal regulators refused to provide any government support in the Lehman sale. On Monday, September 15, 2008, Lehman Brothers, a 158-year-old investment bank, filed for Chapter 11 bankruptcy protection.

Allowing a large financial institution to fail may cause a chain reaction that spreads panicky moods to other parts of the financial markets. Lehman's demise caused tremors throughout the financial system, especially in the money markets. Money markets are markets for short-term, often unsecured debt. When investors in the money markets lose confidence in potential borrowers, they stop lending and start hoarding cash. The stakes are simply too high to take risks. A business that does not have enough cash to meet its immediate needs (such as a bank not having enough cash to meet deposit withdrawals) may fail due to illiquidity, even if it is otherwise a perfectly sound enterprise.

Lehman Brothers was not a sound enterprise by the time of its bankruptcy. Large write-downs of assets coupled with very high leverage left it practically insolvent by September 2008. However, the bankruptcy's ripple effect caused many other businesses, both financial and nonfinancial, much trouble over the next several months. The markets for different money market instruments, such as commercial paper, repurchase agreements, and even short-term interbank loans known as federal funds, were all profoundly affected by this catastrophic event.

When money market investors lose confidence, borrowers lose access to funds. The vicious circle is complete. In late 2008 and 2009, it took some extraordinary measures to break it. ■

The purpose of this chapter is to explain how money markets work and to describe how businesses, governmental units, and individuals use and participate in these important markets. The **money markets** are where depository institutions and other businesses adjust their liquidity positions by borrowing or investing for short periods of time. In addition, the Federal Reserve System conducts monetary policy in the money markets, and the U.S. Treasury finances the day-to-day operations of the federal government in the money markets. The instruments traded in the money markets typically have short-term maturities, low default risk, and high liquidity. The name *money markets* comes from the fact that money market instruments have characteristics very similar to money. Exhibit 7.1 lists the major money market instruments and the dollar amounts of each outstanding. U.S. Treasury bills are the ideal money market instrument. We will discuss in this chapter the general characteristics of the money markets, different classes of money market instruments and the markets they trade in, major money markets participants, interrelations between money market interest rates, and the impact of the global financial crisis of 2007–2009 on the money markets.

LEARNING OBJECTIVES

1 Explain the economic role of the money markets and why they are important to business firms.

2 Identify the key characteristics of money market instruments and why each characteristic is important.

3 Discuss the market for Treasury bills and short-term agency securities.

4 Explain the fed funds market and explain why it is one of the most important financial markets in the United States.

5 Identify other money market instruments that play an important role in liquidity markets.

6 Describe the relationship among yields on the various money market instruments.

7 Discuss how markets for different money market instruments were affected by the global financial crisis of 2007–2009.

EXHIBIT 7.1
Major Money Market Instruments Outstanding ($ billions)

Instrument	December 2005	October 2010
U.S. Treasury bills	963.9	1,768.5
Short-term municipal securities	105.9	129.3
Large, negotiable CDs	1,789.5	1,835.0
Commercial paper	1,640.1	1,050.5
Federal funds and security repurchase agreements	1,723.9	1,313.4

As U.S. budget deficits grow, Treasury bills outstanding grow. Following the crisis in the commercial paper market, however, the volume of commercial paper issues has shrunk substantially. Likewise, as banks hold more deposits in their reserve accounts at the Federal Reserve, there is less demand for federal funds.

Source: Board of Governors, Federal Reserve System, Flow of Funds Accounts (http://www.federalreserve.gov/releases/); Monthly Statement of the Public Debt of the United States.

7.1 HOW THE MONEY MARKETS WORK

The money market consists of a collection of markets, each trading a distinctly different financial instrument. There is no formal organization for money markets, such as the New York Stock Exchange for the equity markets. Central to the activity of the money markets are the dealers and brokers who specialize in one or more money market instruments. Dealers buy securities for their own positions and sell from their security inventories when a trade takes place. Transactions are completed electronically or by telephone. The market is centered in New York City, in downtown Manhattan, because of the concentration of financial firms in that area. The major participants are electronically linked all over the United States and in major European and Asian financial centers.

The money markets are also distinct from other financial markets because they are wholesale markets and because of the large transactions involved. Although some small transactions do take place, most involve $1 million or more. Money market transactions are called *open-market transactions* because of their impersonal and competitive nature. For example, a bank trading in federal funds asks for bids from a number of brokers, selling at the highest price and buying at the lowest. However, not all money market transactions are as open as the federal funds market. For example, money market banks often "accommodate" dealers who are good customers of the bank by selling them negotiable certificates of deposit even though the bank is not actively seeking funds at the prevailing market interest rate. Thus, in the money markets, we find some give, not so much in the form of price concessions but in the form of accommodations.

The hubs of money market transactions are the trading rooms of dealers and brokers. When the market is open, these rooms are characterized by tension and a frenzy of activity. Each trader sits in front of a battery of phones and computers that link the dealer to other dealers and their major customers.

Payment for securities traded in the money market is as simple as making the transaction over the telephone. Most transactions are settled in *immediately available* funds, with parties involved instructing the Federal Reserve to transfer funds from the account of one customer's bank to the other party's bank. The physical transfer of securities is also simplified by the availability of safekeeping facilities in New York City banks. Securities are rarely physically shipped between buyer and seller.

7.2 ECONOMIC ROLE OF THE MONEY MARKETS

The most important economic function of the money market is to provide an efficient means for economic units to adjust their liquidity positions. Almost every economic unit—financial institution, business, or governmental body—has a recurring problem of liquidity management. The problem occurs because the timing of cash receipts and cash expenditures is rarely perfectly synchronized. Money market instruments allow economic units to bridge the gap between cash receipts and cash expenditures, thereby solving their liquidity problems. For example, a business firm has a temporary surplus of cash. Rather than leaving the funds idle in a checking account and earning no interest, the firm can invest in the money markets safely for a period of 1 to 30 days, or longer if needed, and earn the market rate of interest. In another situation, if a bank is temporarily short of reserves in its account at the Fed, it can go to the money markets to purchase (borrow) federal funds from another institution to deposit in its Federal Reserve account overnight and meet its reserve requirements. The key notion here is that participants are adjusting their liquidity in these markets—they are lending idle cash or borrowing for short periods of time.

7.3 FEATURES OF MONEY MARKET INSTRUMENTS

Given the economic role of money markets—to provide liquidity adjustments—it is not difficult to determine the feaures of the "ideal" money market instrument and the types of firms that could issue them. Specifically, investors in money market instruments want to take as little risk as possible. Thus, these instruments are characterized by (1) low default risk, (2) low price risk (because of short term to maturity), (3) high liquidity (i.e., they can be turned into cash quickly), and (4) large denominations so the per-dollar cost for executing transactions is very low. Let us examine in more detail why money market instruments have these characteristics.

First, if you have money to invest temporarily, you want to purchase financial claims only of issuers with the highest credit standing and minimize any loss of principal due to default. Thus, money market instruments are issued by economic units of the highest credit standing (i.e., the lowest default risk).

Second, you do not want to hold long-term securities because they have greater price fluctuations (interest rate risk) compared to short-term securities if interest rates change. Furthermore, if interest rates do change significantly, maturity is not far away for short-term securities, when they will be redeemed for their face value.

Third, temporary investments must be highly marketable in the event that the funds are unexpectedly needed before maturity. Thus, most money market instruments have active secondary markets. To be highly marketable, money market instruments must have standardized features (no surprises). The issuers must be well known in the market and have good reputations. Finally, the transaction costs must be low. Thus, money market instruments are generally sold in large

EXHIBIT 7.2
Characteristics of Money Market Instruments

Instrument	Typical Maturity	Liquidity	Default Risk	Pricing	Secondary Market
U.S. Treasury bills	4–52 weeks	Excellent	Extremely low	Discount	Yes
Federal agency securities maturing within a year	Up to 1 year	Good	Very low	Discount	Yes
Commercial paper	1–270 days	Limited	Low	Discount	Yes
Banker's acceptances	30–180 days	Limited	Low	Discount	Yes
Negotiable certificates of deposit	2–52 weeks	Good	Low	Add-on	Yes
Federal funds	1–7 days	Excellent	Low	Add-on	No
Repurchase agreements	1–15 days	Good	Low	Add-on	No

Money market instruments are typically characterized by short maturities, high liquidity, and low default risk.

wholesale denominations—usually in units of $1 million to $10 million. For example, it costs between 50¢ and $1 to trade $1 million worth of Treasury securities.

Next, we discuss in detail the individual money market instruments and the characteristics of their markets. Exhibit 7.2 summarizes the characteristics of the most important money market instruments. *Discount instruments* (Treasury bills, short-term federal agency debt, commercial paper and banker's acceptances) are sold at a discount to par value and pay par value at maturity. *Add-on instruments* (negotiable certificates of deposit, federal funds, and repurchase agreements) are sold at par value and pay par value plus interest at maturity. While federal funds and repurchase agreements do not have a secondary market, they are considered highly liquid instruments due to their short maturities.

To finance the operations of the federal government, the U.S. Treasury Department issues various types of debt. The most important of these are **Treasury bills (T-bills)**, which are issued by the federal government to cover current deficits (i.e., expenses exceed revenues) and to refinance maturing government debt. Treasury bills are sold regularly through an auction process (described later) and have standard maturities of 4 weeks (28 days), 13 weeks (91 days), 26 weeks (182 days), and 52 weeks (364 days). Sometimes the Treasury issues bills of different maturities, called *cash management bills*. The bills are typically issued in large denominations. However, the minimum denomination is $100; it is a political concession by the federal government to individual investors. Individuals can purchase small-denomination T-bills directly from the Treasury or they can purchase them from dealers in the secondary market. Overall, however, the market for Treasury securities is a wholesale market; a round lot in the interdealer market is $5 million.

Because the U.S. government backs Treasury bills, they are perceived by many to have almost no default risk. In fact, the yield on Treasury bills is often

7.4 TREASURY BILLS

referred to as the *risk-free rate*. Of course, in reality, there is no risk-free rate, but U.S. T-bill yields are the best proxy available. Treasury bills also have little price risk because of their short maturity, and they can be readily converted into cash at very low transaction costs because of their large and active secondary market. Thus, U.S. Treasury bills are considered the ideal money market instrument.

AUCTIONING NEW T-BILLS

The Treasury Department has a systematic procedure for auctioning and redeeming Treasury bills. Each Thursday, the regular weekly offering of 13-week and 26-week bills is announced. Bids, or *tenders*, must be received on the following Monday by 1:00 P.M. New York time. In the case of 4-week bills, the offerings are announced weekly on Mondays and the auctions are conducted on Tuesdays. Bills of the longest maturity, 52 weeks, are offered every 4 weeks; the announcement is made on Thursday and the auction is conducted the following Tuesday. The new bills of all maturities are then issued on Thursday following the auction.

A computer application called TAAPS (Treasury Automated Auction Processing System) processes all submitted bids and prepares a summary data file of the auction results. Institutions submit bids via the Internet. Individual investors must have *TreasuryDirect* accounts, which they can open by registering at *www.treasurydirect.gov*, and may submit bids by mail, telephone, and Internet applications that ultimately reach TAAPS. The electronic bid submission and processing allows for the auction results to be available within 2 minutes of the close of bidding. The short release time reduces the amount of time that bidders are exposed to uncertainty with respect to changes in interest rates. The reduced uncertainty favors both investors and dealers and thus lowers the government's borrowing cost.

Competitive Bids.   Bids can be submitted as either competitive or noncompetitive bids. *Competitive bids* are usually made by large investors who actively participate in money markets on a regular basis, such as Wall Street brokerage firms and large commercial banks. An investor can enter more than one competitive bid, but the total of the bids cannot exceed 35 percent of the Treasury bills offered in the auction. The reason for the *35 percent rule* is to prevent any single bidder from squeezing the market. That is, if a single dealer controls a significant portion of a particular maturity, the dealer may be able to sell the bills at prices higher than otherwise would be the case in competitive markets.

In making a competitive bid, the investor states the desired amount of the face value of bills and the interest rate the investor is willing to accept. In T-bill auctions, the rate specified is the discount yield (we will learn later in this chapter how to compute it). In awarding the Treasury bills, the highest bidder (i.e., the bidder who submits the *lowest* interest rate) receives the first allocation of T-bills, and subsequent bids are filled in decreasing order of price until all of the bills auctioned that week are distributed. Historically, it meant that all successful bidders paid different prices for the same bills. Beginning in November 1998, however, the Treasury switched to *uniform-price auctions* where all bidders pay the same price. Under the uniform-price auctions, competitive and noncompetitive bids are made and accepted as in the past, but once accepted, all bidders pay the same price based on the so-called *stop-out rate* for the auction (the highest rate accepted). The switch to uniform-price auctions eliminated the winner's curse (highest bidders paying the highest price), which characterizes the *multiple-price auction* process.

EXHIBIT 7.3
Department of the Treasury's T-Bill Auction Results, January 10–11, 2011 ($ Millions)

	4-Week T-Bills	13-Week T-Bills	26-Week T-Bills	52-Week T-Bills
CUSIP number	912795V40	9127952L4	9127952Z3	9127952Y6
Competitive bids tendered	$122,406.80	$124,716.50	$125,641.30	$117,358.40
Competitive bids accepted	$24,727.30	$27,486.10	$26,768.70	$21,802.10
Noncompetitive bids accepted	$273.80	$1,515.40	$1,231.40	$198.10
Bid-to-cover ratio	4.91	4.35	4.53	5.34
High rate	0.145%	0.15%	0.18%	0.275%
Price	99.989	99.962	99.909	99.722
Issue date	1/13/2011	1/13/2011	1/13/2011	1/13/2011
Maturity date	2/10/2011	4/14/2011	7/14/2011	1/12/2012

Noncompetitive bids are usually submitted by individuals, small corporations, and small financial institutions. These bids are accepted before any competitive bids are awarded, and noncompetitive bidders earn the highest accepted rate.

Source: Department of the Treasury, http://www.treasurydirect.gov/instit/annceresult/press/press.htm.

Noncompetitive Bids. In making a *noncompetitive bid*, the investor indicates the quantity of bills desired and agrees to accept the price based on the stop-out discount rate of the auction (before the switch to uniform-price auctions in 1998, it was based on the average discount rate of all accepted competitive bids). All noncompetitive bids are accepted before the award of any competitive bids. The minimum noncompetitive bid is for $100 of the face value of T-bills and the maximum is $5 million. Individuals, small corporations, and small financial institutions usually enter them. Noncompetitive bids were designed to allow small investors who are not familiar with money market interest rate movements to purchase Treasury securities to avoid the risks of (1) bidding a price too low to receive any bills or (2) bidding a price substantially higher than the market equilibrium. The latter was a major concern under multiple-price auctions conducted prior to November 1998, but it has been greatly alleviated by uniform-price auctions.

Exhibit 7.3 shows the results of the 4-week, 13-week, 26-week, and 52-week Treasury bill auctions held on January 10–11, 2011. CUSIP numbers are unique identifiers for securities issues. For the 13-week (91-day) bills, competitive bids for over $124.7 billion of T-bills were tendered, and the Treasury Department accepted $27.5 billion of the bids. More than $1.5 billion of noncompetitive bids were tendered and accepted. The **bid-to-cover ratio** of 4.35 indicates that the amount of tendered bids (competitive and noncompetitive) was 4.35 times the amount of accepted bids. All winning bidders were awarded T-bills at the "high rate" of 0.15%. After the close of bidding, the Treasury first accepts all noncompetitive bids and subtracts them from the total amount of securities offered (it was $29 billion for this auction and could be deduced by adding up the accepted competitive and noncompetitive bids and rounding to the nearest $10 million). It then accepts competitive bids, in order of increasing rate, until it has exhausted the offering. This is why the highest accepted rate is known as the **stop**, or the **stop-out rate**. All bids at the stop-out rate of 0.15% were filled on a pro rata basis. All bids above this rate were rejected. The annual yield of 0.15% (which in the case of T-bills is discount yield) results in the price of $99.962 per $100 of face value. We will learn in the next few pages how to compute T-bill prices based on yields, and vice versa.

BOOK-ENTRY SECURITIES

In 1976, the Treasury began switching the entire marketable portion of the federal debt over to book-entry securities in lieu of engraved pieces of paper. Treasury securities owned or held by banks that have accounts with the Federal Reserve System would exist only in the Fed's computer. Treasury Direct accounts for individuals are also book-entry accounts that record the owners of the securities purchased and credit the owners with interest or principal when these payments are made. All marketable government securities (Treasury and agency) may be held in book-entry form, and the bulk of the Treasury's marketable debt is now held in this form.

For example, in New York City, the major banks are linked by wire, and all securities transactions among them are by wire. Thus, if J.P. Morgan were to sell securities to Wells Fargo, it would make delivery by instructing the Fed to debit its Treasury bill account for the amount sold and to credit Wells Fargo's account simultaneously for the same amount. In that way, securities can be quickly transferred by electronic impulses over the Fed wire rather than by cumbersome physical transfers.

PRICING TREASURY BILLS

Treasury bills are sold to investors on a discount basis because T-bills pay no coupon interest; thus, the interest income to the investors is the difference between the purchase price and face value of the bill paid at maturity. Exhibit 7.4 shows the Treasury bill rates as quoted in the *Wall Street Journal* on February 4, 2011.

EXHIBIT 7.4
Treasury Bill Quotations

(1) Maturity	(2) Days to Maturity	(3) Bid	(4) Asked	(5) Change	(6) Asked Yield
2/10/11	6	0.11	0.105	−0.003	0.107
3/17/11	41	0.135	0.13	0.003	0.132
4/28/11	83	0.143	0.138	0.005	0.14
6/9/11	125	0.155	0.15	0.005	0.152
7/28/11	174	0.16	0.155	unch.	0.157
10/20/11	258	0.205	0.2	0.002	0.201
1/12/12	342	0.275	0.27	0.008	0.271

Treasury bill yield quotations are listed in terms of the security's *bank discount yield*. This practice tends to understate the actual yield. In order to compare the yield on Treasury bills to other bonds, Treasury bill quotations often include the bond equivalent yield, as shown in column (6).

Source: Wall Street Journal Online, Treasury Quotes, February 4, 2011.

Column 1 lists the maturity dates for the bills. Column 2 specifies the number of days until a particular T-bill matures. For example, at the close of the trading day on February 4, 2011, the T-bills maturing on March 17, 2011, would trade for 41 more days before they would be retired by the Treasury Department. Note that the securities all have maturities of less than 1 year. Column 3 is the discount yield (defined later) on T-bills and reflects the price at which dealers are willing to buy T-bills from investors. Column 4 is the discount yield set by dealers and reflects the price at which dealers are willing to sell T-bills to investors. The difference between the bid yield and the asked yield is the spread. The *spread* is the dealers' profit for buying and selling T-bills and represents the transaction costs incurred by investors for trading. Column 5 is the change in the ask yield from the previous day's close. The last column is the asked bond equivalent yield, which we discuss later. All yields are expressed in percent; that is, 0.11 means a 0.11% annualized yield.

The *discount yield* (y_d), also called *bank discount yield*, on a Treasury bill is computed by multiplying the percentage price discount on the Treasury bill's face value (P_f) by 360 and dividing by the number of days (n) to the T-bill's maturity. Thus, the formula for calculating the discount rate (y_d) is:

$$y_d = \frac{P_f - P_0}{P_f} \times \frac{360}{n} \times 100\% \tag{7.1}$$

where

y_d = discount yield on an annualized basis
P_f = face value (amount paid to the investor at maturity)
P_0 = purchase price of the T-bill
n = number of days to maturity

LEARNING BY DOING 7.1
Calculating the Discount Yield

PROBLEM: You are an analyst for a money market mutual fund, the J. R. Richardson Short-Term Yield Fund. The fund is considering whether to purchase 6-month (182-day) Treasury bills. So that you can compare the yield on the T-bills with other securities in the portfolio, the portfolio manager that you report to has asked you to calculate the yield. Here is what you know. The T-bills have a face value of $10,000 and are selling at 99 percent of face value.

APPROACH: You recognize that this situation requires you to calculate the *discount yield*, which is a straightforward application of Equation 7.1.

SOLUTION:

$$y_d = \frac{\$10,000 - \$9,900}{\$10,000} \times \frac{360}{182} \times 100\%$$

$$= 1.98\%$$

Note that the discount yield understates the true rate of return on a Treasury bill for two reasons. First, it assumes that the full face value was paid for the T-bill instead of a discounted price. This overstates the investment required to buy the T-bill and thus understates the discount as a percentage of the amount of money actually invested. Second, by using a 360-day year to annualize the yield, the formula ignores the fact that if interest were earned for the full 365- or 366-day year, a higher rate of return would be obtained. Thus, interest can be earned on the interest received on the T-bill. The market convention to quote T-bill yields on the discount basis originated before the widespread use of computers or calculators. When T-bill yields are reported in financial publications such as the *Wall Street Journal*, a *bond equivalent yield is often reported in addition to* the discount yield (see Exhibit 7.4).

The bond equivalent yield assumes a 365-day year and uses the price rather than the face value of the T-bill as the basis for the computation. Because of these assumptions, the bond equivalent yield on a T-bill is always higher than the bank discount yield (see Exhibit 7.4). The formula for the bond equivalent yield is

$$y_{be} = \frac{P_f - P_0}{P_0} \times \frac{365}{n} \times 100\% \tag{7.2}$$

LEARNING BY DOING 7.2
Calculating the Bond Equivalent Yield

PROBLEM: You are an analyst at the J. R. Richardson Short-Term Yield Fund. Your portfolio manager comes back to your cubicle with another request in the process of analyzing the proposed T-bill purchase. She asks you to calculate the bond equivalent yield.

APPROACH: You recognize this as a straightforward application of the formula to calculate the bond equivalent yield, which appears in Equation 7.2.

SOLUTION:

$$y_{be} = \frac{\$10,000 - \$9,900}{\$9,900} \times \frac{365}{182} \times 100\%$$

$$= 2.03\%$$

Notice that the bond equivalent yield is greater than the discount yield because of the reasons discussed above.

A Treasury bill's price can be computed from data in the financial press (see Exhibit 7.4) by taking Equation 7.1 or 7.2 and solving for the price (P_0). Using the discount yield, the equation to solve for the price is

$$P_0 = P_f - \left(y_d \times \frac{n}{360} \times P_f \right) \tag{7.3}$$

Using the bond equivalent yield, the price is

$$P_0 = \frac{P_f}{1 + \left(y_{be} \times \frac{n}{365} \right)} \tag{7.4}$$

You can see how these two formulas work by taking an example from Exhibit 7.4. Let's look at the T-bill maturing on October 20, 2011, as of the date of the *Wall Street Journal* listing, February 4, 2011 (see the next-to-last row of the exhibit). We have the following information, which we substitute into Equation 7.3 to obtain the price:

$$P_f = \$10,000$$
$$y_d = 0.2\% \text{ (see column 4 of Exhibit 7.4)}$$
$$n = 258 \text{ days (see column 2 of Exhibit 7.4)}$$

Thus,

$$P_0 = \$10,000 - \left(0.002 \times \frac{258}{360} \times \$10,000\right)$$
$$= \$1,000,000 - \$1,433,33$$
$$= \$9,985.67$$

Alternatively, we can use the bond equivalent yield of 0.201% (reported in the last column of Exhibit 7.4) to find the price:

$$P_0 = \frac{\$10,000}{1 + \left(0.00201 \times \frac{258}{365}\right)}$$
$$= \frac{\$1,000,000}{1.0014}$$
$$= \$9,985.81$$

The small discrepancy between the prices found using the discount yield and the bond equivalent yield ($0.14) is due to rounding of the yields reported in the *Wall Street Journal*.

DO YOU UNDERSTAND?

1. Given the economic role of the money market, explain the importance of the typical characteristics of money market securities.

2. Using the discount yield in Exhibit 7.3 (reported as "high rate"), confirm that the *price* of a 364-day T-bill is 99.722% of its face value.

3. Refer to Exhibit 7.4. On February 4, 2011, what is the price of the T-bill maturing on April 28, 2011? Calculate the price two ways, using both the bid discount yield and the asked discount yield reported in columns 3 and 4, respectively. Assume a face value of $100,000.

4. Assuming a face value of $10,000, what is the price of a T-bill with 161 days to maturity if its bond equivalent yield is 1.99 percent?

5. Why is the bond equivalent yield of a T-bill higher than the yield calculated on a discount basis?

A **federal agency** is an independent federal department or federally chartered corporation established by Congress and owned or underwritten by the U.S. government. Because some of these agencies are privately owned companies, they are called government-sponsored enterprises (GSEs). Federal agency securities result

7.5 FEDERAL AGENCY SECURITIES

from selected government lending programs. Initially these programs were designed to attract private capital to sectors of the economy where credit flows were considered to be insufficient. Housing and agriculture were traditionally the principal beneficiaries of federal credit programs. In recent years, the objectives of federal credit programs have expanded to include social and economic goals and to promote conservation and resource utilization.

TYPES OF FEDERAL AGENCIES

Exhibit 7.5 provides a list of the major government agencies authorized to issue debt. Many of them issue only long-term debt; however, as these issues approach maturity, they are traded in the money markets. With regard to short-term issues, about 25 percent of all new agency issues have an original maturity of 1 year or less. Next we discuss some important federal agencies.

The Farm Credit System. The Farm Credit System (FCS) is a cooperatively owned system of banks and associations that provides credit and related services to farmers and agricultural cooperatives. The system holds about one-fourth of total farm debt in the United States (about $160 billion in loans made to almost 500,000 borrowers as of the end of 2010). The oldest government debt-issuing agency in the system is the federal land bank (FLB), created by the Federal Farm Loan Act of 1916. Today there are 12 FLBs throughout the country that make credit available to farmers to purchase and develop land and to buy farm equipment and livestock. In addition, farmers can obtain credit from federal intermediate credit banks (FICBs), established in 1923, and from banks for cooperatives (co-ops), organized in 1933.

The financial crisis in the farm sector during the 1980s raised concern over the riskiness of debt issued by farm credit agencies. This led to the passage of the 1985 Farm Bill, which allows Congress to provide direct federal aid to the FCS through a line of credit with the Treasury as well as direct borrowing by the Farm Credit Bank. The act strengthened the market's perception of an implicit federal guarantee of agency debt in the event of default.

EXHIBIT 7.5
Selected U.S. Federal Agencies Authorized to Issue Debt

Farm Credit Bank System

Federal Financing Bank

Federal Home Loan Bank

Federal Home Loan Mortgage Corporation (Freddie Mac)

Federal National Mortgage Association (Fannie Mae)

Export-Import Bank (Eximbank)

Federal Housing Administration

Government National Mortgage Association (Ginnie Mae)

Small Business Administration

Veterans Administration

The first five agencies on the list are privately owned, government-sponsored enterprises, while the last five are U.S. federal government departments.

Housing Credit Agencies.   Another major group of federal agencies is involved in financing purchases of homes. The largest among these agencies are the Federal Home Loan Bank (FHLB), the Federal National Mortgage Association (FNMA, or *Fannie Mae*), and the Federal Home Loan Mortgage Corporation (FHLMC, or *Freddie Mac*). Fannie Mae was chartered by the federal government in 1938 initially to buy federally insured mortgage loans. FNMA's objective is to provide a secondary market for home mortgages. Freddie Mac is similar to Fannie Mae except it was initially established to buy conventional (not federally insured) mortgage loans. Even though Fannie Mae and Freddie Mac have received much more media attention over the past 2 decades, FHLB, which is a system of twelve regional banks established in 1932, has had more debt outstanding than either Fannie or Freddie. Together, FHLB, Fannie Mae, and Freddie Mac account for over 90 percent of the total amount of outstanding federal agency debt. As of 2008, Fannie Mae and Freddie Mac owned or guaranteed about half of the U.S. $12-trillion mortgage market.

Federal Financing Bank.   In the past, most agency securities were sold through financial specialists known as *fiscal agents*. Each agency had one, usually located in New York City, whose job was to assemble a group of investment banking firms to distribute the agency's securities to retail buyers. Today this method of selling new issues is used primarily by federally sponsored agencies that issue large amounts of securities, such as the housing and farm credit agencies. Other government agencies now acquire most of their funds directly from the Treasury or from the Federal Financing Bank (FFB), established in 1973 to coordinate and consolidate the federal financing activities of agencies that issue small amounts of debt or infrequently enter the money and capital markets. Even though the debt of small GSEs would be considered safe, small offering sizes would result in lower marketability and higher yields for these agencies. The goal of the FFB is to lower the borrowing cost of participating agencies. The FFB purchases the securities of participating agencies and, in turn, issues its own obligations. In November 2010, the FFB had $52 billion of debt outstanding. None of its debt is held by the public because the FFB borrows directly from the Treasury.

CHARACTERISTICS OF AGENCY DEBT

Debt securities of government-owned agencies (such as the Government National Mortgage Association, Eximbank, or Federal Housing Administration) are guaranteed by *full faith and credit* of the U.S. government and thus are as safe as U.S. Treasury debt. Government-sponsored agency securities are *not explicitly* guaranteed by the federal government against default. However, some form of federal backing is implied. First, it is unlikely that the federal government would allow one of its sponsored agencies to default. For some issues, the Treasury Department and the Federal Reserve are authorized to purchase securities in the event that market support is needed. For other issues, the agency can borrow from the Treasury up to certain limits.

Events during the global financial crisis of 2007–2009 confirm that the federal government is not willing to allow its sponsored agencies to default. Fannie Mae and Freddie Mac became much more aggressive in the 2000s in conducting their business; they guaranteed or acquired many mortgages of subprime (i.e., low) credit quality. As the subprime mortgage default rates increased significantly, mounting losses of the two agencies in 2007 and 2008 gave rise to fears among

EXHIBIT 7.6
EXHIBIT 7.6
Characteristics of Short-Term Agency Securities

Issuer	Type	Maturities	Offering Schedule	Minimum Denomination ($)
Farm credit banks	Bonds, discount notes	3 and 6 months 1–365 days	Monthly Daily	5,000 5,000
Federal home loan banks	Discount notes	1–360 days	Twice weekly	100,000
Federal National Mortgage Association	Benchmark bills, discount notes	3 and 6 months 1–360 days	Weekly Daily	1,000 1,000

The majority of the federal agencies most active in issuing short-term debt offer securities daily, with maturities typically in the 3- to 6-month range.

investors worldwide that Fannie and Freddie would default on their debt. On September 7, 2008, Fannie Mae and Freddie Mac were placed into conservatorship of the Federal Housing Finance Agency (FHFA). The U.S. government guaranteed the debt issued by the two agencies. While the agencies technically remain privately owned corporations, as of February 2011, the U.S. government is the major owner because, after placing the firms into conservatorship and dismissing their CEOs and boards of directors in September 2008, it forced the issuance to the Treasury of new senior preferred stock and common stock warrants amounting to 79.9 percent of each GSE.

The marketability of agency securities varies with each type of security. The securities of the federal land banks, federal home loan banks, and Federal National Mortgage Association have well-established secondary markets. In recent years, the yield on agency securities has been 1 to 20 basis points above the yield on similar Treasury securities (100 basis points equal 1 percent). Although some of the yield spread difference results from the agency securities' higher default risk, most is attributable to their lower marketability. For example, on January 12, 2011, Fannie Mae issued $2 billion of 3-month benchmark bills and $1 billion of 6-month benchmark bills. These securities are auctioned similarly to T-bills. The stop-out rates at the auction were 0.166 percent and 0.2 percent for the 3- and 6-month benchmark bills, respectively. Both were within 2 basis points of Treasury bill yields of similar maturities reported in Exhibit 7.3. Because Fannie Mae debt is currently guaranteed by the U.S. government, this small spread over T-bill yields must be due to the slightly lower marketability of the agency debt. Exhibit 7.6 shows a list of federal agencies most active in issuing short-term debt and the characteristics of that debt.

7.6 FED FUNDS

The market for **federal funds** (typically called *fed funds*) is one of the most important financial markets in the United States. It provides the means by which commercial banks and a limited number of other financial institutions trade large amounts of liquid funds with one another, usually for a period of 1 day. The fed funds rate is of particular interest because (1) it measures the return on the most liquid of all financial assets; (2) it is closely related to the conduct of monetary policy; and (3) it measures directly the availability of excess reserves within the banking system, which, in turn, influences commercial banks' decisions concerning loans to businesses, consumers, and other borrowers.

Traditionally, the federal funds market has been described as one in which commercial banks borrow and lend excess reserve balances held at the Federal Reserve. The institution that borrows the funds incurs a liability on its balance sheet, called *fed funds purchased*, and the institution that lends the fed funds records an asset, *fed funds sold*. The overnight (or 1-day) interest rate to borrow the funds is called the fed funds rate. Also note that the name *federal funds* or *fed funds* is misleading. Federal funds have nothing to do with the federal government. When the market for fed funds originated in the 1920s, the interest rate was close to the rate paid when borrowing from the Federal Reserve Bank; hence, the term *fed funds*.

Interbank borrowing and lending make up the majority of federal funds transactions. They are essentially 1-day unsecured loans between banks. The typical unit of trade in the brokered fed funds market is $1 million or more. It is possible to borrow for longer than 1 day; however, longer-term borrowing makes up a very small part of the overall fed funds market. With respect to transaction size, some banks will trade smaller amounts, but trades of less than $500,000 are infrequent. In most cases, the only step necessary to arrange a fed funds transaction is a telephone call and wire transfer. No physical transfer of funds occurs.

The quoted yield on fed funds, y_{ff}, assumes a 360-day year. To compare yields in the fed funds market with those of other money market instruments, the fed funds rate must be converted into a bond equivalent yield, y_{be}. For example, if the overnight fed funds rate is 2.00 percent, the bond equivalent funds rate is calculated as follows:

$$y_{be} = y_{ff}(365/360)$$
$$= 2.00\%\,(365/360) = 2.028\%$$

GROWTH IN THE FED FUNDS MARKET

The recent growth and change in the fed funds market makes the traditional description of the fed funds market as the market for short-term interbank loans overly simplified. Today, many active participants in the fed funds market do not hold balances at the Federal Reserve, such as federal agencies and securities firms.

A more appropriate definition of a federal funds transaction is that of an overnight loan (1 day) that is settled in immediately available funds. **Immediately available funds** are defined as (1) deposit liabilities of Federal Reserve banks and (2) liabilities of commercial banks that may be transferred or withdrawn during a business day. A large portion of the fed funds market has consisted of large regional and money-center banks borrowing correspondent balances from smaller banks. At one time, these correspondent balances earned no interest and were held as payment for services. Smaller banks often intentionally accumulate large balances in order to sell the excess to the larger correspondent banks with which they have relationships for investment in the fed funds market. The amounts are usually less than needed for transactions in the brokered market, which start at $1 million. However, the large bank accumulates these balances from its various smaller respondent banks to reach trading-lot size. The correspondent earns a fee for this service.

Nonbank financial institutions have also become increasingly active in this market. These institutions may engage in certain types of immediate fund transactions because of federal regulations governing commercial bank funds that are subject to reserve requirements. They include federal agencies, savings and loan associations, mutual savings banks, branches of foreign banks, and government securities dealers. For example, a savings and loan association may lend federal funds to a foreign bank, or a commercial bank can borrow federal funds from an array of institutions, rather than just reallocating reserves among banks.

Depository institutions have historically attempted to minimize the amount of excess reserves they held with the Fed because the Fed did not pay interest on required and excess reserve balances, and holding excess reserves would constitute a lost investment opportunity. Depositories have actively used the federal funds market to lend excess funds. Starting in October 2008, however, the Fed has paid interest on required and excess reserve balances of depository institutions. As of February 2011, the annual interest rate banks earn on reserves is 0.25 percent; it has been at this level since December 2008. Meanwhile, the *effective federal funds rate* (the weighted average rate on brokered fed funds transactions) was somewhat lower during the same period, between 0.1 percent and 0.2 percent on most of the days. Consequently, depository institutions have an incentive to hold excess funds with the Fed rather than lend them overnight to other institutions. The amount of bank reserves skyrocketed from about $30 billion in 2007, before the global financial crisis gained strength, to around $1 trillion throughout most of 2009 and 2010. While it is not clear whether depositories would be holding as much excess reserves if they did not earn interest on these balances, the financial crisis made many institutions much more cautious and conservative about their lending decisions.

While the amount of money traded in the fed funds market has declined from 2008 to 2010 compared to a pre-crisis period, it remains a large, active market, with many participants lending and borrowing on a daily basis.

7.7 OTHER MAJOR MONEY MARKET INSTRUMENTS

REPURCHASE AGREEMENTS

Closely associated with the functioning of the federal funds market is the negotiation of **repurchase agreements (RPs).** A repurchase agreement consists of the sale of a short-term security (collateral) with the condition that, after a period of time, the original seller buys it back at a predetermined price. The collateral used most frequently is U.S. Treasury securities such as T-bills or agency securities. However, it is possible to use any of the better-known money market instruments. This dual transaction, which in market jargon is called a **repo**, has developed into a meaningful money market instrument in its own right.

Repurchase agreements are most commonly made for 1 day or for very short terms. However, it is not uncommon to see 1- to 3-month (and even longer) repo transactions. The smallest customary denomination for a repo is $1 million. As with other money market instruments, repurchase agreement transactions are settled in immediately available funds. A **reverse repurchase agreement (reverse repo)** involves the purchase of short-term securities with the promise to sell the securities back to the original seller at a predetermined price at a given date in the future. Thus, a borrower in the transaction is in a repo, while a lender is in a reverse repo.

A Repo Transaction.   The definition of a repo in the preceding section may seem a little mind-boggling. However, repos are really very simple transactions. A repo is just a loan that is *secured* by a money market instrument of the same or larger dollar value. Thus, if the borrower defaults on the loan, the lender keeps the collateral, usually a short-term Treasury security. Repos are considered very-low-risk investments because the collateral is of equivalent or larger dollar value and is a short-term security, meaning it has little price risk. Let's work through an example so you can see how repos work. Suppose that a corporate treasurer has $1 million of excess cash for a 2-day period. The treasurer, wishing to earn interest on the funds, arranges to purchase $1 million worth of government securities from a bank with an accompanying agreement that the bank repurchases the securities in 2 days. The interest paid to the corporation is the difference between the purchase price and repurchase price of the collateralized securities. The transactions for both the bank and the corporation are as follows:

	Bank		Corporate Customer	
	Assets	Liabilities	Assets	Liabilities
Before RP		$1 million deposit	$1 million deposit	
Creation of RP		−$1 million deposit	−$1 million deposit	
		+$1 million RP borrowing	+$1 million collateralized loan (RP)	
Completion of RP		+$1 million deposit	+$1 million deposit	
		−$1 million RP borrowing	−$1 million loan (RP)	

Notice that, from the standpoint of the temporary seller of securities, repurchase agreements represent a source of funds; for the buyer, they represent an interest-earning investment. As our example illustrates, a commercial bank may buy idle funds from a corporate customer by selling Treasury securities on a repurchase basis. Or a commercial bank can sell immediately available funds to a dealer in U.S. government securities by purchasing the securities through a repurchase agreement. The dealer thereby finances its security inventory with funds purchased by the bank, and the bank receives interest income from the dealer at money market rates of return.

Because the value of the collateral may fall, repos are typically overcollateralized through a mechanism known as a **haircut**. For example, a 3 percent haircut means that the seller (borrower) receives 97 percent of the market value of the securities. If the value of the collateral is $1 million and the haircut is 3 percent, the borrower will receive $970,000 and the interest will be calculated on this amount.

The unique feature that distinguishes repurchase agreements from other money market instruments is that they may be used to shorten the actual maturity of a security to meet the needs of the borrower and lender. For example, an investor may wish to invest funds for a very short period of time, say, 3 days. A Treasury bill maturing in 3 days could be purchased, but often a 3-day bill is not available. A longer-maturity bill could be purchased, held for 3 days, and then resold in the secondary market. However, this alternative involves price risk. If interest rates rise during the 3-day interval, the investor would suffer a capital loss. A 3-day repo provides the investor with a money market instrument with the precisely needed maturity, thus eliminating all price risk on the repo.

Calculation of the Yield on a Repo.   The rate charged in repurchase agreements is negotiated between the buyers and sellers of funds, but it must be competitive with other money market rates. Transactions are arranged by telephone either directly between the two parties supplying and acquiring funds or through a small group of market specialists, usually government securities dealers.

The credit risk (*default*) on repos is very low because repo transactions are collateralized by securities with low credit and interest rate risk. As a result, the 1-day repo rate is less than the 1-day fed funds rate, which is an uncollateralized loan. The spread between the two rates is typically 20 to 25 basis points. The yield on a repo is calculated as the annualized difference between the initial selling price and the repurchase price, which includes the interest paid, using a 360-day year. The formula for the repo yield or interest rate is

$$y_{repo} = \frac{P_{repo} - P_0}{P_0} \times \frac{360}{n} \times 100\% \tag{7.5}$$

where:

P_{repo} = repurchase price of the security, which equals the selling price plus interest
P_0 = sale price of the security
n = number of days to maturity

For example, a commercial bank does a reverse repurchase agreement (or reverse repo) with a corporate customer who needs funds for 3 days. The bank agrees to buy Treasury securities from the corporation at a price of $1,000,000 and promises to sell the securities back to the corporate customer for $1,000,145 (includes $145 of interest) after 3 days. The yield on the reverse repo is calculated as follows, using Equation 7.5:

$$y_{repo} = \frac{\$1,000,145 - \$1,000,000}{\$1,000,000} \times \frac{360}{3} \times 100\%$$
$$= 1.74\%$$

Note that the bank corporate customer was able to borrow $1 million for 3 days for $145; not a bad deal! Also notice that repos and reverse repos are just opposite sides of the same deal. For the bank, the transaction was a reverse repo and for the corporate customer the deal was a repo.

> ## PEOPLE & EVENTS
>
> ## Lehman Brothers' "Creative" Accounting: Repos 105 and 108
>
> In a series of seemingly innocuous transactions, repos were used by the now defunct investment bank Lehman Brothers to mislead investors in several quarters prior to its bankruptcy filing in September 2008. Lehman employed so-called (within Lehman) Repo 105 and Repo 108 transactions to temporarily remove securities inventory from the balance sheet in late 2007 and 2008. The "105" and "108" refer to the haircuts of 5 percent and 8 percent necessary to account for the transaction as a "sale" under financial accounting standards. Lehman utilized Treasury and agency securities in Repo 105 transactions and equity securities in Repo 108 transactions. Lehman accounted for Repo 105 and Repo 108 transactions as "sales" rather than as financing transactions based on the overcollateralization or higher than normal haircut in such transactions. By classifying these transactions as sales, Lehman removed the inventory of securities sold in these repos from its balance sheet in the days prior to reporting dates.
>
> The cash borrowed through the repos was then used to pay down other short-term liabilities, thereby reducing both the total liabilities and the total assets reported on its balance sheet and lowering its leverage ratios. For example, in the first quarter of 2008, Lehman's reported net leverage ratio (net assets to equity) was 15.4. If Repos 105 and 108 had not been classified as sales, it would have been 17.3. A few days after the reporting date, Lehman would borrow the necessary funds to repay the cash borrowed in the repo transactions plus interest due, repurchase the securities, and restore the assets to its balance sheet. Lehman did not publicly disclose its use of Repo 105s, its accounting treatment for these transactions, the increase in Repo 105 usage in late 2007 and 2008, or the impact on the leverage ratios reported along with quarterly financial statements. The examiner in the Lehman bankruptcy case concluded that, by doing so, Lehman had intentionally misled investors and regulators.
>
> *Source:* Based on Section III.A.4 of the *Report of Anton R. Valukas, Examiner* in the Lehman bankruptcy case. Consult the report, accessible at http://lehmanreport.jenner.com, for details.

COMMERCIAL PAPER

Commercial paper is a short-term promissory note historically issued by large corporations to finance short-term working capital needs. In recent years, some firms have also used commercial paper as a source of interim financing for major construction projects. The basic reason firms issue commercial paper is to achieve interest rate savings as an alternative to bank borrowing. Because commercial paper is typically an unsecured promissory note, the issuer pledges no assets to protect the investor in the event of default. As a result, only large, well-known firms of the highest credit standing (lowest default risk) can issue commercial paper.

The commercial paper market is almost entirely a wholesale money market. Most commercial paper is sold in denominations of $100,000, $250,000, $500,000, and $1 million. Maturities on commercial paper range from 1 to 270 days, but most commercial paper has maturities of 1 to 90 days. Longer maturities are infrequent because issues with maturities greater than 270 days must comply with the costly and time-consuming Securities and Exchange Commission (SEC) registration and prospectus requirements.

History of Commercial Paper. Commercial paper is one of the oldest money market instruments; its use can be traced back to the early 1800s. Early issuers were mainly nonfinancial business firms, such as textile mills, railroads, and tobacco companies. The principal buyers were commercial banks. Beginning in the 1920s, the nature of the commercial paper market began to change. The introduction of the automobile and other consumer durables created a demand by consumers for short-term personal loans. This led to the rapid growth of consumer finance companies that needed funds to finance consumer purchases. The first large consumer finance company to issue commercial paper was General Motors Acceptance Corporation (GMAC), which was established to finance the purchase of General Motors' automobiles. An innovation by GMAC was to sell its paper directly to investors rather than placing it through commercial paper dealers. Commercial paper issued by nonfinancial corporations is known as nonfinancial commercial paper, while that issued by financial institutions, including bank holding companies and finance companies, is called financial commercial paper.

Historically, commercial paper has been unsecured (i.e., backed only by a firm's ability to generate cash flows). With the advent of securitization and asset-backed securities, asset-backed commercial paper (ABCP) has become a significant part of the market. An institution issuing ABCP sells its assets to a bankruptcy-remote (limited liability) special-purpose vehicle (SPV) or structured investment vehicle (SIV), allowing for the issuing institution to be legally separated from the SPV. The financial assets serving as collateral may be accounts receivable or a mix of many different assets (including or limited to subprime mortgages), which are jointly judged to have a low risk of default by a ratings agency.

The Commercial Paper Market.   Historically, commercial banks were the major purchasers of commercial paper. In the early 1950s, many other firms began purchasing commercial paper because of its combination of low default risk, short maturity, and relatively high yields. Today, the major investors in commercial paper are money market mutual funds, large insurance companies, nonfinancial business firms, bank trust departments, and state and local government pension funds. Commercial banks still purchase commercial paper for their own accounts, but they are not a dominant force in the market. Commercial banks remain important to the operation of the commercial paper market, however, because they act as agents in issuing paper, hold it for safekeeping, and facilitate payment in immediately available funds. They also provide backup lines of credit to corporate issuers of commercial paper.

Throughout the 2000s, 1,000 to 2,000 firms issued commercial paper at any given point in time. The precise amount issued varies depending on economic and market conditions; it was smaller during high-interest periods and larger when money was more readily available. Most of these firms sell their paper through dealers. There are about 30 commercial paper dealers, most of whom are located in New York City. Dealers maintain an inventory of the commercial paper they sell and stand ready to buy paper back from their customers at the going market rate plus a one-eighth of 1 percent commission fee. Also, issuing firms repurchase their own commercial paper within limits. Thus, there is a secondary market for commercial paper, but it is not nearly as liquid as that for negotiable bank CDs. Dealers report that only about 2 percent of all commercial paper is redeemed prior to maturity.

The financial crisis of 2007–2009 had a profound impact on the commercial paper market. We will discuss it in the last section of the chapter.

Credit Ratings in the Commercial Paper Market. Both Moody's Investors Service and Standard & Poor's (S&P) rate commercial paper. From highest to lowest, paper ratings run P-1, P-2, and P-3 for Moody's, and A-1, A-2, and A-3 for S&P. Nearly all firms that issue commercial paper obtain credit ratings, and most obtain ratings from both Moody's and S&P. In addition, firms that buy significant amounts of commercial paper have their own credit analysts who assess the risks of purchasing a particular firm's commercial paper. Most commercial paper receives the highest rating. It is extremely difficult to sell commercial paper with the lowest rating, especially during hard economic times. Companies of less than great creditworthiness are therefore unable to use the commercial paper market and have to resort to alternative sources of short-term financing, such as bank loans.

Issuing Commercial Paper. Firms issuing commercial paper can sell it either directly to investors using their own sales force or indirectly using commercial paper dealers. Several dozen firms sell their commercial paper through direct placement. Most of these are large finance companies and bank holding companies, their volume accounting for about 60 percent of all commercial paper sold. Some of the major companies issuing paper directly are GE Capital, Bank of America, and Ford Motor Credit.

The major incentive for direct placement is that the issuer is able to save approximately one-tenth to one-eighth of a percent for the dealer's underwriting commission. For the commission, dealers can perform a number of services. First, dealers price the securities, given current market conditions, and also guarantee the sale of the entire issue. Dealers are able to do this because they transact in and monitor the commercial paper market on a daily basis, maintain contact with a large number of firms, and have a sales force in place. They also provide all of the legal work and administrative assistance to bring a new issue to market. Unless a firm is a regular participant in the market, it is less expensive to issue commercial paper through a dealer.

For example, if a firm places $100 million in commercial paper through a dealer, the commission cost would be $125,000. However, to achieve the $125,000 savings, the issuer must maintain a small sales force—usually three to six employees plus a manager. Thus, most firms find that it pays to deal directly when the average annual amount issuance exceeds $500 million.

Terms on directly placed commercial paper are negotiated directly between the borrower and the supplier of funds. When an agreement is reached as to the rate, maturity date, and amount to be borrowed, the borrower prints the agreement (often over a direct computer linkage to the supplier of funds), and the supplier of funds wires the money to the borrower's bank account.

In most cases, issuers back up their commercial paper with a line of credit from a commercial bank because there is always the risk that an issuer might not be able to pay off or roll over the maturing paper. *Rolling over paper* means that the issuer sells new commercial paper to get the funds to retire maturing paper. Therefore, backup credit lines ensure a source of funds in the event that the firm experiences a cash-flow problem or if credit market conditions become tight. Most investors do not buy commercial paper unless it is backed by a bank credit line. Banks receive a fee for providing backup credit lines. Most banks include a clause that allows them to refuse to lend via the back-up line of credit in the case of *adverse material change* in the borrower's financial conditions.

On August 16, 2007, Countrywide Financial (the largest U.S. mortgage lender at the time) announced the intent to draw on its entire $11.5 billion credit line from a group of 40 banks. The loan was necessitated by Countrywide's inability to borrow in the commercial paper market, as it had done regularly in the past. When Countrywide made mortgage loans, it usually packaged them for sale to large investors as mortgage-backed securities. Amid mounting concerns about credit quality of the mortgages made by Countrywide and other mortgage lenders, the market for many categories of mortgage-backed securities froze in the beginning of August 2007. Credit rating agencies Fitch, Moody's, and Standard & Poor's downgraded Countrywide's debt. The side effect of the downgrades was Countrywide's inability to access the commercial paper market. After struggling for several more months, Countrywide was acquired in 2008 by Bank of America in an all-stock transaction for $4 billion, a small fraction of its market value 2 years prior to the transaction.

Commercial Paper Yields. Like Treasury bills, commercial paper is sold on a discount basis (i.e., it pays no coupon interest). Equations 7.1 and 7.2 can be used to compute the discount yield and the bond equivalent yield on commercial paper.

Let's work through an example using Equations 7.1 and 7.2. Suppose a company purchases $1 million of 45-day commercial paper issued by GE Capital, a large finance company, for a price of $997,200. The discount yield on the commercial paper is calculated as follows:

$$y_d = \frac{\$1,000,000 - \$997,200}{\$1,000,000} \times \frac{360}{45} \times 100\%$$
$$= 2.24\%$$

On a bond equivalent basis, the yield is

$$y_{be} = \frac{\$1,000,000 - \$997,200}{\$997,200} \times \frac{365}{45} \times 100\%$$
$$= 2.28\%$$

As is the case with T-bills, note that the bond equivalent yield is higher than the discount yield.

NEGOTIABLE CERTIFICATES OF DEPOSIT

A *negotiable certificate of deposit (CD)* is a time deposit, issued by a bank or a thrift institution such as a savings bank, that is negotiable (i.e., transferrable). Thus, it can be traded in the secondary market before maturity. The denominations of CDs range from $100,000 to $10 million. However, few negotiable CDs have denominations of less than $1 million because smaller denominations are not as marketable and sell at concession prices. The normal round-lot trading unit among dealers is $1 million. Due to large denominations, negotiable CDs are also known as *jumbo* CDs (as opposed to smaller *retail* CDs).

Negotiable CDs typically have maturities of 2 weeks to 6 months. Beyond the 6-month maturity, the volume is small and there is not an active secondary market. Most negotiable CDs, regardless of where the issuer is located, are payable in New York City in immediately available funds. This eliminates the problem of customers having to ship securities out of New York City to be presented to the issuing bank for payment.

Background of the CD Market.   The idea of a certificate of deposit is not really new. CDs, in one form or another, were sold by banks early in the 1900s to attract consumer and business deposits. Before 1960, however, CDs were rarely issued in negotiable form. In 1961, Citibank announced that it would issue negotiable CDs in large denominations and that major government security dealers had agreed to make a secondary market in them. Other money-center banks and dealers quickly followed Citibank's lead, paving the way for what proved to be a major innovation in the manner in which today's large banks manage their liquidity.

One reason for the development of negotiable CDs was the long-term trend of declining demand for business demand deposits at large banks. Banks are prohibited from paying interest on these accounts. Corporate treasurers, in managing their cash balances, were minimizing demand deposit balances and investing these funds in safe, income-generating money market instruments, such as Treasury bills and commercial paper. Large New York City banks, which are the principal banks for most large corporations, experienced substantial reductions in deposits. Negotiable CDs were designed to recapture lost corporate deposits by allowing commercial banks to pay competitive interest rates for short-term funds.

The primary purchasers of CDs are corporate treasurers interested in maximizing the return of their firms' excess funds while maintaining the liquidity and safety of their principal. The existence of a large secondary market is one of the major reasons money-center banks can attract a large quantity of corporate funds. The secondary market allows corporate treasurers to enter the market at any time and on either side—selling when they want to raise cash quickly or realize profits (accrued interest), or buying when they want maturities shorter than can be acquired in the primary market. Surveys by the Federal Reserve System indicate that between 70 and 80 percent of CDs are purchased by corporate customers.

Negotiable CD Yields.   In the United States, bank deposits are currently insured by the Federal Deposit Insurance Corporation (FDIC) for up to $250,000 per depositor per bank. However, because most NCDs have denominations much larger than $250,000, they are not risk-free instruments. The underlying factors that determine the yield are current money market conditions; rates paid by competing banks on their CDs; yield on other similar short-term instruments; and the characteristics of the issue, such as the default risk and marketability of the CD. If a bank is eager to attract funds, it may offer a rate above the yields on NCDs with similar default risk and marketability issued by other banks.

Large money-center banks are usually able to issue NCDs at lower interest rates than smaller regional banks. The reason for this tiering of interest rates is the lower perceived default risk and greater marketability of prime-name banks' NCDs. This difference is also justified by past handling of failing banks by bank regulators. For example, the largest banks in the United States were all provided government support during the peak of the financial crisis in the fall of 2008 through the Troubled Asset Relief Program (TARP). Also, the FDIC has typically not allowed large banks to fail (most failures are small banks). A failing large bank is usually merged with another bank, and uninsured depositors rarely lose any money. In the largest U.S. bank failure to date, the failed institution Washington Mutual was merged with J.P. Morgan in September 2008; no depositors lost money. In general, smaller regional banks pay a premium of 5 to 25 basis points to sell their CDs.

Similarly to fed funds and repos, negotiable CDs are add-on instruments, with interest paid over and above the principal balance (i.e., face value) using a 360-day year. To make CD yields comparable to bond equivalent rates, an adjustment must be made to allow for a 365-day year.

BANKER'S ACCEPTANCE

A **banker's acceptance** is a time draft drawn on and accepted by a commercial bank. *Time drafts* are orders to pay a specified amount of money to the bearer on a given future date. They are different from *sight drafts*, which are orders to pay immediately (bank checks are sight drafts). By accepting a time draft, a bank unconditionally promises to pay to the holder the face amount of the draft at maturity, even if the bank encounters difficulty collecting from its customers. It is the act of the bank substituting its creditworthiness for that of the issuer that makes banker's acceptances marketable instruments.

Most banker's acceptances arise in international transactions between exporters and importers of different countries. The accepting bank can be either a U.S. or a foreign bank, and the transaction can be denominated in any currency. The U.S. secondary market consists primarily of dollar acceptance financing, in which the acceptor is a U.S. bank and the draft is denominated in dollars.

Banker's acceptances, like T-bills, are discount instruments, with yields quoted on a discount basis. They trade in round lots, typically between $100,000 and $500,000. The maturities are typically between 30 and 180 days. The default risk involved is quite low: During more than 70 years that banker's acceptances have been traded in the United States, no investor has ever suffered a loss of principal.

History of Banker's Acceptances.   Banker's acceptances date back as far as the twelfth century. Early acceptances were used primarily in Europe to finance international trade. In the United States, they were not widely used until after the establishment of the Federal Reserve System in 1913. At that time, the Federal Reserve wanted to develop a dollar-based acceptance market to enhance the role of New York City as a center for international trade and finance.

Until the 1960s, banker's acceptances were not a major money market instrument. Their use depended on world economic conditions and the extent of U.S. foreign trade. Beginning in the 1960s, with the tremendous expansion of international trade, the volume of acceptances grew exponentially and peaked at above $70 billion in the early 1980s. However, over the next 2 decades, the volume declined significantly. First, in 1984, the Federal Reserve announced it would no longer accept banker's acceptances as collateral for repurchase agreements in its open-market operations, which decreased the instrument's attractiveness to its potential holders. The Fed also stopped buying and selling banker's acceptances for its own account. Second, borrowers have come to rely less on banker's acceptances and more on alternative sources of financing such as bank loans and commercial paper (including asset-backed commercial paper). As of October 2010, the volume of outstanding banker's acceptances in the United States (excluding banks' holdings of their own acceptances) was less than $100 million. Banker's acceptances have fallen out of active use because they are relatively cumbersome instruments and may not be well suited to modern finance.

Creating a Banker's Acceptance.   To illustrate how banker's acceptances are created, the following example is helpful. The sequence of events for our transaction
can be followed in Exhibit 7.7. Assume that a U.S. importer wishes to finance the
importation of Colombian coffee and pay for the coffee in 90 days. To obtain
financing, the importer has an American bank write an irrevocable **letter of
credit** for the amount of the sale, which is sent to the Colombian exporter. The
letter specifies the details of the shipment and authorizes the Colombian exporter
to draw a time draft for the sale price on the importer's bank. When the coffee is
shipped, the exporter draws the draft on the American bank and then transfers the
draft at a discount to its local bank, thereby receiving immediate cash payment for
the coffee. The exporter's bank then sends the time draft, along with the proper
shipping documents, to the American bank. The American bank accepts the draft
by stamping "ACCEPTED" on its face and signs the instrument. The bank either
returns the stamped time draft (acceptance) to the exporter's bank or immediately
pays the exporter's bank for it at a discounted price that reflects the time value of
money during the waiting period. If the American bank pays the exporter's bank
for the acceptance, it can then either hold the accepted draft as an investment or
sell it in the open market as a source of funds. When the draft matures, the
American importer is responsible for paying the accepting bank. The American
bank thus earns the difference between the discounted value it paid to the exporter's
bank and the face value of the time draft. The American bank also earns a fee for

---

EXHIBIT 7.7

The Sequence of a Banker's Acceptance Transaction

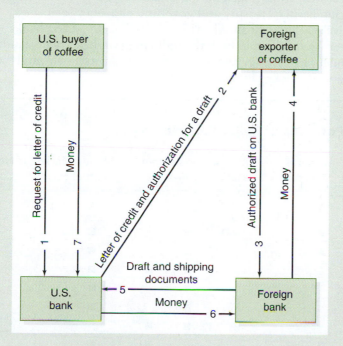

This exhibit shows a possible sequence for creating a banker's acceptance. However, there are
many ways to create acceptances, and to do so requires a great deal of specialized knowledge
on the part of the accepting bank.

providing the letter of credit, typically between 0.1 percent and 0.25 percent of the face amount. If for some reason the importer fails to pay, the accepting bank has legal recourse to collect from it.

7.8 MONEY MARKET PARTICIPANTS

To explain more fully how money markets operate, we discuss the major players in the money market, why they are in the market, and their typical balance sheet position. Exhibit 7.8 presents the major money market participants and the instruments most important to their operation.

COMMERCIAL BANKS

Commercial banks are by far the most important class of buyers and sellers of money market instruments. As Exhibit 7.8 shows, banks engage actively in all the money markets. They are continuously in the process of adjusting their liquidity because of the short-term nature of their liabilities, wide variations in loan demand, and legal reserve requirements imposed on banks by regulations. During periods of cyclical boom, banks are typically faced with the problem of reserve deficiencies because of heavy loan demand. Needed reserves can be obtained by selling securities, such as short-term Treasury securities, from their investment portfolio, or banks can borrow reserves from other banks (federal funds), sell negotiable CDs, sell commercial paper, or borrow in the Eurodollar market. At other times, particularly during recessions, a major bank problem is that of investing excess reserves. During such periods, banks typically build up their secondary reserves by purchasing Treasury and government agency securities.

In the wake of the financial crisis of 2007–2009, U.S. banks significantly decreased their lending due to both the tightening of their credit standards and the lower demand for loans in a recessionary economic environment, and they increased

EXHIBIT 7.8
Money Market Balance Sheet Positions of Major Participants

Instrument	Commercial Banks A	Commercial Banks L	Federal Reserve A	Federal Reserve L	U.S. Treasury A	U.S. Treasury L	Dealers and Brokers A	Dealers and Brokers L	Money Market Mutual Funds A	Money Market Mutual Funds L	Nonfinancial Corporations A	Nonfinancial Corporations L
Treasury bills	■		■			■	■		■		■	
Agency securities	■		■				■		■		■	
Commercial paper	■	■					■	■	■		■	■
Banker's acceptances	■	■					■		■		■	
Negotiable CDs	■	■					■				■	
Federal funds	■	■					■	■				
Repurchase agreements	■	■	■	■			■	■	■		■	

Commercial banks are both important investors and issuers of money market instruments.

Note: A = assets, L = liabilities.

their cash holdings. As of January 26, 2011, banks in the United States held $1.166 trillion of cash assets, or 9.75 percent of the total assets of $11.961 trillion, which represented an uncharacteristically high level by historical standards. Most of these cash assets were reserve balances held on accounts at the Federal Reserve Banks, which have earned interest (albeit small) since October 2008.

THE FEDERAL RESERVE SYSTEM

Although commercial banks are the largest class of participants in the money markets, the Federal Reserve is ultimately the most important participant because of its position as manager of the nation's money supply. The Federal Reserve System has no liquidity problems because of its ability to create money—its monetary power. Monetary policy is implemented by controlling the amount of reserve balances that member banks hold at the Federal Reserve. Changes in reserve balances are usually accomplished by open-market operations—the sale or purchase of Treasury securities by the Federal Reserve Bank. Thus, direct intervention by the Federal Reserve in the Treasury securities market affects the liquidity of the nation's banking system by altering banks' reserve positions, which indirectly affects the liquidity of all economic units in the economy by its impact on general business conditions.

During and after the financial crisis of 2007–2009, the Fed undertook some unorthodox measures to stabilize the money markets. We will discuss some of these measures in the last section of the chapter.

THE U.S. TREASURY AND TREASURY SECURITY DEALERS

Unlike the Federal Reserve System, the Treasury Department has a major liquidity problem. Tax receipts tend to be concentrated around the scheduled tax payment dates, but government expenditures tend to be more evenly distributed throughout the year. Total government expenditures rarely equal, and often exceed, total receipts. The Treasury Department is given the job of financing the federal government's large debt; thus, it issues both long- and short-term securities.

The economic function of primary government security dealers is to "make a market" for Treasury securities by maintaining an active position in most of the maturities issued. That is, dealers maintain an inventory of these securities at their own risk and stand ready to buy or sell from these inventories almost any quantity of Treasury securities at their quoted bid or offer price. Making a market greatly increases the liquidity of Treasury securities because the brokerage function of matching buyers and sellers in multimillion-dollar transactions would prove to be difficult, if not impossible, without it.

Most large dealers also trade in other money and capital market instruments. For example, some large dealers make markets in federal agency securities, negotiable CDs, and state and local government bonds. Still others specialize in commercial paper, corporate bonds, and over-the-counter stocks. Many securities dealers finance their holdings of securities by borrowing in the repurchase agreement or fed funds markets. Thus, dealers help link the nation's money and capital markets together.

The lure of becoming a bond market dealer is based in the immense leverage available in the government securities market. Favorable interest rate movements can mean substantial profits. However, high leverage means higher risk, and unfavorable interest rate swings of only a few basis points can mean catastrophic losses.

Before 2008, the five largest independent U.S. investment banks—Goldman Sachs, Morgan Stanley, Bear Stearns, Merrill Lynch, and Lehman Brothers—were all big players in the securities trading business. Investment banks could use more leverage than bank holding companies such as Citigroup and Bank of America, which also have securities trading businesses. By the end of 2008, Goldman Sachs and Morgan Stanley converted to bank holding companies to be able to receive help from the Federal Reserve; they had to significantly reduce their leverage. Bear Stearns was forced by regulators into a merger with J.P. Morgan in the spring of 2008 because it had experienced large losses, and investors' confidence eroded to the point when the company had difficulty borrowing short-term funds, practically a death sentence for a trading shop. Merrill Lynch, which also had experienced large losses in several consecutive quarters, announced its merger with Bank of America in September 2008 (completed in January 2009). Lehman Brothers did not get as lucky as Bear Stearns or Merrill Lynch and had to file for bankruptcy in September 2008, also after a streak of big losses and counterparties' unwillingness to lend to Lehman. This is not to suggest that these institutions suffered because they traded money market instruments and bonds. They made risky bets involving mortgage-backed securities and more complex instruments, and some of them took multibillion dollar losses as a result. Combined with very high leverage, it brought the investment banking industry to its knees. Throughout the crisis, only Goldman Sachs remained profitable among major trading firms.

MONEY MARKET MUTUAL FUNDS

Money market mutual funds (MMMFs) are investment funds that pool funds from numerous investors and invest in money market instruments. Being portfolios of liquid investments with low default risk, MMMFs often provide investors with check-writing abilities and thus may be viewed as an alternative to bank deposits. Some MMMFs cater to institutional (corporate) investors; they set high minimum invest-ment levels (e.g., $50,000). Others are known as retail MMMFs; their minimum investments are within reach of most individuals. Some MMMFs specialize in invest-ing in Treasury bills only, while others invest in a variety of money market instru-ments. Total assets of retail and institutional MMMFs were $2.26 trillion as of the end of 2010. This represents a very large fraction of total money market instruments (see Exhibit 7.1), making MMMFs, as a group, one of the most important money market investors. These institutions will be covered in more detail in Chapter 19.

NONFINANCIAL CORPORATIONS

Although not as severe as the liquidity problems facing commercial banks, liquid-ity management problems also plague nonfinancial corporations. For them, the inflow of cash usually comes from the collection of accounts receivable that have been generated from sales. Corporate cash disbursements take place in various forms, such as expenditures for tax obligations, payrolls, inventory purchases, and payments for services necessary to do business.

Because cash flows rarely balance, corporate treasuries are constantly juggling their cash positions. The focal point of corporate cash management strategy is the relationship with commercial banks. Some cash balances are held at commercial banks for liquidity needs and others are held as compensating balances as payment for bank services. Because compensating balance service contracts are usually based on monthly averages, corporate treasuries can use these bank balances as a day-to-day buffer for small, unexpected variations in cash flows. For larger, more persistent cash demands, corporate treasuries arrange for lines of credit or seasonal bank loans. If the corporation is large enough, it may find that commercial paper is a less expensive source of short-term credit than borrowing from a bank.

Although the various money market instruments have their individual differences, under normal market conditions, they serve as close substitutes for each other in investment portfolios. For this reason, the interest rates on different money market instruments tend to fluctuate closely together over time. Temporary spread divergences set off arbitrage forces that restore the rates to their normal spread. Specifically, arbitrageurs buy money market securities with relatively attractive yields and sell securities with less attractive yields. The implicit assumption in this argument is that the different money market securities have relatively similar levels of default risk and liquidity; thus, they can be viewed as close substitutes for each other. This, as we mentioned, holds under normal market conditions. But the period from August 2007 through early 2009 was anything but normal in the money markets.

The crisis started in the U.S. subprime mortgage market and spread to other parts of financial markets in 2007. Many financial institutions in the United States made numerous mortgage loans to borrowers of subprime (i.e., low) credit quality between 2002 and 2006. A low interest rate environment and the quest for more profits by financial institutions relying on an overly optimistic assumption of ever-increasing real estate prices led to subprime mortgages amounting to a significant fraction of total mortgage loans. It all worked well as long as real estate prices were rising, but it resulted in catastrophic losses to many investors as the economy started slowing down at the peak of the business cycle, the overbuilt housing market could not absorb many more properties, and subprime borrowers started to default on their mortgages. The problem was that many, if not most, of these loans had been securitized and sold to investors other than the originating institutions, spreading the risk through most financial markets.

The bad news compounded as more and more major financial institutions announced large losses in 2006 and 2007. Then a forced sale of the investment bank Bear Stearns to J.P. Morgan followed in March 2008. It was deemed by regulators that Bear Stearns would not be able to survive on its own. The culmination came in September 2008, when several major negative events took place:

- Due to large continuing losses, the U.S. government placed Fannie Mae and Freddie Mac, the two large government-sponsored enterprises that heavily invest in and insure mortgages, into conservatorship and guaranteed their debt.
- Merrill Lynch was sold to Bank of America amid concerns about Merrill Lynch's ability to survive on its own.
- The investment bank Lehman Brothers filed for bankruptcy due to its inability to roll over debt. Government rescue was discussed but eventually not provided.
- The Reserve Primary money market mutual fund "broke the buck" (i.e., had a negative return on its investment portfolio) due to its holdings of the Lehman Brothers commercial paper; it was only the second such occurrence in the 35-year history of MMMFs.
- The Federal Reserve bailed out a large insurance company, AIG, with an $85 billion loan.

7.9 THE IMPACT OF THE 2007– 2009 FINANCIAL CRISIS ON THE MONEY MARKETS

As a result, many market participants lost confidence in many institutions and the overall health of the financial system. This is a simple description of a complex matter, but it provides the minimum background for the discussion of the impact of the crisis on the markets for different money market instruments, which follows. We also discuss what measures the Federal Reserve undertook to combat the crisis in the money markets.

TREASURY BILLS

When there is a crisis of confidence (i.e., concerns about increased default risk), investors often move to less risky securities in what is described as a flight to quality, flight to safety, or flight from risk. U.S. Treasury securities have the lowest perceived credit risk, and such flights increase the demand for T-bills, thus increasing their prices and decreasing yields. Starting in August 2007, T-bill yields decreased steadily until December 2008. On December 8–9, 2008, the stop-out yields in the Treasury auctions were 0 percent and 0.005 percent for 4-week and 13-week bills, respectively. Investors willing to accept a yield of zero on a safe investment clearly worry about preserving their capital and not about earning positive return on their money. T-bill yields remained very low as of January 2011 (see Exhibit 7.3). The U.S. Treasury significantly increased issuance of bills, notes, and bonds during the crisis to raise the funds needed to stimulate the economy. Exhibit 7.1 showed almost a twofold increase in outstanding T-bills from the end of 2005 to October 2010. This increase in the supply of bills was easily absorbed by an even greater increase in the demand for safe securities, which resulted in very low yields, that is, a very low cost of short-term borrowing for the U.S. government.

The other side of a flight to quality is a flight from risk. Investors move their money to safe havens, such as U.S. T-bills, from riskier asset classes, such as equities, corporate bonds, and even money market instruments issued by borrowers with higher perceived credit risk than the U.S. government.

COMMERCIAL PAPER

In the money markets, asset-backed commercial paper (ABCP) took the first major hit of the crisis in August 2007. Much of ABCP had been issued by financial institutions to finance purchases of longer-term assets. That is, a bank would issue commercial paper and use the proceeds to either make or buy longer-term investments with higher yields (including subprime mortgages). These longer-term investments would be pledged against the commercial paper (hence the term *asset-backed paper*). This strategy relies on the ability of the issuer to *roll over* the paper (i.e., to issue new paper to repay the maturing one) at a low cost. In 2007, many of the assets backing ABCP issues performed poorly, making investors much less willing to purchase ABCP. As markets became unwilling to purchase ABCP because of valuation issues, cash flow issues arose for financial institutions relying on rolling over their ABCP to obtain funds for use in longer-term investments. On August 8, 2007, ABCP yields rose dramatically, as investors started selling off the paper. Some institutions were forced to liquidate their longer-term investments quickly, sometimes at substantial losses, when they were unable to sell new issues of ABCP. The outstanding amount of ABCP declined from its peak of $1.21 trillion in August 2007 to $0.39 trillion in November 2010.

The outstanding amount of financial commercial paper (unsecured paper issued by finance companies and bank holding companies) also declined, from the peak of $0.86 trillion in March 2008 to $0.52 trillion in November 2010. This dramatic decline means that some borrowers could no longer issue the instrument at acceptable rates and had to resort to other sources of funds or, in the worst case, default. The bankruptcy of Lehman Brothers in September 2008 raised questions about the viability of major U.S. financial institutions and the federal government's willingness (or lack thereof) to rescue large institutions from failure. Some investors, including money market mutual funds, started avoiding commercial paper issued by financials as well as asset-backed commercial paper (see the People & Events feature to learn more about the role of MMMFs in the commercial paper market). Another reason for the decline is a slowdown in economic activity resulting in a lower need for short-term financing. As of the end of the third quarter of 2010, total outstanding commercial paper was $1.05 trillion, down by more than a half from the peak of $2.2 trillion in July 2007.

Highly rated issuers of nonfinancial commercial paper felt the impact of the crisis the least: The outstanding amount did not decline and the yields did not deviate much from the Treasury bill yield at the height of the crisis. The outstandings declined in 2009, but it was due to the lower demand for short-term financing in a recessionary environment rather than difficulties in selling commercial paper. This segment of the commercial paper market is the smallest, however, with the outstanding amount below $0.2 trillion.

FEDERAL FUNDS AND REPURCHASE AGREEMENTS

We already mentioned in the section on federal funds that the market shrank because depositories decreased their lending and increased holdings of cash assets; however, the fed funds market remains large and active. Federal funds are different from repos because federal funds are unsecured loans. Therefore, it is the characteristics of the borrower that matter most. While there were no dramatic spikes in the average fed funds rate at the height of the crisis in the fall of 2008, banks that had experienced poor operating performance had to pay higher rates for fed funds loans in the few days following the Lehman Brothers bankruptcy. The rates went back down after the bailout of AIG was announced, likely because of the government's implied support.

Repurchase agreements (repos) are one of the largest sources of funds for securities dealers. As the financial crisis unfolded, concerns about securities firms' financial conditions mounted to the point where Bears Stern became illiquid (i.e., could not raise short-term financing). At this point, lenders were concerned about the ability to be repaid and, in the case of default, the ability to attach and liquidate collateral (especially risky collateral, such as mortgage-backed securities) in a timely and orderly manner. With these heightened concerns over risky collateral, the repo market saw a form of flight to quality as it moved increasingly toward demanding T-bills as collateral. For risky collateral, haircuts increased dramatically, in some cases to 50 percent. As the crisis progressed, the rate on U.S. government-backed repos declined, while the rate on riskier collateral repos rose relative to the appropriate benchmark. It became increasingly difficult for securities dealers to continue to operate in their usual manner.

The crisis led to significant deleveraging (i.e., decreasing the use of debt), by securities firms. The use of repos has fallen significantly relative to the pre-crisis levels. In spite of the crisis, the repo market remains large and active, similar to the fed funds market.

THE FEDERAL RESERVE AND THE CRISIS IN THE MONEY MARKETS

During and after the financial crisis of 2007–2009, the Fed undertook some unorthodox measures that are subject to significant debates among financial market participants and analysts. The measures that directly affected the money markets included expanding access to the discount window, auctioning short-term loans to depository institutions through the Term Auction Facility (TAF), paying

---

PEOPLE & EVENTS

How Breaking the Buck (Almost) Broke the Commercial Paper Market

After the Lehman Brothers bankruptcy on September 15, 2008, a large institutional money market mutual fund, Reserve Primary, "broke the buck." What does that expression mean? MMMFs invest in money market instruments such as T-bills and commercial paper. Most MMMFs strive to maintain a value per share of $1. The increase in the value of investments is paid out monthly as a dividend (which is automatically reinvested unless the investor withdraws money). "Breaking the buck" simply means that the share price has fallen below $1. It takes a write-off of some of the fund's holdings to break the buck. The Reserve Primary Fund had its share price decline to $0.971, or 2.9 percent below $1, due to its holdings of $785 million of the Lehman Brothers commercial paper. This was only the second occurrence of breaking the buck in the 37-year history of the money market fund industry. Ironically, Reserve Primary, established in 1971, was the very first money market mutual fund in the United States.

You might think that a 2.9 percent loss on invested capital is far from extraordinary and should not make waves. This is the case in capital markets, where investors are willing to risk their money in exchange for potentially high returns. Money market investors, however, usually have cash obligations in the near future and do not want to take any risks with their temporary cash excesses. The event caused a panic among institutional money fund investors, who started making large withdrawals, not just from Reserve Primary, which had to close temporarily for redemptions because it was overwhelmed by redemption requests and was eventually liquidated, but also from other institutional MMMFs, causing them to liquidate some assets quickly. The event had serious consequences for the commercial paper market.

Since the 1970s, the development of MMMFs and the commercial paper market have gone hand in

hand: MMMFs bought commercial paper in search of superior returns on relatively safe assets, and firms were encouraged to issue commercial paper because MMMFs were willing to buy it. While all money market securities are fairly liquid, commercial paper is one of the least liquid classes held by MMMFs, and the one considered riskiest, a fact the investors were reminded of by the Lehman failure. Consequently, MMMFs started avoiding commercial paper, specifically asset-backed, financial, and lower-rated nonfinancial issues, and switched instead to safe havens such as U.S. T-bills, driving the demand for commercial paper down and yields up.

The Treasury Department reacted quickly and announced on September 19, 2008, an optional program that would prevent MMMFs from breaking the buck, which helped stop the wave of withdrawals from institutional MMMFs. The Federal Reserve, for its part, started operating the Asset Backed Commercial Paper Money Market Mutual Fund Liquidity Facility (AMLF) on September 22, 2008, which financed purchases of asset-backed commercial paper by banks and other institutions from MMMFs that faced large withdrawals. On October 27, 2008, the Fed started operating the Commercial Paper Funding Facility (CPFF), which purchased commercial paper directly from qualified issuers. It may have been a necessary step because MMMFs mostly continued to avoid commercial paper, causing difficulties to the issuers in placing their paper. The CPFF became a major investor in the commercial paper market because it accommodated more than 22 percent of all commercial paper outstanding at its peak in January 2009. As the market stabilized, the use of CPFF declined. The facility was closed in February 2010. And the Fed made a few billion dollars because no commercial paper bought by the CPFF defaulted!

interest on required and excess reserves of depository institutions, and buying commercial paper directly from issuers through the Commercial Paper Funding Facility (CPFF). The CPFF represented a major departure from the Fed's traditional ways because this facility, which was closed in February 2010, provided funds to firms that included nonfinancial corporations (central banks normally deal only with financial institutions). In December 2008, the Fed set the target federal funds rate as a range between 0 and 0.25 percent and started focusing on acquiring long-term assets, such as mortgage-backed securities, agency debt, and Treasury notes and bonds. The main goal was to stimulate economic activity by not only keeping short-term interest rates at extremely low levels (this is achieved in the money markets), but also reducing long-term interest rates to encourage borrowing and capital investments. To invest in these assets, the Fed has used the enormous amounts of excess bank reserves kept on accounts with the Fed (over $1 trillion as of February 2011) and has also borrowed from the Treasury. As the financial markets return to normalcy, banks expand lending and invest more in assets such as bonds and mortgage-backed securities, and investors' appetite for risk comes back, the challenge for the Fed may be to unwind its large portfolios of long-term assets without causing any disruptions to economic activity and normal functioning of financial markets. At the same time, increased money supply and very low interest rates have a potential to cause high inflation, posing another challenge to the U.S. central bank.

RELATIONSHIPS AMONG MONEY MARKET INTEREST RATES

Exhibit 7.9 shows yields on different money market securities as well as the target fed funds rate before, during, and after the crisis. First, we see that all yields moved closely together before the middle of 2007 and followed the target fed funds rate. The target fed funds rate is set by the Fed as a monetary policy goal. When the Fed increases the target, it tightens the money supply, which results in higher short-term interest rates. As we see, it was done from mid-2004 to mid-2006. The market-determined effective fed funds rate followed the target closely, so we did not plot it in Exhibit 7.9. Second, we see that NCD and financial commercial paper yields first increase noticeably above the target fed funds rates, while T-bill yields fall very fast in the second half of 2007. These are the first signs of flight to safety by money market investors. Third, NCD and financial commercial paper yields did not go down with T-bill yields and the fed funds target rate in March 2008, and then spiked in the fall of 2008. Both of these instruments are issued by financial institutions, and market participants had major concerns about the soundness of many financial firms and the financial services industry in general. The increased cost of short-term debt for financial firms reflected these concerns. It was not until mid-2009 before these yields moved closer to the other rates. The reduction in NCD and financial commercial paper yields indicates not only that investors became more optimistic and lowered their risk assessments of these securities but also that the weakest borrowers exited the market (these yields series represent average yields on all transactions reported by dealers or brokers). Finally, note that the nonfinancial commercial paper yield remained close to the T-bill yield and the fed funds target throughout the crisis, indicating that investors were not worried about credit quality and marketability of this asset class, and the market functioned normally.

The lesson is that different money market instruments are usually viewed as close substitutes. When investors are confident that all instruments have low credit risk and high marketability, interest rates will move closely together. However, if

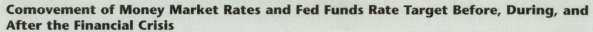

EXHIBIT 7.9

Comovement of Money Market Rates and Fed Funds Rate Target Before, During, and After the Financial Crisis

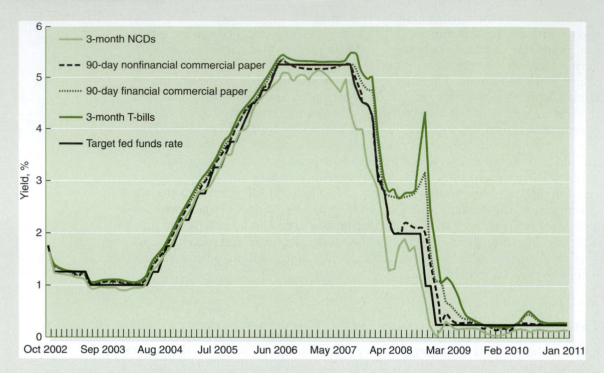

Yields in the money markets fluctuate together closely when instruments are viewed as close substitutes and diverge when some instruments are considered more risky or less marketable than others.

Source: Federal Reserve Board of Governors, H.15 Statistical Release.

concerns arise about credit quality or marketability of an instrument class, investors exit it by selling their holdings or not purchasing new issues. Money market investors are primarily concerned with preservation of their capital and have little desire to take risks.

DO YOU UNDERSTAND?

1. Why do issues of securities by U.S. government agencies tend to have higher interest rates than similar issues of debt by the U.S. Treasury?

2. Why would you never observe a U.S. Treasury bill paying the same quoted rate of interest as a negotiable CD with the same maturity?

3. Why is a repo like a secured loan?

4. How and why do banker's acceptances frequently arise in international trade transactions?

5. What is flight to quality and how did it manifest itself in the money markets from 2007 to 2009?

SUMMARY OF LEARNING OBJECTIVES

1 Explain the economic role of the money markets and why they are important to business firms. The money markets are where financial and nonfinancial businesses adjust their liquidity positions by borrowing or investing for short periods of time. The most important economic function of the money market is to provide an efficient means for economic units to conduct liquidity management when their cash expenditures and receipts are not perfectly synchronized. Commercial banks, nonfinancial corporations, and the U.S. Treasury use the money markets extensively, continuously adjusting their liquidity positions. The Federal Reserve System, perhaps the most important participant in the money market, controls the nation's money supply through open-market operations whereby it buys and sells Treasury securities.

2 Identify the key characteristics of money market instruments and why each characteristic is important. Investors in money market instruments want to take as little risk as possible given the temporary nature of their cash surplus. Issuers of money market instruments are trying to deal with temporary cash deficits. Thus, money market instruments (1) have low default risk; (2) have low price risk because of their short terms-to-maturity; (3) are highly marketable because they can be bought or sold quickly; and (4) are sold in large denominations, typically $1 million or more, so that the cost of executing transactions is low.

3 Discuss the market for Treasury bills and short-term agency securities. The most important security issued by the U.S. Treasury Department is the Treasury bill, or T-bill. T-bills have maturities of 1 year or less, are highly marketable, and are almost free of default risk because they are backed by the U.S. government. T-bills have the most active secondary market of any security and can be bought and sold at very low transaction costs. T-bills are considered to be the ideal money market instrument. Government-sponsored enterprises and federal government agencies also issue short-term debt in the money markets. They trade in active secondary markets and offer many of the advantages of T-bills, but at slightly higher yields, because of the small perceived amount of default risk and lower marketability.

4 Explain the fed funds market and explain why it is one of the most important financial markets in the United States. One of the most important financial markets in the United States, the fed funds market, is the market in which commercial banks and other financial institutions lend each other excess funds overnight. Essentially, fed funds transactions are unsecured loans between banks for 1 to 7 days, in denominations of $1 million or more. The most important role of the fed funds market is that it facilitates the conduct of monetary policy by the Federal Reserve when it conducts open-market operations.

5 Identify other money market instruments that play an important role in liquidity markets. A *repurchase agreement* (*repo*) consists of the sale of a security, usually a U.S. Treasury security, with the condition that, after a specified period of time, the original seller will buy the security back at a predetermined price. In effect, a repo is a short-term loan collateralized by a Treasury security. *Commercial paper* is a short-term promissory note issued by a large corporation to finance short-term capital needs. Commercial paper is viewed as an open-market alternative to bank borrowing, and firms use the commercial paper market to achieve interest savings over otherwise similar bank loans. A *negotiable CD* is a bank deposit that can be traded in the secondary market before its maturity. A *banker's acceptance* is a time draft drawn on and accepted by a commercial bank. Most banker's acceptances arise in international trade.

6 Describe the relationship among yields on the various money market instruments. Money market instruments share many common characteristics; therefore, they serve as close substitutes for one another. For this reason, the yields on money market instruments are highly correlated with one another. However, when concerns about credit quality or marketability of an instrument arise, investors quickly exit the market in a flight to quality, which happened during the financial crisis of 2007–2009.

7 Discuss how markets for different money market instruments were affected by the global financial crisis of 2007–2009. A result of the financial crisis was a loss in confidence in the ability of money market participants to meet their short-term obligations.

In response, investors shifted to even less risky securities. This effect increased the demand and price for T-bills to the point that yields on T-bills were at or near zero. The diminished confidence in the ability of major financial institutions to meet their obligations meant that yields on other money market instruments experienced upward pressure because of a reluctance by investors to put money into securities other than T-bills.

KEY TERMS

Money market	Federal agency	Repurchase agreement (RP)	Haircut
Treasury bill (T-bill)	Federal funds	Repo	Commercial paper
Bid-to-cover ratio	Immediately available	Reverse repurchase	Banker's acceptance
Stop (stop-out rate)	funds	agreement (reverse repo)	Letter of credit

QUESTIONS AND PROBLEMS

1. Calculate the bond equivalent yield for a 180-day T-bill that is purchased at a 6 percent asked yield. If the bill has a face value of $10,000, calculate its price.

2. What are the characteristics of money market instruments? Why must a financial claim possess these characteristics to function as a money market instrument?

3. How are U.S. Treasury and federal agency securities different? What difference primarily explains the yield differential between the two securities?

4. What types of firms issue commercial paper? What are the characteristics critical to being able to issue commercial paper?

5. Why is a bank line of credit necessary to back up an issue of commercial paper?

6. Describe the steps in a typical banker's acceptance transaction. Why is the banker's acceptance form of financing ideal in foreign transactions?

7. Explain how repurchase agreement transactions provide short-term loans to businesses. In what sense is a repo a collateralized loan?

8. Suppose Fargood Corporation engages in a repurchase agreement with The National Bank of Nebraska. In the agreement, Fargood sells $9,987,950 worth of Treasury securities to the bank and agrees to repurchase the securities in 30 days for $10,000,000.

a. Is this transaction a loan, and if so, who is the borrower and who is the lender? Defend your answer.

b. Is the loan collateralized? What is the collateral? Who holds the collateral during the term of the agreement?

c. What interest rate (or yield) is earned by the lender?

d. Draw T-accounts, similar to the example in the chapter, for this transaction. Show the assets and liabilities for each party before and after the transaction.

9. Suppose 7-day fed funds trade at 1.65 percent annually. What is the yield on fed funds on a bond-equivalent basis?

10. Why did many asset-backed and financial commercial paper issuers find it difficult to raise funds from 2007 to 2009 but nonfinancial commercial paper issuers did not?

11. What did the Federal Reserve do to stabilize the money markets from 2007 to 2009?

INTERNET EXERCISE

For purposes of this assignment, you can pretend that you are an analyst reporting to the treasurer of a Fortune 500 firm. Your boss needs to understand the status of the commercial paper market because she is considering issuing commercial paper in the near future.

1. Go to http://www.federalreserve.gov. On the left side of the Web page, select Economic Research and Data.

2. Next, choose Statistics: Releases and Historical Data.

3. Under Business Finance, choose Commercial Paper.

4. Select Outstandings, then scroll down to Month-end levels, a table of data that shows the monthly commercial paper outstanding, seasonally adjusted.

5. Using a spreadsheet program, graph the monthly amounts outstanding for both financial and nonfinancial issuers and answer the following questions:

    (a) What happened to the amount outstanding in the commercial paper market for nonfinancial issues during the past few months? What happened with respect to financial and asset-backed issues?

    (b) Why do you think there are significant differences among financial, nonfinancial, and asset-backed commercial paper?

    (c) Can you find any online articles from the *Wall Street Journal*, the *New York Times*, or *The Economist* that help you answer the questions above? What do these articles have to say about developments in the commercial paper market?

CHAPTER EIGHT

Bond Markets

Bondholders around the world had a tough year in 2009. The debt rating agency Standard & Poor's reported a record 264 global defaults, with a record $628 billion of debt affected by these defaults for the year. Almost 40 percent of the defaults and more than 50 percent of the affected amount were accounted for by so-called distressed exchanges, such as the one executed by Ford.

IT IS WEDNESDAY, MARCH 4, 2009, and you are starting the day with a headache. The value of your equity portfolio, whose composition is similar to the S&P 500 index, is below what it was 12 years ago. Adding to your headache is the worry that Ford Motor Corporation will soon default on various issues of its debt, of which you also have significant holdings. You are hardly alone in this apprehension: Ford's bonds trade at very deep discounts, below 30 cents on the dollar, reflecting the expectations of imminent default among investors. The severe recession badly hurt the North American automakers, who were already struggling in the battle with the leaner Japanese competitors.

Later in the day Ford announces a major debt-restructuring initiative. Holders of the $4.88 billion of face value of convertible notes due December 15, 2036, are offered 108 shares of Ford common stock and a cash incentive of $80 for each $1,000 in notes to be exchanged. You have until April 3 to decide. Ford's already depressed common stock price falls a little more upon the announcement due to the potential dilution effect of the conversion and closes the day at $1.87 per share. You quickly compute that, at the current stock price, the value of the offer is an unimpressive $282 per $1,000 of par value of the convertible notes, even with the $80 cash incentive. However, you also understand that converting debt to equity will reduce Ford's interest payments as well as the probability of bankruptcy, and it may allow the company to focus more on its core business. You sharpen your pencil and sit down to think seriously about the offer.

Ford also made offers to holders of nonconvertible debt, offering between 30 and 55 cents in cash on the dollar, depending on the issue. Ford had $25.8 billion in outstanding debt at the end of 2008, of which $20.7 billion was eligible to be restructured through these offers. On April 6, 2009, the company announced that it was able to reduce debt by $9.9 billion and annual interest expense by $500 million through this restructuring effort. Of the $4.88 billion of face value of the convertible notes, $4.3 billion were converted to stock. In total, Ford used $2.4 billion in cash and issued 468 million shares of common stock in this debt-reducing campaign.

Why did so many of Ford's debt holders accept far less than the face value of their holdings? Apparently, they considered it a better deal than letting the company default and go through a costly bankruptcy. While bondholders could likely recover between 20 and 50 cents on the dollar after the hypothetical bankruptcy, many of them preferred the certainty of the cash offers to the uncertainties of the bankruptcy process.

By the way, 108 shares of Ford were worth $1,738.80 at the market close on February 15, 2011. ■

Chapter 7 discussed money market instruments that have minimal credit risk. These instruments are reasonably homogeneous and are issued and held by economic units as a means to adjust liquidity. This chapter, in contrast, discusses capital market instruments whose terms, conditions, and risk vary substantially.

Capital market instruments are defined as long-term financial instruments with an original maturity of greater than 1 year. As the name implies, the proceeds from the sale of capital market instruments are usually invested in long-term assets such as industrial plants, equipment, buildings, and inventory. The chapter begins with a discussion of the function of the major participants in capital markets. We then turn our discussion to the bond markets: the markets for long-term Treasury and agency securities, state and local government tax-exempt bonds, and corporate bonds. We then discuss junk bonds, the securitization of debt, and the globalization of long-term debt markets. Finally, we look at institutional arrangements that increase the market efficiency of capital markets such as regulatory bodies and the bond-rating agencies. The market for mortgages is discussed in Chapter 9, and the market for equities is discussed in Chapter 10. ∎

LEARNING OBJECTIVES

1 Explain the role and function of capital markets. How does their role differ from that of the money markets?

2 Explain what STRIPs are and how they can be helpful in immunizing a bond portfolio against interest rate risk.

3 Discuss how the municipal bond market differs from the market for corporate bonds and the instruments traded in each market.

4 Explain what junk bonds are and why the market for them developed in the late 1980s.

5 Explain what is meant by the term *securitization of debt*.

6 Identify some of the reasons that bond markets are becoming global.

7 Discuss how the bond markets were affected by the global financial crisis of 2007–2009.

8.1 FUNCTIONS OF THE CAPITAL MARKETS

In the capital markets, the motive of firms issuing or buying securities is very different than in the money markets. In the money markets, firms are warehousing idle funds until needed for some business activity or borrowing temporarily until cash is collected. Firms buy capital goods such as plant and equipment to produce some product to earn a profit. Most of these investments are central to the firm's core business activities. Capital goods normally have a long economic life, ranging from a few years to 30 years or more. Capital assets usually are not highly marketable. As a result, most firms attempt to finance capital goods with long-term debt or equity to lock in their borrowing cost for the life of the project and to eliminate the problems associated with periodically refinancing assets.

For example, a firm buys a plant with an expected economic life of 15 years. Because short-term rates are typically lower than long-term rates, at first glance, short-term financing may look like a real deal. However, if interest rates rise dramatically, as they did in the early 1980s, the firm may find its borrowing cost skyrocketing as it has to refinance its short-term debt. And in the worst case, the firm may find it does not have adequate cash flows to support the debt and thus may be forced into bankruptcy. Similarly, if market conditions become unsettled, as they did during the 2007–2009 crisis, issuers may find themselves unable to refinance their short-term debt; if no other lenders are found, bankruptcy could again be the result.

However, if long-term securities such as bonds are used, the cost of funds is known for the life of the asset and there should be fewer refinancing problems. It should be no surprise, then, that when issuing debt for capital expenditures, firms often try to match the expected asset life with the maturity of the debt. However, there is a price to reduce interest rate and reinvestment risk: Long-term interest rates tend to be higher than short-term rates due to risk premiums.

CAPITAL MARKET PARTICIPANTS

Capital markets bring together borrowers and suppliers of long-term funds. The market also allows investors who hold previously issued securities to trade those securities for cash in the secondary capital markets.

As Exhibit 8.1 shows, the largest net purchasers of capital market securities are households. Financial institutions are a distant second because their net position (assets minus liabilities) is small, which in turn is because of their role as financial intermediaries. However, their asset and liability holdings are the largest of any capital market participant. That is, they purchase funds from individuals and others, and then issue their own securities in exchange. Hence, individuals and households may invest directly in the capital markets but, more than likely, they purchase stocks and bonds through financial institutions such as commercial banks, insurance companies, mutual funds, and pension funds.

EXHIBIT 8.1
Net Financial Positions of Major Sectors of the Economy, October 2010 ($ billions)

Sector	Financial Assets	Financial Liabilities	Net Financial Position	
			Surplus	Deficit
Households and nonprofits	$45,681.9	$13,942.4	$31,739.5	
Nonfinancial businesses	17,238.4	18,858.1		$1,619.7
State and local governments	2,672.0	3,062.9		$390.9
Federal government	1,631.8	10,710.7		9,078.9
Federal Reserve System	2,327.7	2,297.4	30.3	
Financial institutions	60,717.6	58,197.4	2,520.2	
Total	$130,269.4	$107,068.9	$23,200.5	$11,089.5

Source: Board of Governors, Federal Reserve System, Flow of Funds Accounts of the United States, December 9, 2010.

EXHIBIT 8.2
Capital Market Instruments Outstanding ($ billions)

Instrument	Year					Annual Growth Rate (%)
	1980	1990	2000	2005	2010	
Treasury notes and bonds	$407	$1,668	$2,320	$3,205	$6,757	9.9%
Federal agency debt	277	1,446	4,345	6,165	7,594	11.8%
Municipal bonds (more than 1 year)	350	956	1,223	1,738	2,259	6.5%
Corporate bonds	459	1,588	4,254	7,682	9,868	10.9%
Corporate stock (at market value)	1,476	3,333	15,722	17,318	16,906	8.5%
Mortgages	1,449	3,808	6,934	12,070	13,947	7.9%
Total	$4,418	$12,799	$34,798	$48,178	$57,331	9.0%

Note: Figures are for the end of October 2010 and the end of the year for other years. Corporate bonds and stock figures exclude holdings of foreign securities by U.S. residents. Federal agency debt includes mortgage pools guaranteed by government-sponsored enterprises.

Source: Board of Governors, Federal Reserve System, Flow of Funds Accounts of the United States, December 9, 2010.

The major issuers of capital market securities are the federal government and government agencies, state and local governments, and corporations. The federal government and its agencies issue notes and bonds to finance their operations or to refinance existing debt that is about to mature. State and local governments issue debt to finance the myriad of capital projects that municipal governments engage in, such as water treatment plants, roads, airports, convention centers, schools, prisons, and professional sports facilities. The list is restrained only by taxpayers' willingness to support these projects at the ballot box and the willingness of Congress to grant tax-exempt status. Government units cannot issue stock because they are not allowed to sell ownership in themselves. Corporations can issue both bonds and stock. The decision to issue debt and what type of debt is complex and depends on management's philosophy toward capital structure, their willingness to bear risk, and the receptivity of lenders to the securities being offered.

SIZE OF CAPITAL MARKETS

The capital markets are massive in scope, exceeding $50 trillion, as you can see in Exhibit 8.2. By 2010, it was nearly $60 trillion. The fastest growing segment of the capital market is federal agency debt, at 11.8 percent, followed by corporate bonds (10.9 percent) and Treasury notes and bonds (9.9 percent).

U.S. TREASURY NOTES AND BONDS

Treasury notes (T-notes) and **bonds** (T-bonds) are similar to T-bills in that they are issued by the U.S. Treasury and are backed by the full faith and credit of the U.S. government. Hence, they are considered to be free of default risk. They differ from bills in that they are coupon issues (paying interest semiannually) and have maturities greater than 1 year. Notes have an original maturity of 1 to 10 years, and

8.2 U.S. GOVERNMENT AND AGENCY SECURITIES

bonds have an original maturity of more than 10 years. Currently, the standard maturities are 2, 3, 5, 7, and 10 years for the notes and 30 years for the bonds. The primary and secondary markets for Treasury notes and bonds are similar to those for bills: New issues are sold at auction by the Treasury Department, and existing issues can be purchased or sold in the secondary market from securities dealers. Interest on all U.S. Treasury securities is not taxable at the state and local levels.

Many of the characteristics of U.S. Treasury securities were discussed in Chapter 7. Government debt is primarily sold in frequent, well-publicized auctions and is bid on by the approximately 30 primary dealers of government securities, who may resell the debt to the public. Other investors, including individuals, may enter *noncompetitive bids* at each Treasury securities auction through the Treasury Direct program run by the Bureau of the Public Debt within the Treasury Department. Because the maximum noncompetitive bid is $5 million for any one bidder, the primary dealers, who buy in large quantities, must bid specific *competitive* rates in increments of a half of a basis point (0.005 percent). The Treasury accepts the best bids (lowest rates) until it sells all the notes or bonds that it has offered to sell. The coupon rate for an issue is set after the auction at the highest level at which the security trades below par, in increments of 12.5 basis points (one-eighth of 1 percent). Thus, newly issued notes and bonds trade very near par immediately after the auction. For example, the February 9, 2011, auction for 10-year T-notes with the issue date of February 15, 2011, and maturity date of February 15, 2021, registered the highest accepted yield of 3.665 percent. As we know from Chapter 7, all successful bidders are allocated the Treasury securities at the highest accepted yield, known as the stop-out yield. The note's coupon was set at 3.625 percent (the nearest one-eighth of 1 percent at which the note would trade below par). To realize an annual yield to maturity of 3.665 percent on a 3.625 percent coupon 10-year note with semiannual coupons, an investor must pay $99.6676 for each $100 of par value. This is the price successful bidders paid for the T-notes.

Exhibit 8.3 shows a sample of price quotes for U.S. Treasury notes and bonds (left side) and for U.S. Treasury STRIPs (right side) from the *Wall Street Journal*

EXHIBIT 8.3
Selected Quotations on Treasury Bonds, Notes, and STRIPs on February 11, 2011

	U.S. Treasury Notes and Bonds					U.S. Treasury STRIPs					
Rate[a]	Maturity	Bid[b]	Asked	Chg	Asked Yield	Maturity	Type[c]	Bid	Asked	Chg	Asked Yield
4.875	4/30/11	100:31	101:00	−1	0.12	3/31/11	ci	99.978	99.988	0.001	0.09
1.125	12/15/11	100:22	100:23	unch.	0.27	8/15/12	ci	98.991	99.001	0.017	0.72
0.750	8/15/13	99:03	99:04	+1	1.11	5/15/17	ci	83.317	83.327	0.292	2.94
1.625 i	1/15/18	105:19	105:20	+7	0.79	2/15/25	ci	52.879	52.889	0.546	4.60
7.875	2/15/21	136:12	136:14	+19	3.52	1/31/14	np	96.076	96.086	0.044	1.35
5.375	2/15/31	111:15	111:17	+26	4.50	11/15/18	np	77.541	77.551	0.368	3.31
4.250	11/15/40	92:15	92:17	+22	4.72	11/15/40	bp	22.830	22.840	0.342	5.03

[a]i designates an inflation-indexed issue; no designation following the maturity date indicates a bond or a note.
[b]Figures after colons in bid and ask quotes represent 32nds; 99:03 means 99 3/32, or 99.09375% of face value.
[c]ci designates stripped coupon interest; np, stripped principal from a note; bp, stripped principal from a bond.

Source: Wall Street Journal Online, February 11, 2011.

on February 15, 2011. (U.S. Treasury STRIPs are discussed later in the chapter.) Column 1 in the exhibit, labeled Rate, lists the coupon rate for the Treasury security. Note that the coupon rates change in increments of one-eighth of a percent and that coupons are paid semiannually. Column 2, Maturity, shows the date on which the security matures; an "i" after the date denotes inflation-indexed securities, which we will discuss next. Column 3, labeled Bid, is the price at the close of the day in percentage of face value at which dealers buy Treasury securities from investors. Prices are quoted as a percentage of the security's face value in increments of 32nds. For example, using a face value of $1,000, the bid price on a 5.375 percent coupon Treasury bond maturing February 2031 was $1,114.69 (111 + 15/32). Column 4, Asked, is the price at the close of the day at which dealers sell securities to investors. Again, coupon increments are in 32nds and the price calculation is similar to that computed for the bid. Column 5, labeled Chg, is the change in the ask price from the previous day's closing price in 32nds. For example, for our August 2013 note, the price increased 1/32 from the previous day. Finally, Column 6, labeled Asked Yield, is the asked price converted into the bond's yield-to-maturity. The yield-to-maturity calculation is the same yield-to-maturity presented in Chapter 5 (using semiannual coupon payments). Conceptually, the yield-to-maturity is the interest rate that makes the price of the security equal to the present value of the coupon payments and the security's face value (principal).

INFLATION-INDEXED NOTES AND BONDS

In addition to the fixed-principal notes and bonds already discussed, the Treasury issues notes and bonds that adjust for inflation. These securities are commonly referred to as **Treasury Inflation Protection Securities (TIPS).** TIPS were first issued in January 1997. TIPS notes have original maturities of 5 and 10 years, and TIPS bonds have original maturities of 20 and 30 years. Just like the fixed-coupon notes and bonds, the coupon rate on a TIPS issue is determined via the auction process. Unlike the fixed-principal securities, however, the principal amount on which the coupon payments are based changes as the inflation rate changes. Specifically, the principal amount adjusts in response to changes in the Consumer Price Index for All Urban Consumers (CPI-U).

For example, consider an investor who purchases a Treasury inflation-indexed note with an original principal amount of $100,000, a 3 percent annual coupon rate (1.5 percent semiannual coupon rate), and 10 years to maturity. If the semiannual inflation rate during the 6 months ending 3 months before the first coupon payment (the 3-month lag is necessary to allow for the release of the official CPI figures) is 1 percent, the principal amount for the first coupon payment is adjusted upward by 1 percent, or $1,000, to $101,000. Therefore, the first coupon payment is $1,515 ($101,000 × 1.5%). This adjustment in principal amount takes place before each and every coupon payment. If inflation is 1.4 percent over the next 6-month period, the principal will be adjusted to $102,414 (1.4 percent above $101,000), and the coupon payment will be $1,536.21 ($102,414 × 1.5%). The yield of the inflation-indexed note quoted in Exhibit 8.3 (0.79 percent) is based on the adjusted principal. In the case of deflation (a negative CPI change), the principal value of a TIPS is adjusted downward. At maturity, the investor receives the greater of either the final principal amount or the initial par amount.

TIPS are sold three times a year and can be bought directly from the Treasury in denominations starting at $100. TIPS are designed to provide investors with a way to protect their investment against inflation. Since their introduction, the inflation-indexed bonds have proved to be popular with investors.

A TIPS coupon rate provides investors and government policymakers with a simple way to calculate the expected rate of inflation in the economy. The reason is that the principal and interest payments on TIPS are adjusted for changes in price levels; hence, the interest rate on these bonds provides a direct measure of the real rate of interest. The expected rate of inflation can be obtained by manipulating the Fisher equation to solve for the expected inflation:

$$\Delta P_e = (1 + i)/(1 + r) - 1$$

which is Equation 4.2 from Chapter 4, algebraically rearranged. We may also use the following approximation to estimate expected inflation:

$$\Delta P_e = i - r$$

For example, assume the yield on a 5-year Treasury note is 3.49 percent and the yield on 5-year TIPS is 1.10 percent. Thus, the implied expected rate of inflation for the next 5 years is

$$\Delta P_e = (1.0349/1.011) - 1 = 2.36\%.$$

Using the approximation, we get $3.49\% - 1.1\% = 2.39\%$. Our calculation tells us that 2.36 percent is the market's best estimate of the annual inflation rate for the next 5 years. Needless to say, this is valuable information for government policymakers, investors, and other persons in the private sector. However, as with any expectations, they may not be realized. Our calculated value of 2.36 percent is the market's best estimate at a point in time. As new information becomes available, the market participants will, more than likely, revise their estimate.

TIPS may not be a good choice for investors who look for significant current income from their investments. First, the increase in the principal due to inflation is taxed every year, even though the investor does not receive the adjusted principal until maturity. Second, coupon rates on TIPS are lower than on non-TIPS Treasury notes and bonds.

STRIPS

The Treasury's **Separate Trading of Registered Interest and Principal of Securities (STRIPS)** program began in 1985. A STRIPS, or a strip, is just a Treasury security that has been separated into its component parts: Each interest payment and the principal payment become a separate zero-coupon security. For example, a 10-year Treasury note consists of one principal payment, which the holder receives at maturity, and 20 semiannual interest payments. When this note is stripped, 21 separate securities are created. Today, most fixed-principal and inflation-indexed T-notes and T-bonds are eligible for the Treasury's STRIP program. The only restriction on STRIPs is that the components of a STRIP must be sold in multiples of $1,000 with the minimum face value of $1,000.

The Treasury does not issue STRIPs directly to investors. Instead, financial institutions or registered dealers and brokers buy Treasury securities whole at auction and then create stripped components to meet the demands of customers. To do this, the firms instruct the Treasury Department to recode each coupon

What Do Negative Yields on TIPS Tell Us?

On April 26, 2010, the Treasury auctioned $11.2 billion of a 5-year TIPS note maturing on April 15, 2015. The stop-out yield was 0.55 percent, so the note was issued with an annual coupon rate of 0.5 percent (the nearest one-eighth of a percent that makes an issue trade below par) at the price of 99.77. There is nothing very unusual here. While the yield is low, it is still positive.

Later that year, on October 25, 2010, the Treasury auctioned an additional $10 billion of the same TIPS note. That is, the note had the same maturity date (April 15, 2015), coupon rate (0.5 percent), and CUSIP (a security registration number) as the one auctioned on April 26. When the Treasury issues additional amounts of an outstanding issue, it is called a *reopening* of the issue. So the October 25, 2010, auction was for the reopening of the original 5-year TIPS note issued back in April. At that time, the note had 4.5 years to maturity.

The October 25, 2010, auction registered a stop-out yield of −0.55%. If a TIPS auction for a new issue has a negative stop-out yield, then the coupon rate will be zero. That is, investors will not have to pay interest to the Treasury. However, this was not a new issue but a reopening. The coupon rate was already set at the April auction at 0.5 percent. In such cases, the price of a reopened issue is set for the security to yield the stop-out rate. Accordingly, the price was set at 105.51. (Secondary market TIPS yields also ventured into the negative territory in the second half of 2010 and the beginning of 2011.)

What does a negative TIPS yield tell us about investors' expectations? Investors are worried about inflation, and they are ready to accept a slightly negative real return to protect their investment from inflation. It also implies that investors are pessimistic about returns on other asset classes such as bonds, stocks, and commodities, and that they do not want to take on risks associated with these assets. In other words, investors are not particularly upbeat about future economic growth, at least in the short term. In the second half of 2010, while the U.S. economy resumed growing after the grueling recession of 2007–2009, the economic growth was not impressive, and many market participants had doubts about the sustainability of the recovery.

To provide a concrete example, assume you expect future annual inflation to be 3 percent. That is, if you do not invest your money, you will be able to buy 3 percent less goods and services for it in a year. You share what appears to be the current consensus among investors that economic growth prospects are bleak. Accordingly, you do not want to invest in risky asset classes such as corporate bonds or equities. To avoid the loss of purchasing power, you submit a noncompetitive bid for a new TIPS issue. The auction's stop-out yield is negative, and the Treasury sets the coupon at zero, so you will actually realize a zero real return on your investment rather than a negative return. However, new TIPS issues are auctioned only a few times a year. Suppose you buy a TIPS note in a *reopening* auction or on the secondary market instead, and its yield is −0.7 percent. Thus, your annual return will be −0.7 percent, but it sure is better than −3 percent!

payment and the face value payment electronically as a separate security in the book entry system. With this done, the firm now can sell the "new" STRIP securities individually or collectively in the secondary market.

Creation of STRIPs. To give you a better feel for how STRIP securities are created and how they work, let's go through an example. Suppose that Barclays Capital decides to buy a T-note and convert it into a STRIP. The T-note has the following characteristics: maturity of 4 years; coupon rate of 6 percent (semiannual); face value of $10,000; and at its purchase price, a yield-to-maturity of

EXHIBIT 8.4
Present Value of STRIP Security Components

Maturity (in years)	CUSIP	Cash Flow at Maturity	PV of Cash Flow at 5.80%
0.5	1	$300	$291.55
1.0	2	$300	$283.33
1.5	3	$300	$275.34
2.0	4	$300	$267.58
2.5	5	$300	$260.04
3.0	6	$300	$252.71
3.5	7	$300	$245.59
4.0	8	$300	$238.67
4.0	9	$10,000	$7,955.67
			$10,070.49

The present value of STRIPS components for a 4-year Treasury note with a 6 percent coupon, a 5.80 percent yield-to-maturity, and a $10,000 face value is $10,070.48, assuming semiannual compounding.

5.8 percent (see Exhibit 8.4). To convert the T-note to STRIPs, Barclays Capital instructs the Treasury to separate the coupon payments from the principal and give each individual cash flow a separate CUSIP number. (CUSIP [Committee on Uniform Security Identification Procedures] numbers are identification numbers given to each individual security.) For illustrative purposes, we have given each cash flow a CUSIP number from 1 to 9 to emphasize the point that the original T-note is now nine separate securities. The price of the original T-note to Barclays Capital was $10,070.48, and it expects to sell the nine stripped securities for a higher price. The reason for the premium is that there are a number of investors who desire zero-coupon bonds to manage their portfolios. In particular, zero-coupon bonds are much easier to use than whole bonds (coupon payments and principal) to immunize portfolios against interest rate risk.

Using STRIPs to Hedge Against Interest Rate Risk.   STRIPs are effective vehicles for immunizing portfolios against interest rate risk. Recall from Chapter 5 that we can eliminate both price risk and reinvestment risk by structuring our bond investment such that the duration of our bond portfolio matches our holding period. Also recall that this is a dynamic problem and that we must rebalance the duration of our bond portfolio periodically to make sure its duration continues to match our holding period as our holding period shortens. By using STRIPs, however, we avoid having to rebalance our portfolio because the duration of a STRIP is the same as its maturity. If we have a holding period of 5 years and we buy a stripped security that matures in 5 years, we are assured of receiving the face amount of the STRIP security in 5 years. Investors in STRIPs must keep one more thing in mind: Accrued interest on stripped securities is taxed every year at the federal level in the United States, even though no cash will be received until maturity (unless, of course, the security is sold). Thus, taxation of STRIPs creates a cash outflow that is not necessarily offset by cash inflows from the same instrument in the same year.

GOVERNMENT AGENCY SECURITIES

Recall from Chapter 7 that a federal agency is an independent federal department or corporation established by Congress and owned or underwritten by the U.S. government. Federal agency securities result from selected government lending programs. Initially these programs were designed to attract private capital to sectors of the economy where credit flows were considered insufficient. Housing and agriculture were traditionally the principal beneficiaries of federal credit programs. In recent years, the objectives of federal credit programs have expanded to include social and economic goals and to promote conservation and resource utilization. See Exhibit 7.5 for a list of the major government agencies authorized to issue debt.

DO YOU UNDERSTAND?

1. Why do businesses use the capital markets?
2. How do T-bills, T-notes, and T-bonds differ?
3. Explain how coupon rates on TIPS are determined and how interest payments are computed.
4. What is a STRIP? Explain how these securities are created.
5. Explain how STRIPs can be used to immunize portfolios against interest rate risk.

State and local government bonds, often called **municipal bonds**, or *munis*, encompass all issues of state governments and their political subdivisions, such as cities, counties, school districts, and transit authorities. The municipal bond market is one of the largest fixed-income securities markets. The market is unique among major capital markets in that the number of issuers is so large. Estimates indicate that more than 50,000 entities have debt outstanding and an additional 30,000 have legal access to the market. No other direct capital market accommodates so many borrowers. In October 2010, there were $2.26 trillion of long-term municipal securities outstanding.

THE TYPE AND USE OF MUNICIPAL BONDS

State and local government debt generally consists of either **general obligation bonds** or **revenue bonds.** General obligation bonds are backed by the "full faith and credit" (the power to tax) of the issuing political entity; there are no assets pledged in the event of default. *Full faith and credit* means that in the event of default, the bankruptcy court requires the city or local government to raise taxes

8.3 STATE AND LOCAL GOVERNMENT BONDS

to pay coupon or principal payments. Thus, the creditworthiness of these bonds depends on the income levels of the households and the financial strength of businesses within the municipality's tax base. General obligation bonds are typically issued to provide basic services to communities, such as education, fire and police protection, and healthcare facilities. They typically require voter approval and, as a result, in recent years the market for general obligation bonds has been the slowest-growing portion of the municipal debt market.

Revenue bonds are sold to finance a specific revenue-producing project; in the event of default, only the revenue generated from the project backs these bonds. Typical revenue projects are toll roads and bridges, water and sewage treatment plants, university dormitories, parking facilities, and port facilities.

Depending on the type of project, revenue bonds may be riskier than general obligation bonds. For instance, Chesapeake Bridge and Tunnel Authority bonds went into default when a section of the bridge was destroyed. When revenue bonds default, bondholders can take control of the assets pledged and liquidate them. Revenue bonds typically do not require voter approval, which can account for their growth in recent years. The ratio of revenue bonds to general obligation bonds tends to rise during difficult economic times, when voters are less likely to approve new bond issues.

Industrial development bonds (IDBs) are a subclass of revenue bonds. IDBs were first issued to help stimulate local businesses following the Great Depression. When issuing an IDB, the municipality merely gives its approval to the sale of the bonds and assumes no legal liability in the event of default. The recipient of the funds benefits because of the lower borrowing cost associated with tax-exempt debt. Because of IDB abuses of the tax-exempt interest privileges, the tax exemption on many IDBs, other than bonds financing airports, water treatment plants, and certain other public works–related projects, was eliminated by the Tax Reform Act of 1986.

Mortgage-backed bonds are another area of abuse in the tax-exempt market. These bonds are issued by city housing authorities based on mortgage pools generated under their jurisdiction. Because interest paid on the bonds is tax-exempt, the issuer can borrow funds at low interest and then make low-interest mortgage loans. Congress intended these bonds to fund homes for low- and moderate-income people. Because of widespread abuse by some municipalities, Congress has restricted the use of mortgage-backed municipal bonds.

The Tax Reform Act of 1986 significantly restricted private-purpose tax-exempt securities. Pollution-control projects of private firms, sports and convention centers, parking facilities, and industrial parks no longer had access to the tax-exempt market. Private colleges and universities and nonprofit organizations other than hospitals were limited to a maximum of $150 million per organization in outstanding tax-exempts. Finally, other private-purpose bonds such as home mortgage bonds became subject to volume restrictions.

THE CHARACTERISTICS OF MUNICIPAL BONDS

Municipal bonds are typically issued in the minimum denomination of $5,000 and are sold as serial issues. A **serial bond issue** contains a range of maturity dates rather than all of the bonds in the issue having the same maturity date. Exhibit 8.5 shows an example of the structure of a typical serial bond issue. In the example, the issue is a serial bond issue of $1 million and has a final maturity of 8 years. The bond issue contains bonds with eight different maturity dates, ranging from

EXHIBIT 8.5
Example Structure of a Serial Tax-Exempt Bond Issue

Maturity (in years)	Coupon Rate (%)	Principal Payment ($)
1	5.00	100,000
2	5.50	100,000
3	5.90	100,000
4	6.20	100,000
5	6.45	100,000
6	6.60	100,000
7	6.70	100,000
8	6.75	300,000
	Total	$1,000,000

This exhibit illustrates the structure of a serial tax-exempt bond issue for an issue size of $1 million and a maturity of 8 years.

1 year to 8 years. Also, notice that each maturity has a different coupon rate. Typically, when the bond issue is sold, the coupon rates are assigned to correspond to the prevailing term structure in the municipal bond market. In the example, the yield curve is upward sloping. The principal payments correspond to the payment schedule that the municipality has decided for the debt service: $100,000 per year for 7 years with a final balloon payment of $300,000 for the final year.

THE TAX-EXEMPT FEATURE

Municipal securities can be distinguished from other types of securities by the fact that coupon interest payments are exempt from U.S. federal income tax. Many states in the United States also exempt their residents from state income taxes on income from munis issued in their home state. This feature lowers the borrowing cost of state and local governments because investors are willing to accept lower pretax yields on municipal bonds than on taxable securities of comparable maturity and risk. To the extent that these securities are substitutes, investors choose the security that provides the greatest after-tax return. Recall from Chapter 6 that the appropriate yield comparison is between after-tax yields on municipal securities and taxable securities:

$$i_m = i_t(1 - t) \tag{8.1}$$

where i_m and i_t are pretax yields on municipal and taxable securities of comparable maturity and risk, and t is the marginal tax rate that equates the after-tax yield on municipals and taxable securities.

Given values for t and i_t, Equation 8.1 determines the minimum municipal yield to induce investors in tax bracket t to buy municipals rather than taxable bonds. If the investor's marginal tax rate is sufficiently high, municipal securities generate higher yields after tax than taxable securities. If the investor's tax rate is sufficiently low, the opposite holds—taxable securities yield relatively more than tax-exempts. For the two markets to clear, tax-exempt and taxable security yields adjust so that at the margin the last investor who views these securities as substitutes is indifferent; the after-tax yields of the two alternatives are equal. Thus, it is the marginal tax rate of the last investor that determines the relative rate relationship between comparable tax-exempt and taxable securities.

INVESTORS IN MUNICIPAL BONDS

Exhibit 8.6 shows amounts and proportions of the total holdings for major groups of municipal debt investors. The demand for tax-exempt securities is concentrated between two groups of investors who face high marginal tax rates: high-income individuals, who may purchase them either directly or through mutual funds, and property and casualty insurance companies.

Historically, commercial banks were the major purchasers of municipal bonds. In the late 1960s and 1970s, banks typically owned more than 50 percent of all outstanding tax-exempt debt. Since then, bank ownership has declined; in 2010, banks owned only 8 percent of outstanding tax-exempt debt. In the past, bank demand for municipal securities was strongly influenced by banks' ability to engage in a form of tax arbitrage. In the past, commercial banks were allowed to deduct from their taxable income the interest expense on debt (e.g., time deposits) used to obtain funds to finance the purchase of tax-exempt securities. As a result, banks had incentives to borrow money and purchase tax-exempt securities as long as the after-tax cost of debt was below the tax-exempt interest rate. The Tax Reform Act of 1986 put an end to the deductibility of bank interest expenses for funds used to purchase tax-exempt securities (except for small issues).

EXHIBIT 8.6
Holders of Municipal Debt (October 31, 2010)

Holder	Amount ($ billions)	Percentage of Total
Households	1,058.8	37.1
Commercial banks	229.1	8.0
Property and casualty insurance companies	371.1	13.0
Money market mutual funds	331.6	11.6
Mutual funds	532.8	18.7
Other	333.2	11.7
Total[a]	2,856.6	100.0

Individuals are the largest purchasers of municipal bonds. They buy them directly and indirectly through the purchase of mutual funds.

[a]The total of $2,856.6 billion consists of $2,259.1 billion of long-term bonds issued by municipalities, $1,29.3 billion of short-term municipal debt, $266.3 billion of nonprofit organizations' debt, and $202 billion of industrial revenue bonds. The last two categories are liabilities of nonprofits and issuing corporations, respectively, but investors consider them municipal debt because they are issued with the help of municipalities and are tax-exempt.

Source: Board of Governors, Federal Reserve System, Flow of Funds Accounts of the United States, December 9, 2010.

Today, bank demand for tax-exempt securities is strongly influenced by bank incentives to purchase tax-exempt securities because of state pledging or collateral requirements for public (that is, state and local government) deposits. That is, many states require banks to collateralize public deposits with in-state tax-exempt securities. In these states, banks have additional incentives to purchase tax-exempt securities issued in the bank's home state.

Demand from property and casualty insurance companies is primarily determined by industry profitability and insurance companies' need to obtain tax-exempt income.

When commercial banks and insurance companies purchase tax-exempt securities, they tend to concentrate their portfolios in maturities that meet their institutional preferences. Specifically, banks tend to emphasize tax-exempts of high credit quality with short maturities for liquidity as well as those with maturities up to 10 years for investment. In contrast, property and casualty insurance companies concentrate on holding securities with longer-term maturities, higher yields, and lower credit ratings. Insurance companies have been especially important buyers in the market for long-term revenue bonds.

Given the supply of tax-exempt securities and the demand from banks and insurance companies, any tax-exempt securities issued in excess of those desired by firms taxed at the full corporate rate must be purchased by individuals. The greater the excess, the higher tax-exempt yields must rise relative to taxable yields to induce individuals to purchase additional tax-exempt securities. With the decline of tax-exempt holdings by insurance companies and banks since 1980, individual holdings increased from 25 percent in 1980 to 37.1 percent of outstanding tax-exempts in 2010.

AFTER-TAX YIELD COMPARISONS

When investors buy bonds, they should always make a comparison between similar taxable and exempt securities to see which option has the highest after-tax yield to the investors. To make this yield comparison, Equation 8.1 can be restated as follows:

$$i_{at} = i_{bt}(1 - t) \qquad (8.2)$$

where

i_{at} = after-tax yield on the taxable security
i_{bt} = before-tax yield on a taxable security
t = marginal tax rate for the investor (the sum of the marginal federal, state, and local tax rates)

This is Equation 6.4 from Chapter 6. To apply the equation properly, the comparison needs to be done between securities that are similar in all respects, except that one is taxable and the other is tax-exempt. That is, both securities should have the same default risk, marketability, and maturity.

Let's say that your father is considering the purchase of some 5-year sewer bonds issued by San Diego County, rated triple-A, at a yield of 4 percent. His broker recommended these bonds. You have an extra $5,000 and are wondering if it would be a good investment for you because you both live in San Diego County. Your father's total marginal tax rates for federal, state, and county tax is 35 percent. Because you are a student and work part time, your total marginal tax rate is only

15 percent. You look in the newspaper and notice that 5-year, triple-A-rated corporate bonds are yielding 5 percent. What is the correct decision for both you and your father?

For your father, the after-tax return on the corporate bond is 3.25 percent [5%(1 − 0.35)]. Thus, the tax-exempt bond yielding 5 percent provides the higher after-tax return for him. Your marginal tax rate is much lower than your father's (15 percent versus 35 percent) and, as a result, your after-tax return on the corporate bond is 4.25 percent [5%(1 − 0.15)], which makes it a better investment for you. In general, people in high-income-tax brackets find it advantageous to buy tax-exempt securities, and investors in lower tax brackets prefer taxable securities.

THE MARKET FOR MUNICIPAL BONDS

Primary Market. The **primary market** for municipal bonds has a large number of relatively small bond issues. These bonds tend to be underwritten by small regional underwriters in the immediate area of the issuing municipality. Bond issues of well-known governmental units—states, state agencies, and large cities—attract bidding syndicates of major underwriters throughout the country and are sold in a national market. The reason for the existence of local markets is the high cost of gathering information about smaller issues and the tax treatment of these bonds (most local buyers are exempt from local as well as federal taxes on their coupons). Most general obligation bonds are sold by competitive bid.

Secondary Market.   In general, the **secondary market** for municipal bonds is thin and is primarily an over-the-counter market. Although the bonds of some large, well-known municipalities do have active secondary markets, small local issues are traded infrequently, with commercial banks and local brokerage houses making the market. Because of the relatively inactive secondary market, dealers (including local banks) find it difficult to match buyers and sellers of such bonds; thus, the bid–ask spreads on municipal bonds are usually large compared to those of corporate bonds. Because of their limited marketability, municipal bonds may have higher yields than one might otherwise expect (given their ratings and tax-exempt interest feature).

8.4 CORPORATE BONDS

Corporate bonds are debt contracts requiring borrowers to make periodic payments of interest and to repay principal at the maturity date. Corporate bonds can be **bearer bonds**, for which coupons are attached that the holder presents for payment when they come due, or **registered bonds**, for which the owner is recorded and payment due is mailed to the owner. Corporate bonds are usually issued in denominations of $1,000 and are coupon-paying bonds paying interest semiannually; their coupon payments are fully taxable to the investor. Corporate debt can be sold in the domestic bond market or in the Eurobond market, which is a market for the debt issued by foreign companies and denominated in foreign currencies. For example, dollar-denominated bonds sold by U.S. corporations in Europe or Asia are Eurobonds. Most corporate bonds are **term bonds**, which means that all of the bonds that comprise a particular issue mature on a single date. In contrast, most municipal bonds are serial issues, which means that the issue contains a variety of maturity dates.

A bond **indenture** is a legal contract that states the rights, privileges, and obligations of the bond issuer and the bondholder. To ensure that the covenants in the bond indenture are carried out and to ensure the timeliness of the coupon payments, the indenture is overseen by a trustee who is appointed as the bondholder's representative. The trustee, who is usually the trust department of a large bank, initiates legal actions on behalf of the bondholders if any provision of the indenture is violated.

The indenture usually specifies the security or assets to which bondholders have prior claim in the event of default. Mortgage bonds pledge land and buildings; equipment trust certificates pledge specific industrial equipment or *rolling stock*, such as railroad cars, trucks, or airplanes; and collateral trust bonds are secured by stocks and bonds issued by other corporations or governmental units. If no assets are pledged, the bonds are secured only by the firm's potential to generate cash flows and are called **debentures**. Bond contracts that pledge assets in the event of default have lower yields than similar bonds that are unsecured.

Corporate bonds can differ in ways other than security. The debentures can be **senior debt**, giving the bondholders first priority to the firm's assets (after secured claims are satisfied) in the event of default, or **subordinated (junior) debt**, in which bondholders' claims to the company's assets rank behind senior debt.

In addition, many corporate bonds have sinking fund provisions, and most have call provisions. A **sinking fund** provision requires that the bond issuer provide funds to a trustee to retire a specific dollar amount (face amount) of bonds each year. The trustee may retire the bonds either by purchasing them in the open market or by calling them if a call provision is present. It is important to notice the distinction between a sinking fund provision and a call provision. With a *sinking fund provision*, the issuer *must* retire a portion of the bond as promised in the bond indenture. In contrast, a **call provision** is an option that grants the issuer the right to retire bonds before their maturity. Most security issues with sinking funds have call provisions because that guarantees the issuer the ability to retire bonds as they come due under the sinking fund retirement schedule.

Convertible bonds are bonds that can be converted into shares of common stock at the discretion of the bondholder. This feature permits the bondholder to share in the good fortune of the firm if the stock price rises above a certain level. That is, if the market value of the stock the bondholder receives at conversion exceeds the market value of the bond's future expected cash flows, it is to the bondholder's advantage to exchange the bonds for stock, thus making a profit. As a result, convertibility is an attractive feature to bondholders because it gives them an option for additional profits that is not available with nonconvertible bonds. Typically the conversion ratio is set so that the stock price must rise substantially, usually 15 to 20 percent, before it is profitable to convert the bond into equity.

Because convertibility gives investors an opportunity for profits not available with nonconvertible bonds, convertible bonds usually have lower yields than similar nonconvertible bonds. In addition, convertible bonds usually include a call provision so that the bond issuer can force conversion by calling the bond rather than continue to pay coupon payments on a security that has greater value on conversion than the face amount of the bond.

INVESTORS IN CORPORATE BONDS

Life insurance companies and pension funds (private and public) are the dominant purchasers of corporate bonds. Households and foreign investors also own large quantities of them. Corporate bonds are attractive to insurance companies and pension funds because of the stability of the cash flows they experience and the long-term nature of their liabilities. That is, by investing in long-term corporate bonds, these firms are able to lock in high market yields with maturities that closely match the maturity structure of their liabilities, thereby reducing their interest rate risk. In addition, both life insurance companies and pension funds are in low marginal tax brackets, and taxable corporate bonds provide them with higher after-tax yields than do tax-exempt bonds. Finally, both federal and state laws require these companies to be prudent in their investment decisions, which usually translates to purchasing investment-grade bonds—bonds rated Baa and above by Moody's and BBB and above by Standard & Poor's.

THE PRIMARY MARKET FOR CORPORATE BONDS

New corporate bond issues may be brought to market by two methods: public sale or private placement. A *public sale* means that the bond issue is offered publicly in the open market to all interested buyers; a *private placement* means that the bonds are sold privately to a limited number of investors.

Public Sales of Bonds. Public offerings of bonds are usually made through an investment banking firm, which *underwrites* them by purchasing the bonds from the issuer at a fixed price and then reselling them to individuals and institutions. The investment banker can purchase the bonds either by competitive sales or through negotiation with the issuer. A **competitive offering** is, in effect, a public auction. The issuer advertises publicly for bids from underwriters, and the bond issue is sold to the investment banker submitting the bid that results in the lowest borrowing cost to the issuer. In contrast, a **negotiated offering** represents a contractual arrangement between the underwriter and the issuer whereby the investment banker obtains the exclusive right to originate, underwrite, and distribute the new bond issue. The major difference between the two methods of sale is that, in a negotiated sale, the investment banker provides the origination and advising services to the issuer as part of the negotiated package. In a competitive sale, the issuer or an outside financial adviser performs origination services. As a rule, most public entities, such as public utility companies, are required by law to sell their bond issues by competitive sale. It is generally believed that issuers receive the lowest possible interest cost through competitive rather than negotiated sales.

Private Placement. **Private placements** emerged as a distinct method of issuing securities because of the Securities and Exchange Act of 1934, which required publicly sold securities to be registered with the Securities and Exchange Commission (SEC). The provisions of the act were intended to protect individual investors by forcing issuing firms to disclose a modicum of information about their securities. Unregistered securities (that is, private placements) could be sold only to large, financially sophisticated investors (in practice, usually large insurance companies or perhaps other institutional investors) as long as fewer than 35 investors were involved and as long as the securities did not change hands quickly. The rationale for exempting private placements from registration and disclosure requirements was that large institutional investors possessed both the resources and the sophistication to analyze the risks of securities.

In the past 20 years, private placements have become very common. The ratio of private placements to public offerings is sensitive to the business cycle. During periods of low interest rates or stable market conditions, many smaller companies of lower credit quality enter the capital markets and obtain financing by a public sale. Consequently, the ratio of private placements to public sales falls. During periods of high interest rates or unstable market conditions, these same firms sell debt privately. However, larger, better-known firms of high credit standing can easily shift between the two markets and select the market with the lower net borrowing cost.

Since the 1980s, the securities markets have become driven by institutions, with individual investors having little influence on market movements. Also, the private placement market has grown rapidly. These trends led the SEC to adopt **Rule 144A** in 1990 to liberalize the regulation of the private placement market. Most significantly, Rule 144A allows secondary trading of private securities by large institutional investors. By increasing liquidity and decreasing regulatory oversight in the capital markets, the rule should lower corporations' cost of capital. Investors such as pension funds and mutual funds, which have traditionally avoided investing in private placements because of their illiquidity, now find private placements more attractive. Furthermore, foreign corporations, which have historically shunned the highly regulated U.S. capital markets, find it more attractive to issue securities in the United States through the private placement market.

THE SECONDARY MARKET FOR CORPORATE BONDS

Most secondary trading of corporate bonds occurs through dealers, although some corporate bonds are traded on the New York Stock Exchange (NYSE). The secondary market for corporate bonds is thin compared to the markets for money market securities or corporate stock. The term **thin** means that secondary market trades of corporate bonds are relatively infrequent. As a result, the bid–ask spread quoted by dealers of corporate bonds is quite high compared to those of other, more marketable securities. The higher bid–ask spread compensates the dealer for holding relatively risky and illiquid securities in inventory.

Corporate bonds are less marketable than money market instruments and corporate equities for at least two reasons. First, corporate bonds have special features such as call provisions or sinking funds that make them difficult to value. Second, corporate bonds are long term; in general, longer-term securities are riskier and less marketable. To buy or sell a corporate bond in the secondary market, one must contact a broker, who in turn contacts a dealer (or the NYSE for exchange-listed bonds) who provides bid–ask quotes.

JUNK BONDS

During the 1980s, junk bonds became a popular form of corporate financing. **Junk bonds** are corporate bonds with high default risk and hence low bond ratings (below Moody's Baa or Standard & Poor's BBB). Junk bonds were not common in the primary market before the late 1970s, although they could be found in the secondary market. These secondary market junk bonds, the so-called fallen angels, were investment grade (Baa/BBB or greater) when originally issued but were subsequently downgraded by the rating agencies because of deterioration in the financial condition of issuing firms.

Why weren't many junk bonds sold in the primary market before the late 1970s? As discussed earlier, higher-risk bonds tend to be less marketable. In 1977, however, Drexel Burnham Lambert innovated the marketing of junk bonds in the primary market by promising investors that they would act as a dealer for junk bonds in the secondary market. Investors, therefore, were willing to take on the extra risk of junk bonds because they knew that Drexel would buy the bonds back at quoted bid prices, thereby providing liquidity to the market. However, the junk bond market experienced difficulties in the late 1980s as prices fell, and Drexel Burnham failed in 1990, thereby causing further price declines. Although prices of many bonds later recovered, this episode showed that junk bonds retain substantial risk.

The supply of junk bonds in the 1980s was part of the trend toward *disintermediation*, a process whereby firms raise capital in the direct financial markets rather than from financial intermediaries such as commercial banks. High-quality firms with investment-grade credit ratings, for example, issued commercial paper rather than borrowing from banks. These firms were able to borrow more cheaply in the commercial paper market because commercial banks incur various costs associated with loan origination and monitoring and also build in some profit margin into loan rates.

Low-quality firms with speculative-grade credit ratings, however, found that they could issue marketable debt in the direct market (that is, the junk bond market) with longer maturities than the debt they could obtain from commercial banks. Before the development of the junk bond market, low-quality firms relied on short-term or floating-rate bank loans. Banks prefer making short-term or floating-rate loans because such a strategy minimizes their interest rate risk by letting loan interest rates change in step with changes in their deposit interest rates. Borrowing firms that use short-term or floating-rate instruments to finance long-term projects, however, experience increased risk because the timing of cash inflows from their projects does not match the pattern of interest payments on short-term or floating-rate debt when short-term interest rates fluctuate.

The demand for junk bonds came from financial institutions such as life insurance companies, savings and loan associations, pension funds, and mutual funds. Junk bonds were attractive investments because investors believed they consistently outperformed high-rated bonds and even Treasury securities on a risk-adjusted basis. In the growing economy of the 1980s, the performance of junk bonds can be explained by the fact that there were far fewer defaults than expected, but during the late 1980s and early 1990s the number of defaults increased substantially. Losses from these defaults reduced the capital of many financial institutions, exacerbating the thrift crisis and contributing to the failure of several major life insurance firms. Default rates for various grades of bonds are shown in Exhibit 8.7. Even though not all is usually lost when a bond defaults (it is not uncommon for investors to recover more than 40 percent of the face value of bonds), the default rates for junk-rated bonds are very high.

Because of these failures, many observers and policymakers associate junk bonds with the so-called financial excesses of the 1980s. More specifically, critics have blamed junk bonds for the merger mania of the 1980s, for the overall rise in corporate leverage encouraged by the 1986 tax reform, and for the increased volatility of the financial markets in the 1980s. These critics called for laws or regulations that would have limited the corporate use of junk bonds and limited the ability of financial institutions to invest in them.

Research suggests that the growth of the junk bond market was coincidental with the trends described previously rather than causing them. Only a small portion

EXHIBIT 8.7

Cumulative Default Rates for U.S. Corporate Bonds Rated by Standard & Poor's, 1981–2009 (%)

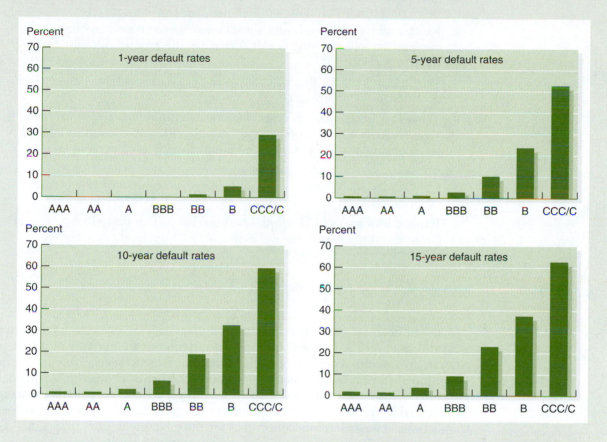

High-rated bonds rarely default in their early years of life. Over time, however, default rates increase. Junk bonds (rated BB or below) have experienced modest default rates even in their first year of existence and have very high cumulative defaults over longer horizons.

Source: Standard & Poor's Global Fixed Income Research and Standard & Poor's CreditPro®.

of mergers were actually financed with junk bonds; most junk bonds were issued to finance capital investment of small, growing companies. Furthermore, researchers have uncovered numerous other causes of the financial market volatility of the 1980s; the evidence suggests little association between junk bonds and volatility. It is true that junk bond defaults may have contributed to the failures of some financial institutions, but in many cases these institutions were in deep financial trouble before investing in junk bonds. The managers of these institutions, attempting to "hit it big" and keep their firms from going under, may not have adequately diversified their investments in junk bonds. In the end, restricting the use of junk bonds might force many small- and medium-size companies back to the more expensive, short-term intermediated credit markets, increasing their cost of capital and financial risk.

DO YOU UNDERSTAND?

1. Explain why sinking funds on corporate bond issues play the same role as the serial structure found on municipal bond issues.

2. Explain why investors should always make a tax-exempt and taxable comparison when buying bonds. What are the ground rules for making the comparison?

3. Why are individuals the major investors in municipal bonds and commercial banks are not?

4. What is your marginal tax rate if you are indifferent between investing in a corporate bond with a 6 percent coupon and a tax-exempt municipal bond of similar risk, maturity, and liquidity with a 4.2 percent coupon rate?

5. How do the secondary markets differ between municipal bonds and corporate bonds?

6. Explain how and why the junk bond market had an impact on commercial bank lending.

8.5 FINANCIAL GUARANTEES

The use of financial guarantees has grown dramatically in recent years. **Financial guarantees** cover the payment of principal and interest to investors in debt securities in the event of a default. So-called monoline (that is, specializing in one line of business) insurance companies or commercial banks provide most financial guarantees. Insurance companies write insurance policies to back bond issues; commercial banks write letters of credit to back commercial paper issues or swap transactions. The guarantors collect fees for the guarantees, usually specified as a certain percentage of the face value of the guaranteed securities.

The quality of the financial guarantee depends on the reputation and financial strength of the guarantor. When an investor buys a guaranteed security, the security issuer with a lower credit standing is, in effect, "leasing" the reputation of the guarantor that has a higher credit standing. Thus, the investor in a guaranteed security is first exposed to the default risk of the guarantor or insurer, and only in the case of their bankruptcy to the default risk of the issuer. Because of the reduction in default risk, guaranteed securities are typically more marketable than similar nonguaranteed securities, and they pay lower yields to investors.

Insurance companies and other providers of financial guarantees need very high credit ratings, most often AAA, to stay in business. A downgrade in the rating will not only increase the cost of funds to the insurer but also cause downgrades in the ratings of all the insured bonds whose ratings are lower than the insurer's original rating.

In the 1990s and early 2000s, monoline insurance companies expanded to insure asset-backed securities and residential mortgage-backed securities. Monolines were hit hard by the subprime mortgage crisis that started in the United States in 2007 and the ensuing global financial crisis.

The problem with monoline insurers was high leverage and, subsequently, low capital. For example, MBIA, the largest municipal bond insurer as of 2007, had insurance on over $1 trillion of debt, but the claims-paying ability of only $14.2 billion before the crisis. Significant delinquencies on subprime mortgages in 2007 and 2008 led to decreasing capital levels of monoline companies as they had to make payments to the holders of the defaulted securities they had insured. The second-largest municipal bond insurer as of 2007, Ambac Financial Group, which introduced municipal bond insurance in 1971, had its credit rating downgraded from AAA to AA in January 2008. It went downward from there for Ambac. After more losses, failing to raise sufficient capital, and missing a debt payment in November 2010, it filed for Chapter 11 bankruptcy protection. MBIA had enough liquidity as of the end of 2010 to meet its obligations for the next few years, but its credit rating had been downgraded by Standard & Poor's to B. This, as you know, is a junk debt rating.

Starting in the late 1970s, many loans have been *securitized* as *mortgage-backed* or *asset-backed* securities. The securities created have been sold in the nation's capital markets in competition with other capital market instruments.

The basic idea involved in securitizing a pool of loans is that separate claims on the principal and interest payments on the loans can be sold to different people. Because different people may be more interested in buying a claim on the first repayments of principal and interest than the last repayments, they may pay a higher price for a security interest in the payments that are most desirable to them. As a result, it may be possible to sell the security interests in separate payments on the pool of loans for more than the initial cost of the loans. This can be done by a process called **securitization**. Securitization involves setting up a trust that buys a large number of loans (a loan *pool*) of similar types. The trust can then sell securities of different types that "pass through" payments of principal and interest on the loans to the investors and may even vary the payments on different securities as interest rates go up or down. By creating attractive pieces, the creator of the trust hopes to sell the restructured pieces of the loans for more than it had to pay to buy the whole pool of loans.

For example, if 100 auto loans worth $2 million were sold to a trust, the trust could sell separate interests in the auto loans. Some interests, called *tranche A*, might receive a predetermined coupon rate plus all principal payments made by people repaying the amount they borrowed on their loans until the tranche was repaid in full. One thousand tranche A units might be created with a face value of $1,000 each, for a total of $1 million. Investors might accept a 7 percent interest payment on that tranche even though the auto loans paid 12 percent interest because they would receive their principal repayments quickly. Another $1 million tranche of security interests would also be created called *tranche B.* That tranche would consist of 1,000 securities that would be repaid only after $1 million in principal repayments had been repaid to holders of tranche A securities. The holders of tranche B might be promised 12.5 percent interest because their repayments would not be as quick or as certain as those of tranche A. Each holder of class B security would receive his or her pro-rated share of principal repayments after the tranche A securities had been repaid in full.

The tranche B securities might receive a premium interest rate, but because the holders of tranche A securities were willing to accept a relatively low interest rate, the trust would pay an *average* interest rate to holders of the tranches that

---

EXHIBIT 8.8
Hypothetical Securitization of Auto Loans

Trust	
Assets	**Liabilities**
100 auto loans worth $2,000,000 in face value (principal amount)	1,000 Tranche A securities with a total value of $1,000,000 at $1,000 each
	1,000 Tranche B securities with a total value of $1,000,000 at $1,000 each

Payments on a pool of loans can be divided into separate tranches. For instance, one tranche might receive only interest payments and the other only principal repayments made on loans in the pool. However, in this simple example we assume that the tranche A securities are repaid in full from the first $1,000,000 in repayments of principal for loans in the pool. Consequently, because of the quick, sure repayment, tranche A securities may need to pay only 7 percent interest to buyers. Tranche B securities are repaid in full only after tranche A securities are fully repaid. Because they have more risk and longer maturities, they may promise to pay 12.5 percent interest. They can pay higher interest than the 12 percent rate paid on the underlying auto loans because tranche A holders receive less. If the average rate paid on both tranches is less than the 12 percent earned, money is left over to pay for loan-servicing costs, losses, and profits.

---

would be less than the amount of interest it earned on the loans. Thus, it would have money left over to pay servicing costs on the loans and tranches, as well as to absorb possible losses and leave a small profit (see Exhibit 8.8). Because the total income on the loans is likely to exceed the total payments to purchasers of the security interests in the loans, the creator of the trust and service provider (collector of payments) for the loans can often make a good profit from securitization. This is particularly true when the creator of the trust securities is able to create securities that are in strong demand, so people are willing to pay a particularly high price for those securities and accept a low rate of return on that tranche.

In the 1990s and early 2000s, a wide variety of asset-backed securities were created—particularly in the mortgage market, where federal government agencies frequently guarantee mortgage loans or securities that pass through payments of principal and interest on the mortgages (see Chapter 9). In addition, the popularity of privately originated asset-backed securities improved as the private sector provided them with a variety of "credit enhancements" to reduce their default risk. The credit enhancements are designed to reduce the risk of default of various tranches and thereby allow them to obtain favorable credit ratings so they need not offer high yields (and low prices) to attract buyers.

Securitization transfers risk from the originators of loans (e.g., banks, mortgage brokers, or finance companies) to the investors and insurers of the asset-backed securities. In 2007, major concerns arose about the quality of assets that backed some such securities, especially subprime mortgage-backed securities. With subprime loan defaults increasing substantially, either investors or insurers of these securities took large losses. As a result, the issuance of asset-backed securities (ABSs) fell dramatically in 2007 and 2008. Credit rating agencies, such as Moody's and Standard & Poor's, were criticized for assigning unjustifiably high ratings (in the opinion of the critics) to structured asset-backed securities. As an example, a structured ABS may include "layers" of loans of different quality (e.g., $100 million of prime-quality mortgages and another $200 million of subprime mortgages). Assigning a rating of AAA to such a structure may be based on overly optimistic assumptions regarding the lower-quality layers. Investors often rely on credit ratings assigned by the rating agencies when making decisions. Overall, the financial crisis that started in 2007 showed that many investors either were overly optimistic regarding the future performance of inherently risky classes of securities or did not understand the risks underlying the asset-backed securities they were buying.

The most important regulator of the U.S. capital markets is the Securities and Exchange Commission (SEC), established in 1933 after the stock market crash of 1929 helped precipitate the Great Depression of the 1930s. The SEC requires that any security sold to the general public be registered with it, and that any potential buyer of the security be provided with a prospectus that fully describes the nature of the security and its issuer and all risks associated with an investment in the security. Issuers of publicly held securities must also file detailed reports with the SEC that provide complete and timely financial information and all relevant information regarding the management of the company, changes in ownership or major policies, and any other information that might materially affect the value of the company's security issues.

Because the registration process is costly and time consuming, many firms prefer to issue private placements. Others issue securities to the public but take advantage of the SEC's "shelf registration" process that allows them to complete much of the general registration procedure early so they can quickly define the terms of the securities and complete the registration process for offering their securities to the public when market conditions are most favorable.

At the state level, state securities laws, sometimes called *blue-sky laws*, require that securities be registered and meet state standards so state residents can't be sold anything under the blue sky without being informed. In some states, securities registration requirements are very restrictive; in others, they are lax.

In addition to state and federal regulation, individuals and firms that participate in the capital markets are subject to regulations imposed by self-regulatory bodies. These bodies are established to preserve the integrity of the market and the reputation of the industry so people will entrust their money to members of the industry. The National Association of Securities Dealers (NASD) is one of the foremost private regulatory authorities. It can fine people or ban them from the industry if they have violated its regulations. In addition, the various securities exchanges each have a detailed set of rules that their members must follow in their dealings with each other and the general public. Violators of the rules can be fined or expelled from membership in the exchange. The self-regulatory bodies are very important to the securities markets because it is essential that the markets retain the trust of the public. If they did not have that trust, people would be reluctant to give them money or do business with them, and their business would decline. That is why extensive private regulation of the capital markets has developed to supplement public regulation of those markets.

8.7 FINANCIAL MARKET REGULATORS

8.8 BOND MARKETS AROUND THE WORLD ARE INCREASINGLY LINKED

With the growth of multinational corporations and the relaxation of international restrictions on capital flows, many companies and government entities have begun to obtain financing in countries other than their home country. When bonds are issued outside the home country of the issuer, they must conform to the regulations imposed by the country in which they are issued. For instance, **Yankee bonds** are bonds issued by foreign entities in the United States. They are denominated in U.S. dollars and must comply with the regulations imposed by the U.S. Securities and Exchange Commission. Some Yankee bonds are traded frequently and are listed as *foreign bonds* at the bottom of the New York Bond Exchange listings in the *Wall Street Journal*.

As of October 2010, U.S. residents owned more than $1.5 trillion of foreign bonds. At the same time, foreigners (including foreign governments) held a staggering $5.5 trillion of U.S. government and agency debt securities and $2.4 trillion of U.S. corporate bonds. In addition, U.S. corporations owed many billions of dollars on debt issued in other countries. U.S. corporations frequently issue dollar-denominated debt in the Eurobond market. A **Eurobond** is a bond denominated in a currency different from the currency of the country where it is issued. Dollar-denominated bonds sold in Germany or Japanese yen–denominated bonds sold in Singapore are examples of Eurobonds. Eurodollar markets originated as a way for large, well-known U.S. borrowers to obtain dollar financing from foreigners who were willing to buy the issuers' bonds and might offer better financing terms than the issuer could obtain in the United States. In the past, some buyers preferred Eurobonds issued in countries that allowed unregistered bearer bonds to be issued and did not require that withholding taxes be levied on interest payments. Such rules might allow some people to avoid taxes. In addition, with relaxed regulations in some countries, it often was cheaper and easier for U.S. corporations to obtain funding abroad than in the United States.

Although most large U.S. corporations have obtained financing from European markets, in recent years they also have obtained financing by issuing Samurai bonds. **Samurai bonds** are yen-denominated bonds issued by foreign companies in Japan. Because the Japanese are possibly the world's most prolific savers, interest rates in Japan tend to be low, but, of course, the borrower incurs foreign exchange risk if it converts the yen to other currencies after borrowing them. Most borrowers simultaneously enter into currency swaps or hedge their foreign exchange risk exposure in other ways. Nonetheless, because yen interest rates have been so low, the Japanese Samurai bond market has expanded dramatically. The market peaked in 1996, when $34 billion of Samurai bonds were issued, which accounted for a quarter of the yen-denominated debt issued in Japan and exceeded the volume of Euroyen debt issues (yen-denominated debt issued outside Japan). U.S. issuers continue to use the Samurai market. For example, Wal-Mart sold 100 billion yen (over $1 billion) of Samurai bonds in July 2008. The coupon on the 5-year portion of the sale was about half what Wal-Mart committed to pay on notes with a similar maturity sold in the United States in April 2008. Samurai bond issuances exceeded $22 billion in 2010.

International credit ratings have become increasingly important in the global bond markets because an important determinant of international credit ratings is *country risk*: Governments sometimes restrict currency flows out of their countries or otherwise cause companies to default on their debts. Thus, it is rare for any corporation to have an international credit rating higher than that of its home country.

Like money markets, bond markets also experienced a flight to quality in 2007–2009. Issuers with lower credit ratings found it expensive and at times difficult to sell new bonds. Secondary market yields on lower-rated issues also increased relative to Treasury bonds. Exhibit 8.9 plots the differences between the yields of Aaa-rated corporate bonds and long-term U.S. Treasury securities, Baa- and Aaa-rated bonds, and Baa-rated bonds and Treasuries. U.S. Treasury securities have the lowest yields because they are considered almost default risk–free. Aaa is the highest corporate debt rating, and Baa is the lowest investment-grade debt rating assigned by Moody's. The differences between yields of debt instruments with different default risk (as measured by ratings) are called **credit spreads**. Of course, we expect bonds with the lower rating (Baa) to have higher yields than bonds with the higher rating (Aaa) and Treasuries. Thus, it is not surprising that all three credit spreads are always positive. However, the spreads are not constant; they change with market conditions and perceived probabilities of default by issuers of certain credit quality. The credit spreads started to widen in the middle of 2007 and peaked in December 2008. However, even at the peak, the Aaa–Treasury spread stayed below 2 percent. The Baa–Treasury spread, however, skyrocketed to over 5 percent, three times its pre-crisis level. This is a manifestation of a flight to quality. The bond markets returned to normalcy in the second half of 2009 and in 2010, when many corporations of various credit ratings issued large amounts of debt because raising debt was much cheaper (given the low interest rate environment) than raising equity, which still traded at the levels well below the highs of 2007. According to Standard & Poor's, corporations around the world issued $3.88 trillion and $3.19 trillion of bonds in 2009 and 2010, respectively. Speculative-grade U.S. issuers sold $162.7 billion of bonds in 2009 and $287 billion in 2010, which were consecutive records.

8.9 THE IMPACT OF THE 2007–2009 FINANCIAL CRISIS ON THE BOND MARKETS

EXHIBIT 8.9
Credit Spreads

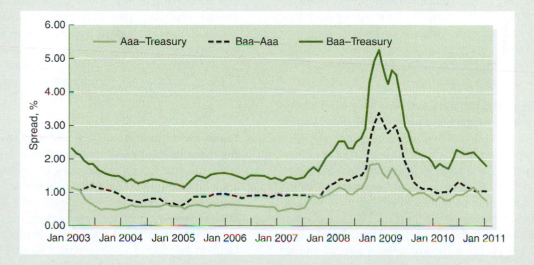

Credit spreads widen as the perceived risk of default of lower-rated borrowers increases.

Source: Federal Reserve Bank of St. Louis.

The drop in the credit spreads is partially explained by the downgrades of many borrowers by rating agencies during the crisis. For example, if a bond's rating is cut from Baa to Ba (the highest junk debt rating), the bond's yield is no longer used to compute the average monthly yields for Baa bonds, which in turn are used to compute the spreads plotted in Exhibit 8.9. The remaining Baa bonds are relatively strong and thus do not deserve a downgrade; plus some other bonds have been downgraded to Baa from higher ratings categories. Thus, the average spread is now lower.

DO YOU UNDERSTAND?

1. Why have asset-backed securities become important in capital markets?
2. Why have financial guarantees become increasingly important in financial markets? Why are guaranteed securities not default risk–free?
3. What types of credit enhancement can be obtained to make asset-backed securities more desirable?
4. Why are financial markets regulated, and who is the principal U.S. regulator?

SUMMARY OF LEARNING OBJECTIVES

1 Explain the role and function of capital markets. How does their role differ from that of the money markets? The *capital markets* are where businesses finance assets that produce core business products for the firm; they produce these products to earn a profit. These assets normally have a long economic life; hence, capital market instruments have long maturities, typically 5 years or longer. *Money markets* are where firms warehouse idle funds until needed or borrow money temporarily until cash is collected.

2 Explain what STRIPs are and how they can be helpful in immunizing a bond portfolio against interest rate risk. A STRIP is a Treasury note or bond that has been separated into two securities: (1) coupon interest payments and (2) principal payments. STRIPs are created from book-entry securities by the Treasury Department at the request of large commercial banks or Wall Street investment firms from Treasury securities purchased at the Treasury auctions. Zero-coupon bonds are excellent for immunizing against interest rate risk. This is done by purchasing zero-coupon bonds with a maturity that matches the duration of the liabilities to be immunized.

3 Discuss how the municipal bond market differs from the market for corporate bonds and the instruments traded in each market. There are two major differences between the municipal and corporate bond markets. First, municipal securities are tax-exempt and corporate securities are taxable. The issuers of corporate bonds are large businesses; in the municipal bond market, there are more than 50,000 issuers. Some of these issuers are large municipalities or states, but the vast majority are small governmental units. The secondary market for municipal bonds of smaller municipalities is quite limited.

4 Explain what junk bonds are and why the market for them developed in the late 1980s. Junk bonds are bonds that have a credit rating below investment grade. Historically, firms with below-investment-grade ratings could not sell public debt and could obtain longer-term financing only through loans from commercial banks. In the 1980s, Drexel Burnham Lambert developed a public market for junk bonds by creating a secondary market for these securities. The attractiveness of this market for corporations was that they could finance their business borrowing at lower interest rates than bank loans of similar maturity.

5 Explain what is meant by the term *securitization of debt*. Securitization of debt is pooling loans such as automobile loans that, by themselves, have no secondary market and creating a financial instrument that can be sold in the secondary markets. Securitization gives financial institutions the opportunity, if they desire, to sell loans that formerly were highly illiquid.

6 Identify some of the reasons that bond markets are becoming global. Some of the reasons that bond markets are becoming more global are the globalization of business, the advent of computer

and telecommunication technology that can move information and financial data around the world in seconds, and the political and economic détente that has allowed the reduction of trade barriers and the standardization of regulations and business practices.

7 Discuss how the bond markets were affected by the global financial crisis of 2007–2009. The financial crisis of 2007–2009 resulted in the widening of bond market credit spreads. After markets returned to relative normalcy in 2009 and 2010, corporations around the world issued large amounts of debt to take advantage of low interest rates.

KEY TERMS

Treasury notes and bonds
Treasury Inflation Protection Securities (TIPS)
Separate Trading of Registered Interest and Principal (STRIP)
Municipal bonds
General obligation bonds
Revenue bonds

Industrial development bonds (IDBs)
Mortgage-backed bonds
Serial bond issue
Primary market
Secondary market
Bearer bonds
Registered bonds
Term bonds
Indenture

Debentures
Senior debt
Subordinated debt (junior debt)
Sinking fund
Call provision
Convertible bonds
Competitive offering
Negotiated offering
Private placements

Rule 144A
Thin
Junk bonds
Financial guarantees
Securitization
Yankee bonds
Eurobond
Samurai bonds
Credit spreads

QUESTIONS AND PROBLEMS

1. Calculate the gross profit that an underwriter would make if it sold $10 million worth of bonds at par (face value) and paid the firm that sold the bonds 99.25 percent of par.

2. If a bond dealer bought a $100,000 municipal bond at 90 percent of par and sold it at 93 percent of par, how much money did the dealer make on the bid–ask spread?

3. If a corporate bond paid 9 percent interest, and you are in the 28 percent income tax bracket, what rate would you have to earn on a general obligation municipal bond of equivalent risk and maturity in order to be equally well off? Given that municipal bonds are often not easily marketable, would you want to earn a higher or lower rate than the rate you just calculated?

4. Suppose a trust is established to securitize $100 million in auto loans that paid 13 percent interest and the average

rate paid on the tranches issued was 10 percent. Suppose also that financial guarantees to protect against default on the loans cost 1.5 percent. How much money would the creator of the trust have available to pay for loan servicing and profits if the financial guarantee was purchased?

5. Why are private placements of securities often popular with both the buyer and the seller of the securities?

6. Give a concise definition of the following types of municipal bonds: (a) general obligation, (b) revenue, (c) industrial development, and (d) mortgage-backed.

7. What features make municipal bonds attractive to certain groups of investors? Why don't other groups invest much in municipal securities?

8. Define the following terms: (a) private placement, (b) asset-backed security, (c) callable securities, (d) sinking fund provisions, and (e) convertible features of securities.

9. Explain how securities are brought to market under (a) a competitive offering and (b) a negotiated offering. How do the two methods of sale differ?

10. Describe the different forms of financial guarantees seen in the bond markets.

11. Are Yankee bonds and Samurai bonds examples of Eurobonds? Why or why not?

12. What is a credit spread? What happened to credit spreads during the financial crisis of 2007–2009?

INTERNET EXERCISE

The Bureau of Public Debt's Web page provides useful information about Treasury securities and the national debt. Go to the Web page (www.treasurydirect.gov/govt/reports/pd/pd.htm) and answer the following questions:

1. Determine to the penny the total U.S. Treasury debt. How much of the debt is held by the public? How much is in the form of intragovernmental holdings?

2. Refer to the Monthly Statement of Public Debt. What is the total amount of marketable securities outstanding? How much is in Treasury bills? Notes? Bonds? Inflation-indexed notes? Inflation-indexed bonds?

3. Look for data on recent Treasury bill auctions at www.treasurydirect.gov/instit/annceresult/auctdata/auctdata.htm. Can you identify any trends in the rates for 10-year Treasury bonds?

Mortgage Markets

THE MORTGAGE MARKET IS THE largest of the long-term debt markets. At year-end 2010, mortgages outstanding in the United States totaled $13.9 trillion, whereas corporate bonds outstanding totaled only $11.4 trillion.

Mortgages are loans for which the borrower pledges real property as collateral to guarantee that the debt will be repaid. If the borrower does not repay the debt as promised, the collateral can be seized and sold through legal foreclosure; proceeds from the sale help repay the debt. Mortgage loans typically are repaid in monthly installments that include both interest due and repayments of a portion of the principal due on the loan. However, mortgage loan borrowers often repay the full amount due early if they move or refinance the loan.

For many years, mortgages were not traded frequently in the nation's capital markets because people found it expensive to check the creditworthiness of individual borrowers and the collateral value of homes located in many different parts of the country. Furthermore, savers often didn't want to buy securities that paid varying amounts of principal and interest from month to month.

Since the mid-1980s, however, the mortgage market has changed dramatically. Federal insurance, federal agencies, and private insurance now guarantee repayments on mortgages to reduce investors' credit risk. In addition, many types of highly marketable **mortgage-backed securities (MBSs)** have been developed. Such securities pass through all or part of the principal and interest payments on "pools" of many mortgages to buyers of the MBSs. MBSs can reduce the illiquidity risk and payment uncer-

Although your home may not be a castle, the mortgage markets are used by Americans to finance the homes of their dreams.

tainties associated with the ownership of individual mortgages. Furthermore, many new mortgages and MBSs are designed to reduce **interest rate risk** and/or **credit risk** for their purchasers. Such securities may have adjustable interest rates or, if they are part of a pool of mortgages, relatively certain repayment patterns. Because the credit risk; liquidity risk; and, for some (but not all) MBSs, interest rate risks have been reduced by the innovations, mortgages are much more attractive investments than they were in the mid-1940s.

As is often the case, however, too much of a good thing can be bad. Many of these mortgage market innovations have been linked to the mortgage market crisis that began in late 2007, but the bad press doesn't diminish their importance. Without these innovations, mortgage borrowing rates would likely be much higher and the availability of mortgage credit would likely be reduced, especially for those borrowers without perfect credit. ■

This chapter describes major mortgage market instruments and major participants in the mortgage markets. It also explains the important role played by government insurance, federal agencies, and regulations in shaping the mortgage market. In addition, it helps you learn how mortgage payments are calculated, how mortgage principal and interest payments typically vary over time, and why mortgage-backed securities have become so popular. ■

LEARNING OBJECTIVES

1 Explain the basic structure of mortgages as debt instruments.

2 Describe the various types of mortgages that exist and discuss how the different types of mortgages allocate interest rate and inflation risks to the borrower or lender.

3 Explain how government and private-market innovations have led to a vastly expanded popularity for mortgages and mortgage-backed securities in the nation's capital markets.

4 Discuss the wide variety of mortgage-backed securities and mortgage-backed debt issues.

5 Describe the key roles that Fannie Mae, Freddie Mac, Ginnie Mae, mortgage bankers, and mortgage insurers have played in developing secondary mortgage markets.

6 Describe the role of mortgage bankers and how they earn profits.

7 Discuss how the nature of mortgage markets has evolved over time.

8 Explain the recent financial crisis and its impact on mortgage markets.

9.1 THE UNIQUE NATURE OF MORTGAGE MARKETS

Mortgage markets exist to help individuals, businesses, and other economic units finance the purchase of a home or other property. It is one of the few markets we discuss in this textbook that you, as an individual, are likely to participate in as an issuer. Unless you are independently wealthy or rent for the rest of your life, you will probably borrow in the mortgage market to finance the purchase of a home.

Fortunately, when you decide to buy a house (if you have not already done so), you will almost certainly find that lenders are eager to lend to you. As you will learn in this chapter, the markets for mortgages and mortgage-backed securities have developed to the point where there is an ample supply of funds for well-qualified borrowers. In fact, until recently there seemed to be an almost limitless supply of funds for all borrowers. Beginning in 2007 with the subprime mortgage crisis, however, the supply of funds in mortgage markets has returned to more rational levels.

Like other capital market segments, mortgage markets bring together borrowers and suppliers of long-term funds. Most of the similarities end there, however, because mortgage markets have several unique characteristics. First, mortgage loans are always secured by the pledge of real property—land or buildings—as collateral. If a borrower defaults on the loan, the lender can foreclose and take ownership of the collateral.

Second, mortgage loans are made for varying amounts and maturities, depending on the borrower's needs. Because of their lack of uniform size, individual mortgages are not readily marketable in secondary markets.

Third, issuers (borrowers) of mortgage loans are typically small, relatively unknown financial entities. Thus, only the mortgage lender benefits from investigating the borrower's financial condition fully. In contrast, corporate securities are often held by many thousands of people. Thus, any changes in the financial condition of a major corporation are widely reported. In short, more people have an incentive to monitor the financial condition of General Motors than that of John and Sue Alvarez.

Fourth, because uniform sizes and types of capital market debt instruments exist and information on the issuers of those instruments is generally widely available, secondary capital markets for stocks and bonds are highly developed and work very efficiently. Even though secondary trading in mortgage market instruments has increased over the past 20 years, particularly for insured mortgages, it is much smaller relative to the value of securities outstanding than is the case in the capital markets.

Finally, mortgage markets are both highly regulated and strongly supported by federal government policies. Federal participation in the operations of other capital markets is much more limited.

9.2 TYPES OF MORTGAGES

One of the most important financial decisions homebuyers face is selecting the type of mortgage that best suits their needs. The traditional 30-year, level-payment, fixed-rate mortgage may make sense for many borrowers, but it may be inappropriate for others. The traditional fixed-rate mortgage is well suited for those borrowers who plan to remain in the same home for many years and prefer the security of fixed monthly payments. It tends to be the mortgage type favored by borrowers with stable and reliable incomes. Other mortgage types may make sense for homebuyers who expect to move in a few years or those who are willing to accept some of the interest rate risk associated with an adjustable-rate mortgage.

The mortgage types described in this section represent the majority of mortgages issued in the United States. If the mortgages described here don't meet a borrower's needs, however, a variety of less common mortgage types exist to meet the needs of just about any borrower.

STANDARD FIXED-RATE MORTGAGES (FRMs)

In a traditional **fixed-rate mortgage (FRM)**, the lender takes a lien on real property and the borrower agrees to make periodic repayments of the principal amount borrowed plus interest on the unpaid balance of the debt for a predetermined period of time. The mortgage is **amortized** over time to the extent that the periodic (usually monthly) payments exceed the interest due; any payment in excess of interest is credited toward repayment of the debt. When the mortgage is fully amortized (that is, repaid), the borrower obtains a clear title to the property. Until then, the lien prevents the borrower from selling the property without first repaying the debt or agreeing to repay the lender from proceeds of the sale. If the borrower fails to make payments on the property before it is fully amortized, the lender may foreclose and, through legal processes, cause the property to be sold or obtain title to the property.

Exhibit 9.1 shows amortization tables for two $200,000 mortgages, one with a 15-year maturity and one with a 30-year maturity. Both mortgages are fixed-rate mortgages that pay 6 percent interest. Thus, the interest charge in the first month is $1,000 for each (which equals $200,000 × 6% divided by 12, because there are 12 months in a year). However, the 15-year mortgage shown in Frame A has a $1,687.71 monthly payment requirement, whereas the 30-year mortgage shown in Frame B has a $1,199.10 payment requirement.

The balance due on the 15-year mortgage falls by $687.71 in the first month, by $691.15 in the second month, and by greater amounts thereafter (because the monthly interest due equals the principal balance due times 6 percent divided by 12—or 0.50 percent—each month, the interest due falls monthly as the balance due on the mortgage declines). Although the balance due falls relatively slowly at first, the mortgage is fully repaid by the end of the fifteenth year. In the last year, the mortgage balance falls sharply because, with a small balance left, interest charges are low and almost all of the $1,687.71 monthly payment can be used to repay the balance due.

Frame B of Exhibit 9.1 shows that the monthly payment on the 30-year $200,000 mortgage is substantially lower, at $1,199.10 per month, even though the interest rate and starting balance of the 30-year and 15-year mortgages are the same. The lower payment is the primary appeal of a 30-year mortgage. However, because the first month's interest is still $1,000, only $199.10 is left over to reduce the balance due on the mortgage after the first payment. Thus, the second month's interest due is $999.00, and the mortgage balance falls only by $200.10 after the second payment is made. Because of the slow repayment of principal on the 30-year mortgage, most of the mortgage balance is still due after 15 years. In the last year of the 30-year mortgage, once again, the mortgage balance is low, so interest charges are low, and most of the mortgage payment is used to repay principal.

The mortgages are fully amortized in both cases when the initial $200,000 mortgage debt has been repaid. Note, however, that total payments are $303,788.46 on the 15-year mortgage and $431,676.38 on the 30-year mortgage. Naturally, the difference in total payments is due to the much higher total interest payment on the 30-year mortgage. Thus, by making higher monthly payments for a shorter period of time, the 15-year-mortgage debtor saves more than $125,000 in total interest due. Consequently, even though the 30-year-mortgage borrower's monthly payment is lower each month, that borrower's interest bill over the life of the mortgage is much greater. (Note that these comparisons are on a pretax basis, however; as long as the government allows mortgage interest payments to be deducted from taxable income, the federal government absorbs part of the extra interest cost.)

ADJUSTABLE-RATE MORTGAGES (ARMs)

As a general rule, fixed-rate mortgages make sense for borrowers who like the certainty of knowing the interest they pay on their mortgages. For borrowers who are willing to accept some uncertainty, however, an **adjustable-rate mortgage (ARM)** may make sense. An ARM is a mortgage with an interest rate that adjusts

EXHIBIT 9.1
Mortgage Balances and Payments

A. 15-year, 6%, $200,000 level-payment, fixed-rate mortgage

Month	Beginning Balance	Monthly Payment	Interest Payment	Principal Payment	Ending Balance
1	$200,000.00	$1,687.71	$1,000.00	$687.71	$199,312.29
2	199,312.29	1,687.71	996.56	691.15	198,621.13
3	198,621.13	1,687.71	993.11	694.61	197,926.53
.	.	.	.	.	.
.	.	.	.	.	.
.	.	.	.	.	.
178	5,012.93	1,687.71	25.06	1,662.65	3,350.28
179	3,350.28	1,687.71	16.75	1,670.96	1,679.32
180	1,679.32	1,687.71	8.40	1,679.32	0.00
Totals:		$303,788.46	$103,788.46	$200,000.00	

B. 30-year, 6%, $200,000 level-payment, fixed-rate mortgage

Month	Beginning Balance	Monthly Payment	Interest Payment	Principal Payment	Ending Balance
1	$200,000.00	$1,199.10	$1,000.00	$199.10	$199,800.90
2	199,800.90	1,199.10	999.00	200.10	199,600.80
3	199,600.80	1,199.10	998.00	201.10	199,399.71
.	.	.	.	.	.
.	.	.	.	.	.
178	143,548.99	1,199.10	717.74	481.36	143,067.63
179	143,067.63	1,199.10	715.34	483.76	142,583.87
180	142,583.87	1,199.10	712.92	486.18	142,097.69
.	.	.	.	.	.
.	.	.	.	.	.
.	.	.	.	.	.
358	3,561.63	1,199.10	17.81	1,181.29	2,380.33
359	2,380.33	1,199.10	11.90	1,187.20	1,193.14
360	1,193.14	1,199.10	5.97	1,193.14	0.00
Totals:		$431,676.38	$231,676.38	$200,000.00	

Both mortgages are fully amortized when the $200,000 mortgage debt has been repaid. Note, however, that the total payments on the 15-year mortgage are $127,887.92 less than the total payments on the 30-year mortgage.

periodically in response to changes in market conditions. The interest rate adjustment is based on a published market index, such as the weekly average yield of 1-year U.S. Treasury securities, the Cost of Funds Index (COFI), or the London Interbank Offer Rate (LIBOR).

ARMs are typically structured so that there is an initial interest rate that remains fixed for a period of time ranging from 1 year to 10 years. After the initial fixed-rate period has ended, the interest rate increases or decreases depending on the reference rate of interest. For example, a 3/1 ARM has a fixed rate of interest for the first 3 years of the mortgage. Each year after that, the interest rate adjusts. The first number tells you the number of years in the fixed-rate period; the second number tells you how frequently the rate adjusts after that. In this case, the 1 tells you that the rate will adjust annually. You might also see advertisements for 3/27 or 5/25 ARMs. For these types of ads, the first number tells you the number of years in the fixed-rate period, and the second number tells you the number of years in the adjustable-rate period. Note that the frequency of adjustment during the adjustable-rate period for these types of ARMs may be every 6 months.

ARMs with an initial fixed rate that last 3 years or longer are often referred to as *hybrid ARMs* because they are a mix of a fixed-rate mortgage and an adjustable-rate mortgage. The initial fixed rate of interest in a hybrid ARM is lower than the rate on a fixed-rate mortgage, which makes hybrid ARMs attractive to borrowers who expect their income levels to increase during the initial fixed-rate period and those homebuyers who expect to move in a few years. Hybrid ARMs are now more popular than traditional 1/1 ARMs in which the interest rate adjusts at the end of the first year and every year thereafter.

ARMs are popular with lenders because they reduce the lender's interest rate risk. Whenever interest rates rise, borrowers' adjustable-rate mortgage payments also rise (after the initial fixed-rate period). That, in turn, makes it easier for lenders to afford the higher interest rates they must pay to their depositors and other creditors at such times.

ARM Rate Adjustments.   Adjustable-rate mortgages use various measures for adjusting their rates, including Treasury security rates, current fixed-rate mortgage indexes, COFIs, the prime rate, and the LIBOR. In addition, ARM rates can be adjusted with varying lags—such as monthly, quarterly, or every year or two. Most ARMs are adjusted annually. In no case, however, can the rate be adjusted solely at the lender's discretion, and in all cases the exact method of rate adjustment must be fully disclosed when the loan is originated. In particular, ARM regulations give flexibility to both the lender and the borrower. They allow contractual rate adjustments to be implemented through changes in payment amounts, the outstanding principal loan balance, or loan maturity, provided that the method of adjustment is specified in the contract. Rates can be adjusted according to any rate index that is readily verifiable to the borrowers and beyond the control of the lender.

ARM Caps.   Although ARMs help lenders reduce their interest rate risk, they might increase lenders' credit risk. If rates rise sufficiently, monthly payments could rise to the point that the borrower is unable to make the monthly payment. The credit risk of the loan would rise and a default could occur. Without limiting the potential increase in monthly payments, the lender incurs greater credit risk on ARMs as interest rates rise. With an interest rate *cap*, however, the likelihood of default is limited. Of course, by limiting the potential increase in interest rates, the lender still bears some interest rate risk. For instance, if the initial rate is 5 percent, a mortgage with a 5 percent lifetime cap could never charge a rate greater than 10 percent.

At first many ARMs had no limit on the amount by which interest rates could increase. For obvious reasons, however, such loans were not very popular with potential borrowers. Borrowers preferred capped ARMs, which may have a payment cap, an interest rate cap, or both.

Payment caps limit the maximum amount by which the monthly payment can increase each year or over the life of the loan. If payments greater than the cap are called for at the new interest rate, the maturity of the loan is increased. If the payment limit is less than the new interest payment, *negative amortization* occurs, and the amount due on the loan increases each month until interest rates fall once again. If interest rates increase without limit and never fall, the borrower may never be able to repay the debt.

Interest rate caps limit the amount that the interest rate on a loan can increase during each interest rate period or over the life of the loan. Interest rate caps typically limit maximum interest rate increases to 1 or 2 percent per year and to 5 percent over the life of the loan; thus, they help keep the monthly payment from rising to a level that the borrower cannot repay. Because many ARMs have initial rates that are lower than the fully indexed ARM rate, however, the first adjustment may not be subject to the same cap as subsequent adjustments.

Because of the popularity of capped ARMs with consumers, in 1987 Congress required that almost all ARMs have a cap. Although capped ARMs have less default risk than uncapped ARMs, they still leave the lender with a small amount of residual interest rate risk.

Pricing Risk Transfers. Lenders like adjustable-rate loans because they reduce their interest rate risk. Thus, lenders are willing to "pay" borrowers to assume interest rate risk by offering lower rates on ARMs than contractual rates for long-term FRMs. However, borrowers incur the interest rate risk that lenders avoid with ARMs. Thus, borrowers are willing to pay higher rates to have the lender assume the interest rate risk inherent in a fixed-rate, long-term mortgage. The market, then, prices risk differences in variable- and fixed-rate obligations by setting the degree of rate reduction for adjustable-rate mortgages that satisfies both borrowers and lenders (see Exhibit 9.2).

Consumers' willingness to assume ARM obligations also varies with their expectations for future interest rate movements. If they think rates are likely to fall, they may be more willing to borrow with ARM mortgages even if ARM rates are close to FRM rates. However, if they expect interest rates to rise, they may want a larger discount from the FRM rate. At such times, the term structure of interest rates is likely to be upward sloping, so lenders may be able to accommodate their wishes. However, some lenders may go further and "sweeten" the initial ARM rate discount from FRM rates by offering especially attractive "teaser rates" for the first year of the ARM. After the first year, the ARM rate adjusts to whatever the rate-setting formula requires. Consumers must be cautious when they take on ARMs with teaser rates because rates on such loans may increase when the initial fixed-rate period is over even if market interest rates don't

EXHIBIT 9.2

Rate Difference Needed for Borrowers to Take the Risk of an Adjustable-Rate Mortgage

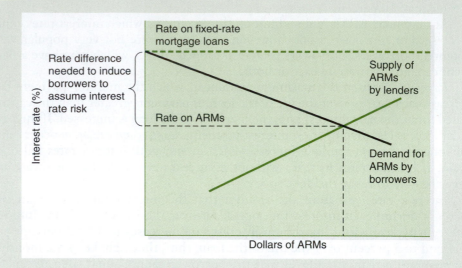

Typically, lenders offer rates on ARMs that are marked up by a certain percentage (usually 2 to 3 percent) over a short-term index rate. One popular type of ARM charges a rate equal to the 1-year T-bill rate plus 2.754 percent. Consumer demand determines the maximum markup lenders can obtain.

Note: When ARM rates equal rates in fixed-rate mortgage loans, it is assumed that the demand will be zero, because the borrower will receive no compensation for taking on the extra risk. As the ARM rate falls further below the fixed-rate loan rate, however, the demand for such loans will increase. At the same time, the supply of ARMs falls when lenders must give up more to reduce their risks.

change. Exhibit 9.3 illustrates the fact that ARM rates are usually well below new FRM rates.

Prepayment Penalties. One of the reasons some borrowers choose an ARM over an FRM is because the payments are, at least initially, more affordable. As a borrower's income increases, it is not uncommon for her to decide that she wants to refinance her ARM by taking out an FRM with a more certain payment stream and using the proceeds from issuing the FRM to pay off the ARM. As you might surmise, however, the ARM lender is not always happy to have its mortgage paid off early, especially if the ARM started with a low initial teaser rate. Lenders that offer low initial rates are counting on those low initial rates to be offset by higher rates over the life of the mortgage. Therefore, some ARMs may require a fee or penalty if you pay off the ARM early. These fees, or prepayment penalties, may apply even if the loan is paid off as a result of selling the home. Generally, there is a trade-off between prepayment penalties and having lower interest rates or origination fees. In any case, any fees or penalties for paying off a loan early must be disclosed in the loan documents.

OTHER MORTGAGES

Although FRMs and ARMs represent the majority of mortgages, other types have been developed to meet the diverse needs of borrowers and lenders or for specific

EXHIBIT 9.3
Fixed and Adjustable Mortgage Rates

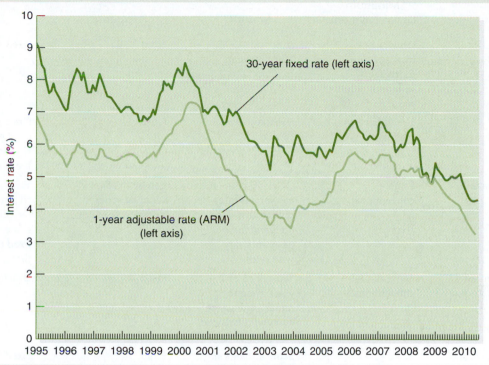

By the end of 2010, both adjustable- and fixed-rate mortgages were at historic lows.

circumstances. We now discuss some of the most widely used. These are also summarized in Exhibit 9.4.

Balloon Payment Mortgages.   Popular in the United States prior to the Great Depression, **balloon payment mortgages** have a relatively low fixed rate of interest for a predetermined period of time (typically 7 years). The remaining balance of the mortgage comes due at the end of that period in the form of a *balloon payment*. Alternatively, the balance can be refinanced at prevailing interest rates. This type of mortgage is popular with borrowers who plan to sell or refinance within a few years and want a low payment until that time. In the event that borrowers choose to refinance, they typically do not need to requalify as long as they have made their payments on time.

Rollover Mortgages (ROMs) and Renegotiated-Rate Mortgages (RRMs).   Like balloon payment mortgages, **rollover mortgages (ROMs)** and **renegotiated-rate mortgages (RRMs)** protect the lender from being locked into a long-term low rate of interest. In ROMs and RRMs, the interest rate is reset to prevailing interest rates at predetermined periods. For example, the interest rate may change every 5 years. Note that this is similar to an ARM except that the number of years between interest rate adjustments is longer than with the typical ARM. This type of mortgage is popular in Canada, but rare in the United States.

EXHIBIT 9.4
Mortgage Characteristics

Type	Minimum Down Payment	Maturity	Payments	Rate
Conventional fixed-rate (FRM)	Usually 3% or more; private mortgage insurance required if <20%	Fixed, usually 15, 20, or 30 years	Fixed	Fixed
FHA and VA	3–10% for FHA; 0% for VA	Fixed, usually 30 years	Fixed	Fixed, cannot exceed government-set limit; insurance fee is extra
Adjustable-rate (ARM)	Same as conventional	Often 30 years, but can vary as rates change; if it does not vary, then payments vary with rates	Can be fixed or variable; varies if maturity does not	Variable according to predetermined rate indexes, but some may have fixed rates for the first 2–10 years
Balloon payment	Same as conventional	Typically 5 or 7 years, then the remaining balance must be refinanced at current rates	Fixed	Usually fixed
Rollover (ROM) and renegotiated-rate (RRM)	Same as conventional	Same as balloon, but the ability to refinance may be guaranteed	Fixed	Fixed for a period, then recontracted
Interest only	Same as conventional	Usually 30 years	Interest only for the first 3–10 years; amortized over the remaining years	Fixed
Construction-to-permanent financing	Same as conventional	Same as conventional once it becomes permanent	Increase over time	Fixed
Reverse annuity (RAM)	None	Usually the lifetime of the borrower	Fixed payments are made to the borrower	Fixed

The various mortgage types have considerably different characteristics. People who deal in the mortgage market often differentiate them by their initials (FRM, ARM, etc.).

Interest-Only Mortgages. Another way for a borrower to secure financing with low payments is to borrow using an **interest-only mortgage**, whereby he or she pays only the interest for the first 3, 5, 7, or 10 years. After the interest-only period, the payments increase so that the loan is fully amortized by the end of 30 years.

Construction-to-Permanent Mortgages. For those homebuyers who are planning to build their own home, a construction-to-permanent mortgage may make the most sense. In these mortgages, the purchase of the land and the construction of the home are financed in increments, with the borrower paying only the interest payments during this phase. Once construction is completed, the outstanding balance is rolled over into an FRM, ARM, or one of the other types of mortgages described previously.

Reverse Annuity Mortgages (RAMs). **Reverse annuity mortgages (RAMs)** are designed for older people who own their homes and need additional funds to meet current living expenses but do not want to sell their homes. RAMs allow people to borrow against the equity in their homes at relatively low interest rates.

RAMs are written so that, instead of making regular monthly payments, the borrower receives them. Many have a lifetime annuity feature guaranteeing that payments will be made for the life of the borrower. The loan plus accrued interest is repaid when the borrower dies, sells the home, or is no longer able to live in the home.

Home Equity Loans and Lines. **Home equity loans** and **home equity lines of credit** were created so that homeowners can borrow against the equity they have accumulated in their home. If the borrower already has a mortgage on the property, the home equity loan or line would be considered a second mortgage. In the event of default and liquidation, the second-mortgage holder gets repaid only after the first-mortgage principal has been repaid in full.

Home equity loans are often used for debt consolidation, home improvement, education, and emergencies (e.g., medical bills). In recent years, some homebuyers have used second mortgages to borrow part of their down payment for their first mortgages and avoid paying for private mortgage insurance (PMI).

After the 1986 tax changes, the popularity of second mortgages increased greatly because interest on such mortgages could be deducted (within limits) from taxes, whereas interest deductions for other types of consumer credit were phased out. Subsequently, many lenders began to offer home equity credit lines that let consumers borrow on a credit line secured with a second mortgage on their homes. Many lenders let borrowers use credit cards to access those credit lines.

9.3 MORTGAGE QUALIFYING

A borrower's ability to qualify for a mortgage depends on several factors, including income level, the amount available for a down payment, credit history, and other financial obligations.

BORROWER INCOME

Like any other lender, mortgage lenders focus on the sources of repayment in determining whether to accept or reject a loan application. In the typical residential mortgage loan, the primary source of repayment is the borrower's income. Lenders use payment-to-income ratios to assess a borrower's ability to repay a loan. Although there is substantial variation in allowable maximums, some conservative rules of thumb are used: (1) a borrower's monthly mortgage payment

(P&I) should be no more than 25 percent of monthly gross income; (2) the monthly P&I plus monthly property tax payments (T), homeowner's insurance premiums (HI), and any mortgage insurance premiums (MI) should be no more than 28 percent of monthly gross income; and (3) the monthly P&I, T, HI, and MI plus other debt service (including car loans, child support, alimony, credit cards, and student loans) should be no more than 33 percent of monthly gross income.

DOWN PAYMENT

Historically, the most important determinant of whether a borrower defaults on a mortgage loan is how much of his or her own money is put toward the purchase of the property. In addition, the equity in a home represents a secondary source of repayment in the event the borrower defaults on the loan. Historically the minimum loan-to-value ratio for a conventional mortgage was 80 percent, meaning that the borrower had to provide a down payment of 20 percent of the purchase price. A borrower who is not able to provide a 20 percent down payment is typically required to purchase private mortgage insurance.

MORTGAGE INSURANCE

Mortgage contracts can be either conventional or federally insured. Mortgages whose ultimate payment is guaranteed by the Federal Housing Administration (FHA) are called **FHA mortgages**. FHA mortgages must have terms that comply with FHA requirements, and a small fee is added to cover the costs of insurance. **Veterans Administration (VA) mortgages** are similar, except that the mortgage and borrower must both meet the requirements of the Veterans Administration. VA and FHA mortgages usually have very low or zero down payment requirements, so people with such mortgages can borrow nearly all the money needed to buy a home.

Conventional mortgages are not insured by a federal government agency. As already described down payment requirements on conventional mortgages are usually much higher than those on federally insured mortgages. If conventional mortgages are privately insured, however, the borrower typically pays an extra charge to cover the mortgage insurance premium and, in turn, can borrow with a low down payment. The use of **private mortgage insurance (PMI)** is illustrated in Exhibit 9.5, which shows that, with insurance, the lender can extend more credit and not bear additional risk. The mortgage insurer accepts the additional risk in return for the insurance premium payment. The consumer pays the insurance premium in addition to the principal and interest on the loan (and thereby pays a higher effective annual percentage rate because the monthly payments include the insurance premium). However, the insurance feature allows the consumer to buy a house with a far lower down payment than would otherwise be possible. Also, if the house rises in value such that the mortgage is less than 80 percent of its value, the borrower is typically able to cancel the PMI.

Exhibit 9.5 illustrates the reallocation of credit risk that is possible with private mortgage insurance. The left side of the exhibit illustrates an uninsured conventional mortgage in which the lender extends a $100,000 mortgage on a house costing $125,000 at 6 percent interest. The consumer makes a down payment of $25,000. In this case, the lender may experience default only if the house value falls by more than $25,000, which is the cushion provided by the borrower's down

EXHIBIT 9.5
Private Mortgage Insurance

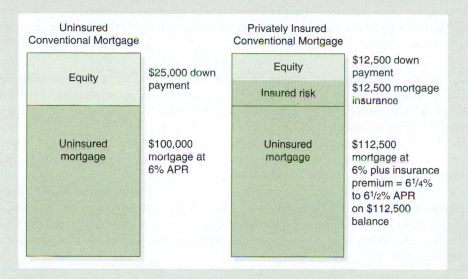

With an uninsured conventional mortgage, the lender extends a $100,000 mortgage at 6 percent interest and is at risk in case of default only if the house value falls by more than $25,000. With a privately insured conventional mortgage, the lender extends a $112,500 mortgage at 6 percent interest and is still at risk only if the house value falls by more than $25,000. In the second case, the private mortgage insurance company bears the risk if the house value falls by $12,500 to $25,000 and the borrower defaults. In return, the insurer receives an insurance premium equal to between 0.25 and 0.5 percent additional interest on the $112,500 debt.

payment. The right side of the exhibit illustrates the effect of private mortgage insurance. In this case, the lender extends a $112,500 mortgage at 6 percent interest and is still at risk only if the house value falls by more than $25,000. In the second case, however, the private mortgage insurance company bears the risk if the house value falls by $12,500 to $25,000 and the borrower defaults. Note, however, that with the insurance the consumer needs a down payment of only $12,500, rather than $25,000, to buy a house worth $125,000. In return for bearing some default risk, the insurer receives an annual insurance premium equal to between 0.25 and 0.5 percent of the $112,500 mortgage.

LEARNING BY DOING 9.1
Determining How Much Home You Can Buy

PROBLEM: Suppose you have saved $50,000 for a down payment on a house. You are considering buying a house by issuing a conventional, 30-year, 5 percent mortgage and you do not want to pay for private mortgage insurance. Your monthly income is $5,000 and you make monthly debt payments of $300. You estimate that homeowner's insurance and property taxes will be about $400 per month. Based on what you have learned so far, how much can you pay for a home and still meet the normal qualification standards?

APPROACH: You can determine the answer to this question by determining the most you can pay for a home using the down payment minimum and the three income ratio maximums.

SOLUTION: According to the down payment minimum of 20 percent, your $50,000 down payment is 20 percent of $250,000; 25 percent of your monthly income is $1,250. This is equivalent to the monthly payment on a 30-year, 5 percent mortgage with a principal amount of $232,852. Twenty-eight percent of your monthly income is $1,400. Subtracting $400 leaves $1,000, which is equivalent to the monthly payment on a 30-year, 5 percent mortgage with a principal amount of $186,282. Thirty-three percent of your monthly income is $1,650. Subtracting your monthly debt payments of $300 and your insurance and taxes of $400 leaves $950. This is equivalent to the monthly payment on a 30-year, 5 percent mortgage with a principal amount of $176,968. This is the smallest figure based on the various qualification formulas; therefore, this is the most that you can borrow using a conventional mortgage.

Subprime Mortgages.   What makes a mortgage subprime? It depends on who you ask. In some cases, a mortgage will be considered subprime because the borrower is subprime, meaning the borrower's credit score is below some lender-determined threshold. Credit scores are numbers representing a borrower's creditworthiness as estimated by a statistical methodology originally developed by Fair Isaac Corporation (FICO). There are several competing credit-scoring methods, but FICO is a leading provider, and the terms *FICO score* and *credit score* are often used interchangeably. FICO scores range from 300 to 850, with those below 650 being considered subprime by many lenders. FICO scores above 650 are usually considered prime. FICO scores are based on a borrower's payment history (35 percent of the overall score), amounts owed (30 percent), length of credit history (15 percent), types of credit (10 percent), and number of credit inquiries (10 percent).

Even if a borrower has a FICO score above 650, there is no guarantee that his or her mortgage will be considered a prime mortgage. Because there is no standard definition, each individual lender determines which borrowers are subprime. In addition, it is not uncommon for prime borrowers to choose mortgage products that were designed for subprime borrowers, have high payment-to-income ratios, or offer low down payments. Depending on the circumstances, these mortgages might be considered subprime even though the borrower is a prime borrower.

Finally, a mortgage may be considered subprime even if it was originated as a prime mortgage, the borrower's credit score has not changed, and payments on the mortgage have been made on a timely basis. If a property being financed by a mortgage is in a geographic region that experiences a substantial decline in property values, the mortgage's loan-to-value ratio will increase. Consequently, the perceived likelihood of default on the mortgage may increase to the point that the mortgage is considered subprime.

DO YOU UNDERSTAND?

1. If you had a 6 percent, $100,000, 15-year mortgage and you paid it as scheduled, how much interest would you pay in the first month of the sixth year on that mortgage? How much principal would you pay?

2. What would your principal and interest payments be if the mortgage were a 30-year mortgage at 6 percent?

3. Suppose you had a mortgage with an initial rate of 2 percent that adjusted its rate once a year to equal the 1-year Treasury bill rate plus 2.75 percent, with a cap on rate increases of 2 percent per year and 5 percent rate increase cap over the life of the mortgage. What rate would you pay in the second year of the mortgage if the 1-year Treasury bill rate was 1.5 percent when the new rate was calculated?

4. In the mortgage described in question 3, what is the maximum rate you could be charged if the Treasury bill rates rose to 10 percent and stayed there?

In the early part of the twentieth century, mortgage markets were very illiquid and inefficient. There was no secondary market for mortgages, so lenders (commercial banks, savings and loans, and mutual savings banks) were forced to hold the mortgages they originated until the loans were repaid. Therefore, mortgage rates and the availability of mortgage credit varied from one region to another and fluctuated over time, depending on loan repayments and new deposits at lending institutions.

In 1934, Congress tried to strengthen the housing market by passing the National Housing Act, which created the Federal Housing Administration (FHA) to provide mortgage insurance on loans made by approved lenders. In addition, a 1938 amendment to the National Housing Act created the Federal National Mortgage Association (FNMA) for the purpose of developing a secondary market for FHA-insured mortgages. FNMA was authorized to purchase FHA-insured mortgages using the funds allocated to it by Congress.

It wasn't until 1968, however, that the secondary market for mortgages began to develop into what it is today. In that year, FNMA was split into two entities, the **Government National Mortgage Association (GNMA–Ginnie Mae)** and the **Federal National Mortgage Association (FNMA–Fannie Mae)**.

GNMA was given the charge of expanding affordable housing by helping lenders access capital markets as a source of funds for government-guaranteed mortgages. Today, GNMA guarantees the timely payment of principal and interest on pools of qualifying FHA, VA, and other government-guaranteed mortgages. Lenders combine qualifying mortgages into pools, acquire a GNMA guarantee on the pool, and then sell security interests in the pool. GNMA does not originate or purchase mortgages. Rather, it provides a guarantee for mortgage-backed securities issued by approved lenders. GNMA was established as a government agency. It is wholly owned by the U.S. government, and its securities are the only

9.4 MORTGAGE-BACKED SECURITIES

mortgage-backed securities explicitly backed by the full faith and credit of the U.S. government.

FNMA, on the other hand, was created to help lenders access capital markets as a source of funds for conventional mortgages. Unlike GNMA, FNMA was established as a stockholder-owned corporation when it was split from GNMA. Also unlike GNMA, FNMA purchases conventional mortgages from lenders. FNMA purchases mortgages for its own account, but it also issues securities backed by pools of the mortgages it purchases.

The **Federal Home Loan Mortgage Corporation (FHLMC–Freddie Mac)** was established by Congress in 1970 as a subsidiary of the Federal Home Loan Bank system. Its initial purpose was to assist savings and loan associations and other mortgage lenders in attracting capital market funds and provide competition for FNMA. Like FNMA, FHLMC was established as a private corporation. Today, FNMA and FHLMC are very similar.

FNMA and FHLMC were referred to as government-sponsored enterprises (GSEs) because they were privately held corporations but they were created by the government, received some government support, and assumed some public responsibilities. Although their securities were not explicitly backed by the full faith and credit of the U.S. government, market participants assumed they had an implied guarantee. In fact, on September 7, 2008, FNMA and FHLMC were placed into the conservatorship of the Federal Housing Finance Association. Dividends to shareholders of the two corporations were suspended, and the U.S. Treasury established a set of arrangements to insure that FNMA and FHLMC would continue meeting their obligations to holders of the mortgage-backed securities that they issued. This effectively extended government guarantees to FNMA- and FHLMC-issued mortgage-backed securities. At the time of this writing, FNMA and FHLMC are still in conservatorship, their shares of stock are no longer listed on the New York Stock Exchange, and their future is a topic of much debate.

CHARACTERISTICS OF MORTGAGE-BACKED SECURITIES

Mortgage-backed securities have attributes that are lacking in individual mortgages but that are desirable for capital market instruments:

1. They are issued in standardized denominations; thus, they are more readily tradable in both the primary and secondary capital markets.

2. They are either issued by large, well-known borrowers or insured by a well-known institution whose credit standing can be checked and evaluated relatively easily. This increases their marketability.

3. They are usually insured and highly collateralized. Thus, they have low degrees of risk and high credit ratings. Many have their principal and interest payments guaranteed by the U.S. government or its agencies.

4. Some have repayment schedules (for principal and interest) more similar to those offered on government or corporate debt issues.

Because of these considerations, secondary mortgage market instruments compete effectively for funds in the conventional capital markets and allow mortgage lending institutions to attract funds more easily. A wide variety of mortgage-backed securities have been developed to allow mortgage lenders to obtain funds from the nation's capital markets. These are summarized in Exhibit 9.6.

EXHIBIT 9.6
Mortgage-Backed Securities

Type	Issuer	Security	Payments	Insurance
Pass-Through Securities				
Ginnie Mae I, II MBSs	Government National Mortgage Association	Pools of government-insured (FHA and VA) mortgages	All principal and interest payments are passed through to security holders	FHA and VA plus GNMA guarantee
Participation certificate (PC)	Federal Home Loan Mortgage Corporation	Pools of new conventional mortgages	Same as GNMA	FHLMC guarantees ultimate payment of principal and interest
Fannie Mae MBS	Federal National Mortgage Association	Pools of government-insured or conventional mortgages	Same as GNMA	FNMA guarantees ultimate payment of principal and interest
Privately issued pass-through (PIP)	Various private institutions	Pools of conventional mortgages—can have varied rates and orginators	Same as GNMA	Privately insured
Other MBSs				
CMOs and REMICs	GNMA, FNMA, FHLMC	Same as pass-through securities	Contractual, according to class or tranche	Same as pass-through securities by the same issuer
IO and PO STRIPped MBSs	FNMA, FHLMC	Same as pass-through securities	IO—interest payments on pool; PO—principal payments on pool	Same as pass-through securities by the same issuer

(continued)

EXHIBIT 9.6
Mortgage-Backed Securities *(continued)*

Type	Issuer	Security	Payments	Insurance
Mortgage-Backed Bonds				
FNMA or FHLMC debt issue	FNMA or FHLMC	FNMA's or FHLMC's assets (mostly mortgages) and government credit line	Regular, contractual payments	None, except FNMA and FHLMC have access to implicit federal guarantees or explicit FHLMC guarantee federal credit lines
Privately issued mortgage-backed bonds, including CMOs (collateralized mortgage obligations) and REMICs (real estate mortgage investment conduits)	Varies with issuer	Pools of mortgages, often overcollateralized (up to 150%) or collateralized with GNMA, FNMA, or FHLMC pass-through securities	Regular, may be on contractual basis; some tranches (subdivision of mortgage pools) are scheduled to receive all principal payments first or second, etc., until fully repaid. Other CMOs may pay only interest to one class of security (IO) and only principal (PO) to another class. The "residual class" is repaid last.	None, but mortgages used as collateral often are insured or backed by government agency guarantees, and pools may be backed with letters of credit
State or local mortgage revenue bond	State housing authorities or municipalities	Mortgage revenues earned on specific housing (finance) programs	Regular contractual payments	None

PASS-THROUGH MORTGAGE SECURITIES

Pass-through mortgage securities pass through all payments of principal and interest on pools of mortgages to holders of security interests in the pool. The security interests represent a fractional share in the pool. Thus, if someone owns a security that represents a 1 percent ownership share in a pool of securities, that person is entitled to receive 1 percent of all principal and interest payments made on the underlying mortgages.

Pass-through mortgage securities are popular because, unlike the underlying mortgages, they are initially sold in standard denominations and, if the guarantor of the pool is well known, they are readily marketable.

Since GNMA began guaranteeing pass-through securities in 1968, their growth has been great. The mortgage-backed security market now exceeds $7 trillion.

Ginnie Mae Pass-Throughs. The Government National Mortgage Association (GNMA–Ginnie Mae) issues securities that pass through all payments of interest and principal received on a pool of federally insured (e.g., FHA, VA) mortgage loans. Ginnie Mae guarantees that all payments of principal and interest are made on a timely basis. Because many mortgages are repaid before maturity, investors in Ginnie Mae MBS pools usually recover most of their principal investment well ahead of schedule.

Ginnie Mae mortgage pools are originated by mortgage bankers, commercial banks, or other mortgage-lending institutions. Once a pool of mortgages is assembled according to Ginnie Mae specifications, pass-through securities are issued that are collateralized by interest and principal payments from the mortgages in the pool and are guaranteed by Ginnie Mae.

Ginnie Mae I MBSs are based on a pool of mortgages of the same type, having the same interest rate, and having the same lender. Ginnie Mae II MBSs allow for the pool of mortgages to be from multiple lenders. In addition, Ginnie Mae II MBSs allow for the interest rate on the underlying mortgages to vary by as much as 0.75 percent. The minimum denomination of both Ginnie Mae MBSs is $25,000. For providing its guarantee and services, GNMA charges a fee, typically equal to $1/2$ of 1 percent (50 basis points). Investors are quite willing to pay the fee by accepting lower yields on GNMAs than on mortgages that are uninsured and less readily marketable.

Fannie Mae and Freddie Mac Pass-Throughs. Freddie Mac issues pass-through securities called *participation certificates* (*PCs*). Fannie Mae offers a variety of pass-through securities similar to FHLMC's PCs. Like Ginnie Mae pass-throughs, the pass-through securities issued by Fannie Mae and Freddie Mac are backed by pools of mortgages and pass through all principal and interest payments made on mortgages in those pools. However, they are unlike Ginnie Mae securities because (1) they may contain conventional mortgages (Fannie Mae MBSs may be backed by conventional or insured mortgages); (2) the mortgages may not be federally insured; (3) the pools are assembled by Fannie Mae or Freddie Mac rather than by private-sector mortgage originators; (4) the mortgages in the pools may be made at more than one interest rate; and (5) the underlying mortgage pools are much larger than GNMA pools, with values ranging up to billions of dollars. In addition, unlike Ginnie Mae securities, Fannie Mae and Freddie Mac securities are not explicitly guaranteed by the U.S. government. They are guaranteed by Fannie Mae or Freddie Mac, but guarantees by these two entities are not perceived to be as safe as those made by Ginnie Mae.

Privately Issued Pass-Throughs (PIPs).   The success of Freddie Mac and Fannie Mae in purchasing mortgages and issuing mortgage-backed securities sparked a number of imitators in the private sector. Some began their operations because private sellers of mortgages thought that FHLMC's insurance and administrative charges were excessively high relative to the risk of default on conventional mortgages.

Privately issued pass-throughs (PIPs) first appeared in 1977. PIPs are issued by private institutions or mortgage bankers, which pool mortgages, obtain private mortgage insurance, obtain ratings for the security issue, and sell the securities using underwriters' services to compete for funds in the bond markets. Privately issued pass-throughs are often used to securitize nonconforming mortgage loans that do not qualify for FHA insurance, often because the mortgage exceeds FNMA's or FHLMC's purchase limit ($417,000 in 2010 for most single-family mortgages) or fails to meet their underwriting standards. Some institutions specialize in high-risk, more than 100 percent loan-to-value ratio mortgages that FNMA and FHLMC do not make; others specialize in "jumbo" mortgages that exceed FNMA's and FHLMC's $417,000 purchase limit.

Unlike FNMA and FHLMC securities, which have an implicit government guarantee, and GNMA securities, which have an explicit government guarantee, privately issued mortgage-backed securities enjoy no such guarantees. Without some type of guarantee, privately issued MBSs can be quite risky because the pools of mortgages on which they are based will often include subprime mortgages. Therefore, to enhance the creditworthiness of the securities and attract more investors, issuers of privately issued mortgage-backed securities often buy insurance against default on the underlying mortgages or they overcollateralize the pool of mortgages such that the principal amount of mortgages in the pool is larger than the principal amount of the mortgage-backed securities. The subprime mortgage crisis that began in 2007 has substantially reduced the volume of mortgage-backed security originations by private institutions.

CMOs AND REMICs

Although pass-through securities have been tremendously successful in attracting capital market funds to mortgage markets, new varieties of mortgage-backed debt securities have been invented to further broaden the appeal of mortgage investing. **Collateralized mortgage obligations (CMOs)** consist of a series of related debt obligations, called **tranches,** which divide up the principal and interest payments made on a pool of mortgages and pay principal and interest to various investors according to a predetermined schedule. For instance, tranche A securities usually receive a fixed interest rate plus all principal payments until the entire tranche is repaid. Each obligation in the debt series except the "residual series" has a fixed maturity priority and interest payments similar to a corporate bond. Wall Street investment banks sell CMOs on behalf of originating thrift institutions and their subsidiaries. CMO tranches typically have a variety of maturity dates that can be tailored to lenders' needs. Some other CMOs may contain interest-only (IO) tranches, coupled with principal-only (PO) tranches; some CMOs may even have tranches that have floating rates if the tranche is backed by a pool of floating-rate mortgages or is paired with an "inverse floater" tranche. Rates on inverse floaters vary inversely with market interest rates.

The major advantage of CMOs is that, except for the interest-only or (residual) class, the size and value of their payments are more certain than payments on their underlying mortgages unless prepayments vary unexpectedly. The major problem with CMOs is that they may create tax problems for various originators because most originators cannot pass through all interest payments tax-free when they issue multiple debt securities. To solve this problem, the 1986 Tax Reform Act authorized the creation of a new form of mortgage-backed security. The new form was called a **real estate mortgage investment conduit (REMIC)**, which was treated like a trust that could pass through all interest and principal payments to buyers of the pass-through securities before taxes were levied. REMICs are similar to CMOs, but they differ in their legal structure. Often, pass-through securities issued by the FHLMC or FNMA are used to back issues of CMOs or REMICs.

CMOs and REMICs are popular because they create securities that have liquidity, payment, or risk characteristics that are more desirable to borrowers than pass-throughs. Because of the attractive attributes of various tranches, the tranches created by a CMO or REMIC can be sold at a higher average price (or with lower average interest rates) than the underlying pool of mortgages.

STRIPped MORTGAGE-BACKED SECURITIES (SMBSs)

Like pass-through securities, **STRIPped mortgage-backed securities (SMBSs)** pass through all payments of principal and interest on pools of mortgages to holders of security interests in the pool. The cash flows received by the holders of the interest-only (IO) security are based solely on the interest payments being made on the underlying pool of mortgages. The interest payments are directly related to the principal amount outstanding on the pool of mortgages. Therefore, the cash flows received by the holders of the IO securities decline as the principal amount declines. The holders of the principal-only (PO) securities, however, receive cash flows based on the principal payments made on the pool of underlying mortgages. Because there is a finite and fixed principal amount associated with the underlying mortgages, the cash flows received by the holders of the PO security total a finite and fixed amount.

The values of IO and PO securities are extremely sensitive to changes in interest rates due to the effect interest rates have on prepayment rates. As interest rates decrease, the holders of a PO security expect to receive the principal amount sooner, and the value of the security increases. When interest rates increase, however, the value of a PO security decreases because its cash flows are deferred further into the future as prepayment rates extend further into the future.

The value of the IO security, however, tends to decline (increase) as interest rates decline (increase). As interest rates decrease, the principal amount outstanding on the pool of underlying mortgages also decreases as a result of the increased rate of prepayments. As the principal amount outstanding declines, the size of the cash flows flowing to the holder of the IO security also declines, causing a decline in the value of the security. If interest rates increase, the expected amount of principal outstanding also increases, so the expected cash flows increase and the value of the IO security increases.

MORTGAGE-BACKED BONDS

Freddie Mac, Fannie Mae, and other institutions that hold large quantities of mortgages often fund their operations by issuing mortgage-backed bonds. A variety of mortgage-backed bonds are available.

FHLMC and FNMA Debt.   In addition to pooling mortgages and securitizing them, Fannie Mae and Freddie Mac issue notes and bonds backed by their mortgage holdings. Because mortgages provide excellent collateral for their note and bond issues and they both have government credit lines, the FNMA and FHLMC are able to issue securities at very favorable rates.

Private Mortgage-Backed Debt.   Mortgage-backed bonds can be issued by any holder of mortgages. They pay interest semiannually and have a fixed maturity (often 5 or 10 years) just like corporate, government, or federal agency bonds. However, they are collateralized by a specific pool of mortgages. The trust agreements associated with such bond issues often call for high collateral maintenance levels (150 percent or more of the value of the bonds). As a result, they obtain very high ratings (often AAA) and can compete effectively for funds in the capital markets.

Mortgage-backed bonds provide financial institutions with an effective way to obtain relatively low-cost funds by issuing bonds when their other sources of funds are expensive or inadequate. These bonds can be particularly helpful when a credit crunch occurs and the term structure of interest rates inverts, so short-term financing is very expensive.

In contrast with private pass-throughs (which are backed by issues of new mortgages) and new GNMA pools (which contain only mortgages written within the previous year), mortgage-backed bonds allow financial institutions to borrow against the value of mortgages already in their portfolios. Such bonds greatly expand those institutions' borrowing potential and eliminate the possibility that they might have to sell (at a loss) some old, low-rate mortgages so that they can obtain more funds during financial crises.

State and Local Government Housing Revenue Bonds.   Mortgage-backed bonds may be issued by particular state and local government agencies, such as state housing finance agencies or municipalities. The interest paid on housing revenue–backed bonds is usually exempt from federal taxes because they are municipal obligations. Thus, they can be sold at advantageous rates, and the proceeds from their sale allow municipalities and housing authorities to provide mortgage credit at relatively low rates.

9.5 MORTGAGE PREPAYMENT RISK

Mortgages usually have interest rates that exceed rates available on Treasury bonds. Because some mortgages and mortgage-backed securities, such as GNMA securities, have a U.S. Treasury guarantee, one might wonder why the mortgage-backed securities have premium interest rates. The reason is that mortgages have a special type of interest rate risk. Unlike U.S. Treasury securities, which typically are not callable, mortgages can be prepaid (in essence, *called*) at the discretion of the borrowers. When interest rates are low, many people **refinance** their old mortgages by obtaining new mortgages with lower interest rates and paying off the balance due on the old mortgages; this exposes the mortgage owner to **call risk** or **prepayment risk** because the mortgage is repaid sooner than expected. If a mortgage-backed security paid a high interest rate, a purchaser might expect to receive high interest payments for a long time and therefore might pay a high price (probably more than face value) for the mortgage-backed security. However, if the mortgages in the pool were prepaid early, before the owner expected, he or she would earn far less interest than expected and would probably lose a substantial amount of money because the mortgages are repaid at face value and the high-interest income ceases.

Conversely, when interest rates are high, people may be reluctant to move and buy a new house when they must borrow money to finance the new house at high interest rates. In addition, they do not want to refinance their old mortgage if they must pay higher interest rates on a new mortgage. Thus, mortgage repayments are slower than normal when interest rates are high; this may expose mortgage owners to **extension risk**. *Extension risk* is the risk that the expected timing of mortgage repayment extends further into the future.

Prepayment risk and extension risk are concerns to mortgage investors because of their impact on mortgage valuations. Unlike noncallable bonds, which increase in value at an increasing rate when interest rates decline, mortgages and mortgage pass-through securities increase in value at a decreasing rate when interest rates decline as a result of the increased likelihood of prepayments and the shortened expected timing of mortgage repayment. When interest rates increase, however, the value of a mortgage or mortgage pass-through security tends to decrease at an increasing rate because borrowers are less likely to prepay their low-interest mortgages.

Repayment rate assumptions make a huge difference in the realized yield a buyer earns on a mortgage-backed security. For instance, a pool of GNMA mortgages with a 7 percent interest rate might be priced at 107 (percent of par) and have a stated yield of 5.5 percent based on an assumed repayment rate. However, if all the mortgages were repaid at par at the end of 1 year, the realized yield would actually be about 0 percent, as the fall in price from 107 percent of par to par (a price of 100) would roughly equal the interest rate earned on the invested funds. Conversely, if a mortgage-backed pool of principal-only (PO) securities were purchased at a price of 80 (percent of par) and repaid at par in a year, the buyer would earn a 25 percent rate of return over that year. However, if the securities were purchased at a price of 80 and not repaid for 20 years, the investor in the POs would actually earn a compound annual rate of return of 1.1 percent, not 25 percent.

Because mortgages contain both prepayment risk and extension risk, financial institutions that provide mortgage financing often securitize the loans by issuing securities that pass through all payments of principal and interest on a pool of mortgages to buyers of the securities. The ultimate buyers of the mortgage-backed securities, then, bear the interest rate risk. The financial institution no longer owns the mortgages or earns interest on them. However, the originating institution usually earns fees for "originating" and "servicing" the mortgages, and it keeps its customers happy by providing mortgage financing when they need it.

Exhibit 9.7 shows that mortgage refinancing activity varies greatly over time, rising sharply when mortgage rates fall and falling sharply when mortgage rates rise again.

EXHIBIT 9.7
Refinancing Activity and Mortgage Rates

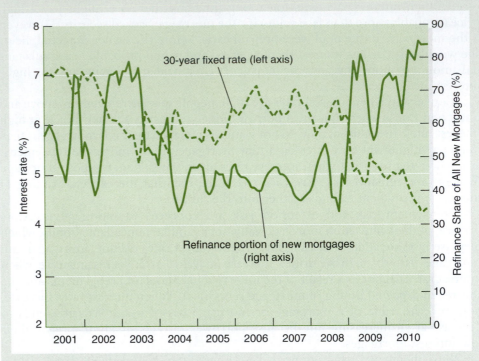

Refinancing activity varies strongly over time, rising sharply when mortgage rates fall and peaking when mortgage rates start to rise again.

DO YOU UNDERSTAND?

1. Suppose you owned a $100,000 security interest in a pass-through mortgage pool that contained $200,000,000 in mortgages and received $20,000,000 in interest payments and $2,000,000 in principal payments in its first year. How much principal and interest would you receive (if there were no mortgage servicing costs) that year?

2. Suppose your security interest in the mortgage pool described in question 1 were a PO security rather than a regular pass-through security. How much would you have received after the first year?

3. Why are securitized mortgage-backed securities often more attractive to investors than pass-through securities on the same pool of mortgages would be?

4. Why is government or private insurance important to the mortgage markets?

MORTGAGE HOLDERS

The major holders of mortgage instruments are shown in Exhibit 9.8. They include thrift institutions, commercial banks, life insurance companies, pension funds, government-sponsored enterprises (GSEs) such as FHLMC and FNMA, holders of government and private pools of mortgage-backed securities, and others.

Thrifts and Banks. Participation in the mortgage markets has been dramatically altered over time. Thrift institutions expanded their presence in the mortgage markets considerably after World War II. A tax and regulatory environment favorable to those institutions, coupled with the requirement that they invest a large portion of their portfolios in mortgages, contributed to that growth. However, beginning in the 1970s, high costs of funds reduced flows of funds to thrift

9.6 PARTICIPANTS IN THE MORTGAGE MARKETS

EXHIBIT 9.8

Mortgages Outstanding by Holder (1978–2010)

	1978	1985	1995	2005	2008	2010
Amount outstanding ($ billions)	$1,169.4	$2,312.3	$4,602.7	$11,942.2	$14,619.0	$14,020.1
Percentage held						
Thrift institutions	45.1%	33.1%	13.0%	9.6%	5.9%	4.4%
Commercial banks	18.3	18.6	23.7	24.8	26.3%	26.4%
Insurance companies and pension funds	10.1	8.8	5.3	2.6	2.5%	2.4%
U.S. government	2.4	2.3	1.3	0.7	0.7%	0.8%
Government-sponsored enterprises (GSEs)	6.2	5.9	5.4	4.0	4.8%	35.9%
Mortgage pools, government agency	6.0	16.0	34.1	30.8	33.9%	7.6%
Mortgage pools, private	—	0.6	6.4	18.0	17.7%	14.5%
Households	8.7	5.4	2.5	1.5	0.8%	0.7%
State and local governments	1.4	3.2	2.5	1.2	1.2%	1.3%
REITs	0.5	0.3	0.3	1.4	0.5%	0.4%
Credit unions	0.3	0.5	1.4	2.1	2.2%	2.3%
Finance companies	—	1.2	1.6	2.4	3.1%	2.6%
Other	1.0	4.1	2.5	0.9	0.6%	0.5%

The rapid growth of mortgage pools has reduced direct holdings of mortgages by many financial intermediaries as these financial intermediaries have substituted more marketable mortgage-backed securities for individual mortgages in their portfolios. For example, in addition to holding 26.4% of outstanding mortgages, commercial banks hold over $1.2 trillion in mortgage-backed securities issued by GSEs or mortgage pools. Note that in 2010, many of the government agency mortgage pools that were previously off the balance sheet were moved on the balance sheets of GSEs to reflect more accurately the true size of the GSEs' obligations.

institutions and reduced their desire to acquire long-term, fixed-rate mortgages. Consequently, thrifts' direct participation in the mortgage markets fell sharply. The decline is overstated, however, because thrifts swapped many of their mortgage holdings for FNMA and FHLMC mortgage-backed securities starting in late 1981.

Government-sponsored agencies (FNMA and FHLMC), mortgage pools, and commercial banks picked up much of the slack as thrifts reduced their participation in the mortgage markets after the 1970s.

Insurance Companies and Pension Funds.   Life insurance companies and pension funds often acquire mortgages to guarantee long-term returns. After World War II they held 11 percent of all mortgages outstanding, and that percentage grew in the postwar years. After the mid-1960s, however, these institutions sharply decreased their participation in the direct mortgage market. Nonetheless, they did not withdraw from the mortgage markets; they mainly acquired highly marketable pass-through securities instead of less-marketable direct mortgages.

Government Holdings.   Federal as well as state and local government agencies play a direct role in the mortgage markets. Federally owned institutions, such as the Federal Land Banks or the Farmers Home Administration, may directly acquire and hold mortgage debt. In addition, state or local housing authorities may issue housing revenue bonds and use the proceeds to acquire mortgage loans.

Government-Sponsored Enterprises (GSEs) and Mortgage Pools.   In 2010, FNMA and FHLMC held over one-third of all outstanding mortgages. Most of these holdings are held in pools to back pass-through securities, participation certificates, and other mortgage-backed securities. Prior to 2010, these pool holdings by FNMA and FHLMC were included in the "mortgage pools, government agency" category, which also includes GNMA pools. In 2010, however, FNMA's and FHLMC's pool holdings were moved on the balance sheets of these GSEs (along with the promised payments to holders of the securities backed by these mortgages) to reflect more accurately the true size of the GSEs' obligations. Now, the government agencies (GSEs) category includes those mortgages held directly by FNMA and FHLMC as well as mortgages being used to back FNMA- and FHLMC-issued mortgage-backed securities. The "Mortgage pools, government agency" category now includes only GNMA pools. Finally, the "Mortgage pools, private" category includes mortgages that back privately issued mortgage-backed securities. Many of these mortgages are subprime mortgages. Not surprisingly, the size of these holdings declined in recent years.

The mortgage markets generate many billions of dollars per year in new mortgages. This vast amount of financing has been facilitated by the operations of mortgage insurers, mortgage bankers, and numerous government agencies.

MORTGAGE INSURERS

FHA Insurance. The federal government pioneered the development of mortgage insurance during the 1930s. As real estate values plummeted and many foreclosures occurred, investors became reluctant to invest in mortgaged property without substantial down payments. Thus, the Federal Housing Administration offered FHA insurance to guarantee lenders against default on mortgage loans. FHA insurance initially had a monthly premium equal to $1/2$ of 1 percent of the outstanding balance on a loan; now the premium is paid in advance and varies with mortgage terms.

Federally insured mortgages were popular. Lenders were willing to make FHA loans to borrowers at favorable interest rates with the minimal down payments required by the FHA because of the insurance.

However, their popularity was hindered at times because the FHA refused to insure loans that (1) were above a certain maximum size, (2) carried an interest rate above what the FHA thought was politically expedient to allow, and (3) did not comply with FHA appraisal and paperwork requirements. Of these, the loan size restrictions and interest rate caps caused the most problems. When FHA-approved interest rate ceilings were below market interest rates, lenders charged discount points on FHA loans. Loan discounts of 10 percent or more were sometimes needed before lenders could earn a market rate of return. As a result, lenders were reluctant to make FHA loans at such times.

VA Insurance. In 1944, the Veterans Administration (VA) was allowed to insure mortgage loans to military veterans on even more lenient terms than the FHA. VA-insured loans can be made for larger amounts and require no down payment at all. However, they require cumbersome paperwork, and they, too, have sometimes been adversely affected by low rate ceilings.

Private Mortgage Insurance. Because of the administrative drawbacks associated with FHA- and VA-insured mortgage lending, many institutions prefer to make conventional mortgage loans. These are often made with down payments that are substantially higher than those for government-insured loans in order to protect the lender against loss. However, their higher down payments make them unpopular with some borrowers.

Private mortgage insurance companies have helped fill the need for low-down-payment conventional mortgages. These companies insure a portion of the total mortgage debt—the riskiest 10 to 20 percent—in return for a relatively high premium on the insured portion (see Exhibit 9.5). This can let a borrower buy real property with as little as 3 percent down. In addition, the overall rate (APR) on the mortgage is not substantially elevated. This is so because the insured portion is only a fraction of the total mortgage.

Effects of Mortgage Insurance. Mortgage insurance has facilitated the development of secondary mortgage markets. The buyer of an insured mortgage need know only the financial strength and credibility of the insurer instead of the financial strength and credibility of the mortgage borrower. This reduces the buyer's information costs considerably—from having to know about thousands of Jane Does' mortgages to merely knowing about the performance of the FHA, VA, or other mortgage insurers. As a result, more investors are willing to buy mortgages, and mortgages are more marketable than would otherwise be the case.

PEOPLE & EVENTS

The Rise and Fall of Fannie and Freddie

In the middle of 2007, the combined market value of equity shares in Fannie Mae and Freddie Mac was over $100 billion. By the end of the decade, the combined value barely topped $1 billion, both companies were being held in conservatorship by the Federal Housing Finance Board, and the only motivation for buying shares in either company was to speculate on its future.

Fannie Mae was created by Congress in 1938 as a federal agency. Its purpose was to help support housing markets by providing liquidity and stability to mortgage markets. In 1968, FNMA was split into two entities, the Government National Mortgage Association (GNMA, or Ginnie Mae) and the Federal National Mortgage Association (FNMA, or Fannie Mae). The Federal Home Loan Mortgage Corporation (FHLMC, or Freddie Mac) was established by Congress in 1970.

GNMA continues as a federal agency and was given the charge of expanding affordable housing by helping lenders access capital markets as a source of funds for government-guaranteed mortgages. Today, GNMA guarantees the timely payment of principal and interest on pools of qualifying FHA, VA, and other government-guaranteed mortgages. Lenders combine qualifying mortgages into pools, acquire a GNMA guarantee on the pool, and then sell security interests in the pool. GNMA does not originate or purchase mortgages. Rather, it provides a guarantee for mortgage-backed securities issued by approved lenders. It is wholly owned by the U.S. government, and its securities are the only mortgage-backed securities backed by the full faith and credit of the U.S. government.

Fannie Mae and Freddie Mac, on the other hand, help lenders access capital markets as a source of funds for conventional mortgages. Unlike GNMA, Fannie Mae and Freddie Mac are stockholder-owned corporations. Their mortgage-backed securities are not explicitly backed by the full faith and credit of the U.S. government. The fact that the two corporations are now being held in conservatorship, however, suggests that they may be receiving some backing by the federal government.

Fannie Mae, Freddie Mac, and Ginnie Mae are significant pieces of the government's broad support for housing and mortgage markets in the United States. After Fannie Mae and Freddie Mac were forced into conservatorship and during the 2007–2009 recession, the Obama administration proposed several options for shrinking the government's support of these markets. Depending on the outcome of deliberations by Congress and the administration, the plans could include phasing out Fannie Mae and Freddie Mac. Whatever their fate, it is clear that policymakers blame Fannie Mae and Freddie Mac, at least in part, for some of the excesses that led to the housing crisis.

It is not clear, however, what will happen to housing and mortgage markets if there is less government support of those markets. Most observers expect that, without government-supported lending programs and secondary market support, the cost of mortgages will go up and homeownership will go down. In addition, many consumer advocates worry that, as the government becomes less involved in housing and mortgage markets, the private sector will fill the void, and some private lenders and investors may not be as scrupulous as the government institutions they are replacing.

MORTGAGE BANKERS

Mortgage bankers have grown in importance since mortgage insurance increased the secondary market for mortgages. **Mortgage bankers**, or mortgage companies, are private firms that originate mortgages and collect payments on them. However, they generally do not hold mortgage loans in their own portfolios for long. Instead, they sell them and obtain their income from "servicing fees" that they charge the ultimate buyers for collecting payments and keeping records on each loan. The service fees, along with loan origination and application fees that they receive when they make the loan, cover their costs of loan origination and collection.

Origination fees can be expressed as *points*, that is, percentages of the mortgage's principal amount and as dollar fees, such as an application fee or document preparation fee. Mortgage bankers typically originate mortgages that meet the *underwriting standards* (loan terms, collateral, and borrower risk requirements) imposed by major purchasers of mortgages. FNMA (Fannie Mae) and FHLMC (Freddie Mac) publish their underwriting standards and give people computer access to see if pending loans qualify for purchase. If a mortgage is *nonconforming* under FNMA and FHLMC standards—primarily because it is for a larger amount or has a lower down payment than FNMA and FHLMC will purchase—it may be sold to a private mortgage purchaser who, in turn, may securitize it—just as FNMA and FHLMC do with most of the mortgages they purchase.

Once a mortgage is sold to a final holder—such as FNMA, FHLMC, a life insurance company, or a pension fund—or to GNMA, a REMIC, or other trust that passes through payments on securitized mortgages, a mortgage banker may continue to profit by servicing the mortgage in exchange for a servicing fee. A *mortgage servicer* collects and records mortgage payments and calculates the portion of payments that are from principal and from interest before passing the payments on to the mortgage owner. The mortgage servicer may also make insurance and tax payments due if such payments are required to be part of the borrowers' mortgage payments. The mortgage servicing fee is usually expressed as a percentage of the principal outstanding. It can range as high as 0.44 percent (44 basis points) and for many years was most often $^3/_8$ (37.5 basis points) percent; however, it has fallen in recent years as computer technology has reduced bookkeeping costs and competition among mortgage servicers has reduced servicing fees. Mortgage bankers must beware that they don't compete too hard, however. The typical mortgage's principal balance and the associated dollar amount of servicing fees tend to fall over time as a mortgage ages. However, a fixed-rate mortgage's payments, and the work required to process those payments, stay the same over time. Thus, servicing fee net income falls over time on aging mortgages. As a result, initially adequate servicing fees may become inadequate when a mortgage gets old. In the past, some mortgage bankers have experienced financial difficulty because they forgot this point.

As you can see from Exhibit 9.9, interest rates on mortgage obligations move in step with those on other capital market obligations, particularly 10-year government securities. Mortgage rates on 30-year fixed-rate mortgages closely track changes in the 10-year Treasury note rate because both have similar durations as a result of the accelerated repayment of mortgages. The mortgage rate is higher than the note rate, however, because mortgages have both call risk and extension risk and, if not government guaranteed, some small credit risk. Long-term fixed-rate mortgages are little affected by changes in short-term interest rates.

9.7 RELATIONSHIP BETWEEN MORTGAGE MARKETS AND THE CAPITAL MARKETS

EXHIBIT 9.9

Mortgage Interest Rates and Other Market Rates

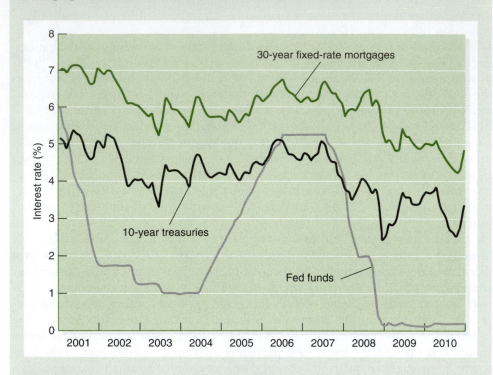

Note that, although interest rates on 30-year fixed-rate mortgages closely track changes in the 10-year Treasury note rate, the spread between mortgage rates and note rates widened substantially during 2008 due to uncertainty in housing and mortgage markets.

SUMMARY OF LEARNING OBJECTIVES

1 **Explain the basic structure of mortgages as debt instruments.** *Mortgages* are collateralized loans that are amortized over time. Monthly mortgage payments include interest and principal. Periodic interest payments are based on the remaining principal balance due—so, in the early years, the mortgage principal declines slowly, and it may take 70–75 percent of the mortgage's life before one-half of the loan is repaid.

2 **Describe the various types of mortgages that exist and discuss how the different types of mortgages allocate interest rate and inflation risks to the**

borrower or lender. A wide variety of mortgages have been developed. Fixed-rate mortgages are common but cannot adjust returns if inflation occurs and interest rates rise. ARMs, flexible ARMs, ROMs, RRMs, and balloon payment mortgages all call for periodic adjustments in interest. Home equity loans, second mortgages, and RAMs allow people to borrow against the accumulated equity in their homes.

3 **Explain how government and private-market innovations have led to a vastly expanded popularity for mortgages and mortgage-backed securities in the nation's capital markets.** After the development of

federal mortgage insurance (FHA, VA, etc.), private mortgage insurance, GNMA, and government-sponsored agencies (FNMA, FHLMC) that guarantee mortgage loans, a national secondary market in mortgages developed. Insurance and other financial guarantees reduce credit risk in the market.

4 Discuss the wide variety of mortgage-backed securities and mortgage-backed debt issues. A wide variety of mortgage-backed securities (MBSs) were developed that increased the appeal of MBSs relative to the original mortgages by reducing *call* (prepayment) risk, extension risk, or payment uncertainties for some types or tranches of MBSs. The development of MBSs increased the ability of mortgage lenders to obtain financing from the nation's capital markets and led to rapid growth in mortgages outstanding and more uniform mortgage rates across the country. These innovations also improved liquidity in the mortgage markets.

5 Describe the key roles that Fannie Mae, Freddie Mac, Ginnie Mae, mortgage bankers, and mortgage insurers have played in developing secondary mortgage markets. The majority of mortgages are now sold in the secondary mortgage markets. Mortgage bankers and government agencies (such as FNMA and FHLMC) facilitate secondary mortgage market operations. These government agencies set underwriting (credit) standards, purchase mortgages, and often securitize pools of mortgages by providing pass-through or other mortgage-backed securities that can be sold or used to back other securities issued in the mortgage markets.

6 Describe the role of mortgage bankers and how they earn profits. Mortgage bankers originate and service mortgage loans. They bear little interest rate risk because they hold on to mortgages only long enough to sell them in the secondary market. Mortgage bankers earn income from two sources. First, on origination of the loan, they receive an origination fee, which can be a fixed percentage of the original loan amount or a set of dollar fees charged for services, such as application or document-preparation fees. Second, they receive servicing fees that are a fixed percentage of the outstanding loan balance.

7 Discuss how the nature of mortgage markets has evolved over time. The nature of the mortgage markets has changed over time. Regional mortgage markets dominated by local lending institutions, such as savings banks or savings and loans, have given way to national mortgage markets dominated by key government agencies, mortgage bankers, and commercial and investment banks (the investment banks help create and sell many of the mortgage-backed securities). Insurance companies and pension funds provide substantial amounts of funding for mortgage loans, but now they are more likely to buy mortgage-backed securities than individual mortgages.

8 Explain the recent financial crisis and its impact on mortgage markets. Fannie Mae's and Freddie Mac's roles in the financial crisis and their takeover by the government raised questions about the government's role in housing and mortgage markets. If government support for housing is reduced, mortgage credit will probably also be reduced.

KEY TERMS

Mortgages
Mortgage-backed securities (MBSs)
Interest rate risk
Credit risk
Fixed-rate mortgage (FRM)
Amortization
Adjustable-rate mortgage (ARM)
Balloon payment mortgages
Rollover mortgages (ROMs)
Renegotiated-rate mortgages (RRMs)
Interest-only mortgage
Reverse annuity mortgages (RAMs)
Home equity loans
Home equity lines of credit
FHA mortgages
Veterans Administration (VA) mortgages
Private mortgage insurance (PMI)
Government National Mortgage Association (GNMA–Ginnie Mae)
Federal National Mortgage Association (FNMA–Fannie Mae)
Federal Home Loan Mortgage Corporation (FHLMC–Freddie Mac)
Privately issued pass-throughs (PIP)
Collateralized mortgage obligations (CMOs)
Tranches
Real estate mortgage investment conduit (REMIC)
STRIPped mortgage-backed securities (SMBSs)
Refinance
Call risk
Prepayment risk
Extension risk
Mortgage bankers

QUESTIONS AND PROBLEMS

1. If you had a 7 percent, $100,000 30-year fixed-rate mortgage, how long would it take before you had repaid half the loan balance due? If you paid an extra $100 per month to reduce the principal due on the mortgage, how long would it take to repay half the principal due? In the case where you paid an extra $100 per month, how long would it take to repay the entire loan? (*Hint:* It probably would help to use a computer spreadsheet program to make these calculations; set it up in the same way that Exhibit 9.1 is set up.)

2. If your bank held 1 percent of the units issued by a unit trust and the mortgages in the trust repaid $10,500,000 in interest and $1,500,000 in principal in its first year, how much principal and interest would your bank receive that year?

3. Suppose your mortgage balance was $60,000 and you had a floating-rate mortgage that called for you to pay interest at an annual rate of 2.75 percent over the 1-year T-bill rate, and the T-bill rate has been averaging 2.05 percent. How much interest would you owe on your mortgage next month?

4. Describe the factors that affect a borrower's ability to qualify for a mortgage.

5. Suppose your gross monthly income is $5,000. Assume that property taxes, homeowner's insurance, and mortgage insurance payments total $200 a month. In addition, assume you have automobile and student loan payments that total $400 a month. If 30-year fixed-rate mortgages have a current annual percentage rate of 6 percent, how much do you qualify to borrow based on the payment-to-income ratios described in the chapter?

6. Suppose you are interested in buying a home valued at $500,000, and 30-year fixed-rate mortgages have an interest rate of 6%. What is your minimum down payment, assuming you will borrow with a conventional mortgage? If property taxes and homeowners' insurance total $500 per month, and you have other loan payments totaling $300 per month, how much do you need to earn on a monthly basis to qualify for a mortgage?

7. Explain why mortgage investors demand a higher yield for investing in securities with call risk and exten-sion risk. Why would a mortgage investor view mortgage prepayments negatively?

8. Assume you set up a REMIC that guaranteed that the class B tranche would bear all the credit risk and the class A tranche would lose only if the class B tranche holders were not repaid. What is the maximum interest rate you could offer the class B tranche holders and still make a profit from securitizing the loans if the class A tranche buyers were willing to accept a 7 percent return on their 90 percent interest in a pool of mortgages that generated an 8 percent interest return? (The class B holders would hold the other 10 percent interest in the pool.)

9. Why was the development of mortgage insurance necessary before secondary mortgage markets could develop?

10. How has the development of secondary mortgage markets allowed mortgage issuers to attract additional funds from the capital markets?

11. Explain how mortgage-related securities have become more similar to capital market instruments over time.

12. Why have mortgage market interest rates become more uniform across the country in recent years?

13. How has the government encouraged the development of secondary mortgage markets?

14. What is the difference between conventional mortgages and FHA and VA mortgages?

15. If you expect prices and incomes to rise, what type of mortgage would you rather have on your house: FRM or ARM? What if you expected prices to fall? Explain your answer. Also explain how your answer would differ if you were a mortgage lender.

16. Why have CMOs and REMICs made it easier for the mortgage markets to compete for funds with corporate bonds? What problems do their residuals pose?

17. If mortgage bankers originate more mortgages than other types of financial institutions, why don't they also hold more mortgages in their asset accounts?

INTERNET EXERCISE

A majority of the mortgages originating in the United States are sold or securi-tized at some time. Mortgage bankers are among the most important originators and sellers of mortgages. Government-sponsored enterprises (GSEs) such as Freddie Mac and Fannie Mae are the most important buyers of mortgages and issuers of mortgage-backed securities. The Web site for the Mortgage Bankers Association of America, http://www.mbaa.org, provides useful news releases on mortgage legislation, mortgage delinquency rates, and mortgage interest rates. The Web sites, www.freddiemac.com and www.fanniemae.com, and www.ginniemae.gov, contain useful descriptions of the various types of mortgage-backed securities one is most likely to encounter in the financial markets.

1. Go to the Fannie Mae Web site. Click on "Mortgage-Backed Securities." Then click on "Basics of Fannie Mae MBSs" and "Basics of REMICs." Finally, click on "Classes." (a) What are three types of tranches that are adversely affected by extension risk? (b) What type of tranche is least likely to be adversely affected by extension risk? (c) What type is most likely to be adversely affected by prepayment (call) risk?

2. The Web site of the Mortgage Bankers Association of America, http://www.mbaa.org, contains useful information on the current state of the mortgage market. Use that site to find the following:

   a. How delinquency rates on mortgages have changed over the last year.

   b. How much the ARM rate differs from the 30-year mortgage rate.

CHAPTER TEN

Equity Markets

EQUITIES (OR STOCKS) REPRESENT ownership of a corporation and are the most visible securities on the financial landscape. At the end of May 2010, the value of stocks around the world totaled more than $45 trillion and were issued by 45,000 different companies (www.world-exchange.org). Every day in newspapers, on television, and on the Internet, reporters eagerly and with rapt interest describe the ups and downs of the stock market because most believe the stock market is an important indicator of the economy's health and because most Americans have money invested in the stock market—through a direct investment, a mutual fund, or a retirement account. In fact, in a recent Gallup/USA Today poll, more than 60 percent of Americans claimed to have some money invested in the stock market at the end of 2009 (www.gallup.com). Investing in stocks, however, can be very risky. As an owner, a stockholder gets a share of the company's profits. Just like if you owned your own business, however, owners get paid only after everyone else gets paid—employees, suppliers, and anyone who has lent the company money. So when things go bad, owners usually suffer the most. According to the 2009 Credit-Suisse Global Investments Returns Year-book, when world equity markets hit lows in November 2008, stocks worldwide had lost more than $21 trillion, or

Equity securities, which represent ownership of corporations, are traded on exchanges such as the New York Stock Exchange.

about $21,000 for every man, woman, and child in the developed world! That wealth simply disappeared—here today, gone tomorrow. ∎

The purpose of this chapter is to answer the following questions about equity securities: What are they? How are they bought and sold? How are stock markets regulated? What determines the prices of equity securities? How do we measure the risk of equities? What is the meaning of various stock indexes such as the Dow Jones Industrial Average or the S&P 500? Do movements in the stock market predict changes in economic activity?

The chapter begins with a description of the types of equity securities: common stock, preferred stock, and convertible securities. We then discuss how equity securities are traded in primary and secondary markets before describing the major venues for trading equities in the United States. Next we briefly describe government regulation of the equity markets. The focus then turns to valuing equity securities and measuring their risks. We then describe the major stock indexes and address whether the stock market is a good predictor of economic activity. ■

LEARNING OBJECTIVES

1 Describe the three types of equity securities.

2 Explain how equity securities are sold in the primary market and the role of underwriters.

3 Explain how equity securities are traded in the secondary markets and be able to understand a stock quote.

4 Describe the basics of equity valuation.

5 Explain how a short sale works.

6 Explain the risks associated with equity securities and discuss how to measure these risks.

7 Describe the major stock market indexes and how they are constructed.

8 Discuss whether the stock market is a good predictor of economic activity.

10.1 WHAT ARE EQUITY SECURITIES?

Although **equity** securities can take several forms, the most prevalent type by far is **common stock**. As its name implies, common stockholders have no special dividend rights and the lowest priority claim if the company goes bankrupt. Owners of **preferred stock**, in contrast, usually receive preferential treatment over common stockholders when it comes to receiving dividends or cash payoffs in bankruptcy. Investors can also purchase convertible bonds that provide an option to trade the debt for stock. Some preferred stock is convertible into common stock.

COMMON STOCK

Common stockholders are the owners of a corporation. If you ask who owns Apple, the answer is whoever owns Apple's common stock. According to Apple's 2010 proxy statement, CEO Steve Jobs holds about 5.5 million shares (less than 1 percent of Apple's ownership). In contrast, Fidelity Management and Research owns about 44 million shares (nearly 5 percent of Apple's outstanding shares). Thus, Fidelity owns about eight times as much of the company as Steve Jobs (i.e., 44/5.5).

The most distinguishing feature of common stock is that it is the **residual claim** against the firm's cash flows or assets. If the firm goes bankrupt, common stockholders cannot be paid until employees, the government, short-term creditors, bondholders, and preferred stockholders are paid first. After these prior claims are satisfied, the stockholders are entitled to what is left over, the residual. Therefore, common stockholders share directly in the firm's profits. The residual nature of common stock, however, means that it is more risky than a firm's bonds or preferred stock.

Legally, common stockholders enjoy **limited liability**, meaning that their losses are limited to the original amount of their investment. In other words, even if the company goes bankrupt, a stockholder's other assets, such as other equity investments, bank savings, and home, are safe. In contrast, a sole proprietor is personally liable for the firm's obligations—if a sole proprietor's company goes bankrupt, creditors can come after the proprietor's other assets. Given limited liability, it is not surprising that most large firms in the United States are organized as corporations.

Dividends. When a company makes money or has positive **earnings**, it can do one of two things: either reinvest the profits in the company (**retained earnings**) for the benefit of the shareholders or pay the money to the shareholders directly (**dividends**). Common stock dividends are not guaranteed, and a corporation does not default if it does not pay them. Dividends, however, are paid out of the firm's after-tax cash flows. Because dividend income is taxable for most investors, corporate profits are doubly taxed—once when the corporation pays the corporate income tax, and once more when the investors pay their personal income taxes.

Voting Rights. Although stockholders own the corporation, they do not exercise control over the firm's day-to-day activities. Control of the firm is in the hands of corporate managers who are supposed to act in the shareholders' interests. Shareholders exercise control over the firm's activities through the election of a board of directors. The board of directors represent the owners and monitor the managers' activities on shareholders' behalf. Shareholders elect directors by voting at an annual meeting. As a practical matter, most shareholders do not physically attend the meeting, voting instead by **proxy**, a process by which shareholders vote by absentee ballot.

In general, one vote is attached to each share of stock, although there are exceptions, called **dual-class firms**. During the 1980s many firms recapitalized with two classes of stock having different voting rights. By issuing stock with limited voting rights compared to existing shares, the managers of a firm can raise equity capital while maintaining voting control of the firm. Needless to say, dual-class firms are controversial. Many view the dual-class recapitalizations as attempts by managers to entrench themselves. Opponents argue that managers of dual-class firms are insulated from the disciplining effects of the proxy or takeover processes, through which ineffective managers can be replaced (i.e., fired). Proponents say that managers of dual-class firms are free to pursue riskier, longer-term strategies that ultimately benefit shareholders without fear of reprisal if the short-term performance of the firm suffers.

There are two procedures for electing directors: cumulative voting and straight voting. In **cumulative voting**, all directors are elected at the same time, and shareholders are granted a number of votes equal to the number of directors being elected times the number of shares owned. In most cumulative voting schemes, shareholders are permitted to distribute their votes across directors as they wish. For example, if five director positions are being voted on and you own 100 shares, you have 500 "votes" to distribute however you want—all 500 votes for a single director or 200 for one director and 300 for another, or any such combination.

The effect of cumulative voting is to give minority shareholders, those owning small proportions of the stock, a voice in the firm's decisions. With cumulative voting, minority shareholders are guaranteed that they will be able to elect the largest percentage of the directors that is less than the percentage of shares the minority shareholders control. For example, if five directors are being elected and the minority shareholders control 42 percent of the shares, they are assured of being able to elect two directors because each director requires 20 percent of the total votes cast to be elected. If only three directors are being elected, then the minority shareholders would be able to elect only one director because each director requires 33.3 percent of the total votes. In **straight voting**, directors are elected one by one. Thus, the maximum number of votes for each director equals the number of shares owned. Under this scheme, it is difficult for minority shareholders to obtain representation on the board of directors because any shareholder who owns even slightly more than 50 percent of the shares can elect the entire board of directors.

PREFERRED STOCK

Preferred stock also represents ownership in the corporation, but as the name implies, it receives preferential treatment over common stock with respect to dividend payments and the claim against the firm's assets in the event of bankruptcy or liquidation. In liquidation, preferred stockholders are entitled to the issue price of the preferred stock plus accumulated dividends after other creditors have been paid and before common stockholders are paid.

Dividends.   Preferred stock is usually designated by the dollar amount of its dividend, which is a fixed obligation of the firm, similar to the interest payments on corporate bonds. Most preferred stock is **nonparticipating** and **cumulative**. Nonparticipating means that the preferred stock dividend is fixed—it doesn't change regardless of how profitable (or unprofitable) the firm may become. Alcoa, for example, has a preferred stock that pays a fixed $3.75 annual dividend ($0.9375/quarter). This dividend will not change. Firms can decide not to pay the dividends on preferred stock without going into default. The cumulative feature of preferred stock means, however, that the firm cannot pay a dividend to its common stockholders until it has paid any dividends it skipped to the preferred stockholders. Some preferred stock is issued with adjustable rates. **Adjustable-rate preferred stock** became popular in the early 1980s when interest rates were rapidly changing. The dividends of adjustable-rate preferred stock are adjusted periodically in response to changing market interest rates (usually Treasury bill rates).

Voting.   Generally, preferred stockholders do not vote for the board of directors. Exceptions to this general rule can occur when the corporation is in arrears on its dividend payments.

CONVERTIBLE SECURITIES

Convertible preferred stock can be converted into common stock at a predetermined ratio (such as two shares of common for each share of preferred stock). By buying such stock, an investor can obtain a good dividend return plus the possibility that, if the price of the common stock increases, the value of the convertible stock will also increase.

Convertible bonds are bonds that can be exchanged for shares of common stock. Until conversion, however, they are corporate debt; thus their interest and principal payments are contractual obligations of the firm and must be made or the corporation will default. Most convertible bonds are subordinated debentures. That means convertible bondholders have lower-ranking claims than most other debt holders, although their claims rank ahead of stockholders.

Because convertible bonds both increase in value with rising stock prices and provide the fixed income and security of bonds, they are popular with investors, who are usually willing to pay more to acquire convertible debt than conventional debt issued by the same corporation. From the corporation's perspective, convertible bonds provide a means by which the corporation can issue debt and later convert it to equity at a price per share that exceeds the stock's present market value. This feature is attractive because it allows the corporation to "sell" stock at a higher future price.

10.2 EQUITY MARKETS

Exhibit 10.1 shows the distribution of ownership for equity securities in the United States at the end of March 2010. Households dominate the holding of equity securities, owning more than 36 percent of outstanding corporate equities. Even though households are the largest single holder of corporate equities, most ownership is by non-households. Mutual funds are the largest institutional holders of equity, followed by foreign investors and pension funds. Investors own equity securities through either primary market or secondary market transactions. In this section, we discuss the primary and secondary markets for equity securities and the costs of buying or selling securities in these markets.

PRIMARY MARKETS

When a company issues equity, it occurs in the **primary market**. This is the only time a company receives money from selling the share. The company can use the funds raised by the sale of equity securities to expand production, enter new markets, further research, and the like. If it is the first time the company has offered a particular type of security to the public, meaning the security is not currently trading in the secondary market, the primary offering is called an unseasoned offering or an **initial public offering (IPO)**. Tesla Motors, for example, raised more than $226 million to pay for factories and development costs in a June 2010 IPO. Otherwise, if the firm already has similar securities trading in the secondary market, the primary issue is known as a **seasoned offering**. In 2009, for example, Goldman Sachs, who already had more than 462 million shares outstanding, sold more than 40 million new shares of common stock (for $5 billion) in a seasoned offering and used the proceeds to repay government aid.

EXHIBIT 10.1
Holders of Corporate Equity Securities (March 31, 2010)

Holder	Amount (Billions)	Percentage of Total
Households	$ 7,793	36.7%
Mutual funds	4,364	20.5
Foreign investors	2,628	12.4
Private pension funds	1,918	9.0
Federal, state, and local retirement funds	1,789	8.4
Insurance companies	1,567	7.4
Exchange traded funds	687	3.2
Others	496	2.3
Total	$ 21,242	100.0%

Although households are the category with the single largest holdings of equity securities, institutional investors, as a group, hold more.

Source: Board of Governors, Federal Reserve System.

New issues of equity securities may be sold directly to investors by the issuing corporation, but they are usually distributed by an investment banker in an underwritten offering, a private placement, or a shelf registration. The most common distribution method is an **underwritten offering** in which the investment banker purchases the securities from the company for a guaranteed amount known as the net proceeds and then resells the securities to investors for a greater amount, called the gross proceeds. The difference between the gross proceeds and the net proceeds is the **underwriter's spread,** which compensates the investment banker for the expenses and risks involved in the offering.

Also, some equity securities are distributed through **private placements**, in which the investment banker acts only as the company's agent and receives a commission for placing the securities with investors. In 2008, for example, Warren Buffet's Berkshire Hathaway purchased $5 billion of preferred stock from Goldman Sachs. In this case, Berkshire Hathaway was the only buyer of the stock. Occasionally a company places equity securities directly with its existing stockholders through a **rights offering**. In a rights offering, a company's stockholders are given the right to purchase additional shares at a slightly below-market price in proportion to their current ownership in the company. Stockholders can exercise their rights or sell them.

Shelf registration is an important method of selling both equity and debt securities. Shelf registration permits a corporation to register a quantity of securities with the SEC and sell them over time rather than all at once. Thus, the issuer is able to save time and money through a single registration. In addition, with shelf registrations, securities can be brought to market with little notice, thereby providing the issuer with maximum flexibility in timing an issue to take advantage of favorable market conditions. Chapter 18 discusses in more detail the process by which investment bankers assist companies in conducting primary offerings of their securities.

FACTORS AFFECTING UNDERWRITER SPREADS

Investment bankers are compensated for the expenses and risks involved in underwriting an issue by earning the underwriting spread—the difference between the gross proceeds (what the underwriter sells the securities for to investors) and net proceeds (what the underwriter pays the company for the security). Several factors affect the size of the spread.

First, the underwriter's spread is inversely related to the size of the offering. In other words, the larger the offering, the smaller the spread tends to be as a percentage of the amount of funds being raised by the company. Second, the more uncertain the investment bankers are concerning the market price of the equity securities being offered, the larger the underwriter's spread. The reason is that in an underwritten offering, especially an unseasoned offering, the investment bankers bear all of the price risk. Third, shelf registrations tend to have lower spreads than ordinary offerings. This is due, in part, to the fact that larger, more well-known companies employ shelf registrations.

SECONDARY MARKETS

Any trade of a security after its primary offering is said to be a secondary market transaction. When an investor buys 100 shares of IBM on the New York Stock Exchange (NYSE), the proceeds of the sale do not go to IBM but rather to the investor who sold the shares. In the United States, most secondary market equity trading is done either on organized exchanges, such as the NYSE, or in the over-the-counter market, such as the NASDAQ.

Have you ever heard a reporter exclaim that "investors were selling today . . ." following a decline in the market? If you think about it, does that make sense? In the secondary market, there's a buyer for every seller—by definition, the number of shares sold equals the number of shares bought. So while many investors were selling, many (other) investors were buying. Just as in any market, prices fall when, at a given price, there are more sellers than buyers. As prices fall, more investors are willing to purchase the security and fewer are willing to sell. Eventually, an equilibrium price is reached where the supply from sellers equals the demand by buyers.

Exhibit 10.2 shows the Google finance quote for IBM on July 9, 2010. Most Web sites (and newspapers) provide similar information. From the exhibit you can see that IBM's stock last traded at a price of \$127.50, down 47¢ from its closing price the previous day. Thus, since trading closed on July 8, the stock price fell 0.37 percent ($-0.47/127.97$). Midway through the trading day on July 9, the stock had traded as low as \$127.37 and as high as \$128.20. Over the previous 52 weeks, the stock had traded as low as \$99.80 and as high as \$134.25. It opened trading on July 9 at \$127.90, and partway through the trading day on July 9, 1.95 million shares of IBM had already been traded (IBM's average daily trading volume is 7.38 million shares). IBM's equity **market capitalization**, or market cap, of \$163.47 billion is the total value of all the outstanding IBM stock and therefore is just the price times the number of shares outstanding (\$127.50 times 1.28 billion shares outstanding). IBM is currently paying a quarterly dividend of 65¢ per share. Thus, if the price never changed, and IBM never changed its dividend, an investor would earn 2.04 percent per year ($[0.65*4]/127.50$), known as the **dividend yield**. Institutional investors, such as pension funds and mutual funds, own 59 percent of IBM's shares. Beta is a risk measure that we will discuss later in the chapter.

EXHIBIT 10.2
IBM Stock Quote (July 9, 2010)

International Business (Public, NYSE: IBM)

127.50 − 0.47 (−0.37%)						
	Range	127.37–128.20	Mkt cap	163.47B	Shares	1.28B
	52 week	99.80–134.25	P/E	12.4	Beta	0.75
	Open	127.90	Div/yield	0.65/2.04	Inst. Own	59%
	Vol/Avg.	1.95M/7.38M	EPS	10.28		

Source: Google Finance, July 9, 2010.

Over the last year, IBM earned $10.28 for every share of common stock. Thus, **earnings per share (EPS)** is simply net income divided by the number of shares outstanding. If IBM did a two-for-one stock split, anyone who held one share would now hold two shares and the number of outstanding shares would double—but the value of the company would not change (i.e., it's still the same company). Instead the stock price would fall to about half its current price. (You can see that a person who trades a $20 bill for two $10 bills is not any better off.) Because any stock's price is a function of how many shares are outstanding, investors can't look at the price to determine if a stock is cheap or expensive. Instead, investors have to standardize the price by some variable such that changes in the number of shares outstanding don't affect the estimate. Although investors use a number of such variables (such as cash flow per share or book value of equity per share), the most common measure is earnings per share. Thus, if IBM doubles the number of shares outstanding, total net income wouldn't change, but EPS (i.e., net income/number of shares), like price, would also fall by half. Therefore, price divided by earnings per share, or the **price/earnings (P/E) ratio**, wouldn't change.

IBM's P/E on July 9, 2010, was 12.4, which is the price ($127.50) divided by the EPS ($10.28). The P/E is used to judge how "expensive" a stock is. Apple's P/E on the same date, for example, was 21.93. Therefore, investors were willing to pay $21.93 per dollar current earnings for Apple versus only $12.40 per dollar of current earnings for IBM. Investors were willing to pay "more" (i.e., a higher P/E) for Apple either because investors believed Apple's future earnings would grow faster than IBM's or because they believed Apple was a safer investment (and therefore they were willing to pay more for less uncertainty).

From an investor's perspective, the function of secondary markets is to provide liquidity at fair prices. Liquidity is achieved if investors can trade large amounts of securities without affecting the prices. Prices are fair if they reflect the underlying value of the security correctly.

There are four types of secondary markets: direct search, brokered, dealer, and auction. Each of these types of secondary markets differs according to the amount of information investors have concerning prices.

Direct Search.   Perhaps the secondary markets furthest from the ideal of complete price information are those in which buyers and sellers must search each other out directly. As an example of a direct search market, imagine if you wanted to purchase a used 2009 Jeep Wrangler from an individual owner. You would scour online (or newspaper) ads and then have to negotiate directly with the current owner. Because the full cost of locating and bargaining with a compatible trading partner is borne by an individual investor, there is only a small incentive to conduct a thorough search among all possible partners for the best possible price. Failure to conduct a search implies a high probability that, at the time a trade is agreed on by the two participants, at least one of the participants could have gotten a better price were he or she in contact with some undiscovered participant. Securities that trade in **direct search markets** are usually bought and sold so infrequently that no third party, such as a broker or a dealer, has an incentive to provide any kind of service to facilitate trading. The common stock of small companies, especially small banks, trades in direct search markets. Buyers and sellers of those issues must rely on word-of-mouth communication of their trading interests to attract compatible trading partners.

Brokered.   When trading in an issue becomes sufficiently heavy, brokers begin to offer specialized search services to market participants. For a fee, called a *commission*, brokers undertake to find compatible trading partners and to negotiate acceptable transaction prices for their clients.

Because brokers are frequently in contact with many market participants on a continuing basis, they are likely to know what constitutes a fair price for a transaction. Brokers usually know whether the offering price of a seller can easily be bettered by looking elsewhere or whether it is close to the lowest offer price likely to be uncovered. Their extensive contacts provide them with a pool of price information that individual investors could not economically duplicate. By charging a commission less than the cost of direct search, they give investors an incentive to make use of that information.

Dealer.   Whatever its advantages over direct search, a **brokered market** has the disadvantage that it cannot guarantee that investor orders will be executed promptly. This uncertainty about the speed of execution creates price risk. During the time a broker is searching out a compatible trading partner for a client, securities prices may change and the client may suffer a loss. However, if trading in an issue is sufficiently active, some market participants may begin to buy and sell their own inventory at their quoted prices. **Dealer markets** eliminate the need for time-consuming searches for trading partners because investors know they can buy or sell immediately at the quotes given by a dealer.

Dealers earn their revenue in part by selling securities at an ask (also known as an offer) price greater than the bid price they pay for the securities. Their **bid–ask spread** compensates them for providing to occasional market participants the liquidity of an immediately available market, and also for the risk dealers incur by holding an issue in their inventory. Not surprisingly, the bid–ask spread tends to be smaller for stocks that trade a lot. That is, the dealer doesn't need to make as much on each individual trade if the dealer has a lot of volume.

In most cases dealers do not quote identical prices for an issue because they disagree about its value or because they have different inventory objectives. A dealer who has recently completed many purchases and therefore has a large inventory, for example, may lower her ask price to reduce inventory. Even in a dealer market, it is incumbent on investors to search for the best prices for their trades. The expense of contacting several dealers to obtain comparative quotations is borne by investors. However, because dealers have an incentive to advertise their willingness to buy and sell, their identity is well known and such contacts can usually be completed quite readily. The ease of searching among dealers guarantees that those dealers quoting the best price are most likely to do business with investors.

Auction.   **Auction markets** provide centralized procedures for the exposure of purchase and sale orders to all market participants simultaneously. By so doing, they nearly eliminate the expense of locating compatible partners and bargaining for a favorable price. The communication of price information in an auction market may be oral if all participants are physically located in the same place or the information can be transmitted electronically.

10.3 EQUITY TRADING

Secondary market transactions can occur in the **over-the-counter (OTC) market** or on a stock exchange such as **NASDAQ** or the **New York Stock Exchange (NYSE)**. Exhibit 10.3 shows the number of companies and their percentage of market value for the NASDAQ and the NYSE.

OVER-THE-COUNTER AND NASDAQ

Most stocks that you've heard of, such as Apple or IBM, trade on an organized exchange (Apple trades on NASDAQ and IBM trades on the New York Stock Exchange). These exchanges, however, list a company's stock only if the company is large enough, there is enough investor interest, and the company meets the minimum listing requirements. Small companies' stock can still be traded, however, in the over-the-counter (OTC) market.

The OTC stock market is primarily a dealer market. Because different OTC issues are not usually close substitutes for each other, a dealer with limited capital can make a successful market even in a relatively narrow range of stocks. As a result, there are a large number of relatively small OTC dealers. OTC dealers, however, often concentrate their trading in particular industry groups or geographic areas.

When a customer places an order to buy or sell a security in the OTC market, the broker or dealer contacts other dealers who have that particular security for sale. Public orders for purchase or sale are often executed by brokers acting as agents for their customers. When handling a public order, a broker contacts several dealers to search out the most favorable price. When a broker is satisfied with a dealer's quoted price, he or she completes the transaction with that dealer and charges his or her customer the same price plus a commission for brokerage services. Investors use brokers to locate the most favorable dealer because they are

EXHIBIT 10.3
U.S. Equity Markets: The NYSE Versus NASDAQ

Exchange	Number of Listed Companies			Percentage of Total Market Value
	Domestic	Foreign	Total	
NASDAQ	2,528	279	2,807	22.0%
NYSE	1,827	499	2,326	78.0%

Source: World Federation of Exchanges (www.world-exchanges.org), July 2010.

usually unfamiliar with the identities of the dealers making markets in specific issues and because brokers can contact dealers at lower cost. More generally, brokers capitalize on economies of scale in search.

Broker-dealers that operate in the OTC market are regulated by the Financial Industry Regulatory Authority (FINRA), a private (i.e., not governmental) self-regulatory organization. There are two major electronic quotation systems inside the OTC market—the OTC Bulletin Board and Pink OTC Markets, Inc. These systems allow members to see real-time quotes, last-sale prices, and volume for many OTC stocks.

The OTC Bulletin Board claims more than 3,500 securities quoted in 2009. OTC Bulletin Board rules require that companies must file current financial reports with the Securities and Exchange Commission (SEC) to be quoted on their system. Pink OTC Markets claims 9,379 securities quoted in July 2010. As the SEC notes on their Web site, many of the companies quoted through Pink OTC Markets do not file reports or audited financial statements with the SEC. Securities quoted through Pink OTC Markets are often referred to as pink-sheet stocks. The name refers to the pre-1971 practice of distributing daily sheets, printed on pink paper, to subscribing dealers listing bid and ask prices submitted by dealers.

Now, many microcap stocks (very small companies) or penny stocks (prices less than $5) trade through the OTC Bulletin Board or Pink OTC Market. As the SEC points out, the lack of public information, listing standards, and high risk imply that investors should be especially diligent when investigating these securities. The SEC notes, for example, that although many microcap stocks are legitimate businesses, fraud can be a problem. For example, a common pump-and-dump trick is for a scam artist to purchase a position in a small company, then leave messages on voicemail where it appears you have received a misdialed number and a message giving you "inside" information or a "hot tip" meant for a friend. As investors respond and drive the stock's price higher, the scam artist sells the stock.

THE NASDAQ STOCK MARKET

A major development in the OTC market occurred in 1971 when the National Association of Securities Dealers (NASD) introduced an automatic computer-based quotation system (NASDAQ). The system provided continuous bid–ask prices for the most actively traded OTC stocks. This system was basically an electronic version of the pink sheets that allowed dealers to see immediately what other dealers were willing to pay for a stock or at what price they were willing to sell a stock. Because the system allowed only price "quotes" and not actual trading, it was an automated (i.e., computerized) quotation system, not a trading system.

Over time, however, NASDAQ has evolved into a major stock exchange. Because the NASDAQ market is electronic—both orders and trades occur through a computer system instead of a physical trading floor—some still refer to NASDAQ as part of the OTC market. That view has changed over time because most now consider NASDAQ a stock exchange, and OTC generally means trading in OTC Bulletin Board or pink-sheet stocks. Even the name *NASDAQ* is changing. *NASDAQ* was originally an acronym for *National Association of Security Dealers Automated Quotation* (note, quotation only, not trading) system. Just like traditional stock exchanges, companies that want to have their stock traded on NASDAQ must meet listing requirements such as sufficient shares outstanding, enough trading volume, and sufficient profit or capitalization. Because

NASDAQ has moved far beyond its quotation system roots, NASDAQ's official stance is that *NASDAQ* is no longer an acronym. As a result, the market is referred to both by the original acronym *NASDAQ* and the proper noun, *Nasdaq*.

NASDAQ remains a dealer market, meaning there are often multiple dealers willing to buy and sell a stock. NASDAQ members can enter orders into the NASDAQ system that are executed against other orders in the system. For example, two dealers enter a bid to buy shares of company ABC. The first dealer is willing to buy up to 500 shares for $30.10 (a bid price of $30.10 for 500 shares). The second dealer is willing to buy up to 400 shares for $30.09. On the other side, a third dealer stands ready to sell 500 shares of ABC for $30.20 (ask price). Because the most anyone is willing to pay (i.e., the highest bid price) is $30.10 and the lowest anyone is willing to sell for (i.e., the lowest ask price) is $30.20, no trading occurs. A broker enters a new order to sell 600 shares at the best possible price. The first 500 shares are purchased by the first dealer for $30.10. The next 100 shares are purchased by the second dealer for $30.09, and the trade is completed. All of this occurs electronically without any direct communication between the broker entering the order or the dealers taking the other side of the trade.

THE NEW YORK STOCK EXCHANGE (NYSE)

The New York Stock Exchange, the preeminent securities exchange in the United States, is an example of an auction market. Unlike NASDAQ stocks, which can have multiple dealers (or market makers) in a given stock, the NYSE has a **specialist** who acts as both a broker and a dealer. Historically, every trade in a given stock was brought through the specialist who acted as both a broker (matching buyers and sellers) and a dealer (who stood ready to buy or sell for his or her own account). Specifically, each stock is traded at a post manned by a specialist. Orders from the public are sent from the brokerage house to brokers located on the floor of the NYSE, who bring the orders to the appropriate posts for execution. There are three major sources of active bids and offerings in an issue available at a post: (1) brokers executing market orders, (2) limit price orders left with the specialist for execution, and (3) the specialist in the issue buying and selling for his or her own account.

In recent years, however, the NYSE has transitioned into a hybrid market that allows traders to choose to execute an order through a specialist or electronically. Specifically, two changes have greatly reduced the loud, frenetic bustle of buying and selling on the floor of the exchange. First, traders no longer need to physically visit the post to submit an order to the specialist. Instead, traders can route orders to the specialist's post electronically for execution (via the NYSE's SuperDOT system). Second, traders can choose to skip the specialist altogether and simply execute the order electronically (similar to NASDAQ) at the best bid or ask price (via the NYSE's Direct+ system).

Hybrid market transactions lack the yelling and hand gestures seen on the floor of the exchange, but they happen much faster—less than a second, compared to nine seconds for a floor trade. In the short-term, floor trading continues because some market customers prefer to have their orders executed on the floor, and the market will probably turn to floor trading during periods of high volatility. In the long run, however, the future of floor trading seems dim. Over time, as market participants become more comfortable with electronic trading, there may be less of a role for floor brokers and specialists.

COMPETITION BETWEEN THE NYSE AND NASDAQ

Historically, smaller companies would begin trading in NASDAQ, move to the American Stock Exchange (which was purchased by, and integrated into, the NYSE in 2009) as they grew, and eventually move to the NYSE. Over time, however, NASDAQ has evolved into the primary NYSE competitor. Many companies that meet NYSE listing standards have remained on NASDAQ, including, for example, Microsoft, Google, Amazon, and Starbucks.

Much of the motivation for the change in the way the NYSE executes transactions can be attributed to increased competition from the NASDAQ. Just because a stock is listed on the NYSE doesn't mean it won't trade on the NASDAQ. In fact, in June 2009, NASDAQ held a 14 percent share of trading in NYSE-listed stocks. As if this didn't cause enough concern for the NYSE, a number of companies have changed their stock's listing from the NYSE to the NASDAQ, including, for example, Mattel and Vodaphone (who claimed they would save $400,000 in listing fees) in 2009. Yet a number of companies have also moved from NASDAQ to the NYSE. Stock brokerage firm Charles Schwab, for example, moved from the NYSE to NASDAQ in 2005 and then from NASDAQ back to the NYSE in 2010.

Regulatory changes are also increasing the competitive pressures on the NYSE. For example, until recently, listing on the NASDAQ meant having a four-letter exchange symbol, such as MSFT for Microsoft or GOOG for Google. For companies like GE, listing on the NASDAQ and being forced to have a four-letter exchange code could have harmed the company's brand identity. Recently, however, the NASDAQ began accepting companies with one-, two-, or three-letter exchange codes.

What does all this mean to investors? First, because increased competition usually leads to better service and more efficiencies, trading costs should go down. Second, reducing trading costs should lead to improved market efficiency as it becomes cheaper for market participants to capitalize on new information. Finally, the days of enjoying watching a frenzied trading floor are probably gone for good.

Exhibit 10.3 reports the number of domestic and foreign stocks listed on each exchange and the fraction of total market capitalization at the end of May 2010. As you can see, there are more companies listed on the NASDAQ exchange than on the NYSE. The NYSE, however, includes many more of the largest companies. As a result, the NYSE still captures more than three-quarters of the total U.S. equity capitalization.

10.4 GLOBAL STOCK MARKETS

The secondary markets for equity securities are becoming increasingly competitive. Improved communications and computer technology have reduced transaction costs, making it easier for other financial intermediaries to compete with securities firms and promoting competition among stock exchanges, including foreign exchanges. Several trends are related to the forces of technology and competition: the emergence of a so-called national market system, the move toward 24-hour trading of equity securities, and the globalization of equity markets.

There is competitive pressure to link international equity markets, too. Both the NYSE and NASDAQ have internationalized their operations. NASDAQ attempted to take over the London Stock Exchange (LSE) between 2006 and 2007, and eventually held a nearly 30 percent interest in the LSE. NASDAQ purchased OMX, a European company that owns eight stock exchanges in Baltic and Nordic countries in 2008. As a result, the parent company of NASDAQ is now called NASDAQ OMX Group (listed, of course, on NASDAQ). Similarly, the NYSE merged with Euronext in 2007. Euronext itself was the result of a merger of several major European exchanges including Paris, Amsterdam, and Brussels. NYSE Euronext is also a publicly traded company listed, of course, on the NYSE.

Many U.S. firms are issuing stocks overseas to take advantage of differences in tax laws and to increase their visibility, liquidity, and reputation. In 1986, the London Stock Exchange created a computer network similar to the U.S. NASDAQ system and permitted U.S. and Japanese investment firms to enter trades on the system. This development was important because it created virtual 24-hour global trading, given the time zone differences among New York, London, and Tokyo. Many U.S. companies are listed on exchanges in all three locations.

Nonetheless, there is some debate regarding whether such cross listings really create value. A recent report by McKinsey & Company ("Why cross-listing doesn't create value"), for example, notes that a number of major corporations have withdrawn their listings from one of the major exchanges. For example, British Airways left the NYSE in 2007 and Boeing left the Tokyo exchange in 2008 to save costs.

Another aspect of the globalization of stock markets is that many foreign companies, such as Sony and Nestlé, have discovered the benefits of trading their stock in the United States. Unfamiliar market practices, confusing tax legislation, incomplete shareholder communications, and the lack of effective avenues for legal recourse tend to discourage U.S. investors from buying equity securities in foreign markets. In addition, the disclosure and reporting requirements mandated by the U.S. SEC historically have discouraged all but the largest foreign firms from directly listing their shares on the NYSE or NASDAQ.

Many foreign companies overcome these obstacles and tap the U.S. equity market by means of **American Depository Receipts (ADRs)**. ADRs are dollar-denominated claims issued by U.S. banks representing ownership of shares of a foreign company's stock held on deposit by the U.S. bank in the issuing firm's home country. Because ADRs are issued in dollars by a U.S. bank to U.S. investors, they are subject to U.S. securities laws.

ADRs have proved to be very popular with U.S. investors, at least partly because they allow investors to diversify internationally. However, they are still holding a claim that is covered by American securities laws and that pays dividends in dollars (dividends on the underlying shares are converted from local currency into dollars and then paid to U.S. investors). Each ADR can represent a fraction or a multiple of a share of the foreign company, so that the price of the ADR is within the range of share prices for comparable companies traded in the United States. Because an ADR can be converted into ownership of the underlying shares, arbitrage ensures rational dollar valuation of this claim against foreign-currency-denominated stock.

SHORT SALES

An investor who believes a stock's price is going to increase can purchase the security today and, if its price rises in the future, sell it for a profit. But what about an investor who believes a stock's price is going to fall? That investor can also trade on her view by selling a stock short. Assume, for example, that an investor believes Valerie's Apparel Lines' (VAL) stock price, currently at $50, is going to fall. The investor can borrow shares from her broker and sell them today (**short sale**) for $50 and promise to buy them back sometime later. The investor must keep the sale proceeds, along with a security deposit (known as a **margin**) on deposit with the broker.

Assume that 1 week later VAL is trading for $55. As a result, the short seller is facing a $5 loss; that is, the investor sold the borrowed stock last week for $50 but will have to pay $55 today to buy the shares back to return them to the broker (cover the short). If, on the other hand, the investor is correct and 1 week later the price has fallen $45, the investor makes a $5 (per share) profit because she can cover the short (i.e., buy back shares to return to the broker) today for $45 after selling the stock last week for $50.

Thus, an investor who holds a company's stock, betting its price will rise, is said to have a long position. Alternatively, an investor who borrows shares she does not own and sells them, hoping to buy them back later at a lower price, has a short position.

MARKET, LIMIT, AND STOP ORDERS

There are three basic kinds of orders an investor can submit to an exchange: a market order, a limit order, or a stop order. A **market order** is an order to buy or sell at the best price available at the time the order reaches the exchange. On an electronic market (such as NASDAQ or NYSE's Direct+), the buy order will be executed against the lowest ask price, and a sell order will be executed against the highest bid price. If a larger order is physically taken to the floor of the NYSE, a broker might execute the order immediately on his arrival, or he might hold back all or part of the order for a short time to see if he can attract a better price than is currently available. He may also choose to quote a price on his transaction that is inside the current bid–ask price, thereby getting in front of other orders at the post and reducing the amount of time he anticipates that he must wait until completing the trade.

A **limit order** is an order to buy or sell at a designated price or at any better price. Thus, a limit order is actually a bid for, or offering of, securities. Assume, for example, that the current highest bid price for company ABC is $30.50 and the current lowest ask price is $30.55. If a broker submits an investor's limit buy order of $30.52, that means the investor is willing to pay up to $30.52 for the stock. In this particular example, no transaction will immediately take place because the lowest anyone is willing to sell for is $30.55. The bid price will increase to $30.52, however, as the new order now represents the most anyone is willing to pay for the stock. If another investor submits a buy order for $30.20, then all limit buy orders for a higher price will have to be executed first, and prices will have to fall, before that investor's order is executed. An investor may use a limit buy order in an attempt to buy on a price dip or a limit sell order in an attempt to maximize profits by selling on a price increase.

A stop order is similar to a limit order except that a sell stop order means an investor wants to sell only if the price drops to the stop price and buy if the price increases to the stop price. An investor may use a stop order to "lock" in profits. Consider, for example, an investor who purchased a stock for $10.00 and the price is currently $20. If the investor puts in a stop order (in this case, also known as a **stop loss order**) for $19.50, then the investor is guaranteed a profit of $9.50 as the stock will sell if the price drops to $19.50.

A **stop buy order** is analogous to a stop loss order except for a short sale. As noted above, an investor who sells a stock short loses money as the price increases. Thus, an investor who is short a stock can submit a stop buy order to purchase the stock if its price rises to a certain level. Consider, for example, an investor who short sells a stock for $30.00. If the price rises to $35, the investor is currently losing $5 a share since it would cost the investor $5 more to purchase the stock to cover her short position. This investor may submit a stop buy order at $36.00 to ensure her maximum loss is $6.00 per share.

10.5 REGULATION OF EQUITY MARKETS

Trading in securities markets in the United States is regulated by several laws. The two major laws are the Securities Act of 1933 and the Securities Exchange Act of 1934. The 1933 act requires full disclosure of relevant information relating to the issue of new securities in the primary market. This is the act that requires registration of new securities and the issuance of a prospectus that details the recent financial history of the company. SEC acceptance of a prospectus or financial report does not mean that it views the security as a good investment. The SEC is concerned only that the relevant facts are disclosed to investors. Investors must make their own evaluations of the security's value. The 1934 act established the SEC to administer the provisions of the 1933 act. It also extended the disclosure of the 1933 act by requiring firms with outstanding securities on secondary exchanges to periodically disclose relevant financial information.

The 1934 act also allowed the SEC to register and regulate securities exchanges, OTC trading, brokers, and dealers. The 1934 act thus established the SEC as the administrative agency responsible for broad oversight of secondary securities markets.

In addition to federal regulations, security trading is subject to state laws. The laws providing for state regulation of securities activities are generally known as *blue-sky laws* because they attempt to prevent the false promotion and sale of securities representing nothing more than blue sky.

DO YOU UNDERSTAND?

1. What characteristics of an asset determine the type of secondary market in which it is most likely to trade?
2. What are the four types of secondary markets?
3. Explain how short selling works.
4. How are the NYSE and NASDAQ different? How are they similar?

10.6 EQUITY VALUATION BASICS

Similar to bond valuation, which we discuss in Chapter 5, *equity valuation* requires us to apply the mathematics of present value. For any security, including common stock or preferred stock, the valuation process involves three steps. First, identify the timing and the size of the cash flows. Second, decide on the appropriate discount rate. The discount rate, which is the interest rate used in the present value calculation, should reflect the opportunity cost of investing in the security. The opportunity cost is the rate of return offered by a security with similar characteristics, including risk, that is trading in the market. Third, apply the discount rate to the cash flows in each period to obtain present values and sum the present values to obtain the price of the security.

COMMON STOCK VALUATION

For a common stock, the expected cash flows are the dividends you expect to receive plus what you expect to be able to sell the stock for in the future. Let P_0 be the current stock price and P_1 be the expected stock price 1 year from now. Assume the firm pays a dividend of D_1 at the end of the first year. Using the present value formula, we write:

$$P_0 = \frac{D_1}{(1 + r)} + \frac{P_1}{(1 + r)} \qquad (10.1)$$

Equation 10.1 assumes that we purchase the stock today, hold it for 1 year, and then sell it after collecting the dividend. One problem with implementing Equation 10.1 is that it requires an estimate of P_1. We can estimate the price 1 year from now in the same way we calculated P_0:

$$P_1 = \frac{D_2}{(1 + r)} + \frac{P_2}{(1 + r)} \qquad (10.2)$$

Substituting Equation 10.2 for P_1 in Equation 10.1 and simplifying, we obtain Equation 10.3:

$$P_0 = \frac{D_1}{(1 + r)} + \frac{D_2}{(1 + r)^2} + \frac{P_2}{(1 + r)^2} \qquad (10.3)$$

Continuing this process, we obtain Equation 10.4, which says that the price of a stock is equal to the present value of all future dividends:

$$P_0 = \frac{D_1}{(1 + r)} + \frac{D_2}{(1 + r)^2} + \cdots = \sum_{t=1}^{\infty} \frac{D_t}{(1 + r)^t} \cdot \qquad (10.4)$$

Of course, Equation 10.4 is difficult to implement in practice because it requires estimates of dividend payments that begin 1 year from now and continue forever. Fortunately, we can make some assumptions about the nature of future dividends that simplify our calculations.

Constant Dividend Growth Rate. Many firms increase their dividends over time. Say we know that a firm just paid a dividend of $2 per share and that this firm's dividends grow at 5 percent per year. The dividend 1 year from today is $D_1 = \$2 \times (1.05) = \$2.10$. Two years from today the dividend will be $D_2 = \$2 \times (1.05)^2 = \$2.21$. In general, if we know that the dividends of a company grow at some rate, g, we can calculate any future dividend as follows:

$$D_t = D_0 \times (1 + g)^t, \qquad (10.5)$$

where D_0 is the dividend just paid.

   If the dividend grows at the same rate forever, the stream of dividends meets the definition of a **growing perpetuity**. As long as the growth rate, g, is less than the discount rate, r, it is easy to determine the present value of all future dividends. Assuming a constant growth rate, we can use Equation 10.5 to rewrite Equation 10.4:

$$P_0 = \frac{D_1}{(1+r)^1} + \frac{D_1(1+g)}{(1+r)^2} + \frac{D_1(1+g)^2}{(1+r)^3} \cdots \qquad (10.6)$$

Now multiplying both sides of Equation 10.6 by $(1+g)/(1+r)$ gives us:

$$P_0\left(\frac{1+g}{1+r}\right) = \frac{D_1(1+g)}{(1+r)^2} + \frac{D_1(1+g)^2}{(1+r)^3} + \frac{D_1(1+g)^3}{(1+r)^4} \cdots \qquad (10.7)$$

Subtracting Equation 10.7 from Equation 10.6 yields:

$$P_0 - P_0\left(\frac{1+g}{1+r}\right) = \left(\frac{D_1}{(1+r)^1} + \frac{D_1(1+g)}{(1+r)^2} + \frac{D_1(1+g)^2}{(1+r)^3} \cdots\right)$$

$$- \left(\frac{D_1(1+g)}{(1+r)^2} + \frac{D_1(1+g)^2}{(1+r)^3} + \frac{D_1(1+g)^3}{(1+r)^4} \cdots\right) \quad (10.8)$$

Note that the second term in the first set of brackets on the right hand side of Equation 10.8 is the same as the first term in the second set of brackets. Thus, those terms cancel. Similarly, the third term in the first set of brackets cancels the second term in the second set of brackets. In fact, except for the very first term in the first set of brackets, every other term in the first set of brackets is canceled by a term in the second set of brackets. Thus, Equation 10.8 can be written as:

$$P_0 - P_0\left(\frac{1+g}{1+r}\right) = \frac{D_1}{(1+r)} \qquad (10.9)$$

Multiplying both sides by $(1+r)$ yields:

$$P_0(1+r) - P_0(1+g) = D_1 \qquad (10.10)$$

Solving for today's price gives us the constant growth model of stock valuation:

$$P_0 = \frac{D_1}{(r-g)} \qquad (10.11)$$

You shouldn't think of Equation 10.11 as the "formula" for determining the value of a stock. The value of a common stock should be the present value of all future dividends (i.e., the present value of the cash flows to an investor). That is, Equation 10.4 is the "formula." However, when a stock's dividend is expected to grow at a constant rate (g) forever, Equation 10.4 simplifies into Equation 10.11. More generally, if a company's dividend is growing at a constant rate g, then the price at time t is given by:

$$P_t = \frac{D_{t+1}}{(r-g)} \qquad (10.12)$$

Continuing with the above example (i.e., the dividend next year is $2.10, and the constant growth rate of 5 percent) and assuming a discount rate of 12 percent, we obtain:

$$P_0 = \frac{\$2 \times (1.05)}{(0.12 - 0.05)} = \frac{\$2.10}{0.07} = \$30$$

The constant dividend growth model gives us a convenient way to summarize the total return on common stock. If we solve Equation 10.12 for r, we obtain

$$r = D_1/P_0 + g \qquad (10.13)$$

The first term of the expression is called the dividend yield, which is the expected dividend expressed as a proportion of the price of the stock. The second term, g, can be interpreted as the **capital-gains yield**, which is the rate at which the value of the firm is expected to grow.

To illustrate, suppose that we have a stock selling for $78 per share that just paid a dividend of $3 per share. The dividend is expected to grow at 6 percent per year forever. What is the required return on this stock? By substituting the information into Equation 10.13, we obtain

$$r = (\$3.18/\$78) + 0.06 \cong 0.04 + 0.06 \cong 0.10$$

or approximately 10 percent.

Variable Dividend Growth Rate.   It may be unreasonable to assume that a firm will grow at the same rate forever. A typical course of events is for growth to proceed rapidly for a period of time, after which the growth rate settles to a more normal level. The present value formulas we have used so far can be easily adapted to deal with situations in which firms grow at different rates over different time periods. If the dividend grows at a constant rate *after t* periods, the price of the stock is

$$P_0 = \frac{D_1}{(1+r)^1} + \frac{D_2}{(1+r)^2} + \cdots + \frac{D_t}{(1+r)^t} + \frac{P_t}{(1+r)^t} \qquad (10.14)$$

where $P_t = [D_t \times (1+g)]/(r-g)$.

LEARNING BY DOING 10.1
Valuing a Stock

PROBLEM: Assume a stock's current dividend (just paid) was $1.50 per share and the dividend is expected to grow at a 15 percent rate for the next 3 years. After the 3-year period, however, dividends are expected to grow at the more normal rate of 8 percent per year indefinitely. If the required return on the stock is 12 percent, what price would you be willing to pay for a share of the stock?

APPROACH: After 3 years, the stock's dividends are expected to grow at a constant rate. Therefore, you can use the constant growth model to estimate the stock's price 3 years from now. The price of the stock today is just the sum of the present value of the dividends in the first 3 years (the abnormal growth period) plus the present value of the stock's estimated price in 3 years.

SOLUTION: First, calculate the dividends in the above-normal period of growth and in the first period of normal growth. In this example, we must calculate the dividends for the first 4 years:

$D_1 = D_0 \times (1 + g) = \$1.50 \times (1.15) = \$1.72$

$D_2 = D_0 \times (1 + g)^2 = \$1.50 \times (1.15)^2 = D_1 \times (1 + g) = \$1.72 \times (1.15) = \$1.98$

$D_3 = D_0 \times (1 + g)^3 = \$1.50 \times (1.15)^3 = D_2 \times (1 + g) = \$1.98 \times (1.15) = \$2.28$

$D_4 = D_0 \times (1 + g)^3(1 + g_{normal}) = \$1.50 \times (1.15)^3(1.08)$

$\qquad = D_3 \times (1 + g_{normal}) = \$2.28 \times (1.08) = \$2.46$

Second, calculate the price at the end of the above-normal growth period. In our example, we must calculate the price of the stock at the end of year 3. After year 3, the dividends grow at a rate of 8 percent forever, so we can use Equation 10.12 to calculate the price at the end of the third year:

$$P_3 = \frac{D_4}{r - g} = \frac{\$2.46}{0.12 - 0.08} = \$61.60$$

Finally, substitute the values for D_1, D_2, D_3, and P_3 into Equation 10.14:

$$P_0 = \frac{1.72}{(1 + 0.12)} + \frac{1.98}{(1 + 0.12)^2} + \frac{2.28}{(1 + 0.12)^3} + \frac{61.60}{(1 + 0.12)^3} = \$48.58$$

Thus, the current stock price is $48.58.

PREFERRED STOCK VALUATION

Preferred stock is relatively simple to value because most preferred shares entitle the holders to regular, fixed dividend payments. Because preferred stock usually has no maturity, the payments are assumed to continue forever. Suppose that a preferred stock promises to pay dividends of D per share forever. Because the dividend never grows, the growth rate is zero. Thus, for a preferred stock, Equation 10.11 simplifies to

$$P_0 = \frac{D}{r} \qquad (10.15)$$

Suppose a firm pays dividends on its preferred stock of $10 at the end of each year and that the required return for the stock is 7.5 percent. The value of the preferred stock from Equation 10.15 is

$$P_0 = \frac{\$10}{0.075} = \$133.33$$

If you know the current market price of the preferred stock and the annual amount of its dividend, you can calculate the required rate of return by solving Equation 10.15 for r:

$$r = \frac{D}{P_0} \qquad (10.16)$$

Suppose the current price per share of preferred stock is $75 and that the firm pays an annual dividend of $6 per share. Applying Equation 10.16, the market's required return on this preferred stock is

$$r = \frac{D}{P_0} = \frac{\$6}{\$75} = 0.08$$

or 8 percent.

10.7 EQUITY RISK

If you put all your money in a savings account at the bank, you will earn a low return, but you will be certain not to lose money. Alternatively, if you invest in stocks, you may lose money or make money. That is, the return is uncertain. Any rational investor will require a higher expected return given greater uncertainty (risk). It is important to recognize that, although investing in stocks should yield a higher expected return, it does not mean the return you actually make—the realized return—will be higher (or even positive) than if you put your money in the bank. In this section, we discuss the types of risk faced in equity markets and how risk is reflected in the required returns of stocks.

SYSTEMATIC AND UNSYSTEMATIC RISK

The total risk of a security can be thought of as the sum of two types of risk: systematic risk and unsystematic risk. To understand the distinction between these two types of risk, we must briefly discuss the benefits of **diversification**, which simply means not putting all of your eggs in one basket.

Investors measure the total risk (or total uncertainty) of a security or a portfolio with the variance or standard deviation of returns. Standard deviation measures the width of a probability distribution of returns. Variance is simply the standard deviation squared. The larger the standard deviation (and therefore the variance), the greater the total risk and the more likely it is that you will have a large price move—either up or down. Roughly speaking, for example, a stock with an expected return of 10 percent and a standard deviation of 20 percent will have a return somewhere between −10 percent and +30 percent (i.e., the expected value plus and minus two standard deviations) two-thirds of the time. One-third of the time, however, the stock will either lose more than 10 percent or gain more than 30 percent. Thus, the higher the standard deviation, the higher the risk.

The good news is that we can reduce the total risk of our investment in equities by diversifying across many securities. Exhibit 10.4 illustrates the effects on a portfolio's total risk of increasing the number of securities in the portfolio. As you can see from the exhibit, the total risk of a portfolio decreases with the number of securities. Also note that Exhibit 10.4 holds only for variance—not for standard deviation—despite what your other finance textbooks may show. Feel free to impress your other finance professors by letting them know the textbook they are using is wrong—the sum of systematic and unsystematic variances equals total variance, but the sum of systematic and unsystematic standard deviations does not equal total standard deviation (e.g., $3^2 + 4^2 = 5^2$, but $3 + 4 \neq 5$). Now aren't you glad you read this far?

Diversification works because **unsystematic risks** (unique or security-specific risks) of different securities tend to partially offset one another in a portfolio. This could occur, for example, because when the price of one stock in the portfolio goes down, the price of another tends to go up, at least partially offsetting the loss. The diversification effect can help even if, when one stock tends to go down, the other stock does not tend to go down by as much, on average. As long as the returns of two securities are *not* perfectly, positively correlated (*perfect positive correlation* means that changes in one stock are matched exactly by changes in the other), one can reduce total risk by combining the securities in a portfolio. By adding enough securities to a portfolio, it is possible to eliminate unsystematic risk. For that reason, unsystematic risk is also called

EXHIBIT 10.4
The Effect of Diversification on Portfolio Risk

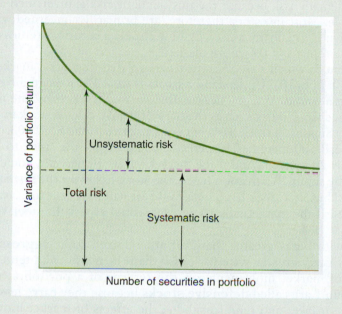

As the number of securities increases, the diversification effect reduces the portfolio's total risk. Total portfolio risk can be reduced, however, only to the level of systematic risk, which cannot be diversified away because it is caused by general market movements that tend to affect all stocks similarly.

diversifiable risk. Examples of unsystematic risks that could reduce a stock's price include unanticipated strikes, lawsuits, changes in government regulation affecting a particular industry, environmental disasters, or changes in production technology.

Note, however, that no matter how many securities we add, the total risk of the portfolio can only be reduced to the level of **systematic risk**. Systematic risk is also called *market risk* or *nondiversifiable risk*. No matter how many securities we add to a portfolio, we cannot reduce systematic risk because it is the risk that tends to affect the entire market in a similar fashion.

Most textbooks will tell you it's easy to eliminate firm-specific risk. They usually claim that holding anywhere from 10 to 30 stocks will result in a well-diversified portfolio that has negligible unsystematic risk. In a paper titled "Portfolio Diversification," published in the *Journal of Investment Management*, however, Bennett and Sias demonstrate that even relatively large portfolios can have substantial unsystematic risk. The authors estimated, for example, that an equal-weighted portfolio of 100 randomly selected stocks would, on average, have an annual standard deviation of unsystematic returns of nearly 6 percent. In other words, an investor holding the average 100 stock portfolio should expect an unsystematic return greater than ± 6 percent at least once every 3 years! Clearly, such portfolios have non-negligible uncertainty regarding unsystematic returns; that is, they are not well diversified.

MEASURING SYSTEMATIC RISK: BETA

If most investors hold reasonably well-diversified portfolios, the relevant measure of risk is systematic risk because the unsystematic risk is diversified away to the extent possible. Most investors, therefore, are primarily concerned with systematic risk, which is usually measured by how closely a security's returns are correlated with the returns of the entire market.

The extent to which a stock's returns are related to general market swings is measured with **beta (β)**. Understanding beta is easy. Let's assign a beta of 1.0 to the market as a whole. As a practical matter, we might represent the market with a broadly based stock index such as the S&P 500. (We discuss stock indexes in the next section.) Suppose a stock has a beta of 2 relative to the S&P 500. This means that if the S&P 500 increases 10 percent, you'd expect the stock to increase by approximately 20 percent. And if the market fell by 10 percent, you'd expect the stock to fall by about 20 percent. Hence, the stock has twice the systematic risk as the market. Thus, if a stock has a beta of 0.5, it will have half the systematic risk of the market. If the market falls 10 percent, you'd expect the stock to fall about 5 percent.

Stocks with betas greater than 1.0 are referred to as **aggressive stocks** because they carry greater systematic risk than the market and tend to magnify the effects of market movements on the returns of a portfolio. Stocks with betas less than 1 are called **defensive stocks** because they carry less systematic risk than the market and tend to subdue the effects of market movements on the returns of a portfolio. The stocks of most U.S. corporations have betas between 0.5 and 1.5. Exhibit 10.5 gives the betas of some well-known U.S. firms. Note that the stock with the lowest beta is Altria—a tobacco company. This makes intuitive sense because demand from smokers is not very sensitive to changes in economic conditions that affect all companies. Although consumers may put off buying a new car (hurting auto stocks) during a recession, smokers keep smoking.

EXHIBIT 10.5
Betas of Selected Firms (July 12, 2010)

Firm	Beta
Amazon.com	1.31
Molson-Coors	0.78
Citigroup	2.65
Dell	1.35
Gap	1.26
Apple	1.49
Altria	0.34
Exxon Mobil	0.48
Starbucks	1.28

Source: Google Finance (www.google.com/finance), July 12, 2010.

THE SECURITY MARKET LINE

Theoretically, the required (or expected) return on a stock depends on the amount of its systematic risk. The **capital asset pricing model (CAPM)** is the most popular model of the relation between systematic risk and expected return. To understand the model, consider the following definition of a **risk premium** (remember that, in Chapter 6, we define the *default risk premium on a bond* as the bond's return, or *yield*, minus the return on a risk-free security):

Risk premium = required (or expected) return on a risky security minus the return on a risk-free security

= total reward for bearing systematic risk

= amount of systematic risk × average reward in the market per unit of systematic risk

Given the definition, we can write an expression for the risk premium on any stock, j.

First let's define some terms:

$E(R_j)$ = expected return on stock j

$E(R_M)$ = expected return on the market portfolio, which consists of all assets in the market (Consider the market portfolio as the ultimate in diversified portfolios.)

R_F = rate of return on a risk-free asset, such as a T-bill

β_j = the beta of stock j

β_M = the beta of the market portfolio

In this case the risk premium is $E(R_j) - R_F = \beta_j \times ([E(R_M) - R_F]/\beta_M)$. The left side of the expression is the total reward for bearing the systematic risk in security j. On the right side, the term β_j is the amount of risk. $[E(R_M) - R_F]/\beta_M$ represents the average reward per unit of risk in the market. The numerator is the risk premium of the market portfolio, also called the **market risk premium**. The denominator is the amount of risk in the market. The expression for the risk premium of stock j simplifies because we know that the beta for the market portfolio is 1. Therefore, the risk premium of security j is

$$E(R_j) - R_F = \beta_j \times [E(R_M) - R_F] \qquad (10.17)$$

which is the equation for the CAPM. The **security market line (SML)** is simply the graph of the CAPM (Exhibit 10.6) showing how expected returns vary with systematic risk:

$$E(R_j) = R_F + \beta_j[E(R_M) - R_F]. \qquad (10.17a)$$

Equation 10.17a shows that the required return on a security equals the return on a risk-free asset plus a premium for bearing systematic risk in the amount β_j. The graph of the SML in Exhibit 10.6 shows that the relationship between risk and return is linear. The slope of the SML is the average reward per unit of risk in the market, $[E(R_M) - R_F]$. This means that an increase in beta increases the required

EXHIBIT 10.6
The Security Market Line

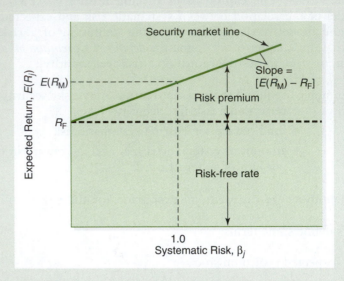

The security market line is the relationship between systematic risk and return. Investors are concerned only with systematic risk, measured by beta, because in a well-diversified portfolio, unsystematic risk is eliminated. As a beta increases, the security's risk premium increases, thereby increasing the security's expected rate or required return.

return on a stock. If, for example, stock A has a beta of 1.0 and stock B has a beta of 1.2, the expected return of stock B will exceed that of stock A by an amount $(0.2) [E(R_M) - R_F]$.

Let's illustrate the use of the SML with an example. Suppose the risk-free rate is 1 percent and the market risk premium, $[E(R_M) - R_F]$, is 8 percent. A stock with a beta of 1.25 would have a required return of $E(Rj) = R_F + \beta_j [E(R_M) - R_F] = 1$ percent $+1.25(8.0 \text{ percent}) = 11$ percent. Using a similar calculation, the required return on a stock with a beta of 1.5 would be 13 percent. More systematic risk implies a higher required return.

DO YOU UNDERSTAND?

1. Describe the general approach to valuing a share of stock.
2. What cash flows are relevant to the value of stock?
3. Describe what happens to the total risk of a portfolio as the number of securities is increased.
4. Suppose a firm's stock has a beta of 1.2. What will probably happen to the value of the stock if the market decreases by 20 percent?

Stock market indexes provide a useful tool to summarize the vast array of information generated by the continuous buying and selling of stocks. At the same time, the use of market indexes presents two problems. First, many different indexes compete for our attention. Second, indexes differ in their composition and construction, and they can often give contradictory information regarding stock market movements.

When constructing a market index, the first decision is what the base index value is and what the starting date is. That is, at what value and on what date does the index begin? The choice is completely arbitrary because absolute index values are meaningless. Only the *relative* changes in index values convey useful information. For example, knowing only that a particular stock market index finished the year at a level of 354.7 is of no value. However, if we also know that the same index finished the previous year at a level of 331.5, then we can calculate that the stock market, as measured by this particular index, rose by approximately 7 percent over the previous year.

The next decision is, which stocks should be included in the index? There are three methods for deciding stock market index composition: (1) the index can represent a stock exchange and include all the stocks traded on the exchange; (2) the organization producing the index can subjectively select the stocks to be included; or (3) the stocks to be included can be selected based on some objective measure such as market capitalization, which, as noted above, is simply the number of shares outstanding times the price per share. The stocks in an index are often divided into groups so that indexes represent the performance of various industry segments such as industrial, transportation, or utility companies. Regardless of the method chosen for selecting the stocks, the composition of an index can change whenever the entity managing the index decides to change it (sometimes as a result of mergers or delistings). In 2009, for example, General Motors and Citigroup were removed from the Dow Jones Industrial Average and replaced by Cisco Systems and Travelers.

Once the stocks to be included in an index are selected, the stocks must be combined in certain proportions to construct the index. Each stock, therefore, must be assigned some relative weight. One of two approaches typically is used to assign relative weights when calculating stock market indexes: (1) weighting by the price of the company's stock or (2) weighting by the market value of the company. After next explaining the calculation of stock indexes, we describe the major stock indexes in the United States. Exhibit 10.7 provides recent statistics on the major stock indexes.

10.8 STOCK MARKET INDEXES

EXHIBIT 10.7
Major Stock Indexes Statistics (July 12, 2010)

Index	High	Low	Daily Close	Today's Change	Percentage Change	52-Week	
						High	Low
Dow Jones Industrial Average	10,220.30	10,146.50	10,216.27	+18.24	0.18%	11,258.00	8,093.31
NASDAQ Composite	2,213.39	2,183.52	2,198.36	+1.91	0.09%	2,535.28	1,736.95
Standard & Poor's 500	1,080.78	1,070.45	1,078.75	+0.79	+0.07%	1,219.80	875.32

Source: Reuters (www.reuters.com), July 12, 2010.

Circuit Breakers, Black Monday, and the Flash Crash

On October 19, 1987 ("Black Monday"), the Dow Jones Industrial Average (DJIA) fell more than 22 percent in a single day. Although the exact causes of the crash are still debated, the SEC responded to the crash with a number of innovations, including **circuit breakers**. Circuit breaker rules require halts to all trading if the DJIA falls by a certain percentage within certain times. If, for example, the DJIA falls more than 10 percent within a trading day, then trading is halted for 1 hour if it's before 2:00 in the afternoon (the NYSE stops trading at 4:00). If it's between 2:00 and 2:30, then trading stops for 30 minutes (thus, ensuring at least 1 more hour of trading). If it is after 2:30, there is no halt. Longer halts (with different time limits) occur with a 20 percent drop. If the DJIA falls 30 percent, trading stops for the day. The idea is that such trading halts may reduce volatility by giving traders time to assimilate and process incoming information.

Although the 1987 crash occurred throughout the entire trading day, May 6, 2010, brought an entirely different type of crash—the flash crash. After falling about 300 points earlier in the day, at about 2:30, the DJIA suffered its largest intraday loss ever—falling a total 999 points for a total intraday decline of about 9.2 percent, most of which occurred in a 15-minute period and erased $800 billion of wealth. Even more amazing, the market came roaring back. According to the SEC testimony, the DJIA recovered 543 points in

approximately 90 seconds! For the day, the DJIA closed down 3.20 percent.

Although the speed with which the flash crash (and recovery) occurred was astonishing, trades in individual stocks were even more puzzling. Procter & Gamble, one of the 30 stocks that make up the DJIA (see below), for example, fell from $60 to less than $40 in under 4 minutes, then recovered to back over $60 in the next minute. Accenture, which opened the day at $41.04, traded for a single penny at one point during the flash crash before recovering to $41.09 by the end of the day!

Even though both Procter & Gamble and Accenture are listed on the NYSE, many of these peculiar trades occurred on other (electronic) exchanges. The Accenture penny trade actually occurred on the CBOE Stock Exchange. In fact, in the end, the most extraordinary trades were canceled. Specifically, the exchanges canceled trades that occurred between 2:40 and 3:00 (EST) that were executed at prices more than 60 percent above or below the 2:40 price. In total, more than 20,000 trades were canceled because they were deemed erroneous.

Just as Black Monday brought circuit breakers to the entire market, the flash crash resulted in circuit breakers to individual stocks. Beginning in June 2010, stocks in the S&P 500 that are traded on the NYSE (a total of 404 stocks) will stop trading for 5 minutes if stock increases or falls by 10 percent within a 5-minute period.

PRICE-WEIGHTED INDEXES

A **price-weighted index** is first computed by summing the prices of the individual stocks composing the index. Then the sum of the prices is divided by a divisor to yield the chosen base index value. Thereafter, as the stock prices change, the divisor remains constant unless there is a stock split, there is a stock dividend, or the composition of the index changes. If such a situation arises, then the divisor is adjusted so that the index value is not affected by the event in question.

For example, if the prices per share of the three stocks A, B, and C in a price-weighted index were $20, $10, and $50, respectively, then the prices would sum to $80. If the base index value is to be 100, then the initial divisor would be 0.8 (100 = 80/0.8). Then on the next trading day, if the prices per share were, respectively, $25, $10, and $40, the sum would now be $75 and the price-weighted index value would be 93.75 ($75/0.8), or 6.25 percent lower.

Now, assume that stock C undergoes a two-for-one stock split after the market closes on the second day such that its price per share declines to $20 ($40/2). The sum of the three prices is now only $55, but the index should remain the same. Thus, the divisor must be adjusted so that the index value continues to be 93.75. The new divisor would be approximately 0.5867 ($55/0.5867 = 93.75), and it would remain constant until it again had to be adjusted.

MARKET VALUE–WEIGHTED INDEXES

A **market value–weighted index** is computed by calculating the total market value of the firms in the index and the total market value of those firms on the previous trading day. The percentage change in the total market value from one day to the next represents the change in the index. Market value–weighted indexes do not require adjustments for stock splits and stock dividends because they do not affect the market capitalization. However, market value–weighted indexes do require adjustment when the composition of the index changes.

For example, if stocks A, B, and C described previously had outstanding shares of 100 million, 200 million, and 10 million, then the total market value for the three stocks on the first day would be $4.5 billion. The total market value on the second day would be $4.9 billion, for an increase of 8.8 percent. If the market value–weighted index began with a base index value of 10 on the first day, then its value on the second day would be 10.88, or 8.8 percent higher.

If we again assume that stock C undergoes a two-for-one stock split after the market closes on the second day such that its price per share declines to $20, we can see that there is no impact on the market value–weighted index. This is because the number of shares outstanding double to 20 million and company C's market value remains at $400 million. Thus, the total market value of the three stocks in the market value–weighted index continues to be $4.9 billion on the second day, and the index remains at 10.88.

Notice the different conclusions concerning the stock market performance given by the price-weighted and market value–weighted indexes in these examples. Both indexes used the same stocks and the same price changes. However, the price-weighted index decreased by 6.25 percent, whereas the market value–weighted index increased by 8.8 percent. This example clearly shows that both the composition of an index and its weighting scheme can have a significant impact on its results.

Both market value–weighted and price-weighted indexes reflect the returns to buy-and-hold investment strategies. If one were to buy each share in an index in proportion to its outstanding market value, the market value–weighted index would perfectly track capital gains on the underlying index, although the return from dividends would not be included. Similarly, a price-weighted index tracks the returns on a portfolio composed of equal shares of each company.

DOW JONES AVERAGES

The most widely cited stock market index is the Dow Jones Industrial Average (DJIA), which was first published in 1896. The DJIA is a price-weighted index that originally consisted of 20 stocks with a divisor of 20; thus, the value of the index was simply the average of the price of the 20 stocks. If a stock split, however, the stock's price, and therefore the DJIA, would fall. To alleviate this problem, the denominator (the Dow divisor) is adjusted downward such that stock splits and dividends don't affect the DJIA.

In 1928, the DJIA was enlarged to encompass 30 of the largest U.S. industrial stocks—so-called blue-chip stocks. The Dow divisor in July 2010 was 0.132319125. Thus, adding up the prices of the 30 DJIA stocks on July 12, 2010, and dividing by 0.13231912 yields the 10,216.27 figure in Exhibit 10.7. Dow Jones also publishes a price-weighted index of 20 transportation companies, a price-weighted index of 15 utility companies, and a composite index that includes the 65 companies making up the industrial, transportation, and utility indexes. None of the Dow Jones indexes are adjusted for stock dividends of less than 10 percent.

STANDARD & POOR'S INDEXES

The Standard & Poor's (S&P) 500 Index is a market value–weighted index that consists of 500 of the largest U.S. stocks drawn from various industries. Because the index is value-weighted, it primarily reflects the performance of the largest stocks. For example, the top 10 stocks (out of the 500 total stocks) accounted for more than 19 percent of the total index at the end of June 2010. The stocks included in the S&P 500 account for more than 75 percent of the total U.S. market capitalization. The base index value for the S&P 500 Index was 10 in 1943. The index is computed on a continuous basis during the trading day and reported to the public. The S&P 500 is divided into two subindexes that follow the performance of industrial and utilities companies.

The S&P 400 MidCap Index is also published by Standard & Poor's. It is market value–weighted and consists of 400 stocks with market values less than those of the stocks in the S&P 500. The S&P 400 MidCap Index is useful for following the performance of medium-size companies.

In addition, Standard & Poor's publishes a market value–weighted SmallCap Index that tracks 600 companies with market values less than those of the companies in its MidCap Index. The S&P 1500 Index includes the companies in the S&P 500, the MidCap 400, and the SmallCap 600.

NASDAQ

The NASDAQ Composite, with a base year of 1970, has been compiled since 1971. Similar to the S&P 500, the index is market-capitalization weighted. It includes all the domestic and international common stocks listed on the NASDAQ stock market (more than 2,800 stocks). Because many large technology stocks and growth companies are listed on NASDAQ, it's widely viewed as a technology and/or growth company index.

OTHER STOCK INDEXES

The Russell 3000 encompasses the largest companies ranked by market capitalization, whereas the Russell 1000 includes the largest 1,000 market capitalization companies. The Russell 2000 includes the bottom 2,000 companies in the Russell 3000, so it represents a small-capitalization market index.

The Wilshire 5000, published since 1971, includes more than 5,000 companies, more common stocks than any other index. It consists of all the U.S. stocks with readily available price data. It is a market value–weighted index.

On October 9, 2007, the DJIA reached 14,164. Exactly 17 months later (March 9, 2009) the DJIA closed at 6,457—a 54 percent decline! Although the stock market certainly declined with the economy, investors seemed to be consistently surprised by the worsening economic conditions. However, because investors should care about future cash flows (i.e., remember how you just learned to value stocks by discounting future expected dividends), the stock market should reflect investors' view of the future. If, for example, investors change their beliefs today and think that economic conditions will be better than what they thought yesterday, their views on expected cash flows should become more positive (bullish) and prices should rise. In addition, the market may forecast economic conditions because stock price declines reduce the wealth of consumers and therefore may lead to reduced consumption spending and a reduction in national income (gross domestic product [GDP]). If consumer confidence is adversely affected by stock price declines, consumption spending may decrease following a decline. Finally, lower stock prices may increase the cost of raising capital and result in a reduction in business investment.

Given this framework, one should expect that the stock market can be used to forecast recessions. The Conference Board (www.conference-board.org), for example, uses the S&P 500 as a leading economic indicator. Empirical evidence suggests, however, that the stock market is not very successful in predicting economic activity. A study by the Federal Reserve Bank of Kansas City showed that only 11 of the 27 recessions between 1900 and 1987 were successfully predicted by stock market declines.[1] The crash of 1987, for example, was followed by 3 more years of economic expansion. The famous economist (and Nobel Prize winner) Paul Samuelson humorously observed, "The stock market has forecasted nine of the last five recessions."

Nonetheless, at the time of this writing, with current unemployment in the United States at 9 percent, the stock market has rallied more than 50 percent since the 2009 low, which is, at a minimum, a hopeful sign for the future. That is, although the economy has improved only slightly over the past year, the market is forecasting a brighter future.

10.9 THE STOCK MARKET AS A PREDICTOR OF ECONOMIC ACTIVITY

SUMMARY OF LEARNING OBJECTIVES

1 Describe the three types of equity securities. There are three general forms of equity securities: common stock, preferred stock, and securities that are convertible into common stock. *Common stock* is the basic form of corporate ownership. Common stockholders typically vote on the corporation's board of directors, may receive periodic cash payments called *dividends*, and are last in priority of payment in the event of bankruptcy. *Preferred stockholders* typically do not vote, but they are given preference in receiving dividend payments over common shareholders. Preferred stockholders are just ahead of common

---

[1]See Bryon Higgins, "Is a Recession Inevitable This Year?" *Economic Review*, Federal Reserve Bank of Kansas City, January 1988, pp. 3–16.

stockholders in priority of payment in bankruptcy. *Convertible securities* are either corporate bonds or preferred stock that converts to common stock at the investor's option.

2 **Explain how equity securities are sold in the primary market and the role of underwriters.** New issues of equity securities may be sold directly to investors by the issuing corporation, but they are usually distributed by an investment banker in an underwritten offering, a private placement, or a shelf registration. The most common distribution method is an underwritten offering in which the investment banker purchases the securities from the company for a guaranteed amount known as the *net proceeds* and then resells the securities to investors for a greater amount, called the *gross proceeds.* The difference between the gross proceeds and the net proceeds is the *underwriter's spread,* which compensates the investment banker for the expenses and risks involved in the offering. Shelf-registered offerings tend to have lower underwriter spreads than those sold by traditional methods.

3 **Explain how equity securities are traded in the secondary markets and be able to understand a stock quote.** Any trade of a security after its primary offering takes place in the secondary market. Secondary markets take four possible forms: direct search, brokered, dealer, and auction markets. Most major U.S. stocks trade on the NASDAQ stock market or the NYSE. Competition between these two exchanges has increased over the past decade. Stocks of major U.S. firms also trade globally on the stock exchanges of other countries.

4 **Describe the basics of equity valuation.** Equity securities are valued similarly to bonds but are more complicated because they are assumed to exist forever and because corporations can change the amount of the dividend at any time. Valuing an equity security requires estimating the future stream of dividend payments. Once the timing and the magnitude of the cash flows (i.e., dividends) are determined, one must determine the discount rate that reflects the risk of holding the stock. This discount rate is then used to calculate the present value of the future cash flows.

5 **Explain how a short sale works.** A short sale is when an investor borrows shares from a broker and

sells those shares today. The investor hopes to buy the shares back in the market (to return to the broker) at some later point for a lower price. Thus, an investor taking a short position is betting on a price decline. If the price rises, the investor will have to repurchase the shares (cover the short) at a higher price and will lose money.

6 **Explain the risks associated with equity securities and discuss how to measure these risks.** The total risk of an equity security (or portfolio) is the sum of unsystematic and systematic risk. Unsystematic risk can be reduced by diversification; systematic risk cannot. Investors measure systematic risk with beta (β), which is an indicator of how closely a security's returns are correlated with the returns of the entire stock market.

7 **Describe the major stock market indexes and how they are constructed.** Stock market indexes track movements of prices in the stock market or in some portion of the stock market, such as a firm size or industry segment. Stock market indexes are constructed by selecting a sample of stocks and calculating the weighted average of stock prices in the sample. The indexes can be price-weighted or market value–weighted. The most visible stock indexes are the Dow Jones Industrial Average and the S&P 500 Index.

8 **Discuss whether the stock market is a good predictor of economic activity.** Market observers believe that changes in the stock market can predict changes in overall economic activity for a number of reasons. First, stock prices should reflect the market's expectation of a firm's future profits. Second, when stock markets go up or down, the wealth of individuals is affected and may, in turn, affect their willingness to spend. Third, the stock market may reflect or affect changes in consumer confidence about the economy. Finally, as the stock market goes up or down, the cost of capital of corporations may be affected, which could influence corporate investment spending. Although some economic recessions have been preceded by declines in the stock market, the empirical evidence suggests that the stock market is generally a poor predictor of economic activity.

KEY TERMS

Equity	Convertible preferred stock	Dealer markets	Capital-gains yield
Common stock		Bid–ask spread	Diversification
Preferred stock	Convertible bonds	Auction markets	Unsystematic risk
Residual claim	Primary market	Over-the-counter (OTC) market	Systematic risk
Limited liability	Initial public offering (IPO)		Beta (β)
Earnings		NASDAQ	Aggressive stocks
Retained earnings	Seasoned offering	New York Stock Exchange (NYSE)	Defensive stocks
Dividends	Underwritten offering		Capital asset pricing model (CAPM)
Proxy	Underwriter's spread	Specialist	
Dual-class firms	Private placements	American Depositary Receipts (ADRs)	Risk premium
Cumulative voting	Rights offering		Market risk premium
Straight voting	Shelf registration	Short sale	Security market line (SML)
Nonparticipating preferred stock	Market capitalization	Margin	
	Dividend yield	Market order	Circuit breakers
Cumulative preferred stock	Earnings per share (EPS)	Limit order	Price-weighted index
	Price/earnings (P/E) ratio	Stop loss order	Market value–weighted index
Adjustable-rate preferred stock	Direct search markets	Stop buy order	
	Brokered market	Growing perpetuity	

QUESTIONS AND PROBLEMS

1. Describe the major differences between common stock and preferred stock.

2. Why are convertible securities more attractive to investors than simply holding a firm's preferred stock or corporate bonds?

3. Valerie Apparel Lines (VAL) has 100 million shares of common stock outstanding, and the company is electing seven directors by means of cumulative voting. If a group of minority shareholders controls 31 million shares, how many directors is the group certain of electing? If straight voting were used, how many directors would the group be certain of electing?

4. Weber Corporation has 10 million shares of a preferred stock issue outstanding that pays a cumulative $6 annual dividend on a quarterly basis. As a result of poor profitability, however, the company has not paid the preferred stock dividend for the previous five quarters. The company also has 20 million shares of common stock outstanding. Weber Corporation's profitability has improved recently, and the board of directors believes that the company can pay $100 million in dividends next quarter. How much of a dividend can the company pay on its common stock?

5. Arbuckle Corporation is selling 2 million shares of common stock in its initial public offering (IPO). The company's investment banker, Jones Securities, offers the stock to the public at $15 per share and charges Arbuckle Corporation an underwriting spread of 7 per-

cent. What are the gross proceeds from the IPO? What are Arbuckle Corporation's net proceeds from the offering? How much does Jones Securities earn for conducting the offering?

6. Explain why investors look at a stock's P/E ratio rather than its price to determine if the stock is cheap or expensive.

7. Briefly describe the role of the NYSE specialist. How does this role differ from that of a dealer?

8. Explain how an American depository receipt (ADR) works.

9. Explain the differences among a market order, limit order, stop loss order, and stop buy order.

10. Rachel and Mary both have decided to buy 100 shares of WWW.COM, a hot Internet stock. The market price is $240 per share when Rachel places a market order and Mary places a limit order at $230 per share. One week later, the price of WWW.COM is $305 per share after having increased. How much profit has Rachel made? How much profit has Mary made?

11. Val believes the price of ABC is too high at $35/share. She shorts 100 shares. A week later, when she covers her short position, the price is $32/share. How much money did Val make?

12. Winters Hi-Hook Inc., a golf club manufacturer, is currently paying dividends of $0.50 per share. These dividends are expected to grow at a 20 percent rate for the next 2 years and at a 3 percent rate thereafter (forever!). What is the value of the stock if the appropriate discount rate is 14 percent?

13. Dolezilek Power Company promises to maintain dividends of $5 per share on its preferred stock, indefinitely. The stock currently sells at $37.50 per share. What is the required return on the stock?

14. Patty's Gardening Supplies is a young startup company. It plans to pay no dividends over the next 5 years because it must reinvest all earnings in the firm to finance planned growth. The firm then plans to begin paying dividends of $3 per share, which are anticipated to grow at 10 percent per year for 3 years and 6 percent per year in perpetuity beyond that. If the required return on Patty's Gardening Supplies stock is 15 percent, what should be today's stock price?

15. You purchase 100 shares of Adams Trading Company stock today for $22.50 per share. At the end of one year, you collect a dividend of $2.75 and then sell the stock at $24.50 per share. What is your total return on the stock? What is the dividend yield? What is the capital gains yield?

16. Farrell Motors stock has a beta of 1.3. If the market has an expected return of 9 percent and the risk-free rate is 1 percent, what is the expected return of the stock according to the security market line?

17. The market's required return on Paul Bunyan Oil Company stock is currently 13.8 percent. If the expected return on the market portfolio is 12.6 percent and the risk-free rate is 3.5 percent, what is the beta of Paul Bunyan stock?

18. Explain the difference between systematic and unsystematic risk. Explain how beta captures systematic risk.

19. You have decided to create stock market indexes using three representative stocks. At the end of day 1, stock X has a price of $20 per share and 20 million shares outstanding, stock Y has a price of $25 per share and 50 million shares outstanding, and stock Z has a price of $35 per share and 40 million shares outstanding. You calculate a price-weighted index and a market capitalization–weighted index. You have decided that the beginning value of each index at the end of day 1 will be 100. What is the value of each index at the end of day 2 if stock X's price is $23 per share, stock Y's price is $22 per share, and stock Z's price is $36 per share?

INTERNET EXERCISE

In this exercise, you learn how to access the DJIA on the Internet and get practice doing some simple analysis of the DJIA.

1. Go to www.reuters.com/finance. Along the right hand side, the market tracker will list the Dow (DJIA) and other indices. Click on "Dow."

2. The resulting page will give you the current level of the DJIA along with a list (and current prices and volume) of the 30 stocks that make up the DJIA. Do you recognize these companies? If you added the prices of these 30 stocks together and divided by the current DJIA divisor (it was 0.132129493 in March 2011), the result will be the DJIA.

3. Now go to www.google.com/finance. Click on the word "Dow" just below the graph. You will get a graph of the DJIA for the past 3 days. Along the top is a "Zoom" row. Click on "Max" to see the DJIA for the past 40 years.

4. As you run your cursor over the line, the top right-hand corner will show you the level of the DJIA and the date. What was the DJIA when you were born?

5. When did the DJIA first cross 10,000? Why do people refer to the 2000s as the lost decade of stock investing? In other words, ignoring dividends, what is the approximate return on the DJIA between 2000 and the end of 2009?

Derivatives Markets

WHAT ARE INTEREST RATES GOING TO DO? What about exchange rates? What about the stock market? Should I bet that interest rates will fall and stocks rise, or should I bet that the exchange rate will fall and stocks fall? How much risk can I take? Should I gamble to try to earn a higher return? Will I lose my job if my portfolio or transactions lose money? How can I protect myself and my transactions and portfolio against loss? Many bond traders, market makers, exporters and importers, and financial institutions and investment funds must ask themselves questions like these daily.

Because many people are concerned with interest rate, exchange rate, or stock market risk, the financial futures markets have grown explosively in recent years. *Financial engineers* developed a wide variety of financial instruments so that individuals and institutions can alter both their risk exposure and return possibilities. The new *financial derivative* securities derive their value from changes in the value of other assets (such as stocks or bonds), values (such as interest rates), or events (such as credit defaults, catastrophes, or even temperature changes in certain localities). Derivative securities also generate substantial fee income for the financial institutions that invent and market them.

Of course, not everyone is a fan of derivatives—especially given the role they played in the 2007–2008 financial crisis. Even back in 2002, legendary

In his 2002 letter to shareholders, Warren Buffett warned, "The derivatives genie is now well out of the bottle, and these instruments will almost certainly multiply in variety and number until some event makes their toxicity clear. . . . Central banks and governments have so far found no effective way to control, or even monitor, the risks posed by these contracts. . . . In our view, however, derivatives are financial weapons of mass destruction, carrying dangers that, while now latent, are potentially lethal."

investor Warren Buffet noted, "The range of derivatives contracts is limited only by the imagination of man (or sometimes, so it seems madmen). At Enron, for example, newsprint and broadband derivatives, due to be settled many years in the future, were put on the books. Or say you want to write a contract speculating on the number of twins to be born in Nebraska in 2020. No problem—at a price, you will easily find an obliging counterparty." ∎

This chapter describes the nature of the most important markets for financial derivatives. It starts with forward and futures markets, then discusses the swaps and options markets. It discusses how markets work, what financial instruments are traded in each, who the major participants are, and how the markets are regulated. It also describes how the financial futures markets can be used to reduce risk—particularly the interest rate risk of financial intermediaries—and how new types of risk, such as basis risk and counterparty risk, may be relevant to claims traded in the financial derivative markets. ■

LEARNING OBJECTIVES

1 Explain the characteristics of forwards, futures, options, and swaps.

2 Explain how market participants use derivative securities.

3 Describe the advantages and disadvantages of each derivative security.

4 Discuss the risks involved in using futures contracts to hedge an underlying risk exposure.

5 Discuss why some people prefer options to forward or futures contracts, and why options protect against risk only if someone pays a price—the option "premium."

6 Explain how swaps work.

7 Explain how the Dodd-Frank Wall Street Reform and Consumer Protection Act affects the way swaps will be traded in the future.

11.1 THE NATURE OF DERIVATIVE SECURITIES

The securities discussed in previous chapters have diverse payoff characteristics, and most financial institutions and other investors pursue their investment objectives by picking and choosing among those securities. At any given point in time, however, these investors may be exposed to more or less risk than they desire in one or more securities or markets. This is where derivative securities come in.

A **derivative security** is a financial instrument whose value depends on, or is derived (hence "derivative") from, some underlying security. For example, the value of a futures contract to buy corn at some future point in time (at a specific price determined today) is derived from the price of corn. The most common types of derivative contracts are forwards, futures, options, and swaps. In fact, almost all derivative securities are some combination of these four basic contracts.

Derivatives are an integral part of a successful risk management program because they offer an inexpensive means of changing a firm's risk profile. A firm's risk profile describes how the firm's value or cash flows change in response to changes in some risk factor. Common risk factors are interest rates, commodity prices, stock market indexes, and foreign exchange rates. By taking a position in a derivative security that offsets the firm's risk profile, the firm can limit the extent to which the firm's value is affected by changes in the risk factor. Similarly, investors can use derivative securities to speculate on these risk factors. In Chapter 19, for example, we discuss how some investment banks' proprietary trading operations used derivatives to make bets on future mortgage values during the subprime crisis. Given the effectiveness of derivative securities in managing a firm's risk exposures and in placing large bets on price increases or decreases, it is not surprising that the markets for derivative securities have seen tremendous growth since the mid-1980s.

Frequently, people enter into contracts that call for future delivery of domestic or foreign currency, a security, or a commodity. Forward markets let people arrange exchanges *forward* in time. A **forward contract**, for example, involves two parties agreeing today on a price, called the **forward price**, at which the purchaser will buy a specified amount of an asset from the seller at a fixed date sometime in the future. This is in contrast to a cash market transaction in which the buyer and seller conduct their transaction today at the **spot price**. The buyer of a forward contract is said to have a **long position** and is obligated to pay the forward price for the asset. The seller of a forward contract is said to have a **short position** and is obligated to sell the asset to the buyer in exchange for the forward price. The future date on which the buyer pays the seller (and the seller delivers the asset to the buyer) is referred to as the **settlement date**.

In a forward market, the person on the other side of the contract (e.g., the person short if you are long) is the **counterparty**. Ordinarily, both parties to the contract are bound by the contract and are not released from that obligation early unless they renegotiate the contract prior to its fulfillment. Individual parties to forward contracts are exposed to potential loss should their counterparty default rather than honor his or her obligation on the settlement date.

The *forward price* for an asset is the price that makes the forward contract have zero net present value. Consider, for example, an asset that does not cost anything to store (a financial asset) and doesn't pay any income (a discount bond). Whether we agree to purchase this asset in 6 months at a certain price (i.e., enter a long forward position), or borrow the current price of the asset, buy it today, and pay back the loan in 6 months, we end up owning the asset in 6 months. Therefore, the forward price must be equal to the current price plus what it would cost us to borrow for 6 months. For instance, consider Hilary, a portfolio manager who plans to buy 1-month Treasury bills in 2 months. The total face amount of securities she plans to buy is $5 million. The current price for 3-month Treasury bills is $992,537 per $1 million face amount. If the current, effective, annual risk-free rate over the 2 months is 3 percent, the fair forward price would be

$$F = \$992,537[1 + (0.03/12)]^2 = \$997,506$$

So the total forward price Hilary should pay is $4,987,530 ($997,506 × 5). If the asset had any storage costs or paid any income, the forward price would be adjusted upward (to incorporate the storage costs) or downward (to incorporate the income).

The forward markets for foreign exchange (money) are the most active forward markets. Markets in foreign currencies let people guarantee a currency exchange

11.2 FORWARD MARKETS

rate at some specific forward point such as 30, 60, or 90 days or more hence. When an exporter wishes to guarantee a forward exchange rate, he or she can go to any one of a number of banks or foreign exchange dealers and enter into a forward contract. The contract guarantees delivery of a certain amount of foreign currency (say, 2 million British pounds) for exchange into a specific amount of dollars ($3.7 million, if the exchange rate is $1.85 = £1) on a specific day (90 days hence).

If a corn exporter sold 1 million bushels of corn at £2 per bushel with payment due in 90 days, the exporter could guarantee the dollar price of the corn by entering into a forward exchange contract with a major bank. The exporter would agree to sell the £2 million it will receive to the bank for $1.85 per pound, or a total of $3.7 million.

A risk of counterparty default exists if, for instance, the exporter does not receive prompt payment of the £2 million and is unable to keep its end of the contract, or if the bank fails (and is not bailed out) before maturity of the contract. Losses as a result of a default are relatively low as long as the pound–dollar exchange rate is close to $1.85 per pound on the designated delivery day because the unfilled end of the contract can be offset in the spot exchange market at a price close to the prearranged rate of exchange. The **spot market** calls for immediate delivery of foreign exchange.

Because the future spot rate is uncertain, exporters do not want to risk their profits by gambling that they can predict it. Furthermore, because the risk of counterparty default on forward exchange contracts is very small, they would rather take that risk and pay their bank a fee for arranging the forward exchange than receive a currency whose future value is uncertain. Forward exchange contracts let importers and exporters offset the price risk inherent in future dealings by guaranteeing future exchange rates and prices.

The individual banks and foreign exchange dealers that make up the forward market balance the supply of and demand for funds by exporters, importers, investors, and speculators in various countries and alter the forward exchange rate as necessary so that the demand for and supply of funds are equal.

Forward exchange dealers make their money on the spread between their buying and asking prices for foreign exchange. For instance, an exchange dealer might exchange dollars supplied by Japanese exporters for yen at ¥86 per dollar and exchange yen supplied by U.S. exporters for dollars at ¥86 per dollar. The dealer profits by buying low and selling high.

11.3 FUTURES MARKETS

Like forward contracts, **futures contracts** involve two parties agreeing today on a price at which the purchaser will buy a given amount of a commodity or financial instrument from the seller at a fixed date sometime in the future. In fact, futures and forwards serve many of the same economic functions. The markets for the two types of instruments are sufficiently different, however, that the two contracts are called by different names.

DIFFERENCES BETWEEN FUTURES AND FORWARD MARKETS

Futures contracts differ from forward contracts in several ways. Many of the differences are attributed to the fact that futures contracts are traded on an organized exchange, such as the Chicago Board of Trade or the Chicago Mercantile Exchange, whereas forward contracts are traded in the informal over-the-counter market.

One of the most important differences between futures and forwards is that futures contracts are standardized in quantities, delivery periods, and grades of deliverable items, whereas forward market contracts are not. Most futures contracts call for the delivery of specific commodities, securities, or currencies either on specific future dates or over limited periods of time. For example, 10-year U.S. Treasury note futures call for a contract size of one U.S. Treasury note having a face value of $100,000. Available delivery months are limited to the nearest March, June, September, and December. This standardization results in a relatively large volume of transactions for a given contract. This makes trading in the contract easy and inexpensive.

In addition, although there must be a buyer and seller when any new contract is initiated, both parties in a futures market transaction hold formal contracts with the **futures exchange**, not with each other. Every major futures exchange operates a clearinghouse that acts as the counterparty to all buyers and all sellers. Although individual traders interact with each other face to face in a futures *pit* (trading area) or trade electronically with each other, the actual contract drawn up to formalize this trade breaks this direct link between buyer and seller and instead inserts the clearinghouse as the opposite party. This means that traders need not worry about the creditworthiness of the party with whom they trade (as forward market traders must), but only about the creditworthiness of the exchange itself. This reduces the risk of default on futures contracts. Forward contracts are riskier because one party may default if prices change dramatically before the delivery date.

The futures exchange is protected from default risk by requiring daily cash settlement of all contracts, called **marking-to-market**. By its very nature, a futures contract is a zero-sum game in that whenever the market price of a commodity changes, the underlying value of a long (purchase) or short (sale) position also changes—and one party's gain is the other party's loss. By requiring each contract's loser to pay the winner the net amount of this change each day, futures exchanges eliminate the possibility that large unrealized losses build up over time. Market participants post **margin** money (if necessary) to take account of gains or losses accruing from daily price fluctuations. In a forward contract, however, there are no cash flows between origination and termination of the contract.

Because the futures exchange acts as the counterparty in all futures contracts and all contracts are marked to market daily, either party in a futures contract can liquidate its future obligation to buy (or deliver) goods by offsetting it with a sale (or purchase) of an identical futures contract prior to the scheduled delivery date. Assume, for example, that you have promised to sell and deliver 5,000 bushels of corn at the end of December (i.e., taken a short position in the corn futures). If you now agree to buy and pick up 5,000 bushels of corn at the end of December (i.e., take a long position), your net position is zero. In contrast, in the forward exchange markets, contracts are ordinarily satisfied by actual delivery of specified items on the specified date. In the futures market, almost all contracts are offset prior to delivery.

EXAMPLE OF A FUTURES MARKET TRANSACTION

The futures markets typically call for delivery of specific items during specific months of the year. For instance, as indicated earlier, a 10-year U.S. Treasury note contract calls for the delivery of $100,000 face amount of 10-year Treasury notes during the months of March, June, September, or December. A person may purchase (or sell) a futures contract for receipt (or delivery) of $100,000 worth of 10-year Treasury notes for any of those months for the next year. Treasury note futures prices are quoted in points and one-half of $1/_{32}$ of a point. For example, a quote of 110'12.5 indicates a futures price of $110,391 (110 12.5/32 percent of $100,000).

Because 10-year U.S. Treasury notes are limited in number, the Chicago Board of Trade allows any U.S. Treasury note maturing in at least 6.5 years, but in no more than 10 years, to be delivered in the event delivery actually takes place. In addition, because there are differences in values between 6.5-year Treasury notes and 10-year Treasury notes, the exchange uses conversion factors to adjust the futures settlement price for these differences. The conversion factors are based on prices that yield 6 percent.

Agreeing to Trade.   Suppose that in December 2010, Paige decides to buy a Treasury note futures contract for delivery in June 2011, at a price of 110'12.5. At the same time, Jake decides to sell a Treasury note futures contract if he can get a price of 110'12.5 or higher. Both place their orders with their brokers, who take them to the trading floor (in practice, the order would probably be executed electronically) at the Chicago Board of Trade. Paige's broker offers to buy one contract and Jake's broker offers to sell one contract. Once they agree on the price, the brokers signal their agreement to buy and sell a June 2011 contract to each other at a price of 110'12.5 and record their orders with the exchange. The exchange, in turn, agrees to sell one Treasury note contract to Paige at 110'12.5 and to buy one contract from Jake at 110'12.5. Because there are both a new buyer and a new seller, the **open interest**, or total number of contracts to deliver a Treasury note in June 2011 through the exchange, increases by one. This process is illustrated in Exhibit 11.1. Note that even though the agreement to buy and

EXHIBIT 11.1

Buyers and Sellers Agree on a Price Through the Futures Exchange

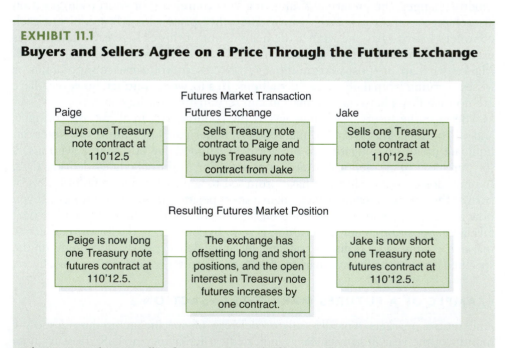

When a person buys or sells a futures contract, the futures exchange is legally the other party to the contract. However, the exchange has a neutral net position because it always simultaneously buys and sells contracts to the public. The total number of long (or short) contracts outstanding in a futures contract is called the *open interest*.

sell was between individuals, the exchange wrote separate contracts with each. This, combined with marking-to-market, allows each participant to liquidate his or her position at will and minimizes the risk of default.

The payoff diagrams for the long and short positions are shown in Exhibit 11.2. If the price of the Treasury note decreases to 110'00.0 ($110,000), Paige is worse off because she must pay $110,391 for Treasury notes that are now worth $110,000 (i.e., a loss of $391). Paige's loss is Jake's gain. Jake now has agreed to sell the Treasury notes for $110,391 and they are only worth $110,000 (i.e., a gain of $391). In contrast, if the price of Treasury notes increases, Paige benefits from the contract because she is guaranteed a price of 110'12.5, or $110,391, and Jake is worse off because he is obligated to sell Treasury notes for

EXHIBIT 11.2
Payoff Diagrams for Treasury Note Futures Contracts

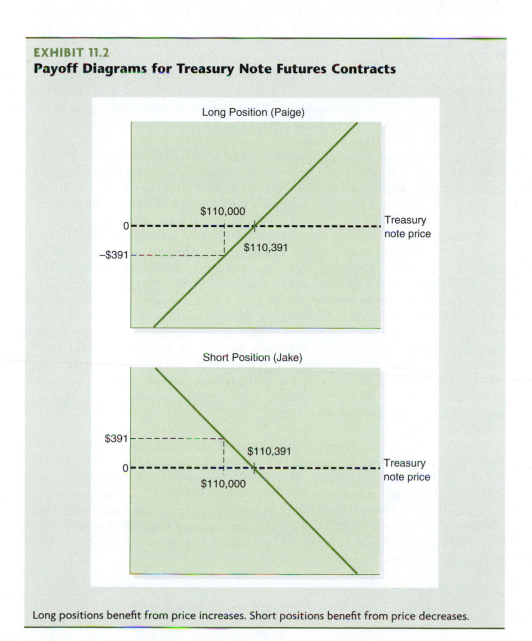

Long positions benefit from price increases. Short positions benefit from price decreases.

110′12.5, or $110,391, which is less than what he could sell them for in the spot market.

Margin Requirements. When Paige and Jake initiate their futures positions (as in forward contracts, an agreement to buy is called a *long position* and an agreement to sell is called a *short position*), they each must deposit money with the exchange to guarantee that they keep their part of the bargain. This deposit is called the **initial margin** requirement. The initial margin for Treasury note futures is $1,890. If the market price of new contracts on the exchange moves adversely, Paige or Jake may have to deposit more money in order to meet the **maintenance margin** requirement imposed on investors by the exchange. Maintenance margin requirements are imposed to ensure that people do not default on their contracts if prices move adversely for them. The Treasury note maintenance margin is $1,400.

Assume that Paige and Jake each posted an initial margin requirement of $1,890 with the exchange, so the exchange holds a total of $3,780 in margin deposits. Now, as before, suppose that the price of the Treasury note futures contract fell to 110′00.0. At that point, Paige's long contract has lost $391 in value and Jake has gained an equal amount. Because futures contracts are marked to market every day, $391 is deducted from Paige's margin account and $391 is deposited in Jake's margin account.

The futures price is set to the new futures price of 110′00.0. After the contracts are marked to market, Paige has a long futures contract with the exchange at the new futures price of 110′00.0. She has $1,499 ($1,890 − $391) in her margin account. Jake has a short position with the exchange at the new futures price of 110′00.0, and $2,281 ($1,890 + $391) in his margin account.

Because she must always post margin equal to or greater than maintenance margin requirements, Paige receives a **margin call** if her margin account balance drops below $1,400. The margin call requires her to add money to her margin account to bring it back up to the initial margin of $1,890. Margin calls are necessary to ensure that futures traders always keep a positive balance in their accounts and do not have an incentive to default on their obligations. Because futures margin requirements may, at any time, require interim cash outlays, they pose more cash-flow risk for investors than do forward contracts. Because margin requirements are continuously maintained, however, they also reduce the risk that a counterparty will default and one party to the transaction will suffer a loss because of credit risk. In the absence of margin requirements, as with over-the-counter trades, traders may take excessive risks.

Suppose the price of the Treasury note futures contract continues to fall to 109′12.5. At that point, Paige has lost a total of $1,000 and must add that much to her account to restore her margin. Jake, however, has a total gain of $1,000. He could withdraw that extra money at will or decide to sell out, take his gain, and withdraw his margin money, too. This is shown in Exhibit 11.3, where we assume that Jake's broker offsets Jake's short position by going to the exchange and buying one Treasury note contract from Carl's broker. Because Carl's broker sold a contract to deliver one Treasury note on Carl's behalf, Carl is now short one Treasury note contract instead of Jake.

Delivery on Futures Contracts. Although the vast majority of all futures contracts are offset before delivery, a few are completed by delivery from the seller to the

EXHIBIT 11.3
Transfer of Futures Contracts

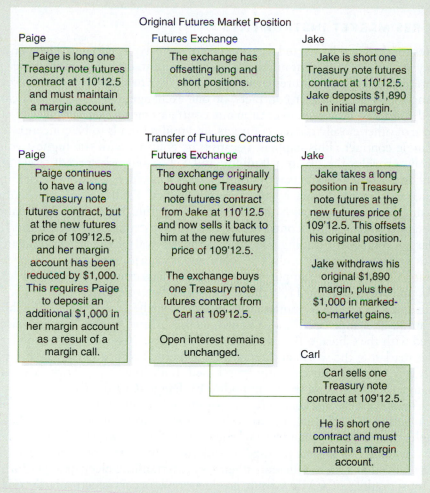

Original Futures Market Position

Paige
Paige is long one Treasury note futures contract at 110'12.5 and must maintain a margin account.

Futures Exchange
The exchange has offsetting long and short positions.

Jake
Jake is short one Treasury note futures contract at 110'12.5. Jake deposits $1,890 in initial margin.

Transfer of Futures Contracts

Paige
Paige continues to have a long Treasury note futures contract, but at the new futures price of 109'12.5, and her margin account has been reduced by $1,000. This requires Paige to deposit an additional $1,000 in her margin account as a result of a margin call.

Futures Exchange
The exchange originally bought one Treasury note futures contract from Jake at 110'12.5 and now sells it back to him at the new futures price of 109'12.5.

The exchange buys one Treasury note futures contract from Carl at 109'12.5.

Open interest remains unchanged.

Jake
Jake takes a long position in Treasury note futures at the new futures price of 109'12.5. This offsets his original position.

Jake withdraws his original $1,890 margin, plus the $1,000 in marked-to-market gains.

Carl
Carl sells one Treasury note contract at 109'12.5.

He is short one contract and must maintain a margin account.

When a person closes out a futures position, a payment is made to settle the change in value that has occurred since the initial purchase, and the contract with the exchange is canceled. This procedure provides liquidity, as it allows one party to the initial trade (Jake) to liquidate his position without requiring the consent of the party who initially took the other side of the contract (Paige). This is one advantage of futures over forward contracts.

buyer. For instance, in Exhibit 11.3, if Carl continues to hold his contract in June 2009, he may fulfill his contract to sell by delivering $100,000 in Treasury notes on any business day of his choosing during the month. The holder of the long (buy side) futures position is invoiced to pay for the Treasury notes at the current settlement price, net of gains or losses, that he or she has accrued on the futures contract. Both the long and the short contracts, then, are canceled by delivery. Note that Paige is not necessarily the buyer. In fact, if she has offset her position, then she is certainly not the buyer. The exchange selects the long position with the oldest outstanding contract to be the buyer of any Treasury notes being delivered.

FUTURES MARKET INSTRUMENTS

Futures markets can be started for any type of security, foreign currency, or commodity for which a sufficient number of people want to exchange future price risk. An interesting aspect of futures contracts is that *the fittest survive.* Initially, several exchanges may issue similar contracts, or one exchange may issue several closely related contracts. However, over time one contract tends to gain popularity at the expense of other closely related contracts, and trading tends to be concentrated in that single contract. This happens because the contract with the highest volume generally provides the greatest liquidity and lowest bid–ask spreads. Eventually, trading in the other contracts is discontinued. For instance, the New York Futures Exchange (since purchased by the Intercontinental Exchange) T-bill contracts were unable to compete with the Chicago Mercantile Exchange's International Monetary Market (IMM) contracts for the same instruments because the IMM had larger volumes of trading. Because of the survival-of-the-fittest tendency of futures contracts, usually only one contract is traded for each type of asset. Exhibit 11.4 lists a few examples of exchange-traded futures contracts.

As shown in Exhibit 11.4, there are a number of futures exchanges. U.S. futures markets changed dramatically, however, in the late 2000s. The Chicago Mercantile Exchange (CME, also known as the "Merc" or the "Chicago Merc") merged with the Chicago Board of Trade (CBOT) in 2007 to become the largest futures market in the world and renamed the merged company the CME Group. The CME Group subsequently purchased both the New York Mercantile Exchange (NYMEX) and the Commodity Exchange (COMEX).

Originally, these markets were pure **open-outcry** markets with traders physically meeting in a "trading pit" to go long or short in futures contracts. See, for example, the Eddie Murphy–Dan Aykroyd classic film *Trading Places* to get an idea of what trading in a futures pit used to look like. Over time, however, more trading has moved to a more efficient, albeit less entertaining, electronic platform. In fact, most trading of CME Group products now occurs electronically (via the CME Globex electronic trading platform). For example, in April 2010, CME Group's daily volume averaged 1.4 million contracts traded in open outcry versus 10.0 million contracts traded electronically. In addition, electronic trading occurs nearly around the clock. The 10-year Treasury notes futures contract, for instance, is traded in an open-outcry trading pit at the Chicago Board of Trade Monday through Friday from 7:20 A.M. to 2:00 P.M. (Central Time). The same contract is also traded on CME Globex every Sunday through Friday from 5:30 P.M. to 4:00 P.M., that is, 22½ hours a day!

Each futures exchange determines the specifications for contracts traded on that exchange. The specifications show delivery dates for each contract, the value of items to be delivered when each contract is exercised, the types of items that can be delivered, and the method of delivery. The exchange also dictates the minimum price change that can occur in the contract and (to prevent panics) the maximum price change that can occur in 1 day. Initial and maintenance margins, trading rules and hours, and trading methods (electronic or pit-traded) for each type of contract are also specified by the exchange. Finally, each exchange enforces trading rules, contract agreements, and margin requirements applicable to that exchange.

EXHIBIT 11.4
Examples of Exchange Traded Futures Contracts

Contract	Exchange	Contract Size
Grains and oilseeds		
Corn	Chicago Board of Trade/CME Globex	5,000 bushels
Oats	Chicago Board of Trade/CME Globex	5,000 bushels
Wheat	Chicago Board of Trade/CME Globex	5,000 bushels
Livestock and meat		
Cattle—feeder	Chicago Mercantile Exchange/CME Globex	50,000 lb.
Cattle—live	Chicago Mercantile Exchange/CME Globex	40,000 lb.
Pork bellies	Chicago Mercantile Exchange/CME Globex	40,000 lb.
Food and fiber		
Cocoa	Intercontinental Exchange (ICE)	10 metric tons
Coffee	Intercontinental Exchange (ICE)	37,500 lb.
Sugar—world	Intercontinental Exchange (ICE)	112,000 lb.
Sugar—domestic	Intercontinental Exchange (ICE)	112,000 lb.
Cotton	Intercontinental Exchange (ICE)	50,000 lb.
Orange juice	Intercontinental Exchange (ICE)	15,000 lb.
Metals and petroleum		
Copper	Comex/CME Globex	25,000 lb.
Gold	Comex/CME Globex	100 troy oz.
Platinum	New York Mercantile Exchange/CME Globex	50 troy oz.
Silver	New York Mercantile Exchange/CME Globex	5,000 troy oz.
Crude oil	New York Mercantile Exchange/CME Globex	1,000 bbl.
Natural gas	New York Mercantile Exchange/CME Globex	10,000 MMBtu
Interest rate		
Treasury bonds	Chicago Board of Trade/CME Globex	$100,000
10-year Treasury notes	Chicago Board of Trade/CME Globex	$100,000
30-day federal funds	Chicago Mercantile Exchange/CME Globex	$5 million
LIBOR	Chicago Mercantile Exchange/CME Globex	$3 million
Eurodollars	Chicago Mercantile Exchange/CME Globex	$1 million
Index		
Dow Jones Industrial Average	Chicago Board of Trade/CME Globex	$10 × avg.
Mini-sized Dow	Chicago Board of Trade/CME Globex	$5 × avg.
S&P 500	Chicago Mercantile Exchange/CME Globex	$250 × avg.
Mini-sized S&P 500	Chicago Mercantile Exchange/CME Globex	$50 × avg.
NIKKEI 225	Chicago Mercantile Exchange/CME Globex	$5 × avg.
Currency		
Japanese yen (Y)	Chicago Mercantile Exchange/CME Globex	Y12.5 million
Euro (EU)	Chicago Mercantile Exchange/CME Globex	EU125,000
British pound (BP)	Chicago Mercantile Exchange/CME Globex	BP62,500

FUTURES MARKET PARTICIPANTS

There are two major types of participants in futures and forward markets: hedgers and speculators. **Hedgers** try to reduce price risk inherent in their balance sheets or future business dealings by guaranteeing buying or selling prices for closely related futures contracts. In our earlier example, Jake may have been holding a portfolio of Treasury securities. If so, his transaction to sell Treasury note futures contracts reduced his price risk; thus, he was a hedger. Other hedgers might try to guarantee their costs of feed (by buying corn futures contracts) or the value of their livestock at market time (by selling cattle or hog futures contracts). By so doing, they can guarantee their costs of raising cattle or hogs and ensure that they make a profit. Similarly, banks can guarantee their cost of funds over the period they make a loan by selling interest rate futures short. Insurance companies can guarantee a return on planned annuity policies by buying Treasury bond futures before they actually sell the policies.

In short, people can use futures contracts in many ways to hedge their financial and business transactions. In the process, some are buyers and some are sellers. The major objective of both is to guarantee a future price that reduces their risk. By doing so, however, they are also limiting their upside potential. A wheat farmer who sells her crop in the forward market today locks in a price today. If wheat prices subsequently rise, she is stuck selling at the lower futures price.

Speculators take risks in the futures markets. They are willing to enter a futures transaction in hopes that the market price moves in a favorable direction. If they are right, like Jake in our example, they can make a great deal of money in a hurry. If prices move unfavorably, however, they can also lose a great deal of money. Speculators may speculate on either a rise in prices by buying futures contracts (*going long*) or a fall in prices by selling futures contracts (*going short*). They also may enter into **spreads** or **straddles**, in which they buy one futures contract and sell a closely related contract (such as a contract for the same commodity that is due in a different month, or a contract for a closely related commodity) in the hope that the price of one contract moves more favorably than the other.

Traders are a special class of speculators who speculate on very short-term changes in prices. Most operate on the floor of the exchange and try to *scalp* short-term changes in market prices by buying and selling quickly when prices seem to be changing. Traders provide a valuable function because their activity adds liquidity to markets and reduces the disparity between bid and ask prices on the exchanges. Consequently, exchanges encourage trading activity in order to broaden the market appeal of their futures contracts.

DO YOU UNDERSTAND?

1. Explain the major differences between *futures contracts* and *forward contracts*.
2. What is the economic role of the margin account on a futures exchange?
3. What determines the size of the margin requirement for a particular futures contract?
4. What is the difference between *hedging* and *speculating*?

Financial futures markets have grown rapidly because they provide a way for financial market participants to insulate themselves against changes in interest rates and asset prices. Financial futures can be used to reduce the systematic risk of stock portfolios or to guarantee future returns or costs. In general, financial futures prices move inversely with interest rates and directly with financial asset prices, so the sale of futures can offset asset price risk.

11.4 USES OF THE FINANCIAL FUTURES MARKETS

REDUCING SYSTEMATIC RISK IN STOCK PORTFOLIOS

In 1982, **stock-index futures contracts** became available. They derive their value from the prices of a basket of underlying stocks that are included in the stock index. The New York Stock Exchange Composite Index includes all stocks listed on the New York Stock Exchange, whereas the S&P 500 Index obtains its value from the 500 stocks included in the Standard & Poor's 500 stock index. The use of stock-index futures has grown rapidly, and they now are among the most actively traded contracts in the U.S. futures markets. There are also stock-index futures (usually traded in foreign markets) that derive their value from foreign stocks. In 2002, futures on individual stocks started to trade in the United States. The primary advantage of stock-index futures contracts is that they let an investor alter the market risk (or systematic risk) intrinsic to his or her portfolio. They can also be tailored to the type of portfolio one holds. People who wish to hedge price movements in stock values in general or in only large stocks may want to use the S&P 500 futures or, possibly, the Dow Jones Index futures, whereas people who wish to hedge price movements in smaller stocks may wish to use the S&P SmallCap 600 futures (the S&P SmallCap 600 is an index comprising smaller stocks).

Systematic risk measures a stock portfolio's tendency to vary relative to the market as a whole. Thus, it is a measure of that part of risk that is common to all stocks (and therefore, often called market risk). It is measured by calculating a stock's return covariance with the market return divided by the variance of the market return, or its *beta*. If the value of a stock or stock portfolio typically moves up or down 1.2 times as much as the general stock market, it is said to have a beta of 1.2. Systematic risk is important because, unlike *unsystematic risk* (which measures the tendency of a stock's price to change due to news about that particular stock rather than news that affects all stocks), systematic risk cannot be diversified away. Thus, before the development of stock-index futures, it was difficult for investors to eliminate systematic risk from their portfolios.

Stock-index futures can be used to control the systematic risk in an investor's portfolio. For instance, assume that an investor has a portfolio worth $30 million with a beta of 1. On average, therefore, the value of the portfolio moves up and down in step with the stock market as a whole. For example, if the stock market falls 5 percent, the portfolio falls 5 percent. Assume further that the S&P 500 futures contract is selling at 1,200. Because the S&P 500 is an index level (versus a price), the value of one contract is the index level times a contract multiplier to convert the index level to a dollar value. In the case of the S&P 500 futures, as shown in Exhibit 11.4, the multiplier is $250

Because one S&P 500 futures contract is worth $250 per point, it is worth $300,000 in stocks ($250 × 1,200) when it is priced at $1,200. Thus, if the investor sold 100 contracts of the S&P 500 futures short, it would have the same effect as selling $30 million worth ($300,000 per contract × 100 contracts) of stocks with an average beta of 1 (the beta of the S&P 500 is usually assumed to be 1 because that index is often used as a measure of market price movements). By selling the 100 futures contracts short, the investor fully offsets the systematic risk in his or her stock portfolio. In sum, the investor is long $30 million worth of stocks with a beta of 1 and short $30 million worth of futures contracts (also with a beta of 1), so the net portfolio beta is zero.

Consider, for example, what happens to this investor if the day after he or she sells the futures contract the stock market falls 2 percent. The investor's stock portfolio value would fall $600,000 (i.e., $-0.02 \times \$30$ million). The futures contract price, however, would also fall by 2 percent, from $1,200 to $1,176. Because the investor agreed to sell the S&P 500 in the future for $1,200 and now the futures price is $1,176, the investor makes $6,000 per contract, that is, the change in the price times the $250 per point ($[1,200 - 1,176] \times \$250$). Multiplying the investor's gain per contract by the 100 future contracts, the investor's profit in the futures market is $600,000, perfectly offsetting his or her loss in the stock portfolio.

By selling futures contracts short, investors need no longer fear that the value of their stock portfolio will change substantially if stock market prices fall. Of course, it's a double-edged sword. If the market rose (instead of fell) 2 percent, the investor's gains in his or her stock portfolio would be perfectly offset by the losses from the futures contract. An investor may want to sell stock-index futures short for several reasons. First, the investor might believe the market is likely to fall, and thus would want to buy portfolio insurance to protect against a possible market decline. Such insurance has a cost because it reduces investors' potential gains as well as their potential losses.

Second, stock investors may also desire to eliminate the systematic risk from their portfolios for several reasons unrelated to portfolio insurance. For instance, stock dealers profit by bidding to buy stocks at a lower price than they offer to sell them. After buying stocks at their bid price, however, dealers take the risk that the price of the stocks they own may decline before they can resell them. Thus, dealers may want to reduce the systematic risk of their portfolios by hedging in the futures markets. In addition, investors who believe that they are superior stock pickers may want to profit by finding undervalued stocks while still protecting themselves from general stock market declines. They too might use stock futures to reduce the systematic risk of their portfolio while still allowing them to capture the excess returns (if any) available to people with superior stock-picking abilities.

LEARNING BY DOING 11.1
Hedging Risk in a Stock Portfolio

PROBLEM: You have recently been hired at a hedge fund. The fund manager believes that securities prices are about to fall and therefore wants to fully hedge the stock portfolio. She has assigned you (yes, you!) the task. Here is what you know:

- Value of hedge fund stock portfolio: $30,000,000
- Beta (systematic risk) of the hedge fund portfolio: 1.20
- Current futures price for the S&P 500 index: $1,200
- S&P 500 index futures multiplier: $250
- If you mess up, you will be fired! (It's $30 million dollars, for crying out loud.)

How do you hedge the portfolio? What happens to the hedge position if the manager is right and, immediately after you place the hedge, markets fall 2 percent?

APPROACH: You know the S&P 500 has a beta of 1 while the hedge fund's beta is 1.20. Thus, if markets fall 2 percent, the S&P 500 futures price will fall 2 percent (everything else equal), but your portfolio will fall approximately 2.4 percent (i.e., 1.2 beta $\times$ 2 percent market decline). Because your portfolio will fall more (in percent) than the market, the dollar value of your S&P 500 futures has to be greater than the dollar value of your hedge fund portfolio so that the dollar value of the loss on your hedge fund (if markets fall) equals the dollar value of your gain from selling the futures contract short.

SOLUTION: First, consider what happens if the market falls 1 percent—your portfolio will fall by 1.2 percent, or $360,000 ($30 million $\times$ -0.012). Next, given a 1 percent decline in the S&P 500 futures price, figure out how many contracts you would need to sell to produce a $360,000 gain. If the S&P 500 futures price falls 1 percent (from 1,200 to 1,188), the gain on each contract sold short is given by the following:

$$\text{Gain on each contract} = (\text{old futures price} - \text{new futures price}) \times \text{futures multiplier}$$
$$= (1,200 - 1,188) \times \$250$$
$$= 3,000$$

Last, determine how many contracts you must sell such that the total gain would be $360,000 (i.e., to fully offset the loss on your equity portfolio):

$$\$3,000 \times \text{number of contracts} = \$360,000$$
$$\text{Number of contracts} = \$360,000$$
$$\$3,000 = 120$$

Therefore, if you sell 120 contracts, the dollar loss on your equity portfolio will be fully offset by the dollar gain on your futures contracts.

Now consider what happens if the portfolio manager is correct and the market falls 2 percent. First, your equity portfolio will lose approximately 2.4 percent because its beta is 1.2 (i.e., 1.2 $\times$ 2 percent) or $720,000 (i.e., $30 million $\times$ -0.024). What happens to the value of the 120 S&P 500 futures contracts you sold short? The S&P futures prices fall by 2 percent (from $1,200 to $1,176), so the gain on each contract is as follows:

$$\text{Gain on each contract} = (\text{old futures price} - \text{new futures price}) \times \text{future multiplier}$$
$$= (1,200 - 1,176) \times \$250$$
$$= \$6,000$$

And the gain on the total futures position is simply the gain on each contract times the number of contracts: $6,000 $\times$ 120 = $720,000. Congratulations, you get to keep your job!

STOCK-INDEX PROGRAM TRADING

Program trading often has substantial short-term effects on stock market price movements. However, many people who engage in program trading do not want to own stocks per se but just want to obtain an investment that generates a higher risk-free rate of return than T-bills. Program traders enter the market when the price of stock-index futures is too far out of line with the prices of the stocks that make up the stock index. For instance, if S&P 500 futures are selling at 1,230 and expire in 3 months, whereas the underlying stocks in the S&P 500 stock index are selling for an equivalent price of 1,200 right now, a person could buy those stocks now, sell futures short, and know that he or she would gain a "riskless" 2.5 percent (1,230/1,200 represents a 2.5 percent gain) in 3 months. The return is guaranteed because the value of the futures must equal the value of the underlying stocks in the stock index when it expires in 3 months. In addition, by owning the stocks for 3 months, the investor might accrue dividends worth an additional 0.5 percent of the stocks' value. Thus, the investor who undertook this arbitrage would earn a riskless return of 3.00 percent (2.5 percent in capital gains plus 0.50 percent in dividends) per quarter, or 12 percent per year. If that return exceeded the T-bill rate, the index arbitrage would be a superior risk-free investment. As a result, when stock-index futures prices rise too far above stock prices, program traders sell the futures index and quickly buy great amounts of stock that replicate the price movement of the underlying stock index (it takes at least 50 stocks to replicate price movements in the S&P 500).

On the downside, if there is mispricing, an investor may be able to earn a greater return through index arbitrage than by holding the stocks in the underlying index. In the previous example, if both stocks and the equivalent stock-index future sold at $1,200, a portfolio manager could buy the futures and sell his or her stocks. If we assume T-bill rates were 1.25 percent per quarter, the stock fund would have 101.25 percent of $1,200, or $1,215 for every $1,200 in stocks sold, by investing the proceeds from the stock sale in T-bills. Because the investor owned a futures contract purchased at a price of $1,200, he or she would be able to reinvest in the same stocks for a net price of $1,200 when the future expired. If we assume the manager gave up dividends totaling 0.50 percent per quarter, the investor would have earned 3/4 percent more in the 3-month period than would have been possible without entering the index arbitrage, that is, 1.25 percent on the T-bills less 0.50 percent dividend yield forgone. If this could be done every quarter, the fund would outperform the index by 3 percent over the course of a year. Consequently, the fund manager would likely earn a bonus for outperforming the stock indexes during the year.

Index arbitrageurs try to profit either by earning a riskless return that is a little greater than the T-bill rate or by selling stocks and investing in T-bills to beat the stock market. To do so, they buy and sell huge quantities of stocks whenever the value of a stock-index futures contract is not equal to the value of its underlying stocks (adjusted for dividend yields and T-bill rate considerations). Through their actions, they provide the socially valuable function of keeping stock-index futures prices in line with the value of underlying stocks. However, when they buy or sell in quantity, they can also cause stock prices to rise or fall sharply in a few minutes.

GUARANTEEING COSTS OF FUNDS

When a corporation plans a major investment, it typically commits itself to major cash outlays for several years in the future. Although a project may be profitable based on forecasted interest rates, it might turn unprofitable if interest rates unexpectedly rise and the corporation has to pay substantially more to borrow the needed funds. One way the corporation can avoid such a risk is by borrowing all the funds at the time the investment is planned and investing excess funds in short-term securities until they are needed. Short-term rates are often lower than long-term rates, however, so it could be costly to borrow long term and invest the temporary excess money at a lower rate. Thus, as an alternative, the corporation may wish to use the futures market to guarantee its future financing costs.

If the corporation usually pays a 2 percent premium over the T-bond rate to borrow, it can use the T-bond market to hedge its cost of funds. Suppose it must borrow $10 million in 1 year. It could sell a T-bond future with a market value of $10 million for a delivery 1 year hence. If it continues to pay 2 percent more interest than T-bonds in 1 year, its hedge allows it to obtain a known interest cost on its future sale of corporate bonds. It would figure its expected interest cost by adding 2 percent (the usual premium it pays over the corporate bond rate) to the yield implied by the T-bond future, which is sold short.

If interest rates rise during the next year, the corporation must pay more to borrow the $10 million. If interest rates rise, however, futures prices fall and the company makes money on its T-bond futures contracts. This gain (assuming it is not taxed) can then be used to reduce borrowing costs. If the corporation had not hedged, the annual interest costs on its debt would have increased when rates went up. By hedging, however, the corporation also loses the possibility of a lower rate if interest rates fall because, even though it might sell its corporate bonds at a lower rate next year, it loses on its sale of the T-bond futures (whose prices would rise as market interest rates fall).

FUNDING FIXED-RATE LOANS

Bank customers often prefer to borrow on a fixed-rate basis so that they know their interest costs in advance. Banks tend to borrow their funds for short periods and therefore, if rates rise, will have to pay more in the future. If you buy a 6-month CD, for instance, the bank is borrowing your money for 6 months. If they use your funds to make a year-long loan (funded by your CD for the first 6 months and another CD 6 months from now), they know their borrowing costs for the first 6 months (what they are paying you), but not for the second 6 months (because they don't know what they will have to pay to get a customer to buy a CD in 6 months). A bank could get rid of this risk in the futures market, however, by selling Eurodollar futures. Exhibit 11.5 illustrates such a case.

In a Eurodollar futures contract, the buyer is agreeing to lend $1,000,000 at a fixed rate for 3 months starting on the settlement date, and the seller is agreeing to borrow $1,000,000 at a fixed rate for 3 months starting on the settlement date. Thus, the bank could sell one 3-month Eurodollar future with settlement in 6 months and one 3-month Eurodollar future with settlement in 9 months and effectively lock in its borrowing costs. (In our example, the bank pays a 25-basis point premium to the Eurodollar rate.) If interest rates rise, the bank will be forced to pay a higher CD rate in 6 months (to attract the funds it needs), but it will gain from its short position in the Eurodollar futures. In sum, the bank offsets its increased interest cost and earns the spread it desires on the

EXHIBIT 11.5
Financing a Fixed-Rate Loan of $1 Million

1. Bank Funding Plan for January 1.

- Sell a 6-month $1 million CD at 3.25% for funding January through June.
- Sell a 3-month $1 million Eurodollar future in June at 96.6 (Eurodollar futures are quoted at 100 minus the Eurodollar interest rate, indicating a Eurodollar rate of 3.40%) guaranteeing funding costs of 3.65% (3.40% plus 25 basis points premium that the bank usually pays on its CDs relative to the Eurodollar rate).
- Sell a 3-month $1 million Eurodollar future in September at 96.4 (a 3.60% rate) to guarantee funding costs of 3.85%.

This gives an average cost of funds per quarter of

$$\frac{3.25\% + 3.25\% + 3.65\% + 3.85\%}{4} = 3.50\%$$

Adding a 2.75% spread, the bank offers to make a fixed-rate, 1-year loan for $1 million at 6.25%.

2. Bank Funding Costs (after the fact)

- First 6 months, 3.25% CD.
- Next 3 months, 3.75% CD (10 basis points more than expected).
- Last 3 months, 4.05% CD (20 basis points more than expected).

Interest costs in the third quarter, then, were $250 ($1,000,000 × 0.10% × ¼ year) more than expected. Interest costs in the fourth quarter were $500 ($1,000,000 × 0.20% × ¼ year) more than expected. Thus, the total interest expenses were $750 more than expected.

- In June, the bank offsets the short Eurodollar futures position at 96.5, for a gain of 10 basis points, or $250 ($1,000,000 × 0.10% × ¼ year).
- In September, the bank offsets the short Eurodollar futures position at 96.2, for a gain of 20 basis points, or $500 ($1,000,000 × 0.20% × ¼ year).

Total gains on futures transactions, then, were $750.

3. Net Result

The gain on the futures transactions offset the increased interest costs (ignoring transaction costs). Thus, the bank realized its expected spread on the loan even though interest rates unexpectedly increased.

fixed-rate loan transaction by hedging the uncertainty regarding what it will have to pay in 6 months to attract an investor to buy a CD.

Banks use futures to provide fixed-rate loans to borrowers who are reluctant to pay variable rates on loans. They can also show such customers how they can lock in their costs of funds by borrowing on a variable-rate basis and selling Eurodollar or Treasury bill futures in the forward markets. The latter approach gained considerable popularity with banks. Consequently, many large banks established futures-trading subsidiaries, called *futures commission merchants (FCMs)*. FCMs provide brokerage services to customers who wish to guarantee their costs of funds or use futures for other purposes.

The previous examples were constructed so that investment in futures perfectly hedges the underlying risk. In practice, however, substantial risks are associated with using futures to hedge. We discuss some of these risks in this section.

BASIS RISK

Basis risk exists because the value of an item being hedged may not always keep the same price relationship to contracts purchased or sold in the futures markets. For instance, in the corporate financing example, the corporation might find that its cost of borrowing was 250 basis points above the Treasury bond rate after 1 year. As a result, a futures hedge would only partially offset its increase in interest costs. The same would be true in the bank cost-of-funds example (Exhibit 11.5) if the bank had to pay 50 basis points more, rather than 25 basis points more than the Eurodollar rate in the futures markets when it issued its CDs.

Frequently, basis risk is the result of **cross-hedging**, which is hedging with a traded futures contract whose characteristics do not exactly match those of the hedger's risk exposure. For instance, a bank that wishes to hedge its assets for more than 1 year may wish to hedge in the Treasury note rather than the mortgage-backed security futures market because trading in distant futures contracts is more active in the former. However, mortgage rates and Treasury note rates, although closely related, do not always move together. As the spread between the rates changes, so does the basis risk. In general, cross-hedges have more basis risk than hedges involving a precise match between the futures contract and the underlying risk exposure.

RELATED-CONTRACT RISK

Hedges can also fail because of a defect in the contract being hedged. In the bank cost-of-funds example, interest rates conceivably could fall (thereby causing a loss on the short sale of the Eurodollar contracts) and the borrower could prepay the loan. Although commercial loan contracts ordinarily do not allow for prepayments, consumer borrowers frequently prepay their debts. Thus, the bank would lose on the futures contract and would not be receiving compensatory loan revenues.

MANIPULATION RISK

The commodity markets are federally regulated because there have been instances of manipulation. Most manipulations involve **short squeezes**, whereby an individual or group tries to make it difficult or impossible for short sellers in the futures markets to liquidate their contracts through delivery of acceptable commodities. Then the "shorts" must buy their contracts back at inflated prices.

Manipulations can take many forms and are hard to predict. In the early 1970s, a strike at grain elevators in Chicago made it impossible to deliver corn to the elevators as called for by the Chicago Board of Trade's corn contract. As a result, futures prices shot upward even though there was a bumper harvest and cash corn prices were low. In another instance, federal regulation of the pork belly market was initiated after a consortium of buyers executed a short squeeze that caused many public losses. In 1977, the activities of the Hunt family of Texas, who, because of their immense wealth, held contracts for more deliverable bushels of soybeans than were readily available in Chicago, caused a short squeeze in soybeans. Then, in 1980 and 1981, the Hunts attempted to squeeze the silver market. Their activities created a short panic that sent the silver price to more than $50 per ounce before it collapsed following changes in exchange rules.

Because manipulations cannot be foreseen and because they cause large price movements, they add an element of risk to trading in some futures contracts. However, futures that use cash settlement procedures, such as Eurodollar or stock-index futures that allow cash instead of an underlying asset to be delivered at expiration, are safe from short squeezes. With cash settlement, futures prices at expiration are simply marked to market to reflect the value of the underlying assets at the designated settlement time. Thus, such contracts are safe from potential short squeezes because holders of short futures positions do not need to obtain physical commodities (which may be hard to obtain) to deliver to satisfy their open futures contracts' requirements on delivery day.

MARGIN RISK

Someone with illiquid assets can also encounter difficulty by hedging in the futures markets if the futures price moves adversely and the individual must constantly post more maintenance margin funds. This could cause a cash shortage that might force him to liquidate his futures contracts at a loss before the illiquid asset matured. The fact that maintenance margin requirements rise when futures prices move adversely should be taken into account lest they cause an unexpected cash squeeze. This is what happens to Duke and Duke in the Eddie Murphy–Dan Aykroyd, film *Trading Places*. A forward contract is sometimes preferred to a futures contract because forwards do not typically have maintenance margins.

DO YOU UNDERSTAND?

1. Suppose you own a well-diversified stock portfolio currently worth $10,000,000. The portfolio has a beta of 0.8. Assume the S&P 500 futures price is $1,200. Describe in detail the futures transaction you would undertake to hedge the value of your portfolio. How many contracts would you buy or sell?

2. Suppose your company needs to borrow $100 million in 6 months. The CFO is concerned that interest rates might rise in the next few months and wants to hedge the risk. How could you hedge this risk? Describe in detail the futures transaction you would undertake to hedge this risk. What futures contract would you use? How many contracts would you buy or sell? If the CFO is wrong and rates fall in the next few months, will the company be better off or worse off as a result of the hedge?

3. Why does cross-hedging lead to basis risk?

11.6 OPTIONS MARKETS

One drawback of hedging with futures is that the hedging process can totally insulate a firm against price changes. Not only does it reduce the firm's losses if prices move adversely, but it also eliminates potential gains if prices move favorably. Because hedging with futures eliminates gains as well as losses, some people prefer to use options rather than futures contracts to insure themselves against various risks. Options have been available on stocks for many years, and they have been traded on organized exchanges since 1973. Options have been available in the United States on financial futures contracts since October 1982.

THE NATURE OF OPTIONS

Options allow people to enter into contracts to buy or sell stocks, commodities, or other securities at a predetermined price, called the **strike** or **exercise price**, until some future time. Unlike futures contracts in which both the long and the short position have agreed to the transaction (i.e., have an obligation to buy or sell), an option buyer has the right to buy or sell, but not the obligation to buy or sell. The person who sells the option, however, must go through with the transaction if the buyer of the option wants to, that is, if the buyer "exercises" the option. Obviously, the option seller won't agree to such an arrangement unless he or she is compensated. We call the price that an option buyer pays the option seller an **option premium**. In addition, an option is good only for a limited time. With an **American-style option**, the option can be exercised at any time prior to and including the expiration date. With a **European-style option**, the option can be exercised only on the expiration date.

An option provides the buyer with a one-sided choice. If price movements are advantageous, the buyer exercises the option and realizes a gain. If price movements are harmful, the buyer can let the option expire unexercised and lose only the option premium he or she paid. As a result, options can insure the buyer against adverse price moves where the option premium is the price of this insurance.

Calls and Puts.   There are two types of options—calls and puts. In addition, each option has both a buyer (who is long the option) and a seller (or writer, who is short the option). **Call options** give the buyer the right (but not obligation) to *buy* a security or futures contract at the strike price. The writer of a call agrees to sell the security (or futures contract) at the strike price if the buyer exercises the option. **Put options** give the buyer the right (but not obligation) to *sell* a security or futures contract at the strike price. The writer of a put agrees to buy the security (or futures contract) for the strike price if the buyer exercises the option to sell the security (or futures contract).

Exhibit 11.6 shows listed call and put option quotations, including quotations on **LEAPS** (**L**ong-term **E**quity **A**ntici**P**ation **S**ecurities), for selected individual stocks (Ford Motor, Wells Fargo, Apple, and Microsoft). The exhibit shows the expiration month, exercise price (*strike*), option price (or option premium, *last* traded price), trading volume, open interest, and current market price of the underlying stock. *Open interest* is the number of option contracts that have not yet been exercised or have not expired. Ordinary stock options (e.g., Ford Motor and Wells Fargo in Exhibit 11.6) typically expire within 9 months. LEAPS (e.g., Apple and Microsoft in Exhibit 11.6) are long-term options that have expirations up to 2½ years.

Many stocks have both ordinary options and LEAPS. For example, Exhibit 11.6 shows us that on September 24, 2010, when Ford was trading for $12.56 per share (last column), an investor could have purchased a right to buy Ford Motor for $12 per share (strike price) any time up to and including the third Friday of October 2010 (October 2010 options expire on this date) for $0.61 per share. Each option contract is for 100 shares. Thus, the total contract premium is $61 ($0.61 per share × 100 shares).

EXHIBIT 11.6
Sample Stock Option Quotations (September 24, 2010)

Sample of Listed Stock Option Quotations

Option	Expiration	Strike	Call			Put			Underlying Stock Price
			Last	Volume	Open Interest	Last	Volume	Open Interest	
Ford Motor	Oct 2010	$12	$0.61	382	282	$0.05	1,771	678	$ 12.56
Ford Motor	Nov 2010	$12	1.02	435	1,734	0.48	484	3,867	12.56
Wells Fargo	Oct 2010	$23	2.60	21	2,219	0.16	107	35,463	25.59
Wells Fargo	Oct 2010	$28	0.09	527	25,591	2.72	235	14,571	25.59

Sample of LEAP Quotations (Long-Term Options)

Option	Expiration	Strike	Call			Put			Underlying Stock Price
			Last	Volume	Open Interest	Last	Volume	Open Interest	
Apple	Jan 2012	$350	$25.01	189	3,425	$81.15	1	629	$292.32
Apple	Jan 2013	350	41.57	111	641	95	9	55	292.32
Microsoft	Jan 2012	30	1.15	1,266	97,790	7	585	24,716	24.78
Microsoft	Jan 2013	30	2.00	16,804	491	8.06	100	117	24.78

Source: Wall Street Journal Online, September 25, 2010.

Later in this chapter we describe how various characteristics of the option (e.g., time remaining to expiration, exercise price) affect the option premium. Exhibit 11.6 provides a preview of these relationships. Look at the first two lines of the exhibit. The two Ford Motor call options have the same exercise prices, but one has more time to expiration than the other (i.e., November is further away than October). Note that the call option with more time to expiration has a higher option premium. This relationship is also true for put options, which you can see from the exhibit. If all other option characteristics are identical, options with more time to expiration are more valuable. In a similar vein, compare the two Wells Fargo call options listed in the exhibit. Both expire in October 2010, but the call option with the lower exercise price has a higher option premium. If all other call option characteristics are identical, call options with lower exercise prices are more valuable. That is, the right to buy Wells Fargo for $23 per share is more valuable than the right to buy it for $28 per share. For two put options with otherwise identical characteristics, a higher exercise price results in a higher premium, which you can see from the Wells Fargo put option data in the exhibit. We discuss these relationships, as well as others, in more detail later in the chapter.

Option Exercise.   Because the Ford Motor November 2010 option is an American-style option, the buyer can exercise the call at any time up to and including the third Friday in November and buy 100 shares of Ford Motor stock for a price of $1,200 ($12 per share). Clearly, the option would be highly valuable if Ford Motor's price rose to $17 per share before the third Friday in November because the option could be exercised and the stock could quickly be sold for a profit of $5 per share.

Stock options like the Ford Motor option are exchanged for stock, for which the exercise price is paid, when they are exercised. However, there are options that trade on a wide variety of financial instruments and indexes, including stocks, stock indexes, stock-index futures, interest rate futures, currencies, and commodity futures. Options on indexes are usually *cash settled*, meaning that the value of the contract, rather than an asset, is exchanged between the buyer and the seller when the option is exercised. For example, options on the NASDAQ 100 index, which are traded on the Chicago Board of Trade, are cash settled at $100 times the difference between the exercise index level and the value of the index at expiration. If an investor owns a call option on the NASDAQ 100 index with a strike level of 2,410 when the index is 2,420, the option would cash settle for $1,000 ([2,420 − 2,410] × $100).

Futures options exercise into a futures position. For example, when a call option is exercised on the S&P 500 future, the owner surrenders the option and obtains a long position in the futures contract at the strike price. If, for instance, the futures contract is trading at $1,250 when the owner of a $1,200 call exercises his or her option, in exchange for the option, he or she receives a futures contract with a cost basis of 1,200. Because S&P 500 futures are based on $250 per index point, his or her account immediately is credited with a mark-to-market gain of $12,500 ([1,250 − 1,200] × $250 per point gained). If a put option is exercised on a futures contract, the option owner surrenders the option and obtains a short position in the futures contract at the strike price. Thus, if the futures price is at $1,180 and a put is exercised with a strike price of $1,200, the owner has a gain of $5,000 ([1,200 − 1,180] × $250).

EXHIBIT 11.7
Gains and Losses on Options and Futures Contracts, if Options Are Exercised at Expiration

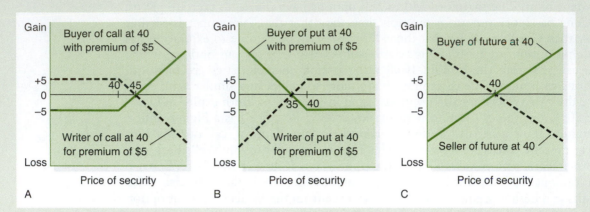

In all of these examples, the gain to the buyer of an option or future equals a loss to the seller (or writer) of the contract, and vice versa. Note that in Frame A, the buyer of a call exercisable at 40 breaks even on the call but loses the $5 premium if the underlying stock is at 40 when the call expires. If the stock is at 45, the $5 gain on the call exactly offsets the $5 premium; thus the net gain is zero. Above 45, the buyer of the call gains, and the writer of the call loses more than the premium and ends up with a loss. In Frame B, puts pay off at expiration in a way that is opposite to calls. Futures, however, have no premium and provide symmetric gains and losses, as shown in Frame C.

Gains and Losses.   Potential gains and losses are quite different for buyers and writers of puts and calls. They also differ for options and futures contracts. Exhibit 11.7 illustrates this. Frame A shows how gains and losses vary as the underlying security price changes for the buyer and the writer of a call option on a security with a strike price of $40 and a premium of $5 if the option is exercised on expiration day. The call buyer's potential gain is unlimited and the writer's potential loss is unlimited if the security price rises. Meanwhile, if the security price falls, the buyer's maximum loss is limited to the premium paid for the option, whereas the call option writer's maximum gain is limited to the premium paid for the option. Put options are similar, as shown in Frame B, except that the put buyer gains when the security price declines and the put buyer loses the amount of the premium if the security price rises. In contrast with options, buyers and sellers of futures gain and lose symmetrically and without limits as futures prices vary. This is illustrated in Frame C.

Covered and Naked Options.   Because the option writer's maximum loss is almost unlimited, many option writers write **covered options** wherein they already own the security that they have agreed to sell or have already sold short the security that they have agreed to buy. Option writers may also write **naked** (that is, uncovered) **options**. In this case, they need not own an offsetting security position. However, writers of naked options typically must deposit margin requirements with the exchange to guarantee that they will honor their commitments. If the underlying security price moves adversely, writers of naked options must deposit additional money to maintain their margin requirements.

The Value of Options. The option premium varies with changes in the price of the underlying asset. For example, a right to buy Wells Fargo for $23 per share is more valuable if Wells Fargo is currently trading for $28 per share than if Wells Fargo is trading for $18 per share. Similarly, for a given strike price, a put increases in value as the price of the stock declines.

Similarly, the right to buy Wells Fargo for $20 per share is more valuable than the right to buy Wells Fargo for $30 per share (holding everything else equal). That is, the lower the strike price, the greater the value of the call. The right to sell Wells Fargo for $20 per share is less valuable than the right to sell Wells Fargo for $30 per share (holding everything else equal). And, as a result, the greater the strike price, the greater the value of the put.

Both put and call values increase with (1) price volatility (variance) of the underlying security and (2) the time to the option's expiration. The greater the price variability of the underlying stock, the greater the chance that the buyer can exercise the option for a larger profit. However, the buyer never exercises the option if it would cause her to take a loss (ignoring the sunk cost of the premium). Consider a simple example of call options (with a $55 strike price) on two hypothetical stocks: A and B both currently sell for $50 per share. Stock A has a 50 percent chance of falling to $40 and a 50 percent chance of rising to $60 prior to expiration. More volatile stock B has a 50 percent chance of rising to $70 and a 50 percent chance of falling to $30. If either stock falls in value (to $40 in the case of stock A or $30 in the case of stock B), you wouldn't exercise the option and simply lose the premium you paid. If either increases, however, you would exercise that option. Stock B would pay out $15 (i.e., $70 less the $55 strike price) while stock A would pay out only $5 (i.e., $60 less the $55 strike price). Clearly, an option on stock B is more valuable, and therefore stock B's call premium would be greater.

The longer the time to expiration, the greater the premium. It is more likely, for example, that Google's price will double (or fall in half) over the next 3 years than over the next 3 days. Thus, longer-term options are more valuable than shorter-term options. As already noted, for instance, the Ford Motor November 2010 calls (selling for $1.02; see Exhibit 11.6) are more valuable than the October 2010 calls (selling for $0.61).

Interest rates also have a small impact on call and put values. Because the purchase of an option allows the buyer to conserve capital until the option is actually exercised and the underlying stock or commodity is purchased, call options on stocks have a higher value when interest rates are high. If a buyer purchases a call option instead of a stock and then invests the money saved, the buyer still shares in the price appreciation of the stock but earns more on the invested funds when interest rates are high. Thus, buyers are willing to pay more for options when interest rates are high, particularly if the option has a long time to maturity. In contrast, put values are inversely related to interest rates.

Finally, because stock options are not protected against dividend payouts, call options lose value (and put options gain value) when a company distributes some of its assets as dividends to shareholders and thereby reduces its stock's price.

The value of an option changes over time in a systematic manner, as shown in Exhibit 11.8, which applies to a call option with a stock price of 100. As shown in line A, just before expiration, the value of a call is equal to its **intrinsic value**, or the value that could be realized by exercising the option immediately. A call option's intrinsic value is equal either to the value of the underlying asset minus the exercise price or to zero (whichever is greater). However, before expiration an option has an additional time value, as shown in line B. The time value of an option usually is

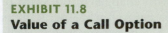

EXHIBIT 11.8
Value of a Call Option

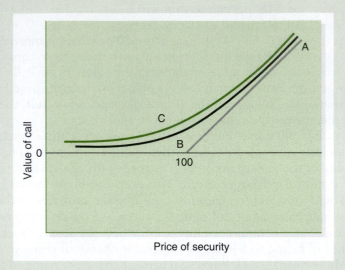

Options have a time premium that exceeds their intrinsic value by a greater amount as the volatility of the underlying security or the time to expiration increases. As an option approaches expiration, its value experiences time decay until it is worth only its intrinsic value.

A—value at expiration (intrinsic value)
B—value shortly before expiration
C—value substantially before expiration

positive prior to expiration. Even if the option has an intrinsic value of zero (as in Exhibit 11.8, when the stock price is 90 and the exercise price is 90 or 100), as long as the underlying asset is sufficiently volatile and there is enough time left until expiration, the option has a chance of becoming valuable before it expires. The time value of an option reflects this chance. Because the chances that an option become valuable before expiration are greater the longer the time to expiration, the option value is higher if there is a longer time to expiration or the stock is more volatile (see line C). Conversely, because there is less chance that the option can still become valuable as expiration approaches, the option value experiences *time decay* and loses value as expiration approaches, shifting from line C to line B. Finally, when the option is due to expire, it retains only its intrinsic value, as shown by line A.

OPTIONS VERSUS FUTURES

The gains and losses to buyers and sellers of futures contracts are quite different from those for buyers and sellers of option contracts (see Exhibit 11.7). For futures, both gains and losses can vary almost without limit. Therefore, some buyers (or sellers) prefer options to futures contracts. For instance, suppose a portfolio manager thinks that interest rates will decline, but he or she is not sure. To take advantage of the rate decline, the manager might want to buy long-term bonds that would increase in value as rates fell. However, if rates rose, the bond would lose value and the manager might lose his or her job. If the manager hedged in the futures market by selling T-bond futures, he or she would be safe if rates rose because the loss on the bonds in the portfolio would be offset by the gain on the short sale of the T-bond futures. If rates fell, however, the gain on the bond portfolio due to the fall in interest rates (that the manager was trying to take advantage of) would be offset by the loss on the T-bond futures.

Thus, this portfolio manager might prefer to buy a T-bond put option. If rates rose and T-bond prices fell, the put option would rise in value and offset the loss on the bond portfolio. However, if rates fell, as expected, the market value of the bonds would rise and the manager could let the T-bond put expire unused—thereby losing only the premium. Similar measures could be used by thrift institution managers who want to buy protection against unexpected rises in interest rates that could lower the value of their mortgage portfolios. Options, then, give a one-sided type of price protection that is not available from futures. The premiums on options may be high, however, and options experience time decay. The potential buyer of the protection must decide whether the insurance value provided by the option is worth its price.

DO YOU UNDERSTAND?

1. What are some considerations in the decision to use futures or options for hedging?

2. Explain the intuition of the relationship between the time to expiration for a put option and the value of the option.

3. Explain the intuition of the relationship between the price volatility of an asset and the value of an option written on that asset.

4. If you hold some shares of stock and would like to protect yourself from a price decline without sacrificing a lot of upside potential, should you purchase call options or put options? Explain.

THE CFTC

The primary regulator of the futures markets is the Commodity Futures Trading Commission (CFTC), a five-member federal commission whose members are appointed to staggered 5-year terms by the president with the consent of the Senate. The CFTC was formed in 1974 to centralize government regulation of the futures markets.

The CFTC monitors futures trading to detect actual or potential manipulation, congestion, and price distortion. It reviews proposed contracts to see if they have an economic purpose and analyzes the terms of proposed trading contracts to ensure that they meet commercial needs and serve the public interest. It also monitors enforcement of exchange rules, registers industry professionals, and audits brokerage houses and clearing associations. Finally, it investigates alleged violations of CFTC regulations and the Commodity Exchange Act and refers apparent violations of federal laws to the Justice Department for prosecution.

The extensive enforcement responsibilities of the CFTC suggest that a major purpose of the commission is to prevent abuse of the public through misrepresentation

11.7
REGULATION OF THE FUTURES AND OPTIONS MARKETS

or market manipulation. In the past, such abuses occurred with some frequency. Because of the low margin requirements relative to the value of futures contracts, it is possible for large amounts of money to be made (or lost) with only small price movements. In addition, the zero-sum nature of the commodity markets means that, unlike the stock market, if one person gains, another loses. Thus wild trading activities sometimes occur in the futures markets, and it is the CFTC's job to ensure that the public is not harmed by violations of exchange rules or federal laws.

THE SEC

The Securities and Exchange Commission (SEC) regulates options markets that have equity securities as underlying assets. Thus, the SEC regulates all individual stock options traded on the Chicago Board Options Exchange as well as all **stock-index options**, which are based on the value of an underlying index of stocks. The CFTC, however, regulates all options that are settled with the delivery of a futures contract, even if that contract is eventually settled based on the value of an index of stocks. For instance, the CFTC regulates the S&P 500 options contracts traded on the Chicago Mercantile Exchange (CME) because those options involve the purchase or sale of futures contracts for the S&P 500 stock index. In contrast, the SEC regulates the S&P 500 index options contracts traded on the Chicago Board Options Exchange (CBOE) because those options involve immediate payments based on the current value of the underlying stocks in the S&P 500 index. However, the SEC and CFTC jointly regulate individual stock futures and narrowly based stock-index futures.

The confusing state of regulation for stock-index products caused turf wars between the SEC and CFTC, particularly after the October 1987 stock market crash, when the SEC maintained that it should be the sole regulator of stocks and all contracts that derived their value from stock price movements. Congress did not go along with the SEC proposal, however, and the CFTC remains the sole regulator of broad-based stock-index futures contracts.

EXCHANGE REGULATION

The commodity exchanges also impose many rules on their members. The rules are designed to ensure that members keep proper accounts, maintain sufficient funds on deposit with the exchange clearinghouse, and do not engage in practices that could affect the ability of the exchange to honor its contracts or otherwise endanger the financial solvency of the exchange. In addition, exchange rules determine trading procedures, contract terms, maximum daily price movements for commodities, margin requirements, and position limits. Position limits impose maximum contract holdings for any one speculator and are designed to prevent manipulation of the futures markets.

Because the commodity exchanges have numerous rules designed to regulate trading behavior, they argue that federal regulation of futures market activities is unnecessary. The counterargument is that the exchanges are organized to serve the purposes of their members, not the public. If push comes to shove, the public may lose.

The exchanges' laxity in enforcing rules was illustrated in early 1989, when an FBI sting operation found that many exchange rules had been violated over a long period of time. As a result, many exchange members and traders were subpoenaed and numerous changes in futures market regulation and monitoring systems were proposed. Subsequently, the exchanges adapted their computer systems to be able to determine more quickly and effectively when all transactions occur and to prevent prearranged trades from taking place.

In recent years, the derivative contract that has had the greatest economic impact is the **swap**—particularly the role of credit default swaps (CDSs) in the financial market meltdown of 2008 and resulting recession. Let's begin, however, with a discussion of traditional swap contracts.

11.8 SWAP MARKETS

In a traditional *swap contract*, two parties agree to exchange payment obligations on two underlying financial liabilities that are equal in principal amount but differ in payment patterns. A swap works much like a forward contract in that it guarantees the exchange of two items of value between counterparties at some time (or at several times) in the future. Unlike the forward market, however, a swap is usually arranged for only a *net* transfer of funds. For instance, if Patty (the first party to a swap) owes JoAnn (the other side of the swap) 4 percent interest on a **notional principal** of $1 million and JoAnn owes Patty 3 percent interest on the same notional principal, they need only exchange the difference, or $10,000, to settle the interest difference due on the $1 million swap. The principal amount is notional (or fictional) in that the $1 million is never actually transferred between counterparties; it serves only as the basis for calculating the swapped interest payments.

Also, unlike a forward contract, the exact terms of trade are usually not pre-specified, but rather they typically vary with interest rates, exchange rates, or some other future price. For instance, Patty may pay a 4 percent fixed-interest rate on the notional principal to JoAnn, whereas JoAnn may pay Patty 2 percent over the T-bill rate, which would be 3 percent if the T-bill rate were 1 percent, but could vary over time.

Swaps are most frequently used to offset interest rate risk by exchanging fixed interest rate payments for variable interest rate payments. In addition, swaps may also be used to offset the risk of future foreign currency flows (such as the income that a firm expects to receive from a foreign subsidiary or foreign investment) or the risk that foreign interest rates may move differently from domestic interest rates.

There is some theoretical debate about why swap opportunities exist. It may be that some institutions have information-cost, transaction-cost, or location advantages in raising or lending funds in certain sectors of the credit markets; however, the sectors that each serves may not be well matched internally. For example, assume that a commercial bank sold $50 million in long-term 10-year individual retirement account (IRA) CDs paying 3 percent interest. This bank's assets (such as commercial loans), however, are short term. Thus, the bank would face interest rate risk. If market rates fell, it would earn lower rates on its short-term assets and might not be able to afford the fixed rate of interest it had agreed to pay to its IRA depositors for the next 10 years.

The bank can offset its potential interest rate risk, however, by entering into a swap with an institution that has too many long-term assets, such as a mortgage-oriented savings association. Thus, let us assume that the bank enters into a swap agreement in which it arranges to make short-term interest payments at a rate equal to the London Interbank Offering Rate (LIBOR) minus $\frac{1}{8}$ percent in exchange for a fixed-interest return of 3¾ percent for 10 years on a notional principal of $50 million. The savings bank, in turn, offers to pay a fixed rate of 3¾ percent for 10 years in return for a variable rate of return equal to LIBOR minus $\frac{1}{8}$ percent on $50 million. The swap is diagrammed in Exhibit 11.9.

EXHIBIT 11.9
Example of a Swap

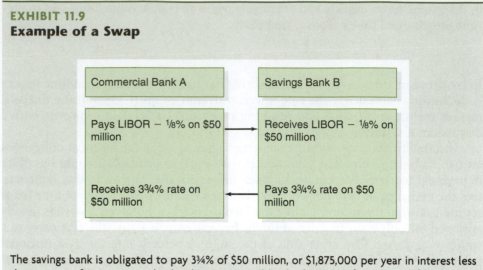

The savings bank is obligated to pay 3¾% of $50 million, or $1,875,000 per year in interest less the amount of interest owed it by the commercial bank. If LIBOR −⅛% equals 3¾%, no net interest payment is required. However, if LIBOR averages 4⅞%, the commercial bank must pay the savings bank 1% (4⅞% − ⅛% − 3¾%) of $50 million ($500,000). Conversely, if LIBOR rates average 1⅞% throughout the year, the savings bank must pay the net difference: (3¾% − [1⅞% − ⅛%]) × $50 million, or $1 million to the commercial bank in that year.

The swap can be advantageous to both parties. For instance, a bank with good credit can usually borrow funds at the LIBOR rate, so it earns a $\frac{1}{8}$ percent profit on its short-term funding of the $50 million (because it pays the savings association $\frac{1}{8}$ percent less than LIBOR). In addition, it earns a $\frac{3}{4}$ percent spread (a 3¾ percent fixed return from the swap less the 3 percent interest cost paid on the CDs) on its long-term IRA deposits. The savings association, in turn, is likely to have a portfolio of mortgages on which it earns 4¾ percent, so it can make a sure profit by agreeing to make 3¾ percent interest payments for 10 years. Furthermore, because savings banks can usually pay as much as 1 percent less than LIBOR to their retail depositors, the savings bank can be assured that it will generally be able to add to its profits by issuing short-term retail deposits to fund its LIBOR minus $\frac{1}{8}$ percent interest rate obligation. The key to making the swap work is that the savings bank has a relative cost advantage in issuing short-term deposits and making long-term mortgage loans, while the commercial bank has a cost advantage in making short-term commercial loans and, temporarily, in issuing long-term IRA deposits.

Theoretically, the risks involved in a traditional swap are not great, as it may first seem. Because only the net difference in interest payments is exchanged, if one party defaults, the potential loss is just a small rate difference, not the entire notional principal. Credit risk does exist, however, and defaults are more likely when the rate movement is disadvantageous to the defaulting party.

SWAP DEALERS

Because credit evaluation of potential counterparties is required to reduce the risks of swaps, and because it is difficult for individual parties to agree on the exact amount, timing, and rate-determination characteristics of swaps, an extensive dealer market has developed in swaps. Historically, commercial banks are among the most active participants in the swaps market (due to their easy access to money markets and foreign currency markets and their ability to assess credit risks), accompanied by investment banks; insurance companies; and, to some degree, foreign exchange dealers. By the end of 2008, the swaps market was estimated to have exceeded $600 trillion (or approximately 10 times the world's total gross domestic product) in notional principal!

Each dealer in the swaps market runs a book of swaps for which it serves as a counterparty. The dealer tries to keep its book as closely matched as possible with respect to short-term or long-term interest rate exposures, foreign currency exposures, or floating-rate-index exposures. If its book is temporarily mismatched, the dealer usually tries to hedge any residual exposure in the financial futures or options markets.

Swap dealers take some risk running their book because they may not be able to match it perfectly or because they may experience the unexpected default of a counterparty at a time when it is expensive to replicate that counterparty's position at low cost. Because of their risks and the fact that they provide a service by matching counterparties' needs, swap dealers usually charge a fee equal to five to ten basis points (0.05 to 0.10 percent) of the notional principal of a swap.

CREDIT DEFAULT SWAPS

Credit default swaps (CDSs) played in important role in the financial crisis of 2008. First, a little background and a lot of acronyms. Recall that most mortgages are securitized. That is, financial institutions (including banks) make loans and then pool those loans to sell to investors through **mortgage-backed securities (MBSs)**. In some cases, these mortgage-backed securities were used to form **collateralized debt obligations (CDOs)**. In a traditional (or cash) collateralized debt obligation, a pool of assets (in this case, mortgage-backed securities) is held by a corporate entity, known as a special purpose entity (SPE). The entity then issues a number of claims (known as **tranches**) to the cash flows created by this pool of assets. Investors in the higher tranches are the first to get paid (i.e., lowest risk). Investors in lower tranches are promised higher yields but face greater risk. Credit agencies provide credit ratings for each tranche.

Of course, the risk to an investor in a collateralized debt obligation is that homeowners start defaulting on the underlying mortgages at a greater rate than expected and the promised payment from the tranches cannot be met. A number of companies, however, were willing to insure this risk in the form of credit default swaps. In a credit default swap, the investors in a collateralized debt obligation paid the counterparty a premium for the counterparty's guarantee that in the event of a credit event (such as a bankruptcy or restructuring), the investors would receive payment for the counterparty. Consider a very simple example: Assume you invest $1,000 in a bond issued by XYZ Corporation and enter a credit default swap with a 2 percent spread for 2 years with a swap dealer. Thus, you pay the swap dealer $20 (0.02 × $1,000) now. If XYZ does not default this year, you pay another $20 to the swap dealer next year. If XYZ *does* default in the second year (and the bond ends up worthless), the swap dealer will pay you $1,000.

Thus, credit default swaps look a lot like insurance—effectively, you are paying someone to take on the risk of default. Technically, however, there are a number of differences between the legal definitions of insurance (which is a highly regulated industry) and credit default swaps (which, as discussed below, is traditionally a highly unregulated industry). First, if credit default swaps were called insurance, they would be subject to insurance regulations. Because they are not technically insurance, there are essentially no capital requirements. Thus, a company

PEOPLE & EVENTS

Swap Market Regulation

Traditionally, swap markets have had very little regulation with no central clearinghouse or regulatory agency. Prior to 2000, there was some legal uncertainty regarding the regulation of swaps. That uncertainty was removed with the Commodity Futures Modernization Act of 2000. Specifically, the act was based on the following arguments: (1) swaps occur primarily in the over-the-counter (OTC) market (as opposed to an organized exchange), (2) swaps occur primarily between sophisticated investors, (3) regulation of the swap market would hurt the United States by driving the swap business offshore, and (4) uncertainty regarding the legal status of swaps may hurt the U.S. economy. As a result, the Commodity Futures Modernization Act made it clear that over-the-counter derivatives (such as swaps) were not subject to the rules of the Commodities Exchange Act (such as exchange trading and clearing) or U.S. securities law as long as the counterparties were "eligible contract participants"

(roughly, those with greater than $10 million in total assets).

Given the role of swaps in the subprime meltdown and ensuing recession, the Dodd-Frank Wall Street Reform and Consumer Protection Act (signed into law in July 2010) completely reshapes the regulation of the swaps market to increase transparency and reduce systemic risk (risk that threatens the entire market). Specifically, the law means five major changes for the swap market. First, most contracts will have to go through a central clearinghouse so that it is clear what, exactly, is each participant's net position. Second, such clearable swaps will have to be executed through an exchange (versus the over-the-counter market). Third, swap dealers will have to post margin (much like futures and options). Fourth, swap dealers and major swap participants will be subject to capital requirements. Fifth, swap dealers and major swap participants will have to register with the CFTC and/or the SEC.

may mistakenly believe that the risk of widespread default on mortgages is extremely unlikely and therefore write a lot of insurance in the form of credit default swaps. Second, unlike traditional insurance, an investor can buy a credit default swap even if the investor does not own the underlying asset. This allows investors to, effectively, make a bet that homeowners would eventually default on the loans. Because these speculators don't hold any of the underlying mortgages they are buying insurance on (i.e., the investors were "naked"), they are simply using credit default swaps to make bets (that homeowners would default) rather than hedge bets (i.e., buying insurance on mortgages they held).

As the real estate market declined dramatically in the post-2007 period, companies who had written credit default swaps were suddenly on the hook for billions of dollars. For example, AIG (at the time one of the largest insurance companies in the world), reported a $13.2 billion loss in the first 6 months of 2008. Because of AIG's size and the government's concern that a major default in the credit default swap market would freeze liquidity, the U.S. government made an $85 billion loan to AIG in September 2008 and, in return, received approximately 80 percent ownership of AIG.

Credit default swaps also played a role in restructuring the investment banking industry (see Chapter 18). For example, some media reports suggest that the rapid increase in the price of insuring Bear Stearns bonds (also known as the Bear Stearns credit default swap spread) made investors concerned that Bear Stearns was going to default and therefore withdrew cash from Bear Stearns. This, in turn, led to a "run on the bank" that caused Bear Stearns to run out of cash.

SUMMARY OF LEARNING OBJECTIVES

1 Explain the characteristics of forwards, futures, options, and swaps. *Forward contracts* and *futures contracts* are agreements between two parties to exchange a specified amount of an asset for a predetermined price at a predetermined point in time in the future. An *option contract* grants the option buyer the right to buy (*call*) or sell (*put*) a specified amount of an asset for a specified price for a specified period of time. A *swap contract* involves two parties exchanging periodic payments for a predetermined length of time.

2 Explain how market participants use derivative securities. *Derivatives markets* allow people to guarantee the price of future transactions with greater certainty. They can be used either by hedgers, to reduce risk, or by speculators, who assume risk in hopes of earning a return.

3 Describe the advantages and disadvantages of each derivative security. Regulated futures and options markets differ from forward markets in that they involve the trading of standardized contracts on organized exchanges by people who typically don't know who has taken the opposite side of their transactions and look only to the exchange to guarantee their contracts.

4 Discuss the risks involved in using futures contracts to hedge an underlying risk exposure. Basis risk, related-contract risk, and manipulation risk may all affect the returns to hedging with standardized exchange-listed contracts. Counterparty default risk must be guarded against in over-the-counter forward and options markets.

5 Discuss why some people prefer options to forward or futures contracts, and why options protect against risk only if someone pays a price—the option "premium." Options markets provide an opportunity for one-sided returns in exchange for the payment of a *premium* to the seller of the option. The premium is much like an insurance premium. Call option premiums increase with uncertainty, interest rates, and the time to maturity of each option. Option prices also increase as an option becomes more *in-the-money*, which means that the intrinsic value is greater than zero.

6 Explain how swaps work. Swaps markets involve two parties agreeing to exchange payment obligations. Swap terms may vary with future foreign or domestic interest rates or foreign exchange rates. Because of their great flexibility in transferring interest rate or currency risk, swaps markets have grown explosively since 1982.

7 Explain how the Dodd-Frank Wall Street Reform and Consumer Protection Act affects the way swaps will be traded in the future. Swaps have traditionally been traded in largely unregulated over-the-counter-markets similar to forward markets. As a result of the Dodd-Frank Wall Street Reform and Consumer Protection Act passed in 2010, however, swap markets will be more like futures and options markets in the future, for example, trading on exchanges, requiring a margin, and centralized clearing.

KEY TERMS

Derivative security	Margin	Basis risk	Naked options
Forward contract	Open interest	Cross-hedging	Intrinsic value
Forward price	Initial margin	Short squeezes	Stock-index options
Spot price	Maintenance margin	Options	Swap
Long position	Margin call	Strike (or exercise) price	Notional principals
Short position	Open-outcry	Option premium	Credit default swaps
Settlement date	Hedgers	American-style option	(CDSs)
Counterparty	Speculators	European-style option	Mortgage-backed
Spot market	Spreads (or straddles)	Call options	securities (MBSs)
Futures contracts	Traders	Put options	Collateralized debt
Futures exchange	Stock-index futures	LEAPS	obligations (CDOs)
Marking-to-market	contracts	Covered options	Tranches

QUESTIONS AND PROBLEMS

1. What are the differences between futures and forward markets? What are the pros and cons associated with using each one?

2. What role does the exchange play in futures market transactions?

3. How can a thrift institution guarantee its costs of funds for a period of time by using the futures markets?

4. Why do you think some futures contracts are more widely traded than others?

5. What agency is the chief regulator of futures markets? Why is federal regulation necessary?

6. Explain the difference between a put and a call. Draw a diagram showing the payoffs of puts and calls at expiration. Draw it from the perspective of both the option buyer and the option seller.

7. Why do you think exchanges are more concerned with writers of naked options than with writers of covered options?

8. Explain the difference in the gain and loss potential of a call option and a long futures position. Under what circumstances do you think someone would prefer the option to the future, or vice versa?

9. Futures contracts on stock indexes are very popular. Why do you think that is so? How do you think they might be used?

10. Assume that, in March, a farmer and a baker enter into a forward contract on 1,000 bushels of wheat at a price of $3.00 per bushel for delivery in September. In September the spot price of wheat is $2.50 per bushel. Who has profited from entering into the forward contract and who has lost? How much is the gain and how much is the loss?

11. Assume the initial margin on a Eurodollar futures contract is $878 and the maintenance margin is $650 (the contract size is $1 million). If the contract price declines by 25 basis points, by how much do the long and short positions' margin balances change? Which position, if any, gets a margin call?

12. Refer to Exhibit 11.6. What is the time value and what is the intrinsic value of a call option on Wells Fargo with a strike price of $23.00 and an October expiration? What is the time value and what is the intrinsic value of a put option on Wells Fargo with a strike price of $23.00 and an October expiration?

13. A bank has entered into an interest rate swap. The swap has a notional principal amount of $100 million and calls for the bank to make annual fixed interest rate payments of 5 percent and to receive an annual floating interest rate payment of LIBOR plus 2 percent. If LIBOR is 1 percent, what payment will the bank make or receive?

14. Do you think swap contracts will have more or less counterparty default risk after the rules in the Dodd-Frank Wall Street Reform and Consumer Protection Act are implemented? Why?

INTERNET EXERCISE

CME Group and the CBOE have excellent Web sites where people can obtain educational information, contract information, delayed quotes, and market volume and open-interest data for the futures and options products traded on their exchanges (www.cmegroup.com and www.cboe.com). Go to each site and find the following:

1. At the CBOE, find out what day of the month the SPX (S&P 500) and the OEX (S&P 100) options, respectively, obtain their settlement prices (look for index options specifications).

2. At the CME, find the principal value for the 1-month Eurodollar futures and the principal value for the 30-day federal funds future.

3. At the CME, there is a futures traded on Non-farm Payroll (under "Economic Events"). Look at the contract speculations and describe what exactly this contract does.

4. At the CME Web site, find the initial and maintenance margin requirements for the 13-week U.S. T-bill futures.

5. At the CME Web site, click on the careers tab and describe what jobs are available for recent college graduates at the CME group.

International Markets

ENGLISH IS THE INTERNATIONAL language for airlines. If there were not a single language, imagine the difficulty pilots would have, with nearly 250 languages spoken in the world. Similarly, for U.S. citizens and businesses, it would be nice if the whole world used the U.S. dollar to conduct business transactions. Then U.S. citizens would never have to worry about the dollar value of revenues denominated in foreign currencies, the dollar value of assets they own abroad, or the dollar cost of materials they obtain from foreign sources. This would make accounting and planning much easier for all people who invest or do business internationally.

Unfortunately, people around the world are not willing to use a foreign currency to conduct their domestic transactions. Consequently, the world's citizens and businesses use many different currencies. The fact that U.S. business firms conduct business in foreign countries introduces additional risks for domestic businesses.

Hong Kong is one of the leading international business centers, best known for its unbridled, free-market, capitalist economy. It is also one of the world's most important foreign exchange markets. Foreign exchange trading is in the trillions of dollars worldwide, and transactions take place 24 hours a day, every day of the year.

This chapter examines the major economic and political forces that influence foreign exchange markets. To reduce currency risk, foreign exchange markets developed so people can convert their cash to different currencies as they conduct business or personal affairs. Furthermore, because payments across borders can be difficult to enforce and creditworthiness can be hard to assess, elaborate credit procedures have developed to facilitate international loans and financing. This chapter discusses how commercial banks play a major role in financing and arranging foreign exchange transactions because of their expertise in financing business, checking credit, and transferring money. In addition, investment banks and foreign exchange dealers play important roles in the foreign currency markets. Finally, a number of organizations have developed to help reduce some of the risks of international trade. ■

LEARNING OBJECTIVES

1 Explain the types of risks that U.S. firms face when engaging in international trade.

2 Explain how a country can run a deficit in its balance of trade and still have a strong currency, given the conventional wisdom suggesting that a trade deficit should lead to a decline in a currency's value.

3 Explain the main functions of foreign exchange markets.

4 Explain why the Eurodollar deposit and Eurobond markets have become so important in recent years.

5 Explain why Europe introduced the euro as its currency.

12.1 THE DIFFICULTIES OF INTERNATIONAL TRADE

When U.S. manufacturers need to buy raw materials, they want to get the best possible deal. Hence, they investigate several potential suppliers to determine the availability and quality of materials from each, how long it takes to receive an order, and the total delivered price. When all potential suppliers are located in the United States, comparison of the alternatives is relatively easy. Both suppliers and customers keep their books, price their goods and services, and pay their employees in the same currency—the U.S. dollar. Furthermore, because the federal government regulates interstate commerce, it is unlikely that there will be any problems in shipping between states. If a dispute arises, the buyer and the seller are governed by the same legal traditions and have access to the same federal court system.

When potential suppliers are not located in the United States, comparisons are more difficult because the evaluation process is complicated by at least three factors. The first problem is that the American buyer prefers to pay for the purchase with dollars, but the foreign supplier must pay employees and other local expenses with its domestic currency. Hence, one of the two parties to the transaction is forced to deal in a foreign currency. The second difficulty is that no single country has total authority over all aspects of the transactions. Nations may erect barriers to control international product and capital flows, such as high tariffs and controls on foreign exchange. Also, countries may have distinctly different legal traditions—such as the English common law used in the United States or the French civil law, which is encountered in many other nations. Finally, banks and other lending agencies often find it difficult to obtain reliable information on which to base credit decisions in many countries.

12.2 EXCHANGE RATES

The first complicating factor mentioned previously—comparing suppliers who price their goods in currency units other than the U.S. dollar—is the easiest to overcome. To make such comparisons, the American buyer can check the appropriate exchange rate quotation in the foreign exchange market. An **exchange rate** is simply the price of one monetary unit, such as the British pound, stated in terms of another currency unit, such as the U.S. dollar.

As an example of how exchange rates facilitate comparisons, assume that the American manufacturer has to pay $190 per ton for steel purchased in the United States and £116 per ton for steel bought from a British supplier. Furthermore, a Japanese steel company is willing to sell steel for ¥20,000 per ton. Which supplier should the American firm choose?

If the exchange rate between dollars and pounds is $1.65/£, British steel costs (£116) × ($1.65/£) = $191.40. At this dollar price, the American firm prefers to buy steel from the American supplier. If the exchange rate between the yen and the dollar is ¥110/$, the Japanese steel costs (¥20,000)/(¥110/$) = $181.82 per ton. Assuming that the price quotation of ¥20,000 includes all transportation costs and tariffs, or that the sum of those costs is less than $8.18, the American manufacturer finds it cheaper to purchase steel from the Japanese supplier. Hence, the contract is awarded to the Japanese steel company, and dollars are exchanged for yen in the foreign exchange market to make the purchase.

However, exchange rates are not constant. Today, most exchange rates are free to move up and down in response to changes in the underlying economic environment. If for some reason the exchange rate between the dollar and the pound falls from $1.65/£ to $1.50/£, British steel could be bought for (£116) × ($1.50/£) = $174.00. Now the British firm becomes the low-cost supplier even though it has done nothing itself to lower its price. See Exhibit 12.1 for a summary of the steel purchase analysis.

Notice that now it takes fewer dollars to buy one British pound, or conversely, more pounds are needed to purchase one U.S. dollar. It is correct to say that the

EXHIBIT 12.1
Foreign Exchange Rates and the Price of Steel in International Markets

Supplier	Price in Local Currency	Foreign Exchange Rate	Conversion to Price in U.S. $	Price of Steel in U.S. $
American	$190	—	—	$190.00
English	£116	$1.65/£	£116 × $1.65/£ =	$191.40
Japanese	¥20,000	¥110/$	¥20,000/¥110/$ =	$181.82
English	£116	$1.50/£	£116 × $1.50/£ =	$174.00

value of the pound has fallen against the dollar or that the value of the dollar has risen against the pound. These two statements are equivalent. Both statements indicate that goods and services priced in pounds are now cheaper to someone holding dollars or that purchases priced in dollars are now more expensive to someone holding pounds. In our example, initially £1 was worth $1.65. As the value of the pound fell relative to the dollar, £1 was now worth only $1.50. Because it has decreased in value relative to the dollar, it has **depreciated**. Conversely, the dollar has **appreciated** because it has increased in value relative to the pound.

Note that if the price of the British steel remains unchanged, the demand for a country's products (British steel) is higher when the country's exchange rate declines relative to other currencies. The reduction in the exchange rate for the pound from $1.65/£ to $1.50/£ led to a reversal of the purchase decisions; at $1.65/£, British steel was the most expensive, but when the exchange rate fell to $1.50/£, it was the cheapest.

CURRENCY QUOTATIONS

Exhibit 12.2 shows the foreign exchange rate quotations for all major currencies as shown in the *Wall Street Journal* on February 14, 2011. Column 2, labeled U.S. $ Equivalent, shows how much U.S. currency exchanges for one British pound or Brazilian real; in other words, it shows how much U.S. currency it takes to buy one unit of foreign currency. For example, it takes $1.60 (rounded to the nearest penny) to buy one British pound today (for now, ignore the forward rates), 60¢ to buy one Brazilian real, and a little over 1¢ to buy a Japanese yen.

Column 3, labeled Currency per U.S. $, shows how much foreign currency trades for one U.S. dollar; that is, how much foreign money it takes to buy one American dollar. For example, $1 would get you about 62 British pence, 1.67 Brazilian reals, or 83.47 Japanese yen.

For the major world currencies such as the U.S. dollar, the British pound, and the Japanese yen, the *Wall Street Journal* lists both the spot rate (current price) and the forward rates for 1 month, 3 months, and 6 months. The spot rate is what you pay to buy currency today—it's today's price for the currency. *Forward prices*, as the name implies, are what you pay for currency if you sign a contract today to buy the currency on a date in the future, such as 1 month or 3 months from now. In making foreign business transactions, many businesses buy currencies forward because they anticipate they will need foreign currencies in the future. By contracting now to buy or sell foreign currencies at some date in the future, the business locks in the cost of foreign exchange at the beginning of the transaction and does not have to worry about the risk of an unfavorable movement in the exchange rate in the future.

The last currency listed in Exhibit 12.2 is the **euro**, which is the common currency for 17 of the 27 member states of the European Union (EU), including Austria, Belgium, Cyprus, Estonia, Finland, France, Germany, Greece, Ireland, Italy, Luxembourg, Malta, the Netherlands, Portugal, Slovakia, Slovenia, and Spain. When the euro was first introduced in January 1999, people could write checks and get loans in the new currency but could not make cash transactions in euros. After a 2-year transition period, national currencies like the French franc and the German mark were taken out of circulation. Today, cash transactions use euro bills and coins.

The original 11 members of the Economic and Monetary Union (EMU) were Austria, Belgium, Finland, France, Germany, Ireland, Italy, Luxembourg, the Netherlands, Portugal, and Spain. On January 1, 2001, Greece became the twelfth member of the EMU. The other three original members of the EU, Denmark, Great Britain, and Sweden, have chosen not to adopt the euro as their currency.

EXHIBIT 12.2
Selected Foreign Exchange Quotations (February 14, 2011)

Country (Currency)	U.S. $ Equivalent	Currency per U.S. $
Argentina (peso)	0.2488	4.0193
Australia (dollar)	1.0021	0.9979
Brazil (real)	0.6004	1.6656
Canada (dollar)	1.0105	0.9896
Chile (peso)	0.0021	472.37
China (yuan)	0.1517	6.5919
Hong Kong (dollar)	0.1283	7.7955
Hungary (forint)	0.005	200.04
India (rupee)	0.0219	45.62
Japan (yen)	0.012	83.47
1 month forward	0.012	83.46
3 months forward	0.012	83.41
6 months forward	0.0231	43.31
Mexico (peso)	0.0831	12.0265
Poland (zloty)	0.3458	2.8918
Russia (ruble)	0.0341	29.308
Singapore (dollar)	0.7801	1.2819
South Korea (won)	0.0009	1126.63
Switzerland (franc)	1.0274	0.9733
1 month forward	1.0277	0.973
3 months forward	1.0283	0.9725
6 months forward	1.0292	0.9716
Taiwan (dollar)	0.0341	29.317
United Kingdom (pound)	1.6005	0.6248
1 month forward	1.6	0.625
3 months forward	1.599	0.6254
6 months forward	1.5964	0.6264
SDR	1.554	0.6435
Euro	0.7382	1.3547

Source: Wall Street Journal, February 14, 2011.

In all three countries there is a great deal of public anxiety that dropping their national currencies would involve giving up too much independence.

By early 2007, membership in the EU had increased to 27. Once a country becomes a member of the EU, it can seek membership in the EMU if it wishes to do so. However, to be admitted into the single-currency community, a prospective EU member must meet strict fiscal and monetary qualifications. On January 1, 2007, Slovenia became the thirteenth country to adopt the euro as its currency.

The EU motivation for adopting a common currency is to make member countries more competitive in global markets by better integrating their national economies and reducing the economic inefficiency caused by large fluctuations in foreign exchange rates. In addition, a European Central Bank (ECB) was established to set a single monetary policy and interest rates for the adopting nations. Finally, the establishment of the EMU is widely regarded as a major step toward European political unification.

For the major world currencies, such as the dollar, the pound, the euro, or the Japanese yen, holdings of one currency can be converted into any other monetary unit. To keep prices consistent among the various currencies, arbitrageurs continually operate in the market to take advantage of any price disparities between currencies or between two trading centers. Thus, if a profit can be made by converting pounds into yen in London and then yen into dollars in New York City, then selling the dollars for pounds in London, an arbitrageur does so and gains the profit. The action of foreign exchange arbitrageurs tends to keep exchange rates among different currencies consistent with each other within narrow limits.

12.3 BALANCE OF PAYMENTS

At the heart of the movement of foreign exchange rates is the change in a county's balance of payments. The *balance of payments* is a convenient way to summarize a country's international balance of investments and trade (imports−exports). Although they look complicated, it is similar to the way a family would keep records of all of its expenditures and receipts. For example, a deficit in the family budget means that family members spent more money than was collected. A trade deficit in the U.S. balance of payments means that, collectively, we are paying out more money abroad for imports than we are collecting from foreigners who buy our exports.

Of course, for the U.S. balance of payments, all of the transactions are between residents of two countries, and the transactions are formally recorded in a set of accounts known as the **balance of payments**. These accounts are kept in accordance with the rules of double-entry bookkeeping; thus debit entries must be offset by corresponding credit entries. This implies that, overall, total debits must equal total credits and that the account must always be in balance. If not, an errors and omissions account is required to balance international flows. Because of smuggling, tax evasion, poor data, and unrecorded transfers, sometimes the international errors and omissions account is quite large.

THE CURRENT ACCOUNT

The **current account** in the balance of payments summarizes foreign trade in goods and services plus investment income and gifts or grants made to other countries. As shown in Exhibit 12.3, line 1, the United States has a substantial merchandise trade deficit (negative sign) because its imports of foreign goods exceeded its exports of goods to foreigners. U.S. consumers may prefer foreign goods for a variety of reasons, such as image or higher quality in the choice of German cars or lower prices in the choice of Chinese textiles or Southeast Asian electronics products.

Although the U.S. merchandise trade balance is strongly negative, the United States often runs a surplus on the "Services" component of the balance-of-payments current accounts, as is shown on line 4 of Exhibit 12.3. The services component includes royalty income, licensing fees, foreign travel and transportation, and some military expenditures and transfers. Because the U.S. services sector generates substantial fee income from transportation, insurance, and other

EXHIBIT 12.3

U.S. Balance of Payments, 2009 (Seasonally Adjusted, millions of $)

Current Accounts

1	Merchandise trade, net		−506,944
2	• Merchandise exports	1,068,499	
3	• Merchandise imports	−1,575,443	
4	Services, net		132,036
5	• Services exports	502,298	
6	• Services imports	−370,262	
7	Investment and other income		121,420
8	• U.S. income from abroad	588,203	
9	• U.S. income payments to foreign investors	−466,783	
10	Unilateral transfers		−124,943
11	Total balance of accounts		−378,431

Capital Accounts

12	U.S. assets abroad, net		−140,466
13	• U.S. official reserve assets	−52,256	
14	• Other U.S. government assets	541,342	
15	• U.S. private assets	−629,552	
16	Foreign assets in the United States		305,736
17	• Foreign official assets	450,030	
18	• Other foreign assets	−144,294	
19	Capital account transactions, net		−140
20	Statistical discrepancy		162,497
21	Other capital account transactions		50,804
22	Total capital accounts		378,431

Current accounts reflect balances on merchandise trade, services, as well as net investment income and the effect of unilateral transfers. Capital accounts reflect changes in U.S. citizens' asset holdings abroad and foreign holdings of U.S. assets. Because of major reporting problems, often a large statistical discrepancy account is needed to balance the current and capital accounts.

Source: U.S. Department of Commerce, Bureau of Economic Analysis.

financial services, and various royalties and licensing fees, the services component usually creates a positive entry in the U.S. balance-of-payments current account.

In the past, net investment income of U.S. citizens contributed positively to the U.S. balance of payments because of large U.S. investments abroad since World War II. However, in the late 1980s the United States changed from a net creditor nation to a net debtor nation as it sold many of its assets, including many U.S. government bonds, to foreign investors to finance its large government deficits and its chronic deficit on its merchandise trade account. Consequently, U.S. net investment income surpluses have narrowed and may become negative in the future. For 2009, however, the investment account was positive, as shown in line 7 of Exhibit 12.3.

EXHIBIT 12.4
U.S. Current Account Trade Deficit

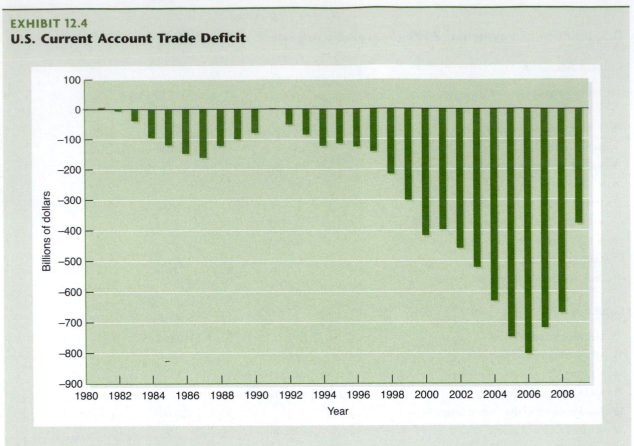

Because of rising imports and falling of stagnant exports, the U.S. deficit on current account rose sharply between 1997 and 2005.

Source: U.S. Department of Commerce, Bureau of Economic Analysis.

Finally, the balance of payments on current account shows that foreign unilateral transfers (line 10) such as foreign aid, for which no compensating payment is received, have consistently been negative. This adds to the net amount of U.S. dollars transferred to foreign investors and makes the total balance of payments on current account more negative than it otherwise would be.

As Exhibit 12.4 shows, in recent years, the U.S. deficit on current account has been very large and increasing. Line 11 in Exhibit 12.3 only confirms this trend. As the exhibit shows, for 2009 the total U.S. deficit for the current account is $378 billion. As in our family analogy, the U.S. balance-of-trade deficit means that, collectively, we are paying out more money abroad to buy imports than we are taking in selling exports.

CAPITAL ACCOUNTS

The balance-of-payments **capital accounts** measure capital flows into or out of the country. Capital flows can be used to finance private long-term investments of more than 1 year, or they may be short-term flows invested in bank deposits or short-term securities. Long-term capital flows often involve investments in land, plant and equipment, real estate, or stocks or bonds in other countries. Such investments occur when long-term potential seems to be substantially greater in one country than another. They may be driven, in part, by breakdowns in purchasing power parity that make it cheaper to buy assets in one country than another. Expectations about future changes in exchange rates could also be a factor.

Government-motivated financial flows often play an important role in the flow-of-funds accounts. If a country is trying to support the value of its currency, its government can sell various reserve assets such as gold or *special drawing rights (SDRs)*, also known as *paper gold*.

The capital accounts therefore keep track of the investment capital flows into and out of a country. A positive balance in these accounts indicates that foreign investors purchased more U.S. assets than U.S. investors purchased foreign assets, creating a capital flow into the United States. A negative balance in these accounts indicates that U.S. investors purchased more foreign assets than foreign investors purchased U.S. assets, creating a capital outflow out of the United States.

Turning to Exhibit 12.3, line 12 shows that net U.S. assets purchased abroad, such as U.S. investors buying stock in a Japanese company, totaled $140.5 billion. The major component of this amount was the $629.6 billion in private assets purchased by U.S. citizens, as shown in line 15. Other factors affecting this account are changes in foreign currency reserves (line 13) and government asset purchases such as special drawing rights (line 14).

Line 16 in Exhibit 12.3 shows that net foreign purchases of assets in the United States, such as the Japanese investors purchasing Treasury securities, total $1,212.3 billion. This account is composed of foreign government assets in the United States (line 17) and other foreign assets in the United States (line 18), which is by far the largest component of this account. The capital account flows (line 22) total $791.5 billion.

Because all current account flows (line 11) must be offset by capital account flows (line 22), these two values should be equal. If they are not equal, the difference is called a *statistical discrepancy* (line 19), which is defined to make the balance-of-payments accounts balance exactly. Unfortunately, because many international transactions are not reported, such as smuggling proceeds, illegal activity transactions, and tax evasion, the statistical discrepancy is often quite large and can be positive or negative. As a result, substantial imprecision exists in the balance-of-payments accounts.

Admittedly, the balance-of-payment accounts are difficult to understand, but it may help our understanding to explain them in terms of a family. If a family spends more money on goods and services than it earns, the family runs a current account deficit balance. To deal with this problem, the family has two choices: (1) it can borrow money to finance the deficit or (2) it can sell off some of the family's financial assets such as stock or bonds. The United States has the same problem when it runs a deficit. *Running a deficit* in the current accounts means that U.S. citizens have bought more foreign goods and services than foreign investors have bought from us; hence, imports exceed exports. In this situation, the United States has two choices: (1) it can borrow abroad or (2) it can sell financial assets such as domestic equities or real estate to foreign entities. Thus, the country must have sufficient net capital inflows to finance the current account deficit. Throughout the 1990s and early 2000s, the United States ran a deficit and financed this trade gap by both borrowing abroad and selling assets such as Treasury securities, stocks, and real estate. The current account surpluses of China and oil-exporting countries have contributed to the widening U.S. deficit since 2001. The economic crisis in 2007 has reduced the U.S. current account deficit through falling imports and a drop in oil prices, but the effect is likely to be short-lived.

Both trade and capital flows affect the supply of and demand for currencies. Thus, they affect prices in the foreign exchange markets, as do other factors, including interest rates and expectations of inflation rates. In the next section, we discuss some of the most important determinants of foreign exchange rates.

12.4 FOREIGN EXCHANGE MARKETS

In foreign exchange markets, individuals, corporations, banks, and governments interact to convert one currency to another. The foreign exchange markets represent the biggest financial markets, with transactions totaling more than $1.5 trillion per day and hundreds of trillions of dollars per year. Foreign exchange markets provide a mechanism for transferring purchasing power from individuals who normally deal in one currency to people who generally transact business using a different monetary unit. Importing and exporting goods and services are facilitated by this conversion service because the parties to the transactions can deal in terms of media of exchange instead of having to rely on bartering. The currencies of some countries are not easily convertible into other currencies. If a corporation chartered in another country wants to do business with a country whose currency is nonconvertible, the corporation may be required to accept locally produced merchandise in lieu of money as payment for goods and services. This practice is known as **countertrade**.

A second reason that efficient foreign exchange markets have developed is that they provide a means for passing the risk associated with changes in exchange rates to professional risk takers. This *hedging* function is particularly important to corporations in the present era of floating exchange rates.

The third important reason for the continuing importance of foreign exchange markets is the provision of credit. The time span between shipment of goods by the exporter and their receipt by the importer can be considerable. Although the goods are in transit, they must be financed. Foreign exchange markets are one device by which financing and related currency conversions can be accomplished efficiently and at low cost.

MARKET STRUCTURE

There is no single formal foreign exchange market such as the one that exists for the sale of stocks and bonds on the New York Stock Exchange. In fact, the foreign exchange market is an over-the-counter market that is similar to the one for money market instruments. More specifically, the foreign exchange market is composed of a group of informal markets closely interlocked through international branch banking and correspondent bank relationships. The participants are linked electronically. It is a truly global market because currencies are traded 24 hours a day around the globe. There are also no written rules governing operation of the foreign exchange markets; however, transactions are conducted according to principles and a code of ethics that have evolved over time. The extent to which a country's currency is traded in the worldwide market depends, in some measure, on local regulations that vary from country to country. Almost every country has some type of active foreign exchange market.

MAJOR PARTICIPANTS

The major participants in the foreign exchange markets are the large, multinational commercial banks, although many investment banking houses have established foreign exchange trading operations in recent years. In the United States, the market is dominated by large money-center banks, with about half of them located in New York City and the remainder in major financial centers such as San Francisco, Chicago, and Atlanta. These banks operate in the foreign exchange market at two levels. First, at the retail level, banks deal with individuals and corporations. Second, at the wholesale level, banks operate in the interbank market. Major banks usually transact directly with the foreign institution involved. However, many transactions are mediated by foreign exchange brokers. These brokers preserve the anonymity of the parties until the transaction is concluded.

The other major participants in the foreign exchange markets are the central banks of various countries. Central banks typically intervene in foreign exchange markets to smooth out fluctuations in currency exchange rates. Additional participants in the foreign exchange markets are nonfinancial businesses and individuals who enter the market through banks for various commercial reasons or to speculate on exchange-rate fluctuations.

TRADING FOREIGN EXCHANGE

In commercial banks, the trading in foreign exchange is usually done by only a few persons. As in the money markets, the pace of transactions is rapid, and traders must be able to make on-the-spot judgments about whether to buy or sell a particular currency. They have a dual responsibility in that, on the one hand, they must maintain the bank's position (inventory) to meet customer needs, but, on the other hand, they must not take large losses if the value of a currency falls. The task is difficult because currency values tend to fluctuate rapidly and often widely, especially because currencies are always subject to possible devaluations by their governments. If a currency is expected to fall in value, however, banks may want to sell it to reduce their foreign exchange losses.

TRANSFER PROCESS

The international funds-transfer process is facilitated by interbank clearing systems. The large multinational banks of each country are linked through international correspondent relationships as well as through their worldwide branching systems. Within each country, regional banks are linked to international banks' main offices, either through nationwide branching systems or through domestic correspondent networks. In the United States, practically every bank has a correspondent relationship with a bank in New York City or with a large bank in a regional financial center. As a result, almost every bank, large or small, is able to provide its customers with international payment services.

There are two types of foreign exchange quotations and trades—spot and forward. In the spot market, delivery of currencies bought or sold is made within no more than 2 business days and often immediately upon agreement. The rate at which a currency is traded in this market is called the **spot rate**. Retail foreign exchange markets are mainly spot markets.

12.5 SPOT AND FORWARD TRANSACTIONS

CURRENCY DERIVATIVES

In addition to the spot market, both parties can agree to exchange a specific amount of one currency for a specific amount of another currency on a certain date in the future. One way of doing this is with futures contracts. Because they are traded on an exchange such as the Chicago Mercantile Exchange (CME) Group, they are standardized in terms of size and delivery date. For example, all CME euro futures contracts are for €125,000 and have a delivery date of the third Wednesday in March, June, September, or December. Another way a firm can exchange currencies is through a forward contract with a bank. These contracts provide much more flexibility than futures contracts. For example, the firm decides how much of the foreign currency it wants to sell to or buy from the bank. The currency is typically delivered 30, 60, 90, or 180 days in the future but can be customized according to the firm's need. The exchange rate the bank offers on these contracts is called the **forward rate**. Note that the forward rate is established on the date on which the agreement is made, even though it represents the exchange rate to be used on the date of the delivery. Thus, by entering into a forward contract, a firm eliminates uncertainty about the home currency value of the amount of the foreign currency to be paid or received in the future. Note in Exhibit 12.2 that forward rates are quoted along with spot rates for major currencies in the *Wall Street Journal*.

LEARNING BY DOING 12.1
Using Forward Contracts to Hedge Exchange Rate Risks

PROBLEM: An American exporter just sold farm equipment to a British firm for £100,000 to be paid in 90 days. The spot rate today is $1.58. The exchange rate in 90 days, according to a specialist forecast, is $1.60. Given the above information and the following scenarios, what will be the expected proceeds from the equipment sale in U.S. dollars in each scenario?

- Scenario 1: The exporter signs a 90-day forward contact with his bank to sell £100,000. The forward rate offered to him is $1.62

- Scenario 2: The exporter signs a 90-day forward contact with his bank to sell £100,000. The forward rate offered to him is $1.57

- Scenario 3: The exporter takes an *unhedged* position; that is, he simply waits 90 days to collect the £100,000 payment. Assume that, in 90 days, it turns out that a pound is worth $1.54.

Would you recommend the exporter hedge through a forward contract? Why?

APPROACH: Even though we know the spot rate today, the exporter does not have £100,000 to trade for dollars at this point. The relevant exchange rate to the firm is the dollar–pound exchange rate in 90 days, which will determine the actual dollar amount to be received for the machinery. The exchange rate in the future is uncertain and may differ from the forecast. Hedging through a forward contract locks in the exchange rate in the future and eliminates uncertainty. If the U.S. firm waits 90 days to collect the £100,000 and then sells it in the spot market for dollars, there is a risk that the dollar price of the pound sterling may drop below the forward rate and the firm will receive lower dollar proceeds. Using the assumed future exchange rates or the forward rates, we can calculate expected proceeds of the unhedged and hedged positions in various scenarios and assess the possible strategies.

SOLUTION:

- Scenario 1: If the exporter sells the pounds to the bank at $1.62, it will secure the dollar proceeds of $1.62 × £100,000 = $162,000 today, to be received in 90 days.

- Scenario 2: If the exporter sells the pounds to the bank at $1.57, it will secure the dollar proceeds of $1.57 × £100,000 = $157,000 today, to be received in 90 days.

- Scenario 3: If the dollar price of a pound decreases to $1.54 in 90 days, the American exporter receives only $1.54 × £100,000 = $154,000 in 90 days by not hedging. The proceeds are lower than those under the forward hedges in scenarios 1 and 2.

Note that hedging decisions have to be made ex ante, before one can observe the actual exchange rate when the payment is due. Ex ante, the dollar proceeds under the forward hedge will be higher than the unhedged position if one expects that, in 90 days, the pound will be worth less than the forward rate. The exporter may be hesitant to hedge if the pound is expected to appreciate more than the forward rate in 90 days. If a firm is averse to the exchange rate risk, however, it may hedge in spite of the exchange rate forecast.

OPTION TRANSACTION

Another alternative for managing foreign exchange risk is a currency option. If the American exporter were to buy a put option on the £100,000 maturing in 90 days at a strike price of $1.60, the firm would be protected against depreciation of the pound below that price. If the spot rate in 90 days is $1.50, the exporter can exercise the put and receive $160,000. However, if the rate goes above $1.60, the American company can let the put expire and sell the sterling at the spot rate. The cost of this asymmetrical protection is the price of the option, paid at the time of purchasing the put. The exporter's commercial banker usually sells the exporter an option that suits the exporter's needs. Commercial banks earn fee income by selling options as well as by arranging forward currency transactions. Options can also be purchased from the major exchanges through brokers.

PURCHASING POWER PARITY

A theory that focuses on international trade flows is purchasing power parity. **Purchasing power parity (PPP)** means that exchange rates tend to move to levels at which the cost of goods in any country is the same in the same currency. For instance, if a Big Mac hamburger costs $3 in the United States and ¥330 in Japan, PPP exists when the ¥/$ exchange rate was ¥110 for $1, as then the Big Mac would cost the same in the same currency in both countries.

If PPP holds for exchange rates, all goods cost the same in the same currency in all countries, so there would be no net cost saving from buying goods in one

PEOPLE & EVENTS

The Big Mac Test of Purchasing Power Parity

As a light-hearted test of purchasing power parity, *The Economist* began publishing the Big Mac Index in 1986. Big Macs are a relatively homogeneous product in that the recipe is roughly the same throughout the 118 countries in which McDonald's conducts business. Comparing a country's PPP rate with the market-determined exchange rate is a test of whether a country's currency is overvalued or undervalued.

The table below shows the price of Big Macs in dollars for select countries from *The Economist*. If PPP holds, the burgernomics test should show the cost of a Big Mac is the same worldwide. Column 2 gives the current price of a Big Mac in a country's local currency. Column 3 converts the correspond-

ing price into dollars at the current market exchange rate. The average price of a Big Mac in major American cities during July 2010 was $3.73. The most expensive burger, priced at $6.56, was in Sweden; the cheapest, at $1.90, was in Hong Kong. As you can see, the prices of Big Macs are hardly the same throughout the world.

To determine how much a currency is over- or undervalued, column 4 calculates a country's PPP rate. For example, dividing the local Hong Kong Big Mac price by the American price gives a dollar PPP of 3.96 HK$ (14.8/3.73). Column 5 shows the prevailing market exchange rate, which is 7.77 HK$. The fact that the market exchange rate is much higher than the PPP exchange rate suggests the

The Hamburger Standard

	Big Mac Prices		Implied PPP* of the Dollar	Actual Dollar Exchange Rate, July 21	Under(−)/Over(+) valuation Against the Dollar, %
	In Local Currency	In Dollars			
United States	$3.73	3.73			
Argentina	Peso 14.0	3.56	3.75	3.93	−5
Brazil	Real 8.71	4.91	2.33	1.77	31
Britain	£2.29	3.48	1.63	1.52	−7
Canada	C$ 4.17	4.00	1.12	1.04	7
China	Yuan 13.2	1.95	3.54	6.78	−48
Denmark	DK 28.5	4.90	7.63	5.81	31
Euro Area	€ 3.38	4.33	1.10	1.28	16
Hong Kong	HK$ 14.8	1.90	3.96	7.77	−49
Japan	¥320.00	3.67	85.70	87.20	−2
Mexico	Peso 32.0	2.50	8.57	12.80	−33
New Zealand	NZ$ 5.00	3.59	1.34	1.39	−4
Poland	Zloty 8.30	2.60	2.22	3.20	−30
Russia	Ruble 71.0	2.33	19.00	30.40	−38
Singapore	S$ 4.23	3.08	1.13	1.37	−18
Sweden	SKr 48.4	6.56	13.00	7.37	76
Switzerland	SFr 6.50	6.19	1.74	1.05	66

* Dollars per pound.

Source: The Economist, July 2010.

HK$ is undervalued by −49 percent ([3.96 − 7.77]/7.77). However, the Swiss franc, SFr, is over-valued 66 percent ([1.74 − 1.05]/1.05). Anyone who has traveled to Switzerland knows, at least for Americans, it is a very expensive place to visit.

Why doesn't burgernomics validate the theory of purchasing power? First, regardless of the Big Mac Index outcome, economists are comfortable with the theory of PPP as the major behavioral force driving exchange rates to PPP equilibrium. The theory assumes products can be traded easily across borders; in the case of perishable Big Macs, this does not seem likely. Furthermore, price variations among countries in the real world are distorted by taxes, tariffs, differences in profit margins, and differences in the cost of nontradable items such as rent. Finally, in the long term, there are a number of other factors influencing exchange rates, such as relative price levels, interest rates, preferences for foreign versus domestic goods, and a country's productivity.

place rather than another. However, if one currency is undervalued, goods produced in that country tend to cost less than similar goods produced elsewhere. As a result, that country's exports grow and its imports diminish unless trade barriers, transportation costs, or the perishability of products makes it infeasible for people to buy the same products in various places. For instance, computer parts are easy and cheap to ship, and we would expect there to be purchasing power parity among countries. However, steel prices may not be equal depending on the source because of high transportation costs, and McDonald's hamburgers would spoil (or, at least, cool off) in transit. Thus, steel and hamburger prices might be less closely equated across various currencies than computer prices.

Because of transportation costs and trade restrictions, PPP does not hold in the short run. Although exchange rates tend to adjust so similar products cost the same amount in the same currency in different countries, the adjustment may not be complete for all products and may take years to happen. Thus, we must look for some additional factors that drive the volatility of foreign exchange rates.

12.6 CAPITAL FLOWS AND EXCHANGE RATES

As Exhibit 12.4 illustrates, the United States has run a deficit in its current account for a number of years. The current account deficit means that foreign citizens increase their holdings of dollars and other claims on U.S. assets. If foreign investors sell their extra dollars to obtain their domestic currency, the value of the dollar falls. Thus, many people think that when the United States runs a deficit on its balance-of-payments current account, the dollar falls in value relative to other currencies.

However, the dollar does not always fall when the United States runs a current account deficit. As Exhibit 12.5 shows, in recent years the deficit grew until the 2001 and 2007 recessions, and the value of the dollar increased in both cases. The reason is that foreign investors can buy U.S. capital assets as well as U.S. manufactured goods and services. If interest rates in the United States are high and U.S. inflation is expected to be low, foreign investors can expect to earn high real returns if they invest in the United States. Thus, net foreign demand for both short- and long-term investments may be great enough to support a high

EXHIBIT 12.5
U.S. Exchange Rates and Current Account Balance

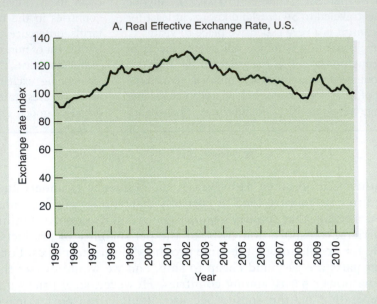

Between 1995 and 2001, the U.S. exchange rate trended upward in terms of the dollar's purchasing power versus the currencies of the major trade partners. U.S. imports rose sharply until the 2001 recession, and exports rose slowly, if at all. After the 2001 recession, imports began to rise even though the dollar's purchasing power was relatively stable. The 2007 global financial crisis was followed by a sudden rise in the dollar's purchasing power and a large decline in both imports and exports.

Source: U.S. Department of Commerce, Bureau of Economic Analysis, Federal Reserve Bank of St. Louis.

price for the dollar even if the United States runs a current account balance-of-payments deficit.

In fact, if the net foreign demand for investments in the United States is high enough, as foreign investors buy dollars to finance investments, they may bid up the value of the dollar and make the U.S. current account merchandise trade deficit even larger. The large trade deficit transfers more dollars to foreign investors' hands so they can afford their desired investments in the United States. As shown in Exhibit 12.6, this has happened since the late 1990s as foreign investors acquired more U.S. stocks, bonds, and investments than U.S. citizens acquired abroad. Thus, it is overly simplistic to say that a large U.S. trade deficit makes the dollar fall in value. The change in the dollar value cannot be predicted unless desired intracountry investment (capital) flows are also taken into account.

It is worth noting that the value of foreign investments in the United States continued to exceed the value of U.S. investments abroad in 2007 and 2008. This difference grew larger in 2008 due to three reasons related to the global financial crisis: (1) a larger decline in prices of U.S.-owned foreign stocks than in foreign-owned U.S. stock prices, (2) the depreciation of most major currencies against the U.S. dollar, and (3) net foreign acquisitions of U.S. financial assets exceeding net U.S. acquisitions of financial assets abroad. As of year-end 2009, the value of foreign investments in the United States exceeded the value of U.S. investments abroad by at least $2.7 trillion.

There are at least two types of international capital flows that affect a currency's exchange rate and explain the volatility of exchange rates. They are investment capital flows and political capital flows.

INVESTMENT CAPITAL FLOWS

Investment capital flows are either short-term money market flows motivated by differences in interest rates or long-term capital investments in a nation's real or financial assets. Changes in long-term investment flows can result either from a change in the perceived attractiveness of investment in a country or from an increase in international holdings of that country's currency. For example, foreign direct investment in the United States increased dramatically during the 1980s because of favorable taxes, a strong currency, and high expected real rates of return on investment. Foreign investors perceived the United States as both a safe and profitable place to invest.

Changes in short-term investment flows usually respond to differences in short-term interest rates in various countries as investors seek to earn the highest possible return on their excess cash. However, high interest rates are usually associated with high expected inflation. Furthermore, higher inflation rates in one country versus another, according to PPP, eventually cause the value of the first country's currency to fall. Consequently, short-term capital flows are most likely to occur only when investors think that *real interest rates* (i.e., interest rates adjusted for expected inflation) are higher in one country than another.

POLITICAL CAPITAL FLOWS

Political capital flows, at times, can alter exchange rates significantly. When a country experiences political instability because of war or domestic upheaval, it

EXHIBIT 12.6
International Investment Position

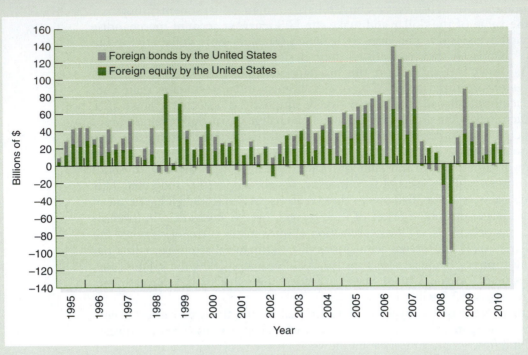

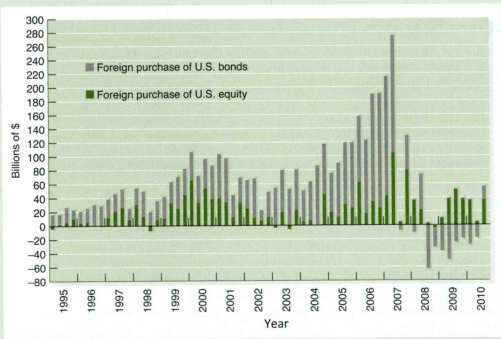

The United States was able to sustain large current account deficits since the late 1990s until the financial crisis of 2007, in part because foreigners' net purchases of U.S. stocks and bonds far exceed U.S. purchases of foreign stocks and bonds.

Source: U.S. Department of Commerce, Bureau of Economic Analysis.

often experiences the phenomenon of **capital flight**, in which owners of capital transfer their wealth out of the country. In addition, when a country adopts socialist economic policies that reduce the value of private investment, private capital "flees" that country. In addition, when people fear war or social disruption, they transfer their investment funds to safer countries. Thus, when an aborted coup against former USSR leader Mikhail Gorbachev occurred in August 1991, European investment funds quickly flowed to the United States; as a result, the dollar's value shot upward temporarily. Large capital outflows also occurred in Argentina in the early 2000s because people feared that the value of their Argentine pesos would fall when Argentina abolished its currency board.

DO YOU UNDERSTAND?

1. Why should purchasing power parity exist? Why might it not hold?
2. What can cause a country to have a deficit in its current account balance of payments?
3. Is it always true that when a country has a deficit in its trade balance the value of its currency will decline? Explain.
4. What types of capital flows exist between countries and what can motivate each type of flow?
5. Why must the balance of payments always balance?

12.7 GOVERNMENT INTERVENTION IN FOREIGN EXCHANGE MARKETS

The equilibrium exchange rate of a given currency is determined by the supply of and demand for the currency. One of the roles of a country's central bank is to influence the value of its currency relative to other currencies. If a government believes its currency is either overvalued or undervalued, the central bank can intervene in the foreign exchange markets by affecting the supply of or demand for its currency.

Exhibit 12.7 shows an initial equilibrium exchange rate of £0.60/$ for dollars that are being exchanged for British pounds in foreign exchange markets. Suppose our government decides this equilibrium exchange rate is contributing to a deficit in our current account with England. How could our central bank, the Federal Reserve, intervene in the dollar and pound foreign exchange markets to remedy this situation? First, the Fed must decide if it should make the £/$ exchange rate increase or decrease in the dollar market. Our current account deficit means we are importing more from England than we are exporting to it. To reduce the deficit, the Fed should take action that decreases the £/$ exchange rate so British products become relatively more expensive compared to American goods and services. That discourages Americans from buying British products, thus reducing our imports. At the same time, British consumers buy more American goods, thus increasing our exports.

What should the Fed do in the currency markets to make the dollar depreciate against the pound? That depends on what it has been doing up to this point in the dollar market. If the Fed has been inactive in the dollar market, it should

EXHIBIT 12.7
Central Bank Intervention

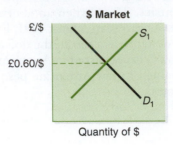

$ Market

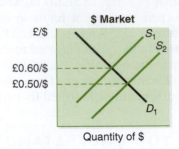

$ Market

To make the dollar depreciate, the Fed should sell dollars, resulting in a lower equilibrium exchange rate.

begin selling dollars in exchange for pounds. This increases the supply curve in the dollar market from S_1 to S_2 (see Exhibit 12.7). Under these new conditions, an exchange rate of £0.60/$ is no longer equilibrium. Market forces lower the £/$ exchange rate to a new equilibrium of £0.50/$.

The Fed pursues a different course of action if it initially decided to make the dollar appreciate against the pound. In this case, it wants the dollar market to reach a new equilibrium exchange rate higher than £0.60/$. To accomplish this, the Fed starts buying dollars in the dollar market while simultaneously selling pounds in the pound market.

FIXED EXCHANGE RATES

Between the end of World War II and 1971, most industrialized nations adhered to a system of **fixed exchange rates** known as the **Bretton Woods system**, under which each country's central bank was obligated to intervene in the foreign exchange markets to keep the exchange rate in a narrow band around a previously agreed on rate. For example, if the rate agreed on between the United States and Britain was £0.60/$ in the dollar, as shown in Exhibit 12.7, then the central banks of the two countries would intervene in the dollar and pound markets to keep the exchange rate within a narrow band above and below £0.60/$. Suppose market forces began shifting the demand and supply curves in these markets, making the £/$ exchange rate increase above the band. If the central banks were inactive up to this point, they would begin selling dollars and buying pounds. They continue doing this until the £/$ exchange rate is back within the acceptable range above/below £0.60/$.

When the Bretton Woods system collapsed in 1971, the central banks of the member nations were no longer required to intervene in the foreign exchange markets to maintain stable exchange rates. Instead, new financial or economic pressures could be relieved by letting the value of the currencies fluctuate in the foreign exchange markets to determine a new equilibrium. For most countries, this is what has happened since the early 1970s.

Nonetheless, if currency fluctuations become too severe and disruptive to the economy, countries may borrow funds from the International Monetary Fund (IMF) to stabilize their currency. Often, the IMF requires that countries reduce their budget deficits and the growth rate of their money supplies as a condition for lending them money. Because such actions not only reduce inflation but also can cause recession, many countries prefer to borrow from the IMF only in emergencies.

INFLATION AND EXCHANGE RATES

One of the most important effects governments have on foreign currency values is through their monetary policies, insofar as those policies affect domestic inflation. A country with high inflation tends to have higher nominal interest rates, often coupled with lower real interest rates and a deteriorating balance of merchandise trade. Because interest rates and trade flows are tied closely to exchange rates, it should not be surprising that exchange rates are materially affected by changes in a country's rate of inflation.

As inflation causes prices to rise in the United States relative to other countries, American buyers are likely to switch from domestic goods to imported foreign goods. Similarly, foreign buyers are likely to switch from American products to those of other countries. Thus, the demand for American goods tends to fall at the same time that Americans supply more dollars in exchange for foreign currencies so that they can buy foreign goods. Thus, these inflation-generated supply and demand shifts cause the dollar's value to fall relative to other currencies. Conversely, as the U.S. inflation rate falls relative to another country, the value of the dollar should rise relative to that country's currency.

LEARNING BY DOING 12.2

Using Purchasing Power Parity to Determine the Expected Exchange Rate

---

PROBLEM: Suppose the spot exchange rate today is \$1.25 = €1.00. The inflation rate is expected to be 3 percent in the United States and 5 percent in the euro zone in the next year. What is the expected exchange rate in 1 year? Is the euro expected to appreciate or depreciate against the U.S. dollar 1 year from now, based on PPP? Further suppose the annual real interest rate will be 2 percent in both economies. What should be the nominal interest rates in both economies?

APPROACH: Exchange rates are effectively ratios of currency prices. Inflation rates, by definition, tell us the change in the currency price level. Hence, we can use purchasing power parity (PPP) to calculate the new currency price levels over the next year to determine the expected exchange rate in 1 year. Then we can infer whether the euro is expected to appreciate or depreciate against the U.S. dollar.

$$\text{nominal interest rates} = (1 + \text{real interest rate}) \times (1 + \text{inflation}) - 1$$

SOLUTION: The expected exchange rate in 1 year should be \$1.25 × (1 + .03) = €1.00 × (1 + .05)

The dollar–euro (\$/€) price = (1.25 × [1 + .03]) ÷ (1.00 × [1 + .05]) = \$1.2262/€

The euro is expected to depreciate against the dollar because one euro will trade for fewer dollars in a year:

$$\text{nominal interest rate in the United States} = (1 + 0.02) \times (1 + 0.03) - 1 = 0.0506$$
$$\text{nominal interest rate in Eurozone} = (1 + 0.02) \times (1 + 0.05) - 1 = 0.0701$$

POLITICS AND EXCHANGE RATES

At times, one hears that the U.S. dollar is overvalued and that its value must fall substantially. In a competitive market such as the foreign exchange market, however, the value is always fair in the sense that it represents the equilibrium point of supply and demand. Thus, what is really meant by the term *overvalued* is that the equilibrium exchange rate established in a competitive currency market results in conditions in the domestic economy that are politically unacceptable. Today, the huge deficit in the current account is thought to result in the exporting of jobs. At a lower value for the dollar, U.S. products are more price-competitive internationally, and both Americans and foreigners shift from foreign products to those produced in the United States. This, it is thought, would increase American employment and stimulate the U.S. economy. Consequently, weak-dollar policies are often supported by businesses, labor unions, and farmers who think a weak dollar increases the demand for domestically produced goods in foreign markets.

However, a strong U.S. dollar makes American capital and financial assets cheap for foreign investors. This may encourage foreign investors to buy into the United States. This may make a strong-dollar policy popular among Wall Street firms that help place foreign investments. However, if the dollar continues to strengthen against other currencies, the dollar returns on American stocks and bonds become less attractive to foreign investors because they receive less of their home currencies when they convert the dollar dividends and interest payments to their home currencies. In addition, because a strong dollar makes foreign goods appear cheap to American consumers, it pressures American producers to lower their prices to meet the foreign competition.

12.8 FINANCING INTERNATIONAL TRADE

One of the most important services provided by international banks is the financing of imports and exports among countries. International transactions are far more complicated than equivalent domestic financing because of the additional sources of risk that are involved. Three problems must be overcome before trade deals can be executed. First, exporters often lack accurate information about the importer's current and past business practices and, hence, the likelihood of payment. Importers are similarly concerned about the ability or inclination of the exporter to fulfill all contractual obligations once payment has been made. Second, before the transaction can be hedged with a forward contract (or an option contract) to reduce foreign exchange risk, the exact amounts and dates of payments must be known. Finally, before a bank is willing to finance an international transaction, a means must be found to insulate the bank from nonfinancial aspects of the transaction that could lead to disputes and to protracted legal proceedings, which delay recovery of its money. A number of specialized financial instruments have been developed to overcome these three problems, thereby minimizing the risk of engaging in international transactions. These instruments are letters of credit, drafts, and bills of lading.

LETTERS OF CREDIT

A **letter of credit (LC)** is a financial instrument issued by an importer's bank that obligates the bank to pay the exporter a specified amount of money once certain conditions are fulfilled. Legally, the bank substitutes its credit standing for that of the importer in that the bank guarantees payment if the correct documents are submitted.

From the perspective of the exporter, letters of credit have several advantages over sales on open account. First, because an exporter's knowledge about a foreign importer is frequently vague, the company is hesitant to ship merchandise without advance payment. With a letter of credit, however, the creditworthiness of the bank is substituted for that of the importer, and exporters see little risk of nonpayment when the bank is the guarantor. Second, as soon as the exporter documents that he or she has met the terms and conditions specified in the LC, payment is assured. This is particularly important because it eliminates the possibility that payment might be held up because of disputes arising from some alleged deficiency in the actual goods. As long as the paper documents are in order, the bank is obligated to pay, even if the importer no longer wants the merchandise. The final advantage of LCs is that they eliminate a major risk facing exporters: the possibility that governments may impose restrictions on payment. There are few cases on record in which governments have prevented banks from honoring LCs that have already been issued.

From the perspective of the importer, there are two definite advantages to using LCs. Because the LC specifies the actions that must be taken before the exporter can be paid, the chance of noncompliance by the seller is reduced. This is most useful when the importer has little knowledge of the business practices of the exporter. The second advantage to the importer is that funds are not paid out until the terms set out in the LC have been met and the documentation is in order.

DRAFTS

A second important document that serves to facilitate international trade is a draft. A **draft** is simply a request for payment that is drawn up by the exporter and sent to the bank that drew up the letter of credit for the importer. If the draft conforms to several legal requirements, it becomes a negotiable instrument that is particularly useful for financing international trade flows.

Drafts can be of two types: sight drafts or time drafts. **Sight drafts**, as the name implies, require the bank to pay on demand, assuming that all documentation is in proper order and that all conditions have been met. **Time drafts**, however, are payable at a particular time in the future, as specified in the letter of credit. When a time draft is presented to the importer's bank for payment, it is checked to make certain that all terms and conditions set forth in the letter of credit have been met, and then it is stamped *Accepted* and dated on the face of the draft. The importer's bank then returns the accepted draft to the exporter or the exporter's bank. Alternatively, the importer's bank may elect to pay the exporter or the exporter's bank a price that reflects the discounted present value of the draft, after which it may hold the acceptance for its own account or sell it in the banker's acceptance market. In either situation, when the time draft matures, the importer must pay the amount due unless other arrangements have been made in advance. The accepting importer's bank must make payment if the importer does not.

BILLS OF LADING

A third document of particular importance for international trade is the bill of lading. The **bill of lading** is a receipt issued to the exporter by a common carrier that acknowledges possession of the goods described on the face of the bill. The bill of lading serves as a contract between the exporter and the shipping company. In this role it specifies the services to be performed, the charges for those services, and the disposition of the goods if they cannot be delivered as instructed.

If it is properly prepared, a bill of lading is also a *document of title* that follows the merchandise throughout the transport process. As a document of title, it can be used by the exporter either as collateral for loans prior to payment or as a means of obtaining payment (or acceptance of a time draft) before the goods are released to the importer.

EXAMPLE OF AN IMPORT TRANSACTION

To better understand how these three documents are used in international trade, let us examine a hypothetical transaction between an American importer and a British exporter. The steps involved in this transaction are shown in Exhibit 12.8. In step 1, the American importer applies for a letter of credit from its American bank. In step 2, if the bank is willing to guarantee payment for the goods on

EXHIBIT 12.8
Steps in a Letter-of-Credit Transaction

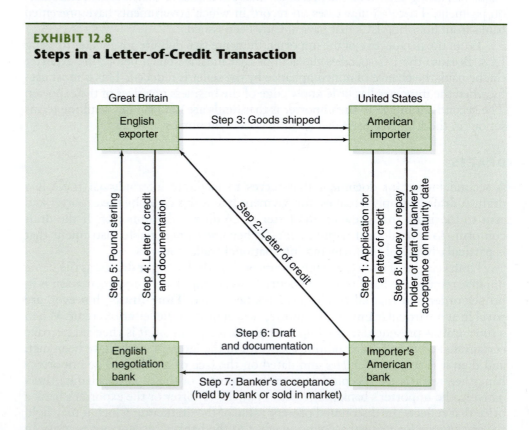

The bank that provides the letter of credit legally substitutes its credit promise for that of the importer and guarantees payment if the correct documents are submitted to prove the right goods were shipped appropriately.

presentation of the required documentation, it prepares a letter of credit and sends it to the exporter in England. The letter specifies the documentation and other conditions that were agreed on to receive payment.

In step 3, the British exporter ships the goods to the American importer and collects the necessary documentation. In step 4, the British exporter prepares a draft in accordance with the terms set out in the letter of credit, and it takes the letter of credit, the draft, and all other required documentation to its London bank. The documentation required may include bills of lading, commercial invoices, certificates of quantity, and certificates of quality or grade, among others. In step 5, the British bank examines the documents carefully for full compliance. If it is satisfied that everything is in proper order, it normally *confirms* the credit (adds its own promise to pay) and pays the exporter. Usually this payment is made in the exporter's own currency (in this case, pounds sterling). Note that the British bank's inspection is limited to an examination of the documents; the bank employees do not physically examine or even see the shipping containers or merchandise. A letter-of-credit transaction does not protect an importer from a dishonest exporter shipping crates of sawdust. However, the documentation may require certifications necessary to prevent such fraud.

In step 6, the British bank sends the draft and documentation to the importer's bank. The American bank examines the draft and accompanying documentation. If the draft is a *sight draft*, the American bank pays on demand and collects from the importer. If it is a *time draft*, the bank stamps it *Accepted*, signs it, and then either returns it to the exporter's bank or pays the exporter's bank a discounted price. If the American bank pays the exporter's bank for a time draft, the draft becomes a **banker's acceptance**. The bank can hold the acceptance and be repaid by the importer when the time draft matures. In this case, the draft acts much like a loan from the bank to the importer. Alternatively, the bank can sell the banker's acceptance in the money markets (step 7)—in which case the time draft is similar to commercial paper issued by the importer and guaranteed by its bank. Because the importer's bank has accepted the time draft, the accepting bank must pay and is at risk if the importer does not pay the obligation at maturity (step 8). Consequently, the banker's acceptance has no more credit risk than other bank obligations, and it might have less (if the importer has a superior credit rating). By selling the banker's acceptance, however, the bank can receive immediate cash to finance the transaction.

DO YOU UNDERSTAND?

1. What could a government do to support the value of its currency in the foreign exchange market?

2. How can a firm reduce its risk by using forward contracts?

3. When a country has high inflation, why is it risky for a foreigner to invest in that country?

4. Why might consumer groups support government policies that maintain a strong U.S. dollar?

5. If the United States has a high rate of inflation, what happens to the value of the dollar? Why?

**12.9 INTER-
NATIONAL
MONEY AND
CAPITAL
MARKETS**

Many business contracts all over the world call for payments in U.S. dollars because the U.S. economy is very large, politically stable, and subject to less regulation than other economies. Consequently, businesses, governments, and individuals choose to hold dollars. Dollar-denominated deposits provide a high degree of liquidity that can be deployed to conduct international trade or exchanged for other currencies.

Prior to World War II, the vast majority of these deposits were in large money-center banks in New York City. However, with the start of the Cold War in the 1950s, the Soviet Union feared that the U.S. government might expropriate deposits held on U.S. soil to repay defaulted czarist bonds that the Soviet government had repudiated. Some large London banks responded to this business opportunity by offering to hold dollar-denominated deposits in British banks. The Soviets withdrew their deposits from American banks and deposited them with European banks. The European banks then issued dollar-denominated deposit liabilities to the Soviets, which were backed by the deposit claims on American banks that the Soviets had transferred. By holding the dollar-denominated claims in Europe, the Soviets were able to avert the threat that the United States might freeze or expropriate their American bank deposits. These deposits were soon dubbed **Eurodollars**. The transaction creating Eurodollars is illustrated in Exhibit 12.9.

Today, the Euromarkets are vast, largely unregulated money and capital markets with centers in Europe, the Middle East, and Asia. The short-term Euromarkets are called **Eurocurrency markets**. A *Eurocurrency* is any currency held in a time deposit account outside its country of origin. Thus, for example, a *Eurodollar* is a dollar-denominated time deposit held in a bank outside the United States. The long-term market is called the **Eurobond market**, and a *Eurobond* is any bond issued and sold outside its country of origin. Thus, a *Eurodollar bond* is a bond issue denominated in U.S. dollars and sold outside the United States.

EXHIBIT 12.9
Transfer of Funds to the Eurocurrency Market

Initial Situation

U.S. Bank		European Bank	
Assets	Liabilities	Assets	Liabilities
	USSR deposits ($)		

Transfer of Deposits to Europe

U.S. Bank		European Bank	
Assets	Liabilities	Assets	Liabilities
	European bank deposits ($)	Deposits in U.S. banks($)	USSR dollar-denominated deposits ($)

The Eurodollar market allows individuals or firms to hold dollars in banks outside the United States. By holding dollar-denominated deposits outside the United States, the deposit holders may be able to avoid restrictions on capital flows or other sanctions imposed by the U.S. government while still owning dollar-denominated deposits.

EUROCURRENCY MARKET

Eurocurrency markets serve three vital functions in international finance. First, they are a particularly attractive source of working capital for multinational corporations. They are attractive because the rates on Eurocurrency loans may be lower than for equivalent loans in the domestic economy. For Eurodollars, the rates are lower in the Euromarkets because (1) there are no reserve requirements or insurance costs associated with the deposits, and thus the overhead costs are lower; and (2) the Euromarkets are wholesale, mainly interbank markets, meaning that all participants are particularly creditworthy, the minimum transaction size is $500,000, and credit-checking and other processing costs are minimal. Because of these factors, lending rates can be lower than in the domestic U.S. market, and deposit rates can be higher without sacrificing profitability.

The second function of the Eurocurrency markets is serving as storehouses for excess liquidity. Corporations, international banks, and central banks find it convenient to hold their idle funds in these markets and earn highly competitive rates of return. There is less regulation in the Eurocurrency markets. This makes them attractive to investors who wish to hold securities in bearer form to preserve their anonymity. The absence of tax withholding on interest earned in some of the Eurocurrency markets also makes them attractive to foreigners.

Finally, the Eurocurrency markets facilitate international trade. Even when trade is financed by letters of credit, banks find it attractive to use Eurocurrency loans to make payments. Corporations sometimes borrow directly in the Eurocurrency markets and pay cash in return for discounts on goods and services. Without this source of capital at very competitive rates, the volume of international trade would be lower because of the higher cost of less flexible financing arrangements.

The outstanding amount of this *stateless money*, as it has been called, is extremely difficult to measure, but the gross size of the Eurocurrency market is many trillions of dollars. Because about half of Eurocurrency deposits are interbank transfers, the net, or *retail*, size of the market is somewhat smaller but still consists of many trillions of dollars. In practice, Eurocurrency deposits are highly liquid because many have maturities ranging from less than a day to a few months. Nearly one-third have a maturity of 8 days or less, and nearly 90 percent have maturities of under 6 months. Relatively few deposits have maturities longer than 1 year.

LIBOR AND EURIBOR

The Eurodollar markets began as wholesale markets for interbank transactions. The markets are now used by banks around the world as a source of overnight borrowing. The interest rate on this borrowing is known as **LIBOR**, the London Interbank Offering Rate. The funds in wholesale Eurodollar markets are a very close substitute for the U.S. federal funds. Loans in both markets are typically 1-day, unsecured loans denominated in U.S. dollars. As a result, the fed funds and LIBOR rates tend to be very closely related and move together, as can be seen in Exhibit 12.10. On the wholesale commercial lending side, LIBOR and the U.S. prime rate are the base rates used to determine the borrower's interest cost in nearly all international lending.

Although the fed funds and LIBOR markets are close substitutes, the fed funds rate tends to be slightly lower because of the relative strength of the U.S.

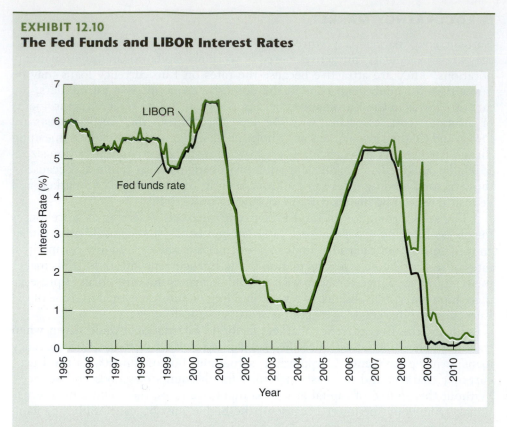

EXHIBIT 12.10

The Fed Funds and LIBOR Interest Rates

The fed funds and LIBOR interest rates are both short-term, unsecured loans denominated in dollars and are close substitutes for one another. The fed funds rate is typically 10 to 20 basis points lower than the LIBOR rate.

Source: The Federal Reserve System, Board of Governors, The Center for Research in Security Prices (CRSP).

banking system and the fact that U.S. bank deposits are covered by deposit insurance. Moreover, there is a perception based on historical action by U.S. bank regulators that U.S. money-center banks are "too big to fail" and that, in effect, the federal government will not allow one of these large banks to fail. Foreign banks have no such guarantees. Historically, the spread between the two rates has been approximately 10 to 12 basis points.

The introduction of the euro in January 1999 created an important new currency market. To provide a benchmark for this new market, **EURIBOR**, or Euro Interbank Offered Rate, was created. This is the rate on euro deposits offered by one prime bank to another prime bank within the EMU.

EUROBOND MARKETS

Eurobonds are long-term bonds issued and sold outside the country of origin. Eurobonds were first sold in 1963 as a way for issuers to avoid taxes and government regulations. At the time, U.S. government currency policy was aimed at keeping domestic dollars invested at home. As a result, U.S. businesses were limited in the amount of funds they could borrow to invest overseas, whereas the bond issues of foreign firms sold in the United States were subject to a 30 percent tax on their coupon interest. The first Eurobonds were denominated in dollars and other currencies and were not subject to U.S. regulations. Even though the U.S. currency regulations were later abandoned, the Eurobond market remained and has grown in popularity. U.S. firms found that, at times, they could sell Eurodollar bonds for domestic investment at substantially lower borrowing costs than similar domestic issues. The savings could be as large as 50 to 100 basis points compared to similar domestic bond issues. Thus, Eurobonds became an alternative source of long-term domestic financing for U.S. multinational firms.

Eurobonds are underwritten by an international syndicate of large commercial banks and securities underwriters. Large selling syndicates then take the bonds to market. Eurobonds tend to be issued in bearer form; pay interest once a year using a 360-day year; are issued in denominations of $5,000 and $10,000; and are traded in the over-the-counter market, mainly in London and Luxembourg. In contrast, bond issues sold in the United States are typically registered bonds and pay coupon interest semiannually. The fact that most Eurobonds are bearer bonds increases their marketability because the identity of the owner is not a matter of public record. In the early years of the market, many of the investors in Eurobonds were wealthy individuals and small investors with an eye toward tax avoidance. During this time, the secondary market for Eurobonds was weak and most of the issues did not have bond ratings. However, in recent years more issues are rated as individual investors are overshadowed in importance by large institutional investors such as mutual funds and pension funds. The fact that most countries regulate securities denominated in foreign currencies only loosely, if at all, means that disclosure requirements and registration costs for Eurobond issues are much lower than those for comparable domestic issues. Hence, Eurobond issues are widely perceived as a cost-effective means of raising long-term debt capital.

12.10 THE GLOBALIZATION OF FINANCIAL MARKETS

Since the mid-1970s, we have witnessed the globalization of business and the exponential growth of international financial markets. Financial instruments and even entire markets that did not exist in the early 1970s have developed and grown to maturity. A complex interaction of historical, political, and economic factors drives the globalization of financial markets. Historical and political factors include the demise of the Bretton Woods system of fixed exchange rates, the economic disruption caused by widely fluctuating oil prices, the large trade deficits experienced by the United States, Japan's rise to financial preeminence during the 1980s and its weakness in the 1990s and early 2000s, the global economic expansion that began in late 1982, the Asian economic crisis in the late 1990s, the fall of the USSR, and the adoption of the euro in 1999. Long-term economic and technological factors that have promoted the internationalization of financial markets include the global trend toward financial deregulation, the standardization of business practices and processes, the ongoing integration of international product and service markets, and breakthroughs in telecommunications and computer technology. We now discuss factors that have led to the globalization of financial markets.

EMERGENCE OF FLOATING EXCHANGE RATES

Under the Bretton Woods fixed exchange rate system, which lasted from 1944 to 1971, corporations had little need for protection against exchange rate movements. The floating exchange rate regime that came about in the 1970s, however, was characterized by rapid and extreme changes in currency values in response to changes in the supply and demand for currencies. This induced an increased demand for foreign exchange and hedging services. International banks quickly developed large, expert, and profitable foreign exchange trading staffs to meet the needs of their corporate clients.

AMERICA AS A DEBTOR NATION

Much has been written about the economic and political consequences of the transformation of the United States from the world's largest creditor in 1980 to the world's largest debtor by 1988. Relatively little, however, has been written about the purely financial impact of this phenomenon. There have been two major effects. First, because corporate capital spending actually rose as the budget and trade deficits mushroomed in the 1980s, the United States had to borrow money from foreigners on a scale never before imagined. This caused the world's most sophisticated financial system to become even larger, more efficient, and more innovative. Second, as the national debt zoomed upward, the U.S. Treasury security market emerged as a truly global bond market of immense size and liquidity.

RISE OF MULTINATIONAL COMPANIES

As the economies of the world have become increasingly interdependent in recent years, large multinational companies have grown ever more powerful. For these companies, capital is almost completely mobile, and their approach to financial management is global in scope and sophisticated in technique. Most large multinational firms have integrated sales and production operations in 100 or more countries, which also require state-of-the-art systems for currency trading, cash management, capital budgeting, and risk management. The financial needs of these companies have been met by the major international banks that have followed their customers as they expanded around the world.

TECHNOLOGY

Breakthroughs in telecommunications and computer technology have transformed international finance at least as much as they have transformed our own lives and careers. Daily international capital movements larger than the gross national products of most countries have now become routine as a result of the speed, reliability, and pervasiveness of information-processing technology. Computers now direct multibillion-dollar program trading systems in equity, futures, and options markets around the world, and a telecommunications *global village* has become a reality for currency traders operating 24 hours a day, 365 days per year from outposts on every continent. The future will certainly bring even more rapid innovation.

THE DOLLAR AS THE "NEW GOLD STANDARD"

One of the problems that currencies encounter is that governments develop reputations for the way they conduct monetary policy. For example, say that a country conducts monetary policy in an irresponsible manner by issuing too much currency, which leads to high rates of domestic inflation and possible devaluation of the currency. People soon become reluctant to hold the currency. Because of the devaluation risk, people who lend money in that currency demand higher interest rates as compensation for risk bearing.

Because people wish to trade with stable currencies that are widely accepted, the U.S. dollar has benefited. For instance, it is estimated that roughly two-thirds of all U.S. currency outstanding is held outside the United States. The reason, in part, is because the U.S. dollar is highly valued for trade and as a store of value because the United States has low inflation relative to most countries. This works out as a good deal for the United States. That is, by printing pieces of paper that are used as currency in many countries around the world, the United States and its citizens are able to obtain valuable goods in exchange. Thus, the United States profits from seigniorage whenever it prints money at low cost and trades its currency for valuable foreign goods. **Seigniorage** is the difference between the cost of the printed currency and the exchange value of the currency.

Some countries have adopted the U.S. currency as a medium of exchange. In Panama, for example, customers pay for their purchases with U.S. dollars. Such countries are said to have *dollarized* their economies. Through **dollarization**, countries can obtain a stable currency widely used in world trade, which makes their accounting and international transactions easier. In addition, their borrowers no longer have to pay an interest rate risk premium to international lenders who fear the currency will be devalued before their loans are paid back.

SUMMARY OF LEARNING OBJECTIVES

1 **Explain the types of risks that U.S. firms face when engaging in international trade.** The major risks for a U.S. firm importing goods are currency risk, country risk due to the fact that the exporter is not a citizen and may be from a country with a different legal system, and the difficulty of getting reliable credit information.

2 **Explain how a country can run a deficit in its balance of trade and still have a strong currency, given the conventional wisdom suggesting that a trade deficit should lead to a decline in a currency's value.** International capital flows by themselves can cause the value of a currency to rise or fall even though the country has a trade deficit. Exchange rates are affected by both trade flows and capital flows, and capital flows can offset trade deficits. For example, starting in the late 1990s, the U.S. dollar rose in value as a result of large capital inflows that more than offset its large current account deficits.

3 **Explain the main functions of foreign exchange markets.** Foreign exchange markets allow one to convert purchasing power in one currency to another. The main functions of the markets include international trade financing, transfer of bank deposits and loans in foreign currencies, and foreign currency derivatives trading.

4 **Explain why the Eurodollar deposit and Eurobond markets have become so important in recent years.** The Eurodollar deposit and Eurobond markets have become important in recent years because the markets provide a large pool of U.S. dollars available for U.S. and foreign firms to borrow or lend. Because of the strength and size of the U.S. economy, the dollar has become an important medium of exchange throughout the world. In addition, more relaxed regulations in these markets have fostered recent growth.

5 **Explain why Europe introduced the euro as its currency.** The euro was introduced to eliminate exchange rate uncertainties so trade and financial planning would become easier among European countries.

KEY TERMS

Exchange rate	Countertrade	Fixed exchange rates	Eurodollars
Depreciates	Spot rate	Bretton Woods system	Eurocurrency markets
Appreciates	Forward rate	Letter of credit (LC)	Eurobond market
Euro	Purchasing power parity	Draft	LIBOR
Balance of	(PPP)	Sight draft	EURIBOR
payments	Investment capital flows	Time draft	Eurobonds
Current account	Political capital flows	Bill of lading	Seigniorage
Capital accounts	Capital flight	Banker's acceptance	Dollarization

QUESTIONS AND PROBLEMS

1. If a bushel of corn costs £3.00, and a British pound is worth $1.50, how many dollars would a person receive for 100,000 bushels of corn sold in Britain in the spot market? If the delivery were to occur in 3 months and the U.S. interest rate exceeded the British rate by 2 percent per year, what would be received in the forward exchange market for a conversion arranged now if the current spot rate is $1.50 per British pound? Explain.

2. If a dollar can buy 98 Japanese yen and a British pound costs $1.50, how many yen would it take to buy £1? If a pound of copper costs £1 in Britain, ¥1,600 per pound in Tokyo, and $1.45 per pound in the United States, where is a pound of copper most expensive and where is it least expensive?

3. Assume that the spot and 1-year forward rates for the British pound are $1.60 and $1.55, respectively, and are $0.90 and $0.92 per euro, respectively. If interest rates are 4 percent in the United States, 6 percent in Britain, and 3 percent in Germany, where can you get the best return on a covered 1-year investment?

4. If the United States runs a deficit in its current account of $100 billion and receives a net inflow of $60 billion on long-term investments in a year, by how much will its short-term capital flows have to change in order to accommodate all these flows?

5. Why are international banks able to earn large fees by providing letters of credit and forward currency transactions?

6. If purchasing power parity applied to Big Macs, and a Big Mac cost $2.50 in the United States, whereas the British pound cost $1.50 and €0.90 could be obtained for $1.00, how much would the Big Mac cost in Britain and Germany, respectively? Why might it actually have a different price?

7. If the Japanese yen were to change from 100 per dollar to 90 per dollar, would the U.S. balance of payments improve (become more positive) or not? Consider what effect this exchange rate change would have on both U.S. exports to and imports from Japan, as well as on purchase decisions made by manufacturers or importers located in other countries.

8. Assume that the United States and Canada are both initially in an economic recession and that the United States begins to recover before Canada. What would you expect to happen to the U.S. dollar–Canadian dollar exchange rate? Why?

9. The newly industrializing countries (NICs) of the Far East, such as Korea, Taiwan, and Hong Kong, dramatically increased their merchandise exports during the 1980s. Based on what you know about the determinants of international trade flows, explain why this export success occurred and what effect it should have on the exchange value of the NICs' currencies.

10. Explain the role that letters of credit and banker's acceptances play in international transactions. Is a banker's acceptance a sight draft? Why or why not?

11. Why do domestic governments often try to limit domestic flows of funds abroad for investment in foreign countries? How did such limitations in the United States contribute to the development of the Eurodollar markets?

12. Will the domestic capital account be helped or hurt if foreign investment inflows into the country increase?

13. How can central bank intervention affect the exchange value of a currency? Will the currency generally rise or fall if a central bank sells its home currency?

14. How does inflation affect a country's spot and forward exchange rates? Why? Is it absolute inflation, or inflation relative to other countries that is important?

15. Describe the factors that promoted the internationalization of financial markets during the previous 15 years. Are any of these factors reversible?

16. Suppose the spot exchange rate today is $1.5/£. The inflation rate is expected to be 3 percent in the United States and 5 percent in the United Kingdom over the next year. The annual real interest rate will be 2 percent in both economies. Calculate the nominal interest rates in both counties next year.

17. Suppose the spot exchange rate today is $1.5/£. The annual inflation rate is expected to be 3 percent in the United States and 5 percent in the United Kingdom in the next 3 years. The annual real interest rate will be 2 percent in both economies in each of the next 3 years. Calculate the nominal interest rates in both countries next year.

18. Suppose the nominal interest rates are 5 percent in the United States and 2 percent in the United Kingdom this year. The inflation rate is 1.5 percent in the United States and 2 percent in the United Kingdom next year. Calculate the real interest rates in both countries. Which country is likely to attract more investment from abroad, everything else holding constant?

19. Suppose the spot exchange rate today is $1.5/£. The inflation rate is expected to be 3 percent in the United States and 5 percent in the United Kingdom over the next year. What is the expected exchange rate in 1 year? Is the pound expected to appreciate or depreciate against the U.S. dollar 1 year from now, based on PPP?

20. Suppose the spot exchange rate today is $1.5/£. The inflation rate is expected to be 3 percent in the United States and 5 percent in the United Kingdom each year over the next 2 years. What is the expected exchange rate at the end of year two? Is the pound expected to appreciate or depreciate against the U.S. dollar at the end of year 2, based on PPP?

21. An American importer needs to pay £100,000 in 30 days and would like to sign a forward contract to hedge the exchange risk. Should the importer buy or sell pounds through a forward contract? Suppose the 30-day forward rate is $1.60/£ and after signing the contract, the spot rate in 30 days turns out to be $1.55. How many dollars does the firm have to pay in 30 days? Should the firm have not hedged?

22. An American exporter is expected to receive ¥10,000,000 in 180 days and would like to sign a forward contract to hedge the exchange risk. Should the exporter buy or sell yen through a forward contract? Suppose the 180-day forward rate is $0.01/£, and the spot rate in 180 days turns out to be $0.0105. How many dollars will she expect to receive in this case? Should she not have hedged?

23. An American importer needs to pay £250,000 in 90 days and would like to use currency options to hedge the risk of appreciation of the pound. Should the importer buy a call or a put option on pounds? Suppose an option on £250,000 maturing in 90 days has a strike price of $1.60/£, and the spot rate in 90 days turns out to be $1.55. Should the importer exercise the option if she has bought the option contract? How many dollars does the firm have to pay in 180 days?

24. An American exporter is expected to receive ¥10,000,000 in 180 days and would like to use currency options to hedge the exchange risk. Should she buy a call or a put option on Japanese yen? Suppose an option on ¥10,000,000 maturing in 180 days has a strike price of $0.01/¥, and the spot rate in 180 days turns out to be $0.0085/¥. Should the exporter exercise the option if she bought the option contract? How many dollars does the firm expect to receive in this case?

25. You noticed the current spot exchange rate is $1.50/£ and the 1-year forward exchange rate is $1.60/£. The 1-year interest rate is 5.4 percent in dollars and 5.2 percent in pounds. Assuming you can borrow at most $1,000,000 or the equivalent pound amount (i.e., £666,667, at the current spot exchange rate), can you make a guaranteed profit? If so, how would you carry out the transaction? If not, why not?

INTERNET EXERCISE

The United States conducts its monetary policy and foreign exchange operations through the Federal Reserve Bank of New York. For this reason, the president of the New York Fed always has a vote on the Federal Open Market Committee. Because it is intimately connected with the U.S. and foreign financial markets, the New York Fed compiles useful data both on U.S. financial markets and on international currency exchange rates. The New York Fed Web page can be reached at http://www.ny.frb.org/, and its daily foreign currency quotes can be obtained from its 12:00 noon foreign exchange (forex) rate site, which can be found easily on its site map. Another useful site is the IMF's site, http://www.imf.org, which contains analyses of the world economy and country conditions, as well as exchange rate data and financial data related to IMF loans.

1. At the New York Fed site, some currencies are stated in terms of the amount of U.S. dollars needed to buy them, and others are priced according to the number of foreign currency units one gets per dollar. List all the currencies priced according to the number of units received per dollar. How do their values seem to differ from those priced the other way?

2. The New York Fed also publishes data on expected currency volatility based on option prices for major currencies. Find that location on the Fed's site map and answer the following:

   a. Over the next 6 months, which currency is expected to be most volatile relative to the U.S. dollar?

   b. Which country do you think has the highest-priced 6-month at-the-money options for its currency quoted in U.S. dollars?

3. Go to the IMF site and find its site map. Use that map to look up countries and find out the last time Argentina was given authority to borrow from the IMF.

PART IV

COMMERCIAL BANKING

Commercial Bank Operations

LIKE OTHER BUSINESSES, BANKS ARE profit-maximizing firms—a fact you are probably reminded of whenever you get charged a fee or service charge. If you are at all like other depositors, you probably do not like paying fees for letting your bank use your money. Banks and other financial intermediaries are unique because their creditors are also their customers. Whenever you deposit money in your bank account, you are effectively lending money to your bank, so it is understandable that you would grumble over paying fees and service charges associated with your checking account. The purpose of this chapter is to explain bank operations. Hopefully, by the time you finish reading this chapter, you will understand why your bank charges those fees and service charges. You probably still won't like the fees, but at least you will understand why the bank charges them. ■

The fundamental business of banking is to accept deposits as a source of funds and then to make loans to consumers and businesses. In the past, most transactions were face to face, with people dropping in on a weekly basis to see the banker and get free coffee and donuts. Today, customers rarely visit their bank, instead conducting most transactions over the phone, by wire, over the Internet, or at an ATM.

This chapter lays the foundation for how commercial banks operate. We begin the chapter by providing an overview of the banking industry. We continue by examining the principal business activities of banks as summarized on their balance sheets. Then we discuss in detail how banks set interest rates and make loans. We also examine the fee-based activities of banks: wealth management and advisory services, correspondent banking, and the off-balance-sheet transactions of loan commitments, letters of credit, loan sales, and derivative securities. Once we have an understanding of the various ways banks earn income, we describe bank income statements and discuss some of the trends in the income and expense items. Finally, we discuss the role of bank holding companies and financial holding companies. ■

LEARNING OBJECTIVES

1 Describe the size and structure of the U.S. banking industry.

2 Discuss banks' sources and uses of funds as reflected on their balance sheets.

3 Explain how banks make lending decisions and how they price their loans.

4 Describe the various fee-based activities of banks.

5 Explain the various off-balance-sheet activities of banks and describe how these activities generate revenue for banks and the conditions under which they become on-balance-sheet activities.

6 Discuss recent trends concerning bank earning and performance.

7 Discuss the development and structure of bank holding companies and the newly formed financial holding companies.

13.1 AN OVERVIEW OF THE BANKING INDUSTRY

Commercial banks are among the most important types of financial institutions because of their size and role in indirect financial markets. They are the largest category of financial institutions, with over $14 trillion in assets. Recall from Chapter 1 that banks and other financial institutions are often called financial intermediaries because they buy financial claims (e.g., mortgages and automobile loans) with one set of characteristics and sell financial claims (e.g., checking account and certificates of deposit) with a different set of characteristics.

Commercial banks' importance was most noticeable during the recent financial crisis, when policymakers considered banks so important that regulators deemed some of them too big to fail and others received government assistance as part of the Troubled Asset Relief Program (TARP). TARP was authorized under the Emergency Economic Stabilization Act of 2008. We will discuss the concept of too big to fail and TARP further in Chapter 15. We refer to them here, however, because they illustrate policymakers' perspective on the importance of the banking industry to the overall health of the economy.

There are currently about 6,600 banks in the United States employing almost 2 million workers. Although this number may seem large, Exhibit 13.1 shows that more than three times as many banks were operating in the 1920s. Frequent bank panics and the collapse of the nation's financial system during the Great Depression (1930–1933) reduced the number of banks from more than 30,000 at the beginning of the 1920s to about 15,000 by 1933. After the Great Depression, the number of banks continued to decline gradually until the 1960s, primarily because of bank mergers rather than bank failures. After 1960, the number of banks increased slightly, stabilizing at around 15,000 until the late 1980s. Then, in the late 1980s and the 1990s the number of banks declined as a result of failures and mergers. Since the early 1980s, however, the number of total banking offices (branches plus main offices) has been increasing despite the downward trend in the number of banks. The reason is the increase in the number of branches. Even though the number of banks has decreased, geographic restrictions on banking have relaxed since the mid-1980s, resulting in more branches per bank.

BRANCHING AND CONSOLIDATION

Although the number of banks has declined in recent years, the number of banking offices has grown dramatically because of a sharp increase in the number of branches. In 1941, there were only 3,564 branch offices in this country. By 2010, there were

EXHIBIT 13.1
Number of Banks and Branches of Commercial Banks (1920–2010)

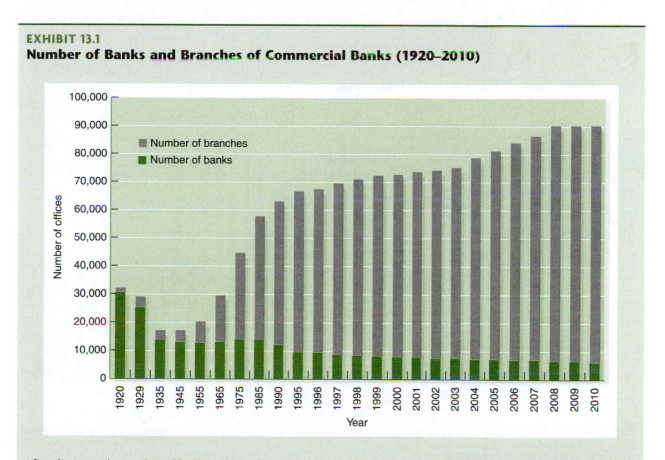

After the 1950s the number of banks and branches increased until the late 1980s. With consolidation and the emergence of electronic banking, the number of banks has declined. The number of branches per bank, however, continues to increase.

Source: FDIC, *Statistics on Banking.*

about 90,000 banking offices, and about 83,000 of these were branch offices. This rapid growth in branches was a result of banks following their customers as they moved from the cities to the suburbs and the easing of state branching restrictions.

Contrary to predictions that improvements in technology would lead to a reduction in the number of bank branches, industry research indicates that locational convenience is still the most important determinant of consumers' bank selection decisions. Even though many consumers do most of their banking online, they are still more likely to choose a bank with a nearby branch. In addition, recent research indicates that some banks invest in branches in an effort to deter other banks from entering the market. Therefore, the number of bank branches continues to increase, albeit at a slower pace than in the past.

The decline in the number of banks can be attributed to the rapid pace of consolidation taking place in the industry since the mid-1980s. The growth in bank mergers is illustrated in Exhibit 13.2. Although many of the mergers that

EXHIBIT 13.2
Mergers in the Banking Industry (1970–2010)

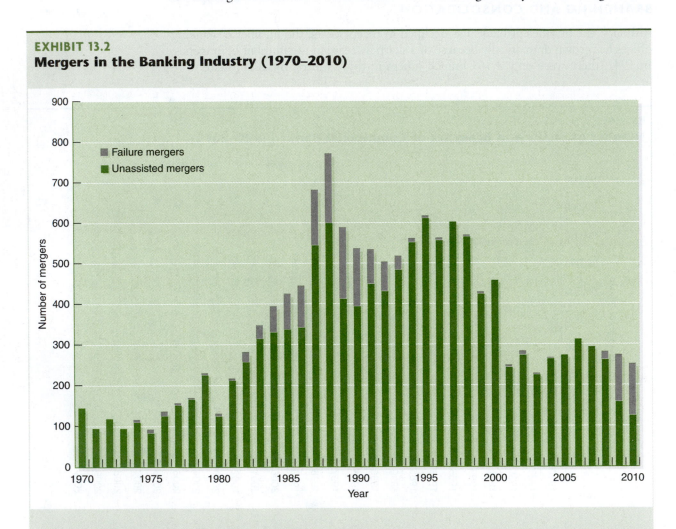

Beginning in the 1980s, the number of mergers in the banking industry grew steadily until the peak in the mid-1990s. The vast majority of these mergers have been voluntary mergers, with the exception of several mergers of failed banks in the late 1980s, early 1990s, and late 2000s.

Note: 2010 figures are estimates.
Source: FDIC, *Statistics on Banking.*

took place during the late 1980s and most recently were the result of failed banks being acquired by healthy banks, the majority of mergers have been the result of deregulation, improvements in technology, and the reduction in geographic restrictions.

In the last 10 years, the pace of consolidation slowed as many banks began to focus more on their internal operations. In addition, there were fewer potential acquisitions to choose from, and many banks were still trying to digest some of their earlier acquisitions. In fact, many banks sold off some of the branches they had previously acquired in order to streamline their operations and reduce redundancies. Finally, deteriorating economic and financial conditions from 2008 to 2010 substantially reduced the number of unassisted mergers.

It seems unlikely, however, that the decline in mergers and acquisitions will continue for very long. Most industry observers view the slowdown as being temporary. As the economy improves and more small banks grow into attractive acquisition targets, the pace of consolidation is likely to accelerate again.

SIZE DISTRIBUTION OF BANKS

We can further increase our understanding of the structure of commercial banking by examining the size distribution of banks. As shown in Exhibit 13.3, the overwhelming majority of U.S. banks are very small. Currently, the smallest 6,495 banks (or about 97 percent of all banks) in this country hold only 21 percent of the deposits in the banking industry. Most of these small banks are located in small one- or two-bank towns. In contrast, the largest 84 banks (about 1 percent of all banks) hold 73 percent of the deposits in the industry.

EXHIBIT 13.3
Deposit Distribution of All Insured Commercial Banks (June 30, 2010)

Asset Size	Number of Banks	Total Deposits (in Millions)	Number of Banks		Total Deposits	
			Percentage	Cumulative Percentage	Percentage	Cumulative Percentage
Less than $25 million	291	$4,263	4	4	0	0
$25 to 50 million	732	23,377	11	15	0	0
$50 to 100 million	1,411	88,115	21	36	1	2
$100 to 300 million	2,500	370,622	37	74	5	7
$300 to 500 million	701	224,540	11	84	3	10
$500 to 1 billion	536	304,041	8	92	4	15
$1 to 3 billion	324	426,476	5	97	6	21
$3 to 10 billion	97	389,289	1	99	6	27
$10 billion or more	84	4,940,163	1	100	73	100
Total	6,676	6,770,886	99		100	

Although there are about 6,676 banks in the United States, the largest 1 percent of the banks control almost three-fourths of all banking deposits.

Source: FDIC, *Statistics on Banking*, June 30, 2010.

EXHIBIT 13.4

The 10 Largest Bank Holding Companies in the United States (September 30, 2010).

Rank	Bank Holding Company	Location	Total Assets (in Millions)
1	Bank of America Corporation	Charlotte, NC	$2,341,160
2	JP Morgan Chase & Co.	New York, NY	$2,141,595
3	Citigroup Inc.	New York, NY	$1,983,280
4	Wells Fargo & Company	San Francisco, CA	$1,220,784
5	Goldman Sachs Group, Inc.	New York, NY	$908,860
6	Morgan Stanley	New York, NY	$841,372
7	Metlife, Inc.	New York, NY	$617,254
8	Taunus Corporation	New York, NY	$389,993
9	HSBC North America Holdings Inc.	New York, NY	$350,102
10	U.S. Bancorp	Minneapolis, MN	$290,654

Bank of America Corporation is the largest bank holding company in the United States. It is almost 10 times larger than the nation's tenth largest bank holding company. Seven of the top 10 bank holding companies are headquartered in New York, the nation's traditional financial center.

Source: Federal Financial Institutions Examination Council, *Top 50 Bank Holding Companies,* September 30, 2010.

Exhibit 13.4 shows the largest bank holding companies (BHCs) in the United States ranked by total assets. Bank holding companies are simply companies that have an ownership interest in at least one bank. Most banks are owned by bank holding companies. At the end of 2009, there were 5,634 bank holding companies that controlled 5,710 commercial banks with about 99 percent of all commercial bank assets. Bank of America Corporation is the largest BHC, with total assets over $2.3 trillion. Seven of the top 10 are located in New York City, the country's financial center.

13.2 BALANCE SHEET FOR A COMMERCIAL BANK

We now turn our attention to examining the operations of a commercial bank. A good place to start is a commercial bank's balance sheet. The balance sheet lists what the business owns (assets), what the firm owes to others (liabilities), and what the owners have invested (capital) as of a given time. The basic balance sheet equation for any organization expresses the relationship between these accounts as

$$\text{Assets} = \text{liabilities} + \text{capital}$$

The capital account (or *net worth*) is a residual that can be calculated by subtracting liabilities owed to creditors from the total assets owned by the organization. The right side of the equation can be viewed as the sources of funds for a bank. Funds are supplied by either creditors (liabilities) or the owners (capital). The left side of the equation shows the uses of funds (assets) that the bank has obtained from the creditors and owners.

In Exhibit 13.5, the major liability and capital items in dollars and percentages are shown for all insured commercial banks and for small, medium, and large banks. The principal source of funds for most banks is deposit accounts—demand, savings, and time deposits. Economically, deposit accounts are similar to other sources of funds borrowed by the bank. Legally, however, deposits take precedence over other sources of funds in case of a bank failure. Furthermore, the

13.3 THE SOURCE OF BANK FUNDS

EXHIBIT 13.5
Liabilities and Capital Accounts of Commercial Banks (September 30, 2010)

Liabilities and Capital Accounts	All Insured Commercial Banks[a]		Small Banks[b]	Medium-Size Banks[c]	Large Banks[d]
	Billions	Percent[e]	Percent[e]	Percent[e]	Percent[e]
Liabilities					
Deposits, Total	$8,373	69	85	83	66
Noninterest-bearing	1,634	13	14	12	14
Interest-bearing	6,739	56	71	71	54
Borrowed Funds, Total	1,902	16	3	6	17
Federal funds purchased and securities sold under repurchase agreements	565	5	0	2	5
Trading liabilities	318	3	0	0	3
Other borrowed money	1,019	8	3	4	9
Subordinated notes and debentures	149	1	0	0	1
All other liabilities	328	3	1	1	3
Total liabilities	$10,752	89	88	90	89
Capital Accounts					
Common and preferred stock	1,091	9	7	6	9
Undivided profits	288	2	5	4	2
Total equity capital	$1,379	11	12	10	11
Total liabilities and equity capital	$12,131	100	100	100	100

Deposits are the largest source of funds for most banks, but they are a much more important source for small and medium-size banks. Borrowed funds are a more important source of funds for large banks. Banks in general are thinly capitalized, but small banks tend to be better capitalized than large ones.

[a]This group consists of 6,622 insured commercial banks.
[b]This group consists of the country's 2,383 smallest banks. These banks have assets of less than $100 million.
[c]This group consists of the country's 3,731 medium-size banks. These banks have assets between $100 million and $1 billion.
[d]This group consists of the country's 508 largest banks. These banks have assets of $1 billion or more.
[e]Columns may not add to 100 percent because of rounding.

Source: FDIC, *Statistics on Banking*, September 30, 2010.

Federal Deposit Insurance Corporation (FDIC) insures the holders of such accounts against any loss up to a maximum of $250,000 per individual depositor.

TRANSACTION ACCOUNTS

Banks offer a number of transaction accounts, which are commonly called *checking accounts*. They serve as the basic medium of exchange in the economy, accounting for about half of the total money supply (M1). Transaction accounts account for about 13 percent of all deposits.

Demand Deposits.   A **demand deposit** is a checking account in which the owner is entitled to receive his or her funds on demand and to write checks on the account, which transfers legal ownership of funds to others. Individuals, government entities, and business organizations can own demand deposits.

The demand deposits of individual corporations and state and local governments are held primarily for transaction purposes. The U.S. Treasury Department also holds deposits in commercial banks.

NOW Accounts.   Until 1980, most banks could not pay explicit interest on checking accounts. Because these deposits provided banks with funds to lend and invest, banks competed for these costless funds by providing individual customers with free services or services sold for less than their cost. Such services include check writing, safekeeping, accounting, and the sale of traveler's checks. These constituted implicit interest payments to the holders of these deposits.

In 1980, the Depository Institutions Deregulation and Monetary Control Act (DIDMCA) allowed all depository financial institutions in the nation to offer NOW (negotiable order of withdrawal) accounts. **NOW accounts** are just demand deposits that pay interest.

SAVINGS DEPOSITS

Historically, savings accounts were the traditional form of savings held by most individuals and nonprofit organizaions. Since the beginning of the deregulation of the financial system in 1980, however, these accounts are becoming a less important source of funds for all banks as consumers switch to higher yielding and more convenient checkable money market deposit accounts.

Savings Accounts.   A blue or green passbook was the standard symbol of savings for generations of Americans. When funds were deposited or withdrawn from a savings account, the passbook had to be presented and the transaction recorded in it. Today most consumers do not receive passbooks. Instead, they receive quarterly statements from the bank and do most of their savings transactions electronically. With the development of money market deposit accounts, savings accounts have become much less important as a source of funds for banks. They now account for about 15 percent of bank deposits.

Money Market Deposit Accounts. To allow banks to be more competitive with money market mutual funds (MMMFs), the Garn–St. Germain Act of 1982 authorized banks to issue accounts directly equivalent to MMMF accounts. In the past, MMMF accounts had grown rapidly whenever market rates of interest rose above the legal limit banks could pay on deposits (Regulation Q). MMMF accounts allowed the public to earn the market rate of interest and offered limited checking features. The regulatory response, in December 1982, was the **money market deposit account (MMDA)**.

MMDAs are federally insured and pay an interest rate that is set at the discretion of the issuing bank. The exact features, such as minimum balance requirements, vary from bank to bank. However, by law depositors are limited to six third-party transfers each month. The account is available to all bank customers, including for-profit corporations. MMDAs quickly proved to be popular with consumers and helped banks attract funds from MMMFs. They account for about 46 percent of bank deposits, making them the largest source of funds for banks.

TIME DEPOSITS

At one time, time deposits were the largest source of funds for banks. With the increased popularity of MMDAs in recent years, however, time deposits are now the second largest source of funds. Time deposits account for 26 percent of bank deposits. Unlike demand deposits, time deposits are not available until their maturity date, and the funds cannot be transferred to another party by a written check. The principal types of bank time deposits are certificates of deposit and negotiable (or jumbo) certificates of deposit.

Certificates of Deposit. Primarily consumers or other small depositors hold **certificates of deposit (CDs)**, which have grown in popularity since the mid-1980s. They are an important source of funds for small, consumer-oriented banks. CDs are bank liabilities issued in a designated amount, specifying a fixed rate of interest and maturity date. The interest rate is generally higher than on savings accounts.

Negotiable Certificates of Deposit. Negotiable certificates of deposit, commonly referred to as *jumbo CDs*, are very large, unsecured liabilities of commercial banks issued in denominations of $100,000 or more to business firms and individuals. They have a fixed maturity date, pay an explicit rate of interest, and are negotiable if they meet certain legal specifications. Negotiable CDs are issued by large, well-known commercial banks of the highest credit standing and are traded actively in a well-organized secondary market.

Negotiable CDs are attractive both to holders of large funds and to commercial banks. They can be redeemed at any time in the secondary market without loss of deposit funds to the bank. CDs allow large commercial banks to attract temporary funds that had previously been invested in other money market instruments. Smaller banks can issue large CDs, but their CDs do not have active secondary markets and thus lose much of their appeal to large investors. The interest rate on CDs is competitive with the rates on comparable money market instruments. Since 1973, there has been no interest rate ceiling on CDs in denominations of $100,000 or more.

BORROWED FUNDS

Borrowed funds are typically short-term borrowings by commercial banks from the wholesale money markets or a Federal Reserve bank. They are economically similar to deposits but are not insured by the FDIC. Although they account for only 16 percent of all bank funds, borrowed funds have grown in importance as high levels of loan demand have increasingly provided banks with the incentive to develop other sources of funds. As loan demand outpaced deposit growth, banks increasingly turned to borrowed funds to fill the funding gap. Exhibit 13.6 illustrates this growth.

EXHIBIT 13.6
Liabilities and Capital Accounts of Commercial Banks (1955–2010)

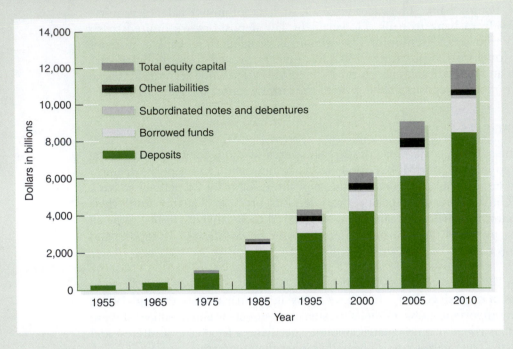

Increased demand for loans at banks has outpaced the growth in deposits at banks. As a result, banks have had to rely more heavily on borrowed funds to finance their operations. Banks made little use of money market sources of funds until the mid-1980s. In recent years, however, banks have made greater use of borrowed funds. They currently account for almost 20 percent of all funds raised by banks.

Source: FDIC, *Statistics on Banking.*

Federal Funds.   For liquidity reasons, banks may hold reserves in excess of those required by law. A bank with more excess reserves than it desires may lend reserves to another bank that does not have its required level of reserves or that desires additional reserves to make more loans. The buying (*borrowing*) and selling (*lending*) of reserves on deposit at the Federal Reserve banks is called *trading in* **federal funds (fed funds)**.

The maturity of fed funds is usually 1 day, but the loans may be continuously renewed with the same or other banks in the fed funds market. Trading units tend to be very large, generally $1 million or more. About 150 large banks participate in the fed funds market regularly, and a number of other large banks participate intermittently.

Repurchase Agreements.   **Repurchase agreements (RPs)** are a form of loan in which the bank sells securities (usually government securities) to the lender but simultaneously contracts to repurchase the same securities either on call or on a specified date at a price that produces an agreed-on yield. For example, a corporation with idle cash balances agrees to buy a 90-day Treasury bill from a bank at a price to yield 2 percent with a contract to sell the bills back 1 day later. Most RP transactions are for $1 million or more and have a maturity of 1 day; however, the

RP can be renewed continuously on a day-to-day basis. There are also term RP transactions that are written for maturities up to 30 days.

Trading Liabilities.   *Trading liabilities* are liabilities because of short positions (from sales of securities that the bank does not own) in financial instruments and the fair value of derivative contracts that are in loss positions. As you might expect, large banks hold the bulk of trading liabilities.

Eurodollars.   Short-term deposits at foreign banks or foreign branches of U.S. banks are called **Eurodollars**. These represent a portion of the "other borrowed money" category in Exhibit 13.5. Eurodollars are denominated in U.S. dollars. U.S. banks may also borrow funds from individuals or other banks in the Eurodollar market for short periods of time. The interbank market is similar to the fed funds market except that interbank loans may be obtained for as long as 6 months. The base rate in this market is the **London Interbank Offer Rate (LIBOR)**. Only large banks actively participate in the Eurodollar market.

Banker's Acceptances.   A **banker's acceptance** is a draft drawn on a bank by a corporation to pay for merchandise. The draft promises payment of a certain sum of money to its holder at some future date. What makes such drafts unique is that a bank accepts them by prearrangement, thereby guaranteeing their payment at the stated time. In effect, the bank has substituted its credit standing for that of the issuer. Banker's acceptances can be held by the bank or sold in the secondary market as a source of funds. Most banker's acceptances arise in foreign trade transactions. Export and import firms find it less risky to deal in drafts guaranteed by well-known banks than those drawn against the bank accounts of firms with whom they are less familiar. Banker's acceptances are primarily a source of funds for large banks.

Federal Home Loan Bank Advances.   Beginning in March 2001, banks that devoted a large percentage of their loan portfolio to mortgage lending were given access to the loans provided by the Federal Home Loan Bank System. Unlike loans from the Federal Reserve Banks, these loans are longer-term in nature. This makes them especially attractive as a source of funds for banks that face an increasingly competitive market for deposits.

Federal Reserve Bank Loans.   Banks can borrow funds from their district Federal Reserve bank for short periods of time. The purpose of this type of borrowing is to cover short-term deficiencies of reserves. The traditional term of a discount loan is 15 days, although loans may be renewed with the approval of the Federal Reserve bank. Borrowing from the discount window requires that the bank apply to the Federal Reserve bank for the loan and receive its approval. Federal Reserve banks exercise close administrative control over this type of borrowing, and the amount of borrowing at the discount window is quite small, representing less than 1 percent of funds for all banks.

CAPITAL NOTES AND BONDS

Issuing bonds to raise funds is a common practice for most industrial firms. It is only in recent years that a few large commercial banks began raising funds by selling short-term capital notes or longer-term bonds. In the early 1960s, the Comptroller of the Currency ruled that debentures subordinate to the claims of depositors could be used to raise funds and that a limited amount of this debt could be counted as part of a bank's capital for regulatory purposes. Subordinated notes and debentures account for only a small percentage of the liabilities of commercial banks.

CAPITAL ACCOUNTS

Bank capital represents the equity or ownership funds of a bank, and it is the account against which bank loan and security losses are charged. The greater the proportion of capital to total funds, the greater the protection to uninsured depositors and creditors. Banks maintain much lower capital levels than other businesses, and currently bank capital accounts for 11 percent of total bank funds.

There are three principal types of capital accounts for a commercial bank: capital stock, undivided profits, and special reserve accounts. *Capital stock* represents the direct investments into the bank in the form of common or preferred stock; *undivided profits* (retained earnings) compose that accumulated portion of the bank's profit that has not been paid out to shareholders as dividends; *special reserve accounts* are set up to cover anticipated losses on loans and investments. Reserve accounts involve no transfers of funds or setting aside of cash. They are merely a form of retained earnings designed to reduce tax liabilities and stockholders' claims on current revenues.

DO YOU UNDERSTAND?

1. Approximately how many banks operate in the United States? Discuss trends in the number of banks versus the number of banking offices. What do these trends tell us about the future structure of the banking industry?

2. The interest rate on borrowed funds is usually higher than the interest rate on small time deposits. Given that, why do large banks continue to rely more heavily on borrowed funds as a source of funds?

3. What are the major sources of bank funds? How do these differ between large and small banks?

4. How does the proportion of capital for a typical bank compare with that of a typical industrial firm? Do you believe banks have adequate capital? Why or why not?

5. Why do you think that small banks are financed by a higher proportion of capital than large banks?

13.4 BANK USES OF FUNDS: BANK INVESTMENTS AND CASH ASSETS

The earning assets of a bank are typically classified as either loans or investments, and there are important differences between these two classes. *Loans* are the primary business of a bank and usually represent an ongoing relationship between the bank and its borrowers. A loan is a highly personalized contract between the borrower and the bank and is tailor-made to the particular needs of the customer. *Investments*, however, are standardized contracts issued by large, well-known borrowers, and their purchase by the bank represents an impersonal or open-market transaction; consequently, they can be resold by

EXHIBIT 13.7
Assets of Commercial Banks (September 30, 2010)

Assets Accounts	All Insured Commercial Banks[a]		Small Banks[b]	Medium-Size Banks[c]	Large Banks[d]
	$ Billions	Percent[e]	Percent[e]	Percent[e]	Percent[e]
Cash assets	$947	8	10	8	8
Federal funds sold and reverse repurchase agreements	$443	4	3	2	4
Investments, total	2,338	19	22	20	19
Loans and lease financing, total	6,613	55	61	66	53
Commercial and industrial	1,112	9	9	9	9
Real estate	3,683	30	40	50	28
Residential	2,103	17	16	17	17
Commercial	963	8	13	21	7
Other real estate	617	5	11	11	4
Agriculture	59	0	7	2	0
Consumer	1,244	10	5	3	11
Credit cards	639	5	0	0	6
Other consumer	605	5	5	3	5
Other	516	4	1	1	5
Less loan loss allowance	228	2	1	1	2
Trading account assets	764	6	0	0	7
Bank premises and fixed assets	109	1	2	2	1
Intangible assets	374	3	0	1	3
Other assets	770	6	3	4	7
Total assets	12,130	100	100	100	100

Loans are the most important earning assets held by banks. They have high yields, but they are typically not very liquid. Investment securities are more important for small banks than for large ones. Large banks concentrate in credit cards and trading account assets, while small and medium-size banks focus on real estate and agricultural loans.

[a]This group consists of 6,622 insured commercial banks.
[b]This group consists of the country's 2,383 smallest banks. These banks have assets of less than $100 million.
[c]This group consists of the country's 3,731 medium-size banks. These banks have assets between $100 million and $1 billion.
[d]This group consists of the country's 508 largest banks. These banks have assets of $1 billion or more.
[e]Columns may not add to 100 percent because of rounding.

Source: FDIC, *Statistics on Banking*, September 30, 2010.

the bank in secondary markets. Unlike loans, investments represent pure financing because the bank provides no service to the ultimate borrower other than the financing. Exhibit 13.7 shows the major asset accounts for all insured commercial banks in the United States and for samples of large and small banks. In this section, we discuss bank investments and other assets. We save our discussion of bank loans for the next section.

CASH ASSETS

Cash items account for 8 percent of the total assets of the commercial banking system. They consist of vault cash, reserves with the Federal Reserve banks, balances held at other banks, and cash items in the process of collection. Cash assets earn little or no interest; banks try to minimize these low-yield balances within their liquidity constraints.

Vault Cash. *Vault cash* consists of coin and currency held in the bank's own vault. Banks typically maintain only minimum amounts of vault cash because of the high cost of security, storage, and transfer. Vault cash does, however, perform two important functions for banks. First, it provides banks with funds to meet the cash needs of the public. Second, banks can count vault cash as part of their legal reserve requirements.

Reserves at Federal Reserve Banks. Deposits held by banks at their district Federal Reserve bank represent the major portion of the banks' legal reserve requirements and serve as check-clearing and collection balances. Rather than physically transferring funds between banks, check clearing and collection can be done by simply debiting or crediting a bank's account at the Federal Reserve bank. Banks may also transfer funds to other banks for reasons other than check clearing. For example, transactions in the fed funds market are performed as bookkeeping entries between banks and are accounted for on the books of the Federal Reserve banks.

In June 2008, commercial banks held just $28 billion in reserve balances at Federal Reserve District banks. In October 2008, the Federal Reserve began paying interest on banks' reserve balances, and by the end of 2008, commercial banks held over $500 billion in balances. As discussed in Chapters 2 and 3, this increase in reserve balances was the result of, among other actions, the Federal Reserve supporting mortgage markets by buying mortgage-backed securities. Rather than lend these increased balances, banks have elected to keep these balances in their reserve accounts at the Federal Reserve in large part due to the fact that they are now earning interest on the balances.

Balances at Other Banks. Banks hold demand deposit balances at other banks for a number of reasons. In most states, small banks that are not members of the Federal Reserve System can usually meet state reserve requirements by holding balances at approved large banks. Also, many small banks use their deposits at other banks to secure correspondent services from large city banks.

FEDERAL FUNDS SOLD AND REVERSE REPURCHASE AGREEMENTS

Federal funds sold correspond to the lending of excess bank reserves in the fed funds market discussed earlier. Banks that sell (lend) excess reserves in the fed funds market acquire assets (fed funds sold) and lose a corresponding amount of reserves on the balance sheet. Banks that borrow fed funds gain reserves but acquire a liability (fed funds purchased). These transactions are reversed when the borrowing bank returns the reserves to the selling bank.

Reverse repurchase agreements are counterparty positions to the repurchase agreements discussed earlier. They are a form of lending in which the bank buys securities (usually government securities) from the borrower and simultaneously contracts to resell the same securities on a specified future date at a price that produces an agreed yield.

INVESTMENTS

The investment portfolios of commercial banks are a major use of funds by the banking system, accounting for 19 percent of total assets. Bank investments consist primarily of U.S. government bonds, municipal securities, and bonds issued by agencies of the U.S. government. Bank investment portfolios serve several important functions. First, they contain short-term, highly marketable securities that provide liquidity to the bank. Second, the investment portfolio contains long-term securities that are purchased for their income potential. Finally, they provide the bank with tax benefits and diversification beyond that possible with only a loan portfolio.

Investment securities are generally more important to the portfolios of smaller banks than to those of larger banks. Larger banks have access to many more sources of liquid funds than do smaller banks, and therefore they do not rely as heavily on investment securities for liquidity.

13.5 BANK USES OF FUNDS: LOANS AND LEASES

Bank loans and leases are the primary business activity of a commercial bank, accounting for about 55 percent of all bank assets. They generate the bulk of a bank's profits and help attract deposits. Although loans are very profitable to banks, they take time to arrange, are subject to greater default risk, and have less liquidity than most bank investments. Also, they do not have the special tax advantage of municipal bonds.

Most bank loans consist of promissory notes. A **promissory note** is an unconditional promise made in writing by the borrower to pay the lender a specific amount of money, usually at some specified future date. Repayment can be made (1) periodically, in installments; (2) in total on a single date; or (3) in some cases, on demand. If the loan is due on demand, either the borrower or the lender can end the contract at any time.

Bank loans may be **secured** or **unsecured**. Most are secured. The security, or **collateral**, may consist of merchandise; inventory; accounts receivable; real estate; plant and equipment; and, in some instances, even stocks or bonds. The purpose of collateral is to reduce the financial injury to the lender if the borrower defaults. An asset's value as collateral depends on its expected resale value. If a borrower fails to meet the terms and conditions of his or her promissory note, the bank may sell the collateralized assets to recover the loan loss.

Banks make either **fixed-rate** or **floating-rate loans**. The interest rate on a fixed-rate loan does not change over the loan's term. The interest rate on a floating-rate loan, however, is periodically adjusted according to changes in a designated short-term interest rate, usually a Treasury rate or LIBOR. In periods of stable interest rates and upward-sloping yield curves, banks are eager to make long-term loans at fixed rates above the rates they pay on their short-term liabilities. As long as rates do not rise too quickly, banks can roll over their deposits at relatively low rates, maintaining a positive spread. When interest rates rise quickly or become more volatile, however, banks have a preference for making short-term or floating-rate loans.

Most bank loans carry fixed rates. Although many commercial loans have floating rates, consumers are generally less willing to bear the interest rate risk of a floating-rate loan. With a fixed-rate loan, the bank assumes all of the interest rate risk. Borrowers shift to floating-rate loans, however, if they are offered sufficient inducement in the form of a lower initial interest rate on the floating-rate loan.

COMMERCIAL AND INDUSTRIAL LOANS

As shown in Exhibit 13.7, loans to commercial and industrial firms constitute 9 percent of total assets. Most are short-term loans with maturities of less than 1 year. The type of loans made by a bank reflect the composition of the bank's customers. Consequently, business lending is typically more important to large banks than to small retail banks.

There are three basic types of business loans, depending on the borrower's need for funds and source of repayment. A **bridge loan** supplies cash for a specific transaction with repayment coming from an identifiable cash flow. Usually, the purpose of the loan and the source of repayment are related; hence the term *bridge loan*. For example, an advertising company enters into a contract to produce a TV commercial for the Ford Motor Company. The total contract is for $850,000; however, the advertising company needs approximately $400,000 in financing to produce the commercial. The loan is a bridge loan because it supports a specific transaction (making the commercial) and the source of repayment is identifiable (completing the commercial).

A **seasonal loan** provides term financing to take care of temporary discrepancies between business revenues and expenses that are the result of the manufacturing or sales cycle of a business. For example, a retail business may borrow money to build inventory in anticipation of heavy Christmas sales and may expect to repay it after the new year begins. The uncertainty in this type of loan is whether the inventory can be sold for a price that covers the loan.

Long-term asset loans are loans that finance the acquisition of an asset or assets. An example would be a manufacturing company purchasing new production equipment with a 7-year expected life. The new equipment should increase the firm's cash flow in future years. The loan would then be repaid over 7 years from the firm's yearly cash flow. Banks' long-term asset loans typically have maturities ranging between 1 and 10 years.

REAL ESTATE

Real estate loans account for 30 percent of banks' total assets. These mortgage loans finance the purchase, construction, and remodeling of both residential housing and commercial facilities. About 60 percent of all mortgage loans are for residential housing, and the remainder is for commercial property and land development.

AGRICULTURAL LOANS

Agricultural loans are both short-term and long-term loans to farmers to finance farming activities. Although agricultural loans make up only 1 percent of all bank assets, they represent an important form of lending at many small rural banks. Small banks (less than $100 million in assets) devote about 7 percent of their assets to agricultural lending. Short-term agricultural loans are generally seasonal and are made primarily to provide farmers with funds to purchase seed, fertilizer, and livestock. In making these loans, specialized knowledge of farming is required, and the lending officer usually inspects the applicant's farming operation once a year.

CONSUMER LOANS

Bank loans to individuals are known as *consumer loans*. Their maturities and conditions vary widely with the type of purchase. Maturities can be as short as 1 month or as long as 5 years for automobile loans. Long-term loans, which are typically paid on an installment basis, are generally secured by the item purchased, as in the case of automobile loans. Short-term loans are usually single-payment loans.

Consumer loans account for about 10 percent of total bank assets. Commercial banks furnish approximately one-half of total consumer installment credit outstanding. Their emergence as a major supplier of consumer credit is a relatively new phenomenon. Prior to the 1930s, commercial banks were primarily engaged in business loans. It was in part the failure of banks to satisfy the growing demand for consumer credit that led to the emergence and rapid growth of consumer-oriented financial institutions such as finance companies, credit unions, and savings and loan associations.

Bank Credit Cards.   The first bank credit card plan was started in 1951 by Franklin National Bank of New York. Early bank credit card plans were local or regional in nature, were run by individual banks, did not provide revolving credit, and did not charge a membership fee. In 1958, revolving credit became a feature of bank credit card plans. In 1966, the first nationwide card plan was started by Bank of America, using the name BankAmericard.

Before 1966, high start-up costs and the acceptance of credit cards only by merchants in the issuing bank's immediate area were obstacles to the growth and widespread use of credit cards. The advent of the nationwide clearing of bank-card slips as well as nationwide licensing of banks to issue credit cards was a turning point in the credit cards' development. These factors transformed local credit cards into national credit cards and made bank cards acceptable to a large number of merchants and consumers. Today, Visa (formerly BankAmericard) and Master-Card (formerly MasterCharge) are the most widely known plans. The merchant who accepts a credit card pays a service charge ranging from 1 to 4 percent, depending on the average sale price and volume generated.

For the consumer, the holder of a credit card is guaranteed a credit limit at the time the card is issued. The dollar amount of the credit lines varies with the cardholder's income and credit rating. The cardholder is entitled to purchase items up to the credit limit without prior approval of the bank. If the purchases are paid for in full within 25 days after the monthly billing by the bank, generally no interest is charged. However, the cardholder does not have to pay the full amount within the billing period and may elect to pay the balance off in installments. The bank sets a minimum monthly payment that must be paid. The interest charged for credit card installments usually varies between 1 and 2 percent per month (12 and 24 percent per annum) on the unpaid balance. The cardholder may receive the card free or may pay an annual membership fee of between $15 and $500, depending on the services the card offers to the cardholder. It is estimated that the annual maintenance cost to the bank for a credit card account ranges between $35 and $55. These costs escalate quickly with the number of delinquent accounts or fraudulent credit card transactions.

LEASE FINANCING

In recent years, leasing has been a fast-growing area of business for commercial banks, particularly large banks. The impetus for bank entry into leasing was provided by a 1963 decision by then–comptroller of the currency James Saxon to allow national banks to purchase property on a customer's request and lease it to a customer. Since then, almost every state allows state-chartered banks to enter into lease-financing arrangements.

The main economic justification for leasing is taxation. When the lessee (e.g., consumer) is in a lower tax bracket than the lessor (e.g., bank), leasing an asset becomes a viable alternative to borrowing and purchasing the asset. This is because with a leasing arrangement, the bank may get a larger tax deduction than the lessee and may pass part of it along to the lessee as a discount on lease payments. Banks enter into leasing because the rate of return on leasing activities is comparable (after risk adjustment) to that earned on bank lending. Leasing is viewed by most bankers as an extension of their commercial lending activities.

OTHER ASSETS

Trading account assets represent the inventory of securities held by banks for resale to investors as part of their securities dealer activities. The types of securities included in the trading account are the same as those included in the investment portfolio. They are listed separately, however, because they are expected to be held for only a short time. Given that trading account assets are held for dealer activities, it is not surprising that trading account assets are concentrated in large banks.

Fixed assets include such real assets as furniture, banking equipment, and the bank's real estate holdings. Other items are intangible assets (e.g., goodwill), prepaid expenses, income earned but not collected, foreign currency holdings, and any direct lease financing. Small banks have a higher proportion of fixed assets than do large banks. Small banks, with a greater consumer/retail emphasis, require more bricks and mortar than do large banks.

13.6 LOAN PRICING

Because most of a bank's assets are loans, loan pricing is one of the most critical decisions made by a bank manager. There are three important facets of loan pricing. First, the bank must earn a high enough interest rate on the loan to cover the costs of funding the loan, whether the funds are from deposits, money market securities, or capital accounts. Second, the rate on the loan must be sufficient to cover the administrative costs of originating and monitoring the loan. Finally, the loan's interest rate must provide adequate compensation for the credit (or default) risk, liquidity risk, and interest rate risk generated by the loan. Of course, the primary concern in loan pricing is the borrower's credit risk.

Historically, the **prime rate** served as a benchmark, or *base rate*, on short-term business and agricultural loans and was the lowest loan rate posted by commercial banks. At that time, the prime rate was the rate banks charged their most creditworthy customers, and all other borrowers were typically quoted rates as some spread above prime, depending on their risk.

Recently, the role of the prime rate has changed. Since the mid-1980s, fewer loans have been priced using the prime rate as a benchmark. Although the prime is still used as a benchmark for certain types of consumer loans, its use in business and agricultural lending has declined. Now, lenders choose from among several other benchmark rates when pricing loans. A common alternative benchmark for pricing loans to large corporate borrowers is the LIBOR, which is the price of short-term Eurodollar deposits. Other popular alternatives include Treasury rates or the fed funds rate. Despite the declining role of the prime rate as a benchmark for loan pricing, the popular media continue to use it as a barometer of conditions in the nation's money markets because banks are the major suppliers of commercial credit in the economy.

BASE-RATE LOAN PRICING

Most banks have adopted a loan-pricing procedure of setting a base interest rate for their most creditworthy customers and then using this rate as the markup base for loans to all other customers. The base rate may be the prime rate, the fed funds rate, LIBOR, or a Treasury rate. It is expected to cover the bank's administrative costs and provide a fair return to the bank's shareholders. The markups include three adjustments. The first is an adjustment for increased default risk above the risk class associated with the base rate. The bank's credit department determines the risk assignment. The second is an adjustment for term-to-maturity. Most business loans are variable rate, with the rate varying with the underlying base rate. Thus, as the base rate increases or decreases, the customer's loan rate is adjusted accordingly. If the customer wants a fixed-rate loan for a certain maturity period, say, 1 year, the bank adjusts the variable-rate loan rate (short-term base rate) by an amount consistent with the current market yield curve (e.g., the Treasury yield curve). Finally, an adjustment is made that takes into account the competitive factor—a customer's ability to borrow from alternative sources. If, for example, a loan officer believes the customer has an alternative source of cheaper funding such as the commercial paper market, the bank may lower the rate to keep the customer's business. The greater the competition, the lower the loan rate. Expressed mathematically, the loan rate to a particular bank customer is

$$r_L = BR + DR + TM + CF \qquad (13.1)$$

where

r_L = individual customer loan rate
BR = the base rate
DR = adjustment for default risk above base-rate customers
TM = adjustment for term-to-maturity
CF = competitive factor

For example, a bank's base rate is 7 percent and two customers—a small firm and a large firm—want loans. The large firm is well known nationally, has sold commercial paper on occasion, and wants a floating-rate loan. The smaller firm wants a 1-year fixed-rate loan. The bank's money market manager reports that 1-year Treasury securities sell for 75 basis points above a 3-month Treasury bill. Given this information, the bank's loan-pricing scheme may be as follows:

Pricing Factor	Small Firm	Large Firm
Prime rate (the base rate)	7.00%	7.00%
Default risk adjustment	3.00	2.00
Term-to-maturity adjustment	0.75	0.00
Competitive factor adjustment	1.00	0.00
Loan rate	11.75%	9.00%

EXHIBIT 13.8

Interest Rate Spread of Commercial and Industrial Loans over the Federal Funds Rate (1986–2010)

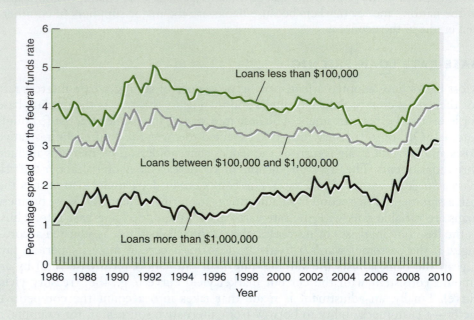

The largest loans tend to be made to the lowest-risk borrowers. Therefore, it is not surprising that the interest rates on these loans are the lowest. During recessions, the yield spread over the federal funds rate tends to remain relatively constant on the largest loans, while the yield spread on smaller, higher-risk loans tends to get larger. During the recession that began in 2007, however, the yield spread on all loans increased dramatically because confidence in the overall economy weakened.

Source: Board of Governors, Federal Reserve System, *E2 Statistical Release.*

The small firm's less favorable borrowing rate is because of greater default risk, a premium for a fixed rate, and the competitive factor—the intensity of competition from other banks or alternative, nonbank borrowing sources such as commercial paper. Exhibit 13.8 shows that the interest rate on small loans is commonly about 200 basis points (2 percent) higher than the rate charged for larger loans.

NONPRICE ADJUSTMENTS

Banks can also make nonprice loan adjustments to alter the effective loan rate. The most common of these are changes in compensating balances. **Compensating balances** are minimum average deposit balances that bank customers must maintain at the bank, usually in the form of non-interest-bearing demand deposits. Compensating balances—usually about 10 percent of the amount of outstanding loans—also encourage borrowers to use other services of the bank and raise effective loan rates. As an example, assume that a firm has a $100,000 line of credit at an 8 percent rate of interest that requires a 10 percent compensating balance.

If the firm borrowed the maximum amount ($100,000) for 1 year, it would have to maintain $10,000 in a deposit account with the bank; because the firm has only $90,000 ($100,000 − $10,000) available to use during the year, the annual effective rate of interest is 8.9 percent ($8,000/$90,000), rather than the stated nominal rate of 8 percent ($8,000/$100,000).

Other methods of adjusting the effective loan rate without altering the nominal rate include reclassifying borrowers from lower to higher credit risk classes (carrying higher loan rates), increasing the amount of collateral (lowering the default risk), and changing the maturity of the loan (moving along the yield curve). Finally, the ability of banks to adjust the effective loan rate and other aspects of the customer relationship explains why the prime rate tends to be more inflexible, or sticky, than other short-term interest rates.

MATCHED-FUNDING LOAN PRICING

One way that banks can control the interest rate risk of fixed-rate loans is through matched funding of loans. **Matched funding** means that fixed-rate loans are funded with deposits or borrowed funds of the same maturity. If, for example, a bank makes a 1-year fixed-rate loan, it might fund the loan with a 1-year CD. Assuming that the cash inflows from the loan match the cash outflows on the CD, the bank is able to reduce interest rate risk because, if interest rates change, the rate on the loan and the CD change by approximately the same amount because they have the same maturity.

13.7 ANALYSIS OF LOAN CREDIT RISK

One of a lending officer's major tasks is to analyze a customer's creditworthiness—that is, to determine a customer's default risk premium. Credit analysis determines whether a loan should be granted and to which credit risk category a customer should be assigned. Of course, in making loans, it is illegal for banks to discriminate on the basis of sex, race, religion, or marital status; only economic factors can be considered.

In attempting to quantify a customer's default risk characteristics, banks typically analyze the *five Cs of credit*:

1. Character (willingness to pay)
2. Capacity (cash flow)
3. Capital (wealth)
4. Collateral (security)
5. Conditions (economic conditions)

Character reflects a borrower's integrity, credit history, and past business relationship with the bank. Basically, banks want to lend to persons who want to repay their debts. *Capacity* analyzes a borrower's projected income statements or cash flow generated from a job. *Capital* looks at a borrower's balance sheet or residual wealth (e.g., stock or landownership). *Collateral* refers to assets that can be taken by the bank and liquidated if a loan is not repaid. Finally, *conditions* refers to economic conditions at the time of the loan and a borrower's vulnerability to an economic downturn or credit crunch.

CREDIT SCORING

Credit scoring is an efficient, inexpensive, and objective method for analyzing a potential borrower's character. Credit scoring involves assigning a potential borrower a score based on the information in the borrower's credit report. The factors and weights that determine the score are based on a statistical analysis of the historical relationships between loan default rates and specific borrower characteristics. A higher credit score indicates a lower risk of default. Generally, credit-scoring models focus on these five factors: (1) the borrower's payment history, (2) the amount owed, (3) the length of the borrower's credit history, (4) the extent of new debt by the borrower, and (5) the type of credit in use. According to Fair, Isaac, and Company (FICO), the following factors are ignored in their credit-scoring model: race, color, religion, national origin, sex, marital status, age, salary, occupation, title, employment history, and any other information not found in a person's credit report.

Most banks and other financial institutions use credit scoring to analyze the character of borrowers in almost all consumer, residential real estate, and small business loan applications. One advantage of credit scoring is that it allows lenders to make very fast loan decisions. Although a conventional analysis and verification of a borrower's character could take days, credit scoring takes only seconds. Thus, lenders are able to provide instant credit for many loan products. A second advantage is that a person's credit score is based on objective criteria, which minimizes the potential for discriminatory lending practices. The disadvantage of credit scoring is that it is impersonal and does not allow for special circumstances. In addition, critics of credit scoring argue that the secretiveness behind credit-scoring models makes it difficult

---

PEOPLE & EVENTS

What's Your Score?

Until the Fair and Accurate Credit Transactions (FACT) Act was passed in 2003, the three major credit-reporting agencies (Equifax, TransUnion, and Experian) were secretive and reluctant to provide consumers with much information about their credit reports. If you were denied credit because of your credit report or you were willing to pay a small fee (typically $8), they would provide you a copy of your credit report. With the passage of the FACT Act, however, you are entitled to a free copy of your credit report annually. Just go to www.annualcreditreport.com and follow the instructions.

It's important to review your credit report periodically to check for mistakes. Increasingly, it is not just lenders that are interested in your credit report. Employers, insurance companies, and others (e.g., apartment managers) are looking at credit reports. They are interested in whether you are a responsible person. What better way to find that out than to look at whether you pay your bills on time? Therefore, it is in your best interest to make

sure there aren't any mistakes on your credit report. If you find a mistake, you are given the opportunity to correct it.

If you are planning a major purchase such as a house or car in the near future and you plan to borrow money for that purchase, you might want to find out your credit score. All of the major credit-reporting agencies make your calculated credit score available for a fee; you just need to decide whether you are willing to pay the fee. If you decide to pay the fee(s), the credit-reporting agencies provide a report to you that tells you your credit score and provides an interpretation of how easy it is for you to borrow. In addition, the report tells you why your score isn't higher and how you might improve your score.

Checking your credit report for errors and knowing your credit score are two of the most important things you can do to make sure future employers, lenders, and insurers view you as favorably as possible.

for potential borrowers to improve their score. For example, consumers who try to improve their rating by consolidating their debt onto one or two cards may actually hurt their rating because credit-scoring models may interpret the behavior as an effort to manipulate their credit rating.

DEFAULT RISK PREMIUMS

Once the five Cs are analyzed, a customer is assigned to a credit-rating category. The default risk premium for each category is determined from an analysis of the bank's credit losses over several business cycles.

For example, a bank with five credit categories may develop the following loan-pricing scheme:

Credit Category	Default Risk Premium
1	Prime-rate customers
2	10–49 basis points
3	50–99 basis points
4	100–200 basis points
5	Reject credit

At some point, however, potential borrowers become too risky, and the bank refuses to grant them credit, as indicated by credit category 5.

Determining the appropriate default risk premium for a given credit category is a delicate process. Lending officers who set their default risk premiums too high tend to drive away the most creditworthy borrowers in a given category because those borrowers are able to borrow more cheaply elsewhere. Lending officers who set their default risk premiums too low eventually lose their jobs because the bank's loan losses exceed the expected loan loss rate, particularly during periods of severe economic downturns.

DO YOU UNDERSTAND?

1. Why do you think small banks have a higher proportion of assets in investments than do large banks?

2. Describe a typical fed funds transaction. Why do you think small banks sell more fed funds as a proportion of total assets than large banks?

3. How does loan portfolio composition differ between large and small banks? Can you provide an explanation?

4. What factors go into setting the loan interest rate? Explain how each factor affects the rate.

5. What customer characteristics do banks typically consider in evaluating consumer loan applications? How do each of these factors influence the decision of the bank to grant credit?

13.8 FEE-BASED SERVICES

Our examination of the balance sheet of a commercial bank has given us a great deal of insight into its business activities. However, some activities in which commercial banks engage are not easily classified, and they do not readily show up in balance-sheet summary accounts. Some of these services are performed directly by banks and others by subsidiaries of bank holding companies. The income from these activities comes in the form of fees rather than interest payments. These fee-based services are subject to less risk and provide more stable income to banks during uncertain conditions in the economy and the financial markets.

CORRESPONDENT BANKING

Correspondent banking involves the sale of bank services to other banks and to nonbank financial institutions. Correspondent banks typically act as agents for respondent banks in check clearing and collection, purchases of securities, the purchase and sale of foreign exchange, and participation in large loans. Traditionally, correspondent services are sold in packages of services, with payment being made by the respondent bank holding compensating balances with the correspondent bank. For example, investing a $100,000 compensating balance from a respondent bank at 12 percent would generate $12,000 gross income for the correspondent bank. If the bundle of services the respondent receives has a fair market value of $12,000, then both parties should be satisfied. In recent years, a trend has developed to unbundle correspondent services and to pay a direct fee for each service. This trend is particularly true in the area of computer and bookkeeping services.

TRUST OPERATIONS

Banks have been involved in trust operations since the early 1900s. The trend in recent years, however, is to call a bank's trust operations something more contemporary, such as *wealth management and advisory services* or *private banking*. Currently, about one-fourth of all banks offer trust services to their customers even if they call them something else. Trust operations involve a bank acting in a fiduciary capacity for an individual or a legal entity, such as a corporation or the estate of a deceased person. This typically involves holding and managing trust assets for the benefit of a third party. Equity investments constitute about two-thirds of the total assets of bank trust departments. Banks administer these securities rather than own them.

INVESTMENT SERVICES, INSURANCE, AND OTHER FINANCIAL PRODUCTS

In the 1980s and 1990s, deposit growth slowed as more people invested in equity shares and **mutual funds**. Rather than allowing depositors to withdraw their funds and invest them elsewhere, however, many banks (through the nonbank affiliates of their bank holding companies) began aggressively marketing mutual funds and offering **brokerage services**. In this way, banks were able to generate noninterest fee income to help offset some of the increased interest costs of relying on borrowed funds to finance their growth.

At the same time that banks have been offering these products and services that have traditionally been the domain of investment companies and investment banks, they have been expanding their offerings of products and services that are traditionally associated with insurance companies. However, the limitations on the allowable activities of banks limited the extent of banks' entry into insurance.

13.9 OFF-BALANCE-SHEET BANKING

Since the mid-1980s, there has been a substantial increase in what is called *off-balance-sheet banking* at large U.S. commercial banks. Like other fee-based activities, off-balance-sheet activities generate fee income for banks. Unlike other fee-based activities, however, off-balance-sheet activities have the feature of representing either contingent assets or contingent liabilities. *Contingent assets* are those off-balance-sheet activities that may ultimately become on-balance-sheet assets. Examples of off-balance-sheet assets are loan commitments and unrealized gains on derivative securities contracts. *Contingent liabilities* are those off-balance-sheet activities that may ultimately become obligations of the bank. Examples of contingent liabilities are letters of credit and unrealized losses on derivative securities contracts.

LOAN COMMITMENTS

Most bank loans begin as loan commitments. A *loan commitment* is a formal promise by a bank to lend money according to the terms outlined in the commitment. The type of loan commitment that most consumers are familiar with is the available credit on their credit cards. At the end of 2010, consumers had drawn on about 19 percent of the available credit on their credit cards, leaving more than $2.7 trillion in available credit. Exhibit 13.9 shows the decline in available credit that resulted from the recession that began in 2007. There are three types of loan commitments that may be agreed on by business borrowers and commercial banks: line of credit, term loan, and revolving credit. Consumers usually do not enter into these types of arrangements. The purpose of the loan commitment is to (1) provide some assurance to the borrower that funds will be available if and when they are needed and (2) provide the lender with a basic format for structuring the customer's loan request properly.

A **line of credit** is an agreement under which a bank customer can borrow up to a predetermined limit on a short-term basis (less than 1 year). The line of credit is a moral obligation, not a legal commitment on the part of a bank. Thus, if a company's circumstances change, a bank may cancel or change the amount of the limit at any time. With a line of credit, it is also customary for a bank to require an annual cleanup period, usually 1 month. This ensures the bank that funds are not being used as permanent capital by the firm. A firm does not have to use a line of credit and incurs a liability only for the amount borrowed.

A **term loan** is a formal legal agreement under which a bank lends a customer a certain dollar amount for a period exceeding 1 year. The loan may be amortized over the life of the loan or paid in a lump sum at maturity. **Revolving credit** is a formal legal agreement under which a bank agrees to lend up to a certain limit for a period exceeding 1 year. A company has the flexibility to borrow, repay, or re-borrow as it sees fit during the revolving credit period. At the end of the period, all outstanding loan balances are payable, or, if stipulated, they may become a binding line of credit.

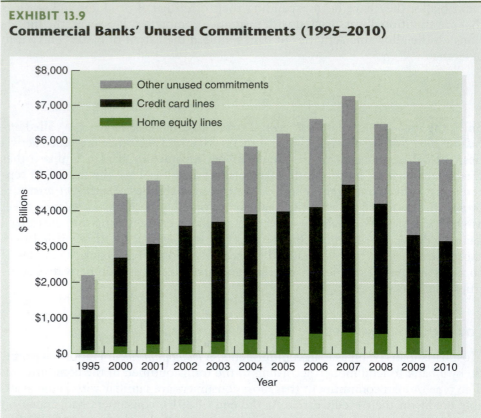

EXHIBIT 13.9
Commercial Banks' Unused Commitments (1995–2010)

Unused credit card lines peaked at almost $4 trillion in 2007 before declining to $2.7 trillion in 2010.

LETTERS OF CREDIT

A *letter of credit* is a contractual agreement issued by a bank that involves three parties: the bank, the bank's customer, and a beneficiary. In a **commercial letter of credit**, the bank guarantees payment for goods in a commercial transaction. The buyer of the goods arranges for the bank to pay the seller of the goods once the terms of the purchase agreement are satisfied. Commercial letters of credit represent only a small part of banks' off-balance-sheet activities.

In a **standby letter of credit (SLC)**, the bank promises to pay a third party in the event the bank's customer fails to perform according to a contract the customer has with the third party. In this way, the bank substitutes its creditworthiness for that of its customer. Thus, if the bank's customer fails to meet the terms and conditions of its contract with the third party, the bank guarantees the performance of the contract as stipulated by the terms of the SLC. The bank's obligation under an SLC is a contingent liability because no funds are advanced unless the contract is breached by the bank's customer and the bank has to make good on its guarantee.

Traditionally, most SLCs are used as backup lines of credit to support commercial paper offerings, municipal bond offerings, and direct loans such as construction lending. These are referred to as *financial SLCs*. Newer applications for financial SLCs, such as for mergers and acquisitions, are emerging. Another type of SLC involves the bank guaranteeing performance of a nonfinancial contract, such as the timely delivery of merchandise or completion of a construction project. These SLCs are called *performance SLCs*.

DERIVATIVE SECURITIES

Banks participate in the markets for interest rate and currency forwards, futures, options, and swaps. Banks participate in these markets for several reasons. First, banks use derivatives to hedge the risks they are exposed to as a result of the asset transformation functions they perform. Second, banks may use derivatives to speculate on the direction of changes in interest rates or currency exchange rates. Bank regulators frown on this type of activity, but it is difficult for outsiders to determine when a bank is using derivatives to hedge and when they are using derivatives to speculate. And finally, some banks act as dealers by serving as the counterparty in derivative contracts for their clients. Derivative securities are both contingent assets and contingent liabilities because they offer potential gains as well as potential losses. In addition, banks that act as derivatives dealers earn fee income by matching up parties that wish to take a long position in a derivative contract and parties that wish to take short positions.

Exhibit 13.10 shows that the notional values of banks' derivative contract positions dwarf the value of banks' assets. Recall from Chapter 11, however, that these notional values are fictional in nature and are used only for calculating the swapped payments. Furthermore, the notional values of the swap contracts shown

EXHIBIT 13.10
Commercial Banks' Interest Rate Derivative Contracts (1995–2010)

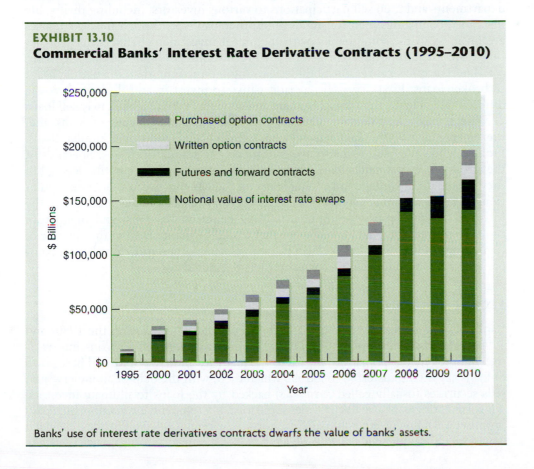

Banks' use of interest rate derivatives contracts dwarfs the value of banks' assets.

in Exhibit 13.10 do not represent net positions, but the sum of the notional value of all the contracts of a given type. Therefore, some banks may have a net position of zero but show a large notional principal amount on their financial statements.

Derivative securities were discussed at length in Chapter 11, so we will not go into detail here about the different types. Many banks, especially large banks, are relying heavily on derivative securities for the purposes mentioned previously. The active use of derivatives by banks and the role of derivative securities in the 2007–2009 financial crisis have prompted recent legislation. The Dodd-Frank Wall Street Reform and Consumer Protection Act, which was passed in 2010 in response to the financial crisis of 2007–2009, includes provisions designed to minimize the potential impact of derivatives trading on the financial system. The implementation details of Dodd-Frank will likely take years, but it is clear that banks' derivatives activities will be subject to much greater scrutiny in the future. In spite of this scrutiny, however, Exhibit 13.10 shows that banks' use of derivative securities continues to grow.

LOAN BROKERAGE

Banks have always sold commercial loan participations to other banks and have entered into syndicated loan agreements when a loan was too large for any single bank. Recently, however, large commercial banks have, to an increasing extent, originated loans with a view to selling them or offering participations. When acting as a loan broker, banks typically negotiate large loans through their credit departments and then sell participations to various investors, including thrifts, life insurance companies, pension funds, and other banks. Although most loan sales are business loans, some banks, with the aid of investment bankers, have structured sales of automobile loans, credit card receivables, and home mortgage loans.

There are several reasons, besides earning fee income, that a bank may want to broker loans. First, loan sales permit banks to invest in and diversify across a different set of loans than they originate and service. Second, a bank may sell loans because it has a competitive advantage in booking certain types of loans and, therefore, can use the funds from loan sales to fund additional similar loans. Finally, banks may sell loans to avoid burdensome regulatory taxes. Specifically, the argument is that banks have a comparative advantage in originating loans, but they are at a disadvantage in keeping loans on their books because of bank regulations. This disadvantage stems from the regulatory tax that banks must pay in the form of federal deposit premiums, holding required reserves, and mandatory capital requirements that exceed those that would be maintained in the absence of regulations. Thus, firms not subject to stringent banking regulations have a comparative advantage in holding loans on their balance sheet.

SECURITIZATION

Banks became increasingly involved in the securitization of loans in the 1980s and 1990s. The **securitization** process begins with banks segregating loans into relatively homogeneous pools with regard to the maturity and type of loan. These pools of loans are then transferred to a trust, which then, with the help of an underwriter, sells securities (usually called *certificates*) backed by the loans to ultimate investors. The originating bank usually provides some form of credit enhancement, which pays promised cash flows to the ultimate investors in the event of default. Also, securitized issues are typically rated for default risk by one of the major rating agencies.

Securitization offers several benefits to banks. First, by selling rather than holding loans, banks reduce the amount of assets and liabilities, thereby reducing reserve requirements, capital requirements, and deposit insurance premiums. Second, securitization provides a source of funding loans that is less expensive than other sources. Finally, banks generate fees from the securitization process. Banks collect origination fees and loan-servicing fees, and recently banks have been permitted to underwrite securitized issues. Thus, banks can also collect underwriting fees in the securitization process.

DO YOU UNDERSTAND?

1. List and describe the major fee-based services offered by commercial banks.
2. Discuss the uses of standby letters of credit (SLCs). What benefits do SLCs offer to a bank's commercial customers?
3. What are the major reasons that banks sell loans?
4. What are the major benefits to banks of securitization?

13.10 BANK EARNINGS

Before we discuss the management problems banks face, let us examine the performance of commercial banks by examining the bank income statement. The major items on the income statement for all federally insured commercial banks and for small, medium, and large banks are shown in Exhibit 13.11. For comparison purposes, we scaled the income and expense items by total assets.

The major source of income for commercial banks is interest on loans, accounting for $485 billion, or 4.00 percent when measured as a percentage of assets. Small banks' interest and fee income on loans is greater than that of large banks (small banks, 4.74 percent; large banks, 3.92 percent). These differences can be attributed to differences in the lending practices of large and small banks. Recall that small banks tend to make more real estate and agricultural loans, whereas large banks tend to hold more trading account assets.

The interest earned on investment securities provides another 0.65 percent. This source of revenue is more important for small banks (0.74 percent of assets) than for large banks (0.64 percent of assets) because small banks hold proportionally more investment securities.

The interest paid on deposits is one of the largest expense items for banks, accounting for $59 billion, or 0.48 percent when measured as a percentage of assets. Small banks pay more interest on their deposits (1.08 percent of assets) than large banks (0.42 percent) because of their greater reliance on deposits as a source of funds (see Exhibit 13.5). Large banks, however, pay more than small banks for federal funds purchased and securities sold under repurchase agreements as well as other borrowed money.

The net interest income (or **net interest margin**) of $394 billion represents the difference between **gross interest income** and **gross interest expense**. Small banks tend to earn a greater net interest income as a percentage of assets than large banks (small banks, 3.57 percent; large banks, 3.22 percent) because small banks generate more interest income than large banks.

EXHIBIT 13.11
Income Statement for Commercial Banks (September 30, 2010)

	All Insured Commercial Banks[a]		Small Banks[b]	Medium-Size Banks[c]	Large Banks[d]
	Millions[e]	Percent of Assets[f]	Percent of Assets[f]	Percent of Assets[f]	Percent of Assets[f]
Total interest income	$485,332	4.00	4.74	4.75	3.92
Loans	378,371	3.12	3.90	4.02	3.02
Lease financing receivables	6,062	0.05	0.02	0.02	0.05
Balances due from dep. institutions	4,246	0.04	0.07	0.03	0.04
Investment securities	78,308	0.65	0.74	0.67	0.64
Assets held in trading accounts	12,262	0.10	0.00	0.00	0.11
Federal funds sold and securities purchased under agreements to resell	3,741	0.03	0.01	0.01	0.03
Other Interest Income	2,342	0.02	0.01	0.01	0.02
Total interest expense	91,719	0.76	1.17	1.25	0.70
Deposits	58,732	0.48	1.08	1.08	0.42
Federal funds purchased and securities sold under agreements to repurchase	2,941	0.02	0.00	0.02	0.03
Other borrowed money	25,303	0.21	0.09	0.15	0.22
Subordinated notes and debentures	4,743	0.04	0.00	0.00	0.04
Net interest income	393,613	3.24	3.57	3.51	3.22
Provisions for loan and lease losses	156,321	1.29	0.50	0.81	1.35
Total noninterest income	221,653	1.83	1.14	0.90	1.93
Fiduciary activities	25,041	0.21	0.39	0.11	0.21
Service charges on deposit accounts	36,837	0.30	0.32	0.31	0.30
Trading account gains and fees	25,552	0.21	0.00	0.00	0.23
All other noninterest income	134,224	1.11	0.44	0.48	1.18
Total noninterest expense	366,164	3.02	3.71	3.12	3.00
Salaries and employee benefits	155,585	1.28	1.72	1.55	1.25
Premises and equipment	40,077	0.33	0.41	0.40	0.32
All other noninterest expense	170,502	1.41	1.59	1.17	1.43
Pre-tax net operating income	92,781	0.76	0.50	0.48	0.80
Gains (losses) on securities	8,247	0.07	0.05	0.06	0.07
Applicable income taxes	34,265	0.28	0.09	0.14	0.30
Income before extraordinary items	66,763	0.55	0.46	0.41	0.57
Extraordinary items, net	−786	−0.01	0.00	0.00	−0.01
Net income	$65,327	0.54	0.46	0.41	0.55

The interest income earned on loans continues to be the most important source of income for banks, especially small banks. Large banks supplement their relatively low net interest income by generating substantial revenue in the form of noninterest income.

[a]This group consists of 6,622 insured commercial banks.
[b]This group consists of the country's 2,383 smallest banks. These banks have assets of less than $100 million.
[c]This group consists of the country's 3,731 medium-size banks. These banks have assets between $100 million and $1 billion.
[d]This group consists of the country's 508 largest banks. These banks have assets of $1 billion or more.
[e]Annualized dollar amounts based on third quarter data.
[f]Columns may not add to 100 percent because of rounding.

Illustrations of the historical trends in interest income and interest expense are shown in Exhibit 13.12. The difference between the two lines in the exhibit represents net interest income. Gross interest income and gross interest expense have been relatively volatile since the mid-1970s and tend to follow market rates of interest. Note that, in 2010, both gross interest income and gross interest expense experienced lows that have not been seen since the 1960s. Fortunately for banks, *interest margins* (the gap between the two lines in Exhibit 13.12) have remained relatively stable.

The **provision for loan losses** is an expense item that adds to a bank's loan loss reserve. The loan loss reserve is a contra-asset account that is deducted from gross loans to determine the net loan amount shown on the bank's balance sheet. Banks add to their loan loss reserve in anticipation of credit quality problems in their loan portfolio. Exhibit 13.11 shows that large banks added more to their loan loss reserve than small banks. The provision for loan and lease losses was 1.35 percent for large banks when measured as a percentage of assets. It was only 0.0.50 percent for small banks. Much of the difference can be attributed to the high delinquency rates on residential mortgage and credit card debt holdings of some large banks.

Exhibit 13.13 gives a historical perspective on the loan loss provisions of commercial banks since 1935. The increase in loan loss provisions in the mid-1980s was the result of many of the loans to less-developed countries (LDCs) that ultimately went bad. The LDC debt crisis in the mid-1980s forced many of the

EXHIBIT 13.12
Interest Income and Expense (1935–2010)

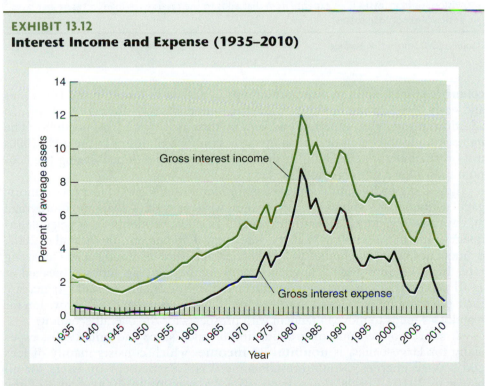

The difference between gross interest income and gross interest expense is net interest income. Net interest income is the traditional source of income for banks.

Source: FDIC, *Statistics on Banking.*

EXHIBIT 13.13
Provision for Loan Losses (1935–2010)

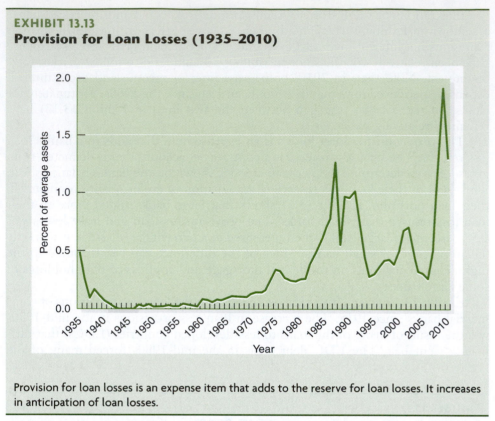

Provision for loan losses is an expense item that adds to the reserve for loan losses. It increases in anticipation of loan losses.

Source: FDIC *Statistics on Banking.*

country's largest banks to write off billions of dollars in loans. In the late 1980s and early 1990s, some banks continued to suffer losses in their LDC loans. In addition, many banks experienced losses in their real estate loan portfolio. The increase and subsequent decline in the provision for loan losses in the early 2000s can be attributed to the credit quality problems that developed during the economic slowdown of the period.

Beginning in 2007, banks' provision for loan losses began to increase as mortgage delinquencies increased. Mortgages with payments that are more than 30 days past due are considered delinquent. In 2005, residential mortgage delinquency rates in the banking industry were about 1.50 percent. By the end of 2007, delinquency rates had climbed to 3.31 percent and were increasing at an increasing rate. In 2010, mortgage delinquency rates in the banking industry peaked at 11.01 percent. This dramatic increase in delinquency rates forced banks to increase their provision for loan losses to record levels. As you can see, banks' provision for loan losses tends to move in tandem with prospects for the overall economy.

A source of revenue of growing importance since the mid-1980s, especially for large banks, is **noninterest income**, which consists mainly of fees and service charges. Noninterest income was 1.83 percent of assets for all banks in 2010. This is down from over 2.5 percent in 2000. Some of the fastest-growing noninterest income items have been those in the "All other noninterest income" category, including ATM surcharges, credit card fees, and fees from the sale of mutual funds and annuities. Exhibit 13.14 shows the

EXHIBIT 13.14
Noninterest Income and Expense (1935–2010)

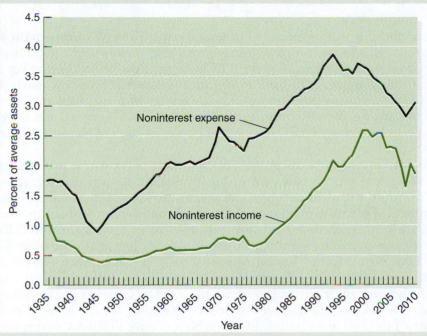

Noninterest income includes fees and service charges earned by the bank. Until recently it has been the fastest growing source of income for banks, especially large banks. Noninterest expense has been declining in recent years due to improvements in efficiencies and economies of scale.

Source: FDIC *Statistics on Banking.*

increase in noninterest income over time. Noninterest income has declined in recent years as economic activity slowed and the market for fee-generating services became more competitive.

Fortunately for banks, as revenue from noninterest income has declined, **noninterest expense** has also declined, and banks have finally started to enjoy the economies of scale promised by the mergers of the 1980s and 1990s. Notice that this long-term trend reversed when noninterest expenses increased over the 2008–2010 period as the expenses associated with servicing loans, especially delinquent loans, increased. Noninterest expenses were about 3.02 percent of assets for all banks in 2010.

Because of differences in scale, resources, and markets, there are significant differences in the noninterest expenses for large and small banks. Most of small banks' noninterest expenses are in the form of salaries and employee benefits, whereas large banks' noninterest expenses are more balanced between the *Salaries and employee benefits* category and the *Other noninterest expense* category, which includes, among other things, merger restructuring charges, marketing expenses, fees for information-processing services, and fees for loan servicing performed by others. Small banks are less automated and have a greater retail emphasis than large banks; therefore, small banks have more employees per dollar of assets than large banks. For the industry as a whole, however, salaries and employee benefits have remained a relatively stable 1.28 percent of assets in recent years.

13.11 BANK PERFORMANCE

Bank profitability can be measured in several ways. The rate of **return on average assets (ROAA)** (net income/average total assets) allows for the comparison of one bank with another. The return on average assets (ROAA) is the key ratio in evaluating the quality of bank management because it tells how much profit bank management can generate with a given amount of assets. Bank management is responsible for the utilization and selection of a bank's assets, and in recent years, ROAA for commercial banks varied between a high of almost 1.40 percent in 2003 to a low of 0.07 percent in 2009.

Another measure of bank profitability is the rate of **return on average equity (ROAE)** capital (net income/average equity capital). Return on average equity (ROAE) tells the bank owners how management has performed on their behalf—the amount of profits in relation to their capital contribution to the firm. Because banks are very highly leveraged (low capital-to-assets ratios), their ROAEs are often quite respectable even though their ROAAs are low relative to other industries. Like ROAA, ROAE has varied substantially in recent years. Exhibit 13.15 shows the ROAA and ROAE capital from 1935 to 2010. The left axis indicates the ROAA, whereas the right axis indicates the ROAE. Changes in the difference between ROAA and ROAE, as illustrated in the exhibit, are the result of changes in banks' capital-to-assets ratios. ROAE is high relative to ROAA during periods when banks have relatively low capital-to-assets ratios (high leverage). For example, banks' capital-to-assets ratios declined during the 1970s and 1980s and, consequently, their ROAEs increased relative to their ROAAs. Since the early 1990s, however, banks' capital-to-assets ratios increased. Consequently, ROAAs increased faster than ROAEs.

Exhibit 13.15 shows the average performance of the whole banking industry. The performance of individual banks will vary relative to the industry depending on a bank's risk exposures. We discuss these risk exposures and banks' efforts to manage the exposures in detail in later chapters. As you will learn in those chapters, however, a bank manager's dilemma is maximizing profit while keeping the risk of failure in check.

DO YOU UNDERSTAND?

1. Suppose a bank's ROAE is 15 percent when ROAA is 1 percent. If the bank's equity capital-to-assets ratio increases, what will happen to the bank's ROAE and ROAA?

2. Exhibit 13.15 shows a dramatic decline in banks' ROAA and ROAE. Use the information in Exhibits 13.11 to 13.14 to explain the drop in banks' performance.

3. Why are changes in gross interest income and gross interest expense highly correlated, while noninterest income and noninterest expense are less highly correlated?

EXHIBIT 13.15
Return on Average Assets and Average Equity (1935–2010)

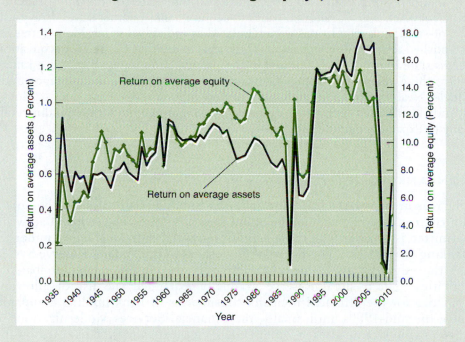

ROAA and ROAE tend to move together over time. When ROAA and ROAE do not move together, it is due to changes in capital-to-assets ratios. ROAE increases relative to ROAA when capital-to-assets ratios decrease, as they did in the late 1960s and 1970s. ROAA increases relative to ROAE when capital-to-asset ratios increase, as they have in the last 20 years.

Source: FDIC *Statistics on Banking.*

13.12 BANK AND FINANCIAL HOLDING COMPANIES

The **bank holding company** is the most common form of organization for banks in the United States. The prominence of the holding company structure is attributable to three important desires on the part of bank management. First is the desire to achieve some form of interstate banking/branching in the face of restrictive laws, almost all of which have been eliminated. Second is the desire by some banks to diversify into nonbanking activities. Finally, bank holding companies can reduce their tax burden relative to the taxes they would pay if they operated as a bank.

DE FACTO BRANCHING

One of the motivations for adopting the holding company structure was to circumvent geographic restrictions on bank branching and acquisitions. By forming multibank holding companies, banks were able to expand beyond regulated geographic boundaries. This organizational form allowed banks to operate in larger units and thereby achieve economies of scale, and it also allowed greater geographic diversification within states for greater safety.

In 1994, Congress passed the Riegle–Neal Interstate Banking and Branching Efficiency Act. This act allowed banks to acquire banks in other states. Previously, out-of-state bank acquisitions were regulated by individual states. Many states had established reciprocal arrangements with other states that allowed for acquisitions across state lines for banks located in the participating states. Beginning June 1, 1997, these reciprocal arrangements were made moot by the passage of the Riegle–Neal Act. In addition, banks can now branch across state lines if allowed by individual states. Consequently, banks no longer need to form a holding company to expand geographically.

NONBANKING ACTIVITIES

The reason many large banks formed bank holding companies was the opportunity to engage in a wide range of business activities. The scope of activities permitted is broader than those activities granted individual banks under the Banking Act of 1933. The Board of Governors of the Federal Reserve System has the authority to define what activities are closely related to banking activities. The Federal Reserve gradually expanded the list of allowable activities for the affiliated nonbank subsidiaries of bank holding companies since the mid-1980s until, finally, the Financial Services Modernization Act of 1999 (the Gramm-Leach-Bliley [GLB] Act) expanded the list of allowable activities for financial holding companies to include almost all financially related businesses.

Under GLB, any well-managed, well-capitalized banking firm that has a satisfactory Community Reinvestment Act rating can convert to a **financial holding company** subject to approval by the Federal Reserve. (The Community Reinvestment Act (CRA) and CRA ratings are discussed in Chapter 15.) Financial holding companies are allowed to own subsidiaries that engage in almost any financial business. Therefore, many bank holding companies have become certified as financial holding companies and acquired insurance and investment banking affiliates. Likewise, some insurance and investment banking firms have acquired bank holding companies and become certified as financial holding companies. A hypothetical structure of a financial holding company is shown in Exhibit 13.16.

TAX AVOIDANCE

One of the most important reasons for smaller banks to form a bank holding company is the tax consideration. For example, approximately 90 percent of bank holding companies are one-bank holding companies, and of these, most are single-subsidiary companies. Product or geographic market motivation cannot account for the existence of these single-subsidiary holding companies. The principal tax benefit of a holding company organization is that interest paid on debt is a tax-deductible expense, and most dividends received from subsidiaries provide tax-exempt revenues for the parent firm. In addition, nonbanking subsidiaries can be structured to avoid local taxes.

EXHIBIT 13.16
Hypothetical Financial Holding Company Structure

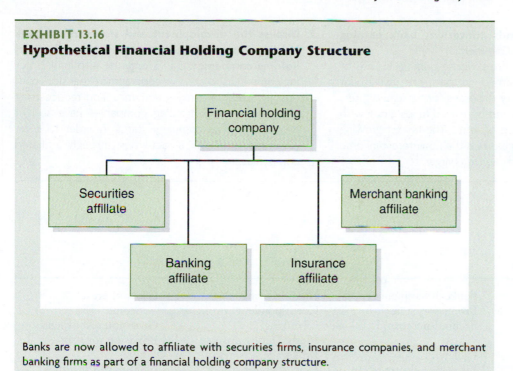

Banks are now allowed to affiliate with securities firms, insurance companies, and merchant banking firms as part of a financial holding company structure.

SUMMARY OF LEARNING OBJECTIVES

1. **Describe the size and structure of the U.S. banking industry.** The elimination of branching restrictions and mergers has reduced the number of commercial banks from about 15,000 in 1985 to about 6,600 today. In addition, the industry is dominated by a small number of very large institutions.

2. **Discuss banks' sources and uses of funds as reflected on their balance sheets.** For most banks, the principal source of funds is deposit accounts. These funds are payable on demand or have very short maturities, and the owners of such accounts are insured by the FDIC against any loss up to $250,000. More than half of the funds obtained by banks are used to make a wide variety of loans. In addition, banks hold large portfolios of investment securities. Short-term investments, such as Treasury securities, afford banks a source of income while also providing liquidity. Long-term securities, such as municipal bonds, are held for their higher after-tax returns. Because cash assets earn no interest, banks keep their cash holdings to a minimum.

3. **Explain how banks make lending decisions and how they price their loans.** Banks' lending decisions and how they price their loans are based largely on the credit risk of borrowers. Credit risk is measured using the five Cs of lending: character, capacity, capital, collateral, and conditions.

4. **Describe the various fee-based activities of banks.** Fee-based services provide stable income during uncertain economic conditions while allowing banks to avoid the usual risks of financial intermediation. These services include correspondent banking, trust services, mutual fund sales, and securities brokerage.

5. **Explain the various off-balance-sheet activities of banks and describe how these activities generate revenue for banks and the conditions under which they become on-balance-sheet activities.** Banks' major off-balance-sheet activities include loan commitments, standby letters of credit, loan brokerage, securitization, and derivative securities. These also generate income for banks in the form of fees or gains in the value of the contracts.

6. **Discuss recent trends concerning bank earning and performance.** Commercial banks are profit-maximizing business firms whose primary source of income is interest earned on loans and investment securities. The primary expenses for banks are interest paid on deposits and borrowed funds along with salaries and employee benefits. The fastest-growing source of income for banks is the noninterest income earned from fees and service charges.

7. **Discuss the development and structure of bank holding companies and the newly formed financial holding companies.** Banks organize into bank holding companies to achieve geographic expansion, conduct limited nonbanking activities, and reduce their taxes. Many bank holding companies have sought financial holding company status in order to offer additional nonbanking activities through affiliated companies.

KEY TERMS

Demand deposit
NOW accounts (negotiable orders of withdrawal)
Money market deposit accounts (MMDA)
Certificates of deposit (CDs)
Borrowed funds
Federal funds (fed funds)
Repurchase agreements (RPs)
Eurodollar
London Interbank Offer Rate (LIBOR)

Banker's acceptance
Promissory note
Secured/unsecured loan
Collateral
Fixed-rate/floating-rate loans
Bridge loan
Seasonal loan
Long-term asset loan
Prime rate
Compensating balances
Matched funding

Credit scoring
Correspondent banking
Mutual funds
Brokerage services
Line of credit
Term loan
Revolving credit
Commercial letter of credit
Standby letter of credit (SLC)
Securitization
Net interest margin

Gross interest income
Gross interest expense
Provision for loan losses
Noninterest income
Noninterest expense
Return on average assets (ROAA)
Return on average equity (ROAE)
Bank holding company
Financial holding company

QUESTIONS AND PROBLEMS

1. What is the primary goal of a commercial bank? Why may this goal be translated into maximizing the firm's stock share price?

2. Why are deposits a more important source of funds for small banks than for large banks? Why are deposits considered to be a more stable source of funds for small banks than for large banks?

3. What are borrowed funds? Give some specific examples. Have borrowed funds become more or less important as a source of funds for banks?

4. Why are negotiable CDs and federal funds primarily sources of funds for very large banks?

5. Define *bank capital*. What is the economic importance of capital to a firm?

6. What are the major uses of funds for a bank? What are the differences between large and small banks? Explain.

7. What are the important differences between investments and loans in a bank portfolio of assets?

8. What are the advantages and disadvantages of using credit scoring to evaluate a loan application?

9. Distinguish between a line of credit and a letter of credit.

10. Give the reasons that banks hold Treasury securities and municipal bonds in their investment portfolios.

11. Explain why banks buy and sell federal funds. Also explain the role of the Federal Reserve System in the fed funds market. Show the T-accounts for a federal funds transaction.

12. Define *correspondent banking*. Why do banks enter into correspondent relationships?

13. What is the prime rate? Why do some banks make loans below the prime rate?

14. What do we mean by *off-balance-sheet activities*? If these things are not on the balance sheet, are they important? What are some off-balance-sheet activities?

15. What are the major benefits of getting assets *off the balance sheet* through either loan sales or securitization?

16. What is a *contingent asset*? What is a *contingent liability*? Provide an example of each.

17. What are the major differences between large banks and small banks on the income statement? Why are there differences between the two groups of banks? For example, why is the net interest income higher for small banks?

18. Describe some of the recent trends affecting bank income statements. For example, has net interest income increased or decreased in recent years? What about other components of the income statement?

19. Give the reasons that banks select the bank holding company form of organization. Why would a bank holding company seek to convert to a financial holding company?

INTERNET EXERCISE

There are several useful Internet sites for gathering information about commercial banks and bank holding companies. In this chapter, we discuss the various sources and uses of funds by commercial banks, the growth in off-balance-sheet activities of banks, and the typical structure of banking organizations. In this Internet exercise, your task is to examine the sources and uses of funds for a specific bank in your local community. Data on the balance sheet, income statement, and structure of individual banks and bank holding companies can be found at the Federal Financial Institutions Examination Council's National Information Center (NIC) Web site, http://www.ffiec.gov/. Click on the "National Information Center (NIC)" link and search for the name of your local bank. Once you have found the bank in the database, you can generate reports on the balance sheet, income statement, performance ratios, deposits, and loan portfolio. In addition, you can determine the organizational hierarchy of the bank. Up-to-date data on the banking industry as a whole can be found at the FDIC's Web site, http://www.fdic.gov.

1. Once you have found your bank on the NIC database, determine which bank regulatory agency is responsible for regulating your bank.

2. Determine whether the bank is part of a holding company structure. If so, determine whether other commercial banks are owned by the same parent company. Are there any nonbank subsidiaries of the parent company?

3. Print out or download data on the balance sheet and income statement of your bank. Import the data into a spreadsheet and determine how your bank compares to industry norms. Do this by calculating the percentages that were calculated in Exhibits 13.5 and 13.7. How do the averages for your bank differ from the averages for other banks of similar size?

4. The performance ratios that you can download from the NIC Web site are useful for analyzing the performance and level of risk faced by your bank relative to its peers. Download or print out the summary performance ratios for your institution.

5. Compare the performance and riskiness of your bank to its peer institutions by examining whether your bank has performed better than its peers in recent periods. Also, look at some of the risk measures to determine whether your bank takes more risk than its peers. Based on the relative performance and relative riskiness of your bank, comment on whether the bank is earning an appropriate return for its shareholders given its risk level.

International Banking

IMAGINE ADVISING A FIRM THAT invests billions of dollars in a foreign currency to gain access to local natural resources and markets. The firm must manage the currency risk that results from changes in the value of the foreign currency relative to the U.S. dollar, as well as political risks, environmental concerns, and cultural differences. This is the situation facing Alcoa, a large U.S. aluminum company.

Alcoa is planning to invest over $10 billion to develop an integrated industrial complex in Saudi Arabia, including a mine, a refinery, and other facilities. The new venture plans to start production in 2013. Given the nature of the Saudi Arabia economy, Alcoa must deal with an infrastructure that is not as developed as the U.S. market with respect to banking, transportation, and most areas related to business.

Alcoa has made great strides in linking overseas investment with their corporate social responsibility plans. Since 2005, Alcoa has consistently achieved the top ranks in the Basic Resources sector in the Covalence Ethical Rankings, an index of ethical performance developed by the Geneva-based company, Covalence. Alcoa has also been a member of the Dow Jones Sustainability Index and a founding member of the U.S. Climate Action Partnership. Philosophical policies and plans such as these represent an

Tokyo, New York, and London are the most important international banking centers and foreign exchange markets. In Asia, most currency conversions are the U.S. dollar to the Japanese yen, the dollar to the euro, the euro to the yen, and the U.S. dollar to the Australian dollar. On most days, exchange rate fluctuations in Tokyo are insignificant, but there are days when the fluctuations are breathtaking.

important departure from some of the early foreign investments abroad, especially in the raw materials industry.

Proposed large investments in Saudi Arabia require Alcoa to undertake purchases and sales of goods in the local currency, the Saudi Arabian riyal. To help manage the currency and economic risks associated with this venture, Alcoa will partner with local firms and financial intermediaries. To the extent that large

U.S. banks have a presence in Saudi Arabia, they are well poised to help Alcoa manage the risks of the international Venture.

Would you like to be an international banker advising Alcoa on methods to manage their risks related to investments in Saudi Arabia? If you were Alcoa's U.S. bank for corporate operations, what advantages would you have in working with Alcoa in Saudi Arabia? ■

This chapter examines international banking—the banking practices, regulations, and market conditions by which American banks compete in the global marketplace and foreign banks operate in the United States.

LEARNING OBJECTIVES

1 Describe the evolution of U.S. overseas banking activities.

2 Explain the reasons for growth in U.S. banking operations overseas.

3 Discuss the regulation of foreign banking activities.

4 Describe the organizational forms that banks can use to conduct overseas operations.

5 Explain the risks involved in foreign lending.

6 Describe the nature of foreign bank activities in the United States.

14.1 DEVELOPMENT OF INTERNATIONAL BANKING

The establishment of an international presence by American banks is a relatively recent development. European financial institutions, however, have conducted overseas activities for centuries. From the twelfth to the mid-sixteenth century, Italian banks dominated international finance. With the establishment of colonial empires, British, Dutch, and Belgian banks became conspicuous by their worldwide presence. Many of them were established in colonial territories, whereas others were in countries having close trading ties to the bank's home country. During this period, Great Britain emerged as the center of international finance, a position it maintained until after World War II.

Until 1960, few American banks had international operations. In fact, national banks were not permitted to establish branches or accept bills of exchange outside the United States until the passage of the Federal Reserve Act of 1913. In an effort to stimulate penetration of American banks into international finance, Congress enacted the Edge Act in 1919. The Edge Act, proposed by Senator Walter E. Edge of New Jersey, provided for federally chartered corporations to be organized that could engage in international banking and financial operations. These activities could be entered into directly by the Edge Act corporation or through subsidiaries that owned or controlled local institutions in foreign countries. Edge Act corporations could make equity investments overseas, an activity denied domestic banks. This and other expanded powers allowed American banks to compete more effectively against stronger and better-established European banking houses.

Although these provisions were important, American banks did not rush into the international banking arena. It was not until after World War II that American banks established any significant foreign presence. This occurred as American corporations began to establish overseas offices and affiliates. These businesses required financial services and expertise that could best be provided by banks located in the host countries, but there was also a need to maintain a strong relationship with the companies' main U.S. banks. This trend toward substantial direct foreign investments forced some large American banks to consider establishing a network of foreign branches or affiliates to serve the expanding needs of their large corporate customers more fully. Although the demand was growing for international banking services, by 1960 only eight American banks had established overseas branches.

THE PERIOD OF EXPANSION

Beginning in 1960, a profound change took place in the international banking activities of American banks. At that time eight large banks, with overseas assets totaling $3.5 billion, dominated U.S. foreign banking. By 1965, there were 13 large banks with 211 branches and foreign assets totaling $9.1 billion. Then the rush to establish foreign branches began in earnest. By 1970, there were 79 banks with foreign branches. By 1980, when the rush slowed, 159 U.S. banks were operating 787 branches overseas, with total assets of $343.5 billion.

Exhibit 14.1 shows that the overseas operations of U.S. banks have declined since the 1980s. The decline in the number of banks and branches is a natural

EXHIBIT 14.1
Foreign Branches of U.S. Commercial Banks*

Year	Number of Banks with Foreign Branches	Number of Foreign Branches
1955	7	115
1960	8	131
1965	13	211
1970	79	532
1980	159	787
1985	162	916
1990	122	833
1995	102	788
2000	91	998
2005	45	713
2006	51	640
2007	52	584
2008	53	509
2009	50	514
2010	44	522

The number of banks with foreign branches peaked in the 1980s, while the number of foreign branches increased substantially between 1955 and 2000 but declined sharply since 2000.

*Data are based on domestically chartered, insured commercial banks with consolidated assets of $300 million or more.
Source: Board of Governors, Federal Reserve System.

consequence of mergers between banks with overseas operations. After the beginning of the most recent economic recession (December 2007), the number of banks with overseas branches declined to 52, whereas the number of foreign branches declined to 584 after peaking at 998 in 2000.

THE REASONS FOR GROWTH

There are a number of reasons for the dramatic growth in American banking overseas, including the overall expansion of U.S. world trade, the growth of multinational corporations, the effects of government regulations on domestic profit opportunities, and the impetus for financing trade deficits as a result of changes in petroleum prices. The 1960s were marked by rapid growth of international trade, full convertibility of most of the world's major currencies, and rapid expansion by major U.S. corporations abroad. As American firms expanded overseas, American banks followed a defensive follow-the-customer strategy. This allowed American banks to maintain relationships with firms in which they fully understood their operations and resultant financing needs. U.S. banks financed this expansion through letters of credit, banker's acceptances, and other credit instruments.

Interest in foreign banking operations has also been encouraged by the regulatory environment in the United States. Specifically, in 1964 and 1965 a set of government programs was introduced to restrain the outflow of funds from the United States and to help the country's balance-of-payments problems. The federal government's capital control program consisted of the Foreign Direct Investment Program (FDIP), the Interest Equalization Tax (IET), and the Voluntary Foreign Credit Restraint (VFCR) program. Under these various programs, U.S. banks and other corporations were limited in the amount of funds they could transfer overseas. As a result of these restrictions, U.S. corporations had to rely on sources outside the United States to finance their growing investments abroad. Thus, to accommodate their overseas corporate customers, many U.S. banks established networks of foreign branches to tap international sources of funds.

Other domestic regulations also accelerated the growth of American banks abroad, such as Regulation Q, which limited the rate that domestic banks were allowed to pay on deposits. In 1966 and again in 1969, when market interest rates increased, U.S. banks were unable to pay rates that were competitive with alternative financial instruments. As a result, banks experienced large runoffs in deposits at domestic offices. To offset these lost funds, U.S. banks turned to foreign branches, which were not subject to the Regulation Q interest rate ceilings. Foreign branches could attract funds because they were free to pay the market rate of interest. Deposits at overseas branches were transferred back to the United States for use by domestic offices. In 1980, the Depository Institutions Deregulation and Monetary Control Act (DIDMCA) phased out Regulation Q.

As a reaction to restrictive domestic regulations and the internationalization of American business operations, the growth in overseas activities by U.S. banks was dramatic. Interestingly, the growth was not limited to banks located in major financial centers, such as New York and San Francisco, which are traditional international trade centers. Banks headquartered in such cities as Chicago, Pittsburgh, Atlanta, Dallas, Seattle, Detroit, and other regional money centers also found it profitable to enter the foreign markets aggressively. Banks without foreign branches soon found themselves at a considerable competitive disadvantage in international as well as domestic business.

RECENT ACTIVITY

Currently, a small number of American banks have a large network of international banking affiliates throughout the world. A larger number of American banks maintain a small number of overseas offices. In addition, the number of U.S. banks having correspondent relationships with foreign banks is in the hundreds.

As many of the largest U.S. banks merged beginning in the mid-1980s and continuing today, the number of banks having overseas operations shrank. We see this in Exhibit 14.1. The relative importance of these institutions increased, however, as the size of the merged institutions increased. Exhibit 14.2 shows the 10 largest banks in the world ranked in terms of total assets at two points in time: December 31, 1990, and November 10, 2010. In 1990, not a single U.S. bank was in the top 10 in terms of total asset holdings. By 2010, however, J.P. Morgan Chase became the eighth largest bank in the world.

In 1990, seven of the 10 largest banks in the world were headquartered in Japan. As of 2010, the composition of the largest banks in the world is very different from that of 1990: Seven of the largest banks in the world are headquartered in Europe. The slowdown of the Japanese economy and the struggling Japanese banking sector resulted in sell-offs of their foreign subsidiaries. In 2010, only one Japanese bank made the list of the top 10. Also in 2010, for the first time, a bank from an emerging market (China) has grown to be one of the 10 largest banks in the world.

14.2 REGULATION OF OVERSEAS BANKING ACTIVITIES

Banking in the United States has traditionally been a highly regulated industry. The broad objectives of federal bank regulations have been (1) to promote bank safety, which fosters economic stability by minimizing economic disturbances originating in the banking sector; (2) to promote competition within the banking system; and (3) to maintain a separation of banking from other business activities in order to promote soundness in banking and to prevent concentration of economic power. For the most part, this overall regulatory framework has been extended to the overseas operations of American banks.

This philosophy is in contrast with that of many other countries, where banks are allowed to engage in a wider range of business activities than are American banks. Japan adopted most of the U.S. financial regulatory system during the postwar American occupation, but most Western nations grant their banks either limited or full merchant banking powers. Furthermore, most bank regulatory authorities, including those in the United States, have historically focused on the domestic operations of banks, often ignoring activities conducted by the banks outside their own national borders.

This stance has changed since the mid-1970s as foreign regulatory authorities began to understand the global nature of financial markets. In particular, the 10-nation agreement on bank capital adequacy standards worked out under the

EXHIBIT 14.2
World's 10 Largest Banks (2010 and 1990)

November 10, 2010

Rank	Company	City	Total Assets (in Billions)
1	BNP Paribas SA	Paris	$2,952.2
2	The Royal Bank of Scotland Group PLC	Edinburgh	2,739.4
3	Crédit Agricole SA	Paris	2,234.4
4	Barclays PLC	London	2,226.6
5	Deutsche Bank AG	Frankfurt	2,153.0
6	Industrial & Commercial Bank of China Ltd	Beijing	1,726.2
7	Lloyds Banking Group PLC	London	1,658.7
8	J.P. Morgan Chase Bank National Association	New York	1,627.7
9	Banco Santander SA	Boadilla del Monte	1,593.3
10	The Bank of Tokyo-Mitsubishi UFJ Ltd	Tokyo	1,494.4

December 31, 1990

Rank	Company	City	Total Assets (in Billions)
1	Dai-Ichi Kangyo Bank	Tokyo	$428.2
2	Sumitomo Bank Ltd.	Osaka	409.2
3	Mitsui Taiyo Kobe Bank	Tokyo	408.8
4	Sanwa Bank	Osaka	402.7
5	Fuji Bank	Tokyo	400.0
6	Mitsubishi Bank	Tokyo	391.5
7	Credit Agricole Mutuel	Paris	305.2
8	Banque Nationale de Paris	Paris	291.9
9	Industrial Bank of Japan	Tokyo	290.1
10	Credit Lyonnais	Paris	287.3

In 1990, Japanese banks dominated other banks in terms of asset holdings. Since then, the struggling Japanese economy combined with consolidation of banks in the United States and Europe resulted in the European and U.S. bank dominance of the top 10.

Source: "World's Largest Banking Companies by Assets," *American Banker*, November, 9, 2006; "Top 50 banks in the world," Bankersalmanac.com, November 10, 2010.

auspices of the Bank for International Settlements (BIS) in July 1988 is tangible evidence that bank regulators are concerned with, and are addressing, international issues. This agreement mandated at least an 8 percent capital-to-assets ratio for all international banks and also defines precisely what is counted as primary (Tier 1) and secondary (Tier 2) capital. At least 4 percent of the 8 percent total must be Tier 1 capital.

THE REGULATORY FRAMEWORK

The regulatory framework for the international operations of U.S. banks can be summarized briefly as follows:

1. The Federal Reserve Act of 1913 allowed federally chartered banks to establish branches outside the United States.
2. The 1916 amendment to the Federal Reserve Act permitted national banks to form agreement corporations.
3. The 1919 Edge Act allowed the formation of federally chartered corporations to engage in foreign banking and such financial operations as owning stock in foreign financial institutions.
4. In 1966, national banks were allowed to invest directly in the stock of foreign banks.
5. In 1970, amendments to the Bank Holding Company Act provided a regulatory framework for international activities of U.S. bank holding companies.
6. In 1978, the International Banking Act extended federal regulation to foreign banks operating in the United States.
7. In 1980, the DIDMCA broadened the scope of the Federal Reserve Board's authority to impose reserve requirements on foreign banks and permitted U.S. banks to establish international banking facilities (IBFs).
8. The International Lending Supervision Act, passed by Congress in late 1983, mandated the reporting of country-specific loan exposure information by commercial banks and established standardized procedures for dealing with problem loans.
9. The Foreign Bank Supervision Enhancement Act (FBSEA) of 1991 provided the Federal Reserve with greater authority over foreign banks and limited the service offerings of foreign banks to those that U.S. banks are allowed to offer.
10. The Financial Services Modernization Act of 1999 allowed commercial banks, investment banks, securities firms, and insurance companies to consolidate. Commercial banks were also permitted to invest in high-risk investment products.
11. In 2010, Title VI of the Dodd-Frank Act (Bank and Savings Association Holding Company and Depository Institution Regulatory Improvements Act of 2010) significantly limited trading activities and speculative investments of insured depository institutions.

The Federal Reserve System and the Office of the Comptroller of the Currency (OCC) have primary responsibility for supervising the activities of U.S. banks' foreign operations. The OCC examines national banks that make up the majority of banks operating overseas, and the Federal Reserve System examines state-chartered member banks, approves national banks' foreign branches, and supervises the operation of Edge Act corporations and IBFs. Also, foreign acquisitions by domestic bank holding companies come under the jurisdiction of the Federal Reserve. The Federal Deposit Insurance Corporation (FDIC) has only a limited role in international banking because few purely international banks are members. However, since enactment of the International Banking Act of 1978, foreign banks operating in the United States have been allowed to establish federally chartered foreign branches, and their deposits up to $100,000 must be insured by the FDIC. Other foreign banking institutions may, at their option, obtain FDIC insurance.

In the past, U.S. bank regulators relied primarily on home office records in conducting examinations of the overseas operations of U.S. banks. This procedure was acceptable as long as the number of banks with overseas operations was small and foreign activities of a bank did not pose a substantial risk to the bank's domestic operations. This is not always true today. On-site examinations are becoming both more necessary and more frequent. The OCC now maintains a permanent staff in London, and both the Federal Reserve Board and the FDIC are increasing the frequency of their overseas on-site examinations. These reviews check the accuracy of head office records and the adequacy of internal controls. The cost of full examinations of all foreign offices' assets would be prohibitive.

ALLOWABLE BANKING ACTIVITIES

In general, U.S. banks abroad can engage in activities not available to domestic banks. This is true even after the repeal of the Glass-Steagall Act of 1933 (which separated commercial banking from investment banking) and the passing of the Financial Services Modernization Act of 1999 (i.e., the Gramm-Leach-Bliley Act). For example, U.S. banks abroad may make limited equity investments in nonfinancial companies in connection with their financing activities. The major reason for the wider latitude in overseas markets has been to enhance the competitive effectiveness of U.S. banks in foreign markets. Most banks in foreign countries have broader powers than those possessed by American banks. Thus, to promote the participation of U.S. banks in overseas markets, Federal Reserve policy has been to broaden powers as long as they did not impinge on domestic policy considerations. Furthermore, because many domestic constraints on banks are concerned with the competitive environment and the concentration of financial resources in the United States, the Federal Reserve has accordingly refrained from restricting the international activities of domestic banks.

Many overseas banking activities have been restrained. Foreign subsidiaries are not allowed to own controlling interests in nonfinancial companies. This restriction stems from the long-standing U.S. concept of separating banking and commerce. Regulatory changes announced in August 1987 weakened these restrictions somewhat by allowing banks to purchase a controlling interest in a foreign nonfinancial corporation, but only if the firm was being sold as part of a privatization program by the foreign government. Affiliates in which U.S. banks have been allowed to own a substantial minority interest have been confined to companies of a predominantly financial nature. Also, investment in foreign companies has been severely limited. It is feared that such investments could indirectly undermine domestic policy objectives, such as the separation of finance-related businesses from other lines of business. Even though Congress effectively repealed the Glass-Steagall Act (which separated commercial and investment banking) by passing the Financial Services Modernization Act of 1999, the activities of U.S. banks, bank holding companies, and financial holding companies are still constrained when compared to banks in some other countries.

PEOPLE & EVENTS

Credit Risk, Subprime Mortgage Crisis of 2007, and Challenges to the Banking Sector

Credit risk is the risk that promised cash flows may not be paid in full. The demand for managing credit risk promoted the fast growth of the credit default swaps (CDS) market. By 2008, the credit default swaps market was worth over $40 trillion, several times bigger than the corporate bond market. After the Financial Services Modernization Act of 1999, traditionally low-risk commercial banks were allowed to engage in high-risk investments, including CDS. Many believe such activities worsened the subprime mortgage crisis of 2007 in the United States.

Starting in the 1970s, U.S. bank mortgage financers started shifting credit risk off their balance sheet through the mortgage-backed securities (MBS) market. (An MBS is a security based on cash flows from a portfolio of mortgage loans.) With low exposure to credit risk, financial institutions had less incentive to screen and monitor the borrowers and thus lowered credit standards. Subprime mortgages, in which borrowers may not qualify for mortgages under more stringent credit standards, quickly became popular. The value of such mortgages rose from $425 billion to $1.8 trillion between 2001 and 2006. Many subprime borrowers took out adjustable-rate mortgages to avoid high initial interest payments. When the Fed increased interest rates in 2006, these borrowers defaulted on the mortgages, leading to huge losses of MBS values and a spike in credit risk.

The credit risk of an MBS, in theory, can be hedged through a CDS. A CDS seller receives fixed amounts of payment in exchange for payments to the buyer in the event of a default. Many of the large insurance companies and banks turned out to be sellers of MBS-based CDSs. As the subprime mortgage crisis deepened, CDS sellers had difficulty covering their exposures. Several top issuers of MBS in 2007 (Countywide Financial, Lehman Brothers, Washington Mutual, and Bear Stearns) were either subsequently sold, declared bankrupt, or put into conservatorship. Lehman Brothers Holding Inc., a 158-year-old investment firm with over $600 billion in assets and over $700 billion in liabilities, filed for the biggest bankruptcy in history.

As part of the regulatory changes in response to the crisis, the Emergency Economic Stabilization Act of 2008 temporarily raised the basic coverage on federal deposit insurance coverage from $100,000 to $250,000 between October 2008 and December 2009. The basic deposit insurance limit was supposed to return to the $100,000 level at the beginning of 2010. However, in 2009, Congress extended the $250,000 limit until 2013. It remains unclear when the new limit will be brought down. Higher deposit insurance is likely to increase the cost of bank operation significantly, with a questionable effect on protection of small depositors. And risk management lessons remain to be learned from the recent crisis.

14.3 DELIVERY OF OVERSEAS BANKING SERVICES

Banks may use a number of organizational forms to deliver international banking services to their customers. The primary forms are (1) representative offices, (2) shell branches, (3) correspondent banks, (4) foreign branches, (5) Edge Act corporations, (6) foreign subsidiaries and affiliates, and (7) international banking facilities. Exhibit 14.3 shows a possible organizational structure for the foreign operations of a U.S. bank. Although possible, all these forms need not exist for any individual bank. We next discuss each organizational form, focusing on its advantages and disadvantages for the parent bank.

REPRESENTATIVE OFFICES

Representative nonbanking offices are established in a foreign country primarily to assist the parent bank's customers in that country. Representative offices

EXHIBIT 14.3

Possible Organizational Structure for a U.S. Bank's International Operations

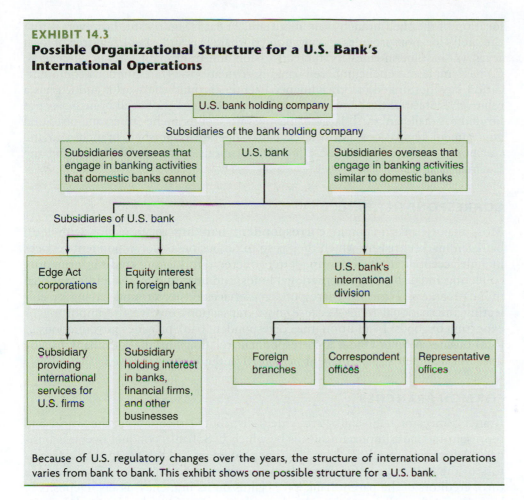

Because of U.S. regulatory changes over the years, the structure of international operations varies from bank to bank. This exhibit shows one possible structure for a U.S. bank.

cannot accept deposits, make loans, transfer funds, accept drafts, transact in the international money market, or commit the parent bank to loans. In fact, they cannot cash a traveler's check drawn on the parent bank. What they may do, however, is provide information and assist the parent bank's clients in their banking and business contacts in the foreign country. For example, a representative office may introduce businesspeople to local bankers, or it may act as an intermediary between U.S. firms and firms located in the country of the representative office. A representative office is a primary vehicle by which an initial presence is established in a country before setting up formal banking operations.

SHELL BRANCHES

The easiest and cheapest way to enter international banking is to establish a **shell branch**. This is a booking office for bank transactions located abroad that has no contact with the public. Activities of shell branches are primarily limited to inter-bank money market transactions (mostly in the Eurodollar market), foreign currency transactions, and the purchase of small shares of syndicate loans. In most cases, transactions at the shell branch reflect banking decisions made at the U.S. head office or at branches around the world. Thus, to some extent, the physical location of the shell branch is unimportant. What is significant, however, is that the shell's location provides an environment that (1) is almost entirely free of local taxes, (2) has liberal rules for the conversion and transfer of foreign currencies, (3) has simple and unencumbered banking regulations, (4) has modern communication facilities linked to other financial centers around the world, and (5) has a relatively stable political environment. The establishment of shell branches is not limited to small banks. All large banks operate shell branches to escape taxes and government regulations. Most U.S. banks operate their shell branches in the Caribbean Basin, with the most popular locations being the Bahamas and the Cayman Islands.

CORRESPONDENT BANKS

Most major banks maintain **correspondent banking** relationships with local banks in market areas in which they wish to do business. Correspondent services include accepting drafts, honoring letters of credit, furnishing credit information, collecting and disbursing international funds, and investing funds in international money markets. Typically, correspondent services center around paying or collecting international funds because most transactions involve the importing or exporting of goods. In addition, the correspondent bank provides introductions to local businesspeople. Under a correspondent relationship, the U.S. bank usually does not maintain any permanent personnel in the foreign country.

FOREIGN BRANCHES

Branch offices of U.S. banks are widely distributed throughout the world and represent the most important means by which U.S. banks conduct overseas business. A **foreign branch** is a legal and operational part of the parent bank. Creditors of the branch have full legal claims on the bank's assets as a whole, and, in turn, creditors of the parent bank have claims on its branches' assets. Deposits of both foreign branches and domestic branches are considered to be total deposits of the bank, and reserve requirements are tied to these total deposits.

Foreign branches are subject to two sets of banking regulations. First, as part of the parent bank, they are subject to all legal limitations that exist for U.S. banks. Second, they are subject to the regulation of the host country. Domestically, the OCC is the overseas regulator and examiner of national banks, whereas state banking authorities and the Federal Reserve Board share the authority for state-chartered member banks. Granting power to open a branch overseas resides with the Board of Governors of the Federal Reserve System. As a practical matter, the Federal Reserve System and the OCC dominate the regulation of foreign branches.

The attitudes of host countries toward establishing and regulating branches of U.S. banks vary widely. Typically, countries that need capital and expertise in lending and investment welcome the establishment of U.S. bank branches and allow them to operate freely within their borders. Other countries allow the establishment of U.S. bank branches but limit their activities relative to domestic banks because of competitive factors. Some foreign governments may fear that branches of large U.S. banks might hamper the growth of their country's domestic banking industry. As a result, growing nationalism and a desire for locally controlled credit have slowed the expansion of American banks abroad in recent years.

The major advantage of foreign branches is a worldwide name identification with the parent bank. Customers of the foreign branch have access to the full range of the parent bank's services, and the value of these services is based on the worldwide value of the client relationship rather than just the local office relationship. Furthermore, deposits are more secure, having their ultimate claim against the much larger parent bank, not just the local office. Similarly, legal loan limits are a function of the size of the parent bank, not of the branch. The major disadvantages of foreign branches are the costs of establishment and the legal limits placed on permissible activities.

EDGE ACT CORPORATIONS

Edge Act corporations are subsidiaries of U.S. banks that were formed to permit U.S. banks to engage in international banking and financing activities and to engage in activities that they could not conduct within the United States. Edge Act corporations operate under federal charter and are not subject to the banking laws of the various states. There are also a number of **agreement corporations** that operate similarly to Edge Act corporations but remain under state charter. At year-end 2009, there were 55 Edge Act and agreement corporations. The principal difference between these two types of organizations is that agreement corporations must engage primarily in banking activities, whereas Edge Act corporations may undertake banking as well as some nonbanking activities. The most important nonbanking activity in which Edge Act and agreement corporations may engage is investing in equities of foreign corporations. Ordinarily, U.S. banks cannot participate in investment activities. Hence, this power has been the main advantage of the Edge Act and agreement corporations' form of organization; it has helped U.S. banks achieve an improved competitive position relative to foreign banks, which are typically allowed to make equity investments. The largest class of these have been investments in foreign banking institutions. Purchases have been made as an alternative to establishing a branch network or to strengthen foreign correspondent relationships. Edge Act and agreement corporations have in recent years also taken equity positions in finance and investment companies.

FOREIGN SUBSIDIARIES AND AFFILIATES

A **foreign subsidiary** bank is a separately incorporated bank owned entirely or in part by a U.S. bank, a U.S. bank holding company, or an Edge Act corporation. A foreign subsidiary provides local identity and visibility of a local bank in the eyes of potential customers in the host country, which often enhances its ability to attract additional local deposits. Furthermore, management is typically composed of local nationals, giving the subsidiary bank better access to the local business community. Thus, foreign-owned subsidiaries are generally in a stronger position to provide domestic and international banking services to residents of the host country.

Closely related to foreign subsidiaries are *foreign affiliate banks*, which are locally incorporated banks owned in part, but not controlled, by an outside parent. The majority of the ownership and control may be local, or it may be other foreign banks.

EU AND CROSS-BORDER M&A

A main objective for the European Union has been to develop a single financial market. Financial integration leads to better financial services at lower costs. The creation of a common European currency and the economic consolidation of Europe present several interesting benefits, challenges, and opportunities for banks around the world.

One of the benefits for banks that operate in Europe is the reduced foreign exchange risk of dealing in a single currency. In the past, banks that lent funds across borders within Europe were subject to foreign exchange risk because of fluctuations in individual currency values. Additional benefits include the increased freedom of capital flows and the increased ability of banks to diversify geographically. With fewer barriers to capital flows, it is easier for banks based in one country to lend to borrowers in other countries. This allows for lower transaction costs and increased allocational efficiency in European financial markets. At the same time, banks become more geographically diversified as they lend to borrowers in more countries.

Increased freedom of capital flows also leads to increased competition in financial markets. The challenge to European banks is to respond to these opportunities more effectively than their competitors do. To be successful in this environment, European banks must do many of the same things that U.S. banks have been doing in recent years: taking advantage of improvements in information technology, trimming excess personnel, eliminating duplicate functions, and merging with other banks when there are opportunities for cost savings.

When interstate branching restrictions were lifted in the United States, it didn't take long for Bank of America to spread nationwide. Now that doing business across national boundaries within the European Union (EU) is relatively easy, it seems like only a matter of time before there is a European version of Bank of America. Surprisingly, there have been relatively few cross-border mergers in Europe. It is not as though there is little room for consolidation. The European banking industry has been consolidating much like the U.S. banking industry, but the vast majority have been within-country mergers.

Although the creation of the EU makes it easier to do business across national borders, a cross-border merger in the EU is still much more challenging than an interstate merger in the United States. Legal, regulatory, political, cultural, and tax differences still exist within the EU. Nonetheless, the benefits of a bank that spans the EU are substantial. A recent high-profile deal was the 2007 acquisition of ABN AMRO, the second largest bank in the Netherlands at the time. After a bidding war with Barclays (in the United Kingdom), a consortium led by the Royal Bank of Scotland Group (also in the United Kingdom), Fortis (headquartered in both Belgium and the Netherlands), and Banco Santander (in Spain) acquired AMRO for more than €71 billion ($100 billion). This was one of the biggest bank takeovers in history. However, the acquisition did not lead to the desired expansion of new markets for the acquirers. Coupled with the high cost of the bid, the Royal Bank of Scotland went into financial trouble soon afterward and was bailed out by the British government in 2008. In the same year, Fortis was nationalized by the Dutch government to avoid a crisis. Subsequently, Fortis, the twentieth largest company (by revenue) in the world as of 2007, sold all businesses except for its insurance division.

Despite the risks and challenges of cross-border mergers and acquisitions (M&As), more than half of the foreign direct investment took the form of cross-border M&A (Organization for Economic Co-operation and Development, 2007). In addition, for the first time recently, cross-border M&As became as important as mergers and acquisitions within a country in 2007. Given the appeal and importance of the EU market, it is reasonable to expect that cross-border M&As of banks in EU will continue to be a crucial part of international investments.

INTERNATIONAL BANKING FACILITIES

Effective in December 1981, the Federal Reserve Board permitted the establishment of **international banking facilities (IBFs)**. These facilities may be established by a U.S.-chartered depository institution, a U.S. branch or agency of a foreign bank, or the U.S. office of an Edge Act or agreement bank. IBFs are not institutions in the organizational sense. They are actually a set of asset and liability accounts segregated on the books of the establishing institutions.

IBFs are allowed to conduct international banking operations that, for the most part, are exempt from U.S. regulation. Deposits, which can be accepted only from non-U.S. residents or other IBFs and must be at least $100,000, are exempt from reserve requirements. The deposits obtained cannot be used domestically; they must be used for making foreign loans. In fact, to ensure that U.S.-based firms and individuals comply with this requirement, borrowers must sign a statement agreeing to this stipulation when taking out the loan.

DO YOU UNDERSTAND?

1. What are the reasons for growth in American banking overseas in recent decades?
2. What are the organizational forms banks use to deliver international banking services to their overseas customers?
3. Compare the U.S. philosophy of bank regulation to that of other countries.
4. In many countries, banks provide broader services than are allowed within the United States. How might an American bank decide to structure its overseas operations to best compete with these financial institutions abroad?

14.4 INTERNATIONAL LENDING

As is the case with domestic operations, the greatest amount of income from international operations is derived from lending. The bulk of the lending is accomplished through foreign branches, subsidiaries, or affiliate banks in foreign countries. The total amount of international lending by U.S. banks is not known precisely because published data are not available on loans made by affiliates of U.S. banks or banks owned jointly by U.S. banks and other foreign banks. However, as of September 2010, the Federal Reserve Board reported that foreign lending by U.S. banks totaled more than $2,297 billion. As Exhibit 14.4 shows, foreign branches are located throughout the world. In amounts of assets, branches in Latin America, Europe, and Japan account for more than 70 percent of all the assets of U.S. branches abroad. However, despite the impressive record of American banks overseas, the market remains dominated by a few giant multinational banks. Currently, a small number of banks dominate the market, and many of the banks operating outside the United States have only single *shell branches* in offshore money markets, such as Nassau or the Cayman Islands. Increasingly, however, regional and superregional banks are increasing their loans and investment activities overseas.

EXHIBIT 14.4
Amount Owed U.S. Banks by Foreign Borrowers (September 2010)

Area	$ Billions	Percentage*
European countries (except those listed here)	505.8	22.0
Germany	301.1	13.1
United Kingdom	419.1	18.2
France	251.9	11.0
Banking centers, international and regional organizations	233.7	10.2
Japan	137.9	6.0
Latin America and Caribbean (except Mexico)	78.3	3.4
Asia (excluding Japan)	191.5	8.3
Canada	74.4	3.2
Australia and New Zealand	63.0	2.7
Mexico	20.8	0.9
Africa	6.6	0.3
Other†	13.5	0.6
Total	2,297.5	100

Although the lending activities of U.S. banks extend worldwide, most U.S. banks' claims are on companies or individuals in Latin America, Europe, or Japan.

*Column adds to less than 100 percent because of rounding.
†Other includes non-G10 developed countries not listed above.

CHARACTERISTICS OF INTERNATIONAL LOANS

In many ways, the loans that banks make to international customers are similar to domestic business loans. Most loans are intermediate-term, floating-rate credits made to moderate- to high-quality borrowers. There are, however, important differences relating to one or more of the following factors: (1) funding, (2) syndication, (3) pricing, and (4) collateral. A further difference is that international loans can be denominated in almost any major currency, although dollars are the overwhelming favorite. International loans tend to be larger in size than typical domestic loans, and borrowers are generally sovereign governments or large multinational companies, so the perceived credit risk tends to be lower.

Most large international loans are negotiated and funded in the Eurocurrency market. International banks operating in this market accept time deposits from nonbank investors and then make short- or intermediate-term loans. Funds can be lent directly to nonbank borrowers, or they can be lent in the interbank market to other international banks if the original bank does not have sufficient loan demand. The interest rate paid to depositors and charged to borrowers is related to the home-country interest rate for the currency in question, but for a variety of reasons, the spread between borrowing and lending rates tends to be smaller in the Eurocurrency market. Most Eurocurrency loans are priced with respect to the **London Interbank Offer Rate (LIBOR)**, which is the rate at which international banks lend to each other in London, historically the center of the Eurocurrency market.

A loan to a nonbank borrower is typically priced at some premium above LIBOR, with the premium being related to the credit risk of the borrower. For example, a loan made to a highly rated multinational company or to a European government might be priced at 0.10 percent above LIBOR, whereas a credit made to a less well-known company or to a developing country might have a premium as high as 1.5 percent or more above LIBOR.

If the loan extends for more than one credit period (such as a month), the interest rate charged on the loan for the coming period is determined by the level of LIBOR at the beginning of the period. These floating-rate loans allow banks to fund the credits in the Eurocurrency market at the beginning of the period and lock in a lending spread for the coming period. At the end of this period, the loan again "rolls over" and is repriced for the subsequent period. This **rollover pricing** mechanism, which was first used in the Eurocurrency market in 1969, allows banks to make intermediate-term loans without exposing themselves to the interest rate risk inherent in fixed-rate loans. The sheer volume of credit available, the low cost of funds, and the sophistication of the banking service provided have also made the Eurocurrency market a favorite source of funds for nonbank borrowers.

Most large (greater than about $50 million) international bank loans are **syndicated**. This means that several banks participate in funding the loan, which is packaged by one or more lead banks. This allows banks to spread their risks among a large number of loans, and it allows borrowers to obtain larger amounts of capital than would be available through other means. This is especially true for *sovereign borrowers* (national governments). Indeed, the intermediate-term, floating-rate, *general obligation* (unsecured and backed by the taxing power of the government), syndicated bank loan was the principal instrument through which financial capital was channeled to developing countries during the 1970s and early 1980s. The total level of such debt grew from essentially nothing in 1971 to more than $300 billion in August 1982, when the Mexican debt moratorium effectively ended voluntary bank lending to **less developed countries (LDCs)** at that time.

Finally, most international bank loans are *unsecured* (made without specific collateral). Business loans are generally made only to large, creditworthy, multinationals and, with public-sector loans, are generally backed by the *full faith and credit* of the borrowing nation. Ironically, during the period when the Organization of the Petroleum Exporting Countries (OPEC) surplus was being recycled to developing countries, bankers comforted themselves with the statement that "Nations don't go bankrupt." Although true in a legal sense, this idea was shown to be tragically misguided when LDCs began experiencing severe financial difficulties during the mid-1980s, and the market value of the creditor banks was reduced to reflect the underlying value of these sovereign loans.

RISK IN INTERNATIONAL LENDING

In many respects, the principles applicable to foreign lending are the same as those applicable to domestic lending—that is, to define and evaluate the credit risk that the borrower will default. In international lending, bankers are exposed to two additional risks: *country risk* and *currency risk*. In this section, we discuss each of these three risks in turn and then suggest ways in which bankers can reduce them.

Although many of the tools used to analyze risk are comparable in international banking circles, bankers must be wary of differences in accounting standards and legal systems around the globe. The general trend toward conformity in international accounting standards ultimately facilitates international commerce, and international banking in particular; however, this convergence is still a number of years away. Similarly, legal standards are also problematic in assessing banking-related risks. For example, when assessing credit risk, we are often concerned with both the likelihood of default and the process that is followed when an entity falls into financial distress. These legal procedures vary substantially in different countries. For example, the German system applies relatively strict rules of default in determining failure. In contrast, many developing countries may be more lax in defining default, and they may even be slow to recognize difficulties in reported financial statements.

Credit Risk. *Credit risk* involves assessing the probability that part of the interest or principal of the loan will not be repaid. The greater the default risk, the higher the loan rate that the bank must charge the borrower. As noted previously, this is the same type of risk that bankers face on the domestic scene. However, it may be more difficult to obtain or assess credit information abroad. U.S. banks are less familiar with local economic conditions and business practices than are domestic banks. It takes time and practice to develop appropriate sources of information and to evaluate such information correctly. As a result, many U.S. banks tend to restrict their foreign lending to major international corporations or financial institutions. This policy reflects the cost of gathering reliable information. A foreign government sometimes offers assurances against default or rescheduling of loans by private borrowers, making such loans more attractive to international lenders.

Country Risk. **Country (sovereign) risk** is closely tied to political developments in a country, particularly the government's attitude toward foreign loans or investments. Some governments attempt to encourage the inflow of foreign funds, whether the funds come from private or public sources. Others, however, make it difficult to maintain profitable lending operations. Minor obstacles, such as wage–price controls, profit controls, additional taxation, and other legal restrictions can inhibit the ability of borrowers to repay loans.

At the extreme, foreign governments may expropriate the assets of foreign investors or prohibit foreign loan repayments, either of which could drastically alter risk exposure. Worldwide, there are only a few cases in which countries have refused to repay or have refused permission for their citizens to repay foreign loans. The reason for this is that the borrowing country does not want to preclude the possibility of obtaining foreign credit in the future. Any nationalization or government refusals to repay international loans may nearly halt the inflow of foreign funds into the country involved. However, rebellions, civil commotions, wars, and unexpected changes in government do occur from time to time, and, as a result, risk is real and must be considered in granting international loans. Somewhat soothing to international lenders is the fact that, with the exception of Chile and Cuba, there have been few large-scale nationalizations by foreign governments in recent years. However, U.S. banks have been forced out of Iran, and some South American countries have taken the properties of some U.S. citizens.

A major problem for banks in the 1980s was the rescheduling of sovereign loans. *Rescheduling* refers to rolling over a loan, often capitalizing interest arrears or extending the loan's maturity. Because of repayment problems, multiyear rescheduling agreements were introduced in 1984. These typically involve (1) a consolidation of several individual public and private loans into a smaller number of standardized debt issues; (2) the extension of government guarantees to private-sector debts; (3) the granting of a grace period of 1 to several years, during which the loans do not need to be serviced; and (4) an extension of the loan maturity date to as long as 15 years.

Although little attention has been paid to LDC debt in recent years, some analysts are raising concerns about the possibility of a crisis similar to that experienced in the 1980s. According to the International Monetary Fund (IMF), emerging country external debt has grown at an average of 11 percent annually from 2006 through 2010. As of 2010, estimates of external debt outstanding in emerging countries exceeded $5.1 trillion.

Currency Risk. **Currency risk** is concerned with currency value changes and exchange controls. More specifically, some loans are denominated in foreign currency rather than dollars, and if the currency in which the loan is made loses value against the dollar during the course of the loan, the repayment is worth fewer dollars. Of course, if the foreign currency has a well-developed market and the maturity is relatively short, the loan may be hedged. However, many world currencies, particularly those in developing nations, do not have well-established foreign currency markets; consequently, these international loans cannot always be hedged to reduce this kind of currency risk.

Another aspect of currency risk concerns exchange controls. *Exchange controls*, which are not uncommon in developing countries, may limit the movement of funds across national borders or restrict a currency's convertibility into dollars for repayment. Thus, exchange risk may occur because of difficulties in the convertibility of a currency or in its exchange rate. Typically, if a country has an active market for its currency and its international payments and receipts are in approximate balance (or it has adequate reserves to pay deficits), currency risk is minimal. However, if a country persistently runs a deficit on its balance of payments, it may establish some form of exchange control. One such example is Mexico, which devalued its currency severely in 1982 and literally suspended exchange operations for a period of time. This was the result of its large balance-of-payments deficit and its inability to make current payments on its sizable international loans.

RISK EVALUATION

When lending abroad, bankers must take into account the same economic factors that they consider domestically—government monetary and fiscal policy, bank regulations, foreign exchange controls, and national and regional economic conditions. Depending on the cost, lenders use different means of evaluating risks in foreign lending. The most direct are in-depth studies prepared by the bank's foreign lending and economic departments. These are based on statistics and other information about a country's economic and financial condition. Information is gathered from government sources and, if available, from the bank's representatives overseas. The analyses often contain careful evaluations of expected inflation, fiscal and monetary policy, the country's trade policies, capital flows, and political stability, as well as an estimate of the credit standing of the individual borrower. Some circumstances affecting sovereign risk cannot be captured in statistical analysis. In such cases, practical judgment and experience play a heavy role while information from government officials in this country and abroad, from branch and representative offices, and from other sources is analyzed carefully.

When international lenders find in-depth analysis too expensive, they may turn to on-site reports, checklists, and statistical indicators to help them assess the risk of lending. However, such methods tend not to be as reliable and may signal false alarms or a false sense of security. Part of the problem with indicators is that they often are not current, and even if current, there is no assurance that they predict the future. Thus, lenders may find it expensive and difficult to gather reliable information about foreign borrowers. Lenders must decide how much information they need to negotiate a loan with a prospective borrower. The higher the cost of gathering information—or the greater the risk of lending because of either lack of information or credit quality—the higher the loan rate. If the risk of making a loan is too great, the loan applicant may be turned down.

METHODS OF REDUCING RISK

Bankers have at their disposal several ways of reducing risk in international lending. The basic avenues open to them are to seek third-party support in the form of insurance or loan guarantees; to share risk exposure by participating in loans with other lenders; or, most important, to diversify their loans among different borrowers and countries.

Third-Party Help.   One way banks may reduce foreign lending risk is to get a third party to agree to pay back the principal and interest in the event that the borrower defaults. Typically, this is done by either foreign governments or central banks. Of course, these guarantees are only as good as the backer's ability and intent to repay. Such a promise from a politically unstable and underdeveloped country may not mean much. Furthermore, if the same government guarantees a number of loans, its ability to repay may be strained if several of these loans are to default simultaneously.

An alternative to foreign government guarantees is an external guarantee from an outside institution. In addition to the credit derivatives discussed in Chapter 13, banks can reduce foreign lending risk by lending to exporters who insure their trade credit with the Foreign Credit Insurance Association (FCIA). The FCIA is an organization of approximately 50 insurance companies throughout the United States. FCIA insurance covers individual transactions up to a certain percentage against nonpayment arising from credit loss and political hazards. Political risks are reinsured by the FCIA through the U.S. Export-Import Bank (Eximbank). The FCIA makes thorough credit investigations of individual borrowers as well as of the sovereign risk. Typically, the insurance covers up to 95 percent of the credit risk and up to 100 percent of the risk associated with political hazards. The insurance premium paid by the exporter depends on the credit rating of the borrower and the rating established for each country. It typically averages about 0.5 percent, but it may be higher for less creditworthy firms and less stable governments.

The Overseas Private Investment Corporation (OPIC) offers programs to insure bank loans against the risk of war, expropriation, and currency inconvertibility. OPIC also finances some loans directly. Similarly, Eximbank guarantees medium-term loans made by commercial banks against both political and credit risks. Eximbank deals with risk beyond the scope that private capital markets or private lenders are willing to assume. The bank's role in financing the high-risk loans may take the form of making a direct loan, participating in a loan with other lenders, or guaranteeing a loan. The Eximbank loan guarantee program is similar to the insurance provided by FCIA described earlier. As a policy matter, Eximbank directs its international lending involvement toward the financing of capital equipment, such as hydroelectric installations, rather than consumer goods.

Pooling Risk.   Banks can also reduce international lending risk for any one institution by making **participation loans**. Under this kind of arrangement, banks join together to provide the funds for a loan and thereby directly reduce the risk exposure for individual banks. Large banks that participate in such arrangements generally make their own assessment of the political and credit risks. Smaller lenders may rely primarily on the reports prepared by large banks. This may lead smaller banks to enter into international loans without fully appreciating or understanding the risk involved. Realistically, however, this is the only means by which smaller banks can enter the international lending arena, but one hopes that they base their decisions on intelligent analysis of the economic returns and risks involved, not on the glamour and prestige of having an international banking department. The decline in international banking activity of some small banks suggests that they have realized they do not have the expertise necessary to compete in international lending.

Another common strategy to reduce political risk is simply to ensure that there are other lenders from well-developed capital markets. When a foreign government or firm considers the implications of default, they are much more hesitant to violate a bond contract that may hamper future relationships with multiple important parties. Simply ensuring that other prominent lenders are included in large loans helps mitigate default risks. The reputation and importance of the other lenders is an important factor in reducing the borrower's likelihood of default and potential expropriation.

Diversification.   Banks may reduce foreign lending risk through portfolio diversification. That is, in the event that a borrower defaults, earnings from other investments minimize the effect of the loan loss on the bank's total earnings. Of course, the extent that diversification reduces risk for a given portfolio of loans depends on how the returns are correlated with one another. The more highly correlated the returns, the less the portfolio risk is reduced. Thus, in a choice between two loans having the same rate of return and riskiness, the loan that is less correlated with the bank's existing portfolio would be the more attractive loan.

Banks pursue portfolio diversification in several ways, with geographic diversification being the most obvious means to reduce risk exposure. Geographic diversification reduces political risk, but such diversification may give rise to other problems. Specifically, a bank develops expertise in certain countries and cultivates sources of primary information that may not be available to other banks. This type of information, plus long-standing experience with a particular borrower, may allow the bank to formulate better estimates of the risk involved in a particular loan. Unfortunately, if a bank specializes in loans that depend on similar risk factors, one large shock can prove to be disastrous. This is what happened to many banks that were heavily exposed in Latin America. Although there may have been good diversification among the various countries, the region's fortunes were tied to a continuation of economic growth in the industrialized countries and to high prices for their export commodities. When these factors started to deteriorate, the entire region suffered, and banks were left with problem loans in many of the countries.

MANAGING RISK: HOW BANKS REDUCE COUNTRY RISK

After suffering huge losses on loans to less developed countries, U.S. banks have been reluctant to make new loans in countries like Mexico and Brazil. These countries and others in Latin America, eastern Europe, and Asia are perceived as being risky places in which to make loans. Bankers are reluctant to lend in these countries because of potential political developments. For example, at the extreme, the government of one of these countries could restrict payment of foreign debt obligations.

This country (sovereign) risk is responsible for keeping U.S. banks from making loans in these countries. This is beginning to change, however, because of innovations that are allowing banks to lend in these countries without bearing substantial country risk. For example, the International Finance Corporation (IFC), a unit of the World Bank, is creating loan syndications to private borrowers in developing countries that make it possible for U.S. banks to make loans in these countries without bearing the country risk normally associated with such loans. These IFC loans are typically for amounts between $5 million and $100 million, with the IFC holding 25 percent of the debt and selling the rest of it to participating banks.

U.S. banks are attracted to these loan participations because they offer attractive yields, typically 2 to 3.5 percent above the LIBOR, and have minimal country risk. Country risk is small for two reasons. First, because the IFC is a unit of the World Bank, it is protected against the risk that a particular country will restrict the payment of debt obligations to foreign banks. And second, because the loans are syndicated, the risk exposure for individual banks is reduced. Note that, although country risk is minimized, these loans still have credit risk associated with them. If the borrower fails, the participants will lose, but it will not be because of political developments in the country; it will be because of the economics of the borrower's underlying business.

DO YOU UNDERSTAND?

1. In what ways may an international loan differ from a domestic loan?
2. What is the difference between *currency risk* and *country risk*?
3. Compare the strategies of pooling risk and diversification as methods of reducing the risks of international lending.

14.5 FOREIGN BANKS IN THE UNITED STATES

Foreign banks have operated in the United States for more than a hundred years. Beginning in the mid-1970s, however, they began to attract attention by their rapid expansion into major U.S. financial centers. Their rapid growth alarmed many U.S. bankers and regulators because, until the passage of the International Banking Act, foreign banks were able to escape federal control almost entirely. Exhibit 14.5 shows the number of foreign banks that have established offices in the United States in recent years. The number of foreign bank offices grew rapidly during the 1980s. Most of the growth in foreign bank offices was the result of the overseas expansion of Japanese banks that was occurring during that period. When the Japanese financial system began experiencing difficulties in the early 1990s, however, many Japanese banks began to consolidate their overseas activities.

GROWTH OF FOREIGN BANKS

Before World War II, the primary motive for foreign banks to establish banking offices in the United States was to facilitate trade and the flow of long-term investments between the United States and their home countries. Following the war, the American dollar emerged as the major world currency, primarily because of the dominance of the U.S. economy relative to the rest of the world. With the importance of U.S. money and capital markets, additional foreign banks began to locate

EXHIBIT 14.5
Number of Foreign Banks in the United States

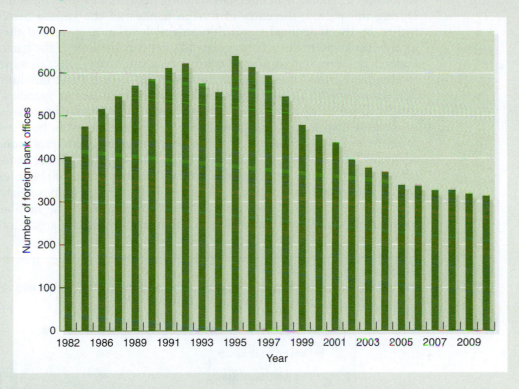

The number of foreign bank offices grew rapidly during the 1980s. Since the mid-1980s, however, home country difficulties and the pace of consolidation in the U.S. banking industry caused a decline in the number of foreign bank offices in the United States.

Source: American Banker, various issues, 1983–1995, and Federal Reserve System, Structure Data for the U.S. Offices of Foreign Banking Organizations, 1997–2010.

here. By 1965, there were 41 foreign banks conducting business in the United States, with assets totaling $7 billion. Most of these foreign banks were located in New York City, the major attraction being the direct access to the city's money and capital markets. Most of the other foreign banks were concentrated in California.

The rapid expansion of foreign banking activities in the United States began in the early 1960s. This spurt can be characterized as a worldwide response by the banking industry to the multinationalization of major manufacturing corporations, as previously discussed. For foreign corporations, the United States represented a major market, and many of these firms made sizable direct investments in the United States. In short, foreign banks followed their corporate customers. The financial services provided were merely a continuation of long-established relationships. Similarly, U.S. corporations also provided some of the impetus for foreign banks to locate in the United States. As American corporations expanded abroad, they established relationships with major local foreign banks, which found it to be good business to extend the banking relationships to the corporate headquarters of U.S. firms by establishing offices in the United States. The banking services that were provided centered on financing the shipment of parts and semi-finished products between the corporate headquarters in the United States and the affiliated suppliers of foreign countries.

However, demand was not the only factor that caused this growth. It was also fostered by both the lack of a federal regulatory framework and the ability of foreign banks to establish an interstate banking network in a form denied U.S. banks. During this period, the entry of foreign banks into the United States was controlled by the individual states. No federal legislation governed their entry. A foreign bank's activities were regulated by federal law only if the bank joined the Federal Reserve System or if it controlled a subsidiary bank, in which case the foreign bank would be subject to the provisions of the Bank Holding Company Act. Thus, as long as the foreign bank operated branches or agencies, it was not subject to federal banking laws. Foreign banks could engage in some nonbanking activities denied to U.S. banks, and they were not required to hold reserves with the Federal Reserve System, a situation that tended to complicate monetary management. For all of the reasons previously discussed, the number of foreign bank offices in the United States increased from 85 to more than 600 between 1965 and 1991. The growth of foreign bank assets in the United States relative to U.S. domestic bank assets is shown in Exhibit 14.6. Although the number of banks operating in the United States increased dramatically, the 50 largest foreign banks

EXHIBIT 14.6

Growth in Foreign Bank Assets in the United States (1985–2010)

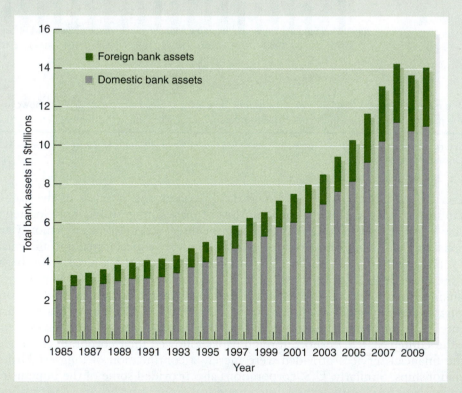

Foreign banks now control about 20 percent of all banking assets in the United States. Foreign bank assets grew rapidly in the 1980s, especially the assets held by branches of Japanese banks. In the 1990s, however, the holdings of U.S. assets by Japanese banks declined. The recent growth in foreign bank assets is the result of increased holdings by Canadian and European banks.

Source: Board of Governors, Federal Reserve System.

EXHIBIT 14.7
Top Foreign Banks in U.S. Assets (September 30, 2010)

Rank	Bank	Headquarters	Total Assets in U.S. Offices ($ Billions)
1	BNP Paribas	France	278.7
2	Toronto-Dominion Bank	Canada	206.3
3	HSBC Overseas Holdings Limited	United Kingdom	193.6
4	Deutsche Bank Aktiengesellschaft	Germany	175.9
5	Bank of Tokyo–Mitsubishi UFJ, Ltd.	Japan	163.0
6	RBSG International Holdings Ltd	United Kingdom	148.5
7	Barclays Bank PLC	United Kingdom	105.6
8	Banco Santander, S.A.	Spain	95.6
9	Royal Bank of Scotland PLC	United Kingdom	93.8
10	UBS Ag	Switzerland	92.0

Most of the U.S. assets held by foreign banks are in European banks. Japanese and Canadian banks also hold substantial U.S. assets.

Source: Board of Governors, Federal Reserve System, *Structure Data for the U.S. Offices of Foreign Banking Organizations,* September 2010.

tend to dominate foreign banking activities in the United States. Exhibit 14.7 shows the foreign banks with the largest U.S. asset holdings. Clearly, a handful of foreign banks dominate the holdings of all foreign banks.

REGULATING THE U.S. OPERATIONS OF FOREIGN BANKS

The lack of regulatory control and the growth of foreign banks in the 1970s led to a recognition by the U.S. government that domestic banks were at a competitive disadvantage against foreign-controlled banks. The result of this realization was the passage of the **International Banking Act (IBA) of 1978**. The broad policy objective of the IBA was to promote competitive equality between domestic and foreign banking institutions in the United States. The policy of national treatment attempted to give foreign banks operating in the United States similar power and to subject them to the same obligations as their domestic counterparts.

There were six major statutory changes implemented under the International Bank Act. First, the IBA allows federal chartering of foreign banking facilities. Second, the ability of foreign banks to accept interstate domestic deposits is limited. Foreign banks are allowed to establish branches in more than one state; however, branches outside the home state of a foreign bank cannot accept deposits and can maintain customer balances only as permitted for Edge Act corporations. Such multistate banking activities were not allowed for domestic banks or bank holding companies at the time, and foreign banks' ability to engage in such activities was viewed as a competitive advantage over domestic banks. Third, the Federal Reserve Board was authorized to impose reserve requirements on foreign banks operating in the United States if they had worldwide assets in excess of $1 billion. This was done to help ensure the integrity of monetary policy actions as well as for competitive equality. Fourth, federal deposit insurance is required for foreign bank operations that engage in retail deposit taking. Fifth, foreign banks were allowed to establish Edge Act corporations to conduct international banking and finance activities. Finally, foreign banks that operate in the United States became subject to the nonbanking prohibitions of the Bank Holding Company Act.

With the passage of the Foreign Bank Supervision Enhancement Act (FBSEA) in 1991, the approval of the Federal Reserve is required before a foreign bank can establish offices in the United States. In addition, the Federal Reserve is required to examine each U.S. office of a foreign bank at least once a year and is given the power to close the office if it is engaging in inappropriate activities. FBSEA was passed shortly after the scandal involving the Bank of Commerce and Credit International (BCCI). Because of the complex organizational structure of BCCI, the bank was operating with very little regulatory oversight. The passage of FBSEA was an attempt to ensure that the Federal Reserve has the authority to oversee the activities of all foreign institutions operating in the United States.

After the Financial Services Modernization Act of 1999 was passed, any well-managed, well-capitalized, banking firm with a satisfactory Community Reinvestment Act rating could convert to a financial holding company, subject to approval by the Federal Reserve. (The Community Reinvestment Act [CRA] and CRA ratings are discussed in Chapter 15.) Financial holding companies are allowed to own subsidiaries that engage in almost any financial business. The provisions of GLB apply to foreign and domestic banks, so it is not surprising that many foreign banks have formed financial holding companies. As of December 31, 2009, 46 of the 525 financial holding companies were foreign owned.

14.6 FUTURE DIRECTIONS OF INTERNATIONAL BANKING

The foreseeable future is almost certain to be a time of dramatic change in international banking. The industry faces several challenges and opportunities:

- The continued consolidation of the European economy into a single market offers both opportunities and challenges for international banks.
- The capital needs of developing nations such as China, India, and Russia are likely to put pressure on world credit markets into the next decade.
- The Asian financial crisis and other shocks to the financial system in the late 1990s and early 2000s have increased financial institutions' awareness of operational risks.
- Increased competition from securities markets for the business of meeting the borrowing needs of large corporate clients is forcing banks to pursue other sources of revenue or develop new ways of competing.
- Finally, the growing interdependence among international economies and financial markets is certain to continue.

These trends have led the major international financial institutions, such as the International Monetary Fund (IMF) and the Bank for International Settlements (BIS), as well as the leading central banks to assume tighter regulatory and supervisory roles regarding the world's banking systems. The results have been a greater awareness of declining capital levels in some countries, some explicit regulations concerning capital adequacy and loan limits, and more supervision in such areas as international lending and foreign exchange trading. Recently the World Bank investigated the possibility of working with private corporations to tap larger pools of capital with which to assist countries with severe debt problems. Under one proposed arrangement, the World Bank would guarantee loans made to corporations for financing the construction of infrastructure projects in developing countries. The IMF is also looking for more ways to reduce the interest burden on developing countries while stimulating their economies to higher levels of output.

SUMMARY OF LEARNING OBJECTIVES

1 Describe the evolution of U.S. overseas banking activities. U.S. banks engaged in very few international banking activities before 1914. It was not until the early 1960s that the rapid expansion of U.S. overseas banking took place.

2 Explain the reasons for growth in U.S. banking operations overseas. The major reasons for this dramatic growth were (1) the overall expansion of U.S. world trade, (2) the growth of multinational corporations, and (3) the effect of government regulations.

3 Discuss the regulation of foreign banking activities. The Federal Reserve Board and the OCC have primary responsibility for supervising the activities of U.S. banks overseas.

4 Describe the organizational forms that banks can use to conduct overseas operations. Banks can use a number of organizational forms to deliver banking services to their international customers. The most important are correspondent relationships, branch offices, Edge Act corporations, and international banking facilities.

5 Explain the risks involved in foreign lending. The basic risk involved in foreign lending is the same as in domestic banking—the customer's default risk. However, there are two additional risks in lending abroad: sovereign risk and currency risk.

6 Describe the nature of foreign bank activities in the United States. Although the number of foreign banks with U.S. operations is in the hundreds, a small number of large institutions tend to dominate the U.S. asset holdings of foreign banks.

KEY TERMS

Representative nonbanking offices
Shell branch
Correspondent banking
Foreign branch
Edge Act corporations
Agreement corporations
Foreign subsidiary
International banking facilities (IBFs)
London Interbank Offer Rate (LIBOR)
Rollover pricing
Syndicated
Less developed countries (LDCs)
Country (sovereign) risk
Currency risk
Participation loans
International Banking Act (IBA) of 1978

QUESTIONS AND PROBLEMS

1. Why were U.S. banks slow in expanding overseas? What changed to encourage overseas expansion?

2. How were the overseas expansion of U.S. nonfinancial corporations and banks related? Discuss the defensive follow-the-customer strategy in your response.

3. Why have the number of U.S. banks operating overseas declined in recent years?

4. What are *Edge Act corporations*? What advantages do they afford American banks that wish to engage in international banking?

5. What is a *shell branch*? What functions do banking shell branches perform in U.S. overseas banking? Why are so many located in Caribbean island nations?

6. What is an *international banking facility*? In what types of business activities can such entities engage? Why did the Federal Reserve Board create these new banking entities?

7. What are the basic objectives of federal bank regulations as they apply to domestic banking? How are these basic regulatory objectives interpreted differently with respect to overseas banking? How do the BIS capital standards affect internationally active U.S. banks?

8. Explain the motivations behind the International Banking Act of 1978.

9. What were the provisions of the International Banking Act? Are some of the provisions no longer relevant? If so, which ones? Explain.

10. The recent development of microfinance led to new ways of looking at banking relationships. Do you believe that microfinance is entirely consistent with bank wealth maximization? If not, what objectives underlie these microloans?

11. What is a *syndicated loan*? In what ways do large international loans differ from typical domestic loans? Define the term *LIBOR*.

12. Consider a large syndicated loan to a firm with close ties to the government in a country with a large degree of political risk. As a large U.S. bank, explain why you might wish to have other reputable lenders from other nations involved before you agree to lend to this firm.

13. What risks must be evaluated in making international loans? Which of these are unique to international lending? How may these risks be reduced?

14. Do you believe that the presence of foreign banks in the United States serves the public's interest? In formulating your answer, consider the issues of bank safety and competition in banking markets.

15. In international lending, what is meant by the phrase *rescheduling of sovereign loans*? Why has rescheduling of loans become a problem to international lenders? What countries are involved?

INTERNET EXERCISE

In Chapter 13, you were asked to use the Federal Financial Institutions Examination Council's National Information Center (NIC) Web site to look up balance-sheet and performance information about a bank in your local community. In this Internet Exercise, your task is to expand on the analysis you have already started. (*Note:* It is not necessary for you to have completed the Internet Exercise in Chapter 13 for you to do this exercise.) Data on the foreign branches of U.S. banks and U.S. branches of foreign banks can be found at the NIC Web site, http://www.ffiec.gov/nic/.

1. Search the NIC Web site to determine whether your bank has any foreign branches. If so, identify the countries in which your bank has branches.

2. Search the NIC Web site to determine whether there are any foreign banks operating in your community. If so, identify the institution that is most similar to the domestic institutions identified in Internet Exercise 1 in terms of asset size.

3. Download or print out the summary performance ratios for the domestic institution and the foreign bank.

4. Compare the activities, performance, and riskiness of your bank to its foreign competitor. Comment on any significant differences between the two institutions.

Regulation of Financial Institutions

In 2008, Washington Mutual was taken over by the Federal Deposit Insurance Corporation (FDIC). With assets over $300 billion, it was the biggest bank failure in history. Its assets and liabilities were eventually acquired by J.P. Morgan Chase.

WHEN WAS THE LAST TIME YOU performed a careful analysis of your bank to make sure it was a safe place to deposit your money? If you are like most people, you have not given much thought to the safety and soundness of your bank. If you had been a student in the early 1900s, however, you would have been keenly aware of your bank's financial strength. At that time, banks had little regulation and bank *liabilities* (paper money or bank accounts) were unsecured. Thus, if your bank failed, you probably lost your money. Given those consequences, it's easy to understand why runs on banks were a common occurrence.

What's a *run* on a bank? Back in the "good old days," when banks had little regulation and some engaged in unscrupulous activities that included cheating or lying, and when you heard a rumor that a bank might fail, you literally ran to the bank to get your money back—either as hard currency (gold or silver coins) or bank notes of a sound bank. The motto of the day about banking was "Better safe than sorry."

Today, people take for granted that banks are safe places to keep their money. Even during the worst days of the recent financial crisis, there were relatively few runs. The reason is, of course, the extensive regulatory system developed over many years of experience and the fact that bank deposits are protected by federal deposit insurance. This chapter discusses the regulation of financial institutions, the reasons for the regulation, and the issues involved. ■

This chapter focuses on the major regulations that affect financial institutions, especially commercial banks. Regulations have a major impact on how financial institutions are managed, how they deal with consumers, the types of products they offer, the structure of the industry, and the types of risks they take. In fact, the interplay between financial institutions and their regulators is so intertwined that one cannot define an institution or understand what it does without understanding the regulations that constrain its behavior.

The chapter begins with a discussion of bank failures and their impact on individual communities and the nation's economy as a whole. Drawing on the lessons from the past, we then discuss the reasons for regulating commercial banks and other financial institutions. Historically, the overriding concern of regulation has been the safety and soundness of the financial system, which includes commercial banks and other financial institutions. The primary tools to achieve safety and soundness are (1) liquidity to the banking system provided by the Federal Reserve banks; (2) federal deposit insurance, which reduces the threat of runs on banks and other depository institutions; (3) minimum capital requirements, which encourage bank owners to take only prudent risks; and (4) the examination process, which monitors compliance with regulations and evaluates the quality of management. In addition, the chapter also discusses other regulations that affect the financial system, such as those affecting competition between institutions, industry structure, and the protection of consumers. The chapter concludes by discussing the powers of various regulators that oversee commercial banks. Subsequent chapters discuss other financial institutions and describe their regulators and the principal regulations that define and limit their business activities: Chapter 16 (Thrift Institutions and Finance Companies), Chapter 17 (Insurance Companies and Pension Funds), Chapter 18 (Investment Banking), and Chapter 19 (Investment Companies).

LEARNING OBJECTIVES

1 Discuss the reasons why banks are regulated.

2 Describe the history of bank failures in the United States, the steps policymakers have taken to reduce the incidence of failure, and the lessons learned from previous bank failures.

3 Explain FDIC insurance and how the FDIC goes about paying off depositors and disposing of the assets of a failed bank.

4 Discuss the issues and concerns created by FDIC insurance.

5 Explain the role of capital requirements and the bank examination process in promoting safety and soundness in the banking system.

6 Explain the limitations on bank activities and discuss recent changes to the limitations.

7 Discuss the various consumer protection regulations with which banks must comply.

8 Describe the responsibilities of the various bank regulatory agencies.

15.1 REASONS FOR REGULATION

Financial institutions are regulated because they provide products and services that the economy needs in order to function well. In addition, they function in an environment where asymmetric information is more the rule than the exception. Most consumers and businesses disclose their financial affairs to a financial institution if it is a necessary condition to obtain services. However, consumers and businesses want their financial affairs to be confidential. As a result, financial institutions are honor bound to keep the information private, but in doing so it is difficult for depositors to have enough information to assess the institution's soundness. Depositors, for example, do not know whether their financial institution has made good loans and entered into sound financial contracts. In fact, in the early 1900s and earlier, this veil of uncertainty caused banks and other depository institutions to experience runs and the financial system as a whole to experience panics as depositors rushed to withdraw funds for fear their bank or the banking system was unsound. When these panics occur, the economy slows down because bank reserves and the money supply shrink abruptly unless the central bank quickly takes action to provide liquidity and restore confidence in the financial system.

Another reason why banks are so heavily regulated is to limit predatory or discriminatory lending practices. Consumers and businesses rely almost exclusively on banks and other financial institutions to provide the loans they need to operate businesses, pay for their educations, buy homes and cars, and pay for other consumer products. In addition, comparison shopping for loan products is made difficult by asymmetric information—a lender must have access to the borrower's confidential financial records to provide an accurate price (interest rate) for a loan product. This reliance on financial institutions and the difficulty of comparison shopping make the consequences of discriminatory lending potentially severe for the borrower and increase the opportunity for lenders to engage in predatory lending practices (for example, charging excessively high interest rates or loan fees or imposing unfair conditions and penalties).

A final reason financial institutions are regulated is that some of the profits earned by financial institutions can be attributed to these financial institutions being able to create money or borrow at low cost because of explicit or implicit government guarantees. Recognizing this, politicians often try to induce financial institutions to surrender some of those profits to further the politicians' social goals. Thus, financial institutions are often coerced into (1) investing in government securities, (2) making loans to classes of customers that otherwise might not qualify, or (3) making certain loans at interest rates lower than the rates that the financial institutions customarily charge on loans of that type and associated risk.

Banks and other depository institutions are willing to accept the regulation as long as they know that the net effect of regulation benefits them by increasing public confidence in their stability and public willingness to accept their liabilities, even if those liabilities pay low interest rates. However, regulated financial institutions also have an incentive to try to avoid regulation if by so doing they can increase their profits even more. Thus, over time a so-called **regulatory dialectic** or regulatory struggle has developed in which regulators impose a regulation—such as limits on activities imposed by the 1933 Glass-Steagall Act— and banks find a way to avoid the regulation, for example, by establishing separate subsidiaries to engage in the prohibited activities. As financial institutions innovate around regulation, the regulators impose new regulations and the regulatory dialectic continues. Overall, however, financial institutions comply with a heavy dose of regulation because the value of the charter to operate as a bank or other financial institution is greater than the cost associated with complying with regulation.

EXHIBIT 15.1
Major Bank Legislation and Regulatory Provisions Since 1900

Federal Reserve Act of 1913

- Establishes the Federal Reserve System

Banking Acts of 1933 (Glass-Steagall) and 1935

- Prohibits payment of interest on demand deposits
- Establishes the FDIC
- Separates commercial banking from investment banking
- Establishes interest rate ceilings on savings and time deposits (note that these ceilings were lifted in 1980)

Bank Holding Company Act of 1956

- Regulates formation of bank holding companies (BHCs)
- Restricts bank holding companies from engaging in insurance or nonfinancial activities.
- Allows nonbank subsidiaries to operate across state lines

Bank Merger Act of 1966

- Establishes merger guidelines and denotes competition as a criterion

Amendment to Bank Holding Company Act of 1970

- Regulates one-bank holding companies

Community Reinvestment Act of 1977

- Requires banks to make loans to all elements of the community—including the inner city and other poor areas

Depository Institutions Deregulation and Monetary Control Act of 1980

- Establishes uniform reserve requirements for all depository institutions
- Phases out deposit rate ceilings by April 1, 1986
- Allows NOW accounts at all depository institutions
- Allows thrifts to make consumer loans and issue credit cards

Depository Institutions Act of 1982 (Garn-St. Germain)

- Allows possibility of interstate and interinstitutional mergers
- Gives thrifts authority to make some commercial loans

Competitive Equality in Banking Act (CEBA) of 1987

- Limits growth of nonbank banks
- Changes definition of *bank* to include FDIC-insured institutions

Financial Institutions Reform, Recovery, and Enforcement Act (FIRREA) of 1989

- Changes structure of thrift institution regulation
- Changes federal deposit insurance structure and financing
- Establishes Resolution Trust Corporation to dispose of assets of failed thrifts

Federal Deposit Insurance Corporation Improvement Act (FDICIA) of 1991

- Provides for additional funding for federal deposit insurance
- Tightens regulations applicable to insured institutions
- Provides for greater capital regulation, early closure, and risk-based deposit insurance premiums

(continues)

Riegle-Neal Interstate Banking and Branching Efficiency Act of 1994

- Allows banks to acquire and merge with out-of-state banks
- Strengthened provisions of the Community Reinvestment Act

Financial Services Modernization Act of 1999 (Gramm-Leach-Bliley)

- Creates financial holding companies that can own commercial banking, securities, and insurance affiliates, thereby effectively removing separation of commercial banking and investment banking

International Money Laundering Abatement and Financial Anti-Terrorism Act of 2001

- Designed to prevent terrorists and others from using the U.S. financial system anonymously to move funds obtained from or destined for illegal activity

Sarbanes-Oxley Act of 2002

- Regulates public accounting firms that audit publicly traded companies
- Prohibits such firms from providing other services to publicly traded companies along with the audit
- Requires that CEOs and CFOs certify the annual and quarterly reports of publicly traded companies

Fair and Accurate Credit Transactions (FACT) Act of 2003

- Designed to improve the accuracy and transparency of the national credit reporting system to prevent identity theft and assist victims

Federal Deposit Insurance Reform Act of 2005

- Merges the Bank Insurance Fund (BIF) and Savings Association Insurance Fund (SAIF) into a single Deposit Insurance Fund (DIF) with a single deposit insurance premium schedule
- Increases coverage limit for retirement accounts to $250,000
- Authorizes FDIC's board to price deposit insurance according to risk for all insured institutions

Dodd-Frank Wall Street Reform and Consumer Protection Act of 2010

- Permanently increases deposit insurance coverage to $250,000
- Merges the Office of Thrift Supervision into the Office of the Comptroller of the Currency
- Gives Federal Reserve authority to impose more rigorous safety and soundness regulations on large bank holding companies
- Creates Financial Stability Oversight Council to monitor and address potential systemic risks
- Creates Bureau of Consumer Financial Protection to regulate mortgage and other consumer lending
- Prohibits banks from engaging in proprietary trading and investing in hedge funds (the Volcker Rule)
- Increases regulation of the market for derivative securities

The major bank legislative actions and their regulatory provisions since 1900 are summarized in Exhibit 15.1, which shows that regulation of financial institutions is broad in scope and quite detailed. The exhibit also shows that banking legislation tends to be cyclical in nature—we tend to go through periods of deregulation (with fewer limits on what banks can do) followed by periods of reregulation (with more limits on what banks can do). The extensive regulation faced by financial institutions and the evolving nature of the regulation make it challenging to manage a financial institution profitably. The next section discusses how bank regulation has changed over time and provides a historical context for the changes.

15.2 BANK FAILURES AND REGULATION

As discussed previously, one of the main reasons that banks are regulated is that policymakers believe the public loses more than the individual bank loses if the bank fails and disrupts the economy or its financial system. For this reason, much of the bank legislation passed during the last two hundred years was an attempt to reduce the number of bank failures or deal with some of the problems caused by bank failures. This section discusses the reasons why banks fail, recent bank legislation, and some of the lessons learned from past bank failures.

Individual bank failures occur for two primary reasons. First, banks fail because of illiquidity. Banks hold fractional reserves and invest in many illiquid assets, such as loans, which in many cases can be resold quickly only at a loss. If many depositors withdraw funds from the bank simultaneously, it forces the bank to liquidate assets at a loss to generate cash to pay depositors. Failures caused by illiquidity can be prevented, however, if a bank can borrow easily in such situations from another institution or, better yet, have a **lender of last resort**. Second, a bank or other financial institution can fail because the bank acquires assets that are too risky relative to the bank's capital base—in other words, inadequate capital. If the investments decline in value or if loans default, the bank's capital can erode to the extent that the bank becomes *insolvent*—that is, its liabilities are greater than its assets. Because banks are highly leveraged, this can happen easily when the value of assets falls by only a small amount.

Unfortunately, the failure of a single bank, whether as the result of inadequate capital or of inadequate liquidity, can create uncertainty about the soundness of other banks. Prior to the creation of federal deposit insurance, this uncertainty would often cause **bank panics**. Thus, one bank's failure often caused the failure of many banks. Consequently, the number of bank failures per year in the United States fluctuates widely. They occur both as isolated local events and in great national waves. For instance, during the business panic of 1893, nearly 500 of the 9,500 banks suspended operations. In contrast, during the recession of 2001, only 3 banks closed.

Exhibit 15.2 shows the number and percentage of all banks failing in the 1921–2010 period. Prior to the 1920s, the number of bank failures averaged about 100 per year, something less than 2 percent of all banks. Beginning in the 1920s, the number of bank failures increased dramatically. The greatest number of failures occurred during the early years of the Great Depression, 1930–1933. All told, more than 14,000 banks failed during the 1921–1933 period.

THE ROLE OF THE FED IN PREVENTING BANK FAILURES

The most important mechanism for preventing bank failures that are the result of inadequate liquidity is the Federal Reserve's discount window. By acting as a lender of last resort, the Federal Reserve reduces the incentive for depositors to panic during a financial crisis, and banks do not have to liquidate assets at substantial losses in order to satisfy depositors' withdrawal requests. In fact, the Federal Reserve often turns to discount window lending to prevent a financial panic. For example, in the days that followed September 11, 2001, discount window borrowing far exceeded normal levels, in part because the Fed encouraged banks to borrow at the discount window in order to ensure that financial markets were sufficiently liquid. Also recall that the Fed never has a liquidity problem because of its power to create money. Through its policy tools of open-market operations and adjusting reserve requirements, the Fed can print all the money needed in a

EXHIBIT 15.2
Number of Banks Failing (1921–2010)

Years	Number of Failures
1921–1933	14,807
1934–1940	328
1941–1950	52
1951–1960	20
1961–1970	49
1971–1980	77
1981–1990	1,178
1991–2000	545
2001–2010	347

FDIC insurance became effective on January 1, 1934, and initially provided depositors with $2,500 in coverage. Its impact on public confidence in the banking system was immediate. The number of bank failures declined dramatically and stayed relatively low, until the rise in banks' deposit interest costs in the early 1980s combined with the regional recessions of the 1980s and early 1990s led to a significant number of bank failures.

Source: FDIC, Annual Report, various issues, and Historical Statistics on Banking.

financial crisis. Refer to Chapters 2 and 3 for a discussion of the Fed's powers to create money.

THE ROLE OF DEPOSIT INSURANCE IN PREVENTING BANK FAILURES

Following the large number of failures in the period 1921–1933, Congress enacted legislation intended to prevent such wholesale bank failures from occurring again. The **Banking Act of 1933** (which is commonly referred to as the **Glass-Steagall Act** in recognition of the senators who sponsored the legislation) restored confidence in the commercial banking system by establishing the **Federal Deposit Insurance Corporation (FDIC)**. By guaranteeing the safety of depositors' funds, federal **deposit insurance** substantially reduced the incidence of banking panics. A potential insolvency at one bank no longer threatens deposits at other banks in the same economic region, thereby putting a stop to the domino effect that had long plagued American banking.

In addition to establishing the FDIC, the Banking Act of 1933 barred banks from paying interest on demand deposits, separated commercial banking from investment banking, and restricted the types of assets that banks could own (e.g., banks can own only investment-grade securities) on the grounds that these and other banking practices were excessively risky. Although the wisdom and effectiveness of some of these restrictions have been questioned and many have since been repealed, the effectiveness of the 1933 Banking Act in reducing bank panics and failures is undisputed.

The effectiveness of federal deposit insurance in reducing bank failures can be seen in Exhibit 15.2. Between 1934 and 1942, bank failures dropped to an average of 54 per year, and many of the banks that failed did not have deposit insurance. Following World War II, the number of bank closings slowed to a trickle, averaging less than 10 per year until the 1980s.

THE 1980s AND 1990s

At first, deposit insurance and the other regulatory initiatives in the 1930s banking acts protected financial institutions against failure. However, during the 1980s, increasing interest rates coupled with increasing competition from non-bank institutions and excessive interest rate risk on the part of thrift (savings and loans and savings banks) institutions led to a sharp increase in depository institution failures. As a result, a number of laws were passed in the 1980s and 1990s in an attempt to strengthen financial institutions and their insurance funds. The laws also broke down traditional barriers between financial institutions by giving them more powers to issue financial liabilities and diversify their assets, in hopes that this would let institutions become more profitable.

The first major law passed was the **Depository Institutions Deregulation and Monetary Control Act (DIDMCA) of 1980**. Basically, DIDMCA tried to "level the playing field" for all depository institutions by giving all of them the right to issue interest-bearing transactions deposits, requiring that all back their transactions deposits with reserves, and requiring that the Fed charge them all equally for the use of check-clearing services (instead of giving such services free to Fed member banks) and give them all equal access to the discount window. Furthermore, the act phased out rate ceilings on deposits and also on certain types of loans (unless the ceilings were reimposed by individual states), and it generally tried to simplify the regulatory environment. It was hoped that the new powers and relaxed loan rate ceilings given thrift institutions and credit unions by the act would enhance their profitability and reduce their interest rate risk.

However, the DIDMCA did not do enough to help the thrift institutions. Thus, Congress passed the **Depository Institutions Act (DIA) of 1982 (Garn–St. Germain)**, which immediately deregulated interest rate ceilings by allowing depository institutions to issue checkable money market deposit accounts that could pay any interest rate and had no reserve requirements as long as the depositor wrote only three checks per month. It also gave thrift institutions the power to issue limited demand deposits and the ability to make commercial loans. This let thrift institutions become more competitive with banks and also made them more attractive as merger candidates for banks. However, the decline in oil prices in the mid-1980s combined with thrifts' already depleted capital led to many thrift failures and an insolvent **Federal Savings and Loan Insurance Corporation (FSLIC)** fund.

After the Garn–St. Germain Act, few regulatory acts were passed until the **Competitive Equality in Banking Act (CEBA) of 1987**. The main provisions of that act were (1) to regulate the activities of *nonbank banks* (banks used by holding companies to evade regulatory restrictions, as they technically were not banks because they either did not have demand deposits or make consumer loans) and (2) to provide funding to bail out the failing FSLIC.

However, the aid for the FSLIC was too little and too late! Thus, in 1989 Congress passed the **Financial Institutions Reform, Recovery, and Enforcement Act (FIRREA)**. The FIRREA made major changes in the financing of deposit insurance and the structure of financial institution regulation. It also provided for the bailout of insolvent thrift institutions. The act recognized that easy accommodation of thrift industry legislative interests, coupled with lax capital, accounting, and regulatory standards, had all contributed to the high rate of failure of thrift institutions and the insolvency of the FSLIC (the thrift institutions' deposit insurance fund until 1989).

The FIRREA dissolved the FSLIC and reorganized the FDIC into two insurance funds—the Bank Insurance Fund (BIF) and the Savings Association Insurance Fund (SAIF). The two funds were recently consolidated into the Deposit Insurance Fund (DIF).

The FIRRE Act also implemented risk-based capital standards and mandated an increase in deposit insurance premiums. The deposit rate premium increases embodied in FIRREA were not sufficient to keep the bank deposit insurance fund solvent, however. Thus, in 1991 Congress passed the **Federal Deposit Insurance Corporation Improvement Act (FDICIA)**. The major purpose of the act was to provide additional funding provisions for the FDIC. However, the act also mandated that major changes be made in financial regulation and compliance procedures in order to reduce the probability of failure and any ensuing cost to the taxpayers.

After the FDICIA was passed, bank failures stayed high for a year or two as the weakest institutions that could not restore their capital were liquidated; then bank failures fell to minuscule levels, falling as low as one failure per year in 1997. A strong economy helped reduce failures but so did the new emphasis on increased examinations and **prompt corrective actions** taken while banks still retained some capital.

After a few years of a booming economy during which bank depositors were withdrawing funds from banks and investing in the stock market, Congress passed the **Financial Services Modernization Act of 1999 (Gramm-Leach-Bliley)**. This act allowed commercial banks to expand further into investment banking activities, and vice versa, thereby formally removing the Glass-Steagall Act's separation of commercial banking and investment banking. Prior to the act being passed, however, regulators had been allowing large financial institutions to engage in activities that they had previously not been allowed to pursue. Therefore, many viewed the Gramm-Leach-Bliley Act as merely formalizing what had already been occurring.

RECENT YEARS

Following the passage of Gramm-Leach-Bliley, the financial services industry experienced consolidation but not at the pace that many expected. It turns out that expertise in one type of financial services does not easily allow expansion into other types of financial services. Nevertheless, the banking industry began to experience substantial growth as the Federal Reserve lowered the target fed funds rate from 6.5 percent in May 2000 to 1.0 percent by June 2003 in response to the economic slowdown at the time. This reduction in interest rates combined with an influx of foreign investments in the United States led to a reduction in credit standards for borrowers.

Low interest rates, easy credit, growth in affordable housing programs, growth in the market for mortgage-backed securities, and increased competition for borrowers led to a dramatic increase in subprime mortgage lending. Not surprisingly, housing values increased substantially in the early to mid-2000s in response to these conditions.

In the mid-2000s, industry experts began to question subprime lending standards and the structure of the market for mortgage-backed securities. Also in the mid-2000s, short-term interest rates increased substantially—the fed funds rate increased from 1.0 percent in June 2004 to 5.25 percent in June 2006. Because many subprime mortgages (and some prime mortgages) have adjustable payments tied to short-term interest rates, many borrowers began to have trouble making their payments, and housing values began to tumble. By 2007, the subprime mortgage industry had collapsed, and those financial institutions with direct or indirect exposure to the industry began to feel the effects of the collapse.

By late 2008, as the value of banks' mortgage loan portfolios continued to decline, their capital base shrank, and their ability (or desire) to make loans was severely limited. As banks stopped lending, consumers and businesses stopped spending. In September 2008, Fannie Mae and Freddie Mac were placed into conservatorship, and Lehman Brothers, a large investment bank, filed for bankruptcy. The financial system was in severe crisis, and fear of another depression was common among many experts.

One of the actions taken by government officials was the **Emergency Economic Stabilization Act of 2008**. Signed into law on October 3, 2008, this legislation established the **Troubled Asset Relief Program (TARP)**, which authorized the U.S. Treasury to purchase or guarantee mortgage-related assets of banks and other financial institutions. TARP has been criticized for bailing out large Wall Street firms that many view as culprits in the financial crisis. Supporters of the program argue that the program was necessary in order to restore stability to the financial system, allow banks to rid their balance sheets of otherwise illiquid assets, and ultimately encourage banks to resume lending in support of economic growth. Ultimately, the vast majority of funds invested in banks as part of TARP have been repaid.

In 2010, President Barack Obama signed into law the **Dodd-Frank Wall Street Reform and Consumer Protection Act** in an effort to reduce the odds of a similar crisis occurring in the future. Dodd-Frank will be implemented over several years as regulatory authorities work out the details, but the primary areas addressed in the act are the structure of the regulatory agencies, enhanced regulation of systemic risk, increased consumer protection regulation, and limits on banks' proprietary trading and use of derivative securities.

LESSONS FROM PAST BANK FAILURES

One of the lessons learned from past bank failures is that by guaranteeing depositors' funds, the FDIC has effectively prevented runs on the banks that it insures. Depositors no longer must operate under the rule of "better first in line than sorry." If their bank fails, depositors know the FDIC will pay them in an orderly manner. When bank runs have occurred in recent years, they have been limited to a single bank and not spread to other insured banks.

Another lesson learned from past bank failures is that poor diversification is often a cause of bank failures. Those banks that lack geographic, industry, or loan-type diversification are at increased risk of failure. From 1921 through 1931, most bank failures involved unit (one-location) banks that were closely tied to local economies. Branch banking over wide geographic areas provides diversification for a bank's loan and deposit portfolio, resulting in reduced business risk compared to a similar unit bank. Regional or industrywide depressions still cause bank failures in states whose economies are poorly diversified. This was shown by numerous bank failures in the oil-dependent Southwest and agriculturally dependent Midwest during the 1980s. Most recently, we have seen examples of banks failing due to their focus on mortgage lending. However, even among banks that concentrate on making certain types of loans or operate in a small geographic region, it is usually only the most poorly managed banks (i.e., the least diversified, most illiquid holders of the poorest quality loans) that fail.

Finally, another lesson learned from past bank failures is that fraud, embezzlement, and poor management are the most notable causes of bank failures. This has been particularly true since the 1940s. For example, of the 54 insured banks that failed between 1959 and 1970, 35 (65 percent) were classified by the FDIC as failing

PEOPLE & EVENTS

WaMu and the Destructive "Power of Yes"

In September 2008, Washington Mutual (WaMu) became the largest bank failure in history. Technically a thrift institution, WaMu had $307 billion in assets, employed 43,000 people, and operated 2,200 branches in 15 states. As a thrift, WaMu focused on mortgage lending and, in the company's quest for growth, it said yes to just about any loan applicant. In fact, the company's advertising slogan was "The Power of Yes," which signaled to potential borrowers that few would be denied credit.

WaMu has come to symbolize the mortgage-lending excesses that contributed to the housing bubble of the mid-2000s and its subsequent collapse. According to company insiders, WaMu became the lender of last resort for borrowers who would not qualify for a mortgage at other lenders. In addition, the company aggressively marketed option ARM mortgages (see Chapter 9). As adjustable rate mortgages, option ARMs are subject to interest charges that adjust in response to market rates of interest. The option part of option ARMs involves the flexibility that borrowers have in making their payments. Some of the payment options were so low that negative amortization often occurred. However, these mortgages are periodically recast so that they become fully amortizing. When this occurred, many borrowers found that they were unable to make the new payments and ended up defaulting, thereby causing WaMu substantial losses. By the time it failed, WaMu held more than $50 billion in option ARMs on its books. In addition to marketing these potentially risky mortgages, WaMu had a reputation for lax documentation and poor processes for verifying income and credit standing.

By the time the subprime mortgage crisis was in full swing, government regulators were increasingly worried about WaMu's future. They began trying quietly to broker a deal for another financial institution to take over the assets and liabilities of the failing WaMu. After the failure of Lehman Brothers in early September 2008, however, WaMu depositors began withdrawing funds at an alarming pace. In an effort to stem deposit outflows, on September 25, 2008, WaMu was placed into FDIC receivership, and its assets and liabilities (except for those that were not insured or secured) were quickly sold to J.P. Morgan Chase. Most of the former WaMu branches are now Chase branches.

The failure of WaMu offers several lessons. First, WaMu did not fail because it made bad investments in complicated financial instruments like hedge funds, private equity funds, or derivative securities. WaMu failed the old-fashioned way. It made risky loans, was poorly diversified, and had poor processes in place to minimize risks. Second, being a big bank doesn't always mean the bank is too big to fail (TBTF). WaMu was allowed to fail because it was not viewed as being systemically important. Finally, the failure of WaMu highlights the potential agency problem faced by bank regulators. WaMu was, by far, the largest institution regulated by the Office of Thrift Supervision (OTS). As much as 15 percent of the OTS's budget came from fees paid by WaMu. Therefore, the OTS had a vested interest in the survival of WaMu. When OTS examiners found potential problems in WaMu's loan portfolio, the OTS did little to correct the problems. As long as WaMu was performing well, any concerns were probably dismissed as being overly worrisome. Naturally, once the loan portfolio started to experience losses, it was too late to fix the problems.

as a consequence of fraud or other irregularities. That percentage fell sharply in the 1980s, however, as bank failures ascribable to weak local economies increased. Nonetheless, among major bank failures, the FDIC blamed the failures of the United States National Bank of San Diego and Franklin National Bank of New York City on irregular banking practices, and the failures of Penn Square Bank of Oklahoma and United American Bank of Knoxville resulted from unusual loan losses.

United American Bank, a large bank that failed in Tennessee in 1983, had made many floater loans that floated down to lower-ranking loan officers from top management with the request that the loans be approved. Many of the loans were to friends or political cronies of the president of the bank, and often the loans were not repaid.

15.3 SAFETY AND SOUNDNESS REGULATION: DEPOSIT INSURANCE

When deposit insurance was first enacted in 1933, it covered only deposits up to $2,500. Its purpose was to protect people with small deposits. People with large deposits were assumed to be sophisticated enough to look after themselves. It was believed, however, that small depositors (those with small amounts of money) were more likely to be unable or unwilling to assess a bank's true financial status. Thus, they were thought to be both more vulnerable to bank failures and more likely to panic and cause a run on a bank to get their deposits back quickly if they heard rumors that a bank might fail.

Over time, federal deposit insurance has been increased from $2,500 per account offered by the FDIC on deposits at insured commercial banks and savings banks in 1934 to more institutions and to $250,000 per depositor. In 1934, the Federal Savings and Loan Insurance Corporation (FSLIC) extended deposit insurance of $5,000 per account to savings and loan depositors. The FSLIC was established by the National Housing Act of 1934 and continued until 1989, when it was eliminated as a separate entity and the responsibility for thrift institutions was transferred to the FDIC. Federal insurance is also extended to credit unions' depositors' shares through the **National Credit Union Share Insurance Fund (NCUSIF)**.

HOW REGULATORS HANDLE BANK FAILURES

When a bank fails, it is closed by its chartering authority and handed over to the FDIC. The FDIC may have a choice of several policies to use when resolving the assets and liabilities of a failed bank. In the past it had some discretion about which policy to use, but the FDICI Act mandates that it use the least-cost method. The most straightforward approach to resolving a failed institution is to *pay off* the insured deposits, take over the failed institution, and *liquidate* the institution's assets. Exhibit 15.3 illustrates the FDIC's payoff policy. Under a **payoff and liquidate policy**, if sufficient funds were not realized from the liquidation of the failed institution, the insured depositors would be paid in full only up to $250,000 per depositor. After that, the depositors would obtain only a partial settlement, or no settlement at all, when the assets of the bank were liquidated. A partial settlement would often be necessary because an insolvent bank has total assets worth less than the total value of its liabilities (see Exhibit 15.3). In such a case, the FDIC would pay insured depositors in full, but the uninsured depositors might receive only 50¢ on the dollar for uninsured deposits.

Exhibit 15.3 involves the simplest possible liquidation scenario. In fact, there may be different levels of financial claims outstanding when a bank is liquidated.

EXHIBIT 15.3
FDIC Payoff Policy

Assets	Liabilities and Net Worth
Value realized from sale of assets = $75 million	Deposits under $100,000 = $50 million
	Uninsured liabilities and deposits over $100,000 = $100 million
	Net worth = −$75 million

In a deposit payoff, the FDIC pays off the $50 million in insured deposits and, in turn, is owed $50 million by the bank. The FDIC then takes possession of the failed bank's assets and liquidates them. It uses the proceeds to pay off the $150 million of deposits and other liabilities (including the $50 million that it is owed in return for paying off the insured deposits). After recovering $75 million from the asset liquidation, the FDIC can pay itself and uninsured liability and deposit holders $0.50 in payoff for each $1 ($75 million/$150 million) of the bank's liabilities that they own. The owners of the bank receive zero dollars back because the bank is insolvent and has no positive net worth.

Formerly, laws differed regarding payoff priorities. However, in the Omnibus Budget Reconciliation Act of 1993, payoff priorities were established for different claimants of the failed bank's assets. Depending on the availability of funds, payoffs would be made in the following order: (1) the administrative expenses of the receiver; (2) the claims of all depositors, including the FDIC in place of the insured depositors whom it had paid off; (3) general creditors; (4) subordinated creditor claims; and, (5) if there are any assets left, the claims of shareholders. Note that subordinated debt holders are not paid off until all claims except shareholder claims have been satisfied.

Because a bank may have more value as a going concern, with valuable customer relations, locations, staff knowledge, and expertise, it may be more valuable if at least part of its operations is maintained than if it is totally liquidated. This has generated a number of alternative methods for resolving bank failures. Most commonly, various forms of *purchase and assumption* transactions are used.

Instead of liquidating a failed bank, the insurance fund can allow another bank to enter into a **purchase and assumption agreement**, in which it would purchase the failed bank and assume all of its liabilities. In that case, the FDIC might provide financial assistance to the acquirer and relieve the bank of some or all of the bad assets in order to induce the new buyer to assume the failed bank's liabilities. Because the failed bank might have more value as an ongoing concern than as a failed bank, it could be less costly for the FDIC to provide financial assistance than to liquidate the failed bank. Furthermore, when all the liabilities were assumed, no depositor would lose a dime, regardless of how large or small the depositor's account was. Thus, the use of the purchase and assumption technique would provide de facto 100 percent deposit insurance.

Exhibit 15.4 illustrates a purchase and assumption in which the acquiring institution injects $5 million in new capital and pays a purchase premium of $5 million to cover past losses. In addition, the FDIC provides $20 million in financial assistance in this example to cover other losses.

The FDIC may use either a *whole bank* purchase and assumption or a *clean bank* purchase and assumption policy. In the latter case, the FDIC retains some of

EXHIBIT 15.4
FDIC-Assisted Purchase and Assumption Transaction: Failed Bank Subsidiary of New Bank

Assets	Liabilities and Net Worth
$75 million, value of old bank's good assets acquired by new bank	$100 million in deposits and other liabilities of old bank assumed by new bank
$20 million in financial assistance provided by FDIC in exchange for some bad assets	
$5 million purchase premium paid by new bank's owners in the form of assumed liabilities	
$5 million in new cash injected by new bank's owners to buy capital	$5 million in new capital in new bank

In a purchase and assumption, the owners of the new bank acquire selected assets of the failed bank and assume all of its liabilities, including its uninsured as well as insured deposits. The new bank's owners may request financial assistance from the FDIC and, in turn, give the FDIC claims on some of the old bank's bad assets (defaulted or doubtful loans). Before they are allowed to acquire and operate the new bank, the owners also may have to (1) inject new money in the form of a purchase premium to make up for asset deficiencies (charged-off loans of the old bank) and (2) inject new capital into the bank. If the old bank has hidden assets, such as a valuable banking franchise, the new bank's owners may be willing to pay a substantial amount to acquire it.

the failed bank's assets and provides the acquirer with an FDIC promissory note to cover the value of the retained assets. Alternatively, the acquirer may acquire all the failed bank's assets but retain an option to "put" some of the assets back to the FDIC in exchange for an FDIC promissory note at some later point in time. It may exercise the put after it has a chance to better evaluate the failed bank's loan portfolio. In such a case, the FDIC is likely to receive all the failed bank's defaulted and doubtful loans when the put is exercised.

Finally, the FDIC may retain the failed bank's assets and transfer the insured deposits of that bank to another financial institution. Because an acquiring institution may find it cheaper to obtain additional deposit liabilities by "buying them" from the FDIC, rather than by advertising, it may be willing to pay the FDIC a small premium for being allowed to assume the failed bank's insured deposit obligations.

DO YOU UNDERSTAND?

1. Why are bank failures considered to be so undesirable that the government should try to prevent them?
2. What has the U.S. trend in bank failures been since 1920?
3. What is the difference between a purchase and assumption and a payoff method for liquidating a failed bank?
4. Why might it be unfair to small banks if all large bank liquidations were accomplished via purchase and assumption rather than payoff transaction?

Although deposit insurance reduces the numbers of bank failures and panics, it is not without its own issues. In fact, because of these issues, some policymakers argue in favor of more limited coverage of deposits. This section describes the issues created by deposit insurance and discusses how policymakers attempt to deal with those issues.

15.4 DEPOSIT INSURANCE ISSUES

MORAL HAZARD PROBLEMS

A major problem resulting from the provision of deposit insurance is that it reduces the incentive of depositors to monitor the health of institutions in which they place their money. This is a **moral hazard** in that the insured individual is less careful, and thus is more likely to incur a loss, than would be the case if he or she were not insured. Thus, since 1983, the FDIC has tried to ensure that *uninsured* depositors police more carefully the banks in which they deposit their funds. It has done so by arranging insured-deposit transfers in cases of bank failure. In such cases, only the insured deposits are transferred to another institution. The uninsured deposits are returned to the old bank, which is liquidated. Consequently, because uninsured depositors may lose some or all of their funds, they have a greater incentive to monitor the safety of the bank than they would if they expected a purchase and assumption to occur in the event of failure.

Deposit insurance can also create a moral hazard for the managers of depository institutions. In particular, even if a depository institution is risky, if it is insured, it can usually continue to issue deposits to obtain funds at much the same rate as less risky institutions. It can do so because most deposit holders do not share the risks of loss (which are primarily borne by the FDIC). Thus, unlike corporation managers, managers of insured depository institutions can usually take greater risk without greatly increasing the price they must pay to obtain (deposit) liabilities. If they do not bear the full cost of their risk taking, they may be encouraged to take more risk than they would if they could only issue uninsured liabilities.

For example, an institution with many bad loans may fear that it will have to write them off and become insolvent. If that were done, it would be liquidated, thereby costing the management team its jobs, salaries, and perquisites. However, if the institution issues more insured deposits paying its usual insured-deposit rate, makes more loans at higher rates, and charges high loan origination or application fees, it may be able to report enough profits on its newly expanded loan portfolio that it will be able to absorb the losses on past loans and still appear to be profitable. This strategy can work only if losses appear on the new loans with a lag while the income from extra fees and higher rates on loans immediately increases reported profits. Such a "profitable" institution can continue to operate. If the new loans are, in fact, sound, the management may have true profits and survive its crisis. However, if the new borrowers were willing to pay high loan rates and large up-front fees only because the borrowers' loan requests were risky, loan losses will ultimately occur as the new loans go bad. Thus, the weak institutions must grow still faster so that reported earnings from new loans grow faster than reported loan losses on old loans.

This moral hazard problem means that managers of troubled institutions have an incentive to gamble. If the gamble fails, they can gamble again in hopes that the gambling process will obscure their losses, buy them more time as managers, and give the institution a chance to grow out of its difficulties. Deposit insurance makes this gambling possible because it allows remotely generated deposits to be funneled to the gamblers by deposit brokers, even if local depositors become wary of an institution that is taking too many risks.

THE TOO BIG TO FAIL PROBLEM

Purchase and assumption policies provide 100 percent coverage for all depositors whose deposits are assumed. A second policy adopted by federal regulators that provided 100 percent deposit insurance was its **too big to fail (TBTF)** policy. For many years it appeared that the FDIC was reluctant to liquidate large banks. Instead, it generally arranged purchase and assumption transactions if a large bank failed. Then in 1984, when Continental Illinois National Bank essentially failed, the Comptroller of the Currency (the regulatory agency responsible for supervising national banks) announced that Continental, as well as 11 other of the largest banks in the country, were too big to fail. Their depositors would be paid off in full regardless of how large the deposit was or how poorly the bank performed. This policy was implemented not only in resolving the Continental Illinois failure but also in conjunction with the 1988 failures of First City Bank Corporation and First Republic Bank Corporation in Texas and with the failure of the Bank of New England in 1991. In each case, federal regulators guaranteed that 100 percent of deposits would be paid off, regardless of the deposits' size.

The reason these large institutions were not allowed to fail is because their failure might lead to other failures based on the interdependent financial relationships these banks have with other financial institutions. Put another way, regulators are worried that the failure of a large bank will cause a run on that bank, not by insured depositors but by uninsured creditors and other financial institutions. In response to these cases and concerns that the failure of one large institution might have a domino effect throughout the financial system, Congress enacted a *systemic risk* provision as part of the FDICI Act of 1991. This provision allows the Treasury secretary to rescue a bank if it is determined that the bank's failure could cause significant damage to the economy. However, the TBTF policy did not escape criticism. First, it has created a two-tiered banking system. All depositors at very large institutions have de facto 100 percent deposit insurance. Depositors at small banks, however, have deposit insurance only up to $100,000 per account. This creates an obvious unfair advantage for larger institutions when it comes to attracting depositors.

A second criticism is that if the federal government stands behind all big-bank liabilities, bank management may be tempted to make riskier loans in an effort to increase profits. This is because uninsured depositors, who are at risk, help monitor the bank's performance, and their willingness (or unwillingness) to purchase the bank's liabilities disciplines the bank to take prudent risks. In recent years, the FDIC has hoped to strengthen market discipline in banking; however, with the TBTF policy in place, large banks' uninsured depositors may now be indifferent to the risks that these banks take because of the willingness of the FDIC or some other government agency to intervene and prevent the banks from suffering any loss. This creates a major moral hazard problem.

Although the criticisms of TBTF are valid, the consequences of allowing a large, systemically important financial institution to fail are potentially catastrophic. The failure of Lehman Brothers in 2008 is an example of a large financial institution that was allowed to fail. That failure created tremendous market turmoil and was the catalyst for many of the systemic risk components in the Dodd-Frank Wall Street Reform and Consumer Protection Act of 2010. For example, because Lehman Brothers was an investment bank and did not own a commercial bank, it was not subject to oversight by the Federal Reserve. Under the Dodd-Frank Act, however, the **Financial Stability Oversight Council (FSOC)** was created to monitor systemic risk, and federal authorities were given greater oversight over systemically important nonbank financial institutions.

In addition to the systemic risk components of Dodd-Frank directed at non-bank financial institutions, the bill subjects bank holding companies with more than $50 billion in assets to enhanced prudence regulations. In addition, Dodd-Frank includes limits on the size of allowable mergers.

There is much debate over whether Dodd-Frank adequately addresses the TBTF issue. Some argue that Dodd-Frank, if implemented correctly, gives regulatory authorities the tools they need to end TBTF without putting the financial system at risk. Others argue that systemic risk is inherent in the modern financial system and that making large financial institutions subject to greater regulatory oversight will not alleviate the TBTF problems.

INSURANCE AGENCIES AS "POLICE"

In the 1940s through the 1960s, deposit insurance seemed to solve the problem of bank failures. During the 1980s, however, more than one-third of all savings institutions disappeared, and bank failures rose consistently to exceed 200 per year before the end of the decade. Clearly, not all problems had been solved.

One factor that changed after deposit insurance became available was that depositors with deposits under the deposit insurance limit at small banks or deposits of any size at too big to fail banks no longer had to fear bank failures. As a result, depositors no longer caused runs on banks based on unsubstantiated rumors. At the same time, most depositors no longer had an incentive to make sure that a depository institution was sound before they put their money in it; all they wanted to know was whether it had federal deposit insurance. As long as depositors know that a depository institution is federally insured for an amount greater than their individual deposits (or know that the bank is too big to fail), the depositors have no incentive to withdraw funds from a financial institution even if that institution is taking many risks. As a result, the deposit insurance funds must have a "police" mentality—as they try to protect members of the public who (by relying on deposit insurance for protection) no longer protect themselves by withdrawing funds from risky institutions.

The FDIC and other bank regulators, therefore, have enacted various policies designed to ensure that insured depository institutions are operated safely. They hire large forces of examiners and examine insured institutions regularly. If an insured institution is found to be violating any of a number of detailed regulations, its board of directors is held responsible and asked to change policies. Such policy changes may include hiring more guards; keeping less money in the vault; providing marked money so that bank robbers can be traced; using surveillance cameras; double-checking all transfers of funds; monitoring all loans made to employees or directors; complying fully with the disclosure and procedural requirements associated with accepting loan applications, granting loans, and documenting all aspects of all loan transactions; and so on.

If a bank is found to score poorly on the examiners' rating system, it is scheduled for more frequent examinations than other banks. If the problems are serious, the institution may be subjected to *cease and desist* orders that force it to change its operations, change directors or principal officers, obtain more capital contributions from stockholders, or cease operations.

STOCKHOLDERS AND DEBT HOLDERS AS "POLICE"

If a bank has inadequate net worth because of operating losses or loan charge-offs, examiners may force it to obtain more capital by selling more common stock or closely related securities, such as preferred stock or mandatory convertible debt. In this case, the bank must sell securities in the nation's capital markets, which entails a risk of loss for the buyers. Thus, if the bank is very risky, the buyers of those securities buy them only if they are promised a very high rate of return. In that way, the capital market imposes a risk premium for risky banks that attempt to sell additional stock or subordinated debt to comply with the insurers' capital requirements.

Although bank examinations are costly and infrequent, the use of uninsured subordinated debt to provide funds for the institution ensures that a group of interested people (the owners of that debt) find it profitable to monitor bank actions and risk-taking on an ongoing basis lest their investment in the bank debt lose value. In that way, the owners of the subordinated debt help police the bank to ensure that it does not take excess risk. Furthermore, if the debt holders believe the institution is taking excess risk, they often sell their debt holdings in the open market, thereby depressing the price of the debt and quickly and inexpensively alerting regulators to the fact that something may be wrong.

ARE DEPOSIT INSURANCE PREMIUMS APPROPRIATE?

One of the problems associated with deposit insurance in the past was that one rate was applied to all institutions insured by the same insurance fund. This aggravated moral hazard problems because riskier institutions did not have to pay more. Unlike auto insurance, where a person's insurance rate is likely to go up after a series of tickets or accidents, riskier institutions could obtain insurance at the same rate as the safest institutions, and this took away the riskier institutions' incentive to "drive safely" in a risky world. To solve this problem, the FDICI Act of 1991 required that the FDIC charge higher deposit insurance premiums for riskier institutions. Consequently, the FDIC adopted and recently updated a grid system to assess different deposit insurance premiums based on the insured institution's examiner ratings and capitalization status. Well-capitalized institutions with good examiner ratings have a low deposit insurance premium, whereas poorly capitalized institutions with low examiner ratings may have to pay substantial premiums to obtain deposit insurance—thereby putting them at a competitive disadvantage in obtaining deposits (because they can't pay as high a rate to depositors if they also have to pay a high insurance premium) and providing them with incentives to increase their capital and reduce their riskiness.

DO YOU UNDERSTAND?

1. What is *moral hazard* and how does deposit insurance contribute to it on the part of both depositors and bank management?
2. How can bank capital and subordinated debt help protect deposit insurance funds against losses?
3. What are the arguments for and against regulators using a too big to fail policy?
4. How do you think risk-based deposit insurance premiums help or hurt any of the situations discussed in this section?

As indicated earlier, one of the ways a bank can fail is for its investments to decline in value or its loans to default such that the bank's capital is eroded to the extent that the bank becomes insolvent—that is, its liabilities are greater than the value of its assets. For this reason, both bank managers and regulators are concerned about banks maintaining adequate amounts of capital. For bank managers, bank capital performs several important roles. First, it provides a financial cushion that enables banks to continue to operate even if they suffer temporary operating losses. Second, capital is a source of funds for the bank's growth and the addition of new products, services, or facilities.

For bank regulators, adequate capital protects the FDIC and uninsured depositors and creditors from losses and consequently helps maintain public confidence in the soundness and safety of individual banks and the banking system. Much like the way the deductible on your automobile insurance protects your insurance company from losses and encourages you to drive safely (to avoid a crash and having to pay the deductible), equity capital protects the FDIC from losses and encourages bank owners to manage the bank in a safe and sound manner. The more equity capital that bank owners have at stake, the less likely they are to take risks that might expose them to losses.

TRENDS IN BANK CAPITAL

In the early 1970s, bank regulators and public officials became concerned about erosion of key capital ratios (Exhibit 15.5). Their concern was heightened by the failure of several large banks in 1973 and 1974 and again during the early 1980s following two back-to-back recessions. The debate over capital adequacy focuses on how much bank capital is necessary to provide a stable and safe banking system. Although opinions differ as to the amount of capital that provides reasonable protection, there is agreement that the capital ratios of the banking system declined appreciably in the 1960s and 1970s. Exhibit 15.5 shows that equity capital declined from about 8 percent of total assets in 1960 to less than 6 percent by 1974. The decline in bank capital is partly attributable to the economic prosperity of the 1960s and early 1970s, which caused banks' assets to grow rapidly while their capital grew more slowly.

Beginning in the 1980s, capital adequacy once more became an issue with bank regulators. Although the number of bank failures was less than 10 per year

---

15.5 SAFETY AND SOUNDNESS REGULATION: CAPITAL REQUIREMENTS

EXHIBIT 15.5

Ratio of Total Equity Capital to Total Assets for Insured Commercial Banks (1934–2010)

Capital levels declined in the late 1960s and early 1970s. The decline in capital levels was due to asset growth exceeding capital growth. In the last 20 years, capital levels have improved in response to more stringent capital adequacy standards. Most recently, the equity capital to total assets ratio has continued to improve in spite of loan defaults. This is due primarily to stagnant asset growth and healthy interest and noninterest margins.

Source: FDIC *Statistics on Banking.*

in 1979, the number of failures reached record numbers in the 1980s, with 118 banks failing in 1985 and more than 200 failing in 1987. Given this environment, bank regulators started increasing bank capital requirements in a series of steps beginning in December 1981. By 1985, the minimum ratio of equity capital to total assets increased to 5.5 percent of total assets.

CAPITAL ADEQUACY REGULATION

Basel I.   In July 1988, the central banks of the major industrial countries adopted a sweeping proposal addressing the capital adequacy of international banks. (The agreement, called the *Basel Accord*, included central banks from the following countries: Belgium, Canada, France, West Germany, Italy, Japan, the Netherlands, Sweden, the United Kingdom, the United States, Switzerland, and Luxembourg.) The central banks reached this agreement as part of an effort to coordinate bank supervisory policies, with the goal of strengthening the international banking system and alleviating competitive inequities. The guidelines define capital uniformly across all nations, apply risk weights to all assets and off-balance-sheet exposures, and set minimum levels of capital for international banks. In the

United States, the effort to develop a risk-based capital measure began in 1985. Of concern was the rapidly growing risk exposure of large money-center banks stemming from their off-balance-sheet activities.

Current capital adequacy requirements in the United States define two forms of capital. **Tier 1 capital** includes the sum of common stock, paid-in-surplus, retained earnings, noncumulative perpetual preferred stock, and minority interest in consolidated subsidiaries minus goodwill and other intangible assets. Tier 1 capital is commonly referred to as *core capital*. **Tier 2 capital** includes cumulative perpetual preferred stock, loan loss reserves, subordinated debt instruments, mandatory convertible debt instruments, and other debt instruments that combine both debt and equity features. Tier 2 capital is commonly referred to as *supplemental capital*. In addition to being measured against total assets, these capital measures are measured against **risk-weighted assets**. Risk-weighted assets is a measure of assets that weights high-risk assets more heavily than low-risk assets. The minimum capital requirements require the following:

1. The ratio of Tier 1 capital to total assets must be at least 3 percent. This is often referred to as the *leverage ratio*.

2. The ratio of Tier 1 capital to risk-weighted assets must be at least 4 percent.

3. The ratio of total capital (Tier 1 capital plus Tier 2 capital) to risk-weighted assets must be at least 8 percent.

Notice that the regulatory definition of Tier 2 capital includes debt. In the economic sense, debt is not capital; operating losses cannot be written off against debt. However, the debt included in Tier 2 capital is not insured by the Federal Deposit Insurance Corporation (FDIC) and represents a residual claim against the assets of the bank. The holders of the debt securities included in Tier 2 capital are ahead of common stockholders in terms of their claim against the assets of the bank, but they are behind the claims of the FDIC, uninsured depositors, secured creditors, and other debt holders. Banks are allowed to include these debt sources of funds as Tier 2 capital because they represent a buffer between losses by the bank and losses by the FDIC Bank Insurance Fund.

The basic purpose of the capital guidelines is to relate a bank's capital to its risk profile so that high-risk activities require relatively more bank capital. The risk weightings applied to bank assets for capital adequacy calculations are shown in Exhibit 15.6. The risk weightings applied to off-balance-sheet activities are slightly more complicated because the off-balance-sheet amounts must be adjusted to reflect their potential on-balance-sheet exposure. In other words, off-balance-sheet amounts must be converted to on-balance-sheet amounts using a conversion factor. The conversion factor is a percentage that reflects the percentage of the off-balance-sheet exposure that potentially ends up on the balance sheet. The current risk weights and conversion factors for sample off-balance sheet activities are shown in Exhibit 15.7.

The degree of regulatory scrutiny faced by a bank depends on the bank's level of capital. As capital declines, regulators clamp down harder on bank activities. The capital requirements are based not only on the risk-based capital ratios described previously, but also on the so-called leverage ratio.

The regulatory implications of declining capital are severe. Critically undercapitalized banks are subject to being seized by the FDIC, the worst possible penalty. All banks in the undercapitalized categories must submit

EXHIBIT 15.6
Risk Weights for Assets

Category 1—Zero Percent Weight

Cash

Balances due from Federal Reserve banks and claims on central banks in other OECD countries[a]

U.S. Treasury and government agency securities and claims on or unconditionally guaranteed by OECD central governments

Federal Reserve stock

Claims collateralized by cash on deposit or by securities issued or guaranteed by OECD central governments or U.S. government agencies

Category 2—20 Percent Weight

Cash items in the process of collection

All claims on or guaranteed by U.S. depository institutions and banks in OECD countries

General obligation bonds of state and local governments

Portions of claims secured by U.S. government agency securities or OECD central government obligations that do not qualify for a zero percent weight

Loans or other claims conditionally guaranteed by the U.S. government

Securities and other claims on U.S. government-sponsored agencies

Category 3—50 Percent Weight

Loans secured by first liens on 1- to 4-family residential property and certain multifamily residential properties

Certain privately issued mortgage-backed securities

Revenue bonds of state and local governments

Category 4—100 Percent Weight

All loans and other claims on private obligors not placed in a lower risk category

Bank premises, fixed assets, and other real estate owned

Industrial development revenue bonds

Intangible assets and investment in unconsolidated subsidiaries, provided they are not deducted from capital

[a]The group of countries associated with the Organization for Economic Cooperation and Development (OECD) includes the United States and 24 other major industrial countries.

Category 1 is the least risky asset category; category 4, the riskiest. The weights reflect that regulators require banks to have more capital set aside to cover riskier activities.

Source: Commercial Bank Examination Manual, Board of Governors, Federal Reserve System, October 2010.

improvement plans to the FDIC within 45 days of falling below the minimum. The FDIC also restricts the asset growth of undercapitalized banks. Banks in the significantly undercapitalized category could face caps on deposit rates, forced sale of subsidiaries, or the firing of bank executives. These banks could also be forced to fire the board of directors and elect new members. Needless to say, the guidelines provide a strong incentive to bank managers to maintain adequate capital.

EXHIBIT 15.7
Risk Weights and Conversion Ratios for Selected Off-Balance-Sheet Activities

Weight (%)	Conversion Factor	Off-Balance-Sheet Item
0	0	Short-term loan commitments
50	0[a]	Short-term interest rate derivatives
50	0.005[a]	Long-term interest rate derivatives
50	0.01[a]	Short-term foreign exchange derivatives
50	0.05[a]	Long-term foreign exchange derivatives
100	0.2	Commercial letters of credit
100	0.5	Long-term loan commitments
100	1	Standby letters of credit

Long-term off-balance-sheet activities require more capital than short-term activities. This is reflected in the weights associated with long-term activities.

[a]In addition to holding capital against potential on-balance-sheet exposures as measured by conversion factors, banks must also hold capital against the current value (replacement cost) of derivative securities.
Source: Commercial Bank Examination Manual, Board of Governors, Federal Reserve System, October 2010.

Basel II. On June 26, 2004, the Basel Committee endorsed Basel II, a 251-page document outlining how capital standards will be implemented over the next several years. Having been in the works for several years, Basel II is an attempt to incorporate credit, market, and operational risks more effectively into capital standards. In the United States, the Federal Reserve implemented regulations based on its interpretation of Basel II. Under Basel II, large international banks are expected to use sophisticated models to measure credit, market, and operational risks and then use those models to determine their regulatory capital requirement.

Basel III. The financial crisis of 2007–2009 revealed some potential shortcomings of the existing capital standards. Therefore the Basel Committee has proposed several measures intended to increase capital level and liquidity levels in banks. The intent of the new Basel accords is to improve the financial system's ability to withstand shocks and improve banks' management of liquidity risk.

DO YOU UNDERSTAND?

1. Explain how bank capital protects a bank from failure.
2. Why has bank capital increased in the last 20 years?
3. Why do bank regulators prefer that banks have more equity capital than bankers would like?

15.6 BANK EXAMINATIONS

Historically, regulatory examinations did not become widespread until the National Bank Act of 1863. The then newly created **Office of the Comptroller of the Currency (OCC)** examined all banks chartered under the federal statute annually. By the early 1900s, every state instituted some sort of bank examination procedure. Today, all commercial banks in the United States are examined by a bank regulatory agency (federal or state). Examinations are more frequent if a bank is believed to be particularly risky.

Regulatory examinations are not equivalent to an audit by an accounting firm. A public accounting firm audit verifies the bank's financial statements and ensures that generally accepted accounting principles are followed consistently from one period to the next. Regulators' examinations are intended to promote and maintain safe and sound bank operating practices and to ensure that all applicable regulations are followed.

THE BANK EXAMINATION PROCESS

The principal purpose of bank examinations is the prevention of bank failures resulting from poor management or dishonesty. There are two principal ways in which information is gathered for bank examinations. First, **call reports** (detailed statements of the operating and financial condition of the bank) are prepared by bank management four times a year. The examination staffs of the various bank regulators conduct second, **on-site bank examinations**. Those visits are unannounced and the examiners remain at the bank or its branches until the examination is completed. Generally, the examiners first control the records of the bank and such assets as cash and marketable securities by securing or taking physical possession of them. At this point in the examination procedure, the examiners are concerned with the possible detection of embezzlement or fraud. Next, the securities portfolio is examined to see if the securities claimed are on hand and if control procedures comply with regulations. Finally, the market value of bonds is determined, with particular attention given to bonds considered to be speculative or in default.

The most important part of the examination, and the one to which the most time is devoted, is the evaluation of the creditworthiness of the bank's loan portfolio. Loans are examined for compliance with or violation of laws or regulations—such as limits on the maximum size loan that may be made to any one borrower or loans to bank officers. Next, loans are examined on a sampling basis as to their quality and are classified in one of four categories: satisfactory, substandard, doubtful, or loss. Loans classified as *loss* are thought to be uncollectible, and the bank is required to write them off (but not to stop trying to collect them). *Doubtful* loans are expected to result in some loan losses, although the exact amount is not precisely determinable. Loans classified as *substandard* have some element of risk and, if not watched closely, may result in losses to the bank. *Satisfactory* loans are those that meet the standards of prudent banking practice and appear to be in no danger of defaulting.

Another important part of the bank examination procedure is the evaluation of the quality of the bank's organizational structure. The supervision by top management and the board of directors; internal controls over bank operations; and, most important, the abilities of management are all appraised.

Based on the call reports and on-site examinations, examiners assess the overall quality of a bank's condition using the **CAMELS** rating system. Exhibit 15.8

EXHIBIT 15.8
The CAMELS Rating System

Rating Category	Primary Rating Criteria
Capital adequacy	• The level and quality of capital and the overall financial condition of the institution • The ability of management to address emerging needs of additional capital • Balance-sheet composition
Asset quality	• The adequacy of underwriting standards • The level, severity, and trend of problem loans • The adequacy of the allowance for loan losses • The diversification and quality of the loan and investment portfolio • The adequacy of loan and investment policies, procedures, and practices • The adequacy of internal controls
Management	• The capability of the board of directors and management to identify, measure, monitor, and control the risks of an institution's activities • The level and quality of oversight and support of all institution activities by the board of directors and management • The accuracy and timeliness of management information and risk-monitoring systems • Management depth and succession • Reasonableness of compensation policies and avoidance of self-dealing
Earnings	• The level, trend, and stability of earnings • The quality and sources of earnings
Liquidity	• The adequacy of liquidity sources compared to present and future needs • The availability of assets that can be converted to cash without undue loss • The trend and stability of deposits • Access to money markets and other sources of liquidity
Sensitivity to market risk	• The sensitivity of earnings or economic value to adverse changes in interest rates, foreign exchange rates, commodity prices, or equity prices • The ability of management to identify, measure, monitor, and control exposure to market risk given the institution's size and complexity

Banks are rated on a scale from 1 (best) to 5 (worst) for each rating category. In addition, a composite rating is formed based on the six component ratings.

Source: Department of Supervision, FDIC, *Manual of Exam Policies.*

summarizes the CAMELS rating system. The S in CAMELS is relatively new and it is intended to reflect how the impact of changes in interest rates, exchange rates, commodity prices, and equity prices can adversely affect a financial institution's earnings or capital.

Finally, a summary of the bank examination report is presented and discussed with the bank's management. If the bank's operations are in violation of the law, if poor operating procedures are detected, or if the bank's capital is below capital requirements, management is requested to bring the violation into compliance over a period of time. The bank's progress in correcting the difficulties is closely monitored. If a bank has a problem that could seriously jeopardize its safety, regulatory agencies can serve *cease and desist* orders on it. These require immediate or speedy compliance under penalty of law.

OTHER BANK EXAMINATIONS

In addition to the safety and soundness examinations discussed previously, banks are subject to other examinations that are intended to determine the success or failure of a bank in satisfying other regulatory requirements. For example, banks are examined periodically with respect to their success in achieving the requirements of the Community Reinvestment Act (CRA). If a bank does not receive a satisfactory rating on its CRA examination, then it has difficulty getting approval from regulators for acquisitions, expansions, and other actions requiring regulatory approval. In addition to CRA-related examinations, banks are also subject to other inquiries concerning their compliance with other consumer protection regulations. The CRA and other consumer protection regulations are discussed later in the chapter. Finally, bank trust departments are also subject to examination so that regulators can ensure that the bank is not violating its fiduciary responsibilities.

15.7 STRUCTURE AND COMPETITION REGULATIONS

Other types of regulation faced by banks include limitations on the activities that banks are allowed to engage in, the geographic boundaries on those activities, and the organizational structures within which the activities can occur. These types of regulation have been the most controversial and the most dynamic since the mid-1980s. In fact, the banking industry has seen these regulations change dramatically just since the mid-1990s. This section provides some history on the initial motivation for these regulations, the arguments for and against the regulations, and the changes in the regulations over time.

BRANCHING LIMITATIONS

Until the McFadden-Pepper Act of 1927, the question of whether federally chartered banks could establish branches was unanswered. The 1927 act answered the question by subjecting national banks to the state branching regulations in their home state. Furthermore, interstate banking was not allowed unless explicitly approved by state governments. These restrictions contributed to the development of bank holding companies as a way to avoid intrastate and interstate branching restrictions. As a result, the Bank Holding Company Act of 1956 and subsequent amendments regulated multibank holding companies and limited the ability of bank holding companies to circumvent branching restrictions.

These restrictions tended to reduce entry of new competition into local banking markets, thereby reducing competition for existing banks and enhancing their profits. However, several states allowed reciprocal operations by bank subsidiaries of bank holding companies under provisions in the Douglas Amendment to the Bank Holding Company Act. Thus, interstate banking through holding company banks developed until, in 1994, the **Interstate Banking and Branching Efficiency Act (IB&BEA)** allowed banks to merge and branch across state lines unless a potential host state "opted out" of interstate branching. As it stands now, all banks are allowed to freely branch across state lines as long as it is done through acquisition of another bank or bank branch. In addition, if allowed by state law, a bank can create a new branch (**de novo branching**) across state lines. Bank branches have become a common feature across the U.S. landscape as four or five brand-name banking conglomerates have raced to take full advantage of under branching privilege.

DEPOSIT RATE CEILINGS

Additional regulations incorporated in the 1933 Banking Act were also designed to restrict risk taking by banks, reduce competition among banks, and enhance bank profitability. The Glass-Steagall Banking Act of 1933, for example, prohibited the payment of interest on demand deposits (checking accounts) and mandated that the Fed regulate maximum interest rates that could be paid on bank time and savings deposits through its **Regulation Q**. Deposit rate regulation was extended to thrift institutions in 1966.

However, these rate-ceiling restrictions subsequently had very disruptive effects in financial markets as they caused financial disintermediation (as people withdrew funds from financial intermediaries) whenever market interest rates exceeded the "Reg Q" ceiling. Consequently, banks and thrifts had to drastically reduce credit availability whenever market interest rates rose. Furthermore, during the high-interest-rate period in the 1970s, disintermediated funds fled to unregulated **money market mutual funds (MMMFs)**. The MMMFs began to offer checking account withdrawals and, as a result, attracted even more funds from banks and thrift institutions. The DIDMCA Act of 1980 provided a phaseout of deposit rate ceilings and allowed banks, thrifts, and credit unions nationwide to offer checkable interest-bearing (NOW and share draft) accounts. Because the phaseout was not fast enough and banks and thrifts had to maintain reserves to back their NOW accounts, the MMMFs still had a competitive advantage. Thus, the 1982 Depository Institutions (Garn-St. Germain) Act accelerated the phaseout of rate ceilings and allowed banks and thrifts to offer checkable **money market deposit accounts (MMDAs)** that had no rate ceiling and no reserve requirement if check transactions were limited.

Deposit rate ceilings are now gone, but they led to substantial financial innovation as people sought ways to avoid them. Consequently, their legacy still exists in the form of MMMFs, MMDAs, and NOW accounts, which would not have come into existence if rate ceilings had not existed.

SEPARATION OF COMMERCIAL AND INVESTMENT BANKING

The Banking Act of 1933 also tried to reduce bank risk taking by separating commercial banking from investment banking. That way commercial banks would not be exposed to price-risk fluctuations in the value of securities that they had underwritten but had not yet sold.

The Glass-Steagall prohibitions against investment banking also prevented banks from acquiring equity securities for their own accounts and from acting as equity securities dealers. The prohibition against owning equity securities not only prevents banks from carrying certain potentially risky assets on their balance sheet, which could increase their risk of failure, but also lessens potential conflicts that can arise when the ownership and creditor functions of banks are combined. Thus, the prohibition reflects, in part, a long-standing American fear that unscrupulous manipulation and exercise of creditor powers could ultimately lead to ownership. In contrast, in countries such as Germany, *universal banking* is allowed in which commercial banks can also serve as investment banks and even appoint directors for businesses in which they own stock.

The U.S. Glass-Steagall restrictions were gradually relaxed during the 1980s and 1990s until the Financial Services Modernization Act of 1999 repealed most of the restrictions. This legislation allows U.S. commercial banks to engage in investment banking, insurance, and other financial activities through affiliated subsidiaries.

FINANCIAL SERVICES MODERNIZATION ACT OF 1999

The major provisions of the Financial Services Modernization Act of 1999 (often referred to as the Gramm-Leach-Bliley Act in recognition of the senators who sponsored the legislation) are (1) banks are allowed to create securities and insurance subsidiaries; (2) a new organizational form, called *financial holding companies (FHCs)*, can establish commercial banking, insurance, security, and merchant banking affiliates; invest in and develop real estate; and engage in other finance-related activities (see Exhibit 13.16); (3) insurance companies and securities firms can acquire commercial banks and form FHCs with Federal Reserve approval; (4) financial service providers must comply with a new set of privacy rules concerning how information about customers is shared within an organization and with others; and (5) the Federal Reserve is the umbrella supervisor over FHCs, whereas the bank and nonbank subsidiaries of the FHC fall under the supervision of other regulators. This approach is referred to as **functional regulation**.

The 1999 act was passed after many years of weakening restrictions on bank activities. Throughout the 1980s and 1990s, bank regulators loosened the restrictions on bank activities. For example, in 1986 the Federal Reserve allowed certain bank holding companies to own subsidiaries that engage in investment banking activities as long as those activities did not generate more than a small percentage of the company's total revenue. Therefore, in many respects, the 1999 act merely formalized well-established regulatory interpretations and positions on already-existing laws. For example, even though the act explicitly allowed affiliation among commercial banks and investment banks, the restrictions on these activities had eroded so much already that there were few real barriers to such affiliation.

In contrast to the securities activities of bank holding companies, the ability to affiliate with insurance companies is new. Except for limited abilities to sell insurance products, banking firms were not allowed to engage in insurance activities, especially insurance underwriting. Following the 1999 act, however, bank and insurance companies can be separate subsidiaries within the same financial holding company.

THE 2007–2009 FINANCIAL CRISIS

The Gramm-Leach-Bliley reforms encouraged financial service providers to affiliate, integrate, and reorganize, but not at the pace originally expected. Although many of the largest commercial banks eagerly adopted the financial holding company structure and entered into direct competition with investment banks, the largest investment banks chose to remain as independent investment banks. Unfortunately, by remaining as independent investment banks, these institutions were not eligible for assistance from the Federal Reserve when the financial crisis occurred. As the crisis revealed weaknesses in the independent investment bank business model, some investment banks failed (e.g., Lehman Brothers), were acquired by a commercial bank (Bank of America bought Merrill Lynch), or were converted to bank holding companies (Morgan Stanley and Goldman Sachs converted to bank holding companies and eventually financial holding companies). With these conversions, the days of the large independent investment bank appear to be over.

Now there are relatively few restrictions on the banking-related activities that can occur within a financial holding company. These activities include insurance underwriting, securities dealing and underwriting, financial and investment advisory services, merchant banking, and generally any nonbanking activity authorized by the Bank Holding Company Act. The one major caveat to this list of allowable activities is that most of these banking-related activities must be conducted within subsidiaries that are separate from the FDIC-insured commercial bank subsidiary.

15.8 CONSUMER PROTECTION REGULATIONS

The final regulations to be discussed are those designed to protect consumers in their transactions with commercial banks and other credit-granting institutions. Since 1968 there has been a trend toward legislation designed to protect consumers in the credit market, precipitated by an active and growing consumer movement. The regulatory philosophy behind many of the consumer regulations is twofold: (1) consumers generally have unequal market power relative to creditors and other market participants, and (2) consumer markets, when left to their own devices, may not allocate credit in the most socially desirable manner. It often is not clear, however, that the regulations have their intended effects.

LOAN RATE CEILINGS

Loan rate ceilings vary widely from state to state and historically have usually applied to consumer and mortgage credit. Rate ceilings pose no problem for banks or consumers as long as the ceiling exceeds the rate of interest that would be charged in a competitive market. When rate ceilings become binding, they may cause serious problems. For instance, it is well documented that mortgage rate ceilings seriously impede the flow of mortgage credit and reduce housing starts when market interest rates rise above the maximum ceiling rate. In the consumer credit markets, because prices of goods sold on credit can be raised, credit is not usually cut off entirely as a result of rising market rates of interest, but it may become unprofitable for banks to make direct loans that are subject to the rate ceilings.

TRUTH-IN-LENDING

In 1969 Congress passed the **Consumer Credit Protection Act** (popularly known as the **Truth-in-Lending Act**) with the intent of ensuring that every borrower obtained meaningful information about the cost of credit. The act applies not only to banks but also to all lenders who extend credit to consumers for personal or agricultural use up to a limit of $25,000. For commercial banks, truth-in-lending is administered by the Board of Governors of the Federal Reserve System under Federal Reserve **Regulation Z**.

The two most important disclosures required by Regulation Z are (1) the annual percentage rate and (2) the total finance charges on a loan. The purpose of the Truth-in-Lending Act is to increase consumers' awareness of true loan rates and charges. The desired result is that consumers shop more wisely for credit and obtain credit from the lowest-rate source. This has helped banks because they often have the lowest rates on consumer loans. Truth-in-Lending also served as the model for Truth-in-Savings, the requirement that institutions disclose the annual percentage yield on interest-bearing deposits.

FAIR CREDIT BILLING ACT

The **Fair Credit Billing Act (FCBA)** of 1974 requires that creditors provide detailed information to consumers on the method of assessing finance charges and

PEOPLE & EVENTS

Dual or Dueling Banking Systems?

In the United States, banks are part of a **dual banking system**, in which both state and federal authorities have significant regulatory authority. The primary federal banking authority is the Office of the Comptroller of the Currency (OCC). The OCC charters, regulates, and examines national banks. Individual states have their own bank regulatory offices. State banking authorities share regulatory authority over state-chartered banks with either the FDIC or the Federal Reserve, depending on whether the bank is a member of the Federal Reserve System.

Preemption actions by the OCC and the reaction by state banking authorities suggest that the dual banking system might be more appropriately called a *dueling banking system*. In February 2004, the OCC issued regulations preempting state regulations concerning national banks' powers and activities. Essentially, the OCC said that any state law that applies to all businesses (property laws, environmental laws, and contract laws) also applies to national banks, but that states may not attempt to regulate the deposit-taking and lending activities of national banks. As you might expect, state banking authorities were not too happy with the OCC.

The current preemption battle stems largely from predatory lending and consumer protection laws passed at the state level. The OCC challenged the applicability of these laws to national banks. Because the National Banking Act of 1863 exempts national banks from state laws and oversight by state officials, the OCC has won most of the court cases concerning preemption.

State banking officials argue that the OCC is pandering to the institutions it regulates and is trying to eliminate the dual banking system. Their concern is that some state banks will drop their state charter in favor of a national charter because, according to some state authorities, the OCC favors banks' interests over consumer interests. The OCC counters that the OCC is interested in consumer issues. For example, it forced national banks to stop providing funds to *pay-day lenders*.

Although the OCC's stance on structure, competition, or consumer regulations has often seemed less stringent than that of several of the largest states, it enforces safety and soundness standards more stringent than those of most state banking authorities. Thus the "dueling" banking system fosters important debate and experimentation while offering meaningful choices to all participants—just as our federal system was intended to do in all areas of public policy.

also that billing complaints be processed promptly. The purpose of the Fair Credit Billing Act is to deal with some of the problems created by the increasing automation of credit and the proliferation of credit card transactions. The act requires that banks and other suppliers of consumer credit send their customers a detailed description of their rights and of the procedures they must follow in making complaints about billing errors. The act is administered by the Federal Reserve System under Regulation Z.

The FCBA raises costs to creditors by increasing legal complexities and mandating quick formal responses to complaints. However, by formalizing procedures for filing and handling complaints, it has also simplified operations and reduced some costs. In addition, because there is no longer a threat of litigation as long as the act is complied with, lenders report that they are now less charitable in awarding disputed claims and can do so in a less costly (more routine) manner than before.

EQUAL CREDIT OPPORTUNITY ACT

In 1974, Congress passed the **Equal Credit Opportunity Act (ECOA)**, which requires that credit be made available to individuals without regard to sex or marital status. In 1976, Congress broadened the scope of that act to forbid discrimination by creditors based on race, age, national origin, or whether credit applicants received part of their income from public assistance benefits. It also requires women's incomes to be treated equally with men's in evaluating credit. The act is implemented through **Regulation B** of the Federal Reserve Board.

THE COMMUNITY REINVESTMENT ACT (CRA)

The **Community Reinvestment Act (CRA)** was created in 1977 to prevent *redlining*, in which a lender draws a hypothetical red line on a map around one part of the community and refuses to make loans in that area. Although some bankers argue that redlining never existed, Congress passed the CRA to make sure that banks make credit available to all people in their market area regardless of where they live. Thus, under the CRA, banks must be able to show that they attempt to serve the credit needs of all people in their area, and they must be able to document their efforts and make the documentation available to regulators and the general public. The upside of the act is that it does ensure that credit is generally available to all people who qualify. The downside of the act is that the documentation requirements of CRA are very expensive to perform, especially after the requirements were increased by the FDIC Improvement Act of 1991 and by the Interstate Banking and Branching Efficiency Act of 1994. Some of the new requirements were intended to ensure that banks channel credit to the neediest people and neediest areas in their communities as well as to politically favored community groups. Because banks that cannot show that they have complied faithfully with the CRA requirements may be prohibited from merging, branching, or taking other actions that require regulatory approval, many banks have made unsound loans to favored groups just to ensure that they would not encounter problems with CRA compliance and the regulators in the future.

FAIR AND ACCURATE CREDIT TRANSACTIONS ACT

In 1970, the **Fair Credit Reporting Act (FCRA)** was passed. It was intended to promote the accuracy, fairness, and privacy of personal information assembled by credit-reporting agencies. The three major credit-reporting agencies are Equifax (www.equifax.com), Experian (www.experian.com), and Trans Union (www.transunion.com). In the 1990s and early 2000s, banks and other financial institutions began relying more and more on credit reports and credit scores to evaluate credit applications. Concerns about potential errors in credit reports and increased worries over identity theft led to the passage of the **Fair and Accurate Credit Transactions (FACT) Act** in 2003.

The FACT Act reauthorized some of the provisions of the FCRA that were expiring. In addition, it preempted individual states from enacting legislation that would impose even greater requirements on credit-granting institutions and credit-reporting agencies. In exchange for the preemptions, however, credit-granting institutions and credit-reporting agencies face increased responsibility for protecting consumers. For example, consumers are entitled to receive a free copy of their credit report once a year. In addition, banks and other lenders are required to tell customers if they report negative information about them to credit bureaus and must notify them when they are granted credit at terms less favorable than most other consumers receive.

DODD-FRANK WALL STREET REFORM AND CONSUMER PROTECTION ACT OF 2010

In response to many of the lending abuses associated with the 2007–2009 financial crisis, the Dodd-Frank Act includes several consumer protection provisions. The act created the **Bureau of Consumer Financial Protection (BCFP)** to enforce consumer finance laws. According to the BCFP's Web page, the bureau will do the following:

- Conduct rule-making, supervision, and enforcement for federal consumer financial protection laws
- Restrict unfair, deceptive, or abusive acts or practices
- Create a center to take consumer complaints
- Promote financial education
- Research consumer behavior
- Monitor financial markets for new risks to consumers
- Enforce laws that outlaw discrimination and other unfair treatment in consumer finance

In addition to creating the BCFP, the Dodd-Frank Act includes several provisions intended to address some of the causes of the subprime mortgage crisis and limit the incidence of predatory lending. Included among these provisions are national underwriting standards for mortgages, limits on allowable fees and interest rates for certain types of mortgages, and enhanced property appraisal requirements.

Finally, the act includes provisions intended to improve access to mainstream financial institutions for low- and middle-income households. The motive behind these provisions is that low- and middle-income households often seek out the types of loans that are readily available from payday lenders (and other high-cost lenders) but are not generally available from mainstream financial institutions (e.g., banks and credit unions). As a result, these households end up paying very high interest rates for short-term loans. The Dodd-Frank Act attempts to address this via education programs and by establishing grants and incentives designed to encourage mainstream financial institutions to develop products that appeal to low- and middle-income households.

Because the U.S. banking system developed over time, and because the United States has a wide variety of other depository institutions that evolved to serve specialized needs over time, the U.S. financial regulatory structure is quite complex. State regulators regulate state-chartered financial institutions. However, federal regulators regulate nationally chartered or insured institutions as well. Several regulators could conceivably all be responsible for the same institution (e.g., a nationally chartered bank that belongs to the Federal Reserve System and has federal deposit insurance could be examined by the Fed, the OCC, or the FDIC). Thus, the federal agencies cooperate so only one of the federal regulators takes on the responsibility for examining the bank to make sure that it complies with all applicable laws. In addition, the FDIC retains the authority to initiate an independent examination of any problem institution that presents a risk to the deposit insurance fund. Furthermore, each of the various regulators remains responsible for regulating branching, mergers, entry, and exit by institutions under its jurisdiction.

Federal supervision of banks is divided among the FDIC, the Federal Reserve, and the Comptroller of the Currency. Exhibit 15.9 summarizes the regulatory responsibilities of each. In addition, state banking commissioners are responsible for the regulation and examination of banks chartered in their states. State banking commissioners also must ensure that branches of out-of-state banks chartered or located in their state comply with all applicable state laws.

Each state has its own agency that is responsible for regulating and supervising commercial banks chartered by the state. These agencies can also regulate other financial institutions in the state, such as savings and loan associations, mutual savings banks, credit unions, finance companies, and out-of-state bank branches that are located in their state. The agency directors may be called *commissioner* or *superintendent of banking*, but, in general, the scope of their duties with respect to state-chartered banks is analogous to that of the Comptroller of the Currency for national banks. Although their functions vary from one state to another, state banking authorities normally have the following responsibilities. First, they approve the charters for new state banks, the opening and closing of branch offices, and the scope of bank holding company operations within the state. Second, they examine financial institutions chartered by the state. Third, state bank agencies have powers to protect the public interest. These powers take the form of regulating the activities of finance companies and enforcing various consumer regulations, such as credit disclosure and usury laws.

It is difficult to make any broad generalizations about the quality of state banking supervision. Perhaps all that can be said fairly is that the quality varies. Some state agencies are comparable to federal agencies in the quality of their bank examinations. Others, unfortunately, are weak. Administrators may be selected by patronage; examiners may be poorly paid, undertrained, and influenced by the institutions that they are supposed to regulate. Generally, state banking agencies are more permissive in the types of banking practices they allow. As a result, we find a large number of both large and small banks preferring state charters. For example, many large New York City banks whose operations are global in scope are state-chartered banks. However, the Federal Reserve regulates bank and financial holding companies.

15.9 BANK REGULATORS

EXHIBIT 15.9
Primary Supervisory Responsibilities for Commercial Bank Regulators

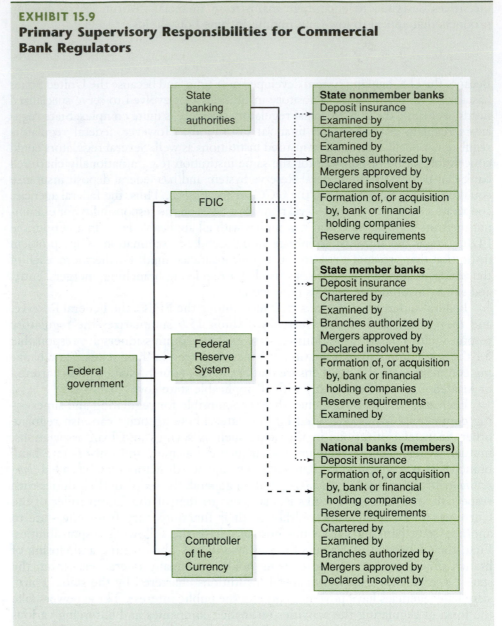

Because there are so many different bank regulators, it is often difficult to determine which regulator is responsible for which different banking activities.

One of the issues addressed by the Financial Services Modernization Act concerns the allocation of regulatory authority within a financial holding company. According to the 1999 act, the Fed has umbrella authority over financial holding companies, but functional regulation is the responsibility of the individual regulators. For example, a financial holding company that owns both a state-chartered commercial bank that is not a member of the Federal Reserve System and an investment bank is subject to regulatory authority from the Federal Reserve, state banking authorities, the FDIC, and the Securities and Exchange

Commission (SEC). Because the Federal Reserve has regulatory authority over financial holding companies, it is responsible for reviewing the activities of the holding company. Because the commercial bank is state chartered, it is subject to regulatory oversight by its state banking authorities. Because the commercial bank is state chartered and not a member of the Federal Reserve System, it is subject to regulation and examination by the FDIC. The investment banking affiliate is subject to oversight by the SEC. In addition, depending on their activities, some of the financial holding company's affiliates may fall under the authority of other regulatory agencies, such as the Commodity Futures Trading Commission.

Understanding the lines of regulatory authority was made even more complicated by the Dodd-Frank Act. As discussed earlier, this act establishes the Financial Stability Oversight Council (FSOC). The FSOC is responsible for monitoring the stability of the financial system, identifying potential systemic risks, and directing the other financial regulatory agencies to address the risks. The act also makes nonbank financial institutions that are considered systemically important subject to regulatory oversight by the Federal Reserve. The FSOC is intended to act as an umbrella regulatory authority over systemic risks while the Federal Reserve maintains umbrella authority over financial holding companies, bank holding companies, and systemically important nonbank financial companies. Functional regulatory authority is the responsibility of the OCC, the FDIC, the SEC, the CFTC, and state banking authorities.

DO YOU UNDERSTAND?

1. In what way did the Financial Services Modernization Act of 1999 merely formalize the regulatory interpretations of existing laws?

2. What was the justification for separating commercial banking from investment banking?

3. Why do bankers probably have more favorable attitudes toward the Truth-in-Lending Act than the Community Reinvestment Act?

4. What does it mean to say that the Federal Reserve is an *umbrella regulator*? What is meant by *functional regulation*?

SUMMARY OF LEARNING OBJECTIVES

1. **Discuss the reasons why banks are regulated.** Financial institutions are heavily regulated because politicians fear that their failures could heavily damage local or national economies.

2. **Describe the history of bank failures in the United States, the steps policymakers have taken to reduce the incidence of failure, and the lessons learned from previous bank failures.** The greatest number of bank failures occurred during the 1930–1933 period. In more recent years, the number of bank failures has been much smaller. The creation of

deposit insurance did more to limit bank panics and failures than any other development.

3. **Explain FDIC insurance and how the FDIC goes about paying off depositors and disposing of the assets of a failed bank.** Deposit insurance was created in 1933. In the event that an insured institution fails, the FDIC attempts to resolve the institution using the least costly approach. Purchase and assumption transactions make the most sense when an institution has value as a going concern. Otherwise, the FDIC pays off depositors and liquidates the assets.

4. **Discuss the issues and concerns created by FDIC insurance.** Deposit insurance creates a moral hazard in that depositors do not fully monitor the riskiness of insured institutions. As a result, the institutions' managers can take more risk without having to pay higher interest rates to attract deposits.

5. **Explain the role of capital requirements and the bank examination process in promoting safety and soundness in the banking system.** By requiring bank owners to invest a minimum amount of their own funds in a bank, it discourages imprudent risk taking. Bank examinations serve to ensure that bank managers are behaving in a safe and sound manner.

6. **Explain the limitations on bank activities and discuss recent changes to the limitations.** Beginning in the 1980s, limitations on interest rates, geographic boundaries, and bank activities have been gradually reduced. Banks are now able to engage in just about any banking-related activity, except those limited by the Dodd-Frank Act, but some of those activities must be conducted in separate subsidiaries.

7. **Discuss the various consumer protection regulations with which banks must comply.** Banks are subject to significant regulations that are intended to protect consumers from bankers who have significant influence over the consumers' quality of life. These regulations help ensure that consumers are not exploited, but they also create an additional regulatory burden for banks and other lenders.

8. **Describe the responsibilities of the various bank regulatory agencies.** Many regulators exist at the federal level both to examine and to provide deposit insurance to various institutions. Important regulators include the FSOC, Fed, FDIC, OCC, OTS, NCUSIF, and state banking commissioners.

KEY TERMS

Regulatory dialectic
Lender of last resort
Bank panics
Banking Act of 1933 (Glass-Steagall Act)
Federal Deposit Insurance Corporation (FDIC)
Deposit insurance
Depository Institutions Deregulation and Monetary Control Act (DIDMCA) of 1980
Depository Institutions Act (DIA) of 1982 (Garn-St. Germain)
Federal Savings and Loan Insurance Corporation (FSLIC)
Competitive Equality in Banking Act (CEBA) of 1987
Financial Institutions Reform, Recovery, and Enforcement Act (FIRREA)

Federal Deposit Insurance Corporation Improvement Act (FDICIA)
Prompt corrective actions
Financial Services Modernization Act of 1999 (Gramm-Leach-Bliley)
Emergency Economic Stabilization Act of 2008
Troubled Asset Relief Program (TARP)
Dodd-Frank Wall Street Reform and Consumer Protection Act
National Credit Union Share Insurance Fund (NCUSIF)
Payoff and liquidate policy
Purchase and assumption agreement
Moral hazard
Too big to fail (TBTF)

Financial Stability Oversight Council (FSOC)
Tier 1 capital
Tier 2 capital
Risk-weighted assets
Office of the Comptroller of the Currency (OCC)
Call reports
On-site bank examinations
CAMELS
Interstate Banking and Branching Efficiency Act (IB&BEA)
De novo branching
Regulation Q
Money market mutual funds (MMMFs)
Money market deposit accounts (MMDAs)
Functional regulation
Consumer Credit Protection Act
Truth-in-Lending Act
Regulation Z

Fair Credit Billing Act (FCBA)
Dual banking system
Equal Credit Opportunity Act (ECOA)
Regulation B
Community Reinvestment Act (CRA)
Fair Credit Reporting Act (FCRA)
Fair and Accurate Credit Transactions (FACT) Act
Bureau of Consumer Financial Protection (BCFP)

QUESTIONS AND PROBLEMS

1. Why are bank failures considered to have a greater effect on the economy than other types of business failures? Do you agree with this conclusion?

2. What are the major lessons learned from past bank failures? Do you think that history can or will repeat itself?

3. Although the FDIC does not grant charters for banks to operate, it is said to have an enormous influence on the charter process. Explain.

4. Which of the bank safety regulations enacted in the 1930s do you believe are most important in actually achieving bank safety? Which of the safety regulations would you classify as being anticompetitive?

5. How would you assess the success of consumer regulation? In what areas has it failed its stated objectives?

6. Bank regulation is considered to be in the public interest. Thus, the more regulation, the better. Explain why you agree or disagree with this statement.

7. What is the purpose of bank examinations? How do they differ from CPA audits?

8. How do failing bank resolution policies differ between large and small banks? Why the difference?

9. Why has Congress passed more regulatory acts for financial institutions in recent years? Cite major acts passed since 1980 and the major provisions of each.

10. What is *moral hazard*, and how is it created by deposit insurance?

11. Why did bank failures increase, with a lag, after deposit insurance became available to banks? What else contributed to the increase in bank failures in the 1980s?

12. How can an effective lender of last resort prevent financial panics from developing? Why was the Fed unable to prevent the Great Depression of the 1930s?

13. Why do banks and other financial institutions willingly comply with financial regulation, even though they may complain about it?

14. How might possibilities for regulatory capture contribute to the large number of financial regulators and deposit insurance funds?

15. What are risk-based capital standards? What are they designed to do?

16. Why is capital adequacy more of a problem for commercial banks than for most other businesses?

17. Explain why bank regulators are so concerned with capital adequacy for the banking industry

INTERNET EXERCISE

All financial institution regulators have Internet sites where people can obtain extensive information on the institutions they regulate and can learn about current and pending regulations. The Internet Exercise for Chapter 13 asked you to look up information on the Federal Financial Institutions Examination Council (FFIEC) Web site. The FFIEC Web site is useful because it has links to all the other bank and thrift regulatory agencies. It also acts as a sort of clearinghouse for information about individual institutions. One of the topics of discussion in this chapter concerns the Community Reinvestment Act. Recall that institutions are examined with respect to how well they satisfy the provisions of the act. Using a bank that is in your local community, do the following:

1. At the FDIC's Web page, http://www.fdic.gov/, click "Consumer Protection." Then click "Community Affairs." Then click "CRA Ratings & Performance Evaluations." Here you can find your bank's CRA ratings. How is your bank doing?

2. Open the institution's CRA evaluation and read the summary of the institution's CRA performance. What criteria were used in evaluating the institution? Under which criteria did the institution do well? Under which criteria did the institution do poorly?

3. Can you identify any reasons why you think your institution did or did not do well on its CRA evaluation?

PART V

FINANCIAL INSTITUTIONS

Thrift Institutions and Finance Companies

IF YOU HAVE EVER SEEN THE MOVIE *It's a Wonderful Life*, starring Jimmy Stewart, then you already have an understanding of why early thrift institutions were created. In the movie, Jimmy Stewart played George Bailey, the president of the Bailey Building and Loan during the late 1930s and early 1940s. **Building societies**, such as the Bailey Building and Loan, were formed by groups of people who pooled their savings so that each could eventually acquire a home. They might draw lots to see who would be first to obtain a home and, as the mortgages were repaid and more funds were deposited, the building societies could finance more home construction for their members.

Prior to World War II, *commercial* banks primarily served business customers, hence the name *commercial* banks. The consumer-focused institutions that emerged during this period were savings and loan associations, mutual savings banks, and credit unions. These institutions are often called *thrift institutions*, a term which is frequently shortened to just *thrifts*. Thrifts historically accommodated

In the Jimmy Stewart movie, once news got around town that the Bailey Building and Loan could not honor deposit withdrawals because of operating losses, the depositors started a run on the bank. Had Bailey had federal deposit insurance, which protects small depositors from bank failures, the run could have been prevented.

the needs of working-class people who typically have small amounts to save and want to make sure that their "thriftiness" is rewarded by earning a respectable rate of interest on their deposits while taking minimal risk of loss. ■

This chapter is about **thrift institutions**, which are consumer-orientated financial institutions that accept deposits from and make loans to consumers. Thrift institutions are composed of savings institutions and credit unions. There are two types of savings institutions that focus on residential mortgage lending: (1) savings associations and (2) savings banks. The chapter also is about **finance companies**, which provide specialized financial services to consumers and businesses. Exhibit 16.1 shows in a diagram the economic roles of each type of institution that we discuss in this chapter. As you read the chapter, you may find it convenient to refer back to Exhibit 16.1, given the complexity of the historical development and regulation of these institutions.

EXHIBIT 16.1

Types of Thrift Institutions and Finance Companies

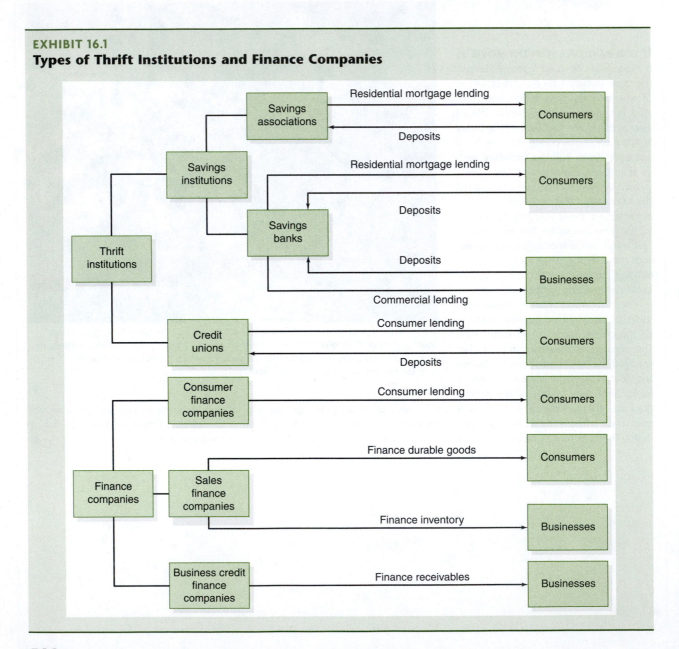

The chapter begins with a discussion of the history of mortgage-oriented thrifts, now called *saving institutions*. Historically, savings associations have specialized in making consumer mortgage loans, whereas savings banks have operated as more diversified institutions with a large concentration of residential mortgages but also holding some commercial loans, corporate bonds, and stocks as well. Because savings institutions, regardless of type, focus on long-term residential mortgages and fund them with short-term consumer savings deposits, they are exposed to considerable interest rate risk, which creates significant management challenges.

We also discuss another class of thrifts, credit unions, which specialize in short-term consumer loans. They are unique because (1) they are nonprofit organizations, (2) they are owned by the depositors (or members), and (3) they have rules that limit their membership.

Finally, we discuss finance companies, which make loans to both consumers and businesses. They differ from thrifts in that they do not accept deposits from the public to obtain funds; instead, they rely on short-term and long-term funding from the sale of commercial paper, notes, bonds, or stock. For each institution, we discuss their regulators, their size and structure, and their operations.

LEARNING OBJECTIVES

1 Discuss the historical development of savings institutions.

2 Describe the balance-sheet composition of savings institutions.

3 Explain the problems faced by savings institutions in the 1980s, how Congress addressed the problems, and the impact of the problems and regulations on the industry today.

4 Describe the operations and organizational structure of credit unions.

5 Explain the various types of finance companies and the roles they play in providing credit.

16.1 HISTORICAL DEVELOPMENT OF SAVINGS INSTITUTIONS

In this section we discuss the economic and political forces that have influenced the development of the two types of savings institutions: savings banks and savings associations. These institutions focus on mortgage lending to consumers.

SAVINGS BANKS

Savings banks were first started in the United States in 1816. They were formed as depository institutions that would allow people with small deposit balances to save and earn a respectable rate of interest on their deposits while taking prudent risk of loss.

The original savings banks in the United States were **mutual institutions** that were technically owned by their depositors and were managed by a public-spirited board of trustees that sought to invest depositors' funds to earn a safe and secure rate of interest. Initially, the savings banks' trustees could invest in stocks, bonds, consumer or mortgage loans, or any other asset they deemed to be a safe investment that would earn interest for their depositors. In the 1900s, however, savings banks began to invest increasingly in mortgage loans because of the desire of their depositors to own their homes. In addition, until 1996 and because of the political importance of homeownership, the federal government gave large tax breaks to mortgage-oriented lenders who invested at least 60 percent of their assets in home-mortgage-related lending.

SAVINGS ASSOCIATIONS

The first savings associations in the United States were chartered as *building societies*. Historically, savings associations were known as **savings and loan associations (SLAs)** or, in brief form, *savings and loans* or *S&Ls*. With the changes in the regulatory structure of the financial services industry, these institutions are now called *savings associations*. The first was the Oxford-Provident Building Society, chartered in 1831 in Philadelphia. Building societies were formed by groups of people who pooled their savings so that each could eventually acquire a home, in some instances drawing lots to see who would be first. As mortgages were repaid and more funds were deposited, the building societies could finance more home construction for their members. In some cases, once all the original members obtained a home, the early building societies would dissolve. In other cases, however, the society would continue to make mortgage loans and would continue to pay interest to its depositors.

Many of these early savings associations were formed as mutual institutions, which technically means that the depositors own the institution. Mutual savings associations were managed by officers who were elected by their depositors on a "one-dollar, one-vote" basis. When depositors started an account, they would typically sign over a proxy statement to the current management that let the management vote on their behalf. Thus, managements of mutual institutions often became self-perpetuating.

An alternative form of savings association was a stockholder-owned and directed **stock association**. Stock associations issue common stock to shareholders and are operated by managers appointed by a board of directors elected by profit-seeking shareholders—just like a commercial bank or any other corporation.

REGULATION OF SAVINGS INSTITUTIONS

Savings associations and savings banks were chartered at the state level in most states until the 1930s. In 1932, because of liquidity problems experienced by mortgage lenders in the Great Depression, the **Federal Home Loan Bank** system was established. That system consisted of 12 regional Federal Home Loan Banks that were empowered to borrow in the national capital markets and make loans, called **advances**, to savings associations in their regions that were members of the Federal Home Loan Bank. Advances were much like discount window loans made by the Federal Reserve banks, with the difference that advances could be made with maturities of many years rather than a few days at rates that were usually only modestly above the Federal Home Loan Banks' borrowing rates. Because the home loan banks are government agencies with minimal credit risk, their borrowing rates are relatively low, and they can make advances at attractive rates.

EXHIBIT 16.2
Three-Month Treasury Bill Rates (1960–February 2011)

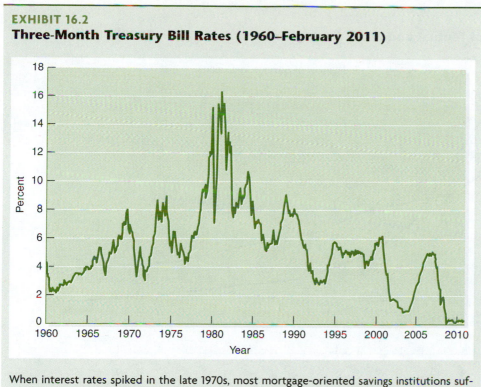

When interest rates spiked in the late 1970s, most mortgage-oriented savings institutions suffered large losses because they were forced to pay higher rates to retain deposits but did not earn additional interest on their loan portfolio.

Source: Federal Reserve Board of Governors, H15 Statistical Release.

When interest rates began to increase sharply in the late 1970s and spiked in the early 1980s, as can be seen in Exhibit 16.2, many savings associations and savings banks encountered severe financial problems. The problem was that these mortgage-oriented thrifts funded themselves by selling short-term deposits to consumers and making long-term fixed-rate home mortgage loans. Thus, when interest rates rose sharply, their cost of funds rose quickly above the interest rate earned on mortgages, which remained relatively constant, causing operating losses. Because many of these institutions took too much interest rate risk, and some took too much credit risk, many thrifts failed during the 1980s. As a result, deposit insurance funds for these institutions were nearly depleted, and Congress established new regulatory agencies to handle the ensuing crisis. Also during this period, it became clear that mortgage-oriented thrifts needed to attract more capital investment from outside shareholders to survive and prosper.

During this thrift crisis, Congress enacted the 1980 Depository Institutions Deregulation and Monetary Control Act (DIDMCA), which permitted thrifts to obtain federal charters rather than state charters and to convert to stockholder ownership. This allowed mortgage-oriented thrifts to attract more capital investment and increased their ability to bear the losses caused by too much interest rate risk. Consequently, many of the largest and healthiest savings institutions are now stockholder-owned and are managed and directed much like commercial banks, rather than as mutual institutions, as they were originally chartered. Exhibit 16.3 shows

EXHIBIT 16.3

Number and Assets of Mutual and Stock Savings Institutions (1989–2009)

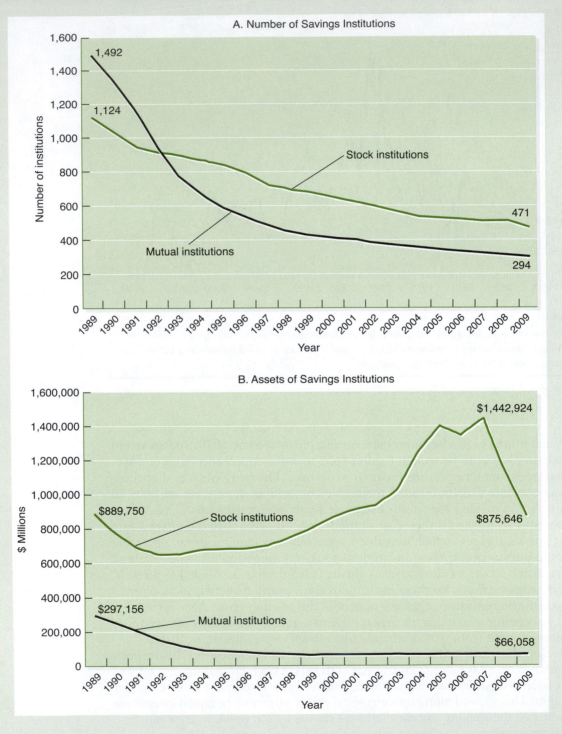

In recent years, the number and size of mutual and stock savings institutions has fallen sharply.

Source: Office of Thrift Supervision, *2009 Fact Book*, March 2010.

that, although the overall number of mortgage-oriented savings institutions declined sharply in the last 20 years, the relative number of stock institutions and their assets has increased.

When the problems of the industry worsened, with continued rising interest rates and too much credit risk being taken on by some thrifts in the 1980s, Congress blamed lax regulation as the source of the problem and abolished the **Federal Home Loan Bank Board (FHLBB)**, which regulated savings and loan associations, and the Federal Savings and Loan Insurance Corporation (FSLIC), which provided deposit insurance to savings and loan associations. Congress replaced those two institutions with two new regulatory institutions: (1) the **Office of Thrift Supervision (OTS)**, which chartered and regulated savings institutions at the federal level, and (2) the FDIC Savings Association Insurance Fund (**FDIC-SAIF**), which was a deposit insurance fund run by the FDIC to provide deposit insurance to member savings associations and savings banks. Eventually, the FDIC-SAIF was combined with the FDIC Bank Insurance Fund to form the Deposit Insurance Fund (DIF), and the OTS was merged into the Office of the Comptroller of the Currency (OCC).

Although the FHLBB was abolished, the Federal Home Loan Bank system still exists. In fact, because Federal Home Loan Banks' lending policies made them politically popular, they have expanded their functions by allowing qualifying commercial banks (banks that make a sufficiently large number of mortgage loans) and a few credit unions to join the Federal Home Loan Bank system.

16.2 OPERATIONS OF SAVINGS INSTITUTIONS

After World War II and until 1996, savings institutions were given substantial federal income tax relief (a **bad-debt deduction**) if at least 60 percent of their assets were related to home mortgage lending. The tax breaks encouraged the mortgage-oriented thrifts to finance the great expansion in homeownership that occurred after World War II.

Because of the tax incentive to conduct residential mortgage lending, these institutions exposed themselves to substantial interest rate risk because they held too many long-term fixed-rate mortgages when interest rates rose sharply in the late 1970s and early 1980s. As discussed previously, by the 1980s, many savings institutions were in severe financial trouble and failed because of the excessive interest rate risk. Exhibit 16.4 shows the major reasons that mortgage-oriented thrifts exited the industry. In the late 1980s and early 1990s, there were a large number of failures and charter conversions. In recent years, merger and acquisition activity is the leading reason for the decrease in the number of institutions.

Because their traditional methods of operation had caused savings institutions to experience problems, the 1980 DIDMCA gave them many additional powers traditionally reserved for commercial banks, such as issuing transactions deposits (i.e., checking accounts) in addition to savings deposits and making shorter-term loans, such as consumer and credit card loans. The reasoning was that banks had broader powers and had experienced fewer problems than mortgage-oriented thrifts in the late 1970s and early 1980s. By giving savings associations additional powers, regulators hoped that savings institutions could diversify more and reduce their dependence on the long-term mortgage lending that had

EXHIBIT 16.4

Contraction of OTS-Regulated Private Sector Savings Institutions as a Result of Failures, Mergers, and Conversion to Bank Charters

	1989	1990	1991	1992	1993	1994	1995	1996–2000	2001–2005	2006–2009
Exits										
Failures	320	213	147	61	8	2	2	3	3	27
Voluntary dissolutions	0	0	6	8	10	3	5	15	66	7
Charter conversions	2	16	43	108	116	66	29	135	76	39
Mergers and acquisitions	46	48	57	71	79	78	93	374	132	90
Total exits	368	277	253	248	213	149	129	527	277	163
Entrants	15	24	6	6	15	11	23	156	72	65
Net change (Exits)	353	253	247	242	198	138	106	371	205	98

In the late 1980s and early 1990s, the major reasons for savings association exit were failures, mergers, and conversions to savings bank or commercial bank charters. In recent years, mergers and charter conversions have been the primary reasons for contraction.

Source: Office of Thrift Supervision, *2009 Fact Book,* March 2010.

exposed them to such great interest rate risk. Savings institutions received additional powers with the passage of the 1982 Depository Institutions Act. The act permitted savings associations to make a limited number of commercial loans and gave them additional powers. Consequently, mortgage-oriented thrifts now own a wider variety of assets than they did in the 1970s, and their operations are more complicated.

ASSETS

Exhibit 16.5 shows that the largest single type of asset held by savings institutions is one- to four-family residential mortgage loans. In addition to one- to four-family residential mortgages, savings institutions hold loans on many other types of real estate, including mortgage loans for multifamily apartments, commercial properties, construction, and land acquisition. Most savings institutions also hold substantial amounts of mortgage-backed securities. Because mortgage-backed securities are more marketable and have more desirable cash-flow characteristics than the underlying mortgages, they have grown in importance in savings institutions' total assets in recent years.

Savings institutions continue to hold many mortgages despite their interest rate risk because they obtain a number of advantages from doing so. First, savings institutions that hold a sufficiently large amount of mortgages and qualifying assets (more than 60 percent) are designated as qualified lenders and are therefore eligible for more favorable regulatory treatment than banks if they are part of a single-depository-institution holding company. This treatment means that they can have commercial affiliates and are not subject to intense

EXHIBIT 16.5
Assets of Thrift Institutions (December 31, 2010)

Asset Accounts	All Insured Thrift Institutions[a]		Small Savings Inst.[b] (Percent[e])	Medium-Size Savings Inst.[c] (Percent[e])	Large Savings Inst.[d] (Percent[e])
	Millions	Percent[e]			
Cash and due from depository institutions	$68,085	5	12	7	5
Securities, total	316,067	25	17	19	27
Federal funds sold and securities purchased under repurchase agreements	5,381	0	1	1	0
Loans and leases, total	767,099	61	64	66	60
Loans secured by real estate, total	616,229	49	60	60	46
Construction and land development	25,805	2	3	4	2
One- to four-family residential	419,887	33	47	38	32
Multifamily residential	57,853	5	2	4	5
Commercial	112,233	9	8	14	8
Commercial and industrial loans	63,295	5	3	4	5
Loans to individuals	89,764	7	2	2	8
Other loans	11,063	1	0	0	1
Less allowance for loan losses	13,435	1	1	1	1
Trading account assets	1,417	0	0	0	0
Bank premises and fixed assets	10,428	1	2	2	1
Other real estate owned	6,119	0	1	1	0
Goodwill and other intangible assets	20,552	2	0	0	2
Other assets	58,631	5	3	4	5
Total assets	**$1,253,780**	**100**	**100**	**100**	**100**

Real estate lending, especially for residential properties, dominates savings institutions' asset portfolios.

[a] This group consists of 1,128 insured savings institutions.
[b] This group consists of the country's 297 smallest savings institutions. These institutions have assets of less than $100 million.
[c] This group consists of the country's 674 medium-size savings institutions. These institutions have assets between $100 million and $1 billion.
[d] This group consists of the country's 157 largest savings institutions. These institutions have assets of $1 billion or more.
[e] Columns may not add to 100 percent because of rounding.
Source: FDIC, *Statistics on Banking,* December 31, 2010.

holding company regulation. Furthermore, savings associations that hold sufficient mortgages can borrow on relatively advantageous terms by joining the Federal Home Loan Bank system and obtaining "advances" from their regional Federal Home Loan Bank.

Savings institutions can also hold nonmortgage loans such as loans to individual consumers, including credit card loans. However, most savings associations do not hold large amounts of such loans, which average only about 7 percent of savings institutions' total assets.

Savings institutions hold cash, deposits with other financial institutions, and investment securities to meet reserve requirements imposed on their transactions deposit holdings, to meet additional needs for liquidity, to obtain clearing and correspondent services from other financial institutions, and to earn additional income. Because of their focus on mortgage lending, their other investments are small relative to their total assets.

LIABILITIES

Deposits.   Exhibit 16.6 shows that the primary source of funds for savings institutions is from deposits—particularly relatively small deposits of $100,000 or less. Initially, passbook savings deposits were the primary sources of funds for savings institutions, but now they issue a wide variety of deposits. Specifically, because of the 1980 and 1982 Depository Institutions Acts, they can issue checkable deposits such as NOW accounts and transaction-limited money market deposit accounts (MMDAs). In addition, they can issue demand deposits to commercial customers with whom they do business, and some savings banks have issued non-interest-bearing checkable accounts. Thus, savings associations can offer a variety of transactions deposits, and they must back those deposits by meeting the same reserve requirements applicable to commercial banks.

Savings institutions typically issue a variety of savings certificates and negotiable certificates of deposit as well as regular savings accounts. The certificates are usually tailored to meet the needs of retail customers and can be issued to customers' retirement accounts.

Borrowed Funds.   Savings institutions supplement their deposits by borrowing from other sources. The most important source of borrowed funds consists of FHLBB advances, which are included in the *other borrowed money* category. FHL Bank advances are available to FHLB member institutions. Advances are available with relatively long maturities, up to 20 years, at rates that are only a little higher than the FHL Banks' government agency borrowing rate. Thus, advances are an attractive source of funding for savings associations with long-term assets. Savings institutions also have expanded their borrowing by obtaining collateralized loans (**reverse repos**) from the repurchase agreement market. Borrowings from Federal Home Loan Banks have expanded greatly, whereas other sources of borrowings have declined in relative importance because of the restructuring of the savings institution industry in 1989.

CAPITAL

The most startling change since the regulatory structure was reformed and weak savings institutions were assigned to the RTC for liquidation in 1989 is that savings institutions now hold substantially more net worth (capital) relative to their assets. Savings institutions' net worth may be either in the form of reserves and surplus, for mutual institutions, or in the form of *stockholders' equity*, for stockholder-owned institutions. By the end of 2010, savings institutions had

EXHIBIT 16.6
Liabilities and Capital Accounts of Savings Institutions (December 31, 2010)

Liability and Capital Accounts	All Insured Thrift Institutions[a]		Small Savings Inst.[b] (Percent[e])	Medium-Size Savings Inst.[c] (Percent[e])	Large Savings Inst.[d] (Percent[e])
	Millions	Percent[e]			
Liabilities					
Deposits	$908,657	72	80	79	71
Borrowed funds, total	178,155	14	5	9	16
Federal funds purchased and securities sold under repurchase agreements	47,610	4	0	1	5
Other borrowed money	130,545	10	5	8	11
Subordinated notes and debentures	2,010	0	0	0	0
Trading liabilities	82.183	0	0	0	0
All other liabilities	17,396	1	1	1	2
Total liabilities	$1,106,301	88	86	89	88
Capital accounts					
Common and preferred stock	$1,240	0	1	0	0
Surplus	96,962	8	5	4	9
Undivided profits	47,008	4	9	7	3
Total equity capital	$147,479	12	14	11	12
Total liabilities and equity capital	**$1,253,780**	**100**	**100**	**100**	**100**

Deposits are the largest source of funds for most savings institutions, but they are a much more important source for small and medium-size institutions. Borrowed funds are a more important source of funds for large banks. Other borrowed money consists largely of FHLB advances.

[a] This group consists of 1,128 insured savings institutions.
[b] This group consists of the country's 297 smallest savings institutions. These institutions have assets of less than $100 million.
[c] This group consists of the country's 674 medium-size savings institutions. These institutions have assets between $100 million and $1 billion.
[d] This group consists of the country's 157 largest savings institutions. These institutions have assets of $1 billion or more.
[e] Columns may not add to 100 percent because of rounding.

Source: FDIC, *Statistics on Banking*, December 31, 2010.

capital-to-assets ratios that averaged 12 percent. This is much higher than it has been in the past and exceeds the capital-to-assets ratios of commercial bank (Exhibit 16.7).

INCOME AND EXPENSES OF SAVINGS ASSOCIATIONS

Exhibit 16.8 shows the trend in savings institutions' net interest margin. Recall that a financial institution's net interest margin is the difference between gross interest income and gross interest expense. The exhibit shows that savings

EXHIBIT 16.7

Trends in Capital Adequacy, Problem Assets, and Savings Institution Earnings

Year-End	1989	1991	1996	1997	2000	2003	2006[b]	2009[b]
Capital Adequacy Ratios for OTS-Supervised Savings Institutions								
Average Tier-I leverage ratio	3.83%	5.27%	7.38%	7.59%	7.39%	7.82%	8.52%	9.60%
Average (total) risk-based capital ratio	7.19	10.16	14.53	14.59	13.32	14.23	14.33	16.7
Problem Assets of OTS-Regulated Savings Institutions								
Total troubled assets as a percentage of assets	NA	3.80%	1.13%	1.00%	0.60%	0.67%	0.70%	3.25%
Noncurrent loans as a percentage of assets	NA	1.87	0.85	0.77	0.5	0.58	0.61	2.76
Noncurrent one- to four-family loans[a]	NA	1.85	1.21	1.11	0.67	0.83	0.89	4.99
Noncurrent multifamily loans[a]	NA	—	1.45	0.79	0.15	0.13	0.21	3.38
Noncurrent commercial loans[a]	NA	5.98	1.38	1.1	1.52	1.21	0.9	2.71
Noncurrent consumer loans[a]	NA	1.32	0.89	0.97	0.81	0.94	0.91	1.59
Return on Assets (ROA) for OTS-Regulated Savings Institutions								
Average ROA for savings institutions	−0.41%	0.13%	0.89%	0.84%	0.90%	1.29%	1.06%	0%
Average ROE for savings institutions	0.97	1.88	11.15	10.44	11.61	14.29	11.18	0.03

After weak savings institutions were liquidated by the RTC in the early 1990s, savings institutions' assets fell, but capital ratios, earnings, and troubled asset ratios improved. Commercial loans and multifamily loans showed the greatest improvement.

NA = not available.

[a] As a percentage of the loan type.

[b] Total noncurrent loans including repurchased GNMA loans.

Source: Office of Thrift Supervision, *2009 Fact Book*, March 2010.

EXHIBIT 16.8

Net Interest Margin of Savings Institutions (1970–2010)

In the late 1970s and early 1980s, savings institutions' net interest margins shrank to almost nothing. In the 1990s, however, savings institutions' net interest margins grew as interest rates declined. Margins have remained relatively stable since then.

Source: FDIC, *Statistics on Banking*, December 31, 2010.

associations' net interest spread declined substantially in the early 1980s. The reason was that savings associations' cost of funds rose sharply while the interest revenue from their mortgage portfolio lagged behind. As a result, savings associations in general suffered large losses in 1981 and 1982 as a result of interest rate risk.

Exhibit 16.9 shows the trend in savings institutions' provision for loan losses over the 1984–2005 period. The dramatic increase in the provision in the late 1980s can be attributed to increased risk taking by many institutions following the deregulation of the industry in the early 1980s. Many savings institutions grew rapidly in the mid-1980s by making risky loans. Recall from Chapter 15 that poorly capitalized depository institutions face a moral hazard. That was certainly the case in the savings institution industry in the early 1980s. Unfortunately, many of these risky loans, especially those that were made in the oil-producing states of Texas, Oklahoma, Louisiana, and elsewhere, ended up in default.

After the FIRRE Act was passed in 1989 and regulators cleaned up the problem savings institutions, and other savings institutions disposed of their bad assets and took care to avoid new problems, savings institutions' provisions for loan losses declined greatly in the 1990s. Consequently, because of widening interest margins, greater fee income, and declining loan losses, savings associations' profits recovered sharply in the 1990s and into the early 2000s. This recovery is shown in Exhibit 16.10.

Unfortunately, much of the industry's profitability in the early 2000s was due to low interest rates and a housing boom. The housing boom eventually led to a bubble that burst in the mid-2000s. Because of savings institutions'

EXHIBIT 16.9
Provision for Loan Losses for Savings Institutions (1984–2010)

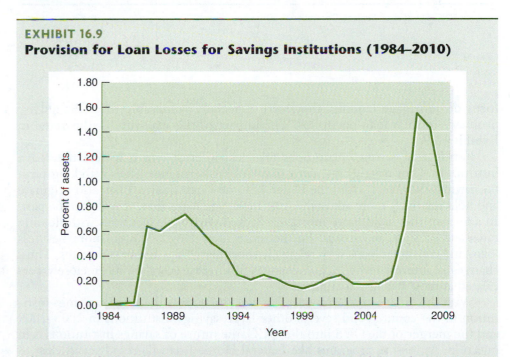

The provision for loan losses at thrift institutions increased substantially in the late 1980s as many savings institutions struggled to absorb losses on their lending portfolio, especially those loans made in oil-producing states such as Texas, Oklahoma, and Louisiana. The housing and mortgage-market crises that began in 2007 led to historic loan losses.

Source: FDIC, *Statistics on Banking*, December 31, 2010.

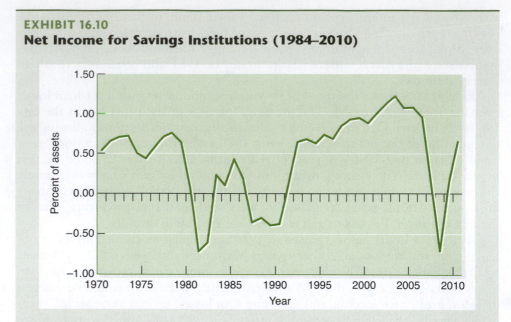

EXHIBIT 16.10
Net Income for Savings Institutions (1984–2010)

The high interest rates of the late 1970s and early 1980s caused substantial losses at savings institutions. After the deregulation of the industry in 1980 and 1982, many savings institutions grew rapidly and the industry began to show a profit again, at least on a book-value basis. When oil prices dropped in the mid-1980s, however, loan defaults mounted quickly in the oil-producing states of Texas, Oklahoma, Louisiana, and elsewhere. More recently, the housing and mortgage-market crises caused record losses for mortgage-oriented thrifts.

Source: FDIC, *Statistics on Banking*, December 31, 2010.

focus on mortgage lending, they were especially vulnerable to credit quality problems in their loan portfolios. The impact of this exposure is illustrated in Exhibit 16.9.

Fortunately, savings institutions take less interest rate risk than they have historically. They match-fund many of their long-term mortgages with long-term borrowings (advances) from the Federal Home Loan Banks. They also originate and hold relatively more adjustable-rate mortgage loans than they did in the past. In addition, they hold more mortgage-backed derivative securities with floating rates and/or short maturities. Furthermore, they have acquired more business loans and consumer loans with relatively short maturities and flexible rates. Thus, changes in interest revenues and changes in interest costs are more closely correlated at most savings institutions.

With the failure of Washington Mutual, which was the largest savings institution in the country, and several other large savings institutions in 2008–2009 and the merger of the OTS into the OCC, the future of savings institutions is in question. As long as programs like Federal Home Loan Bank Advances exist to provide incentives for financial institutions to support housing markets, however, it seems likely that at least some financial institutions will continue to focus on mortgage lending.

DO YOU UNDERSTAND?

1. When and why were the various types of thrift institutions started in the United States?
2. Name the present federal regulators of savings institutions. Also, explain which ones no longer exist and why.
3. What are savings institutions' most important assets and liabilities?
4. What trends have recently occurred in savings institutions' capital adequacy, earnings, and numbers, and why?

16.3 CREDIT UNIONS

Originating in Germany in the mid-1800s, the first credit union in the United States, St. Mary's Cooperative Credit Association, was organized in New Hampshire in 1909. Like savings institutions, credit unions were started both to provide an outlet for savers to deposit small amounts of funds and as organizations that would provide loans on relatively lenient terms to their members. Unlike savings institutions, however, credit unions were not instituted for the purpose of providing mortgage financing for their members. Instead, credit unions tend to focus on consumer lending.

Credit unions are strictly mutual institutions. They are organized like clubs whose members pool their savings and loan them to one another. Each member has one vote to elect members of the board of directors. Every member of a credit union must have one or more savings *shares* in the credit union in order to use its facilities, borrow funds from it, or vote for its board of directors. Often a minimum share (deposit) of $25 is required of each member who joins a credit union, but the minimum amount varies at different credit unions. The board of directors establishes major credit union policies, chooses the management of the credit union, and can change the management if necessary. To be a member of a credit union, a person must qualify under the credit union's **common bond requirements**. Most common bonds (more than 80 percent) are *occupational* (e.g., members work for the same employers or in the same industry); some (around 10 percent) are *associational* (e.g., members belong to the same religion, trade association, or trade union). The rest are *residential* (e.g., members live in a qualifying sparsely populated rural county or in specified low-income areas).

The common bond requirement gives credit unions several advantages that are not available to other depository institutions. First, like other clubs, their income is not subject to federal income tax before it is paid out as *dividends*. Savers who own shares (which are equivalent to other institutions' deposits) in the credit union receive dividends instead of interest as a return on their savings shares (deposits). Second, because their common bond requirement prevents credit unions from competing for the same customers (members), they are not subject to antitrust laws that otherwise might keep them from engaging in cooperative ventures. Consequently, they developed strong trade associations that provide them with many jointly provided services and help them coordinate their activities. Their trade associations, cooperative ventures, and tax exemption give them advantages that are not available to other depository institutions. Thus, although the mortgage-oriented thrifts are becoming more like commercial banks, credit unions are likely to remain a distinctive form of financial institution.

Demographic Change Brings Opportunity

Between 1980 and 2000, the minority share of households increased from 17 percent to 26 percent. Over the same period, the number of households headed by unmarried women increased by almost 10 million. Both of these trends are expected to continue well into the future. This represents a tremendous opportunity for those thrifts and finance companies that make their products and services appealing to these growing segments of the consumer and mortgage markets.

Thrifts (savings institutions and credit unions) have a tradition of serving the credit-related needs of consumers, so it is natural to expect thrifts to capitalize on this opportunity. However, commercial banks are also interested in serving minorities. Recently, the Credit Union National Association (CUNA) published the *Hispanic National Resource Guide* to help credit unions develop strategies to meet the needs of Hispanics. The American Bankers Association (ABA) published its *Best Practices in Immigrant Lending*. Not surprisingly, the two documents have much in common.

According to the CUNA and ABA, financial institutions should develop an outreach strategy to help establish contacts with members of the minority community. For example, many banks and credit unions have developed a partnership with local churches or community groups to offer financial literacy training. Another key to success is developing products that meet the needs of the minority community. For example, many immigrants do not have a credit history, so some lenders offer secured credit cards that are a low-risk way for the lender to help an immigrant establish a credit history. Other lenders have developed unique loan products targeted at Muslims. Islamic law prohibits the payment of interest, so the loan product must be carefully structured to incorporate an allowable profit that is not in the form of interest.

Although these practices make sense, a financial institution's success also depends on who is implementing the practices. Many minorities are distrustful of the financial system because of language barriers and a lack of familiarity with how the system works. The best way to overcome these barriers is for financial institutions to hire employees who are representative of the groups they are trying to serve.

CREDIT UNION REGULATORS

At first, credit unions were chartered and regulated only by individual states. It was not until 1934 that the Federal Credit Union Act was approved by Congress. That act allowed for the regulation and supervision of credit unions at the federal level. Most deposit insurance, if any, was provided by state insurance funds. Federal deposit (share) insurance became available only in 1970. At that time the **National Credit Union Administration (NCUA)** was established to regulate federally chartered credit unions and the new **National Credit Union Share Insurance Fund (NCUSIF)**. The NCUSIF provided federal insurance to members who owned shares (had deposits) in federally chartered credit unions and in qualifying state-chartered credit unions that elected to obtain federal insurance for their shareholders. The coverage of NCUSIF insurance was similar to that of FDIC and FSLIC insurance. Presently, NCUSIF insurance insures members' shares in a credit union up to $250,000, just like the FDIC. The NCUSIF also uses a CAMELS (capital adequacy, asset quality, management, earnings, liquidity and sensitivity to market risk) rating system, adapted from the FDIC, when examining credit unions to determine their soundness.

The NCUA is the most important credit union regulator. It not only charters federal credit unions, it also regulates the NCUSIF, which oversees all federally insured credit unions, including state-chartered credit unions that have federal share insurance. In addition, it oversees the **Central Liquidity Facility (CLF)** for credit unions.

The CLF is empowered to make loans to credit unions that have a liquidity need. The Central Liquidity Facility can borrow funds through the Federal Financing Bank, which helps finance government agencies' funding needs, and lends the funds either directly to credit unions or indirectly, through credit unions' privately run central credit union system. Although the CLF rarely uses its lending authority, it was authorized by Congress in 1978 so credit unions could be assured that they would always have access to funds, if necessary, in the event of a liquidity crisis.

Like many banks and savings associations, some credit unions had substantial mortgage holdings and consequently were affected by the housing and mortgage-market crises that began in 2006. Shortly after Congress established the Troubled Asset Relief Program (TARP) for banks and other banking-related institutions in October 2008, the NCUA established the Credit Union Homeowners Affordability Relief Program (HARP). HARP was intended to help member institutions deal with the financial crisis by encouraging credit unions to modify the terms of delinquent mortgages.

CREDIT UNIONS' OPERATIONS AND BALANCE SHEETS

By the end of 2009, 7,554 federally insured credit unions had almost $900 billion in total assets, 90 million members, and $575 billion in loans outstanding (Exhibit 16.11). The amount of credit union shares and assets outstanding has grown rapidly, even though the number of credit unions has shrunk by more than 35 percent since 1988, because many credit unions have merged with others. The surviving institutions have grown rapidly because they have exploited their access to new powers, such as the issuance of checkable (share-draft) accounts and credit card loans, and they have expanded their common bonds so each credit union can serve more members. Credit unions can often allow retirees in the area they serve to join even if they do not meet the credit union's common bond. In addition, they can stretch their common bonds by allowing family members of those who meet the common bond to join and by letting people retain their membership even if they move or change jobs and no longer meet the common bond requirement. Credit unions can also extend their common bonds through mergers and by extending their common bond requirement to additional groups that could not muster more than 3,000 members if they were to charter a separate credit union.

Exhibit 16.12 shows selected ratios for the credit union industry as a whole and for the smallest and largest credit unions. As you might expect, the smallest credit unions have higher operating costs, as a percentage of assets, than larger credit unions. The smallest ones have operating expenses that equal nearly 4 percent of assets each year, whereas the largest credit unions' operating expenses are less than 3 percent of assets. Because of their high operating costs, the smallest credit unions pay lower rates of return to their members who hold shares. Because of higher operating costs, lower fee income, and more loan delinquencies, however, smaller credit unions have substantially lower returns on average assets than larger credit unions. They also offer their members fewer liability services because almost all of their savings shares are in traditional (passbook-type) regular share accounts (Exhibit 16.13). Thus, members of small credit unions have a strong

EXHIBIT 16.11

Trends in Credit Union Assets, Members, Loans, Investments, and Profits

	1993	1997	2001	2005	2009
Credit union trends					
Numbers	12,317	11,238	9,984	8,695	7,554
Members (million)	63.5	71.4	79.4	84.8	89.9
Assets (billion $)	277.1	351.2	501.6	678.7	884.8
Share growth (%)	11.8	7.1	15.3	3.8	10.5
Loan growth (%)	9.2	8.6	7	10.6	1.14
Key ratios (% of assets)					
Loans	55	66.1	64.3	67.52	64.7
Investments	40.7	28.5	22.3	21.8	23.81
Capital (reserves)	9	11.1	10.8	11.2	9.81
Return (ROAA)	1.4	1.03	0.96	0.85	0.2
Memo: loan delinquency					
Rate delinquency (%)	1	1.01	0.84	0.73	1.82

Credit unions experienced constant growth in assets and membership even though the number of credit unions has fallen consistently in recent years. Because credit unions try to accommodate members' financial needs, they reduce their investments when loan demand exceeds share growth and increase their investments when share growth exceeds member loan growth.

Source: National Credit Union Administration, *2009 Year-End Statistics for Federally Insured Credit Unions,* Washington, DC, 2009.

incentive to merge or otherwise expand their common bonds so they can gain economies of scale and more services. If they reduce their costs by increasing their size, credit unions can pay higher dividend rates on their shares and/or charge lower loan rates to their members.

CREDIT UNION ASSETS

Credit unions have relatively simple balance sheets. Their assets consist primarily of loans to members. At year-end 2009, almost 65 percent of their assets consisted of loans (see Exhibits 16.11 and 16.13). Because their members are consumers, their loans are consumer and mortgage loans. Exhibit 16.13 shows that the most important type of credit union lending consists of first- and second-mortgage loans (35 percent of assets), followed closely by new- and used-auto loans (20 percent of assets). For many years credit unions did not make many mortgage loans, but they have increasingly done so to accommodate members' needs and to try to take advantage of an upward-sloping yield curve to earn extra income. Because many of their real estate–secured loans consist of first or second mortgages and many of their liabilities are of shorter maturity than their assets, credit unions are exposed to interest rate risk. Additional assets of credit unions consist of unsecured personal loans, credit card loans (at larger and more

EXHIBIT 16.12

Selected Ratios by Asset Size for Federally Insured Credit Unions (December 31, 2009)

	All Credit Unions	Small Credit Unions (Less Than $2 Million)	Large Credit Unions (Greater Than $500 Million)
Profitability (%)			
Return on average assets	0.20	−0.61	0.35
Cost of funds to average assets	1.74	1.02	1.91
Operating expenses to average assets	3.18	3.99	2.80
Provision for loan losses to average assets	1.11	0.53	1.30
Net operating expenses to average assets	3.21	3.62	3.10
Capital adequacy			
Capital to total assets	9.92	18.83	9.33
Asset quality			
Delinquent loans to assets	1.18	2.33	1.23
Asset/liability management			
Net long-term assets to total assets	31.49	2.96	34.12
As a percentage of total gross income			
Interest on loans (net of interest refunds)	66.80	77.62	67.62
Income from investments	11.70	14.44	11.10
Fee income	13.15	5.74	11.61

Source: National Credit Union Administration, *2009 Year-End Statistics for Federally Insured Credit Unions,* Washington, DC, 2009.

sophisticated credit unions), and investments. Credit unions held 24 percent of their assets in the form of investments at the end of 2009.

Credit union investments can take a variety of forms. Most invest in relatively safe government or government agency securities. Other credit union investments include bank or savings institution CDs and mutual fund shares. In addition, many credit unions invest large portions of their excess funds with one of the corporate central credit unions that serve credit unions (credit unions in each state can join the appropriate corporate central credit union that serves credit unions in that state). The central credit unions issue certificates of deposit or savings accounts to their member credit unions and utilize their acquired funds by making loans to credit unions that need additional liquidity or by investing their excess funds. In effect, the corporate central credit unions are the credit unions for credit unions.

The central credit unions are members of the U.S. Central Credit Union, the nation's only wholesale corporate credit union. The U.S. Central Credit Union has a commercial bank charter in the state of Kansas, so it has access to the nation's check payment system and can invest in a variety of ways—in the securities repo market or in the Eurodollar deposit market, for instance. The U.S. Central Credit Union can also lend money to credit unions, or their centrals, in the event they need excess liquidity, and it is empowered to borrow from the Central Liquidity Facility operated by the NCUA on behalf of its members. Thus, by investing idle funds in the credit union central system, credit unions can channel their funds across their state or across the nation to fill the liquidity needs of other credit unions. In a sense, credit unions in general operate like a giant branch bank through their network of central credit unions. They can also borrow from government agencies if necessary, through their centrals, and can use their centrals as intermediaries that help them clear checks and maintain any required reserves on their checkable (share-draft) deposits with the Federal Reserve.

Although many credit unions do not have to maintain reserve deposits, those that hold a large enough quantity of transactions deposits are subject to the same reserve requirements as commercial banks. Unlike banks, however, they can deposit their required reserves with their central credit unions, which in turn can maintain reserve accounts with the Federal Reserve.

CREDIT UNION LIABILITIES

Credit unions' liabilities consist primarily of member savings share accounts. Originally, shares were in the form of passbook savings accounts. However, since the 1970s and particularly since the DIDMCA was passed in 1980, credit unions have offered a variety of savings vehicles. Exhibit 16.13 shows that, whereas regular savings shares are still the largest source of credit union funds, they now account for only 23 percent of all member savings. Checkable share-draft accounts (credit unions' version of interest-paying NOW accounts), money market shares (which allow limited numbers of checks to be written and pay higher rates of interest, like MMDA), share certificates (similar to certificates of deposit at banks), and IRA or Keogh retirement savings accounts together account for a larger portion of credit unions' total liabilities than regular savings shares.

CREDIT UNION CAPITAL

Credit unions are mutual institutions that do not hold shareholders' equity. Instead, their net worth account consists of reserves and surplus and **undivided earnings**. They must set aside a portion of their earnings as reserves, until their reserves are sufficiently large relative to their assets. In addition, they may retain additional undivided earnings similar to retained earnings if their dividend payments and additions to reserves are less than their total net earnings.

Credit union capital requirements are similar to those of other thrift institutions at the national level. Because of the general national emphasis on improved capital holdings, credit unions have increased their capital in recent years. By year-end 2009, they held equity capital equal to 10 percent of their assets.

CREDIT UNION TRADE AND SERVICE ASSOCIATIONS

Because they are exempt from antitrust restrictions as a result of their nonoverlapping common bonds, credit unions have developed a large number of service organizations that allow them to cooperate greatly. Their major trade associations are the **Credit Union National Association (CUNA)**, which serves all credit unions, and the **National Association of Federal Credit Unions (NAFCU)**, which serves the interests of the generally larger, federally chartered credit unions.

EXHIBIT 16.13
Credit Union Assets and Liabilities (December 31, 2009)

	All Credit Unions		Small Credit Unions (less than $2 m)	Large Credit Unions (greater than $500 m)
	Millions	Percent	Percent	Percent
Assets				
Cash and equivalents	$ 67,710	8	23	7
Total investments	210,679	24	26	23
U.S. government obligations	7,053	1	0	1
Federal agency securities	107,589	12	0	15
Other investments	96,037	11	26	7
Total loans outstanding	572,437	65	51	67
Unsecured credit card loans	34,864	4	0	5
All other unsecured loans	25,553	3	13	2
New-vehicle loans	75,263	9	13	8
Used-vehicle loans	98,132	11	17	10
First mortgage real estate loans	217,100	25	1	28
Other real estate loans	92,418	10	1	11
Other loans	29,107	3	5	3
Allowance for loan losses	8,767	1	1	1
Other assets	42,299	5	1	5
Total assets	$884,753	100	100	100
Liabilities/equity/savings				
Total liabilities	$ 45,323	5	1	7
Total savings	752,667	85	80	84
Share drafts	85,090	10	1	9
Regular shares	199,772	23	69	19
Money market shares	158,661	18	1	21
Share certificates/CDs	225,790	26	7	26
IRA/Keogh accounts	73,388	8	1	9
All other shares and deposits	9,966	1	2	1
Total equity	86,763	10	19	9
Reserves	27,095	3	5	3
Undivided earnings	59,668	7	14	6
Total liabilities/equity/savings	$884,753	100	100	100

Source: National Credit Union Administration, *2009 Year-End Statistics for Federally Insured Credit Unions,* Washington, DC, 2009.

PEOPLE & EVENTS

Commercial Banks Versus Credit Unions

As credit unions gained more powers, banks increasingly came to view them as competitors that they wanted to discourage. When credit unions developed *share-draft*—that is, checkable savings—accounts that paid interest in the late 1970s, banks sued to prevent them from offering checkable accounts. A federal judge found that checkable accounts other than bank demand deposits were not legal, but allowed that Congress could pass a law making them legal. Congress did so in the DIDMCA of 1980.

Later, as credit unions tried to expand their common bonds to obtain larger memberships and economies of scale, banks sued to try to limit their ability to extend their common bonds. They won a case against an ATT credit union in North Carolina that had aggressively expanded its membership criteria. However, Congress quickly passed the Credit Union Membership Access Act in 1998, empowering the NCUA to expand the common bond requirement for credit unions starting in 1999. However, as soon as the NCUA proposed its new credit union membership rules, the American Bankers Association sued again to prevent them from becoming effective immediately. That suit did not get very far because, as in the case of share-draft accounts, Congress typically has been very friendly to credit unions.

Credit unions have more than 89 million members and are well organized in letting Congress know their wishes. In addition, they are nonprofit institutions with a good public image as service organizations, so Congress usually supports their endeavors. Congress had already relaxed common bond requirements when it allowed residential credit union common bonds to be used in areas that served low-income customers and customers who were not adequately serviced by more profit-oriented institutions. Thus, in general, Congress supported the interests of credit unions over the interests of commercial banks even when the banks succeed in winning court cases against credit unions.

However, banks are not done with their efforts to hamstring their potential competitors. They have consistently advocated that Congress take away credit unions' federal income tax exemption. Congress may eventually be sympathetic to the banks' argument on taxes because it is always on the lookout for ways to obtain more tax revenues. In defense, credit unions must emphasize the following points: (1) Unlike stockholder-owned institutions like commercial banks, they cannot sell stock to expand or acquire additional capital when needed and they cannot merge freely with other publicly traded firms; (2) unlike profit-oriented institutions, their main goal is to provide service to the public at low cost, and thus they do not raise prices when able just to make the maximum possible profit; and (3) they frequently provide financial services to people who otherwise might not have access to them because credit unions' common bond requirements and membership knowledge may allow them to make loans or issue checking accounts to people that other institutions might consider to be too risky.

Both associations have considerable influence with Congress because credit unions, in total, have more than 89 million members in the United States. That is one reason they may continue to receive more favorable tax and regulatory treatment than other depository institutions.

In addition to lobbying, however, their trade associations, particularly CUNA, have developed additional services for credit unions. For instance, CUNA supported the development of the central credit unions and the U.S. Central Credit Union, which help credit unions manage their liquidity, clear their checks, and obtain various investment and funds-management services. It also developed CUNA Mortgage to serve as a mortgage bank to pool and resell mortgages originated by credit unions, CUNA Mutual to provide deposit and credit insurance to credit union members, CUNA Strategic Services, Inc., to provide data-processing services to credit unions that are members, and a variety of other services. By providing services that can be used by many credit unions at low cost, CUNA has helped credit unions overcome the disadvantages of small individual size that otherwise might make it impossible for them to afford sophisticated services for their members.

16.4 THRIFT INSTITUTIONS AROUND THE GLOBE

The United States is not alone in having thrift institutions. Many foreign countries also have thrift institutions similar to those found in the United States. The United States, in fact, has often copied the form of financial institutions that were first developed in other countries. England, for instance, has *building and loan societies* that provide real estate finance much like U.S. savings and loan associations. In recent years, just like the United States, the British institutions have developed more retail banking powers and have become somewhat more like commercial banks—some have even converted from mutual to stock ownership.

The first credit union was developed in Germany, and mutual savings banks also developed in Europe before they were copied in the United States. Although commercial banks play a dominant role in banking in most European countries, many of the European savings banks also are large and economically quite important institutions: Some of them make a wide variety of loans and employ large numbers of people. Savings banks are quite popular in Scandinavia and other countries that favor mutual ownership forms for financial organizations. The International Savings Bank Association, headquartered in Finland, has member institutions in Norway, Sweden, Austria, Germany, Italy, Spain, the United Kingdom (building societies), the United States, and other countries. Although many savings banks make a broad range of loans, in many countries, including the United States, building societies, savings and loans, and other specialized mortgage lenders are popular because construction interests, potential borrowers, and their political friends perceived a need to make mortgage credit more readily available to a broader range of borrowers than might otherwise be the case.

DO YOU UNDERSTAND?

1. What are credit unions' most important assets and liabilities?
2. Why is the credit union common bond requirement changing? How and why is it changing?
3. How does the common bond requirement affect credit unions' credit risk?

16.5 FINANCE COMPANIES

Compared to thrift institutions, which tend to specialize in making certain types of loans (mortgages for savings institutions and consumer loans for credit unions), finance companies are more diverse. Many specialize in consumer finance, particularly small loans; others specialize in business loans, purchasing business accounts receivable (factoring), or leasing. Their business structure includes partnerships, privately owned corporations, publicly owned independent corporations, and wholly owned subsidiaries of manufacturers, commercial bank holding companies, life insurance companies, or other corporate entities.

Captive sales finance companies help finance goods sold by their parent companies. Other finance companies, such as GE Capital, finance goods sold by their parent company and a wide variety of other goods and services as well. Among the largest finance companies are **sales finance companies** that are "captives" of major retailers and auto manufacturers that help finance sales of their parents' goods. Examples are Ford Credit and Ally Financial (formerly General Motors Acceptance Corporation [GMAC]).

Other large finance companies are large factoring finance companies (such as CIT Group) that are subsidiaries of commercial bank holding companies and "lend" to their clients by buying and collecting their accounts receivable. Some large finance companies, such as GE Capital or IBM Global Financing, are owned by nonfinancial firms. Some of these finance companies started by financing goods sold by their parent organization, then broadened their lending and leasing activities. Other finance companies are independent lenders, which largely make personal loans to consumers and are known as **consumer finance companies**. Still other finance companies are diversified lending and leasing subsidiaries of major commercial bank holding companies. Thus, finance companies come in many varieties and are owned by many different types of parent organizations.

In contrast to depository institutions, finance companies obtain most of their funds in large amounts by borrowing from banks or selling securities in the capital markets rather than by issuing many small deposits. In addition, they often make many small loans rather than a few large ones. A few finance companies have industrial bank charters that allow them to accept deposits from the public. Others have started consumer banks, which accept deposits from the public and make loans to consumers but not to businesses.

Traditionally, finance companies lent to consumers. However, such lending is strictly regulated by state loan rate ceilings, debt collection restrictions, and many other consumer protection or credit control regulations. This strict regulation caused severe operating problems, especially for small finance companies. Thus, in recent years, finance companies increasingly consolidated; as a result of their consolidation, the number of finance companies has declined sharply and their average size has increased. They have also shifted their portfolios toward business lending, leasing, and second-mortgage credit, where regulations are less burdensome.

ASSETS OF FINANCE COMPANIES

Although some finance companies make only business loans or leases, and others make only consumer loans or leases, overall, finance companies divide their lending between consumer and business lending. Finance companies' loan and lease receivables usually amount to more than 70 percent of their net assets. Other assets consist of cash, time deposits, investment securities, buildings, and computers. Investment securities, which provide both a secondary source of liquidity and direct earnings, usually account for less than 10 percent of assets. Real assets, such as real estate, computers, and equipment, and loans made to foreign borrowers account for the remainder of finance companies' assets.

Types of receivables held by finance companies vary greatly. Some companies, such as GE Capital, make all types of loans to all types of borrowers. Others, such as factors or local consumer loan companies, specialize in only a few types of loans.

CONSUMER RECEIVABLES

Personal Loans. Traditionally, consumer-oriented finance companies have attempted to serve consumers by extending credit with more lenient terms, making smaller loans, taking more risk, and providing more personal service than other lenders. Consequently, they make many **personal loans**. Consumer finance companies, in fact, usually specialize in personal loans. Personal loans are the largest single category of finance company receivables at smaller finance companies; they are also important at large companies. Because of rising risks and costs of funds, in recent years many finance companies have increasingly made personal loans secured with second mortgages on home equity. Some home equity loans provide a revolving line of credit that can be used many times and often can be accessed with a credit card. However, most second-mortgage consumer loans are for a fixed term and must be renegotiated if the customer wishes to borrow more. Because of the growing importance of home equity–secured loans, finance companies' real estate–secured loans have grown rapidly in recent years.

Automobile Credit. Finance company subsidiaries of the major automobile manufacturers make a large number of loans to finance the new and used automobiles their dealers sell. Because the business of auto manufacturers' finance company subsidiaries is to help manufacturers profit by selling cars, they can often provide credit on more favorable terms (with 2.9 or even 0 percent financing) than consumers can find elsewhere. Smaller finance companies do little new-car financing because they do not profit from auto sales per se. However, they often finance consumers' used-car purchases. Increasingly, finance companies provided lease financing for new-car acquisitions.

Mobile Home Credit. Finance companies expanded rapidly in the mobile home credit market in the early 1970s because such credit was relatively profitable. However, in the mid-1970s many finance companies experienced substantial losses from defaults on their mobile home loans. Meanwhile, their costs of funds rose. As a result, many finance companies slowed their rate of expansion of mobile home lending, and others abandoned the field entirely. However, some companies with a large stake in business credit financing for mobile home dealers continued to make such loans. Therefore, mobile home loans continue to provide an important use of assets for some finance companies.

Revolving Consumer Installment Credit. Revolving credit has become increasingly important to finance companies. Once a finance company extends credit on a revolving basis, a consumer can borrow up to his or her credit limit many times. Revolving credit origination costs are less costly per dollar of credit extended than small loans. It also may be offered through electronic funds transfer systems and can be secured through home equity lines of credit. Many finance companies also offer revolving credit to serve retailers' needs.

Several major finance companies operate **private-label credit** plans for retailers. Here all correspondence with the consumer is carried on using the retailer's name. However, the finance company is responsible for approving all credit card applications. In addition, the finance company bills the customers, receives all interest revenues, and incurs all losses (above a predetermined amount) applicable to credit card purchases made at the retailer's store. Thus, under such plans, the consumer who uses a credit card appears to borrow from the retailer but actually borrows from the finance company.

By offering a private-label credit plan, the retailer is able to gain customer loyalty by offering his or her own credit card plan. In return for providing the expertise and personnel needed to run the credit operations, the finance company usually receives a fee equal to a stated percentage of credit sales, compensation for some losses, and interest revenues on credit balances extended under the plan.

Revolving credit has been one of the most rapidly growing areas of finance company lending in recent years. Finance companies developed dealer plans, offered credit cards directly to their customers, and offered revolving credit lines tied to second mortgages. Because such credit is compatible with electronic funds transfer systems and reduces the overhead costs of lending, it is likely to continue to grow.

Other Consumer Installment Loans.   Many consumer loans are used to finance purchases of retail goods other than automobiles and mobile homes. Many finance companies obtain potential personal loan customers and solidify dealer relationships by buying consumer receivables from furniture and appliance dealers. Customers who must borrow to finance a furniture or appliance purchase may also need to borrow to finance other consumer expenditures. Many such borrowers are in the stage of their life cycle where they are fairly heavily indebted. In particular, they may be young people who anticipate rising incomes in the future and have strong needs to buy particular goods (houses, cars, washers and dryers, furniture, and so on) now. Such customers may be prime candidates for finance company personal loans in the near future. Thus, finance companies buy retail credit contracts and later usually try to make the borrowers aware that they can obtain additional cash credit if they need it. Because of the growth of revolving credit plans at retailers and the fact that consumer installment loans of other types are relatively small and thus not very profitable, these loans have declined at finance companies in recent years.

REAL ESTATE LENDING

For several years, the fastest-growing area of finance company lending was real estate lending secured by second mortgages. Finance companies rapidly expanded their **second-mortgage lending** for several reasons. First, inflation increased both consumers' demands for credit and the equity value of people's homes. For many people, home equity became their largest single asset. The only way they could tap that asset, however, was either to sell their homes or to borrow against their equity with second mortgages. This phenomenon increased the demand for second mortgages. Second, revisions in consumer protection laws, particularly the Federal Bankruptcy Reform Act of 1978, made it difficult to collect defaulted debts if the debts were unsecured. Thus, bankruptcy filings increased greatly. Although personal loans often are discharged in bankruptcy and are hard to collect in general, second mortgages provide excellent security for finance company loans in the event of default. As a result, losses on such loans are very low compared to those on unsecured personal loans. Consequently, many finance companies converted much of their personal lending to second-mortgage lending. Third, by making larger, longer-maturity loans, finance companies could obtain a higher rate of return (*net of costs*) on their loans. At the same time, they could offer lower rates and larger amounts of credit to consumers and thereby attract more customers. Finally, second mortgages have substantial tax advantages relative to other consumer credit. The 1986 income tax reforms phased out consumers' ability to deduct consumer credit interest payments from their federal income tax; however, mortgage interest, including limited amounts of interest paid on second mortgages, retained its tax-deductible status. As you probably surmised, finance companies that were actively involved in real estate lending suffered substantial losses during the housing crisis that began in 2006.

BUSINESS CREDIT

Business financing activities of finance companies include the wholesale financing of inventories held by businesses prior to sale, the retail financing of durable goods purchased by firms, lease financing, and other business financing—including the financing of customer receivables held by firms or factored (sold) to the finance company. Business credit in general has expanded much more rapidly than consumer lending in recent years. Consumer lending is highly regulated, whereas business lending is not. As a result, business lending has been more profitable than consumer lending. The various types of business lending by finance companies are described in the following sections.

Wholesale Paper. **Wholesale paper** is generated when a finance company helps a dealer finance the purchase of goods. For instance, retail dealers must pay for the automobiles or washers and dryers kept in stock. Dealers need the stock for display purposes and to guarantee prompt delivery, yet they receive no cash for the goods until they are sold.

A finance company may provide a dealer with interim financing called **wholesale** or **floor-plan financing**. A floor-plan financing arrangement is one in which the finance company pays the manufacturer when the goods are delivered to the dealer. The finance company then holds a lien on the goods as long as the dealer keeps them in inventory. The dealer pays interest on the value of goods financed by floor-plan financing, and when the goods are sold, the dealer uses the proceeds of the sale to repay the finance company.

Because finance companies have close ties with auto or retail goods dealers for whom they provide floor-plan financing, they may also provide retail financing for the consumers who buy the dealers' goods. In that way, their wholesale financing activities help generate retail financing business, and vice versa, because a dealer is more likely to do business with a finance company that also provides retail financing for his or her customers.

Retail Paper. Sales of goods used for business purposes may be financed with installment sales contracts (such as auto credit contracts) provided by finance companies. Business purchases of vans, light or heavy trucks, and other commercial vehicles are often financed this way. In addition, retail sales of industrial and farm equipment to businesses and farmers may be financed with installment contracts.

Lease Paper.   In recent years, leasing of durable goods has been popular for a number of reasons. First, accelerated depreciation and investment tax credits make it profitable for a firm in a high tax bracket to buy and lease durable investment goods at favorable rates compared to firms in low or zero tax brackets, which cannot profit as much from possible tax savings. Second, an institution that leases a durable good need not borrow the funds required to buy it outright. Third, a lessor retains an equity interest in the good and can regain possession of it more easily and cheaply if the lessee defaults on payments than would be possible if the good were sold under an installment sales contract. This advantage is particularly valuable because consumer protection and bankruptcy laws have given far greater protection to consumers and businesses that fall behind on their debt payments. Fourth, leases can be written so that the good is available when desired, and the good need not be disposed of by a purchaser who is relatively unsophisticated in the marketing of used durable goods. Finally, the lessor can maintain the good under an *operating lease*, which provides valuable time and cost savings for the lessee.

In summary, leasing often provides greater tax advantages, protection of ownership rights, and financial flexibility or convenience. Consequently, many finance companies have rapidly expanded their leasing activities in recent years.

Other Business Credit.   Other business credit makes up a substantial portion of finance companies' total assets. Two forms of that credit are particularly interesting because they illustrate the long and close relationship that many finance companies maintain with business firms.

First, the largest single source of other business credit is loans on commercial accounts receivable. These are secured by the accounts receivable of the business firm to which the finance company extends credit. In many cases, a finance company takes possession of the accounts receivable as collateral for its loan and collects payments on the accounts as they come due. As it collects payments, it reduces the loan balance its business customer owes.

Second, factored accounts receivable are accounts due that are directly purchased from the business firm by the finance company. The purchase price is discounted to allow for potential losses and also to allow for the fact that the finance company will not receive full payment until some time in the future. To make an adequate assessment of potential losses and repayment lags, a finance company dealing in **factoring** must have a close working knowledge of the operations of a business firm and the nature of its customers.

Once factored, the accounts receivable become the property of the finance company. It is its responsibility to collect all remaining balances due on factored accounts receivable. In return for selling its accounts receivable at a discount, the selling business firm immediately obtains cash from the finance company. Most of the largest factoring firms are owned by commercial bank holding companies because banks have considerable expertise in evaluating accounts receivable.

SECURITIZATION OF RECEIVABLES

In the past 15 years finance companies have securitized an increasing portion of their receivables. Recall from Chapter 13 that, by securitizing assets, loan originators can reduce financing costs, reduce their interest rate risk, and earn servicing fee income. As asset-backed securities have become more popular in financial markets, finance companies have securitized leases as well as credit card loans, automobile loans, and automobile leases. Larger finance companies may securitize as much as 25 percent or more of some types of receivables. Shorter-term and nonstandard loans are less frequently securitized than longer-term standardized loans (like real estate, automobile, mobile home, or business equipment loans and leases). Small business loans and small personal installment loans are less likely to be securitized than larger and more standardized types of loans and leases.

LIABILITIES AND NET WORTH OF FINANCE COMPANIES

Net Worth.   One of the most striking aspects of finance company balance sheets is that their overall net worth is very small relative to their total assets. Their total capital, surplus, and undivided profits account for around 10 percent of total assets. Thus finance companies are highly leveraged institutions. Consequently, their income can fluctuate substantially if they experience loan losses or if interest rate changes have different effects on their assets and liabilities.

Because finance companies must have adequate capital so they can maintain their credit ratings and borrow easily from banks, many smaller finance companies back their asset holdings with much higher capital ratios than large finance companies. Only those with strong parent companies (such as GE, Ford, or IBM) are likely to have capital ratios below 10 percent of assets. Smaller finance companies may hold capital equal to 25 percent or more of their total assets.

Finance Company Debt.   Even though most finance company assets are relatively short term, some, such as leases and certain installment credit contracts, are long-term assets. On the liability side of the balance sheet, finance companies hold a mixture of both short-term and long-term debt. However, the major portion of their liabilities, like the major portions of their assets, usually consists of short-term obligations. These may take several forms.

Many small finance companies that do not have access to national capital markets borrow from banks to obtain a reliable and relatively low-cost source of funds. Large finance companies often use bank lines of credit to back up their commercial paper and thereby obtain higher ratings on their commercial paper. Others may borrow seasonally from banks or even obtain long-term loans. Overall, bank loans are less than 3 percent of liabilities of finance companies, but they amount to more than 40 percent for small finance companies.

Finance companies obtain almost 20 percent of their funds by issuing **commercial paper**. Because commercial paper is unsecured, only large, top-rated borrowers have direct access to that market. Less well-known issuers must either place their commercial paper through dealers for a small fee or obtain their short-term financing from other sources. Commercial paper was one of the most rapidly growing sources of finance company funds since 1980. Recall from Chapter 7, however, that the commercial paper market shrank dramatically in response to the 2007–2009 financial crisis. As a result, some finance companies found it difficult to raise the necessary funds and had to scale back their lending.

One valuable source of credit for smaller companies is **transfer credit** in the form of funding provided by their larger parent companies. Transfer credit from finance companies' parents accounts for 7 to 8 percent of their total liabilities.

A few finance companies have outstanding deposit liabilities and thrift certificates among their other liabilities. Finance companies may sell debt obligations directly to the public, provided that those debt issues are approved by securities regulators. In the past, finance companies often have had difficulty getting small-denomination debt issues approved because such debt certificates would compete with savings certificates issued by depository institutions. However, limited amounts of small-denomination debt have been sold to the public by finance companies as thrift certificates.

In about 20 states, finance companies can, if they meet certain requirements, obtain charters as **industrial banks**. Industrial banks can accept savings deposits and make loans for specified purposes, such as consumer loans. By obtaining charters as industrial banks, finance companies are better able to compete for the relatively low-cost sources of funds that are available to banks, credit unions, and savings institutions. Nonetheless, because the largest finance companies primarily obtain their funds from other sources, deposit liabilities and thrift certificates outstanding account for a very small percentage of liabilities for all finance companies combined.

Long-term debt is one of the largest liabilities of large finance companies. However, long-term debt waxes and wanes in relative importance as a source of finance company funds. When interest rates are low, finance companies may issue more long-term debt. By doing so, they hope to hold down future increases in their costs of funds if interest rates should rise. They may also sell long-term debt to reduce their interest rate risk when they acquire long-term loans or lease contracts. Finance companies' capital market debt (*debt owed mkt., n.e.c.*) amounts to nearly 40 percent of their assets.

REGULATION OF FINANCE COMPANIES

Finance company consumer lending is heavily regulated, although finance company business lending generally is not. The reason is that businesspeople are presumed to be better able to act in their own interest than consumers. However, finance company business and consumer lending can both be affected by regulations affecting mergers, branching, and market entry.

Rate Ceilings.   The most influential regulations on finance company operations are those affecting rates that can be charged on loans of different types, sizes, and maturities. Most states have regulations that limit rates charged by consumer or sales finance companies. Frequently, higher rates are permitted on small loans and short-maturity loans. In addition, **rate ceilings** may vary with the type of loan or type of lender. Finance companies often are allowed to charge higher rates than other lenders. However, they also are frequently allowed to make only small loans. If the rate ceilings are too restrictive, consumer finance companies leave the market, as they have in several states.

Sales finance companies, however, can continue to operate in states with low rate ceilings. They can compensate for losses in interest revenues by discounting the consumer finance paper they buy from retail sales outlets. By paying less than face value for consumer credit contracts, sales finance companies can earn a profitable rate of return on their invested funds.

Creditor Remedy Regulation.   States or the federal government impose various restrictions on finance companies' abilities to collect on delinquent or defaulted debts. These restrictions include limitations on creditors' abilities to charge late fees or to garnishee (i.e., to collect a portion of an employee's wages from an employer) a borrower who falls behind on payments. They also may require that certain legal processes be followed and that the lender bear the full expense of collecting on the bad debts.

Creditor remedy restrictions are of particular importance to finance companies that serve customers who are likely to default or fall behind in their payments. If finance companies have few remedies to induce customers to pay their debts (or few remedies to recover the money if a customer stops paying entirely), they will lose more whenever a customer defaults. This means that they must either stop serving high-risk borrowers or charge higher rates to make up for increased operating expenses and losses.

Branching, Chartering, and Merger Restrictions. State departments of financial institutions and banks are responsible for enforcing restrictions on finance company chartering and branching within their states. Convenience and advantage restrictions require a finance company that wishes to organize or form a new office to show that the office offers a convenience to the local community and is to the community's advantage. Often such restrictions reduce competition by preventing new entrants from establishing offices in a market if that market is already served by an existing finance company. Although local market entry can be restricted by antitrust or convenience and advantage regulations, no federal regulations prevent finance companies from operating in many states. Thus, the major finance companies have a nationwide presence. Because of this, in the past many bank holding companies acquired finance companies to gain access to interstate markets.

Consumer Protection Regulations. Since 1968, Congress and various state legislatures passed a large number of consumer protection bills. Many of the regulations in these bills had a considerable impact on the costs and operations of consumer finance companies. The most important regulations include Regulation Z (truth-in-lending) and the 1978 revisions in the bankruptcy laws. Regulation Z made finance companies disclose their annual percentage rates rather than *add-on* or *discount* loan rates that understated the true rates charged. Subsequently, finance companies lost some of their market share in the consumer credit markets to banks and credit unions. Nonetheless, even though many consumers acknowledge that finance companies are not the cheapest place to borrow, many still patronize them. Because many finance companies offer fast, convenient, and personal service and grant loans on lenient terms, they attract loyal customers who are not highly sensitive to interest rate differences.

The liberalization of federal consumer bankruptcy laws in October 1979 gave increased protection to consumers who declared bankruptcy. Under the law, consumers who declared bankruptcy could eliminate their debts and still retain many thousands of dollars of their assets. Unsecured creditors, such as finance companies, rarely were able to collect their debts once an insolvent debtor declared bankruptcy under the new law. Consequently, the law substantially increased potential finance company losses.

Because of the liberalization of bankruptcy law, finance companies could not afford to take as many risks as before without raising their loan rates, which they often could not do because of rate ceilings. As a result, many finance companies switched to second-mortgage lending because larger loans allowed them to increase their returns, net of operating costs, without raising their loan rates. Furthermore, the security provided by second mortgages reduced the finance companies' losses substantially.

The creation of the Bureau for Consumer Financial Protection (BCFP) by the Dodd-Frank Wall Street Reform and Consumer Protection Act of 2010 (see Chapter 15) will likely have a significant impact on the consumer protection regulations faced by finance companies. At this early stage in the bureau's existence, however, it is too early to know the extent of its impact.

DO YOU UNDERSTAND?

1. What types of finance companies exist and what does each do?
2. How do finance companies fund their operations?
3. Why are good credit ratings important to finance companies?
4. What regulations have caused finance companies to deemphasize their unsecured personal lending?

SUMMARY OF LEARNING OBJECTIVES

1 Discuss the historical development of savings institutions. Thrift institutions were established to serve the needs of savers who had relatively small deposits.

2 Describe the balance-sheet composition of savings institutions. Savings institutions (savings associations and savings banks) are the mortgage-oriented thrifts that hold a large portion of their assets in mortgage loans or mortgage-backed securities.

3 Explain the problems faced by savings institutions in the 1980s, how Congress addressed the problems, and the impact of the problems and regulations on the industry today. After suffering many losses in the 1980s as a result of excessive interest rate risk, savings associations received new regulators, had to comply with stricter accounting and capital requirements, and reduced their risk taking. As a result, the industry is financially much stronger than it was in the 1980s, when many institutions were weakened because they took too much interest rate risk or credit risk.

4 Describe the operations and organizational structure of credit unions. Credit unions make consumer loans to their members, each of which must have a savings deposit at the credit union and share a *common bond*. All credit unions and many savings institutions are *mutual* institutions that are technically owned by their depositors or members rather than stockholders.

5 Explain the various types of finance companies and the roles they play in providing credit. Finance companies are highly diverse institutions. They can be consumer finance companies, sales finance companies, factors, or leasing companies. The major roles of finance companies include making personal loans to consumers, helping retailers to finance inventory, assisting with equipment leasing, and financing a firm's accounts receivable.

KEY TERMS

Building societies
Thrift institutions
Finance companies
Mutual institution
Savings and loan
  associations (SLAs)
Stock association

Federal Home Loan Bank
  Advances
Federal Home Loan Bank
  Board (FHLBB)
Office of Thrift
  Supervision (OTS)
FDIC-SAIF

Bad-debt deduction
Reverse repos
Common bond
  requirements
National Credit Union
  Administration
  (NCUA)

National Credit Union
  Share Insurance Fund
  (NCUSIF)
Central Liquidity Facility
  (CLF)
Undivided earnings

Credit Union National
  Association (CUNA)
National Association of
  Federal Credit Unions
  (NAFCU)

Captive sales finance
  companies
Sales finance companies
Consumer finance
  companies
Personal loans

Private-label credit
Second-mortgage lending
Wholesale paper
Wholesale financing
Floor-plan financing
Factoring

Commercial paper
Transfer credit
Industrial banks
Rate ceilings

QUESTIONS AND PROBLEMS

1. Why were each of the U.S. thrift institutions started, and when? Why are they now greater competitors with commercial banks than they were originally?

2. What were the two major types of problems that caused savings institution failures during the 1980s?

3. How did regulatory weakness contribute to some of the savings institutions' problems?

4. What changes in market interest rates can hurt savings institutions? Why? What can savings institutions do to minimize their problems? Explain the kind of market interest rate changes that might help savings institutions.

5. What are (a) the major regulations and (b) the major regulatory bodies that affect savings institution operations? How do these regulations and regulatory bodies affect them?

6. How have savings institutions altered their deposit and liability structures to reduce their interest rate risk exposure in recent years? Would you say they have totally eliminated their interest rate risk? Why or why not?

7. How do finance companies differ from banks and thrift institutions?

8. Why have finance companies shifted from consumer to real estate and business lending in recent years?

9. Why have second mortgages grown in popularity with finance company consumer lenders?

10. What effect have growing consumer credit regulations had on finance companies' lines of business? What about their future opportunities?

11. How can finance companies manage their interest rate, liquidity, and credit risks? What are their advantages or disadvantages vis-à-vis depository institutions?

12. What are the major asset and liability accounts for credit unions?

13. What are share-drafts? Why are they important to credit unions?

14. What are the advantages and disadvantages of the credit union common bond requirement?

15. Compare and contrast the retail operations of a commercial bank with those of a typical credit union in operation today. Taking into account the expanded powers of credit unions, how will they compare in the future?

16. Individual credit unions are very small in size. If there is going to be increased competition in the consumer credit market and greater regulatory equalization among competing institutions, how do you expect credit unions to survive?

17. What is the U.S. Central Credit Union? Why is it important to the future development of the credit union industry?

INTERNET EXERCISE

The major U.S. regulators compile extensive information on the thrift industry. The FDIC http://www.fdic.gov/ site is the primary source of information because it collects detailed statistics on all federally insured thrift institutions. The main source of information on finance companies is the Federal Reserve. Every month it publishes information on finance companies in the Federal Reserve *Bulletin* and a G.20 statistical release, which is available through the Fed's Web site on the Internet, http://www.federalreserve.gov. The main source of information on credit unions is the National Credit Union Administration, which is their primary regulator and supervises their insurer. The NCUA Web site can be found at http://www.ncua.gov. It publishes regular NEWS items on current events as well as historical data on credit union balance sheets and income, based on call report data.

1. Go to the FDIC Web site, access its databank (www.fdic.gov/databank/index. html), and find the most recent quarterly data on savings institutions. Find out how many savings institutions were insured by the FDIC in the last reporting period and how many assets they held.

2. Go to the Federal Reserve Web site, access its statistical releases, find the latest G.20 release, and find information on the terms of auto loans. Find the latest interest rate, maturity, loan-to-value ratios, and average loan sizes for new- and used-auto loans. Which has the highest loan rate, which has the longest maturity, which has the lowest average balance, and which has the highest loan size? Given what you know, explain why the loan rate is higher on used- than on new-auto loans.

3. Access the NCUA Web site and find the most recent NCUA NEWS or Quick Facts publication that provides information from the latest credit union call reports. How many credit unions are there, and how have their numbers changed from the previous year? How many members and assets do they have, and how have their members and assets changed from the previous year? If the number of credit unions, members, and assets are not all changing in the same manner (i.e., all increasing or all decreasing by about the same percentage amounts), how do you explain the disparity?

Insurance Companies and Pension Funds

Insurance companies protect people and companies from the financial consequences of events whose risks are actuarially determinable. For those buying insurance, the financial health of the insurance company is the single most important purchase criterion because an insurance contract is a promise by the insurance company to pay the insured if an event occurs. Examples of such events include the unexpected death of a family member, an automobile accident, the crash of a passenger jet, or an extended hospital stay.

INSURANCE HAS BEEN DESCRIBED AS "the product everyone buys, but no one wants to use." In the same vein, insurance contracts are often described as "least-read best sellers." Everybody buys insurance, but few people ever take the time to read the contract unless, of course, a loss occurs.

Although insurance is often taken for granted, try to imagine a world without it. The death of the family bread-winner might condemn a family to poverty without life insurance proceeds to replace the lost income. Want to buy a new car or a home? Then you had better have enough cash to pay the full purchase price because there's no property insurance available to insure the car or home, which usually serves as collateral for the loan. What about the risk of being sued? Are you willing to operate a motor vehicle knowing that if you are negligent and injure or kill someone you don't have liability insurance to protect against a lawsuit?

Insurance is a necessity for individuals, small businesses, and large corporations. Insurance has had a prominent impact on some major recent events that occurred in the United States. The 9/11 terrorist attacks and Hurricane Katrina created the largest insured losses for human-made and natural disasters in history. The Insurance Information Institute estimates that insurers paid $39.4 billion and $41.1 billion

(in 2009 dollars), respectively, in claims following these events. The financial crisis of 2007–2009 was not limited to banks, mortgage lenders, and investment companies. Without a government bailout, American International Group (AIG), one of the largest insurers in the United States, would have become insolvent.

The company issued credit default swaps, derivatives that guaranteed mortgage-backed securities consisting of substandard mortgages, through its financial products division. Major health insurance reform was enacted by Congress in 2010 with passage of the Patient Protection and Affordable Care Act. ◼

This chapter covers insurance, insurance companies, and pensions. Insurance and retirement plans play an important role in providing economic security. They are also important in the capital formation and financial intermediation process. The purposes of this chapter include (1) to explain how the insurance mechanism works; (2) to provide an overview of the insurance industry, including the market structure, organizational structures, types of coverages sold, and asset holdings; (3) to discuss the role and importance of insurers as financial intermediaries; (4) to provide an overview of the field of retirement plans, including Social Security and private pensions; and (5) to discuss the role and importance of pension funds as financial intermediaries. ■

LEARNING OBJECTIVES

1 Explain how the insurance mechanism works, including the concepts of pooling and risk transfer, and the requisites of privately insurable risks.

2 Define *objective risk* and explain the ways in which insurers can reduce the objective risk of their operations.

3 Discuss the economic structure of the insurance industry, the various forms of organizations that operate in the insurance industry, and how and why the insurance industry is regulated.

4 Describe the major products marketed by life and health insurers.

5 Describe the major products marketed by property and liability insurers.

6 Describe the balance sheet of life and health insurers and property and liability insurers, and explain the differences in their asset holdings.

7 Discuss retirement plans, including the various types of government and private pension plans and the regulation of retirement plans.

17.1 INSURANCE

Individuals and businesses face **risk**, which is uncertainty concerning the occurrence of loss. Risk takes many forms, including the risk of premature death or poor health, the risk of damage to property, the risk of legal liability, and the risk of individuals outliving their accumulated assets. Certain risks can simply be avoided. Other risks, however, must be effectively managed. Methods of dealing with these risks include retention, loss control, and risk transfer.

Use of *retention* means that the individual or business is responsible for the loss. An uninsured risk and the physical damage deductible on your automobile collision insurance are examples of retention. Loss control includes any effort to reduce the frequency and severity of loss. Loss control can take many forms. Some examples include seat belts, sprinkler systems, smoke detectors, nonflammable building materials, and ergonomically designed workstations. Finally, risk may be transferred to another party through a contract. The most widely used form of contractual risk transfer is insurance.

THE INSURANCE MECHANISM

Insurance is the transfer of a pure risk to an entity that pools the risk of loss and provides payment if a loss occurs. **Risk transfer** means shifting the responsibility of bearing the risk from one party to another party. **Pooling** means that losses suffered by a small number of insureds are spread over the entire group of insureds so insurance purchasers substitute the average loss (a small amount) in place of the uncertainty that they might suffer a large loss. **Pure risks** are situations in which two outcomes are possible: loss or no loss. Examples of pure risk include the risk of poor health, the risk of premature death, the risk of legal liability, and the risk of damage to property. **Speculative risks** have three possible outcomes: loss, no loss, or gain. The *entity* that pools the risk and provides indemnification is usually a private insurance company; however, for some risks, government involvement is necessary to insure the risks.

Insurance benefits society in several important ways. First, it reduces fear and worry because if a loss occurs the insurer provides a payment to mitigate the loss. Insurance also provides an incentive for loss control because insurance premiums are determined by the chance of loss, and loss control reduces the chance of loss. Insurance helps facilitate credit by protecting collateral pledged to secure loans. This benefit is especially important in commerce because it helps facilitate the shipment of raw materials and finished goods. Finally, the insurance industry plays an important role in capital formation. Insurance companies collect small amounts of money from many insurance purchasers. They pool these funds and then make large blocks of funds available in the capital markets.

INSURERS AND OBJECTIVE RISK

If individuals and businesses are unable to bear individual pure risk exposures and transfer them away, how can insurance companies bear the risk of hundreds or thousands of pure risk exposures? The risk that an insurer faces once it has accepted the transfer of risk from insurance purchasers is called objective risk. **Objective risk** is the deviation between actual losses and expected losses. Insurance is priced to cover the cost of expected losses and expenses. If loss levels are as predicted, the insurance mechanism works well. If loss levels are greater than expected, the insurer loses money. If catastrophic losses occur, the solvency of the insurer may be threatened.

METHODS OF REDUCING OBJECTIVE RISK

Insurance companies use an important mathematical principle, the law of large numbers, to reduce the objective risk of their operations. The **law of large numbers** states that, as the number of insured risks increases, the deviation between actual and expected results declines. A simple coin-flipping example demonstrates this mathematical principle. If you flip a fair coin twice, you might get two heads or two tails. However, if you continue flipping the coin, the result grows closer to 50 percent heads and 50 percent tails as the number of repetitions increases. Although an insurance company's business risk increases as more units are insured (there are more potential claims to pay), objective risk declines as the sample size increases.

A second way in which insurance companies reduce objective risk is through careful underwriting. **Underwriting** is the selection and classification of insurable

9/11 and Katrina: Insurance Coverage Disputes

While the phrase *insurance policy* is popular, *insurance contract* is more appropriate, especially when disputes over terminology arise. Indeed, many claims arising out of the two largest loss-causing events in the last 15 years hinged upon meaning assigned to terminology used in insurance contracts. The interpretation of key words had billion-dollar implications for property owners and insurers.

On September 11, 2001, terrorists hijacked two planes and slammed into the World Trade Center towers. Hours later, both towers collapsed. Was the attack on the World Trade Center one event, or two separate events? Although it may sound like a trivial question, it was crucial for the owner of the property, Silverstein Properties, Inc. Silverstein insured the two towers for $3.5 billion, using several insurers to obtain the necessary capacity. After the towers were leveled, Silverstein sought to collect $7.0 billion, arguing that two separate events had occurred. Insurers, of course, claimed the attacks constituted a single occurrence.

This settlement dispute went to court. The first trial ended in April 2004, in which the federal court determined that, under the form used by several insurers, loss of the two towers constituted a single event. These insurers were ordered to pay $1.8 billion, the aggregate per-occurrence limit of liability. This award was upheld in the U.S. Court of Appeals in October 2006. However, the same court ruled that under the form used by another group of insurers, the attacks constituted two separate events. These insurers, who provided about $1.0 billion of property coverage, were ordered to pay the limit of liability twice ($1.0 billion for each

tower) because the court held that two separate events had occurred.

On August 28 and 29, 2005, Hurricane Katrina ravaged the U.S. Gulf Coast. Especially hard-hit were Mississippi and Louisiana. In the wake of the storm, a number of coverage disputes arose between property owners and insurers. Some issues at the heart of many of the claims were: attributing loss causation to wind (covered) and flood (excluded), the wording used in the flood exclusion, and insurer's denial of claims when two or more perils concurrently cause a loss and at least one peril is excluded (the "concurrent causation" exclusion).

Insurers often exclude perils where the resulting losses could be catastrophic. Homeowners insurance, for example, commonly excludes floods and earthquakes. After Hurricane Katrina, property owners began to file claims with their insurers. But was the water damage caused by flooding (excluded), or did hurricane winds damage the structure, thus permitting wind-driven rain to damage the premises (covered)? Many homes were so badly damaged it was difficult to determine the actual cause of loss.

Disputes also arose where flooding was the obvious cause of loss. Many homes were not flooded initially, but later were flooded when the levees failed. A watertight definition of *flood* and/or a clearly worded concurrent causation exclusion permitted some insurers to deny liability for claims. Claimants had some success against insurers that did not use *regardless of cause* wording in their flood exclusion and against insurers where the concurrent causation exclusion wording was deemed to be ambiguous.

risks. Although insurance agents and brokers solicit applications and coverages for prospective insureds, there is no guarantee that the insurer will agree to insure the risk. Insurance underwriters review applications and decide which applicants are acceptable. Underwriters also assign acceptable risks to underwriting classes. For example, an auto insurer may have three categories: superior, average, and substandard. Based on underwriting information, the applicant may be assigned to one of these categories or the application may be rejected.

Another way of reducing objective risk is to make the insured pay a portion of any loss that occurs. Insurers use a variety of approaches to make the insured participate in the loss. The most common loss-sharing provision is a deductible. **Deductibles** make the insured responsible for the first portion of any loss that occurs. Deductibles are used in property insurance, health insurance, and disability income insurance. Another loss-sharing provision is called **coinsurance**. In the case of health insurance, coinsurance is simple loss sharing after the deductible has been satisfied. In the case of property insurance, if the insured does not carry adequate insurance, coinsurance requires the insured to pay a portion of the loss. Insurance policy exclusions and limits on certain types of losses also make the insured bear some or all of the loss.

A final way in which insurers reduce objective risk is through the use of **reinsurance**. Just as individuals and businesses purchase insurance, insurers can also shift some of the risk that they have insured to another insurance company. This process, called *reinsurance*, is crucial for some insurers and in certain lines of insurance where objective risk is greater. Reinsurance can be arranged in several ways. For example, an insurer and a reinsurer may share premiums and losses based on a predetermined percentage basis, such as 50–50 or 25–75. Alternatively, the original insurer may place a limit on losses, and the reinsurer is required only to pay losses that exceed that limit. Although the primary insurer is ultimately responsible for losses, reinsurance recoveries help mitigate the fear of greater-than-expected losses. Reinsurers were crucial in paying for losses from the 9/11 terrorist attacks.

REQUIREMENTS OF PRIVATELY INSURABLE RISKS

Certain conditions must be present before a private company can insure a risk. First, there must be a large number of similar exposure units. This requirement is necessary so that similar exposures can be placed in the same underwriting category and losses can be predicted based on the law of large numbers. Second, losses that occur should be accidental and unintentional. As the law of large numbers assumes random events, this condition is important. Third, the losses must not be catastrophic. Fourth, losses should be determinable and measurable. Fifth, the chance of loss must be calculable. Finally, the premium for insurance must be affordable.

A review of insurer practices and contractual provisions demonstrates how these requirements are satisfied. Insurers use underwriting categories to group similar risks. For example, one underwriting category might be wood-frame dwellings, whereas another may be masonry homes. The underwriting category for an auto insurer may be female drivers ages 30–40, whereas a life insurer may group all standard male applicants age 25 in one underwriting class. Heterogeneous loss exposures must seek specialty insurers. For example, a famous racehorse or a professional quarterback's arm may be insured through Lloyd's of London.

Losses that are intentionally caused and perils where the intent is to destroy property (e.g., war) are usually excluded from coverage under insurance contracts. To help assure that only fortuitous losses are covered, insurers often require the insured to bear a portion of any loss through a deductible or other loss-sharing provision. Catastrophic losses are also usually excluded. Floods and earthquakes could have a simultaneous impact on thousands of insureds. Compounding the problem is the fact that only insureds susceptible to these risks (e.g., insureds who live in floodplains or near fault lines) purchase the insurance. Insureds are often required to pay additional premiums and assume responsibility for more of the loss to obtain coverage for earthquakes. The federal government assists in making flood insurance available to the general public.

To make sure a covered loss has occurred, insurers employ workers called *claims adjusters* whose job it is to verify that an insured loss has occurred and to try to set a value on the amount of the loss. Credible data are necessary to determine insurance premiums, and unless the premiums are affordable, no one will purchase insurance.

PRICING INSURANCE

The goal of the insurer when developing an insurance rate is to charge enough to cover claims and expenses and still make a profit. Insurers participate in competitive markets, so the rate must be competitive with other insurers and satisfy any rate regulation. Ordinarily, the states do not regulate life insurance rates, but automobile insurance and workers' compensation rates are often regulated. Health insurance rates often must be filed with the department of insurance and approved by the state insurance commissioner. Insurance regulators require that rates be adequate to pay losses, with the goal of insurer solvency in mind. The insurance code also requires that rates not be unfairly discriminatory.

Highly skilled mathematicians and statisticians called *actuaries* determine insurance premiums. Actuaries work for insurance companies and for rating bureaus that provide rates to insurance companies. Rates are based on the likelihood of loss for a given risk. For life and health insurance, for example, to determine the probable number of people in a group who will die or become disabled at any age, statistics on large numbers of people are collected and developed into mortality and morbidity tables. For property and liability insurance, past losses, premiums, and expense statistics are furnished to rating bureaus, and the bureau furnishes advisory rates based on the statistics. When pricing insurance, actuaries take into consideration investment income that will be earned on premium dollars received. Thus, if interest rates are expected to be high and investment income is expected to be large, a lower rate is charged. If interest rates are expected to decline and investment income is expected to be lower, rates charged are higher.

INTEREST RATE RISK AND INSURANCE COMPANIES

Interest rates are an important consideration in insurance pricing, especially in commercial property and liability insurance. For many years, a cyclical pattern, called the **underwriting cycle**, has been observed in commercial property and liability insurance. Property and liability insurance markets fluctuate between periods of high premiums and tight underwriting standards (called a *hard insurance market*) and periods of low premiums and loose underwriting standards (called a *soft insurance market*). Interest rates and the rate of return on invested assets help determine the state of the insurance market.

During the early 1980s, many insurers expected interest rates to continue rising as sharply as they had in the late 1970s, and the companies charged much lower premiums than they should have for certain lines of insurance, especially commercial liability insurance. In addition, because interest rates were high, it was attractive for the companies to take in as many premium dollars as possible for investment purposes. Insurers wrote some exposures that were not good risks from an underwriting standpoint. These companies were engaging in **cash-flow underwriting**, in other words, writing insurance at a discounted price in order to get the premium dollars to invest at high interest rates.

The commercial property and liability insurance markets were soft throughout most of the 1990s. Insurers could charge lower premiums and rely on investment income, especially returns on the equity portion of the portfolio, to offset underwriting losses. The market was hardening in the late 1990s because of low rates of return on newly invested funds and adverse equity returns. The terrorist attacks on September 11, 2001, accelerated the hardening of the market because the surplus of the industry was used to pay the large, unanticipated losses. Although reinsurers paid most of these losses, the reinsurers increased the price of reinsurance to primary companies. The primary companies, in turn, passed along these rate increases to insurance purchasers. Surplus was restored through higher premiums and tighter underwriting. The increased surplus set the stage for a prolonged soft market in the latter half of the decade.

Life insurance contracts are long term in nature, and the assets backing these products are also long term. Insurers protect themselves from interest rate risk through the large spread between the rate of return earned on invested assets and the guaranteed rate of interest credited to the cash value. It is when insurers assume that high interest rates will continue and guarantee high interest rates for long periods that they can get into trouble. Executive Life Insurance Company of California and Baldwin United are two examples of insolvencies that occurred because of interest rate guarantees that could not be met by the insurer.

MARKET STRUCTURE OF THE INSURANCE INDUSTRY

The insurance industry approximates a model of pure competition. There are a large number of buyers and sellers, individual buyers and sellers cannot exert pricing pressure, the commodity bought and sold is rather homogeneous, and the barriers to entry are not severe. The first two of these points are self-explanatory, but the latter two points deserve additional explanation. Although it is true that there are many different types of insurance products available, there are great similarities between the contracts used to insure specific risks. States, for example, have adopted sets of mandatory provisions that must appear in each life insurance contract. Whereas insurers are free to develop their own forms, many companies simply use forms developed by organizations such as the Insurance Services Office (ISO). With regard to barriers to entry, it is important to remember that the insurance industry is based on financial capital (money) rather than physical capital (e.g., bricks and mortar). Although it might take General Motors 2 years to build a $200 million production facility, $200 million in new capital may be added to the insurance industry overnight.

ORGANIZATIONAL FORMS

It's difficult to name an industry in which there are more types of business organizations. Insurers may be organized as stock companies, mutual companies, reciprocals, and Lloyd's associations.

Stock Companies. A **stock insurance company** is a corporation owned by its shareholders. This form of organization is the most popular one used in the insurance industry in the United States. The oldest U.S. stock insurer is the Insurance Company of North America (INA), which began operations in Philadelphia in 1792. The objective of a stock insurer is to maximize the value of the firm, which will produce positive returns for stockholders. The shareholders elect a board, and the board appoints a management team. Note that at stock companies the owners and customers (policyowners) are separate groups of claim holders.

The types of insurance that a stock insurer may sell depend on the company's charter. A stock insurer must meet minimum capital and surplus requirements of the state in which it is domiciled. Stock insurers dominate in the property and liability insurance industry, especially in the commercial lines market. Some stock companies write only nonparticipating, or *nonpar*, policies, whereas others issue par and nonpar policies. **Participating policies** are those that pay dividends to policyowners. Dividends to policyowners are not guaranteed and depend on the profitability of the insurer.

Mutual Companies.   A **mutual insurance company** is an insurer that is owned by its policyowners—there are no stockholders. The owner and customer functions are merged into a single group of claim holders. The objective of this type of organization is to minimize the cost of insurance to the policyowners. The oldest mutual insurer in the United States is The Philadelphia Contributionship for the Insurance of Houses from Loss by Fire, which began in 1752 and continues to operate to this day.

Mutual insurers issue participating policies and pay policyowners' dividends if their operations are profitable. The ability to pay dividends is determined by a mutual insurer's loss experience, expenses, and investment returns. Unlike dividends paid to stockholders, policyowner dividends are not considered taxable income. Under the Internal Revenue Code, policyowner dividends are considered a refund of overcharged premiums. Although there are many large mutual companies marketing property and liability insurance, mutual insurers account for a disproportionately large (compared to the number and percentage of all organizations) amount of life and health insurance in force.

Several large mutual life insurance companies have gone public, converting to stock organizations through a process called **demutualization**. The primary motivation for these companies is access to capital. The stock form of organization permits insurers to sell additional shares of stock if capital is needed. John Hancock (1998), Metropolitan (2000), and Prudential (2001) are examples of insurers that have demutualized in recent years.

Reciprocals.   Another type of insurance organization is a **reciprocal** or **reciprocal exchange**. These organizations operate like unincorporated mutuals, and their objective is to minimize the cost of the insurance. Each member of a reciprocal insures the other members and, in return, is insured by the other members. Reciprocals are managed by an attorney-in-fact, which is usually a corporation authorized to collect premiums, pay losses, invest premiums, and arrange reinsurance. Most of the remaining pure reciprocals now operating are found in the automobile insurance market. Farmers Insurance Exchange is the largest reciprocal. Most reciprocal business is now written by interinsurance associations, which are more like mutuals than the pure reciprocals. Separate accounts are not kept for each member, and insureds do not have a claim to any portion of surplus funds. Also, expenses and losses are not prorated among insureds. USAA is an example of an interinsurance association.

Lloyd's Associations.   **Lloyd's associations** are organizations that do not directly write insurance but instead provide a marketplace and services to members of an association who write insurance as individuals. In this respect, Lloyd's is similar to the New York Stock Exchange, which does not buy or sell securities but provides a trading floor and services to stock traders.

The most famous Lloyd's association is **Lloyd's of London**, where the members (called *names*) have unlimited liability for the risks they underwrite. In England, *unlimited liability* means one stands to lose everything but "his bed linens and the tools of his trade." Groups of names are organized into *syndicates*, and what type of insurance the syndicate writes and how much premium is charged are determined by the syndicate's underwriters. Although Lloyd's of London is well known for writing high-profile risks (e.g., a star quarterback's arm, a diva's voice), the organization is an important player in international insurance and reinsurance markets, insuring space ventures, oil tankers, and many other risks.

Lloyd's of London is admitted to do business as a primary insurer in the United States only in Kentucky and Illinois. Lloyd's was admitted first in Kentucky because of its long association with the thoroughbred horse industry. Illinois is the "backup" state for Lloyd's, in case, for some reason, the organization is no longer permitted to write business in Kentucky. In other states, Lloyd's may be used only when a particular coverage is not available from any insurer admitted in the state. In those states, Lloyd's is a surplus lines insurer.

Because it experienced underwriting losses beginning in the mid-1980s, Lloyd's of London instituted a *corporate membership* in 1994. This membership allows for limited liability, attracts capital, and changed the makeup of the underwriters and syndicates at Lloyd's of London.

Private underwriters in the United States formed associations similar to Lloyd's of London over the years. However, several American Lloyd's associations have failed, and some states, including New York, forbid the formation of new American Lloyd's associations.

PEOPLE & EVENTS

The Rise, Fall, and Return of American International Group (AIG)

The financial crisis of 2007–2009 led to a monumental reorganization of the financial sector: Bank of America purchased Countrywide; Bear Stearns was sold to JPMorgan Chase, which later acquired Washington Mutual; Merrill Lynch was taken over by Bank of America. The subprime mortgage problem nearly led to the bankruptcy of American International Group (AIG), one of the largest insurers in the world.

Before the financial crisis, AIG was well known and widely respected. In 2004, AIG was added to the Dow Jones Industrial Average. When it was added to the Dow 30, AIG stock was selling for $76 per share. While best known for its insurance operations, AIG's financial products division engaged in the sale of derivatives called credit default swaps. AIG sold these guarantees to investors (e.g., European banks), which purchased financial securities backed by pools of mortgages, many of which were subprime loans. When mortgage defaults increased, AIG lacked the capital to make good on its guarantees.

In September 2008, the U.S. government invested $85 billion in AIG to keep the company solvent, receiving an 80 percent equity stake in return. By then, AIG's stock was selling for less than $2 per share. AIG was removed from the Dow 30 and replaced by Kraft. AIG's tenure in the Dow 30 was the briefest of any stock since the Great Depression.

Subsequent investments and credit lines increased the total cost of the government bailout of AIG to $182.5 billion. Starting in 2009, AIG began to sell some of its operations to raise money to repay the loans it received. The bailout of AIG was one of the more controversial actions taken by the federal government during the financial crisis.

THE SIZE AND NUMBER OF INSURANCE COMPANIES

According to the American Council of Life Insurers, there were 709 stock insurance organizations operating in the United States in 2009. These companies had assets of $3.714 trillion, and life insurance in force of $12.977 trillion. There were 136 mutual life insurers operating in the United States in 2009. These companies had assets of $1.110 trillion and were responsible for $4.707 trillion of life insurance in force. The largest U.S. life insurer was MetLife (Metropolitan Life Insurance Company). Other life and health insurance providers include fraternal societies and Blue Cross/Blue Shield health plans. The 18 largest life and health insurance companies in the United States, ranked by revenues in 2009, are shown in Exhibit 17.1.

According to A. M. Best, at year-end 2009, there were 1,876 property and liability insurers doing business in the United States that were organized as stock companies. The largest of these companies, by revenues, was Berkshire Hathaway, led by billionaire CEO Warren Buffet. Berkshire Hathaway's insurance holdings include

EXHIBIT 17.1
Top U.S. Life/Health Insurance Groups By Revenues, 2009 ($ Millions)

Rank	Group	Revenues	Assets
1	MetLife	$41,098	$539,314
2	New York Life Insurance	$34,014	$187,772
3	Prudential Financial	$32,688	$480,203
4	TIAA-CREF	$26,278	$383,595
5	Massachusetts Mutual Life Insurance	$25,424	$173,776
6	Northwestern Mutual	$21,603	$167,180
7	AFLAC	$18,254	$84,106
8	Unum Group	$10,091	$54,477
9	Guardian Life Ins. Co. of America	$10,041	$42,683
10	Lincoln National	$9,072	$177,433
11	Genworth Financial	$9,069	$108,187
12	Principal Financial	$8,849	$137,759
13	Reinsurance Group of America	$7,067	$25,250
14	Thrivent Financial for Lutherans	$6,515	$57,752
15	Pacific Life	$5,211	$109,954
16	Mutual of Omaha Insurance	$5,150	$22,197
17	Western & Southern Financial Group	$5,014	$33,674
18	Conseco	$4,341	$30,344

Revenues for insurance companies include premium and annuity income, investment income, and capital gains or losses but exclude deposits. Based on companies and categories in the Fortune 500. Each company is assigned only one category, even if it is involved in several industries. Data are from Fortune.

Source: Insurance Information Institute, *The Financial Services Fact Book,* 2010.
See: http://www.financialservicesfacts.org.

EXHIBIT 17.2
Top Twenty U.S. Property/Casualty Companies by Revenues, 2009 ($ Millions)

Rank	Group	Revenues	Assets
1	Berkshire Hathaway	$112,493	$297,119
2	American International Group	$103,189	$847,585
3	State Farm Insurance Cos.	$61,480	$183,785
4	Allstate	$32,013	$132,652
5	Liberty Mutual Insurance Group	$31,094	$109,475
6	Hartford Financial Services	$24,701	$307,717
7	Travelers Cos.	$24,680	$109,560
8	Nationwide	$20,751	$140,084
9	United Services Automobile Association (USAA)	$17,558	$79,906
10	Progressive	$14,564	$20,049
11	Loews (CNA)	$14,123	$74,070
12	Chubb	$13,016	$50,449
13	Assurant	$8,701	$25,842
14	American Family Insurance Group	$6,453	$16,251
15	First American Corp.	$5,973	$8,723
16	Fidelity National Financial	$5,858	$7,934
17	Auto-Owners Insurance	$5,017	$14,300
18	W.R. Berkley	$4,431	$17,329
19	American Financial Group	$4,321	$27,683
20	Erie Insurance Group	$4,255	$13,359

Revenues for insurance companies include premium and annuity income, investment income, and capital gains or losses but exclude deposits. Data are from Fortune.

Source: Insurance Information Institute, *The Financial Services Fact Book,* 2010. See http://financialservicesfacts.org.

General Reinsurance (Gen Re) and GEICO Insurance. The largest of the stock companies by total assets was American International Group (AIG). AIG gained great notoriety during the financial crisis. There were 385 mutual property and casualty organizations at year-end 2009. Although fewer in number, there are some large mutual companies such as State Farm Insurance, Nationwide, and Liberty Mutual Insurance Company. Each of these companies ranks in the top 10 largest property and casualty companies, by assets and revenues. The 20 largest property and casualty U.S. insurers, ranked by revenues in 2009, are displayed in Exhibit 17.2.

REGULATION OF THE INSURANCE INDUSTRY

Insurance companies are regulated primarily by the states in which they do business. Federal legislation enacted in 1945, the **McCarran–Ferguson Act (Public**

Law 15), stated that the continued regulation of insurers at the state level was in the best interest of the public and that federal law applies only to the extent that state law does not apply. The debate over whether insurance should be regulated at the state or federal level continues to this day.

Insurance is regulated for several reasons. Regulation is designed to help assure the solvency of insurers, protect consumers who may have inadequate knowledge of insurance, make sure that rates charged are reasonable, and help make sure that needed insurance coverages are available.

The three main sources of insurance regulation are legislation, court decisions, and state insurance departments. State legislatures pass laws that regulate the operations of insurers. Such laws address a number of factors, including surplus and capital requirements, licensing of agents, taxation of insurers, insurance rate regulations, and sales and claims practices. In addition to rules passed by state legislatures, insurers are also subject to regulation by certain federal agencies and are required to follow certain federal acts. For example, the Civil Rights Act bars discrimination on the basis of race, religion, or national origin. Insurers that market products with an investment element (e.g., variable life insurance and variable annuities) are subject to rules of the Securities and Exchange Commission (SEC). Insurers must follow the guidelines for private pensions detailed in the Employee Retirement Income Security Act of 1974 (ERISA) and subsequent acts.

The second method of regulating the industry is through the courts. When a court decision is rendered in a case relating to insurance, a legal precedent is established that can be cited and relied upon in future litigation. If the court decision is adverse to the interests of insurers, exclusions are added when new policies are issued and when contracts are renewed. A 1980s court decision illustrates this point. In this case, two perils jointly brought about a loss. One peril was excluded and the other peril was not excluded. The insurer denied the claim and the policyowner filed suit. When the court ruled that in such case losses are covered, insurers added an exclusion to new policies designed to address this issue.

All states have an agency charged with the regulation of insurance. The first state to establish a separate insurance department was New Hampshire in 1841. This state regulatory agency is headed by the insurance commissioner, who is either appointed by the governor or elected. Insurance commissioners have considerable power. They can issue, revoke, or deny licenses; hold hearings; and place insurers in rehabilitation or liquidation.

State insurance commissioners are members of the **National Association of Insurance Commissioners (NAIC)**. This organization was founded in 1871 to help set uniform regulatory standards among the states. The NAIC is not a statutory body but an organization of insurance commissioners who meet regularly to discuss regulatory issues and to prepare model legislation for recommendation to their state legislatures. The commissioners have developed systems for cooperative company audits, simultaneous investigations of interstate problems, and information exchanges that increase efficiency in the regulatory process. By virtue of its high degree of cooperation, the NAIC has overcome some of the burden of conflicting regulation in different states.

Several important aspects of insurance companies and insurance operations are regulated. After formation, an insurer must be licensed before it can do business in a state. Insurers must meet minimum capital and surplus requirements to obtain a license if they are stock insurers and minimum surplus requirements if they are mutuals.

Every year, insurers must file a series of financial statements called a *Convention Blank* with the commissioner's office in every state in which they operate. An insurer must have sufficient assets to offset its liabilities. Loss reserves must be shown on the balance sheet, and states regulate the methods that may be used to calculate the reserves. The surplus position of each company is also regulated. Policyholders' surplus is the difference between the insurer's assets and liabilities. This surplus is especially important in property and liability insurance. The amount of new business an insurer is allowed to write is limited by its policyholders' surplus. For example, a conservative rule is that an insurer can write only $2 of net new premiums for each $1 of policyholders' surplus. Also, surplus is necessary to offset any underwriting or investment losses or deficiencies in loss reserves over time.

States regulate the types and quality of investments that insurers make and also establish the maximum percentage of total assets that can be invested in certain instruments. Life insurers, for example, are limited in the percentage of total assets that can be invested in common stocks. In New York, for example, common stock investments are limited to 10 percent of total assets or 100 percent of surplus, whichever is lower. Property and liability insurers are subject to fewer investment restrictions.

Liquidation of insurers is also regulated, and if a company becomes technically insolvent, the state insurance commissioner assumes control of the company with the intent of rehabilitating it. If it cannot be saved, it is liquidated. All states have *guaranty funds* that pay the claims of insolvent property and liability insurers. Some states have guaranty funds for insolvent life and health insurers. Often the commissioner can find another insurer to buy a troubled company to avoid liquidation.

Rates, policy forms, sales practices, commission rates, and claims practices are also regulated in varying degrees by the states. In some states, rates must be filed and approved before the insurer can use them; in others rates must just be filed. The commissioner must also approve some policy forms before they can be used. All states regulate the licensing of agents and brokers, requiring the agent to pass an exam before selling insurance. State insurance departments have a complaint division to handle consumer complaints about unfair treatment by insurers.

GLOBALIZATION OF INSURANCE

There is a continuing trend toward globalization in insurance company operations. U.S.-based insurance companies often enter foreign markets. For example, Georgia-based AFLAC earns the majority of its revenues by selling insurance in Japan, and a New England–based insurer writes disability coverage in England. Foreign insurers may also enter the U.S. market, as evidenced by Sun Life Insurance Company of Canada marketing coverages in the United States. Foreign ownership of U.S. insurance companies is not uncommon, and mergers and acquisitions often occur across borders. In 2003, for example, Toronto-based Manulife acquired Boston-based John Hancock, creating the second-largest insurance company in North America by market capitalization. Reinsurance markets are truly global in nature. Indeed, three of the reinsurers with the greatest liability for claims arising out of the 9/11 terrorist attacks were from Europe (Lloyd's of London, Munich Re, and Swiss Re).

One other international aspect of insurance deserves mention. Most Fortune 500 companies have formed a subsidiary called a **captive insurance company**. Captive insurers are formed for the purpose of insuring the parent company's loss exposures and provide direct access to the reinsurance market. Although captive insurers may be based in the United States, they are often domiciled offshore to avoid domestic surplus and capital requirements and other regulations. Bermuda and the Cayman Islands in the Caribbean are popular domiciles for captive insurers.

SECURITIZATION OF RISK

A development likely to have an increasing impact on the insurance industry is the securitization of risk. **Securitization of risk** means that insurable risk is transferred to the capital markets through the creation of a financial instrument, such as a catastrophe bond, futures contract, or options contract. Securitization of risk increases the capacity of the industry. Rather than simply relying on insurers and reinsurers to bear risk, securitization opens the door for other capital market participants, such as bond investors, to share risk.

Securitization is especially important in addressing potentially catastrophic losses (earthquakes, hurricanes, etc.). An example demonstrates how securitization works. Assume that a property insurer concentrated its underwriting efforts in an area where hurricanes are likely to occur. The insurer is concerned about the financial impact of a large hurricane. The insurer could issue catastrophe bonds, borrowing money from a group of investors. The promise to repay principal and interest, however, may be contingent on catastrophic hurricane losses not occurring. If hurricane losses exceed a specified amount, some or all of the principal and interest payments would be waived, and the insurer could use the funds saved by not having to pay the bondholders to pay the catastrophic losses. USAA Insurance Company issued catastrophe bonds through a subsidiary in 1997 to protect the company from catastrophic hurricane losses.

DO YOU UNDERSTAND?

1. Define *insurance*. What are the requirements for privately insurable risks?
2. What is meant by the term *objective risk*, and why is it so important to insurers?
3. What are the various types of insurance organizations?
4. What are the sources of regulation for the insurance industry, and what areas are regulated?
5. How does securitization of risk increase insurance industry capacity?

17.3 LIFE AND HEALTH INSURANCE

Life and health insurers offer a wide variety of financial services products, including life insurance, health insurance, annuities, IRAs, mutual funds, and money market accounts. A few traditional products, however, account for a substantial portion of life insurer revenues. These products are life insurance, health insurance, and annuities. These products are designed to protect against the economic risk of premature death, poor health, and living too long.

The primary purpose of life insurance is to provide financial support to dependents in the case of premature death. Although all deaths may seem premature, from an economic standpoint, **premature death** means loss of life while others are financially dependent on the person who died. Life insurance proceeds replace the lost income and cover expenses that may coincide with death (e.g., uninsured medical bills, the cost of a funeral, estate/probate costs).

TERM INSURANCE

Term insurance is pure life insurance protection for a specified period of time, less than all of life. If the insured dies while the policy is in force, the insurer pays the face value of the policy to the beneficiary. If the insured survives the coverage period, the policy expires and there are no further benefit rights. Term insurance is the purest form of life insurance, as it provides death protection only and does not develop a savings reserve or *cash value*. The premiums for term insurance track the probability of death, so they are low at younger ages but increase, at an increasing rate, as the insured grows older.

Term insurance policies may be classified broadly by the duration of coverage, whether the face value varies, and expiration protection. *Straight term insurance* is written for a certain time period and then terminates. Popular policy durations are 1-year, 5-year, and 10-year periods. Most term insurance polices have a face value that remains constant during the duration of the coverage. *Decreasing term* has a face amount that decreases yearly or monthly, although the premium stays level. This type of term insurance is often used to cover the outstanding mortgage if the insured dies. Some insurers market *increasing term*, which provides coverage that increases monthly or yearly. This type of coverage may be used to maintain the purchasing power of the death benefit for the beneficiary. Two provisions are often included in term insurance policies to address the problem of continuing life insurance after the period of coverage expires. These provisions are the renewability and convertibility provisions.

Renewable term insurance policies may be placed back in force again at the end of the coverage period. The insured does not have to provide evidence that he or she is still insurable. The premium increases when the policy is renewed, reflecting the increase in mortality risk to the insurer. The number of renewals permitted is usually limited so that the coverage cannot be renewed beyond a specified age, such as 65 or 70. This limitation is designed to protect against adverse selection. **Adverse selection** occurs when those most likely to suffer a loss seek to purchase insurance. Because term insurance premiums increase with the insured's age, by the time the insured reaches age 65 or 70, premiums may have become prohibitively expensive and only those in poor health would renew their coverage. Limiting the number of renewals reduces the risk of adverse claims experience for the insurer.

Convertible term insurance permits the term insurance coverage to be switched to whole life insurance without providing evidence of insurability. Conversion must be done within some given time period, such as the first 5 years. This is an attractive provision because often those who purchase term insurance do so because of the low cost at younger ages. As the insured ages, his or her income may increase and the need for permanent life insurance may develop.

WHOLE LIFE INSURANCE

Some individuals want permanent life insurance protection. **Whole life insurance** provides coverage for all of life, up to and in some cases beyond age 100.

Several premium payment plans are available. Under the most popular, *continuous premium whole life*, a premium is paid each year for the duration of the coverage. Some policyowners prefer to limit premiums to a specified period, such as 20 years or until they reach age 65. These limited-payment options permit policyowners to pay the entire cost of the coverage earlier, while enjoying life insurance protection until they die.

How can an insurer offer coverage for all of life under a level-premium policy? Simply put, policyowners overpay the cost of mortality in early years and underpay in later years. Life insurance actuaries first calculate the net single premium for the coverage (the present value of the death benefit payable) and then level the premium by amortizing it over the premium payment period. Leveling the premium makes the policy affordable. As the policyowner overpays the cost of mortality in early years, a saving reserve called the **cash value** develops.

Insurers pay interest on the cash value. The cash value also increases because of a survivorship benefit that is added each year. When members of the insured's pool of insureds die, their cash values are divided among the insureds who are still alive. Every year, a mortality charge is deducted from the cash value to pay the claims of those insureds who died. Then the cash value in the policies of deceased insureds is distributed to those who are still alive, along with interest income. The sum of interest income and the survivorship benefit is greater than the mortality charge, so the savings element increases each year. The interest accumulated on the cash values is not taxed as income unless the policy is surrendered. This tax benefit, along with the idea of forced savings, makes whole life insurance attractive to some consumers. The cash value serves as a savings account for the policyowner. He or she may borrow the cash value at reasonable interest rates (traditionally between 5 and 8 percent), or the insured may surrender the policy and receive the entire cash value.

Often people purchase whole life insurance with the idea that if they survive until retirement age, they can use the accumulated cash value to purchase a retirement annuity. In these situations, life insurance protects against the peril of premature death during the income-earning years and against the risk of **superannuation** (that is, living too long) after retirement.

Whole life insurance has historically been a popular form of life insurance. Whole life premiums are a large source of funds for life insurers because of the long-term nature of the product and the cash values that accumulate. As with banks, life insurance companies can make money on the difference between the guaranteed fixed rate of return paid on whole life insurance and the rate of return the insurer can earn by investing the funds. Although whole life insurance does not provide a high rate of interest, the cash value accumulates tax free and is guaranteed by the insurer.

UNIVERSAL LIFE INSURANCE

In the late 1970s and early 1980s, short-term interest rates were quite high. Many life insurance policyowners looked at the low rate of return they were earning on their whole life policies and compared it to the rate of return on CDs, money market mutual funds, and other money market alternatives. Many policyowners questioned why they should accept a 4 or 5 percent rate of return on their whole life insurance cash value when they could earn a 15 percent rate of return in the money market. Many policyowners either surrendered their cash value policies or borrowed the cash value and invested in money market alternatives. This flow of funds away from the life insurance industry, financial disintermediation, led to the introduction and success of a number of products touted as *interest-sensitive life insurance*.

Universal life insurance was the most successful interest-sensitive product during the 1980s. **Universal life insurance** is flexible-premium, nonparticipating life insurance that provides a market-based rate of return on the savings or cash value account. Policyowners pay premiums at their discretion, and each month the insurer deducts a mortality charge from the cash value and adds an interest credit. A minimum interest rate is guaranteed, but the rate credited is pegged to some observable market interest rate. Thus, the interest rate paid by the insurer fluctuates with changing interest rates. As with traditional life insurance, interest credited to the cash value is not currently taxable provided the policy satisfies IRS requirements to qualify as life insurance.

Universal life insurance offers lifetime protection, competitive interest rates, and deferred taxation. The product was so successful that by 1984, universal life accounted for 32 percent of the life insurance sold. When interest rates began to fall, the product became less attractive. By 1990, universal life accounted for 20 percent of all life insurance sold, and by 1997, new universal life sales accounted for only 10.5 percent of sales.

Some insurers that marketed universal life insurance became the targets of policyowner litigation. As only a minimum interest rate was guaranteed and the actual rate paid was determined by market rates, life insurance agents could illustrate universal life policies using alternative interest rate assumptions. Agents wishing to make sales often did not illustrate the impact that low interest rates would have on the cash value element, instead illustrating unreasonably high interest rates. Some policyowners sued life insurers, alleging that the policies failed to perform as illustrated when interest rates declined.

VARIABLE LIFE INSURANCE

The low interest rates of the 1990s helped to fuel the bull market. Facing declining universal life sales and superior equity returns, some insurers began offering another form of interest-sensitive life insurance called variable life insurance. **Variable life insurance** is fixed-premium life insurance that permits the policyowner to invest the cash value in a mutual fund offered by the insurer. Variable life insurance guarantees a minimum death benefit, but the death benefit can be higher if investment returns are favorable. Insurers offering variable life insurance offer a number of mutual fund alternatives for the cash value. Under this type of life insurance, there are no cash value guarantees. Some insurers offer variable–universal life or universal–variable life, which offers all the characteristics of variable life along with the premium payment flexibility of universal life.

ANNUITIES

Annuities are products sold by life insurers that can be thought of as the opposite of life insurance. Life insurance creates an immediate estate and protects against the economic consequences of premature death. Life annuities are a means of systematically liquidating an accumulated estate and protecting the annuitant against the economic consequences of living too long. Annuities are nice companion products for life insurance insurers. Both products, life insurance and annuities, address personal risks and have obvious similarities in premium calculations (i.e., one minus the probability of death equals the probability of survival), and life annuities are sometimes used as a means of paying the death benefit to the beneficiary after the insured has died.

A life annuity purchaser pays the insurer a premium for the annuity. In return, the insurer promises to make periodic payments to the annuitant until he or she dies. The annuity income the insurer pays is made up of three components: return of the annuity purchaser's money, interest income, and a survivorship benefit (from those in the pool who die during the year). Each year, the interest income becomes a smaller portion of the annuity payment and the survivorship benefit and liquidation proportion increase, whereas the total payment to the annuitant is level. As annuities are purchased with after-tax dollars, only the portion of payment received that is attributable to investment income is taxable. Once the annuitant recovers his or her entire investment in the annuity, then the entire annuity payment is taxable. Obviously some annuitants die before receiving back what they paid for the annuity, whereas others live far beyond life expectancy and collect far more than what they paid for the annuity.

Annuities offer great flexibility. They can be purchased through installment premiums or through a lump-sum purchase. The benefit payments can begin immediately or can be deferred to a later date. The purchaser may also add some type of guarantee feature to the annuity. For example, the annuitant may select a "life income with 10 years for certain" option. Under this option, annuity payments are made for life. If the annuitant dies before receiving payments for 10 years, the remaining payments are made to a beneficiary. Finally, an annuity can be purchased on more than one life. A retired husband and wife, for example, may purchase a *joint-and-survivor annuity*. This type of annuity provides payments until the last of the two annuitants has died.

Annuities are big business for insurers, especially as baby boomers approach retirement age. In 1986, premiums and annuity considerations for individual annuities were $26.1 billion; in 1990, they were $49.0 billion; in 1999, they were $115.6 billion; and in 2009, they were $128.9 billion.

HEALTH INSURANCE

Medical expenses can be catastrophic. The perils insured against in **health insurance** are the medical costs associated with illness and injury and the loss of income. Specific medical costs include the costs of a hospital room, surgical procedures, miscellaneous expenses (e.g., lab tests, X-rays), nonsurgical care, and long-term care. These expenses can be paid through hospital–surgical expense policies, major medical insurance, and long-term care insurance.

Often overlooked in a personal risk management program is the risk of disability. The economic consequences of a long-term, permanent disability can be greater than the economic consequences of premature death. Disability income insurance replaces lost income during a period of temporary or permanent disability caused by illness or injury.

Health insurance can be purchased individually or made available through a group insurance plan. Health insurance providers include insurance companies, Blue Cross/Blue Shield organizations (the *Blues*), and health maintenance organizations (HMOs). Some group health plans entered into agreements with care providers through which the care provider offers its services at a discount. Members of the group health plan are given a financial incentive to use the preferred provider organization (PPO) for their care. PPOs and other forms of managed care plans are popular because of continued healthcare-sector inflation.

Concerns over rising medical costs and the large number of people who were uninsured led Congress to pass the **Patient Protection and Affordable Care Act** of 2010. This act extends coverage to many uninsured Americans by providing subsidies to individuals and small businesses. The act includes provisions designed to reduce healthcare costs in the long-run. It also places limits on certain insurer practices, such as the use of preexisting conditions exclusions and rescinding individual health policies. The act is controversial, and the enforceability of the act upon the states was immediately called into question.

THE BALANCE SHEET OF LIFE INSURANCE COMPANIES

Life insurance company funds originate primarily from the sale of financial services products. Selling these products creates liabilities, similar to accounts payable for other types of businesses. These liabilities are called *reserves*. Exhibit 17.3 shows the composite balance sheet for life insurers in 2009.

One is struck immediately by the magnitude of the assets. In 2009, life insurers had assets of $4.94 trillion dollars. Notice that the bulk of the assets are financial assets—$2.35 trillion in bonds, $77.7 billion in corporate stock, $324.9 billion in mortgages, and $19.7 billion in real estate. Clearly, life insurers are important financial intermediaries. They collect small amounts of money from millions of policyowners, package the premiums, and make large blocks of funds available in the capital markets.

Several important points deserve mention. First, the long-term nature of life insurance contracts and the steady cash flows they generate motivate insurers toward long-term investments. As Exhibit 17.3 shows, corporate bonds and mortgages are the most important investments backing traditional life insurance products. The second largest asset holding is "Separate account assets." This category of assets is segregated from general assets and is exempt from most investment rules. Separate account assets back life insurer products that have an investment nature—variable life insurance, variable annuities, and pension plans.

One item listed as an asset that you may find surprising is "Policy loans." Recall that a cash value policy (e.g., whole life insurance) permits the policyowner to borrow the cash value from the policy. So why are policy loans an asset? Policy loans are analogous to accounts receivable. If the insurer had not loaned the money to the policyowners, it would have invested the funds elsewhere in interest-earning assets. As interest is payable on policy loans, and loans must either be repaid or the outstanding balance is deducted from the death benefit when it is payable, policy loans are interest-earning assets for life insurers.

Exhibit 17.3 shows that policy loans were 2.5 percent of total assets in 2009. Policy loans vary with economic conditions. During the Great Depression, policy loans reached 18 percent of company assets. In 1981, when interest rates in the market were high, policy loans accounted for 9 percent of insurer assets. Policy loans have historically been made at low rates of interest, usually 5 to 8 percent. In 1981, market interest rates greatly exceeded the low interest rates on policy loans, so insureds borrowed their cash values to reinvest in higher-yielding instruments. Since then, all states have enacted insurance legislation called the Model Bill on Policy Loan Rates, or a similar law, that allows life insurers to use a variable policy loan rate tied to a market interest rate.

EXHIBIT 17.3
Life Insurance Companies' Balance Sheet, 2009

Type of Account	Amount ($ in Billions)	Percentage
Assets		
Bonds	2,345.9	47.5
Corporate stock	77.7	1.6
Mortgage loans	324.9	6.6
Real estate	19.7	0.4
Policy loans	122.6	2.5
Cash and short-term investments	123.4	2.5
Other assets	287.9	5.8
Separate account assets	1,634.4	33.1
Total	4,936.5	100.0
Liabilities and net worth		
Policy reserves liability	2,358.5	47.8
Policy claims	42.1	.9
Deposit-type contracts	287.1	5.8
Other liabilities	320.2	6.5
Separate account business	1,631.2	33.0
Surplus and net worth	297.4	6.0
Total	4,936.4	100.0

Source: Best's Aggregates and Averages, Life/Health, 2006 Edition; Total U.S. Life/Health and Fraternal Balance Sheet.

The liabilities of insurance companies are interesting. Most businesses know exactly what they owe to creditors. The best an insurance company can do, however, is to estimate what it will owe in claims payments in the future. This estimate is called the policy reserves or **loss reserves**. The balancing figure on an insurance company's balance sheet is **policyholders' surplus**, which is analogous to owners' equity. Policyholders' surplus is what would remain if the company used its assets to repay all of its liabilities. Surplus is a cushion that an insurer can rely upon if losses are higher than anticipated.

LEARNING BY DOING 17.1
Calculating Policyholders' Surplus

PROBLEM: You are an analyst with Rock Solid Life Insurance Company. The assistant comptroller is working on revising the company's balance sheet and has asked you to do two tasks: (1) Calculate policyholders' surplus and (2) determine the impact on policyholders' surplus if the company takes a $20 million charge to correct underestimated loss reserves. Rock Solid has total assets of $900 million and its estimated liabilities are $810 million.

APPROACH: You recognize that you can find the answers with a simple application of the balance sheet identity for a life insurance company (see, for example, Exhibit 17.3).

SOLUTION:

1. By the balance sheet equation, you know that total assets = total liabilities + policyholders' surplus. For Rock Solid, $900 million = $810 million + policyholders' surplus; therefore, policyholders' surplus = $90 million.

2. If the company takes a $20 million charge to correct the loss reserve estimate, its policyholders' surplus declines to $20 million: $900 million = $830 million + policyholders' surplus; therefore policyholders' surplus = $70 million.

An increase in loss reserves means a reduction in net worth (surplus).

DO YOU UNDERSTAND?

1. How do term life insurance and whole life insurance differ with respect to the duration of coverage and savings accumulation?

2. Why was universal life insurance popular in the 1980s? What made variable life insurance popular in the 1990s?

3. Why are life insurance and life annuities often described as opposites?

4. What are the largest asset categories on a life insurance company balance sheet?

17.4 PROPERTY AND LIABILITY INSURANCE

Property and liability insurers sell policies that offer protection from direct and indirect loss caused by **perils**. Some perils that could cause direct loss to property include a fire, wind, an explosion, a flood, or an earthquake. Some indirect losses are also insurable. For example, a successful restaurant that is damaged by a fire may be forced to close while repairs are made. The profits that could have been earned if the restaurant were operating would be an indirect loss that could be covered by business income insurance. Property insurance indemnifies policyowners for the financial loss associated with the destruction and loss of use of their property. Liability insurance protects against the peril of legal liability. An insured that is negligent and causes bodily injury, property damage, or personal injury (such as libel or slander) may be called on to pay damages to the injured party. Liability insurance pays such awards on the behalf of the insured. Most liability policies also cover the insured's legal defense costs.

PROPERTY INSURANCE

Property insurance is purchased by individuals and organizations to protect against direct or indirect loss to property they own. Perils, causes of loss, are insured against under property insurance policies. Some property insurance policies provide **named-perils coverage**. These policies provide a listing of perils that are covered. If a loss is caused by a peril not listed, the loss is not covered. An alternative to naming perils is to provide **all-risk coverage** (also called *open perils*).

This type of coverage insures against all losses except those that are excluded. So if a loss is not excluded, it is covered. An insurer's loss exposure in property insurance is easier to predict than its liability loss exposures because it is generally not difficult to determine the value of the property damaged or destroyed.

LIABILITY INSURANCE

Liability insurance is purchased by individuals and businesses to protect against financial loss because of legal responsibility for bodily injury, property damage, and personal injury. Insurers selling liability insurance also agree to defend the insured against suits alleging negligence and to pay damages awarded by the court for bodily injury, property damage, and sometimes personal injury such as libel or slander. The liability exposure is much more difficult to gauge because there is no upper limit on the damages that may be awarded. Liability claims often take years to settle. Some states have enacted tort reform statutes that may limit punitive damages, but special damages and general damages are not limited. A liability loss, therefore, can be catastrophic.

MARINE INSURANCE

Marine insurance is a special classification of property and liability insurance. Marine contracts, which cover losses related to transportation exposures, are divided into two categories: ocean marine and inland marine. Ocean marine policies include hull coverage for damage to the vessel and indemnity (liability) coverage. The policies can be endorsed to provide cargo coverage, longshore and harbor worker coverage, and other supplemental coverages. Inland marine policies include coverage for such exposures as goods transported by rail, motor vehicles, and armored cars, as well as *instrumentalities of transportation* such as bridges, tunnels, and pipelines. Floater policies that cover scheduled items of high value such as fine arts, jewelry, furs, and antiques also fall under the classification of inland marine insurance.

MULTIPLE LINE POLICIES

Multiple line policies, frequently written by property and liability insurers, combine property and liability insurance coverage in a single contract. The homeowner's policy is an excellent example. This policy was developed in the 1950s and continues to be widely popular. The homeowner's form provides six coverages: damage to the dwelling, damage to other structures, damage to personal property, loss of use, personal liability, and medical payments to others. Like the homeowner's policy, the personal auto policy (PAP) combines several coverages, including bodily injury and property damage liability, medical payments coverage, uninsured motorists coverage, and physical damage coverage for the insured auto.

Some forms used to insure businesses also combine property and liability insurance coverage. The business owner's policy (BOP) used by small businesses provides coverage for the building, business personal property, and general liability insurance in one contract. The commercial package policy (CPP) used by large businesses insures the plant, equipment, other property, as well as general liability loss exposures of the organization.

Multiple line policies offer a number of advantages. Purchasing coverages combined in a single policy is less expensive than purchasing the coverages separately. A multiple line policy is underwritten once, whereas separate policies require individual underwriting and individual issue costs. Multiple line policies provide more complete coverage, have a common expiration date, and are convenient for the insured, who faces only one common policy expiration date and deals with only one agent and one insurer.

THE BALANCE SHEET OF PROPERTY AND LIABILITY INSURANCE COMPANIES

The operations and investment practices of property and liability insurers differ from those of life insurers for several reasons. First, property and liability insurance policies have a much shorter duration than life insurance policies. Typically, property and liability policies are written for 6 months or a year. Second, the probability of loss is higher under these policies, and property claims are often paid during the policy period. Thus, the insurer can invest premium revenue for a shorter period of time. Finally, the objective risk of the property and liability insurer is greater than that faced by life insurers. Claims against property and liability insurers are greatly affected by economic conditions and are often much greater than predicted. For example, inflation affects workers' compensation losses, the cost of replacing property, and amounts awarded in liability suits. Property and liability insurers invest a larger proportion of their funds in corporate stocks for higher returns and in municipal bonds for tax advantages. The balance sheet for all property and liability insurers for 2009 is shown in Exhibit 17.4.

EXHIBIT 17.4
Property/Liability Companies' Balance Sheet, 2009

Type of Account	Amount ($ in Billions)	Percentage
Assets		
Bonds	895.6	58.1
Corporate stock	166.8	10.8
Real estate, offices	9.3	0.6
Real estate investment	1.4	0.1
Cash and short-term investments	92.3	6.0
Investments in affiliates	86.5	5.6
Premium balances	118.5	7.7
Other assets	170.7	11.1
Total	1,541.1	100.0
Liabilities and net worth		
Losses and loss adjustment expenses	592.8	38.5
Conditional reserves	12.1	0.8
Unearned premiums	200.2	13.0
Other liabilities	204.5	13.3
Surplus and net worth	531.6	34.5
Total	1,541.1	100.0

Source: *Best's Aggregates and Averages*, Property/Casualty, 2010 Edition; *Total U.S. P.C. Industry Balance Sheet*, p. 2.

Just as in the case of the balance sheet for life insurance companies, you are immediately struck by the magnitude of the funds. In 2009, U.S. property and liability insurance companies controlled $1.54 trillion in assets. Again, note the financial nature of the assets that appear on the balance sheet. Property and liability insurers held $895.6 billion in bonds and $166.8 billion in common and preferred stock. Also note the higher relative position in cash and short-term investments (6.0 percent of total assets) as compared to life insurance companies (2.5 percent of total assets), demonstrating the desire for liquidity.

The liabilities of property and liability insurers are quite logical. They consist of reserves for losses, for loss adjustment expenses, and for unearned premiums. Also of interest is the relatively larger surplus position of property and liability insurers (34.5 percent) as compared to life insurers (6.0 percent). Surplus represents a cushion that can be drawn upon if losses are higher than anticipated. Property and liability insurers must maintain larger relative surplus positions because of objective risk and the higher frequency of loss.

LEARNING BY DOING 17.2
Measuring Insurance Company Profitability with the Combined Ratio

PROBLEM: You are a financial analyst with the Gonzales Hedge Fund. The fund is considering an investment in Bedrock Property and Casualty Insurance Company. The fund manager has asked you to determine the profitability of Bedrock.

APPROACH: One way to measure the profitability of property and casualty insurers is the combined ratio. The ratio compares the premiums earned relative to claims and expenses. Bedrock had premium income of $200 million, paid claims of $140 million, and had expenses of $70 million. The combined ratio is calculated as claims plus expenses divided by premium income.

SOLUTION: For Bedrock, the combined ratio = (claims + expenses)/premium income = ($140 million + $70 million)/$200 million = 1.05.

A combined ratio exceeding 1.0 (or 100 percent) indicates an insurer paid more in claims and expenses than it earned in premiums. A combined ratio of less than 1.0 (or 100 percent) indicates underwriting profitability—less was paid in claims and expenses than was collected in premiums.

Bedrock's combined ratio exceeds 1.0. So why might Bedrock have to pay income taxes? It's because insurance companies have two sources of income—underwriting risks and investment income. An insurer could lose money underwriting risks, as Bedrock did, but if its investment income offsets the underwriting loss, the company will report a profit.

DO YOU UNDERSTAND?

1. Property insurance is available for both *direct* and *indirect* losses. Differentiate between these two types of losses.
2. Why is the liability loss exposure more difficult to gauge than the property loss exposure?

3. What are major benefits of purchasing coverage through a multiple line policy as opposed to purchasing the same coverages separately?

4. What are the major classes of asset holdings on a property and liability insurance company balance sheet? How do the asset holdings of property and liability insurance companies differ from the holdings of life and health insurance companies?

17.5 PENSIONS

Pensions are used to protect against the risk of *superannuation*, which can be defined as outliving your ability to earn a living to support yourself. Most individuals do not save enough for retirement, relying on Social Security old-age benefits for the bulk of their retirement income. Social Security was never meant to be the sole source of retirement income. Numerous tax advantages have been made available under the tax code to encourage retirement savings.

Several problems currently exist with retirement savings. Many individuals delay retirement saving, spending financial resources today for current consumption rather than saving for retirement. Some individuals do not earn enough to be able to afford retirement savings. During the recent recession, some workers, especially those who found themselves unemployed, were forced to spend their retirement funds early. Finally, the period of retirement saving is shortening while the period that the funds are required to last is lengthening. Many individuals delay entry to the workforce until completing college. These same individuals may elect to retire early, shortening the period over which retirement savings can be set aside and earn investment income. Americans, on average, are living longer. Therefore, retirement funds that have been accumulated must last, on average, a longer period of time.

Even with these problems, pension plans have been among the fastest-growing financial intermediaries since the mid-1970s. Like insurance companies, pension plans collect small contributions from many employees or larger contributions from employers. The plan pools these contributions and makes large blocks of funds available to purchase stocks, bonds, real estate–related investments, and other securities. The pension fund uses the funds plus investment income to make retirement benefits available.

A BRIEF HISTORY OF PENSIONS

The earliest pension programs were established by the railroads, the first in the United States in 1875 by the American Express Company and the second by the Baltimore & Ohio Railroad in 1880. Railroads were the first to establish pensions because they were the first business organizations to become large enough and, more important, because the work was hazardous and some type of relief was needed, particularly for the disabled. By 1929, there were only 400 assorted pension funds in operation with pension assets of less than $500 million, covering fewer than 4 million workers and their families.

During the Great Depression many business firms went bankrupt. Their pension funds often failed, too, because pension benefits were frequently paid out of current income. These nonfunded, pay-as-you-go plans operated without regulation, and participants had few, if any, rights. Pension plans underwritten by insurance companies, however, were actuarially funded and were far superior in weathering the rough financial times of the 1930s.

EXHIBIT 17.5
Pension Fund Assets in 2010 ($ Billions)

Private funds	.	$8,072
Insured	$2,411	
Noninsured	5,661	
State and local government employees		2,729
Federal government		1,336
Total		$12,137

Source: The Federal Reserve. See http://www.federalreserve.gov/RELEASSES/zl/Current/Zl.pdf.

The financial hardships of the Great Depression underscored the need for some type of universal retirement and disability program, and the passage of the Social Security Act in 1935 helped meet the need for financial security. The program's purpose was to provide a minimum floor of retirement income, with the balance supplied through private savings. It wasn't until World War II that private pension plans became an important factor in the economy. By 1945, private pension plans covered 6.4 million workers, up 50 percent from the number that had been covered 5 years earlier. The number of Americans covered by pension plans continued to grow, with 9.8 million covered in 1950 and 21 million by 1960. More recently, there were 85.8 million active participants in private pension plans in 2006. Private pension fund assets totaled $8.1 trillion in 2010. Exhibit 17.5 shows pension fund assets in 2010 for private plans, state and local government plans, and federal government plans.

Various laws have addressed specific provisions of pension plans and attempted to safeguard pension benefits. Some of these include the Self-Employed Individuals Tax Retirement Act of 1962, the Employee Retirement Income Security Act of 1974 (ERISA), the Pension Reform Act of 1978, the Economic Recovery Tax Act of 1981 (ERTA), the Tax Equity and Fiscal Responsibility Act of 1982 (TEFRA), and the Tax Reform Act of 1986. The Economic Growth and Tax Relief Reconciliation Act of 2001 increased the tax advantages of private pension plans for employers and employees.

GOVERNMENT PENSION PLANS

State and local government employee pension plans are designed to cover teachers, police officers, firefighters, and other employees of states, counties, and cities. Tax deductibility of pension contributions is not an issue for government entities, so such plans are typically exempt from ERISA and other rules that apply to private pensions. The federal government operates a number of pension funds. Some are large retirement funds of civil service and military employees; others are small separate funds for employees of the foreign service, the federal judiciary, the Tennessee Valley Authority, and the Board of Governors of the Federal Reserve System.

The largest government retirement plan is Social Security, formally referred to as Old Age, Survivors, and Disability Insurance (OASDI). **Social Security old-age benefits** are financed through a payroll tax on employers, employees, and the self-employed. Retirement benefits are paid to those workers who have earned enough credits under the system through paying the payroll tax. Social Security retirement benefits were paid to 34.6 million retired workers in 2010. The benefits totaled $487.9 billion, with an average monthly benefit of $1,175.

Social Security old-age benefits are intended to provide a minimum floor of retirement income for those covered by the plan. Participants do not contribute directly to their own benefits; instead, retirement benefits are paid from the Social Security taxes of those currently working. Under the current system, individuals may elect to retire at age 65 and receive full retirement benefits. Retirement benefits are available as early as age 62, but the benefit is permanently reduced to 80 percent of the full retirement benefit. For those born after 1960, the age for full retirement benefits is 67. Retirement benefits are available at age 62, but the benefit is permanently reduced to 70 percent of the full benefit.

Social Security is a social insurance program. Social insurance programs combine elements of private insurance and welfare. Social Security benefits stress **social adequacy**, slanting benefits in favor of certain groups (e.g., lower-paid workers) in order to achieve a broader social goal, a minimum floor of income for everyone. Private pension plans and insurance plans stress **individual equity**, paying benefits in direct relation to contributions.

PRIVATE PENSION PLANS

Private pension plans are plans established by private-sector groups, such as industrial, commercial, union, or service organizations, as well as plans established by individuals that are not employment related. Private pension plans are afforded significant tax advantages if they satisfy a number of rules. Plans may be organized in a number of ways, depending on how the plan is funded, benefit or contribution guarantees, and whether the plan is insured.

Significant tax advantages are available to employers and employees through private pension plans. However, to enjoy these tax advantages the plan must satisfy a lengthy list of rules. **Qualified plans** are plans that satisfy the rules and are therefore granted favorable tax treatment. Employers are permitted to deduct pension contributions as a business expense. Employees do not have to pay tax currently on employer contributions. If the employee contributes to the plan, pretax dollars as opposed to after-tax dollars are used. The employee's pension benefit accumulates on a tax-deferred basis, with distributions not taxed until the money is distributed.

Another characteristic of private pension plans is how the plans are funded. **Noncontributory plans** are funded through employer contributions only. **Contributory plans** use employer and employee contributions. A 401(k) plan, in which an employee makes a contribution and the employer matches the contribution, is an example of a contributory plan. Some plans are fully contributory. Under a **fully contributory plan**, only the employee makes contributions to the plan.

An important consideration in a private pension plan is the promise made by the employer. Older, larger plans tend to be defined benefit plans. Under a **defined benefit plan**, the employer states the benefit that the employee receives at retirement. The benefit may be a flat dollar amount, a percentage of average salary over a specified period, or a unit benefit formula based on period of employment and salary. An example of a unit benefit plan would be an employer who awards 2.5 percent per year of service, with the total multiplied by average salary during the three highest consecutive years. So an employee who worked for the company for 20 years would receive 50 percent (20×2.5 percent) of the average salary for those 3 years as his or her pension benefit.

Defined benefit plans are difficult to administer and place the investment risk squarely on the employer. Consider determining the appropriate annual pension contribution for the employee in the previous unit benefit example. How long will the employee be with the company? What will his or her average salary be? How long will he or she live after employment when the company terminates? What rate of return will be earned on pension assets? Under a defined benefit plan, the employer promises a benefit and then must fund the plan so that the benefit can be paid.

Defined contribution plans have increased in importance in recent years. Indeed, most of the new plans being started today are defined contribution plans. Employers like these plans because they are easy to administer and they shift the investment risk to the employee/retiree. Under a defined contribution plan, all the employer states is what is set aside for the employee. For example, an employer may promise to contribute 4 percent of an employee's salary to the employee's pension account. For an employee who earns $50,000 per year, the employer contributes $2,000. No guarantees are offered about the actual benefit payable at retirement. If the investment performance is favorable, a larger benefit is payable. If the performance is not favorable, a smaller benefit is payable. Defined contribution plans often permit employees to decide where to invest their retirement funds, and several funds are often available.

Another way in which pension funds can be characterized is whether the plan is insured or noninsured. An **insured pension plan** is established with a life insurance company. A **noninsured pension plan** is managed by a trustee appointed by the sponsoring organization, such as a business or union. The trustee is usually a commercial bank or trust company, which holds and invests the contributions and pays retirement benefits in accordance with the terms of the trust. In some instances, the investment procedure is handled directly by the sponsoring organization, as in the case of large companies or unions. Pension funds constitute more than one-third of the assets of commercial banks' trust departments, and there is intense competition among financial institutions for the business of managing these large sums of money. Total assets held by all private and government-administered pension funds, excluding Social Security, exceeded $12.1 trillion in 2010. Private pension funds accounted for the majority of this total.

PROVISIONS OF ERISA AND SUBSEQUENT LEGISLATION

The **Employee Retirement Income Security Act (ERISA)** was signed into law on Labor Day, 1974. The law does not require employers to establish a pension program for their employees; it does, however, require that certain standards be observed if the plan is to receive favorable tax treatment. ERISA was passed because Congress had become concerned that many workers with long years of service were failing to receive pension benefits. In some instances, workers were forced out of work before retirement age. In other situations, pension funds failed in their fiduciary responsibilities to their participants because the firms failed, pension plans were inadequately funded, or pension assets were mismanaged.

Some of ERISA's more important provisions attempted to (1) strengthen the fiduciary responsibilities of a pension fund's trustees, (2) establish reporting and disclosure requirements, (3) provide for insurance of the retirees' pension benefits in the event of default or termination of the plan, and (4) allow self-employed persons to make tax-deferred pension contributions. Because of the importance of ERISA and its far-reaching implications for pension fund operations, some of its more important provisions are discussed below.

To prevent employers from designing plans that cover only highly compensated employees, certain minimum coverage rules must be observed to receive favorable tax treatment. ERISA also established **minimum funding standards** for the funding of benefits under qualified plans. *Funding* refers to employers setting aside money to pay future pension benefits. To remain qualified, contributions to pension plans must be sufficient to both meet current costs and amortize past service liabilities and payments over not more than 40 years. Employers who fail to meet the funding requirements are subject to substantial tax penalties.

Portability is the workers' right to take pension benefits with them when changing jobs. Workers changing jobs may defer taxes on a lump-sum distribution of vested credits from their employers by investing them in a tax-qualified individual retirement account (IRA) or by depositing them in the new employer's plan. The law does not require any specific portability provisions from plan to plan.

Vesting refers to an employee's right to employer-promised pension benefits or employer contributions. To remain qualified under the tax code, defined benefit plans and some defined contribution plans must satisfy one of two standards: complete vesting after 5 years (called *cliff vesting*, as it is all-or-nothing) or 20 percent vesting after 3 years, with an additional 20 percent per year vested over the next 4 years so vesting is complete after 7 years (*graduated vesting*). The Economic Growth and Tax Relief Reconciliation Act of 2001 tightens the vesting standards for defined contribution plans in which employers match employee contributions. Such plans must be fully vested after 3 years (cliff vesting) or achieve full vesting under a graduated schedule after 6 years. It's important to recall that these standards are minimums—employers are free to be more generous with vesting if they prefer.

A federal insurance agency, the **Pension Benefit Guarantee Corporation (PBGC)**, was established under ERISA. The PBGC insures defined benefit plans up to a specified amount per month. Only benefits that are vested under a plan prior to termination are guaranteed by the PBGC. If a plan is overfunded when it is terminated, the employer is entitled to receive a reversion of surplus assets. The Tax Reform Act of 1986 imposed a 10 percent tax on reversions to reduce the incentive for terminating such plans.

A **plan fiduciary** is any trustee, investment adviser, or other person who has discretionary authority or responsibility in the management of the plan or its assets. Fiduciaries are required to perform their duties solely in the interest of plan participants and beneficiaries as defined in the pension law. ERISA imposes personal liability on plan fiduciaries who do not render the standard of care required.

All plans are required to file a report (Form 5500) with the Department of Labor annually. This report discloses information about pension and welfare plans, their operations, and their financial conditions to the secretary of labor and to plan participants and their beneficiaries.

Overall, ERISA is viewed as a milestone in pension legislation. The creation of the PBGC was particularly important from the employee's standpoint. Before ERISA, when an employer went bankrupt, the employee could not collect anything beyond what was in the pension fund. The PBGC relieves employees of the risk of losing pension benefits up to the established maximum amount per month. ERISA's provisions have been strengthened by subsequent legislation, including ERTA, TEFRA, the Tax Reform Act of 1986, and the Economic Growth and Tax Relief Reconciliation Act of 2001. This legislation tightens vesting standards, penalizes companies for asset reversions, and reduces discrimination favoring highly compensated employees.

DO YOU UNDERSTAND?

1. How are Social Security old-age benefits funded? Are these benefits based on social adequacy or individual equity?
2. What are the tax advantages of qualified private pension plans?
3. Explain the difference between *contributory* and *noncontributory* pension plans. Differentiate between *defined benefit* and *defined contribution* pension plans.
4. ERISA and subsequent acts regulate several features of qualified private pensions. What is meant by *portability*, *vesting*, and *fiduciary standards*?

SUMMARY OF LEARNING OBJECTIVES

1 Explain how the insurance mechanism works, including the concepts of pooling and risk transfer, and the requisites of privately insurable risks. *Insurance* involves the transfer of a pure risk from one party to an entity that pools the risk and provides payment if a loss occurs. Risk is transferred, and the party accepting the risk becomes responsible for payment should a loss occur. The risk is pooled in that the party transferring risk bears the average loss of the group of insureds instead of a large uncertain loss. Not all risks are privately insurable. For a risk to be privately insurable, the following conditions must be met: (1) there must be a large number of similar exposure units, (2) losses should be accidental and unintentional, (3) losses must not be catastrophic, (4) losses should be determinable and measurable, (5) chance of loss must be calculable, and (6) the premium for the coverage must be affordable.

2 Define *objective risk* and explain the ways in which insurers can reduce the objective risk of their operations. *Objective risk* is the variation between expected losses and actual losses. An insurance company does not know up-front what its loss experience will be. There are several ways in which insurers reduce objective risk: (1) insuring many risks, thereby applying the law of large numbers; (2) carefully underwriting the risks; (3) making the insured pay a portion of the loss through deductibles, co-payments, internal policy limits, and exclusions; and (4) reinsuring some or all of the insurance written.

3 Discuss the economic structure of the insurance industry, the various forms of organizations that operate in the insurance industry, and how and why the insurance industry is regulated. The market structure of the insurance industry is a pure competition model. There are a large number of buyers and sellers, no buyers and sellers are dominant, the product bought and sold is relatively homogeneous, and the barriers to entry (financial capital rather than physical capital) are not severe. The insurance industry is characterized by the presence of diverse forms of organizations. There are stock companies, mutual companies that are owned by their policyowners, reciprocals, and Lloyd's associations. The insurance industry is regulated primarily at the state level. The sources of regulation include legislation, court decisions, and state insurance departments. The industry is regulated to protect against the insolvency of insurers, to protect consumers who may have inadequate knowledge, to make sure that insurance rates are not excessive, and to make insurance available.

4 Describe the major products marketed by life and health insurers. Life and health insurance companies market a number of financial services products to protect insureds and their dependents from financial loss. Life insurance products marketed include term insurance, whole life insurance, universal life insurance, variable life insurance, medical expense coverage, disability income insurance, annuities, and other products.

5 Describe the major products marketed by property and liability insurers. Property and liability insurance companies market a wide array of products for individuals, small businesses, and large corporations. These products protect against direct loss (damage, destruction, or theft of property), indirect loss (loss of profits or increased expenses after a direct loss has occurred), and the consequences of legal liability. If an insured is alleged to be responsible for bodily injury, property damage, or personal injury, the insurer provides for the cost of a legal defense and pays up to the limit of liability if the insured is judged responsible.

6 Describe the balance sheet of life and health insurers and property and liability insurers, and explain the differences in their asset holdings. The balance sheet of life and health insurance companies and property and liability insurance companies is very different from the balance sheet of nonfinancial organizations. The major assets listed are various holdings of financial assets as opposed to plant and equipment. Life and health insurers invest in longer-term assets, matching asset duration with the contracts

issued. Property and liability insurance companies invest in shorter-duration assets. They have a larger relative position in corporate stocks and much smaller holdings in real estate and mortgages. Life insurers list loans to policyowners as an interest-bearing asset. Property and liability insurers have larger relative positions in cash and short-term investments, providing necessary liquidity, and a large surplus position reflecting the riskiness of their operations.

7 Discuss retirement plans, including the various types of government and private pension plans and the regulation of retirement plans. Both government and private-sector pension plans are available. Social Security is the largest government plan, and it is designed to provide a minimum floor of income that should be supplemented with a private pension. Private pensions offer significant tax advantages to employers and employees. Private pension plans may be contributory or noncontributory, and defined benefit or defined contribution. Significant assets accumulate in government and private pension plans. The assets are used to purchase a variety of financial assets, including stocks and bonds.

KEY TERMS

Risk
Insurance
Risk transfer
Pooling
Pure risks
Speculative risks
Objective risk
Law of large numbers
Underwriting
Deductibles
Coinsurance
Reinsurance
Underwriting cycle
Cash-flow underwriting
Stock insurance company
Participating policies
Mutual insurance company
Demutualization

Reciprocal or reciprocal exchange
Lloyd's association
Lloyd's of London
McCarran–Ferguson Act (Public Law 15)
National Association of Insurance Commissioners (NAIC)
Captive insurance company
Securitization of risk
Premature death
Term insurance
Renewable term insurance
Adverse selection
Convertible term insurance
Whole life insurance
Cash value

Superannuation
Universal life insurance
Variable life insurance
Annuities
Health insurance
Patient Protection and Affordable Care Act
Loss reserves
Policyholders' surplus
Perils
Property insurance
Named-perils coverage
All-risk coverage
Liability insurance
Marine insurance
Multiple line policies
Social Security old-age benefits
Social adequacy
Individual equity

Private pension plans
Qualified plans
Noncontributory plans
Contributory plans
Fully contributory plan
Defined benefit plan
Defined contribution plans
Insured pension plan
Noninsured pension plan
Employee Retirement Income Security Act (ERISA)
Minimum funding standards
Portability
Vesting
Pension Benefit Guarantee Corporation (PBGC)
Plan fiduciary

QUESTIONS AND PROBLEMS

1. Throughout this chapter, the role of insurance companies and pension funds as financial intermediaries was stressed. Discuss the financial intermediation process as it applies to insurance companies and pension funds.

2. What is the difference between *pure risk* and *speculative risk*? Provide an example of each of these types of risk.

3. According to the law of large numbers, as the number of insureds increases, risk is reduced. However, as an insurance company writes more policies, it exposes itself to the potential for greater insured losses, which is riskier. Explain this apparent contradiction.

4. To what extent do (a) the risk of unemployment and (b) the risk of war satisfy the requirements of privately insurable risks?

5. What problem is likely to develop for a stock life insurance company that issues participating policies?

6. What are the primary sources of insurance regulation? What areas are regulated?

7. What is meant by the phrase *adverse selection* in insurance? Although discussed in this chapter in connection with term insurance, adverse selection is a problem in all insurance markets. What is the adverse selection risk for insurers marketing life annuities?

8. Term insurance becomes cost prohibitive for older individuals. However, the same insurance companies that do not offer term policies at advanced ages sell whole life insurance. How are these insurers able to offer life insurance for all of life under whole life insurance but not under term insurance?

9. Why did universal life insurance become popular in the 1980s? What explains the popularity of variable life insurance in the 1990s?

10. Why are *annuities* and *life insurance* often described as opposites? If they are opposites, then why do insurance companies marketing life insurance also commonly market life annuities?

11. What is the relationship between the level of life insurance policy loans taken by policyowners and the level of interest rates in the general economy?

12. Why is the liability risk much more difficult to gauge than the property risk?

13. What are the advantages of purchasing a package policy versus purchasing the same coverages included in a package policy separately?

14. What are the major similarities between the balance sheets of life insurance companies and property and liability insurance companies? What are the major differences?

15. How are Social Security old-age benefits funded? What is the age for full retirement benefits for those retiring under Social Security today? What is the age under current law for full retirement benefits when someone who is 20 years old today retires?

16. Differentiate between *defined benefit* and *defined contribution* pension plans. Who bears the investment risk under each of these alternatives? Which type of plan is easier to fund and manage?

17. An insurance company's total assets were $400 million. Its total liabilities were $340 million. What was this insurer's policyholder surplus?

18. Assume it was determined that the insurer in question 17 had overestimated its loss reserves by $20 million. If the loss reserve estimate was corrected, what is the impact on policyholders' surplus?

19. Granite Insurance Company had claims and expenses of $425 million last year. The company's premium income was $450 million. What was the company's combined ratio?

20. Granite Insurance Company's combined ratio 2 years ago was 1.035. A review of that year's financial statements showed the company paid $4.5 million in income taxes. Why was the company required to pay income taxes when its underwriting activities produced a loss, as measured by the combined ratio found in question 19?

INTERNET EXERCISE

There are many useful Web sites with information about insurers and insurance products. However, many of these sites are marketing tools designed to interest you in purchasing financial services products from the sponsor. An excellent site for objective information about insurance is provided by the Insurance Information Institute (http://www.iii.org/). Although the Institute's primary concern is property and liability insurance, some excellent information about life insurance, health insurance, and annuities is also provided. Access the site, and use the links provided in the lower left margin of the home page to answer the following questions.

1. Click on the "Auto Insurance" link in the left margin of the home page.

   a. What six coverages may an auto insurance policy include? (Click on the link for "What is covered by a basic auto policy?")

   b. The average American driver spends about $850 per year on auto insurance. How can you lower your auto insurance premium? (Click on the "How can I save money?" link.)

2. Click on the "Homeowners and Renters Insurance" link in the left margin of the home page.

   a. What four essential coverages are found in a standard homeowner's policy? (See the "What is in a standard homeowner's insurance policy?" link.)

   b. A homeowner should purchase enough insurance to cover the cost of rebuilding the home. What factors determine the cost to rebuild? (See the "How much homeowner's insurance do I need?" link.)

3. Click on the "Life Insurance" link in the left margin of the home page.

   a. What are six reasons for purchasing life insurance? (See the "Why should I buy life insurance?" link.)

   b. What are some factors that you should take into consideration when deciding on the amount of life insurance to purchase? (See the "How much life insurance do I need?" link.)

4. Click on the "Disability Insurance " link in the left margin of the home page.

   a. What are three important sources of income replacement for those who experience a nonoccupational disability? (See the "How can I insure against loss of income?" link.)

   b. What key factors should you look for when shopping for a disability income insurance policy? (See the "How can I purchase disability insurance?" link.)

5. Click on the "Business Insurance—General" link at the bottom of the home page.

   a. Small businesses, like large corporations, have loss exposures. What four types of insurance are essential for small businesses? (See the "Small Business Insurance Basics" link.)

   b. Small businesses often insure their loss exposures by purchasing a business owner's policy (BOP). What coverage is provided through a BOP and what does the BOP not cover? (See the "What does a Business Owners Policy Cover?" link.)

Investment Banking

INVESTMENT BANKING HAS THE allure of allowing one to make lots of money. Careers-in-finance.com recently reported that the typical pay (salary plus bonus) for a first-year associate (which usually requires an MBA) in investment banking was $180,000. Many investment bankers make millions each year as partners in prestigious Wall Street firms. Where else can you even come close to making that much money outside professional athletics or Hollywood? Glamorous profession? Yes, but the job can have its downside.

Unfortunately, the industry has suffered a few black eyes over the years. Investment banks, for example, are frequently accused of having a conflict of interest. In 2002, for instance, Merrill Lynch agreed to a $100 million settlement with New York and other states after being investigated by Eliot Spitzer, the attorney general for New York. Spitzer accused Merrill Lynch and other Wall Street firms of providing its customers with overly rosy research reports about the stocks that the firm's investment banking division was underwriting.

In spite of these black marks on the industry's reputation, few careers offer the same kind of excitement, prestige, and money-making opportunities as investment banking. Analysts work long hours in a high-energy, fast-paced environment where success is quickly rewarded and failure means the end of a

All investment bankers wear red suspenders. They really do! But we have no idea why. The core business activities of investment banks are bringing new securities to the market and participating in secondary markets for those securities. Investment banks also innovate cutting-edge financial products for corporations.

career. It is not uncommon to hear of 20-hour work days, ridiculously large salaries and bonuses, and lavish lifestyles. It is also not uncommon, however, to hear of very short careers because many investment bankers leave the industry quickly. The industry is all about risk and reward, and those who work in the industry face the same trade-off in their own careers: substantial risk and the potential for substantial rewards. ■

This chapter is about Wall Street firms and highlights what are typically referred to as investment banks, the premier players in the capital markets. We discuss investment banks' original primary business activities of underwriting new securities sold in the primary markets and their role as dealers and brokers in the secondary markets. We also discuss other services they provide, such as merger and acquisition advising, private placement financing, asset management, and prime brokerage. Our story is also about large money-center banks and their historical competition with investment banks for products and customers. Commercial banks can now freely engage in investment banking with the relaxation of the depression-era legislation during the 1990s. As a result of the financial crisis of 2007–2009, several of the historically independent large investment banks merged with, or were purchased by, commercial banks (e.g., Bank of America bought Merrill Lynch). The remaining large "independent" investment banks (e.g., Goldman Sachs) converted to bank holding companies or went bankrupt (e.g., Lehman Brothers). As a result, these companies are now regulated and supervised by the Board of Governors of the Federal Reserve. Finally, we discuss the role of private equity, including both venture capitalists and buyout firms. Venture capitalists are often at the heart of the new business formation process. They supply the capital for these high-risk invest-ments in exchange for a share of the ownership. These fledgling businesses are too risky to receive financing through traditional funding sources. Buyout firms likewise play an increasingly important role in capital markets. ■

LEARNING OBJECTIVES

1 Explain the core business activities of investment banks.

2 Explain the reasons for the enactment of the Glass-Steagall Act of 1933 and discuss its impact on commercial and investment banking.

3 Explain the Gramm-Leach-Bliley Act of 1999 and discuss how it is likely to affect the structure of the financial services industry.

4 Explain what happened to most large independent investment banks during the 2007–2009 financial crisis.

5 Explain why investment bankers typically underprice new securities when they are sold in the primary markets.

6 Describe what private equity funds do.

As we discuss in Chapter 1, there are two basic ways that new financial claims can be brought to market: direct or indirect (intermediation) financing. In the indirect credit market, **commercial banks** are the most important participants; in the direct market, **investment banks** are the most important participants. *Investment banks* are firms that specialize in helping businesses and governments sell their new security issues (debt or equity) in the primary markets to finance capital expenditures. In addition, after the securities are sold, investment bankers make secondary markets for the securities as brokers and dealers.

The term *investment bank* is somewhat misleading because those involved have little to do with *commercial banking* (accepting deposits and making com-mercial loans). The Banking Act of 1933, or the Glass-Steagall Act as it is more commonly known, separated the investment-banking and commercial-banking

18.1 THE RELATIONSHIP BETWEEN COMMERCIAL AND INVESTMENT BANKING

industries. The act, however, did allow commercial banks some securities activities, such as underwriting and trading in U.S. government securities and some state and local government bonds. Thus, in the area of public securities, investment banks and commercial banks do compete.

The legislated separation of commercial banking and investment banking in the United States was somewhat unusual. In countries where there is no legislation, commercial banks provide investment-banking services as part of their normal range of business activities. The notable exception to this rule is Japan, which has securities laws that closely resemble those of the United States. Countries where investment banking and commercial banking are combined have what is called a *universal-banking system*. **Universal banks** are institutions that can accept deposits, make loans, underwrite securities, engage in brokerage activities, and sell and manufacture other financial services such as insurance. Most European countries allow universal banks.

During the 1980s and 1990s, commercial banks and investment banks came into competitive conflict. Large money-center and regional commercial banks saw their largest and most profitable customers increasingly switching from intermediation services, such as bank loans, to direct credit-market transactions, such as commercial paper. As a result, large commercial banks in the United States sought to break down the legal barrier to investment banking established by Glass-Steagall. Ultimately, they were successful in breaking down the barriers, but the barriers worked both ways. With the passage of the Financial Service Modernization Act in 1999, commercial banks were allowed to engage in more investment banking activities. At the same time, however, investment banks were allowed to engage in more commercial banking activities. As we see later in the chapter, the story of investment banking is inextricably interwined with that of commercial banking.

STRUCTURE OF THE INDUSTRY

There are hundreds of investment-banking firms doing some underwriting business in the United States. However, the industry is dominated by the 50 largest firms, most of which have their head offices located in New York City. The balance are headquartered in major regional financial centers such as Chicago and Los Angeles.

Exhibit 18.1 lists the 10 largest investment banks ranked by investment banking fees earned in the first half of 2010. The largest investment banking firm (in terms of deals in the first 6 months of 2010) was JPMorgan, who earned more than $2.3 billion in fees. JPMorgan is owned by the bank holding company JPMorgan Chase. JPMorgan is the investment banking side of JPMorgan Chase, while Chase is the commercial and consumer banking business side. Similarly, the second biggest investment banker was Bank of America Merrill Lynch. The "Bank of America" part of the company is, of course, a commercial bank. Goldman Sachs, the third largest investment banker, is the first that doesn't have a direct tie to a traditional commercial bank.

EARLY HISTORY

Investment banks in the United States trace their origins to the prominent investment houses in Europe, and many early investment banks were branches or affiliates of European firms. Early investment banks in the United States

EXHIBIT 18.1

Ten Largest Investment Banks (Based on Fees Earned in the First Half of 2010)

	Fees ($ Millions)	Percentage of Fees Earned			
		Mergers and Acquisitions	Equity	Bonds	Loans
JPMorgan	2,319.99	28	27	30	15
Bank of America Merrill Lynch	2,001.48	18	26	35	21
Goldman Sachs	1,736.88	41	31	23	4
Morgan Stanley	1,703.28	42	33	23	2
Credit Suisse	1,420.71	33	25	36	6
Deutsche Bank	1,387.51	31	21	39	10
Citi	1,350.41	28	25	37	10
Barclays Capital	1,131.86	28	17	44	11
UBS	1,045.14	35	36	26	3
BNP Paribas	602.23	22	14	44	21

JPMorgan was the top investment banker in the first half of 2010. The fees it earned were spread relatively evenly over mergers and acquisitions, equity offerings, bond offerings, and loans.

Source: Financial Times Investment Banking Review, August 28, 2010.

differed from commercial banks. Commercial banks were corporations that were chartered exclusively to issue banknotes (money) and make short-term business loans; early investment banks were partnerships and, therefore, were not subject to the regulations that apply to corporations. As such, investment banks, referred to as **private banks** at the time, could engage in any business activity they wished and could have offices in any location. Although investment banks could not issue banknotes, they could accept deposits as well as underwrite and trade in securities.

The golden era of investment banking began after the Civil War. Following the war, the United States began to build a railroad system that linked the country together and provided the infrastructure for industrialization. Modern investment-banking houses acted as intermediaries between the railroad firms—which needed massive amounts of capital to finance roadbeds, track, bridges, and rolling stock—and investors located primarily on the East Coast and in Europe. Because of the distance between investors and the investment project, investors found it difficult to estimate the value of the securities offered. The reputation of investment bankers to price securities fairly made these transactions possible.

With the rapid industrialization of the United States, companies began selling new securities publicly, and outstanding securities were traded on organized exchanges. The demand for financial services led to the growth of powerful investment-banking firms like those led by Jay Cooke, J. Pierpont Morgan,

Marcus Goldman, and Solomon Loeb. These organizations created some of the giant businesses of the 20th century, such as United States Steel.

As it turned out, investment banking was a very profitable business. Firms discovered innumerable ways to make money, such as charging fees for underwriting, financial consulting, trading securities, redeployment of a client's deposited funds, private placements, doing mergers and acquisitions, and so on. Early commercial banks, which were chartered exclusively to issue banknotes and make short-term loans, soon began to covet a wider range of financial activities, especially those that were highly profitable. Over time, because of competitive pressures, states began to permit their state-chartered commercial banks to engage in selected investment-banking activities.

National banks, which were regulated by the comptroller of the currency, began pressuring the comptroller for expanded powers. At first, national banks could underwrite and trade only in securities that they were permitted to invest in, which were primarily federal and municipal securities. With time, competitive pressure from state banks, which gained expanded powers more quickly, forced the comptroller to grant national banks the authority to underwrite and trade in corporate bonds and equities. Finally, national banks were allowed to organize state-chartered security affiliates that could engage in full-service investment banking. Thus, by 1930, commercial banks and investment banks were almost fully integrated, and they or their security affiliates were underwriting more than 50 percent of all new bond issues sold.

THE GLASS-STEAGALL ACT AND ITS AFTERMATH

In the 1930s, the long history of suspicion and questionable practices caught up with the investment-banking industry. On October 28, 1929, the stock market declined 12.8 percent, signaling the "Crash of 1929" and the beginning of the Great Depression. During the Great Depression (1929–1933), output declined 30.5 percent compared to the beginning of 1929, and unemployment rose to more than 20 percent of the workforce. More than 9,000 commercial banks failed. The country and the financial system were devastated. To deal with the crisis at hand, Congress enacted legislation. To regulate investment banks and Wall Street, Congress enacted the Securities Act of 1933; the Securities Exchange Act of 1934; and, of course, the Glass-Steagall Act of 1933 to regulate the banking system. Thus, after years of functioning with little regulation, the financial sector—the securities industry and commercial banking system—became one of the most heavily regulated sectors in the economy.

The Glass-Steagall Act of 1933 effectively separated commercial banking from investment banking. The Glass-Steagall Act is technically known as the *Banking Act of 1933*. The act's popular name comes from its major sponsors, Senator Carter Glass, who sponsored the Senate bill on commercial and investment banking, and Representative Henry Steagall, who sponsored the House bill on federal deposit insurance. The Banking Act of 1933 combined the two bills. The act did the following:

- It prohibited commercial banks from underwriting or trading (for their own account) stocks, bonds, or other securities. The major exceptions were U.S. government securities, general obligation bonds of state and local governments, and bank securities such as CDs.

- It limited the debt securities that commercial banks could purchase for their own account to those approved by bank regulatory authorities.
- It prohibited individuals and firms engaged in investment banking from simultaneously engaging in commercial banking.

Thus, commercial banks and investment banks were given a choice of being one or the other, but not both. Most firms elected to stay in their primary line of business and divested themselves of the prohibited activity. However, not all firms did this. For example, Citibank, Chase Manhattan Bank, and Harris Trust took the most common route and dissolved their security affiliates. The investment-banking firm of JPMorgan decided to maintain a position as a commercial bank through its subsidiary, Morgan Guaranty and Trust Co. However, some senior partners left the firm to form the investment house of Morgan Stanley. The First Boston Corporation was patched together out of the cast-off security affiliates of several commercial banks, one of which was the affiliate of the First National Bank of Boston.

The Glass-Steagall Act, when passed, had three basic objectives: (1) to discourage speculation in financial markets, (2) to prevent conflict of interest and self-dealing, and (3) to restore confidence in the safety and soundness of the banking system. Regarding speculation, the act's proponents argued that if banks were affiliated with securities dealers, banks would have incentives to lend to customers of the security affiliates, who would use the money to buy stock on credit. Thus, banks engaged in investment banking were channeling money into speculative investment rather than into what was believed to be more productive investments. The conflict-of-interest rationale hinged on the fear that commercial banks might make imprudent loans to firms it had underwritten securities for in order to gain additional securities business. Thus, the quality of the bank's loan portfolio could be compromised by the bank's dual role of lender and investment banker.

Perhaps the most important reason for the Glass-Steagall Act was the fear concerning bank safety and the desire to prevent bank failures. Simply stated, investment banking is a risky business. Debt and equity markets are inherently subject to large price fluctuations, with the risk of such fluctuations being borne by security dealers and underwriters. The act insulated commercial banks from that risk by prohibiting them from acting as dealers, underwriters of securities, and investors in private-sector companies.

THE COMPETITION BETWEEN COMMERCIAL AND INVESTMENT BANKING

Beginning in the 1980s, large U.S. commercial banks increasingly pursued their desire to engage in investment banking. These banks discovered that commercial banking was not as profitable as it once was, whereas some investment-banking activities were becoming extremely profitable. At the same time, many of their best customers were turning to investment banks for short-term financing, the traditional business of commercial banks. Commercial banks wanted the flexibility, as other financial firms have, to shift to other, more profitable product lines as business conditions change. Because of the lack of flexibility, some large commercial banks in New York City, most notably Chase Manhattan (now JPMorgan Chase), threatened to give up their banking charters so that they could operate as investment banks.

Two primary factors changed the relation between commercial and investment banking. First, new electronic information-processing technology reduced the cost of gathering data, manufacturing, and transmitting financial products to the ultimate user. The technology not only made it possible to provide traditional financial services at reduced cost, but also made the creation of new financial products feasible. Lower transaction costs favor direct-credit-market rather than intermediation transactions.

A second reason working against intermediation financing is the regulatory taxes that commercial banks must pay relative to other financial firms. Most important are the requirement to hold non-interest-earning reserves against deposits and the mandatory capital requirements that exceed those that would exist in the absence of regulation. Banks find that they are at a disadvantage in financing and keeping loans on their books, although they still have a comparative advantage in analyzing credit risk and originating transactions. As a result of these forces (economic, technological, and regulatory), there is a trend for borrowers to place debt directly with investors and, correspondingly, to do fewer transactions with intermediaries such as commercial banks. Evidence of declining information costs is found in the shrinking amount of bank borrowing by large and middle-market corporate companies that once relied on banks as their primary source of funds.

SECURITIES ACTIVITIES OF COMMERCIAL BANKS

For many years, banks have been able to underwrite and trade (dealer and broker) U.S. government securities and general obligation bonds, to trade financial futures, to do private placement deals, and to do merger and acquisition work. The securities activities denied commercial banks under the Glass-Steagall Act were underwriting and trading corporate bonds, equities, and commercial paper; underwriting and selling mutual funds; and being a full-service broker and investment adviser.

The 1980s, however, marked the beginning of the crumbling of Glass-Steagall's power to limit banks' securities activities. The most important action of the decade may be the U.S. Supreme Court decision on July 13, 1988, to let stand the Federal Reserve Board's approval for commercial banks to underwrite three new kinds of securities: commercial paper, municipal revenue bonds, and securities backed by mortgages or consumer debt. The new securities activities had to be handled through a separate subsidiary of a bank holding company, and underwriting activities could not account for more than 5 percent of the subsidiary's gross revenues. The Fed's approval of the new powers was based on its interpretation that the percentage limit on underwriting would keep the bank affiliate from being "engaged principally" in securities, which was barred by the Glass-Steagall Act.

At the same time, investment banks began encroaching on activities that were traditionally the preserves of commercial banks. For example, one of the most damaging moves into retail banking was the introduction of money market mutual funds that drew billions of dollars away from commercial banks during the high-interest-rate periods of the late 1970s and early 1980s. It was not until banks were allowed to offer money market deposit accounts that banks regained a portion of their customers. At the commercial level, investment banks moved into short-term business financing with commercial paper, which drew corporate borrowers away from banks to the securities houses that marketed the paper. Finally, investment banks entered the foreign exchange market, which was traditionally a bank activity.

THE FINANCIAL SERVICES MODERNIZATION ACT OF 1999

By the late 1990s, commercial banks became free to acquire investment banks in spite of the Glass-Steagall Act because of various rulings by regulators and the passage of the Financial Services Modernization Act of 1999 (the Gramm-Leach-Bliley Act). Recall from Chapter 15 that the Gramm-Leach-Bliley Act allows commercial banks, investment banks, and insurance companies to affiliate with each other as part of a *financial holding company* organizational structure. The first acquisition of a major investment bank by a commercial bank occurred in 1997, when Bankers Trust of New York, now part of Deutsche Bank, bought Alex Brown for $2.1 billion. This acquisition, for practical purposes, signaled the end of the Depression-era legislation—Glass-Steagall Act. Large commercial banks are now able to freely enter into investment banking. Today, nearly every large commercial bank has a significant investment-banking affiliate. Likewise, investment banks (and insurance companies) are able to acquire commercial-banking affiliates and form financial holding companies.

PEOPLE & EVENTS

Where, Oh, Where Have All the Investment Banks Gone?

At the beginning of 2008 there were five major independent investment banks—Bear Stearns, Lehman Brothers, Merrill Lynch, Morgan Stanley, and Goldman Sachs. By the end of 2008, there were none. The first to go was Bear Stearns. In January 2007, Bear Stearns sold for more than $171 per share. A little more than a year later (in March 2008), commercial bank JPMorgan Chase agreed to buy Bear Stearns for $2 per share—and even then only with a guarantee from the Federal Reserve to cover losses associated with Bear Stearns' investments. (Due to investor outrage, JPMorgan Chase eventually paid $10 per share for Bear Stearns.) Bear Stearns' problem arose from heavy subprime mortgage investments and clients' concerns that Bear Stearns would run out of cash. This created a run on the bank and, effectively, Bear Stearns did run out of cash. JPMorgan Chase's purchase was orchestrated, at least in part, by the Federal Reserve and Treasury Department.

And then there were four.

Like Bear Stearns, Merrill Lynch and Lehman Brothers had also invested heavily in mortgage-backed securities (primarily collateralized debt obligations [CDOs]). As losses mounted, a liquidity crisis developed. In the middle of September 2008, Bank of America agreed to buy Merrill Lynch, ultimately paying about $29 per share for a stock that sold for $75 per share a year earlier. Lehman Brothers, on the other hand, found no suitor and was forced to file for bankruptcy.

And then there were two.

Near the end of September 2008, the last two major independent investment banks, Goldman Sachs and Morgan Stanley, announced they would reorganize as bank holding companies—resulting in greater regulation and supervision but also access to the Fed's discount window.

And then there were none.

Goldman Sachs and Morgan Stanley's transformation to bank holding companies was timely. A few weeks after their transformation, the Treasury began the Troubled Asset Relief Program (TARP), which allowed the Treasury to purchase troubled assets from bank holding companies, including Goldman Sachs and Morgan Stanley. *Troubled assets* were defined as basically mortgages and securities whose value depends on mortgages. In fact, a number of firms, not just investment banks, decided to become bank holding companies in late 2008, including insurance giant American International Group (AIG); GM's financing arm (GMAC Financial Services); and credit card giant, American Express.

18.2 PRIMARY SERVICES OF AN INVESTMENT BANK

Although still called investment banks, the major players in the investment-banking business engage in a number of activities. Exhibit 18.2, for example, lists segment and subsegment revenue for Goldman Sachs in 2009. As you can see, at least for Goldman Sachs, investment banking represents a relatively small portion of their business, accounting for less than 11 percent of their 2009 revenue (i.e., $4,797 million investment-banking revenue versus $45,173 million total revenue). This section describes the major business activities of investment-banking firms. We begin with the investment-banking portion of the business, which consists of bringing new securities to the public market, private placements, and mergers and acquisitions. In the case of Goldman Sachs, the first two fall under the underwriting business, while the last one falls under the financial advisory business.

BRINGING NEW SECURITIES TO MARKET

One of the basic services offered by an investment-banking firm is to bring to market new debt and equity securities issued by private firms or governmental units. New issues of stocks or bonds are called **primary offerings**. If the company has never before offered securities to the public, the primary offering is called an **unseasoned offering** or an **initial public offering (IPO)**. Otherwise, if the firm already has similar securities trading in the market, the primary issue is called a **seasoned offering**.

EXHIBIT 18.2
Goldman Sachs' Revenue by Segment (2009, in Millions)

Segment	Business	$ Millions	$ Millions
Investment banking			
	Underwriting	2,904	
	Financial advisory	1,893	
	Total (investment banking)		$4,797
Trading and principal investments			
	Fixed income, currency, and commodities (FICC)	23,316	
	Equities	9,886	
	Principal investments	1,171	
	Total (trading and principal investments)		34,373
Asset management and security services			
	Asset management	3,970	
	Security services	2,033	
	Total (asset management and security services)		6,003
Total		45,173	45,173

In 2009, less than 11 percent of Goldman Sachs' revenue came from its investment banking business.

Source: Goldman Sachs 2009 Annual Report.

An offering can be either a **public offering** or a **private placement**. If a company decides to make a public offering, it must then decide whether to have the issue underwritten or sold through a **best-efforts offering**. As the terms imply, in an underwritten issue, the investment banker is guaranteeing (or **underwriting**) that the issuer receives a fixed amount of money whether the securities are all sold to investors or not. In a best-efforts issue, the investment banker makes no such guarantee and instead promises only to make its best sales effort. In this case, the investment banker does not take on the risk associated with underwriting, and compensation is based on the number of securities sold. Not surprisingly, most issuing corporations prefer underwritten to best-efforts contracts, so the actual decision on issue type falls to the investment banker, who usually forces only the smallest and riskiest issues to be handled on a best-efforts basis.

Another decision that must be made by a corporation is whether to solicit investment-banking services through **competitive bidding**. With competitive bidding, the issuer publicly announces a desire to sell securities and solicits offers from several investment-banking firms. The alternative is direct negotiation with a single investment banker. Almost all corporations that have a real choice (utilities frequently are legally required to use competitive bidding) choose **negotiated offering** procedures.

The seemingly irrational choice of negotiated offerings can be explained by the fact that investment bankers must invest in performing due diligence examinations of potential security issuers. This means that they are legally required to diligently search out and disclose all relevant information about an issuer before securities are sold to the public, or the underwriter can be held legally responsible for investor losses that occur after the issue is sold. Because investors understand that the most prestigious investment bankers have the most to lose from inadequate due diligence, the mere fact that these firms are willing to underwrite an issue provides valuable certification that the issuing company is in fact disclosing all material information. With so much to lose, top-tier investment bankers are unlikely to be enticed by competitive bid issues that entail the same risk, but far less profit, as negotiated bids. Thus, issuing firms are willing to pay the higher direct issuance costs of a negotiated bid to obtain the services of a prestigious underwriter.

One of the problems investment bankers face with IPOs is how to price them because they are securities that have never been traded. The price for which a security is sold is important to the issuer because the higher the price, the more money the company gets. If the security is priced too high, however, there may not be sufficient demand for the security, and the offering may be canceled or the underwriter may not be able to sell the issue at the proposed offering price. In this case, the investment banker suffers a loss.

The average IPO suffers from **underpricing**. Shares are typically sold to investors at an offering price that is, on average, about 15 percent below the closing price of the shares after the first day of trading. This implies that underwriters deliberately (and consistently) sell shares to investors for only six-sevenths of their value. Exhibit 18.3 gives information on the number of IPOs per year since 1980, the average initial return to investors, and the gross proceeds raised.

In bringing securities to market, investment bankers take clients through three steps: origination, underwriting (risk bearing), and distribution. Depending on the method of sale and the client's needs, an investment banker may provide these services.

EXHIBIT 18.3
Initial Public Offerings and Returns

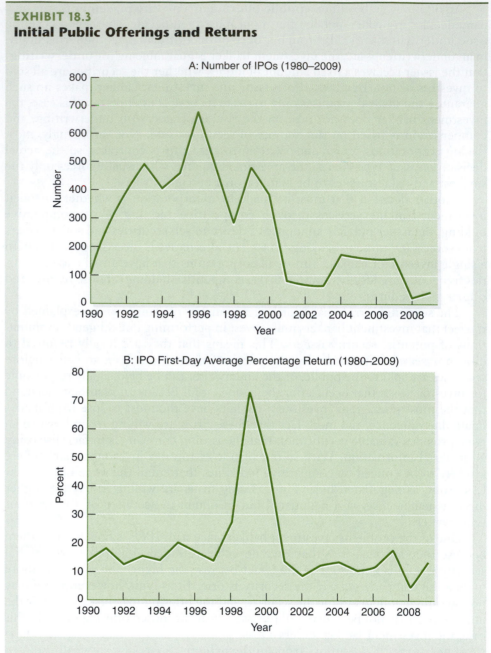

Initial public offerings (IPOs) usually earn large, positive initial returns for investors who are allocated shares. Note that these graphs exclude offerings with an initial price of less than $5 per share.

Source: Jay Ritter's Web page (http://bear.warrington.ufl.edu/ritter/ipodata.htm).

Origination. During the origination of a new security issue, the investment banker can help the issuer analyze the feasibility of the project and determine the amount of money to raise; decide on the type of financing needed (debt, equity); design the characteristics of securities to be issued, such as maturity, coupon rate, and the presence of a call provision and/or sinking fund for debt issues; and provide advice on the best sale date so that the issuer can get the highest possible price.

Once the decision to issue the securities is made, the investment banker can help the client prepare the official sale documents. If the securities are to be sold publicly, security laws require that a **registration statement** be filed with the Securities and Exchange Commission (SEC). A portion of this statement, called the **preliminary prospectus**, contains detailed information about the issuer's financial condition, business activities, industry competition, management and their experience, the project for which the funds will be used, the characteristics of the securities to be issued, and the risks of the securities. After approval by the SEC, the **final prospectus** is reproduced in quantity and distributed to all potential investors. By law, investors must have a final prospectus before they can invest. The information in the prospectus allows investors to make intelligent decisions about the proposed project and its risk. SEC approval implies only that the information presented is timely and fair; approval is not an endorsement by the SEC as to investment quality. Exhibit 18.4 shows the front page of a final prospectus.

During the registration process for a debt issue, the investment banker can also help secure a credit rating; coordinate the activities of a bond counsel, who passes an opinion about the legality of the security issue; select a transfer agent for secondary market sales; select a trustee, who sees that the issuer fulfills its obligation under the security contract; and arrange for printing of the securities so that they can be distributed to investors. For an equity issue, the investment banker can arrange for the securities to be listed on a stock exchange or traded in the over-the-counter market.

Underwriting. *Underwriting*, or bearing price risk, is what most people think that investment bankers do in a firm-commitment offering. Underwriting is the process whereby the investment banker guarantees to buy the new securities for a fixed price. The risk exists between the time the investment banker purchases the securities from the issuer and the time they are resold to the public. The risk (inventory risk) is that the securities may be sold for less than the **underwriting syndicate** paid for them. In seasoned offerings, there is a risk of unforeseen price changes as a result of changes in market conditions. For example, in October 1979, IBM issued $1 billion in bonds through a syndicate of underwriters. As the issue was coming to market, interest rates suddenly jumped upward, causing bond prices to tumble, and the underwriters lost in excess of $10 million. In unseasoned offerings, there is no prior market price on which to base the offering price.

To decrease the price risk of any one primary issue, underwriters form syndicates comprising other investment-banking firms. Each member of the syndicate is responsible for its pro rata share of the securities being issued. By participating in the syndicate, each underwriter receives a portion of the underwriting fee as well as an allocation of the securities being sold that it can sell to its own customers. In addition, other investment-banking firms, known as the *selling group*, can be enlisted to assist in the sale of the securities being issued. Members of the selling group bear no underwriting responsibility but receive a commission for whatever securities they sell.

Distribution. Once the investment banker purchases the securities, they must be resold to investors. The syndicate's primary concern is to sell the securities as quickly as possible at the offering price. If the securities are not sold within a few days, the underwriting syndicate disbands, and members sell the securities at whatever price they can get.

EXHIBIT 18.4

The Front Page of a Final Prospectus

Filed Pursuant to Rule 424(b)(4)
Registration No. 333-114442-01,
333-117324

Prospectus
24,221,929 shares

Domino's Pizza, Inc.

Common stock

Domino's Pizza, Inc., the parent company of Domino's, Inc., is selling 9,375,000 shares of common stock, and the selling stockholders identified in this prospectus are selling an additional 14,846,929 shares. We will not receive any of the proceeds from the sale of the shares by the selling stockholders. This is the initial public offering of our common stock.

Prior to this offering, there has been no public market for our common stock. Our common stock has been approved for listing on the New York Stock Exchange under the symbol "DPZ."

	Per share	Total
Initial public offering price	$ 14.00	$339,107,006
Underwriting discount	$ 0.96	$ 23,253,052
Proceeds to Domino's Pizza, Inc., before expenses	$ 13.04	$122,250,000
Proceeds to selling stockholders, before expenses	$ 13.04	$193,603,954

The selling stockholders have granted the underwriters an option for a period of 30 days to purchase up to 3,633,289 additional shares of our common stock on the same terms and conditions set forth above to cover overallotments, if any.

Investing in our common stock involves a high degree of risk. See "Risk factors" beginning on page 9.

Neither the Securities and Exchange Commission nor any state securities commission has approved or disapproved of these securities or passed upon the adequacy or accuracy of this prospectus. Any representation to the contrary is a criminal offense.

The offering is being made on a firm commitment basis, and the underwriters expect to deliver the shares of common stock to investors on July 16, 2004.

JPMorgan   ### Citigroup

Bear, Stearns & Co. Inc.

Credit Suisse First Boston

Lehman Brothers

July 12, 2004

The prospectus provides full disclosure of relevant information to prospective investors in compliance with U.S. securities laws.

The sales function is divided into institutional sales and retail sales. Retail sales involve selling the securities to individual investors and firms that purchase in small quantities. Examples of national investment-banking firms with a strong retail presence are Merrill Lynch, with an extensive network of 950 branches, and Morgan Stanley Smith Barney, with 920 offices. Most regional investment-banking firms specialize in retail sales. Institutional sales involve the sale of a large block of securities to institutional purchasers, such as pension funds, insurance companies, endowment trusts, or mutual funds.

Private Placements. The other portion of Goldman Sachs' underwriting business is arranging private placements. A private placement is a method of issuing securities in which the issuer sells the securities directly to the ultimate investors. Because there is usually no underwriting in a private placement deal, the investment banker's role is to bring buyer and seller together, help determine a fair price for the securities, and execute the transaction. For these services, the investment banker earns a fee. Firms choose between a private placement and public sale depending on which method of sale offers to the issuer the highest possible price for the securities after transaction costs.

To qualify for a private placement exemption, the sale of the securities must be restricted to a small group of **accredited investors**. To qualify as an accredited investor, the individual or institution must meet certain income and wealth requirements. The reasoning for the private placement exemption is that accredited investors are financially sophisticated and do not need the protection afforded by the registration process. Typical institutional accredited investors include insurance companies, pension funds, mutual funds, and venture capitalists.

Private placements have several advantages over public securities offerings. They are less costly in terms of time and money than registering with the SEC, and the issuers do not have to reveal confidential information. Also, because there are typically far fewer investors, the terms of a private placement are easier to renegotiate, if necessary. The disadvantage of private placements is that the securities have no readily available market price, they are less liquid, and there is a smaller group of potential investors compared to the public market.

One of the restrictions the Securities Act of 1933 imposed on buyers of private placements was that they hold the securities for at least 2 years. At the time, it was feared that firms would sell their new securities issues through the private placement market as a means to circumvent the new regulations requiring that securities sold in the public markets be registered with the SEC. The legislation was designed to protect less-sophisticated investors with small portfolios from being duped into purchasing risky or fraudulent unregistered securities. Rule 144A removes this restriction and allows large institutions to trade private placements among themselves without having to hold the securities for 2 years or register them with the SEC. *Large institutions* are defined as firms that hold a security portfolio of at least $100 million. The rule significantly improves the liquidity of private placements and, hence, reduces the cost of raising funds.

Mergers and Acquisitions. Mergers and acquisitions also fall under the Investment-Banking segment (see Exhibit 18.2). Beginning in the 1980s, mergers and acquisitions (M&As) became an important and highly profitable business activity for investment-banking firms. Growth in the M&A market resulted from the large number of business consolidations driven by technology and the globalization of business. Although the level of M&A activity ebbs and flows with economic conditions, M&A work continues to be an important part of investment banks' business.

Investment banks provide four categories of M&A services for which they earn fees. First, investment bankers help firms identify M&A candidates that match the acquiring firm's needs. Large investment banks have a global network of industry and regional contacts that can quickly identify potential acquisition candidates and assess their interest in being acquired.

Second, the investment bank does all of the analysis necessary to price the deal once an acquisition candidate firm is located. These activities include reviewing the target firm's financial statements and financial projections; estimating the expected future cash flows; evaluating the firm's management team; performing due diligence; and, finally, determining the estimated value (price) of the firm. **Due diligence** is checking the validity of all the important information the firm provided the potential buyers. The potential buyers want to make sure that if a firm is purchased, they get what they are promised. The expected cash flows are the heart of the valuation process. Two cash flows must be estimated: (1) the cash flows of the acquired firm as a stand-alone business and (2) the additional cash flow that the acquiring firm can generate if it purchases the business. For example, if you're a food-processing firm such as Kraft foods and you buy a regional firm that manufactures egg rolls, you may be able to generate significant additional sales (and cash flows) by selling the egg rolls through your national distribution system. In theory, the acquiring firm that can generate the largest net cash flow should be the firm willing to pay the highest price for the firm.

Third, the investment bankers work with the acquiring firm management, provide advice, and help them negotiate the deal. Finally, once the deal is complete, investment banks assist the acquiring firm in obtaining the funds to finance the purchase. These activities range anywhere from arranging bank loans to arranging bridge financing, underwriting the sale of equity or debt, or arranging a leveraged buyout (LBO) deal. *Bridge financing* is just a temporary loan until permanent financing is obtained. An *LBO* is where a firm is acquired by issuing debt and then taken private. Both buying and selling firms may seek the services of investment bankers because, for most firms, M&As are occasional or intermittent events. Thus, hiring expert counsel is good business practice.

The fee charged by investment-banking firms depends on the extent of the work they perform and the complexity of the tasks they are asked to perform. In some cases, the investment banker may simply receive an advisory fee or retainer. In most cases, however, the banker receives a fee based on the percentage of the selling price. In one fee structure used by investment bankers, called the 5-4-3-2-1 formula, the investment banker receives 5 percent on the first $1 million, 4 percent on the second $1 million, 3 percent on the third $1 million, 2 percent on the fourth $1 million, and 1 percent on the remaining amount. The flat rate for investment banks' sales is typically 2 to 3 percent of the selling price.

The entire process of origination, underwriting, and sales falls under the underwriting business segment at Goldman Sachs. As you can see from Exhibit 18.2, underwriting accounted for less than 7 percent of Goldman Sachs's 2009 revenue.

TRADING AND PRINCIPAL INVESTMENTS

As shown in Exhibit 18.2, trading and principal investments is actually the largest portion of Goldman Sachs's business, accounting for more than three-quarters of its 2009 total revenue. This business consists of acting as brokers or dealers for existing securities in the aftermarket and Goldman Sachs's own proprietary trading and investing. In the case of Goldman Sachs, this business is broken into two divisions. The FICC group focuses on fixed income (bonds) trading, currency trading, and commodity trading. The equities group focuses on stocks and stock derivatives (such as equity options) trading. The principal investments division represents Goldman Sachs's direct investment into real estate or other business. Goldman Sachs, for example, has a substantial investment in Industrial and Commercial Bank of China (ICBC), which is the largest wholesale and retail bank in China.

Broker-Dealers. Aftermarket activities may involve a simple brokerage function, in which the firm earns a commission for bringing buyers and sellers together; or it may involve a dealer function, in which the investment bank carries an inventory of securities from which it executes buy and sell orders and trades for its own account (**broker-dealer** function). When an investment bank acts as a dealer for a security, it is said to be *making a market* in the security and is known as a *market maker*. The **market maker** is willing to buy the security at one price, known as the *bid price*, and sell it at a higher price, the *ask price*. The market maker makes a profit based on the difference between the bid and the ask prices. The price difference is known as the **bid–ask spread**. Of course, with ownership of the asset comes the risk of price fluctuations caused by changes in economic and market conditions.

Brokerage houses compete for investors' business by offering a variety of services that are sold by stockbrokers or account executives. Stockbrokers must be licensed by the Financial Industry Regulatory Authority (FINRA). FINRA is the successor to the National Association of Securities Dealers (NASD), and some people still refer to FINRA licensing as NASD licensing. Stockbrokers must also abide by the ethical guidelines of FINRA and the exchanges on which they place orders. FINRA is a self-regulating body largely comprising brokerage houses. For their services, stockbrokers receive commission rates that vary with the service provided or take a fee as a percentage of assets managed.

Brokers also provide investors a convenient way to store their securities. That is, investors can leave securities with a broker for safekeeping and thus do not have to rent a safety-deposit box or physically transfer securities to and from the broker's office when a transaction is made. In fact, most securities are registered in the broker's **street name**. This means the security is registered in the broker's name in the issuer's records, but the broker keeps track that the investor is the ultimate beneficial owner. Investors do this because it makes it much easier to hold and transfer securities. In fact, street-name registration is the default holding method at most brokerage firms—which means that, if you have an account at a brokerage firm, your securities are probably held in the broker's street name. Investors are protected against loss of the securities or cash held by brokers by the Security Investor Protection Corporation (SIPC). Note, however, that the SIPC does not guarantee the dollar value of securities but guarantees only that the securities themselves will be returned.

If you open an account at a brokerage firm, you will have the choice of either a cash account application or a margin account application. **Margin trading** simply means that the investor can buy securities partly with borrowed money. For example, if a customer uses a 40 percent margin, it means that 40 percent of the investment is being financed with the investor's own money and the remaining 60 percent is financed with money borrowed from the brokerage house. Most types of securities can be purchased on margin—for example, common and preferred stock, corporate and Treasury bonds, convertible bonds, warrants, commodities, financial futures, and mutual funds. Margin requirements are set by the Board of Governors of the Federal Reserve System, and they currently are 50 percent for both equity and debt securities. The rate of interest charged is usually marked up 1 to 2 percent above the *broker's call loan rate* (the rate at which brokers borrow from commercial banks), which is usually slightly below the commercial bank prime rate.

Brokers are traditionally classified as either full-service brokers or discount brokers. **Full-service brokers** offer research staff, individual financial planning, and a specific broker dedicated to handling your account. Most **discount brokers** simply take and execute customers' orders and do not, in general, offer investment advice. Of course, because they offer fewer services the fee is much lower. Because discount brokers have become so popular, most large full-service brokers now offer some sort of affiliated discount brokerage option. In 2010, for example, Bank of America began offering a discount online brokerage service called Merrill Edge in addition to its full-service brokerage, Merrill Lynch.

Proprietary Trading and Investing. Historically, most large investment banks also engage in **proprietary trading** (also known as "prop trading" or the "prop desk"). In proprietary trading, the investment bank uses its own capital to make bets. Investment banks' proprietary trading is, essentially, an internal hedge fund. An investment bank, for example, may bet the U.S. dollar will appreciate against the yen. If they are right, the bank can make a substantial return.

There are potential conflicts of interest, however. In 2010, for example, Senator Charles Levin claimed that Goldman Sachs was betting mortgage-backed securities would decline in value while selling mortgage-backed securities to its clients: "The subcommittee has determined that, contrary to its public pronouncements, in 2007 Goldman Sachs shifted direction, and placed heavy bets against mortgage-backed securities that it had created and that it was selling to its clients." Information gathered as part of a Senate investigation into the housing crisis revealed one email from Goldman Sachs CEO Lloyd Blankfein to CFO David Viniar claiming, "Of course we didn't dodge the mortgage mess. We lost money, then made more than we lost because of shorts." Those short positions (i.e., betting the housing market and related securities would fall in value) were part of Goldman Sachs's proprietary trading. Of course, one may argue that there is nothing wrong with Goldman Sachs taking a position opposite of some of their clients—different investors can have different views.

Although proprietary trading can entail pure bets (e.g., betting on a decline in the housing market or a rise in inflation), proprietary traders also engage in **arbitrage** activities. In pure arbitrage, an investor has no money invested, takes no risk, and makes a profit. If, for example, Wal-Mart shares are trading for $53 per share on the New York Stock Exchange (NYSE) and $52 per share on NASDAQ, a smart investor could buy a share on NASDAQ for $52, immediately sell it for $53 on the NYSE, and make $1. If there was no risk involved (i.e., the trades occurred simultaneously), then an investor would keep doing this until the prices came together. That is, the investor buying on NASDAQ and selling on the NYSE would tend to increase the price on NASDAQ and lower the price on the NYSE.

Most of what traders call arbitrage, however, is not pure arbitrage. That is, in practice, these arbitrage trades typically involve some risk. One strategy, for example, is merger arbitrage. Say, for example, that Julia's School Supply is selling for $5 per share and Michelle's Baby Store is selling for $10 per share. If Michelle's Baby Store wants to take over Julia's School Supply and offers to trade one share of Michelle's Baby Store for each share of Julia's School Supply, Julia's School Supply will increase in price and Michelle's Baby Store will (typically) decrease in price (markets may believe they are overpaying for Julia's School Supply because the market had thought Julia's School Supply was worth only $5 per share and Michelle's Baby Store is paying $10 per share).

For simplicity, assume Julia's School Supply price rises to $8 per share and Michelle's Baby Store falls to $9 per share. If the deal goes through, each share of Julia's School Supply will convert into one share of Michelle's Baby Store. As a result, if the deal is completed, one share of Julia's School Supply must have the same price as one share of Michelle's Baby Store. An investor engaging in merger arbitrage can sell short one share of Michelle's Baby Store and purchase one share of Julia's School Supply. If the deal does not fall apart, the investor will make money regardless of whether both Julia's School Supply and Michelle's Baby Store rise or fall in value. The investor has only bet that the prices will come together. If there was no uncertainty regarding the deal, the investor would have an arbitrage profit. In the real world, however, there is the possibility that the merger may not occur. Thus, although often called arbitrage, it is not pure arbitrage.

The future of proprietary trading within investment banks is unclear. Because all the large investment banks are now bank holding companies (or parts of bank holding companies), they are subject to bank holding company regulations. As part of the Dodd-Frank Wall Street Reform and Consumer Protection Act passed in July 2010, bank holding companies are now limited to investing no more than 3 percent of their Tier I assets in proprietary trading, private equity, or hedge funds (called the Volcker Rule after former Federal Reserve chair Paul Volcker). As a result, proprietary trading divisions in investment banks were in a state of transition in the summer and fall of 2010. Some investment banks were reportedly attempting to sell their proprietary trading divisions to non–bank holding companies not subject to such regulations. Others were reportedly moving their proprietary trading business to their asset management side. Fox Business News, for example, reported that by the end of July 2010, Goldman Sachs had moved about half of its proprietary traders to the asset management side of the business where these traders would engage in similar bets by acting as dealers for clients. If, for example, an investment banker wanted to take a large bet in a security and a client wanted to sell a large position in a security, the investment banker, acting as a dealer, may still get the position desired despite labeling it as a client-related trade.

ASSET MANAGEMENT AND SECURITY SERVICES

As shown in Exhibit 18.2, asset management and security services business accounted for the second largest portion of Goldman Sachs's revenue.

Asset Management. Goldman Sachs, like most large investment banks, provides a wide range of investment information and advice to its clients, ranging from simple stock and bond guides to detailed research reports written by a security analyst on a particular investment. In addition, most large investment banks publish periodic publications or newsletters that analyze economic, market, and industry conditions and provide lists of securities or investments that the firm's analyst recommends investors buy or sell. Clients include individual investors and institutions (e.g., pension funds, university endowments). The asset management business generates revenue through management and/or incentive fees.

Security Services.   Security services provide a number of services to institutional investors (including mutual funds, hedge funds, pension funds, foundations) and very wealthy individual investors. Hedge funds, for example, typically use a **prime broker**. The prime broker lends money (so the hedge fund can leverage its investments) and securities (so the hedge fund can sell the securities short) to the hedge fund. The prime broker also usually takes care of clearing trades and retains custody of the securities on behalf of the hedge fund. In addition, most prime brokers offer risk management services for hedge funds.

DO YOU UNDERSTAND?

1. What was the purpose of the Glass-Steagall Act?
2. Describe the steps entailed in underwriting a new security issue.
3. In what activities, other than underwriting new securities, are investment banks involved?

18.3 PRIVATE EQUITY

As opposed to the public offerings most often associated with investment banks, a number of firms specialize in private equity. Similar to public equity, private equity represents ownership of a company (i.e., both public and private equity investors are stockholders). Unlike public equity, however, private equity cannot be traded on a public stock exchange. Many investment banks are also involved in private equity. Goldman Sachs's principal investments (see Exhibit 18.2), for example, include private equity investments. As noted above, however, the so-called Volcker rule (part of the Dodd-Frank Wall Street Reform and Consumer Protection Act passed in July 2010) means that bank holding companies are limited to investing no more than 3 percent of their Tier I assets in proprietary trading, private equity, or hedge funds. Although the investment banks have been given some time to comply with this limit, the rule may change the importance of private equity at traditional investment banks.

Nevertheless, private equity has become an important source of financing for many companies. In 2007, for example, according to TheCityUK estimates (www. TheCityUK.com), nearly $500 billion was raised in the private equity market worldwide. Since that time, however, the market has cooled substantially—only $150 billion was raised in 2009. North America accounted for 66 percent of all private equity funds raised worldwide in 2009. Private equity can be broken down into two primary groups: **venture capital private equity** and **buyout private equity**. According to TheCityUk, venture capital accounted for 43 percent of private equity investments in 2009 versus 57 percent for buyouts.

PRIVATE EQUITY ORGANIZATIONAL STRUCTURE

Most private equity funds have a fixed life (often 10 years). The funds are usually set up as a limited partnership, with the private equity firm as the general partner and the investors as the limited partners. The fund begins with the manager raising **commitments** from investors who agree to provide up to a given amount of capital for the private equity capital investments as needed. As the private equity manager (general partner) finds investments, the limited partners' commitments are drawn down (known as a **drawdown**). Assume, for example, that an investor commits $10 million to a private equity fund partnership that has total commitments of $100 million. If the manager invests $20 million in a startup firm, the investor's drawdown will be $2 million and the investor's remaining commitment will be $8 million.

PRIVATE EQUITY FEE STRUCTURE

The general partners at most private equity funds are compensated in two ways: a management fee and **carried interest**. The management fee typically is 1 or 2 percent of the value of the fund and covers the cost of operating the private equity fund such as salaries, offices, and travel to investigate potential investments. The carried interest represents the incentive portion of the private equity manager's compensation. Typically, the general partner receives 20 percent of the profits that the fund generates. In some cases, the general partner gets 20 percent of the profits only after the investors have received some nominal rate of return on their investment, for example, 5 percent per year. If a private equity general partner is paid a 2 percent management fee and 20 percent of the profits, the fee structure is referred to as 2 and 20.

VENTURE CAPITAL

New corporations raise funds from a variety of sources. Initial financing typically is provided by the firm's founders and their friends, and later financing often comes from individuals and perhaps banks. Eventually, a successful venture may raise funds from a public offering of its stock or be acquired by a larger corporation. Venture capital is yet another source of funds to finance growth. Venture capitalists are equity-oriented investors who also provide management expertise to the company. They are most likely to invest after the enterprise has exhausted capital provided by its founders but before it is merged into a larger firm or makes an initial public offering of its stock.

According to the National Venture Capital Association, nearly 2,400 companies received venture capital financing in 2009. There were just under 800 venture capital firms in the United States managing $179 billion in 2009. The average fund size was just over $150 million. Venture capital funds raise capital from a variety of sources, but most comes from institutional investors, including pension funds, endowments, sovereign wealth funds, and insurance companies.

The Types of Business Invested in by Venture Capitalists. Venture capitalists typically prefer to invest in technology-based businesses in areas such as electronics, computer software and services, biotechnology, medical care, communications, and industrial products. For several reasons manufacturing businesses are more intense users of venture capital than most service businesses. The lag between formation of a business and initial sales is usually longer in manufacturing than in services. This development cycle is especially long for innovative products and those manufactured with high-technology processes. Also, the minimum efficient scale is typically larger in a manufacturing business. These factors increase the required level of financing and decrease the liquidity of the investment, thus increasing the need for outside equity financing. Tesla Motors, for example, received substantial venture capital financing.

The Stages of Venture Capital Investments.

Although venture capitalists generally work with younger firms, there can be wide variation in "how young." As a result, investments are usually classified into three stages: (1) **Seed financing** is capital provided at the idea stage. The capital goes for product development and market research. (2) **Startup financing** is used to develop the product and begin marketing. (3) **Expansion financing** is for growth and expansion. Tesla Motors, for example, has a product and has been opening a number of dealerships around the world.

How Venture Capitalists Differ from Public Equity Investors.

The form of investment varies from company to company, but investments tend to feature three characteristics: substantial control over management decisions, some protection against downside risks, and a share in capital appreciation. Typically, venture capitalists have a seat on the board of directors. A popular vehicle for investing in startup companies is preferred stock that carries the right to purchase or convert into common stock. Preferred stockholders have priority over common stockholders in liquidation proceedings. The convertibility feature enables venture capitalists to participate in the high gains associated with successful ventures that go public or are acquired. In general, venture capitalists are less likely to provide debt financing. If they do, however, they usually combine the debt with an instrument that has equity features such as warrants or convertibility into common stock at a later date.

Rates of Return Earned by Venture Capitalists.

Venture capitalists often think of their required rate of return in terms of multiples of the amount of money they invest in a company. For example, a venture capitalist might expect to receive a return of 10 times the money invested in a startup company over a 6-year investment horizon, which equals a rate of return of 47 percent per year. A less risky third-stage investment in a profitable company might be expected to return five times the money invested over a 4-year investment horizon, which equals a rate of return of 41 percent per year. This does not mean that venture capital funds generate returns for their investors in the 40 percent range. Some of the companies in which the venture capitalist invests fail and generate a rate of return of −100 percent. Others are only moderately successful.

According to the National Venture Capital Association, 40 percent of firms invested in by venture capitalists fail, 40 percent earn modest returns, and the remaining 20 percent earn high returns. Thus, the distribution is highly skewed— a venture capitalist may earn a strong return on average only because a few investments do very well, but nearly half the investments lose 100 percent of the investment.

How Venture Capital Investments Are Valued.

The most important aspect of the venture capital process is the company's valuation. Various valuation methods can be used to price the transaction, with the two most common methods being comparable companies and multiple scenarios.

Many issues are inherent in the valuation process. First, return expectations typically are defined by the internal rate of return based on the return objectives of the portfolio and the risk expected to be assumed. Risks that affect valuation might not be easily quantified—for example, the risk of poor management. Other issues that affect valuation are (1) the development stage of the company, that is, whether it is an early or expansion-stage investment; (2) the valuation of industry comparables; (3) the financial history of the company, its growth rate, and its profitability; (4) the amount of influence that can be exercised by the venture capitalist; and (5) the amount of future dilution expected if additional venture capital financing is required.

Industry multiples typically create a backdrop for the valuation process. The commonly used multiples are based on revenue and earnings. Valuations of companies in an early stage of development are more likely to be based on revenue, and valuations for companies in later stages of development are more likely to be based on earnings and cash flow. These multiples are influenced by the attractiveness of the market in which the company operates, competition among other investors to be part of this financing, the stage of the company's development, and how other relevant or comparable public companies are valued. Learning by Doing 18.1 provides an example of the multiple-scenario valuation technique.

LEARNING BY DOING 18.1

Evaluating a Venture Capital Investment

PROBLEM: You have recently been hired at a venture capital firm (for a really exorbitant salary) and have just been assigned to determine if your fund should invest in a company (Mark's Soccer Supply) that is seeking $3 million in venture capital financing. After much analysis, you decide there are three possible scenarios—pessimistic, expected, and optimistic—representing different profitability, growth, and valuation expectations. Given the riskiness of this young company, assume that you decide the required rate of return is 30 percent. Given the following information, determine whether your fund invests in Mark's Soccer Supply:

	Pessimistic	Expected	Optimistic
Probability of outcome	30%	50%	20%
Revenue in year 6 (millions)	$10	$25	$40
Profit margin	5%	8%	10%
Price/earnings ratio at sale	6	10	15

What is the expected value of the company in 6 years? Given the required rate of return, do you recommend that your fund invest in Mark's Soccer Supply?

APPROACH: Begin by determining the company's earnings under each of the scenarios. Then multiply expected earnings by the price/earnings ratio to estimate the value of the company in 6 years under each scenario. Next compute the weighted-average company value (based on the probability of each scenario) to estimate the expected value of Mark's Soccer Supply in 6 years. Last, determine the present value (based on the required rate of return) of the expected value of the company to determine if your fund should make the investment.

SOLUTION: First, compute total company earnings (i.e., net income) as revenue times the profit margin under each scenario:

	Pessimistic	Expected	Optimistic
Probability of outcome	30%	50%	20%
Revenue in year 6 (millions)	$10	$25	$40
Profit margin	5%	8%	10%
Earnings = revenue × profit margin (millions)	$ 0.5	$ 2	$ 4

Next, the price/earnings ratio for any company is the share price divided by earnings per share. Multiplying earnings per share by the number of shares outstanding yields total earnings: EPS × number of shares = total earnings. Similarly, multiplying price by number of shares yields the total value of the company's equity: price × number of shares = total equity value of company. Thus, the [price/earnings (per share)] ratio is the same as (total equity value of company)/(total earnings) ratio. As a result, multiplying the price/earnings ratio by total earnings generates the total equity value of the company:

$$\frac{\text{Price}}{\text{earnings (per share)} \times \text{total earnings}} = \text{total equity value of company}$$

Using the above formula, determine the expected value of the company in year 6 under each scenario:

	Pessimistic	Expected	Optimistic
Probability of outcome	30%	50%	20%
Price/earnings ratio at sale	6	10	15
Earnings = revenue × profit margin (millions)	$0.5	$ 2	$ 4
Company equity value = P/E × earnings (millions)	$ 3	$20	$60

Next, compute the expected equity value of the company in year 6 as the weighted (by the probabilities) average value:

Expected equity value = (0.30 × $3) + (0.50 × $20) + (0.20 × $60) = $22.90 million

Then determine the present value of the expected value by discounting it back at the 30 percent required return for 6 years:

$$\text{Present value} = \frac{22.90}{(1 + 0.30)^6} = \$4.74 \text{ million}$$

Given the expected value of $4.74 million and the initial investment of $3 million, the investment has a net present value of $1.74 million and you should make the investment. Hope it works out!

BUYOUT PRIVATE EQUITY

In the case of venture capital, the goal is to invest in a young private company and eventually sell it once it becomes successful—often by turning it into a public company (i.e., an initial public offering). In contrast, buyout firms often take public companies and make them private companies. As private companies, the owners have direct control over management and strategy. In addition, because the companies are not publicly traded, they are not required to provide detailed public financial statements to the public (and, therefore, their competitors).

CKE Restaurants, owners of Carl's Jr. (home of the 1,040 calorie Guacamole Bacon Six Dollar Burger) and Hardee's, became a publically traded company in 1981. In 2010, a private equity fund (Apollo Management VII, L.P.) purchased the entire company for $12.55 per share in cash. Thus, Apollo bought out the company. Because the buyouts are typically more mature firms, the largest private equity deals are usually buyouts. The Carlyle Group, one of the largest private equity firms, for example, owns AMC Entertainment (movie theaters), Dunkin' Brands (Dunkin' Donuts and Baskin-Robbins), and Hertz (car and equipment rental). All together, The Carlyle Group held over 900 corporate and real estate investments as of 2010.

Although buyout targets can be public companies (e.g., CKE Restaurants), they can also be part of a public company or a private company. For example, a group of three private equity firms (The Carlyle Group, Bain Capital, and Thomas H. Lee Partners) bought Dunkin' Brands from Pernod Ricard SA, a publicly traded French company that primarily focuses on alcoholic beverages, including Chivas Regal, Seagram's gin, Absolut vodka, and Beefeaters gin, in 2006.

Ironically, several of the largest private equity companies have become publicly traded themselves. The Blackstone Group sold a 12.3 percent stake in the company in a 2006 IPO and now trades on the New York Stock Exchange (NYSE) under the ticker BX. Thus, an investor can purchase the security and participate in the private equity partnership as an owner of the company that serves as the general partner. Kohlberg Kravis Roberts (KKR), another large private equity firm, began trading on the NYSE in July 2010 (ticker: KKR). Apollo Global Management also listed its shares on the NYSE in March 2011.

Leveraged Buyouts (LBOs). Although in many buyouts, the private equity firm pays cash for the shares, sometimes the private equity firm also borrows money to purchase the shares. Assume, for example, that the private equity fund is paying $100 per share for a target. The fund may raise the $30 (per share) directly from private equity investors and borrow the remaining $70 (per share). In such a case, the buyout is leveraged with debt, hence, a **leveraged buyout (LBO)**. The interest paid on the debt (hopefully) comes from the cash flow generated by the company.

Perhaps the most famous LBO was Kohlberg Kravis Roberts's (KKR) purchase of RJR Nabisco in 1988. RJR Nabisco was a tobacco (including Camel, Kool, Winston, Salem) and snack food (including Oreos, Ritz, Chips Ahoy!) conglomerate. The takeover battle for the company began when the CEO first proposed to buy out the company (a management buyout). The ensuing drama, when KKR outbid the management and others, was captured in the very engaging best-selling book *Barbarians at the Gate* and later made into an HBO movie starring James Garner (of TV's *Rockford Files* fame—ask your parents).

DO YOU UNDERSTAND?

1. What is the difference between public equity and private equity?
2. What are the two major types of public equity and how do they differ?
3. What are the advantages and disadvantages of having a company's equity traded publicly versus held privately?

SUMMARY OF LEARNING OBJECTIVES

1. **Explain the core business activities of investment banks.** The primary businesses of investment banks are raising capital and underwriting in the primary market (the investment banking portion of an investment bank), the trading of securities (equity, fixed income, currency and commodities) in the secondary market (broker/dealer), proprietary trading, asset management, and security services (such as lending money or securities to hedge funds).

2. **Explain the reasons for the enactment of the Glass-Steagall Act of 1933 and discuss its impact on commercial and investment banking.** The Glass-Steagall Act of 1933 separated commercial banking from investment banking and said that financial institutions can do one or the other, but not both. At the time, it was thought that the stock market crash of 1929 and the subsequent collapse of the banking system led to the Great Depression of the 1930s. The reason the Glass-Steagall Act was passed was the belief that investment banking was too risky for banks to engage in and, in part, that the commercial-banking and investment-banking activities of the times contributed to the collapse of the banking system.

3. **Explain the Gramm-Leach-Bliley Act of 1999 and discuss how it is likely to affect the structure of the financial services industry.** The Gramm-Leach-Bliley Act of 1999 repealed much of the Glass-Steagall Act by allowing commercial banks, investment banks, and insurance companies to affiliate with each other as part of a financial holding company structure.

4. **Explain what happened to most large independent investment banks during the 2007–2009 financial crisis.** During the housing bubble meltdown in 2007–2009, the major investment banks were either purchased by commercial banks (e.g., JPMorgan Chase's purchase of Bear Sterns), went bankrupt (e.g., Lehman Brothers), or converted to bank holding companies (e.g., Goldman Sachs). As a result, by the end of 2008, there were no large independent investment banks left in the United States.

5. **Explain why investment bankers typically underprice new securities when they are sold in the primary markets.** Most new securities issues sold in the primary market are *underpriced*, meaning that their new offer price is below their closing price after the first day of trading. Investment bankers do this to ensure that the issues sell quickly, thus ensuring the issuing firm of a successful issue and reducing its underwriting risk.

6. **Describe what private equity funds do.** Private equity has become a major force in financial markets. The two primary categories of private equity funds are venture capital (which provides capital and expertise to small, fast-growing businesses) and buyout firms (which purchase, and typically restructure, more mature businesses).

KEY TERMS

Commercial banks	underwriting	Broker	Venture capital private
Investment banks	Best-efforts offering	Dealer	equity
Universal banks	Competitive bidding	Market maker	Buyout private equity
Private banks	Negotiated offering	Bid–ask spread	Commitments
Primary offerings	Underpricing	Street name	Drawdown
Unseasoned offering	Registration statement	Margin trading	Carried interest
Initial public offering	Preliminary prospectus	Full-service brokers	Seed financing
(IPO)	Final prospectus	Discount brokers	Startup financing
Seasoned offering	Underwriting syndicate	Proprietary trading	Expansion financing
Public offering	Accredited investors	Arbitrage	Leveraged buyout (LBO)
Private placements	Due diligence	Prime broker	

QUESTIONS AND PROBLEMS

1. What are the major business activities of investment banks?

2. Explain why issuing new securities can be a risky business.

3. Explain each of the following parts of bringing a new issue to market: origination, underwriting, and distribution.

4. Explain why there were no large independent investment banks left in the United States at the end of 2008.

5. How does a private placement differ from a public offering?

6. What is the difference between an IPO and a seasoned offering?

7. What does a broker-dealer do? How does a broker-dealer make money?

8. What is proprietary trading?

9. What is prime brokerage?

10. How does private equity differ from public equity?

11. What are the two primary categories of private equity? How do they differ?

12. Assume a venture capitalist requires a 40 percent rate of return per year. If the venture capitalist thinks that a company will be worth $50 million in 5 years, what percentage of ownership in the company will the venture capitalist require today in exchange for a $3 million investment?

INTERNET EXERCISE

1. Go to Morgan Stanley's Web page (www.morganstanley.com) and download its most recent annual report. Select the "About Morgan Stanley" tab, then select the "Investor Relations" tab, then select "Annual Reports" on the left. Select the most recent "10-K" disclosure (which is the SEC identifier for the annual report). Once the annual report is open, search the document for "Business Segments." What are Morgan Stanley's business segments? What does each segment do? Find the page titled "Institutional Securities—Income Statement Information." Of the income from its Institutional Securities segment, how much of Morgan Stanley's income arises from investment banking and how much arises from trading (broker-dealer)?

2. From Morgan Stanley's Web page, link to the "Careers" page. What careers are available to recent college graduates?

CHAPTER NINETEEN

Investment Companies

IN 2009, MORE THAN 50 million U.S. households, representing 87 million people and 43 percent of the households in the United States, owned mutual funds, according to the Investment Company Institute. The median age of a mutual fund owner is 50. Seventy-six percent of mutual fund owners are married or living with a partner, and 47 percent have a college degree. The median financial assets of this group are $150,000, and, at retirement age, 99 percent wish they had saved or invested more.

Okay, we made up the last statistic, but just about everyone wishes he or she had saved or invested more when they were younger. As a college student, you are probably relatively young and will soon face decisions about how much to spend versus how much to save and invest. As we will learn in this chapter, mutual funds hold more assets than any other type of financial institution in the United States. Therefore, if you don't already own any mutual fund shares, it is probably just a matter of time. In fact, the sooner you begin learning about and using mutual funds, the sooner you will accumulate wealth in them. For example, if you begin investing $675 a month (about $22 a day) in a mutual fund that earns 8 percent per year, compounded monthly, after 5 years, you will have accumulated $49,597. After 10 years, you will have accumulated $123,489; after

Most households in the United States invest in mutual funds. In addition to serving as an important investment vehicle for retirement, mutual funds are used by many parents to invest money for their children's college educations.

20 years, $397,589; and after 30 years, you're a millionaire ($1,005,992)! Clearly, the sooner you invest and the more you invest, the more money you should have when it is time to retire.

Of course, as you learned in Chapter 10, regardless of what you expect, the future return you actually earn in the stock market is uncertain. If your older sister graduated in 2000 and invested the same $675 a month for the next 10 years in the S&P 500, she would have lost money! Although the above example demonstrates the magic of compounding and potential rewards, investing in the stock market is risky—which is just another way of saying that, despite what

markets have averaged in the past, nobody really knows what will happen in the future.

Nonetheless, mutual funds are attractive investments for small investors because they offer the benefits of diversification, professional management, and small denominations. In addition, in recent years, another type of investment company—the exchange-traded fund (ETF)—has become a popular alternative to mutual funds. Other types of investment companies offer specialized investment products targeted to particular investors. For example, hedge funds are targeted at wealthy, sophisticated investors.

In this chapter, we describe the functions of various types of investment funds: open-end mutual funds, exchange-traded funds, closed-end mutual funds, and unit investment trusts. We also delve into the world of two other investment vehicles that are not technically investment companies—hedge funds and real estate investment trusts (REITs). We explain the characteristics of each and note how these institutions have waxed or waned as market conditions, the regulatory environment, and/or competitive conditions have changed. ∎

LEARNING OBJECTIVES

1 Explain open-end mutual funds and how they work.

2 Explain the role of money market mutual funds and how they differ from money market deposit accounts.

3 Explain closed-end mutual funds and how they differ from open-end mutual funds.

4 Explain how exchange-traded funds (ETFs) work and how they differ from mutual funds.

5 Explain how hedge funds work and how they differ from mutual funds.

6 Describe the operations of real estate investment trusts (REITs).

19.1 INVESTMENT COMPANIES

Investment company is a legal term defined in the Investment Company Act of 1940. There are four major types of investment companies: open-end mutual funds, closed-end mutual funds, exchange-traded funds, and unit investment trusts. Investors, like you, give these companies money to invest on their behalf. Most investment companies specialize in long-term investments (e.g., a stock mutual fund), but others focus on short-term investments (e.g., a money market fund). Investment companies provide a number of potential benefits to investors, including the ability to invest small amounts of money into a professionally managed broadly diversified portfolio.

Exhibit 19.1 reports the total net assets for the four major types of investment companies at the end of 1995 and 2009. In 1995, investment companies, in aggregate, controlled just over $3 trillion in assets. Fourteen years later (in 2009), investment company assets had more than quadrupled, to over $12 trillion. To get an idea of how large a number that is, consider that the value of all the stocks listed on the NASDAQ and NYSE totaled just over $15 trillion at the end of 2009.

EXHIBIT 19.1
Growing Importance of Investment Companies

Type	Total Net Assets ($ Billions) 1995	2009
Open-end mutual funds	$2,811	$11,121
Exchange-traded funds	1	777
Closed-end funds	143	228
Unit investment trusts	73	38
Total	$3,028	$12,164

Source: 2010 Investment Company Institute Fact Book.

Investment companies are regulated by the Securities and Exchange Commission (SEC) and are also subject to state securities regulations. Regulations require that funds provide full and honest disclosure to actual and potential customers, diversify their portfolios, avoid questionable sales compensation or kickback schemes, and avoid conflicts of interest between advisers or management companies and fund shareholders. Federal regulations are embodied in the Investment Company Act of 1940 as subsequently amended. More recently, the National Securities Markets Improvement Act of 1996 assigned federal regulators sole jurisdiction over the structure and operations of mutual funds and over mutual fund prospectuses and advertising. State regulators retained their ability to prosecute fraud and sales practice abuses.

Under the conduit theory of taxation, mutual funds are not subject to direct taxes on their income provided that they distribute to their shareholders at least 90 percent of all income received. Most distribute 100 percent minus expenses. The fund investor must then pay tax on the capital gains, interest, and dividend income that is distributed to the investor by the fund each year.

19.2 OPEN-END MUTUAL FUNDS

As shown in Exhibit 19.1, **open-end mutual funds** (more commonly known simply as mutual funds), hold by far the largest share of investment company assets, accounting for more than 90 percent of total net assets held by all investment companies. Mutual funds offer a plethora of investing options, investing in stocks and bonds (including money markets) both domestically and internationally. At the end of 2009, there were over 8,600 mutual funds in the United States!

MUTUAL FUND PRICING

Let's consider a hypothetical mutual fund—Alta Mesa Fund—that holds only two stocks: seven shares of Hardy Pizza, currently selling for $100/share, and 31 shares of Dolezilek Power currently selling for $10/share. Thus, altogether, Alta Mesa's portfolio is worth $1,010: (7 shares × $100) + (31 shares × $10) = $1,010. Alta Mesa Fund, however, owes $10 in management fees that have yet to be paid. Thus, given Alta Mesa's assets total of $1,010 and their liabilities total of $10, the *net* value of the fund is $1,000.

Now assume that Alta Mesa Fund has a total of five shares outstanding. Each mutual fund share is worth the net value of the fund divided by the number of shares, or $1,000/5 = $200. That figure is known as the **net asset value** (**NAV**). Technically, it's really the net asset value per share, but it's almost always simply called the net asset value. Basically, the NAV is how much each mutual fund shareholder would receive if the fund liquidated today.

Open-end mutual funds stand ready to buy or sell their shares based on the current NAV at any time. When an investor buys shares in an open-end fund, the fund fills the purchase order by issuing new shares in the fund. Both buy and sell transactions are carried out at a price based on the current market value (which is the NAV) of all securities held in the fund's portfolio, which is calculated daily. Assume, for example, you decide to invest in Alta Mesa Fund. If you give Alta Mesa Fund $200, you will get one share of Alta Mesa Fund. The total number of Alta Mesa shares outstanding increases from five to six, and Alta Mesa will use your cash to purchase additional equity securities. Alta Mesa, for example, may purchase two additional shares of Hardy Pizza. Similarly, assume that 2 weeks later you decide to sell your one share of Alta Mesa Fund. If the NAV at that point is $205, the following three events would happen: (1) Alta Mesa would sell stocks to raise $205 in cash, (2) you would receive $205 in cash, and (3) the number of outstanding Alta Mesa shares would fall from six to five.

LEARNING BY DOING 19.1
Calculating Net Asset Value

PROBLEM: You have recently been hired at a mutual fund (for an exorbitant salary) and were just assigned to calculate the fund's net asset value per share. Yesterday, the fund had 400 mutual fund shares outstanding, held $210 in cash, had accrued a management fee of $40, and held the following four stocks:

Stock	Number of Shares	Price
Phil's Firefighting Supply Company	100	$15
Terri's Pet Supply Company	50	30
Mary's Travel Supply Company	220	12
Mike's Baseball Supply Company	30	45

What is the fund's NAV (per share)? Next, assume that at the end of the day, an investor wants to redeem two shares. How does the fund's NAV (per share) change as a result of the redemption?

APPROACH: The fund's net asset value per share is the sum of its assets less its liabilities divided by the number of shares outstanding. To compute the effect of the redemption, simply determine how much cash the fund gives the shareholder (and the resulting total value of the fund) and decrease the number of shares outstanding by 2.

SOLUTION: First, calculate the value of the stock portfolio by computing the sum of the value of each position (price times number of shares):

Stock	Number of Shares	Price	Value
Phil's Firefighting Supply Company	100	$15	$1,500
Terri's Pet Supply Company	50	30	1,500
Mary's Travel Supply Company	220	12	2,640
Mike's Baseball Supply Company	30	45	1,350
Total stock portfolio value			$6,990

Next, add cash to the portfolio value to compute total gross assets:

$6,990 (stock portfolio value) + $210 (cash) = $7,200 (total gross assets)

Then subtract the fund's one liability to compute the fund's total net assets:

$7,200 (total gross assets) − $40 (accrued management fee)
= $7,160 (total net assets)

Last, divide total net assets by the number of mutual fund shares outstanding to calculate the fund's net asset value per share:

$$\frac{\$7,160 \text{ (total net assets)}}{400 \text{ mutual fund shares}} = \$17.90$$

Thus, the fund's net asset value per share is $17.90. If a shareholder redeems two shares, the fund would give the investor $35.80 (2 × $17.90) and the fund's total net assets would decline by that amount of cash. The number of shares would fall to 398. Thus, the net asset value would not change:

$$\frac{\$7,160 - \$35.80}{398 \text{ mutual fund shares}} = \$17.90$$

MUTUAL FUND CASH HOLDINGS AND REDEMPTION POLICIES

Because some investors will likely redeem shares each day, mutual funds generally hold a portion of their assets in cash. Funds may hold very liquid assets (such as bank CDs) because they want "cash" for later investments. Conventional mutual funds' holdings of liquid assets vary, typically ranging from 4 percent to 6 percent of total asset holdings.

Many investors and security analysts use mutual fund cash and liquid asset holdings as a stock market indicator. They believe that large mutual fund cash holdings are a bullish (i.e., good) sign for the stock market because mutual fund managers have a lot of money to invest, which could fuel higher stock prices. Alternatively, low mutual fund cash levels are a bearish sign. Mutual fund managers selling off stocks to increase their cash holdings drive prices downward. Implicitly (and ever so rarely, explicitly), this argument requires that the investors providing liquidity to mutual fund managers require lower prices to be incentivized to buy the securities that mutual funds are selling. That is, because there is a buyer for every seller, a mutual fund manager buying a stock must mean another investor is selling a stock.

The financial crisis of 2008–2009 seemed to follow this pattern. In July 2007, when the Dow Jones Industrial Average (DJIA) was nearly 14,000, equity mutual fund cash levels were at a record low of 3.5 percent of assets. In January 2009, with the DJIA down to 8,000, mutual fund cash levels were nearly 6 percent. As the markets rebounded strongly over the next year, mutual fund cash levels dropped once again, to near-record lows (3.6 percent). Keep in mind, however, that if a fund keeps a constant dollar amount invested in cash, then cash as a fraction of assets will vary inversely with stock prices. If a manager holds $100 in cash and if a stock portfolio is worth $900, then cash holdings are 10 percent of assets. If the manager keeps the same amount in cash and if stock prices increase, causing the portfolio value to increase to $1,900, then cash holdings decline to 5 percent of assets, even though the manager did not trade any securities.

TYPES OF MUTUAL FUNDS

The four major mutual fund classifications are equity funds, bond funds, hybrid funds, and money market funds. Exhibit 19.2 shows the net assets of each type. At year-end 2009, mutual funds, in total, held assets worth more than $11 trillion. Equity mutual funds accounted for nearly 45 percent of those assets, bond and hybrid funds accounted for approximately 26 percent, and money market funds held nearly 30 percent of all mutual fund assets.

EXHIBIT 19.2
U.S. Mutual Fund Net Assets

Year	Total Net Assets ($ Billions)	Percentage of Net Assets			
		Equity Funds	Hybrid Funds	Bond Funds	Money Market Funds
2000	$ 6,964.63	56.9	5.0	11.6	26.5
2001	6,974.91	49.0	5.0	13.3	32.8
2002	6,383.48	41.7	5.1	17.7	35.5
2003	7,402.42	49.8	5.8	16.9	27.6
2004	8,095.08	54.2	6.4	15.9	23.5
2005	8,891.11	55.6	6.4	15.3	22.8
2006	10,396.51	56.9	6.3	14.4	22.5
2007	12,000.64	54.3	6.0	14.0	25.7
2008	9,602.60	38.6	5.2	16.3	39.9
2009	11,120.73	44.6	5.8	19.8	29.8

Mutual fund holdings totaled more than $11 trillion in assets by the end of 2009. Equity funds accounted for the largest portion, followed by money market funds.

Source: 2010 Investment Company Institute Fact Book.

EXHIBIT 19.3
Portfolio Holdings of Long-Term U.S. Mutual Funds

Year	Total Net Assets ($ Billions)	Percentage of Net Assets					
		Common and Preferred Stock	U.S. Government Bonds	Corporate Bonds	Municipal Bonds	Liquid Assets	Other
2000	5,119,386	76.4	6.0	6.8	5.3	5.4	0.1
2001	4,689,603	73.0	8.1	7.9	6.2	4.7	0.0
2002	4,118,402	65.3	11.7	10.1	7.8	5.1	0.0
2003	5,362,398	70.1	9.4	9.3	6.2	4.8	0.1
2004	6,193,746	72.5	8.7	8.6	5.1	5.0	0.1
2005	6,864,287	73.6	8.9	8.0	4.8	4.4	0.2
2006	8,058,057	74.8	8.0	8.3	4.5	4.3	0.2
2007	8,914,884	74.2	8.4	8.8	4.1	4.3	0.2
2008	5,770,368	64.7	12.2	11.7	5.8	5.1	0.4
2009	7,804,530	65.3	10.9	13.2	5.8	4.7	0.2

Source: 2010 Investment Company Institute Fact Book.

Exhibit 19.3 presents data on the asset holdings of non–money market mutual funds. In recent years, mutual fund holdings of equity securities have dominated bond holdings, but there can be dramatic shifts between investments in equities and bonds, depending on investors' perceptions of the relative attractiveness of the risk–return trade-off across the two markets. In the 1950s and 1960s, for example, equities made up more than 80 percent of mutual fund assets. The relative importance of stock and bond mutual funds also varies with market returns. In 2008, equity markets suffered large negative returns. As a result, the value of the assets held by equity funds also suffered. In contrast, at the end of 2000, the top of the so-called tech bubble, more than 76 percent of mutual funds assets were held in equities.

EQUITY FUNDS

Equity funds are also classified by their **Morningstar style box**. Specifically, Morningstar classifies mutual funds into one of nine categories along two dimensions based on the portfolio of stocks the fund holds: the market capitalization and the value/growth characteristics. Basically, every stock is classified by its market capitalization (small-, mid-, and large-capitalization stocks) and its value/growth characteristics (value, blend, and growth). Morningstar then classifies the mutual fund's style based on the capitalization and value/growth characteristics of the fund's portfolio—which is just the weighted average of the individual stocks in the portfolio. For example, a fund that primarily holds large-capitalization growth stocks would be classified as a large-cap/growth fund, while a fund that primarily holds an equal amount of small-value stocks and small-growth stocks would be classified as a small-cap/blend fund. These style boxes have become ubiquitous in mutual fund descriptions.

As their names suggest, **equity funds** primarily invest in stocks. There are many different types of equity funds, including growth and income funds, growth funds, aggressive growth funds, income-equity funds, international and global equity funds, specialized funds, and index funds.

Growth and Income Funds.

Growth and income funds seek a balanced return consisting of both capital gains and current income. These funds place most of their assets in high-quality common stocks. Such funds may be appropriate for investors who need some current income but want the opportunity to participate in the growth of the economy.

Growth Funds.

The investment goal of a growth fund is capital appreciation. Such funds primarily invest in companies that are judged to have above-average growth potential, for example, high P/E ratio growth stocks. Growth funds are most suitable for aggressive investors with long-term investment horizons. Most high-growth companies pay no dividends (instead reinvesting earnings back into the company to fund the growth), and thus a growth fund would not be suitable for investors who need current income.

Aggressive Growth Funds.

Aggressive growth funds are speculative investments that strive for big profits from capital gains. Their portfolios typically consist of the stocks of small companies with high P/E ratios or companies whose stock prices are highly volatile.

Income-Equity Funds.

Income-equity funds seek to obtain higher equity income by investing in stocks with relatively high dividend yields. Usually these securities represent older, more mature, and slower growing companies.

International and Global Equity Funds.

International and global equity funds are useful for investors who want to diversify their asset holdings internationally. Global funds can invest anywhere in the world, whereas international funds tend to invest outside the United States. An international fund can diversify broadly across countries or invest only in a specific country or group of countries. Potential investors must read the fund's prospectus to determine where it is likely to invest and how its current investments are distributed. Dreyfus (a large mutual fund company), for example, offers an Emerging Asia Fund, a Brazil Equity Fund, and a Greater China Fund.

Specialized Funds.

Specialized funds restrict their investments to a single segment of the market, such as precious metals funds. Sector funds may concentrate on special industries, such as telecommunications, oil, oil drilling, biotechnology, healthcare, and electric utilities. Specialty funds are like international funds in that they are created in response to the demands of investors who want to concentrate their investments in particular areas but do not want to acquire the expertise or the amount of funds necessary to do so themselves.

Index Funds.

Index funds are managed to match the return from a particular market index such as the S&P 500. Index funds offer very low fees because the portfolio is passively managed. That is, an index fund manager does not have to worry about selecting stocks that she believes will outperform the market or reduce the risk of her portfolio. Instead, an index manager tracking the S&P 500 can simply buy and hold the 500 stocks that make up S&P 500 in proportion to their weights (remember that the S&P 500 is a market-capitalization weighted index) in the S&P 500 index. According to the Investment Company Institute, the fraction of equity funds' total net assets managed by index funds grew from 4 percent in 1995 to nearly 14 percent in 2009.

BOND FUNDS

Similar to their equity style box, Morningstar also classified bond funds into one of nine categories along two dimensions based on the portfolio of bonds the fund holds: the credit rating of the bonds and the interest rate sensitivity (duration) of the bonds. For example, a fund that primarily holds intermediate-term high-yield ("junk") bonds would be classified as an intermediate term/low credit quality fund.

Bond funds, not surprisingly, primarily invest in bonds. As you know by now, however, there are many different types of bonds and, as a result, many different types of bond funds. Some of the major bond fund types include corporate, high-yield, global and international, government, strategic income, and municipal bond funds.

Corporate Bond Funds.   Corporate bond funds invest in the debt issued by corporations. Thus, investors in corporate bond funds run the risk that the corporation may default on its debt. Most bond funds classified as corporate bond funds hold investment-grade debt—which means the bonds have a rating from one of the major ratings firms (e.g., Moody's, Standard & Poor's) that indicates the bond has low default risk.

High-Yield Bond Funds.   In contrast, high-yield bond funds (also known as junk bond funds) primarily hold bonds that are below investment grade. Because of the higher default risk, these bonds (and funds) offer a higher promised yield.

Global and International Bond Funds.   Global and international bond funds (also known as world bond funds) invest in corporate and government bonds around the world, in a specific region (e.g., an Asia bond fund), or a specific country (e.g., Brazil). These funds are powerful tools for investors wanting to diversify their bond holdings outside the United States.

Government Bond Funds.   Government bond funds hold bonds issued by governments or government-sponsored enterprises (such as bonds issued by Federal National Mortgage Association [FNMA]). Government can mean federal, state, or local. Some government bond funds hold all types—federal, state, and local bonds.

Strategic Income Bond Funds.   Strategic income bond funds hold a combination of different types of bonds. For example, a strategic income fund may hold U.S. Treasury bonds, U.S. corporate bonds, mortgage pass-through bonds, and foreign corporate bonds. The weights in each of these areas (or others) can be highly dynamic or relatively static.

Municipal Bond Funds.   **Municipal bond funds** hold debt issued by states, cities, counties, and municipalities. Unlike corporate bonds or federal government bonds, income from municipal bonds is exempt from federal income tax. If the municipal bond is issued from a municipality in your state, then income from the bond may also be exempt from state and local income taxes. As a result, several municipal bond funds hold only bonds from a single state and thus are geared to investors in that state.

HYBRID FUNDS

Hybrid funds invest in both stocks and bonds. There are two major types of hybrid funds: asset allocation funds and balanced funds.

Asset Allocation Funds.

Asset allocation funds change their stock and bond (including cash) weights over time as market conditions change. Vanguard's Asset Allocation Fund, for example, uses a computer model to evaluate expected returns and risks of stocks, bonds, and cash. Then it changes weights over time based on those forecasts. As of March 2009, for example, the fund held 20 percent in cash, 78 percent in stock, and none in bonds (2 percent in others). A year later, in March 2010, the fund held 22 percent in cash, 60 percent in stocks, and 17 percent in bonds. Thus, over the course of the year, the fund moved about 17 percent of the assets from stocks to bonds.

Balanced Funds.

Balanced funds invest in both stocks and bonds and in relatively constant proportions. Vanguard's Balanced Index Fund Investor Shares, for example, invests approximately 60 percent of their assets in the U.S. stock market and 40 percent in the U.S. bond markets.

MONEY MARKET MUTUAL FUNDS

Money market mutual funds invest in very liquid, short-term assets (typically less than 120 days) whose prices are not significantly affected by changes in market interest rates (i.e., very short duration) and have little credit risk. In addition, they provide shareholders with ready access to their funds via wire transfers, transfers among stock and bond accounts, check writing, or credit card capabilities. Because money market mutual funds are extremely liquid, they are included in M2 and M3 money supply definitions.

Money market funds come in three main varieties: taxable government money market funds, taxable nongovernment money market funds, and tax-exempt money market funds. Similar to municipal bond funds, tax-exempt money market funds invest in high-quality, short-term municipal bonds issued by states and local municipalities. Taxable government money market funds primarily invest in T-bills, short-term government agency debt (e.g., Fannie Mae), and repurchase agreements that are backed by some sort of government debt. Taxable nongovernment money market funds invest in short-term government securities (despite the nongovernment title) in addition to riskier short-term debt, including certificates of deposit and short-term corporate debt (so-called commercial paper). Because nongovernment funds hold riskier assets, they generally have a higher yield. Exhibit 19.4 reports asset composition for taxable government and nongovernment money market funds at the end of 2009.

Even though many banks sell money market mutual funds and the names are similar, it is important to recognize that money market mutual funds are different

EXHIBIT 19.4

What Money Market Mutual Funds Hold in Their Portfolios

	PERCENTAGE OF TOTAL ASSETS	
	Taxable Nongovernment Money Market Funds	Taxable Government Money Market Funds
T-bills	2.7%	25.8%
Other treasury securities	1.2	6.3
U.S. government agency debt	10.0	34.7
Repurchase agreements	8.6	31.1
Certificates of deposit	30.8	0
Eurodollar CDs	5.3	0
Commercial paper	27.6	0.9
Bank notes	2.8	0.2
Corporate notes	6.2	0.3
Other assets	4.7	0.8
Average maturity (days)	50.0	47.0
Total net assets ($ millions)	$1,854,287	$1,064,464

Most of nongovernment money market mutual fund assets are invested in certificates of deposit and commercial paper. In contrast, most government money fund assets are invested in government agency debt and repurchase agreements backed by government debt.

Source: 2010 Investment Company Institute Fact Book.

than money market deposit accounts at a bank. Money market mutual funds, although low risk, are not federally insured deposits. Although rare, investors can, and have, lost money by investing in a money market mutual fund. In contrast, money market deposit accounts are FDIC insured.

Nonetheless, money market mutual funds are formidable competition for banks. Although they cannot pay out higher rates of interest than they earn on their holdings of money market instruments, they have been able to offer a variety of transactional conveniences. First, by cooperating with banks, many allow people to write checks on their money market mutual fund accounts that clear through the banking system. Second, by cooperating with card-issuing organizations, many allow their customers to use debit cards (and even credit cards for customers who hold cash management accounts with brokerage firms) to access the funds in their accounts for transaction purposes. Third, many funds allow customers to obtain wire transfers to designated parties from the balances in their money market mutual fund accounts. Fourth, customers who hold other assets with the parent company of the money market mutual fund may be allowed to sweep excess cash balances into their money market mutual fund (if, for instance, they sell stock at the parent brokerage firm). Conversely, the parent firm may also make automatic transfers of funds out of the money market mutual fund on the day that payment is needed for stock market transactions or when funds are needed for transfer into another mutual fund managed by the same fund family.

These features allow investors to earn the maximum possible interest on their cash balances by ensuring that their idle cash is always invested in their money market mutual fund until it is needed.

RELATIVE SIZES OF MUTUAL FUNDS

Exhibit 19.5 reports the fraction of total mutual fund assets held by various fund types in 1990, 2000, and 2009. As you can see, equity funds grew from about 22 percent of total mutual fund assets in 1990 to over 55 percent in 2000 (near the peak of the technology bubble), while bond funds fell from 27 percent to 11 percent, and money market funds fell from 47 percent to 27 percent of total mutual fund assets. Since 2000, equity's portion of total mutual fund assets has fallen to just under half of all mutual fund assets. Note also that equity investors have been more willing to hold international assets—world equity funds increased from just under 3 percent of total mutual fund assets in 1990 to nearly 12 percent by 2009.

EXHIBIT 19.5
Mutual Fund Assets by Fund Type

	PERCENTAGE OF TOTAL MUTUAL FUND ASSETS		
	1990	**2000**	**2009**
Equity Funds			
Capital appreciation	10.6	30.9	19.9
World	2.7	7.8	11.5
Total return	9.2	18.2	13.2
Total Equity Funds	**22.5**	**56.9**	**44.6**
Hybrid Funds	**3.4**	**5.0**	**5.8**
Bond Funds			
Corporate	2.4	2.0	3.2
High-yield	1.8	1.3	1.7
World	1.2	0.3	1.1
Government	9.8	1.9	2.4
Strategic income	0.8	2.1	7.3
State muni	4.7	1.9	1.4
National muni	6.6	2.1	2.7
Total Bond Funds	**27.3**	**11.6**	**19.8**
Money Market Funds			
Taxable	38.9	23.1	26.2
Tax-exempt	7.9	3.3	3.6
Total Money Market Funds	**46.8**	**26.5**	**29.8**

Money moves not only between mutual fund classes, but also within classes. Equity fund investors, for example, have become more willing to hold world equity funds over time.

Source: 2010 Investment Company Institute Fact Book.

Money Market Mutual Funds Breaking the Buck

Unlike other mutual funds, where NAVs vary every day (as the value of the portfolio rises or falls), money market mutual funds try to maintain their NAV at $1.00. The idea is pretty straightforward. The instruments they invest in are so safe, short term, and liquid, an investor who invests $1.00 should be able to get $1.00 out of the fund; that is, the fund should never lose money. To maintain the $1.00 NAV, money market funds adjust their yields. So if short-term rates increase, a money market mutual fund's yield will rise (as it invests in new, higher-yielding assets), but its NAV will stay at $1.00.

Although the assets that money market mutual funds invest in are very safe compared to equities or longer-term debt, they are not always risk free. For example, if the assets held by the money market mutual fund fall sufficiently in value, the fund's NAV could fall below $1.00. If this happens, the fund is said to have "broken the buck." Prior to September 2008, breaking the buck was an extremely rare occurrence. The economic tsunami in the fall of 2008, however, changed all that.

On Monday, September 15, 2008, Lehman Brothers declared bankruptcy. Reserve Primary Fund (a money market mutual fund) held approximately $785 million of Lehman Brothers debt in the form of commercial paper and floating rate notes. As a result of the bankruptcy, the value of the Lehman Brothers debt declined sharply, and on Tuesday, September 16, 2008, Reserve Primary Fund broke the buck when it lowered its NAV to $0.97. That meant investors, who may have erroneously believed they couldn't lose money in a money market mutual fund, faced a 3 percent loss of capital.

After news hit the market that Reserve Primary Fund broke the buck, investors rushed to remove money from their money market mutual funds—approximately $170 billion were removed from money market funds over the next week. As a result, demand for commercial paper fell dramatically as money market funds sold assets to fund redemptions. And as a result of that, companies suddenly had a hard time "rolling over" their commercial paper. When they did, it was at much higher rates. The *Wall Street Journal* reported, for example, that commercial paper rates increased from around 2 percent to nearly 8 percent within a week.[1]

To restore investor confidence, the Treasury Department announced, just 4 days following Lehman Brothers' bankruptcy, a temporary program to insure money market mutual fund assets (i.e., guarantee $1.00 NAV) to those funds that paid a fee to participate in the program (much like FDIC insurance). Some in the press referred to the program as the money market mutual fund bailout. As the Treasury intended, the program worked in restoring investor confidence in money market mutual funds. Banking groups, such as the American Bankers Association, not surprisingly expressed displeasure at the Treasury insuring money market fund assets. That is, banks' competitive advantage over money market mutual funds is that banks' money market deposit accounts were FDIC insured, while money market mutual funds were uninsured. The temporary Treasury insurance program ended in September 2009. As before, money market mutual funds are no longer insured.

As a result of the crisis, however, the SEC adopted strict new rules for money market mutual funds that went into effect in May 2010. These rules included liquidity requirements (10 percent of the assets have to be liquid within 1 day and 30 percent within 1 week), a reduction in the maximum weighted average maturity from 90 days to 60 days, a requirement to post holdings on the fund's Web site monthly, and a requirement that funds be able to process purchases and redemptions at prices other than $1.00 to allow orderly redemptions in case a fund breaks the buck.

[1]"Bailout of Money Funds Seems to Stanch Outflow" *Wall Street Journal*, September 8, 2008.

MUTUAL FUND FEES

Mutual funds are also classified by their fee structure. A **load fund** charges a fee to invest in the fund that is used to pay the broker (or financial adviser). Basically it's a commission to the broker. Most load funds charge the fee when you purchase the mutual fund (a **front-end load**). The Financial Industry Regulatory Authority (FINRA), a private, self-regulatory organization (not a government agency), sets the maximum front-end load of 8.5 percent of the net asset value. A front-end load, of course, reduces the amount of money that will be invested in the fund. If you pay $1,000 and there is a 5 percent up-front load, $950 will be invested and $50 will be paid to the broker who sold you the fund.

Some load funds charge a **back-end load** (also known as a **contingent deferred sales charge**). The *back-end load* is subtracted from the net asset value of the redeemed shares before payment is made to the shareholder who redeems shares. If, for example, your fund has a 5 percent bank-end load, and you redeem $1,000 worth of the fund, you will receive only $950. As with a front-end load, the remaining $50 is used to compensate the salesperson who sold you the fund. Most contingent deferred sales charges are temporary, however, and may diminish or disappear over time. For instance, a fund may levy a 5 percent contingent deferred sales charge if shares are redeemed within a year of purchase, with the charge falling by 1 percent per year until no charge is levied on people who have held their shares in the fund for 5 years on more.

Mutual funds that charge no sales load are called, not surprisingly, **no-load funds**. A no-load fund, however, does not mean that a salesperson won't be compensated or that you won't pay any fees. Specifically, most funds charge **12b-1 fees** to cover distribution expenses, which usually include compensation to the broker who sold you the fund. The name *12b-1 fees* comes from the SEC statute that allows funds to charge them. In addition, FINRA allows mutual funds to call themselves no-load funds as long as the combined 12b-1 fees and shareholder service fees are no greater than 0.25 percent of the fund's net asset value. To make matters even more confusing, many, if not most, load funds also charge 12b-1 fees. In July 2010, however, the SEC voted to change the rules for 12b-1 fees, including doing away with the 12b-1 name. Under the new proposal, funds will be allowed to change a "marketing and service" fee of up to 0.25 percent.

Both no-load and load funds can charge other fees. A redemption fee is similar to a back-end load, but it is paid to the fund instead of the broker. An investor is sometimes charged an exchange fee when he or she moves money from one fund (i.e., redeems shares) to another related (i.e., managed by the same company) fund. In addition, some funds charge account maintenance fees, especially on low-balance accounts.

The largest portion of the annual fee, however, is typically the annual **management fees** or **advisory fees** that are paid to the company that manages the fund's portfolio. Such fees may amount to 1 percent or more of the fund's annual average net assets. They can be as low as 0.2 percent for index funds that are not required to make portfolio decisions or trade actively, or they can be as high as 2 or 3 percent or more for funds that operate in markets where information is costly to obtain and considerable expertise is needed to invest wisely.

To make matters more confusing, many mutual funds now offer multiple **mutual fund share classes**. A multiclass fund has the same manager and portfolio, but shareholders in different fund classes pay different fees. Class A shareholders pay an up-front load but lower annual fees. Class B shareholders pay higher annual fees and a back-end load but no up-front load. If held long enough, class B shares may convert class A shares. Class C shareholders pay no up-front load and may have a small back-end load (usually only if they sell within 1 year), but they have higher expenses than class A shares. In addition, unlike some class B shares, class C shares do not convert to class A shares regardless of how long an investor owns the fund. Clearly, which class of shares you purchase will depend on your holding period. For example, although class A shares charge an up-front load, an investor may still be better off buying class A shares if the investor's holding period is long enough because of the lower annual expenses. Fortunately, all mutual funds issue a prospectus for investors (available on nearly all mutual fund Web sites). The prospectus provides an easy-to-read and -understand fee table that shows exactly what loads and fees the fund charges for each share class.

Sometimes it may be worth paying a high management fee to obtain access to particular markets and superior investment management skills, but the payment of a high management fee doesn't guarantee superior performance. In fact, one of the classic problems with judging mutual fund managers is that it's hard to distinguish skill from luck. (If your neighbor wins the lottery, do you consult her on how to pick the best lottery numbers?) If anything, the academic literature seems to suggest that the worst-performing mutual funds levy the highest fees. That result is not totally unexpected because the return to the investor is reduced by the amount of the management fees paid. Remember, they mean it when they say past performance does not necessarily predict future returns.

One reason many academics advocate investment in index funds (where the fund's performance is approximately equal to the matched stock index) is that the low management fees for such funds have little negative effect on the investor's returns. Although the investor in an index fund does not do much better (or worse) than the market index the fund is matching, he or she may still outperform actively managed funds that do only marginally better than the index after accounting for the higher management fees of funds that are not index funds.

MUTUAL FUND FAMILIES

Mutual funds proliferated in the 1990s in part because of the creation of **mutual fund families**. Part of the motivation for creating mutual fund families is to service retirement accounts, particularly 401k, 403b, IRA, and Keogh accounts that are self-directed by the employee or employer. Mutual fund families, or groups of mutual funds under control of the same company but with different investment philosophies, appeal to people who may want to change how they invest their money—moving assets from domestic to foreign stocks, or from stocks to bonds to cash, or from long-term bonds to short-term bonds or back, and so on. By allowing people to shift their assets around within the fund family, a fund family reduces transaction costs and hassles for their customers, particularly for customers who hold their assets in retirement accounts that are subject to extensive government regulation and restriction. The Investment Company Institute reports that at the end of 2009, the top 25 fund families controlled 74 percent of total mutual fund assets.

Fidelity funds, for example, offer dozens of domestic equity funds (e.g., Fidelity Magellan Fund), international equity funds (e.g., Fidelity Emerging Markets Fund), domestic and international bond funds (e.g., Fidelity Corporate Bond Fund), index funds (e.g., Spartan 500 fund), money market funds (e.g., Fidelity Cash Reserves), and hybrid funds (e.g., Fidelity Balanced Fund). By keeping many assets in one fund family, a customer can easily change his or her investment objectives and holdings with a mouse click or phone call. Some funds allow cash to be transferred among various funds electronically. Thus, it is very easy for consumers to change the nature of their investments as they see fit. In addition, by dealing with only one fund family, a person can comply with all applicable retirement account regulations more easily as assets are shifted from one fund to another.

Let's start with a fictional closed-end fund that has no liabilities: McKinnon Fund has five mutual fund shares outstanding, and the entire portfolio consists of only one stock—100 shares of Yukon Dog Food (YDF) selling for $10 per share. The total value of the McKinnon Fund is simply the total value of the Yukon Dog Food holdings: 100 shares × $10 = $1,000. Because the McKinnon Fund has five shares outstanding, the fund's NAV is $200 ($1,000/5). If McKinnon was an open-end fund, a shareholder could redeem shares for $200 (and the McKinnon Fund would shrink) or purchase additional shares for $200 (meaning the McKinnon Fund would issue more shares and increase in size).

Closed-end funds differ from open-end funds, however, in one really important way: In general, the fund manager will not redeem or issue shares. That is, as a closed-end fund, McKinnon Fund will always have 5 shares outstanding. The NAV, of course, could change as the price of Yukon Dog Food company's stock rises and falls. An investor who wants to leave the McKinnon Fund, therefore, has to sell shares to another investor. And, similarly, an investor who wants to own McKinnon Fund will have to buy shares from another investor. Thus, unlike open-end funds, where an investor buys shares from the manager (who issues additional shares) or sells shares to the manager (redeeming shares), closed-end fund shares are traded between investors just as any other stock is traded between investors in the secondary market. Therefore, closed-end fund share prices, just like any other stock, are set by supply and demand.

So what price should McKinnon Fund shares trade for? If McKinnon Fund shut down today, selling all its assets and distributing the proceeds to its shareholders, each share would get $200. That is, the NAV is nothing more than the liquidation value of the fund to each shareholder. As a result, many argue the "fair" value of a closed-end fund share is the NAV. After all, ignoring potential fees, that's what the shareholder could "sell" the shares to the manager for if it were an open-end fund.

Somewhat surprisingly, however, most closed-end fund prices are usually substantially below their net asset values. When a closed-end fund's shares trade for less than its net asset value, the fund is said to be trading at a **discount**. On the other hand, sometimes a fund's shares will trade at a price higher than the net asset value. When that occurs, the fund is said to be trading at a **premium**. Exhibit 19.6 reports premiums or discounts from net asset values (on July 21, 2010) of selected U.S. closed-end funds—two domestic equity funds, two bond funds, and two international equity funds. As you can see, prices can differ substantially from net asset values. First Opportunity Fund, for example, had net assets worth $7.92 per share, yet it was trading for $6.01 per share—a 24 percent discount.

Some people think that the fact that a fund's NAV does not equal its market price may indicate that market inefficiencies exist because the value of the whole should equal the value of the sum of its parts. Others maintain that there are rational explanations for the price discrepancies. For instance, in some foreign

19.3 CLOSED-END MUTUAL FUNDS

EXHIBIT 19.6
Data on Selected Closed-End Funds (July 21, 2010)

Fund	Ticker/ Exchange	Strategy	Net Asset Value (NAV)	Market Price	Total Net Asset ($ Millions)	Premium/ Discount (%)
Nuveen Core Equity Alpha Fund	JCE/NYSE	US equity—general	$12.34	$11.61	$ 197.62	−5.92
First Opportunity Fund	FOFI/pink sheets	US equity—general	7.92	6.01	227.54	−24.12
Rivus Bond	BDF/NYSE	Taxable income—investment grade	19.63	18.06	128.05	−8.00
PIMCO Corporate Opportunity	PTY/NYSE	Taxable income—investment grade	15.00	16.80	1,498.34	12.00
ING Asia Pacific High Dividend	IAE/NYSE	Non-U.S./other—Asia equity	16.40	16.73	205.14	2.01
Thai Fund	TTF/NYSE	Non-U.S./other—Asia equity	12.00	10.19	190.33	−15.08

Source: Closed-End Fund Connect, www.cefconnect.com.

countries, investment funds are allowed to invest in shares, but individuals are not. Thus, individuals who want to invest in that country may be willing to pay a premium to obtain assets in that country by buying shares in the fund. Also, investors may be willing to pay a premium because they believe the fund manager has superior ability. People may not be willing to pay full NAV for a fund with poor managers who cannot be replaced easily or for a fund that has high management costs and fees relative to its expected returns. In these cases, a fund may sell at a discount to its NAV for good reasons, not because of market inefficiencies.

Some investors also believe they can earn abnormal returns from buying closed-end funds that are selling at a large discount. As noted above, for example, First Opportunity Fund had a net asset value of $7.92 and a price of $6.01 in July 2010. Thus, the fund was selling at a 24 percent discount: $7.92 − 0.24($7.92) = $6.01. That means an investor buying $1 worth of First Opportunity Fund is getting a claim to assets worth $1.32: $1.32 − 0.24($1.32) = $1. The risk, of course, is that the discount could get even bigger. In addition, the investor would have to pay a management fee. Last, it is possible the manager may substantially underperform in the market.

As shown in Exhibit 19.7, there was $228 billion invested in closed-end funds at the end of 2009 versus more than $11 trillion invested in open-end funds (refer back to Exhibit 19.2). Although small relative to open-end funds, there is a lot of

EXHIBIT 19.7

Assets and Number of Closed-End Funds by Type of Fund (*End of Year*)

Year	Total	Equity Funds			Bond Funds			
		Total Equity	Domestic	Global/ International	Total Bond	Domestic Taxable	Domestic Municipal	Global/ International
Assets ($ Millions)								
2002	$158,805	$33,724	$26,596	$ 7,128	$125,081	$25,643	$90,024	$ 9,414
2003	214,088	53,019	42,987	10,032	161,069	55,428	94,102	11,539
2004	254,296	82,327	63,762	18,565	171,969	64,230	94,884	12,855
2005	277,017	105,588	77,124	28,464	171,430	64,119	94,606	12,705
2006	298,328	122,477	87,772	34,705	175,851	68,051	94,569	13,231
2007	312,795	146,174	87,569	58,604	166,622	62,281	88,659	15,682
2008	187,986	75,658	46,807	28,851	112,328	33,727	67,710	10,891
2009	228,174	92,599	53,969	38,630	135,575	43,973	77,942	13,660
Number of Funds								
2002	545	123	63	60	422	105	292	25
2003	584	131	75	56	453	129	297	27
2004	619	158	96	62	461	136	295	30
2005	635	193	121	72	442	131	280	31
2006	647	204	129	75	443	134	276	33
2007	664	230	137	93	434	131	269	34
2008	642	221	127	94	421	128	260	33
2009	627	208	116	92	419	127	260	32

Source: 2010 Investment Company Institute Fact Book.

money invested in a lot of closed-end funds. Exhibit 19.7 reports assets under management and number of funds over time by the type of fund. At the end of 2009, there were 627 closed-end funds traded in the United States: 208 equity funds and 419 bond funds. Equity funds were approximately evenly split between domestic and global/international. Municipal bond funds dominate the closed-end bond fund market.

19.4 EXCHANGE-TRADED FUNDS

First introduced in the United States in 1993, **exchange-traded funds (ETFs)** are investment companies whose shares trade on stock exchanges similar to closed-end funds. Unlike closed-end funds, however, ETFs have a unique creation and redemption feature that prevents large premiums or discounts from the NAV. Basically, a so-called authorized participant (usually a large institutional investor) can exchange ETF shares for shares of the underlying portfolio (a redemption) or can exchange the securities that make up the underlying portfolio for ETF shares (thus, creating new ETF shares). As a result, if the value of the ETF share is substantially smaller than the value of the underlying assets, an authorized participant will buy ETF shares in the market and exchange them for underlying assets. Thus, authorized participants will buy ETFs that are selling at a substantial discount, driving their price higher until the discount disappears. Similarly, if the ETF share price is higher than the net asset value, an authorized participant will buy the securities that the ETF holds, exchange them for more valuable ETF shares, and immediately sell those shares in the market.

Consider a simple example. Assume that the Rachel ETF only holds shares in PepsiCo. The Rachel ETF holds 1,000 shares of PepsiCo that are currently selling for $100/share. The Rachel ETF has 500 shares outstanding. Thus, each share of the Rachel ETF should be worth $(1,000 \times \$100)/500 = \$200$. In addition, each share of the Rachel ETF has a claim to two shares of PepsiCo (i.e., 1,000 shares of PepsiCo/500 shares of Rachel ETF). Assume, however, that the Rachel ETF is selling for $205. How could an authorized participant exploit this opportunity? Because the Rachel ETF is worth more than the underlying stocks, the authorized participant would purchase shares of PepsiCo, exchange them for Rachel ETF shares, and then sell the Rachel ETF shares. For example, if the manager purchased 2 shares of PepsiCo (for a total cost of $200) and gave them to the ETF trustee, the ETF trustee would issue 1 new share of the Rachel ETF, which the authorized participant would sell for $205, thus making a $5 profit. Because large investors are constantly looking for opportunities to earn a quick profit, ETF share values stay pretty close to their NAVs.

Most ETFs are designed to track a domestic stock index, an international index, or an industry sector. For example, there are ETFs designed to track the S&P 500, Nasdaq 100, Fortune 500, S&P 500 financials, Dow Jones Industrial Average, Russell 3000, S&P Europe 350, S&P Latin America 40, and countless others. As you can see from Exhibit 19.8, the growth in ETFs has been explosive since they appeared on the scene in the early 1990s. At the end of 2009, there were nearly 800 ETFs with more than $777 billion in net assets.

Although most ETFs are based on broad-based domestic equity indexes (such as the S&P 500), specific sectors (such as a consumer cyclicals ETF) or an international index or sector (such as a small capitalization Japan index) commodity funds have grown in popularity in recent years. As their name implies, commodity ETFs typically hold a physical asset (e.g., a gold ETF) or futures contracts on a physical

EXHIBIT 19.8
Assets and Number of ETFs by Type of Fund (*End of Year*)

Year	Total	Domestic Broad-Based	Equity Domestic Sector	Global/ International	Commodities	Hybrid	Bond
Assets ($ Millions)							
2002	$ 102,143	$ 86,985	$ 5,919	$ 5,324			$ 3,915
2003	150,983	120,430	11,901	13,984			4,667
2004	227,540	163,730	20,315	33,644	$ 1,335		8,516
2005	300,820	186,832	28,975	65,210	4,798		15,004
2006	422,550	232,487	43,655	111,194	14,699		20,514
2007	608,422	300,930	64,117	179,702	28,906	$119	34,648
2008	531,288	266,161	58,374	113,684	35,728	132	57,209
2009	777,128	304,044	82,073	209,315	74,508	169	107,018
Number of ETFs							
2002	113	34	32	39			8
2003	119	39	33	41			6
2004	152	60	42	43	1		6
2005	204	81	65	49	3		6
2006	359	133	119	85	16		6
2007	629	197	191	159	28	5	49
2008	728	204	186	225	45	6	62
2009	797	222	181	244	47	5	98

There has been explosive growth in ETFs since they first appeared in the early 1990s. Most of the growth has been in equity ETFs.

Source: 2010 Investment Company Institute Fact Book.

commodity (e.g., a natural gas ETF). These commodity ETFs provide an easy way for investors to make (or hedge) bets on the price of nearly any commodity.

Legally, ETFs are not a unique type of investment company. Instead, most ETFs are legally organized as mutual funds or unit investment trusts (discussed later in this chapter). In addition, commodity ETFs are not investment companies at all; that is, they are not registered with the SEC under the Investment Company Act of 1940. Instead, because they invest in commodity futures, they are regulated by the Commodity Futures and Trading Commission (CFTC).

Just a few of the most popular ETFs are listed in Exhibit 19.9. As you can see, these ETFs are very large. Even the smallest (Diamonds, tracking the DJIA) holds a portfolio worth $8.29 billion. ETFs have very low expense ratios. Spiders (tracking the S&P 500 index), for example, average an annual expense ratio of less than one-tenth of 1 percent. There are a number of other reasons for the growing popularity of ETFs compared to an open-end index mutual fund. First, if a mutual fund manager sells some securities in the portfolio, those realized capital gains or losses are passed on to the mutual fund shareholder. In contrast, an ETF rarely sells securities; instead, it trades one set of securities for another set (e.g., an authorized investor receives the underlying stocks in exchange for the ETF

EXHIBIT 19.9
Selected Exchange-Traded Funds (March 2010)

Name	Ticker/ Exchange	Nickname and Index or Representative Holdings	Market Capitalization ($ Billions)	Expense Ratio (Percent)
SPDR S&P 500 ETF	SPY/NYSE	"Spiders" track the S&P 500 index and are the largest ETF.	$93.36	0.09
SPDR Dow Jones Industrial Average ETF	DIA/NYSE	"Diamonds" track the Dow Jones Industrial Average.	8.29	0.17
PowerShare QQQ	QQQQ/NASDAQ	"Cubes" track the Nasdaq-100 index.	18.58	0.20
iShares MSCI Brazil Index Fund	EWZ/NYSE	EWZ tracks the Brazil equity market.	10.44	0.65
SPDR Gold Shares	GLD/NYSE	GLD tracks the price of gold bullion.	45.38	0.40

Source: Fund fact sheets.

share). Second, similar to any other stock, you can purchase ETFs anytime during the trading day from any brokerage account. In contrast, a mutual fund can be redeemed or issued only at the end of the trading day. Third, ETFs can be sold short. If, for example, you wanted to bet that gold will fall in value, you could sell short the SPDR Gold Shares ETF. If you are right, then, as the price of gold bullion falls, so will SPDR Gold Shares, thus allowing you to profit when you cover the short position (i.e., buying back the shares you borrowed) at a lower price.

UNIT INVESTMENT TRUSTS

Investment trusts are often used to invest in assets, such as municipal bonds, that cannot be bought or sold easily in the market. An investment trust (or **unit investment trust**) consists of pro rata interests in an unmanaged pool of assets. More specifically, shares or *units* in a trust are sold to the public to obtain the funds needed to invest in a portfolio of securities. The securities are held in safekeeping in accordance with a set of conditions spelled out in a trust agreement. The securities purchased are typically government notes and bonds; corporate and municipal bonds; and, on occasion, preferred stock and money market instruments. Once the securities are purchased, no new securities are added, and with rare exceptions, no securities are sold. Because there is no trading of securities by the trustee and most securities purchased have a fixed return, the return (or *yield*) on an investment trust is fairly predictable. For instance, each unit in a trust with 100,000 units has a 1/100,000th interest in each security owned by the trust and is entitled to receive 1/100,000th of the income generated by that security.

There are three types of unit investment trusts: equity (invests in stocks), taxable debt (invests in Treasury bonds, agency bonds, corporate bonds, etc.), and tax-free debt (invests in municipal bonds). As shown in Exhibit 19.10, the importance of equity unit investment trusts has increased in recent years, and the importance of tax-free debt unit investment trusts has declined. As with open-end mutual funds, unit investment trust investors often pay a front-end sales load when purchasing unit investment trusts. Unlike actively managed mutual funds, however, unit investment trusts have a specific time in existence and a fixed portfolio. As shown in Exhibit 19.10, however, unit investment trusts are only a very small portion of the investment company universe.

EXHIBIT 19.10
Assets and Number of Unit Investment Trusts by Type (*End of Year*)

Year	Total Trusts	Equity	Taxable Debt	Tax-Free Debt
Assets ($ Millions)				
2002	$36,016	$14,651	$4,020	$17,345
2003	35,826	19,024	3,311	13,491
2004	37,267	23,201	2,635	11,432
2005	40,894	28,634	2,280	9,980
2006	49,662	38,809	2,142	8,711
2007	53,040	43,295	2,066	7,680
2008	28,543	20,080	2,007	6,456
2009	38,336	24,774	3,668	9,894
Number of Trusts				
2002	8,303	1,247	366	6,690
2003	7,233	1,206	320	5,707
2004	6,499	1,166	295	5,038
2005	6,019	1,251	304	4,464
2006	5,907	1,566	319	4,022
2007	6,030	1,964	327	3,739
2008	5,984	2,175	343	3,466
2009	6,049	2,145	438	3,466

Source: 2010 Investment Company Institute Fact Book.

Unit trusts are usually formed and sold by brokerage houses to investors with limited resources who want to acquire a diversified portfolio of fixed-income securities and earn a monthly income. Although there is no active secondary market for trust shares, investors can usually sell them back to the sponsor at a price equal to the prevailing net asset value per unit minus a sales commission if the sponsor can find another buyer.

DO YOU UNDERSTAND?

1. What type of investment company—an open-end mutual fund, a closed-end mutual fund, or an exchange-traded fund—is most likely to sell at a price that differs the most from its net asset value (NAV)? Which type is most likely to sell at a price that differs the least from its NAV? Explain why each type of fund might or might not sell at a price that diverges from its NAV.

2. What are the pros and cons on investments in mutual funds that try to match a general market index?

3. What are the various types of fees and charges that may be levied by different mutual funds?

4. Why is it essential that potential investors thoroughly read the prospectus for any mutual fund they are considering as an investment?

19.5 HEDGE FUNDS

Despite the name of this chapter, most **hedge funds** are not investment companies. According to the SEC, companies (such as hedge funds) that are exempt from registering as investment companies as part of the Investment Company Act of 1940 are not considered investment companies. Hedge funds are similar to investment companies, however, in the sense that they pool investors' money to invest in a range of assets. Hedge funds are typically organized as limited partnerships, with the fund manager serving as the general partner and the investors serving as the limited partners.

Most hedge funds avoid registering as investment companies by either a Section 3(c)(1) exemption or a Section 3(c)(7) exemption. This turns out to be important because it greatly restricts who can invest in a hedge fund and how the fund can be offered. First, hedge funds cannot make a public offering of their securities. You don't see, for example, newspaper ads for hedge funds. A hedge fund that has a 3(c)(1) exemption can have no more than 100 investors, and these investors must be accredited. In July 2010, an accredited investor was roughly defined as a person with a net worth of more than $1 million or at least $200,000 income in the past 2 years and reasonable expectation of the same this year. The Dodd-Frank Wall Street Reform and Consumer Protection Act passed in July 2010 refined the definition of an accredited individual to be $1 million in net worth excluding the person's residence. Certain business (e.g., banks, insurance companies) and non-profit organizations are also accredited investors.

Hedge funds that claim a (3)(c)(7) exemption can have only qualified purchasers and no more than 499 investors. These funds also cannot make their securities publicly available. A qualified purchaser is an individual with net worth of at least $5 million or an institution with net worth of at least $25 million. In short, hedge fund investors are either institutions with substantial assets or wealthy individuals. Your university's foundation, for example, may be invested in hedge funds.

It is estimated that, as of 2010, there was approximately $1.6 trillion invested in hedge funds. According to Exhibit 19.1, this means that money invested in hedge funds is only about 14 percent of the money invested in mutual funds. Nonetheless, there is more money invested in hedge funds than in exchange-traded funds, closed-end funds, and unit investment trusts combined.

HOW DO HEDGE FUNDS DIFFER FROM MUTUAL FUNDS

Hedging, of course, means to reduce your risk. Thus, hedge funds began as a "safer" alternative. Alfred Jones started the first hedge fund in 1949. His basic idea of a long-short fund is still used today. Basically, Jones wanted to bet on the relative performance of companies. Say, for example, you believed Microsoft's stock will outperform Apple's stock over the next few months. If you buy Microsoft, you still run the risk of losing money, even if Microsoft outperforms Apple. In 2008, for example, Microsoft had a total return of approximately −44 percent, while Apple had a total return of −57 percent. Thus, even if you predicted Microsoft would beat Apple, you still lost money.

Jones's insight was that one could remove the market risk and bet only on the relative performance of Microsoft and Apple by taking a long position in Microsoft and a short position in Apple. If you had been able to employ that strategy in 2008, for example, your gains from the Apple short sale would have more than offset your losses on holding Microsoft and you would have made money. Jones's "hedged" fund had two other unique characteristics. First, Jones also borrowed

---

PEOPLE & EVENTS

Hedge Funds and the Dodd-Frank Wall Street Reform and Consumer Protection Act

Historically, hedge fund managers have enjoyed their privacy. In 2005, the SEC adopted a rule that would have required hedge fund managers to register with the SEC. A hedge fund manager successfully sued the SEC, however, and the registration requirement was struck down. As a result, registration with the SEC was voluntary for hedge funds. The 2010 Dodd-Frank Wall Street Reform and Consumer Protection Act, however, has changed the rules. Specifically, the act eliminated the "Private Advisor" exemption to the Investment Advisor Act of 1940 (which, again to make life confusing, is different than the Investment Company Act of 1940).

As a result of the new rules, hedge funds with more than $150 million in assets under management must register with the SEC. Although specific rules are not clear at this point, the SEC will have the power to require advisers to give information on their trades and portfolios as necessary to assess systemic risk (risk that threatens the entire market). Systemic risk could arise, for example, if a group of highly leveraged funds made bets that went sour and then did not have enough equity to cover the bets. The organization on the other side of the bet (the counterparty), which could be, for example, a bank, therefore could face substantial losses even though it made the "right" bet.

---

money, which allowed him to use leverage to magnify (good or bad) his returns. He believed that because he had greatly reduced market risk (by hedging long positions with short positions), he could take on more firm-specific risk (e.g., the risk that Apple outperforms Microsoft). Second, instead of taking a flat fee similar to most mutual funds (e.g., 1 percent of assets as a management fee), Jones (and his team) took 20 percent of the profits. Reportedly, Jones based this figure on the argument that Phoenician ship captains took 20 percent of the profits from a successful voyage. (Phoenicia was an ancient civilization from about 1550 B.C. to 300 B.C. in present-day Lebanon, Syria, and Israel.)

As with Jones's original fund, most hedge funds continue to use short positions and leverage. In contrast, most mutual funds do not take short positions (although some do, and a few specialize in short positions) and in general don't use leverage. Hedge funds also differ from mutual funds in their fee structure. Most take a management fee (e.g., 2 percent of assets under management) and also, following Jones's original fund, a performance fee (e.g., 20 percent of profits). Thus, a hedge fund's fee structure may be quoted as 2 and 20. As a result of hedge funds' unique fee structure, the pay can be incredible. Even with a −37 percent total return on the S&P 500 in 2008, for example, James Simons of Renaissance Technologies reportedly earned $2.5 billion in 2008. It's kind of funny to think that hedge fund pay today is based on the pay structure of Phoenician ship captains literally thousands of years ago.

HEDGE FUND INVESTMENT STRATEGIES

Hedge funds fall into two primary categories: absolute return and directional. An absolute return fund attempts to eliminate all market risk and bets only on relative performance. Roughly speaking, for example, a fund that sold an equal amount of stocks short as it had invested long would be making a pure relative bet, assuming that the beta (see Chapter 10) of the long portfolio was the same as the beta of the short portfolio. A fund that does not fully eliminate market risk is a directional fund. For example, a number of hedge funds made a directional bet on the decline of the euro relative to the U.S. dollar in 2010.

Global Macro Strategies. The strategy of macro fund managers is based on shifts in global economies. Macro managers speculate on changes in countries' economic policies and shifts in currency and interest rates by the use of derivatives and leverage. Portfolios tend to be concentrated in a small number of investment positions. The investments are often specifically designed to take advantage of artificial imbalances in the marketplace brought on by central bank activities.

Market-Neutral Strategies. A market-neutral strategy seeks to eliminate market risk by balancing long and short positions equally. Exposure to the market is reduced because short and long portfolio losses and gains as a result of market fluctuations typically offset one another. If the longs selected are undervalued and the shorts are overvalued, a profit results when the market recognizes the mispricing.

Sector Strategies. Sector funds invest long and short in specific sectors of the economy. Examples of such sector specialization include technology companies, financial institutions, healthcare, utilities, real estate investment trusts, and energy companies. Managers construct portfolios of long and short positions based on intensive research.

Short Selling. This strategy is based on the sale of securities that are overvalued from either a technical or a fundamental viewpoint. The investor does not own the shares sold but instead borrows them from a broker in anticipation that the share price will fall and the shares may be bought later at a lower price to replace those borrowed from the broker earlier. Short sellers typically focus on situations in which they believe stock prices are being supported by unrealistic expectations.

Fixed-Income Arbitrage. This strategy involves taking long and short positions in bonds with the expectation that the yield spreads between them will return to historical levels. When combined, these positions approximate one another in terms of rate and maturity but suffer from price inefficiencies. Risk varies with the level of leverage used and the types of trades.

Index Arbitrage. Index arbitrage involves buying and selling a "basket" of stocks or other securities and taking a counterposition in index futures contracts to capture differences as a result of inefficiencies in the market. This process is also known as *program trading*.

Closed-End Fund Arbitrage. In closed-end fund arbitrage, like stock index arbitrage, the fund manager buys or sells a basket of stocks. In this case, the basket replicates the holding of a closed-end mutual fund. The manager seeks to identify closed-end mutual funds that are trading at prices substantially different from their net asset value.

Convertible Arbitrage. In convertible arbitrage, the fund manager simultaneously goes long in the convertible securities and short in the underlying equities of the same issuers, thereby working the spread between the two types of securities. Returns result from the convergence of valuations between the two securities.

Event-Driven Investing. Event-driven investing is a strategy that seeks to profit from price imbalances or fluctuations. The event-driven investing strategies are risk arbitrage, distressed securities, and special situations.

Risk Arbitrage. In risk arbitrage, fund managers take a long position in the stock of a company being acquired in a merger, leveraged buyout, or takeover and a simultaneous short position in the stock of the acquiring firm. If the takeover fails, this strategy may result in large losses because the target company's stock price likely will return to its previous price.

Distressed Securities. In this strategy, fund managers, sometimes referred to as "vulture capitalists," typically invest in the securities of companies undergoing bankruptcy or reorganization. Managers tend to focus on companies that are undergoing financial rather than operational distress.

Special Situations. Special-situation managers attempt to take advantage of unusual events with a significant position in the equity or debt of a firm. Special-situation managers tend to focus on areas such as depressed stocks, impending mergers or acquisitions, or emerging bad news that may temporarily cause a company's stock or bond prices to decline.

HEDGE FUND PERFORMANCE

The performance of the various hedge fund strategies varies from year to year. Exhibit 19.11 shows the cumulative performance of the Hennessee Hedge Fund Index for 1993 through 2009. Note that, during the period when the technology bubble burst, the S&P 500 suffered large negative returns, while hedge funds continued, on average, to gain ground. A few other important thoughts on hedge fund performance: First, unlike investment companies, hedge funds are not required to report returns. As a result, hedge fund indexes are based on voluntary filings and therefore likely have some biases. For example, a fund that had such bad performance last quarter that it was forced to liquidate would likely not voluntarily report its results (this is known as a survivorship bias). Second, although the graph in Exhibit 19.11 suggests that hedge funds, on average, have done well, there is a lot of cross-sectional variation in hedge fund returns—some funds have done very well and others have done very poorly.

DO YOU UNDERSTAND?

1. Why would an investor want to invest in a hedge fund?
2. How are hedge funds different from closed-end funds and mutual funds?
3. Why do hedge fund managers follow such specialized strategies?

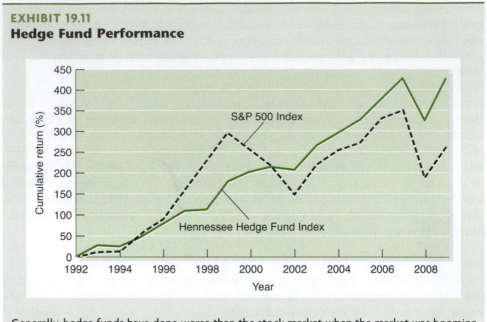

EXHIBIT 19.11
Hedge Fund Performance

Generally, hedge funds have done worse than the stock market when the market was booming (e.g., late 1990s) but better than the stock market when the market was falling (e.g., early 2000s).

Source: Hennessee Group, LLC, www.hennesseegroup.com.

19.6 REAL ESTATE INVESTMENT TRUSTS

A **real estate investment trust (REIT)** is similar to a closed-end fund that invests in real estate. It may hold income-generating properties (e.g., apartment buildings, office buildings, or even in one case, prisons), acquire mortgages, finance real estate developments, provide interim financing to builders, or acquire and lease property to real estate developers. As with hedge funds, real estate investment trusts are not technically investment companies. Specifically, the Investment Company Act of 1940 excludes companies that are primarily in the business of "purchasing or otherwise acquiring mortgages and other liens on and interests in real estate."

REITs must abide by the Real Estate Investment Act of 1960, however, which governs their formation and business operations. REITs are exempt from federal income tax provided that they derive at least three-fourths of their income from operations related to real estate and pass through more than 90 percent of their net income to shareholders. According to the National Association of Real Estate Investment Trusts (NAREIT), at the end of 2009, there were 142 REITS with a total market capitalization of $271 billion. Comparing that figure with Exhibit 19.1 reveals that the total market capitalization for REITs is greater than that for closed-end funds but only about 2.5 percent of the total market capitalization for open-end mutual funds.

REITs grew slowly until the late 1960s, when their growth exploded. New favorable tax treatment, federal encouragement of real estate investment, a strong economy, and rising real estate prices all contributed to their growth. Although they were growing rapidly, many REITs took excessive risks, making highly leveraged or speculative investments on the assumption that rising real estate prices would soon increase builders' and owners' equity. Furthermore,

REITs that provided construction and interim financing to speculative builders (builders who erected properties without first having firm contracts from end users) took the most risk. Those taking the least risk provided long-term mortgage financing to ultimate users of properties or were *equity trusts* that owned and leased real properties.

When interest rates rose and housing construction sagged during the money crunch of 1973 and 1974, numerous owners could not find permanent tenants for their properties. Many construction and development projects were left uncompleted or deferred as builders saw the market for their project dry up. As a result of these developments, numerous REITs had bad loans and experienced well-publicized financial distress. Many failed. To prevent failure of REITs associated with bank holding companies bearing their names, some commercial banks knowingly purchased bad mortgage loans from their affiliated REITs. This, in turn, jeopardized the banks. Before regulators could stop this practice, several large banks failed.

The bad publicity and financial distress surrounding REITs in the early and mid-1970s halted their rapid growth and started a substantial decline. Many of those that survived the 1973–1974 money crunch were the REITs that held relatively low-risk physical assets. Although most survivors own sound assets, the bad publicity that REITs in general experienced in the mid-1970s made it difficult for them to attract new shareholders and lenders. Starting in the mid-1980s, however, REITs began to play a more important role in the economy once again, in part because tax reforms made other forms of real estate investment less attractive and enhanced the attractiveness of REITs as a source of passive real estate income. Newly formed mortgage REITs bought pools of high-yielding mortgages. In the 1990s, the growth in REITs was fueled by Wall Street's desire to securitize real estate and by favorable changes in the tax laws that allow institutional ownership of REIT shares. As a result, REITs expanded rapidly once again.

Exhibit 19.12 provides historical data on the number and total capitalization of REITs overall and by type. In 1971, there were only 34 REITs with market capitalization totaling approximately $1.5 billion. REITs were also fairly evenly divided among equity REITs (that hold real estate interests directly), mortgage REITs (that hold mortgages), and hybrid REITs (that hold both direct interests and mortgages). Over the next 19 years (from 1971 to 1990), the number of REITs increased to 119 with total market capitalization of nearly $9 billion. Over the next 16 years (from 1990 to 2006), the total number of REITs increased by only 64, but the market capitalization of REITs grew from about $9 billion to over $438 billion—an annual growth rate of 27.72 percent! This growth coincided with the dramatic growth in U.S. real estate values (U.S. housing prices peaked in 2005). Note also that tremendous growth over this period was in equity REITs. At the end of 2006, equity REITs accounted for more than 90 percent of total market capitalization of all REITs. Since the housing market bubble burst, the value of these REITs has declined dramatically, and at the end of 2009, total market capitalization was $271 billion.

Exhibit 19.13 shows how publicly traded REITs performed relative to the S&P 500. As shown, REIT returns closely tracked that of the stock market indexes from 1990 until the late 1990s, when REIT returns were below the broader market. Between 2002 and 2006, REITs had tremendous performance, which coincided with the dramatic rise in U.S. (and world) real estate values. Over the next 2 years (2007 and 2008), REITs suffered large losses as the real estate bubble burst.

EXHIBIT 19.12
Assets and Number of REITs (End of Year)

Year	All REITs		Equity REITs		Mortgage REITs		Hybrid REITs	
	Number of REITs	Market Capitalization ($ Millions)	Number of REITs	Market Capitalization ($ Millions)	Number of REITs	Market Capitalization ($ Millions)	Number of REITs	Market Capitalization ($ Millions)
1971	34	1,494	12	332	12	571	10	592
1975	46	900	12	276	22	312	12	312
1980	75	2,299	35	942	21	510	19	847
1985	82	7,674	37	3,270	32	3,162	13	1,241
1990	119	8,737	58	5,552	43	2,549	18	636
1995	219	57,541	178	49,913	24	3,395	17	4,233
2000	189	138,715	158	134,431	22	1,632	9	2,652
2005	197	330,691	152	301,491	37	23,394	8	5,807
2006	183	438,071	138	400,741	38	29,195	7	8,134
2007	152	312,009	118	288,695	29	19,054	5	4,260
2008	136	191,651	113	176,238	20	14,281	3	1,133
2009	142	271,199	115	248,355	23	22,103	4	741

The number and total value of REITS expanded and contracted with the real estate boom and crash between 2005 and 2009.

Source: National Association of Real Estate Investment Trusts, www.reit.com.

EXHIBIT 19.13
REIT Performance

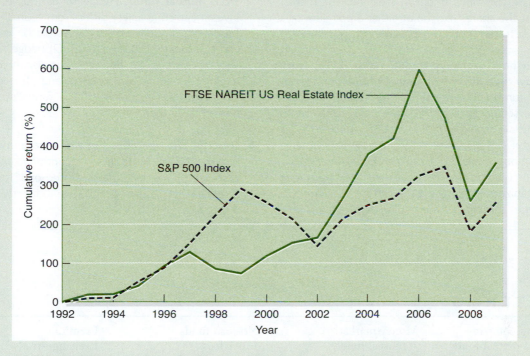

REITs strongly outperformed the stock market during the real estate boom (2002–2006) but fell dramatically during the real estate crash (2007–2008).

Source: National Association of Real Estate Investment Trusts, www.reit.com.

SUMMARY OF LEARNING OBJECTIVES

1 Explain open-end mutual funds and how they work. Mutual funds account for more than 90 percent of investment company assets. They invest in a wide range of securities (stocks, long-term debt, short-term debt) and provide investors a number of benefits, including the ability to invest a small amount of money with a professional manager in a broadly diversified portfolio, sophisticated risk controls, easy liquidity, and easy access to any portion of stock and bond markets (e.g., the ability to invest in small capitalization Japanese stocks). In addition, the investor is guaranteed that she can buy or sell shares at the NAV (plus or minus applicable fees such as a front-end or back-end load) from the fund manager.

2 Explain the role of money market mutual funds and how they differ from money market deposit accounts. Money market mutual funds, although very safe, are neither risk-free nor insured. These funds hold short-term debt and are considered so liquid that they are included in M2 and M3 money supply definitions. These funds are in direct competition with FDIC-insured money market deposit accounts at banks.

3 Explain closed-end mutual funds and how they differ from open-end mutual funds. Closed-end mutual funds will not, in general, issue or redeem shares at NAV. Instead, closed-end fund shareholders must sell their shares in the market if they wish to terminate their investment in the fund. The market price of the shares may be at either a premium or a discount to the fund's net asset value.

4 Explain how exchange-traded funds (ETFs) work and how they differ from mutual funds. Exchange-traded funds (ETFs) are similar to closed-end funds but are set up so that the share price rarely varies substantially from the NAV. Most ETFs track an index or sector. This allows investors to make investments in a number of markets, industries, countries, sectors, or even commodities. Because the shares are traded on organized exchanges, ETFs can be purchased or sold short throughout the trading day.

5 Explain how hedge funds work and how they differ from mutual funds. Hedge funds (not technically investment companies) differ from mutual funds in four ways: (1) Only wealthy investors or institutions can participate in hedge funds, (2) hedge funds use short positions, (3) hedge funds use leverage to magnify (good or bad) returns, and (4) hedge fund managers take a portion of the fund's profits (the performance fee).

6 Describe the operations of real estate investment trusts (REITs). REITs (not technically investment companies) are essentially closed-end funds that invest in real estate directly or indirectly through mortgages.

KEY TERMS

Investment company	Money market	No-load funds	Premium
Open-end mutual funds	mutual funds	12b-1 fees	Exchange-traded
Net asset value (NAV)	Load fund	Management fees	funds (ETFs)
Morningstar style box	Front-end load	Advisory fees	Unit investment trust
Equity funds	Back-end load	Mutual fund share classes	Hedge funds
Index funds	Contingent deferred	Mutual fund families	Real estate investment
Municipal bond funds	sales charge	Discounts	trust (REIT)

QUESTIONS AND PROBLEMS

1. How can the pricing of closed-end funds possibly indicate that market inefficiencies exist? What are the pros and cons of that argument? If market inefficiencies exist, how can they be exploited to make money? Explain, and think of any possible problems that might occur.

2. What type of fund would you want to buy if you believed that stock markets were always fully and completely efficient? Explain why. Why do you think people don't all buy the same kinds of funds?

3. If you invested $10,000 in a mutual fund that charged a 1 percent of net assets management advisory fee and a 1 percent 12b-1 fee, and the fund matched the stock market's returns of 10 percent per year for 10 years, how much would your shares in the fund be worth at the end of that time (assuming no taxes, all income net of fees was reinvested at year-end, and all fund charges were levied at the end of each year)?

4. If you invested $10,000 in a closed-end fund that invested in stocks that matched the market return of 10 percent per year for 10 years, levied a management fee of 2 percent of net assets per year, and sold at a 15 percent discount to its NAV both when you bought it and when you sold it 10 years later, how much would you have at the end of that time (assuming no taxes, all income was reinvested, and all fund charges were levied at the end of each year)?

5. If you invested $10,000 in an index fund that matched the market return of 10 percent per year for 10 years and levied a 0.25 percent management fee but no other fees, how much would you have at the end of the 10 years (assuming no taxes, all income was reinvested, and all fund charges were levied at the end of each year)?

6. (a) If you earned 3 percent per year in a tax-free money market fund and you were in the 31 percent federal income tax bracket and were fortunate enough to live in a state that had no state income tax, what interest rate would you have to earn in a taxable money market fund or bank account to be equally well-off? (b) What if your state had a 6 percent income tax but did not levy it on interest earned on municipal security obligations issued in your state—which were the only type of securities that your tax-exempt fund bought?

7. What is the major difference between open-end and closed-end investment companies? Why have open-end companies been more popular?

8. Why have ETFs grown so popular so quickly? What advantages do ETFs have over open-end index funds?

9. Why are money market funds included in the broader measures of the money supply (M2 and M3) that the Federal Reserve introduced in 1980?

10. Give examples from this chapter to illustrate how different forms of financial institutions may either grow rapidly or decline as economic and regulatory conditions change.

11. Explain how a hedge fund differs from a mutual fund.

12. What is an REIT? How did REITs perform during the most recent U.S. real estate bubble and crash?

INTERNET EXERCISE

One of the best sources of information on mutual funds and investment companies is the Investment Company Institute Web site, http://www.ici.org. It contains voluminous data on the four major types of investment companies: open-end funds, closed-end funds, ETFs, and unit investment trusts. Its annual *ICI Fact Book*, which is available on its site, is especially interesting.

Go to the Investment Company Institute Web site and find the latest facts and figures on mutual funds (click on "Research & Statistics," then select the "Statistics" tab). Look for the latest statistical releases.

1. Find the current quarterly "Worldwide Mutual Fund Assets and Flows" report and look for "Net Sale of Mutual Funds Worldwide." What patterns do you see for the past few years? Are the patterns different for equity funds, bond funds, and money market funds? Can you explain what may be driving these flows?

2. Find the most recent "Weekly Money Market Fund Assets" report. What fraction of money market mutual fund assets is held by retail investors versus institutional investors?

3. Find the most recent "Trends in Mutual Fund Investing" report. What is the most recent percentage of stock mutual fund assets held in liquid assets? Has this increased or decreased since last year? Given this information, do you forecast an increase or decrease in mutual fund demand for stocks?

Risk Management in Financial Institutions

IN THE 1960S AND 1970S, bankers managed by the so-called 3-6-3 rule. According to this rule, a smart banker would borrow at 3 percent from depositors, lend at 6 percent to borrowers, and be on the golf course by 3 o'clock. Banking was a much simpler business at the time.

For better or worse, the financial services industry has evolved into a much more challenging business. Just as it was in the 1960s and 1970s, financial institution managers are in a constant quest for profits. However, profits must be earned without sacrificing safety; that is, managers must maintain adequate liquidity and capital. Furthermore, banks and other financial institutions must manage the risks they face in order to protect their liquidity and capital positions. Failure to manage these risks effectively can lead to, at a minimum, greater regulatory scrutiny. At worst, a failure to maintain adequate capital and liquidity can lead to a financial institution being taken over by regulators, shareholders losing their investments, and managers being the target of

Risk management is about balancing the desire to generate profits against the need for safety.

legal action. A financial institution that takes very little risk, however, will not generate enough profits to satisfy the demands of shareholders.

Among the differences between today and the 1960s and 1970s are that the competition for profitable lending and investment opportunities is much greater, interest rates are more volatile, attracting and keeping depositors and other creditors are more difficult, and shareholders are more demanding. Consequently, the challenges of managing a profitable financial institution are more difficult. Fortunately, the tools that managers use in their quest to maximize profits and minimize risk have also evolved. ■

The last several chapters have discussed what banks and other financial institutions do to generate profits. In simple terms, financial institutions sell financial claims with one set of characteristics and buy financial claims with a different set of characteristics. These differences in characteristics give rise to risk. This chapter examines these risks and discusses how financial institution managers address these risks. We begin by discussing the trade-off that managers face in balancing the desire for profit against the need for safety. Next, we discuss the major risks faced by almost all financial institutions, including liquidity risk, interest rate risk, and credit risk, and how financial institutions manage these risks. ■

LEARNING OBJECTIVES

1 Explain the profitability-versus-safety trade-off faced by banks and other financial institutions.

2 Discuss how banks and other financial institutions manage their liquidity risk.

3 Describe the methods used to manage credit risk.

4 Explain the process used to measure and manage interest rate and other market risks.

5 Discuss how financial institutions measure interest rate risk.

6 Describe the various approaches to minimizing interest rate risk.

As profit-maximizing firms, financial institutions can increase expected profits by taking on more credit risk, interest rate risk, or liquidity risk, all of which jeopardize financial institution safety. *Financial institution safety* refers to the ability to survive as a going concern—staying in business. For a financial institution to survive, it must balance the demands of three constituencies: shareholders, creditors (including depositors for some financial institutions), and regulators. If financial institution managers do not generate adequate profits, shareholders may become dissatisfied with management and sell their stock, driving the stock price lower. If managers take on too much risk, creditors may become concerned about the safety of their funds and they may remove them, creating a liquidity crisis. If regulators believe that the actions of managers are imprudent, they may intervene in the management of the institution or, at the extreme, revoke the institution's charter. Managers can avoid the problems of taking too many risks by taking very little risk, but then the institution would not be very profitable. In this section, we discuss the trade-offs faced by managers in balancing profitability against liquidity and solvency.

20.1 THE DILEMMA: PROFITABILITY VERSUS SAFETY

SOLVENCY

As discussed in Chapter 13, the capital–total assets ratio for a commercial bank is about 10 percent, which is low compared to other industries. Other financial institutions also tend to have low capital–assets ratios. What are the managerial implications of having such low capital–assets ratios? First, it means that the owners provide only a small portion of the funds necessary to operate a financial institution. The remaining funds are furnished by the bank's creditors. Second, and more important, a relatively small depreciation in the value of the institution's assets could make it insolvent. A firm is **insolvent** when the value of its liabilities exceeds the value of its assets; the firm is legally bankrupt. For example, if a commercial bank invests all of its funds in Treasury bonds that fall in price by 10 percent, the bank becomes bankrupt. Thus, given commercial banks' extremely low capital position, they are vulnerable to failure if they accept excessive credit risk or interest rate risk.

LIQUIDITY

Another risk facing financial institutions is that of inadequate liquidity. A financial institution's **liquidity** refers to its ability to accommodate deposit withdrawals (in the case of banks and other depository institutions) and loan requests, and pay off other liabilities as they come due. Normally, some depositors withdraw funds or write checks, and others add to their deposit accounts. Similarly, some borrowers pay off loans, whereas other borrowers take lines of credit or other loan commitments. On some occasions, however, a large number of depositors withdraw their funds simultaneously, such as occurred in the 1920s and 1930s. If a bank has insufficient funds to meet its depositors' demands, it must close its doors. Financial institutions fail, therefore, because they are unable to meet their legal obligations to depositors, other creditors, and borrowers.

THE DILEMMA

As suggested by the discussion in this chapter so far, a financial institution can fail in two ways. First, it can become insolvent by suffering losses on its loans or investment portfolio (i.e., credit risk or interest rate risk), resulting in a depletion of its capital. Second, it can be a profitable business operation but fail because it cannot meet the liquidity demands of its depositors, creditors, or borrowers (i.e., liquidity risk). Exhibit 20.1 summarizes the profitability-versus-safety dilemma facing financial institution managers. The central problem for management is reconciling the conflicting goals of solvency and liquidity on the one hand, and profitability on the other. Unfortunately, it is a set of conflicts not easily resolved. For example, liquidity could be achieved by holding only Treasury securities. In this strategy, management would sleep well but eat poorly because profits would be low. At the other extreme, the financial institution could shift its asset portfolio into high-yielding, high-risk loans at the expense of better-quality loans or liquid investments. Management would eat well temporarily because of increased profits but would sleep poorly because of the possibility of a failure later caused by large loan losses or inadequate liquidity. Finally, it is worth noting that liquidity and solvency are interrelated. For example, most bank runs are triggered by depositors' and other creditors' expectations of extraordinary losses in the bank's loan or investment portfolios.

EXHIBIT 20.1
Profitability Goal Versus Liquidity and Solvency

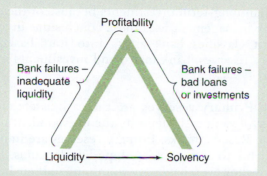

The goal of bank management is to maximize the value of the firm. However, higher profits must not be achieved at the expense of bank safety

Identifying the right level of risk tolerance for a given financial institution is a strategic decision made by managers and the board of directors as they balance the demands of the various stakeholders identified above. Once identified, however, it is up to the financial institution's managers and employees to (1) identify potential risk exposures, (2) measure the exposures, (3) assess the potential impact of the exposures on the financial institution's safety and soundness, and (4) manage the exposures within the identified risk tolerances. We focus on these responsibilities in this chapter.

We begin with how financial institutions manage their liquidity risk. We focus on the liquidity management approach used by banks, but other financial institutions adopt similar strategies.

20.2 LIQUIDITY MANAGEMENT

Banks and other financial institutions use certain strategies to maintain sufficient liquidity while maximizing overall bank profits. There are two primary approaches to managing liquidity risk. The first is **asset management**—relying on available cash and sellable assets to meet demands for liquidity. The second is **liability management**—acquiring liquidity from the liability side of the balance sheet. In practice, of course, financial institutions obtain liquidity from both sides of the balance sheet.

ASSET MANAGEMENT

A commercial bank requires liquidity to accommodate deposit withdrawals, pay other liabilities as they become due, and accommodate loan requests. Sources of liquidity are new deposits, increases in other liabilities, loan repayments, and the sale of assets. Cash accounts are available to the bank for payment of immediate withdrawals at no cost to the bank. All other assets must be converted into cash assets before they can be used for liquidity purposes. The conversion process involves the time and expense to sell the assets as well as the risk that they may be sold below their purchase price (price risk).

We can draw the following general conclusions when examining the assets held by commercial banks: (1) investment securities are more liquid than bank loans because of their superior marketability, and (2) short-term investments are more liquid than long-term investments because of the smaller price risk. Let's see how bank management uses these conclusions in asset management. Asset management classifies bank assets into four basic groups: primary reserves, secondary reserves, bank loans, and investments for income and tax shields.

Primary Reserves. **Primary reserves** are the cash assets on a bank's balance sheet. They consist of vault cash, deposits at correspondent banks, and deposits held at the Federal Reserve banks. Primary reserves are immediately available at no cost to the bank to accommodate liquidity demands. Because they yield little or no interest, however, banks try to minimize their holdings of primary reserves.

Secondary Reserves. **Secondary reserves** are short-term assets that can be converted quickly into cash at a price near their purchase price. Their main purpose is to provide the bank with additional liquidity while safely earning some interest income. Treasury bills and short-term government agency securities make up the majority of the bank's secondary reserves. Because the securities that compose secondary reserves are highly marketable and have low default risk, they typically have yields below the yields of loans and other investment securities held by the bank.

Bank Loans. After the bank has satisfied its potential liquidity needs, bank management can concentrate on its primary business—making loans to business firms and individuals. Business loans are generally less liquid and riskier than other bank assets and, as a result, typically carry the highest yield of all bank assets and offer the greatest potential for profit.

Investments. After the bank has satisfied its loan demand, the remaining funds are then available for open-market investments. The primary function of the investment portfolio is to provide income and tax advantages to the bank rather than liquidity. Open-market investments are typically longer-term securities that are less marketable and have higher default risk than secondary reserves. Therefore, these investments offer greater income potential to the bank. Investments for income include long-term Treasury securities, municipal bonds, and government agency securities. Banks usually prefer to hold municipal instead of corporate bonds because they offer a higher after-tax yield.

The Asset Mix. The proportion of liquid assets a bank should hold brings us back to the dilemma between bank profitability and liquidity. The greater the proportion of primary and secondary reserves the bank holds, the greater the liquidity of its portfolio. Unfortunately, highly liquid assets that are low in default risk typically have low interest returns. Overall bank strategy, then, is to hold the minimum amounts of primary and secondary reserves consistent with bank safety. Exhibit 20.2 shows assets commonly held in bank asset management strategy and the liquidity–yield trade-off that bank management must make. The exhibit provides a useful review of the concepts involved in asset management.

EXHIBIT 20.2
Summary of Asset Management Strategy

Category and Type of Asset	Purpose	Liquidity	Yield
Primary Reserves	Immediately available funds	Highest	None
Vault cash			
Deposits at the Fed			
Deposits at other banks			
Secondary Reserves	Easily marketable funds	High	Low
Treasury bills			
Fed funds sold			
Short-term agency securities			
Bank Loans	Income	Lowest	Highest
Business loans			
Consumer loans			
Real estate loans			
Agriculture loans			
Investments	Income when safe loans are unavailable as well as tax advantages	Medium	Medium
Treasury securities			
Agency securities			
Municipal bonds			

To maintain adequate liquidity, banks hold both primary and secondary reserves. Secondary reserves allow banks to earn some interest income while still meeting their liquidity needs.

At a minimum, banks are required to hold enough primary reserves to satisfy reserve requirements and expected liquidity needs. Banks usually hold additional primary and secondary reserves to address at least part of any unexpected liquidity demands. The total amount of primary and secondary reserves that a bank holds is related to reserve requirements, deposit variability, other sources of liquidity, loan commitments outstanding, bank regulations, and the risk posture of the bank's management. Deposit variability is often determined by examining past deposit behavior, particularly in regard to deposit inflows and outflows. Deposit variability also depends on the type of account and bank customer. For example, demand deposits are more variable than time deposits. Therefore, a bank with a relatively large percentage of demand deposits typically holds more primary and secondary reserves.

LIABILITY MANAGEMENT

Prior to the 1960s, banks and other financial institutions relied almost exclusively on their assets to meet their liquidity demands. Over time, however, many banks relied increasingly on liability management. Liability management relies on financial institutions using the liability side of their balance sheets for liquidity. Historically, banks had always treated their liability structure as a fixed pool of funds, at least in the short run. Bank asset holdings were tailored to the deposit variability characteristics of their liabilities. Under liability management, however, banks take asset growth as given and then adjust their liabilities as needed. Thus, when a bank needs additional funds for liquidity or any other purpose, it merely buys the funds in the money markets. When we say a bank *buys* funds in the money market, we mean they are borrowing the funds. We say *buy* because they are paying for the short-term use of the funds.

Liability Management Theory. *Liability management* is based on the assumption that certain types of liabilities are very sensitive to interest rate changes. Thus, by raising the interest rate paid on these liabilities above the market rate, a financial institution can immediately attract additional funds. By lowering the rate paid on these liabilities, however, a financial institution may allow funds to run off as the liabilities mature.

Some of the liabilities employed in liability management are negotiable certificates of deposit (CDs), federal funds, repurchase agreements, commercial paper, and Eurodollar borrowings. These securities are sensitive to interest rates and have markets large enough to accommodate the activities of the commercial banking system. Other liabilities, such as savings accounts or demand deposits, are not as sensitive to interest rates, and changes in the posted offering rate do not result in notable immediate inflows or outflows of funds. Long-term debt and capital are not appropriate for use in liability management because of the time it takes to bring these securities to market.

Using Liability Management. The liquidity gained by liability management is useful to a financial institution in several ways. First, it can be used to counteract deposit inflows and outflows and reduce their variability. Sudden or unexpected deposit outflows can be offset immediately by the purchase of new funds. Second, funds attracted by liability management may be used to meet increases in loan demand by the financial institution's customers. Customers need not be denied loans because of a lack of funds. As long as the expected marginal return of the new loans exceeds the expected marginal cost of funds, the financial institution can increase its income by acquiring the additional funds through liability management. Third, the ability to immediately attract additional funds allows financial institutions to engage in more off-balance-sheet activities. As discussed in Chapter 13, off-balance-sheet activities generate fees for banks but also represent contingent commitments of the bank. Banks that use liability management have the funding flexibility that allows them to participate safely in contingent commitments.

Summary. Liability management supplements asset management but does not replace it as a source of liquidity. Asset management still remains the primary source of liquidity for financial institutions, particularly smaller institutions. If used properly, liability management allows financial institutions to reduce their secondary reserve holdings and invest these funds in higher-yield assets, such as loans or long-term municipal bonds. Liability management is not well suited to smaller institutions because they do not have direct access to the wholesale money markets where liability management is practiced.

The discussion here has focused on commercial banks, but the same principles apply to nonbank financial institutions. Commercial banks, insurance companies, and investment banks all must manage their liquidity risk. Almost all use asset management, and the larger institutions with good credit ratings are able to use liability management.

PEOPLE & EVENTS

Operational Risk

Although interest rate, credit, and liquidity risks are the primary risks that financial instituions worry about, there are plenty of other risks that get their attention. For example, operational risk has been drawing much of the industry's attention in recent years. For banks, this is the result, in part, of the endorsement of the Basel II Accord on June 26, 2004. The Basel Committee defines *operational risk* as "the risk of direct or indirect loss resulting from inadequate or failed internal processes, people, and systems, or from external events." This catchall risk category includes losses from fraud, theft, terrorism, litigation, and even reputation problems. According to the Basel II Accord, large international banks are required to hold capital against their operational risk.

These risks have been around for a long time but have taken on new importance in recent years.

Some of the increased focus on these risks can be blamed on the tragedy of September 11, 2001, and, more recently, on some well-publicized corporate scandals. In addition to these reasons, however, financial institutions are increasingly concerned about these risks because of increased reliance on technology, increased complexity in organizational structures, and the ever-increasing pace of change in the industry.

The biggest worries faced by financial institutions concern the infrastructure costs associated with developing an operational risk management system, a lack of operational risk data with which to measure the risk, and lack of sufficient regulatory guidance on implementation issues. Fortunately, most financial institutions believe that improving their operational risk management systems will help them be competitive and improve their profitability.

However, liability management is not a panacea for liquidity problems. There may be times when financial institutions are unable to attract or retain funds through liability management because of tight credit periods or because of uncertainty about the soundness of a particular institution. This is what happened during the financial crisis of late 2008. Uncertainty about the health of individual banks and the overall financial system caused money market participants to stop lending to each other. Consequently, the system suffered a liquidity crisis, forcing the Federal Reserve to intervene.

DO YOU UNDERSTAND?

1. Explain how liquidity risk can lead to a financial institution's failure.

2. What defines a financial institution's insolvency? What characteristic of a commercial bank's balance sheet makes it vulnerable to insolvency?

3. Explain some simple strategies banks can follow to avoid insolvency or illiquidity. Why don't more banks adopt these strategies?

4. Why do banks and other financial institutions try to minimize their holdings of primary reserves in the practice of asset management?

5. What asset accounts make up secondary reserves? What role do these accounts serve in an asset management strategy?

20.3 MANAGING CREDIT RISK

Historically, the primary risk that banks and other lenders dealt with was the risk of loan defaults. In fact, although few banks failed in the late 1990s through the mid-2000s, most modern-day bank failures can be attributed to credit risk losses. The recent subprime mortgage crisis illustrates this far too well. In response to these failures, financial institution managers and regulators have increased efforts to monitor and manage credit risk exposures more effectively. The credit risk associated with an individual loan concerns the losses that the lender can experience in the event that the borrower does not repay the loan.

The credit risk associated with a bank's loan portfolio concerns the aggregate credit risk of all the loans in the lender's portfolio. Obviously, the lender's shareholders and regulators are most concerned about the overall risk exposure, but managers must also focus on managing the credit risk of individual loans if they are to be successful. It is important that lenders manage both dimensions of credit risk effectively.

This section describes strategies for how lenders can manage the credit risk associated with individual loans as well as strategies for managing the credit risk associated with loan portfolios. In addition, we also provide a brief discussion of how credit derivatives can be used to supplement these strategies.

MANAGING THE CREDIT RISK OF INDIVIDUAL LOANS

Managing credit risk begins with the lending decision, as discussed in Chapter 13. Once a loan is on the books, managers are responsible for ensuring that the performance of an individual loan is monitored closely, that problem loans are identified as quickly as possible, and that as much as possible is recovered from problem loans.

Identifying Problem Loans. Banks and other financial institutions rely on several indicators to identify problem loans. Obviously, the first of these is failing to make promised payments on the loan. In addition, other events can cause financial institution managers to become concerned about a borrower's risk of default. Some of these additional indicators of potential problem loans are (1) adverse changes in the customer's credit rating, (2) adverse changes in deposit balances, (3) adverse changes in sales or earnings, and (4) delays in supplying financial statements or other documents.

Loan Workouts. Once a problem loan is identified, the goal of the financial institution is to recover as much as possible from the borrower. In many cases, it is possible for the lender to recover all or most of the loan amount by restructuring the loan so that the borrower has a greater chance of making the payments on the new loan successfully. Some of the issues that the lender is concerned about in the loan recovery process are (1) other creditors and other claims against the borrower's assets, (2) the ability of the borrower to service the debt if it is restructured, and (3) the losses to the bank if the loan is not restructured.

MANAGING THE CREDIT RISK OF LOAN PORTFOLIOS

Traditionally, monitoring the performance of each individual borrower was sufficient for successful credit risk management in most financial institutions. In recent years, however, several developments in the financial services industry have forced banks and other financial institutions to become more sophisticated about their management of credit risk. For example, banks are larger, are more geographically dispersed, and offer a wider range of loan products than ever before. These developments have led to increased complexity in banks' loan portfolios and increased challenges for bank managers.

Internal Credit Risk Ratings. Financial institutions are relying more and more on **internal credit risk ratings** to measure and manage the credit risk of loan portfolios. Much like the credit rating assigned to bonds by Moody's and Standard & Poor's, many financial institutions assign internal credit risk ratings to the loans in their portfolios. Some lenders have as few as three grades, whereas others have as many as eight or ten. The rating systems with only a few grades typically base their ratings on whether the loan is delinquent and how long it has been delinquent. More sophisticated credit risk rating systems also consider some of the variables discussed in number one of the following numbered list: "Identifying problem loans." For example, if a borrower's external credit rating changes, the internal credit risk rating assigned by the financial institution to that borrower's loan may also change. These internal credit risk ratings are used for a range of purposes, including the following:

1. **Identifying problem loans.** The credit risk rating of an individual loan is based on the probability of default on the loan and may also consider the dollar amount likely to be recovered in the event of default. By having several gradations in potential credit risk ratings, lenders can identify the quantity and volume of loans that are most likely and least likely to become problem loans. If the lender has only a few credit risk rating grades, managers are limited in their use of the rating system. For general monitoring and management reporting, having only a few gradations is fine. For more sophisticated use of the rating system, however, the more gradations, the better.

2. **Determining the adequacy of loan loss reserves.** Credit risk ratings can also be used to assess whether a lender's loan loss reserves are sufficient for the level of substandard or doubtful loans in its portfolio. In addition, if the credit risk ratings have several gradations, managers may use the ratings to forecast future loan losses.

3. **Loan pricing and profitability analysis.** Many financial institutions use their internal credit risk ratings to analyze the profitability of loan types. The ratings can be used to identify the expected losses and expenses associated with individual loans. The expected losses and expenses can be subtracted from the yield on the loan or loan type to determine the net yield. This type of analysis is especially useful to managers who are responsible for deciding the types of loans a financial institution should pursue and the types to avoid. For example, a bank may change its marketing strategy to attract more loans that tend to generate a high net yield. This type of profitability analysis can also be a useful input into loan officers' compensation packages. Finally, managers can use the results of this profitability analysis to price future loans of a given type. For example, if a certain type of loan consistently generates a low net yield, managers may want to raise the interest rate they charge on loans of that type.

Loan Portfolio Analysis. Banks and other lenders recognize the need to consider the performance of the loan portfolio as a whole in addition to the performance of individual loans. Modern portfolio theory teaches us that there are benefits to holding a well-diversified portfolio of assets. We can apply the same principles to loan portfolios as long as the default rates on individual loans are less than perfectly correlated. Lenders can minimize portfolio credit risk by minimizing the degree of correlation among default rates on the loans in their portfolios.

The most common way of monitoring and managing loan portfolios is by using concentration ratios. **Concentration ratios** measure the percentage of loans or loan commitments allocated to a given geographic location, loan type, or business type. Higher concentration ratios imply higher correlation among default rates for loan portfolios. For example, a bank that makes all of its loans to businesses and individuals in a small town has a higher geographic concentration ratio, and higher portfolio credit risk, than a bank that makes loans to similar businesses and individuals throughout the state. If a business in that small town goes bankrupt and closes, not only are the individuals employed by that company more likely to default on their loans from the bank, but other businesses in the town are also more likely to default because of a decline in revenue.

Similarly, financial institutions that concentrate on making certain types of loans are exposed to more portfolio credit risk than banks that make a variety of loans. For example, the bursting of the housing bubble led to a dramatic increase in mortgage delinquincies. Consequently, those banks that specialized in mortgage lending had much more portfolio credit risk than other banks that were better diversified in terms of the variety of loan products in their portfolios.

Finally, financial institutions also avoid concentrating on making too many business loans to any single industry. Lenders use either Standard Industrial Classification (SIC) codes or North American Industry Classification System (NAICS) codes to monitor their business lending concentration ratios. Lenders that concentrate on lending to a specific industry have a relatively high loan portfolio credit risk because of the high correlation among default rates within specific industries. Some lenders have gone so far as to use sophisticated modeling of macroeconomic variables to arrive at default rate probabilities for specific industries that can be applied to their business loan portfolios. Managers can develop comprehensive estimates of overall loan portfolio credit risk using these macroeconomic forecasts, the correlation among historical or projected default rates within industries, and lending concentration ratios.

LOAN SALES, SECURITIZATIONS, AND BROKERAGE

Recall from Chapter 13 that banks and other financial institutions can reduce the amount of funds devoted to a given loan or loan type in several ways. In Chapter 9, we discussed mortgage-backed securities. By originating mortgages and then securitizing them, lenders are able to exploit the comparative advantage they have in originating loans while not committing to fund the loan (or bear the credit risk) for the entire term of the loan. Selling loans to the secondary market is another way that financial institutions may reduce their credit risk exposure. In addition, it is not uncommon for financial institutions to form syndicates for the purpose of funding a large loan. All of these approaches are common methods for reducing the credit risk exposure of a financial institution to a given loan type or individual borrower.

PEOPLE & EVENTS

Counterparty Controversy: AIG and Its Risky Risk Management

With $850 billion of assets, American International Group (AIG) had grown to become one of the largest insurance companies in the world by 2004. Its biggest asset was its AAA credit rating. Only a handful of private-sector companies ever achieve the prized AAA rating.

Because of its AAA rating, AIG was able to help other financial institutions (for a "small" fee) manage the credit risk of loan portfolios through writing (or selling) over-the-counter credit default swaps (CDSs), which were discussed earlier in this chapter and in Chapter 11. CDSs work much like insurance. The purchaser of the CDS renders periodic payments, similar to insurance premiums, to the writer (or seller) of the CDS. In exchange for the payments, the seller of the CDS reimburses the financial institution in the event of a default in the institution's loan portfolio. AIG's AAA credit rating was instrumental in its ability to write credit default swaps because purchasers of the "insurance" would be concerned about AIG's ability to make good on its obligations in the event of defaults. The AAA rating gave purchasers of CDSs confidence that AIG would be able to meet those obligations.

As a result of the rapid creation of collateralized debt obligations (CDOs) backed by subprime mortgages in the mid-2000s (essentially securitized portfolios of high credit-risk mortgages), there was great demand for credit default swaps on CDOs. With the credit-risk protection afforded by the CDSs, banks and other financial institutions could add securities (CDOs) with potentially high returns to their portfolios without a requirement for adding additional capital. In essence, the writer of the CDS was guaranteeing the performance of the CDOs, thereby allowing other financial institutions to earn higher returns for risky investments without having to add additional capital to absorb the potential bad outcomes from those investments. Because of its AAA rating, AIG was able to attract a huge amount of business selling credit risk "insurance" on CDOs. By the peak of the subprime market, AIG had written ("sold") nearly $80 billion of CDSs ("insurance") on subprime CDOs.

Technically, the CDSs were not insurance contracts from a regulatory perspective, so AIG was not required to provide much additional capital or to provide collateral to support the CDSs. AIG did agree to provide collateral to its counterparties, however, if the value of the subprime mortgages underlying the CDOs dropped or if AIG's credit rating was reduced. In fact, AIG lost its AAA rating in 2005 when the company had to issue a corrective earnings disclosure because it had been found to have inappropriately manipulated its reported earnings. Despite losing its AAA credit rating, AIG continued to write credit default swaps until 2006.

One of AIG's biggest customers was Goldman Sachs, which held over $20 billion of AIG's CDSs. As one of the largest underwriters of CDOs, Goldman Sachs facilitated over $250 billion of mortgage-backed securities from 2004 to 2006. It stands to reason that Goldman Sachs would have required a large volume of CDSs to protect its position in these deals. As a large purchaser of CDSs from AIG, Goldman Sachs was greatly exposed to AIG credit risk. AIG's loss of its AAA rating triggered the requirement that AIG provide collateral to its counterparties in the CDS contracts. Goldman Sachs started issuing invoices to AIG to post collateral—the first invoice requested $1.8 billion! Given the diminution of AIG's credit quality, Goldman Sachs also purchased credit default swaps to protect itself against a potential default of one of its largest counterparties, AIG. To this day, AIG and Goldman Sachs dispute the amount of collateral that AIG should have posted to cover potential losses on CDS contracts. Goldman keeps sending invoices and AIG continues to dispute them.

Other counterparties to AIG in many over-the-counter CDS deals also sent invoices to AIG to provide collateral to cover potential losses from the reduction in AIG's credit standing and from the mounting subprime mortgage defaults in 2007 and 2008. The invoices totaled billions and billions of dollars. With its deteriorating credit standing, AIG found it nearly impossible to raise funds to meet the collateral obligations. In effect, AIG's declining credit quality prevented it from accessing the liquidity it needed to post collateral.

Ultimately, the lethal combination of credit risk and liquidity risk killed AIG. Unable to meet demands for collateral from CDS counterparties, AIG was bailed out with an $85 billion loan from the federal government. To this day, counterparties are disputing the required posting of collateral on CDS contracts with AIG!

CREDIT DERIVATIVES

Even if they are trying to minimize credit risk by effectively monitoring individual loans, minimizing loan concentration ratios, and securitizing or selling some loans, many banks still feel that they have too much credit risk exposure. Alternatively, many banks tend to specialize in making certain types of loans and therefore have relatively high concentration ratios. Under these circumstances, both types of banks may turn to the market for derivative securities for help in reducing their credit risk.

The market for credit derivatives offers a variety of instruments that lenders can use to minimize their credit risk exposure. These instruments are called **credit derivatives** because, just like the derivative securities discussed in Chapter 11, credit derivatives have cash flows tied to some underlying asset. In the case of credit derivatives, the underlying asset is a loan or portfolio of loans. In a **credit default swap**, for example, the holder of a loan makes periodic payments to the seller of the swap in exchange for a promise to pay the holder of the loan the face amount of the loan in the event the borrower defaults. **Credit insurance** offers the same kind of protection that a credit default swap offers but in the form of an insurance contract. This form of credit protection is useful for lenders that are either unwilling or unable to trade in derivatives because of regulatory or tax reasons.

The market for credit derivatives grew rapidly until the 2008 financial crisis. Recall from Chapter 11 that credit derivatives played a significant role in the financial meltdown; consequently, their use is being more heavily scrutinized. The market for credit derivatives has not grown much since then. It has not shrunk much either, however, suggesting that these types of instruments are here to stay. One thing seems certain—credit derivatives are certain to draw increased regulatory scrutiny from now on.

In spite of their role in the financial meltdown, using a credit swap, credit insurance, or other credit derivative to reduce or eliminate the credit risk associated with a lending relationship has several advantages. First, and most important, is the reduction in credit risk. Second, in addition to reducing the credit risk of a loan, the lender can do so while maintaining the relationship with the borrower. Unlike a loan sale, which typically requires borrower notification, the borrower does not need to be notified when a credit default swap is used to insure against the risk of default by that borrower.

DO YOU UNDERSTAND?

1. Explain how financial institutions identify problem loans.
2. If a bank has a problem loan in its portfolio, what is its objective in dealing with the loan?
3. What does a concentration ratio measure?
4. Explain why the credit risk associated with a loan portfolio is less than the sum of the credit risk associated with each of the loans in the portfolio.
5. Explain how credit derivatives can be used to reduce concentration ratios.

In response to increased volatility in interest rates over the past 40 years, interest rate risk has become as much of a concern to financial institution managers and regulators as credit risk. Similarly, other market risks (commodity price risk, equity market risk, and foreign exchange risk) have grown in importance. We focus on interest rate risk here, but many of the same principles apply to managing other types of market risks. In addition, we focus on interest rate risk management by commercial banks, but other financial institutions use very similar approaches.

The first step in any risk management process is to identify the exposure. The risk of unexpected interest rate changes affects both sides of a bank's balance sheet. It arises because of differences in the sensitivity of bank assets and liabilities to changes in market rates of interest. To make a profit, banks must earn higher rates of return on their loans and investments (assets) than they pay out to attract deposits and other funds (liabilities). The essence of managing interest rate risk is to ensure that the bank will always be able to profit from the spread between its borrowing (and deposit) rates and its rates of return on investment, even if market interest rates change.

If a financial institution has identified interest rate risk as potentially affecting its profitability, the typical next step is to measure the exposure. In other words, managers want to know how much profitability might be affected by a given change in interest rates. Once a manager knows how sensitive profitability (or firm value) is to changes in interest rates, she can estimate how much profitability is likely to be affected if interest rates change as much as might be possible within a given period of time and confidence level. This section describes how financial institutions go through this process.

20.4 MEASURING AND ASSESSING INTEREST RATE RISK

EFFECTS OF CHANGING INTEREST RATES ON COMMERCIAL BANKS

Recall from our examination of the typical bank balance sheet in Chapter 13 that most banks operate by using shorter-term deposits to fund longer-term (or fixed-rate) loans. This strategy takes advantage of the fact that long-term interest rates usually exceed short-term interest rates (i.e., the term structure is usually upward sloping) and earns the bank a positive spread, or net interest income. But the strategy exposes the bank to decreasing earnings when interest rates rise because the liabilities reprice before the assets, on average.

To illustrate the effects of changing interest rates (*interest rate risk*), let us examine what happens to the cash flows of a commercial bank that borrows short and lends long if interest rates increase. We use a simple example, which is given in Exhibit 20.3. Suppose that a bank makes a 1-year, single-payment loan at the beginning of the year. This loan has a face value of $1,000 and pays 9 percent interest; thus, at the end of 1 year the borrower pays the bank $1,090 ($1,000 principal plus $90 interest). The bank funds this loan by issuing a $500 denomination, 3-month certificate of deposit (CD) with the idea of renewing the CD every 3 months over the life of the 1-year loan. The bank funds the other $500 of the loan with a $500-denomination, 6-month CD with the idea of renewing the CD every 6 months over the life of the loan. Initially the 3-month CD pays 5 percent interest and the 6-month CD pays 6 percent.

After 3, 6, and 9 months the bank must "roll over" the 3-month CD. The 6-month CD rolls over after 6 and 12 months. Thus, every 3 months the bank

EXHIBIT 20.3
Net Cash Flow Example Assuming No Change in Interest Rates

Action	Elapsed Time (Months)				
	0	3	6	9	12
Cash Inflows					
Issue 3-month CD	$500	$506	$513	$519	
(percent)	(5)	(5)	(5)	(5)	
Issue 6-month CD	500		515		
(percent)	(6)		(6)		
1-year loan					$1,090
Total cash inflow	$1,000	$506	$1,028	$519	$1,090
Cash Outflows					
1-year loan	1,000				
(percent)	(9)				
Payoff 3-month CD		506	513	519	525
Payoff 6-month CD			515		530
Total cash outflow	$1,000	$506	$1,028	$519	$1,055
Net cash flow =	$0	$0	$0	$0	$35
Total cash inflow − Total cash outflow					

Net cash flow from funding a $1,000 loan with a 3-month CD and a 6-month CD (assuming no change in interest rates).

issues a new CD in an amount sufficient to pay off the principal and interest on the old CD. At the end of the first 3 months of the year, for example, the bank would issue one 3-month CD of $506 [$500 × (1.05)^{0.25}] to pay off the first 3-month CD (see Exhibit 20.3). At the end of 6 months, the bank would issue another 3-month CD to retire the second 3-month CD and a 6-month CD of $515 [$500 × (1.06)^{0.5}] to retire the first 6-month CD. Assuming that interest rates do not change over the year, Exhibit 20.3 shows that the anticipated net cash flow (that is, the loan repayment plus interest minus the amount required to pay off the last two CDs) from funding the 1-year loan with a portfolio of 3-month and 6-month CDs is $35, or a net yield of 3.5 percent on an investment of $1,000 over the year. Notice that the 3.5 percent figure is the difference between the average yield on assets of 9 percent and the average cost of liabilities of 5.5 percent [(5% + 6%)/2].

What happens to the bank's net cash flow if, immediately after making the loan and issuing the first batch of CDs, all interest rates in the market rise by 100 basis points, or 1 percent? The bank's cash inflows from the loan are not affected because the loan is fixed-rate; assuming no default risk, the loan pays $1,090 after 1 year. Unfortunately, the rates on 3-month and 6-month CDs rise by 1 percent so that when they are rolled over, the bank's cost of funds increases. Exhibit 20.4

EXHIBIT 20.4
Net Cash Flow Example Assuming a 1 Percent Change in Interest Rates

Action	Elapsed Time (Months)				
	0	3	6	9	12
Cash Inflows					
Issue 3-month CD	$500	$506	$514	$521	
(percent)	(5)	(6)	(6)	(6)	
Issue 6-month CD	500		515		
(percent)	(6)		(7)		
1-year loan					$1,090
Total cash inflow	$1,000	$506	$1,029	$521	$1,090
Cash Outflows					
1-year loan	1,000				
(percent)	(9)				
Payoff		506	514	521	529
3-month CD					
Payoff			515		533
6-month CD					
Total cash outflow	$1,000	$506	$1,029	$521	$1,062
Net cash flow =	$0	$0	$0	$0	$28
Total cash inflow − Total cash outflow					

Net cash flow from funding a $1,000 loan with a 3-month CD and a 6-month CD (assuming a 1 percent increase in interest rates).

shows that the bank's anticipated net cash flow at the end of 1 year falls to $28 if interest rates rise by 100 basis points. It is easy to show that the bank's cash flows would have increased had interest rates declined.

MEASURING INTEREST RATE RISK

In the preceding example, why did the bank's net cash flow decline when interest rates increased? Because the liabilities were shorter term than the assets (4.5 months on average versus 1 year), the liabilities repriced before the assets. Thus, the cost of liabilities increased faster than the yields on assets with the interest rate increase; the liabilities were more rate sensitive than the assets. The rate sensitivity of bank earnings can be measured by the gap between the maturity or duration of assets and liabilities (hereafter referred to as *GAP*).

Maturity GAP Analysis.   In a typical GAP management process, bank management divides all assets and liabilities on the balance sheet according to their interest rate sensitivity. An asset or a liability with an interest rate subject to change within a year is considered *rate sensitive*. One whose interest rate cannot change for more than a year is considered *fixed*. The GAP between **rate-sensitive assets (RSAs)** and **rate-sensitive liabilities (RSLs)** is defined as:

$$GAP = RSA - RSL \qquad (20.1)$$

The GAP can be expressed either as dollars or as a percentage of total earning assets. If RSA is greater than RSL, the GAP is positive; if RSA is less than RSL, the GAP is negative; and if RSA equals RSL, the GAP is zero. Exhibit 20.5 shows the rate-sensitive GAP for a bank balance sheet and identifies the most important rate-sensitive and fixed-rate financial instruments. For the balance sheet shown, the GAP = 50% − 20% = 30%.

Controlling the size of the GAP is an important decision that depends both on the degree of risk that a bank's management is willing to accept and on its forecast of future interest rate movements. For example, assume that we are at the bottom of a business cycle and that interest rates are low and expected to rise. Under such circumstances, bank management would want a large positive GAP. The reason is that, given expected higher interest rates in the future, the bank wants to hold rate-sensitive assets in order to take advantage of future higher interest rates and to hold fixed-rate liabilities in order to lock in the current low

EXHIBIT 20.5
Rate-Sensitive GAP for a Bank Balance Sheet

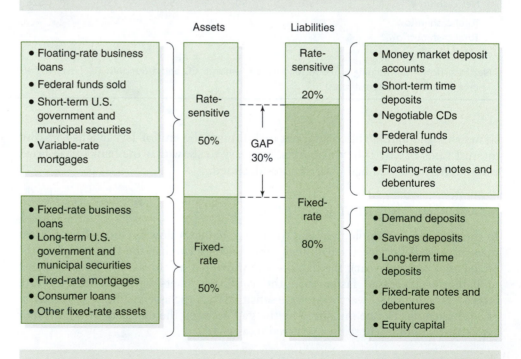

GAP management helps banks manage their interest rate risk exposure. The larger the GAP, the greater the risk exposure.

interest rates—thus a positive GAP. However, at the top of the business cycle, when interest rates are high and expected to decline, a negative GAP is desirable. In this case, the desired balance-sheet portfolio consists of fixed-rate assets and rate-sensitive liabilities. Finally, if the bank's management wishes to minimize interest rate risk, a zero GAP is the desired portfolio strategy. In sum, the greater the GAP—either positive or negative—the greater the bank's exposure to interest rate risk.

The size of the GAP has a major influence on the volatility of bank earnings. If, for example, all variable interest rates changed by 1 percent, a 30 percent GAP would have a $9 million effect on the pretax earnings of a bank with $3 billion in assets. The size of a bank's GAP, then, varies with the bank management's expectations of future interest rates and the risk it is willing to take.

The tendency is for banks that are expecting higher interest rates to accept large positive GAPs and to plan to decrease the GAPs as interest rates turn down. However, because the demand for short-term (or variable-rate) loans is usually heaviest when interest rates are high, most banks cannot close the GAP when they want to. To overcome this problem, bank fund managers are increasingly turning to the use of financial futures contracts to hedge exposed asset and liability risk positions.

The technique just discussed is **maturity GAP** analysis. It is probably the most widely used technique for assessing interest rate risk. It compares the value of assets that either mature or are repriced within a given time interval to the value of liabilities that either mature or are repriced during the same time period. It is possible to calculate cumulative GAPs for assets and liabilities as a result of being repriced during any period desired, such as 1 day, 1 week, 1 month, 1 quarter, 6 months, or 1 year. Large banks compute GAPs on a daily basis, whereas smaller banks often compute monthly GAPs.

In addition to cumulative GAPs, a financial institution may wish to compute *incremental GAPs*. Incremental GAPs show how much the cumulative GAP will change during a future interval. For instance, bank A may have a cumulative GAP of +$40 million over 1 year, with incremental GAPs of +$30 million in the first quarter, +$15 million in the second quarter, −$10 million in the third quarter, and +$5 million in the final quarter. Incremental GAPs can be useful for determining how and when a bank should offset interest rate risk. Thus, bank A's risk-offset strategy would likely be quite different from the strategy undertaken by bank B, which also had a cumulative GAP of +$40 million over 1 year, but had incremental GAPs of +$10 million per quarter.

Maturity GAP analysis is widely used by banks because it is relatively easy to compute and it makes good intuitive sense. By ensuring that its assets have maturities similar to its liabilities, a financial institution can ensure that its assets mature or are repriced at the same time that an approximately equal amount of liabilities is repriced.

Duration GAP Analysis.   Maturity GAP provides only an approximate rule for analyzing interest rate risk. Consider, for instance, a bank that issues a $10,000 zero-coupon deposit that promises to double the depositor's money in 7 years (i.e., pays interest at an annual compound rate of 10.4 percent) and uses the proceeds to buy a $10,000 7-year bond paying annual interest at a 12 percent rate. Provided that the bank reinvests all interest coupons paid on the bond each year-end at a 12 percent rate, it would have $22,107 at the end of 7 years— more than enough to pay back the depositor and to book a gross profit of over $2,000 before costs. However, if interest rates fell to the extent that the coupon interest could be reinvested only at a 5.5 percent rate (recall reinvestment risk from Chapter 5), at the end of 7 years the institution would have accumulated only $19,920—not enough to repay the $20,000 obligation to the depositor, even before costs. Clearly, then, matching the maturities of liabilities and assets is not sufficient to guarantee that an institution does not bear interest rate risk.

To reduce the reinvestment risk, banks try to match the durations of their assets and liabilities, not their maturities. (See Chapter 5 for a detailed discussion of duration and its use as a measure of interest rate risk.) As discussed in Chapter 5, *duration* is a measure of the average time it takes for a security (or portfolio) to return its present value to the owner, and it can also be viewed as the effective time until an asset reprices. Although duration is a complicated concept, it is quite useful for immunizing an institution's balance sheet against interest rate risk. If an institution's assets and liabilities have equal values and the same durations, their values change similarly as interest rates change. Thus, by matching the duration of its assets to the duration of its liabilities, an institution can immunize its balance sheet against changes in value caused by interest rate changes.

If an institution wants to use duration GAP analysis to immunize the value of its equity against interest rate changes, it computes and sets at zero its duration GAP, D_G. Its *duration GAP* accounts for differences in the respective market values of a firm's assets and liabilities, MV_A and MV_L. The formula for **duration GAP** is

$$D_G = D_A - (MV_L/MV_A) \times D_L \tag{20.2}$$

where D_A is the weighted average duration of assets, and D_L is the weighted average duration of liabilities. When a bank adjusts its asset and liability durations such that $D_G = 0$, interest rate changes affect the value of the firm's assets and its liabilities similarly, leaving the market value of its equity unchanged.

Duration GAPs are opposite in sign from maturity GAPs for the same risk exposure. For instance, if an institution is *asset sensitive*—in other words, subject to income declines if interest rates fall—its assets have shorter duration than its liabilities. Thus, it has a *negative duration GAP*. At the same time, it ordinarily has more rate-sensitive (short-maturity) assets than rate-sensitive liabilities, so it has a *positive maturity GAP*.

Duration matching to immunize against interest rate risk is complicated, however, because asset and liability durations change every day. Except for zero-coupon securities, asset and liability durations change whenever interest rates change, just as bond present values change whenever interest rates change. Furthermore, it is difficult to assess the duration of loans on which customers have the option to prepay or the duration of deposits that customers can withdraw at any time. These customer options pose problems for computing both duration and maturity GAPs.

Because it requires a great deal of computation on a continuing basis, only the largest institutions use duration GAP analysis. Most smaller institutions prefer to use maturity GAP analysis to reduce interest rate risk because of its greater simplicity. These banks should recognize, however, that their management of interest rate risk is less precise by using maturity GAP instead of duration GAP because maturity GAP ignores the reinvestment risk associated with intermediate cash flows.

To illustrate how duration GAP works, let's return to the example presented earlier, Exhibits 20.3 and 20.4. Recall in our example that the bank funded a $1,000 fixed-rate, single-payment, 1-year loan with a 3-month and a 6-month CD having face values of $500.

The duration GAP calculation is simple in this case because the assets and liabilities have no intermediate cash flows (i.e., they are zero-coupon instruments); thus, their durations equal their maturities (0.25 years for the 3-month CD and 0.5 years for the 6-month CD). The duration GAP is calculated as

$$
\begin{aligned}
D_G &= D_A - (MV_L/MV_A) \times D_L \\
&= 1 - (1 \times 0.375) \\
&= 0.625
\end{aligned}
$$

Note that D_L is the weighted average of the durations of the two CDs:

$$
\begin{aligned}
D_L &= [(\$500/\$1,000) \times 0.25] + [(\$500/\$1,000) \times 0.5] \\
&= 0.375 \text{ years}
\end{aligned}
$$

The duration of assets exceeds the duration of liabilities in this case, suggesting that the liabilities reprice before the assets. The average dollar of liabilities reprices after 0.375 years (4.5 months), whereas the assets do not reprice until the end of the year. Thus, an interest rate increase results in declining earnings for this bank.

However, had the bank issued a 6-month CD and an 18-month (1.5 years) CD, the duration of the liabilities would have equaled 1 year:

$$
\begin{aligned}
D_L &= [(\$500/\$1,000) \times 0.5] + [(\$500/\$1,000) \times 1.5] \\
&= 1 \text{ year}
\end{aligned}
$$

Thus, the duration of the assets equals the duration of the liabilities, the duration GAP is zero, and the bank's cash flows are immunized from interest rate changes.

ASSESSING RISK: VALUE AT RISK

The interest rate risk measures discussed so far are commonly used to measure the extent to which a financial institution's profitability or value will be affected by a given change in interest rates. What these measures don't tell us, however, is how much we might lose. **Value at risk (VAR)** is a common approach to assessing risk in financial firms' trading accounts and is gaining popularity in evaluating overall riskiness for banks. VAR measures the loss potential up to a certain probability within a given time period. It allows us to estimate how much a change in interest rates might affect the firm's value within a given confidence limit.

Using recent historical data, we can estimate the mean and standard deviation of changes in the underlying risk factors (e.g., interest rates) that affect the value of the assets in our trading account. After estimating the mean and standard deviation of the risk factor, we can use the asset's duration to estimate the change in asset values for the maximum, probable change in the risk factor. The VAR is calculated as follows:

$$
VAR = \frac{\Delta V}{\Delta r} \times \Delta r^* \tag{20.3}
$$

where

$\Delta V / \Delta r$ = the sensitivity of changes in asset values to changes in the risk factor.[1]

Δr^* = the potential adverse change in the risk factor within the relevant time period for a given confidence level. For example, a 95 percent confidence level implies that $\Delta r^* = 1.65\ \sigma$, where σ is the standard deviation of changes in the risk factor.[2]

For example, consider Bank of Pullman, which holds a portfolio of Treasury bills in its trading account. The trading desk manager of Bank of Pullman has estimated that the mean change in the Treasury bill yield over the next month is 0 basis points with a standard deviation of 50 basis points. Based on a 95 percent confidence level, this implies that the potential change in the Treasury bill yield is 82.5 basis points, or 0.00825 (1.65 × 0.005). The duration for the Treasury bills is 0.50 years. The bank holds $10,000,000 in Treasury bills, and the expected Treasury bill yield in 1 month is 7 percent per year. Based on this information, the VAR is calculated as follows:

$$VAR = -\frac{0.5}{(1 + 0.035)} \times \$10,000,000 \times 0.00825 = -\$39,855$$

Put another way, we can say with 95 percent confidence that the worst loss Bank of Pullman can expect to experience in the next month as a result of changes in the Treasury bill yield is $39,855.

The advantage of VAR as a method for assessing the extent of a firm's risk exposure is that it summarizes the potential for bad outcomes in a single number. However, there are several limitations to VAR. First, VAR relies on a normal distribution. Changes in risk factors may not be normally distributed, and the standard deviation we estimate for the risk factor is subject to estimation error. Second, VAR is sensitive to the time horizon we choose. A VAR that is accurate over a 1-month period may not be accurate when it is extended over a year.

The disadvantage of VAR is that it does not account for the kinds of events that occur outside most firms' confidence intervals. For example, if a bank determines that, with 95 percent confidence, the most it stands to lose due to interest

---

[1] Recall from Chapter 5 that we can use duration to estimate the sensitivity of fixed-income security values to changes in interest rates:

$$\%\,\Delta PB = -D\left[\frac{\Delta i}{(1 + i)}\right] \times 100$$

or, stating it slightly differently,

$$\Delta PB = -D\left[\frac{\Delta i}{(1 + i)}\right] \times PB$$

So, rearranging, we get

$$\frac{\Delta PB}{\Delta i} = -\left[\frac{D}{(1 + i)}\right] \times PB$$

Notice that $\Delta PB/\Delta i$ can be thought of as the $\Delta V/\Delta r$ for a fixed income security in the VAR equation. Therefore, the VAR equation for a fixed-income security can be written as

$$VAR = -\left[\frac{D}{(1 + i)}\right] \times PB \times \Delta i^*$$

[2] Recall from the principles of statistics that 95 percent of the area under a normal probability distribution is below +1.65 standard deviations from the mean.

rate risk in a given month is $1 million, this means that it probably will not lose more than $1 million in a month because of changes in interest rates. Unfortunately, it also means that there is a 5 percent chance that the bank might lose more than $1 million. VAR does not account for these extreme possibilities.

If a financial institution determines that its interest rate risk exposure is sufficiently large that the potential losses it might incur exceed the institution's risk tolerances, then it will take steps to hedge (or minimize) the exposure. The next section discusses some of the approaches a financial institution might take to limit its potential losses.

Hedging means taking actions to reduce or eliminate risk. The simplest form of hedging is matched funding of loans. With matched funding, the bank funds a loan with a CD (or other liability) that has exactly the same maturity (or duration, if the instruments involved have intermediate cash flows). Matched funding means that the interest rate sensitivity of the loan and the CD are identical, or that they have the same effective time to repricing. Thus, changes in cash flows of the asset as a result of interest rate changes are matched exactly by changes in the cost of financing the asset. One should remember, however, that by hedging the bank not only eliminates downside risk, it also eliminates upside potential.

Matched funding is a form of **microhedging**, which is hedging a specific transaction. **Macrohedging**, however, involves using instruments of risk management, such as financial futures, options on financial futures, and interest rate swaps (see Chapter 11) to reduce the interest rate risk of the firm's entire balance sheet. We now discuss how financial futures, options on financial futures, and interest rate swaps can be used in managing interest rate risk.

20.5 HEDGING INTEREST RATE RISK

FINANCIAL FUTURES

The interest rate risk of a bank with a negative maturity GAP or positive duration GAP (in either case, recall that the assets are more rate sensitive than the liabilities) can be reduced through the use of financial futures. In Chapter 11, we showed that the prices of financial futures behave similarly to those of bonds when interest rates change; thus, there is an inverse relationship between the price of a financial futures contract and interest rates.

A short-funded bank experiences a decline in earnings with a rise in interest rates, as shown in our earlier example. To offset this risk, the bank sells (or *shorts*) financial futures. Recall from Chapter 11 that if interest rates rise, a short position in financial futures increases in value. A short position in the futures market, therefore, offsets the decline in the bank's earnings should interest rates rise.

Exhibit 20.6 illustrates the effects of macrohedging on a typical bank with financial futures. The graph shows that as interest rates increase, the bank's net cash flow declines. At the same time, the value of the short futures position increases. The logic here is simple. Recall that when a bank sells futures contracts, it does so at a given price for the underlying security. As interest rates rise, the price of the underlying security declines, as does the value of the futures contract. To get out of the short position, the bank does not have to deliver the underlying security; it simply purchases an identical futures contract in the secondary market. With an interest rate increase (that is, a price decrease), therefore, the bank has *sold high and bought low* in the futures market, making a profit that offsets the decline in bank cash flows. Notice from Exhibit 20.6 that after hedging with

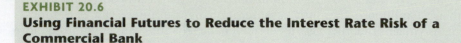

EXHIBIT 20.6

Using Financial Futures to Reduce the Interest Rate Risk of a Commercial Bank

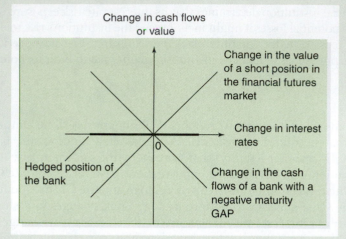

Banks can reduce interest rate risk by selling short financial futures. Notice, however, that by hedging, the bank eliminates the upside potential that comes from a decline in interest rates.

futures, the bank's cash flows do not fluctuate with changes in interest rates. Chapter 11 (see Exhibit 11.5) provided a detailed example of how financial futures can be used to microhedge a fixed-rate loan.

OPTIONS ON FINANCIAL FUTURES

Banks can develop more sophisticated hedges against interest rate risk by using options on financial futures. Recall from Chapter 11 that options on financial assets can reduce downside risk without eliminating all of the upside potential. A common use of options on financial futures is to create so-called **caps**, **floors**, and **collars** on interest rates. A *cap* on interest rates is created by purchasing a put option (that is, an option to sell) on a financial futures contract. Banks can use caps to limit increases in the cost of their liabilities without sacrificing the possibility of benefiting from interest rate declines. However, a *floor* on interest rates is created by selling a *call option* (i.e., an option to buy) on a financial futures contract. The *floor* sets a lower limit for liability costs.

By simultaneously buying a cap and selling a floor, the bank creates a *collar*. Collars limit the movement of a bank's liability costs within a specified range. If, for example, a bank purchases a cap at 9 percent and sells a floor at 5 percent, the bank's liability costs fluctuate between 5 and 9 percent. Exhibit 20.7 shows the cash flows of caps, floors, and collars. As shown in Frame A of Exhibit 20.7, if interest rates rise above the cap rate, the bank purchasing the cap receives a cash flow from the writer (seller) of the cap (or the value of the put option on the futures contract increases). Frame B shows that if the bank has written (sold) a floor, it must pay the purchaser of the floor a cash flow if rates decrease below the floor rate. Frame C shows the cash flows from the collar.

Exhibit 20.8 shows the cash flows of a bank with a negative maturity GAP (or *positive duration GAP*) after creating a collar. Notice that if rates increase beyond the cap rate or decrease below the floor rate, the bank's cash flows are

EXHIBIT 20.7

Using Options on Financial Futures to Create Caps, Floors, and Collars

Panel A: Cash flows from buying an interest rate cap

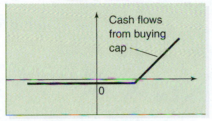

Change in cash flows or value

Cash flows from buying cap

Change in interest rates

0

Panel B: Cash flows from selling an interest rate floor

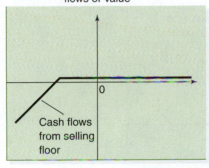

Change in cash flows or value

Change in interest rates

0

Cash flows from selling floor

Panel C: Cash flows from simultaneously buying an interest rate cap and selling an interest rate floor (interest rate collar)

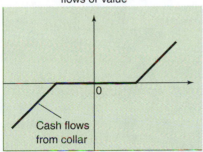

Change in cash flows or value

Change in interest rates

0

Cash flows from collar

By simultaneously buying a put option on financial futures (a *cap*) and selling a call option on financial futures (a *floor*), a bank creates a *collar*, which limits the movements of a bank's liability costs within a specified range.

EXHIBIT 20.8
Using Collars to Manage Interest Rate Risk

Panel A: Cash flows of a bank with a negative maturity GAP

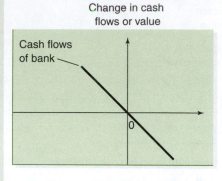

Panel B: Cash flows from a collar

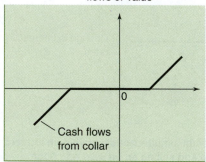

Panel C: Cash flows of bank with collar

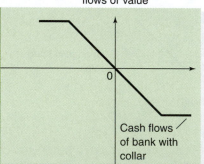

A collar eliminates the effects of extreme movements in interest rates, allowing the bank's cash flows to fluctuate within a specified range.

unchanged. The caps and floors illustrated here eliminate only the effects of extreme movements in interest rates, allowing the bank's cash flows to fluctuate within a specified range.

Exhibits 20.7 and 20.8 naturally raise the question, Why would a bank want to limit reductions in its liability costs by selling a floor? To understand the answer to this question, one must understand that purchasing a cap is equivalent to buying an insurance policy against increasing interest rates, and that selling a floor is equivalent to selling an insurance policy to someone who fears a decline in interest rates. As everyone knows, insurance is not free. We all must pay premiums for insurance protection. By simultaneously selling insurance (in the form of a floor) to a third party, a bank generates "premium" income that offsets the cost of obtaining the cap. Thus, banks are willing to give up some of their upside potential from decreasing interest rates as a way of reducing the cost of downside protection.

Although caps, floors, and collars can be created by buying and selling options on financial futures, this strategy is difficult because exchange-traded options with sufficiently long maturities do not exist. Most caps, floors, and collars, therefore, are privately negotiated agreements (that is, over the counter) between buyers and sellers of interest rate "insurance." These privately negotiated agreements are called *interest rate options*.

INTEREST RATE SWAPS

Banks also use interest rate swaps (see Chapter 11) to manage interest rate risk. Recall from Chapter 11 that in an interest rate swap, two counterparties literally swap cash flows based on relative movements of two interest rates that are agreed on in the swap agreement. In the simplest and most common form, parties to a swap periodically exchange cash flows (monthly, quarterly, or semiannually) based on the difference between an agreed-on fixed interest rate and a variable interest rate.

To illustrate, consider the case of a short-funded bank, one whose liabilities are more rate sensitive than its assets. Such a bank has a problem with rising interest rates because liability costs are "variable" compared to the relatively "fixed" asset returns. Thus, liability costs increase faster than yields on assets. The bank, therefore, pays out variable cash flows and receives relatively fixed cash flows with respect to interest rate changes. This logic leads to the same cash flow profile of a bank shown in Exhibit 20.6. What a short-funded bank needs to offset the risk position, therefore, is to receive a variable cash flow and pay a fixed cash flow.

To hedge interest rate risk, the bank enters into an interest rate swap in which the bank receives cash flows based on a floating interest rate and pays cash flows based on a fixed interest rate. In an interest rate swap, the cash flows are based on what is called a *notional amount of principal*. The principal is *notional* in that it never actually changes hands. The counterparties to the swap simply pay each other difference checks based on the interest rate changes as applied to the notional amount of principal.

Suppose a bank enters into a swap and agrees to pay a fixed rate and receive a cash flow based on a variable rate. If interest rates rise in the first settlement period, the bank would receive a difference check because the variable interest rate increased relative to the fixed interest rate. If, for example, the variable rate is 100 basis points higher than the fixed rate on the settlement date, the bank would receive a difference check from the counterparty of $1 million on a notional principal of $100 million. If the variable interest rate declines, the bank would have to pay a difference check to the counterparty. This type of interest rate swap results in a net cash inflow to the bank if interest rates rise, offsetting the decrease in net interest income that occurs when liability costs increase faster than asset yields. Of course, the swap also eliminates the upside potential from an interest rate decline because, even though a bank with a negative maturity GAP would ordinarily benefit from the decline, it must pay a difference check that offsets that benefit.

If we were to draw the cash-flow profile of the type of interest rate swap just described, it would be identical to the change in value of a short position in the financial futures market shown in Exhibit 20.6. If financial futures and interest rate swaps can accomplish essentially the same objective, why do they both exist? Recall from Chapter 11 that financial futures are standardized agreements, trading on organized exchanges. Financial futures are *cash-settled* (or marked to market) daily. Unfortunately, there is not a corresponding financial futures contract for every financial instrument. Interest rate swaps, however, are privately negotiated agreements that can be tailor-made to fit the circumstances of particular counterparties. Swaps can be made for more varied maturities than is possible with futures, tailored to particular interest rates, and the settlement dates can be designed to fit the cash-flow patterns of the counterparties. The trade-off for the increased flexibility of designing swaps is that swaps are less marketable and carry more default risk than financial futures.

As you can see, there are a variety of possibilities for managing a financial institution's interest rate risk exposure. The specific approach chosen depends on a financial institution's circumstances. Learning by Doing 20.1 takes us through one bank's situation and discusses the advantages and disadvantages of the different approaches from this bank's perspective.

LEARNING BY DOING 20.1
Measuring Interest Rate Risk

PROBLEM: Consider a bank with the balance sheet shown below. You have been asked to measure the extent to which this bank is exposed to interest rate risk and suggest some ways the bank can minimize its exposure.

Assets		Liabilities and Equity Capital	
Cash assets	$10 m	Demand deposits	$40 m
3-month Treasury bills ($D = 0.25$ year)	25 m	Money market deposit accounts ($D = 0.25$ year)	30 m
6-month Treasury notes ($D = 0.50$ year)	30 m	3-month CDs ($D = 0.25$ year)	40 m
3-year Treasury bonds ($D = 2.7$ years)	70 m	3-month banker's acceptances ($D = 0.25$)	20 m
Short-term business loans ($D = 0.43$ year)	50 m	6-month commercial paper ($D = 0.5$)	60 m
Long-term consumer loans ($D = 2.45$ years)	25 m	1-year CDs ($D = 1.0$ year)	20 m
10-year fixed rate mortgages ($D = 8.9$ years)	20 m	2-year CDs ($D = 2.0$ years)	40 m
30-year floating rate mortgages ($D = 0.6$ year)	40 m	Equity capital	20 m
Total assets	$270 m	Total liability and equity	$270 m

APPROACH: Using maturity GAP and duration GAP and the information given on the balance sheet, you can calculate those two measures of interest rate risk. Based on these measures, you can also suggest potential approaches to minimizing the risk exposure.

SOLUTION: The first step is to determine the bank's rate-sensitive assets. Recall that rate-sensitive assets are assets that mature or are repriced within a year, as follows:

Rate-sensitive assets (RSA)	
3-month T-bills	25 m
6-month T-notes	30 m
Short-term business loans	50 m
30-year floating-rate mortgages	40 m
Total RSA or 53.7% of total assets	145 m

The-rate sensitive liabilities are liabilities that mature or reprice within a year, as follows:

Rate-sensitive liabilities (RSL)	
Money market deposits	30 m
3-month CDs	40 m
3-month banker's acceptances	20 m
6-month commercial paper	60 m
1-year CDs	20 m
Total RSL or 63.0% of total liabilities and equity capital	170 m

The difference between rate-sensitive assets and rate-sensitive liabilities is maturity GAP:

$$\text{Maturity GAP} = \text{RSA} - \text{RSL}$$
$$= \$145 \text{ m} - \$170 \text{ m}$$
$$= -\$25 \text{ m or } -9.3\% \text{ of total assets}$$

Interpreting this negative maturity GAP is straightforward. The bank has $25 million more in rate-sensitive liabilities than rate-sensitive assets. If interest rates increase by 100 basis points in the next year, the bank will earn 100 basis points more on $145 million of its assets. Unfortunately, it will also be paying 100 basis points more on $170 million of its liabilities. The net effect is that it will be paying 100 basis points more on the difference of $25 million. This is obviously a crude calculation, and we have made several assumptions to arrive at this estimate. Nevertheless, knowing a bank's maturity GAP is helpful in understanding its interest rate risk exposure.

As explained earlier in the chapter, maturity GAP is useful, but it suffers from several problems. An additional measure of interest rate risk is duration GAP. Duration GAP is not perfect either, but it is probably better than maturity GAP for estimating the market value impact of a change in interest rates. The first step in calculating duration GAP is to determine the duration of your assets. It is just the weighted average of the durations of all assets:

Asset	D	Weight	D * Wt
Cash assets	0	10/270	0.000
3-month Treasury bills	0.25	25/270	0.023
6-month Treasury notes	0.5	30/270	0.056
3-year Treasury bonds	2.7	70/270	0.700
Short-term business loans	0.43	50/270	0.080
Long-term consumer loans	2.45	25/270	0.227
10-year fixed-rate mortgages	8.9	20/270	0.659
30-year floating-rate mortgages	0.6	40/270	0.089
Weighted average duration of assets			1.833

Similarly, you can calculate the weighted average duration of liabilities:

Liability	D	Weight	D*Wt
Demand deposits	0	40/250	0.000
Money market deposits	0.25	30/250	0,030
3-month CDs	0.25	40/250	0.040
3-month banker's acceptance	0.25	20/250	0.020
6-month commercial paper	0.5	60/250	0.120
1-year time deposits	1	20/250	0.080
2-year time deposits	2	40/250	0.320
Weight average duration of liabilities			0.610

Next we take the difference between the weighted average duration of assets and weighted average duration of liabilities, after adjusting for the fact that there are more assets than liabilities:

$$\text{Duration GAP} = D_A - (MV_L/MV_A) \times D_L$$
$$= 1.833 - (250/270) \times 0.610$$
$$= 1.268$$

The fact that the weighted average duration of assets is greater than the weighted average duration of liabilities indicates that the bank's assets tend to be longer-term in nature than its liabilities. Consequently, if interest rates increase, the bank's assets will lose value at a greater rate than its liabilities, thereby causing a decline in the value of equity. Note that the interpretation of duration GAP is somewhat different from the interpretation of the maturity GAP calculation, but the interpretations are consistent with each other. Using either measure, it is clear that this bank will not be as profitable if interest rates increase.

So how do you minimize this risk? As suggested earlier in the chapter, you can enter into a short position in financial futures. Any change in interest rates will affect the balance sheet and a short position in financial futures contracts in opposite directions. Any gains or losses on the balance sheet as a result of changes in interest rates will be offset by gains or losses in the financial futures position. Specifically, if interest rates increase, the bank will lose profitability on its balance sheet as already described. The financial futures position, on the other hand, will gain because you will have secured a selling price for the underlying assets in the futures contract. If interest rates increase, the market value of the underlying assets will go down and the value of having a secured selling price will increase.

Alternatively, if you are interested in preserving the potential gains associated with a decrease in interest rates, you might purchase a put option on financial futures. This will give you the ability to profit in the event that interest rates increase (and the value of the underlying asset in the futures contract goes down), but only lose the option premium if interest rates decrease. Obviously, the advantage of this approach is that the bank's losses will be minimized if interest rates increase, and it preserves the ability to enjoy increased profits if interest rates go down. The disadvantage is that options are not free. The bank will have to pay a premium for such an option, and the cost of the option may be substantial.

A third option is to enter into an interest rate swap agreement. If the bank agrees to pay fixed and receive floating in a fixed-for-floating swap, its gains or losses on the balance sheet as a result of changes in interest rates will be offset by the cash flows associated with the swap agreement. This approach works well for financial institutions that have risk exposures of an ongoing nature. If the exposure is temporary, however, a swap may not make sense.

DO YOU UNDERSTAND?

1. What is meant by *repricing*? What happens to the cash flows of a bank whose liabilities reprice before assets as interest rates increase?

2. If a bank's liability costs increase faster than yields on assets as interest rates rise, does the bank have a positive or negative maturity GAP? What kind of duration GAP would such a bank tend to have—positive or negative? Explain.

3. Should banks use maturity GAP or duration GAP to manage interest rate risk? What are the important considerations in this decision?

4. Explain how financial futures can be used by banks to reduce interest rate risk.

5. What trade-offs should banks consider when choosing between a cap and a collar to manage interest rate risk?

SUMMARY OF LEARNING OBJECTIVES

1 **Explain the profitability-versus-safety trade-off faced by banks and other financial institutions.** Like all business firms, banks and other financial institutions strive for higher profits consistent with safety. The trade-off between profitability and safety is more acute for financial institutions than for most other businesses because financial institutions tend to have low capital–assets ratios and because most of their liabilities are short term. Banks can fail because of inadequate liquidity and inadequate capital.

2 **Discuss how banks and other financial institutions manage their liquidity risk.** Financial institutions have two basic tools for maintaining sufficient liquidity: (1) asset management and (2) liability management. Under asset management, financial institutions use liquidity stored on the asset side of the balance sheet in the form of primary reserves and marketable securities. Under liability management, financial institutions obtain liquidity by increasing liabilities such as fed funds purchased or by issuing certificates of deposit.

3 Describe the methods used to manage credit risk. Financial institutions manage the credit risk associated with individual loans by closely monitoring loan performance, identifying problem loans quickly, and recovering as much as possible in the event of default. Financial institutions manage the credit risk of loan portfolios by diversifying across geographic regions, loan type, and borrower type. Financial institutions supplement these efforts by using credit derivatives, securitizing loans, and performing loan brokerage.

4 Explain the process used to measure and manage interest rate and other market risks. Financial institutions must first identify the nature of their risk exposures. Once identified, the risks must be measured and assessed to estimate the extent to which firm value might be affected by the risk factor. Finally, managers must determine whether the risk is sufficiently large to justify expending resources to minimize the exposure.

5 Discuss how financial institutions measure interest rate risk. Financial institutions measure interest rate risk by estimating their maturity and duration GAPs. The greater the size of the GAP, the greater the financial institution's interest rate risk exposure.

6 Describe the various approaches to minimizing interest rate risk. When interest rates are expected to rise, the proper strategy is to have a positive maturity GAP. If interest rates are expected to decline, there should be a negative maturity GAP. If a bank wishes to minimize interest rate risk, it should strive for a zero GAP. Banks use futures, options on futures, and interest rate swaps to manage interest rate risk.

KEY TERMS

Insolvent	Internal credit risk ratings	Rate-sensitive liabilities (RSLs)	Macrohedging
Liquidity	Concentration ratios		Caps
Asset management	Credit derivatives	Maturity GAP	Floors
Liability management	Credit default swap	Duration GAP	Collars
Primary reserves	Credit insurance	Value at risk (VAR)	
Secondary reserves	Rate-sensitive assets (RSAs)	Microhedging	

QUESTIONS AND PROBLEMS

1. Explain the profitability versus solvency and liquidity dilemma facing bank management.

2. What are the two ways a bank can fail? Explain how these two conditions cause failure. Give examples of times when we have had the two different types of failures.

3. Liquidity management can be practiced on either side of the balance sheet. How are asset and liability management similar and how do they differ? Why do smaller banks have limited access to liability management?

4. Discuss the debt instruments used in liability management. What are the common characteristics of these debt instruments, and what type of bank is most likely to issue them?

5. How do banks decide on the proper amount of primary and secondary reserves to hold?

6. Assume you are the manager of a bank with the following balance sheet. Determine the maturity GAP and duration GAP for the bank. What happens to the value or net income for the bank if interest rates go up or down?

Assets		Liabilities and Equity Capital	
Cash assets	$15 M	Demand deposits	$10 M
Short-term investments ($D = 0.35$ years)	$30 M	Interest-bearing deposits maturing in less than 1 year ($D = 0.40$ years)	$10 M
Long-term investments ($D = 5.00$ years)	$5 M	Interest-bearing deposits maturing in more than 1 year ($D = 2.5$ years)	$45 M
Loans maturing in less than 1 year ($D = 0.5$ years)	$25 M	Borrowed funds ($D = 0.25$ years)	$5 M
Loans maturing in more than 1 year ($D = 10.0$ years)	$5 M	Equity capital	$10 M
Total assets	$80 M	Total liabilities and equity capital	$80 M

7. Distinguish between the credit risk of individual loans and the credit risk of loan portfolios. How are they related? Which is most important?

8. How do financial institutions identify problem loans?

9. Describe what banks do when they identify a problem loan.

10. Describe how internal credit risk ratings can be used to allocate funds to different types of loans.

11. Describe how credit default swaps can be used to manage credit risk exposure.

12. Explain what happens to the cash flows or market value of a typical bank when interest rates decline. What happens if interest rates increase?

13. Suppose a financial institution holds a portfolio of bonds with a value of $50,000,000 and duration of 3.5. The portfolio currently yields 4 percent, and you don't anticipate any changes in the yield over the next month. If the standard deviation of changes in the yield over the next month is 75 basis points, what is the portfolio's VAR for the month?

14. Explain how financial futures are used to reduce bank interest rate risk. How does the value of a futures contract change when interest rates change?

15. Explain how one can use options on financial futures to manage interest rate risk.

16. A bank economist projects that interest rates in the future are expected to decline. What is the bank's proper funds management strategy? Why?

INTERNET EXERCISE

Two of the strategies identified in this chapter for hedging interest rate risk exposure are using either financial futures or options on financial futures. For example, if a financial institution is worried that interest rates might increase in the next few months, it might either sell financial futures or buy a put option on financial futures. Suppose the financial institution is trying to decide between the two possibilities. Your job is to determine how much it will cost the financial institution to hedge using options versus futures.

1. Go to the CME Group Web page at www.cmegroup.com. Select the "Interest Rates" tab, and click on "10-year U.S. Treasury Notes." This will bring up quotes for futures contracts on 10-year U.S. Treasury Notes. Use the links on this page (including the "Contract Specifications" and "Market Data Explanations" links) to determine the futures price of the nearest term futures contract.

2. Click on the "OPT" link to determine the option prices for the option contracts tied to the futures contract. What is the put option price for the option with an exercise price nearest to the current futures price?

3. Based on the futures and options prices, how much would the futures price need to change for the cost of the option contract to be worth the additional cost?

accredited investors   Individuals who are considered to be sophisticated investors and who do not need the protection afforded to regular investors by the securities laws.

actual reserves   The reserve amount computed by a bank by summing its holdings of vault cash with its holdings of reserve deposits at Federal Reserve banks over a 2-week reserve maintenance period.

adjustable-rate mortgage (ARM)   Mortgages on which the contractual interest rate changes when market rates change.

adjustable-rate preferred stock   Preferred stock issued with adjustable rates; the dividends are adjusted periodically in response to changing market interest rates.

ADR   *See* **American Depository Receipts.**

advances   Loans by the Federal Home Loan Bank to its member institutions.

adverse selection   Problem of hidden information in general. For instance, the tendency of the most risky people to buy insurance or apply for loans.

advisory fees   *See* **management fees.**

aggressive stocks   Stocks with betas greater than 1.0 that carry greater systematic risk than the market.

agreement corporations   Corporations that operate similarly to Edge Act corporations but remain under state charter.

allocative function of interest rates   The function of interest rates in the economy whereby they allocate funds between surplus spending units (SSUs) and deficit spending units (DSUs) in the financial markets.

all-risk coverage   Property insurance coverage that insures against all losses except those that are excluded.

American Depository Receipts (ADRs)   Dollar-denominated claims issued by U.S. banks representing ownership of shares of a foreign company's stock held on deposit by the U.S. bank in the issuing firm's home country.

American-style option   The right to buy (or sell) and receive (or deliver) the underlying asset at the strike price at any time prior to and including the expiration date.

amortization   To pay the principal amount due on a loan in stages over a period of time. When the full amount is repaid, the loan is fully amortized.

amortized loan   A loan repaid over the life of the loan, using a contractual rate of interest; each payment includes both interest and principal.

annuities   Products sold by life insurers that can be thought of as the mirror image of life insurance. The function of an annuity is to liquidate an estate.

appreciated   For a currency that has increased in value relative to another currency.

arbitrage   The process of simultaneously selling overvalued assets and buying similar undervalued assets.

ARMs   *See* **adjustable-rate mortgages.**

asset management   A financial institution's management of its asset structure to provide both liquidity and desirable rates of return.

asymmetric information   A situation in which a party (for instance, a buyer) does not have the same information as the other (for instance, a seller).

auction market   A market that provides centralized procedures for the exposure of purchase and sale orders to all market participants simultaneously, thereby eliminating the expense of locating compatible partners and bargaining for a favorable price.

back-end load   Fees charged when investors take money out of a mutual fund by redeeming shares; the fees can be either redemption fees or contingent deferred sales charges.

bad-debt deduction   Federal income tax savings given to savings banks and savings associations after World War II until 1996 that reduced federal income tax obligations of these institutions.

balance of payments   A set of accounts that summarizes a country's international balance of trade and the payments to and the receipts from foreigners.

balloon payment mortgages   Mortgages on which the final scheduled payment is substantially larger than preceding payments.

banker's acceptance   A draft issued by a company, drawn on and accepted by a bank. The draft promises payment of a certain sum of money to its holder at some future date. In effect, the bank substitutes its credit standing for that of the issuing corporation.

bank holding company   A major form of organization for banks in the United States in which 25 percent or more of the voting stock of one or more banks is held by a single entity.

Banking Act of 1933 (Glass-Steagall Act)   Legislation that barred banks from paying interest on demand deposits, separated commercial banking from investment banking, and restricted the types of assets that banks could own.

bank panic.   *See* **panic**.

bank run.   *See* **run**.

basis risk   A risk that exists because the value of an item being hedged may not always keep the same price relationship to contracts purchased or sold in the futures markets.

BCFP   *See* **Bureau of Consumer Financial Protection**.

bearer bonds   Bonds for which coupons are attached; the holder presents them for payment when they come due.

best-efforts offering   The distribution of registered securities in which the investment banker acts only as the company's agent and receives a commission for placing the securities with investors.

beta   The measurement of the extent to which a stock's returns are related to general market returns.

bid–ask spread   The difference between the bid price at which a dealer is willing to buy a security and the ask price at which the dealer is willing to sell the security; dealers make a profit by selling at a higher price than the price they paid to buy the security.

bid-to-cover ratio   The ratio of the dollar amount of tendered bids (competitive and noncompetitive) to the amount of accepted bids.

bill of lading   An international trade document that is a receipt issued to the exporter by a common carrier that acknowledges possession of the goods described on the face of the bill; a contract between the exporter and the shipping company.

BIS   *See* **Bank for International Settlements**.

bond   A contractual obligation of a borrower to make cash payments to a lender for a fixed number of years; upon maturity, the lender is paid the face value of the security.

bondholder   The lender in a bond contract.

bond issuer   The borrower of a bond contract.

bond price volatility   The percentage change in bond price for a given change in yield.

bond ratings   Published rankings of bonds based on relative default risk.

borrowed funds   Short-term funds borrowed by commercial banks from the wholesale money market (or the Federal Reserve).

breadth.   *See* **market breadth**.

Bretton Woods system   Before 1971, a system of fixed currency exchange rates under which a government was obligated to intervene in the foreign exchange markets to keep the value of its currency within a narrow range.

bridge–finanancing   *See* **bridge loan**.

bridge loan   A loan supplying cash for a specific transaction; repayment is made from cash fiows from an identifiable source. Usually, the purpose of the loan and the source of repayment are related.

broker   One who acts as an intermediary between buyers and sellers but does not take title to the securities traded.

brokerage services   A function of an investment firm in which the firm earns a commission for bringing a buyer and seller together.

brokered market   A market in which trading in an issue becomes sufficiently heavy that brokers begin to offer specialized search services to market participants for a fee (commission); brokers find compatible trading partners and negotiate acceptable transaction prices for their clients.

building societies   The first savings associations.

Bureau of Consumer Financial Protection (BCFP)   An independent bureau created by the Dodd-Frank Act within the Federal Reserve System to enforce consumer finance laws and to promote fairness and transparency for consumer financial products and services.

buyout private equity Private equity investments made by firms specializing in leveraged buyouts.

call feature. *See* **call option (call provision)**.

call interest premium The difference in interest rates between callable and comparable noncallable bonds.

call loans Usually, a loan that either the borrower or the lender can terminate upon request.

call options A contract giving the buyer the right but not the obligation to buy the underlying asset at a predetermined price (known as the strike or exercise price).

call price A prespecified price at which a bond issuer can buy back the bond before maturity. Usually it is set at par or slightly above par.

call provision The option of the bond issuer to buy back the bond at a specified price in advance of the maturity date; the price (call price) is usually set at the bond's par value or slightly above par.

call reports Detailed statements of the operating and financial condition of a bank.

call risk *See* **prepayment risk**.

CAMELS **C**apital adequacy, **A**sset quality, **M**anagement competence and control, **E**arnings, **L**iquidity, and **S**ensitivity to market risk rating system used by financial institution examiners.

caps A cap on interest rates is created by purchasing a put option (i.e., an option to sell) on a financial futures contract.

capital accounts In the balance of payments accounts, capital accounts measure capital flows into and out of the country.

capital asset pricing model (CAPM) A model of the relation between systematic risk and expected return. It suggests return on a security equals the return on a risk-free asset plus a premium for bearing systematic risk.

capital flight When owners of capital transfer their wealth out of the country, typically in response to political instability.

capital-gains yield The rate at which the value of the firm is expected to grow.

capital markets Financial markets in which financial claims with maturities greater than 1 year are traded. Capital markets channel savings into long-term productive investments.

captive insurance company Insurance company created by a parent company for the purpose of insuring the parent company's loss exposures.

captive sales finance companies Sales finance companies that are owned by a manufacturer and help finance the sale of the manufacturer's goods.

carried interest The portion of the profits of a private equity fund that the fund manager earns.

cash-flow underwriting Writing insurance on just about any risk in order to get the premium dollars to invest at high interest rates.

cash items in the process of collection (CIPC) An account that is the value of checks drawn on other banks but not yet collected.

cash value In the language of insurance, because of overpayment of whole life insurance premiums in the early policy years, the premiums paid by the insured earn interest, and cash values develop within the policy.

CEBA *See* **Competitive Equality in Banking Act**.

Central Liquidity Facility (CLF) An organization empowered to make loans to credit unions that have a liquidity need; the CLF is overseen by the National Credit Union Administration (NCUA).

certificates of deposit (CDs) Bank liabilities issued in a designated amount with a fixed interest rate and maturity date.

CIPC *See* **cash items in the process of collection**.

circuit breakers SEC rules aimed at reducing market volatility by requiring halts to all trading if the DJIA falls by a certain percentage within certain times.

CLF *See* **Central Liquidity Facility**.

closed-end fund *See* **investment company**.

CMO *See* **collateralized mortgage obligation**.

coinsurance Loss-sharing provision in insurance. In health insurance, coinsurance is the loss-sharing percentages after the deductible is satisfied. In property insurance, coinsurance requires the insured to bear a portion of the loss if property is not insured for a specified percentage of value.

collars Limiting the movement of interest costs within a specified range by simultaneously buying a cap and selling a floor.

collateral Assets that are used to secure a loan. Title to them will pass to the lender if the borrower defaults.

collateralized debt obligation (CDO) A debt security collateralized by cash flows from a pool of assets such as loans and bonds. Buyers receive returns on CDOs paid in tranches.

collateralized mortgage obligations (CMOs) Securities issued by a trust or finance subsidiary that promises to pass through specified portions of the principal and interest payments on pools of underlying mortgages.

commercial banks The most important participant in the indirect credit markets. Commercial banks issue checkable demand deposits and make loans.

commercial letter of credit A promise by a bank to pay for goods in a commercial transaction. The letter of credit is written by the bank for a customer that is engaged in commercial transactions. The buyer of the goods arranges for the bank to pay the seller of the goods once the terms of the purchase agreement are satisfied.

commercial paper An unsecured, short-term promissory note issued by a large creditworthy business or financial institution. Commercial paper has maturities ranging from a day to 270 days and is usually issued in denominations of $1 million or more. Direct-placed commercial paper is sold by the seller to the buyer. Terms are negotiable. Dealer-placed commercial paper is sold through dealers with terms similar to those offered on banks' CDs.

commission Compensation for brokers that is usually based on the number of items sold or their value, or else on a share of the profits that their brokerage firm earned on the transaction they helped arrange.

commitments Agreements from investors to provide up to a certain amount of capital for the private equity capital investments as needed.

common bond requirement A requirement of a credit union that members share a "common bond" such as an occupational bond, an associational bond, or a residential bond.

common stock Basic ownership claim in a corporation. Stockholders share in the distributed earnings and net worth of a corporation and select its directors.

Community Reinvestment Act (CRA) Legislation created to prevent redlining, where a lender draws a hypothetical red line on a map around one part of a community and refuses to make loans in that area. Requires that lenders keep records to show they lend in all areas of their community.

compensating balances Minimum average deposit balances that customers must maintain at the bank, usually in the form of non-interest-bearing demand deposits.

competitive bidding A type of public offering in which the company selects the investment banker who will conduct the offering based on which investment banker offers to pay the highest net proceeds for the securities.

Competitive Equality in Banking Act (CEBA) of 1987 A regulatory act that (1) redefined nonbank banks and (2) provided funding to bail out the failing FSLIC.

competitive offering *See* **competitive bidding**.

compounding The calculation of future value based on the assumption that all interest earned will be reinvested to earn additional interest.

computerized exchanges Stock exchanges that use computerized trading and automated exchange facilities.

concentration ratios Concentration ratios measure the percentage of loans or loan commitments allocated to a given geographic location, loan type, or business type by a lender.

Consumer Credit Protection Act (Truth-in-Lending Act) Legislation passed with the intent of ensuring that every borrower obtained meaningful information about the cost of credit, especially (1) the annual percentage rate and (2) the total finance charges on a loan.

consumer finance companies Finance companies that specialize in making cash loans to consumers.

contemporaneous reserve accounting system A procedure under which reserves are posted 2 days after a 2-week reserve computational period.

contingent deferred sales charge A fee assessed when people redeem shares in a mutual fund; the fee is usually lower or absent if the money has been in the fund for longer periods of time.

contributory plans A pension plan funded by both employer and employee contributions.

conversion option The option allowing the investor to convert a security into another type of security at a predetermined price.

conversion yield discount The difference in yield between convertible bonds with the conversion option and similar bonds without this option.

convertible bonds Bonds that can be exchanged for shares of common stock.

convertible preferred stock Preferred stock that can be converted into common stock at a predetermined ratio.

convertible term insurance Term insurance that may be switched to whole life insurance without providing evidence of insurability.

convexity The curve representing T-bonds' price/yield relationship is convex. Thus, convexity is the adjustment for the shape of the curve in the formula for estimating the percentage change in the price of the bond corresponding to a given change in the market interest rate.

corporate bonds Long-term financial claims issued by corporations against the firm's assets.

correspondent balances Deposits that banks hold at other banks to clear checks and provide compensation for correspondent services.

correspondent banking A business arrangement between two banks in which one (the correspondent bank) agrees to provide the other (respondent bank) with special services, such as check-clearing or trust department services. International correspondent relationships provide international banking services such as accepting drafts, honoring letters of credit, furnishing credit information, collecting and disbursing international funds, and investing funds in international money markets.

counterparty In a forward market, the contracted party that exchanges one item for another for a predetermined price at a predetermined point in time. Ordinarily, both parties to the contract are bound by the contract.

countertrade In international trade transactions, the practice of accepting locally produced merchandise in lieu of money as payment for goods and services.

country (sovereign) risk The risk tied to political developments in a country that affects the return on loans or investments.

coupon payment The periodic interest payment in a bond contract.

coupon rate The amount of coupon payments received in a year stated as a percentage of the face value.

covered options Option writers' position if they already own the securities that they have agreed to sell or have already sold short the securities that they have agreed to buy.

CRA *See* **Community Reinvestment Act**.

credit default swaps (CDSs) A swap contract transferring risk of default from the buyer to the seller.

credit derivatives A derivative security with a payoff that is tied to credit-related events such as default or bankruptcy.

credit insurance An insurance policy that pays the holder of a loan in the event the borrower defaults.

credit risk (default risk) The possibility that the borrower will not pay back all or part of the interest or principal as promised.

credit scoring A method for analyzing a potential borrower's risk by assigning the borrower a score based on information in her credit report. Higher score indicates lower default risk.

credit spreads Differences between yields of debt instruments with different default risk (measured by ratings).

Credit Union National Association (CUNA) A major trade and service association of credit unions that lobbies in Congress, supports the development of the central credit unions and the U.S. Central Credit Union, and helps credit unions manage their liquidity, clear their checks, and obtain various investment and funds-management services.

cross-hedging Hedging with a traded futures contract whose characteristics do not exactly match those of the hedger's risk exposure.

cumulative preferred stock The cumulative feature of preferred stock means that the firm cannot pay a dividend on its common stock until it has paid the preferred shareholders the dividends in arrears.

cumulative voting A procedure for electing directors in which all directors are elected at the same time and shareholders are granted a number of votes equal to the number of directors being elected times the number of shares owned.

CUNA *See* **Credit Union National Association**.

currency risk Risk resulting from changes in currency exchange values that affect the return on loans or investments denominated in other currencies.

current account The balance of payments account that summarizes foreign trade in goods and services plus investment income and gifts or grants made to other countries.

DACI *See* **deferred availability cash items**.

de novo branching Creating a new bank branch.

dealer One who is in the security business acting as a principal rather than an agent. The dealer buys for his or her own account and sells to customers from his or her inventory.

dealer markets Markets in which trading in an issue is sufficiently active that some market participants maintain bid and offer quotations of their own; such dealers buy for, and sell for, their own inventory at their quoted prices. Dealer markets eliminate the need to search for trading partners.

debentures Bonds for which no assets have been pledged as collateral. These bonds are secured only by the firm's potential to generate positive cash flows.

deductibles Insurance contract provisions requiring the insured to bear a portion of an insured loss.

default The failure on the part of the borrower to meet any condition of the bond contract.

default risk (credit risk) *See* **credit risk (default risk)**.

default risk premium The amount of additional compensation investors must receive for purchasing securities that are not free of default risk. The rate on U.S. Treasury securities is used as the default-free rate.

defensive stocks Stocks with betas less than 1 that carry less systematic risk than the market.

deferred availability cash items (DACIs) Federal Reserve balance-sheet item representing the value of checks deposited at the Fed by depository institutions that have not yet been credited to the institution's accounts.

deficit spending unit (DSU) An economic unit that has expenditures exceeding current income. A DSU sells financial claims on itself (liabilities) or sells equity to obtain needed funds.

defined benefit plan A pension plan in which the employer states the benefit the employee will receive at retirement.

defined contribution plans Pension plans in which the employer offers no guarantees about the actual benefit at retirement, only the periodic contributions that will be made on behalf of the employee.

demand deposit Deposits held at banks that the owner can withdraw instantly upon demand—either with checks or electronically.

demutualization The term applied to the trend in the insurance and thrift industries of large numbers of mutual companies converting to stock companies.

deposit insurance Funds established with the purpose of protecting depositors in the event of a bank failure.

Depository Institutions Act (DIA) of 1982 (Garn–St. Germain Bill) Extended the 1980 revisions in banking regulation by authorizing MMDA accounts, accelerating the phaseout of deposit rate ceilings, granting thrift institutions broader powers, and providing for acquisitions of failing institutions by different types of institutions located in different states.

Depository Institutions Deregulation and Monetary Control Act of 1980 (DIDMCA) The first major 1980s banking act. It deregulated financial institution deposit and loan rate ceilings and allowed nonbank institutions to have checking accounts (NOWs) and offer other services in competition with banks. It also extended reserve requirements to all institutions that offered transactions deposits.

depreciated For a currency that has decreased in value relative to another currency.

depth *See* **market depth**.

derivative security A financial instrument whose value depends on its underlying security.

DIDMCA *See* **Deregulation and Monetary Control Act of 1980**

direct financing Financing wherein DSUs issue financial claims on themselves and sell them for money directly to SSUs. The SSU's claim is against the DSU, not a financial intermediary.

direct search markets Secondary markets in which buyers and sellers must search each other out directly.

discount A pricing situation in which a closed-end fund trades below its net asset value.

discount bond A bond that sells below its par or face value. A bond sells at a discount when the market rate of interest is above the bond's fixed coupon rate.

discount brokers Brokerage firm that competes against full-service brokerage firms by offering fewer brokerage services and passing the savings on to investors.

discounting The calculation for finding the present value of some future sum of money.

discount rate The interest rate a financial institution must pay to borrow reserve deposits from its regional Federal Reserve bank.

discount window An operation of the Federal Reserve System whereby banks may borrow temporary reserves from the Federal Reserve System as an alternative to selling secondary reserves or borrowing federal funds to cover legal reserve deficiencies; the discount window is part of the mechanism for adjusting short-term required reserve deficiencies.

diversification The process of acquiring a portfolio of securities that have dissimilar risk–return characteristics in order to reduce overall portfolio risk.

dividends Corporate payments to stockholders.

dividend yield The expected dividend expressed as a proportion of the price of the stock.

Dodd-Frank Wall Street Reform and Consumer Protection Act A law in 2010 designed to reduce the likelihood of a similar financial crisis in the future by addressing the structure of the regulatory agencies, enhanced regulation of systemic risk, consumer protection, and limits on bank's proprietary trading and use of derivative securities.

dollarization The practice by some countries of adopting the U.S. currency as a medium of exchange.

draft In international trade, a request for payment that is drawn up by the exporter (or the exporter's bank) and sent to the bank that drew up a letter of credit for the importer.

drawdown Committed capital from the investors paid into private equity funds.

DSU *See* **deficit spending unit.**

dual banking system A term referring to the fact that U.S. banks can be chartered either by the federal government (national banks) or by state governments—with each system having different laws.

dual-class firms Firms that recapitalize with two classes of stock having different voting rights.

due diligence The process through which an investment banker investigates a company conducting a security offering to ensure that all the information in the prospectus is true.

duration A measure of interest rate risk (or bond price volatility) that considers both coupon rate and maturity; it is the weighted average of the number of years until the present value of each of the bond's cash flows is received.

duration GAP A GAP analysis measure of the sensitivity of a portfolio to interest rate changes.

earnings The amount of profit that a company produces during a period. Also known as net income.

earnings per share (EPS) Net income divided by the number of shares outstanding.

easy money Situations in which it is easy for banks to issue banknotes when businesses want loans (easy credit).

ECOA *See* **Equal Credit Opportunity Act.**

Edge Act Corporations Subsidiaries of a U.S. bank formed to engage in international banking and financial activities that domestic banks cannot conduct in the United States.

elastic money supply A flexible supply of currency that can accommodate changing public demand for cash.

Emergency Economic Stabilization Act of 2008 One of the actions taken to alleviate the financial crisis that started in the United States in 2007. The legislation established the Troubled Asset Relief Program (TARP).

Employee Retirement Income Security Act (ERISA) A 1974 law that requires employers to observe certain standards if their pension programs are to retain an advantageous tax status. ERISA was passed because Congress became concerned that many workers with long years of service would fail to receive pension benefits.

Equal Credit Opportunity Act (ECOA) A law that requires that credit be made available to individuals without regard to sex or marital status. In 1976 Congress broadened the scope of the act to forbid discrimination by creditors based on race, age, national origin, or whether credit applicants received part of their income from public assistance benefits. It requires women's incomes to be treated equally with men's in evaluating credit.

equity A term implying an owner's claim against a corporation's cash flows as opposed to the claim of a creditor (or lender).

equity funds A mutual fund primarily investing in stocks.

ERISA *See* **Employee Retirement Income Security Act.**

ETF *See* **exchange traded fund.**

EURIBOR Euro Interbank Offered Rate, the rate on euro deposits offered by one prime bank to another prime bank in the European Monetary Union.

euro The common currency for the countries that are members of the European Union.

Eurobonds Any bonds issued and sold outside their country of origin.

Eurobond market The market for long-term borrowing or lending of large amounts of U.S. dollars that have been deposited in overseas banks.

Eurocurrency markets Markets for short-term borrowing or lending of large amounts of any currency held in a time deposit account outside its country of origin.

Eurodollar expansion The expansion of dollar-denominated bank deposits in banks outside the United States.

Eurodollar U.S. dollar–denominated deposits issued by banks located outside the United States.

European-style option An option that can be exercised only at expiration. The buyer of the option pays the seller (writer) a premium. The writer keeps the premium regardless of whether the option is exercised. An option need not be exercised if it is not to the buyer's advantage to do so.

excess reserves The amount arrived at when required reserves are subtracted from a bank's actual reserves.

exchange rate The rate at which one nation's currency can be exchanged for another's at the present time.

exchange-traded funds (ETFs) An investment company whose shares are traded on organized exchanges at market determined prices. Unlike closed-end funds, however, ETFs have unique creation and redemption features that prevent large premiums or discounts from net asset value.

exercise price *See* **strike price**.

expansion financing Venture capital investments for growth and expansion.

expected yield The expected return on a bond at the end of a relevant holding period based on predictions made from interest rate forecasts.

extension risk The risk that mortgage prepayments are slower than expected.

face value *See* **par value**.

factoring Selling accounts receivable to a third party at a discount in exchange for immediate funds.

Fair and Accurate Credit Transactions (FACT) Act Passed in 2003 as an amendment to the Fair Credit Reporting Act to help reduce identity theft.

Fair Credit Billing Act (FCBA) Requires that creditors provide detailed information to consumers on the method of assessing finance charges and also that billing complaints be processed promptly.

Fair Credit Reporting Act (FCRA) Intends to promote the accuracy, fairness, and privacy of personal information assembled by credit-report agencies.

Fannie Mae *See* **Federal National Mortgage Association**.

FACT Act *See* **Fair and Accurate Credit Transactions Act**.

FCBA *See* **Fair Credit Billing Act**.

FCRA *See* **Fair Credit Reporting Act**.

FDIC *See* **Federal Deposit Insurance Corporation**.

FDICIA *See* **Federal Deposit Insurance Corporation Improvement Act**.

FDIC-SAIF A deposit insurance fund run by the FDIC to provide deposit insurance to member savings associations and savings banks.

federal agency An independent federal department or federally chartered corporation established by Congress and owned or underwritten by the U.S. government.

Federal Deposit Insurance Corporation (FDIC) A government agency that provides federal insurance for depositors of qualified banks and supervises both the Bank Insurance Fund (BIF) and the Savings Association Insurance Fund (SAIF).

Federal Deposit Insurance Corporation Improvement Act (FDICIA) This act went beyond the FIRRE Act in tightening bank and thrift institutions'

capital requirements. It allowed "well-capitalized commercial banks" to enter investment banking in a limited way through subsidiaries.

federal funds (fed funds) Immediately available funds that can be lent on an overnight basis to financial institutions. Banks may lend their deposits at the Fed to other financial institutions by transferring them through federal funds market loans.

federal funds rate (fed funds rate) The rate at which banks and other depository institutions lend excess reserves or other immediately available cash deposits to each other overnight; the rate is determined by negotiation between the private borrowers and lenders of reserves.

Federal Home Loan Bank A system of twelve regional banks empowered to borrow in the national capital markets and make loans, called advances, to savings and loans in their regions that are members of the Federal Home Loan Bank.

Federal Home Loan Bank Board (FHLBB) Until 1989, the primary regulatory agency for savings and loan associations. It controlled the Federal Home Loan Bank system, the Federal Home Loan Mortgage Corporation, and the Federal Savings and Loan Insurance Corporation. Its regulations affected all federally chartered and federally insured savings associations.

Federal Home Loan Mortgage Corporation (FHLMC, or Freddie Mac) A federal agency initially established by Congress in 1970 as a subsidiary of the Federal Home Loan Bank System. Now a quasi-private government agency, it assists savings and loan associations and other mortgage lenders. It provides a secondary market for conventional mortgages and issues mortgage-backed securities.

Federal National Mortgage Association (FNMA, or Fannie Mae) An agency that provides a secondary market for insured mortgages by issuing and executing purchase commitments for mortgages.

Federal Open Market Committee (FOMC) A committee that consists of seven members of the Board of Governors of the Federal Reserve System plus five presidents of Federal Reserve banks and that determines the nation's monetary policy and financial institutions' reserve balances.

Federal Savings and Loan Insurance Corporation (FSLIC) An agency that insured savings association and federal savings bank deposits until 1989, when deposit insurance responsibilities passed to the Savings Association Insurance Fund supervised by the FDIC.

fed funds *See* **federal funds**.

FHA mortgages   Mortgages whose ultimate payment is guaranteed by the Federal Housing Administration (FHA).

FHC   *See* **financial holding company.**

FHLBB   *See* **Federal Home Loan Bank Board.**

FHLMC   *See* **Federal Home Loan Mortgage Corporation**.

final prospectus   After approval by the Securities and Exchange (SEC), information provided about a new issue; by law, investors must have a final prospectus before they can invest.

finance companies   Companies that extend short- and intermediate-term loans and lease credit to individuals and business firms that cannot obtain credit as cheaply or easily elsewhere; nonbank financial institutions that make loans to both consumers and business but are not federally insured.

financial claim   A written promise to pay a specific sum of money (the principal) plus interest for the privilege of borrowing money over a period of time. Financial claims are issued by DSUs (liabilities) and purchased by SSUs (assets).

financial guarantees   Guarantees by third parties such as commercial banks or insurance companies to cover the payment of interest and principal to investors in debt securities in the event of a default by the borrower.

financial holding company (FHC)   A designation applied to bank holding companies that have been approved for "financial holding company" status by the Federal Reserve. FHCs are allowed to own subsidiaries that engage in almost any financial business.

financial institution   An institution that issues deposits and other financial liabilities and invests predominantly in loans and other financial assets.

Financial Institutions Reform, Recovery, and Enforcement Act (FIRREA)   This act made major changes in the structure of financial regulation. It abolished the FHLBB and FSLIC and established the OTS, FDIC-SAIF, and RTC as their replacements. It required that deposit insurance premiums be raised and that thrift institutions adopt stricter accounting standards. It also imposed "tangible capital" requirements that disallowed the counting of goodwill and various other intangible assets toward a thrift's capital adequacy requirements.

financial intermediaries   Institution that issues liabilities to SSUs and use the funds so obtained to acquire liabilities of DSUs.

financial intermediation   *See* **indirect financing**.

financial markets   The markets for buying and selling financial claims.

Financial Services Modernization Act of 1999 (Gramm-Leach-Bliley)   Legislation that repealed many of the Glass-Steagall restrictions on commercial banking and investment banking.

Financial Stability Oversight Council (FSOC)   A U.S. federal government organization created under the Dodd-Frank Act to monitor systemic risk of the financial system.

FIRREA   *See* **Financial Institutions Reform, Recovery, and Enforcement Act**.

Fisher equation   The inflation premium component of the nominal rate of interest; it equals the difference between the nominal rate of interest and expected inflation.

fixed exchange rates   A constant rate of exchange between currencies. Governments try to fix their exchange rate by buying or selling their currency whenever its exchange value starts to vary.

fixed-rate/floating rate loans   Loans with a fixed (variable) interest rate over their life.

fixed-rate mortgage (FRM)   A standard mortgage agreement in which the lender takes a lien on real property and the borrower agrees to make periodic repayments of the principal amount of money borrowed plus a fixed interest rate on the unpaid balance of the debt for a predetermined period of time.

flight to quality   A phenomenon in which investors buy bonds with high credit rating (low default risk) and sell bonds with low credit rating (high default risk) during a recession because of concerns for safety in their investment.

floors   A floor on interest rates by is created selling a call option (that is, an option to buy) on a financial futures contract.

floor-plan financing   Also known as wholesale financing; interim financing provided to a dealer by a finance company.

FNMA   *See* **Federal National Mortgage Association**.

FOMC   *See* **Federal Open Market Committee**.

foreign branch   A legal and operational part of the parent bank. Creditors of the branch have full legal claims on the bank's assets as a whole and, in turn, creditors of the parent bank have claims on its branches' assets.

foreign exchange   Markets developed so that people can convert their cash to different currencies as their needs for different currencies vary in their business affairs and operations.

foreign exchange risk The fluctuation in the earnings or value of a financial institution that arises from fluctuations in exchange rates; responsible for gains or losses in the currency positions of financial institutions and changes in U.S. dollar values of non-U.S. financial investments.

foreign subsidiary A separately incorporated bank owned entirely or in part by a U.S. bank, a U.S. bank holding company, or an Edge Act corporation.

fortuitous loss Exposure units used to predict losses must be homogeneous for the law of large numbers to work; the losses that occur must be fortuitous, meaning that the loss is unexpected and happens as a result of chance.

forward contract A contract that guarantees delivery of a certain amount of goods, such as a foreign currency, for exchange into a specific amount of another currency, such as dollars, on a specific day in the future.

forward price In a forward contract, the price at which the purchaser will buy a specified amount of an asset from the seller at a fixed date sometime in the future.

forward rate (1) The interest rate that is expected to exist in the future. (2) The exchange rate for future purchase or sale of currencies.

Freddie Mac *See* **Federal Home Loan Mortgage Corporation**.

frictional unemployment A term indicating that a portion of those who are unemployed are in transition between jobs.

FRM *See* **fixed-rate mortgage**.

front-end load Fees paid at the time people invest money in a mutual fund.

FSLIC *See* **Federal Savings and Loan Insurance Corporation**.

FSOC *See* **Financial Stability Oversight Council**.

full employment Term implying that every person of working age who wishes to work can find employment.

full-service brokers Investment firms serving as brokers that offer investment advice, research, individual financial planning, and a specific broker dedicated to a customer's account.

fully contributory plan A pension plan in which only the employee makes contributions to the plan.

functional regulation An approach to financial institution regulation in which the Federal Reserve acts as the umbrella regulator while the bank and nonbank subsidiaries fall under the supervision of other regulators.

futures contract A contract to buy (or sell) a particular type of security or commodity from (or to) the futures exchange during a predetermined future time period.

futures exchange A place where buyers and sellers can exchange futures contracts. The exchange keeps the books for buyers and sellers when contracts are initiated or liquidated.

future value The worth in the future of a currently held amount of money if it is invested and reinvested at known interest rates.

Garn–St. Germain *See* **Depository Institutions Act (DIA) of 1982**.

general obligation bonds State and local government bonds backed by the "full faith and credit" (the power to tax) of the issuing political entity; they require voter approval.

Ginnie Mae *See* **Government National Mortgage Association**.

Glass-Steagall Act *See* **Banking Act of 1933**.

GNMA *See* **Government National Mortgage Association**.

Government National Mortgage Association (GNMA, or Ginnie Mae) Organized in 1968, a federal agency that helps issuers of mortgages obtain capital market financing to support their mortgage holdings. It does so by creating government-guaranteed securities that pass through all interest and principal repayments from pools of mortgages to purchasers of the pass-through securities.

Gramm-Leach-Bliley Act *See* **Financial Services Modernization Act of 1999**.

gross interest expense The total interest paid on deposits and other borrowings.

gross interest income The total interest income earned on loans and investment securities.

growing perpetuity A cash flow grows forever at a constant rate.

haircut A term referring to the mechanism of over collateralizing repos. An x percent of haircut means the borrower receives $1 - x$ percent of the market value of securities.

health insurance Protection against medical costs associated with illness and injury and the loss of income.

hedge funds Pools of investment capital that use a combination of market philosophies and analytical techniques to identify, evaluate, and execute trading decisions.

hedgers Individuals or firms that engage in financial market transactions to reduce price risk.

home equity lines of credit Agreements secured by a mortgage on a borrower's home under which a bank customer can borrow up to a predetermined limit on a short-term basis.

home equity loans Personal loans that are secured by a mortgage on the borrower's home.

Humphrey-Hawkins Act Passed in 1978, this legislation specifies the primary objectives of monetary policy—full employment, stable prices, and moderate long-term interest rates. In addition, it requires that the Board of Governors of the Federal Reserve System submit a report on the economy and the conduct of monetary policy to Congress by February 20 and July 20 of each year.

IBF *See* **international banking facility**.

IB&BEA *See* **Interstate Banking and Branching Efficiency Act**.

Immediately available funds Deposit liabilities of Federal Reserve banks, and liabilities of commercial banks that may be transferred or withdrawn during a business day.

implied forward rate The forward rate of interest implied by the difference in a short-term interest rate and a longer-term interest. The implied forward rate is the rate necessary to make funds invested at the short rate and reinvested at the implied forward rate generate a return equal to that which could be obtained by buying the longer-term security.

indenture The legal contract that states the rights, privileges, and obligations of the bond issuer and the bondholder.

index funds Mutual funds that try to match the performance of a specific stock or bond market index, such as the S&P 500 Index, by buying similar or identical securities.

indirect financing (financial intermediation) The purchase of direct claims (IOUs) with one set of characteristics from DSUs and the transformation of them into indirect claims (IOUs) with a different set of characteristics

individual equity In a pension plan, the concept of paying benefits in direct relation to contributions.

industrial banks Financial institutions chartered under industrial banking laws in a state. Industrial banks make loans and issue savings deposits. Finance companies may obtain charters as industrial banks so that they can issue savings deposits to obtain funds.

industrial development bonds (IDBs) Municipal revenue bonds that are issued by private companies. The municipality assumes no legal liability in the event of default.

inflation The continuous rise in the average price level.

inflation targeting An economic policy wherein a central bank estimates and makes public a projected or target inflation rate, and then steers the actual rate of inflation in the economy toward the target rate through use of monetary policy tools.

initial margin A deposit of money or other valuable assets with a futures exchange to guarantee that buyers will keep their part of a bargain.

initial public offering (IPO) The primary offering of a company that has never before offered a particular type of security to the public, meaning the security is not currently trading in the secondary market; an unseasoned offering.

insolvent When the value of a firm's liabilities exceeds the value of its assets.

insurance The transfer of pure risk to an entity that pools the risk of loss and provides payment if a loss occurs.

insured pension plan A pension plan established with a life insurance company.

interest The rental price of money, usually expressed as an annual percentage of the nominal amount of money borrowed; the price of borrowing money for the use of its purchasing power.

interest-only mortgage A mortgage whereby a borrower pays only the interest for the first few years, after which payments increase so that the loan is fully amortized by the end.

interest rate *See* **interest**.

interest rate cap *See* **cap**.

interest rate collar *See* **collar**.

interest rate floor *See* **floor**.

interest rate risk The risk that changes in interest rates will cause an asset's price and realized yield to differ from the purchase price and initially anticipated yield.

internal credit risk ratings Internal credit risk ratings are ratings systems that some banks use to identify the credit risk associated with the loans in their portfolios.

International Banking Act (IBA) of 1978 Legislation that created a federal regulatory structure for the operation of foreign banks in the United States.

international banking facilities (IBFs) U.S. branches or agencies of a foreign bank, or the U.S. office of an Edge Act or agreement bank, established by a U.S.-chartered depository institution. An IBF is not an institution in the organizational sense; It is actually a set of asset and liability accounts segregated on the books of the establishing institutions.

Interstate Banking and Branching Efficiency Act (IB&BEA)   Legislation allowing U.S. banks to merge and branch across state lines unless a potential host state opted out of interstate branching.

intrinsic value   The value that could be realized by exercising an option immediately.

investment banks   The most important participant in the direct credit market; firms that specialize in helping businesses and governments sell their new security issues in the primary markets to finance capital expenditures.

investment capital flows   Capital flows that are either short-term money market flows motivated by differences in interest rates or long-term capital investments in a nation's real or financial assets.

investment company   A nonbank financial institution that invests the pooled capital of investors in long-term and short-term securities.

investment-grade bonds   The bonds rated in the top four major rating categories by Moody's and Standard & Poor's (i.e., bonds rated Baa or BBB or better).

IPO   See **initial public offering**.

junior debt   See **subordinated debt**.

junk (speculative-grade) bonds   See **speculative-grade (junk) bonds**.

law of large numbers   A mathematical law that applies to the loss exposures of insurers; the larger the number of loss exposures, the more predictable the average losses become.

LBO   See **leveraged buyout**.

LEAPS (Long-term Equity Anticipation Securities)   Long-term equity or index options.

lender of last resort   The role of the Fed as a lender to banks experiencing difficulties to prevent the banks from failing due to a lack of liquidity.

less developed country (LDC)   Countries whose political and financial conditions make loans risky; because most international bank loans are unsecured, business loans are generally made only to large, creditworthy multinationals and are backed by the "full faith and credit" of the borrowing LDC nation.

letter of credit (LC)   A financial instrument issued by an importer's bank that obligates the bank to pay the exporter (or other designated beneficiary) a specified amount of money once certain conditions are fulfilled.

leveraged buyout (LBO)   Buying a company using a significant amount of borrowed money.

liability insurance   Insurance against financial loss due to legal responsibility for bodily injury, property damage, or personal injury.

liability management   A bank's management of its liability structure to increase or decrease its source of funds as needed.

LIBOR   See **London Interbank Offer Rate**.

limited liability   A legal concept meaning that losses of common stockholders are limited to the original amount of their investment; it also implies that the personal assets of a shareholder cannot be obtained to satisfy the obligations of the corporation.

limit order   An order to buy or sell at a designated price or at any better price.

line of credit   An agreement under which a bank customer can borrow up to a predetermined limit on a short-term basis.

liquidity   Ability of an institution to hold sufficient amounts of cash and liquid assets to allow it to easily meet requests from its liability holders for cash payment.

liquidity premium   Additional interest paid by borrowers who issue illiquid securities to obtain long-term funds; the interest premium compensates lenders who acquire a security that cannot be resold easily or quickly at par value.

liquidity risk   The risk that a financial institution will be unable to generate sufficient cash inflow to meet required cash outflows.

liquidity trap   In Keynesian theory, an occurrence during major depressions when people already have so much money relative to their needs that any extra money is hoarded and will no longer drive down interest rates.

Lloyd's associations   Organizations that do not directly write insurance but that provide services for members of the association who write insurance as individuals.

Lloyd's of London   The most famous Lloyd's association, where members (names) have unlimited liability for the risks they underwrite.

load fund   An investment (mutual) fund that charges a commission when shares in the fund are purchased.

London Interbank Offer Rate (LIBOR)   The lending rate between large international banks; often the lowest lending rate in the market because of low credit risk.

long position   An agreement to buy an asset such as security, commodity, or currency.

long-term asset loan   A loan that finances the acquisition of an asset or assets. Maturities of the loan are typically between 1 and 10 years.

loss reserves   Also known as policy reserves. An estimate of an insurance policy on what it will owe in claims payments in the future.

macrohedging   Using instruments of risk management, such as financial futures, options on financial futures, and interest rate swaps, to reduce the interest rate risk of the firm's entire balance sheet.

maintenance margin   In the futures market, a margin requirement imposed to ensure that people do not default on their contracts if prices move adversely for them.

management fees   Also known as an advisory fee. In mutual funds, the fee paid to the company that manages a fund's portfolio, usually expressed as a percentage of the fund's annual average net assets.

margin   (1) A security deposit that a customer keeps with a broker when borrowing to buy securities. (2) In futures markets, money posted to guarantee contracts will be honored and to take account of gains or losses accruing from daily price movements.

margin call   In the futures market, when the funds in an investor's margin account fall below the investor's maintenance margin, the investor is required to add enough funds to the account to get it back up to the initial margin.

margin requirements   The amount of money people can borrow so they can buy stocks; this amount is restricted by Federal Reserve Regulations G, T, U, and X in order to prevent excessive speculation in the stock market.

margin trading   Trading in which an investor can buy securities partly with borrowed money.

marine insurance   Insurance against losses related to transportation exposures.

marketability   The cost and quickness with which a financial claim can be resold. The greater the marketability of a financial security, the lower its interest rate.

market capitalization   Also known as market cap. Total market value of outstanding shares of a company.

market economy   An economy in which consumers have a free choice to buy or not buy whatever goods or services they want.

market failure   Condition in the loan markets where banks decide not to make loans to businesses or consumers because reliable information is not available at a reasonable cost.

market maker   Term applied to an individual who regularly quotes bid and ask prices in a stock and trades for his or her own account at those prices.

market order   An order to buy or sell at the best price available at the time the order reaches the exchange.

market risk premium   The risk premium of the market portfolio.

market-segmentation theory   The theory that maintains that market participants have strong preferences for securities of a particular maturity and holds that they buy and sell securities consistent with these maturity preferences, resulting in the yield curve being determined by the supply of and demand for securities at or near a particular maturity.

market value–weighted index   A stock market index that is computed by calculating the total market value of the firms in the index and the total market value of those firms on the previous trading day; the percentage change in the total market value from one day to the next represents the change in the index.

marking-to-market   In futures markets, a requirement that all gains or losses on futures positions be taken into account in determining the value of all contracts each day.

matched funding   A circumstance in which fixed-rate loans are funded with deposits or borrowed funds of the same maturity.

maturity GAP   Interest rate risk measure comparing the value of assets that will either mature or be repriced within a given time interval to the value of liabilities that will either mature or be repriced during the same time period.

McCarran-Ferguson Act (Public Law 15)   Federal legislation that specifies that insurance companies should be regulated at the state level.

microhedging   Hedging a specific transaction. Matched funding is an example.

minimum funding standards   ERISA rules on how much money employers should set aside to pay future pension benefits under qualified plans.

MMDA   *See* **money market deposit account**.

MMMF   *See* **money market mutual funds**.

M1, M2   Alternative definitions of the money supply as designated by the Federal Reserve System.

monetary base   Currency in circulation plus financial institution reserve deposits at the Federal Reserve. The monetary base consists of all assets that can be used to satisfy legal reserve requirements. Thus, if it grows, financial institution reserves (and financial institution deposits) usually grow, too.

money center bank   A large commercial bank located in a major financial center that directly transacts in the money market.

money market A financial market in which financial claims with maturities of less than a year are sold. The most important money market is that for U.S. Treasury bills.

money market deposit accounts (MMDAs) Federally insured deposits that have a legal limit of six third-party transactions each month. Their interest rates and other features are determined by the issuing bank.

money market mutual funds (MMMFs) Open-ended mutual funds that invest in short-term debt, collect an annual account fee, and offer checking account withdrawals.

moral hazard Problems of hidden actions. For instance, in the case of deposit insurance, insured individuals have less incentive to monitor the health of the deposit institutions and thus are more likely to incur a loss than when their deposit institution does not carry insurance.

Morningstar Style Box Morningstar's classifications of equity funds based on the market cap and the value/growth characteristics of the stock portfolios the fund holds.

mortgage-backed bonds Tax-exempt bonds issued by city housing authorities based on mortgage pools generated under their jurisdiction.

mortgage-backed securities (MBSs) Securities such as pass-through securities and "collateralized mortgage obligations" that pass through all or part of the principal and interest payments on pools of many mortgages to buyers of the mortgage-backed securities.

mortgage bankers Also called mortgage companies. An institution that originates mortgages and collects payments on them.

mortgages Loans for which the borrower pledges real property as collateral to guarantee that the debt will be repaid.

M2 multiplier The ratio of M2 money to bank reserves (or the monetary base).

multiple line policies Insurance policies that combine property and liability coverage in one contract.

municipal bonds Bonds issued by state and local government bodies; they represent one of the largest fixed-income securities markets.

municipal bond funds Funds holding debt issued by states, cities, counties, and municipalities.

municipal securities Securities issued by state and local governments that sell for lower market yields than comparable securities issued by the U.S. Treasury and private corporations; they are exempt from federal taxes.

mutual funds An open-ended investment company; the most common type of investment company that stands ready to buy or sell its shares at the current net asset value at any time.

mutual fund families Cluster of related mutual funds that have similar names and related marketing strategies, and allow funds to be transferred easily among themselves. They facilitate asset gathering by mutual fund management companies.

mutual fund share classes Types of shares with different expenses investing in the same portfolio of securities within a mutual fund.

mutual institution Financial institutions technically owned by their liability holders (depositors) and managed by an elected manager or a public-spirited board of trustees that seek to invest depositors' and liability-holders' funds to earn a safe and secure rate of return.

mutual insurance company An insurer owned by its policyowners. The goal of the company is to minimize the cost of insurance to its policyowners because there are no stockholders.

NAFCU *See* **National Association of Federal Credit Unions**.

naked options An option writer's position if he or she does not own the securities that he or she has agreed to sell or has not sold short the securities that he or she has agreed to buy.

named-perils coverage Property insurance that provides a specific list of perils that are covered.

NAIC *See* **National Association of Insurance Commissioners**.

NASDAQ *See* **National Association of Securities Dealers Automated Quotation System**.

National Association of Federal Credit Unions (NAFCU) A credit union trade and service association that serves the interests of the generally larger, federally chartered credit unions.

National Association of Insurance Commissioners (NAIC) An organization founded in 1871 to set uniform regulatory standards among the states.

National Association of Securities Dealers (NASD) Private regulatory authority participating in the determination of rules that financial market participants must follow when they issue and exchange securities.

National Association of Securities Dealers Automated Quotation System (NASDAQ) A computerized communications system that provides continuous bid-and-ask prices on the most actively traded OTC stocks.

National Credit Union Administration (NCUA) The regulatory body that sets standards for all federally chartered and federally insured credit unions.

National Credit Union Share Insurance Fund (NCUSIF) An organization providing federal insurance to members who own shares (deposits) in federally chartered credit unions and in qualifying state-chartered credit unions.

natural rate of unemployment Level of unemployment that policymakers are willing to tolerate—a sort of "full employment unemployment rate."

NAV *See* **net asset value**.

NCUA *See* **National Credit Union Administration**.

NCUSIF *See* **National Credit Union Share Insurance Fund**.

negotiable certificates of deposit (NCDs) Unsecured liabilities of banks that can be resold before their maturity in a dealer-operated secondary market.

negotiated offering A type of public offering in which the company selects the investment banker who will conduct the offering and then negotiates the net proceeds that the company will receive for the securities.

net asset value (NAV) A price based on the current market value of all securities held in a mutual fund's portfolio divided by the number of outstanding shares in the fund, and quoted as NAV per share.

net interest margin The difference between gross interest income and gross interest expense.

New York Stock Exchange (NYSE) The preeminent securities exchange located in New York City.

no-load fund An investment fund that does not levy a sales charge when the fund is purchased.

nominal rate of interest The interest rates that are observed in the marketplace.

noncontributory plans Pension plans funded through employer contributions only.

noninsured pension plan A pension plan managed by a trustee rather than an insurance company.

noninterest expense Salaries, employee benefits, technology-related expenses, and other expenses for a financial institution.

noninterest income Income for a financial institution that consists mainly of fees and service charges.

nonparticipating preferred stock Preferred stock is nonparticipating in that the preferred dividend remains constant regardless of any increase in the firm's earnings.

notional principal The face value amount for which interest payment obligations are computed under a "swap" agreement. Because the principal is never repaid, it is only "notional" for the duration of the swap.

NOW account Deposit account that pays explicit interest and can be withdrawn by "negotiable orders of withdrawal" (checks) on demand.

NYSE *See* **New York Stock Exchange**.

objective risk An insurer's risk that is the deviation of actual losses from expected losses; objective risk can be measured statistically.

OCC *See* **Office of the Comptroller of the Currency**.

Office of the Comptroller of the Currency (OCC) Created in 1863 by the National Bank Act, the OCC is a subsidiary of the Treasury Department and is responsible for supervising national banks.

Office of Thrift Supervision (OTS) Created in 1989 as a subsidiary of the Treasury Department. Assumed the chartering and many of the supervisory powers of the Federal Home Loan Bank Board, which it replaced.

on-site bank examinations Unannounced visits by bank examiners to a bank or its branches.

open-end mutual funds *See* **mutual funds**.

open interest The total number of futures contracts for delivery of a specific good at a futures exchange.

open-market operations The purchase or sale of government securities by the Federal Reserve. Open market operations are used to increase or decrease bank reserves and the monetary base. When the Fed purchases securities, the monetary base expands.

open-outcry Method of communication involving traders in a "trading pit" shouting and using hand signals to convey information about buy and sell orders.

opportunity cost The interest rate on the next best alternative investment.

options A contractual agreement that allows the holder to buy (or sell) a specified asset at a predetermined price on or prior to its expiration date. The predetermined price is called the strike price. Options to buy assets are call options. Options to sell assets are put options.

option contract *See* **option**.

option premium The price of the option.

OTC *See* **over-the-counter market**.

OTS *See* **Office of Thrift Supervision**.

over-the-counter market (OTC) Primarily a dealer market where securities not sold on one of the organized exchanges are traded.

panics The events that occur when depositors lose confidence in banks in general and "run" many banks to redeem their deposits quickly.

par bond A bond that is selling at its par value.

participating policies Policies issued by stock companies in which policyholders receive dividends; thus policyholders "participate" in the profitability of the insurance company.

par value (principal, face value) The stated or face value of a stock or bond. For debt instruments, the par value is usually the final principal payment.

participation loans A means of reducing international lending risk; an arrangement under which banks participate by joining together so each provides only part of the funds for a loan; the participation thereby reduces the risk exposure for each individual bank.

Patient Protection and Affordable Care Act A legislation passed in 2010 that extends coverage to many uninsured Americans by providing subsidies to individuals and small businesses.

payoff and liquidate policy An approach for resolving a bank failure by paying off insured deposits and liquidating the bank's assets.

PBGC *See* **Pension Benefit Guarantee Corporation.**

Pension Benefit Guarantee Corporation (PBGC) Federal insurance agency that insures defined benefit plans up to a specified amount per month.

perils Fire, windstorm, theft, explosion, and negligence—conditions against which property and liability insurers offer protection policies.

personal loans Credit to individuals not related to credit financing of specific assets.

Phoenix merger Merger of two or more failing thrift institutions to create a new (and seemingly more sound) institution.

plan fiduciary Any trustee, investment adviser, or other person who has discretionary authority or responsibility in the management of a pension plan or its assets.

PMI *See* **private mortgage insurance.**

policyholders' surplus An item in the Liabilities and Net Worth of an insurance company. Analogous to owners' equity, it is the difference between assets and liabilities.

political capital flows International capital flows that respond to changed political conditions in a country.

political risk Country or sovereign risks that can result in financial claims of foreigners being repudiated or becoming unenforceable because of a change of government, or of government policy, in a country.

pooling Losses suffered by a small number of insureds are spread over the entire group so insurance purchasers substitute the average loss in place of the uncertainty that they might suffer a large loss.

portability In pension plans, workers' right to take pension benefits with them when changing jobs.

positive time preference The preference of people to consume goods today rather than tomorrow.

PPP *See* **purchasing power parity.**

preferred-habitat theory The theory of the term structure of interest rates that suggests investors leave their preferred maturity range only if adequately compensated for the additional risk of investing in a security whose maturity does not match the investors' investment horizon. This theory is an extension of the market segmentation theory.

preferred stock Corporate stock that has certain "preferences" relative to the interests of common stockholders. Usually, dividend payments are predetermined and must be made before dividends can be distributed to common stockholders.

preliminary prospectus A portion of the registration statement that contains detailed information about the issuer's financial condition, business activities, industry competition, management and their experience, the project for which the funds will be used, the characteristics of the securities to be issued, and the risks of the securities.

premature death Loss of life while others are financially dependent on the person who died.

premium A pricing situation in which a closed-end fund trades above its net asset value.

premium bond A bond whose market price is above its par or face value. A bond sells at a premium when the market rate of interest is below the bond's fixed coupon rate.

prepayment risk The risk that a mortgage will be repaid sooner than expected.

present value The value today of a future stream of cash payments discounted at the appropriate discount rate.

price/earnings (P/E) ratio Ratio of market price per share to earnings per share.

price indexes Indexes (CPI, PPI, GDP deflator) constructed by selecting a representative group or "basket" of commodities and tracing their price changes from period to period. Price indexes demonstrate whether prices in general are rising or falling.

price risk   Interest rate changes can cause the market price of a bond to rise or fall, resulting in gains or losses for an investor.

price stability   The stability of the average price of all goods and services in the economy.

price-weighted index   A stock market index that is first computed by summing the prices of the individual stocks composing the index; then the sum of the prices is divided by a "divisor" to yield the chosen base index value.

primary market   Financial market in which financial claims are first sold as new issues. All financial claims have a primary market.

primary offering   Offerings of new issues of stocks or bonds.

primary reserves   Cash assets on a bank balance sheet that are immediately available to accommodate deposit withdrawals or meet reserve requirements.

prime broker   An investment bank that lends money and securities to hedge funds, clears trades and retains custody of securities on behalf of hedge funds, and often performs risk management services for hedge funds.

prime rate   The interest rate banks charge their most creditworthy customers on short-term loans. It was historically an important benchmark for loan pricing.

principal (par value)   *See* **par value**.

private banks   After the Civil War and before the 1930s, privately owned investment banks that could engage in any business activity and could have offices at any location.

private-label credit   Plans offered by major finance companies for retailers; all correspondence with the consumer is carried on using the retailer's name, but the credit is provided by the finance company.

privately issued pass-throughs (PIPs)   Securities issued by private institutions or mortgage bankers by pooling (often nonconforming) mortgages, obtaining private mortgage insurance, and security ratings, and sold using underwriter's services.

private mortgage insurance (PMI)   Insurance for mortgages not insured by a federal agency; the consumer pays the insurance premium in addition to the loan rate, thus allowing the consumer to buy a house with a lower down payment.

private pension plans   Plans established by private-sector groups such as industrial, commercial, union, and service organizations, or individuals who are most employment related.

private placements   The distribution of equity securities in which the investment banker acts only as the company's agent and receives a commission for placing the securities with investors.

promised yield (yield to maturity)   *See* **yield to maturity**.

promissory note   Unconditional promise in writing by the borrower to pay the lender a specific amount of money at some specified date.

prompt corrective actions   A policy of intervening in the management of a financial institution quickly when the institution begins showing signs of financial distress.

property insurance   Protection against direct and indirect loss to property.

proprietary trading   Trading of financial instruments by a firm with the firm's own capital instead of its customers' capital.

provision for loan losses   An expense item that adds to a financial institution's loan loss reserve.

proxy   A process in which shareholders vote for the corporation's board of directors by absentee ballot rather than at the annual shareholders' meeting.

Public Law 15   *See* **McCarran–Ferguson Act**.

public markets   Organized financial markets where securities registered with the SEC are bought and sold.

public offering   The offering of securities publicly in the open market to all interested buyers. Public offerings are usually made through an investment-banking firm.

purchase and assumption agreement   A policy of the deposit insurance fund covering bank failures. The insurance fund can sell the assets of the failed institution to another institution that "purchases" the assets and "assumes" the responsibility for repaying the liabilities of the failed institution.

purchasing power parity (PPP)   An economic concept that says the purchasing power of a currency should be equal in every country if goods, services, labor, capital, and other resources can flow freely between countries. However, because there are impediments to free trade, purchasing power parity conditions often do not hold. Thus, goods often cost more in one country than in another.

pure risks   In the language of insurance, a risk in which the outcome is either a loss or no loss; there is no possibility for gain. Pure risks arise from events over which one has little or no control.

put interest discount   The difference in interest rates between putable and similar nonputable bonds.

put options The option allowing the investor to sell an asset to the put seller at a predetermined price.

pyramiding of reserves System by which smaller country banks counted their deposits in large city banks as part of their reserves; when the country banks needed currency, they exchanged their reserves at larger banks for cash, thus depleting the larger banks' holdings. Pyramiding of reserves often led to a liquidity squeeze and financial panics.

qualified plans Pension plans that satisfy certain rules to be granted favorable tax treatment.

rate ceilings Regulations limiting the maximum interest rates that can be charged on different types of loans.

rate-sensitive assets (RSAs) Assets that either will mature or can be repriced within a specific period of time (often 1 year).

rate-sensitive liabilities (RSLs) Liabilities that either will mature or be prepriced within a specific period of time (usually one year).

real estate investment trust (REIT) A type of closed-end investment company that invests in real estate.

real estate mortgage investment conduit (REMIC) A legal entity that issues multiple classes of securities that pass through principal and interest payments made on mortgages or CMOs. Like CMOs, most REMIC securities pay structured principal and interest payments.

real GDP The quantity of goods and services produced in the economy, as opposed to nominal GDP, which is the value (price times quantity) of goods and services produced in the economy.

realized real rate of return The nominal rate of return on an investment adjusted for the actual rate of inflation that occurred after the investment was undertaken; the realized real rate can be either negative or positive.

realized yield The rate of return earned on a bond given the price paid and the cash flows actually received by the investor.

real rate of interest The nominal rate of interest prevailing in the marketplace adjusted for the expected rate of inflation; the equilibrium rate of interest if no inflation occurs.

reciprocal (reciprocal exchange) A form of insuring organization that operates like unincorporated mutuals and whose objective is to minimize the cost of the insurance product.

refinance Obtaining new financing with a lower interest rate and using the proceeds to pay off the balance due on old financing.

registered bonds Bonds for which the bondholder's name is recorded and coupon payments are mailed to the bondholders. No coupons are physically attached to the bond.

registration statement A statement filed with the Securities and Exchange Commission (SEC) when securities are to be sold publicly.

Regulation B Regulation through which the Federal Reserve Board implements the Equal Credit Opportunity Act of 1974.

Regulation Q A historical Federal Reserve regulation that set a maximum interest rate that banks could pay on deposits. All interest rate ceilings on time and savings were phased out on April 1, 1986, by federal law.

Regulation Z Regulation requiring disclosures about (1) the annual percentage rate and (2) the total finance charges and other terms of a loan.

regulatory dialectic The process by which regulations are evaded, new regulations are enacted to close the loopholes, new evasion strategies and products are developed, new regulations are adopted to curb the innovations, and so on.

reinsurance Risk sharing between the original insurer and another insurance company, the reinsurer.

reinvestment risk The risk resulting from market interest rate changes that cause a bond investor to have to reinvest coupon payments at interest rates different from the bond's promised yield.

REIT *See* **real estate investment trust.**

REMIC *See* **real estate mortgage investment conduit.**

renegotiated-rate mortgages (RRMs) Mortgage whose rate must be renegotiated periodically. Renewal at the new rate is guaranteed and the maximum rate change is limited.

renewable term insurance An insurance policy that may be placed in force again at the end of the coverage period. The insured does not have to provide evidence of insurability.

repo *See* **repurchase agreement.**

representative money Legal tender (such as silver certificates) issued by the government and representing a specified amount of precious metal held on deposit that could be withdrawn on request.

representative nonbanking offices Offices established in a foreign country primarily to assist the parent bank's customers in that country. Representative offices cannot accept deposits, make loans, transfer funds, accept drafts, transact in the international money market, or commit the parent bank to loans.

repurchase agreements (RPs) Also known a repo. A form of loan in which the borrower sells securities (usually government securities) and simultaneously contracts to repurchase the same securities, either on call or on a specified date, at a price that will produce a specified yield.

required reserves Financial institutions are required by law to maintain minimum reserves equal to a percentage of specified deposit liabilities. Reserve requirements vary with the deposit size of the institution and the type of deposit. They are held at Federal Reserve banks or as cash in financial institutions' vaults.

residual claim A feature of common stock that is a claim against the firm's cash flow or assets; in the event of the firm's liquidation, those with prior claims are paid first and the common stockholders are entitled to what is left over, the residual.

retained earnings Portion of net income kept by the corporation instead of being distributed to owners.

return on average assets (ROAA) An institution's annual net income divided by its average assets during the year.

return on average equity (ROAE) An institution's annual net income divided by its average book value of equity during the year.

return on investment The future additional real output generated by investment in productive capital projects.

revenue bonds State and local government bonds sold to finance a specific revenue-producing project; in the event of default, these bonds are backed only by the revenue generated from the project.

reverse annuity mortgages (RAMs) Mortgages designed for older people who own their homes and need additional funds to meet current living expenses but do not want to sell their homes. RAMs allow people to borrow against the equity in their homes at relatively low interest rates. The borrower receives monthly payments.

reverse repurchase agreement Also known as reverse repo. The reverse (lending) side of a repurchase agreement.

reverse repo *See* **reverse repurchase agreement**.

revolving credit A formal legal agreement under which a bank agrees to lend up to a certain limit for a period exceeding 1 year.

rights offering The placement of equity securities directly with the company's existing stockholders; existing stockholders are given "rights" to purchase additional shares at a slightly below-market price in proportion to their current ownership in the company. Stockholders can exercise their rights or sell them.

risk Uncertainty concerning the occurrence of loss.

risk premium Required (or expected) return on a risky security minus the return on a similar risk-free security.

risk transfer Shifting the responsibility of bearing risk from one party to another party.

risk-weighted assets A measure of total assets that weights high-risk assets more heavily than low-risk assets.

ROAA *See* **return on average assets**.

ROAE *See* **return on average equity**.

rollover mortgages (ROMs) Mortgages that mature before full amortization. At that time the borrower may elect to renew (roll over) the mortgage at the prevailing mortgage rate. Thus, the borrower may pay several different rates on the mortgage before it is fully amortized.

rollover pricing Floating-rate loans that allow banks to fund credits in the Eurocurrency market at the beginning of the period and lock in a lending spread for the coming period. At the end of this period, the loan will again roll over and be repriced for the subsequent period.

Rule 144A SEC rule that allows secondary trading of private securities by large institutional investors.

sales finance company A company that finances the credit sales of retailers and dealers by purchasing the installment credit contracts that they acquire when they sell goods on credit.

Samurai bonds Bonds issued in Japan by foreign companies.

savings and loan associations (SLAs) Also known as savings associations, savings and loans, or S&Ls. Financial institutions that specialize in accepting savings deposits and making mortgage and other loans.

seasonal loan A loan providing term financing to take care of temporary discrepancies between business revenues and expenses that are due to the manufacturing or sales cycle of a business.

seasoned offering The primary issue of securities of a type already trading in the secondary market.

secondary market Financial market in which participants buy or sell previously issued financial claims.

secondary reserves Short-term assets (often Treasury bills) that banks can quickly convert to cash at a price near their purchase price.

second-mortgage lending Mortgage lending in which real estate lending is secured by second mortgages.

secured/unsecured loan A bank loan guaranteed (not guaranteed) by collateral consisting of merchandise, inventory, accounts receivable, plant and equipment, real estate, or stocks and bonds.

securitization The process of setting up a trust that buys a large number of loans of similar types and then sells securities of different types that "pass through" payments of principal and interest on the loans to the investors and may even vary the payments on different securities as interest rates change. The creator of the trust creates attractive pieces in the hope of selling them for more than it had to pay to buy the whole pool of loans.

securitization of risk Transfer of insurable risk to the capital markets through the creation of a financial instrument.

security market line (SML) The linear relationship between systematic risk (beta) and expected return.

seed financing Capital provided to a company at the idea stage that goes to market research and product development.

seigniorage Difference between cost of the printed currency and the exchange value of the currency.

senior debt In the event of liquidation of a firm, senior debt holders must be paid first.

Separate Trading of Registered Interest and Principal (STRIPs) A Treasury security that has been separated into its component parts; each interest payment and the principal payment become a separate zero-coupon security.

serial bond issue A municipal bond issue that contains a range of maturity dates rather than all of the bonds in the issue having the same maturity date.

settlement date In a forward contract, the future date on which the buyer pays the seller and the seller delivers the assets to the buyer.

shelf registration An innovation in the sale of new corporate securities that permits a corporation to register a quantity of securities with the SEC and sell them over a 2-year period rather than all at once.

shell branches A booking office for bank transactions located abroad that has no contact with the public; the easiest and cheapest way to enter international banking.

short position An agreement to sell an asset such as a security, commodity, or currency.

short sale Sales of security (e.g., equity) borrowing from the broker.

short squeezes Circumstances in which an individual or group tries to make it difficult or impossible for short sellers in futures markets to liquidate their contracts through delivery of acceptable commodities.

sight draft A draft that requires the bank to pay on demand, assuming that all documentation is in proper order and that all conditions have been met.

sinking fund A corporate bond provision that requires the bond issuer to provide funds to a trustee to retire a specific dollar amount (face amount) of bonds each year.

SLAs *See* **savings and loan associations**.

social adequacy The concept of slanting pension benefits in favor of certain groups to achieve broader social goals.

Social Security old-age benefits Retirement benefits paid to workers who have earned enough credits under the Social Security plan through paying the payroll tax.

sovereign risk *See* **country risk**.

specialist Members of the exchange who combine the attributes of both dealers and order clerks; they have an affirmative obligation to maintain both bid and offer quotations at all times for listed securities.

speculative-grade (junk) bonds The bonds rated below Baa (or BBB) by bond rating agencies such as Moody's or Standard & Poor's.

speculative risks In the language of insurance, a risk that can result in either a gain or a loss.

speculators Individuals who assume price risk in the expectation of earning a high return.

spot market The market in which securities are traded for immediate delivery and payment.

spot price An observed price at which current transactions take place.

spot rate (1) Actual market interest rate today. (2) The foreign exchange rate at which a currency is traded in the spot market (i.e., for almost immediate delivery).

spreads (or straddles) A position in options that combines two or more options (i.e., two or more calls or puts).

SSU *See* **surplus spending unit**.

standby letter of credit A guarantee that a financial institution will make a payment (in return for advancing a loan to its customer) if the customer should fail to do so.

startup financing Capital used to develop a product and initiate marketing.

stock association   A form of savings and loan association that issues common stock to shareholders and is managed by managers appointed by a board of directors elected by profit-seeking shareholders.

stock-index futures contracts   Futures contracts written on the value of a stock index.

stock-index options   Options contracts written on the value of stock indexes.

stock insurance company   A corporation owned by its shareholders. It's the most popular organizational form in the U.S. insurance industry.

stop buy order   An investor's order that buys a stock only if the price rises above the market price to a certain level. The order is designed to protect profits that have already been made or limit losses in a short sale.

stop loss order   An investor's order that sells a stock only if the price drops below the market price to a certain level. The order locks in the profits that have already been made to limit losses.

stop (stop-out) rate   The highest accepted rate in Treasury bill auctions.

straight voting   A procedure for electing directors in which directors are elected one by one; thus, the maximum number of votes a shareholder has for each director equals the number of shares owned.

street name   Registering a security in the issuer's records under the name of the brokerage firm instead of the customer's own name.

strike price (exercise price)   The price at which an option can be exercised.

STRIPped mortgage-backed securities (SMBSs)   Mortgage-backed securities that represent separated interest and principal payments.

STRIPs   *See* **Separate Trading of Registered Interest and Principal**.

structural unemployment   A portion of those who are unemployed are unemployed because there is a mismatch between their skill levels and available jobs, or there are jobs in one region of the country but few in another region.

subordinated debt   Also known as junior debt. In the event of default, subordinated debt holders' claims to the company's assets rank behind senior debt.

superannuation   Living too long; outliving your income.

surplus spending unit (SSU)   An economic unit whose income for the period exceeds expenditures. SSUs often purchase financial claims issued by deficit spending units (DSUs).

swap   An exchange of assets or income streams for equivalent assets or income streams with slightly different characteristics.

syndicated   A group of banks packaging and participating to fund a large international bank loan.

systematic risk   Also known as market risk or nondiversifiable risk. The risk that tends to affect the entire market in a similar fashion.

systemic risk   Risk of the failure of the entire financial system resulting from the interdependencies among financial institutions.

T bill   *See* **Treasury bill**.

TARP   *See* **Troubled Asset Relief Program**.

TBTF   *See* **too big to fail**.

technical factors   Factors outside the control of the Federal Reserve (e.g., cash drains, float, and Treasury deposits) that affect the monetary base.

term bonds   A bond issue in which all of the bonds that make up the issue mature on a single date.

term insurance   A product that provides a death benefit to the beneficiary if the insured dies within a specified time. Such policies provide only death protection and no savings element.

term loan   A loan from a bank with a specific maturity. Typically, term loans have maturities greater than 1 year.

term structure of interest rates   The relationship between yield and term to maturity on securities that differ only in length of time to maturity; graphically approximated by the yield curve.

term-to-maturity   The length of time until the final payment of a debt security.

thin   A term describing a market where trades are relatively infrequent.

thrift institutions   Consumer-oriented financial institutions that accept deposits from and make loans to consumers. They include savings institutions and credit unions.

Tier 1 capital   A measure of bank capital that includes the sum of common stock, paid-in-surplus, retained earnings, noncumulative perpetual preferred stock, and minority interest in consolidated subsidiaries minus goodwill and other intangible assets. Tier 1 capital is commonly referred to as core capital.

Tier 2 capital   A measure of bank capital that includes cumulative perpetual preferred stock, loan loss reserves, subordinated debt instruments, mandatory convertible debt instruments, and other debt instruments that combine both debt and equity features. Tier 2 capital is commonly referred to as supplemental capital.

time draft A draft payable at a particular time in the future, as specified in a letter of credit.

time value of money The concept based on the belief that people have a positive time preference for consumption, preferring to consume goods today rather than consume similar goods in the future; thus, a dollar today is worth more than a dollar received at some future date.

TIPS *See* **Treasury Inflation Protection Securities**.

too big to fail (TBTF) Policy adopted by federal regulators that the failure of certain financial institutions would have too much of an adverse effect on the economy and so those institutions will not be allowed to fail.

total reserves *See* **actual reserves**.

total return The return to a bond investor that reflects coupon payments, capital gains or losses, and potential changes in the interest rate at which coupon payments are reinvested.

toxic securities A term for subprime mortgages during the 2008 financial crisis because of their toxic effect on a firm's capital and solvency.

traders Individuals who buy or sell securities in the hope of profiting quickly from expected price movements.

tranches Specific portions of a security issue; for example, mortgage-backed securities may have interest-only or principal-only tranches.

transaction costs The costs involved in buying or selling securities.

transfer credit A source of credit for smaller subsidiaries in a holding company; a form of funding provided by their larger parent companies.

Treasury bill (T-bill) Direct obligation of the federal government with initial maturities ranging from 3 months to 1 year. They are considered to have no default risk and are the most marketable of any security issued.

Treasury Inflation Protection Securities (TIPS) Treasury securities that have a fixed coupon rate but a principal amount that changes in response to changes in the inflation rate.

Treasury notes and bonds Similar to Treasury bills in that they are issued by the Treasury and are considered free of default risk; they differ from bills in that they are coupon issues, redeemable at face value upon maturity,

and have initial maturities greater than 1 year and no more than 10 years.

Troubled Asset Relief Program (TARP) A program established in 2008 that allows the U.S. Treasury to purchase or guarantee mortgage-related assets of banks and other financial institutions.

Truth-in-Lending Act *See* **Consumer Credit Protection Act**.

12b-1 fees Annual fees assessed by a mutual fund, over and above its fund management or advisory fees, specifically to pay for the sales and marketing expenses incurred by the fund.

underpricing The situation that occurs when securities sold in a public offering immediately begin trading at a price higher than the offering price.

underwriter's spread The difference between the fixed price paid for securities and the price at which they are resold, constituting the investment banker's (or underwriter's) gross profit.

underwriting The risk-bearing function of the investment banker. Underwriting occurs when the investment banker guarantees fixed proceeds to security issuers while uncertain of the eventual resale price.

underwriting cycle In insurance, a cyclical pattern in commercial property and liability insurance.

underwriting syndicate A group of investment bankers who underwrite a security issue.

underwritten offering The most common distribution method for new issues of equity securities in which the investment banker purchases the securities from the company for a guaranteed amount known as the net proceeds and then resells the securities to investors for a greater amount, called the gross proceeds.

undivided earnings Part of a credit union's net worth; credit unions must set aside a portion of their earnings as reserves until their reserves are sufficiently large relative to their assets; similar to retained earnings of a corporation.

U.S. Central Credit Union An organization whose members include central credit unions. The U.S. Central Credit Union has a commercial bank charter in the state of Kansas and has access to the nation's check payment system. The union can invest in a wide variety of assets and can lend money to credit unions or their centrals.

unit investment trust A group of assets purchased by investment-banking firms and formed into a trust; units in the trust are sold to individual investors. The trust is passively managed, passing through payments of interest and principal on the initial asset pool until all assets are liquidated.

universal banks Institution that can accept deposits, make loans, underwrite securities, engage in brokerage activities, and sell and manufacture other financial services such as insurance.

universal life insurance Flexible-premium, nonparticipating life insurance that provides a market-based rate of return on the savings or cash value account.

unseasoned offering The name for a primary offering if the company has never before offered securities to the public.

unsystematic risk The unique or security-specific risks that tend to partially offset one another in a portfolio.

value at risk (VAR) A method for determining the interest rate risk exposure of a financial institution based on a determination of the amount that the institution might lose if interest rates were to vary by a sufficiently large amount that such a change would occur only about 1 percent of the time. Recommended capital requirements to control for interest rate risk are several times VAR.

VAR *See* **value at risk**.

variable life insurance Fixed-premium life insurance that permits the policyowner to select where the cash value is invested.

velocity of money Measures of the number of dollars of national income that are supported with each dollar of money in circulation. When velocity rises, more income can be generated with the same amount of money in circulation. The converse holds if velocity declines.

venture capital private equity Private equity investments made by venture capital firms.

vesting An employee's right to employer-promised pension benefits or employer contributions, usually after a specified period of time.

Veterans Administration (VA) mortgages Mortgages whose payment is guaranteed by the Veterans Administration.

whole life insurance An insurance contract that provides periodic payment of premiums and protection as long as the insured lives. Upon death or a specific age (usually 65), the face amount of the policy is paid to the policyholder or beneficiary.

wholesale financing Interim financing provided to a dealer by a finance company.

wholesale paper Finance company business lending in which a finance company helps a dealer finance the purchase of goods.

Wildcat banks Banks opened by dishonest bankers who intended to defraud the public by issuing banknotes far in excess of their reserves (gold or silver).

Yankee bonds Bonds issued by foreign entities in the United States.

yield curve The graph of the relationship between interest rates on particular securities and their yield to maturity. To construct yield curves, bonds must be as similar in as many other characteristics as possible.

yield spread Difference in yields between various issues of securities, for instance, yields between the 10-year and 3-month Treasury securities.

yield-to-maturity (promised yield) The discount rate that equates the present value of all cash flows from a bond (interest payments plus principal) to the market price of the bond.

zero coupon bonds Bonds that have no coupon payment but promise a single payment at maturity.

Credits and Acknowledgments

Part Openers GlowImages/Superstock.

Chapter Openers

Chapter 1 Cyberimage/Taxi/Getty Images.

Chapter 2 © Bettmann/Corbis.

Chapter 3 Photo by Chris Kleponis/ZUMA KPA (©) Copyright 2005 by Chris Kleponis.

Chapter 4 Fredrik Skold/The Image Bank/Getty Images.

Chapter 5 Photo by Tim Boyle/Bloomberg via Getty Images.

Chapter 6 Lawrence Migdale/Photo Researchers, Inc.

Chapter 7 AP Photo/Mary Altaffer.

Chapter 8 UPPA/Photoshot.

Chapter 9 Robert Harding/Digital Vision/Getty Images, Inc.

Chapter 10 UPI Photo/Monica Graff/Landov LLC.

Chapter 11 © Globe Photos/ZUMAPRESS.com.

Chapter 12 Travel Pix//Taxi/Getty Images.

Chapter 13 © Bettmann/Corbis.

Chapter 14 © B.S.P.I./Corbis.

Chapter 15 Brendan McDermid/Reuters/Landov LLC.

Chapter 16 RKO Pictures/MoviePix/Getty Images.

Chapter 17 Alan R. Moller/Stone/Getty Images.

Chapter 18 Cusp/SuperStock.

Chapter 19 Image Source/Punchstock.

Chapter 20 AURORA OPEN/Image Source Limited.

Exhibit 10.7 *Wall Street Journal Online*, February 26, 2007. Copyright © 2007 by Dow Jones & Co., Inc. Reproduced with Permission of Dow Jones & Co., Inc., via Copyright Clearance Center.

Exhibit 17.3 "Total U.S. Life/Health and Fraternal Companies' Balance Sheet, 2009," from *Best's Aggregates and Averages, Life/Health*, 2010 ed. © A. M. Best Company. Used with permission.

692 Credits and Acknowledgments

Exhibit 17.4   "Total U.S. PC Industry Companies' Balance Sheet, 2009," from *Best's Aggregates and Averages, Property/Casualty*, 2010 ed. © A. M. Best Company. Used with permission.

Exhibit 18.1   "Top Twenty U.S. Life/Health Insurance Groups and Companies by Revenues, 2005," from the Insurance Information Institute's *The Financial Services Fact Book*, 2007 ed. © A. M. Best Company. Used with permission. Data from *Fortune*.

Exhibit 18.2   "Top Twenty U.S. Property/Casualty Insurance Groups and Companies by Revenues, 2005," from the Insurance Information Institute's *The Financial Services Fact Book*, 2007 ed. © A. M. Best Company. Used with permission. Data from *Fortune*.

Exhibit 18.3   "Total U.S. Life/Health and Fraternal Companies' Balance Sheet, 2005," from *Best's Aggregates and Averages, Life/Health*, 2006 ed. © A. M. Best Company. Used with permission.

Exhibit 18.4   "Total U.S. PC Industry Companies' Balance Sheet, 2005," from *Best's Aggregates and Averages, Property/Casualty*, 2006 ed. © A. M. Best Company. Used with permission.

Exhibit 20.8   "How to Read Mutual Fund Quotes in Newspapers," *Source:* 2001 *Mutual Fund Fact Book*. Copyright © 2001 Investment Company Institute. Reprinted by permission of the Investment Company Institute (www.ici.org).

Exhibit 20.12   "Major Stock Total Return Indexes," from the National Association of Real Estate Investment Trusts *Chart Book*, March 2007.

Index